MAP FINDER

SIXTH EDITION

International Business

The Challenge of Global Competition

SIXTH EDITION

International Business

The Challenge of Global Competition

DONALD A. BALL
University of Texas–Pan American

WENDELL H. McCULLOCH, JR.
California State University, Long Beach

IRWIN

Chicago • Bogotá • Boston • Buenos Aires • Caracas
London • Madrid • Mexico City • Sydney • Toronto

© Richard D. Irwin, a Times Mirror Higher Education Group, Inc. company, 1982, 1985, 1988, 1990, 1993, and 1996

Executive editor:	*Craig S. Beytien*
Developmental editor:	*Jennifer R. McBride*
Marketing manager:	*Michael Campbell*
Project editor:	*Ethel Shiell*
Production supervisor:	*Lara Feinberg*
Graphics supervisor:	*Heather D. Burbridge*
Assistant manager, graphics:	*Charlene R. Breeden*
Interior designer:	*Lucy Lesiak*
Cover designer:	*Lucy Lesiak*
Cover photographer:	*Sharon Hoogestraten/Lucy Lesiak*
Art studio:	*Carlisle Communications, Ltd./Maryland CartoGraphics*
Compositor:	*Carlisle Communications, Ltd.*
Typeface:	*10/12 New Aster*
Printer:	*Webcrafters, Inc.*

Library of Congress Cataloging-in-Publication Data

Ball, Donald A.
    International business : the challenge of competition / Donald A.
Ball, Wendell H. McCulloch, Jr. —6th ed.
      p.   cm.
    Includes index.
    ISBN 0-256-16601-3. — ISBN 0-256-16606-4 (annotated instructor's ed.)
    1. International business enterprises—Management.
2. International business enterprises. 3. International economic relations. I. McCulloch, Wendell H. II. Title.
HD62.4.B34 1996
658'.049—dc20

                  95–18497

Printed in the United States of America
1 2 3 4 5 6 7 8 9 0   2 1 0 9 8 7 6 5

To Vicky and Sally

Don, Jr., Dulce, Lianne, Susan, Jim,

Kevin, and Malinda

About the Authors

Don Ball is director of the doctoral program in international business and a professor of marketing and international business at the University of Texas–Pan American and a consultant to international companies. He has a degree in mechanical engineering from Ohio State University and a Ph.D. in business administration from the University of Florida. Ball has published articles in the *Journal of International Business Studies* and other publications. Before obtaining the doctorate, he spent 15 years in various marketing and production management positions in Mexico, South America, and Europe.

Wendell McCulloch is a professor of international business, finance, and law and director of international business programs at California State University, Long Beach. He earned a bachelor's degree in economics and political science from George Washington University and a J.D. from Yale University. He has published articles in *The Wall Street Journal*, the *Journal of International Business Studies*, and the *Collegiate Forum*. The results of McCulloch's research have appeared in publications by the Joint Economic Committee of the U.S. Congress and the Heritage Foundation. Before beginning his academic career, McCulloch spent 19 years as an executive for American and European multinationals that offered banking, insurance, and investment products in many countries. While teaching and writing, he continues to act as an international business consultant.

Preface

We are pleased to present the sixth edition of *International Business: The Challenge of Global Competition*. We thank all of you who have taken the time to call or write us with suggestions for improving this edition.

Purpose and Scope of This Text

The text is written for the first course in international business taken either at the undergraduate level or in an M.B.A. program. A growing number of schools are permitting students to take the international business course *before* they have all the required basic courses so they are better prepared to discuss worldwide aspects of each business function. This enables professors to take a more global approach in the presentation of their material.

In schools that do not yet require an international business course, many professors recommend this text as a supplementary book for international courses in finance, management, marketing, and so forth. Numerous executive seminars include this book as part of their handouts in programs on the various aspects of international business, and many business executives buy it as a reference book.

We begin the text by describing the nature of international business and the three environments in which an international businessperson works. In Section Two we examine the increasingly important international organizations, the international monetary system, and their impact on business. In Section Three we discuss the uncontrollable forces that make up the foreign environments and illustrate their effect on business practice. In the final section we reverse the procedure and deal with the functions of management, showing how managers deal with the uncontrollable forces.

Changes in the Sixth Edition

Suggestions for improving this edition came from a number of sources: detailed chapter-by-chapter reviews by international business professors, calls and letters from professors and students, comments by businesspeople who attended executive seminars or who bought the book for their personal libraries, and students in our own classes, both graduate and undergraduate.

We have retained many of the features people liked in the fifth edition. We begin each chapter with a quotation, followed by an article relating to the material presented in the chapter. Margin definitions help students learn the language of international business, and indented examples further clarify the concepts being taught. The Worldview boxes contain readings pertinent to the chapter material, and a minicase finishes each chapter. Three comprehensive cases are once again located at the end of the book.

We have used every effort, including calling government officials, to bring you the latest information available. We invite you to compare data in our tables with those of other textbooks published in the same year. In addition to up-to-date tables, we have made an effort to use more graphs and maps to convey important information. Pictures are used since they often present a concept more vividly than we can describe it, and an occasional cartoon appears—international business does have its lighter side.

New Features and Areas of Substantive Change

We have added some exciting new features to this edition.

1. **Small Business in the Global Economy boxes.** Because international business can involve all sizes of businesses, from sole proprietorships to multinational corporations, we have added a feature focusing on small businesses involved in international business. Small businesses are often ignored in traditional international business texts; however, many students will work for small- to medium-sized companies and should be aware of the international involvement possible to firms of all sizes.

2. **Videocases.** We now offer you four integrated videocases, one found at the end of each of the four sections of the text. These videocases were written to expand on the material presented in each of the four videos. The videocases are Vanguard Pollution Control Company, a look at how and why Vanguard decided to enter foreign markets; International Finance, a look at the prospects of monetary union in Europe; Trading Attitudes, a discussion of the different attitudes held by Americans and Japanese; and The Evolution of Ogre Mills, what the evolution from a Soviet enterprise to a private company means to Ogre Mills.

3. **Maps.** This edition has twice as many illustrative maps as the fifth edition. We find maps can be used to convey information as well as teach geography.

4. **Graphs.** In response to your requests, we have replaced many statistical tables with graphs since illustrative representations convey the same information in a quicker and easier-to-read format.

In addition, we have updated the material in each chapter to reflect recent world events and their ramifications on international business.

1. In Chapter 1 we have expanded the appendix, Careers in International Business, to include information on numerous employment opportunities with the federal government.

2. In Chapter 2 we introduce a new concept, "reverse maquila." Also, responding to professors' requests, we now have a map showing locations of in-bond plants (maquiladoras) in Mexico.

3. Chapter 3 includes discussions of the Leontieff paradox, learning curve, Linder Theory of Overlapping Demand, Porter's Comparative Advantage of Nations, and four new kinds of dumping.

4. In Chapter 4 we describe a new trend in the World Bank and IMF: more encouragement of and support for investment by the private sector. There is expanded coverage of the European Bank for Reconstruction and Development and an update on the GATT Uruguay Round, which resulted in the World Trade Organization replacing GATT.

5. In Chapter 5 the Big MacCurrencies illustration of purchasing power parity is brought up to date, as are European efforts to implement the Maastricht Treaty. National difficulties in maintaining desired currency exchange rates in the face of the huge amounts of money being traded in the foreign exchange markets are presented.

6. In Chapter 6 we update the effects of inflation and currency exchange controls on business.

7. Chapter 7 presents an economic analysis showing why India is an important new market. More graphs are also used in this chapter.

8. In Chapter 8 we introduce a new concept, passive processing. There is also new information on the progress of burning water and hydrogen in internal combustion engines.

9. In Chapter 9 we discuss the cultural successes and failures of Disney theme parks and present Geert Hofstede's work on understanding national cultures.

10. Chapter 10 includes a discussion of the transition from centrally planned to market economies and a privatization update. There is new material on country risk assessment (CRA).

11. Chapter 11 includes a new application of antitrust law as well as material on intellectual property protection.

12. Chapter 12 contains material on new developments affecting refugee and guest workers and progress for females in the work force.

13. In Chapter 13 we present the impact of foreign direct investment on the U.S. trade position and show that who owns the company *does* matter, contrary to arguments by members of the Clinton administration. There is new information on U.S. competitiveness and discount retailing in Japan.

14. Chapter 14 includes information on the UN *Industrial Statistics Yearbook* and how to use it.

15. In Chapter 15 we have expanded the discussion on regional and global brands and added accounts of two expensive sales promotions that went wrong, Hoover in the United Kingdom and Pepsi-Cola in the Philippines.

16. Chapter 16 includes a new section on sources of export counseling and the new Trade Point Global Network.

17. Chapter 17 has been completely rewritten to deal with the evolution from dictatorships and centrally planned economies toward democracy and market economies.

18. Chapter 18 presents the latest practices in staffing and human resource management.

19. Chapter 19 includes a section on global outsourcing. We discuss concurrent engineering, computer integrated manufacturing, delayering, and soft manufacturing.

20. Chapter 20 contains new material on derivatives and other international finance management devices.

21. In Chapter 21 we discuss the virtual corporation, the horizontal corporation, and other ways CEOs' are seeking to make their firms leaner, flatter, more innovative, and quicker to respond.

22. Chapter 22 deals with international business control and changes being driven by new technology.

Advantages of Using This Book in Your Class

This book is the result of teamwork between many professors and their students who have used previous editions. One aspect constantly mentioned is its readability. Because students understand what they read in this book, professors can spend less time clarifying basic points and more time discussing emerging issues, of which there is no lack in this fast-moving field. However, don't be misled by the writing style. We have compared this book with others and have yet to find one as comprehensive. Note that we have included a complete chapter on the physical forces, to strengthen what is generally a weak area of students' education. There are also complete chapters on exporting-importing and production. We invite comparisons of our treatment of marketing, financial management, and international organizations, all important topics for international businesspeople. The many tables and their analyses enable students to make important comparisons of markets, and the numerous listed sources of additional information facilitate the research process for students' projects.

Our 34 combined years in international business, in both the home offices of worldwide firms and their subsidiaries, have influenced our writing. We wanted a book that would describe what managers have to face in international business and how they respond to the uncontrollable environmental forces; in short, the kind of book people would like to have if they were suddenly told by the boss that they were going overseas. In fact, this happened to one of us—who found no such book at that time.

The Ball and McCulloch International Business Package

1. **Annotated Instructor's Edition.** The annotated instructor's edition includes three types of annotations for your convenience:
   a. Supplementary readings—Selected supplementary readings are placed in the margin near the topic they relate to. A complete list of supplementary readings is provided in the instructor's manual.
   b. Concept previews—The concept previews are restated in the margin where they are first discussed.
   c. Acetate references—This annotation identifies which maps and figures are available as four-color acetates.

2. **Instructor's Manual.** The manual will help you save valuable time preparing for the course and provide you with suggestions for heightening your students' interest in the material. Each chapter-by-chapter discussion presents the concept previews, an overview of the chapter, suggestions and comments, student involvement exercises, suggestions for guest lecturers, and a detailed chapter outline. Suggestions for videotapes and films are included.

3. **Testbank.** The testbank is available in a number of formats: (1) a printed manual, (2) computerized testing software, available in DOS, Windows, and Macintosh formats, and (3) Teletest, a customized, phone-in service.

4. **Instructor's Resource Box.** The box includes 22 file folders, one for each chapter of the text. Each folder is filled with the Instructor's Manual and Testbank material for that chapter.

5. **Acetates.** The acetate package includes 65 four-color acetates of maps and significant figures from the text.

6. **Videos.** Upon request, adopters of the sixth edition will receive four new videos, each with an accompanying videocase found at the end of each of the four sections of the text.
   a. How to Enter Foreign Markets—an overview of the Taiwan market and a case study of Karen Wolters, inventor and entrepreneur in Taiwan.
   b. International Finance—a brief history of the gold standard and a look at present-day currency trading.

    c. Forces Affecting International Business—examples of cultural, socio-economic, political, and legal forces influencing trade between the United States and Japan.

    d. East-West Relations—the transition of a former Soviet textile firm to a private company in a free market economy.

7. **World Atlas CD-ROM.** Upon request, adopters of the sixth edition will receive the new World Atlas CD-ROM. It includes:

- Political, topographical, and statistical maps of the world's countries.
- A database that includes more than 60,000 statistics on world economy, agriculture, demographics, and much more.
- More than 150 videoclips of landmarks from major world cities.
- Over 1,000 high-resolution photographs from all over the world.
- Flags from over 200 countries and recordings of their national anthems.

Acknowledgments

To the long list of people to whom we are indebted, we want to add professors Robert T. Aubey, University of Wisconsin-Madison; Mark C. Baetz, Wilfrid Laurier University; Rufus Barton, Murray State University; S. A. Billon, University of Delaware; James R. Bradshaw, Brigham Young University; Sharon Browning, Northwest Missouri State University; Dennis Carter, University of North Carolina–Wilmington; Mark Chadwin, Old Dominion University; Refik Culpan, Pennsylvania State University; Peter DeWitt, University of Central Florida; Galpira Eshigi, Illinois State University; Prem Gandhi, State University of New York at Plattsburgh; Stanley D. Guzell, Youngstown State University; Gary Hankem, Mankato State University; Baban Hasnat, State University of New York at Brockport; Paul Jenner, Southwest Missouri State University; Bruce H. Johnson, Gustavus Adolphus College; Michael Kublin, University of New Haven; Eddie Lewis, University of Southern Mississippi; Lois Ann McElroy Lindell, Wartburg College; Carol Lopilato, California State University–Dominguez Hills; Gary Oddon, San Jose State University; John Setnicky, Mobile College; Jesse S. Tarleton, William and Mary College; John Thanopoulos, Akron University; Kenneth Tillery, Middle Tennessee State University; Hsin-Min Tong, Redford University; Dennis Vanden Bloomen, University of Wisconsin–Stout; and George Westacott, State University of New York at Binghamton. Attorney Mary C. Tolton, Esq., of the law firm Parker, Poe, Adams & Bernstein of Raleigh, North Carolina, provided valuable supplementary readings for the legal forces chapter. Professor Michael Minor, University of Texas–Pan American, made many valuable comments.

    We are also indebted to the following reviewers for helping us fine-tune the text to better meet market needs: Suhail Abboushi, Duquesne University; C. G. Alexandrides, Georgia State University; Christopher Clott, St. Xavier University; Budd H. Herbert, Harding University; David Kelson, Ferris State University; Robert Letovsky, Saint Michael's College; John Petrakis, Webster University–Kansas City; John A. C. Stanbury, Indiana University–Kokomo; Dennis R. Vanden Bloomen, University of Tennessee; and Alan Wright, Henderson State University.

    We continue to invite your suggestions for making this a more useful text and thank you for your interest and input.

Donald A. Ball
Wendell H. McCulloch, Jr.

Contents in Brief

Contents

SECTION II
THE INTERNATIONAL ENVIRONMENT: ORGANIZATIONS AND MONETARY SYSTEM

SECTION III
FOREIGN ENVIRONMENT

Worldview
Pointing Way to Prosperity for
East Europe Countries, 557

The Nature of International Business

International Business: Diversity and Competitiveness

> There is no longer any such thing as a purely national economy. The rest of the world is just too big to ignore, either as a market or as a competitor. If business schools do nothing other than to train their students to think internationally, they would have accomplished an important task.
>
> John Young, CEO, Hewlett-Packard

CONCEPT PREVIEWS

After reading this chapter, you should be able to:

1. **appreciate** the dramatic internationalization of markets

2. **understand** the various names given to firms that have substantial operations in more than one country

3. **distinguish** between firms of the early 1900s and present-day companies

4. **comprehend** why international business differs from domestic business

5. **describe** the three environments—domestic, foreign, international—in which an international company operates

Why Study International Business?

Eric Phillips, age 40 and a 10-year veteran with American Telephone & Telegraph, was eager to return to company headquarters in New Jersey and get on with his career after spending two years serving a White House fellowship. His superiors, however, asked him to move to Belgium to be AT&T's European sales manager. "I didn't want to move my family, but the company was going global. I had to go," he said. • Phillips is one of an escalating number of American executives facing this situation because more American firms are going abroad after new markets. As their companies' overseas business grows, many fast-track executives feel it is necessary to do a foreign tour of duty to further their careers. For example, the chief executive officer (CEO) of Gerber, which is expanding markets in Latin America and Europe, says his company will emphasize foreign assignments as part of normal career development for executives. The vice president for human resources of FMC Corporation, a heavy machinery and chemicals producer, says his company believes that "no one will be in a general management job by the end of the decade who didn't have international exposure and experience.[a] • Until the decade of the 1990s, most businesspeople did not view an overseas job as a career enhancer. Top managements focused primarily on the vigorous U.S. economy, and middle managers felt that taking a foreign assignment would remove them from where the action was, causing their careers to suffer. However, this has changed with the increased globalization of American industry. As overseas business has become a more significant part of many firms' total operations, the importance of experience in foreign markets for managers has increased. Now, for example, all of the Big Three automakers have CEOs with extensive foreign experience. Recently, firms such as General Electric, Nynex, Dell Computer, and Motorola have increased the number of U.S. managers overseas. Nynex has 105 American executives overseas compared with practically none five years ago. General Motors has 485 American managers overseas, an increase of 15 percent over the previous year.[b] • It is apparent that American managements want their top executives at company headquarters to have years of foreign experience, and they are sending young executives abroad to acquire that experience. But, do CEOs of the major American firms generally recognize the value of an internationalized business education for *all* employees in management? Do they, in fact, believe it is important that all business graduates they hire have some education in the international aspects of business? How important is the knowledge of foreign languages? • To find out, we surveyed the CEOs of *Forbes* "100 Largest Multinational Firms" and *Fortune*'s "America's 50 Biggest Exporters." We found that: (1) Seventy-nine percent believed that all business majors should take an introduction to international business course. (2) About 70 percent

Sources: [a]"Path to Top Job Now Twists and Turns," *The Wall Street Journal,* March 15, 1993, p. B1. [b]"The Fast Track Leads Overseas," *Business Week,* November 1, 1993, pp. 64–68. [c]Donald A. Ball and Wendell H. McCulloch, Jr., "The Views of American Multinational CEOs on Internationalized Business Education for Perspective Employees," *Journal of International Business Studies,* 2nd Quarter, 1993, pp. 383–91. [d]"Prospects," *The New York Times,* January 3, 1988, p. F1.

felt that business graduates' expertise in foreign languages, international aspects of functional areas (e.g., marketing, finance), and business, human, or political relations outside the United States is an important consideration when making hiring decisions. (3) A majority of the respondents believed that a number of courses in the international business curriculum (e.g., international marketing, international finance, export–import, international management) are relevant to their companies. • It appears from our study, then, that the CEOs of the major American firms doing business overseas are convinced that the business graduates they hire should have some education in the international aspects of business.[c] Most seem to agree with the executive vice president of Texas Instruments who said, "Managers must become familiar with other markets, cultures, and customs. That is because we operate under the notion that it is 'one world, one market,' and we must be able to compete with—and sell to—the best companies around the world."[d] • Clearly, the top executives from some of the largest corporations in the world are saying that they prefer business graduates who know something about markets, customs, and cultures in other countries. Companies that do business overseas have always needed some people who could work and live successfully outside their own countries, but now it seems that managers wanting to advance in their firms must have some foreign experience. • Did you note the reason for this emphasis on foreign experience for managers—increased involvement of the firm in international business? The top executives of many corporations want their employees to have a global business perspective. What about companies that have no foreign operations of any kind? Do their managers need this global perspective? They do indeed, because it will help them not only to be alert for both sales and sourcing opportunities in foreign markets but also to be watchful for new foreign competitors preparing to invade their domestic market. • Indicators of this expanding competition are the increases in import penetration and the buildup of foreign investment. Imports as a percentage of the gross national product (GNP) have increased markedly for four of the five major importing nations over the past two decades (Table 1–1), and the world's stock of foreign investment has more than tripled over the last 10 years. • In summary, we can say that every company, whether or not it has any foreign involvement, needs to be aware of what is occurring globally in its markets and its industry.

TABLE 1–1
Merchandise imports as a percentage of GNP, 1970 versus 1992 ($ billions)

	Imports		GNP		Imports/GNP (%)	
	1992	1970	1992	1970	1992	1970
United States	$552	$43	$5,904	$975	9.3%	4.4%
Germany	407	30	1,846	180	22.0	16.6
France	238	19	1,279	157	18.6	12.1
Japan	231	19	3,508	199	3.5	9.5
United Kingdom	222	22	1,025	127	21.7	17.3

Sources: *World Bank Atlas*, 1971; *UN Statistical Yearbook*, 1988; *World Bank Development Report*, 1994; *World Bank Atlas*, 1994.

What about you? Are you involved in the global economy yet? Think back to how you began your day. After you awoke, you may have looked at your Timex watch for the time and turned on your RCA TV for the news and weather while you showered. After drying your hair with a Conair dryer, you quickly swallowed some Carnation Instant Breakfast and Sanka coffee, brushed your teeth with Close-Up toothpaste, and drove off to class in your Honda with its Firestone tires and a tank full of Shell gasoline.

Meanwhile, on the other side of the world, a group of Japanese students dressed in Lacoste shirts, Levi's jeans, and New Balance shoes may be turning off their IBMs in the computer lab and debating whether they should stop for hamburgers and Cokes at McDonald's or coffee and doughnuts at Mister Donut. They get into their Ford Mustangs with Goodyear tires and drive off.

What do you and the Japanese students have in common? You are all consuming products made by *foreign-owned companies*. This is international business.

To further see the point we're making, answer this question: Which of the following companies or brands are foreign owned?

1. Norelco (electric razors).
2. Chesebrough-Pond (Vaseline).
3. Electrolux (household appliances).
4. Lever Brothers (Lux, Whisk, Close-Up).
5. Pearle Eyecare (glasses).
6. Del Monte.
7. BF Goodrich (tires).
8. Burger King.
9. Holiday Inn.
10. Nabisco (crackers and cereal).
11. Scott Paper (Kleenex).
12. CBS records.
13. General Tire (tires).
14. A&W Brands (root beer).
15. Motel 6.
16. Pillsbury.[1]

All that you have read so far points to one salient fact: *There is an emphatic need for all businesspeople to have some knowledge of international business.* As you increase your knowledge of international business, you will add dozens of words to your vocabulary. Let's look at some important terms.

International business, like every field of study, has its own terminology. To assist you in learning the special vocabulary, an important function of every introductory course, we've included a glossary at the end of the book and listed the most important terms at the end of each chapter.

INTERNATIONAL BUSINESS TERMINOLOGY

Multinational, Global, International, and Transnational

As with any new discipline, definitions of a number of words vary among users. For example, some people use the words *world* and *global* interchangeably with *multinational* to describe a business with widespread international operations; but others define a global firm as one that attempts to standardize

Globalization: What Is It?

"There is too much competition in the United States. To increase our sales, we'll have to sell outside the country. We have to globalize," said the owner of a small Ohio company that makes home barbecue grills. However, the president of Goodyear, remarking about his firm's global strategy, stated, "We have globalized our product line to service automakers and their customers no matter where they are. It doesn't matter if a car was built in Sydney or São Bernardo and then shipped to London or Laramie. When a replacement tire is needed, Goodyear will have one on hand locally to match the Goodyear already on the car."

Both are using the same term, but are they talking about the same thing? Unfortunately, globalization and its root, global, are overused and misused in international business. For example, global marketing strategy for some people, such as the Ohio grill manufacturer, means a plan to sell in markets all over the world (*where* the company does business). For others, a global marketing strategy is one that focuses on customer similarities and uses large-scale manufacturing and superior quality to standardize products and services worldwide (*how* the company does business).

More recently, globalization is taking on a new meaning. After talking about having to be a multinational firm in order to gain a competitive advantage during the 1960s, managements turned to the buzzword *globalization* in the 1980s as a strategy for beating their competitors. Over time, however, globalizing firms are becoming more significant than their predecessors, the multinationals, for two reasons.

One is that there are many of them—37,000 worldwide, with 24,000 in 14 industrial nations compared with 7,000 in 1969, according to the United Nations Conference on Trade and Development. Second, they are placing production plants all over the world to gain the benefits of lower-cost labor and better-educated workers. Managements are removing the barriers within their companies to allow the free flow of ideas and people. For cultural diversity, many are offering top management positions to citizens from countries other than the home country.

There is already a new name for this type of company—*multicultural multinational*—that is based on two propositions:

- Because innovation is the key to success, managers are looking everywhere in the global organization for new ideas, hence the name, multicultural. No longer do they treat foreign subsidiaries as pure factories subject to orders and ideas that come from the single culture at headquarters. Managements speak about eradicating the "not invented here" syndrome, meaning that the headquarters staff members are being educated to give serious consideration to ideas and suggestions that originate from overseas affiliates.
- Communications technology is making it possible for people from subsidiaries around the world to work together on projects. For example, teleconferencing and computer networks enabled Ford designers in Europe and the United States to work jointly on the design of its new global car, the Mondeo.

The aims of the multicultural multinational are (1) to be responsive to local markets, (2) to produce and market its products globally, and (3) to exploit its technology on a global basis, an elusive objective attained by few companies so far.

Sources: "Goodyear's Perspective on Mergers and Acquisitions and Running an MNC Today," *Business International,* January 23, 1989, p. 19; Coskin Samli, Richard Still, and John S. Hill, *International Marketing* (New York: Macmillan, 1993), p. 210; and "The Discreet Charm of the Multicultural Multinational," *The Economist,* July 30, 1994, p. 37.

operations in all functional areas but that responds to national market differences when necessary. (See the Worldview in this chapter for a discussion of *globalization* and *multicultural multinational*.

According to this definition, a global firm's management:

1. Searches the world for (*a*) market opportunities, (*b*) threats from competitors, (*c*) sources of products, raw materials, and financing, and (*d*) personnel. In other words, it has global vision.
2. Seeks to maintain a presence in key markets.
3. Looks for similarities, not differences, among markets.

Those who use *global* in this manner are defining a multinational company as a kind of holding company with a number of overseas operations, each of which is left to adapt its products and marketing strategy to what local managers perceive to be unique aspects of their individual markets. Some academic writers suggest using terms such as *multidomestic* and *multilocal* as synonyms for this definition of multinational.[2] You will also find those who consider *multinational corporation* to be synonymous with *multinational enterprise* and *transnational corporation*.

The United Nations and the governments of most developing nations have been using *transnational* instead of *multinational* for decades to describe a firm doing business in more than one country. Recently, some academic writers have employed the term for a company that combines the characteristics of global and multinational firms: (1) trying to achieve economies of scale through global integration of its functional areas while at the same time (2) being highly responsive to different local environments (a newer name is *multicultural multinational*).[3] You recognize, of course, that this is similar to the definition of a global company mentioned earlier. To be able to use this definition for transnational, these writers have simply redefined a global firm as one that responds weakly to local environments.

Businesspeople, though, usually define a transnational as a company formed by a merger (not a joint venture) of two firms of approximately the same size that are from different countries. Four of the largest are Unilever (Dutch-English), Shell (Dutch-English), Azko-Enka (Dutch-German), and ABB, a merger of ASEA (Swedish) and Brown-Bovari (Swiss). *Binational* is another name for this kind of company.

Perhaps the Japanese have the solution to the usage of terms with multiple definitions; they call the technique of adapting to local conditions, *dochakuka*, meaning "global localization." The word comes from Japanese agriculture where it means adjusting the planting, fertilizing, and harvesting methods to meet local soil conditions.

To complete this discussion, we need to mention that the term *supranational corporation* was described in a publication of the United Nations as one in which both the operation and ownership are multinational; yet many reserve this term for a corporate form that does not now exist—one that would be chartered by an international agency such as the United Nations.

Definitions Used in This Text

In this text, we will employ the definitions listed below, which are generally accepted by businesspeople. Although we primarily use the terms *global, multinational,* and *international* firms or companies, at times we may use *multinational enterprise (MNE)* interchangeably with *international company (IC)* inasmuch as both terms are employed in the literature and in practice.

1. *International business* is business whose activities involve crossing national borders. This definition includes not only international trade and foreign manufacturing but also the growing service industry in such areas as transportation, tourism, banking, advertising, construction, retailing, wholesaling, and mass communications. Figure 1–1 demonstrates how widespread one service corporation has become.

2. *Foreign business* denotes the domestic operations within a foreign country. This term is sometimes used interchangeably with international business by some writers.

3. **Multinational company** (MNC) is an organization with multicountry affiliates, each of which formulates its own business strategy based on perceived market differences.

multinational company
An organization with multicountry affiliates, each of which formulates its own business strategy based on perceived market differences

FIGURE 1-1 Overseas locations of an international service company, McDonald's (countries/number of stores opened as of July 26, 1994)

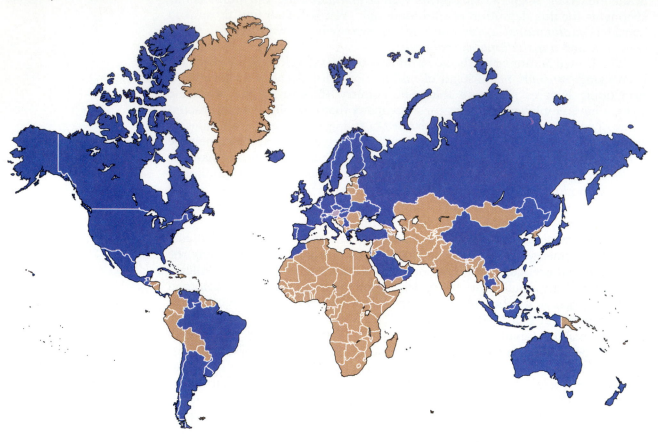

● COUNTRIES WITH McDONALD'S RESTAURANTS

ANDORRA (1)	CHILE (6)	GREECE (5)	JAPAN (1,058)	NETHERLANDS (105)	RUSSIA (3)	TAIWAN (80)
ARGENTINA (30)	CHINA (19)	GUADELOUPE (1)	KOREA (25)	NEW CALEDONIA (1)	SAIPAN (1)	THAILAND (22)
ARUBA (1)	COSTA RICA (9)	GUAM (4)	KUWAIT (1)	NEW ZEALAND (72)	SAUDI ARABIA (4)	TURKEY (22)
AUSTRALIA (405)	CUBA (1)	GUATEMALA (8)	LUXEMBOURG (3)	NORTHERN IRELAND (4)	SCOTLAND (28)	UNITED STATES (9,912)
AUSTRIA (48)	CZECH REPUBLIC (5)	HONG KONG (80)	MACAO (4)	NORWAY (14)	SERBIA (6)	URUGUAY (3)
BAHAMAS (4)	DENMARK (32)	HUNGARY (20)	MALAYSIA (44)	OMAN (1)	SINGAPORE (54)	VENEZUELA (9)
BELGIUM (23)	EL SALVADOR (3)	ICELAND (1)	MARTINIQUE (1)	PANAMA (11)	SLOVAKIA (5)	VIRGIN ISLANDS (4)
BERMUDA (1)	ENGLAND (474)	INDONESIA (19)	MEXICO (87)	PHILIPPINES (57)	SLOVENIA (1)	WALES (18)
BRAZIL (126)	FINLAND (24)	IRELAND (19)	MONACO (1)	POLAND (12)	SPAIN (68)	
BRUNEI (1)	FRANCE (298)	ISRAEL (1)	MOROCCO (1)	PORTUGAL (5)	SWEDEN (72)	
CANADA (727)	GERMANY (524)	ITALY (20)	NETHERLAND ANTILLES (3)	PUERTO RICO (51)	SWITZERLAND (41)	

Source: McDonald's Corporation.

global company
An organization that attempts to standardize operations worldwide in all functional areas

international company
Either a global or a multinational company

4. **Global company** (GC) is an organization that attempts to standardize operations worldwide in all functional areas.

5. **International company** (IC) refers to both global and multinational companies.

While international business as a discipline is relatively new, international business as a business practice is not, as we shall see in the next section, "History of International Business."

Well before the time of Christ, Phoenician and Greek merchants were sending representatives abroad to sell their goods. In 1600, the British East India Company, a newly formed trading firm, established foreign branches throughout Asia. At about the same time, a number of Dutch companies, which had organized in 1590 to open shipping routes to the East, joined together to form the Dutch East India Company and also opened branch offices in Asia.[4] American colonial traders began operating in a similar fashion in the 1700s.

Early examples of American foreign direct investment are the English plants set up by Colt Fire Arms and Ford* (vulcanized rubber), which were established before the Civil War. Both operations failed, however, after only a few years.

The first successful American venture into foreign production was the Scotch factory built by Singer Sewing Machine in 1868. By 1880, Singer had become a worldwide organization with an outstanding foreign sales organization and several overseas manufacturing plants. Other firms soon followed, and by 1914, at least 37 American companies had production facilities in two or more overseas locations.

Among those firms already established overseas were National Cash Register and Burroughs, with manufacturing plants in Europe; Parke-Davis, with a plant near London (1902); and Ford Motor Company, which had assembly plants or distribution outlets in 14 countries. General Motors and Chrysler followed soon afterward, so that by the 1920s, all three companies had sizable foreign operations. Interestingly, and quite the reverse of today's situation, in the 1920s, *all* cars sold in Japan were made in the United States by Ford and General Motors and sent to Japan in knocked-down kits to be assembled locally. Another early overseas investor was General Electric, which, by 1919, had plants in Europe, Latin America, and Asia.[5] Other well-known American firms in Europe at that time were Alcoa, American Tobacco, Armour, Coca-Cola, Eastman Kodak, Gillette, Quaker Oats, Western Electric, and Westinghouse.

Interestingly, American business moving overseas caused similar consternation among Europeans that Japanese investments in the United States cause today. One author wrote, "The invasion goes on unceasingly and without noise or show in 500 industries at once. From shaving soap to electric motors, and from shirtwaists to telephones, the American is clearing the field."[6]

Although American firms were by far the largest foreign investors, European companies were also moving overseas. Friedrich Bayer purchased an interest in a New York plant in 1865, two years after setting up his plant in Germany. Then, because of high import duties in his overseas markets, he proceeded to establish plants in Russia (1876), France (1882), and Belgium (1908).[7] Bayer, now one of the three largest chemical companies in the world ($25 billion in sales), has operations in 70 countries. Its annual sales in the United States alone are over $4 billion. Interestingly, Bayer, after many years of trying, was able recently to buy the over-the-counter drug division of Eastman Kodak, present manufacturer and owner of the brand name Bayer aspirin.[8]

Although international firms existed well before World War I, they have only recently become the object of much discussion and investigation, especially concerning the increasing globalization of their production and markets. What are the reasons for globalization?

HISTORY OF INTERNATIONAL BUSINESS

---

*This Ford was no relation to Henry Ford.

Globalization Forces

Three interrelated forces are leading international firms to the globalization of their production and marketing:[9]

1. Advances in computer and communications technology permit an increased flow of ideas and information across borders, enabling customers to learn about foreign goods. Cable systems in Europe and Asia, for example, allow an advertiser to reach numerous countries simultaneously, thus creating a regional and sometimes global demand. Global communications networks enable manufacturing personnel to coordinate production and design functions worldwide so that plants in many parts of the world may be working on the same product.

2. The progressive reduction of barriers to investment and trade by most governments are hastening the opening of new markets by international firms that are both exporting to them and building production facilities for local manufacture.

3. There is a trend toward the unification and socialization of the global community. Preferential trading arrangements, such as the North American Free Trade Agreement and the European Union, that group several nations into a single market have presented firms with significant marketing opportunities. Many have moved swiftly to enter, either through exporting or by producing in the area.

The impact of this rush to globalization had been an explosive growth in international business.

Explosive Growth

There has been an explosive growth in both the size and the number of U.S. and foreign international concerns. One variable commonly used to measure where and how fast internationalization is taking place is the increase in total foreign direct investment (FDI).* For example, the world stock of FDI is estimated to have risen from $105 billion in 1967 to $1,932 billion in 1992, an eighteenfold increase in just 25 years.[10] During the same period, U.S. FDI based on historical cost went from $59 billion to $488 billion—8.3 times the 1967 amount. Despite this sizable increase, international firms in Japan and Europe have, since the beginning of the 1980s, increased their share of the total foreign investment.

Consider this. In 1980, the stock of U.S. FDI amounted to 43.5 percent of all foreign direct investment, yet by 1992, it was only 25.3 percent. During the same period, however, the Japanese percentage quadrupled (3.3 percent to 13.0 percent) and European foreign investment went from 40.7 percent to 43.7 percent (see Figure 1–2).[11] Table 1–2 reveals that a great part of this foreign investment was made in the United States.

As you can see, international firms from all these nations have made major investments in the United States. Note the especially high percentages of the total FDI coming from the United Kingdom, Japan, Germany, and France. Although American international companies were not withdrawing from foreign markets during this period, they seem to have focused more on the U.S. domestic market, in great part because the expansion of Japanese and European firms in the United States increased domestic competition.

Foreign direct investment is sufficient investment to obtain significant management control. In the United States, 10 percent of the stockholders' equity is sufficient; in other countries, it is not considered a direct investment until a share of 20 or 25 percent is reached.

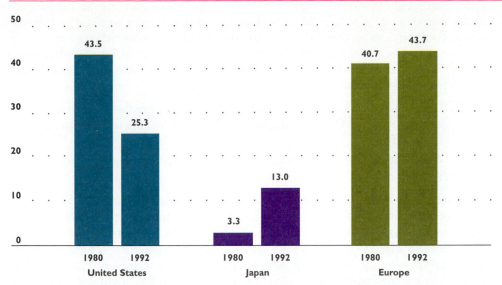

FIGURE 1–2
Country FDI as percentage of global FDI, 1980 versus 1992

We also have estimates of the importance of the globals and multinationals in the world economy. The Division on Transnational Corporations and Investment, a specialized agency of the United Nations, estimates there are at least 37,000 international firms in the world. They control over 206,000 foreign affiliates, which generated sales of over $4.8 trillion in 1991. Moreover, the 600 largest multinational or global firms account for between one-fifth and one-fourth of the value added in the production of *all the goods in the world's market economies.*[12] In Japan, just nine general trading companies account for 34.2 and 55.6 percent of all the exports and imports, respectively.[13]

As a result of this expansion, the foreign company's subsidiaries have become increasingly important in the industrial and economic life of many nations, developed and developing. This situation is in sharp contrast to the one that existed when the dominant economic interests were in the hands of local citizens. The expanding importance of foreign-owned firms in local economies came to be viewed by a number of governments as a threat to their autonomy. However, beginning in the 1980s, there has been a marked liberalization of government policies and attitudes toward foreign investment in both developed and developing nations. Leaders of these governments

	Global FDI		Increase	FDI in U.S.		Increase	ΔFDI in U.S.
	1980	1992	1992–1980	1980	1992	1992–1980	ΔGlobal FDI
	(1)		(2)	(3)		(4)	(4)/(2)
Japan	$ 16.6	$250.4	$233.8	$ 4.2	$96.7	$92.5	39.6%
United Kingdom	80.7	221.2	140.5	12.2	94.7	82.5	58.7
Germany	43.1	178.7	135.6	5.4	29.2	23.8	17.6
Netherlands	42.1	131.7	89.6	16.9	61.3	44.4	49.6
France	23.6	160.9	137.3	3.0	23.2	20.2	14.7
Canada	22.6	87.5	64.9	10.1	39.0	28.9	44.5
Others	277.9	901.9	624.0	16.6	78.8	62.2	10.0

TABLE 1–2
U.S. FDI increase as a percentage of global FDI increase, 1980 versus 1992 ($ billion)

Note: Δ = increase.

Sources: Division on Transnational Corporations and Investment, *World Investment Report 1994* (New York: United Nations, 1994), p. 419; and *Survey of Current Business*, August 1982, p. 36, August 1992, p. 95, and May 1994, p. 55.

know that local firms must obtain modern commercial technology in the form of direct investment, purchase of capital goods, and the right to use the international company's expertise if they are to be competitive in world markets.*

Despite this change in attitude, there are still critics of large global firms who cite such statistics as the following to "prove" that host governments are powerless before them:

1. Only 21 nations have gross national products greater than the total annual sales of General Motors, the world's largest international company.
2. GM's total sales surpass the *sum* of the gross national products of 70 nations.[14]

As Table 1–3 illustrates, these statements are certainly true. In fact, when nations and industrial firms are ranked by gross national product and total sales, respectively, 56 of the first 100 on the list are industrial firms. While a nation's GNP and a company's sales are not comparable, they are indicators of potential power, as you shall see in Chapter 10, Political Forces. Also, regardless of the parent firm's size, each subsidiary is a local company that must comply with the laws in the country where it is located. If not, it can be subject to legal action or even government seizure. From 1970 to 1975, there were 336 acts of seizure, but a decade later, this number had dropped to just 15. Now most differences are settled by arbitration.[†15]

Recent Developments

Lessening of American Dominance. You may have noticed in Table 1–3 that there are as many European international firms as there are American. It was not always this way. Until the 1960s, American internationals clearly dominated world business, but then the situation began to change. European firms started challenging American multinationals, first in their home countries and then in third-country markets dominated by U.S. companies. By the 1970s, large European and Japanese businesses were expanding their overseas production facilities faster than were the American multinationals. To realize the change in the relative importance of American, European, and Japanese multinationals, it is helpful to compare *Fortune*'s lists of the top 100 industrial firms in the world ranked according to sales for 1980 and 1993:[16]

1980		1993	
45	United States	32	United States
42	Western Europe	38	Western Europe
8	Japan	23	Japan
1	South Korea	4	South Korea
1	Brazil	1	Brazil
1	Mexico	1	Mexico
1	Venezuela	1	Venezuela
1	Canada		

Interestingly, *Fortune* explains that the extremely strong yen as compared to the dollar was responsible for putting 10 of the 23 Japanese firms on the 1993 list. The strong yen also changed the sales declines of 70 percent of the Japanese firms on the list to gains when they were expressed in dollars. The magazine used a rate of 124.8 yen to the dollar in 1992; in 1993, the rate was only 107.9.[17]

---

*Granting the right to use a firm's expertise for a fee is called *licensing*. See Chapter 2 for more details.

†These and related subjects are discussed in Chapters 10 and 11.

Ranking	Nation or Firm	GNP or Total Sales for 1993 ($ billion)
21.	Denmark	133.9
22.	*General Motors*	132.8
23.	Iran	130.9
24.	Saudi Arabia	126.4
25.	Indonesia	122.8
26.	Finland	116.3
27.	Turkey	114.2
28.	Norway	110.5
29.	Thailand	106.6
30.	South Africa	106.0
31.	*Exxon*	103.5
32.	*Ford*	100.8
33.	*Royal Dutch Shell*	98.9
34.	*Hong Kong*	89.3
35.	*Toyota Motor*	79.1
36.	Poland	75.3
37.	Greece	75.1
38.	Portugal	73.3
39.	Israel	67.7
40.	*IRI (Italy)*	67.5
41.	*IBM*	65.1
42.	*Daimler-Benz*	63.3
43.	*General Electric*	62.2
44.	*Hitachi*	61.5
45.	*British Petroleum*	59.2
46.	Venezuela	58.9
47.	*Matushita Electrical*	57.5
48.	*Mobil*	57.4
49.	*Volkswagen*	56.7
50.	Malaysia	51.9
51.	*Siemens*	51.4
52.	*Nissan*	50.2
53.	*Philip Morris*	50.2
54.	*Samsung*	49.6
55.	Philippines	49.5
56.	Pakistan	49.4
57.	Algeria	48.3
58.	*Fiat*	47.9
59.	Colombia	44.6
60.	Singapore	44.3
61.	*Unilever*	44.0
62.	Ireland	42.8
63.	New Zealand	41.2
64	*ENI (Italy)*	40.4
65.	*Elf Aquitane* (France)	39.7
66.	*Nestlé*	39.1
67.	*Chevron*	38.5
68.	*Toshiba*	37.5
69.	*Du Pont*	37.4
70.	Chile	37.1
71.	*Texaco*	37.1
72.	United Arab Emirates	37.1
73.	Egypt	34.5
74.	*Chrysler*	36.9

TABLE 1–3

Ranking of international companies and nations according to GNP or total sales

Notes: Does not include nations that do not report GNPs to World Bank.

Country name in italics indicates the firm's nationality.

Sources: *The World Bank Atlas 1994* (Washington, DC: World Bank, 1994), pp. 18–19; and "The World's Largest Corporations," *Fortune*, July 25, 1994, pp. 143–52.

The lists show that although the United States is still the world's preeminent economic power, it has lost some of its superiority. Note that firms from developing nations such as Mexico, Brazil, and Venezuela are among the world's top 100 industrial concerns. We can also compare lists over time of the largest firms in a number of industries to see if there has been a change of leadership in sales volume. Following is an analysis of the automobile industry.

1959	1981	1993
1. General Motors (U.S.)	1. General Motors (U.S.)	1. General Motors (U.S.)
2. Ford (U.S.)	2. Ford (U.S.)	2. Ford (U.S.)
3. Chrysler (U.S.)	3. Fiat (Italy)	3. Toyota (Japan)
4. American Motors (U.S.)	4. Renault (France)	4. Daimler Benz (Germany)
5. Volkswagen (Germany)	5. Volkswagen (Germany)	5. Nissan (Japan)
6. British Motor (U.K.)	6. Daimler Benz (Germany)	6. Volkswagen (Germany)
7. Fiat (Italy)	7. Peugeot (France)	7. Chrysler (U.S.)
8. Daimler-Benz (Germany)	8. Toyota (Japan)	8. Honda (Japan)
9. Renault (France)	9. Nissan (Japan)	9. Fiat (Italy)
10. Simca (France)	10. Mitsubishi (Japan)	10. Renault (France)

A similar analysis of the top 10 firms in six other industries that American firms dominated in 1959 showed that by 1993, they continued to lead in only two of them.[18]

Industry	1959	1993
Aerospace	8 United States	7 United States
	2 European	3 European
Chemicals	7 United States	2 United States
	3 European	6 European
		2 Japanese
Metal products	4 United States	1 United States
	4 European	2 European
	2 Canada	1 Canada
		6 Japanese
Electronics	7 United States	1 United States
	2 European	2 European
		5 Japanese
		2 South Korean
Metal manufacturing	9 United States	0 United States
	1 European	7 European
		3 Japanese
Pharmaceuticals	7 United States	6 United States
	3 European	4 European

Mini-Nationals.   Small and medium-sized firms of a special kind are entering world markets in growing numbers, not just by exporting as many small firms do, but by opening factories, research facilities, and sales offices overseas in the manner of the large multinational and global enterprises. Because not much is known about these firms called *mini-nationals* (also *mini-multinationals, micro-multinationals,* or *mini-globals*), *Business Week* analyzed hundreds of smaller internationally active firms and identified 50 that it considered to be the best. Each is a U.S. manufacturing company that has a minimum of $200 million in sales. At least 20 percent of their sales are international, including both exports from the United States and goods

Tennessee to Japan?

Can a four-employee Tennessee manufacturer successfully sell its products in the fiercely competitive market of Japan?

Quality Control Instruments (QCI) of Oak Ridge, Tennessee, not only can, it is selling there. Japan is the largest of its 26 foreign-country markets. The company, which started six years ago in a one-room warehouse, makes products for the metal-plating and metallurgy industries that have a wide variety of applications, such as the molds for Barbie dolls and instruments for the aircraft and electronic industries. The company now exports one-third of its production. The Japanese business started

with an advertisement in a trade journal that was spotted by executives of Nippon Steel. They arranged to meet with Roger Derby, the QCI president, at a trade show in Philadelphia. The meeting, which lasted three hours, led to regular orders, currently running at about $5,000 a month.

Derby, confident that his products can compete technologically overseas, says the company now needs to emphasize marketing. He has sales agents in Japan, Hong Kong, South Korea, the Philippines, and Taiwan and is looking for more. The company is also exploring the Chinese market. To get ready, Derby is studying Chinese.

---

manufactured overseas. The average total annual sales of one of these firms is $600 million, growing at an average of 22.9 percent annually. International sales amount to 44 percent of total sales. *Business Week* surveyed these companies and found that they had the following characteristics:

1. Products often unique because of their technology, design, or cost.
2. Sharply focused. Their goal is to be first or second globally in a technology niche.
3. Lean operations to save money and speed decision making. Because of relatively open trading regions and newer technologies, they are able to service the global market with a small number of manufacturing locations, resulting in a smaller bureaucracy.
4. Open to ideas and technologies from around the world. Many establish research laboratories in other countries.
5. Using foreigners to head foreign operations and also fill senior positions at headquarters.

These younger, more agile midsize firms are remaking the global corporation for the 1990s and beyond. As Christopher Bartlett, expert on multinational enterprises, says, "The newcomers have the huge advantage of starting fresh. They can develop much more flexible structures."[19]

International business differs from domestic business in that a firm operating across borders must deal with the forces of three kinds of environments—domestic, foreign, and international. In contrast, a firm whose business activities are carried out within the borders of one country needs to be concerned essentially with only the domestic environment. However, no domestic firm is entirely free from foreign or international environmental forces because the possibility of having to face competition from foreign imports or from foreign competitors that set up operations in its own market is always present. Let us first examine these forces and then see how they operate in the three environments.

WHY IS INTERNATIONAL BUSINESS DIFFERENT?

Forces in the Environments

Environment as used here is the sum of all the forces surrounding and influencing the life and development of the firm. The forces themselves can be classified as *external* or *internal*. Furthermore, management has no direct

environment
All the forces surrounding and influencing the life and development of the firm

control over them, though it can exert influences such as lobbying for a change in a law, heavily promoting a new product that requires a change in a cultural attitude, and so on. The external forces are commonly called **uncontrollable forces** and consist of the following:

1. *Competitive*—kinds and numbers of competitors, their locations, and their activities.
2. *Distributive*—national and international agencies available for distributing goods and services.
3. *Economic*—variables (such as GNP, unit labor cost, and personal consumption expenditure) that influence a firm's ability to do business.
4. *Socioeconomic*—characteristics and distribution of the human population.
5. *Financial*—variables such as interest rates, inflation rates, and taxation.
6. *Legal*—the many kinds of foreign and domestic laws by which international firms must operate.
7. *Physical*—elements of nature such as topography, climate, and natural resources.
8. *Political*—elements of nations' political climates such as nationalism, forms of government, and international organizations.
9. *Sociocultural*—elements of culture (such as attitudes, beliefs, and opinions) important to international businesspeople.
10. *Labor*—composition, skills, and attitudes of labor.
11. *Technological*—the technical skills and equipment that affect how resources are converted to products.

The elements over which management does have some command are the internal forces, such as the factors of production (capital, raw material, and people) and the activities of the organization (personnel, finance, production, and marketing). These are the **controllable forces** management must administer in order to adapt to changes in the uncontrollable environmental variables. Look at how one change in the political force—the passage of the North American Free Trade Agreement—is affecting all of the controllable forces of firms worldwide that do business in or with the three member-nations, the United States, Mexico, and Canada. Suddenly these companies must examine their business practices and change those affected by this new law. For example, some American concerns and foreign subsidiaries in the United States are relocating part of their operations to Mexico to exploit the lower wages there. There are European and Asian companies setting up production in one of the member-countries to supply this giant free trade region. By doing this, they will avoid paying import duties on products coming from their home countries.

The Domestic Environment

The **domestic environment** is composed of all the uncontrollable forces originating in the home country that surround and influence the life and development of the firm. Obviously, these are the forces with which managers are most familiar. Being domestic forces does not preclude their affecting foreign operations, however. For example, if the home country is suffering from a shortage of foreign currency, the government may place restrictions on overseas investment to reduce its outflow. As a result, manage-

uncontrollable forces
External forces over which management has no direct control, although it can exert an influence

controllable forces
Internal forces that management administers to adapt to changes in the uncontrollable forces

domestic environment
All the uncontrollable forces originating in the home country that surround and influence the firm's life and development

Charles Gupton/Tony Stone Images

Domestic firms are always facing the possibility of competition from foreign imports.

ments of multinationals find that they cannot expand overseas facilities as they would like to do. In another instance from real life, a labor union striking the home-based plants learned that management was supplying parts from its foreign subsidiaries. The strikers contacted the foreign unions, which pledged not to work overtime to supply what the struck plants could not. The impact of this domestic environmental force was felt overseas as well as at home.

The Foreign Environment

The forces in the **foreign environment** are the same as those in the domestic environment except that they occur in foreign nations.* However, they operate differently for several reasons, including the following:

foreign environment
All the uncontrollable forces originating outside the home country that surround and influence the firm

Different Force Values.   Even though the kinds of forces in the two environments are identical, their values often differ widely, and at times they are completely opposed to each other. A good example of diametrically opposed political force values and the bewilderment they create for multinational managers is the case of Dresser Industries and the Soviet pipeline. When President Reagan extended the American embargo against shipments of equipment for the pipeline to include foreign companies manufacturing equipment under license from U.S. firms, the Dresser home office instructed its French subsidiary to stop work on an order for compressors. Meanwhile, the French government ordered Dresser-France to defy the embargo and begin scheduled deliveries under penalty of both civil and criminal sanctions. As a Dresser's vice president put it, "The order put Dresser between a rock and a hard place."

Foreign has multiple definitions according to the *American Heritage Dictionary,* including (1) originating from the outside—external, (2) originating from a country other than one's own, and (3) conducted or involved with other nations or governments. *Extrinsic* is a synonym. Note that we are not using another definition—unfamiliar or strange. Some writers have this last definition in mind when they state that overseas markets in which the firm does business are not foreign because their managers know them well. However, according to any of the first three definitions, the degree of familiarity has no bearing.

Changes Difficult to Assess.   Another problem with the foreign forces is that they are frequently difficult to assess, especially their legal and political elements. A highly nationalistic law may be passed to appease a section of the population. To all outward appearances, a government may appear to be against foreign investment, yet pragmatic leaders may actually encourage it. A good example is Mexico, which, until 1988, had a law prohibiting foreigners from owning a majority interest in a Mexican company. However, a clause permitted exceptions "if the investment contributes to the welfare of the nation." IBM, Eaton, and others were successful in obtaining permission to establish a wholly owned subsidiary under this clause.

Forces Interrelated.   In the chapters that follow, it will be evident that the forces are often interrelated. This in itself is no novelty, because the same situation confronts the domestic manager. Often different, however, are the types and degrees of interaction that occur. For instance, the combination of high-cost capital and an abundance of unskilled labor in many developing countries may lead to the use of a lower level of technology than would be employed in the more industrialized nations. In other words, given a choice between installing costly, specialized machinery needing few workers or less expensive, general-purpose machinery requiring a larger labor force, management will frequently choose the latter when faced with high interest rates and a large pool of available workers. Another example is the interaction between physical and sociocultural forces. Barriers to the free movement of a nation's people, such as mountain ranges or deserts, help maintain pockets of distinct cultures within a country.

The International Environment

international environment
Interaction between the domestic and foreign environmental forces or between sets of foreign environmental forces

The **international environment** is the interactions (1) between the domestic environmental forces and the foreign environmental forces and (2) between the foreign environmental forces of two countries when an affiliate in one country does business with customers in another. This agrees with the definition of international business—business that involves the crossing of national borders.

For example, personnel at the headquarters of a multinational or global company work in the international environment if they are involved in any way with another nation, whereas those in a foreign subsidiary do not unless they too are engaged in international business through exporting or management of other foreign affiliates. In other words, the sales manager of Goodyear-Chile does *not* work in the international environment if he or she sells tires only in Chile. Should Goodyear-Chile export tires to Bolivia, then the sales manager is affected by forces of both the domestic environment of Chile and the foreign environment of Bolivia and therefore is working in the international environment. International organizations whose actions affect the international environment are also properly part of it. These organizations include (1) worldwide bodies (e.g., World Bank), (2) regional economic groupings of nations (e.g., North American Free Trade Agreement), and (3) organizations bound by industry agreements (e.g., Organization of Petroleum Exporting Countries).

Decision Making More Complex

Those who work in the international environment find that decision making is more complex than it is in a purely domestic environment. Consider managers in the home office who must make decisions affecting subsidiaries in just 10 different countries (many multinationals or globals are in 20 or more countries). They must not only take into account the domestic forces, but they must also evaluate the influence of 10 foreign national environments. Instead of having to consider the effects of a single set of 10 forces, as do their domestic counterparts, they have to contend with 10 sets of 10 forces, *both individually and collectively,* because there may be some interaction.

For example, if management agrees to labor's demands at one foreign subsidiary, chances are it will have to offer a similar settlement at another subsidiary because of the tendency of unions to exchange information across borders. Furthermore, as we shall observe throughout the text, not only are there many sets of forces, but there are also extreme differences among them.

Another common cause of the added complexity of foreign environments is managers' unfamiliarity with other cultures. To make matters worse, they will ascribe to others their own preferences and reactions. Thus, the foreign production manager, facing a backlog of orders, offers the workers extra pay for overtime. When they fail to show up, the manager is perplexed. "Back home, they always want to earn more money." This manager has failed to understand that the workers preferred time off to more money. This unconscious reference to the manager's own cultural values, called **self-reference criterion,** is probably the biggest cause of international business blunders. Successful administrators are careful to examine a problem in terms of the local cultural traits as well as their own.

self-reference criterion
Unconscious reference to one's own cultural values when judging behavioral actions of others in a new and different environment

INTERNATIONAL BUSINESS MODEL

The relationships of the forces in the three environments we have been discussing form the basis for our international business model shown in Figure 1–3. The external or uncontrollable forces in both the domestic and the foreign environments surround the internal forces controlled by management. The domestic environment of the international firm's home country is surrounded by as many sets of foreign environments as there are countries in which the company does business. Solid lines connecting the internal forces at the home office to the internal forces in the foreign affiliates indicate the lines of control. The circles with the broken lines indicate the international environment in which personnel in the headquarters of the international firm work. If, for example, the affiliate in foreign environment A exports to or manages the affiliate in foreign environment B, then its personnel are also working in the international environment, as shown by the straight dashed lines.

We shall be using this model throughout the book. After describing the nature of international business in Section One, we examine the international organizations and the international monetary system in Section Two. In Section Three, we analyze the uncontrollable forces that make up the foreign and domestic environments and illustrate their effect on management functions. Finally, we reverse the procedure in Section Four and deal with the management functions, demonstrating how they are influenced by the uncontrollable forces.

CENTRAL THEME OF THIS BOOK

A solid understanding of the business concepts and techniques employed in the United States and other advanced industrial nations is a requisite for success in international business. However, because transactions take place across national borders, three environments—domestic, foreign, and international—may be involved instead of just one; thus in international business, the international manager has three choices in what to do with a concept or a technique employed in domestic operations: (1) transfer it intact, (2) adapt it to local conditions, or (3) not use it overseas. International managers who have discovered that there are differences in the environmental forces are

FIGURE 1–3
International business model

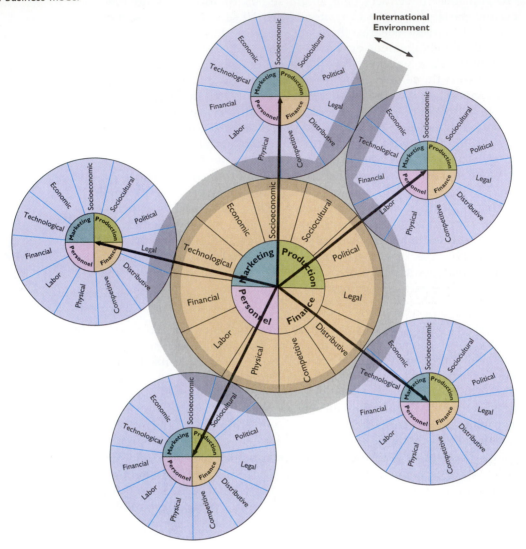

● DOMESTIC ENVIRONMENT
(INCLUDES SOCIOECONOMIC, SOCIOCULTURAL, POLITICAL, LEGAL, DISTRIBUTIVE, COMPETITIVE, PHYSICAL, LABOR, FINANCIAL, TECHNOLOGICAL,
AND ECONOMIC ENVIRONMENTS)

● FOREIGN ENVIRONMENT
(INCLUDES SOCIOECONOMIC, SOCIOCULTURAL, POLITICAL, LEGAL, DISTRIBUTIVE, COMPETITIVE, PHYSICAL, LABOR, FINANCIAL, TECHNOLOGICAL,
AND ECONOMIC ENVIRONMENTS)

better prepared to decide which option to follow. To be sure, no one can be an expert on all these forces for all nations, but just knowing that differences may exist will cause people to "work with their antennas extended." In other words, when they enter international business, they will know they must look out for important variations in many of the forces that they take as given in the domestic environment. It is to the study of the three environments that this text is directed.

SUMMARY

1. **Appreciate the dramatic internationalization of markets.** Global competition is mounting. The huge increase in import penetration, plus the massive amounts of overseas investment, mean that firms of all sizes face competitors from everywhere in the world. This increasing internationalization of business is requiring managers to have a global business perspective gained through experience, education, or both.

2. **Understand the various names given to firms that have substantial operations in more than one country.** Although the definitions vary among users, a *global company* is an organization that attempts to standardize operations worldwide in all functional areas. A *multinational firm,* on the other hand, is an organization with multicountry affiliates, each of which formulates its own business strategy based on perceived market differences. The term *international company* is often used to refer to both global and multinational firms.

3. **Distinguish between firms of the early 1900s and present-day companies.** American and foreign international companies have existed for over a century, but their explosive growth and the increasing globalization of their products and markets are more recent phenomena. The total stock of foreign direct investment, for example, has risen from $105 billion in 1967 to $1,932 billion in 1992. Since the 1980s, Japanese and German firms have increased their share of worldwide foreign

investment, while the U.S. share has fallen from 43.5 percent in 1980 to 25.3 percent in 1992. The United States has become a major recipient of their FDI.

4. **Comprehend why international business differs from domestic business.** International business differs from its domestic counterpart in that it involves three environments—domestic, foreign, and international—instead of one. Although the kinds of forces are the same in the domestic and foreign environments, their values often differ, and changes in the values of foreign forces are at times more difficult to assess. The international environment is defined as the interactions (1) between the domestic environmental forces and the foreign environmental forces and (2) between the foreign environmental forces of two countries when an affiliate in one country does business with customers in another. An international business model helps to explain this relationship.

5. **Describe the three environments—domestic, foreign, international—in which an international company operates.** While international businesspersons must understand business concepts and techniques employed in industrialized nations, they must also know enough about the differences in the environmental forces of the markets in which they operate to be able to decide if a concept or a technique (1) can be transferred to another country as is, (2) must be adapted to local conditions, or (3) cannot be used elsewhere.

KEY WORDS

- multinational company   7
- global company   8
- globalization   6
- international company   8
- environment   15
- uncontrollable forces   16

- controllable forces   16
- domestic environment   16
- foreign environment   17
- international environment   18
- self-reference criterion   19

QUESTIONS

1. What are the differences between international, global, and multinational companies?

2. Give examples to show how an international business manager might manipulate one of

the controllable forces in answer to a change in the uncontrollable forces.

3. A nation whose GNP is smaller than the sales volume of a global firm is in no position to enforce its wishes on the local subsidiary of that firm. True or false? Explain.

4. Discuss the forces that are leading international firms to the globalization of their production and marketing.

5. Business is business, and every firm has to produce and market its goods. Why, then, cannot the managers apply the techniques and concepts they have learned in their own country to other areas of the world?

6. What do you believe makes foreign business activities more complex than purely domestic ones?

7. Discuss some possible conflicts between host governments and foreign-owned companies.

8. Why, in your opinion, do the authors regard the use of the self-reference criterion as "probably the biggest cause of international business blunders?" Can you think of an example?

9. You have decided to take a job after graduation in your hometown. Why should you study international business?

10. Although forces in the foreign environment are the same as those in the domestic environment, they operate differently. Why is this so?

MINICASE 1–1   Key Differences between the Global and the Multinational Corporation

They seem to be similar, but in fact, the concepts of the global corporation and the multinational are dissimilar. The multinational firm sells to several countries, but adjusts its products, manufacturing processes, and business strategies to local conditions. The global firm also sells to several countries, but does so with the same products, same manufacturing processes, and a single business strategy. Management regards the entire world as a single market.

Which of the following characteristics commonly define the global corporation and which are attributes of the multinational corporation as defined in Chapter One?

1. Localized decision making.

2. Home country the major market.

3. Research and design implemented wherever necessary, often in foreign laboratories.

4. Shareholders spread around the world.

5. Trade barriers not a threat to the company's business.

6. Company stock listed on home country stock exchange only.

7. Has no legal nationality and home tax authority.

8. Considerable number of foreign directors on company board of directors.

9. Research conducted principally in home (headquarters) country.

10. Headquarters makes the major decisions, not the overseas subsidiaries.

11. Global image bolstered, not confined, by a strong home-country identity (if it has one).

12. Products designed at headquarters.

13. Decision making is greatly affected by national borders and barriers to trade.

14. Multiple identities and loyalties successfully managed through a fluid chain of command.

15. Less than 50 percent of the company's sales come from overseas.

16. Overseas management staffed and directed chiefly from headquarters with few nonnationals on fast track to upper management.

17. A significant amount of non–home-country nationals on the board of directors.

18. Company stock generally listed on stock exchanges in several countries.

19. Clear, unambiguous chain of command.

20. Global ownership and control at the level of the parent company.

Source: "Globalization Starts with Company's Own View of Itself," *Business International*, June 10, 1991, pp. 197–98; and Yao-Su-Hu, "Global or Stateless Corporations Are National Firms with International Operations," *California Management Review*," Winter 1992, pp. 107–26.

Careers in International Business

Frequently, students ask us how they can get jobs in international business. Traveling, meeting new people with different customs, seeing and living in places they have only heard about—these exciting activities stir the imagination, and students want to partake in the experience.

We agree with them. Living and working overseas is exciting. Between us, we have spent a total of 34 years living and working in countries other than our own, and it has been rewarding. However, with the possible exception of international banking, there are few opportunities for recent graduates to be assigned overseas even when they have the basic business skills and can speak at least one foreign language. Why? They must first learn how their employer does business and become skilled in some functional area of the firm, such as marketing or finance. To rise in the firm, employees then need to acquire experience in various functional areas, not just in one. Furthermore, some of this experience should be international. Remember the discussion at the beginning of this chapter? Make sure that your employer knows you are interested in acquiring international experience. In fact, some firms screen out people who state they do not want an overseas assignment.

If you want immediate employment in international business, how can you get it? You realize, of course, this is not the same as asking how you can get a job working overseas. Why isn't it the same? Because there are many home-based jobs in international business, some of which require occasional international travel. There are also international jobs in the federal government, especially in the Department of State and the Department of Commerce.

Home-Based Jobs in International Business

EMPLOYMENT IN INDUSTRY

Most home-based jobs in international business are connected with exporting. For example, every port city has banks with international departments that work with export financing; far fewer banks are involved in international lending. Here are some of the home-based jobs available in international business:

1. Export companies—office personnel and sales personnel who travel periodically to overseas markets.
2. International departments of banks—staff who handle clients' export financing.
3. Steamship companies—office and sales personnel.
4. International airlines—office and sales personnel.
5. Marine insurance firms—office and sales personnel to service exporters.
6. Container operators (own cargo containers)—office and salespeople.
7. Foreign freight forwarders and customhouse brokers—agents who facilitate export and import shipments.

FIGURE A–1
Coca-Cola job profile

The Coca-Cola Company

Job Profile: International Opportunities

COMPANY | The Coca-Cola Company is the world's largest producer and distributor of syrups and concentrates for soft drinks. Company products include Coca-Cola classic, diet Coke, cherry Coke, Sprite, Fanta, and Minute Maid Orange. Independent research confirmed Coca-Cola as far and away the world's best known and most admired trademark. Coca-Cola products are sold in more than 170 countries around the globe. Our international soft drink business has grown at an average annual rate of 9 percent over the last five years and now accounts for 80 percent of the Coca-Cola Company's operating income.

OPPORTUNITIES | The Coca-Cola Company recruits for interns and trainees for each of our international business units: The European Community, Latin America, Northeast Europe/Africa, and the Pacific. International opportunities typically exist for candidates in the areas of marketing research, brand management, financial analysis, accounting, and auditing.

Key Background And Attributes Required

EDUCATION | First year MBA students are recruited for internship opportunities. Recent MBA graduates are recruited for traineeships.

EXPERIENCE | 2-5 years of marketing, finance, or technical/engineering experience is preferred.

ATTRIBUTES | Nationalists desired for opportunities in their home countries; multicultural and multilingual candidates preferred; proficiency in English required; willingness to work and travel abroad preferred.

Mail Resume To: | The Coca-Cola Company
Attn: Corporate Staffing
P.O. Drawer 1734
Atlanta, GA 30301

An Equal Opportunity Employer

Prolonged Overseas Employment

The entry-level job of staff person in an international area often leads to prolonged overseas employment. The firm may organize the international area as a separate company, a department for each product division, or a regional division. Some of these jobs are essentially training positions, and some companies might have them in all functional areas.

Figure A–1 is an actual job profile from Coca-Cola with which the firm is recruiting for both interns and trainees, many of whom will eventually work overseas. The trainees would first be employed in a headquarters unit responsible for a given geographical area in one of the functional areas listed.

After training, during which the trainees learn about the company and how work in the various functional areas is done, those wishing to work overseas may get the opportunity to do so.

Although some graduates who want to go overseas may be fortunate to find employment with the division or group in the home office that is responsible for overseas business, others may first have to acquire the technical expertise in the domestic operation. If you are in this second group, we recommend that after working for the company for two to three years, you inform both the personnel department and the head of the international group in your functional area that you are interested in working with them. Meanwhile, you can study another foreign language or take a course related to international business. Not only will this improve your knowledge, but it will also demonstrate your continued interest in foreign business to your employer.

Some people have gotten into international business by first acquiring industrial experience in the domestic operations of one company and then obtaining employment in the international operations of another firm in the same industry. Note that Coca-Cola prefers from two to five years of marketing, finance, or engineering experience even for these training jobs.

As you can imagine, there is considerable competition for these jobs, but there are ways to improve your employment possibilities.

Enhancing Your Employment Possibilities

Many employers like to hire people for international business positions who have shown they can live overseas successfully. You're probably thinking that that's not a very helpful piece of advice. But there are ways to acquire this experience *before* getting the employment you are seeking. For example, many American universities have options that permit students to take a substantial part of their programs overseas. An international firm that offers 6- to 12-month overseas internships is another possibility, as is service with the Peace Corps.[1] The student organization, AIESEC, arranges internships with foreign companies. Check to see if your school has a chapter.

Another way to enhance your employment possibilities is to enroll in an international business graduate program. A number of American and Canadian universities have them, and a few include overseas internships in their programs. A way to show a prospective employer that you have had experience living overseas is to study for an MBA in a European management school such as INSEAD (France), IMEDE (Switzerland), the London Business School, or IESE (Barcelona).[2] The tuition is as expensive as that charged by the best American schools, however. Interestingly, some American international firms are considering graduates from European schools for both domestic and overseas jobs. The MBA recruitment coordinator at Sara Lee Corporation, a large consumer products multinational, says, "It makes sense that people running our international businesses have an international background, perspective, and focus."[3]

EMPLOYMENT IN GOVERNMENT

A number of federal government agencies have jobs related to international business. The Department of State and the Department of Commerce offer numerous opportunities.

Department of Commerce

International Trade Administration.   The Commerce Department's International Trade Administration (ITA) is the primary U.S. government agency responsible for assisting exporters. Its activities include export counseling, develop-

Maria Patterson

Maria Patterson graduated in 1989 with a BS in business administration and a major in marketing from the University of Texas Pan American in Edinburg, Texas.

In February 1990, she was hired by Fruit of the Loom as a quality control supervisor for its manufacturing plant in Texas. In November 1990, she was promoted to assistant plant manager for the company's first plant in Mexico.

From the beginning, the most challenging task for the plant manager and Maria was to instill a work ethic in the new employees, most of whom had never before worked indoors in a factory. They also had to fight a common belief among Mexicans that foreign companies come to Mexico only to take advantage of low labor costs without any regard for the environment or the welfare of the Mexican workers. She found that in nonindustrial areas this myth is even stronger than in big cities where foreign companies are common. Her plant is located in a small agricultural town, and it has taken them years to overcome this belief and be accepted as part of the community.

In 1992, Fruit of the Loom began building a plant with a capacity for 1,200 employees, and Maria learned that her company was looking for locations to set up more plants in Mexico. Obviously, the company considered the "Mexican experiment" a success. Maria was promoted to plant manager the same year. In 1993, the company opened a second plant.

Currently, her plant has 1,100 employees and her regular working day lasts 13 to 14 hours. Maria says, "Working in Mexico can be frustrating, challenging, and demanding. However, the beauty of it is that we have proved that you don't have to be born on the other side of the border to succeed. I have witnessed positive changes in many peoples' lives and I have learned that it does not matter what your background is. You can excel as long as you are committed to a goal."

Courtesy Maria Patterson

ment of marketing opportunities, analyses of overseas markets and impediments to market entry, and sales representation through export promotion events. ITA has four units: (1) International Economic Policy, (2) Trade Development, (3) U.S. and Foreign Commercial Service, and (4) Import Administration.

ITA states that the following types of positions are available: international trade specialist, trade specialist, trade assistant, commodity industry specialist, international economist, economist, and import compliance specialist.

The requirements are (1) a college degree (BA, BS, MA, MS, MBA) in international economics, international finance, international business, public administration, international trade, international relations, or business administration; or (2) appropriate work experience, which can qualify you for some positions such as market research, sales promotion, advertising, industrial production operations, or application of investigative skills in determining compliance with or violation of laws, rules, or regulations in the international arena.

Note that there are some occupations for which you may substitute education for experience. If you have a bachelor's degree related to the position, you will generally qualify for a GS-5 level; for a GS-7, with one year of related graduate education; and for a GS-9, with a related master's degree. If you have a bachelor's degree in a field related to the position and a grade point average of 3.0 or higher, you may qualify for a GS-7.

Civil Service Eligibility.   Most of these positions are filled through the competitive process. You may inquire about this procedure by contacting the Federal Job Information Center or the Office of Personnel Management nearest you.

You can call (202) 482-1533 for information concerning current vacancies in the International Trade Administration. On request, the ITA will mail you copies of current vacancy announcements.

Student Volunteer Program.   The ITA utilizes the services of student volunteers to benefit both the student and the agency. A student volunteer can work in any of the ITA areas described at the beginning of this section. The agency is interested in students majoring in economics, business administration, international affairs, and political science. Good writing skills are important. To be eligible, the student must be an American citizen and currently enrolled in an accredited academic degree program. Although you will not receive any remuneration for participating in this program, the experience you get will be extremely valuable for future employment either in industry or with the federal government. For information, call Linda Blanks, Coordinator, Student Volunteer Program at (202) 482-3301.

U.S. and Foreign Commercial Service.   The U.S. and Foreign Commercial (U.S. & F.C.) Service is another area of the Department of Commerce that places people in overseas posts. It operates 47 district offices and 22 branch offices in the United States as well as 128 posts in 67 countries around the world. In these locations, U.S.&F.C. personnel advise U.S. firms on export markets and the implementation of export strategies. They also carry out trade promotion activities, do market research, and provide representation to foreign governments on behalf of American companies. You can contact the personnel unit of the Office of Foreign Service at this address: Personnel Unit, 14th & Constitution Ave., N.W., Room 3813-HCHB, Washington, DC 20230, Telephone: (202) 482-4701.

Other Federal Government Agencies

Other government agencies offer international job opportunities. You can contact the Department of Commerce, the Central Intelligence Agency, and the U.S. Information Agency, for example. There is the U.S. Office of Personnel Management with 16 offices outside of Washington, DC, that you can call or visit. If you do not know their locations, you may call the Office of Affirmative Recruiting and Employment 24 hours daily at (202) 606-0023. Or you can talk with information specialists during business hours (8:00 AM–4:00 PM Eastern Standard Time) and also request forms 24 hours a day at (202) 606-2700. In addition, there is the Federal College Hotline, 1-(900)-990-9200, open 24 hours per day, seven days per week. This, however, costs 40 cents per minute.

International Trade and Foreign Investment

Exporting isn't always possible . . . *Usually our approach has been to begin with direct export of goods and services. With the EC, we began with direct investment. EC restrictions are very efficient at controlling trade.*

Kim Song Whan, international finance director, Lucky-Goldstar One of the top five Korean conglomerates (over $25 billion annual sales)

CONCEPT PREVIEWS

After reading this chapter, you should be able to:

1. **appreciate** the magnitude of international trade and how it has grown

2. **identify** the direction of trade, or who trades with whom

3. **recognize** the value of analyzing trade statistics

4. **explain** the size, growth, and direction of U.S. foreign direct investment

5. **identify** who invests and how much is invested in the United States

6. **understand** the reasons for entering foreign markets

7. **recognize** the weaknesses in using GNP per capita as a basis for comparing economies

8. **understand** the international market entry methods

9. **explain** the many forms of strategic alliances

International Firms Invest Overseas, but They Also Export

Although the media scarcely mention it, the United States has been in an export boom for some time. Since 1986, total exports have been growing four times as fast as the gross domestic product—9 percent annually when adjusted for inflation. Are small firms, large firms, or both kinds responsible for this growth? • Many believe that small and medium-sized firms, because they lack the financial and human resources, service their foreign markets by exporting rather than manufacturing in them and that large international companies do just the opposite. However, the latest annual study by *Fortune* shows that there are at least 50 Fortune 500 concerns whose annual exports range from $14.9 billion to a minimum of $750 million. Of these 50 companies, 33 also have foreign sales (excluding exports) ranging from $76 billion to $2 billion. The percentage of foreign sales to total sales varied from 77.3 percent for Exxon to 13.2 percent for Chrysler (see Table 2–1). Many large international corporations are marketing to as many as 100 different countries, but none can manufacture in all these markets. The foreign investment is too great and many markets are too small to support local manufacturing. They must be served by exports. • To see the importance of international trade and foreign investment for these companies, examine the last column, which shows the percentage of export sales and foreign sales to their total sales. Intel, the computer chip maker, depends on them for 88.6 percent of its sales, and 19 of the 33 companies (58 percent) derive more than 50 percent of their sales from international business. Without it, many of them could not remain in business.

Sources: "Strategies for the New Export Boom," *Fortune*, August 22, 1994, pp. 124–30; and "Getting the Welcome Carpet," *Forbes*, July 18, 1994, pp. 276–79.

TABLE 2–1 Exports and foreign sales of top U.S. exporters ($ billions)

Company	U.S. Exports	Rank in Fortune 50	Foreign Sales	Rank in Forbes 100	Total Sales	Rank in Fortune 500	Exports Total Sales	Foreign Sales Total Sales	Exports + Foreign Sales Total Sales
General Motors	$14.91	1	$38.65	2	$133.62	1	11.2%	28.9%	40.1%
Ford	9.48	3	32.86	5	108.52	2	8.7	30.3	39.0
General Electric	8.50	4	10.04	14	60.82	5	14.1	16.6	30.7
Chrysler	8.40	5	5.75	27	43.60	8	19.3	13.2	32.5
IBM	7.30	6	37.01	4	62.72	4	11.6	59.0	70.6
Motorola	4.99	7	7.45	21	16.96	23	29.4	43.9	73.3
Hewlett-Packard	4.74	8	10.97	12	20.32	19	23.3	54.0	77.3
Philip Morris	4.11	9	15.32	11	50.62	7	8.1	30.3	38.4
Caterpillar	3.74	10	2.30	85	11.62	41	32.2	19.8	52.0
United Technologies	3.50	11	8.15	19	20.74	18	16.9	39.3	56.2
Du Pont	3.50	12	16.76	8	32.62	10	10.7	51.4	62.1
Intel	3.41	13	4.37	40	8.78	56	38.8	49.8	88.6
Archer Daniels Midland	2.90	15	2.55	76	9.81	48	29.6	26.0	55.6
Eastman Kodak	2.24	16	7.98	20	20.06	20	11.2	39.8	50.9
Compaq Computer	1.92	18	3.52	55	7.19	76	26.7	49.0	75.7
Digital Equipment	1.80	19	9.15	17	14.37	29	12.5	63.7	76.2
Allied Signal	1.70	21	2.61	72	11.83	38	14.4	22.1	36.4
Minnesota Mining & Manufacturing	1.49	23	6.89	24	14.02	31	10.6	49.1	59.8
Dow Chemical	1.44	25	8.78	18	18.06	21	8.0	48.6	56.6
Unisys	1.34	28	3.67	50	7.74	71	17.3	47.4	64.7
Sun Microsystems	1.27	29	1.99	97	4.31	120	29.5	46.2	75.6
Xerox	1.10	31	9.24	16	14.98	26	7.3	61.7	69.0
International Paper	1.10	32	2.86	16	13.69	33	8.0	20.9	28.9
Abbott Laboratories	1.01	35	3.06	63	8.41	59	12.0	36.4	48.4
Merck	1.00	36	4.58	38	10.50	46	9.5	43.6	53.1
Deere	0.96	37	2.12	91	7.69	72	12.5	27.6	40.1
Monsanto	0.93	38	2.74	70	7.90	70	11.8	34.7	46.5
Bristol-Myers Squibb	0.92	39	4.69	36	11.41	44	8.1	41.1	49.2
Alcoa	0.90	42	3.78	49	9.06	54	9.9	41.7	51.7
RJR Nabisco	0.88	44	4.20	43	15.10	25	5.8	27.8	33.6
Honeywell	0.77	48	2.07	93	5.96	89	12.9	34.7	47.7
Tenneco	0.75	49	3.37	61	13.26	34	5.7	25.4	31.1
Exxon	0.74	50	75.64	1	97.83	3	0.8	77.3	78.1

Note: Because of rounding, values in the last column do not always equal the sum of the values of the next two columns to the left.
Forbes defines foreign sales as sales from foreign production and excludes exports and intercompany sales.

Sources: Fortune 50—"Top 50 U.S. Industrial Exporters," *Fortune*, August 22, 1994, p. 132. Forbes 100—"The 100 Largest U.S. Multinationals," *Forbes*, July 18, 1994, pp. 276–79. Fortune 500—"Fortune 500 Largest Industrial Corporations," *Fortune* April 18, 1994, pp. 220–44.

The opening section of this chapter illustrates that both means of supplying overseas markets—*exporting* to and *production* in those markets—are essential to most major U.S. corporations. Moreover, these two international business activities are not confined to manufacturing concerns. Of the Forbes 100 largest multinationals, 24 are service companies in banking, finance, construction, insurance, entertainment, transportation, and retailing. But

smaller firms also have operations overseas. According to the *World Investment Report 1993*, small and medium-sized international firms comprise 28.3
percent of the total 3,000 U.S. international corporations.*[1]

In this chapter, we shall examine two topics directly related to exporting
and production in foreign countries: (1) *international trade*, which includes
exports and imports, and (2) *foreign direct investment*, which internationals
must make to establish and expand their overseas operations.[2] Later, in the
chapters on production and importing, we shall discuss the third activity of
international business—**foreign sourcing**, the overseas procurement of raw
materials, components, and products.

foreign sourcing
*The overseas procurement of
raw materials, components,
and products*

Volume of Trade

**INTERNATIONAL
TRADE**

In 1990, a milestone was reached when the volume of international trade in
goods and services measured in current dollars surpassed $4 trillion. Yet, only
three years later, it was approaching $5 trillion.[3] Of this, exports of merchan-
dise were $3.75 trillion, 12 times what they were just 23 years earlier (see
Table 2–2). The dollar value of total world exports in 1993 was greater than
the gross national product of every nation in the world except the United
States. One-fourth of everything grown or made in the world is now exported,
another measure of the significance of international trade.

TABLE 2–2
World trade in merchandise exports (FOB values; in billions of current U.S. dollars)

	1970	1980	1990	1992	1993	Average Annual Percentage Increase
Total world exports	$314	$2,001	$3,392	$3,686	$3,751	11.4%
Developed countries	225	1,269	2,441	2,669	2,664	11.3
Germany[a]	35	193	398	385	368	10.8
United States	43	217	394	425	439	10.6
Japan	19	130	287	340	358	13.6
France	18	111	210	185	206	11.2
Great Britain	19	110	186	157	180	10.3
Italy	13	78	169	159	153	11.3
Developing countries[b]	56	587	779	927	1,006	13.4
EU	88[c]	690[d]	1,342[e]	1,445[e]	1,410[e]	12.8
EFTA	51[f]	112[g]	225	228	216	6.5
LAIA	13	80	113	116	125	10.3

Notes: EU = European Union.
EFTA = European Free Trade Association.
LAIA = Latin American Integration Association (formerly LAFTA).
[a]Includes exports to East Germany before reunification.
[b]Defined by the World Bank as low- and middle-level income nations as indicated by GNP/capita.
[c]Original six members only (Belgium, Luxembourg, France, West Germany, Italy, and the Netherlands).
[d]Includes original six plus Denmark, Ireland, and Great Britain.
[e]Includes Greece, Spain, and Portugal.
[f]Includes Finland as associate member with the original seven states—Austria, Denmark, Norway, Portugal, Sweden, Great Britain, and Switzerland.
[g]Includes Iceland and excludes Great Britain and Denmark.

Sources: *Monthly Bulletin of Statistics*, June 1994, pp. 256–59; July 1994, pp. 98–101; and various earlier issues.

---

*The United Nations defines small and medium-sized international firms for this study as
nonbank parents of nonbank affiliates with *affiliate* assets, sales, or income greater than $3
million with fewer than 500 employees in the parent firm.

FIGURE 2–1 1993/1970 Export ratios based on current dollars and quantum indexes

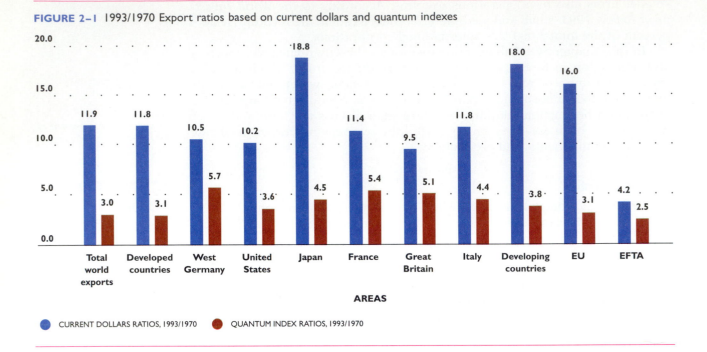

● CURRENT DOLLARS RATIOS, 1993/1970   ● QUANTUM INDEX RATIOS, 1993/1970

True, inflation was responsible for a large part of this trade increase, but using a quantum index that eliminates the effects of inflation from the data, we see that the volume of world trade in 1993 was triple what it was in 1970 (4.9 percent annual increase). Figure 2–1 compares the increase in exports measured in current dollars, including the effects of inflation, with volume increases measured by quantum indexes that eliminate the effects of inflation for the entries in Table 2–2.

How even has this growth been? Have some nations fared better than others? Although there are some differences, the exports of most of the major exporting nations have increased at about the same rate as the world average. However, Japan, the European Union (EU), and the developing nations as a whole did surpass the world rate. Note that much of the EU's increase has come from the admission of six new members, and the relatively slow growth rate of the European Free Trade Agreement (EFTA) is the result of losing Denmark, Great Britain, and Portugal to the EU.

Significance to Business. The tripling of world exports in only 23 years indicates that opportunities to export continue to grow, but the export growth of individual nations also signifies increasing competition from imports in domestic markets. Figure 2–2 shows some of the American industries in which this has occurred. For example, U.S. exports of computers and peripherals increased by $2.1 billion from 1993 to 1994, but imports increased by $3.9 billion. In other words, even though the export volume of these products increased from 1993 to 1994, so did the deficit in this account. Nevertheless, the aerospace and aircraft industries continue to export far more than they import.

Direction of Trade

What are the destinations of these nearly $5 trillion in exports? If you never have examined trade flows, you may think that international trade consists mainly of manufactured goods exported by the industrialized nations to the

FIGURE 2–2 Exports and imports of selected products, 1993 versus 1994 ($ billions)

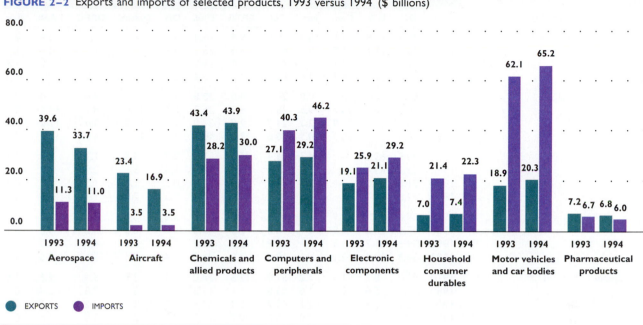

developing nations in return for raw materials. However, Table 2–3 shows that this is only partially correct. More than half of the exports from developing nations do go to developed countries, but nearly three-fourths of the latter's exports, with two exceptions, go to other industrialized nations, not to developing countries.

The Two Exceptions—Japan and the United States.   One reason Japan sells more to developing nations than most developed nations do is that it has had an extensive distribution system in these markets since the early 1900s. Because the country has no local sources of raw materials, it has used general trading companies (*sogo-shosha* in Japanese) to import much of the raw materials and components necessary for Japanese industry. The trading companies' offices in developing nations where these materials are obtained also market Japanese manufactured products to those nations. Moreover, when other industrialized nations have imposed import restrictions on Japanese exports to protect their home industries, the Japanese trading companies have expanded their efforts to sell to developing nations.[4] Table 2–3 shows that their efforts have succeeded.

The United States also exported a smaller proportion to other developed countries (DCs) and more to the developing nations than did developed countries generally, but for somewhat different reasons than Japan. American firms have significantly more subsidiaries in developing nations than Japanese companies do; these subsidiaries are captive customers for their American owners. In addition, some buyers in Southeast Asian countries, remembering that Japan was an aggressor nation, prefer to buy from American firms. Notice, also, the high percentage of American exports that go to Latin America. The United States exports to Latin America are 2.3 times the dollar value of what all the Latin American nations export to each other.[5] As a percentage of total exports, the United States exports are 3.4 times the percentage of all developed nations (17.1 percent versus 5.1 percent).

TABLE 2–3 Direction of trade for selected regions and countries (Percentage of region's or country's total merchandise exports to regions or country in columns)

Exports from	Year	DC	U.S.	Can.	Jap.	EU	EFTA	Dev.	DA	D. Am.	OPEC	LAIA	Aus.
Developed countries (DC)	1970	76.9	12.8	5.1	6.9	39.5	9.4	18.4	4.1	6.2	3.4%	4.4	2.0
	1980	70.8	19.1	4.0	9.9	43.1	8.4	25.1	5.2	6.1	7.9	4.8	1.4
	1990	71.1	19.5	4.5	8.2	46.2	7.9	19.5	2.4	3.9	3.3	2.9	1.8
	1993	71.0	21.4	4.7	7.6	42.2	7.1	23.4	2.2	5.1	3.8	3.9	1.3
United States (U.S.)	1970	69.5	—	20.7	10.8	26.6	4.0	28.8	2.3	15.2	4.8	11.4	2.6
	1980	59.5	—	15.7	9.5	26.7	3.3	36.2	2.1	17.6	8.1	14.6	2.1
	1990	64.7	—	20.9	12.3	24.8	2.8	34.0	1.6	14.0	3.6	11.2	2.5
	1993	58.4	—	20.9	10.5	20.8	2.7	40.3	1.6	17.1	4.6	14.2	2.1
Canada (Can.)	1970	90.9	65.4	—	4.7	16.4	1.8	7.4	0.7	4.3	1.1	2.3	1.5
	1980	85.1	63.4	—	5.7	13.2	1.4	11.7	1.4	5.1	2.9	3.7	1.0
	1990	91.1	75.0	—	5.5	8.1	1.5	8.0	0.7	1.8	1.3	1.3	0.7
	1993	92.6	80.7	—	4.5	5.7	1.0	7.0	0.5	2.0	1.1	1.6	0.5
Japan (Jap.)	1970	54.6	31.1	2.9	—	11.2	3.0	39.2	5.6	5.8	5.1	3.5	3.6
	1980	47.5	24.5	1.9	—	14.0	2.5	49.8	4.6	6.6	14.2	4.6	3.1
	1990	59.3	31.7	2.3	—	18.8	2.9	39.5	1.3	3.4	4.7	1.9	2.8
	1993	54.8	28.4	2.1	—	18.5	2.5	44.9	1.4	4.4	5.6	2.6	2.4
European Union (EU)**	1970	81.0	8.2	1.3	1.2	51.0	12.5	14.0	4.9	3.9	3.4	2.6	1.6
	1980	76.5	5.6	0.7	1.0	55.8	11.1	19.2	6.6	3.2	7.8	2.4	0.8
	1990	83.1	7.1	0.9	2.1	60.7	10.3	13.3	3.2	1.9	3.2	1.3	0.8
	1993	79.8	7.2	0.7	2.0	58.0	9.7	15.5	2.9	2.6	3.5	1.8	0.7
European Free Trade Association (EFTA)†	1970	82.2	6.6	1.3	1.3	49.4	18.6	10.7	3.5	3.6	1.8	2.9	1.0
	1980	78.4	4.8	0.7	1.4	54.7	14.7	14.9	3.5	2.9	5.2	2.2	0.7
	1990	83.8	6.8	1.2	2.6	57.9	13.4	11.2	1.4	1.4	2.4	1.3	0.9
	1993	80.7	7.2	1.1	2.9	56.8	11.3	13.5	1.4	2.1	2.6	1.5	0.9
Developing countries (Dev.)	1970	72.3	18.4	1.8	10.8	33.9	3.0	19.8	2.8	6.7	1.9	3.1	1.4
	1980	68.4	19.8	1.2	14.0	29.4	2.3	26.5	2.6	7.6	3.9	3.8	1.2
	1990	60.5	21.3	1.3	12.4	22.0	2.0	33.1	2.5	3.7	3.7	2.2	1.3
	1993	56.8	22.1	1.2	9.9	20.2	1.6	40.6	2.0	5.2	4.4	3.6	1.3
Developing Africa (DA)	1970	81.2	6.7	0.7	4.0	61.2	4.3	10.7	5.6	2.0	1.2	0.6	6.5
	1980	82.9	26.1	0.2	2.1	46.2	2.5	13.7	3.1	6.4	1.1	1.6	2.6
	1990	82.8	18.4	1.1	2.2	58.9	1.4	13.2	5.9	1.6	2.4	0.7	4.3
	1993	82.6	18.0	0.3	2.5	58.6	1.8	15.0	7.6	1.5	2.5	1.3	
Developing America (D. Am.)	1970	74.2	32.4	3.4	5.4	26.3	3.4	19.1	0.7	17.3	0.9	7.7	0.2
	1980	64.3	32.2	2.6	4.2	22.2	1.9	27.5	2.2	21.3	3.3	10.2	0.2
	1990	62.8	32.6	1.2	5.3	21.0	1.6	21.4	1.0	13.6	3.0	8.9	0.5
	1993	66.0	36.4	1.6	4.7	20.7	1.6	32.5	1.3	22.5	0.9	15.7	0.3
Latin American Integration Association (LAIA)	1970	76.5	30.0	3.4	5.7	30.2	3.3	20.8	0.6	19.0	1.0	10.1	0.1
	1980	65.2	29.4	3.1	5.2	24.1	2.0	29.6	2.2	23.1	3.6	13.8	0.2
	1990	63.3	32.2	1.0	6.0	21.7	1.3	22.2	1.4	13.8	4.6	16.3	0.5
	1993	67.1	37.6	1.5	5.2	20.8	1.1	31.2	1.3	22.3	3.8	17.4	0.3
Organization of Petroleum Exporting Countries (OPEC)‡	1970	75.3	9.7	2.5	13.1	43.4	2.0	19.3	1.5	9.1	0.7	0.7	1.3
	1980	75.3	18.4	1.5	17.3	34.6	2.6	22.8	1.4	8.4	1.3	1.3	1.0
	1990	63.9	14.1	0.9	19.4	27.1	1.6	25.4	3.5	2.8	2.7	2.7	0.8
	1993	66.4	19.0	0.6	18.3	26.5	1.2	31.8	2.0	4.6	5.7	5.7	1.1
Australia and New Zealand (Aus.)	1970	76.9	13.8	3.0	23.9	27.1	0.7	17.8	1.5	1.4	1.8	0.8	—
	1980	58.2	10.5	2.0	22.7	15.6	0.6	31.1	2.3	1.3	6.8	1.0	—
	1990	61.8	11.5	1.6	24.9	14.3	2.2	35.0	1.3	1.5	5.6	1.3	—
	1993	55.7	8.7	1.8	22.9	12.5	1.1	41.8	1.0	1.7	8.3	1.5	—

Note: The European Union, European Free Trade Association, and the Latin American Integration Association are three different forms of regional trading groups. The member-nations in each one of them have reduced or eliminated their import duties on goods and services from the other members.
*1980 data include Denmark, Great Britain, and Ireland. Greece, Spain, and Portugal are included in 1990 data.
†Excludes Denmark and Great Britain and includes Iceland in 1980.
‡OPEC includes Algeria, Ecuador, Gabon, Indonesia, Iran, Iraq, Kuwait, Libya, Nigeria, Qatar, Saudi Arabia, United Arab Emirates, and Venezuela.

Sources: *Monthly Bulletin of Statistics* (New York: United Nations, June 1994), pp. 256–60; June 1993, pp. 256–60; and *Statistical Yearbook, 1969* (New York: United Nations), pp. 376–83.

The Changing Direction of Trade.   The percentages in Table 2–3 also demonstrate how the direction of trade is changing. The percentage of total exports of all the categories of developed nations to other developed nations is declining with the exception of Canada's. However, in the column to the right, you see that most of that country's exports to DCs actually go to the United States. This percentage has increased in part as a result of the progressive removal of import duties since the U.S.–Canada Free Trade Agreement went into effect in 1989. Although the percentage of total American exports to Canada did not change during the same period, their dollar value in 1993 was 2.7 times the 1980 value.

Another interesting observation is that the developing nations as a group are selling a smaller percentage of their exports to the DCs (the United States is an exception), but more to each other. This is due in part to their increasing ability to export manufactured goods and the growing intercompany trade among multinationals' subsidiaries. Note too that members of the Latin American Integration Association are selling more to each other.

It also appears that the percentages of Japan and the United States are converging. An example is the narrowing over the years of the percentage differences between both nations' exports to the DCs. The change from 11.2 to 18.5 percent of Japan's exports to the European Union is evidence of its efforts to penetrate this important market. In contrast, the American percentages of total exports to the EU have been dropping and are approaching the Japanese values.

Major Trading Partners

An analysis of the major trading partners of the firm's home country and those of the nations where it has affiliates that export can provide valuable insights to management.

Why Focus on Major Trading Partners?   There are a number of advantages in focusing attention on a nation that is already a sizable purchaser of goods coming from the would-be exporter's country:

1. Business climate in importing nation is relatively favorable.
2. Export and import regulations are not insurmountable.
3. There should be no strong cultural objections to buying that nation's goods.
4. Satisfactory transportation facilities have already been established.
5. Import channel members (merchants, banks, and customs brokers) are experienced in handling import shipments from the exporter's area.
6. Foreign exchange to pay for the exports is available.
7. The government of a trading partner may be applying pressure on importers to buy from countries that are good customers for that nation's exports. We have seen the efforts of the Japanese, Korean, and Taiwanese governments to persuade their citizens to buy more American goods. They have also sent buying missions to the United States.

Major Trading Partners of the United States.   Table 2–4 shows the major trading partners of the United States. The data indicate that the United States, an industrialized nation, generally follows the tendency we found in Table 2–3; that is, developed nations trade with one another. Mexico and Canada are major trading partners in great part because they share a common border with the United States. Freight charges are lower, delivery times are shorter,

TABLE 2–4 Major trading partners of the United States ($ billions in current dollars)

1965		1993		1965		1993	
Imports from	Amount	Imports from	Amount	Exports to	Amount	Exports to	Amount
1. Canada	$4.83	1. Canada	$113.31	1. Canada	$5.64	1. Canada	$101.19
2. Japan	2.41	2. Japan	107.23	2. Japan	2.08	2. Japan	46.68
3. U.K.	1.41	3. Mexico	40.43	3. W. Germany	1.65	3. Mexico	41.48
4. W. Germany	1.34	4. China	31.54	4. U.K.	1.62	4. U.K.	25.66
5. Venezuela	1.02	5. Germany	28.49	5. Mexico	1.11	5. Germany	18.44
6. Mexico	0.64	6. Taiwan	25.10	6. Netherlands	1.09	6. Taiwan	15.34
7. Italy	0.62	7. U.K.	21.49	7. France	0.97	7. S. Korea	14.07
8. France	0.62	8. S. Korea	17.09	8. India	0.93	8. France	13.23
9. Brazil	0.51	9. France	15.22	9. Italy	0.89	9. Netherlands	12.64
10. Bel. & Lux.	0.49	10. Italy	13.20	10. Australia	0.80	10. Singapore	10.83
11. Philippines	0.37	11. Singapore	12.80	11. Bel. & Lux.	0.65	11. Hong Kong	9.84
12. India	0.35	12. Hong Kong	9.56	12. Venezuela	0.63	12. Bel. & Lux.	9.35
13. Hong Kong	0.34	13. Netherlands	8.48	13. Spain	0.47	13. China	8.73
14. Neth. Ant.	0.32	14. Venezuela	8.42	14. S. Africa	0.44	14. Australia	8.11
15. Australia	0.31	15. Brazil	7.48	15. Switzerland	0.37	15. Italy	6.31

Notes: Exports are stated on an f.a.s. (free alongside ship) value basis. Services not included.
Imports are stated on CIF (Cost, Insurance, Freight) value basis. Services not included.
U.K. = United Kingdom
Bel. & Lux. = Belgium and Luxembourg. Their export and import statistics are reported jointly.
Neth. Ant. = Netherlands Antilles.

Source: Department of Commerce, *Survey of Current Business*, June 1994, pp. 102–4.

and contact between buyers and sellers is easier and less expensive. Now that both nations are joined with the United States in the North American Free Trade Agreement, we can be confident that their importance as trading partners will grow.

Note the marked change in the rankings of America's trading partners in just three decades. Not only have the rankings changed, but nations have been added while others have become relatively less important. South Korea, Taiwan, and Singapore are supplying the United States with huge quantities of electronic products and components and other labor-intensive goods, much of which is produced by affiliates of American internationals. By 1993 China had risen to 4th place in exports to the United States ($31.54 billion) although it was only in 13th place as an importer ($8.73 billion).

These same countries appear as importers of American goods as well because (1) their rising levels of living enable their people to afford more imported products, and the countries' export earnings provide the foreign exchange to pay for them; (2) they are purchasing large amounts of capital goods to further their industrial expansion; and (3) their governments, pressured by the American government to lower their trade surpluses with the United States, have sent buying missions to this country to look for products to import.

Utility of These Data

The analysis of foreign trade that we have described would be helpful to anyone just starting to search outside the home market for new business opportunities. The preliminary steps of (1) studying the general growth and direction of trade (Table 2–3) and (2) analyzing major trading partners (Table 2–4) would provide an idea of where the trading activity is. What kinds of products do these countries import from the United States? The Department of Commerce annual publication, *U.S. Foreign Trade Highlights*, reports the top 40 U.S. exports to and imports from 90 countries. Another Department of Commerce publication, the *FT 925*, details the quantities, dollar values, and destinations of specific products. We shall discuss this in greater detail in Chapter 14.

The topic we have been examining, international trade, exists because firms export. As you know, however, exporting is only one aspect of international business. Another, overseas production, requires foreign investment, the topic of the next section.

Foreign investment can be divided into two components: **portfolio investment,** which is the purchase of stocks and bonds solely for the purpose of obtaining a return on the funds invested, and **direct investment,** by which the investors participate in the management of the firm in addition to receiving a return on their money.

Portfolio Investment

Although portfolio investors are not directly concerned with control of a firm, they invest immense amounts in stocks and bonds from other countries. Data from the U.S. Department of Commerce show that persons residing outside the United States hold American stocks and bonds valued at $733 billion ($340 billion in stocks).[6] Of this, 57 percent is owned by European residents, 13 percent by Japanese residents, and 10 percent by Canadian residents.[7] American residents, on the other hand, own $518 billion in foreign securities, of which $298 billion is in corporate stocks.[8] As you can see, foreign portfolio investment is sizable and will continue to grow as more international firms list their bonds and equities on foreign exchanges.

Foreign Direct Investment

Volume.   In Chapter 1, we stated that the book value of all foreign investments is almost $2 trillion. Table 2–5 indicates how this total is divided among the largest investor nations. The United States has almost double the foreign direct investment of the next largest, Japan, which in turn has invested 13 percent more than the United Kingdom, the third largest.

One factor that has contributed to the increase of foreign investment in the United States has been the U.S. dollar's loss of value in terms of other currencies. For example, in dollar terms, Japan's American investment in 1992

FOREIGN INVESTMENT

portfolio investment
The purchase of stocks and bonds to obtain a return on the funds invested

direct investment
The purchase of sufficient stock in a firm to obtain significant management control

Country	1992		1980	
	Amount	Share	Amount	Share
United States	$ 488.8	25.3%	$220.2	43.5%
Japan	250.4	13.0	16.6	3.3
United Kingdom	221.2	11.4	80.7	15.9
Germany	178.7	9.2	43.1	8.5
France	160.9	8.3	23.6	4.7
Netherlands	131.7	6.8	42.1	8.3
Canada	87.5	4.5	22.6	4.5
Other	413.1	21.5	57.7	11.4
World total	$1,932.3	100.0%	$506.6	100.0%

TABLE 2–5
Direct overseas investment, 1992 and 1980 ($ billions in current dollars)

Source: Division on Transnational Corporations and Investment, *World Investment Report 1994* (New York: United Nations, 1994), p. 419.

was 23.02 times as large as it was in 1980. However, this investment cost Japanese investors only 12.85 times as many yen because by 1992, the yen was worth nearly twice as much in U.S. dollars as it had been in 1980.

	Yen/US$	Investment ($ billions)	1992/1980 ratio	Investment (yen billions)	1992/1980 ratio
1980	226.74	4.2		952	
1992	126.51	96.7	23.02×	12,234	12.85×

Direction.   Even though it is impossible to make an accurate determination of the present value of foreign investments, we can get an idea of the rate and amounts of such investments and of the places in which they are being made. This is the kind of information that interests managers and government leaders. It is analogous to what is sought in the analysis of international trade. If a nation is continuing to receive appreciable amounts of foreign investment, its investment climate must be favorable. This means that the political forces of the foreign environment are relatively attractive and that the opportunity to earn a profit is greater there than elsewhere. Other reasons for investing exist, to be sure, but if the above are absent, foreign investment is not likely to occur.

In which countries are investments being made, and where do the investments come from? Table 2–6 indicates that the industrialized nations invest primarily in one another just as they trade more with one another.

Actually, foreign investment follows foreign trade. Managements observe that the kinds of products they manufacture are being imported in sizable quantities by a country, and they begin to study the feasibility of setting up production facilities there. They are spurred to action because it is common knowledge that competitors are making similar analyses and may arrive at the same conclusion. Often the local market is not large enough to support local production of all the firms exporting to it, and the situation becomes one of seeing who can become established first. Experienced managers know, too, that governments often limit the number of local firms producing a given product so that those who do set up operations will be assured of having a profitable and continuing business.

U.S. Foreign Direct Investment

The United States is by far the largest investor abroad (about one-fourth of the total; see Table 2–5), and as you can see from Table 2–7, American firms have invested much more in the developed than in the developing countries. Also, as with international trade, the relative importance of regions and countries has been changing. In a period of 30 years, the percentage of American foreign investment in the developed nations has risen from 61 percent to 77 percent. Europe's share has more than doubled, and of the European countries, Great Britain and Germany have obtained the greatest dollar increase. Note that although the developing nations as a group have suffered a large percentage decrease, the percentage of investment in the Other Asia and Pacific region—which includes fast growing countries such as Singapore and Hong Kong has more than doubled.

Foreign Direct Investment in the United States

Rapid Increase.   Foreign direct investment in the United States has risen rapidly from about $6.9 billion in 1960 to $445 billion in 1993 (see Table 2–8). Of this, companies in the industrialized nations of Europe account for 60.8 percent of the total foreign investment and firms in the United Kingdom and the Netherlands own 21.4 and 15.4 percent, respectively. Observe how concen-

	1973	1979	1992
Where funds originate (net investment)			
World	$23.44	$48.37	$170.95*
Industrial nations	23.13	48.08	161.13
United States	11.53	24.84	34.79
United Kingdom	4.01	5.91	14.69
Japan	1.92	2.95	17.24
Germany	1.69	4.73	15.78
France	0.94	2.07	30.99
Netherlands	0.93	2.35	11.25
Canada	0.77	1.89	5.74
Belgium and Luxembourg	0.27	1.36	11.18
Italy	0.26	0.55	6.02
Switzerland	0.30	0.64	4.90
Developing nations (oil export)	0.16	−0.15	0.62
Developing nations (nonoil)	0.15	0.41	9.20
Where funds go (net investment)			
Industrial nations	10.62	24.60	99.54
United States	2.85	9.92	2.37
United Kingdom	1.80	2.76	18.05
France	1.14	2.59	21.84
Spain	0.39	1.43	1.3
Canada	0.83	1.50	7.76
Italy	0.63	0.37	3.07
Belgium and Luxembourg	0.73	1.08	11.07
Netherlands	0.87	1.24	5.32
Germany	2.06	1.13	6.80
Japan	0.21†	0.24	2.72
Developing nations (oil export)	0.27	0.09	3.56
Developing nations (nonoil)	4.04	8.42	46.82
Africa	0.32	0.36	2.70
Asia	0.80	2.14	27.64
People's Republic of China	n.a.	0.43‡	11.16
Singapore	0.39	0.83	5.64
Malaysia	0.17	0.89	4.12
Western hemisphere	2.50	4.38	14.53
Mexico	0.46	0.68	5.37
Brazil	1.39	2.46	1.45
Colombia	0.02	0.16	0.79
Argentina	0.01	0.18	4.18

TABLE 2–6

Direction of foreign direct investment for selected regions and countries ($ billions in current dollars)

Note: n.a. = Not available.
*Amounts do not coincide because of reporting lag.
†1974.
‡1982.

Sources: International Monetary Fund, *Balance of Payments Yearbook Supplement to Volumes 31 and 33* (Washington, DC: December 1980); and *Balance of Payments Statistics Yearbook*, vol. 38, part 2, 1992, pp. 66–67.

trated foreign direct investment is in the United States. Firms from just five nations: the United Kingdom, Japan, the Netherlands, Germany, and Canada own over 75 percent of the total.

Notice too that Japanese firms now have a slightly higher stock of direct investments in the United States than do the British. The nationwide distribution and the growth in the number of their manufacturing sites is impressive (Figures 2–3 and 2–4 on page 42).

TABLE 2–7 U.S. direct investment position overseas on a historical-cost basis ($ billions)

Country or Region	1960		1993							
	Total	Percent of Total	Total	Percent of Total	Manufacturing	Percent of Manufacturing	Finance[a]	Percent of Finance	Other[b]	Percent of Other
Total	$31.87	100 %	$548.64	100%	$199.46	100%	$182.32	100%	$202.86	100%
Developed countries	19.32	61	393.34	72	153.20	77	118.10	65	122.04	60
Canada	11.18	35	70.40	13	34.06	17	13.07	7	23.27	11
Europe[c]	6.69	21	269.16	49	96.75	49	96.48	53	75.93	37
EC[d]	2.65	8	224.59	38	91.04	46	75.11	41	58.44	29
Belgium & Luxembourg	0.23	0.7	13.87	3	6.85	3	3.83	2	3.19	2
France	0.74	2	23.57	4	13.26	7	2.74	2	7.57	4
Germany	1.01	3	37.52	7	22.28	11	7.34	4	7.90	4
Italy	0.38	1	13.92	3	8.75	4	2.00	1	3.17	2
Netherlands	0.28	0.9	19.89	4	7.78	4	5.33	3	6.78	3
Great Britain	3.23	10	96.43	18	22.86	11	48.52	27	25.05	12
Denmark and Ireland	n.a.	—	11.37	2	5.33	3	S	—	S	—
Greece	n.a.	—	0.42	<1	0.13	<1	S	—	S	—
Japan	0.25	0.8	31.39	6	13.61	7	5.09	3	12.69	6
Aust. and S.A.[e]	1.20	4	22.40	4	8.40	4	3.46	2	10.54	5
Developing countries	11.13	35	152.47	28	46.63	23	64.22	35	41.62	21
Latin America	7.48	23	101.94	19	29.64	15	55.51	30	16.79	8
Brazil	0.95	3	16.91	3	12.57	6	3.09	2	1.25	<1
Venezuela	2.57	8	2.30	<1	1.37	<1	S	—	S	—
Mexico and Central America	1.54	5	28.97	5	11.57	6	11.97	7	5.43	3
Other western hemisphere	0.88	3	42.05	8	0.94	<1	35.99	20	5.12	3
Africa[f]	0.64	2	4.37	<1	0.52	<1	0.76	<1	3.09	2
Middle East	1.14	4	6.46	1	2.09	1	1.40	<1	5.18	3
Other Asia and Pacific	0.98	3	39.40	7	14.38	7	7.55	4	2.97	1
International[g]	1.42	4	3.13	<1	—	—	—	—	—	—

Notes: n.a. = Not applicable.
S = Suppressed to avoid disclosure of individual firm.
[a]Includes finance, banking, real estate, and insurance.
[b]Other includes transportation, communications, public utilities, petroleum, mining, and wholesale trade.
[c]No East European investment included.
[d]Great Britain, Ireland, Denmark, and Greece not in EC in 1960. Are included in 1993.
[e]Australia, New Zealand, and South Africa.
[f]Does not include South Africa.
[g]Shipping companies operating under flags of convenience, primarily those of Panama and Liberia, and investments not allocated to any specific country by reporting firms.

Sources: *Survey of Current Business*, June 1994, p. 74; and *Statistical Abstract of the United States* 1977, p. 755.

Largest Investors. When the president and government officials talked down the value of the dollar in 1993 in order to lower the prices stated in other currencies of American exports, they may not have realized that they were

TABLE 2–8 Foreign direct investment position in United States on a historical-cost basis, 1993 ($ billions)

Country	All Industries	Percent of Total	Manufac-turing	Percent of Total	Trade	Percent of Total	Real Estate	Percent of Total	Finance*	Percent of Total
Total	445.27	100.0%	166.70	100 %	69.72	100 %	28.61	100 %	57.57	100.0%
Europe	270.77	60.8	122.59	73.5	27.99	40.1	10.85	37.9	22.50	39.1
United Kingdom	95.42	21.4	42.54	25.5	6.93	9.9	4.42	15.4	8.56	14.9
Japan	96.21	21.6	17.75	10.6	34.75	49.8	9.46	34.8	20.95	36.4
Netherlands	68.48	15.4	22.86	13.7	7.71	11.1	4.49	15.7	6.13	10.6
Germany	34.67	7.8	17.85	10.7	7.30	10.5	1.07	3.7	2.01	3.5
Canada	39.41	8.9	16.60	10.0	1.84	2.6	4.69	16.4	5.64	9.8
France	28.47	6.4	16.94	10.2	1.88	2.7	0.05	0.2	1.84	3.2
Switzerland	21.38	4.8	11.30	6.8	0.71	1.0	†	‡	2.67	4.6
Netherland Antilles	6.98	1.6	3.27	2.0	1.32	1.9	0.27	0.9	0.35	0.6
Australia	7.28	1.6	2.23	1.3	S	S	0.18	0.6	S	S
Sweden	8.08	1.8	5.38	3.2	0.77	1.1	0.43	1.5	§	—
Belgium	4.59	1.0	1.88	1.1	0.98	1.4	0.06	0.2	S	S
Panama	4.75	1.1	0.45	0.3	‖	—	0.11	0.4	S	S
Bermuda	1.44	0.3	0.53	0.3	0.45	0.6	0.16	0.6	S	S
Luxembourg	0.99	0.2	0.82	0.5	S	S	0.11	0.4	0.11	0.2
Saudi Arabia	1.59	0.4	S	S	S	S	0.02	0.1	0.03	†
Finland	1.50	0.3	1.09	0.7	0.2	0.3	S	S	S	S
Kuwait	1.56	0.4	S	S	S	S	1.07	3.7	S	S
Italy	1.23	0.3	0.44	0.3	0.51	0.7	S	S	0.07	0.1
Bahamas	1.18	0.3	†	‡	S	S	0.06	0.2	0.79	1.4

Note: S = Suppressed to avoid disclosure of individual companies.
*Finance includes banking.
†Less than $10 million.
‡<0.01%
§ = Negative position.
‖ Disinvestment.

Source: *Survey of Current Business*, June 1994, p. 77.

talking down the prices of American assets as well. Foreign investors, however, did notice the difference and responded by spending twice as much to acquire American firms in 1993 as they did in 1992 ($23 versus $11 billion).[9] The 20 largest foreign investors in the United States are ranked by revenue in Table 2–9 (on page 43). Observe how the rankings have changed in only three years. Although a few firms, such as Shell, Nestlé, and Unilever have been in this country for years, many of these investments are recent. You can tell from the names of the American affiliates that their major investment strategy has been to acquire existing firms rather than start from the ground up. In 1993, foreign investors spent $23.1 billion on acquisitions and only $3.1 billion to establish new companies.[10]

International firms enter foreign markets for a number of reasons, all of which are linked to the desire to either increase profits and sales or protect them from being eroded by competition.

WHY ENTER FOREIGN MARKETS?

Increase Profits and Sales

Enter New Markets. Managers are always under pressure to increase the sales and profits of their firms, and when they face a mature, saturated market at home, they begin to search for new markets outside their home country. They find that (1) a rising GNP per capita and population growth appear to be

FIGURE 2–3 Distribution of Japanese manufacturers' factory sites in the United States (September 1992 versus May 1988)

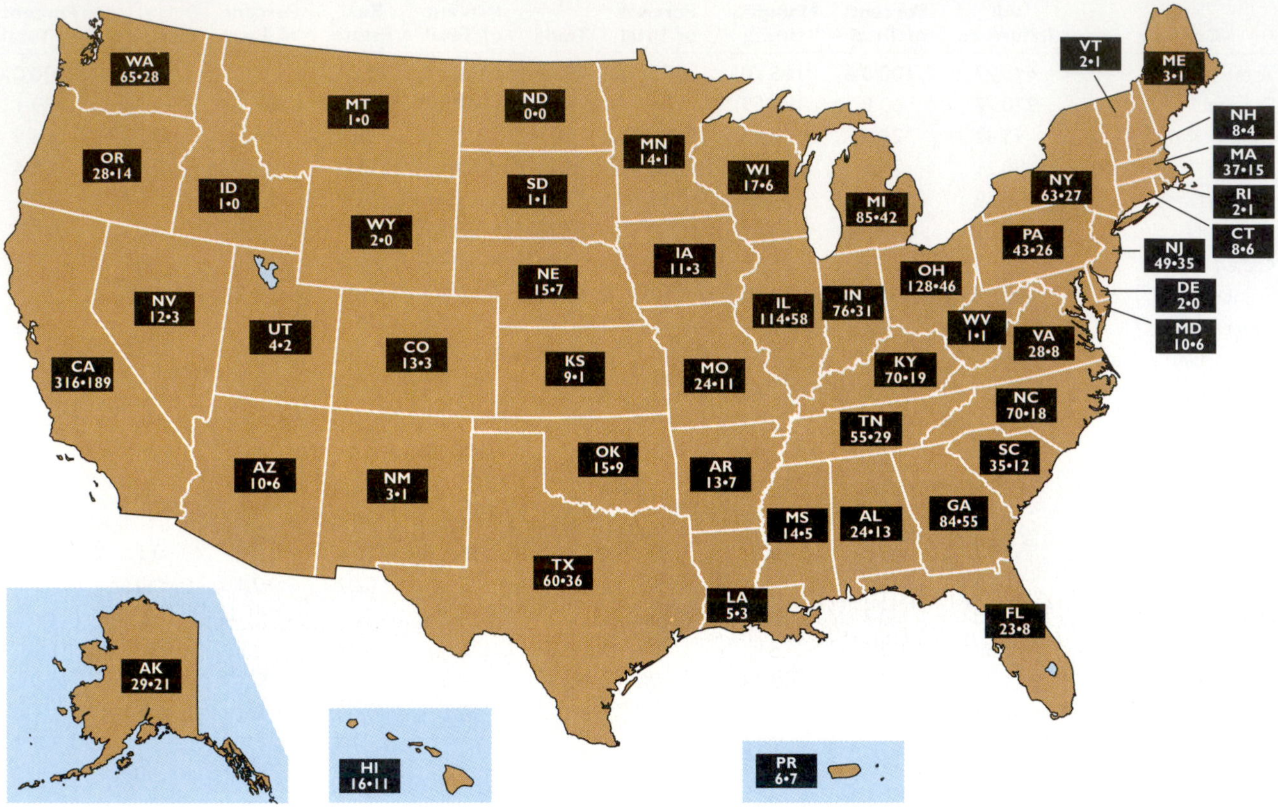

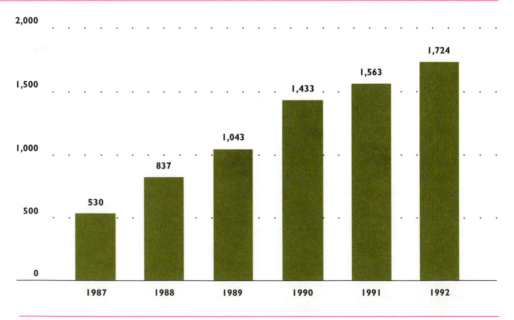

WA 65•28
OR 28•14
ID 1•0
MT 1•0
ND 0•0
MN 14•1
WI 17•6
MI 85•42
VT 2•1
ME 3•1
NH 8•4
MA 37•15
NY 63•27
RI 2•1
CT 8•6
WY 2•0
SD 1•1
IA 11•3
IL 114•58
IN 76•31
OH 128•46
PA 43•26
NJ 49•35
DE 2•0
MD 10•6
NV 12•3
UT 4•2
CO 13•3
NE 15•7
KS 9•1
MO 24•11
KY 70•19
WV 1•1
VA 28•8
CA 316•189
AZ 10•6
NM 3•1
OK 15•9
AR 13•7
TN 55•29
NC 70•18
SC 35•12
MS 14•5
AL 24•13
GA 84•55
TX 60•36
LA 5•3
FL 23•8
AK 29•21
HI 16•11
PR 6•7

FIGURE 2–4
Number of Japanese plants in the United States

Year	Number
1987	530
1988	837
1989	1,043
1990	1,433
1991	1,563
1992	1,724

TABLE 2–9 Twenty largest foreign investments in the United States ($ millions)

1993 Rank	1992 Rank	Foreign Investor	Country	U.S. Investment	Percent Owned	Industry	Revenue	Assets
1	1	Seagram Co. Ltd.	Canada	E I du Pont de Nemours	24	Chemicals, energy	32,732	37,053
				JE Seagram	100	Beverages	3,784	9,182
							36,516	
2	2	Royal Dutch/Shell Group	Netherlands/U.K.	Shell Oil	100	Energy, chemicals	20,853	26,851
3	3	British Petroleum Plc	U.K.	BP America	100	Energy	16,006	18,293
4	11	Sony Corp.	Japan	Sony Music Entertainment	100	Music entertainment		
				Sony Picture Entertainment	100	Movies	12,195	12,657
				Sony Electronics	100	Consumer electronics		
5	4	Grand Metropolitan Ltd.	U.K.	Burger King	100	Fast food	5,250	
				Pillsbury	100	Food processing	3,700	
							8,950	
				Heublein	100	Wines and spirits	1,600	6,131
				Pearle Vision	100	Eye care retailing	600	
				Other companies	100	Wines and spirits	625	
							11,775	
6	10	Hanson	U.K.	Hanson Industries	100	Mining, aggregates, chemicals	7,975	18,700
				Quantum Chemical	100	Petrochemicals	2,294	4,980
				Smith Corona	48	Office supplies	309	198
				Ground Round Restaurants	33	Restaurant chain	233	152
				Marine Harvest International	27	Food processing	137	104
							10,948	
7	5	Tengelmann Group	Germany	Great A&P Tea	53	Supermarkets	10,384	3,099
8	12	Nestlé	Switzerland	Nestlé USA	100	Food processing	8,646	n.a.
				Alcon Laboratories	100	Pharmaceuticals		
		L'Oreal	France	Cosmair	>50	Cosmetics	1,347	n.a.
							9,993	
9	9	B.A.T. Industries	U.K.	Brown & Williamson Tobacco	100	Tobacco	2,774	n.a.
				Farmers Group	100	Insurance	1,709	6,999
		Imasco	Canada	Hardee's Food Systems	100	Fast food	4,957	843
							9,440	
10	22	Toyota Motor Corp.	Japan	Toyota Motor Mfg.	100	Automotive	4,000E	n.a.
				New United Motor Mfg.	50	Automotive	3,600E	n.a.
		Nippondenso	Japan	Nippondenso America	100	Auto parts	1,800	n.a.
							9,400	
11	7	Petroleos de Venezuela	Venezuela	Citgo Petroleum	100	Refining, marketing	9,107	3,866

continued

TABLE 2–9 Twenty largest foreign investments in the United States—*continued*

1993 Rank	1992 Rank	Foreign Investor	Country	U.S. Investment	Percent Owned	Industry	Revenue	Assets
12	8	Unilever NV	Netherlands	Unilever United States	100	Food processing, personal prods	8,970	8,560
		Unilever Plc	U.K.					
13	20	Delhaize "Le Lion"	Belgium	Food Lion	25	Supermarkets	7,610	2,504
14	29	Ahold	Netherlands	First National Supermarkets	100	Supermarkets	2,158	
				BI-LO	100	Supermarkets	1,828	2,137
				Tops Markets	100	Supermarkets	1,565	
				Giant Food Stores	100	Supermarkets	1,133	
				Red Food Stores	100	Supermarkets	585	n.a.
							7,269	
15	13	Philips Electronics NV	Netherlands	Philips Electronics NA	100	Electronics	5,955	3,028
				Whittle Communications LP	25	Publishing	250E	n.a.
		PolyGram NV	Netherlands	PolyGram Records	100	Music	909	n.a.
							7,114	
16	17	Hoechst AG	Germany	Hoechst Celanese	100	Chemicals	6,899	7,917
17	34	Siemens AG	Germany	Siemens Corp.	100	Electronics	5,579	n.a.
				Osram Sylvania	100	Lighting products	958	n.a.
							6,537	
18	n.a.	AXA	France	Equitable Cos.	49	Insurance	6,480	98,991
19	16	Bayer	Germany	Miles	100	Chemicals, health care	6,459	5,242
20	37	Matsushita Electric Industrial	Japan	Matsushita Elec. Corp. (Am)	100	Electronics	2,200	1,000
				MCA	100	Entertainment	4,100	n.a.
							6,300	

Notes: E = Estimated.
n.a. = Not available.

Source: "The 100 Largest Foreign Investors in the U.S.," *Forbes*, July 18, 1994, pp. 266–70.

creating markets that are reaching the critical mass necessary to become viable candidates for their operations and (2) the economies of some nations where they are not doing business are growing at a considerably faster rate than is the economy of their own market.

New Market Creation. Table 2–10 illustrates the great variety in growth rates among the top and bottom countries ranked by GNP per capita. Note the disparity among and between the two groups. You can also compare the (green) countries with the (brown) in Figure 2–5.

Although nearly everyone looks to GNP per capita as a basis for making comparisons of nations' economies, extreme care must be exercised to avoid drawing unwarranted conclusions. In the first place, because the statistical systems in many developing nations are deficient, the reliability of the data provided by such nations is questionable.

Second, to arrive at a common base of U.S. dollars, the World Bank and other international agencies convert local currencies to dollars. The Bank uses

TABLE 2–10
Population (1992),
GNP/capita (1992), and
average growth rates of
GNP/capita and population
(1980–1992) (Countries
with populations of 1 million
or more)

Ranking	Country*	1992 GNP/Capita (current US$)	1992 Population (millions)	Annual Growth Rates (percentage) GNP/Capita[†]	Annual Growth Rates (percentage) Population
1	Switzerland	$36,080	6.9	1.4%	0.7%
2	Japan	28,190	124.5	3.6	0.5
3	Sweden	27,010	8.7	1.5	0.4
4	Denmark	26,000	5.2	2.1	0.1
5	Norway	25,820	4.3	2.2	0.4
6	United States	23,240	255.4	1.7	1.0
7	Germany	23,030	80.6	2.4[‡]	0.2
8	Austria	22,380	7.9	2.0	0.4
9	France	22,260	57.4	1.7	0.5
10	United Arab Emirates	22,020	1.7	−4.3	4.0
11	Finland	21,970	5.0	2.0	0.5
12	Belgium	20,880	10.0	2.0	0.2
13	Canada	20,710	27.4	1.8	1.1
14	Netherlands	20,480	15.2	1.7	0.6
15	Italy	20,460	57.8	2.2	0.2
16	United Kingdom	17,790	57.8	2.4	0.2
17	Australia	17,260	17.5	1.6	1.4
18	Singapore	15,730	2.8	5.3	1.8
19	Hong Kong	15,360[§]	5.8	5.5	1.2
20	Spain	13,970	39.1	2.9	0.4
21	Israel	13,220	5.1	1.9	2.3
22	New Zealand	12,300	3.4	0.6	0.8
23	Ireland	12,210	3.5	3.4	0.4
24	Saudi Arabia	7,510	16.8	−3.3	4.9
25	Portugal	7,450	9.8	3.1	0.1
26	Greece	7,290	10.3	1.0	0.5
27	South Korea	6,790	43.7	8.5	1.1
108	Central African Republic	410	3.2	−1.5	2.6
109	Benin	410	5.0	−0.7	3.1
110	Togo	390	3.9	−1.8	3.3
111	Nicaraugua	340	3.9	−5.3	2.7
112	Nigeria	320	101.9	−0.4	3.0
113	Mali	310	9.0	−2.7	2.6
114	Kenya	310	25.7	0.2	3.6
115	India	310	883.6	3.1	2.1
116	Burkina Faso	300	9.5	1.0	2.6
117	Niger	280	8.2	−4.3	3.3
118	Rwanda	250	7.3	−0.6	2.9
119	Laos, PDR	250	4.4	n.a.	2.6
120	Madagascar	230	12.4	−2.4	2.9
121	Guinea-Bissau	220	1.0	1.6	1.9
122	Chad	220	6.0	3.4	2.4
123	Bangladesh	220	114.4	1.8	2.3
124	Malawi	210	9.1	−0.1	3.2
125	Burundi	210	5.8	1.3	2.8
126	Bhutan	180	1.5	6.3	2.1
127	Uganda	170	17.5	n.a.	2.6
128	Nepal	170	19.9	2.0	2.6
129	Sierra Leone	160	4.4	−1.4	2.4
130	Tanzania	110	25.9	0.0	3.0
131	Ethiopia	110	54.8	−1.9	3.1
132	Mozambique	60	16.5	−3.6	2.6

Notes: n.a. = Not available.
*Only countries for which data were reported to the World Bank are listed.
[†]GNP/capita growth rates are real.
[‡]Refers to former Federal Republic of Germany.
[§]GNP data refer to GDP.

Source: *World Development Report,* 1994 (Washington, DC: World Bank, 1994).

FIGURE 2–5 GNP per capita

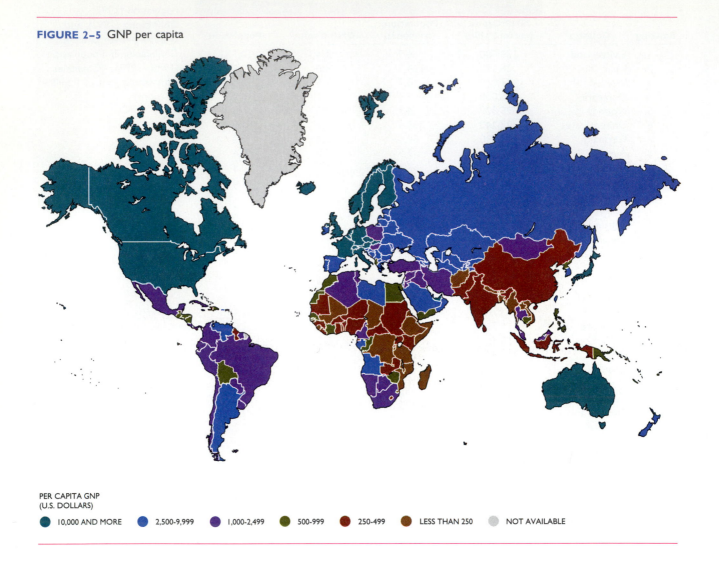

PER CAPITA GNP
(U.S. DOLLARS)

● 10,000 AND MORE   ● 2,500-9,999   ● 1,000-2,499   ● 500-999   ● 250-499   ● LESS THAN 250   ● NOT AVAILABLE

an average of the exchange rate for that year and the previous two years, after adjusting for differences in relative inflation between the particular country and the United States.[11] World Bank economists admit that official exchange rates do not reflect the relative domestic purchasing powers of currencies, "However," they say, "exchange rates remain the only generally available means of converting GNP from national currencies to U.S. dollars."[12]

Finally, you must remember that GNP per capita is merely an arithmetic mean obtained by dividing GNP by the total population. However, a nation with a lower GNP but more evenly distributed income may be a more desirable market than one whose GNP is higher. On the other hand, as you will note in the chapter on the economic forces, a skewed distribution of income in a nation with a low GNP per capita may indicate that there is a viable market, especially for luxury goods. People do drive Cadillacs in Bolivia.

The data from Table 2–10 indicate that, from a macro viewpoint, markets around the world are growing, but this does not mean that equally good opportunities exist for all kinds of business. Perhaps surprisingly, economic growth in a nation causes markets for some products to be lost forever while

WORLDVIEW

Misleading Data

Much of the data reported by the Department of Commerce is understated; but probably the data about U.S. trade flows and international financial transactions are among the poorest. Before 1970, the volume of exports and imports was so small that reporting errors were of little consequence for the balance-of-payments statistics. However, the value of the U.S. international trade has risen since then and now amounts to over 11 percent of GDP.

One reason trade data are understated is that exporters declare values below the true values in order to reduce their reported profits for lower income taxes. Lower declared values will also cost the exporter less in insurance premiums. For example, producers of software will declare the value of plain computer disks rather than the much higher value of the programs on them.

The National Academy of Sciences, which recently examined the quality of American trade data, declared that the most underreported area is service exports. Government statisticians have little idea what their true value is. Official estimates for 1993, the latest year available, show that the United States had a surplus in service exports of $59 billion. The true value is probably far larger.

Sources: "Why the Economic Data Mislead Us," *Fortune*, March 8, 1993, pp. 112–13; and *Survey of Current Business*, June 1994, p. 110.

---

simultaneously markets for other products are being created. Take the case of a country in the initial stage of development. With little local manufacturing, it is a good market for exporters of consumer goods. As economic development continues, however, businesspeople see profit-making opportunities in (1) producing locally the kinds of consumer goods that require simple technology or (2) assembling from imported parts the products that demand a more advanced technology. Given the tendency of governments to protect local industry, the importation of goods being produced in that country will normally be prohibited. Thus, the exporters of the easy-to-manufacture consumer goods, such as paint, adhesives, toilet articles, clothing, and almost anything made of plastic, will begin to lose this market, which now becomes a new market to producers of the inputs to these "infant industries."

Preferential Trading Arrangements. The fact that most nations have experienced population and GNP per capita growth does not necessarily mean they have attained sufficient size to warrant investment by an international firm in either (1) an organization for marketing exports from the home country or (2) in a local manufacturing plant. For many products, a number of these nations still lack sufficient market potential. However, when such nations have made some kind of a **preferential trading arrangement** (for example, the European Union and the European Free Trade Association), the resultant market has been so much larger that firms frequently have bypassed what is often the initial step of exporting to make their initial market entry with local manufacturing facilities.

preferential trading arrangement
An agreement by a small group of nations to establish free trade among themselves while maintaining trade restrictions with all other nations

Faster-Growing Markets. Not only are new foreign markets appearing, but many of them are growing at a faster rate than the home market. One outstanding example has been the growth of Japan's GNP per capita from $9,890 in 1980 to $28,220 in 1992. Table 2–10 shows that Japan's real annual growth rate for that period averaged 3.6 percent compared to Switzerland's

Not Too Small to Export

Artais Weather Check, a manufacturer of weather-observation systems for small airports, is a small business ($3.5 million sales in 1993) that already dominates the American market. To increase sales, management decided to enter new markets overseas.

It now is experiencing an export boom and expects foreign sales to reach $3.7 million in 1994, which is two-thirds of the total projected sales of $5.5 million. To obtain these orders, the firm has had to overcome difficulties that it never had encountered in the home market. Nevertheless, the company has proved that being a small business is not necessarily a handicap in foreign markets.

For example, the firm found a lack of recognition in overseas markets in spite of its being the market leader in the United States. It also had to face foreign competitors that received subsidies such as export rebates from their governments. Having to adapt their products to local markets was another novelty for the Artais management.

The effort to export has brought excellent results. The sales that the company has made in China, Taiwan, Ecuador, Saudi Arabia, and Egypt are more lucrative because of the extra spare parts and installation fees. The prices for domestic sales range from $45,000 to $60,000 while foreign contracts have varied from $200,000 to nearly $2 million.

Artais is one of many small and medium-sized firms that have realized good profits in export sales. One survey found that 46 percent of companies with annual sales of less than $100 million reported exporting in 1992. This is 10 percent higher than what was reported in 1990.

Source: "Artais Finds Smallness Isn't Handicap in Global Market," *The Wall Street Journal*, June 23, 1994, p. B2.

Courtesy Greencrest Marketing/Photography by Larry Hamill

1.4 percent or Sweden's 1.5 percent. Note the annual growth rates of the Asian nations: Singapore, 5.3 percent; Hong Kong, 5.5 percent; and South Korea, 8.5 percent, the highest growth rate listed by the World Bank. China and Thailand, with growth rates of 7.6 and 6.0 percent respectively, are other Asian markets attracting the attention of multinationals.[13] Of the 132 nations listed in the World Bank table on which Table 2–10 is based, 34 had average annual growth rates higher than the American growth rate for the period from 1980 to 1992.

Improved Communications.   This might be considered a supportive reason for opening up new markets overseas, because certainly the ability to communicate with subordinates and customers by telex and telephone has given managers confidence in their ability to control foreign operations if they should undertake them. In addition, improved transportation enables managers to either send home-office personnel to help with local problems or be there themselves within a few hours if necessary.

Good, relatively inexpensive international communication enables large insurance, banking, and software firms to "body shop," that is, transmit computer-oriented tasks worldwide to a cheap but skilled labor force. New York Life, for example, employs 50 people in Ireland to process insurance claims in a computer linked to the firm's computer in New Jersey. American employees coming to work in the morning find the claims processed during the night in Ireland have been transmitted to their computer in the United States. Some computer consultants in the United States are earning $75 an hour while their Indian counterparts are working for the same firms via an overseas telecommunications link for $5 an hour.[14]

Shorter travel time has also been responsible for numerous business opportunities because foreign businesspersons have come to the home country to look for new products to import or new technology to buy. The Department of Commerce, in *Business America,* regularly publishes a list of arrivals who desire to contact suppliers.

Faster growth in the markets of developing nations frequently occurs for another reason. When a firm that has supplied the market by exports builds a factory for local production, the host government generally prohibits imports. The firm, which may have had to share the market with 10 or 20 competitors during its exporting days, now has the local market all to itself or shares it with only a small number of other local producers. Before General Tire began manufacturing tires in Chile, probably a dozen exporters, including General Tire, were competing in the market. However, once local production got under way, there was only one supplier for the entire market—General Tire. That is growth.

Obtain Greater Profits.   As you know, greater profits may be obtained by either increasing total revenue or decreasing the cost of goods sold, and often conditions are such that a firm can do both.

Greater Revenue.   Rarely will all of a firm's domestic competitors be in every foreign market in which it is located. Where there is less competition, the firm may be able to obtain a better price for its goods or services. For example, General Tire had only three competitors in Spain for its V-belt line when dozens of brands were available in the United States.

Increasingly, firms are obtaining greater revenue by introducing products in overseas markets and their domestic markets simultaneously. This results in greater sales volume while lowering the cost of goods sold.

Lower Cost of Goods Sold.   Going abroad, whether by exporting or by producing overseas, can frequently lower the cost of goods sold. Increasing total sales by exporting will not only reduce R&D costs per unit, but will also make other economies of scale possible. The president of a Westinghouse division stated, "The people who can spread their R&D and engineering and manufacturing development costs across those three markets [Europe, Japan, and North America] have a substantial advantage." Westinghouse, like many companies, obtains lower unit costs through long production runs made possible by having one factory supply one product internationally.[15] The management of Warner-Lambert, a global health care and consumer products manufacturer, evidently agrees as it states, "Warner-Lambert is addressing each new product as a global opportunity, particularly pharmaceuticals. Only in the context of a worldwide marketplace can Warner-Lambert hope to recapture the escalating costs of bringing new drugs to market. Estimates conservatively place development costs at more than $230 million for a single drug."[16] The president of Bristol-Myers Squibb, the second-largest pharmaceuticals manufacturer in the United States, claims that "only 1 in 5,000 compounds synthesized in the laboratory makes it to the marketplace. It costs an average of $359 million to develop a new drug and can take up to 12 years to reach the marketplace."[17]

Another factor that can positively affect the cost of goods sold is the inducements that some governments offer to attract new investment. For example, Greece offers the following to new investors: (1) investment grants of up to 50 percent of the investment, (2) interest subsidies to cover up to 50 percent of the interest cost of bank loans, and (3) reduction of up to 90 percent of a firm's taxes on profits. Incentives such as these are designed to attract prospective investors and generally are not a sufficient motive for foreign investment. Nevertheless, they do have a positive influence on the cost of goods sold.

Higher Overseas Profits as an Investment Motive.   There is no question that greater profits on overseas investments were a strong motive for going abroad in the early 1970s and 1980s. *Business International* reported that 90 percent of 140 Fortune 500 companies surveyed had achieved higher profitably on foreign assets in 1974, for example. The survey showed that for the period from 1978 to 1985 the average growth in foreign earnings outpaced foreign sales growth (5.9 percent versus 4.1 percent), whereas domestic earnings were down an average of 27 percent despite a domestic sales growth of 5.2 percent.[18] American firms continue to earn more on their foreign sales. In 1993, of the 100 largest U.S. multinationals, only 18 earned more than 50 percent of their revenue overseas, but 33 earned over 50 percent of their profits from their foreign operations. Look at the statistics for General Motors, the industrial firm with greatest sales. While only 28 percent of its revenue came from foreign operations, 91 percent of its profit did.[19]

Acquire Products for the Home Market.   The relative ease of foreign travel has both created markets for new products and facilitated the search for new products to be introduced in the U.S. market. Americans travel overseas in unprecedented numbers, and in their travels they frequently encounter products and customs previously unknown to them. When they return home, they want to continue to use them. American marketers, sensitive to this market, have sent buyers around the world to search for those new products, and many manufacturers have begun to produce them here.

> Minnetonka executives were browsing in a German supermarket when they came across an intriguing product—toothpaste in a pump dispenser, which had not yet appeared in the United States—so they contacted the German manufacturer. This was the beginning of Check-Up toothpaste. A marketing vice president stated, "We make grocery shopping a regular part of our business trips to Europe. It helps give us a jump on our bigger competitors."
>
> American firms have found products such as aseptic beverage cartons (which permit storage without refrigeration), hair-styling mousses, and body fragrance sprays. "The search across oceans and borders for new products is heating up," said the president of General Food's international division.[20]

Let's now look at some reasons for going abroad that are more related to the protection of present markets, profits, and sales.

Protect Markets, Profits, and Sales

Protect Domestic Market.   Frequently, a firm will go abroad to protect its home market.

Follow Customers Overseas.   Service companies (accounting, advertising, marketing research, banks, law) will establish foreign operations in markets where their principal accounts are, to prevent competitors from gaining access to those accounts. They know that once a competitor has been able to demonstrate to top management what it can do by servicing a foreign subsidiary, it may be able to take over the entire account. Similarly, suppliers to original equipment manufacturers (for example, battery manufacturers to automobile producers) often follow their large customers. These suppliers have an added advantage in that they are moving into new markets with a guaranteed customer base.

This is true for the over 250 Japanese auto parts makers that have come to the United States, the world's largest auto parts producer, to supply the eight Japanese auto plants in this country. For example, Tokyo Seat has established a subsidiary to make seats, exhaust systems, and other parts for Honda, which also asked Nippondenso, a Japanese producer of radiators and heaters, to set up an American plant.

Companies from the Mitsubishi group in Japan created a version of the Japanese supplier network in Ohio to supply the plant of the Mitsubishi-Chrysler joint venture, Diamond Star. In addition, there are captive suppliers that are not part of the Mitsubishi group. Just an hour's drive away from the Diamond Star factory, now wholly owned by Mitsubishi, a cooperative of 16 nonaffiliated suppliers to Mitsubishi in Japan built a $37 million plant to produce components such as engine mounts and bumpers. "We had a direct request from Mitsubishi to build this project here in the United States," said the cooperative's president Isamu Kawasaki.[21] According to a University of Michigan study, a similar situation exists in Honda's Marysville, Ohio, plant. Researchers found that U.S. companies supplied only 16 percent of the parts; the other 84 percent is supplied either by Japanese plants or by Japanese-owned plants in the United States.[22] Of 63 U.S. parts suppliers to Toyota's American plant, only 32 are American-owned.[23] And it is not only parts suppliers—Mitsubishi bank, the lead bank for Toyota in Japan, opened an office in Columbus, Ohio, to serve Honda's Ohio plant.[24]

Occasionally, a firm will set up an operation in the home country of a major competitor with the idea of keeping it so occupied defending that market that it will have less energy to compete in the home country of the first company. Although Kodak claimed its decision to open a manufacturing plant in Japan had nothing to do with its Japanese competitor (Fuji), its announcement came just 10 days after Fuji began construction of its first manufacturing facility in the United States.[25]

Using Foreign Production to Lower Costs.   A company may also go abroad to protect its domestic market when it faces competition from lower-priced foreign imports. By moving part or all of its production facilities to the countries from which its competition is coming, it can enjoy such advantages as less costly labor, raw materials, or energy. Management may decide to produce certain components abroad and assemble them in the home country; or, if the final product requires considerable labor in the final assembly, it may send the components overseas for this final operation.

Zenith Electronics, the last American-owned producer of television sets in the United States, announced in 1992 that it would move its television assembly operations from Missouri to Mexico. Zenith, which has not earned a profit since 1984, expected to save many millions of dollars in annual labor costs from the move. A spokesman said the cutbacks in Missouri should help the company remain competitive in areas such as color picture tubes.[26]

Zenith was able to take advantage of the lower-cost Mexican labor because of the in-bond (*maquiladora* in Mexico) program, a version of the export processing zones that began in the 1960s in Hong Kong, Taiwan, and Singapore. These all pertain to using foreign production to lower costs.

In-bond (maquiladora) industry. **In-bond plants (maquiladoras)** came into existence because of an arrangement between Mexico and the United States. The Mexican government permitted plants in the in-bond area to import parts and processed materials to be assembled, packaged, and pro-

In-bond plants (maquiladoras) *Production facilities in Mexico that temporarily import raw materials, components, or parts duty-free to be manufactured, processed, or assembled with less expensive local labor; the finished or semifinished product is then exported.*

cessed without paying import duties, provided that the finished products were reexported; the American government permitted the finished product containing the American-made parts and materials to be imported with import duty being paid only on the value added in Mexico. Originally, the in-bond plant program was called the *twin-plant program* because it was thought that a plant on the Mexican side would do the labor-intensive processes for a twin located on the American side. However, fewer than 10 percent of the Mexican plants have a twin on the U.S. side.

Although Mexican law required the in-bond plants to locate on the border in the beginning, later they were permitted into the interior of the country. Despite this relaxation on location restrictions, about 80 percent of in-bond plant employment is still in the border area. Presently, there are over 2,100 in-bond plants employing nearly one-half million workers[27] (see Figure 2–6). Their exports, led by electronics, electronic machinery, transportation equipment, and textiles, amounted to $19.8 billion in 1993.

North American Free Trade Agreement (NAFTA)
A treaty establishing a free trade area consisting of the United States, Mexico, and Canada; quotas on each other's goods were eliminated January 1994, and import duties will be phased out over 10 years.

Because of the **North American Free Trade Agreement (NAFTA),** in the year 2001, in-bond plants will have to pay Mexican import duties on components coming from outside the NAFTA member-nations. As a result, the advantage in using an in-bond plant will be lost to the hundreds of Japanese and Korean firms that presently import most of their raw materials, especially for electronic products, from Asia. Because Mexican suppliers currently provide only 2 percent of the total inputs used by the in-bond plants, Japanese companies are concerned that they will then have to purchase components from American manufacturers. To avoid this, Japan has sent experts to advise Mexico on how to foster greater development of suppliers to Japanese industry.[28]

Another factor will change the way the in-bond plants operate. Since the beginning of 1994, they can sell 50 percent of their production in Mexico. However, because most plants produce subassemblies that are sent out of Mexico to the parent company for further processing, they have practically nothing to sell locally. Most home offices are only beginning to realize the import of this change in the Mexican law. Eventually, they will have to change the scope of the in-bond plants to include the production of finished products.[29]

Caribbean Basin Initiative. This was started by President Reagan to stimulate investment in the Caribbean nations. The advantages are similar to those enjoyed by Mexican in-bond industries, but the Caribbean Basin has more liberal American textile and apparel import quotas. The American apparel industry sends precut pieces to these countries where they are assembled and returned for sale in the United States. This work has created over 100,000 jobs in Haiti, the Dominican Republic, Jamaica, and other nearby countries.[30]

Andean Trade Preference Act (ATPA). This is a unilateral trade benefit program similar to the Caribbean Basin Initiative, but it is designed to promote economic development in Bolivia, Colombia, Ecuador, and Peru. It is a major component of President Bush's Andean Trade Initiative that is designed to combat the production of coca by offering broader access to the U.S. market. ATPA's provisions are similar to those of the Caribbean Basin Initiative with some limitations.[31]

growth triangles
Transnational economic zones spread over large, geographically proximate areas covering three or more countries where differences in factor endowments are exploited to promote external trade and investment.

Growth triangles. To remain competitive in attracting new industry in the face of rising wages, Singapore introduced the concept of localized economic cooperation zones, or growth triangles. They consist of a group of countries that complement each other economically and are close to each other geographically. The original one is the Southern Growth Triangle covering a 30-mile radius encompassing Singapore, the Malaysian state of Johore, and Indonesia's Riau Islands. Singapore furnishes management,

FIGURE 2-6 Location and number of Mexican in-bond plants

Aguascalientes (10)

Baja California
Ensenada (49)
Mexicali (125)
Tecate (92)
Tijuana (529)

Baja California Sur
La Paz (8)

Campeche (3)

Chihuahua
Cd. Chihuahua (66)
Cd. Juárez (278)

Ojinaga (1)
Palomas (5)
Other cities (17)

Coahuila
Cd. Acuña (50)
Monclova (3)
Piedras Negras (43)
Saltillo (6)
Torreón (40)
Other cities (28)

Durango
Gómez Palacio (50)

Guanajuato (36)

Hidalgo (13)

Jalisco
Guadalajara (45)

Mexico, D.F. (27)

Michoacan (2)

Morelos (15)

Nuevo Leon
Monterrey (95)*

San Luis Potosi (9)

Sinaloa (5)

Sonora
Agua Prieta (32)
Cd. Obregón (3)
Guaymas (2)
Hermosillo (15)
Naco (4)
Nogales (76)*
San Luis Rio Colorado (25)
Other cities (39)

Tamaulipas
Matamoros (111)
Nuevo Laredo (54)

Reynosa (78)
Valle Hermoso (13)

Veracruz (2)

Yucatan
Mérida (31)*

Zacatecas (4)

*Total includes surrounding areas.

financing, transportation, and telecommunications capabilities, while Riau and Johore provide land, labor, and natural resources. At least five other growth triangles in Asia are being organized.[32]

Export processing zones. Many developing nations have a form of the export processing zone in which firms, mostly foreign manufacturers, enjoy almost a complete absence of taxation and regulation of materials brought into the zones for processing and subsequent reexport.

WORLDVIEW

Reverse Maquila, a New Concept

A new concept called *reverse maquila* is gaining attention in the Rio Grande Valley on the Texas–Mexican border, where over 200 in-bond plants (maquiladoras) are located. The term is so new that its definition is still fluid. Users are applying it to two different manufacturing situations: (1) a Mexican firm sets up production on the American side of the border and produces for sale in Mexico, and (2) a Mexican firm establishes production facilities on the American side of the border and sells the output in the United States.

Anyone familiar with the maquiladora concept recognizes that the first situation is the reverse of the usual maquiladora operation, in which an American or other non-Mexican company builds a plant on the Mexican side of the border to produce products using foreign-made components and the cheaper Mexican labor and then exports them to the United States. Here is an example of the reverse of that operation. A Mexican snack company owned by Pepsico International is building a plant in the Texas border city of Weslaco to make snacks that will be sold in Mexico. Why build the plant on the American side of the border where labor is more expensive?

There are a number of reasons being offered for locating on the U.S. side:

1. Many of the American materials used in the manufacturing process are of consistently superior quality to what the firm can obtain in Mexico. According to Pepsico, the quality of the American potatoes is better for their needs.

2. There are far fewer problems with organized labor on the American side.

3. Operational services such as electricity and waste disposal are less expensive.

4. NAFTA-level import duties for both nations are becoming progressively lower.

5. Less bureaucracy and less corruption exist on the American side.

6. The finished product does not have to undergo what can be a time-consuming process: passing through U.S. customs.

7. Roads, telecommunications, and waste disposal on American side are far superior.

8. There has been a lessening of the difference in effective hourly wages: $6 average in Mexico compared with less than $16 in American border area. For products produced by automated manufacturing processes, labor costs commonly range from 15 to 20 percent of production costs compared with 45 to 55 percent of production costs for raw materials.

9. Workers on American side of the border are better educated and more accustomed to factory work. They are bilingual.

10. Far less housing is available on the Mexican side for the workers, many of whom literally live in cardboard boxes. Because of the poor living conditions, a large number leave after a short time, causing the turnover of the workers to be much higher on the Mexican side of the border.

An example of the second situation is the case of a Mexican manufacturer of elastic for the underwear industry. The company, Select Elastics of America, is now constructing a plant in McAllen, Texas, also in the Rio Grande Valley and near the Pepsico plant mentioned above. This firm has been supplying elastic to American producers of underwear, such as Playtex and VF, from Mexican production using Mexican raw materials. To maintain these customers, the company recognizes that it must deliver, on time, a consistently top-quality product. To do so, it must have raw materials of superior quality and they must be constantly available. Because the production process is labor-intensive, the labor cost is 16 to 18 percent of the production cost compared to 48 to 52 percent for the raw materials cost. Thus, the savings in labor costs are insignificant compared to the expense caused by the factors listed above. A company representative believed that the management chose a location close to the border and still far from its clients in the North because the Mexican owners felt more comfortable with an operation in an area with a strong Mexican culture and where most people speak both Spanish and English. It is also much closer to their headquarters in Mexico City.

Representatives of the McAllen Economic Development Corporation are talking with numerous companies from both sides of the border about moving to the area and are finding a high level of interest because of the reasons stated above.

Source: Personal interviews.

Protect Foreign Markets.   Changing the method of going abroad from exporting to overseas production is often necessary to protect foreign markets. The management of a firm supplying a profitable overseas market by exports may begin to note some ominous signs that this market is being threatened.

Lack of Foreign Exchange.   One of the first signs is a delay in payment by the importers. The importers may have sufficient local currency but may be facing delays in buying foreign exchange (currency) from the government's central bank. The credit manager in the exporting firm, by checking with his bank and other exporters, learns that this condition is becoming endemic—a reliable sign that the country is facing a lack of foreign exchange. In examining the country's balance of payments, the financial manager may find that its export revenue has declined while the import volume remains high. Experienced exporters know that import and foreign exchange controls are in the offing and that there is a good chance of losing the market, especially if they sell consumer products. In times of foreign exchange scarcity, governments will invariably give priority to the importation of raw materials and capital goods.

If the advantages of making the investment outweigh the disadvantages, the company may decide to protect this market by producing locally. Managers know that once the company has a plant in the country, the government will do its utmost to provide foreign exchange for raw materials to keep the plant, a source of employment, in operation. Because imports of competing products are prohibited, the only competition, if any, will have to come from other local manufacturers.

Local Production by Competitors.   Lack of foreign exchange is not the only reason a company might change from exporting to manufacturing in a market. For instance, while a firm might enjoy a growing export business and prompt payments, it still may be forced to set up a plant in the market. It may be that its competitors have also noticed their export volumes will support local production.

Should a competing firm move to put up a factory in the market, management must decide rapidly whether to follow suit or risk losing the market forever. Managers know that many governments, especially those in developing nations, will not only prohibit further imports once the product is produced in the country but will also permit only two or three other companies to enter so as to maintain a sufficient market for these local firms. General Motors tried for years to enter Spain, but the Spanish government, believing there were already enough automobile manufacturers in the country, refused the company entry. Only when Spain joined the European Community was General Motors permitted to enter.

Downstream Markets.   A number of OPEC nations have invested in refining and marketing outlets, such as filling stations and heating oil distributors, to guarantee a market for their crude oil at more favorable prices. As shown in Table 2–9, Petroleos de Venezuela, owner of Citgo, is one of the largest foreign investors in the United States. Kuwait bought Gulf Oil's refining and marketing network in three European countries and also owns 20 percent of British Petroleum, which has the third-largest foreign investment in this country. These are just two examples.

Protectionism.   When a government sees that local industry is threatened by imports, it may erect import barriers to stop or reduce them.* Even threats to do this can be sufficient to induce the exporter to invest in production facilities in the importing country. This and the high-priced yen, which makes it difficult for Japanese exports to compete with American products, are the principal reasons for Japanese investment in the United States.

---

*See Chapter 3 for a discussion of import barriers.

Guarantee Supply of Raw Materials.   Few developed nations possess sufficient domestic supplies of raw materials (see Figure 2–7). Japan and Europe are almost totally dependent on foreign sources, and even the United States depends on imports for more than half of its aluminum, chromium, manganese, nickel, tin, and zinc. Furthermore, the Department of the Interior estimates that by the end of the century, iron, lead, tungsten, copper, potassium, and sulfur will be added to the critical list.

To ensure a continuous supply, manufacturers in the industrialized countries are being forced to invest primarily in the developing nations, where most new deposits are being discovered. Interestingly, although Japan does this as well, for years it has also looked to the United States as a source of raw materials. A Japanese deputy general consul once stated,

> The United States offers an abundance of raw materials. Because Japan has long depended on the United States for various materials, such as grain, coking coal, and lumber, it is entirely logical for Japanese firms to establish facilities close to the sources of these essential raw materials.

Some analysts claim that the Japanese-American trade flows approximate those between an industrialized and a developing country: the industrialized nation sends manufactured goods to the developing nation in return for raw materials. This is somewhat exaggerated, but in 1992, 97.4 percent of Japan's exports to the United States consisted of manufactured goods, and over 40 percent of American exports to Japan were foodstuffs, raw materials, and mineral fuels.[33]

Acquire Technology and Management Know-How.   A reason often cited by foreign firms for investing in this country is the acquisition of technology and management know-how. Nippon Mining, for example, a copper mining company, came to Illinois and paid $1 billion for Gould Inc. to acquire technology leadership and market share in producing the copper foil used in printed circuit boards. In a similar situation, Taiwan's Acer Inc. wanted to learn about small business computers so it bought Counterpoint Computers in California for $20 million, saving millions in research.

Geographic Diversification.   Many managements have chosen geographic diversification as a means of maintaining stable sales and earnings when the domestic economy or their industry goes into a slump. Generally, when one economy or industry (building materials, for example) is in a trough, it is at its peak elsewhere in the world. In the early 1980s, the foreign operations of American multinationals were outperforming their domestic counterparts. Sunbeam and Ford, for example, reported that their Mexican business was unusually strong, and Twin-Disc, a transmission manufacturer, said that the slowdown in the European market "wasn't nearly as bad as in the United States."[34] In 1987, earnings jumped 32 percent for Hoechst, the German chemical producer, solely because of the earnings of its American subsidiary, Celanese. "Without those earnings, the company would have shown a profit decline," declared Hoechst's chairman.[35]

Satisfy Management's Desire for Expansion.   The faster growth mentioned previously helps fulfill management's desire for expansion. Stockholders and financial analysts also expect firms to continue to grow, and those companies operating only in the domestic market have found it increasingly difficult to sustain that expectation. As a result, many firms have expanded into foreign markets. This, of course, is what companies based in small countries, such as Nestlé (Switzerland), SKF Bearing (Sweden), and Shell (Great Britain and the Netherlands), discovered decades ago.

FIGURE 2–7 Mineral wealth

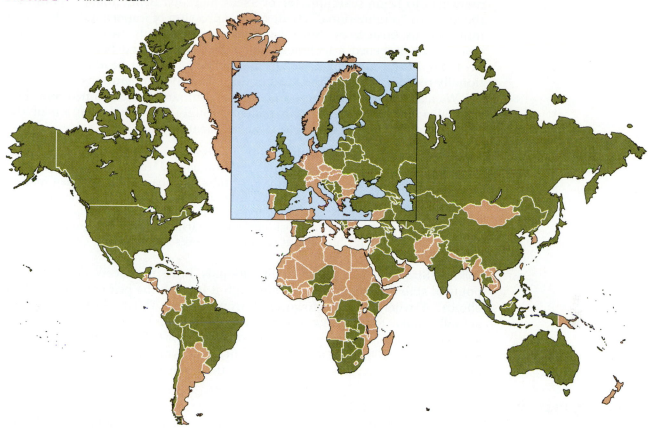

ALBANIA:
Chromium 6.4%

AUSTRALIA:
Bauxite 36.0%
Coal 4.0%
Diamonds 37.5%
Gold 8.7%
Iron 9.9%
Lead 13.6%
Nickel 7.5%
Silver 7.7%
Tin 3.4%
Uranium 9.8%
Zinc 10.6%

BOLIVIA:
Tin 5.1%

BOTSWANA:
Diamonds 16.4%

BRAZIL:
Bauxite 7.7%
Iron 14.9%
Lumber 7.3%
Tin 21.6%

CANADA:
Copper 8.4%
Gold 7.5%
Iron 4.1%
Lead 10.9%
Lumber 5.5%
Nickel 23.7%
Silver 9.8%
Uranium 33.5%
Zinc 18.7%

CHILE:
Copper 12.7%
Silver 3.4%

CHINA:
Bauxite 3.5%
Coal 23.0%
Copper 4.1%
Gold 4.3%
Iron 16.8%
Lead 9.2%
Lumber 8.3%
Nickel 3.4%
Oil 5.0%
Tin 14.7%
Zinc 7.3%

CUBA:
Nickel 5.0%

DOMINICAN REPUBLIC:
Nickel 3.5%

ETHIOPIA:
Lumber 1.2%

FINLAND:
Chromium 4.6%
Lumber 1.3%

FORMER SOVIET UNION:
Bauxite 5.9%
Chromium 27.7%
Coal 14.0%
Copper 11.0%
Diamonds 11.8%
Gold 15.6%
Iron 25.7%
Lead 15.3%
Lumber 11.6%
Nickel 24.4%
Oil 20.0%
Silver 10.7%
Tin 7.4%
Zinc 13.3%

FORMER YUGOSLAVIA:
Bauxite 3.0%
Lead 3.0%

FRANCE:
Uranium 9.4%

GUINEA:
Bauxite 16.8%

INDIA:
Bauxite 3.4%
Chromium 6.5%
Coal 4.0%
Iron 5.4%
Lumber 7.7%

INDONESIA:
Copper 3.3%
Lumber 4.9%
Nickel 7.1%
Tin 14.5%

IRAN:
Oil 5.0%

IRAQ:
Oil 5.0%

JAMAICA:
Bauxite 7.3%

JAPAN:
Lumber 1.0%

KENYA:
Lumber 1.0%

MALAYSIA:
Lumber 1.2%
Tin 14.2%

MEXICO:
Copper 3.0%
Lead 5.0%
Oil 5.0%
Silver 16.0%
Zinc 3.6%

NAMIBIA:
Uranium 9.6%

NEW CALEDONIA:
Nickel 7.4%

NIGER:
Uranium 8.2%

NIGERIA:
Lumber 3.0%

NORTH KOREA:
Zinc 3.1%

PERU:
Copper 3.3%
Lead 4.4%
Silver 10.5%
Zinc 6.7%

PHILIPPINES:
Lumber 1.1%

POLAND:
Copper 4.9%
Coal 5.0%
Silver 7.2%

SAUDI ARABIA:
Oil 8.0%

SOUTH AFRICA:
Chromium 36.3%
Diamonds 9.2%
Gold 34.5%
Nickel 4.1%
Uranium 10.6%

SPAIN:
Silver 3.6%
Zinc 3.8%

SURINAME:
Bauxite 3.4%

SWEDEN:
Lumber 1.6%

THAILAND:
Lumber 1.1%
Tin 7.0%

TURKEY:
Chromium 6.8%

UNITED KINGDOM:
Oil 3.0%

UNITED STATES:
Coal 24.0%
Copper 15.8%
Gold 11.2%
Iron 5.9%
Lead 11.6%
Lumber 14.9%
Oil 14.0%
Silver 11.3%
Uranium 13.9%
Zinc 3.6%

VENEZUELA:
Oil 3.0%

ZAIRE:
Diamonds 19.6%

ZAMBIA:
Copper 5.8%

ZIMBABWE:
Chromium 4.8%
Copper 5.2%

Another aspect of this reason sometimes motivates a company's top managers to begin searching for overseas markets. Being able to claim that the firm is a "multinational" creates the impression of importance, which can influence its customers. Sun Microsystems, a manufacturer of computer workstations, opened a technical center in Germany and built a factory in Scotland. "To be a major player in the marketplace, you have to be internationally recognized," said the head of Sun's European operations.[36]

We also know of instances in which a company has examined and then entered a market because its president brought it to the attention of the market planners after enjoying a pleasant vacation there.

> How else can you explain the fact that in pre-Castro Cuba, there were three American tire factories in Havana, the "fun capital" of the world, with Miami just 90 miles away? Delivery of tires to Cuba could have been made in hours and at better prices. One of the authors found out why when he spent a winter in Akron working for a tire company. That was the time of the year when the Cuban subsidiary customarily had financial, marketing, and production problems that required the presence of Akron executives.

Political Stability.　　U.S.-based multinationals have not been motivated by political stability to go overseas, although it is often the prime factor in their choice of where to go. However, European and Third World firms may actually make foreign investments (usually in the United States) for that reason. "The U.S. is a very safe place to invest," says Gilbert de Botton, head of London-based Global Asset Management, which manages $1.6 billion. "You are as comfortable there, if not more so, than you are in your own home."[37]

HOW TO ENTER FOREIGN MARKETS

As you learned in Chapter 1, all of the means for supplying foreign markets may be subsumed in just two activities: (1) exporting to a foreign market or (2) manufacturing in it.

Exporting

Most firms began their involvement in overseas business by exporting—that is, selling some of their regular production overseas. This method requires little investment and is relatively free of risks. It is an excellent means of getting a feel for international business without committing any great amount of human or financial resources. If management does decide to export, it must choose between *direct* and *indirect* exporting.

indirect exporting
The exporting of goods and services through various types of home-based exporters

Indirect Exporting.　　**Indirect exporting** is simpler than direct exporting because it requires neither special expertise nor large cash outlays. Exporters based in their home country will do the work. Management merely follows instructions. Among the exporters available are (1) *manufacturers' export agents*, who sell for the manufacturer; (2) *export commission agents*, who buy for their overseas customers; (3) *export merchants*, who purchase and sell for their own account; and (4) *international firms*, which use the goods overseas (mining, construction, and petroleum companies are examples).

Indirect exporters, however, pay a price for such service: (1) they will pay a commission to the first three kinds of exporters; (2) foreign business can be lost if exporters decide to change their sources of supply; and (3) firms gain little experience from these transactions. This is why many managements that begin in this manner generally change to direct exporting.

direct exporting
The exporting of goods and services by the firm that produces them

Direct Exporting.　　To engage in **direct exporting**, management must assign the job of handling the export business to someone within the firm. The simplest arrangement is to give someone, usually the sales manager, the responsibility for developing the export business. Domestic employees may handle the billing, credit, and shipping initially, and if the business expands, a separate export department may be set up. A firm that has been exporting to wholesale importers in an area and servicing them by visits from either home office personnel or foreign-based sales representatives frequently finds that sales have grown to a point that will support a complete marketing organization.

Management may then decide to set up a **sales company** in the area. The sales company will import in its own name from the parent and will invoice in local currency. It may employ the same channels of distribution, though the new organization may permit the use of a more profitable arrangement. This type of organization can grow quite large, often invoicing several millions of dollars annually. Before building a plant in Mexico, for many years Eastman Kodak imported and resold cameras and photographic supplies while doing a large business in local film developing. Many firms that began with local repair facilities later expanded to produce simple components. Gradually, they produced more of the product locally until, after a period of time, they were manufacturing all of the components in the country.

sales company
A business established for the purpose of marketing goods and services, not producing them

A firm's foreign business may evolve sequentially over the path just traced, or a company may move directly to foreign production (nonsequentially) for any of the reasons discussed previously in the section "Why Enter Foreign Markets?"

Before examining foreign manufacturing, we want to describe briefly the *turnkey project,* which is an export of technology, management expertise, and in some cases, capital equipment. The contractor agrees to design and erect a plant, supply the process technology, provide the necessary suppliers of raw materials and other production inputs, and then train the operating personnel. After a trial run, the facility is turned over to the purchaser.

The exporter may be a contractor that specializes in designing and erecting plants in a particular industry such as petroleum refining or steel production. It may also be a company in the industry that wishes to earn money from its expertise by delivering a plant ready to run rather than merely selling its technology. Chemical companies sold numerous turnkey projects to the communist countries, for example. Another kind of supplier of turnkey projects is the producer of a key input that sells a complete plant in order to obtain a contract to provide its product to the finished factory.

> One of the writers used to sell Goodyear latex to a U.S. manufacturer of paint driers. The client found it could lock in contracts to supply its products overseas by selling investors in developing countries a complete paint factory. It designed the plant, hired a contractor to erect it, trained the people to operate it, and provided ongoing technical assistance after the factory was delivered to the owners. The company also acted as a distributor for American producers of other inputs and manufacturers of paint-making machinery.

Foreign Manufacturing

When management does decide to become involved in foreign manufacturing, it generally has five distinct alternatives available, though not all of them may be feasible in a particular country. These are:

1. Wholly owned subsidiary.
2. Joint venture.
3. Licensing agreement.
4. Franchising.
5. Contract manufacturing.

A sixth arrangement, the *management contract,* is utilized by both manufacturing and service companies to earn income by providing management expertise for a fee.

Wholly Owned Subsidiary.   The company that wishes to own a foreign subsidiary outright may (1) start from the ground up by building a new plant, (2) acquire a going concern, or (3) purchase its distributor, thus obtaining a distribution network familiar with its products. In this last case, of course, production facilities will have to be built. American companies certainly prefer wholly owned subsidiaries, but they do not have a marked preference for any of the three means of obtaining them.

However, this is not the case for foreign investors in the United States, who prefer to acquire going concerns for the instant access to the market they provide. Moreover, they also have one less competitor after the purchase.

> Rather than build a U.S. plant, YKK, a leading Japanese zipper manufacturer, paid $50 million for Universal Fasteners, a competitor based in Kentucky. "They bought instant market share with no headaches," said a banker familiar with the transaction.[38]

In 1993, as in previous years, nearly 90 percent of the $26.2 billion spent by foreign investors was for acquiring American firms. Only $3.1 billion was spent to establish new companies. Figure 2–8 points out an interesting fact. The average size of an acquisition in 1993 was six times that of an investment in a new firm ($41.7 million versus $6.9 million).

Sometimes it is not possible to have a wholly owned foreign subsidiary. The host government may not permit it, the firm may lack either capital or expertise to undertake the investment alone, or there may be tax and other advantages that favor a joint venture.

FIGURE 2–8 Investment outlays and number of investments, 1985–1993

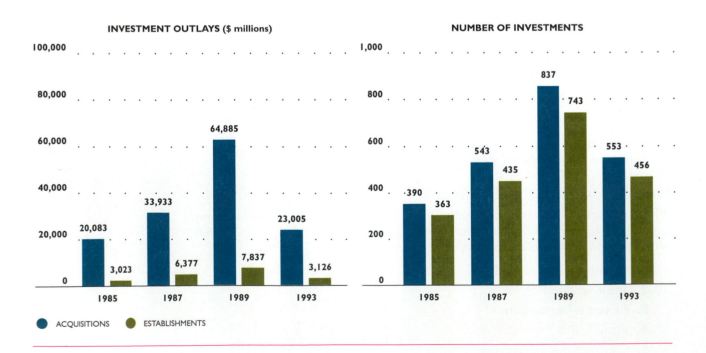

Joint Venture.   A **joint venture** may be (1) a corporate entity formed by an international company and local owners, (2) a corporate entity formed by two international companies for the purpose of doing business in a third market, (3) a corporate entity formed by a government agency (usually in the country of investment) and an international firm, or (4) a cooperative undertaking between two or more firms of a limited-duration project. Large construction jobs such as a dam or an airport are frequently handled by this last form.

In 1987, Ford and Volkswagen formed a novel joint venture in which their operations in Argentina and Brazil were merged into a holding company, Autolatina, in an effort to eliminate losses suffered by both. The joint venture, owned 51 percent by Volkswagen and 49 percent by Ford, assembled products based on VW and Ford designs, but both companies marketed the vehicles through their own distribution channels. Although 1993 sales reached $7.58 billion, the companies decided to terminate the operation. One industry expert says that Ford wanted to leave because Autolatina did not fit its new global strategy of having global vehicles. The two companies clashed about sharing models when they are facing increasing pressure from General Motors, which has sold so many of its Corsa subcompacts that it undertook an ad campaign telling consumers not to be in a hurry to buy the car. In 1994, Volkswagen dealers refused to share the company's new subcompact with Ford, prompting Ford to rush its program to produce the small Fiesta. In a news release, the companies said the termination of the joint venture reflects "the necessity of the companies to make better use of the force and resources of their worldwide organizations."[39]

When the CEO of General Mills decided to enter the European market where a very tough rival, Kelloggs, was entrenched, he knew it would be very expensive to set up manufacturing facilities and a huge marketing force. However, he knew that another food giant, Nestlé, the world's largest food company, has a famous name in Europe, a number of manufacturing plants, and a strong distribution system. It also lacked strong cereal brand names, something that General Mills, the number two American cereal company, has. Just three weeks after the initial discussions, General Mills and Nestlé formed a joint venture, Cereal Partners Worldwide. General Mills provides the cereal technology, brand names, and its cereal marketing expertise. Nestlé supplies its name, distribution channels, and production capacity. Cereal Partners Worldwide will distribute worldwide, except in the United States, where it is excluded.[40]

When the government of a host country requires companies to have some local participation, foreign firms must engage in a joint venture with local owners to do business in that country. In some situations, however, a foreign firm will seek local partners even when there is no local requirement to do so.

Strong Nationalism.   Strong nationalistic sentiment may cause the foreign firm to try to lose its identity by joining with local investors. Care must be taken with this strategy, however. Although a large number of people in many developing countries dislike multinationals for "exploiting" them, they still believe, often with good reason, that the products of the foreign companies are superior to those of purely national firms. One solution to this ambivalence has been to form a joint venture in which the local partners are highly visible, give it an indigenous name, and then advertise that a foreign firm (actually the partner) is supplying the technology. Even wholly owned subsidiaries have followed this strategy.

Eastman Kodak has eliminated the word *Kodak* from the names of its 100-percent-owned subsidiaries in Venezuela, Mexico, Chile, Peru, and Colombia. Kodak-Venezuela has become Foto Interamericana, and Kodak's

joint venture
A cooperative effort among two or more organizations who share a common interest in a business enterprise or undertaking

large manufacturing company in Mexico is now called Industria Fotografica Interamericana.

Acquire Expertise, Tax, and Other Benefits.   Other factors that influence managements to enter joint ventures are the ability to acquire an expertise that is lacking, special tax benefits some governments extend to companies with local partners, or the need for additional capital and experienced personnel.

> Merck, the largest U.S. maker of ethical drugs, spent $313 million to acquire 50.5 percent of Banyu Pharmaceutical in Japan. Management had been dissatisfied with the performance of Merck's Japanese subsidiary in the world's second-largest ethical drug market. With this acquisition, the 600-person sales force of Merck-Japan was augmented by Banyu's 350 sales representatives. Merck's chairman said, "To bring new products effectively to market in Japan required a larger and more effective marketing organization. With a controlling interest in Banyu, I would hope for a better penetration of the Japanese market."[41]
>
> To take advantage of Israel's lower labor costs and the 1985 U.S.–Israel Trade Agreement, which (1) reduced import duties on Israeli-made shirts and (2) permitted them quota-free access to the United States, Van Heusen decided to buy the production facilities of an insolvent Israeli clothing manufacturer. When the government refused to sell on Van Heusen's terms, the company formed a joint venture with another Israeli textile-and-apparel conglomerate. Van Heusen will purchase the plant's output for five years, with the option to extend the agreement if satisfied with the local partner's performance, and will have exclusive control over marketing. Although it has trained Israeli engineers and will maintain its own engineers at the operation, the Israeli partner has had to invest all of the capital to expand an existing plant.[42]

Some firms, as a matter of policy, enter joint ventures to reduce investment risk. Their strategy is to enter into a joint venture with either native partners or another worldwide company. Still others, such as Ford and Volkswagen, have joined together to achieve economies of scale. Incidentally, any division of ownership in a joint venture is possible unless there are specific legal requirements.

Disadvantages.   Although a joint venture arrangement offers the advantage of less commitment of financial and managerial resources, and thus less risk, there are some disadvantages for the foreign firm. One, obviously, is that profits must be shared. Furthermore, if the law allows the foreign investors to have no more than a 49 percent participation (common in developing countries), they may not have control. This is because the stock markets in these countries are either small or nonexistent, so it is generally impossible to distribute the shares widely enough to permit the foreign firm with its 49 percent to be the largest stockholder.

Lack of control over the joint venture is why many managements resist making such arrangements. They feel that they must have tight control of their foreign subsidiaries to obtain an efficient allocation of investments and production and to maintain a coordinated marketing plan worldwide. For example, local partners might wish to export to markets that the global company serves from its own plants, or they might want to make the complete product locally when the global company's strategy is to produce only certain components there and import the rest from other subsidiaries.[43]

In recent years, numerous governments of developing nations have passed laws requiring local majority ownership for the purpose of giving control of firms within their borders to their own citizens. Despite these laws, control with a minority ownership is still feasible.

Control with Minority Ownership.   There have been occasions when the foreign partner has been able to circumvent the spirit of the law and ensure its control by taking 49 percent of the shares and giving 2 percent to its local law firm or some other trusted national.

Another method is to take in a local majority partner, such as a government agency, an insurance company, or a financial institution, that is content to invest merely for a return while leaving the venture's management to the foreign partner. If neither arrangement can be made, the foreign company may still control the joint venture, at least in the areas of major concern, by means of a *management contract.*

Management Contract.   The **management contract** is an arrangement under which a company provides managerial know-how in some or all functional areas to another party for a fee that ranges from 2 to 5 percent of sales. International companies make such contracts with (1) firms in which they have no ownership (examples: Hilton Hotel provides management for non-owned overseas hotels that use the Hilton name, and Delta provides management assistance to foreign airlines), (2) joint venture partners, and (3) wholly owned subsidiaries. The last arrangement is made solely for the purpose of allowing the parent to siphon off some of the subsidiary's profits. This becomes extremely important when, as in many foreign exchange–poor nations, the parent firm is limited in the amount of profits it can repatriate. Moreover, because the fee is an expense, the subsidiary receives a tax benefit.

management contract
An arrangement by which one firm provides management in all or specific areas to another firm

Used in Joint Ventures.   Management contracts can enable the global partner to control many aspects of a joint venture even when holding only a minority position. If it supplies key personnel, such as the production and technical managers, the global company can be assured of product quality with which its name may be associated as well as be able to earn additional income by selling the joint venture inputs manufactured in the home plant. This is possible because the larger global company is more vertically integrated. A local paint factory, for example, might have to import certain semiprocessed pigments and driers that the foreign partner produces in its home country for domestic operations. If these can be purchased elsewhere at a lower price, the local majority could insist on other sources of supply. This rarely happens, because the production and technical managers can argue that only inputs from their employer will produce a satisfactory product. They are the experts, and they generally have the final word.

Purchasing Commission.   There is another source of income that a global or multinational company derives not only from firms with which it has a management contract but also from joint ventures and wholly owned subsidiaries. That source is a commission for acting as purchasing agent of imported raw materials and equipment. This relieves the affiliates of having to establish credit lines with foreign suppliers and assures them that they will receive the same materials used by the foreign partner. The commission received for this service averages about 5 percent of invoice value and is in addition to the management contract fee.

Licensing.   Frequently, worldwide companies are called on to furnish technical assistance to firms that have sufficient capital and management strength. By means of a **licensing** agreement, one firm (the licensor) will grant to another firm (the licensee) the right to use any kind of expertise, such as manufacturing processes (patented or unpatented), marketing procedures, and trademarks for one or more of the licensor's products.

licensing
A contractual arrangement in which one firm grants access to its patents, trade secrets, or technology to another for a fee

General Tire, before being bought by Continental, the German tire manufacturer, was both a licensor and a licensee. It licensed some firms to use its tire technology and others to use its know-how to produce plastic film. At the same time, it made licensing agreements with manufacturers of conveyor belting, V belting, and car batteries to use their technology in General Tire plants overseas.

The licensee generally pays a fixed sum when signing the licensing agreement and then pays a royalty of from 2 to 5 percent of sales over the life of the contract (five to seven years, with option for renewal). The exact amount of the royalty will depend on the amount of assistance given and the relative bargaining power of the two parties.

In the past, licensing was not a primary source of income for international firms. This changed in the 1980s, however, especially in this country, because (1) the courts began upholding patent infringement claims more than they used to, (2) patent holders became more vigilant in suing violators, and (3) the federal government pressed foreign governments to enforce their patent laws.[44]

This forced foreign companies to obtain licenses instead of making illegal copies. Texas Instruments, for example, sued nine Japanese electronics manufacturers for using its patented processes without paying licensing fees. The defendants have paid the company over $1 billion since 1986 ($260 million in 1991 alone).[45] It is estimated that Union Carbide, which has a special division to sell its technology and services, added 5 percent to its pre-tax profit just by licensing its process to make a single product—polystyrene, a plastic. According to the Department of Commerce, American firms received $20.4 billion in payment of royalties and license fees from foreign customers in 1993 and paid out only $4.8 billion.[46]

However, more than know-how is licensed. In the fashion industry, a number of designers license the use of their names. Pierre Cardin, the largest such licensor, has 840 licenses worldwide on everything from skis to frying pans. These earn the company $75 million annually, including $12 million from 32 American licensees. Even Russia pays the firm three-quarters of a million dollars every year.

Are you giving Coca-Cola free advertising on your T-shirt? The company's manager for merchandise licensing expects the company to make millions from an agreement with the founder of Gloria Vanderbilt. He says the firm agreed to the arrangement because "clothes enhance our image. The money is not important."

Another industry, magazine publishing, is licensing overseas editions. You can buy *Cosmopolitan* in the native language in over 12 countries, *Playboy* in 10, and *Penthouse* in 5. For some reason, *High Technology* appears only in Japan.

Despite the opportunity to obtain a sizable income from licensing, many firms, especially those that produce high-tech products, will not grant licenses. They fear that a licensee will become a competitor upon expiration of the agreement or that it will aggressively seek to market the products outside of its territory. At one time, licensors routinely inserted a clause in the licensing agreement that prohibited exports, but most governments will not accept such a prohibition.

franchising
A form of licensing in which one firm contracts with another to operate a certain type of business under an established name according to specific rules

Franchising.   In recent years, American firms have gone overseas with a new kind of licensing—**franchising**. Franchising permits the franchisee to sell products or services under a highly publicized brand name and a well-proven set of procedures with a carefully developed and controlled marketing strategy. Of the 35,000 overseas outlets operated by 374 American franchising companies, fast-food operations (such as McDonald's, Kentucky Fried

FIGURE 2–9 International franchising (U.S. firms) in 1988

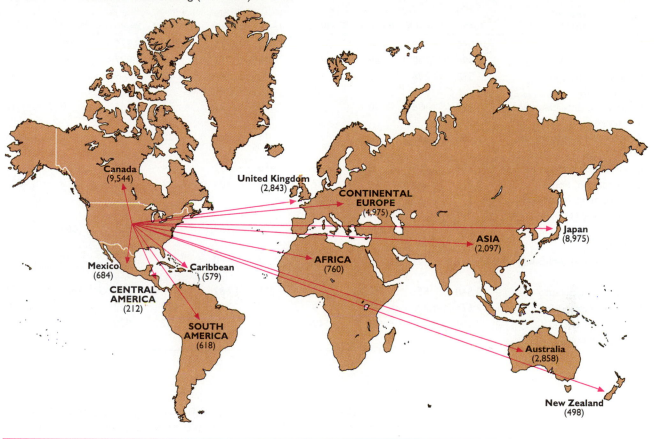

Notes: Franchising companies (374).
Number of franchising outlets (35,046).

Chicken, and Tastee-Freeze) are the most numerous—McDonald's alone has about 2,500 outlets in 40 countries (see Figure 2–9). As Table 2–11 indicates, Canada is the dominant market with 9,544 units, Japan is second with 8,975, and Australia is third with 2,858. These data are for 1988. No later data are available.

   Other types of franchisors are hotels (Hilton, Holiday Inn), business services (Muzak, Manpower), soft drinks (Coca-Cola, Orange Crush), home maintenance (Servicemaster, Nationwide Exterminating), and automotive products (Midas).

Contract Manufacturing.   International firms employ **contract manufacturing** in two ways. One way is as a means of entering a foreign market without investing in plant facilities. The firm contracts with a local manufacturer to produce products for it according to its specifications. The firm's sales organization markets the products under its own brand, just as Montgomery Ward sells washing machines made by Norge.

contract manufacturing
An arrangement in which one firm contracts with another to produce products to its specifications but assumes responsibility for marketing

   When Gates Rubber licensed its V belt technology to General Tire's Chilean plant, it drew up a novel licensing agreement that included contract manufacturing. General Tire was obliged to produce part of its output with the Gates label. Gates executives knew that in Chile, once General Tire began production, the government would stop the importation of all V belts,

TABLE 2–11 Location of international franchisees of American franchisors

Types of Franchises	Total	Canada	Mexico	Caribbean	U.K.	Other Europe	Australia	Japan	Other Asia	Other
Total	35,046	9,544	684	579	2,843	4,975	2,858	8,975	2,097	2,491
Restaurants (all kinds)	6,996	1,338	146	213	726	772	750	1,827	546	678
Hotels, motels and campgrounds	518	238	22	19	28	77	13	9	31	81
Recreation, entertainment, and travel	327	194	0	1	17	25	34	41	0	15
Automotive products and services	1,708	683	25	31	15	505	128	143	49	129
Business aids and services	5,851	2,762	8	8	459	732	774	890	103	113
Construction, home improvement, maintenance, and cleaning services	2,813	1,188	0	7	502	104	27	647	17	321
Educational products and services	5,583	520	124	7	106	183	262	1,591	665	43
Laundry and dry-cleaning services	27	21	0	0	1	0	0	0	5	0
Rental services (auto-truck)	5,548	553	268	265	378	1,682	417	579	471	935
Retailing (nonfood)	3,574	1,378	78	9	548	720	429	227	81	104
Retailing (food, nonconvenience)	2,101	669	13	19	63	175	22	939	129	72

Source: Exhibit 127, *Franchising in the Economy 1988–1990*, p. 100.

including theirs. Gates would gain in a number of ways: (1) it would earn a royalty on all belts made in Chile, (2) it would have belts made in Chile to Gates specifications without making any investment in production facilities, and (3) competition from a dozen importers would be eliminated. There would be only one local competitor, General Tire. General Tire gained because it increased its product mix and offered another product to its present channels of distribution.

The second way is to subcontract assembly work or the production of parts to independent companies overseas. Although the international firm has no equity in the subcontractor, this practice does resemble foreign direct investment. When the international firm is the largest or only customer of the subcontractors, it has in effect created in another country a new company that generates employment and foreign exchange for the host nation. Frequently, the international firm will lend capital to the foreign contractor in the same way that a global or multinational firm will lend funds to its subsidiary. Because of these similarities, this practice is called *foreign direct investment without investment.*

Strategic Alliances. Faced with (1) expanding global competition, (2) the growing cost of research, product development, and marketing, and (3) the need to move faster in carrying out their global strategies, many firms are forming **strategic alliances** with competitors (called *competitive alliances*), suppliers, and customers. Their aim is to achieve faster market entry and start-up; to gain access to new products, technologies, and markets; and to share costs, resources, and risks.

Alliances include various types of partnerships. Companies wanting to share technology will cross-license their technology (each will license its technology to the other). If their aim is to pool research and design resources,

strategic alliance
Partnerships between competitors, customers, or suppliers that may take one or more of various forms

they will form an R&D partnership. For example, Texas Instruments and Hitachi, which have had a technical information exchange since 1988, agreed in 1991 to develop together a common design and manufacturing process for 64-megabit DRAMs. Each firm will handle its own mass production and marketing.[47]

Alliances May Be Joint Ventures.   Other companies carry the cooperation further by forming joint ventures in manufacturing and marketing. In 1986, Westinghouse and Toshiba formed an equity joint venture to produce color display tubes for computer terminals and picture tubes for TV sets. Westinghouse, which was making monochrome tubes, formed the alliance to get the technology to produce color tubes. The joint venture gave Toshiba an opportunity to be involved in a manufacturing facility that could supply tubes to its TV plant in Tennessee. The Japanese also expected that another U.S.-based venture would help deflect protectionist pressure from Toshiba.[48] Toshiba provided the technology and Westinghouse provided a factory building and helped arrange financing, including $46 million in low-cost public loans. However, within just two years, Westinghouse had sold its interest to Toshiba, which then became the sole owner of the facility.[49]

Alliances Can Be Mergers and Acquisitions.   Swedish ASEA and Swiss Brown Bovari, both energy generation and transmission specialists, merged to form an $18 billion company. The reason, according to the CEO of the new firm, was that the two firms individually were too small to compete with U.S. and Japanese rivals such as Westinghouse, General Electric, Hitachi, and Toshiba.

Future of Alliances.   There is no question that some alliances have accomplished what they set out to accomplish. CFM International, the alliance between General Electric and France's Snecma, has been producing jet engines for two decades. Airbus Industrie, an alliance among British, French, German, and Spanish aircraft manufacturers, is now the world's second-largest commercial aircraft producer.

Nevertheless, many alliances fail or are taken over by one of the partners. The management consulting firm, McKinsey & Co., surveyed 150 companies involved in alliances that had been terminated. It found that three-quarters of the alliances had been taken over by Japanese partners.[50] Professor Chalmers Johnson, an expert on Japan, warns, "I find the idea of joint ventures no longer makes any sense at all. They are a way for the Japanese to acquire technology."[51]

PATHS TO MULTINATIONALISM

Many large global and multinational firms with numerous manufacturing subsidiaries all over the world began their foreign operations by exporting. Once succeeding at this stage, they established sales companies overseas to market their exports. Where sales companies were able to develop sufficiently large markets, their firms set up plants to assemble imported parts. Finally, complete products were manufactured locally. However, this sequence does not represent the only way firms can enter foreign markets. In some countries, conditions may require a complete manufacturing plant as the means of initial entry. International companies today are simultaneously employing all of the methods we have discussed to reach their worldwide markets.

> Gillette, in its 1992 annual report, stated that "manufacturing operations are conducted at 57 facilities in 28 countries, and products are distributed through wholesalers, retailers, and agents in over 200 countries and territories."

SUMMARY

1. **Appreciate the magnitude of international trade and how it has grown.** The volume of international trade in goods and services measured in current dollars approached $5 trillion in 1994. Merchandise exports at $3.75 trillion were 12 times what they were in 1970.

2. **Identify the direction of trade, or who trades with whom.** The percentage of total exports of all the categories of developed nations to other developed nations is declining with the exception of Canada's. Most of Canada's exports to DCs go to the United States, and they have been increasing since the U.S.–Canada Free Trade Agreement went into effect. Developing nations are selling more to each other, as are members of the LAIA.

3. **Recognize the value of analyzing trade statistics.** The analysis of trade statistics is useful to anyone starting to search outside the home market for new trade opportunities. Studying the general growth and direction of trade and analyzing the major trading partners will give an idea as to where the trading activity is.

4. **Explain the size, growth, and direction of U.S. foreign direct investment.** Foreign direct investment (FDI) has also grown rapidly and now totals almost $2 trillion. The American FDI is almost double that of Japan, the next largest foreign investor, which is closely followed by that of the United Kingdom. The direction of foreign direct investment follows the direction of international trade; that is, developed nations invest in each other just as they trade with each other.

5. **Identify who invests and how much is invested in the United States.** Foreign direct investment in the United States has risen from $7 billion in 1960 to $445 billion in 1992. Companies from just five nations—the United Kingdom, Japan, the Netherlands, Germany, and Canada—own over 75 percent of the total

FDI. Japanese firms now own slightly more in the United States than do English firms.

6. **Understand the reasons for entering foreign markets.** Companies enter foreign markets (exporting to and manufacturing in) to increase sales and profits and to protect markets, sales, and profits. Foreign firms often buy American firms to acquire technology and marketing know-how. Foreign investment also enables a company to diversify geographically.

7. **Recognize the weaknesses in using GNP per capita as a basis for comparing economies.** One must be careful in using GNP blindly as a basis for comparing nations' economies. First, the reliability of the data is questionable. Second, the World Bank and other international agencies convert national currencies to dollars, the unit that usually appears in their statistics. Official exchange rates do not reflect the relative domestic purchasing powers of currencies. To overcome this deficiency, the agencies use exchange rates based on purchasing power parity of the currencies.

8. **Understand the international market entry methods.** The two basic methods of entering foreign markets is through exporting to or manufacturing in them. Exporting may be done directly or indirectly. A firm may become involved in foreign production through various methods: (1) wholly owned subsidiaries, (2) joint ventures, (3) licensing, (4) franchising, and (5) contract manufacturing.

9. **Explain the many forms of strategic alliances.** Many firms are forming strategic alliances with competing companies, suppliers, and customers to gain access to new products, technology, and markets and to share resources, costs, and risks. Strategic alliances take many forms, including licensing, mergers, joint ventures, and joint research and development contracts.

KEY WORDS

QUESTIONS

1. The greater part of international trade consists of an exchange of raw materials from developing nations for the manufactured goods from developed nations. True or false? Explain.

2. The volume of exports has increased, but the ranking of U.S. trading partners in order of importance remains the same year after year. True or false? Of what use is this information to a businessperson?

3. What is the value of analyzing foreign trade data? For example, what should the tripling of world exports in just 23 years indicate to businesspeople?

4. Knowing that a nation is a major trading partner of another signifies what to a marketing analyst?

5. You saw in the text that Japan's foreign direct investment in the United States went from $4.2 billion in 1980 to $96.7 billion in 1992, an increase of 2,300 percent. Yet, the Japanese invested only 12.85 times as many yen in 1992 as they did in 1980. How is this possible? Government officials have tried to talk down the value of the dollar because a cheaper dollar would make U.S. exports cheaper in other currencies. How does this affect Japanese investment in the United States?

6. How can a firm protect its domestic market by investing overseas?

7. Why might management decide to bypass indirect exporting and go to direct exporting right from the start?

8. Under what conditions might a company prefer a joint venture to a wholly owned subsidiary when making a foreign investment?

9. *a.* Why would the foreign partner in a joint venture wish to have a management contract with the local partner?

   b. Why would a global or multinational require a wholly owned foreign subsidiary to sign a management contract when it already owns the subsidiary?

10. *a.* What are in-bond plants?

   b. What simple act by Congress probably would put them out of business?

MINICASE 2–1   Quick Research—The Stanton Bearing Company

The Stanton Bearing Company is a medium-sized manufacturer of tapered, needle, and cylindrical roller bearings. Bill Stanton, the president, is dissatisfied with the company's growth and has been thinking about exporting to increase sales. At a university seminar, Stanton heard about the exporting successes of some small firms whose sales are about the same as those of the Stanton Bearing Company ($25 million annually). He learned that the U.S. Department of Commerce gathers statistics on exports and imports and publishes them in *U.S. Merchandise Trade: Exports, General Imports, and Imports for Consumption, FT925.* A copy is available in the government documents section of the local university.

He calls in Jane Anderson, the marketing manager, and asks her to do some quick research. "Jane, perhaps there is a market overseas for our products. I heard that the university has a Department of Commerce publication called *FT925*, which gives the monthly and cumulative totals by product for countries importing that product from the United States and for countries exporting it to the United States. The December issue will give you the total for the whole year (see page 70). Please send your assistant to the university to make a copy of the data for our products from this *FT925*. This will tell us which countries are now buying our American competitors' bearings and which countries are our major competitors here in this market. Of course, I think we already know our competitors. Still, it won't hurt to check."

1. What countries seem to be good markets for Stanton Bearing?

2. What percentage of the total market do these countries represent?

3. Are there any other product or geographical markets represented on this page of the *FT925* that could be of interest to Stanton?

4. What other information about these potential markets will Jane Anderson want to gather?

Table 2. VALUE OF EXPORTS AND GENERAL IMPORTS BY SITC COMMODITY GROUPINGS BY COUNTRY – Con.

[IN THOUSANDS OF DOLLARS, SEE EXPLANATION OF STATISTICS FOR ADDITIONAL INFORMATION ON COVERAGE, DEFINITION OF EXPORT AND IMPORT VALUATIONS, ESTIMATING PROCEDURES, AND SOURCES OF ERROR IN THE DATA.]

Column 1

COUNTRY	ANNUAL EXPORTS F.A.S. VALUE BASIS	ANNUAL GENERAL IMPORTS CUSTOMS VALUE BASIS
74595 AUTOMATIC GOODS-VENDING MACHS, INCL MONEY-CHG MACHS–Con.		
SINGARP	1 733	-
SPAIN	8 684	-
SWITZLD	48	2 095
TURKEY	2 652	-
U KING	19 088	3 877
OTH CTY	10 002	97
TOTAL	140 331	24 347
74597 PARTS FOR AUTOMATIC GOODS-VENDING MACHINES		
AUSTRAL....	948	23
CANADA	9 613	1 324
CHINA T	287	3 544
DENMARK ...	3 336	135
FR GERM	2 750	421
FRANCE	1 329	92
HUNGARY ...	769	241
ITALY	824	62
JAPAN	342	6 581
MEXICO	1 491	856
SWITZLD....	58	733
U KING	3 099	3 348
OTH CTY	4 242	593
TOTAL	29 088	17 954
74610 BALL BEARINGS		
AUSTRAL....	3 078	34
AUSTRIA	222	1 174
BELGIUM	940	43
BRAZIL	2 163	2 525
CANADA	136 075	60 579
CHINA M	1 156	37 688
CHINA T	719	17 927
COLOMB	1 030	-
FR GERM	5 599	49 342
FRANCE	2 275	17 805
HG KONG ...	744	1 654
HUNGARY ...	116	1 300
INDIA	199	4 248
IRELAND	708	14
ISRAEL	892	5
ITALY	1 369	13 150
JAPAN	10 132	224 622
KOR REP	2 229	12 862
MEXICO	14 823	6 516
NETHLDS....	4 373	184
POLAND	74	7 899
PORTUGL ...	-	1 122
REP SAF	864	535
RUSSIA	21	3 566
SINGARP	4 911	61 191
SPAIN	621	3 294
SWEDEN	232	3 980
SWITZLD....	1 231	4 743
THAILND....	233	9 043
U KING	4 828	10 705
VENEZ	1 990	-
OTH CTY	5 658	2 201
TOTAL	209 506	559 950
74620 TAPERED ROLLER BEARINGS		
ARGENT	2 198	3
AUSTRAL....	7 793	2 678
BELGIUM	1 970	27
BRAZIL	5 510	943
CANADA	40 555	11 470
CHILE	794	-
CHINA M	301	18 274
CHINA T	1 475	58
COLOMB	2 937	-
FR GERM	11 745	21 226
FRANCE	3 843	5 501
HG KONG ...	740	298
HUNGARY ...	1 541	426
INDIA	2 301	-
ITALY	2 195	209
JAPAN	6 059	31 260
KOR REP....	4 589	194
MEXICO	20 542	5 898
PAKISTN	701	-
PHIL R	623	-
POLAND	33	3 018
REP SAF	3 487	399
SINGARP	2 264	180
SPAIN	749	259
U KING	4 757	6 920
VENEZ	4 470	-

Column 2

COUNTRY	ANNUAL EXPORTS F.A.S. VALUE BASIS	ANNUAL GENERAL IMPORTS CUSTOMS VALUE BASIS
74620 TAPERED ROLLER BEARINGS– Con.		
OTH CTY	5 238	1 293
TOTAL	139 408	110 532
74630 SPHERICAL ROLLER BEARINGS		
AUSTRAL....	880	4
AUSTRIA	29	781
BRAZIL	938	16
CANADA	13 310	169
FR GERM	798	13 987
HG KONG ...	1 690	-
ITALY	173	5 747
JAPAN	646	5 830
MEXICO	1 358	1
REP SAF	924	23
SINGARP ...	886	2
SWEDEN	126	10 311
U KING	793	6 053
OTH CTY	2 647	2 396
TOTAL	25 197	45 318
74640 NEEDLE ROLLER BEARINGS		
AUSTRAL....	916	-
CANADA	8 151	2 277
CHINA T	227	965
FR GERM	4 735	7 776
FRANCE	572	698
JAPAN	1 220	16 656
KOR REP	938	12
MEXICO	683	7
SINGARP ...	819	12
U KING	1 476	126
OTH CTY	2 560	971
TOTAL	22 297	29 499
74650 CYLINDRICAL ROLLER BEARINGS NES		
AUSTRAL....	1 198	-
AUSTRIA	12	3 341
BELGIUM	933	-
CANADA	20 088	3 356
FR GERM	932	22 631
FRANCE	195	2 749
ITALY	80	818
JAPAN	959	19 542
MEXICO	2 452	51
SWEDEN	436	1 060
SWITZLD....	21	2 468
U KING	790	4 996
VENEZ	719	-
OTH CTY	4 181	1 261
TOTAL	32 995	62 272
74680 BALL OR ROLLER BEARINGS NES		
AUSTRAL....	772	-
CANADA	32 362	280
CHINA T	1 037	45
FR GERM	865	2 161
FRANCE	973	353
JAPAN	1 101	447
KOR REP	1 424	19
MEXICO	1 760	28
SINGARP ...	1 272	22
U KING	1 059	314
OTH CTY	4 585	1 024
TOTAL	47 209	4 692
74691 BALLS, NEEDLES AND ROLLERS (BEARINGS PARTS)		
AUSTRAL....	3 041	-
BELGIUM	1 393	43
BRAZIL	1 444	522
CANADA	14 237	4 280
CHINA M	271	867
CHINA T	1 034	2 065
FR GERM	2 184	4 931
FRANCE	4 938	144
ITALY	782	523
JAPAN	2 001	2 959
KOR REP	1 824	-
MEXICO	3 477	146
NETHLDS....	1 148	22
SINGARP ...	902	-
SPAIN	13 140	2 389
SWEDEN	921	902
SWITZLD....	111	779

Column 3

COUNTRY	ANNUAL EXPORTS F.A.S. VALUE BASIS	ANNUAL GENERAL IMPORTS CUSTOMS VALUE BASIS
74691 BALLS, NEEDLES AND ROLLERS (BEARING PARTS) – Con.		
U KING	5 317	2 429
OTH CTY	4 055	626
TOTAL	62 218	23 628
74699 PTS OF BALL AND ROLLER BEARINGS NES		
ARGENT	853	-
AUSTRAL	3 895	372
BRAZIL	2 653	2 457
CANADA	22 412	16 931
CHINA M	606	4 077
COLOMB	1 264	-
FR GERM	2 188	14 706
FRANCE	1 304	4 475
INDIA	6 097	19
JAPAN	4 502	92 590
KOR REP	2 798	23
MEXICO	6 865	882
NORWAY ...	24	3 017
PAKISTN	2 562	-
REP SAF	2 280	-
SINGARP	1 059	95
SWEDEN	359	3 143
SWITZLD	63	1 308
U KING	2 671	3 404
VENEZ	1 243	-
OTH CTY	4 742	1 458
TOTAL	70 440	148 957
74710 PRESSURE-REDUCING VALVES		
ANGOLA	609	-
ARGENT	667	3
AUSTRAL	3 037	16
BELGIUM	907	151
BRAZIL	963	1 822
CANADA	44 585	12 592
CHILE	942	-
CHINA M	3 310	114
CHINA T	2 337	2 712
COLOMB ...	1 198	-
DOM REP	805	-
FR GERM	2 513	24 910
FRANCE	3 072	785
HG KONG ...	921	113
INDNSIA ...	680	99
ISRAEL	688	605
ITALY	2 030	2 625
JAPAN	4 724	6 739
KOR REP	4 602	41
MEXICO	6 059	17 009
N ZEAL	1 416	32
NETHLDS....	3 277	990
REP SAF	822	284
S ARAB	1 214	-
SINGARP ...	2 545	7
SPAIN	656	159
SWEDEN	628	512
SWITZLD ...	292	1 053
THAILAND ..	1 249	-
TURKEY ...	1 131	-
U KING	8 300	5 313
VENEZ	3 188	-
OTH CTY	6 965	881
TOTAL	116 331	79 567
74720 VALVES FOR OLEOHYDRAULIC OR PNEUMATIC TRANSMISSIONS		
AUSTRAL	2 794	56
BELGIUM	1 599	8 662
BRAZIL	720	229
CANADA	29 766	1 269
CHINA M	1 154	25
CHINA T	2 246	1 505
COLOMB ...	1 115	7
DENMARK ..	13	4 601
FR GERM	7 917	26 643
FRANCE	2 117	1 884
HG KONG ...	3 300	170
ITALY	586	2 545
JAPAN	13 271	17 867
KOR REP	3 339	48
MEXICO	10 659	12 521
NETHLDS....	2 163	155
REP SAF	721	65
SINGARP ...	7 659	283
SWEDEN	331	6 027
SWITZLD	18 716	1 772

Economic Theories on International Trade, Development, and Investment

If a foreign country can supply us with a commodity cheaper than we ourselves can make it, better buy it of them with some part of our own industry, employed in a way in which we have some advantage.

Adam Smith, The Wealth of Nations

CONCEPT PREVIEWS

After reading this chapter, you should be able to:

1. **understand** the theories that attempt to explain why certain goods are traded internationally

2. **comprehend** the arguments for imposing trade restrictions

3. **explain** the two basic kinds of restrictions: tariff and nontariff trade barriers

4. **recognize** the weaknesses of GNP/capita as an economic indicator

5. **identify** the common characteristics of developing nations

6. **understand** the new definition of economic development, which includes more than economic growth

7. **understand** why some governments are changing from an import substitution strategy to one of export promotion and the implications of this change for businesspeople

8. **explain** some of the theories of foreign direct investment

The Advantage of Knowing Economic Theory

When Chile's new government took over from the Marxist regime of Salvador Allende, the country's economy was in a shambles. Inflation was running at more than 1,000 percent annually and the country's external debt load was totally unmanageable. The previous government had been following the policy of many developing nations at that time—heavy involvement in the economy. This included placing high duties on imports to protect local industry, levying high income taxes on the private sector to obtain funds for government-directed investment, and granting huge subsidies for selected industries. • Recognizing that drastic changes had to made, the new government appointed a group of Chilean conservative economists to design a new program. Known as the Chicago Boys, they were followers of the free-market teachings of former University of Chicago economics professor and Nobel Prize winner Milton Freidman. • The contents of the Chicago Boys' economic program and its impact on business should not have surprised anyone with a knowledge of economic theory. In fact, much of what they proposed was based on the theory of comparative advantage. Their most important reform was to reduce import duties, which were as high as 1,000 percent, to a basic level of 10 percent. This forced Chile into becoming a free-market economy where manufacturers and growers had to compete in world markets to stay in business. The lower import duties also reduced the costs of imported capital equipment, which encouraged business investment. • The president of Chile's largest appliance manufacturer, whose industry had been protected from foreign competition by a 1,000 percent import duty, gave his opinion of the new program: "We used to have 5,000 workers and an annual productivity of only $9,000 per worker. Now we have 1,860 workers and a productivity of $43,000 per worker, and we are finally showing a profit." The firm has invested $20 million in new equipment and plans to hire 300 new workers. • There was, however, a disadvantage to lowering the high protectionist import duties. Although the leading appliance maker mentioned above was able to compete after losing its import protection, a number of other local appliance makers were forced to either go out of business or contract their operations. "We're going to lose a large part of our appliance industry," conceded Alvaro Bardon, a 37-year-old Chicago Boy, then head of the Central Bank of Chile, "and also our electronics industry and our automobile assembly plants." Mr. Bardon was hardly disappointed, however. "Those are products we should be importing," he said. "We have other things based on our own farm products, our timberlands, our fisheries, and our mineral resources that we should be making because they give us a natural advantage over other countries." • How successful were the measures taken by the new government? Exports certainly increased—from 14 percent of the gross domestic product in

Sources: Various tables in *World Development Report 1994* (Washington, DC: World Bank, 1994); "Preliminary Overview of the Economy of Latin America and the Caribbean 1993," *Notas Sobre la Economia y el Desarrollo* (Santiago, Chile: United Nations, December 1993); "Why Chile's Economy Roared while the World's Slumbered," *The Wall Street Journal*, January 22, 1993, p. A11, "Osmosis," *Forbes*, October 10, 1994, p. 47.

1965 to 31 percent in 1992. Not only are Chilean firms exporting more, they are acquiring some large companies in other Latin American countries. For example, Chile's largest Coca-Cola bottler paid $120 million to buy Brazil's second-largest bottler, and the country's second-largest supermarket chain became Peru's second-largest supermarket chain after buying two chains in Lima. Moreover, since 1985, the annual growth of the gross domestic product has averaged 6.1 percent, the highest in the region. Chile's GNP/capita as measured by the World Bank is approaching $3,000, and its purchasing power parity GNP estimate is over $8,000. Unemployment during 1993 was 4.5 percent, the lowest in 30 years and the horrendous 1,000 percent annual inflation rate of the 1970s was down to just 12 percent in 1993. • An indication of the confidence that world investors have in Chile's economic policies is the price of its external debt paper in the New York secondary market. Offer prices that were 60 percent of face value in 1989 have risen to 92 percent, the highest percentage of all Latin American countries. Uruguay, with 80 percent, is second highest.

The economic program that the Chilean economists put into effect is a practical application of the keystone of international trade theory—the law of comparative advantage. Note, too, the education of the head of Chile's central bank. This is typical of government policymakers and advisors worldwide. When they have a particularly strong influence in government affairs, they are frequently dubbed with such names as the "Chicago Boys" in Chile, "tecnicos" in Mexico, or "Berkeley Mafia" (economists educated at the University of California–Berkeley) in Indonesia. In fact, the people currently running Mexico are probably the most economically literate group to ever lead a country. There was a saying when Salinas was president that cabinet ministers who do not have doctorates in economics from the best American universities, as did President Salinas and others in the government, show up at meetings with young aides who do.[1]

What is the significance for international businesspeople? For one thing, since they frequently will be dealing with government officials trained in economics, they must be prepared to speak their language. When presenting plans requiring governmental approval, businesspeople must take care that the plans are economically sound, for they are almost certain to be studied by economists and will often need to be approved by them. Marketers proposing large projects to government planners must be aware that the key determinant now is economic efficiency rather than mere financial soundness.[2] Moreover, as you have seen in the case of Chile, knowledge of economic concepts, especially in the areas of (1) international trade, (2) economic development, and (3) foreign direct investment, frequently will provide insights as to future government action.

INTERNATIONAL TRADE THEORY

Why do nations trade? This question and the equally important proposition of predicting the direction, composition, and volume of goods traded are what international trade theory attempts to address. Interestingly, as is the case with numerous economic writings, the first formulation of international trade theory was politically motivated. Adam Smith, incensed by government intervention and control over both domestic and foreign trade, published *An Inquiry into the Nature and Causes of the Wealth of Nations* (1776), in which he tried to destroy the mercantilist philosophy.

Mercantilism

Mercantilism, the economic philosophy Smith attacked, held that it was essential to a nation's welfare to accumulate a stock of precious metals. These were, in the mercantilists' view, the only source of wealth. Because England had no mines, the mercantilists looked to international trade to supply gold and silver. The government established economic policies that promoted exports and stifled imports, resulting in a trade surplus to be paid for in gold and silver. Import restrictions such as import duties reduced imports while government subsidies to exporters increased exports. These acts created a trade surplus.

Although the mercantilist era ended in the late 1700s, its arguments live on. A "favorable" trade balance still means that a nation exports more goods and services than it imports. In balance-of-payment accounting, an export that brings dollars to this country is called *positive,* but imports that cause dollar outflow are labeled *negative.*

An example of modern-day mercantilism, called *economic nationalism* by some, was the industrial policy based on heavy state intervention that the socialists were creating for France. They nationalized key industries and banks so as to use the power of the state as both (1) stockholder and financier and (2) customer and marketer to revitalize the nation's industrial base. With nearly one-third of France's productive capacity and 70 percent of its high-tech electronic capabilities in the hands of the government, its power was approaching the level of state intervention in the 17th century. Some writers were calling this *high-tech mercantilism.* In 1986, after five years of little growth and high unemployment, the government reversed its policy when a conservative was elected premier.

In the United States, many businesspeople believe that Japan, because of its protectionism, remains largely a nearly impenetrable market—a present-day "fortress of mercantilism." American businesspeople are concerned that Japan's barriers to their imports are the result of Japanese insularity, traditional preoccupation with self-sufficiency, and an "us against them" mentality. A U.S. secretary of commerce once said, "They tell us they have to protect their markets because of their culture. They haven't joined the world yet." Comments from the Japanese seem to confirm what some Americans are saying. "The public is not in favor of perfect markets," says a Japanese bank manager. "We would like to preserve the substance of our culture. If we move to free trade, we may lose Japanese virtue in the process."[3]

Theory of Absolute Advantage

Adam Smith claimed that market forces, not government controls, should determine the direction, volume, and composition of international trade. He argued that under free, unregulated trade, each nation should specialize in producing those goods it could produce most efficiently (had an absolute advantage, either natural or acquired). Some of these would be exported to pay for the imports of goods that could be produced more efficiently elsewhere. Smith showed by his example of **absolute advantage** that both nations would gain from trade.

An Example.   Assume there is perfect competition and no transportation costs in a world of two countries and two products. Suppose that (1) one unit of input (combination of land, labor, and capital) can produce the following quantities of rice and automobiles in the United States and Japan, (2) each nation has two input units it can use to produce either rice or automobiles,

mercantilism
An economic philosophy based on the belief that a nation's wealth depends on accumulated treasure, usually gold; to increase wealth, government policies should promote exports and discourage imports

absolute advantage
The capability of one nation to produce more of a good with the same amount of input than another country

and (3) each country uses one unit of input to produce each product. If neither country imports or exports, the quantities shown in the table are also what is available for local consumption. The total output of both nations is 4 tons of rice and 6 automobiles.

Commodity	United States	Japan	Total
Tons of rice	3	1	4
Automobiles	2	4	6

In the United States, three tons of rice or two automobiles can be produced with one unit of output. Therefore, three tons of rice should have the same price as two automobiles. In Japan, however, since only one ton of rice can be produced with the input unit that can produce four automobiles, one ton of rice should cost as much as four automobiles.

The United States has an absolute advantage in rice production (3 to 1), while Japan's absolute advantage is in automobile manufacturing (4 to 2). Will anyone anywhere give the Japanese automaker more than one ton of rice for his four automobiles? According to the example, all American rice producers should because they can get only two automobiles for three tons of rice at home. Similarly, Japanese automakers, once they learn that they can obtain more than one ton of rice for every four automobiles in the United States, will be eager to trade Japanese autos for American rice.

Each Country Specializes.   Suppose each nation decides to use its resources to produce only the product at which it is more efficient. The following table shows each nation's output. Note that with the same quantity of input units, the total output is now greater.

Commodity	United States	Japan	Total
Tons of rice	6	0	6
Automobiles	0	8	8

Terms of Trade (ratio of international prices).   With specialization, now the total production of both goods is greater, but to consume both products, the two countries must trade some of their surplus. What are the limits within which both countries are willing to trade? Clearly, the Japanese automakers will trade some of their cars for rice if they can get more than the one ton of rice that they get for four cars in Japan. Likewise, the American rice growers will trade their rice for Japanese automobiles if they get a car for less than the 1.5 tons of rice it costs them in the United States.

If the two nations take the mean of the two trading limits so that each shares equally in the benefits of trade, they will agree to swap 1.25 tons of rice for one car. Both will gain from specialization because each now has the following quantities:

Commodity	United States	Japan	Total
Tons of rice	3	3	6
Automobiles	4	4	8

Gains from Specialization and Trade.   Because each nation specialized in producing the product at which it was more efficient and then traded its surplus for goods that it cannot produce as efficiently, both gained the following:

Commodity	United States	Japan
Tons of rice		2
Automobiles	2	

Certainly, both nations have gained by trading. But what if one country has an absolute advantage in the production of *both* rice and automobiles? Will there still be a basis for trade?

Theory of Comparative Advantage

Ricardo demonstrated in 1817 that even though a nation held an absolute advantage in the production of two goods, the two countries could still trade with advantages for each as long as the less efficient nation was not *equally* less efficient in the production of both goods.[4] Let us slightly change our first example so that now the United States has an absolute advantage in producing *both* rice and automobiles. Note, that compared to the United States, Japan is less inefficient in automaking than in producing rice. Therefore, it has a relative advantage, or **comparative advantage**, according to Ricardo, in producing automobiles.

comparative advantage
A nation having absolute disadvantages in the production of two goods with respect to another nation has a comparative or relative advantage in the production of the good in which its absolute disadvantage is less

Commodity	United States	Japan	Total
Tons of rice	6	3	9
Automobiles	5	4	9

Each Country Specializes.   If each country specializes in what it does best, its output will be as follows:

Commodity	United States	Japan	Total
Tons of rice	12	0	12
Automobiles	0	8	8

Terms of Trade.   In this case, the terms of trade will be somewhere between the one ton of rice for five-sixths of an auto that American rice growers must pay in the United States and the one and one-third automobiles Japanese automakers must pay for one ton of Japanese rice.

Let us assume that the traders agree on an exchange rate of one car for one ton of rice. Both will gain from this exchange and specialization, as the following shows:

Commodity	United States	Japan
Tons of rice	8	4
Automobiles	4	4

Note that this trade left the United States with some surplus rice and one less automobile than it had before. Japan has more rice and the same quantity of automobiles. However, the American rice growers should be able to trade the two tons of surplus rice for two automobiles elsewhere. Then the final result will be:

Commodity	United States	Japan
Tons of rice	6	4
Automobiles	6	4

Gains from Specialization and Trade.   Gains from specialization and trade in this case are the following:

Commodity	United States	Japan
Tons of rice		1
Automobiles	1	

Production Possibility Frontiers.   We can also illustrate the gains from trade graphically using production possibility frontiers. Figure 3–1 graphs the Japanese and U.S. production possibility frontiers using constant costs for simplicity.

FIGURE 3–1
Production and consumption possibility frontiers before and after trade

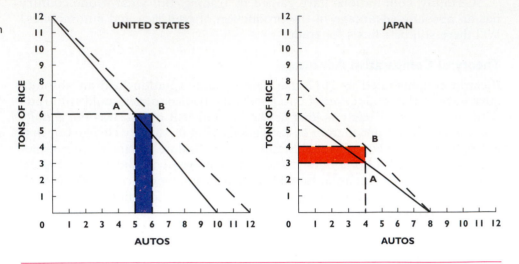

These curves, in the absence of trade, also illustrate the possible combinations of goods for consumption. Before trade, the United States might be producing and consuming six tons of rice and five automobiles (point A), while Japan is producing and consuming three tons of rice and four automobiles (point A).

With each nation specializing in the production of the goods in which it has a comparative advantage and trading its surplus with the other, both nations are able to consume at point B. The shaded areas under each curve indicate the gains from trade.

The simple concept of comparative advantage is the basis for international trade.

Notice that in our examples we mentioned a unit of input. This is a more modern version of the examples of Ricardo and Smith, who used only labor input. They did so because at that time only labor was considered important in calculating production costs.[5] Also, no consideration was given to the possibility of producing the same goods with different combinations of factors and no explanation was given as to why production costs differed. Not until 1933 did Ohlin, a Swedish economist building on work begun by the economist Heckscher, develop the theory of **factor endowment**.[6]

Heckscher-Ohlin Theory of Factor Endowment

The Heckscher-Ohlin theory states that international and interregional differences in production costs occur because of differences in the supply of production factors. Those goods that require a large amount of the abundant—thus less costly—factor will have lower production costs, enabling them to be sold for less in international markets. For example, China, relatively well endowed with labor compared to the Netherlands, ought to concentrate on producing labor-intensive goods; the Netherlands, with relatively more capital than labor, should specialize in capital-intensive products. When these countries trade, each will obtain the goods that require large amounts of the relatively scarce production factor at a lower price, and both will benefit from the transaction.

How useful is this theory for explaining present-day trading patterns? Countries with relatively large amounts of land (such as Australia) do export land-intensive products (such as grain and cattle), whereas Hong Kong exports labor-intensive goods.[7] There are exceptions, however, due in part to

factor endowment
Heckscher-Ohlin theory that countries export products requiring large amounts of their abundant production factors and import products requiring large amounts of their scarce production factors

Chapter 3 / Economic Theories on International Trade, Development, and Investment **79**

Ohlin's assumptions. One assumption was that the prices of the factors depend only on the factor endowment. We know this is untrue. Factor prices are not set in a perfect market. Legislated minimum wages and benefits force the cost of labor to rise to a point greater than the value of the product that many workers can produce. Investment tax credits reduce the cost of capital below market cost, and so forth. As a result, factor prices do not fully reflect factor supply.

Ohlin also assumed that a given technology is universally available, but this is not so. There is always a lag between the introduction of a new production method and its worldwide application. As a result, superior technology often permits a nation to produce goods at a cost lower than that of a country better endowed with the required factor. A closely related assumption was that a given product is either labor or capital intensive. Yet anyone who has watched construction methods in less developed nations knows that wet concrete can be poured either by a gang of laborers with buckets or a crane and its operator.

A study made in 1953 by the economist Wassily Leontief disputed the usefulness of the Heckscher-Ohlin theory as a predictor of the direction of trade. The study, known as the *Leontief paradox,* found that the United States, one of the most capital-intensive countries in the world, was exporting labor-intensive products. Economists have speculated that this occurred because the United States exports technology-intensive products produced by highly skilled labor requiring a large capital investment to educate and train and imports goods made with mature technology requiring capital-intensive mass production processes operated by unskilled labor. A study by Harvard economists Sachs and Shatz in 1994 did in fact show that the United States has increased its exports of skill-intensive goods to developing nations while reducing its production of unskilled goods.[8] Another possible explanation is that many products may be produced by either capital- or labor-intensive processes, as noted in the previous paragraph.

Heckscher-Ohlin also ignored transportation costs, but there are goods for which freight charges are so high that the landed cost (export sales price plus transportation charges) is greater than the cost of a locally made product. In that case, there will be little trade. Why not say there will be no trade?

It is because of a demand-side construct that is always difficult to deal with in economic theory and that we have so far neglected—*differences in taste.* Businesspeople, however, cannot neglect this difference, which enables trade to flow in a direction completely contrary to that predicted by the theory of comparative advantage—from high- to low-cost nations. France sells us wine, cosmetics, clothing, and even drinking water, all of which are produced here and generally sold at lower prices. Germany and Italy send Porsches and Maseratis to one of the largest automobile producers in the world. We buy these goods not only on the basis of price, the implied independent variable in the theory we have been examining, but also because of taste preferences.

We have presented the theory of comparative advantage without mentioning money; however, a nation's comparative advantage can be affected by differences between the costs of production factors in that country's currency and their costs in other currencies. As we shall see in the next section, money can change the direction of trade.

Introducing Money

Suppose the total cost of land, labor, and capital to produce either the daily output of rice or automobiles in the example on absolute advantage is $10,000 in the United States or 2.5 million yen in Japan. The cost per unit is as follows:

	Price per Unit	
Commodity	United States	Japan
Tons of rice	$\dfrac{\$10,000}{3} = \$3,330/\text{ton}$	$\dfrac{2.5 \text{ million yen}}{1} = 2.5 \text{ million yen/ton}$
Automobiles	$\dfrac{\$10,000}{2} = \$5,000/\text{auto}$	$\dfrac{2.5 \text{ million yen}}{4} = 0.625 \text{ million yen/auto}$

To determine if it is more advantageous to buy locally or to import, the traders need to know the prices in their own currencies. To convert from foreign to domestic currency, they use the *exchange rate.*

exchange rate
The price of one currency stated in terms of another currency

Exchange Rate.   The **exchange rate** is the price of one currency stated in terms of the other. If the prevailing rate is $1 = 250 yen, then 1 yen must be worth 0.004 dollar.* Using the exchange rate of $1 = 250 yen, the prices in the preceding example appear to the U.S. trader as follows:

	Price per Unit (dollars)	
Commodity	United States	Japan
Ton of rice	$3,330	$10,000
Automobiles	5,000	2,500

The American rice producers can earn $6,670 more by exporting rice to Japan than they can by selling locally; but can the Japanese automakers gain by exporting to the United States? To find out, they must convert the American prices to Japanese yen.

	Price per Unit (yen)	
Commodity	United States	Japan
Ton of rice	0.83 million yen	2.5 million yen
Automobiles	1.25 million yen	0.625 million yen

It is apparent that the Japanese automakers will export cars to the United States because they can earn a greater profit, 0.625 million yen. The American automobile manufacturers, however, will need some very strong sales arguments to sell in the United States if they are to overcome the $2,500 price differential. Ricardo did not consider this possibility; in his time, products were considered homogeneous and therefore were sold primarily on the basis of price.

Influence of Exchange Rate.   Rice to Japan and cars to the United States will be the direction of trade as long as the exchange rate remains in a range around $1 = 250 yen. But if the dollar strengthens to $1 = 750 yen, the American rice will cost as much in yen as the Japanese rice, and importation will cease. On the other hand, should the dollar weaken to $1 = 125 yen, then a Japanese car will cost $5,000 to American traders, and they will have little reason to import.

Actually, when the dollar reached 100 yen in 1993, sales of Japanese cars dropped as the manufacturers were forced to increase sharply the dollar prices of their exports to the United States in order to maintain their yen profits. Because their cars produced in the United States contain so many Japanese parts, they had to increase these prices as well. Analysts figure that

---

*If $1 = 250 yen, to find the value of 1 yen in dollars, divide both sides of the equation by 250. Then 1 yen = $\dfrac{1}{250}$ = $0.004.

Japanese cars now cost $2,500 more than their American counterparts.[9] The following example demonstrates the impact of the yen's appreciation against the dollar on the dollar prices of Japanese imports.

> Suppose Toyota wanted 3,000,000 yen for its Camry in 1985. At an exchange rate of 250 yen = $1, the company would have had to charge $12,000 for the car. To get 3,000,000 yen for the car in 1994 with the exchange rate at 100 yen = $1, it would have to charge $30,000 (3,000,000 yen ÷ 100 yen/$).

Another way a nation can avoid losing markets and regain competitiveness in world markets is through **currency devaluation** (lowering its price in terms of other currencies). Notice that this leaves the domestic prices unchanged.

currency devaluation
Lowering its price in terms of other currencies

> In the 1980s, Mexico, which depends on American tourists for a large part of its foreign exchange earnings, was faced with losing this business because inflation had driven peso prices so high that at the rate of 12.5 pesos = $1, dollar prices to the Americans were excessive. Mexican officials had three alternatives: (1) deflate to drive peso prices down (time consuming and painful to the Mexicans); (2) lower prices by government edict (bureaucratic difficulties as with any system of price controls); or (3) devalue the peso. Overnight the rate was decreased to 25 pesos = $1, and without disturbing the peso prices, the prices in dollars were halved. Suddenly, trips to Mexico were a bargain for Americans.

The international trade theory we have been discussing was the only explanation of trade available to us until the 1960s, when a new concept—the international product life cycle—was formulated.[10] Note that this concept, unlike the Heckscher-Ohlin theory, applies only to manufactured goods.

International Product Life Cycle (IPLC)

This concept, related to the product life cycle, concerns the role of innovation in trade patterns. It can be applied to new product introduction by firms in any of the industrialized nations, but because more new products have been successfully introduced on a commercial scale in the United States, let us examine the **international product life cycle (IPLC)** as it applies to this country. The four stages through which a new product is said to pass are illustrated in Figure 3–2 and described as follows.

international product life cycle (IPLC)
A theory explaining why a product that begins as a nation's export eventually becomes its import

1. *U.S. exports.* Because the United States possesses the largest population of high-income consumers in the world, competition for their patronage is intense. Manufacturers are therefore forced to search constantly for better ways to satisfy their customers' needs. To provide new products, companies maintain large research and development laboratories, which must be in constant contact with suppliers of the materials they need for product development. That their suppliers are also in this country facilitates the contact.[11] In the early stages of the product life cycle, the design and the production methods are changing. By being close to the market, management can react quickly to customer feedback. These factors combine to make the United States a leader in new product introduction. For a while, American firms will be the only manufacturers of the product; overseas customers, as they learn of the product, will therefore have to buy from American firms. The export market develops.

2. *Foreign production begins.* Overseas consumers, especially those in developed nations, have similar needs and the capability to purchase the product. Export volume grows and becomes large enough to support local production. If the innovator is a multinational firm, it will be sending its subsidiaries new product information with complete details on how to

FIGURE 3–2

International product life cycle

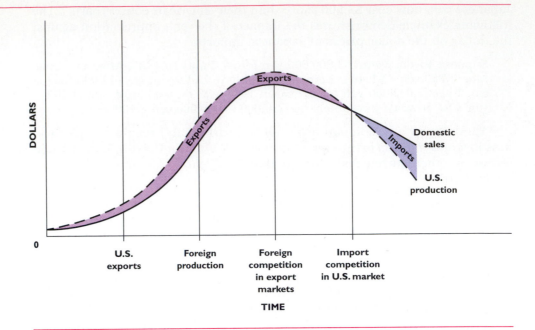

produce it. Where there are no affiliates, foreign businesspeople, as they learn of the product, will obtain licenses for its production. Foreign production will begin. The American firm will still be exporting to those markets where there is no production, but its export growth will diminish.

3. *Foreign competition in export markets.* Later, as early foreign manufacturers gain experience in marketing and production, their costs will fall. Saturation of their local markets will cause them to look for buyers elsewhere. They may even be able to undersell the American producers if they enjoy an advantage in labor or raw material costs. In this stage, foreign firms are competing in export markets, and as a result, American export sales will continue to decline.

4. *Import competition in the United States.* If domestic and export sales enable foreign producers to attain the economies of scale enjoyed by the American firm, they may reach a point where they can compete in quality and undersell American firms in the American market. From that point on, the U.S. market will be served by imports only. Black-and-white television sets are an example of such a product.

The authors of the IPLC concept also claim that this cycle may be repeated as the less developed countries with still lower labor costs obtain the technology and thus acquire a cost advantage over the more industrialized nations. Although little research has been done to substantiate the IPLC concept, the World Bank study mentioned previously seems to provide a plausible reason for these changes in production locations.

With countries progressing on the comparative advantage scale, their exports can supplement the exports of countries that graduate to a higher level. . . . A case in point is Japan, whose comparative advantage has shifted towards highly capital-intensive exports. In turn, developing countries with a relatively high human capital endowment, such as Korea and Taiwan, can take Japan's place in exporting relatively human capital-intensive products, and countries with a relatively high physical capital endowment, such as Brazil and Mexico, can take Japan's place in exporting relatively physical capital-intensive products. Finally, countries at lower levels of development can supplant the middle-level countries in exporting unskilled labor-intensive commodities.[12]

Some Newer Explanations for the Direction of Trade

Economies of Scale and the Experience Curve.   In the 1920s, economists began to consider the fact that most industries benefit from economies of scale; that is, as a plant gets larger and output increases, the unit cost of production decreases. This is because larger and more efficient equipment can be employed, companies can obtain volume discounts on their larger volume purchases, and fixed costs such as those of research and design and administrative overheads can be allocated over a larger quantity of output. Production costs also drop because of the *learning curve*. As firms produce more products, they learn ways to improve production efficiency causing production costs to decline by a predictable amount[13]

Economies of scale and the experience curve affect international trade because they permit a nation's industries to become low-cost producers without having an abundance of a certain class of production factors. Then, just as in the case of comparative advantage, nations specialize in the production of a few products and trade with others to supply the rest of their needs.

This also illustrates the importance of **market share**, especially in an oligopoly. Japanese manufacturers have been particularly proficient in employing this concept. By being one of the first to enter the market (an *early mover*) or by "buying market share" with low entry-level prices when competitors are already in the market, the firm strives to attain a large sales volume rapidly. This enables it to take advantage of the economies of scale and experience curve, to become the lowest-cost producer.

market share
A firm's sales as a percentage of the total sales of the industry in that market

The Linder Theory of Overlapping Demand.   Another Swedish economist, Stefan Linder, recognized that although the supply-oriented Heckscher-Ohlin theory, which depended on factor endowments, was adequate to explain international trade in primary products, another explanation was needed for trade in manufactured goods. His demand-oriented theory stated that customers' tastes are strongly affected by income levels and therefore a nation's income per capita level determines the kinds of goods they will demand. Because industry will produce goods to meet this demand, the kinds of products manufactured reflect the country's income per capita level. Goods produced for domestic consumption will eventually be exported.

The Linder theory deduces that international trade in manufactured goods will be greater between nations with similar levels of per capita income than between those with dissimilar per capita income levels. The goods that will be traded are those for which there is an *overlapping demand* (consumers in both countries are demanding the same good).[14] Note that the Linder model differs from the model of comparative advantage in that it does not specify in which direction a given good will go. In fact, Linder specified that a good may go in either direction. You recognize, of course, that this intraindustry trade occurs because of *product differentiation;* for example, Ford exports its Mustangs to Japan and Nissan sends its 300ZXs to the United States because consumers in both countries perceive a difference in the brands.

Porter's *Competitive Advantage of Nations*.   Michael Porter, an economics professor at Harvard, studied 100 firms in ten developed nations to learn if a nation's prominence in an industry can be explained more adequately by variables other than the factors of production on which the theories of comparative advantage and Heckscher-Ohlin are based. The Porter theory claims that four kinds of variables will have an impact on the ability of the local firms in a country to utilize the country's resources to gain a competitive advantage:

1. Demand conditions—nature of the domestic demand.
2. Factor conditions—level and composition of factors of production.
3. Related and supporting industries—suppliers and industry support services.
4. Firm strategy, structure, and rivalry—extent of domestic competition, the existence of barriers to entry, and the firm's management style and organization.

Porter's work complements the theories of Ricardo and Heckscher-Ohlin. However, as one scholar stated, there is nothing new in Porter's analysis; but Porter does set out a model in which the determinants of national competitiveness may be identified. One other problem is that Porter's evidence is anecdotal. There is no empirical evidence as yet.[15]

Summary of International Trade Theory

In summary, we can say that international trade occurs primarily because of relative price differences among nations. These differences stem from differences in production costs, which result from:

1. Differences in the endowments of the factors of production.
2. Differences in the levels of technology that determine the factor intensities used.
3. Differences in the efficiencies with which these are utilized.
4. Foreign exchange rates.

However, taste differences, a demand variable, can reverse the direction of trade predicted by the theory.

International trade theory clearly shows that nations will attain a higher level of living by specializing in goods for which they possess a comparative advantage and importing those for which they have a comparative disadvantage. Generally, trade restrictions that stop this free flow of goods will harm a nation's welfare. If this is true, why is every nation in the world surrounded by trade restrictions?

TRADE RESTRICTIONS

This apparent contradiction occurs because government officials who make decisions about import restrictions are particularly sensitive to the interest groups that will be hurt by the international competition. These groups consist of a small, easily identified body of people—as contrasted to the huge, widespread number of consumers who gain from free trade. In any political debate over a proposed import restriction, the protectionist group will be united in exerting pressure on government officials, whereas pro-trade consumers rarely mount an organized effort. For example, steel companies and steelworker unions have protested vehemently to Congress and government officials about lower-priced imported steel, yet consumer organizations have said nothing. In other words, if you are employed by a chemical manufacturer, you probably are not going to fight for unrestricted steel imports even though you may believe they contribute to a lower price for your automobile.

In the next section, note the importance of special interest groups.

Arguments for Trade Restrictions and Their Rebuttal

One argument for trade restrictions involves national defense.

National Defense.   Certain industries need protection from imports because they are vital to the national defense and must be kept operating even though they are at a comparative disadvantage with respect to foreign competitors. If competition from foreign firms drives these companies out of business and leaves this country dependent on imports, those imports may not be available in wartime.

One problem with this argument is that the armed forces require hundreds of products, ranging from panty hose to bombs.

> In 1984, the U.S. shoe industry, after failing to obtain relief from imports with arguments about loss of jobs, requested Congress to impose restrictions based on the fact that growing reliance on imported footwear is "jeopardizing the national security of the United States." In the event of war, shoemakers claim that there would be insufficient manufacturing capacity in this country.
> A Defense Department spokesman said he knew of no plan to investigate the prospects of a wartime shoe crisis. Furthermore, federal law already requires the armed forces to buy U.S.-made footwear exclusively.[16]

Critics of the defense argument claim it would be far more efficient for the government to subsidize a number of firms to maintain sufficient capacity for wartime use only. The output of these companies could be varied according to the calculated defense needs. Moreover, a subsidy would clearly indicate to taxpayers the cost of maintaining these companies in the name of national security—something, however, that some interests do not want known. Currently, most American steamship companies receive government subsidies without which they could not remain in business because of the competition from foreign firms with lower operating costs. In this way, we have a merchant marine ready in case of hostility, and we know what this state of readiness costs us.

Protect Infant Industry.   Advocates for the protection of an infant industry may claim that in the long run, the industry will have a comparative advantage, but that its firms need protection from imports until the labor force is trained, production techniques are mastered, and they achieve economies of scale. When these objectives are met, import protection will no longer be necessary. Without the protection, they argue, a firm will not be able to survive because lower-cost imports from more mature foreign competitors will underprice it in its local market.

The protection is meant to be temporary; but realistically, a firm will rarely admit it has matured and no longer needs this assistance. Protected from foreign competition by high import duties, the company's managers have little reason to improve efficiency or product quality.

International businesspeople will find that the infant-industry argument is readily accepted by the governments of most developing nations. The first firm in an industry new to the country generally gets protection with no date stipulated for its removal. However, some of the larger developing nations, such as Brazil and Mexico, have been reducing their protection to force these companies to lower their prices and become more competitive in world markets.

Protect Domestic Jobs from Cheap Foreign Labor.   The protectionists who use this argument will compare lower foreign hourly wage rates to those paid here and conclude that exporters from these countries can flood the United States with low-priced goods and put America out of work. The first fallacy of this argument is that wage costs are neither all of the production costs nor all of the labor costs. In many less developed countries, the legislated fringe benefits are a much higher percentage of the direct wages than they are in this country.

In Mexico, the base pay of the typical worker is the peso equivalent of US$1.80, less than half of the American minimum wage. This is deceiving, however, as the base pay is less than 30 percent of the total hourly pay, whereas in the United States, it amounts to over 70 percent. The difference is due to the pay supplements that the Mexicans receive—a month's pay for Christmas, up to 80 percent extra pay at vacation time, and punctuality bonuses. With these supplements, the hourly rate rises to around US$6.00 per hour. In addition, Mexican employers are required to pay workers for 365 days annually, even though they do not work weekends; that is, their weekly income is the US$6.00 hourly rate times eight hours daily times seven days, not five. This raises the hourly rate on a weekly basis to about US$8.40.[17]

Furthermore, the productivity per worker is frequently so much greater in developed countries because of more capital per worker, superior management, and advanced technology that the labor cost is lower even though wages are higher.

The second fallacy results from failure to consider the costs of the other factors of production. Where wage rates are low, the capital costs are usually high, and thus production costs may actually be higher in a low-wage nation. Ironically, one of the arguments for protection used by manufacturers in developing nations is that they cannot compete against the low-cost, highly productive firms in the industrialized countries. Those who might be persuaded by this argument to stop imports to save domestic jobs should remember that American exports create jobs—every $1 billion in exports creates 25,000 new jobs. If we stop a country's imports, its government may retaliate with greater import duties on our exports. The result could be a net loss of jobs rather than the gain that was anticipated.

Scientific Tariff or Fair Competition.   Supporters of this argument say they believe in fair competition. They simply want an import duty that will bring the cost of the imported goods up to the cost of the domestically produced article. This will eliminate any "unfair" advantage that a foreign competitor might have because of superior technology, lower raw material costs, lower taxes, or lower labor costs. It is not their intent to ban exports; they wish only to equalize the process for "fair" competition. If this were law, no doubt the rate of duty would be set to protect the least efficient American producer, thereby enabling the more efficient domestic manufacturers to earn large profits. The efficient foreign producers would be penalized, and, of course, their comparative advantage would be nullified.

Retaliation.   Representatives of an industry whose exports have had import restrictions placed on them by another country may request their government to retaliate with similar restrictions. An example of how retaliation begins is the ban by the European Union (EU) on imports of hormone-treated beef from the United States on January 1, 1989. Because the use of hormones is considered a health hazard in the EU, it closed the market to $100 million worth of beef (12 percent of total U.S. meat exports). American beef producers complained that no scientific evidence supports the claim, and the United States promptly retaliated by putting import duties on about $100 million worth of EU products, including boneless beef and pork, fruit juices, wine coolers, tomatoes, French cheese, and instant coffee. The EU then threatened to ban U.S. imports of honey, canned corn, walnuts, and dried fruit worth $140 million. In reply, the United States announced that it would follow the EU ban with a ban of all European meat. If that had happened, about $500 million in U.S.–EU trade would have been affected.[18]

In late 1989, a joint EU/U.S. hormones task force agreed to "lift retaliation on EU products to the extent that U.S. meat exports to the EU resumed." Two small reductions were made in 1989 on that basis. In 1994, the EU requested in writing that the United States make a further reduction. The American government replied that after examining the trade data, it did not consider an adjustment of retaliation measures to be warranted. The EU raised the issue again during the final GATT negotiations, but the United States was not prepared to give a commitment to reduce the retaliation.[19]

Dumping. Retaliation will also be made for **dumping**. This is the selling of a product abroad for less than (1) the cost of production, (2) the price in the home market, or (3) the price to third countries.

A foreign manufacturer may take this action because it wishes to sell excess production without disrupting prices in its domestic market, or it may have lowered the export price to force all domestic producers in the importing nation out of business. The exporter expects to raise prices in the market once that objective is accomplished. This is *predatory dumping*.

In the United States, when a manufacturer believes a foreign producer is dumping a product, it can ask the Office of Investigation in the Department of Commerce to make a preliminary investigation. If Commerce finds that products have been dumped, the case goes to the International Trade Commission* to determine if the imports are injuring U.S. producers. If the commission finds that they are, U.S. Customs is authorized to levy antidumping duties.

Most governments retaliate when dumping injures local industry. The EU, for example, levied dumping duties ranging from 23 to 43 percent on Japanese computer printers when investigators found that they were priced 20 percent lower in the EU than in Japan.[20] In fact, antidumping suits have become the favorite means of manufacturers in the EU, the United States, and increasingly, other nations to protect themselves from less expensive imports. In 1980, only 8 nations had antidumping laws, but now over 40 countries (including the EU as one nation) have them.

> Mexico's Cemex is the fourth-largest cement producer in the world. It has bought cement plants in the United States, Spain, and more recently, Venezuela. Cemex cement from Mexico is subject to American antidumping duties imposed by the Bush administration to protect American producers whose costs are 30 percent higher. In spite of the North American Free Trade Agreement and a GATT ruling in favor of Cemex, the Clinton administration has continued the duties. However, the company is avoiding the antidumping duties by supplying the United States from its Spanish plants. Cemex increased its sales by 45 percent in the first quarter of 1994 compared with the same period in 1993.[21]

New Types of Dumping. There are at least four new kinds of dumping for which fair-trade lobbies consider sanctions to be justified in order to level the playing field for international trade. In reality, these special interest groups calling for the level playing fields are seeking to raise the production costs of their overseas competitors to protect their local high-cost manufacturers. The classes of dumping are:

1. *Social dumping*—Unfair competition by firms in developing nations that have lower labor costs and poorer working conditions.

dumping
Selling a product abroad for less than the cost of production, the price in the home market, or the price to third countries

*The International Trade Commission is a government agency that provides technical assistance and advice to the president and Congress on matters of international trade and tariffs.

2. *Environmental dumping*—Unfair competition caused by a country's lax environmental standards.

3. *Financial services dumping*—Unfair competition caused by a nation's low requirements for bank capital/asset ratios.

4. *Cultural dumping*—Unfair competition caused by cultural barriers aiding local firms.[22]

subsidies
financial contribution provided directly or indirectly by a government and which confers a benefit. Include grants, preferential tax treatments, and government assumption of normal business expenses.

Subsidies.   Another cause of retaliation may be **subsidies** that a government makes to a domestic firm either to encourage exports or help protect it from imports. Some examples are cash payments, government participation in ownership, low-cost loans to foreign buyers and exporters, and preferential tax treatment. For example, Airbus, the European consortium that produces passenger jet aircraft, has, according to a U.S. Department of Commerce study, received over $13.5 billion in government subsidies, without which the company could not have been established nor survived. Airbus did not make a profit during its first 20 years of operation.[23]

countervailing duties
Additional import taxes levied on imports that have benefited from export subsidies

Competitors in importing nations frequently request their governments to impose **countervailing duties** to offset the effects of a subsidy. In the United States, when the Department of Commerce receives a petition from an American firm claiming that imports from a particular country are subsidized, it first determines if a subsidy actually was given. If the findings are positive, Commerce proceeds to impose countervailing duties equal to the subsidy's amount. In most cases involving GATT members, another independent government agency, the U.S. International Trade Commission, must determine if the firm has been injured by the subsidy before Commerce assesses the duty.

Other Arguments.   The arguments we have examined are probably the most often given. Others include the use of protection from imports to (1) permit diversification of the domestic economy or (2) improve the balance of trade. You should have gathered from this discussion that protection from imports generally serves the narrow interests of a special group at the expense of many. Although their application can sometimes buy time for the protected industry to modernize and become more competitive in the world market, a real danger exists that a nation's trading partners will retaliate with restrictions causing injury to industries that have received no protection. Let's examine these restrictions.

Kinds of Restrictions

Import restrictions are commonly classified as *tariff* (import duties) and *nontariff* barriers (see Table 3–1).

tariffs
Taxes on imported goods for the purpose of raising their price to reduce competition for local producers or stimulate their local production

Tariff Barriers.   **Tariffs,** or import duties, are taxes levied on imported goods primarily for the purpose of raising their selling price in the importing nation's market to reduce competition for domestic producers. A few smaller nations also use them to raise revenue on both imports and exports. Export of commodities such as coffee and copper are commonly taxed in developing nations.

ad valorem duty
An import duty levied as a percentage of the invoice value of imported goods

Ad Valorem, Specific, and Compound Duties.   Import duties are either (1) *ad valorem,* (2) *specific,* or (3) a combination of the two called *compound.* An **ad valorem duty** is stated as a percentage of the invoice value. For example, the U.S. tariff schedule states that flavoring extracts and fruit flavors not containing alcohol are subject to a 6 percent ad valorem duty. Therefore, when a shipment of flavoring extract invoiced at $10,000 arrives in the United States,

Tariff Barriers	Nontariff Barriers	TABLE 3–1
Import Duties	Quantitative	Kinds of import restrictions
Ad valorem	Quotas	
Specific	• Tariff-rate quotas	
Compound	• Global	
Variable levies	• Discriminatory	
Official prices	Voluntary export restraints	
	Orderly marketing arrangements	
	Nonquantitative	
	Direct government participation in trade	
	• Subsidy	
	• Buy domestically	
	• Import licenses	
	• Manipulation of exchange rates	
	• Local content	
	Customs and other administrative procedures	
	• Tariff classifications	
	• Documentation requirements	
	• Product valuation	
	Standards	
	• Health, safety, and product quality	
	• Packaging and labeling	
	• Product testing methods	

the importer is required to pay $600 to U.S. Customs before taking possession of the goods. A **specific duty** is a fixed sum of money charged for a physical unit. A company importing dynamite in cartridges or sticks suitable for blasting would have to pay $.37 per pound, irrespective of the invoice value. When the flavoring extracts and fruit flavors mentioned above contain over 50 percent alcohol by weight, they are charged $.12 per pound plus 3 percent ad valorem. On a $10,000 shipment weighing 5,000 pounds, the importer would have to pay a **compound duty** of $900 ($.12 × 5,000 pounds + 0.03 × $10,000 = $600 + $300). Note that a specific duty, unless changed frequently in an inflationary period, soon loses its importance, whereas the amount collected from an ad valorem duty increases as the invoice price rises. Sometimes, however, an exporter may charge prices so much lower than domestic prices that the ad valorem duty fails to close the gap. Some governments set *official prices* or use *variable levies* to correct this deficiency.

specific duty
A fixed sum levied on a physical unit of an imported good

compound duty
A combination of specific and ad valorem duties

Official Prices.   These prices are included in the customs tariff of some nations and are the basis for ad valorem duty calculations whenever the actual invoice price is lower. The official price guarantees that a certain minimum import duty will be paid irrespective of the actual invoice price. It thwarts a fairly common arrangement that numerous importers living in high-duty nations have with their foreign suppliers whereby a false low invoice is issued to reduce the amount of duty to be paid. The importer sends the difference between the false invoice price and the true price separately.

Variable Levy.   One form of **variable levy,** which guarantees that the market price of the import will be the same as that of domestically produced goods, is used by the EU for imported grains. Calculated daily, the duty level is set at the difference between world market prices and the support price for domestic producers.

variable levy
An import duty set at the difference between world market prices and local government-supported prices

WORLDVIEW

Our Taxing Tariff Code

In 1790, the U.S. tariff code was written on just one page; it now requires two volumes with 8,753 different rates. Although it's true that the average American import duty is only 5 percent of the product's value—one of the lowest average duty levels in the world—the United States still levies over 100 percent duty on some products. Why must importers pay a 35 percent duty rate for apricot jam when they pay only 3 percent on jam made with currants? Has an apricot jam cartel gotten to Congress? How do you explain this difference? Although vitamin B12 is no longer produced in this country, it carries a 16.2 percent duty rate while vitamin E is levied less than half that amount, 7.9 percent, and vitamin C only 3.1 percent. The reason, of course, is that the government adds new tariffs to satisfy interest groups and no one is vitally interested in removing a tariff just because nobody is benefiting from it now.

Besides Congress, the U.S. Customs Service also has the ability to raise import duties or even keep some products from entering the country. It does this by putting goods in more restrictive tariff classifications. For example, an American importer had been bringing in girls' ski jackets at a 10.6 percent import duty. Suddenly, Customs declared that a shipment of 33,000 jackets should now pay 27.5 percent of the invoice value plus 17 cents per pound because they had small strips of corduroy trim on the sleeves. The strips, which comprised only 2 percent of the jacket's materials, were ruled to have changed the jackets from being "garments designed for rainwear, hunting, fishing, or similar uses" (skiing might be one) to the more expensive category, "other girls' wearing apparel, not ornamented." The importer brought this case to the Court of International Trade (the U.S. court that

Frank Grant/International Stock

Courtesy U.S. Customs Service/Photography by Billy L. Mason

handles such disputes), and the judge not only ruled against Customs, but he also ordered the government to refund all the extra duty that the importer had paid.

Tariff classification disputes and the thousands of import categories are the bases for these absurd situations. They also make it difficult for the United States to call for other nations to reduce their tariff and nontariff barriers. In fact, every year, since 1984, the European Union publishes its *Report on United States Barriers to Trade and Investment.* This 115-page publication lists, as the EU puts it, "a significant number of barriers and impediments to international trade that the European Union wants the United States to remove. These barriers, some of which have been in existence for decades, reduce the benefits which can be gained from free trade, they cause distortions to the efficient flow of capital and investment, and in many cases cause significant market distortions and losses of business to European firms in the U.S." To give you an idea of the contents, the topics cover such areas as public procurement, tariffs as trade impediments, standards, testing, labeling, and the application of countervailing duty legislation.

It is apparent that while the United States pursues the reduction of tariff and nontariff barriers that other nations have erected, there are also many in this country that must be eliminated.

Sources: James Bovard, *The Wall Street Journal,* March 28, 1990, p. A14; "The Customs Service's Fickle Philosophers," *The Wall Street Journal,* July 3, 1991, p. A10; "Trade Barriers' Cost Put at $19 Billion," *The Press Democrat (Santa Rosa),* November 27, 1993, p. E3; and *Report on United States Barriers to Trade and Investment 1994* (Brussels: Services of the European Commission, 1994).

Lower Duty for More Local Input.   Import duties are set by many nations in such a way as to encourage local input. For example, the finished product ready for sale to the consumer may have a 70 percent ad valorem duty. However, if the product is imported in bulk so that it must be packaged in the importing nation, the duty level may be at 30 percent. To encourage some local production, the government may charge only 10 percent duty on the semifinished inputs. These situations can provide opportunities for foreign manufacturers of low-technology products, such as paint articles and toiletries, to get behind a high tariff wall with very modest investments.

Nontariff Barriers.   **Nontariff barriers (NTBs)** are all forms of discrimination against imports other than the import duties we have been examining. As nations have reduced duties, nontariff barriers, which are either quantitative or nonquantitative, have assumed greater importance.

A study of 16 major industrial nations compared the percentage of world trade covered by nontariff barriers in 1981 and 1986. The average percentage increase was 17.2 percent for all 16 nations, but for the United States alone, it was 51.8 percent (Table 3–2).

nontariff barriers (NTBs)
All forms of discrimination against imports other than import duties

Quantitative.   **Quotas,** one type of quantitative barrier, are numerical limits for a specific kind of good that a country will permit to be imported without restriction during a specified period. If the quota is *absolute*, once the specified amount has been imported, further importation for the rest of the period (usually a year) is prohibited.

quotas
Numerical limits placed on specific classes of imports.

> China is the biggest clothing supplier of the American market, a market ruled by quotas. And when it comes to evading quotas, China has no equal. For example, China is notorious for overshipping, that is, sending goods after the quota is filled. Because of overshipping, China's quotas are often filled after only six months into the new year.

Importer	Trade Coverage Ratio†		
	1981	**1986**	**Percentage Increase**
Belgium-Luxembourg	12.6%	14.3%	13.5%
Denmark	6.7	7.9	17.9
Germany	11.8	15.4	30.5
France	15.7	18.6	26.8
Greece	16.2	20.1	24.1
Great Britain	11.2	12.8	14.3
Ireland	8.2	9.7	18.3
Italy	17.2	18.2	5.8
Netherlands	19.9	21.4	7.5
Switzerland	19.5	19.6	0.5
Finland	7.9	8.0	1.3
Japan	24.4	24.3	−0.4
Norway	15.2	14.2	−6.6
New Zealand	46.4	32.4	−30.2
United States	11.4	17.3	51.8
All above	15.1	17.7	17.2

TABLE 3–2

Nontariff trade coverage ratios for 16 industrialized nations*

*Nontariff measures include variable import levies, quotas, and nonautomatic import authorizations including restrictive import licensing requirements, quantitative voluntary export restraints, and trade restraints under the Multifiber Arrangement.
†The share of total imports (by value) subject to hardcore nontariff measures. In computing this index, the researchers applied 1981 and 1986 nontariff measures to a constant 1981 trade base. petroleum products and European Union intratrade were excluded.

Source: "An Introduction to Nontariff Barriers to Trade," *Federal Reserve Bank of St. Louis Review*, January–February 1989, pp. 32–46.

Another kind of quota evasion—transshipping—is plain fraud. Chinese producers ship finished goods to other countries with unfilled quotas where they are labeled as a product of that country. This deceptive labeling scheme brings $2 billion in illegal clothing imports from China into the United States annually. Gitano, for example, pled guilty to charges of fraud for importing Chinese blouses labeled "Made in the Maldive Islands." The firm was expected to pay $2 million in fines.[24]

Some goods are subject to *tariff-rate quotas,* which permit a stipulated amount to enter the country duty free or at a low rate, but when that quantity is reached, a much higher duty is charged for subsequent importations. This process is repeated annually.

Quotas are generally *global;* that is, a total amount is fixed without regard to source. They may also be *allocated,* in which case the government of the importing nation assigns quantities to specific countries. For example, the United States allocates quotas for specific tonnages of sugar to 25 nations. Because of their nature, allocated quotas are sometimes called *discriminatory* quotas.

voluntary export restraints (VERs)
Export quotas imposed by the exporting nation

Recently, because of the general agreement among nations against imposing quotas unilaterally, governments have negotiated **voluntary export restraints (VERs)** with other countries. Although a VER is a generic term for all bilaterally agreed measures to restrict exports, it has a stricter legal definition in the United States: "an action unilaterally taken to restrict the volume or number of items to be exported during a given period and administered by the exporting country. It is 'voluntary' in the sense that the country has a formal right to eliminate or modify it."[25] It is also voluntary in that the exporting nation may prefer its consequences to any trade barriers the importing nation might impose.

To avoid having the United States place quotas on imports of Japanese automobiles, the Japanese government has limited its annual exports to the United States to 1.65 million units. However, because of the expensive yen, U.S. imports from Japan have dropped considerably. Honda, for example, announced it would cut exports to this country by 20 percent in the 1994 fiscal year. A Honda official said that with the exchange rate at 105 yen to the dollar, it makes no sense to make cars in Japan and send them to the United States. For every one yen the dollar falls, Honda will lose $62 million in export sales. In 1993, Honda exported 41,000 cars from its American plants, including 23,000 to Japan. It exported 321,000 cars to the United States from Japan.[26]

orderly marketing arrangements
Formal agreements between exporting and importing countries that stipulate the import or export quotas each nation will have for a good

Orderly Marketing Arrangements. **Orderly marketing arrangements** are VERs consisting of formal agreements between governments to restrict international competition and preserve some of the national market for local producers. They differ from unilaterally imposed quotas and other trade barriers in that they result from negotiations between exporting and importing countries. Usually, they stipulate the size of import or export quotas that each nation will have for a particular good. Arrangements that involve industry participation are often called *voluntary restraint agreements.*

The largest and oldest such arrangement is the Multifiber Arrangement (MFA), which began in 1973 and has subsequently been renewed every four years. The pact includes 54 exporting and importing nations. It regulates about 80 percent of the world's textile and clothing exports to the industrialized nations.

In 1986, Japanese computer chip manufacturers slashed prices on a common chip, the DRAM, because of high inventories. The two American producers appealed to the government for help, and an accord was made that fixed minimum prices and established voluntary import quotas. Although the American chip manufacturers increased their profits, the makers of products containing the chips and the consumers who bought those products lost. The Brookings

Institution, a famous "think tank," estimates that the DRAM's price rose from $2.50 in 1986 to $10 in 1988 and, as a result, added more than $100 to the price of a $500 personal computer. The arrangement helped American firms, but it benefited Japanese chip makers much more. Instead of having to cut their prices to compete, they were able to put their monopoly profits into research on higher-technology products where Americans still lead. "What we did was pretty stupid," said a trade analyst at the Institute for International Economics.[27]

In 1991, a new five-year semiconductor accord between Japan and the United States specified that sales of foreign-made semiconductors in Japan should reach at least a 20 percent market share by the end of 1992. Japan finally reached that goal the last quarter of 1992. The United States and other foreign computer chip producers captured a record 21.9 percent of the Japanese market during 1994.[28]

Nonquantitative Nontariff Barriers. Many international trade specialists claim that the most significant nontariff barriers are the nonquantitative type. Governments have tended to establish nontariff barriers to obtain the protection formerly afforded by import duties. A study of the nonquantitative barriers revealed over 800 distinct forms, which may be classified under three major headings: (1) direct government participation in trade, (2) customs and other administrative procedures, and (3) standards.

1. *Direct government participation in trade.* The most common form of direct government participation is the *subsidy.* Besides protecting industries through subsidies, as mentioned earlier, nearly all governments subsidize agriculture. The EU, for example, paid European farmers an export refund of $150 per ton to get them to sell their wheat in the export markets for the world price of $80 per ton when the government-guaranteed price within the EU was $230. In 1992, the total of EU farm subsidies amounted to $85.4 billion, 47 percent of the total farm output.[29] Figure 3–3 shows that although the American subsidies amount to over $30 billion annually, those of the Japanese and the EU are even higher. Note too that the subsidies paid by the governments of Australia and New Zealand, two

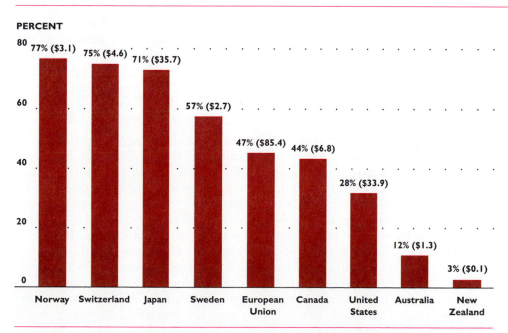

PERCENT

FIGURE 3–3
Value of farm subsidies
($ billions)

Norway 77% ($3.1)
Switzerland 75% ($4.6)
Japan 71% ($35.7)
Sweden 57% ($2.7)
European Union 47% ($85.4)
Canada 44% ($6.8)
United States 28% ($33.9)
Australia 12% ($1.3)
New Zealand 3% ($0.1)

Source: "Producer Subsidy Equivalents," *Agricultural Policies, Markets, and Trade* (Paris: OECD, 1993), Table II.1.

major exporters of agricultural products, are extremely small percentages of the total production value, unlike those of the United States and other developed nations.

Government procurement policies also are trade barriers because they usually favor domestic producers and severely restrict purchases of imported goods by government agencies. Policies may also require that products purchased by government agencies have a stipulated minimum *local content*. A recent law slightly related to local content stipulations requires American car dealers to put labels on new cars showing the percentage of Canadian and American parts as well as indicating the final assembly point. Japanese and European carmakers as well as American dealers of foreign cars are complaining bitterly, and the EU thinks "this constitutes an unjustifiable discrimination."[30]

Governments also try to restrict imports by the *manipulation of foreign exchange rates*. The U.S. government at various times has tried to drive down the dollar's price in foreign currencies for the purpose of improving American price competitiveness in world markets. This monetary policy has not been too successful, partly because much of international trade is between parent companies and foreign subsidiaries. For example, intercompany trade accounts for almost 80 percent of the two-way trade between Japan and the United States, 40 percent of the U.S.–EU trade, and 55 percent of the Japan–EU trade. Sales between unaffiliated firms are decreasing.[31]

2. *Customs and other administrative procedures.* These cover a large variety of government policies and procedures that either discriminate against imports or favor exports. For example, in France, the time of the year when customs officials take longer to process the documentation necessary to import sweaters coincides with the buying season. Italy permits textiles to be imported through only 10 specified ports, thus creating delays in passing goods through customs. When U.S. Customs was ordered by a federal court to change the classification of the two-door Nissan Pathfinder from truck to passenger car in 1994, the import duty level dropped from 25 percent to 2.5 percent. The government then owed the carmaker a refund of between $50 million to $75 million.[32]

Governments have also found ways to discriminate against the exportation of services. Overseas, U.S. airlines face a number of situations in which the national airline receives preferential treatment such as in the provision of airport services, airport counter locations, and number of landing slots. Other examples of discrimination are the Canadian government's giving tax deductions to local businesses that advertise on Canadian TV, but not when they use American stations across the border, or Australia's requiring television commercials to be shot in Australia.

3. *Standards.* Both governmental and private standards to protect the health and safety of a nation's citizens certainly are desirable, but for years exporting firms have been plagued by many that are complex and discriminatory. France, for example, prohibits the advertising of bourbon, alleging that grain spirits are injurious to health; but of course, spirits made from grapes are exempt from the ban. Australia, like most countries, requires imported livestock to be quarantined but has no quarantine facilities.

The United States recently stopped the sale of and recalled Indian skirts made of rayon. According to the U.S. Consumer Product Safety Commission, it did so to protect the American consumer. However, the Indian government claimed "it was a deliberate, anti-import measure and is one of the many nontariff barriers that can be expected." Annually, India exports nearly 20 million skirts worth $48 million.[33]

Will Revised Product Standards in the EU Hurt American Small Businesses?

Since January 1, 1993, the EU has been phasing in hundreds of new product standards concerned with health, safety, and environmental protection, and any American firm wanting to sell in Europe must meet these standards. Will they help or hinder small business?

That there will be one common set of standards for all 12 EU countries is an advantage for all companies, but especially for small firms that could not afford to produce different versions of their products for different European nations. A common set of standards will open up the entire EU to many small manufacturers for the first time. American companies, both exporters to and manufacturers in the EU, are beginning to face a single market with uniform standards and certification and testing procedures.

At the same time, however, they are experiencing increased competition from EU-based manufacturers. Many EU firms that formerly stayed in their own country because of the differences in standards are now expanding to other markets within the EU. Harmonization of standards and the simultaneous reduction of physical barriers at border crossings have made intra-EU exporting considerably less expensive. Estimates are that physical barriers added 45 percent to the prices of goods produced by EU firms employing less than 250 employees.

American companies worry that the new standards will keep them out of the European market by requiring them to retool and make expensive design changes. Moreover, new standards cover many products that heretofore have not been regulated. For example, Zimmer, a U.S. manufacturer of orthopedic devices, sells one-third of its output in Europe. New standards on the smoothness and roundness of hip socket balls forced the firm to buy production and testing equipment costing $5 million and add 10 people to its 6-person standards staff. Said the senior vice president, "There was no quality benefit, but we didn't want to be outflanked on a technical barrier to trade."

Another set of standards preoccupying American firms is the ISO 9000 series published by the International Standards Organization and adopted by over 95 nations, including the United States and members of the EU. EU directives make manufacturers liable if they supply defective products that cause harm to a person or damage property. For this reason, manufacturers and product users in the EU demand certification that the components or finished products they acquire have no defects. Although ISO 9000 certification does not protect a firm from being sued for a defective product, quality system documentation will prove useful in a legal defense.

More and more firms are realizing that ISO 9000 certification will not only make it easier to enter the European market, but also will bring them important cost savings. Conversely, if they are already in that market and are not certified, they probably will lose it to competitors that are.

Sources: "Quality Standards the World Agrees On," *Nation's Business*, May 1994, pp. 71–73; "Quality Certification," *Business America*, July 12, 1993, pp. 19–20; Jack G. Kaikati, "Opportunities for Smaller Industrial Firms in Europe," *Industrial Marketing Management* 19, 1990, pp. 339–48; and Saeed Samiee, "Strategic Considerations of the EC 1992 Plan for Small Exporters," *Business Horizons*, March–April 1990, pp. 48–52.

"Uniqueness" is the reason Japan has cited in its efforts to keep out various imports. Japanese skin is different, so foreign cosmetics companies must test their products in Japan before they can sell them there. Imports of tangerines have been limited because Japanese stomachs are small and thus have room only for small Japanese tangerines. However, their intestines are longer, so they have a harder time digesting American beef than Americans do, argued the head of Japan's agricultural committee. He said that the Japanese market should be closed to imports of American beef.[34] One of the strangest claims was that made by Japan's Ministry of Health, who told an American towel manufacturer that importation of the towels was restricted because the nap was too thick to dry smaller Japanese ears.[35]

Denmark, Finland, Norway, and Sweden each apply separate standards for electrical equipment and require individual testing in the country prior to certifying imports. Imagine the plight of the American manufacturer that must make special products for each of these countries to comply with its special standards. The cost of compliance may price the company out of the market. This could be and frequently is the reason such standards were set up in the first place.

Product Group	Cost per American Job Saved	Number of Jobs Involved	Total Cost ($ millions)
Benezoid chemicals	$1,000,000	216	$ 216
Luggage	933,628	226	211
Softwood lumber	758,678	605	459
Sugar	600,177	2,261	1,357
Polyethelene resins	590,604	298	176
Dairy products	497,897	2,378	1,184
Frozen concentrated orange juice	461,412	609	281
Ball bearings	438,356	146	64
Maritime	415,325	4,411	1,832
Ceramic tiles	400,576	347	139
Machine tools	348,349	169	59
Apparel and textiles	340,727	12,624	4,301

Source: Gary C. Hufbauer and Kimberly Ann Elliott, *Measuring the Cost of Protection in the United States* (Washington, DC: Institute for International Economics, 1994), pp. 11–13.

These few examples will give an idea of the complexity involved in trying to eliminate nontariff barriers. Some progress is being made, but it is slow. Meanwhile, the international businessperson should look for such barriers before attempting to conduct business in a foreign country.

Costs of Barriers to Trade

You read previously that the computer chip voluntary trade restraint agreement has proven costly to the final consumer, and you might have been amazed at how costly it was. But this is a small part of what trade restraints cost consumers. Economists of the Institute for International Economics studied 21 product groups, each of which has a domestic market of at least $1 billion and, after removal of import restraints, potential imports of $100 million. They estimate that the average consumer cost per job saved is $170,000 per year. This means that consumers pay over six times the average annual compensation of manufacturing workers to preserve jobs through import restraints. With the exception of lumber and machine tools, the sectors studied have been shielded from imports for 35 years or more. Table 3–3 summarizes the findings for the 12 product groups most affected.

This is why your jeans cost you what they do. Protection makes sugar, a commodity for which the United States has no comparative advantage, cost you 50 percent more than the world price. The United States has lost valuable wetlands in the Florida Everglades to sugar growers. One single family controls most of the Florida sugar industry, and annually American consumers make involuntary contributions to that family.[36] Note, too, how much it costs to save one American job. Studies done in other countries show similar results.[37]

ECONOMIC DEVELOPMENT

When businesspeople move from domestic to international business, they encounter markets with far greater differences in levels of economic development than those in which they have been working. It is important to understand this because a nation's level of economic development affects all aspects of business—marketing, production, and finance. Although nations vary greatly with respect to economic development levels, we commonly group them into the categories of developed, newly industrializing, developing, less developed, or least developed.

Categories Based on Levels of Economic Development

Developed is the name given to industrialized nations of Western Europe, Japan, Australia, New Zealand, Canada, and the United States. There is less agreement as to which nations should be included in another category, the **newly industrializing countries (NICs).** Commonly, this group includes Brazil, Mexico, the four Asian tigers (South Korea, Taiwan, Hong Kong, and Singapore), and three emerging NICs—Malaysia, Thailand, and Chile. These countries (1) have what the World Bank considers to be middle-income economies or higher, (2) possess a heavy concentration of foreign investment, (3) export large quantities of manufactured goods, including high-tech products, and (4) have fast-growing economies. Some economic experts do not include Brazil, Argentina, nor Mexico in this category because of their slow economic growth rates. Generally, Indonesia and south China are not yet considered to be NICs; however, they are not far behind.

Because the economies of the four tigers, as measured by GNP/capita, have grown faster than those of the other NICs and are approximating the size of the industrialized nations' economies, these countries are becoming known as **newly industrialized economies (NIEs).**[38] The NIEs are in the World Bank's classifications of either high-income or upper-middle-income economies. **Developing,** less developed (LDCs), and least developed are names used to categorize the rest of the world. See Table 3–4.

Intergovernmental agencies such as the UN and the World Bank tend to employ low-, middle-, and high-income designations rather than developed and less developed. However, since the latter are commonly used in industry as a kind of shorthand to describe the characteristics of two distinct groups of nations, we shall also use them in this text. Note that GNP/capita is the basis for both methods of classification.

developed
A classification for all industrialized nations, which are most technically developed

newly industrializing countries (NICs)
The middle-income economies of Brazil, Mexico, Malaysia, Chile and Thailand

newly industrialized economies (NIEs)
Fast growing upper middle-income and high-income economies of South Korea, Taiwan, Hong Kong, and Singapore

developing
A classification for the world's lower-income nations, which are less technically developed

GNP/Capita as an Indicator

We mentioned in Chapter 2 that although GNP/capita is widely used to compare countries with respect to the well-being of their citizens and for market or investment potential, businesspeople must use it with caution. What does this value signify? Is a country with an $800 GNP/capita a better market for a firm's products than one whose GNP/capita is only $750? To assume this gives excessive credence to its accuracy. For example, to arrive at

Category	Member-Nations	Characteristics
Developed	United States, Western Europe, Japan, Australia, New Zealand, and Canada	Most industrially advanced and technically developed nations
Newly industrialized economies (NIEs)	South Korea, Taiwan, Hong Kong, and Singapore	Fast-growing upper-middle-income and high-income economies; possess high concentration of foreign investment and are fast-growing exporters of manufactured goods including a large percentage of high-tech products.
Newly industrializing countries (NICs)	Mexico, Brazil, Malaysia, Chile, and Thailand	Middle-income economies with fast-growing manufacturing sector; attracting sizable new foreign investment and exporting sizable quantities of manufactured goods, including high-tech products
Developing	Remaining noncommunist countries	Lower-income nations; less technically developed

TABLE 3–4
Categories of nations based on level of economic development

the GNP, government economists must impute monetary values to various goods and services not sold in the marketplace, such as food grown for personal consumption. Moreover, many goods and services are bartered in both low-income nations (because people have little cash) and high-income countries (because they wish to reduce reported income and thus pay less income tax). Transactions of this type are said to be part of the *underground economy*.

underground economy
The part of a nation's income that, because of unreporting or underreporting, is not measured by official statistics

Underground Economy.   Much has been written about the part of the national income that is not measured by official statistics because it is either underreported or unreported. Included in this **underground** (black, parallel, submerged, shadow) **economy** are undeclared legal production, production of illegal goods and services, and concealed income in kind (barter). As a rule, the higher the level of taxation and the more onerous the government red tape, the bigger the underground economy will be.[39] Figure 3–4 shows estimates of some underground economies. They vary widely because of different methodologies used to compile them; also, people who have undeclared income will not likely admit it and be liable to prosecution for tax evasion. But there are many humorous incidents that people tell about others.

> In Bonn, a gardener completed a large landscaping job and when asked for a bill replied, "If you want one, it will be DM1,500 plus 14 percent tax. If you don't need one, just pay me DM1,400 cash." In Greece, when a patient tried to pay with a check, the physician was reluctant to accept one or to give a receipt, and when he opened his desk drawer, it was crammed with cash. A visitor to an Italian company was talking to the chief executive when his secretary announced the unexpected arrival of a tax inspector. He told her to stall the inspector and then called the company's financial director. A few minutes later, the visitor looked out the window and saw the financial director running across the field with an armload of ledgers.[40]

FIGURE 3–4 Underground economies (percentage of GNP)

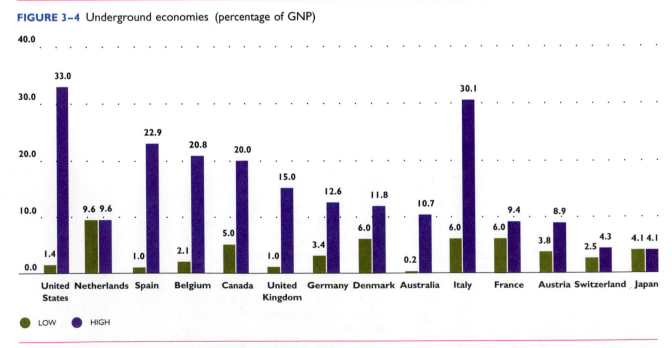

Source: "La Economía Subterránia en Estados Unidos," *Comercio Exterior*, May 1994, p. 451.

In addition to reducing the total taxes paid to government, the underground economy is responsible for all kinds of distortions of economic data. In Italy, for example, there was no record that a single pair of gloves was produced in Naples, yet it is now known that Naples is one of Italy's biggest glove-making centers—the unreported output is produced by small groups of workers in kitchens and garages. The official government statistical agency estimates that the GDP is at least 15 percent greater than the official figure. Italians are proud to say that, because of their underground economy, their per capita income has now overtaken that of the British. The *black work* in France is believed to be the reason 50 percent of all the cement produced vanishes into thin air as far as official records are concerned. Mexico's underground economy involved 23 percent of the work force in 1990, up from 13 percent in 1986. The value of enterprises working without records and paying no taxes accounted for 10 percent of Mexico's GNP in 1990.[41]

Currency Conversion.   Another problem with GNP estimates is that to compare them, the GNPs in local currency must be converted to a common currency— conventionally the dollar—by using an exchange rate. If the relative values of the two currencies accurately reflected consumer purchasing power, this conversion would be acceptable. However, the World Bank recognizes that "the use of official exchange rates to convert national currency figures to U.S. dollars does not reflect domestic purchasing powers of currencies."[42]

To overcome this deficiency, the UN International Comparison Program (ICP) has developed a method of comparing the GNP based on **purchasing power parity (PPP)** rather than on the international demand for currency (exchange rates). Here is how purchasing power parity rates are calculated.[43]

purchasing power parity (PPP)
The number of units of a currency required to buy the same amounts of goods and services in the domestic market as one dollar would buy in the United States

Suppose Thailand reports to the World Bank that its GNP per capita for last year is 46,370 baht/capita. The Bank must translate this value to U.S. dollars. It uses the current exchange rate of 25.2 baht = $1 to convert 46,370 baht to $1,840 (46,370/25.2). How well does this measure Thailand's welfare? What can a Thai citizen consume with the 46,370 baht as compared with what an American can consume with the $23,240 per capita income of the United States?

Compare local prices in both countries of the same basket of goods.

Goods	Thailand (baht)	U.S. ($)
Soap (bar)	15	0.45
Rice (lb.)	10	0.30
Shoes (pair)	450	60.00
Dress	350	45.00
Socks (pair)	25	2.00
	850	$107.75

850 baht buys in Thailand what $107.75 buys in the United States. Therefore comparing purchasing power of the currencies, 850 baht/$107.75 = 7.9 baht per $1. Using the exchange rate of 7.9 baht per dollar, Thailand's GNP/capita is now 46,370/7.9 = $5,870. At the official exchange rate of 25.2 baht/$1, Thailand's GNP is $1,840. At the purchasing power parity rate of 7.9 baht/$1, Thailand's GNP is $5,870.

Table 3–5 illustrates that comparisons based on purchasing power parity result in GNP/capita that are considerably higher than those regularly given for developing nations and lower for most developed nations; that is, when considering purchasing power, the differences between the GNPs of developing and developed nations are smaller than those generally published. Note how the smaller buying power of the yen compared to that of the U.S. dollar affects the GNP/capita based on PPP.

TABLE 3–5
GNP/capita based on UN
ICP for selected countries
1992

Country	GNP/Capita in US$s Converted at World Bank Adjusted Exchange Rates	GNP/Capita in US$s Based on Purchasing Power Parity
Switzerland	$36,080	$22,100
Japan	28,190	20,160
Sweden	27,010	17,610
Denmark	26,000	18,650
Norway	25,820	18,040
United States	23,240	23,120
Sri Lanka	540	2,810
Pakistan	420	2,130
India	310	1,210
Nepal	170	1,100

Source: *World Development Report 1994*, Tables 1 and 30, pp. 162 and 220.

More than GNP/Capita Is Required

Even if the problems we have examined did not exist, businesspeople still would not obtain a true picture of the relative strengths of markets by comparing GNP/capita alone. Remember that GNP/capita is a mean, which infers that every inhabitant receives an equal share of the national income. This is patently untrue, especially in developing nations, where the national income is much less evenly divided than it is in developed countries. Thus, businesspeople who conclude from a low GNP/capita that a nation is too poor to buy their products will certainly miss some lucrative markets.

The dissatisfaction with GNP/capita as an indicator of a nation's level of living (it is an index of production, not consumption) has led to various attempts to create indexes by combining variables such as the consumption of steel, concrete, newsprint, and electricity with the ownership of automobiles, telephones, TVs, and radios. In Chapter 14 on market analysis, we shall examine an index to compare market size that *Business International* has constructed by combining population and GDP with the consumption and production of certain key commodities. Although GNP/capita is an imperfect yardstick for comparing the purchasing power and market size of nations, it does serve as a rough indicator of whether a country is in the developed or developing category. This is valuable because it gives a set of common characteristics that provide some insight to the approximately 140 nations belonging to the **Third World*** of developing nations.

Third World
The developing nations

Characteristics of Developing Nations

Although there is great diversity among the many developing nations, most share the following common characteristics:

1. GNP/capita of less than $2,000.
2. Unequal distribution of income, with a very small middle class.
3. *Technological dualism*—a mix of firms employing the latest technology and companies using very primitive methods.
4. *Regional dualism*—high productivity and incomes in some regions and little economic development in others.
5. A preponderance (80 to 85 percent) of the population earning its living in a relatively unproductive agricultural sector.

---

*First World refers to industrial nations, Second World to the communist bloc, Third World to developing nations, and Fourth World to the bottom 30 nations of the Third World.

6. Disguised unemployment or underemployment—two people doing a job that one person can do.

7. High population growth (2.5 to 4 percent annually).

8. High rate of illiteracy and insufficient educational facilities.

9. Widespread malnutrition and a wide range of health problems.

10. Political instability.

11. High dependence on a few products for export, generally agricultural products or minerals.

12. Inhospitable topography, such as deserts, mountains, and tropical forests.

13. Low saving rates and inadequate banking facilities.

You can see from these characteristics that a tremendous gap exists between the levels of living of Third World inhabitants and those of industrialized nations. Although economists have studied and theorized about the various aspects of economic development for over two centuries, their preoccupation with the poor nations of the world really began only after World War II.

A Human-Needs Approach to Economic Development

Until the 1970s, economists generally considered economic growth synonymous with economic development. A nation was considered to be developing economically if its real output per capita as measured by GNP/capita was increasing over time. However, the realization that economic growth does not necessarily imply development—because the benefits of this growth so often have occurred to only a few—has led to the widespread adoption of a new, more comprehensive definition of economic development.

The **human-needs approach** defines economic development as the reduction of poverty, unemployment, and inequality in the distribution of income. The definition of poverty also has been broadened. Instead of being defined in terms of income, as is common in developed countries, a reduction in poverty has come to mean less illiteracy, less malnutrition, less disease and early death, and a shift from agricultural to industrial production.[44]

human-needs approach *Defines economic development as the elimination of poverty and unemployment as well as an increase in income*

Because of the increased emphasis on human welfare and the lack of a clear link between income growth and human progress, the United Nations Development Program has devised a Human Development Index (HDI) based on three essential elements of human life: (1) a long and healthy life, (2) the ability to acquire knowledge, and (3) access to resources needed for a decent standard of living.[45] These elements are measured by (1) life expectancy, (2) adult literacy, and (3) GDP/capita, adjusted for differences in purchasing power (see Figures 3–5 and 3–6). In its latest report, the program ranked Japan as the most developed with respect to social progress (HDI = 0.983); the United States ranked sixth (HDI = 0.976), below Japan, Canada, Norway, Switzerland, and Sweden. The primary reason for this ranking was the lower American adult literacy rate.[46]

No Accepted General Theory.   The inclusion of noneconomic variables has made it impossible to formulate a widely accepted general theory of development. Instead of pursuing a general theory, development economists are concentrating on specific problem areas, such as population growth, income distribution, unemployment, transfer of technology, the role of government in the process, and investment in human versus physical capital.

Relevance for Businesspeople.   What is the relevance of a lack of consensus among specialists about development theory? If a particular theory has fallen into disfavor among the experts, can businesspeople neglect it when dealing

FIGURE 3–5 World literacy rates as a percentage of the population, 1990–1991

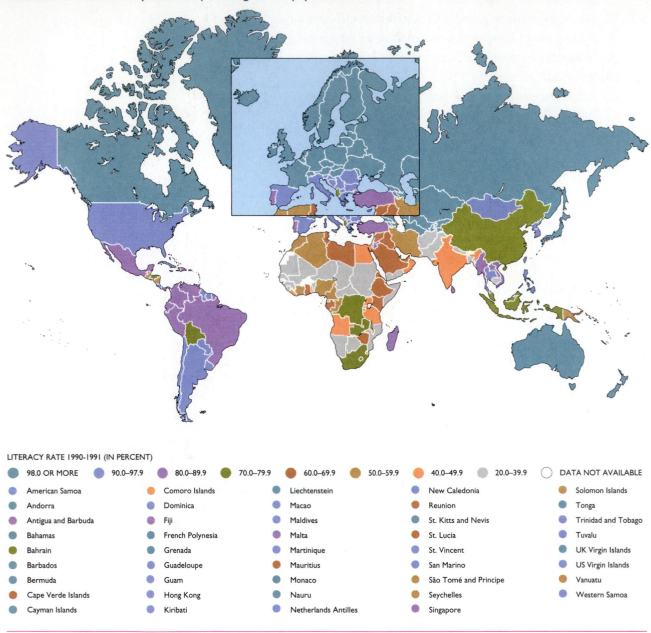

LITERACY RATE 1990-1991 (IN PERCENT)

● 98.0 OR MORE   ● 90.0–97.9   ● 80.0–89.9   ● 70.0–79.9   ● 60.0–69.9   ● 50.0–59.9   ● 40.0–49.9   ● 20.0–39.9   ○ DATA NOT AVAILABLE

American Samoa	Comoro Islands	Liechtenstein	New Caledonia	Solomon Islands
Andorra	Dominica	Macao	Reunion	Tonga
Antigua and Barbuda	Fiji	Maldives	St. Kitts and Nevis	Trinidad and Tobago
Bahamas	French Polynesia	Malta	St. Lucia	Tuvalu
Bahrain	Grenada	Martinique	St. Vincent	UK Virgin Islands
Barbados	Guadeloupe	Mauritius	San Marino	US Virgin Islands
Bermuda	Guam	Monaco	São Tomé and Principe	Vanuatu
Cape Verde Islands	Hong Kong	Nauru	Seychelles	Western Samoa
Cayman Islands	Kiribati	Netherlands Antilles	Singapore	

with government officials? That depends. Perhaps those officials still subscribe to it. In that case, businesspeople should emphasize the parts of their proposals that are germane to the theory, which is generally not too difficult because nearly every proposal will provide not only investment in physical capital but also training of employees, providing employment, and transferring technology. There will even be some redistribution of income through the creation of a middle class composed of managers and highly skilled technicians. As an example, let's look at how businesspeople might emphasize investment in human capital when making a proposal.

Investment in Human Capital.   This recent development in theory recognizes that more than just capital accumulation is needed for growth. There must also be investment in the education of people so there will be managers to

FIGURE 3–6 GDP per capita (in US$)

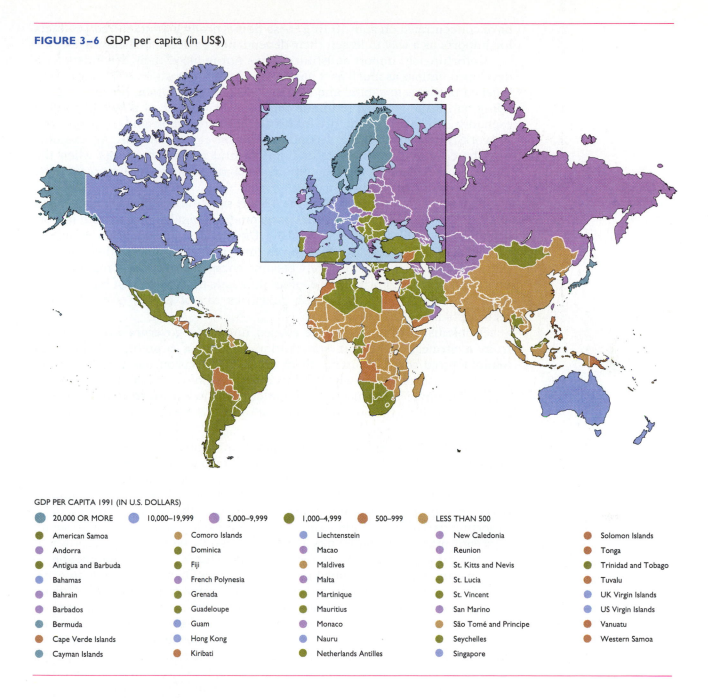

GDP PER CAPITA 1991 (IN U.S. DOLLARS)

● 20,000 OR MORE   ● 10,000–19,999   ● 5,000–9,999   ● 1,000–4,999   ● 500–999   ● LESS THAN 500

● American Samoa	● Comoro Islands	● Liechtenstein	● New Caledonia	● Solomon Islands
● Andorra	● Dominica	● Macao	● Reunion	● Tonga
● Antigua and Barbuda	● Fiji	● Maldives	● St. Kitts and Nevis	● Trinidad and Tobago
● Bahamas	● French Polynesia	● Malta	● St. Lucia	● Tuvalu
● Bahrain	● Grenada	● Martinique	● St. Vincent	● UK Virgin Islands
● Barbados	● Guadeloupe	● Mauritius	● San Marino	● US Virgin Islands
● Bermuda	● Guam	● Monaco	● São Tomé and Principe	● Vanuatu
● Cape Verde Islands	● Hong Kong	● Nauru	● Seychelles	● Western Samoa
● Cayman Islands	● Kiribati	● Netherlands Antilles	● Singapore	

ensure that the capital is productive and skilled workers to operate and maintain the capital equipment.

If managers know that this theory has strong acceptance in the country where they have an operation or are seeking permission to establish one, they should emphasize this aspect of their investment. A multinational or global firm that does not have training programs for workers is rare, and nearly all send local managers to the home office to update their skills.

Import Substitution versus Export Promotion.   Another strategy followed by some developing nations has been **import substitution**. Although developing nations have long considered the exporting of primary products (agricultural and raw materials) an important facet of their development strategy, they have not aggressively promoted the exporting of manufactured goods. Instead, they

import substitution
The local production of goods to replace imports

have concentrated on substituting these domestically manufactured products for imports as a way to lessen their dependence on developed countries.

Unfortunately, import substitution has not reduced their dependence on developed nations as much as it has changed the composition of imports from finished products to capital and semiprocessed inputs. Often, however, developing nations are unable to obtain these inputs because of a lack of foreign exchange, which can stop entire industries and throw thousands of people out of work, further increasing dependence on developed nations. An example was the closing of automobile and agricultural machinery plants when the Turkish government could not obtain foreign exchange for importing the necessary intermediate products.

Another serious problem with the import substitution strategy stems from the protection to local industry that governments grant by levying high import duties on goods also made domestically. Under this umbrella, local manufacturers feel no pressure to either lower their costs or improve their quality. Without such pressure, they rarely become competitive in world markets and thus cannot export. Furthermore, other domestic firms that must buy imports from these high-priced, protected industries cannot export either because their costs are excessive.

Problems such as these have caused numerous governments to change from a strategy of import substitution to one of promoting exports of manufactured goods. Spurring them on to this decision has been the rapid export growth of the newly industrializing nations, which we mentioned earlier. To force companies to become competitive in world markets, some governments limit the amount and duration of the protection they provide.

Relevance for Businesspeople.　　This change in strategy affects international firms in a variety of ways. First, local affiliate managers must be prepared for demands to export by government officials. They may even be given ultimatums, as were automobile manufacturers in Mexico: "If you need to import parts for your output, you must earn the foreign exchange to pay for them by exporting part of your production." A company asking for permission to set up a foreign manufacturing facility now will certainly be asked by government administrators about its plans for exporting. This is a new phenomenon to longtime managers accustomed to restricting an affiliate's sales to its internal market to save the export market for home country production. Second, managers can no longer count on having permanent protection from competing imports, as they once could. In some countries, they are likely to be told that after a certain date, they will lose their protection and will be expected to compete internationally. Last, in a situation where two firms are competing for permission to establish a plant, the deciding factor may be that one offers its multinational channels of distribution to the affiliate's exports.

The Importance of Keeping Current.　　These few examples illustrate (1) some of the concepts that underlie the strategies and policies of developing nations and (2) the relationship between the theories of international trade and development. Moreover, they show why experienced international businesspeople keep abreast of developments in both areas.

INTERNATIONAL INVESTMENT THEORIES

Contemporary international investment theory has been expanded considerably from the classical theory, which postulated that differences in interest rates for investments of equal risk are the reason international capital moves from one nation to another. For this to happen, there had to be perfect competition; but as Kindleberger, a noted economist, stated, "Under perfect competition, foreign direct investment would not occur, nor would it be likely to occur in a world wherein the conditions were even approximately competitive."[47]

Contemporary Theories of Foreign Direct Investment

Monopolistic Advantage Theory.   The modern **monopolistic advantage theory** stems from Stephen Hymer's dissertation in the 1960s, in which he demonstrated that foreign direct investment occurred largely in oligopolistic industries rather than in industries operating under near-perfect competition. This meant that the firms in these industries must possess advantages not available to local firms. Hymer reasoned that the advantages must be economies of scale, superior technology, or superior knowledge in marketing, management, or finance. Foreign direct investment takes place because of these product and factor market imperfections.[48]

monopolistic advantage theory
Foreign direct investment is made by firms in oligopolistic industries possessing technical and other advantages over indigenous firms

Product and Factor Market Imperfections.   Caves, a Harvard economist, expanded Hymer's work to show that superior knowledge permitted the investing firm to produce differentiated products that the consumers would prefer to similar locally made goods and thus would give the firm some control over the selling price and an advantage over indigenous firms. To support these contentions, he noted that companies investing overseas were in industries that typically engaged in heavy product research and marketing effort.[49]

International Product Life Cycle (IPLC).   We have already examined this theory to help explain international trade flows, but as we said, there is a close relationship between international trade and international investment. As you saw, the IPLC concept also explains that foreign direct investment is a natural stage in the life of a product. To avoid losing a market that it services by exporting, a company is forced to invest in overseas production facilities when other companies begin to offer similar products. This move overseas will be heightened during the third and fourth stages as the company that introduced the product strives to remain competitive, first in its export markets (stage 3) and later in its home market (stage 4), by locating in countries where the factors of production are less expensive. In-bond factories on the Mexican–American border are an example.

Other Theories.   Another theory was developed by Knickerbocker, who noted that when one firm, especially the leader in an oligopolistic industry, entered a market, other firms in the industry followed. The follow-the-leader theory is considered defensive because competitors invest to avoid losing the markets served by exports when the initial investor begins local production. They may also fear that the initiator will achieve some advantage of risk diversification that they will not have unless they also enter the market.[50] In addition, suspecting that the initiator knows something they do not, they may feel it is better to be safe than sorry.

Graham noted a tendency for **cross investment** by European and American firms in certain oligopolistic industries; that is, European firms tended to invest in the United States when American companies had gone to Europe. He postulated that such investments would permit the American subsidiaries of European firms to retaliate in the home market of U.S. companies if the European subsidiaries of these companies initiated some aggressive tactic, such as price cutting, in the European market.[51] Of course, as we noted in Chapter 2, there are a number of other reasons investment in the United States by foreign multinationals takes place, such as *following the customer*

cross investment
Foreign direct investment by oligopolistic firms in each other's home country as a defense measure

(Japanese parts manufacturers following Japanese auto manufacturers), *seeking knowledge* (Japanese and European investment in the Silicon Valley), and *benefiting from the stability of the American government.*

internalization theory
An extension of the market imperfection theory: to obtain a higher return on its investment, a firm will transfer its superior knowledge to a foreign subsidiary rather than sell it in the open market

The **internalization theory** is an extension of the market imperfection theory. A firm has superior knowledge, but it may obtain a higher price for that knowledge by using it than by selling it in the open market. By investing in a foreign subsidiary rather than licensing, the company is able to send the knowledge across borders while maintaining it within the firm, presumably realizing a better return on the investment made to produce it.[52]

Other theories relate to financial factors. Aliber believes the imperfections in the foreign exchange markets may be responsible for foreign investment. Companies in nations with overvalued currencies are attracted to invest in countries whose currencies are undervalued.[53] Although empirical tests are inconclusive, it does seem that a sizable number of U.S. takeovers by European globals and multinationals occurred during the late 1970s, when the dollar was relatively weak. One other financially based theory (portfolio theory) suggests that international operations allow for a diversification of risk and therefore tend to maximize the expected return on investment.[54]

Dunning's Eclectic Theory of International Production. This theory combines elements of some of those we have discussed. Dunning maintains that if a firm is going to invest in production facilities overseas, it must have three kinds of advantages.

1. *Ownership-specific*—This is the extent that a firm has or can get tangible and intangible assets not available to other firms.
2. *Internalization*—It is in the firm's best interests to use its ownership-specific advantages (internalize) rather than license them to foreign owners (externalize).
3. *Location-specific*—The firm will profit by locating part of its production facilities overseas.

eclectic theory of international production
For a firm to invest overseas, it must have three kinds of advantages: ownership-specific, internalization, and location-specific

The **eclectic theory of international production** provides an explanation for an international firm's choice of its overseas production facilities. The firm must have both location and ownership advantages to invest in a foreign plant. It will invest where it is most profitable to internalize its monopolistic advantage.[55]

There is one commonality to nearly all of these theories that is supported by empirical tests—the major part of direct foreign investment is made by large, research-intensive firms in oligopolistic industries. Also, all these theories offer reasons companies find it *profitable* to invest overseas. However, as we stated in Chapter 2, all motives can be linked in some way to the desire to increase or protect not only profits, but also *sales* and *markets*.

SUMMARY

1. **Understand the theories that attempt to explain why certain goods are traded internationally.** Why do nations trade? Mercantilists did so to build up storehouses of gold. Later, Adam Smith showed that a nation would export goods that it could produce with less labor than other nations. Ricardo then proved that even though it was less efficient than other nations, a country could still profit by exporting goods if it held a comparative advantage in the production of those goods.

The idea that a nation would tend to export products requiring a large amount of a relatively abundant factor was offered by Heckscher and Ohlin in their theory of factor endowment. The international product life cycle theory states that many products first produced in the United States or other developed countries are eventually produced in less developed nations and become imports to the very countries in which their production began.

In the 1920s, economists realized that economies of scale affect international trade because they permit industries of a nation to become low-cost producers without having an abundance of a class of production factors. As in the case of comparative advantage, nations specialize in the production of a few products and trade to supply the rest. The Linder theory of overlapping demand states that because customers' tastes are strongly affected by income levels, a nation's income level per capita determined the kind of goods they will demand. The kinds of goods produced to meet this demand reflect the country's income per capita level. International trade in manufactured goods will be greater between nations with similar levels of per capita income. Porter claims that four classes of variables affect a country's ability to gain a competitive advantage: demand conditions, factor conditions, related and supporting industries, and firm strategy, structure, and rivalry.

2. **Comprehend the arguments for imposing trade restrictions.** Special interest groups demand protection for defense industries and new firms. Others want fair competition. Companies will also demand that their government retaliate against dumping and subsidies offered by their competitors in other countries.

3. **Explain the two basic kinds of restrictions: tariff and nontariff trade barriers.** In response to demands for protection, governments impose import duties (tariff barriers) and nontariff barriers, such as quotas, voluntary export restraints, and orderly marketing arrangements; and nonquantitative nontariff barriers, such as direct government participation in trade, customs and other administrative procedures, and standards for health, safety, and product quality.

4. **Recognize the weaknesses of GNP/capita as an economic indicator.** For a number of reasons, GNP/capita is a weak market indicator. Transactions worth billions of dollars go unrecorded because people do business in the underground economy, paying cash without demanding receipts and invoices. Exchange rates for converting economic data usually do not reflect consumer purchasing power. International institutions such as the World Bank and the United Nations have developed a method of comparing GNPs that is based on purchasing power parity.

5. **Identify the common characteristics of developing nations.** Developing nations have certain common characteristics: unequal distribution of income, technological and regional dualism, large percentage of population in agriculture, high population growth, high illiteracy rate, insufficient education, and low saving rates.

6. **Understand the new definition of economic development, which includes more than economic growth.** The human-needs approach defines economic development as the reduction of poverty, unemployment, and inequality in the distribution of income.

7. **Understand why some governments are changing from an import substitution strategy to one of export promotion and the implications of this change for businesspeople.** Governments are changing from using an import substitution strategy to one of export promotion to become less dependent on developed nations. Also, governments are opening their borders to imports to force local producers to raise quality and improve prices so they can enter world markets. Managers of foreign-owned affiliates can be expected to export even though the multinational may prefer to keep exporting and the profits for the home office.

8. **Explain some of the theories of foreign direct investment.** International investment theory attempts to explain why foreign direct investment (FDI) takes place. Product and factor market imperfections provide firms, primarily in oligopolistic industries, with advantages not open to indigenous companies. The international product life cycle theory explains international investment as well as international trade. Some firms follow the industry leader, and the tendency of European firms to invest in the United States and vice versa seems to indicate that cross-investment is done for defensive reasons. The internalization theory states that firms will seek to invest in foreign subsidiaries rather than license their superior knowledge to receive a better return on the investment used to develop that knowledge.

There are two financially based explanations of foreign direct investment. One holds that foreign exchange market imperfections attract firms from nations with overvalued currencies to invest in nations with undervalued currencies. The second theory postulates that FDI is made to diversify risk. Empirical tests reveal that most FDI is made by large, research-intensive firms in oligopolistic industries.

The eclectic theory of international production explains an international firm's choice of its overseas production facilities. The firm must have location and ownership advantages to invest in a foreign plant. It will invest where it is most profitable to internalize its monopolistic advantage.

KEY WORDS

- mercantilism   75
- absolute advantage   75
- comparative advantage   77
- factor endowment   78
- exchange rate   80
- currency devaluation   81
- international product life cycle (IPLC)   81
- market share   83
- dumping   87
- subsidies   88
- countervailing duties   88
- tariffs   88
- ad valorem duty   88
- specific duty   89
- compound duty   89
- variable levy   89
- nontariff barriers (NTBs)   91

- quotas   91
- voluntary export restraints (VERs)   92
- orderly marketing arrangements   92
- developed   97
- newly industrializing countries (NICs)   97
- developing   97
- underground economy   98
- purchasing power parity (PPP)   99
- Third World   100
- human-needs approach   101
- import substitution   103
- monopolistic advantage theory   105
- cross investment   105
- internalization theory   106
- eclectic theory of international production   106

QUESTIONS

1. *a.* Explain Adam Smith's theory of absolute advantage.
   b. How does Ricardo's theory of comparative advantage differ from the theory of absolute advantage?

2. What is the relationship between the Heckscher-Ohlin factor endowment theory and the theories in question 1?

3. Name some products that you believe have passed through the four stages of the international product life cycle.

4. It seems that free, unrestricted international trade, in which each nation produces and exports products for which it has a comparative advantage, will enable everyone to have a higher level of living. Why, then, does every country have import duty restrictions?

5. We certainly need defense industries, and we must protect them from import competition by placing restrictions on competitive imports. True or false? Is there an alternative to trade restrictions that might make more economic sense?

6. "Workers are paid $20 an hour in the United States but only $4 in Taiwan. Of course we can't compete. We need to protect our jobs from cheap foreign labor." What are some possible problems with this statement?

7. There are two general classifications of import duties: tariff and nontariff barriers.
   a. Describe the various types of tariff barriers.
   b. What are some of the nontariff barriers?

8. Of what importance to marketers is a nation's level of economic development?

9. What problems with the import substitution strategy have caused some governments to increase their emphasis on export promotion?

10. *a.* What do economies of scale have to do with international trade?
    b. What is the importance of market share in international trade?

MINICASE 3–1   Tarus Manufacturing

John Baker, vice president of Tarus Manufacturing, called in Ed Anderson, the export manager, to discuss the sales results for the new adhesive that Tarus was exporting to its sales subsidiary in Colombia.

Baker: Ed, How is Tarus Colombiana doing with the new adhesive we're sending them?

Anderson: They're doing well. In the first six months they've sold 6,000 quarts at 1,800 pesos or $3 a quart.

Baker: Not bad for a small operation. If they keep it up, that cement is going to be a best-seller.

Anderson: That's true, and our profit is good. Moreover, I've been studying Colombia's import tariff and I think I've found a way to improve our profit.

Baker: Great. How are you going to do it? It has to be honest, Ed.

Anderson: Well, you know that they have to pay a 40 percent ad valorem import duty on our $1.60 invoice price plus 60 pesos per quart specific duty. If, however, we send them the adhesive in 55-gallon drums, the import duty drops to 30 percent ad valorem plus a specific duty of 6,600 pesos per drum.

Baker: Yes, but then they'll have to buy one-quart cans and labels and fill them in Colombia. This adds to their expense.

Anderson: True, but because we won't have to fill the cans or charge them for cans and labels, we will save 20 cents per quart, which we'll pass on to them.

Baker: How much will it cost to fill the cans locally?

Anderson: They tell me the cans, labels, and labor to fill the cans will come to 180 pesos per can, and the only investment required is a shutoff valve, which they screw in the drumhead when the cans are filled.

Baker: I'm not sure I see the advantage, Ed. The cans, labels, and labor are more expensive in Colombia than they are here. Where is the advantage?

Anderson: Let me show you, John.

Show Ed Anderson's calculations. Disregard any possible freight savings for shipping in bulk.

Vanguard Pollution Control Company

Five years ago, Diane Alber, applications engineer with Dickson Environmental Engineering Company, decided to start her own firm. She was confident that the public's demand for cleaner air and water as well as for relief from the dangers of hazardous waste would be met by a rapid growth in the environmental equipment industry. She judged correctly that the Clean Air Act Amendments of 1990 would require manufacturing, refining, and mining companies to make massive investments in equipment to monitor and reduce air pollution. Moreover, the dwindling number of municipal landfills was forcing firms to seek new ways to treat and recycle their solid waste. Table I–1 shows just how correct Alber's forecast was. U.S. industry's 1991 investment in pollution reduction equipment increased by 23 percent over the amount spent in 1990. The industries that are the largest purchasers are: (1) utilities, (2) chemicals, (3) petroleum and coal, (4) paper, and (5) mining.

By the end of 1994, Alber's company, Vanguard Pollution Control, was producing fabric filters and electrostatic precipitators to remove pollutants from gaseous streams before factories discharged them into the atmosphere. During that year, Vanguard began to design and build hazardous waste incinerators. The company's laboratory is experimenting with pyrolysis to gasify medical waste, a worldwide disposal problem. The resultant gas is then burned in high temperature, leaving a fine, sterile powder. The volume and the weight are reduced to 1 percent of the original amounts. If this process can be carried out successfully on a commercial scale, Vanguard will have a virtual monopoly on the handling of medical waste.

The company is perfectly positioned to participate in areas of fast growth: air pollution control and waste management. By 1995, the first was expected to double in sales volume, whereas the amount spent on waste management control would increase by 50 percent. In 1994, total sales of Vanguard Pollution Control had reached one million dollars and the firm had 21 employees. Presently, about 80 percent of the sales revenues are derived from air pollution control equipment, with the rest coming from waste management. Although Alber had made no effort to do business overseas, she was supplying some products to a number of in-bond plants in Reynosa, Mexico, that belonged to her customers.

Recently, however, the vice president for production of one of Alber's customers, a multinational with sizable operations in Europe, called Alber to tell her about his visit to his company's European plants. He said that many of Vanguard's products his company used in the United States were better than what his European subsidiaries could get. The vice president then asked her when Vanguard was going to enter the European market.

TABLE I–1
U.S. industry capital expenditures for pollution reduction ($ billions)

	1988	1989	1990	1991
Air	$1.524	$1.819	$2.562	$3.706
Water	1.289	1.825	2.651	2.815
Solid waste	0.610	0.666	0.818	0.869
Total	$3.423	$4.310	$6.031	$7.390

Source: U.S. Department of Commerce, Bureau of Census.

Alber laughed and said, "any day now." However, after the conversation, she began to think about the possibilities of entering foreign markets. She decided to ask her industry association, the Air & Waste Management Association (A&WMA), about the potential of foreign markets. This is what she learned. In 1992, the OECD estimated that the global market for environmental technologies, including goods and services, was about $200 billion in 1990 and would reach $300 billion by the year 2000 (see Table I–2). The A&WMA believes the United States comprises about 40 percent, or $80 billion, of the world market.

The A&WMA also gave her the results of a study by the Environmental Protection Agency (EPA), which shows that the United States is a major exporter of environmental equipment. Between 1989 and 1991, American exports increased 70 percent while imports grew by only 45 percent. The EPA describes the U.S. environmental industry as one of the most competitive in the world and declares it has an excellent potential for increasing exports despite strong German and Japanese competition. Currently, American industry exports 10 percent of its output.

Taiwan, Hong Kong, and the Republic of Korea are said to present the best market opportunities in Asia. The governments of both Taiwan and Hong Kong encourage the importation of environmental equipment, and neither country levies import duties on it. The governments of all three nations are highly committed to environmental cleanup. However, there is strong competition from Japanese firms that offer attractive financing.

The U.S. Department of Commerce estimated that the Association of Southeast Asian Nations (ASEAN) was a market worth nearly $2 billion in 1993. They further estimated that the sales of filtration and purification equipment for water and wastewater treatment will grow at a rate of 30 to 40 percent annually for the next three years. The sales of instrumentation and monitoring equipment will increase at a rate of 20 percent for the next few years. Mexico represents the largest market in Latin America, in part because of NAFTA, but also because it has heavy air and water pollution as well as hazardous waste disposal problems in its major cities. The new countries of Eastern Europe are also faced with major pollution problems, providing another major market. Long-term prospects are good, although these nations have very limited resources in the short run. The Department of Commerce expects American firms to capture 10 to 15 percent of the market even though there is strong competition from Western European countries.

	1990	2000
Water treatment	$ 60	$ 83
Waste management	40	63
Air quality control	30	42
Other	22	32
Services	48	80
Total	$200	$300

TABLE I–2

Forecast of world market for environmental industry equipment ($ billions)

Source: *The OECD Environment Industry: Situation, Prospects, and Government Policies* (Paris: OECD, 1992).

After studying all this information, Alber concluded that her company should enter this huge international market. The Asian market looked especially appealing. She also understood that she needed help from someone with international experience and wondered how she could locate that person. The company was limited in what it could afford. She then called her friend, a business professor at the university. Without making any definite recommendations, after considerable discussion of Alber's requirements, the professor suggested she talk with a Taiwanese MBA student who was about to graduate and was looking for a job.

The next day Diane met Zhen Xi-pei, the MBA student. She told him that she wanted someone to learn about the global market in environmental pollution equipment, assess the potential for Vanguard Pollution Control, and recommend a plan of action for the firm. The student replied that he had worked as a manager's assistant in Taiwan and was confident he could handle the kind of responsibility she was describing. Alber told him to come to work the following Monday.

On Monday, Zhen Xi-pei was there when Alber opened the office. It was early and Alber invited him to have some coffee. After a few minutes of small talk, Zhen said he had been thinking about Alber's comments concerning the Asian market. Remembering the needs of his own country, he had called the Taiwanese trade officer in Houston for recent information about the Taiwan market. He told Alber what he had learned.

The trade officer had confirmed that Asia is a major market for all American Exports. In fact, the United States now trades more with the Pacific Rim nations that with Europe (see Table I–3).

These are some specific facts about Taiwan:

1. Taiwan's economy experienced real growth of 5.9 percent in 1993 and expected a higher rate of 6.2 percent in 1994.

2. Taiwan's GNP/capita was expected to rise from US$10,566 in 1993 to US$11,236 in 1994.

TABLE I–3

Top 20 export markets for U.S. manufactured products

Markets	Rank		U.S. 1992 Exports		
	1992	1991	Value ($ billions)	Share of U.S. Exports	Share of Top 20 Markets
Top 20 markets			$302.1	82.0%	100.0%
Canada	1	1	80.8	21.9	26.8
Mexico	2	3	34.6	9.4	11.4
Japan	3	2	30.3	8.2	10.0
United Kingdom	4	4	21.0	5.7	7.0
Germany	5	5	19.2	5.2	6.4
France	6	6	13.1	3.6	4.3
Taiwan	7	9	12.2	3.3	4.0
Netherlands	8	8	10.6	2.9	3.5
Republic of Korea	9	7	10.2	2.8	3.4
Singapore	10	10	9.0	2.5	3.0
Australia	11	12	8.3	2.3	2.8
Hong Kong	12	13	7.6	2.1	2.5
Belgium/Luxembourg	13	11	7.5	2.0	2.5
Italy	14	14	6.7	1.8	2.2
Saudi Arabia	15	15	6.5	1.8	2.1
China	16	18	6.3	1.7	2.1
Brazil	17	17	5.0	1.3	1.6
Venezuela	18	19	4.8	1.3	1.6
Switzerland	19	16	4.3	1.2	1.4
Malaysia	20	21	4.2	1.1	1.4
World total			$368.5		

Source: U.S Department of Commerce, *U.S. Industrial Outlook 1994*, p. 15.

	Exports to (US$ billions)			Imports from (US$ billions)		
	1994	1993	Percent Change	1994	1993	Percent Change
United States	$11.24	$11.42	−1.6%	$ 9.18	$ 8.52	7.7%
Europe	6.28	6.62	−5.1	7.60	6.83	11.2
Asia	21.12	19.23	9.8	19.40	17.86	8.6
Hong Kong*	9.93	8.93	11.2	0.73	0.88	−17.1
Japan	4.64	4.53	2.4	11.99	11.49	4.4
ASEAN	4.84	4.40	9.9	3.97	3.36	18.0
Others	4.78	4.68	2.1	4.86	5.38	−9.8
Total	$43.42	$41.95	3.5%	$41.03	$38.60	6.3%

TABLE I–4
Taiwan's destinations of exports and origins of imports (1993–1994)

*Final destination is the People's Republic of China.

Source: Ministry of Finance, Taiwan.

3. Despite placing import barriers on Japanese products to reverse its trade deficit with Japan, Taiwan still imports more from Japan than from any other nation; the United States is second (see Table I–4).

4. Foreign direct investment flows to Taiwan for 1986 to 1992 ($ millions) were:

1986	1987	1988	1989	1990	1991
$326	$715	$959	$1,604	$1,330	$1,271

Source: UNCTAD, *World Investment Report 1994* (New York: United Nations, 1994), p. 14.

5. An American Week '94, with theme "American My Partner" was held in Taipei from July 2 to 17. The program was planned by the American Institute in Taiwan to promote American products and technology while emphasizing how Taiwan and the United States can work together to overcome Taiwan's environmental protection difficulties. The U.S. product exhibition introduced a wide range of products and new-to-market (NTM) companies. The show generated over $500,000 in sales and received 120,000 visitors. All NTM exhibitors found local distributors or agents to represent them in Taiwan.

The trade official did not have the data on the imports of environmental equipment, but he promised to request them from Taiwan and would call Zhen as soon as they arrived. But he did send a videotape on Taiwan, which Zhen gave to Alber who put it in the office VCR.

1. The U.S. market for environmental equipment is huge and Vanguard is small. Should the company risk entering an unknown market instead of expanding in the United States?

2. Do you believe there is a market in Taiwan for Vanguard's products? Why or why not?

3. How useful are the recommendations of the secretary general of CETRA?

4. Will it be possible for a woman such as Diane Alber to do business personally with Taiwanese businessmen?

5. If there is a market in Taiwan, how should Vanguard supply it—export to it, set up a wholly owned company to manufacture in it, set up a sales organization and arrange with a local firm to produce for it under contract, enter into a joint venture, or license its technology to a Taiwanese firm?

6. Do Zhen and Alber have enough information to make such a decision?

7. If not, what else do they need to know?

Sources: U.S. Department of Commerce, *U.S. Industrial Outlook 1994*, pp. 19–1 through 19–7; various market research reports from the National Trade Data Bank, U.S. Department of Commerce, International Trade Administration, November 1994; and "A Study of the R.O.C.'s Economic Development Experience," *Economic Review*, May–June 1994, pp. 1–9.

The International Environment: Organizations and Monetary System

International Organizations

In several areas such as environment and external trade, the commission has too few staff to cope with the work load. Elsewhere, people have time to twiddle their thumbs. The personnel department . . . is grossly overstaffed. The directorate-general, laughingly called Information, has not got the communications skills to sell ice cream in a heat wave. The research establishments of the commission, parked in Italy, are known . . . as the holiday camp on Lake Maggiore. They have cost the European taxpayer a fortune and have produced little more than a suntan for those working there. . . .

"A Fly on the Berlaymont Wall," The Economist, *June 1, 1991, p. 48*

CONCEPT PREVIEWS

After reading this chapter, you should be able to:

1. **explain** the activities of the United Nations in the economic and social fields as well as those as a peacekeeper

2. **explain** the three major parts of the World Bank: its regular loan window, its International Finance Corporation, and its International Development Association

3. **explain** the original and changed activities of the International Monetary Fund

4. **understand** how the European Bank for Reconstruction and Development started in the wrong direction but has been turned around

5. **compare** the successes and failures of the regional development banks,

6. **explain** recent developments at the Bank for International Settlements

7. **compare** the powers and activities of the World Trade Organization with those of the General Agreement on Tariffs and Trade, which it replaced, and understand the importance of the WTO to world business and trade

8. **understand** the opportunities for business presented by the European Union, and the political and cultural obstacles facing the EU members in reaching the goals of full union

9. **understand** the potential for the North American Free Trade Agreement

10. **understand** uses of the Organization for Economic Cooperation and Development for business and students

The International Finance Corporation Succeeds

Michael Barth has learned that experts can be wrong. In the early 1980s, he helped organize a fund in the United States for investing in South Korean stocks. Wall Street experts said the fund would fail for want of investor interest. • Wall Street was wrong. Investors liked the potential of the South Korean economy and bought Korea Fund shares. It was listed on the New York Stock Exchange in 1984 and has since been one of the best-performing country investment funds. • Mr. Barth works for the International Finance Corporation (IFC) capital markets department. The Korea Fund has been followed by a $50 million emerging-markets growth fund, a $30 million Thailand Fund, and an $86 million Malaysia Fund.[a] • Fifty new country funds were created in 1990, and by the end of that year there were 150 such funds listed on the New York or London stock exchanges. They had net assets of $12 billion and offered investment opportunities in Asia, Eastern Europe, and Latin America.[b] • The continuing success of the IFC caused it to be emulated in 1992 by creation of a profit-making entrepreneurial version, the Emerging Market Corporation (EMC). Based in Washington, DC, the EMC's purpose is to take advantage of growing opportunities for direct and portfolio investment in developing countries, Eastern Europe, and the former Soviet Union.[c]

Sources: [a]Cheah Cheng Hye, "IFC's Pioneering Investment Funds Funnel Capital to Asian Equity Markets," *Asian Wall Street Journal,* September 21, 1987, p. 28; [b]*The Economist,* June 1, 1991, p. 77; [c]Michael Prowse, "IFC-Style Investment Company Launched," *Financial Times,* February 13, 1992, p. 6.

Given the immense and growing numbers and importance of private and governmental international transactions, it is not surprising that a variety of international organizations have sprung up to facilitate, regulate, measure, or finance them. It behooves the business student—who is likely to be exposed to international opportunities and problems soon after graduation—to be aware of the existence and functions of a number of these organizations.

Some are worldwide organizations, and some are regional organizations with members from only one geographic area. Some are large, some small. Most are groupings of governments, but some are private.

The element common to all the organizations discussed in this chapter is that they all can be important to businesses. They may be sources of orders or sources of financing. They may be regulatory, or they may aim at standardization of weights and measurements. And, last but not least, they may be sources of jobs for you (see Figure 4–1).

THE UNITED NATIONS

Possibly the best-known worldwide organization is the United Nations (UN). Conceived and born amid the idealism and hopes that came with peace following World War II (1939–45), the UN has been a disappointment to many of its original supporters. Others foresaw more accurately what the UN's strengths and weaknesses would probably be.

> During the early UN years, one international law scholar, Professor Edwin Borchard of Yale Law School, cautioned his classes, which contained a number of World War II veterans, not to be too sanguine about enduring peace resulting from the UN. He told them, in effect, to keep their powder dry, and indeed the education or early careers of many of them were interrupted by the Korean War. In fact, one side in that war fought in the name of the UN.

Of course, there have been many other wars, declared and undeclared, between nations, colonies, provinces, tribes, and ethnic groups since the days of great expectation in the mid-1940s. These wars were waged despite the UN's peacekeeping efforts, and many despaired of the UN as a keeper of the peace. During the late 1980s and into the 1990s, it enjoyed some relative successes and some dismal failures. Iraqi troops were chased out of Kuwait, which they had invaded, and the UN oversaw a fairly peaceful election in Cambodia, although an important Cambodian force, the Khmer Rouge, boycotted the election.

In the former Yugoslavia, despite the presence of UN troops, bitter fighting and "ethnic cleansing" continued between Serbs, Croats, and Muslims. A UN intervention into Somalia was begun by American troops with the objective of stopping fighting between forces of opposing Somali warlords in order to distribute food to starving Somalis. Troops from other countries, notably Italy and Pakistan, joined the Americans in the UN force, and in the beginning the goals of curbing the fighting and feeding the people were being met. However, in 1993, the warriors of one of the warlords ambushed and killed several Pakistani UN soldiers, whereupon the UN, led by American forces, launched an unsuccessful effort to capture the "bad" warlord. There were American casualties, and pressure grew in the U.S. Congress to withdraw U.S. troops, which President Clinton did in 1994.[1]

In addition to its peacekeeping functions, the UN also conducts many activities potentially of great importance to businesspeople and students. It spends over $750 million annually for goods and services from businesses worldwide, and its agencies advise member-countries as they contract to buy goods and services in amounts that annually exceed $20 billion.

ASIAN DEVELOPMENT BANK

The **ASIAN DEVELOPMENT BANK** is an international development finance institution owned by 53 member governments consisting of 37 regional members from Asia and the Pacific, and 16 non-regional members from Europe and North America. The Bank, which was established in 1966, is based in Manila, Philippines. It seeks to accelerate economic and social development in the Asian and Pacific region through policy dialogue with its member governments as well as through loans and equity investments, technical assistance and promotion of investment of public and private capital for development.

Applications are invited from highly qualified professionals for the following current and anticipated staff positions:

* **ECONOMISTS**
* **STATISTICIAN**
* **PROJECT ENGINEERS**
* **FINANCIAL ANALYSTS**
* **ENVIRONMENT SPECIALISTS**
* **ENERGY SPECIALISTS**
* **EDUCATION SPECIALISTS**
* **PERSONNEL OFFICERS**
  (Career Counselling, Compensation, Training and Development)
* **LEGAL COUNSELS**
* **SOCIOLOGISTS/ANTHROPOLOGISTS**
* **ARCHIVIST/LIBRARIAN**

GENERAL REQUIREMENTS: It is expected that candidates have, preferably, a Master's degree or its equivalent in their appropriate field, at least eight years of relevant experience and familiarity with the developing countries in Asia. They must be nationals of the Bank's member countries and proficient in written and spoken English, the working language of the Bank. Excellent analytical and interpersonal skills as well as the ability to draft reports and undertake negotiations are essential. The possession of multidisciplinary skills such as in economics cum sociology or engineering cum finance would be an advantage to the successful applicants.

WOMEN ARE ACTIVELY ENCOURAGED TO APPLY.

The Bank offers a competitive salary paid in US Dollars (normally free of tax) and an excellent benefits package tailored to the needs of those living outside their home country.

Interested persons may send their curriculum vitae to **REF. NO 9319-B, HUMAN RESOURCES DIVISION, ASIAN DEVELOPMENT BANK, P.O. BOX 789, 1099 MANILA, PHILIPPINES.** FAX NOS. (63-2)741-7961; (63-2)632-6816; (63-2)631-7961; and (63-2)631-6816.

FIGURE 4–1
International organization job opportunities

Source: *The Economist*, January 8, 1994, p. 7.

The UN is characterized by decentralization, which can be a source of frustration for the student or businessperson. To help businesses approach the UN, the Interagency Procurement Services Unit (IAPSU) was established in 1985. It is an information clearinghouse that helps match up suppliers and UN customers.* To help you better understand the UN's structure, Figure 4–2 presents an organizational chart.

---

*To contact the IAPSU and other UN agencies directly, see the fax, telephone, and telex numbers and addresses in *Business International*, January 6, 1995, p. 275.

FIGURE 4–2 UN organizational chart

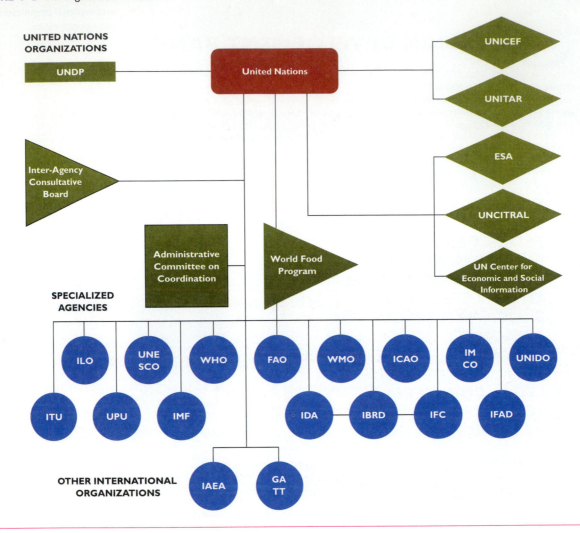

UN Growth and Change

All UN member-nations are members of the **General Assembly,** in which each nation has one vote regardless of its size, wealth, or power. The number of members has grown rapidly since the UN's establishment in 1945, and new nations continue to join as they gain independence and become sovereign in their territory. To understand recent, current, and probable future developments at the UN, it is necessary to bear in mind one fundamental fact about almost all the new members: they are poor.

Their relative poverty, combined with their numbers (they have far more votes than the wealthier, more developed countries can muster) has radically altered the UN's complexion and operational directions. These alterations are being expressed in the multiplication of projects aimed at raising the income of the **less developed countries (LDCs).** Among the many such projects are education, irrigation, health, agriculture, raw materials, industrialization, and technological transfers from the **developed countries (DCs).**

The LDCs are best able to exert their influence in the UN's General Assembly, where it is one country, one vote regardless of the tremendously different characteristics of the countries. The other major body of the UN is the **Security Council.** It is composed of 15 members—5 permanent members and 10 chosen (5 each year) for two-year terms by the General Assembly. The five permanent members—the People's Republic of China, France, Russia, the United Kingdom, and the United States—each have the power to veto any measure even though all other members voted for it.

Security Council
Body of UN composed of 5 permanent members with veto power and 10 chosen (5 each year) for two-year terms

UN Specialized Agencies

Most of these agencies were created to do research and to publish information in particular subject areas, but all are now active in providing aid to LDCs. The UN Conference on Trade and Development was established by the LDCs in the UN General Assembly for the sole purpose of helping them.

We shall name the specialized agencies here without discussion. Their names indicate their areas of activity, and if they interest you as potential customers for your company or for research, you can easily find considerable information about them.

UN Children's Fund

World Health Organization

Food and Agriculture Organization

UN Industrial Development Organization

International Labor Organization

UN Educational, Scientific, and Cultural Organization

UN Development Program

International Civil Aviation Organization

International Telecommunications Union

Universal Postal Union

World Meteorological Organization

International Atomic Energy Agency

International Fund for Agricultural Development

UN Conference on Trade and Development

Career Opportunities

Having read the list of UN specialized agencies, you can imagine that they hire thousands of people as do the UN secretariat and the national delegations. The medium- to high-level jobs at these places pay very well and frequently carry tax, travel, and prestige perquisites. You should not ignore them when job hunting.

The UN is far from the only international organization that offers job opportunities. Figure 4–1 is an advertisement by one of the regional development banks for employees in 11 fields. That bank and a number of other international organizations are discussed in this chapter.

UN Publications Useful to Businesses

In 1992, the United Nations Centre on Transnational Corporations inaugurated a new periodical, *Transnational Corporations.* For information, phone (212) 963-6901. Numerous other publications are available from the Centre. From UN publications, (212) 963-8302, you can get "The Impact of Trade-Related Investment Measures on Trade and Development."

UN Future

By and large, the UN's record in peacemaking and peacekeeping has been dismal, as the headline for an article in *The Economist* reflects: "Shamed are the peacekeepers."[2] Figure 4–3 presents a map of the largest peacekeeping operations in mid-1994. As you see, the largest UN force is in the former Yugoslav federation, but it has not been able to prevent the ethnic cleansing referred to above.

FIGURE 4–3 Largest peacekeeping operations

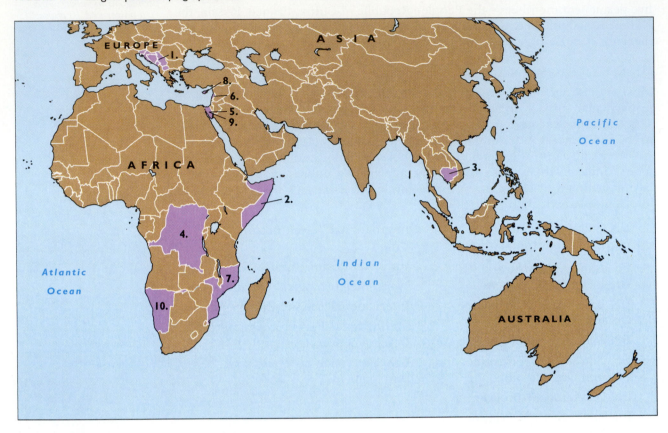

● COUNTRIES WITH THE LARGEST PEACEKEEPING OPERATIONS

1. Former Yugoslav Federation
Force size: 30,500
Fatalities: 77
Dates: March 1992 to present
Result: Unresolved

2. Somalia
Force size: 22,300
Fatalities: 100
Dates: May 1993 to 1995
Result: Unresolved

3. Cambodia
Force size: 22,000
Fatalities: 55
Dates: March 1992 to September 1993
Result: Elections

4. Zaire (Former Belgian Congo)
Force size: 19,800
Fatalities: 234
Dates: July 1960 to June 1964
Result: Secession put down

5. Sinai Desert (between Egyptian and Israeli forces)
Force size: 7,000
Fatalities: 52
Dates: October 1973 to July 1979
Result: Peace treaty

6. Lebanon
Force size: 6,900 maximum strength (now 5,200)
Fatalities: 195
Dates: March 1978 to present
Result: Still keeping peace after 16 years

7. Mozambique
Force size: 6,800
Fatalities: 10
Dates: December 1992 to present
Result: Heading toward elections

8. Cyprus
Force size: 6,400 maximum strength (now 1,200)
Fatalities: 163
Dates: March 1964 to present
Result: Still keeping peace after 30 years

9. Sinai Desert (between Egyptian and Israeli forces)
Force size: 6,100
Fatalities: 90
Dates: November 1956 to June 1967
Result: Six-Day War followed their removal

10. Namibia
Force size: 4,400
Fatalities: 6
Dates: April 1989 to March 1990
Result: Elections

Source: Victor Horowitz, "Largest Peacekeeping Operations," *Los Angeles Times*, May 3, 1994. Reprinted by permission. Copyright 1994.

In the central African countries of Burundi and Rwanda, the majority Hutu tribe and the minority Tutsi have fought with differing degrees of ferocity for centuries. In the most recent outbreak of violence in Rwanda, at least a half-million people, mostly Tutsis, were slaughtered by the middle of 1994, and fighting continued with the Tutsi retaliation.

When the UN secretary-general, Boutros-Ghali, told the UN Security Council members that they should choose either to send several thousand blue-helmets* to Rwanda or to cut the force there to symbolic size, their decision was never in doubt. They had found it equally easy to decide not to send peacekeepers to Burundi during the massacres there six months earlier. Boutros-Ghali was contemptuous of the Security Council countries, particularly the United States, being the strongest; but they found the risks of casualties to their soldiers, financial costs, and hostile domestic political reactions too great.

One author says, "The UN is a legalistic absurdity, deeply flawed from birth. The accident of history that made the USSR the West's glorious ally also made it a permanent member of the UN Security Council. . . . Furthermore, since the UN was the creation of the victorious allies, the emerging major democracies, Germany and Japan, were excluded from the role to which their economic power and military potential have long entitled them."[3]

We named some UN specialized agencies. While saying some of them are doing good work, one article charges that too many "have become private worlds of cronyism, sloth, and incompetence."[4]

A minority of writers favor abolishing or at least ignoring the UN and turning instead to an organization of democracies that one author would name the Association of Free Nations.[5] Most believe such drastic changes would be impracticable and instead advocate more forceful efforts to improve the efficiency of the UN and its agencies.

The International Bank for Reconstruction and Development is usually referred to—in its own publications and elsewhere—as the World Bank. The World Bank Group consists of the Bank itself, the International Finance Corporation (IFC), and the International Development Association (IDA).

THE WORLD BANK

Applicable to the entire Group is the preference of most, if not all, governmental borrowers for multinational or international agency loans and assistance rather than bilateral loans or aid. Visions of imperialism, real or imagined, are less likely if the lender/donor is multinational or international.[6] The great majority of Group loans or credits† are made to LDCs, frequently referred to as emerging economies.

Importance to Business

Businesspeople should be aware of the World Bank Group's activities for a number of reasons:

1. Many companies are suppliers to borrowers in Group-financed projects, and these borrowers spend billions of dollars each year buying goods and services from businesses.

2. The development finance institutions in LDCs, which are partly financed and technically assisted by the Group, are potential capital sources for businesses selling or working in LDCs.

3. The World Bank's center for arbitration may be able to resolve difficulties encountered by business in a foreign country.

4. Projects financed by the Group tend to be mutually supportive (for example, general benefits resulting from improved infrastructure, and better economic resource inventories).

5. The information that the Group gathers about a nation's or a project's finances, uses of funds, management abilities, and so forth

---

*Troops from whatever nation, when they are on a UN mission, wear identical blue helmets.
†In World Bank terminology, moneys lent by the bank are called *loans,* while those lent by the IDA are referred to as *credits.*

tends to be more complete and accurate than the information likely to be available to a private, foreign business.

6. The Multilateral Investment Guarantee Agency (MIGA) was set up as a World Bank affiliate in 1988. Its insurance-type agreements will protect companies against expropriation, currency inconvertibility, wars, revolutions or civil disturbances, and other noncommercial risks to their new investments in LDCs that are signatories to the MIGA charter. MIGA has $780 million in subscribed capital and began writing agreements in 1990.

Hard Loans

hard loans
Made and repayable in hard, convertible currencies at market interest rates with normal market maturities

The World Bank makes **hard loans**. This means its loans are at prevailing market interest rates and are granted only to sound borrowers for periods not exceeding 25 years. The Bank must make relatively safe loans with high assurance of repayment because its own funds are acquired through the sale of securities that must compete with government and private business offerings of all sorts. Investors would not buy World Bank securities, even at advantagous interest rates, if they felt the Bank's loans were insecure, because the Bank must repay the buyers of its securities out of proceeds and profits on its loans.

To date, there have been no defaults on loans made by the World Bank, and its bonds carry the highest quality rating available, that is, AAA. The World Bank has operated at a profit every year since 1947. That profit has been used to make additional loans and to furnish funds for the IDA, a part of the World Bank about which we shall talk shortly.

Although no World Bank loans have been officially declared to be in default, some countries have been unable to make payments when called for by the original loan terms. The Bank has rescheduled many of those loans, giving the debtor countries more time to repay them; however, it is quite possible that unless economic conditions improve for debtor LDCs, some World Bank loans will have to be recognized as in default.

Business Opportunities and Information Sources

The billions of dollars and other currencies lent by the World Bank create many opportunities for businesses to sell their products and services to the borrowers. International competitive bidding is a Bank requirement. However, although the Bank announces the signing of each loan, it does not invite bids or tenders from potential suppliers to the financed projects. Such invitations are the responsibility of the government or agency executing the project. Thus, a company desiring to sell to a project must watch for the loan announcements and then contact appropriate officials in the borrowing country or at that country's embassy in its own country.[7]

Evidently, that procedure poses difficulties for firms, particularly smaller ones, that would like to sell their products or services to a Bank-financed project. In recognition of this, the UN began in 1978 to furnish procurement information. The UN Center for Economic and Social Information in Geneva publishes *Development Forum Business Edition*, a biweekly newspaper that gives details of all major business opportunities opened by World Bank loans. The newspaper publishes requirements for each project and instructions on how to bid for the business.

Among World Bank reports and publications that can be helpful to businesspersons and students are its *Annual Report, Statement of Loans* (quarterly), *Guidelines Relating to Procurement under World Bank Loans and IDA Credits, Uses of Consultants by the World Bank and Its Borrowers,* and *World Bank Atlas of Per Capita Product and Population.* Also available are reports of the World Bank's various General Survey Missions regarding certain countries or areas. World Bank publications deal with many areas, countries, and subjects, and the Bank issues a periodic *Publications Update*. You can get it from the World Bank Book Store, 1818 H Street N.W., Washington, DC , 20433, telephone (202) 473-2941.

International Finance Corporation (IFC)

The International Finance Corporation (IFC) is the World Bank Group's investment banker. Its sphere is exclusively private risk ventures in the LDCs. The purpose of the IFC is to further economic development by encouraging the growth of productive enterprise in member-countries, thus supplementing the activities of the World Bank.[8]

Joint Ventures Favored. The IFC's policy is to favor joint ventures that have some local capital committed at the outset, or at least the probability of local capital involvement in the foreseeable future.[9] This is not to say that the IFC will not cooperate with capital sources outside the host country (the country in which the investment is being made), and there are many examples of such cooperation. Among the industries thus capitalized have been fertilizers, synthetic fibers, tourism, paper, and cotton fabric. The outside capital sources, if in related lines of business, are usually international companies (ICs). A few ICs that have cooperated with the IFC have been Phillips Petroleum, AKV Netherlands, ICI, Intercontinental Hotels, and Pechiney-Gobain.

Creation of Local Capital Markets. In return for its investment in a company, the IFC takes securities in the form of stock (equity ownership) or bonds (debt). One objective of the IFC is to sell its securities into a local capital market. To do that, it will help create and nurture such a market. For example, the IFC extended a $5 million credit line to a syndicate of private Brazilian investment banks to provide support for those banks' securities underwriting activities. The banks work with Fondo do Desenvolvimento do Mercado de Capitais, a revolving capital market development fund maintained by the Brazilian central bank. The objectives are (1) to induce the investment banks to assume a greater role in underwriting Brazilian securities in Brazil, (2) to improve the access of Brazilian companies to long-term domestic source capital, and (3) to encourage Brazilians to invest in sound domestic securities.

As you saw at the beginning of this chapter, thanks to the IFC, investors from both poor and rich countries can now buy and sell securities (stocks and bonds) of companies operating in the developing countries through funds traded on the New York, London, and other stock exchanges. In addition, stock markets are playing an increasing part in supplying and pricing fresh capital in emerging economies.

The Third World's growing trend towards privatization will help its stock markets. As governments, especially in Latin America, trim back public sectors, they will deepen their markets with extra stock and open them to foreign capital and liquidity.[10]

Several recent developments and successes for IFC include:

- IFC investments soared from $400 million in fiscal year 1984 to $2.1 billion in 1993, and its profits rose from $25 million to over $200 million.[11]

- Although at present more than 60 percent of IFC's loan and equity portfolio is located in Latin America and Asia, it expects the weighting to shift to Eastern Europe and the Middle East as those regions adopt market-oriented economic policies.[12]

■ In February 1994, the IFC joined George Soros, the U.S. investor and speculator who manages the Quantum Group of funds, in launching a $1 billion fund to invest in Asian infrastructure projects. The Asian Development Bank, discussed later in this chapter, is also part of this launch.[13]

■ The IFC is having success coaxing commercial banks to lend more to developing countries. By June 30, 1994, it had $2 billion in joint financing deals with banks as co-lenders. Well-capitalized European banks are increasingly willing to participate in such loans, as are insurers, which often are willing to make longer-term loans than are banks.[14]

Figure 4–4 is an announcement of a project financed by the IFC together with private banks from various countries and the Export–Import Bank of the United States.

International Development Association (IDA)

The IDA is the *soft* loan (or *credit*, as an IDA loan is called) section of the World Bank. Although it shares the Bank's administrative staff and grants credits for projects covering the same sorts of projects in LDCs as the Bank's loans, its **soft loans** differ from the hard loans of the Bank in several important ways. They have up to 40-year maturities, compared to 15- to 25-year maturities of the Bank. The IDA may grant 10-year grace periods before repayment of principal or interest must begin, whereas the grace periods of the World Bank usually do not exceed 5 years. The IDA charges only three-fourths of 1 percent as a service charge on disbursed loan balances plus one-half of 1 percent on undisbursed balances. As is evident from these differences, borrowers from the IDA are the poorest of the poor LDCs, which need credit for development projects but cannot carry the burden on their economies or foreign exchange reserve positions that would result from normal commercial term loans. Determination of which countries qualify as poor enough for IDA credits is based on per capita incomes. The maximum per capita income to qualify for an IDA credit is $765. To the extent possible, the credits are made in the currency of the borrowing member-country.

soft loans
May be repayable in soft, nonconvertible currencies; carry low or no interest obligations; are frequently long term, up to 40 years; and may grant grace periods of up to 10 years during which no payments are required

IDA Capital Sources.   Unlike the World Bank, the IDA cannot raise capital in competitive capital markets and depends instead on subscriptions donated by the DCs and some LDCs. Generally, the DC members make contributions in convertible currencies; the LDC members donate their own currencies.

IDA resources are renewed periodically by a process called *replenishment,* whereby supporting nations donate money. In 1993, the tenth replenishment of IDA resources, covering the three years starting July 1993, provided contributions of SDR* 13 billion ($13.3 billion) at the June 7, 1994 exchange rate). Although this represents a small increase over the SDR 11.7 billion provided by the previous IDA replenishment, in per capita terms it is less generous because the funds will have to be spread over more recipients, including newly qualifying nations such as several former Soviet republics.[15]

Privatize the World Bank?

The World Bank was designed to serve the nationalized industries and state sectors of developing nations. But as one author argues, "it is being made obsolete by privatization in the Third World. . . . Opportunities for loans to

---

*Special drawing rights are explained in Chapter 5.

This announcement appears as a matter of record only.

Mobil Producing Nigeria

U.S. $265,000,000
Project/Export Credit Facilities
for the
Oso Condensate Field Development Project

U.S. $170,000,000
Project Loan Facility
Funds Provided by

International Finance Corporation
and through IFC Participations by

Morgan Guaranty Trust Company	Union Bank of Switzerland
Banque Nationale de Paris	Crédit Lyonnais
ABN AMRO	Banque Française du Commerce Extérieur
Banque Indosuez	Banque Worms
The Long-Term Credit Bank of Japan, Ltd.	Morgan Grenfell & Co. Limited
New York Branch	Österreichische Länderbank
NMB Bank	Aktiengesellschaft

U.S. $95,000,000
Export Credit Facility
Guaranteed by

The Export-Import Bank of the United States
Funds Provided by

Morgan Guaranty Trust Company	Union Bank of Switzerland
Banque Nationale de Paris	Crédit Lyonnais
ABN AMRO	Banque Française du Commerce Extérieur
Banque Indosuez	Morgan Grenfell & Co. Limited
NMB Bank	Österreichische Länderbank
	Aktiengesellschaft

Documentation Agent	Administrative Agent
Morgan Guaranty Trust Compnay	Union Bank of Switzerland

April, 1991

Source: *The Economist*, May 11, 1991, p. 78.

FIGURE 4–4
Announcement of an IFC financing together with private banks and the U.S. Export–Import Bank

finance state enterprise, the reason for being of the World Bank and of other multilateral development banks, will become scarcer if developing nation governments continue to sell state companies."

State companies already sold or leased and now owned or operated by private enterprises include those managing telephones, airports, bridges, highways, tunnels, ports, railroads, water systems, and many other assets and operations. While the IFC efforts to aid private-sector companies have been generally successful, the Bank's efforts to direct its hard loans to private enterprise have created "a record of decades of botched lending."[16]

This is largely because the Bank's charter permits it to lend only to governments. To get around this, it has had to create lending intermediaries called development finance institutions (DFIs) run by local governments to relend World Bank funds to private borrowers. A Bank study found nearly 50 percent of those loans in arrears and said few DFIs have become financially viable.[17]

INTERNATIONAL MONETARY FUND (IMF)

Although the IMF deals solely with governments, its policies and actions have profound impact on business worldwide. Its influence may become even greater. Before explaining that statement, we should look briefly at the objectives and activities of the IMF and how they developed. Most of them continue to be important.

The IMF Articles of Agreement were adopted at the Bretton Woods Conference in 1944.[18] In general terms, the IMF's objectives were, and continue to be, to foster (1) orderly foreign exchange arrangements, (2) convertible currencies, and (3) a shorter duration and lesser degree of balance-of-payments disequilibria. The premise of the IMF is that the common interest of all nations in a workable international monetary system far transcends conflicting national interests.[19] One of the IMF's original objectives, since abandoned, was the maintenance of fixed exchange rates among member-countries' currencies, with par value related to the U.S. dollar, which was valued at $35 per ounce of gold.

Each member-country has a quota equal to the amount it subscribes to the IMF. Votes at IMF meetings are weighted according to quota size, and the amount a member can draw is related to its quota.[20]

The IMF agreement was entered prior to the founding conference of the United Nations, and when the UN was formed, the IMF was brought into relationship with the UN by an agreement. This agreement preserved the IMF's independence, which was justified by the need for independent control of monetary management. This need results from the temptations of every government to overspend and cause inflation.[21]

Changes in the IMF

The 1970s and 1980s saw some fundamental changes in the IMF's activities and roles. As stated above, the IMF abandoned the objective of maintaining the fixed exchange rate system. More accurately stated, the obligation of maintaining such a system remained in the Articles of Agreement, but the IMF was powerless to uphold it in the face of a situation in which all major currencies were floating* rather than fixed in value. In recognition of reality, the articles were amended to legalize the actual current practice, that is, floating exchange rates.

firm surveillance
Permits the IMF to influence or even dictate fiscal and monetary policies of member-countries if the economically strong countries allow such intrusion.

Greater Power for the IMF?   The amended articles also included a new Article IV, which, among other things, empowers the IMF to "exercise **firm surveillance** over the exchange rate policies" of members. Some observers feel that this new surveillance power may permit the IMF to move toward the position in the world occupied by central banks nationally.[22] That, of course, would require the member-countries to surrender a great deal of sovereignty, which many governments will stoutly resist.

The IMF fulfills its surveillance responsibilities in two principal ways. First, its board of governors regularly examines in depth each member's

---

*Discussion of floating exchange rates as compared to fixed exchange rates appears in Chapter 5.

INTERNATIONAL MONETARY

"OK, I'm sorry we called you a dirty capitalist imperialist swine — now can we have the money?"

Source: Reprinted from *The Wall Street Journal:* permission of Cartoon Features Syndicate.

economic policies and performance and the interaction of those policies with economic developments in other countries. Second, the board holds regular discussions on the world economic outlook and periodic discussions on exchange rate developments in the major industrial countries.

The IMF contributes to policy coordination among the major industrial countries through its work on the economic indicators and the medium-term economic outlook. Those major industrial countries (Canada, France, Germany, Italy, Japan, the United Kingdom, and the United States) are sometimes referred to as the **Group of Seven** and the IMF managing director participates in the group's meetings. There are 172 other IMF member-countries, making a total of 179.

Group of Seven (G7)
The major industrial countries, namely, Canada, France, Germany, Italy, Japan, the United Kingdom, and the United States

World Debt Crisis and the IMF.   Over the years, countries have occasionally been unable or unwilling to pay their debts. When the countries were unable to pay debts that came due (**debt default**), the debts were sometimes rescheduled to give the countries more time to pay (**debt rescheduling**). Debts of Peru, Zaire, and Turkey are among those that were rescheduled.

Usually due to government changes, countries sometimes refuse to pay the debts of previous governments; the new government repudiates the old debt. This occurred when communist governments assumed power in the former Soviet Union, the People's Republic of China, and Cuba.

Before 1981, such reschedulings and repudiations were relatively unusual. Suddenly that all changed. First Poland and other Soviet-bloc countries, then Mexico, followed by Brazil, Argentina, and other Latin American countries as well as countries in Africa and Asia found themselves short of money to repay their debts.

debt default
Occurs when a debtor will not or cannot repay a loan when payment is due

debt rescheduling
Involves the debtor and creditor agreeing to permit a longer payment period, lower interest rate or forgiveness of some of the debt

Financial and Economic Disaster?   Some observers foresaw massive debt repudiations, bank failures, world trade breakdown, and deep depressions with high unemployment. The debts of the non-OPEC developing countries totaled some $520 billion at the end of 1982, and the disaster scenario had all of them defaulting at once—perhaps after forming a "debt OPEC" to coordinate their debt repudiation.

Enter the IMF. While Mexico was negotiating its emergency IMF loan in November 1982, it was preparing to inaugurate a new president in December. The outgoing president wanted no part of the austerity programs being insisted on by the IMF, and the incoming president had no official power until December. Jacques de Larosière, the IMF's managing director, prodded both presidents into cooperation.

De Larosière's problems did not end there. The some 1,400 large and small creditor banks of Mexico wanted no more to do with Mexico, so he called a creditors' meeting in New York, at which he bluntly warned them that unless they came up with $5 billion more for Mexico, the IMF would pull out. Knowing they would lose their entire loans if it did that, the creditors went along with the IMF plan.

Such aggressiveness by the IMF was a sharp departure from its previous low-key approach.[23] Add to that the large increases in lending resources provided by industrial member-countries and the IMF has become a major new world force.

Conditionality and Cooperation with the World Bank.   Scarcity of trained personnel and lack of political will or strength are reasons countries are unable or unwilling to take steps necessary to correct their economic problems. To ensure better use of their funds, the IMF and the World Bank now cooperate with each other in working with borrowing member-countries in what are called *structural adjustment facilities* (SAFs) or, if the problems are greater, enhanced structural adjustment facilities (ESAFs).

Funding by the IMF or Bank is conditional and linked to the member's progress in implementing policies geared to restoring balance-of-payment viability and sustainable economic growth. The borrowing member must file a policy framework paper that details annual programs it will undertake to reach the established goal. The Bank and IMF monitor the progress of the programs.

EUROPEAN BANK FOR RECONSTRUCTION AND DEVELOPMENT

This bank, known by its acronym EBRD, was created in 1990 to assist the countries of the ex-Soviet Union and its former Eastern European satellites. There were 42 founding member-countries, and its initial capitalization was $13 billion.

Jacques Attali, who had been an aide to François Mitterrand, president of France, became the first EBRD president, and the world soon learned of Attali's lavish tastes.

- During 1992, the bank spent some $900,000 hiring private jet aircraft for him.
- Attali did not like the marble in the bank building's head office, so he had it changed at a cost of $1.125 million.
- The 1992 EBRD staff Christmas party was held at the swank Grosvenor House Hotel in London, which cost the bank $78,000.

Attali denied that such expenditures were excessive; but the purpose of the EBRD was to make capital available to the countries of Eastern Europe and the former Soviet Union. The comparisons were not favorable for Attali's argument. From April 1991 to the end of 1992, the bank had disbursed loans and investments of $151.5 million compared to $302.25 million spent on furnishing and equipping its offices and paying staff travel and administrative overheads.[24]

Those numbers raised eyebrows of the bank's board of directors, who raised Attali out of the president's chair and replaced him with Jacques de Larosière—as mentioned earlier, de Larosière was the president of the IMF who, in 1982, was instrumental in getting Mexico and its credit banks together to renegotiate the Mexican debts, averting what could have been a disastrous series of defaults. He turned EBRD's priorities around, and by the spring of 1994, it had committed $3.7 billion to 156 projects.[25]

Through co-financing with private lenders, the total value of EBRD-linked projects had reached $11.7 billion. The EBRD is also using local banks as agents for lending money; as the banks add some of their own money to the credits, this is proving to be an effective device for efficient use of capital.[26]

Regional development banks are regional versions of the World Bank. There are three major ones: the African Development Bank, the Asian Development Bank, and the Inter-American Development Bank. Their function is to lend money in less developed countries to build infrastructure, support agriculture and industry, and create jobs. The sources of their funds are several. All get contributions from their member-countries, and all get money from developed countries that are permitted to be members even though they are not located in the geographic areas. They also raise money in the international capital markets, in the Eurocurrency market, and in the Eurobond market.

REGIONAL DEVELOPMENT BANKS

regional development banks
Regional versions of the World Bank

The African Development Bank (AFDB) has tried to lower the percentage of loans it makes to governments, because of public-sector mismanagement, and to increase the percentage to private companies, some of which have been privatized recently by the governments. The bank is also channeling more money to two of Africa's most vital human resources, largely ignored in the past. They are rural women who produce more than two-thirds of Africa's food and small-business entrepreneurs who keep many national economies afloat with their informal market trading.

However, by 1994, the AFDB was in deep trouble. A report by external consultants, chaired by David Knox, former vice president of the World Bank, found a chaotic, top-heavy bureaucracy riddled with political intrigue and suspicion. The consultants could not assess the quality of AFDB loans because of unreliable and insufficient data. They could not find a central file on any project.

One thing the consultants did find was mounting arrears and defaults of loan repayments. Africa's growing impoverishment is placing greater demands on the African Development Fund, which is the soft-loan arm of the AFDB as the IDA is of the World Bank. But its coffers are empty, and industrial countries that donate funds every three years are refusing to replenish the AFDB until it streamlines its bureaucracy and tightens its lending policies.[27] The AFDB has tried to raise money by selling bonds. Figure 4–5 presents the announcement of a 1991 bond placement by the AFDB. As you can observe, some very prominent international investment banks were involved. The lead bank was Barings, one of the oldest and most prestigious British banks, one of whose customers was the queen of England. Although the AFDB was not affected, it should be mentioned that Barings was destroyed in 1995 by one of its traders' dealings in derivitives. They are dealt with in Chapter 20.

At the Asian Development Bank (ADB)—the senior management of which is dominated by the Japanese—there is disagreement between Japan and the United States, the two largest shareholders. Washington wants to bring the ADB more in line with the World Bank, requiring borrowers to reform their economic policies before loans are granted, especially in countries where bloated government financial institutions are perpetuating inefficiency. While Tokyo pays lip service to this, it appears most interested in turning the ADB into a better channel for recycling its huge trade surplus and financing Japanese exports.[28]

FIGURE 4–5
Announcement of 1991
bond placement by the
African Development Bank

This announcement appears as a matter of record only.

AFRICAN DEVELOPMENT BANK

£100,000,000

11¼ per cent. Bonds due 2001

Issue price 99.63 per cent.

Baring Brothers & Co., Limited

IBJ International Limited	◆ Barclays de Zoete Wedd Limited
Credit Suisse First Boston Limited	◆ Deutsche Bank Capital Markets Limited
Goldman Sachs International Limited	◆ Samuel Montagu & Co. Limited
J.P. Morgan Securities Ltd.	◆ Nomura International
Salomon Brothers International Limited	◆ Lehman Brothers International
UBS Phillips & Drew Securities Limited	◆ S.G. Warburg Securities

BARINGS

July, 1991

Source: *Financial Times*, August 8, 1991, p. 13.

In a move to direct more loans to private-sector borrowers, the ADB created a separate bank, the Asian Finance and Investment Corporation (AFIC), in August 1989. The AFIC is 30 percent owned by the ADB, the other shareholders being 25 commercial banks and securities companies. The AFIC is smaller than the ADB and therefore can act faster and consider much smaller projects.[29]

The ADB raises money by selling bonds in Europe, North America, and Australia and so-called dragon bonds in Hong Kong, Singapore, and Taipei, thus developing regional capital markets.[30]

The United States questioned the ADB lending policies that have financed a number of failed projects. The bank admitted to an "approval culture" under which the emphasis was on meeting annual lending targets without adequate risk assessment, and it promised to tighten policies. With that, agreement was reached to double the bank's capital to $46 billion.[31]

The Inter-American Development Bank (IDB) created the Multilateral Investment Fund in 1992 to strengthen the role of the private sector, provide worker training, and increase financing for small businesses. In addition, an IDB affiliate, the Inter-American Investment Corporation, formed in 1989, had by 1994 approved $467 million in loans and investments for private enterprises in 21 countries.[32]

In April 1994, the IDB held its 35th annual meeting in Guadalajara, Mexico. One author characterized this meeting as having "had a touch of history."[33]

- It was the first IDB meeting with the North American Free Trade Agreement in force.
- The bank's capital was increased from $61 billion to over $100 billion.
- Latin American countries gave up their majority 53 percent stake in the bank, the United States agreed to reduce its 34.7 percent to 30 percent, while European countries and Japan got larger stakes.
- It was agreed that 40 percent, up from a third previously, should go to "social" projects, which means help for the poor.

The World Bank aims to put about a third of its lending in the region to the same end, but there is one big doubt about all this enthusiasm. Most loans will go through the government departments, such as education or health, of the recipient countries, and these are "among the weakest institutions in the world," riddled with corruption, weakened by low investment, and burdened by hordes of employees and labor laws that prevent anyone from being sacked.[34]

For our purposes, the importance of the regional development bank loans is that LDCs use much of the money they borrow to purchase goods and services from companies in other countries. The alert business management can earn some of that money. *The IDB*, a publication of the IDB, gives information on how to bid on projects financed by the organization.

BANK FOR INTERNATIONAL SETTLEMENTS (BIS)

The round tower of the BIS is the first landmark in Basel, Switzerland, for anyone leaving the main railway station and heading toward the city center. There is, however, no sign saying "BIS" because this is the most discreet financial institution in the world, the place where the central bankers of the major industrial countries meet 10 times a year to discuss the global financial system.

The BIS is such a convenient meeting place for central banker groups that one needs a program to sort them out. The BIS board of directors consists of the governors of several European central banks. A second group that meets in Basel consists of the central bank governors of the Group of 10—which has 11 members now that Switzerland has joined but is still called the Group of 10. The original 10 are Belgium, Britain, Canada, France, Holland, Italy, Japan, Sweden, Germany, and the United States. A third group is that of the European Union (EU) countries. Yet another group is the annual general meeting of the governors of the 29 central banks that are BIS shareholders.

In addition to providing a congenial and confidential meeting place for central bankers, the BIS provides secure, anonymous cover for shareholder countries as they transfer large amounts of currency or gold among themselves. When they do this through the BIS, the currency and gold traders may not be able to figure out the identity of the real buyers and sellers.

The world financial strains in 1982 that enhanced the IMF's role also caused some changes for the BIS. In 1982 and 1983, the BIS made loans to cash-strapped Hungary, Mexico, Argentina, Brazil, and Yugoslavia. These were called *bridge* loans because they were intended to bridge those debtor countries over a period until IMF, World Bank, government, and private bank loans could be mobilized. The first BIS bridge loans were made in 1931 to Spain, Hungary, Austria, Germany, and Yugoslavia to relieve the financial turmoil of the Great Depression. Even in those days, BIS understood how to adapt to pressing circumstances and to act quickly.

The BIS has four main functions. It serves as (1) a forum for international monetary cooperation, (2) a center for research, (3) a banker for central banks, and (4) an agent or trustee with regard to various international financial arrangements.

1. The forum function was touched on in the second and third paragraphs of this section.

2. Applied economic research finds an outlet in the series of economic papers published by the BIS. Probably the best known is the BIS *Annual Report,* published in June of each year.

3. Some 80 central banks from around the world have deposits with the BIS. In addition to placing surplus funds in the international markets, the BIS occasionally makes liquid resources available to central banks. The bridge loans referred to above and more traditional types of lending are other banking services the BIS provides.

4. As an agent and trustee, the BIS books and settles the balances that arise from currency exchange market interventions by EU* central banks in observation of European Monetary System (EMS) rules. Officially, the BIS is agent for the European Monetary Co-operation Fund, which holds 20 percent of EU countries' gold and dollar reserves.

    The Bank also serves as agent for the private European Currency Unit (ECU)† clearing and settlement system. Large amounts of bonds and other securities and credits are denominated in ECUs, and the BIS-operated clearing and settlement system permits them to be efficiently bought and sold, transferred from seller to buyer, and paid at maturity.[35]

Since several Eastern European countries broke out of the Soviet empire in 1989, a fifth function has been developed. A number of their central bankers now meet their Western counterparts at BIS headquarters to study free-market banking. Training courses have been established.[36]

WORLD TRADE ORGANIZATION (WTO), PREVIOUSLY THE GENERAL AGREEMENT ON TARIFFS AND TRADE (GATT)

How GATT Was Conceived

Arising from the optimism among the Western allies following World War II was the ideal of an international organization that would function in the trade areas much as it was hoped the UN would function in the political and peacekeeping areas. A charter was drawn for an International Trade Organization (ITO) at the Havana Conference in 1948. However, the ITO never came into existence because not enough governments ratified its charter.

---

*The EU is introduced later in this chapter.
†The EMS, European Monetary Co-operation Fund, and ECU are discussed in Chapter 5.

At what were thought of as preliminaries to and preparations for an ITO, the American negotiators presented what they envisioned as a step toward an acceptable ITO treaty, which was to embody the numerous bilateral trade treaties into one multilateral treaty. They suggested, in the absence of any established international trade rules, that the commercial policy rules of the draft ITO charter be incorporated into a general agreement on tariffs and trade as an interim measure pending ITO ratification. The American suggestions were accepted, and so the General Agreement on Tariffs and Trade (GATT) was born in 1947.[37] Differently stated, the ITO was not ratified as a de jure organization, and GATT became a de facto international trade organization.[38]

Some observers felt GATT to be a "slender reed" on which to base world progress toward free international trade. Nevertheless, it still exists and has been extremely successful in some areas of tariff reduction as well as in other fields.[39]

GATT 1947–1995: RIP

GATT set up business in the Palais des Nations of the old League of Nations, which was superseded by the UN. The Palais is in Geneva, where GATT has since erected its own headquarters building to house its secretariat.

GATT negotiations to reduce tariffs and other trade obstacles were conducted in sessions referred to as *rounds*, of which there were eight, from the first in 1947, through the Uruguay Round, launched in 1986 in Punta del Este, Uruguay. A main achievement of the first seven rounds was reduction of tariffs among industrial countries from an average of 40 percent to 5 percent. In addition, 9 out of 10 disputes among trading nations brought to GATT were settled satisfactorily, discretely, without publicity. The volume of trade in manufactured goods multiplied twentyfold.

The Uruguay Round.   This was a hugely ambitious undertaking. As indicated, the seven preceding rounds had reduced industrial product tariffs from 40 to 5 percent, and the Uruguay negotiators succeeded in lowering them by more than their target of one-third more. But, Uruguay broke new GATT ground by writing new international rules for trade in services and agriculture and for protection of intellectual properties. Agreement was reached to phase out the multifiber arrangement, which is Byzantine and the oldest managed-trade system. It covers textiles and clothing. Procedures to speed settlements of trade disputes were agreed as were means to reduce trade subsidies.

Many regarded a successful conclusion of the Uruguay Round as hopelessly overambitious, but the negotiators met a GATT-imposed December 15, 1993, deadline by initialing an agreement late on that day. There was disappointment that antidumping laws were not limited, and the American entertainment industry wanted greater access to the European markets than the agreement allowed. Presumably, these and many other carryover and new issues will be brought up in the new World Trade Organization (WTO).[40] Figure 4–6 presents a map of WTO members.

The U.S. Trade Representative forecasts that the new WTO measures will expand the U.S. economy by about a trillion dollars over the coming decade, creating as many as two million new jobs. But there is still work to be done. Among the most important matters to be faced are:

- Restrictions on foreign direct investment.
- Government protection of new technology to protect domestic industry.
- Antidumping laws.
- Environmentalists' opposition to increased trade.[41]

FIGURE 4-6 Map of WTO members

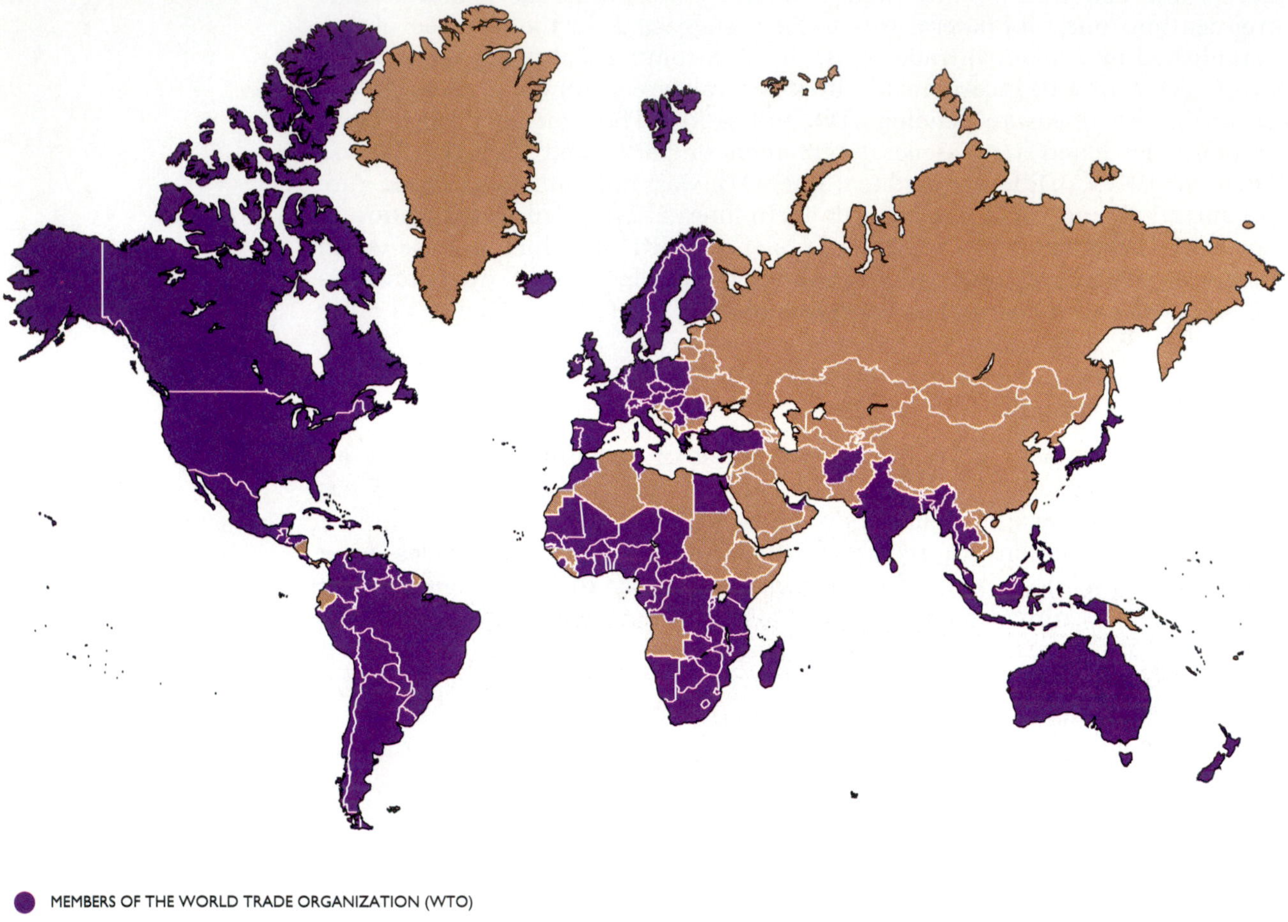

● MEMBERS OF THE WORLD TRADE ORGANIZATION (WTO)

The World Trade Organization

As provided by the successful conclusion of the Uruguay Round GATT negotiations, on January 1, 1995, the WTO replaced the GATT secretariat and began to administrate the system of international trade law. A trade policy review mechanism will raise issues for discussion on a regular agenda, replacing the previous practice of periodic rounds of negotiation with a permanent process of revising the rules of international trade.[42]

ORGANIZATION OF PETROLEUM EXPORTING COUNTRIES (OPEC)

Realizing that if the oil-exporting countries were united they could bargain more effectively with the large oil companies, Iran and Venezuela joined the Arab Petroleum Congress at a Cairo meeting in 1959. Discussions and secret agreements at that meeting became the seeds for the Organization of Petroleum Exporting Countries (OPEC).[43] Figure 4–7 presents a map of OPEC members.

Oil Companies Should Have Listened

Early in 1960, the Venezuelan minister of mines and hydrocarbons and the Saudi oil minister wrote to the oil companies operating in Venezuela and the Middle East, requesting that they consult with the host governments before making any price changes. In August 1960, the oil companies reduced oil

FIGURE 4–7 Map of OPEC members

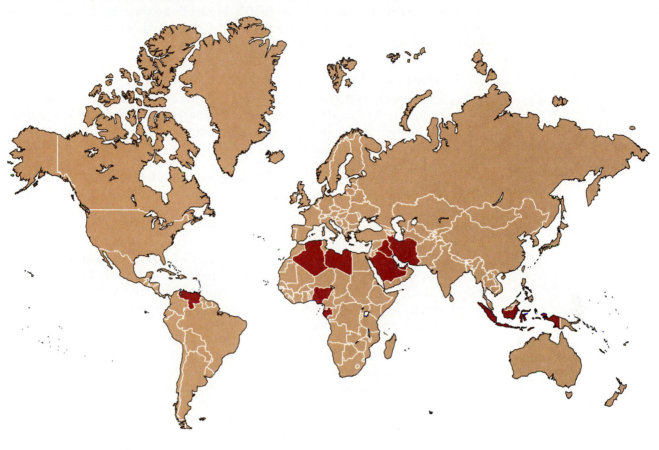

● MEMBERS OF THE ORGANIZATION OF PETROLEUM EXPORTING COUNTRIES (OPEC)

prices, and it is said that the host governments learned of it only when they read it in the newspapers. In any event, they had not been consulted. This made them angry and also increased their anxiety about the control and conservation of their natural resources. In that atmosphere, they called a meeting on September 14, 1960, in Baghdad.

Attending the meeting were representatives of Iran, Iraq, Kuwait, Saudi Arabia, and Venezuela. OPEC was formed., and the OPEC members took charge of pricing.

> This first headquarters of OPEC was in a relatively small apartment in Geneva. There was general skepticism as to the durability of the new organization and hesitancy on the part of some potential employees to take what they feared would be short-term jobs.
>
> Clearly, the skeptics have been proved wrong. OPEC's headquarters have been moved to Vienna, and its members, in addition to the founders named above, include Qatar, Libya, Indonesia, Abu Dhabi, Algeria, Ecuador, and Gabon.[44]

Economic Muscle and Political Strength

OPEC soon began to test its strength, and the price of petroleum began to rise. At the end of 1973 and in early 1974, OPEC demonstrated its potentially devastating strength with the oil embargo by its Arab members against the

Netherlands and the United States, accompanied by very large price increases to all customers. Its strength stemmed from the comparative cohesiveness of the members and from the fact that it controlled some 68 percent of the world's known petroleum reserves.[45] OPEC supplied some 84 percent of Europe's oil needs and over 90 percent of Japan's.[46]

OPEC Downs and Ups

Using its strength, OPEC drove up petroleum prices from about $3 a barrel in 1973 to close to $35 in 1980. Such a drastic increase in energy prices caused recession and unemployment in oil-importing countries, but it also sparked conservation measures, increased oil exploration in non-OPEC countries and research for alternate energy sources.

Thanks to these initiatives, OPEC's market weakened, but its members refused to cut their production and thus an oversupply developed. OPEC had seized control of pricing in the mid-1970s, but by the early 1980s, the free markets were setting prices with major markets in Rotterdam, New York, and Chicago.[47]

"Isn't it time to regain control of the price of oil?" asked Arrieta Valera, Venezuela's new oil minister, at an OPEC meeting in March 1994. But that may be difficult to achieve, considering the huge oil and gas projects being developed in such former Soviet republics as Kazakhstan and Azerbaijan and even bigger ones in Russia.[48]

On the other hand, as shown in the bottom left-hand chart in Figure 4–8, the OPEC share of world supply of oil is up to 40 percent from just over 20 percent in 1984. In addition, sustained low oil prices have weakened conservation efforts and have made exploration, investment, and extraction unprofitable; moreover, demand is increasing in developing countries, with China and Indonesia becoming net importers by the year 2000, so OPEC may have a shot at regaining oil price control.[49]

The top chart in Figure 4–8 shows the spot price of oil below $15 a barrel. The "real" price in 1980 U.S. dollars, adjusted for inflation, is below $10, as you can see in the bottom right-hand chart.

THE EUROPEAN UNION (EU)

Background

In the aftermath of the Second World War, Europe was in shambles as a result of the fighting and the devotion of all efforts and investments to the war. To assist Europeans back to their feet and to encourage strong, friendly governments, U.S. Secretary of State George C. Marshall recommended the United States give financial aid to and work with European countries in their reconstruction.

Marshall Plan
Named for American Secretary of State George C. Marshall, who suggested using U.S. capital and cooperation in Europe's reconstruction after WW II

Thus was born the **Marshall Plan,** which was immensely successful. It swung into action in 1948, and by the first quarter of 1950, European industrial production was already 138 percent ahead of the level reached in the last year of peace, 1938. Europeans achieved this success by working together, and they continued to do so. One milestone in this relationship was the Treaty of Rome. Signed in 1957, it created the European Community (EC), sometimes called the European Economic Community (EEC) or the European Common Market. The first six Common Market members were Belgium, the Federal Republic of Germany, France, Italy, Luxembourg, and the Netherlands. Chronologically, the next to sign the treaty were Denmark, Ireland, the United Kingdom, Greece, Portugal, and Spain, making a total of 12 member-nations. Then on January 1, 1995, Austria, Finland, and Sweden became members and there were 15.

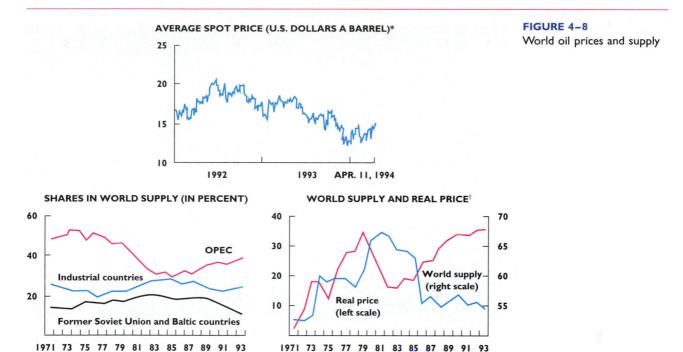

FIGURE 4–8
World oil prices and supply

Sources: *Petroleum Market Intelligence* (New York): other oil industry sources; and International Energy Agency.
*Simple average of daily U.S. dollar spot prices of U.K. Brent, Dubai, and Alaska North Slope crude oil, equally weighted.
†Oil supply is in millions of barrels a day. The price of oil is deflated by consumer prices in industrial countries and is in constant 1980 U.S. dollars.

Source: *IMF World Economic Outlook,* May 1994, p. 21.

EU objectives were to remove trade obstacles among members and to cooperate in many other ways. Brussels was established as headquarters, housing the EU Commission. The 17 commissioners are each responsible for a subject area somewhat similar to U.S. cabinet positions: labor, transportation, trade, and so forth.

The policy-setting body of the EU is the Council of Ministers. The prime ministers of the 15 member-nations meet periodically to establish policy to be executed by the commissioners and the other Eurocrats, as the bureaucrats who work in Brussels are called.

The European Parliament (part of the EU) has its seat in Strasbourg and is popularly elected by voters in each member-country. It has broad but very blunt powers; for example, it can fire all the commissioners but not fewer than all, and it can veto the entire EU budget but not a portion thereof. On one occasion, it did veto the budget—much to everyone's astonishment—and since then the commission and others have taken the parliament more seriously. Some feel if the parliament is given wider and more discreet powers, it could become the heart of an ultimate United States of Europe. The Single European Act of 1987 gave the European Parliament some power to amend legislation drafted by the commission.

The EU Court of Justice decides all cases arising under the Treaty of Rome, and its authority supersedes that of the member-countries' courts. Because the treaty covers many subjects and more and more cases are being decided by the Court of Justice, its influence is growing steadily.

From 1957 until the early 1970s, cooperation continued and measurable progress was made in eliminating tariff barriers among EU countries. Then

The EU Court of Justice in session.

Courtesy European Commission Delegation, Washington, DC.

the Bretton Woods currency exchange regime collapsed;* the OPEC price increases hit; inflation, unemployment, and recession gripped the EU; and progress slowed considerably. (The community languished for several years until it was jolted to life by Project 1992.) Project 1992 did not achieve all its goals. See the "A United States of Europe?" section, below, for a continuation of the saga.

The EU joins most of the economic and industrial might of Western Europe and most of its population. The EU is the largest import and export market in the world. It is second only to the United States in the size of its gross domestic product, and it accounts for 20 percent of world trade, compared with 14 percent for the United States and 9 percent for Japan. Table 4–1 gives some comparisons between the EU and other industrialized countries.

A United States of Europe?

The countries involved have made great strides toward union, and the EU is now a major world force. There is a historic dream among Europeans of a United States of Europe in which movement of people, money, and goods would be as free as it is in the America; but a wall of obstacles stands in the way of realizing that dream.

There are 15 sovereign nations in the EU—and more want to join—with long, proud histories and loyalties and different cultures and languages; and of course, there have been bitter, bloody wars among Europeans. Each country has its own laws, taxes, armed forces, and police. And several of the countries have shown strong and growing reluctance to surrender their national currency, central bank, and other powers to a "distant" authority, particularly an unelected authority.

---

*The Bretton Woods system is discussed in Chapter 5.

TABLE 4-1 Industrial countries: Real GDP, consumer prices, and unemployment (in percent)

	Real GDP*				Consumer Prices*				Unemployment			
	1991	1992	1993	1994	1991	1992	1993	1994	1991	1992	1993	1994
All industrial countries	0.6	1.6	1.2	2.4	4.5	3.3	2.9	2.5	7.0	7.8	8.2	8.3
Major industrial countries	0.5	1.7	1.4	2.5	4.4	3.1	2.8	2.4	6.6	7.3	7.3	7.4
United States†	−0.7	2.6	3.0	3.9	4.2	3.0	3.0	2.8	6.7	7.4	6.8	6.2
Japan	4.3	1.1	0.1	0.7	3.3	1.7	1.3	0.9	2.1	2.2	2.5	3.0
Germany	1.0	2.1	−1.2	0.9	4.5	4.9	4.7	3.0	6.7	7.7	8.9	10.0
France	0.7	1.4	−0.7	1.2	3.2	2.4	2.1	1.9	9.4	10.1	11.7	12.4
Italy‡	1.2	0.7	−0.7	1.1	6.3	5.2	4.3	3.8	10.9	11.5	10.4	11.3
United Kingdom§	−2.2	−0.6	1.9	2.5	6.8	4.7	3.0	3.2	8.1	9.8	10.3	10.0
Canada	−1.7	0.7	2.4	3.5	5.6	1.5	1.9	0.5	10.3	11.3	11.2	10.8
Other Industrial Countries	0.9	0.9	—	1.6	5.5	4.2	3.7	3.2	9.1	10.4	12.3	12.9
Belgium	1.9	0.6	−1.3	1.0	3.2	2.4	2.8	2.7	7.5	8.2	9.4	10.2
Denmark	1.0	1.2	0.3	2.4	2.4	2.1	1.3	2.2	10.6	11.4	12.3	12.1
Greece	1.8	0.9	—	0.5	19.5	15.8	14.4	11.2	7.7	9.2	9.8	10.0
Ireland	2.6	4.9	2.5	4.0	3.2	3.1	1.5	2.5	14.7	15.5	15.8	15.3
Netherlands	2.1	1.4	0.3	0.8	3.9	3.7	2.1	2.3	7.2	6.9	7.8	8.9
Portugal	2.3	1.5	−0.8	1.1	11.4	8.9	6.5	5.5	4.1	4.1	5.5	6.8
Spain	2.2	0.8	−1.0	1.0	5.9	5.9	4.6	4.3	16.3	18.4	22.7	24.0
Austria	2.7	1.6	−0.5	1.4	3.3	4.1	3.6	2.7	5.8	5.9	7.3	7.5
Finland	−7.1	−3.8	−2.6	1.6	4.2	2.9	2.2	2.8	7.6	13.1	17.9	19.8
Norway	1.6	3.3	1.8	3.1	3.2	2.3	2.3	1.8	5.5	5.9	6.1	6.0
Sweden	−1.1	−1.9	−1.7	2.2	9.3	2.3	4.7	2.7	2.9	5.3	8.3	8.4
Switzerland	—	−0.1	−0.7	1.2	5.8	4.0	3.3	1.5	1.1	2.6	5.1	5.3
Australia	−0.8	2.0	3.0	2.6	3.2	1.0	1.9	2.3	9.6	10.8	10.8	10.4
New Zealand	−2.7	2.1	3.7	3.6	2.6	1.0	1.4	1.2	10.6	10.3	9.4	9.0
Memorandum												
European Union	0.7	1.0	−0.3	1.3	5.3	4.6	3.7	3.2	9.1	10.1	11.2	11.9
West Germany	4.5	1.6	−1.9	0.5	3.5	4.0	4.1	2.7	5.5	5.8	7.3	8.6

*Annual percent change.
†To maintain comparability with the historical data, the projections are not adjusted to the higher unemployment level implied by the new survey techniques adopted by the U.S. Bureau of Labor Statistics in January 1994.
‡The unemployment rate presents a new series starting in 1993, reflecting revisions in the labor force surveys and the definition of unemployment to bring data in line with those of other industrial countries.
§Data for consumer prices based on the retail price index excluding mortgage interest.

Source: *IMF World Economic Outlook*, May 1994, p. 13.

Maastricht. In December 1991, representatives of the then 12 EU member-nations met in the Dutch city of Maastricht where they signed a treaty that bears the city's name. This treaty has numerous provisions, but it is the broad sweep that fits this "United States of Europe" discussion. Its goals include economic and monetary union, with a European central bank to replace the national central banks and a European currency instead of the national ones.

In national referenda, the Maastricht treaty was approved in Italy, approved in Denmark after first being turned down, and approved narrowly in France. In Britain, Prime Minister Major has been able to avoid the popular vote demanded by his predecessor, Margaret Thatcher, who opposed Maastricht. An organization, L'Autre Europe, was formed to coordinate anti-Maastricht groups across Europe, but its aims are more than just to dismantle the treaty; it wants to do away with majority voting in the EU, give back veto power to each country, and reverse the principle that European law is supreme over national law.[50]

Fortress Europe?   The term *Fortress Europe* was used by outsiders, Americans, Japanese, and others to express their fears that the EU would deny its privileges to them, their companies, and their products.[51] Although those fears persist, the term is now being used in another context: prevention of countries to join as new EU members.

Austria, Finland, and Sweden got membership in 1995, and a number of other countries also want in, notably Turkey, the Czech Republic, Slovakia, Poland, Hungary and the countries that were republics of the Soviet Union.[52] Figure 4–9 presents a map of EU members and other countries interested in joining.

Some current EU members want a "wider" organization and would admit any European democracy that met certain criteria such as stable prices, sound public finances and monetary conditions, and a sustainable balance of payments. Other current members want a "deeper" organization giving EU

FIGURE 4–9
EU and other European countries

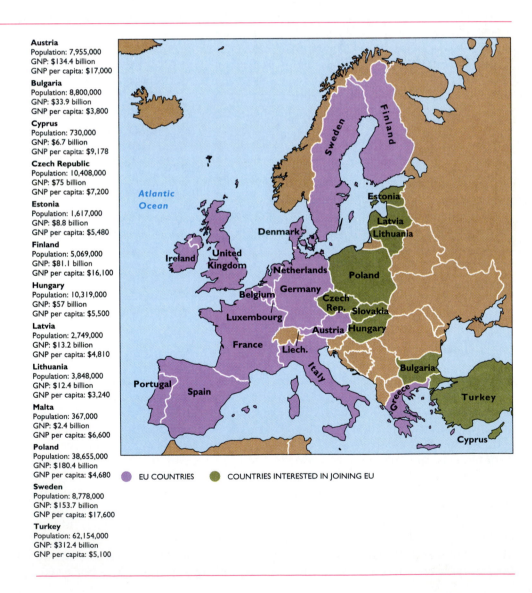

Austria
Population: 7,955,000
GNP: $134.4 billion
GNP per capita: $17,000

Bulgaria
Population: 8,800,000
GNP: $33.9 billion
GNP per capita: $3,800

Cyprus
Population: 730,000
GNP: $6.7 billion
GNP per capita: $9,178

Czech Republic
Population: 10,408,000
GNP: $75 billion
GNP per capita: $7,200

Estonia
Population: 1,617,000
GNP: $8.8 billion
GNP per capita: $5,480

Finland
Population: 5,069,000
GNP: $81.1 billion
GNP per capita: $16,100

Hungary
Population: 10,319,000
GNP: $57 billion
GNP per capita: $5,500

Latvia
Population: 2,749,000
GNP: $13.2 billion
GNP per capita: $4,810

Lithuania
Population: 3,848,000
GNP: $12.4 billion
GNP per capita: $3,240

Malta
Population: 367,000
GNP: $2.4 billion
GNP per capita: $6,600

Poland
Population: 38,655,000
GNP: $180.4 billion
GNP per capita: $4,680

Sweden
Population: 8,778,000
GNP: $153.7 billion
GNP per capita: $17,600

Turkey
Population: 62,154,000
GNP: $312.4 billion
GNP per capita: $5,100

EU COUNTRIES   COUNTRIES INTERESTED IN JOINING EU

members and institutions time to digest Maastricht before bringing in new members. One point of view is that the EU should substitute qualified new members for present members that are not playing by EU rules.[53]

Fraud.   EU members can't agree whether they want to implement Maastricht and have a centralized federal system with most of the power held by the EU institutions (e.g., the parliament, council, and commission) or leave the power with the member-countries in a Europe-of-countries form. They disagree whether to admit new member-countries, which ones, or when.

But one subject about which there is unhappy agreement is that fraud is costing the EU about $7 billion a year, with most of the leakage from the agriculture budget, which at 48.6 percent, is the largest item of the EU budget. The EU itself has little power to track down and punish cheats; there is no EU criminal law equivalent to the federal statutes that American officials enforce. In addition, national authorities often decline to notify Brussels of fraud because they are embarrassed to admit its existence and may have to turn back fraud-fighting money they have received from the EU.[54] More fraud-fighting money is on the way, and there is hope it will be better utilized.[55]

Will the EU Succeed?

There are skeptics.[56] But real progress has been made, and much of it is irreversible. Companies are merging, buying competitors, or creating joint ventures in order to be large enough to compete effectively in the vastly enlarged market. The European Monetary System (see Chapter 5), which many observers left for dead in 1993 after large currency value adjustments, is operating. There may not be a United States of Europe in the near future, or ever, but much unification has been achieved. Moreover, efforts toward more unification and harmonization are continuing, and the EU is an enhanced and growing power with which Japan, the United States, and the rest of the world must come to terms.[57]

The U.S. government and the governments of several American states take the EU seriously. They encourage their companies to trade with and invest in the EU, and want the EU to reciprocate. Table 4–2 gives U.S. government contacts for doing business in and with the EU, while Table 4–3 shows state activities.

OTHER REGIONAL GROUPINGS OF NATIONS

The success of the EU has led nations to form a number of other groupings with similar, but usually more limited, objectives. None of those groupings has come as close to being a true common market as has the EU; however, some have become customs unions and others free trade areas. A free trade area exists when a group of countries abolishes restrictions on mutual trade but each country keeps its own quotas and tariffs on trade with countries outside the group. An *industrial* free trade area, such as the European Free Trade Association, has free trade in industrial products only.

In the following section, we shall talk briefly about the European Free Trade Association, the European Economic Area, the Association of Southeast Asian Nations, African Trade Agreements, the North American Free Trade Agreement, and the Free Trade Agreement of the Americas. Of course, the World Trade Organization is the worldwide group for liberalization and encouragement of trade and investment. There are other groups, each important in its area and for companies doing business there. We shall name some, but space does not permit us to describe them all. Among the important ones are Asia-Pacific Economic Cooperation, Andean Group, Australia-New

TABLE 4–2 Key contacts in the U.S. government on the EU

Key Contacts in the U.S. Government on EU

The Interagency Task Force on EU
U.S. Trade Representative
Agriculture
Council of Economic Advisers
Securities and Exchange Commission
Office of Management and Budget
Energy
Commerce
Justice
Central Intelligence Agency
Environmental Protection Agency
Customs
Census
State
Labor
U.S. International Trade Commission
Transportation
Small Business Administration
Interior
Treasury
Defense
Food and Drug Administration
U.S. Information Agency
National Security Council
U.S. OCA
(ITC participates as an observer)

Working Groups (chaired by)
Services (Commerce)
Rules of Origin (USTR)
Residual Quantitative Restrictions (USTR)
U.S. Treaty Rights (State)
Standards Development, Testing &
    Certification (Commerce)
Third Country Relations (State)
Civil Aviation Issues (Transportation)
Health & Environment (FDA)
Investment Issues (Treasury)
Agriculture (Agriculture)
Social Dimension (Labor)

For more information on the Interagency
Task Force or the U.S. Government
policy response, contact Mark Orr or
Michael Brownrigg, Office of the U.S.
Trade Representative
(202) 395-3320 or 3211

Economic and Policy Council
For more information on the EPC and
European Monetary Reform, contact
Helen Walsh
Industrial and Global Analysis
Department of the Treasury
(202) 566-2856

EU
U.S. Mission to the EU
40 Boulevard du Regent
B-1000 Brussels
or APO New York 09667

Tel.: 32-2-513-4450;
ELEX: 846-21336

Commerce Department
Single Internal Market: 1992 Information
Service
Office of European Community Affairs
U.S. Department of Commerce
Room 3036
14th & Constitution Avenue, N.W.
Washington, D.C. 20230
Charles Ludolph or Mary Saunders,
(202) 377-5276

Industry Sector Outreach Coordinator
Debra Miller, Office of Industrial
Trade, (202) 377-3703

**Trade Development Industry Experts
at Commerce**
Textiles and Apparel
Michael Hutchinson, (202) 377-2043

Service Industries
Fred Elliot, (202) 377-3734

Information Technology, Instrumentation
and Electronics
Myles Denny-Brown, (202) 377-4466

Chemicals, Construction Industry
Products, and Basic Industries
Maryanne Smith, (202) 377-0614

Autos and Consumer Goods
Bruce Miller, (202) 377-2762

Construction Projects and Industrial
Machinery
Kay Thompson, (202) 377-2474

Aerospace
Marci Kenney, (202) 377-8228

Office of Industrial Trade
Debra Miller, (202) 377-3733

State Department
For more information, contact
The Department of State
Bureau of European and Canadian Affairs
Regional Political-Economic Affairs (RPE)
Richard Kauziarich or Ann Carey
(202) 647-2395
For Information on Residual Quantitative
Restrictions, contact
Robert Pollard, Bureau of Economics
and Business Affiars, (202) 647-2742

**Other U.S. Government Agency
Contacts**
Department of the Treasury
Industrial and Global Analyses

Helen Walsh, 566-2856 or Office of
International Trade
Wes McGrew, (202) 566-8106

Department of Agriculture
Foreign Agricultural Service
Western Europe and Inter-America
Group
Carol Harvey, Director (202) 447-2144

Department of Defense
Office of International Economics and
Energy Affairs
Dave Tarbell, Director (202) 695-2659

Environmental Protection Agency
Office of International Activities
Carol Deck (202) 475-8199

Food and Drug Administration
Office of International Affairs
Walter Batts, Acting Director
(301) 443-4480

United States Information Agency
Office of European Affairs
Bernard F. Skinkman, E.C. Desk Officer,
(202) 485-8853

U.S. International Trade Commission
Office of Executive and International
Liaison
Eliza Patterson, Deputy Director,
(202) 252-1146

Department of Justice
Public Affairs
David Runkel, Director
(202) 633-2007
Antitrust Division, Foreign Commerce
Section
Charles S. Stark, Director,
(202) 633-2464

Department of Labor
Bureau of International Labor Affairs
Richard Schulman, E.C.-92 Affairs,
(202) 523-9548

Securities and Exchange Commission
Public Affairs
Mary McCue, Director, (202) 272-2650
Office of International Affairs
Michael D. Mann, Director,
(202) 272-2306

Small Business Administration
Office of International Trade
Antony Korenstein, Director,
(202) 653-7794

Department of Transportation
International Aviation
Paul Gretch, Director, (202) 366-2423

Source: *Europe,* April 1990, p. 16.

State	Brussels Office	Other Offices in the EU	Export Value to EU* ($ millions)	Rank
Alabama		Frankfurt	560.4	27
Alaska			52.8	44
Arizona			979.3	20
Arkansas	X		153.1	39
California		Frankfurt, London	10,679.5	1
Colorado			728.9	24
Connecticut		Frankfurt	1,295.6	16
Delaware		The Hague	110.3	40
Florida	X		2,065.0	10
Georgia	X		1,097.5	17
Hawaii			10.1	50
Idaho			104.2	42
Illinois	X		3,046.5	6
Indiana		Amstelween (Netherlands)	1,034.9	19
Iowa		Frankfurt	469.6	29
Kansas		Stuttgart	371.4	31
Kentucky	X		938.9	22
Louisiana			1,785.5	12
Maine			186.2	36
Maryland	X	London	527.5	28
Massachusetts			3,971.3	4
Michigan	X		1,835.6	11
Minnesota	X	London	1,588.1	15
Mississippi		Frankfurt	359.7	32
Missouri		Düsseldorf	703.0	25
Montana			32.2	46
Nebraska			124.4	41
Nevada			70.4	43
New Hampshire			359.1	33
New Jersey			2,562.8	8
New Mexico			38.8	45
New York		Frankfurt, London	5,871.9	2
North Carolina		Düsseldorf	1,704.9	14
North Dakota			18.2	49
Ohio	X		2,946.2	7
Oklahoma			409.8	30
Oregon			690.2	26
Pennsylvania	X	Frankfurt	1,747.1	13
Rhode Island		Antwerp	159.5	37
South Carolina		Frankfurt	942.0	21
South Dakota			26.2	47
Tennessee			845.7	23
Texas			4,979.0	3
Utah			187.4	35
Vermont			153.7	38
Virginia	X		2,371.7	9
Washington			3,810.7	5
West Virginia			307.9	34
Wisconsin		Frankfurt	1,078.1	18
Wyoming		Eze-Village (France)	23.7	48

TABLE 4–3
State-level activities

*Exports are to the EU and are for commercial commodities, including processed foods. Figures do not include crops, livestock, minerals, fish, forestry products, and scrap.

Source: *Europe*, April 1990, p. 19.

Zealand Closer Economic Relations, Caribbean Community and Common Market, Central American Common Market, Southern African Development Community, and Southern (American) Common Market (Mercosur).

European Free Trade Association (EFTA) and European Economic Area (EEA)

The EFTA, created in 1960 in reaction to the EU, consisted of almost all the European countries that were not EU members. EFTA countries wanted to stimulate trade among themselves and enable bargaining with the EU as an organization rather than as individual countries. As EFTA countries observed EU progress toward unification, they realized that a potentially powerful European force was in the making. They feared being excluded from it and are reacting in different ways.

On January 1, 1994, a new organization came into being that incorporates the EU countries and most EFTA members. It is called the European Economic Area (EEA); the EFTA countries that signed the EEA treaty are Austria, Finland, Iceland, Norway, and Sweden. The only EFTA countries not to join the EEA are Liechtenstein and Switzerland, and Liechtenstein will as soon as it completes negotiations amending its customs union with Switzerland. The five current EEA countries have adopted all EU rules and laws except those pertaining to agriculture, fisheries, energy, and transport. Agreements on those politically sensitive subjects must still be negotiated.

Austria, Finland, and Sweden achieved full EU membership, and EEA was a stepping-stone. For those that do not succeed, or do not want EU membership, the EEA at least represents a realistic economic alternative, or a "safety net" as it has been called.[58] Central and eastern European countries and states of the former Soviet Union now think of the EEA as their possible stepping stone. Israel and Turkey desire EU membership and are in negotiations with the EU, EFTA, and the EEA in efforts to move in that direction.

Association of Southeast Asian Nations (ASEAN)

Created in 1967, ASEAN, with 325 million citizens, is one of the most dynamic and fastest-developing economic regions in the world. Taken together, its members—Brunei, Indonesia, Malaysia, the Philippines, Singapore, and Thailand—are the fifth-largest trading partner of the United States. Figure 4–10 presents a map of ASEAN members.

However, because many of the products of ASEAN countries compete with each other, intra-ASEAN trade has not grown rapidly. To remedy that, the members formed the ASEAN Free Trade Area in 1992, with the aim of creating a common market by the year 2008.[59] By the end of 1993, intra-ASEAN trade growth was already apparent, and observers expected the additional benefit of the member-countries being more attractive for investments from America, Europe, and Japan.[60]

African Trade Agreements (AFA)

In order to generate similar benefits for themselves, a number of African countries have formed trade and investment groups. Three of them are the Economic Community of West African States (ECOWAS), the Southern African Development Coordination Conference (SADCC), and the Preferential Trade Area for Eastern and Southern Africa (PTA). For a look at their locations in Africa and names of their member countries, see Figure 4–11.

FIGURE 4–10 Map of ASEAN members

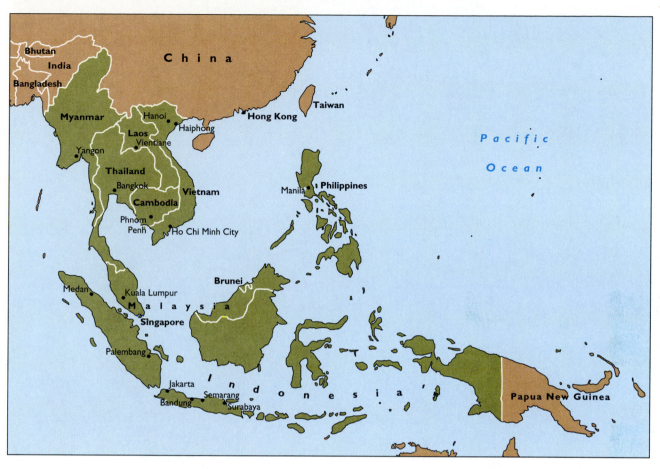

⬤ MEMBERS OF THE ASSOCIATION OF SOUTHEAST ASIAN NATIONS (ASEAN)

North American Free Trade Agreement (NAFTA)—Add the Western Hemisphere? The World?

In 1990, President George Bush proclaimed as a goal, "Enterprise for the Americas," envisioning a free trade zone from Alaska to Tierra del Fuego. Canada and the United States began implementation of their free trade area in 1989, and negotiations began in 1991 to add Mexico.[61]

Despite fierce opposition from organized labor and some politicians, the negotiations succeeded, and the legislatures of Canada, Mexico, and the United States approved the NAFTA treaty. The stated basis of labor's opposition to NAFTA was the fear of job losses to lower-wage-level Mexico, and some U.S. companies have opened plants in Mexico. But as one author put it, "dozens of their Mexican counterparts are charging north," including banks, tire manufacturers, truck and bus makers, broadcasters, and apparel and food companies.[62]

Chile wants an agreement with the United States.[63] Argentina, Brazil, Paraguay, and Uruguay are banding together economically, as are Bolivia, Colombia, Ecuador, Peru, and Venezuela; and the United States has or is negotiating bilateral trade pacts with a number of Western Hemisphere countries.[64]

FIGURE 4–11
African trade agreements

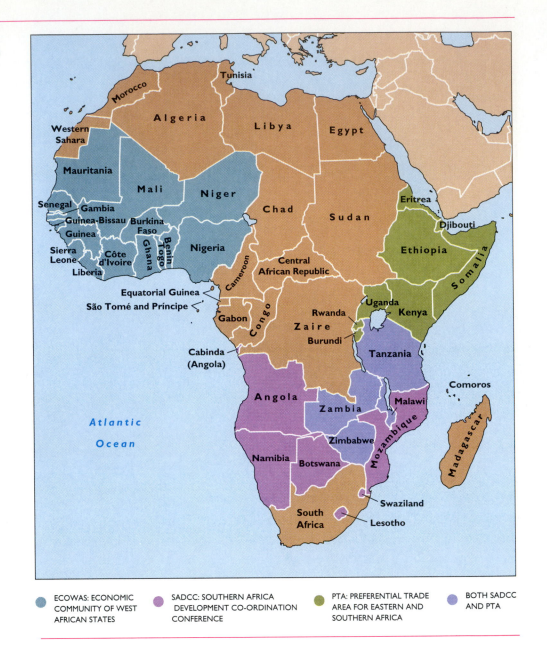

- ● ECOWAS: ECONOMIC COMMUNITY OF WEST AFRICAN STATES
- ● SADCC: SOUTHERN AFRICA DEVELOPMENT CO-ORDINATION CONFERENCE
- ● PTA: PREFERENTIAL TRADE AREA FOR EASTERN AND SOUTHERN AFRICA
- ● BOTH SADCC AND PTA

As stated above, President Bush called for an "enterprise for the Americas" in the Western Hemisphere. The Canadians have enlarged the picture in a big way, calling for NAFTA membership to be open to the world. Roy MacLaren, the Canadian trade minister, envisions NAFTA as the nucleus of an association of free trade countries wherever they are situated.[65] Some non–Western Hemisphere countries, such as Australia, New Zealand, Singapore, and South Korea, have indicated interest in membership. NAFTA continues to be developed as the nations involved agree on new rules in ongoing negotiations. See Table 4–4 for names, addresses, and phone numbers of information sources on NAFTA.

Free Trade Agreement of the Americas (FTAA)

Will NAFTA be extended to include the entire Western Hemisphere? A major step in that direction was taken at a Summit of the Americas meeting in

For assistance in conducting business in the United States, Canada, or Mexico under NAFTA, contact the following organizations:

TABLE 4–4 Resources

U.S. Department of Commerce
14th and Constitution Avenue NW
Washington, DC 20230

Office of Canada, (202) 377-3103
Office of Mexico, (202) 482-4464
Latin America/Caribbean Business
Development Center, (202) 482-0841
Trade Info. Center, (800) USA-TRADE
(Industry-related questions will be referred to Industry Desks)

NAFTA Help Desk
U.S. Department of Customs
(202) 927-0066

U.S. Trade and Development Agency (Latin America)
SA-16, Room 309
Washington, DC 20523 (703) 875-4357

Office of the U.S. Trade Representative
600 17th St. NW Washington, DC 20506
(202) 395-3230

Canadian Council for the Americas
145 Richmond St. W., 3rd floor
Toronto, ON Canada M5H 2L2
(416) 367-4313

Offices of the Trade Commission of Mexico:
New York: (212) 826-2916
Chicago: (312) 856-0316
Dallas: (214) 688-4095

Beverly Hills: (213) 655-6421
Atlanta: (404) 522-5373
Miami: (305) 372-9929
Seattle: (206) 441-2833

Mexican Chamber of Commerce
(202) 296-5198

American Economic Association
Journal of Economic Literature
Economic Literature Index
P.O. Box 7320 Pittsburgh, PA 15213
(412) 268-3869

International Trade Communications Group/World Information Network
Department of External Affairs (Canada)
Canada–U.S. Free Trade Agreement
125 Sussex Dr.
Ottawa, ON Canada K1A 0G2
(613) 944-4000

***The Economics* Intelligence Unit**
111 W. 57th St. New York, NY 10019
(212) 554-0600

Journal of Commerce, Inc.
Trade Information Service
2 World Trade Center, 27th floor.
New York, NY 10048
(212) 837-7000

Trade Data Reports, Inc. *The Exporter*
34 W. 37th St. New York, NY 10018
(212) 563-2772

Source: *Global Competitor*, Spring 1994, p. 63.

Miami, in December 1994. The head of every Western Hemisphere government, except one,* attended, and they signed a potentially important agreement.

They agreed to begin negotiations immediately on a Free Trade Agreement of the Americas (FTAA), which would create a free trade area from Alaska and Canada in the north, through Argentina and Chile in the south. Presumably, the FTAA would supersede the existing regional groupings such as the Andean Pact, the Central American Common Market, Mercosur, and NAFTA, and the goal is to have it in full effect by 2005. Figure 4–12 presents a map of existing regional trade agreements in Central and South America.

The acronym FTAA for Free Trade Agreement Americas did not please some. They considered the name Americas Free Trade Agreement, the acronym for which would be AFTA, but abandoned AFTA for two reasons. First, there is already in process of formation an Asian Free Trade Agreement, which will use AFTA. Second, AFTA means cold sore in Spanish, and of course, Spanish is the language of many Latin American countries.

*Cuba was not invited because of the long-standing hostility between Fidel Castro's communist government and the United States.

FIGURE 4–12
Regional trade agreements in Central America and South America

REGIONAL TRADE AGREEMENTS IN CENTRAL AMERICA AND SOUTH AMERICA

● ANDEAN PACT   ● CENTRAL AMERICAN COMMON MARKET   ● MERCOSUR

ORGANIZATION FOR ECONOMIC COOPERATION AND DEVELOPMENT (OECD)

The members of the Organization for Economic Cooperation and Development (OECD) are the industrialized DCs. The OECD originated in Europe, and most of its members are European. However, among its members now are Australia, Canada, Japan, New Zealand, Turkey, the United States, and Mexico, which was admitted in 1994. Negotiations were underway to admit South Korea, the Czech Republic, Hungary, Poland, and Slovakia. In addition, the OECD signed a cooperation agreement with Russia to provide expertise to help build a market economy.

You should be familiar with the OECD because it produces and publishes extensive research and statistics on numerous international business and

Feeling the Benefits of NAFTA

"We need blood and chicken shit?" asks an incredulous Richard Heckman of U.S. Filter Corporation, speaking to Ursula Oswald Spring, the environmental development minister for the Mexican state of Morelos. She tells him not to worry, because the mayor of the state's largest city, Cuernavaca, will organize the region's farmers to deliver the stuff. It will be mixed with sludge from a local wastewater treatment plant to make fertilizer. U.S. Filter, which got a contract to build a fertilizer plant, figures that a price markup on the fertilizer produced at the plant could be greater than 100 percent and still undercut import competition.

Another American company profiting from NAFTA is Bennett X-Ray Technologies. Before 1993, the Copiague, New York, company rarely had any sales in Mexico. In 1993, $500,000 of Bennett equipment was sold there, and it estimates 1994 sales of $5 million. NAFTA abolished a 12 percent tariff on Bennett products from the United States, but that tax still applies to products of its main competition, Germany's Siemens and Japan's Toshiba.

economic subjects. Also, it produced a declaration of guidelines of good business practices for firms operating in OECD countries.[66]

Material from and about the OECD may be obtained from OECD Publications and Information Center, 1750 Pennsylvania Avenue, NW, Washington, DC 20006.

SUMMARY

1. **Explain the activities of the United Nations (UN) in the economic and social fields as well as those as a peacekeeper/peacemaker in the world's trouble spots.** The UN organization consists of (1) a 15-member Security Council, of which 5 are permanent members, which is responsible for the UN's peacekeeping operations, (2) the General Assembly, of which every country is a member and every country has one vote, and (3) specialized agencies that conduct studies and assist LDC member countries in many fields, including labor, agriculture, meteorology, and health.

2. **Explain the three major parts of the World Bank: its regular loan window, its International Finance Corporation (IFC), and its International Development Association (IDA).** The World Bank lends money to LDCs for projects and has begun to insist that the borrowers put their economic houses in order as a condition to getting loans. The International Finance Corporation, a very successful arm of the Bank, encourages private business in LDCs.

3. **Explain the original and changed activities of the International Monetary Fund (IMF).** The International Monetary Fund helps LDCs with balance-of-payments deficits and cooperates with the World Bank's efforts to correct borrowers' fiscal and monetary policies. It began the LDC/banks loan renegotiation procedures that have helped deal with the sovereign debt crisis that came to light in the 1980s.

4. **Understand how the European Bank for Reconstruction and Development started in the wrong direction but has been turned around.** The European Bank for Reconstruction and Development has straightened out its act and is getting capital to the countries of eastern Europe and the former Soviet Union it was created to assist.

5. **Compare the successes and failures of the regional development banks, African, Asian and Inter-American.** The African Development Bank is in trouble, as an investigating team was unable to find records about projects supposedly financed by its loans, and large amounts of the loans are in arrears or default. The Asian Development Bank and the Inter-American Bank, by contrast, seem comparatively well run and are financing projects in their areas.

6. **Explain recent developments at the Bank for International Settlements (BIS).** The

Bank for International Settlements continues to find useful, new functions (e.g., the clearinghouse for Eurobonds and a school for eastern European bankers.

7. **Compare the powers and activities of the World Trade Organization (WTO) with those of the General Agreement on Tariffs and Trade (GATT), which it replaced, and understand the importance of the WTO to world business and trade.** The Uruguay Round of GATT was concluded, and GATT was replaced by the WTO. The WTO addresses areas not subject to GATT, including agriculture, intellectual properties, and services.

8. **Understand the opportunities for business presented by the European Union (EU), and the political and cultural obstacles facing the EU member-countries in reaching the goals of full union.** The EU countries signed the Maastricht treaty, which committed them to submit to a European central bank instead of their national banks and to use a European currency in place of their current national moneys. These and other moves to centralize powers away from the countries' governments have stirred great hostility and resistance, and there is doubt that the Maastricht goals will be met, at least during this century.

9. **Understand the potential for the North American Free Trade Agreement (NAFTA).** NAFTA was ratified by Canada, Mexico, and the United States. Negotiations are afoot to admit all Western Hemisphere countries, and some want to open it to the world.

10. **Understand uses of the Organization for Economic Cooperation and Development (OECD) for business and students.** The OECD is an excellent source of research on many subjects. New member-countries are joining as they become more affluent democracies.

KEY WORDS

- General Assembly   120
- less developed country (LDC)   120
- developed country   120
- Security Council   121
- hard loans   124
- soft loans   126

- firm surveillance   128
- Group of Seven (G7)   129
- debt default   129
- debt rescheduling   129
- regional development banks   131
- Marshall Plan   137

QUESTIONS

1. What are some reasons businesspeople and business students should be aware of the more important international organizations?

2. What is the feature common to all or almost all new UN member-countries?

3. When the World Bank makes a loan, how can a business, which would like to sell products or services to the borrower, go about making sales?

4. *a.* Which part of the World Bank Group is referred to as its investment banker?
   b. Why?

5. How do IDA credits differ from World Bank loans?

6. Why do outsiders fear a fortress Europe?

7. What is the importance of the OECD for business and students?

8. *a.* Stock and other securities markets are expanding in several LDCs. True or false?
   b. How are those markets likely to be affected by privatization of government-owned companies in the LDCs?

9. What changes have been made at the European Bank for Reconstruction and Development? Why?

10. The North American Free Trade Agreement passed the U.S. Congress despite strong opposition from organized labor. What motivated labor's stand? Have labor's forecasts turned out to be correct?

MINICASE 4–1 Use of International Organizations—Setting Up a 100-Percent-Owned Subsidiary

You are an international business consultant in the United States. Your specialty is exporting to and investing, licensing, or franchising in LDCs.

One of your clients is a hotel company that wants to build, operate, and 100 percent own a hotel in Guatemala. Your client is willing to put up about half of the original capital but wants to be assured that its share of the profits can be converted to U.S. dollars and repatriated as dividends.

To what organizations discussed in Chapter 4 might you look for assistance in raising the rest of the needed capital? To what organizations might you look for information concerning a Guatemalan company's ability to convert profits into U.S. dollars and remit them to the United States?

International Monetary System and Balance of Payments

> *Ninety percent of what we do is based on perception. It doesn't matter if that perception is right or wrong or real. It only matters that other people in the market believe it. I may know it's crazy. I may think it's wrong. But I lose my shirt by ignoring it. This business turns on decisions made in seconds. If you wait a minute to reflect on things, you're lost.*
>
> James Hohorst, head of foreign exchange trading in North America, Manufacturers Hanover Trust

CONCEPT PREVIEWS

After reading this chapter, you should be able to:

1. **understand** the historical and present uses and attractiveness of gold

2. **explain** the developments shaping the world monetary system from the end of World War II to the present

3. **understand** balance of payments (BOP)

4. **compare** the relative strengths and weaknesses of currencies and reasons for them

5. **understand** how "Big MacCurrencies" and the purchasing power parity theory are related

6. **identify** the major foreign exchange (Fx) markets of the world

7. **understand** the central reserve asset/national currency conflict of the U.S. dollar and the reasons and uses for special drawing rights (SDRs)

8. **discuss** the European Monetary System's (EMS) purposes and difficulties

9. **explain** the purpose of the European Currency Unit (ECU)

Politics Moves Money

 One of the phone-line lights flashed and was quickly answered by a currency dealer. As soon as the caller spoke, the dealer responded quietly, "1010," and replaced his phone on its hook. He then stated in a voice that could be heard around the trading room, "I've got 2 million at 1010." • Another trader was on her phone and said "1000." She then announced, "Got a million at 1000." • In the course of a few seconds, two customers had traded their French francs for 3 million U.S. dollars. The trades were made at exchange rates of 5.1010 and 5.1000 francs per dollar. The action took place in the trading room of a bank in the City, London's financial center, shortly after the news was flashed that Vladimir Zhirinovsky's party had achieved by far the largest number of votes in the Russian election for the State Duma. The party believes that Russia should at least reconquer the space formerly occupied by the Soviet Union.

Since the end of World War II in 1945, the U.S. dollar has been a central currency in the world's transactions. In the beginning it was dominant because the U.S. economy emerged from the war relatively undamaged and far and away the most powerful. Fairly rapidly in historical context, however, Japan and countries in western Europe and elsewhere developed powerful economies, and their currencies were increasingly used together with or instead of the U.S. dollar.

Although the American consumer pays U.S. dollars (US$s) for a German car or Scotch woolens purchased in the United States, the car manufacturer in Germany and the wool processor in Scotland must have, respectively, deutsche marks (DM) and pounds sterling (£) in order to meet their local expenses. At some point, the US$s must be exchanged for the necessary DM and £. Underlying the mechanics and rates of exchange (both of which are discussed in some detail in Chapter 6) is the international monetary system. The currencies mentioned above are **convertible currencies** (that is, they are readily convertible in the market), but most currencies are not. For example, the currencies of most less developed countries (LDCs) and communist countries are either not convertible or legally convertible only at artificial, government-established rates.

The international businessperson or student should have some knowledge of the history and current state of the international monetary system. We discuss history in this chapter because of its lessons and also because a vocal minority wants to resurrect elements of it, namely the *gold standard* and *fixed currency exchange rates*. We then look at post–gold standard, 20th-century developments before examining current practices of businesspeople, economists, governments, and institutions. The forecasting and planning that each of those groups must do involve informed guesses about the future.

convertible currencies
Also called hard currencies; exchangeable for any other currency at uniform rates at financial centers worldwide

A BRIEF GOLD STANDARD HISTORY AND COMMENT

From about A.D. 1200 to the present, the direction of the price of gold has been generally up.[1] True, there have been wide fluctuations in that price, and an investor in gold should have steady nerves, though law-abiding American investors were for a time spared that source of nervousness because it was illegal for them to own gold bullion between 1933 and 1976. During that period, the price of gold rose from about $21 per ounce to just under $200 in December 1976, when Americans were again legally free to own gold in bullion form. As it developed, Americans did not rush into the market, and the price has fluctuated between a bit over $100 and over $800 per ounce since 1976.

On December 22, 1717, Sir Isaac Newton, master of the English mint, established the price of gold at 3 pounds, 17 shillings, 10.5 pence per ounce. England was then on the gold standard and stood willing to convert gold to currency, or vice versa, until World War I, except during the Napoleonic Wars. During that period, London was the dominant center of international finance. It has been estimated that more than 90 percent of world trade was financed in London.[2]

gold standard
When countries agree to buy or sell gold for an established number of currency units

Most trading or industrial countries adopted the **gold standard**. Each country set a certain number of units of its currency per ounce of gold, and the comparison of the numbers of units per ounce from country to country was the exchange rate between any two currencies on the gold standard.

The financial burdens of World War I forced Britain to sell a substantial portion of its gold, and the gold standard ended. Between the First and Second World Wars, there was a short-lived flirtation with the gold standard, but it was not successfully reestablished.

Andy Caulfield/The Image Bank

Return to the Gold Standard?

Although the gold standard has not been the international monetary system for many years, it has had some ardent and influential advocates recently. One of the staunchest was Jacques Rueff, who until his death in 1978 was a member of the French Academy and an adviser to the French government. The heart of Rueff's argument may be expressed by one word: *discipline.*

Under the gold standard, a government cannot create money that is not backed by gold. Therefore, no matter how great the temptation to create more money for political advantage, without regard for economic results, a government cannot do so without the established amount of gold. This is the discipline that Jacques Rueff argued is the only effective means of avoiding inflation.[3]

One argument for a return to the gold standard, thus making gold the reserve asset of nations, is based on the premise that the current situation, in which the U.S. dollar is the reserve asset, is unsustainable. As world trade, investment, and economies grow, countries need more reserves. With the US$ as the reserve asset, other countries can increase their reserves only if the United States increases its net reserve indebtedness with a balance-of-payments (BOP) deficit. The United States can increase its liquidity only at the expense of other countries; a U.S. BOP surplus would drain US$ reserves from other countries. Thus, under the present system, the reserves of other countries can increase only if the largest debtor nation in the world—the United States—goes further into debt.

It has been suggested that the five nations with the largest economies should agree to settle their accounts with one another in gold, not US$s.[4] If a gold standard were established, what should be the price of gold? Lewis Lehrman advocates $500 an ounce, based on production costs. Arthur Laffer picks a price in the $200 range, based on the increase in the consumer price level since gold was $35 an ounce. A third school of thought, identified with Robert Mundell, suggests pegging the price where it happens to be on the day that the five nations agree to institute a gold standard.[5]

Present-Day Uses of Gold

In addition to its uses in jewelry and dentistry, gold has some industrial uses. It is an excellent conductor of heat and is used as protective insulation in the space programs.

In India, gold is a very popular dowry at weddings; at a typical wedding, about $500 worth is given. It also serves as a currency in the pervasive black market in India.[6] The Indian government also has uses for gold. In 1991, it shipped 45 tons to Switzerland and London. This Swiss shipment was to secure a $200 million loan from a Swiss bank. The Indian gold in London would permit India to borrow from the Bank of England and serves to "shore up the confidence of the international community."[7]

A new gold standard-type use has been suggested by former Federal Reserve governor Wayne Angell and several economists. Speaking first about the Soviet Union and then the Russian Republic, they argue that the ruble—or whatever the currency is called—should be backed by gold.

To protect Russia against changes in the price of gold—if the price rises, there would be inflation, if it declines, deflation—they advocate gold-backed U.S. dollars, convertible into rubles and vice versa. The United States would cooperate with Russia to establish a stable international currency backed by gold.

A major objective is to bring about price stability and attract foreign investment in Russia. The political objective is to avoid economic chaos, which could cause social upheaval and the overthrow of the democratically elected government.

The world's interest in gold remains high. Figure 5–1 is a notice of and invitation to a World Gold Conference held in London in 1994.

BRETTON WOODS AND THE GOLD EXCHANGE STANDARD

Bretton Woods
A New Hampshire town where treasury and central bank representatives met near the end of World War II; they established the IMF, the World Bank, and the gold exchange standard

During World War II, the countries of the world were much too involved with the hostilities to consider the gold standard or any other monetary system. However, many officials realized some system must be established to operate when peace returned. Actually, consideration of it did not await the firing of the last shot. Before that, in 1944, representatives of the major Allied powers, with the United States and Britain assuming the dominant roles, met at **Bretton Woods**, New Hampshire, to plan for the future.

There was general consensus that (1) stable exchange rates were desirable, but experience might dictate adjustments; (2) floating* or fluctuating exchange rates had proved unsatisfactory, though the reasons for this opinion were little discussed; and (3) the government controls of trade, exchange, production, and so forth that had developed from 1931 through World War II were wasteful, discriminatory, and detrimental to expansion of world trade and investment. Despite the third consensus, the conferees recognized that some conditions—for example, reconstruction from war damage or development of less developed countries (LDCs)†—would require government controls.

To achieve its goals, the Bretton Woods Conference established the International Monetary Fund (IMF). Article I of the IMF Articles of Agreement set forth its purposes, which reflected the consensus referred to above.[8] The IMF Articles of Agreement entered into force in December 1945.

The IMF agreement was the basis for the international monetary system from 1945 until 1971. It is doubtful, however, that the future role assumed by,

---

*A currency is said to float freely when the governments do nothing to affect its value in the world currency markets. Other varieties of floating are discussed later in this chapter.

†As we move through the 1990s, new terminology is developing, and less developed countries are sometimes called *developing countries* and more recently *emerging economies*.

Source: *Financial Times*, March 11, 1994, p. 9.

FIGURE 5–1
Notice of World Gold Conference

or thrust upon, the US$—which became the major **central reserve asset**— was fully foreseen.[9]

The US$ was agreed to be the only currency directly convertible into gold for official monetary purposes. An ounce of gold was agreed to be worth US$35, and other currencies were assigned so-called par values in relationship to the US$. For example, the British pound's par value was US$2.40, the French franc's was US$0.18, and the German mark's was US$0.2732.[10]

It was recognized that each member-country would be subject to different pressures at different times. The pressures could be caused by political or economic events or trends and could render the par values (currency ex-

central reserve assets
Gold, SDRs, or hard currencies held in a nation's treasury

change rates) established at Bretton Woods unrealistic. A major force that affects currency exchange rates is the balance of payments (BOP) of the member-countries.

Balance of Payments

One task assumed by the IMF was assistance to member-countries having difficulty keeping their balance of payments (BOP) out of deficit.* A country's BOP is a very important indicator of what may happen to the country's economy, including what the government may cause to happen. If the BOP is in deficit, inflation is often the cause, and a company doing business there must adjust its pricing, inventory, accounting, and other practices to inflationary conditions. The government may take measures to deal with inflation and the deficit. These may be so-called **market measures,** such as deflating the economy or devaluing the currency, or **nonmarket measures,** such as currency controls, tariffs, or quotas.

Even if a company does not consider itself international, it will be affected by inflation and by the government's methods of combating inflation and a BOP deficit. All of those methods have the common goals of causing the country's residents to buy fewer foreign goods and services and to sell more to foreigners.

Debits and Credits in International Transactions.
International debit transactions involve payments by domestic residents to foreign residents, and international credit transactions are the opposite. Taking America as the domestic economy, a list of debit transactions would include:

1. Dividend, interest, and debt repayment services on foreign-owned capital in America.
2. Merchandise imports.
3. Purchases by Americans traveling abroad.
4. Transportation services bought by Americans on foreign carriers.
5. Foreign investment by Americans.
6. Gifts by Americans to foreign residents.
7. Imports of gold.

The opposite would be examples of credit transactions. For example, dividend, interest, and debt repayment services on American-owned capital abroad are credits on the American ledger.

Double-Entry Accounting.
Although writers use debit and credit transaction language, each international transaction is an exchange of assets with a debit and credit side. Thus, the BOP is presented as a double-entry accounting statement in which total credits and debits are always equal. The statement of a country's BOP is divided into several accounts (see Table 5–1).

Current account. Three subaccounts are included in the current account: (*a*) goods or merchandise, (*b*) services, and (*c*) unilateral transfers. The first two subaccounts are sometimes treated together, and they include the real (as opposed to the financial) international transactions, that is, exports and imports.

---

*A deficit occurs when the residents of a country are paying nonresidents more than they are earning or otherwise getting from nonresidents. The opposite is a surplus.

market measures
Steps taken to end a BOP deficit, including deflating the economy, or devaluing the currency

nonmarket measures
Steps taken to end a BOP deficit, such as setting tariffs, quotas, and currency exchange controls

	Debits	Credits	**TABLE 5–1**
			Balance-of-payments
			accounts

1. Current account
   a. Goods or merchandise—imports and exports
   b. Services
       Net goods and services balance
   c. Unilateral transfers
       To abroad
       From abroad
           Net current account balance
2. Capital account
   a. Direct investment
       To abroad
       From abroad
   b. Portfolio investment
       To abroad
       From abroad
   c. Short-term capital
       To abroad
       From abroad
           Net capital account balance
3. Official reserves account
   a. Gold export or import (net)
   b. Increase or decrease in foreign exchange (net)
   c. Increase or decrease in liabilities to foreign central banks (net)
         Net official reserves
4. Net statistical discrepancy

a. The goods or merchandise account deals with "visibles," such as autos, grain, machinery, or equipment, that can be seen and felt as they are exported or imported. The net balance on merchandise transactions is referred to as the country's trade balance.

b. The services account deals with "invisibles" that are exchanged or bought internationally. Examples include dividends or interest on foreign investments, royalties on patents or trademarks held abroad, travel, insurance, banking, and transportation.

c. Unilateral transfers are transactions with no quid pro quo; some of these transfers are made by private persons or institutions and some by governments. Some private unilateral transfers are for charitable, educational, or missionary purposes; others are gifts from migrant workers to their families in their home countries and bequests or the transfer of capital by people migrating from one country to another. The largest government unilateral transfers are aid—which may be in money or kind—from developed countries to developing countries. Pension payments to nonresidents and tax receipts from nonresidents are two other government-related unilateral transfers.

Capital account. The capital account records the net changes in a nation's international financial assets and liabilities over the BOP period, which is usually one year. A capital inflow—a credit entry—occurs when a resident sells stock, bonds, or other financial assets to nonresidents. Money flows to the resident, while at the same time the resident's long-term international liabilities are increased, because dividends (profit) may be paid on the stock, rent will be paid on other assets, and interest must be paid on the bonds. And at maturity the bonds' face amounts must be repaid.

Subaccounts under the capital account are (*a*) direct investment, (*b*) portfolio investment, and (*c*) international movements of short-term capital.

a. Direct investments are investments in enterprises or properties located in one country that are effectively controlled by residents of another country. Effective control is assumed for BOP purposes (1) when residents of one country own 50 percent or more of the voting stock of a company in another country or (2) when one resident or an organized group of residents of one country own 25 percent or more of the voting stock of a company in another country.

b. Portfolio investments include all long-term—more than one year—investments that do not give the investors effective control over the object of the investment. Such transactions typically involve the purchase of stocks or bonds of foreign issuers for investment—not control—purposes, and they also include long-term commercial credits to finance trade.

c. Short-term capital flows involve changes in international assets and liabilities with an original maturity of one year or less. Some of the fastest-growing types of short-term flows are for currency exchange rate and interest rate hedging in the forward, futures, option, and swap markets. (These subjects are dealt with in Chapter 20, Financial Management.) Among the more traditional types of short-term capital flow are payments and receipts for international finance and trade, short-term borrowings from foreign banks, exchanges of foreign notes or coins, and purchases of foreign commercial paper or foreign government bills or notes.

The volatility, private nature, and wide varieties of short-term capital flows make them the most difficult BOP items to measure—and therefore the least reliable. The wide fluctuations of currency exchange rates and interest rates during the 1980s and into the 90s have caused the surge in hedging activities mentioned above, with attendant surges in short-term capital movements.

Official reserves account.   The official reserves account deals with (*a*) gold imports and exports, (*b*) increases or decreases of foreign exchange (foreign currencies) held by the government, and (*c*) decreases or increases in liabilities to foreign central banks.

Total credits and debits must be equal because of the double-entry accounting system used to report the BOP. Because some BOP figures are inaccurate and incomplete (notably true of the short-term capital flows item), the statistical discrepancy item is plugged in to bring total credits and debits into accounting balance.

Balance-of-Payment Equilibrium and Disequilibrium

Although the BOP is always in accounting balance, the odds are astronomical that it would be so without the statistical discrepancy item. There would be a surplus or a deficit in almost every case, but the BOP would nevertheless be considered in equilibrium if over a three- to five-year period the surpluses more or less canceled out the deficits.

monetary policies
These regulate the amount of growth or contraction of a nation's monetary stock

fiscal policies
These regulate a government's money receipts through taxes and its expenditure

Temporary and Fundamental BOP Deficits.   In IMF terminology, a *temporary* BOP deficit is one that can be corrected by the country's **monetary policies** or **fiscal policies** and perhaps by short-term IMF loans and advice.

A *fundamental* BOP deficit is too severe to be repaired by any monetary or fiscal policies the country can apply; there are economic, social, and political limits to how much a country can deflate its economy, which causes unemployment, or devalue its currency, which causes higher prices for imports.

In these cases, the IMF rules permitted the countries' currencies to be devalued from the par values per US$ set at Bretton Woods; the amount of the devaluation was agreed by the country and the IMF. Although many par value changes occurred between 1946 and 1971, none led to international financial crises of the kind that followed the devaluations of 1931. This was due at least in part to the performance of the IMF; it was able to maintain generally stable exchange rates, and when changes became necessary, it was able to prevent the competitive devaluations that proved so futile and destructive in the 1930s.

The devaluations of the 1946–71 period were in terms of the US$, so its relative value went up in terms of the devalued currencies. This caused the prices of American goods and services to go up in terms of other currencies, because after devaluation, more units of those currencies were required to buy US$s. This, in turn, was one cause of an American BOP deficit that began in 1958.

American BOP Deficit

From the end of World War II until about 1958, there was a shortage of US$s for the development of world trade and investment. Even during that era, many dollars flowed abroad due to government aid, private investment, and tourism. Around 1958, the United States began to run a series of BOP deficits, the flow of dollars became a flood, and the US$ shortage ended. The United States could have tried market methods (deflating its economy or devaluing the US$) to slow or reverse the deficit, but it did not, and its trading partner countries did not urge it to do so.

Why Market Methods Were Not Attempted.
Vivid recollections of the hunger and hardships of the 1930s Depression caused U.S. leaders to see deflation as the greater danger, and until the late 1960s the U.S. government did not perceive inflation as a possible cause of another depression. The US$ had been enshrined at Bretton Woods as the key currency in the gold exchange standard and had become, along with gold, the central reserve asset of most countries. Those countries were understandably reluctant to see a reduction in the value of part of their reserves, and U.S. authorities seemed to feel that this nation's prestige would be tarnished by a devaluation of the US$.[11]

Moreover, foreign competitors of U.S. exports derived a price advantage from the overvaluation of the US$. As pointed out above, almost all of the 1946–71 currency value changes were devaluations in terms of the US$. Thus, foreign goods and services became relatively less expensive for holders of US$s; but at the same time, U.S. exports were becoming relatively more expensive for holders of other currencies, who bought fewer of those more expensive goods and services. The foreign competitors of U.S. firms did not want to lose that advantage, and their governments discouraged any U.S. inclination to devalue the US$.

Raising the US$ price of gold would amount to a dollar devaluation in terms of other currencies unless they also devalued. It was generally recognized that the US$ was overvalued and that, if permitted to float, its value would fall vis-à-vis the currencies of most industrialized countries.

The United States had thousands of troops stationed in Europe and Asia and could have saved billions of dollars in expenditures abroad by bringing them home. But the host countries—for example, Germany, Japan, South Korea, and South Vietnam—brought strong pressure on the U.S. government not to reduce its forces, and the United States felt obliged to maintain them.

Gold Exchange Standard

As the United States failed to even try market methods to end its BOP deficit, and other rather halfhearted attempts had little success, dollars piled up in foreign hands, including those of government **central banks.** At this point,

central bank
A government institution that manages the monetary policy of a country

gold exchange standard
Cast the U.S. dollar as the central currency at $35 per ounce of gold, at which price the U.S. agreed to buy gold from or sell to other central banks

beginning in 1958, the "exchange" part of the **gold exchange standard** began to function.

Gold for Dollars.   The exchange feature agreed on at Bretton Woods required the United States to deliver an ounce of gold to any central bank of an IMF member-country that presented US$35 to the U.S. Treasury. As dollars accumulated in foreign hands in amounts greater than were needed for trade and investment, the central banks began turning them in to the U.S. Treasury for gold.

Gold and Dollars Go Abroad.   From 1958 through 1971, the United States ran up a cumulative deficit of $56 billion. The deficit was financed partly by use of the U.S. gold reserves, which shrank from $24.8 billion to $12.2 billion,[12] and partly by incurring liabilities to foreign central banks. During this period, those liabilities increased from $13.6 billion to $62.2 billion.[13] This is illustrated by Figure 5–2.

The foreign central banks were willing to accept so many dollars primarily because those dollars were treated as a central reserve asset; they provided liquidity growth to support growing world trade and finance. But in the late 1960s and into 1971, the central banks became increasingly nervous at the volume of US$ accumulation. A number of them turned in excess dollars for gold, but by the mid-1960s, the banks held more dollars than there was gold left in the U.S. Treasury. By 1971, the Treasury held only 22 cents' worth of gold for each US$ held by those banks.[14]

As indicated, another reason foreigners accepted so many US$ was that these dollars provided liquidity to support world trade and investment, which grew rapidly in the post–World War II era. Of course, this meant liquidity growth depended on U.S. BOP deficits, but such deficits could not continue indefinitely without deterioration of confidence in the strength of the U.S. economy and of the US$. Here is illustrated the inherent contradiction of the gold exchange standard. Foreigners needed and wanted growing numbers of dollars for many purposes but became nervous when the amounts of dollars they held exceeded the amount of gold held by the United States at the established price of $35 per ounce of gold.[15]

FIGURE 5–2
Accumulation of US$s in non–U.S. resident hands and loss of U.S. gold

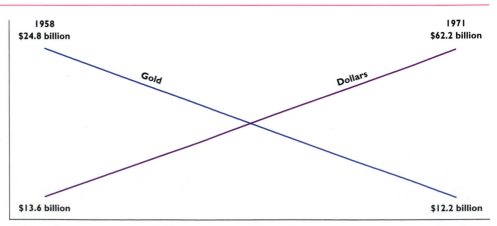

The gold value was set at $35/ounce

As noted above, by 1971, many more dollars were in the hands of foreign central banks than the gold held by the U.S. Treasury could cover. The event said to have triggered the drastic decisions made at Camp David* on the weekend beginning Friday, August 13, 1971, was a request by the British government that the United States cover US$3 billion of its reserve against loss.[16] President Nixon, with Treasury Secretary John Connally, Treasury Undersecretary Paul Volcker, and others, made the decisions that the president announced on Sunday night (the 15th). Those decisions shook the international monetary system to its roots.[17]

The president announced that the United States would no longer exchange gold for the paper dollars held by foreign central banks. He was said to have "closed the gold window."

The shock caused currency exchange markets to remain closed for several days, and when they reopened, they began playing a new game for which few rules existed. Currencies were floating, and the stated US$ value of 35 dollars per ounce of gold was now meaningless because the United States would no longer exchange any of its gold for dollars. The gold exchange standard was ended.

The president also imposed and announced a 10 percent surcharge on imports from all industrial countries except Canada. He demanded those countries lower their obstacles to imports from the United States in return for canceling the surcharges. Agreement on trade obstacles was reached in December 1971 along with new currency exchange rates that devalued the US$. The agreement was called the Smithsonian Accord because the final negotiations and signing ceremonies were held at the Smithsonian Institution in Washington, DC. The new rates could not be maintained, and by 1973, currencies were floating.

Politicians versus Speculators

Two attempts were made to agree on durable, new sets of **fixed currency exchange rates**, one in December 1971 and the other in February 1973. Both times, however, banks, businesses, and individuals (collectively referred to as speculators by unhappy politicians) felt that the central banks had pegged the rates incorrectly, and the speculators proved correct each time. Of course, the speculators' prophecies could be said to have been self-fulfilling in that they put billions of units of the major currencies into the currencies they felt to be strong—for example, the deutsche mark (DM), the Dutch guilder, and the Swiss franc—thereby making them even stronger. The speculators profited, and one writer commented, "It wasn't a holdup. It was more like an invited robbery."[18]

In March 1973, the major currencies began to float in the foreign exchange markets, and the system of **floating currency exchange rates** still prevails.[19] However, Western Europe has moved back toward a fixed system, the European Monetary System, which is discussed later in this chapter.

The two kinds of currency floats are referred to by various commentators as free or managed or as clean or dirty. The free (clean) float is one of the world's closest approaches to perfect competition, because there is no government intervention and because billions of the product (units of money) are being traded by thousands of buyers and sellers. Buyers and sellers may change

AUGUST 15, 1971, AND THE NEXT TWO YEARS

fixed currency exchange rates
When two or more countries agree on the exchange rate(s) of their currencies and undertake to maintain those rates

floating currency exchange rates
Values are not set by governments but by markets, although governments intervene frequently

1973 TO THE PRESENT

---

*Camp David is a relatively isolated retreat in the Maryland mountains that U.S. presidents frequently use to escape the pressures of Washington.

sides on short notice as information, rumors, or moods change or as their clients' needs differ. In the managed (dirty) float, governments intervene in the currency markets as they perceive their national interests to be served. Nations may explain their interventions in the currency market in terms of "smoothing market irregularities" or "assuring orderly markets."[20]

Beginning in September 1985, governments' reasons for intervening in currency markets have been expressed more forthrightly. The US$ soared in value from 1981 to its peak in February 1985, gaining some 80 percent against a trade-weighted basket of other major currencies. Although there were many other reasons for the huge growth of the American trade deficit, the powerful US$ was probably the biggest single reason.[21]

The unprecedented U.S. trade deficit, which was $134 billion in 1985 and reached $170 billion at its peak in 1987, greatly concerned the United States and its trading partners. To seek a solution, the finance ministers of the Group of Five (Britain, France, Germany, Japan, and the United States) met at the Plaza Hotel in New York in September 1985. Although the US$ exchange rate had begun to move down in March, they decided it was still too high and agreed in the so-called Plaza Accord to cooperate in bringing its rate lower. The Plaza meeting was the first of several—including one in Paris at the Louvre in February 1987—whose objective was to set the US$ at the "right" exchange rate, particularly in terms of the Japanese yen and the German deutsche mark (the currencies of the other two major world economies). And so, since 1985, the governments of the Group of Five have been intervening in currency markets to maintain their currencies' exchange rates at the "right" levels or within "target zones."

The Group of Five grew to be the Group of Seven (G7)* as Canada and Italy joined the meetings and deliberations. The G7 heads of state meet each year, and between those summits there are frequent private discussions among G7 finance ministers and central bankers on economic policy issues.[22] This is one of the important uses of the Bank for International Settlements: Its low-key facilities in Basel permit private, confidential meetings and discussions.

Economic policy coordination as practiced by the G7 has emerged as a key factor in the foreign exchange (Fx) markets. And although there is little doubt the G7 central banks have become more adept in influencing currency movements, another development can overwhelm their efforts. That is the explosive growth in the volume of currencies being traded in the world's foreign exchange markets. From an annual volume of roughly $18 trillion in 1979, Fx transactions are now estimated at more than $1.2 trillion daily.[23]

Even the richest countries have government reserves of "only" a few billion dollars available to influence exchange rates. Obviously, that is a lot of money, but it pales in the light of over a trillion being traded every day. For example, if the Fx market players believe the Japanese yen should be stronger in US$ terms, the yen will strengthen in spite of government market intervention. That occurred in June 1994 and continued into 1995.

Currency Areas

The U.S. dollar, Canadian dollar, Japanese yen (¥), Swiss franc, and several other currencies are floating in value against one another and against the European Currency Unit (ECU), a grouping of Western European currencies. Most currencies of developing countries (LDCs) are pegged (fixed) in value to

---

*The July 1994 G7 meeting in Naples, Italy, was attended by President Yeltsin of Russia, and some writers began to refer to the G8.

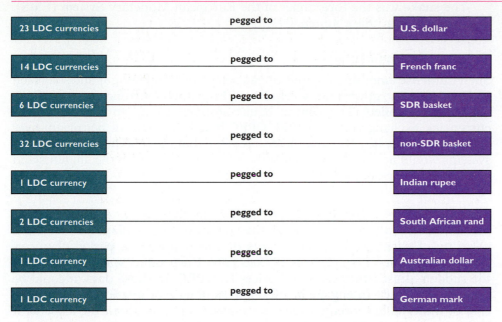

Source: *IMF Survey*, June 8, 1992, p. 185.

FIGURE 5–3
Pegged LDC currencies

one of the major currencies or to currency baskets such as the ECU, special drawing rights (SDRs), or some specially chosen currency mix or basket (see Figure 5–3).

Current developments may make the growth of currency areas, trading blocs, and currency blocs more likely. The most important of those developments are the continuing EU progress toward unification and enlargement, the implementation and extension of the NAFTA throughout the Western Hemisphere, and the growing economic importance of Pacific Rim countries.

Snake

In Europe during the mid-1970s, a currency grouping called the *snake* was created. The snake comprised several European currencies, led by the German deutsche mark. There was an agreed central exchange rate, but currencies' values could fluctuate up or down to a ceiling or floor exchange rate shown by the solid lines.

The snake was so called because of how it appeared in a graph showing the member currencies floating against nonmember currencies, such as the yen or the Canadian or U.S. dollar.

The reptile's health was damaged by the departure of several currencies, including the pound sterling, the Italian lira, and the Swedish krona, and by the in-and-out relationship of the French franc.[24] The system's inflexibility, the major reason those currencies were removed, explains the snake's ultimate demise. Each member-country was responsible for keeping its currency's value within the agreed relationship to the other members' currencies, but each country had different inflation rates, fiscal and monetary policies, and BOP balances. Thus, market pressures pushed currency exchange rates out of the agreed ranges, and the countries lacked the political will or resources to restore the agreed exchange rate. Then, the currency automatically fell out of the system.

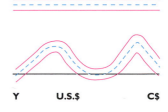

The snake was the forerunner of the European Monetary System (EMS), discussed later in this chapter.

Experience with Floating

Such immense amounts of major currencies were being bought and sold each trading day that governments' efforts to keep their currencies at fixed exchange rates failed. The central banks stopped trying to peg the major currencies' exchange rates in 1973. OPEC hiked the price of petroleum over 400 percent early in 1974, and there were fears that the banking and monetary systems would not be able to handle the resulting changes in the amounts and directions of currency flows.[25]

Fears not Realized.   However, despite occasional flare-ups and sharp changes in the relative values of currencies, the system did not collapse. Indeed, the volatility of exchange rate movements diminished after a period of uncertainty with the new system, from 1973 to 1974. Uncertainty was heightened by the sudden, drastic increase of oil prices by OPEC. In those days, it could be difficult and costly to engage in a foreign exchange transaction. By 1977, the cost of undertaking foreign exchange transactions was about the same as it had been under the Bretton Woods system.[26]

The system has still not collapsed, even though the value of the US$ fluctuated widely between 1977 and 1994. Beginning in June 1977, the US$ fell in value about 28 percent against the Swiss franc, 20 percent against the Japanese yen, and some 15 percent against the deutsche mark within a year. Many laid the blame for the dollar's weakness on inflationary American fiscal and monetary policies, particularly the latter.

In 1979, the American Federal Reserve System (Fed) slowed the rate of monetary growth, and the US$ began to move up in value. The new administration that took office in 1981 continued the anti-inflationary policies instituted by Fed chairman Paul A. Volcker in 1979, and indeed inflation did fall. As it fell, the value of the US$ rose, and by the beginning of 1985, it had risen about 80 percent against a trade-weighted basket of other major currencies.

Then, beginning in March 1985, the dollar exchange rate reversed its climb, and by 1988, it had dropped about 40 percent. Into the mid-1990s, the US$ continued to lose value vis-à-vis the German mark, Japanese yen, and the United Kingdom pound, as illustrated by Figure 5–4. Politicians and economists have given different explanations for this US$ performance since 1985. They include the continuing U.S. government budget deficit, which causes the national debt to continue rising; the balance-of-payments deficits, which result in more and more dollars in foreign hands; and the recovery from recession by the United States sooner than Europe or Japan began their recoveries, resulting in strong import demands in the United States and weak demands in Europe and Japan. A political explanation given by some is uncertain and contradictory leadership by American government administrations, which diminished confidence of foreign businesspeople and governments in American reliability and performance.

In terms of currencies other than Japanese or European, the US$ has held its own or gained in value. You may remember that the currencies of 23 countries are pegged to the dollar. In relation to the Mexican peso and the Canadian dollar—and recall that Canada is America's biggest trading partner—the US$ gained during 1994. Why would the US$ show strength against the peso and Canadian dollar while losing value against European and Japanese currencies?

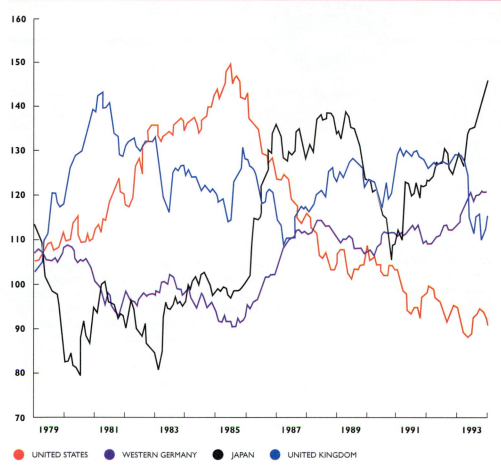

FIGURE 5–4
Real effective exchange rates
in major countries

At the end of 1993, one US$ would buy 3.11 new pesos; by the beginning of 1995, the exchange rate was 1 to 7. A combination of political and financial factors were blamed. On the political side, there was the January 1, 1994, uprising and continuing unrest in Mexico's state of Chiapas. That was followed by the assassinations of the ruling party's presidential candidate and of another leader in the party, the combination of which introduced an element of political instability that undermined confidence in the Mexican economy. That was exacerbated by an official peso devaluation in December 1994.

Financial factors included increasing interest rates in the United States, which could divert money that would have been invested in Mexico, and inflation. The Mexican inflation rate in mid-1994 was officially about 8 percent compared to some 3 percent in the United States.[27]

In mid-1994, the Canadian dollar bought 72 U.S. cents, down 4 cents from the beginning of the year, 6 cents from mid-1993, and 11 cents since 1989. The major reason for that decline, which analysts expected to continue, was political. In Quebec, the Parti Quebecois won September 1994 elections, and the Parti Quebecois is dedicated to the independence of Quebec from Canada. If it takes that province out of Canada, the political and economic ramifications will be great.[28]

Forecasting Float Direction. Such large changes in short time periods prompt efforts by everyone affected to forecast currency value changes. Such changes have many causes, including political events and expectations and govern-

WORLDVIEW

Big MacCurrencies

Rumors in the foreign exchange markets that *The Economist* has shorted the Big Mac, ahead of plans to replace its Big Mac currency unit by a Burger King index, are untrue. It is, however, time for our annual feast of burgernomics. Our Big Mac index was launched in 1986 as a lighthearted guide to whether currencies are at their correct level.

Burgernomics is based upon the theory of purchasing power parity (PPP)—the notion that a dollar should buy the same amount in all countries. In the long run, argue PPP supporters, the exchange rate between two currencies should move toward the rate that would equate the price of an identical basket of traded goods in the respective countries.

Our "basket" is a McDonald's Big Mac, which is produced locally in 68 countries. The Big Mac PPP is the exchange rate that would leave hamburgers costing the same in America as in, say, Japan.

The first column of the table shows the local-currency price of a Big Mac. The second column shows prices in dollar terms. The cheapest is in China, where a burger costs a bargain $1.03. Switzerland's Big Mac is the most expensive, at $3.96. These figures imply that the yuan is the most undervalued currency, the Swiss franc the most overvalued.

The average price of a Big Mac in four American cities is $2.30 (including sales tax). Dividing the Swiss price (SFr5.70) by the American price gives a Big Mac PPP for the dollar of SFr2.48 (i.e., at this exchange rate a Swiss burger would cost the same as an American one). This compares with a current exchange rate of SFr1.44, implying that the Swiss franc is overvalued against the dollar by a hefty 72 percent. On the same basis, the yen is overvalued by 64 percent, the DM by a modest 17 percent.

Compared with a year ago, European currencies have moved closer to their PPPs: they are now less overvalued against the dollar. The yen, however, is more overvalued. In general, rich countries' currencies are overvalued against the dollar (Canada and Australia are the notable exceptions).

Most developing countries' currencies, however, seem to be undervalued according to the Big Mac standard. The currencies of Brazil, China, Hong Kong, Malaysia, and Poland are all undervalued by

more than 30 percent. The Mexican peso, however, is more or less at its "correct" level against the dollar. Only two emerging market currencies are noticeably overvalued: the South Korean won (by 24 percent) and the Argentine peso (57 percent).

According to the Big Mac index, the dollar has been undervalued against the other main currencies for many years. Some readers have therefore had the temerity to complain that the theory of burgernomics is flawed because:

- It assumes that there are no trade barriers. However, price differences between countries may, in part, reflect different levels of farm support. The currencies of places which keep out cheap beef—e.g., Western Europe and Japan—will appear overvalued; Hong Kong and Singapore, which import food at world prices, will seem to have undervalued currencies.
- High rates of value-added tax in countries such as Sweden and Denmark inflate prices and so exaggerate the degree of overvaluation.
- Profit margins vary with the strength of competition. In Buenos Aires, for example, McDonalds restaurants are in prime spots and appeal to upper middle-class families, who are eager to pay a big premium to enjoy the American way of life.

Yet the Big Mac does provide a rough and ready measure of PPP. Using far more sophisticated methods, Goldman Sachs, an investment bank, estimates the dollar's PPP to be ¥189 (compared with our ¥170). This suggests that the dollar is even more undervalued than the Big Mac suggests.

Cheesed Off

Most forecasters have been expecting the dollar to strengthen

Reuters/Bettmann

sharply for more than a year. So why has it weakened against the yen and risen only modestly against the DM? One reason is that America's trade dispute with Japan raised fears that the Americans would use the exchange rate to put pressure on the Japanese. Another is that the markets have been disappointed by the glacial pace at which Germany's central bank has cut interest rates.

Yet economic fundamentals still seem to favor a dollar appreciation. Not only is the currency cheap, but American interest rates are likely to rise further this year, while in Germany and Japan rates should fall. The Big Mac index is not a perfect

currency forecaster, but it still gives dealers something to chew over.

Source: *The Economist,* April 9, 1994, p. 88.

	Big Mac Prices		Actual $ Exchange Rate 5/4/94	Implied PPP[b] of The Dollar	Local Currency Under(−)/over(+) Valuation[c] (%)
	In Local Currency[a]	In Dollars			
UNITED STATES[d]	$2.30	$2.30	—	—	—
Argentina	Peso3.60	3.60	1.00	1.57	+57
Australia	A$2.45	1.72	1.42	1.07	−25
Austria	Sch34.00	2.84	12.0	14.8	+23
Belgium	BFr109	3.10	35.2	47.39	+35
Brazil	Cr1,500	1.58	949	652	−31
Britain	£1.81	2.65	1.46[e]	1.27[e]	+15
Canada	C$2.86	2.06	1.39	1.24	−10
Chile	Peso948	2.28	414	412	−1
China	Yuan9.00	1.03	8.70	3.91	−55
Czech Rep	CKr50	1.71	29.7	21.7	−27
Denmark	DKr25.75	3.85	6.69	11.2	+67
France	FFr18.5	3.17	5.83	8.04	+38
Germany	DM4.60	2.69	1.71	2.00	+17
Greece	Dr620	2.47	251	270	+8
Holland	Fl5.45	2.85	1.91	2.37	+24
Hong Kong	HK$9.20	1.19	7.73	4.00	−48
Hungary	Forint169	1.66	103	73.48	−29
Italy	Lire4,550	2.77	1,641	1,978	+21
Japan	¥391	3.77	104	170	+64
Malaysia	M$3.77	1.40	2.69	1.64	−39
Mexico	Peso8.10	2.41	3.36	3.52	+5
Poland	Zloty31,000	1.40	22,433	13.478	−40
Portugal	Esc440	2.53	174	191	+10
Russia	Rouble2,900	1.66	1,775	1,261	−29
Singapore	$2.98	1.90	1.57	1.30	−17
S Korea	Won2,300	2.84	810	1,000	+24
Spain	Ptas345	2.50	138	150	+9
Sweden	Skr25.5	3.20	7.97	11.1	+39
Switzerland	SFr5.70	3.96	1.44	2.48	+72
Taiwan	NT$62	2.35	26.4	26.96	+2
Thailand	Baht48	1.90	25.3	20.87	−17

[a]Prices vary locally. [b]Purchasing-power parity; local price divided by price in United States. [c]Against dollar. [d]Average of New York, Chicago, San Francisco, and Atlanta. [e]Dollars per pound.

Source: McDonald's.

ment economic policies. A major cause is present and forecast relative inflation from country to country. One means of measuring relative inflation is purchasing power parity (PPP), the theory of which is that an exchange rate between the currencies of two countries is in equilibrium when it equates the prices of a basket of goods and services in both countries.

One product sold worldwide that is, or is supposed to be, the same everywhere is McDonald's Big Mac hamburger. In 1989, *The Economist* published the first of what became an annual study of worldwide PPP using the price of a Big Mac as its "basket" of goods. The Worldview entitled "Big MacCurrencies" presents the 1994 update of this hamburger index.

Money Markets, Foreign Exchange

money markets
Places where moneys can be bought, sold, or borrowed

The daily volume of foreign exchange trading in the world's three leading **money markets** has grown at a rapid pace. London is the largest Fx market, trading over $300 billion a day; but its role could slip when the new European Central Bank gets into full operation as London lost out to Frankfurt as the bank's headquarters. New York has the second-largest Fx market with some $200 billion daily, and Tokyo comes in third with about $130 billion. Further down the league is Singapore in fourth place, followed by Zurich, Hong Kong, Frankfurt, and Paris.[29]

The US$ is the most traded currency. The US$-deutsche mark market is the busiest, closely followed by that of the US$-yen. Third, fourth, and fifth are US$-sterling, US$-Swiss franc, and mark-yen.[30]

Although the US$ is the most traded currency, it need not be a part of every transaction. As indicated, the mark-yen market is big, and other major currencies are traded without going through the US$. Therefore, they are quoted in terms of each other, referred to as cross-rates of exchange.

London has a pivotal role in world currency trading. Because the London market shares trading hours with markets in Asia and the Middle East during its morning session and with the New York market during its afternoon session, it has more transaction opportunities than do the New York or Tokyo markets. Figure 5–5 shows the trading hours of major financial centers.

The growth of foreign exchange trading in recent years has greatly outpaced world trade, even though trade has also expanded. This has been due to the near explosions in international investment and in hedge and swap transactions. Hedges and swaps are explained in Chapter 20.

London, New York, and Tokyo have the biggest currency markets but by no means the only ones. Other important markets are in Los Angeles and San Francisco, Hong Kong, Singapore, Bahrain, Frankfurt, Zurich, and Paris. Trades can be made 24 hours a day at one or more of these markets.

Billions of US$s are traded around the world in the various currency markets. Smaller—but still large—amounts of the other currencies of major market countries are also traded outside the borders of the issuing countries, and all of these currencies are used as countries' national reserve assets as well as in trade, investments, hedges, and swaps.

Beginning in the 1960s, there was a growing feeling that national currencies or gold should be replaced as central reserve assets. In 1970, the IMF established special drawing rights for that purpose.

SDRs in the Future

special drawing rights (SDRs)
Established by the IMF as units of value to replace the dollar as a reserve asset

Special drawing rights (SDRs) may be a step toward a truly international currency. The US$ has been the closest thing to such a currency since gold in the pre–World War I gold standard system, but the US$ must also serve as a national currency, and the roles sometimes conflict (see the Worldview on p. 175).

FIGURE 5–5 Trading hours of the world's major financial centers

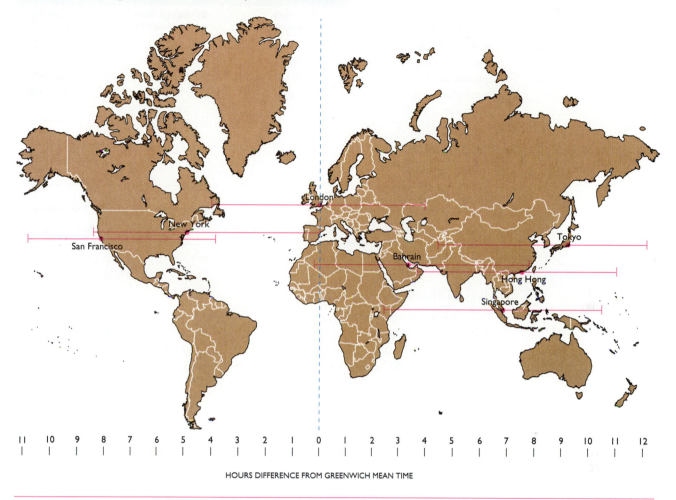

HOURS DIFFERENCE FROM GREENWICH MEAN TIME

Source: *Bank for International Settlements, 63rd Annual Report, June 14, 1993, p. 194.*

SDRs, bookkeeping entries at the IMF, were created in 1970 by agreement of the IMF members, whose accounts are credited with certain amounts of SDRs from time to time. The objective was to make the SDR the principal reserve asset in the international monetary system.[31]

Value of the SDR.   The SDR's value is based on a basket of the following five currencies (the percentage of each currency is in parentheses): U.S. dollar (40), German mark (21), Japanese yen (17), British pound sterling (11), and the French franc (11). The weights broadly reflect the relative importance of the currencies in trade and payments, based on the value of the exports of goods and services by the member-countries issuing these currencies. In 1990, the percentages were changed to those indicated above; the previous percentages were US$ 42, mark 19, yen 15, and the pound and franc 12 each.

The value of the SDR in US$ terms is calculated daily by the IMF as the sum of the values in US$s based on market exchange rates of specified amounts of the currencies in the valuation basket.

An illustrative calculation of the SDR's value in terms of the US$ is shown in Table 5–2. Inasmuch as exchange rates fluctuate, so too does the SDR value from day to day.[32]

TABLE 5–2
SDR valuation on October 11, 1993

Currency	1 Currency Amount	2 Exchange Rate on October 11	3 US $ Equivalent
Deutsche mark	0.4530	1.60120	0.282913
French franc	0.8000	5.61850	0.142387
Japanese yen	31.8000	106.10000	0.299717
Pound sterling	0.0812	1.53670	0.124780
U.S. dollar	0.5720	1.00000	0.572000
Total			1.421797

SDR 1 = US$1.42180
US$1 = SDR 0.703335

Column 1: The currency components of the SDR basket.
Column 2: Exchange rates in terms of currency units per U.S. dollar except for the pound sterling, which is expressed in U.S. dollars per pound.
Column 3: The U.S. dollar equivalents of the currency amounts in Column 1 at the exchange rates in Column 2—that is, Column 1 divided by Column 2.

Source: IMF Treasurer's Department.

Uses of the SDR

The SDR's value remains more stable than that of any single currency, and that stability has made the SDR increasingly attractive as a unit for denominating international transactions. Future payment under a contract, for example, may be agreed to be made in a national currency at its rate in terms of the SDR on the payment date, and some Swiss and British banks will now accept accounts denominated in SDRs.

Holders of SDRs.   SDRs are held by the IMF, its 179 members, and 16 official institutions, which typically are regional development or banking institutions prescribed by the IMF. All holders can buy and sell SDRs both spot and forward* and receive or use SDRs in loans, pledges, swaps, grants, or settlement of financial obligations. Holders receive interest at a rate determined weekly by reference to the weighted-average interest rate on short-term obligations in the money markets of the five countries with currencies in the SDR valuation basket.

SDRs as Central Reserve Assets.   A major purpose envisioned for SDRs was to replace currencies and gold as central reserve assets of nations. That has not happened. After the first allocation of 9 billion SDRs to members in 1972, they constituted 6.1 percent of the central reserves, while foreign exchange made up 65.3 percent and gold 24.5 percent at $35 per ounce. There was a second SDR allocation in 1979 of 13 billion, but total reserves went up faster, so that by 1983, SDRs constituted only 3.4 percent of the central reserves. Currencies had increased to 78.7 percent, and gold had fallen to 8.2 percent, but that was on the basis of valuing gold at $35 per ounce. In the gold markets, the price of gold had soared to over $800 in 1980, and gold traded between $300 and $465 per ounce from then into 1992.

The most recent SDR allocation to the 141 IMF member-countries at that time was on January 1, 1981, in the amount of SDR 4.1 billion. As of the end of 1993, the IMF had allocated a total of SDR 21.4 billion in six allocations, but SDR holdings by member-countries amounted to only 4 percent of their total nongold reserves.

_____
*Spot and forward rates are discussed in Chapter 6.

Central Reserve/National Currency Conflict

The US$ has been the most used central reserve asset in the world since the end of World War II. Somewhat analogous to a savings account, the dollars were available when needed to finance trade or investments or to intervene in currency markets. Held in the form of U.S. Treasury bonds, the US$s earn interest, and the more held in the savings/central reserve account, the better. But the countries don't want their central reserve asset US$s to lose value, and there lies a contradiction: at some point, greater numbers of US$s (or any other product) in supply cause them to lose value—supply and demand.

At the same time, the US$ is the national currency of the United States of America, whose government must deal with inflation, recession, interest rates, unemployment, and other national, internal problems. The U.S. government uses fiscal and monetary policies to meet those problems—higher or lower taxes, decisions as to how to spend available revenue, growth or contraction of the money supply, and rate of its growth or contraction.

It would be only accidental if the national interests of the United States in dealing with its internal problems coincided with the interests of the multitude of countries holding US$s in their central reserve asset accounts. The United States may be slowing money supply growth and raising taxes to combat U.S. inflation while the world needs more liquidity, in the form of US$s, to finance growth, trade, or investment. Or, the United States may be stimulating its economy by faster money supply growth and lower taxes at a time when so many US$s are already outstanding that their value is dropping—not a happy state of affairs for countries holding US$s.

It was a quirk of history that thrust the US$ into this conflicting role. It was the hope of the IMF that a nonnational asset, the SDR, would rescue the US$ and the world from the conflict.

Such lack of enthusiasm for SDRs as central reserve assets may have several explanations. Dollars and other hard currencies are more flexible and have more uses, usually yield higher interest returns, and can officially be credited and debited by anyone—in contrast to the limited numbers with official access to SDRs.

European Monetary System (EMS)

As evidenced by the snake, the European countries prefer fixed currency exchange rates to floating ones. Due to inflexibility and weaknesses, the snake expired in the mid-1970s. Not daunted, a larger group of European countries banded together in 1979 and created the **European Monetary System (EMS),** which is a large step back toward fixed currency exchange rates. It is an enlarged and improved version of the snake.

The EMS member-countries agreed to maintain their currency values within a specified range in relation to one another. An important feature, not available to the old snake, is the European Monetary Cooperation Fund (EMCF). Composed of dollars, gold, and member-country currencies, it is used to support the efforts of member-countries to keep their currency values within the agreed relationship to the other currencies. The EMCF has the equivalent of about $32 billion with which to work.

Another difference between the EMS and its ancestor, the snake, is that the exchange rates of the EMS are flexible. If one currency proves weaker than another and the governments cannot or will not take steps to correct the situation, the EMS exchange rates can be changed. There have been several rate rearrangements since 1979. If a snake member-country could not keep its currency up to the agreed strength, it dropped out and ceased to be a member.

European Monetary System (EMS)

A grouping of most Western European nations cooperating to maintain their currencies at fixed exchange rates

Two of the EMS fathers, former French president Valery Giscard d'Estaing and former West German chancellor Helmut Schmidt, think it's time their child was allowed to grow up. They are pushing hard for the never-implemented second stage of their plan, the economic and monetary union of Europe. This union would be accomplished through a European Central Bank and free use of the European Currency Unit (see the next section) by banks, companies, and consumers in all 15 EU countries.

Despite opposition from the German central bank (the Bundesbank) and the British government, the two men are optimistic the European Bank will be created. Schmidt says, "All the talk about European union will be rubbish if we don't do anything. We must create a European Central Bank because we must have a currency with which you could as easily buy a dress or a train ticket in Paris or Madrid."[33]

The EU took large steps toward those goals at a summit meeting in Maastricht, the Netherlands, during December 1991. There, the then members signed a commitment to proceed toward economic and monetary union (EMU) involving a single currency governed by a European Central Bank by 1999.

But, does Maastricht make sense? In Chapter 4, we discussed the growing opposition to Maastricht goals (e.g., a European central bank and a single European currency). And, during 1993, the EMS, a step toward those goals, suffered a blow as several countries were unable to keep their currencies close in value to the deutsche mark; they were devalued, and the permissible range of values was enlarged to 15 percent below and 15 percent above the agreed central exchange rate, a range so wide it almost constitutes a free currency float system.[34] Nonetheless, the EMS survived, and in 1994 an embryo European central bank came into existence. It is called the European Monetary Institute, and it is subject to all the intense hostilities and strong support of the other Maastricht goals.[35]

European Currency Unit (ECU)

European Currency Unit (ECU)
A value established by the EMS for intra-EMS bookkeeping

The **European Currency Unit (ECU)** was established as the EMS bookkeeping currency. Its value is determined by reference to a basket of European currencies. The weights of each currency in the ECU are shown in Figure 5–6. The weights changed in 1989 when Portugal and Spain joined the EMS. The Portuguese escudo was accorded a 1 percent weight while the Spanish peseta was given 5 percent. The 6 percent loss was shared among the other currencies.[36]

The international market for ECU-denominated bonds increased dramatically in liquidity and issuance during 1990 and 1991. All sorts of borrowers entered the market: international agencies such as the World Bank, numerous national governments, municipalities, and public and private companies. In the first six months of 1991, more bonds were denominated in ECUs than any currency except the US$.[37] Uses of ECUs have surpassed those of SDRs, which were discussed earlier in this chapter. Figure 5–7 is an announcement of an ECU Eurobond placement.

One reason the ECU has become more popular than the SDR is that neither the US$ nor the yen is included in the currency basket that determines its value. The exchange rates of the US$ and the yen have fluctuated much more widely than have those of the European currencies in the ECU basket. Both the US$ and the yen are in the SDR basket, so the SDR's value has been less stable than that of the ECU.

Another reason the ECU's use has surpassed that of the SDR is active sponsorship of the ECU by European governments, banks, and businesses;

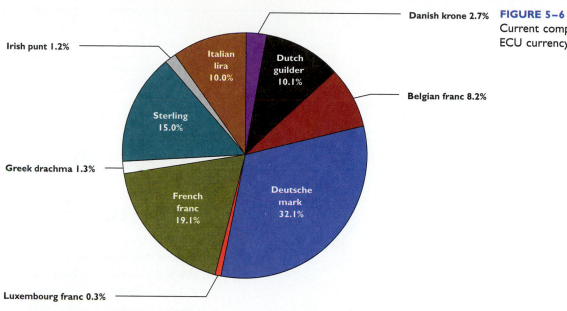

FIGURE 5–6
Current composition of the ECU currency weightings

The ECU is a "basket currency" composed of a combination of the currencies of 12 European Union member-states, mixed in proportion to the relative strength of each country's economy.

Source: "Bulletin," *Swiss Banking Magazine*, November 1989.

the SDR has received no such support. The ECU is being used for various purposes, and support and supplementary networks have been put in place. Bank accounts can be denominated in ECUs, and ECU traveler's checks are available. Between units of some international companies, debits and credits are denominated in ECUs as they buy, sell, or borrow from one another.

The ECU regains its popularity; trading in ECU denominated bonds on the rise

Courtesy European Commission Delegation, Washington, DC

FIGURE 5–7
ECU denominated
euro-notes

This announcement appears as a matter of record only. These Securities have not been registered under the United States Securities Act of 1933 and may not, as part of the distribution, be offered, sold or delivered, directly or indirectly, in the United States or to United States persons

New Issue / April, 1986

ECU 100,000,000

Phibro-Salomon Inc

**8$^1/2$% Series A Note Due February 24, 1996
and 100,000 Warrants to Purchase
ECU 100,000,000 8$^1/2$% Series B
Notes Due February 24, 1996**

Salomon Brothers International Limited

Banque Nationale de Paris   **Banque Bruxelles Lambert S.A.**

Banque Générale du Luxembourg S.A.		**Banque Indosuez**
Banque Internationale a Luxembourg S.A.		**Bayerische Hypotheken-und Wechsel-Bank** Aktiengesellschaft
Commerzbank Aktiengesellschaft		**Crédit Commercial de France**
Crédit Lyonnais	**Crédit Agricole**	**Deutsche Bank Capital Markets Limited**
Fuji International Finance Limited	**Daiwa Europe Limited**	**Goldman Sachs International Corp.**
Kredietbank International Group	**Generale Bank**	**Morgan Guaranty Ltd.**
Morgan Stanley International		**Nippon Credit International (HK) Ltd.**
Nippon European Bank S.A./LTCB Group		**Nomura International Limited**
Orion Royal Bank Limited		**Shearson Lehman Brothers International**
Swiss Bank Corporation International Limited		**The Taiyo Kobe Bank (Luxembourg) S.A.**
Takugin International Bank (Europe) S.A.		**S.G. Warburg & Co. Ltd.**

Source: © 1989 The Economist Newspaper Ltd.

Countries outside the European Union have begun to utilize ECUs (e.g., Cameroon, Romania, Sweden, and New Zealand), and American companies have recently issued bonds denominated in ECUs. ECU futures and options contracts are available at markets in Amsterdam, Chicago, and Philadelphia. And last but not least, an association of banks together with the European Investment Bank (a unit of the European Union) has begun a multilateral, electronic clearing system for ECU transactions. It will be administered by the Bank for International Settlements, which will perform functions for the ECU similar to the U.S. Federal Reserve's clearing of dollar transactions.

In addition, the ECU is now the third-biggest reserve currency behind the US$ and the deutsche mark. At the end of 1990, the US$ share of countries' foreign exchange reserves was 51 percent, the DM 19 percent, the ECU 17 percent, and the yen 9 percent.[38] Some influential Europeans forecast and advocate still another ECU use: the role as EU's central currency.[39]

During 1992 and 1993, as we have noted, opposition grew to the EU's unification programs, and the close unity of currencies within the EMS was lost at least temporarily. Because the ECU is so closely identified with EU unification and the EMS, the ECU's popularity plummeted during those years.[40]

The ECU's road to recovery was started by the EU in the autumn of 1993 with its own $1.16 billion offering of bonds. Then, early in 1994, the Portuguese government made a successful global offering of ECU dominated bonds, becoming only the second EU currency after the deutsche mark to have the prestige of being sold worldwide. The signs are that ECU financial markets have recovered much of their former popularity.[41]

SUMMARY

1. **Understand the historical and present uses and attractiveness of gold.** Since the earliest recorded times, gold has held an allure. People have used it, and continue to use it, for many purposes, including jewelry, coinage, store-of-value, and protection against inflation and political unrest.

2. **Explain the developments shaping the world monetary system from the end of World War II to the present.** The gold exchange standard, established at Bretton Woods after World War II, worked until the 1970s when it collapsed due to inflation and the surplus of U.S. dollars held outside the United States.

3. **Understand balance of payments (BOP).** BOP accounts measure and compare the amount of money coming into a country with the amount going out.

4. **Compare the relative strengths and weaknesses of currencies and reasons for them.** Causes for a currency's relative strengths and weaknesses include relative inflation, balance of payments, political developments, and confidence in the country's leaders.

5. **Understand how "Big MacCurrencies" and the purchasing power parity theory are related.** A Big Mac hamburger is supposed to be the same at every McDonald's around the world. Therefore, according to the PPP theory, its cost in the currency of one country compared with its cost in the currency of a second country should equal the exchange rate between those currencies.

6. **Identify the major foreign exchange markets of the world.** London is the largest Fx market, New York the second, and Tokyo the third. With major markets located around the world, so that you can trade 24 hours on most days.

7. **Understand the central reserve asset/national currency conflict of the U.S. dollar and the reasons and uses for special drawing rights (SDRs).** The U.S. dollar is the currency of the United States, but it is also the major reserve asset of other countries. It is usually desirable for countries to increase their reserve assets, but that depends on growing amounts of US$s being in the hands of foreign holders, which may not be in the best interest of the United States. SDRs were established by the IMF to replace the U.S. dollar as the main central reserve asset.

8. **Discuss the European Monetary System's (EMS) purposes and difficulties.** The EMS is the effort by the EU to keep the values of their currencies close to an agreed exchange rate. For that to be achieved, countries must accept discipline and uniformity in their economic and political policies. Some countries are reluctant to do that, so that the closely bound EMS exchange rates came apart in 1992 and 1993. The EMS survives, but there is a 30 percent range from the floor to the ceiling rates.

9. **Explain the purpose of the European Currency Unit (ECU).** The ECU was established by the EMS as an intra-Europe value. They are both used to denominate bonds and other long-term obligations. Because their values are a composite of several national currencies, their value fluctuations are not as great as individual currencies.

KEY WORDS

QUESTIONS

1. Explain the appeal gold holds for people. Discuss the pros and cons of a gold standard.

2. Identify and discuss causes for currencies to strengthen or weaken in Fx markets.

3. Why were SDRs created? Discuss their success in their original mission and their current uses.

4. The ECU has risen and fallen in popularity. Why?

5. Explain the national currency/central reserve conflict.

6. The Maastricht objectives to unify Europe are being opposed. By whom and why?

7. What difficulties are the EMS encountering? Why?

8. Why should managers be aware and wary of the BOP of the country in which their business operates?

MINICASE 5–1   SDR Exchange Risk

The Bowling Green National Bank has made loans denominated in SDRs to several of its MNE customers. It has built up a portfolio to the amount of SDR 8 million. Management decides to hedge by selling in the forward market the currencies that make up the SDR basket. How much of each currency must be hedged?

"May I have my allowance in Deutsche Marks, Dad?"

Reprinted from The Wall Street Journal; permission Cartoon Features Syndicate.

International Finance

Chapter 5 and the video for Section II presented the modern history of the international monetary system, and some of the institutions discussed in Chapter 4 were and are involved with that system. Here we shall get into the sequel to the story, particularly in regard to Europe, which affects planning by Asian, North American, and all other firms doing or planning European operations.

From the days of the gold exchange standard through those of the snake and into the European Monetary System (EMS), the European countries have demonstrated their preference for fixed currency exchange regimes instead of any sort of float. With the Maastricht Treaty, Europe is trying to go all the way to the ultimate fix, that is, one single currency for all Europeans, plus a European central bank.

In 1994 it got its bank, the European Monetary Institute (EMI), but there are fundamental differences of opinion about EMI's role. One position is that it should force integration of European countries and become *the* central bank above the current national banks. Belgium and the EU Commission hold this position. Opposing this are notably the Bank of England and the German Bundesbank, which want EMI's role to be mainly advisory.

A Maastricht goal is economic and monetary union (EMU), and five criteria were set to have been met by European countries by December 31, 1998. They were (1) a low inflation rate, (2) a low long-term government bond rate, (3) a deficit that does not exceed 3 percent of GDP, (4) government debt that does not exceed 60 percent of GDP, and (5) a currency exchange rate that has remained within the ± 2.25 percent bands of the exchange rate mechanism (ERM) for at least two years.

By the middle of 1994, only Luxembourg of the then 12 EU members met the criteria, and the ERM had fallen apart as the EMS finance ministers abandoned the ± 2.25 percent band, widening it to ±15 percent, so wide it almost constitutes a free float.

As a company executive who wants to do business in Europe, how can you plan intelligently amid all this confusion? There is conflicting advice. The *Financial Times* says, "the prospect of EMU by the end of the century is no longer laughed out of court," but it goes on to cite "formidable obstacles." Among the obstacles cited are (1) the EU has done little to ensure that bank notes, coinage, or payment systems are ready for a single European currency, (2) both the United Kingdom and Denmark have reserved the right not to join EMU, and (3) there are signs that tight EU integration is losing support among electors in several countries, including France and Germany.

The publication, *Euromoney*, in an article entitled "Why EMU Will Happen," points to "passionately keen" support in some countries, notably Belgium and Portugal, as well as creation of the embryo central bank, the EMI. It says the convergence process is slow but is happening and suggests an EMS with exchange rates adjusted to reflect inflation differentials and a fluctuation ban that narrows over time. This article also mentions the political capital EU heads of government have invested in a European EMU.

Pointing the other direction is an article published by the Federal Reserve Bank of St. Louis. It says that at the time Maastricht was signed, only two countries qualified by meeting the five criteria; they were France and Luxembourg. All countries vowed to bring their economies in line with the convergence criteria, but they have moved the other direction primarily because of the European recession. This article concludes there is little evidence that the EU will be able to implement monetary union even by the end of the century.

So, as the executive responsible for planning and implementing your company's European operation, how will you proceed? The deutsche mark has been Europe's strongest currency, reflecting the size and strength of the German economy and the determination of the Bundesbank to prevent inflation. The British are reluctant to give up their pound sterling. The European Currency Unit (ECU) is envisioned by many as the European currency. The U.S. dollar is still the most widely used currency in the world.

In raising money for your European operations, which currency will you choose? Would your decision vary for operations in different European countries?

Foreign Environment

Financial Forces

> *Do the wrong thing. That's the best advice anyone could possibly offer an ambitious young person eager to get ahead in banking.*
>
> Alan Abelson, *Barron's*

CONCEPT PREVIEWS

After reading this chapter, you should be able to:

1. **realize** that much money is made, and lost, in the foreign exchange (Fx) markets

2. **understand** Fx quotations, including cross-rates

3. **recognize** currency exchange risks

4. **expect** currency exchange controls

5. **anticipate** financial forces such as balance of payments, tariffs, taxes, inflation, fiscal and monetary policies, and differing accounting practices that affect business

6. **understand** sovereign debt, its causes and solutions

7. **know** that a Third World vegetable stand might be a better credit risk than a Third World government

8. **know** that Third World governments are not the only ones in debt; the largest debt is that of the United States

Currency Loss Bombs Explode

 In 1993, Showa Shell Sekiyu, a Japanese oil refiner and distributor, disclosed that it had an unrealized loss in 1992 of 125 billion yen ($1.05 billion), equal to 82 percent of its shareholders' equity. The losses stemmed from $6.4 billion worth of speculative foreign exchange contracts made by people in the firm's treasury department, apparently without informing Showa's top management until the losses became too big to ignore. • Japanese banks, which were the counterparties in the contracts, had routinely allowed their customers to defer settlement of loss-making contracts by rolling them over, until Japan's finance ministry warned the banks in 1993 about the risks involved. And one of the risk bombs exploded, as Showa covered some of its foreign exchange losses by selling assets, prominent among which were bank shares.

The "uncontrollable" financial forces on which we shall touch include foreign currency exchange risks, national balances of payment, taxation, tariffs, national monetary and fiscal policies, inflation, and national business accounting rules. *Uncontrollable* means that these forces originate outside the business enterprise. It does not mean that the financial management of a company is helpless to minimize its disadvantages; those disadvantages may even be turned to the company's advantage.

We shall have a look at what causes exchange rates to change and at how governments sometimes intervene in foreign exchange markets. We shall emphasize the importance for management to remain aware of BOP developments, exchange rate forecasts, inflation forecasts, government fiscal and monetary policies, and other financial forces. And at the end of the chapter, we look at the sovereign debt of developing countries, such as Brazil and Mexico. And not to be outdone, the United States has run up the biggest net negative international investment position in the world.

FLUCTUATING CURRENCY VALUES

An attempt is being made to bind together the values of most European currencies in the European Monetary System (EMS). In Chapter 5, we spoke of the Maastricht efforts to unify European countries with a central bank and a single currency, and we learned there is powerful opposition in some countries to give up their own historic—and in some cases strong—currency as well as the powers of their national central bank. Efforts toward unification are continuing, but progress is slow and uncertain.

Permissible currency value fluctuations within the EMS were increased to 30 percent from 4.5 percent in 1993. Outside the EMS, there are no comparable efforts by countries to tie major currency values to each other, so now, inside and outside, currency values are free to fluctuate.

Financial managers must understand how to protect against losses or optimize gains from such fluctuations. Another level of currency exchange risk is encountered when a nation suspends or limits convertibility of its

Currency exchange, an uncontrollable financial force seen here at the International Monetary Exchange Trading Floor in Singapore.

Ann Rippy/The Image Bank

currency, and managers must try to foresee and minimize or avoid losses resulting from large holdings of inconvertible and otherwise limitedly useful currencies.

When you want to convert one currency into another currency, you might first look for the value of the currency you have in terms of the one you want. You can find international currency exchange quotations in business publications such as *The Wall Street Journal* or the *Financial Times* and in the business section of most major newspapers.

FOREIGN EXCHANGE QUOTATIONS

The foreign exchange quotations—the price of one currency expressed in terms of another—can be confusing until you have examined how they are reported. In the world's currency exchange markets, the U.S. dollar (US$) is the common unit being exchanged for other currencies. Even if a holder of Japanese yen (¥) wants British pounds (£), the trade, particularly if it involves a large amount, usually will be to buy US$s with the ¥ and then to buy £s with the US$s. The reasons for this procedure are historical and practical.

Historically, the international monetary system established at Bretton Woods just before the end of World War II set the value of the US$ in terms of gold at $35 per ounce. The values of all the other major currencies were then stated in terms of the US$; for example, the yen was worth 0.28 of a U.S. penny, the French franc (Ff) was worth 18 cents, the German mark (DM) was worth 27 cents, and the £ was worth $2.40. In other words, the US$ was established as the keystone currency at the center of the world's monetary system.

The practical reasons for the continuing central position of the US$ are the several functions it has come to perform in the world. It is the main central reserve asset of many countries. It is the most used **vehicle currency** and **intervention currency**.

Liberia and Panama use the US$ as their official currency, and Israel uses it as a parallel currency to its shekel. One of the authors did some consulting and research in parts of South America during 1990; in most countries, and particularly in Argentina, the US$ was preferred to local currencies and even to other equally hard, convertible currencies. It has been the preferred medium of exchange and store of value also in Poland, the former Soviet Union, and many other countries.

Among the reasons the US$ is in great demand worldwide are its so-called **safe haven** aspect and its universal acceptance. Even if U.S. interest rates and investment opportunities were less attractive, many would still feel that money is safe in American securities or property. Inflation has been brought to a low level, and the country is seen as less likely than others to be invaded or to elect a socialist government. It is seen as a safe haven.

As to universal acceptance, if you have traveled internationally with US$s, you have found them welcome everywhere. A dramatic example was the scene in the film *The Killing Fields*, based on a true story, in which the Cambodian doctor/prisoner was asked by the Vietnamese officer for whom he worked to take the officer's young son and try to escape with the boy to Thailand. The officer gave the doctor a small emergency kit whose contents included a roll of American $20 bills.

Although the US$ remains the most used currency, the currencies of the other industrial countries are also important in world transactions and growing more so. This is particularly true of the German deutsche mark and the Japanese yen. And, although most large currency exchanges go through the US$ (see the ¥–£ example above), it is also possible to directly trade yen for pounds. The exchange rates for trading directly between non-US$ currencies are called **cross-rates**. See Figure 6–1 for the cross-rate quotes on July 19, 1994.

vehicle currency
A currency used as a vehicle for international trade or investment

intervention currency
A currency used by a country to intervene in the foreign currency exchange markets (e.g., using some of its U.S. dollar reserve to buy—and thus strengthen—its own currency)

safe haven
In reference to the U.S. dollar, a political concept based on the belief that the United States is less likely than most countries to elect a socialist or communist government or to be subjected to a military coup or revolution

cross-rates
Currency exchange rates directly between non-US$ currencies; usually determined by comparing the US$ exchange rates of the other currencies

FIGURE 6–1 Key currency cross-rates (late New York trading July 19, 1994)

	Dollar	Pound	SFranc	Guilder	Peso	Yen	Lira	DMark	FFranc	CdnDlr
Canada	1.3762	2.1310	1.03669	.78255	.40530	.01387	.00088	.87757	.25611	—
France	5.3735	8.321	4.0478	3.0556	1.58254	.05414	.00342	3.4265	—	3.9046
Germany	1.5682	2.4284	1.1813	.89173	.46185	.01580	.00100	—	.29184	1.1395
Italy	1569.6	2430.4	1182.34	892.50	462.24	15.814	—	1000.86	292.09	1140.5
Japan	99.25	153.69	74.765	56.437	29.230	—	.06323	63.289	18.470	72.12
Mexico	3.3955	5.2579	2.5578	1.9308	—	.03421	.00216	2.1652	.6319	2.4673
Netherlands	1.7586	2.7232	1.3247	—	.51792	.01772	.00112	1.1214	.32727	1.2779
Switzerland	1.3275	2.0556	—	.75486	.39096	.01338	.00085	.84651	.24705	.9646
United Kingdom	.64579	—	.48647	.36722	.19019	.00651	.00041	.41180	.12018	.46925
United States	—	1.5485	.75330	.56863	.29451	.01008	.00064	.63767	.18610	.72664

Source: *The Wall Street Journal*, July 20, 1994, p. C12.

Exchange Rates

Figure 6–2 shows that the price for one German deutsche mark was .6380. This means that one DM costs US$ 0.6380. For a less expensive currency, look at the Japanese yen, quoted at .010186; each yen costs that fraction of a dollar. Two currencies that cost more than US$1 on July 19, 1994, were the Bahrain dinar at $2.6522 and the British pound at $1.5487.

DM1.5675 = US$1.00

There is more to be learned from reading the exchange rates quotes. Using Figure 6–2, you will see the figure .6466 to the right of the "Germany (mark)" .6380 quote. Now look at the tops of the columns in which those numbers appear, and you will find the abbreviations, "Tues." and "Mon." As you probably have surmised, the .6380 quote is the price at the close of trading on Tuesday, July 19, 1994, while .6466 was the quote at the close of the previous trading day. Those two prices tell you the US$ strengthened vis-à-vis the German mark during Tuesday's trading; one DM cost US$.6380 at Tuesday's close, while it had cost more, US$.6466, at Monday's close.

There is another way of expressing the value relationships between currencies. Look again at the "Germany (mark)" line in Figure 6–2, and move to the right of the number about which we spoke. There you find another "Tues." and another "Mon." column; the quote in the "Tues." column is 1.5675, while it is 1.5465 under "Mon." These quotes inform us how many German marks it took to buy one US$ at the close of trading on each of those days, and they are the mirror images of the two quotes to the left. Observe that about two more German pfennig were needed to buy one US$ after Tuesday's trading than was needed after Monday's trading; in other words, the DM had weakened a little vis-à-vis the US$.

spot rate
The exchange rate between two currencies for delivery within two business days

Spot Rates. The **spot rate** is the exchange rate between two currencies for their immediate trade for delivery within two days. The rate on the same line as the name of the country is the spot rate. You will note in Figure 6–2 that the spot rate for German marks was .6380.

forward rate
The exchange rate between two currencies for delivery in the future, commonly 30, 60, 90, or 180 days

Forward Rates. The **forward rate** is the cost today for a commitment by one party to deliver to or take from another party an agreed amount of a currency at a fixed, future date. The commitment is a forward contract, and for frequently traded currencies such contracts are usually available on a 30-, 60-,

The New York foreign exchange selling rates below apply to trading among banks in amounts of $1 million and more, as quoted at 3 P.M. Eastern time by Bankers Trust Co., Dow Jones Telerate Inc., and other sources. Retail transactions provide fewer units of foreign currency per dollar.

FIGURE 6–2
Exchange rates (Tuesday, July 19, 1994)

Country (currency)	US $ Equivalent		Currency per US$	
	Tues.	Mon.	Tues.	Mon.
Argentina (peso)	1.01	1.01	.99	.99
Australia (dollar)	.7345	.7303	1.3615	1.3693
Austria (shilling)	.09068	.09187	11.03	10.88
Bahrain (dinar)	2.6522	2.6522	.3771	.3771
Belgium (franc)	.03096	.03137	32.30	31.88
Brazil (real)	1.0752688	1.0989011	.93	.91
Britain (pound)	1.5487	1.5615	.6457	.6404
30-day forward	1.5477	1.5609	.6461	.6407
90-day forward	1.5465	1.5605	.6466	.6408
180-day forward	1.5459	1.5603	.6469	.6409
Canada (dollar)	.7261	.7265	1.3772	1.3765
30-day forward	.7252	.7256	1.3789	1.3782
90-day forward	.7237	.7236	1.3817	1.3820
180-day forward	.7209	.7196	1.3871	1.3896
Czech. Rep. (koruna)				
Commercial rate	.0357603	.0359028	27.9640	27.8530
Chile (peso)	.002442	.002442	409.51	409.51
China (renminbi)	.115221	.115221	8.6790	8.6790
Colombia (peso)	.001226	.001226	815.90	815.90
Denmark (krone)	.1625	.1645	6.1540	6.0777
Ecuador (sucre)				
Floating rate	.000461	.000461	2169.00	2169.00
Finland (markka)	.19248	.19521	5.1955	5.1228
France (franc)	.18622	.18848	5.3700	5.3055
30-day forward	.18604	.18829	5.3753	5.3110
90-day forward	.18580	.18809	5.3821	5.3167
180-day forward	.18562	.18795	5.3873	5.3205
Germany (mark)	.6380	.6466	1.5675	1.5465
30-day forward	.6377	.6450	1.5681	1.5505
90-day forward	.6382	.6467	1.5670	1.5462
180-day forward	.6386	.6480	1.5660	1.5431
Greece (drachma)	.004222	.004280	236.85	233.65
Hong Kong (dollar)	.12945	.12945	7.7250	7.7250
Hungary (forint)	.0099810	.0100281	100.1900	99.7200
India (rupee)	.03212	.03212	31.13	31.13
Indonesia (rupiah)	.0004619	.0004619	2165.00	2165.00
Ireland (punt)	1.5279	1.5406	.6545	.6491
Israel (shekel)	.3298	.3298	3.0320	3.0320
Italy (lira)	.0006361	.0006447	1572.20	1551.14
Japan (yen)	.010086	.010168	99.15	98.35
30-day forward	.010106	.010191	98.95	98.13
90-day forward	.010149	.010240	98.53	97.66
180-day forward	.010230	.010333	97.75	96.78
Jordan (dinar)	1.4810	1.4810	.6752	.6752
Kuwait (dinar)	3.3792	3.3792	.2959	.2959
Lebanon (pound)	.000596	.000596	1678.00	1678.00
Malaysia (ringgit)	.3854	.3854	2.5947	2.5945
Malta (lira)	2.7397	2.7397	.3650	.3650
Mexico (peso)				
Floating rate	.2945074	.2943341	3.3955	3.3975
Netherland (guilder)	.5687	.5765	1.7583	1.7346
New Zealand (dollar)	.5990	.5971	1.6694	1.6748

continued

FIGURE 6–2
Exchange rates (Tuesday, July 19, 1994)—continued.

Country (currency)	US $ Equivalent		Currency per US$	
	Tues.	Mon.	Tues.	Mon.
Norway (krone)	.1459	.1477	6.8555	6.7721
Pakistan (rupee)	.0328	.0328	30.52	30.52
Peru (new sol)	.4679	.4679	2.14	2.14
Philippines (peso)	.03821	.03821	26.17	26.17
Poland (zloty)	.00004469	.00004453	22375.00	22456.00
Portugal (escudo)	.006203	.006277	161.22	159.30
Saudi Arabia (riyal)	.26667	.26667	3.7500	3.7500
Singapore (dollar)	.6612	.6620	1.5125	1.5105
Slovak Rep. (koruna)	.0319183	.0319183	31.3300	31.3300
South Africa (rand)				
Commercial rate	.2726	.2733	3.6685	3.6595
Financial rate	.2208	.2240	4.5300	4.4650
South Korea (won)	.0012387	.0012392	807.30	807.00
Spain (peseta)	.007738	.007824	129.24	127.82
Sweden (krona)	.1288	.1300	7.7615	76.900
Switzerland (franc)	.7539	.7664	1.3265	1.3048
30-day forward	.7541	.7667	1.3261	1.3043
90-day forward	.7549	.7676	1.3247	1.3027
180-day forward	.7570	.7699	1.3210	1.2988
Taiwan (dollar)	.037622	.037622	26.58	26.58
Thailand (baht)	.04005	.04005	24.97	24.97
Turkey (lira)	.0000325	.0000326	30776.20	30695.28
United Arab (dirham)	.2723	.2723	3.6725	3.6725
Uruguay (new peso)				
Financial	.199601	.199601	5.01	5.01
Venezuela (bolivar)	.00588	.00588	170.00	170.00
SDR*	1.46463	1.46680	.68277	.68276
ECU†	1.21820	1.23320	—	—

*Special drawing rights (SDR) are based on exchange rates for the U.S., German, British, French and Japanese currencies.
†European Currency Unit (ECU) is based on a basket of community currencies.

Source: *The Wall Street Journal*, July 20, 1994, p. C15.

90-, or 180-day basis. You may be able to negotiate with banks for different time periods or for contracts in other currencies.

Refer to the "Germany (mark) 30-day forward" quotation in Figure 6–2, and you will see that it is .6377. Compare that with the spot rate of .6380, and you can see that it would cost less in US$s to buy DMs for delivery in 30 days than for delivery today. The DM is said to be **trading at a discount** in the 30-day forward market. Look then at the 90- and 180-day trade reports and you see the DM costs .6382 cents for 90-day delivery and .6386 for 180 days, more expensive than the .6380 spot report. The DM is said to be **trading at a premium** in the 90- and 180-day trade reports.

trading at a discount
When a currency's forward rate quotes are weaker than spot

So Many Yen, So Few Pounds

trading at a premium
When a currency's forward rate quotes are stronger than spot

Look again at Figure 6–2, and you will see that it took about 99 yen to buy 1 US$, whereas less than 1 pound was enough for a dollar. Glancing up and down the column, you find that an Indonesian rupiah holder would need 2,165 rupiahs for US$1 and that a different number is required by holders of each of the other currencies quoted. It might seem that the fewer units of a currency required to buy a dollar, the "harder" or better that currency is compared to the others, but that is not necessarily correct.

As we have seen, the currencies of the world's major countries were set in value relative to the US$ at the end of World War II. Those exchange rates were the rates in the markets at that time; they were historical accidents. Since then, and particularly since 1973, the relative values of currencies, their convertibility, and their hardness or softness have been set by the supply and demand volumes of the foreign exchange markets. Those volumes are influenced by the policies of the various governments—their monetary and fiscal policies, their trade policies, and so on. Thus, the number of units of a currency per US$ on any given day does not indicate the relative strength of that currency. Many other factors must be examined to determine that.

The cost of a forward contract is the premium or discount compared to the spot rate. Whether there is a premium or a discount and its size depend on the expectations of the world financial community, businesses, individuals, and governments about what the future will bring. These expectations factor in such considerations as supply and demand forecasts for the two currencies, relative inflation in the two countries, relative productivity and unit labor cost changes, expected election results or other political developments, and expected government fiscal, monetary, and currency exchange market actions.

Bid and Asked Prices. When travelers or businesses contact a bank or an exchange agency to buy or sell a currency, they find a bid price and an asked price. The bid is the lower. The quotation for the French franc may be .16 bid and .17 asked. If the customer has francs to sell, the bank or agency is bidding—offering—16 cents (U.S. pennies) for each franc. If the customer wants to buy francs, the bank or agency is asking 17 cents, a higher price. The difference provides a margin—profit—for the bank or agency.

Commercial and Financial Rates. In Figure 6–2, you will note two spot reports for South Africa. They give commercial and financial rates. The commercial rate is for import/export transactions, and the financial rate is for all other transactions. In 1995, that was ended, and there is now only one rate for the rand.

Fluctuating Exchange Rates Create Risk

When your activities involve more than one country, you must deal with more than one currency. For example, an American company exporting to France will, in most cases, want to receive US$s. If credit is involved, payment is not made when the goods are delivered, and one of the parties will have a currency exchange risk. If the French importer agrees to pay French francs, then the American exporter bears a risk that the value of the French franc will fall and thus the French francs will buy fewer US$s when received than they would have at the earlier goods delivery date. On the other hand, if the French importer agrees to pay in US$ at a future time, then the importer bears that risk (see Figure 6–3.)

Company financial managers are not without weapons for dealing with this type of risk. These are presented in Chapter 20. A greater potential hazard for a company is that a country in which it has assets may institute exchange controls.

Currency exchange controls limit or prohibit the legal use of a currency in international transactions. Typically, the value of the currency is arbitrarily fixed at a rate higher than its value in the free market, and it is decreed that all purchases or sales of other currencies be made through a government agency. A black market inevitably springs up, but it is of little use to a finance manager, who usually wants to avoid breaking the laws of a country in which the company is operating. In addition, the black market is rarely able to accommodate transactions of the size involved in a multinational business.

CURRENCY EXCHANGE CONTROLS

FIGURE 6–3
Currency exchange risk

February 1	Goods delivery date exchange rate	August 1	Payment date exchange rate
Suppose:	US$1 = Ff6		US$1 = Ff6
	Whichever party bore the currency exchange risk, neither gained nor lost.		
Suppose:	US$1 = Ff6		US$1 = Ff7
	Whichever party bore the currency exchange risk lost. It now requires Ff7 to buy the US$1, which could have been bought for Ff6 at the time the goods were delivered.		
Suppose:	US$1 = Ff6		US$1 = Ff5
	Whichever party bore the currency exchange risk gained. It now requires only Ff5 to buy the US$1, which would have cost Ff6 at the time the goods were delivered.		

currency exchange controls
Government controls that limit the legal uses of a currency in international transactions

Thus, the company, along with all other holders of the controlled or blocked currency, must pay more than the free market rate if the government grants permission to buy foreign currency. If permission is not granted or if the cost of foreign currency is uneconomically high, the blocked currency can be used only within the country. This usually presents problems of finding suitable products to buy or investments to make within the country.

People will go to remarkable extremes to get blocked money out of exchange-controlled countries. A few years ago, in the west of France, an employee of a company operating in France strapped on a big money belt packed with large-denomination French franc banknotes. He then put on hang glider wings and glided into Switzerland, where he bought Swiss francs and deposited them in a Swiss bank account.

In New Delhi, the local manager of a major international airline gave a case of Scotch to a government official. Shortly thereafter, the agency for which that official worked granted the airline permission to use blocked rupees to buy almost US$20 million and transfer them to the airline's home country.

Those were extreme methods of converting blocked currencies to convertible currencies; the methods were, of course, also illegal. Most financial managers do not resort to such methods, but they can take legal steps to protect their firms from the adverse effects of currency exchange controls. Those steps are considered in Chapter 20.

Table 6–1 shows the currency exchange control laws and regulations of several countries.* You can see that the controls differ greatly from country to country and even within a country, depending on the type of transaction. As a generality, only the relatively rich industrialized countries have few or no currency exchange controls. They are a minority of the world's countries, and thus the great majority of the countries do impose exchange controls. The international businessperson must carefully study those laws and regulations both before and while doing business in any country. Even the industrialized countries may have some restrictions.

BALANCE OF PAYMENTS

Balance of payments (BOP) was discussed in some detail in Chapter 5, but we would be remiss not to mention it as a major financial force. The state of a nation's BOP will tell observant management much of value. If the BOP is slipping into deficit, the government is probably considering one or more

*The information in Table 6–1 comes from *Business International Money Report*, July 26, 1990, pp. 210–15. Many more countries are covered in that publication; we have presented only a few to give you an idea of the types of controls and how countries differ. As of 1995, *Business International Money Report* had not updated the table, but for the countries named in this book, there had been few changes, so the information is still accurate.

market or nonmarket measures to correct or suppress that deficit. Management should be alert for either currency devaluation or restrictive monetary or fiscal policies to induce deflation. Another possibility is that currency or trade controls may be coming. With foresight, the firm's management can adjust to the changing government policies or at least soften their impact.

On the export side, the company may start shopping for **export incentives**—government incentives to make exporting easier or more profitable. Lower-cost capital may be available if the company can demonstrate that exports will be boosted.

One of the most common export incentives is the financing of exports by a government agency that offers foreign buyers lower interest rates than they could get from other money sources. Sometimes the agency's loans are accompanied by an aid grant, which need not be repaid.

Countries that levy value-added taxes (see Chapter 11) are permitted by WTO rules to rebate them to exporters. This makes the exports less expensive and thus more competitive.

When firms are engaged in tough competition for major export contracts, their home governments may intervene to assist. Often, the potential customer is a government agency, and the intervention may be contact with the customer's decision makers by their counterparts in the home government.

export incentives
Tax breaks, lower-cost financing, foreign aid, or other advantages that governments give to encourage businesses to export and foreign customers to buy goods and services

TARIFFS OR DUTIES

The words *tariffs* and *duties* are used interchangeably. These can be high or low, and it is of great importance to business to minimize them. They are discussed in the "Trade Restrictions" section of Chapter 3 and as one of the legal forces in Chapter 11, but they can certainly be classified as financial forces and therefore should be mentioned in this chapter.

The European Union (EU) and the other groupings of nations that we discussed in Chapter 4 have lowered or abolished tariffs on trade among member-countries. Such developments add new dimensions to the decision-making processes of companies located outside the groupings. For example, would the expenses and legal and personnel problems involved in establishing operations within a grouping be justified by tariff savings?

TAXATION

Inasmuch as most international business is conducted by corporations, we are concerned with tariffs paid by and taxes levied on corporations. The point may be made that corporations don't pay taxes; they only collect them. In the end, people pay taxes.[1] The taxes may be collected from customers in higher prices, from employees in lower wages, from stockholders in lower dividends or capital gains, or from suppliers in smaller orders. However, even though corporations act as tax collectors rather than bearing the ultimate burden, it is very much in their best interest to minimize taxes. If a corporation can achieve a lower tax burden than its competitors, it can lower prices to its customers or make higher profits with which to pay higher wages and dividends. The price of its stock tends to rise, and it can be a better customer for the suppliers of its components and raw materials.

All of this is true for all corporations, but international companies have more taxes—more countries—to consider, and therefore more risks. They also have more opportunities to save taxes.

Different Taxes in Different Countries

In almost every country, the income tax is the biggest revenue earner for governments. Then there are sales or value-added taxes on goods or services, capital gains taxes, property taxes, and social security. A company must study carefully the tax laws of each country in which it operates. This subject is dealt with further in Chapter 11, and in Chapter 20 we shall see how financial

TABLE 6–1 Comparative table of worldwide exchange controls

Country (currency)	Regulatory Environment	Borrowing from Abroad	Incoming Direct Investment	Incoming Portfolio Investment
Argentina (austral, A)	Two FX* tiers since October; official rate for trade and foreign loans; free market rate for other transactions.	Terms must be fixed in advance, with minimum of 1 year.	Amounts under $5 million and equity injections under 30% of firm's capital freely permitted.	Freely permitted for listed shares of amounts under $2 million.
Chile (peso, $)	Ongoing liberalization; official FX rate set by Banco Central used for most transactions.	Registration and approval of loan required.	Investments over $5 million or in certain sectors require approval.	Freely permitted.
China (renminbi, RmB)	Severe FX shortage; new foreign exchange centers offer minimal volume and high premiums.	A few local entities may borrow abroad, subject to restrictions.	Time-consuming approval process; minimum foreign equity, 25%.	No markets exist.
Egypt (pound, £E)	All transactions are at the free market rate, except basic commodity imports, traditional exports (e.g., cotton), and oil company transactions. These are at a rate of E0.7:US$1.	Permitted for new projects if within approved financing plan and for ongoing projects if they generate FX to service the debt.	Approval required; freely given in sectors needing foreign expertise or capital.	Approval required; foreign ownership limited in banking, insurance; priority given to export-oriented and import-substitution projects.
France (franc, F)	In the process of eliminating remaining controls.	Freely permitted.	Freely permitted, but advance notification required so authorities can check source of funds.	Regulations gradually being relaxed.
Germany (deutsche mark, DM)	Extremely liberal	Freely permitted.	No approval needed; stringent antitrust laws should be considered.	Freely permitted.
Hong Kong (dollar, $)	All controls abolished in December 1972.	Freely permitted.	Freely permitted; local business-registration procedures must be followed.	Freely permitted.

managers can sometimes use different tax regimes and other measures to lower their taxes legally. Figure 6–4 (page 200) shows the tax revenues as a percentage of GDP* for OECD nations.

The amount of taxes paid is affected by inflation. At one time, some thought that inflation was a problem limited to LDCs and that industrialized countries need not worry about it. Recent experience has shown how erroneous that view was.

INFLATION

The phenomenon of increasing prices for almost everything over a period of time is familiar. Contagious inflation was probably the major cause of the end of the unprecedented world economic boom that lasted from the end of World War II until 1973. As prices of internationally traded goods rose because of a combination of rising demand and increased money supplies in all the DCs, inflation fever spread from one DC to the others.[2]

---

*The GDP (gross domestic product) of a country is the gross national product minus net property invisible payments, such as dividends, interest, and royalty, paid to and received from other countries.

Remittance of Dividends and Profits	Remittance of Interest and Principal	Remittance of Royalties and Fees	Repatriation of Capital	Documentation for Remittances
Freely permitted at free market rate; heavy taxes on excess over 12% of capital base.	Freely permitted at commercial rate for approved loans.	Freely permitted at free market rate; fees must reflect market value.	Fully remittable 3 years after initial investment at free rate.	Authorization forms must be filed with the CB.[†]
Freely permitted.	Freely permitted for registered loans.	Freely permitted for approved contracts.	Freely permitted for full amount after 3 years.	Requests must be filed with the CB.
FX income and expense must be balanced before remitting.	FX income and expense must be balanced before remitting.	Limited to 4% and 10-year period; low FX priority for fees.	Freely permitted, but FX shortage makes conversion difficult.	Onerous and complex requirements.
Approval required; 20% reserve required; firms without FX to cover remittance must apply to banks for FX allocation.	Freely permitted if the project generates sufficient FX to cover payment; if not approval required.	Freely permitted if the project generates FX for payment; if not, approval required.	Allowed after 5 years, to be remitted in 5 equal annual payments; exceptions sometimes made.	Accountant's certificate of source of funds and proof of tax payment required.
No restrictions if minimum capital and reserve requirements met.	No restrictions on bonds or loans; prepayment requires approval.	No restrictions, but the CB requires the account number.	Freely permitted, if repatriated within 3 months of liquidation.	Notification needed; local bank must run transaction.
Freely permitted.	Freely permitted.	Freely permitted.	Freely permitted.	Notification required for statistical purposes.
Freely permitted.	Freely permitted.	Freely permitted.	Freely permitted.	No official requirements.

continued

Inflation's Effects on Interest Rates

Inflation is clearly a financial force external to companies that finance managers must deal with as best they can. Almost every company must borrow money occasionally, and the inflation rate determines the real cost of borrowing. Real interest rates are found by subtracting inflation from the nominal interest rates. Figure 6–5 shows the difference between the real and nominal rates in 15 countries. When borrowed money is repaid in the future after inflation, it is worth that much less to the lender and, of course, is that much cheaper to the borrower.

Figure 6–6 illustrates that most of the OECD countries have succeeded in lowering their inflation rates since 1992. Turkey is the worst exception, while Greece has seen the greatest decline.

Monetary and Fiscal Policies Affect Inflation

Nations may conduct their monetary policies and fiscal policies in ways that cause inflation or cut it. *Monetary policies* control the amount of money in circulation, whether it is growing and, if so, at what pace. *Fiscal policies* address the collecting and spending of money by governments. What kinds of taxes at what rates? On what and in what amounts does the government spend money?

TABLE 6–1 *Continued*

Country (currency)	Regulatory Environment	Borrowing from Abroad	Incoming Direct Investment	Incoming Portfolio Investment
India (rupee, Rs)	Strict controls; managed FX rate; parallel market exists, at 15–20% premium.	Approval required; borrowing usually limited to capital investments.	Approval required; maximum foreign equity; 40% in most cases.	Limited to authorized mutual funds.
Japan (yen ¥)	Liberalization continuing; controls persist in certain areas (e.g., netting).	Freely permitted; must be reported to Ministry of Finance.	3 months' prior notice required.	Notification usually required.
Nigeria (naira, N)	Highly controlled; two different exchange rates—interbank rate and FEM‡ rate. FEM rate determined at fortnightly auctions.	Subject to Finance Ministry approval.	Approval needed from Finance Ministry and Ministry of Internal Affairs; limits on foreign equity vary, 100% ownership not allowed.	Finance Ministry approval required.
Saudi Arabia (riyal, Sr)	No restrictions are placed on the inward or outward movement of funds.	Freely permitted.	Freely permitted	Freely permitted.
Switzerland (franc SwF)	Controls usually avoided, but government has applied restrictions in the past.	Freely permitted.	Freely permitted, except for a few public services.	Freely permitted for registered shares.
United Kingdom (pound sterling, £)	All controls have been removed.	Freely permitted.	Freely permitted, although takeovers scrutinized by Department of Trade.	Freely permitted.
United States (dollar $)	Virtually no controls	Freely permitted.	Freely permitted in most sectors; some states have their own restrictions.	Freely permitted in most sectors.

*Fx = Foreign exchange, †CB = National central bank; ‡FEM = Foreign exchange market.

Source: *Business International Money Report*, July 26, 1990. This table includes only a partial listing. For a more comprehensive list of countries and restrictions, see the *Business International Money Report*.

Successful policies have two common denominators: (1) they remove artificial economic controls, such as wage and price controls, and (2) they apply fiscal and monetary restraint. The restraint includes lower taxes and slower growth in the nation's money supply.[3]

Japan, Germany, and the United States have had relatively good records in keeping inflation down in recent years. At the other extreme, many believe the infamous hyperinflation of the German mark in 1923 is the world's record. It is not. That dubious distinction belongs to the Hungarian pengö; inflation in Hungary in 1946 was a thousand times worse than the earlier German inflation. In 1939, 1 US$ bought 3.38 Hungarian pengös; in July 1946, the same dollar was worth 500 million trillion pengös. Never before or since has so much official money been worth so little.

Most Latin American countries have inflation troubles, although not as drastic as the Hungarian example. From 1970 into the 1990s, the worst inflation in Latin America occurred in Bolivia in 1985 at a rate of 11,750 percent. That far outstripped Brazil, in second place with 3,118 percent in 1990.

In a dramatic turn around, Bolivia slashed its inflation to only 8.5 percent in 1993, and in that year, Brazil replaced Bolivia at the top of the Latin inflation league with 1,933 percent. Chile is a Latin American economic

Remittance of Dividends and Profits	Remittance of Interest and Principal	Remittance of Royalties and Fees	Repatriation of Capital	Documentation for Remittances
Approval required; no ceiling on amount.	Freely permitted for approved loans.	Approval required; generally restricted to 4% of sales.	Approval required; amounts may be limited.	Onerous; FX must be obtained from authorized banks.
Freely permitted.	Freely permitted for approved loans.	Freely permitted for approved contracts; tax authorities monitor rate changes.	Freely permitted.	Handled by FX banks; mainly for reporting purposes.
Finance Ministry approval required; frequent delays. No ceilings if paid out of current-year after-tax profits.	Finance Ministry approval required.	Finance Ministry approval required; royalties limited to 1% of sales, fees to 2% of pretax profits.	Finance Ministry approval required, followed by authorized FX dealer's approval.	Onerous and complex requirements; transfers via authorized dealers only.
Freely permitted.	Freely permitted.	Freely permitted.	Freely permitted.	No official requirements.
No restrictions, except for reserve requirements.	Freely permitted.	Freely permitted.	Freely permitted.	Only that needed for ordinary bank transactions.
Freely permitted.	Freely permitted.	Freely permitted.	Freely permitted.	No official requirements.
Freely permitted.	Freely permitted.	Freely permitted.	Freely permitted.	Foreign bank transaction records must be kept for 5 years.

success story, decreasing inflation from 505 percent in 1974 to 12.7 percent in 1993 while increasing per capita income substantially. Argentina reduced inflation from 3,080 percent in 1989 to 10.5 percent in 1993 while achieving a slight increase in per capita income; Mexico brought down inflation from 132 percent in 1988 to 9.8 percent in 1993, although Mexico's per capita income also came down.[4] Mexico's economic—and perhaps social—progress was thrown in to doubt by an accumulation of debt, which became evident in 1994 and a devaluation of its peso in December 1994. Inflation started back up in 1995.

Importance of Inflation to Business

Even within a single country, inflation is of concern to management. Should it raise capital at all, and if so, should this be done through equity or debt? High inflation rates encourage borrowing because the loan will be repaid with cheaper money. But high inflation rates bring high interest rates or may discourage lending. Potential lenders may fear that even with high interest rates, the amount repaid plus interest will be worth less than the amount lent. Instead of lending, the money holder may buy something that is expected to increase in value, thereby further fueling inflation.

Lenders have begun to use variable interest rates, which rise or fall with inflation, to shift the risk to the borrower. Of course, that risk requires the

FIGURE 6–4 Tax revenues as a percent of GDP, 1992

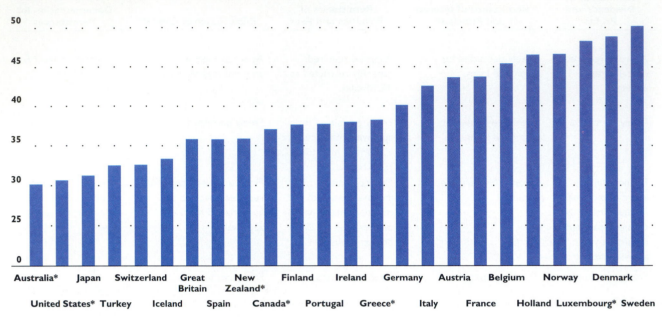

Australia*   Japan   Switzerland   Great   New   Finland   Ireland   Germany   Austria   Belgium   Norway   Denmark
                                      Britain   Zealand*

United States*   Turkey   Iceland   Spain   Canada*   Portugal   Greece*   Italy   France   Holland   Luxembourg*   Sweden

The ratio of tax revenues to GDP is a measure of a country's tax burden. Sweden continues to top the list of OECD nations, with taxes that amounted to 50 percent of GDP in 1992. This was, however, far less than its peak of 57 percent in 1990. Since 1980, Spain has seen its tax burden rise from 24 percent of GDP to 36 percent in 1992. Italians were also badly stung: their taxes went up from 30 percent to 42 percent of GDP over the same period. Norway is the only OECD country where taxes accounted for a smaller share of GDP last year than in 1980; yet at 47 percent it still has the fourth-highest tax burden. Australia, America and Japan continue to enjoy the lowest taxes in the OECD, with tax-to-GDP ratios of 29 percent (in 1991, the latest figure), 30 percent (in 1991), and 30 percent respectively.

*1991.

Source: *The Economist,* September 4, 1993, p. 103.

FIGURE 6–5 Nominal and real interest rates (April 5, 1994)

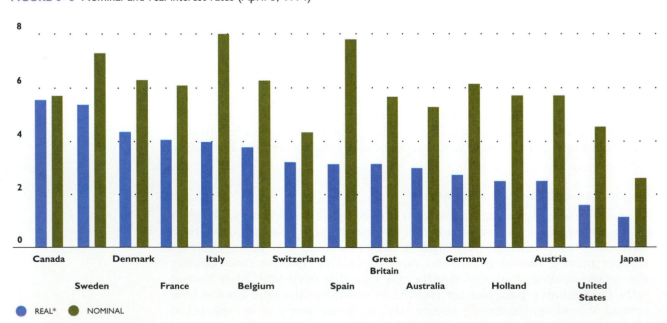

Canada   Denmark   Italy   Switzerland   Great   Germany   Austria   Japan
                                                             Britain

      Sweden   France   Belgium   Spain   Australia   Holland   United
                                                                                              States

● REAL*   ● NOMINAL

*Deflated by consumer price inflation.

Source: *The Economist,* April 9, 1994, p. 115.

FIGURE 6–6 Inflation rates in OECD countries *

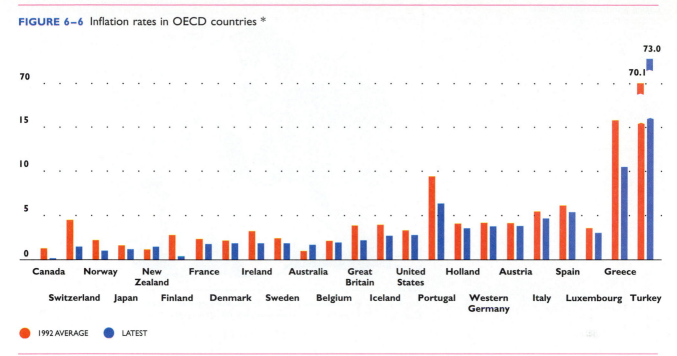

Since 1992 consumer price inflation has fallen in all but two of the 24 OECD countries shown in the chart. One exception is Australia, where inflation has risen from 1 percent to 1.9 percent. The other is Turkey, which has the highest inflation rate. At 73 percent., its consumer prices are rising more than seven times faster than in Greece, which has the second-highest rate. Since 1992, Greece has seen the biggest decline in its consumer price inflation rate: from 15.9 percent to 10.2 percent. Portugal (6.0 percent), Spain (5.0 percent), and Italy (4.2 percent) are the only other countries where inflation is running at more than 4 percent. Inflation is now below 2 percent in 11 countries. Prices are almost flat in Canada (where inflation is 0.2 percent) and Finland (0.4 percent).

* Consumer prices percentage increase on a year earlier.

Source: *The Economist*, April 30, 1994, p. 118.

borrower to be much more careful about borrowing. The original rate and any future changes are based on a reference interest rate, such as the U.S. prime rate or the London Interbank Offer Rate (LIBOR).

High inflation rates make capital expenditure planning more difficult. Management may allocate $1 million for a plant and be forced to pay much more to complete construction.

Inflation and the International Company.   All of this also applies to international business, with the complication that inflation rates differ in different countries. For this reason, management of an international company must try to forecast the rates for each of the countries in which it is active. The comparative inflation rates will affect the comparative currency values as the currencies of high-inflation countries weaken vis-à-vis the currencies of the countries with lower inflation rates. Management will try to minimize holdings of the weaker currencies.

Higher inflation rates cause the prices of the goods and services produced or offered by a country to rise, and thus the goods and services become less competitive. The company's affiliate in that country finds it more difficult to sell its products in export, as do all other producers there. Such conditions tend to cause balance-of-payments (BOP) deficits, and management must be alert to changes in government policy to correct the deficit. Such changes could include more restrictive fiscal or monetary policies, currency controls, export incentives, and import obstacles.

Coping with treble-digit inflation

Relative inflation rates affect where the international company raises and invests capital. Interest rates tend to be higher where inflation is higher, and high inflation discourages new investment for all of the reasons we have seen.

The Misery Index

The term *misery index* had its origin in American politics during the 1980 presidential campaign, when both inflation and unemployment were high. A simple total of a country's unemployment and inflation rates, it is a sort of indicator of economic success; the higher the total score, the worse the misery. Figure 6–7 is a comparison of the misery levels of various countries. It also indicates for each whether misery had increased or diminished from September 1989 to the end of 1990.

ACCOUNTING PRACTICES

Accounting practices vary widely from country to country. When dealing with its foreign subsidiaries, an international company must be prepared to use the accounting practices of the host country. It must then translate these results into home country practices so home country investors, creditors, and government regulators understand them. Accounting practices are financial forces, which is why we include the topic here. In Chapter 20 we shall examine some of management's solutions.

COUNTRIES WENT BUST

sovereign debt
The debt of a government or government agency

During the lending binge by banks to developing countries (LDCs) in the 1970s, the chairman of a major bank said, "Countries don't go bust." He was proved wrong, and a new and ominous financial force hit international business: **sovereign debt**. Contrary to many expectations, a number of developing countries found themselves unable to pay even the interest, much less the principal, on their debts. The sovereign debt crisis for Poland occurred in 1981; for Mexico, Brazil, Argentina, and others it occurred in 1982 and thereafter.

We examined this matter in Chapter 4 from the point of view of the International Monetary Fund (IMF) and the Bank for International Settlements (BIS). As discussed, the IMF has taken the lead role in trying to resolve

FIGURE 6–7 Misery index

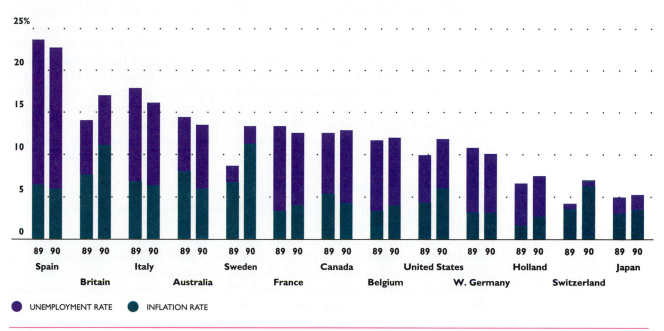

Source: *The Economist*, November 10, 1990, p. 123.

these crises as they arise, and the BIS has made bridge loans while the IMF was preparing to act.

Because these crises were so important and still affect international business, we shall discuss some of the background in this chapter. Also, we can suggest some possible solutions.

Causes of Increasing LDC Indebtedness

The immediate causes of the growing debts were the jumps in oil prices (crude oil represents an average of 16 percent of the merchandise imports of the nonoil LDCs). In 1973–74, oil prices quadrupled; they then doubled in 1979–80, and that increase from a higher base represented an even larger increase in absolute terms than the 1973–74 rise.

Those oil price increases made the already severe inflation that much worse, and the combination brought on a worldwide recession. The resulting drop in prices of primary nonoil commodities, which account for 45 percent of LDC (excluding Mexico and OPEC LDCs) exports, was a serious blow to LDCs' economies and abilities to pay their heavy debts. Mexico and the OPEC LDCs were hurt by the drops in oil prices beginning in 1981 as well as by uneconomic uses of the oil revenue and borrowed moneys they received during the 1970s and in the early 1980s.

Then, after the 1979–80 oil price jump, interest rates increased. That increase affected all new loans and the many existing loans that carried variable rather than fixed interest rates. Every 1 percent increase in US$ interest rates costs the LDCs some $2.5 billion per year more in interest payments.

On top of all that, the US$ began to strengthen in value in the foreign exchange markets during 1980. It continued up into 1985 and gained over 80 percent on a trade-weighted basis by March 1985. LDCs borrow mainly in dollars but export in many currencies, so the rise in the value of the US$

created new burdens; they had to earn that much more in deutsche marks, yen, francs, and so on to pay the US$ debts.

The US$ peaked in value in terms of the yen and West European currencies in February 1985. At that time, it began to move down in terms of those currencies, and by January 1988, it had fallen some 45 percent against the yen and the deutsche mark and 30 percent against the British pound. However, the US$ weakened little or even continued to gain in exchange for currencies of Canada, Asian newly industrializing countries (NICs), and Mexico and other Latin American countries, all of which are important trading partners of the United States. From 1988 into the 1990s, the US$ weakened in terms of the currencies of most OECD countries and the NICs, but the Latin American countries' currencies continued to weaken in US$ terms.

Debt Problem Solutions

The IMF, the BIS, national central banks, and commercial banks have been scrambling for solutions.

Short-Term Solutions.   The short-term answers have included rescheduling of debts that countries were unable to pay as they came due. But renegotiations are becoming more and more difficult. The BIS, the commercial banks, and the central banks are reluctant to come up with more money, and the IMF's resources are finite.

The debtor countries are balking at the stringent austerity programs being insisted on by the IMF. The economic growth of some LDCs has halted as they must use new money they receive from exports or loans to repay debt rather than for productive investments. Social unrest, including rioting, has broken out in several countries, notably Venezuela, Argentina, and Brazil.

The debtor countries are in desperate straits, but the industrialized countries are also being damaged. As the debtor-countries use money to repay debts, they do not buy goods and services from the developed countries. As a result, the developed countries have lost billions of dollars of export business and thousands of jobs.

The LDC debtor countries can reduce their debts only by exporting more than they import and thus running BOP surpluses. Some of the LDC debtor countries have been able to run BOP surpluses and make debt payments. However, these surpluses have been achieved as much by cutting imports as by expanding exports, and that has slowed or stopped economic development in the debtor countries and also hurt exports from countries that had been suppliers before the imports were curtailed.

Most of the LDC debtor countries have needed more money from private banks and international agencies and have been lent more. This has caused the debt burdens of these countries to increase at the same time that their economic development has been retarded, a process that cannot be sustained.

All is Not Lost.   The debt renegotiations accompanied by stringent austerity were part of the first phase of the world's efforts to solve the debt problems. This phase led to declines in living standards and curtailed economic growth and exports.

The second phase saw a growing awareness that short-term adjustment policies would not do the job alone. The problem for the LDCs was not the outstanding debt per se but the economic policies they followed and the cultural and attitudinal barriers they faced.

Recognizing this, the Baker Plan (named for then U.S. secretary of the treasury James Baker) called for market-oriented strategies to encourage growth and bring inflation under control. Measures were needed to rebuild confidence in and lure flight capital and new investment back to debtor countries.[5]

The Baker Plan was followed by the Brady Plan, which built on its predecessor and made debt relief conditional on the debtor country's pursuit of an IMF-approved economic adjustment program. The plan called on private banks for more money backed by funds from the IMF, the World Bank, and developed country governments.

Brady debt relief is provided through three mechanisms: (1) the exchange of old debt for new at a discount, (2) the exchange of old debt for new at a lower interest rate, and (3) the buying back of debt from creditor banks at a discount.[6]

Growing LDC Debt Market. The third mechanism has resulted in debtor countries buying their own debt and retiring it. The creditor banks have also sold LDC debt to other banks and investors, resulting in a large LDC debt market.[7] The debts are traded in bond forms, referred to as Brady bonds, and the prices of several of them went up sharply during 1993. Figure 6–8 shows the price increases on Brady bonds of nine countries and reasons for those increases.

Even as the Latin American debt market has flourished, LDC debt traders have begun to focus on Eastern Europe, and those prices also rose during 1993. The list of major players reflects how important the financial commu-

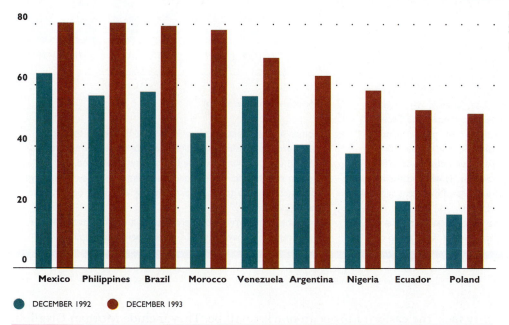

FIGURE 6–8
Secondary-market debt prices

● DECEMBER 1992   ● DECEMBER 1993

The prices of developing countries' restructured debts, or Brady bonds, increased sharply in 1993. Mexican bonds now fetch 82 percent of their face value, up from 65 percent at the end of 1992. The price of Morocco's debt has risen from 47 percent to 80 percent. And Polish debt has doubled in price, to 50 percent. According to Joyce Chang of Salomon Brothers, an investment bank, three factors have been at work. First, low yields on American Treasury bonds have made Brady bonds, which have higher yields, more attractive. Second, more investors, especially in Europe and Asia, are showing an interest in developing-country debt. And third, many countries' economic policies and performances are boosting investors' confidence: privatization plans and reduced inflation have helped lift the prices of Moroccan and Latin American debt.

Source: *The Economist,* December 18, 1993, p. 100.

Third World Debt That Is Almost Always Paid in Full

You think it would be utter folly to lend money to a Third World nation? So, how about a Third World vegetable stand?

U.S. development organizations are finding that some of the world's poorest entrepreneurs repay their debts at rates approaching 100 percent. To encourage grass-roots private business in Latin America, Asia, and Africa, these organizations are expanding programs that already lend thousands of these struggling entrepreneurs amounts ranging from $50 to several hundred dollars.

Tiny Third World businesses commonly repay these "microloans" faithfully because they crave the security of a favorable credit rating. This rescues them from the clutches of loan sharks—microloans typically charge the prevailing commercial loan rate—and lets them borrow again in hard times. The money helps them start or expand their businesses—selling vegetables, sewing, repairing shoes, making furniture, and the like—and boosts their local economies.

Their repayment performance shines when compared with that of many sovereign nations. It also looks good compared with a default rate of 17 percent by U.S. recipients of federally guaranteed student loans.

Though microlending has been around for years, it is now booming. With the decline of communism, U.S. development groups believe they are exporting free-market economics to tiny businesses that can fuel growth in the developing world.

"Micro-enterprise lending is the hottest thing in development since the Green Revolution. Everybody does it," says Accion International spokeswoman Gabriela Romanow. The Green Revolution sent farm output surging in many poor nations.

Romanow cites the case of Aaron Aguilar, an unemployed factory worker in Monterrey, Mexico, who borrowed $100 to buy clay and glazes for making figurines with his wife in their backyard. In six years, the couple took out and repaid five loans and built their business to 18 full-time employees.

Sometimes borrowers have to struggle against setbacks that might seem comical in the prosperous West. One group of

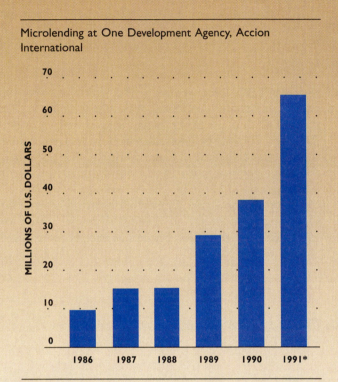

Microlending at One Development Agency, Accion International

*Projection.

Source: Accion International.

women in Cameroon received $100 from Trickle Up to start a rabbit-breeding business, but the rabbit ate her offspring, recalls Mildred Leet, cofounder of the U.S. agency. Undaunted, the women switched to chickens and made enough money selling eggs to branch out into tomatoes and tailoring, ultimately opening two shops, Leet says.

Some Third World commercial banks are taking note of poor entrepreneurs' repayment rates. Accion persuaded family-owned

nity feels the eastern European market will be. They include Morgan Grenfell, Indosuez, Salomon Brothers, Merrill Lynch, Chase Manhattan, J. P. Morgan, Chemical, and Continental Bank of London.

So far, debts of Russia and Poland are the most traded of the eastern European countries, with some Bulgarian issues thrown in. The other eastern European countries are described by one banker as "flies on the back of the elephant." Strangely enough, Latin American money has been going into Russia as investors seek yield and capital appreciation, demonstrating how small a financial world it has become.[8]

Multi Credit Bank of Panama City, Panama, to start making microloans two months ago. Isaac Btesh, a director and son of the founder, says the bank has lent $80,000 to 100 people so far on 60-day, rotating lines of credit—with a 100 percent repayment rate. "When we got in touch with Accion, we were incredulous," Btesh says. "We couldn't believe their figures. But everything they said is true."

Poverty lending has such promise that Multi Credit plans to make it the bank's number one activity, ahead of trade financing, consumer loans, and merchant loans, the official adds.

Average Loan: $303

Accion, a Cambridge, Massachusetts–based nonprofit international development group and a leader in the U.S. microloan movement, says it plans to increase its microlending this year to $66.5 million from $37.8 million in 1990 and $9.8 million five years ago. It says it plans to add 64,000 new clients, up from 40,000 last year and 9,000 five years ago. Its average loan is $303.

Accion's Romanow says the group, which serves Latin America, plans to expand the lending to a total of between $500 million and $1 billion over the next five years. The payback rate is 98 percent.

CARE, New York, perhaps the world's largest private international development group, says small economic activity development—primarily microlending—is its fastest-growing portfolio. "There's energy and creativity out there, people bootstrapping who aren't waiting for the next handout," says Larry Frankel of CARE.

Trickle Up, which makes thousands of $100 loans annually, says its budget rose to $1 million this year from $800,000 in 1989 after doubling almost every year throughout the 1980s. Trickle Up makes $100 loans in two installments of $50 each to small groups of individuals. "We feel private enterprise is the way to help the poor," says Leet, who founded Trickle Up with her husband in 1979. The group started a program in China in 1989 and moved into Laos, Vietnam, and Namibia last year.

Betsy Campbell, economic development manager of Westport, Connecticut–based Save the Children, says her group underwent a shift in the 1980s "from being primarily a charitable organization" to being one oriented towards helping profit-making activities. She says microlending to individuals in 20 nations is rising sharply, with more than $3 million in circulation at the moment. Repayment rates in most nations exceed 90 percent. "These people value access to credit so highly that default isn't really a problem," she says.

Some Third World banks, notably in Asia, have been making microloans for years. Grameen Rural Bank of Bangladesh is considered a pioneer. However, most such banks were set up with state support specifically to target the poor.

Some Detractors

Not every charity group in the United States has joined the microloan bandwagon. The Christian Children's Fund of Richmond, Virginia, sticks to relief efforts and to person-to-person sponsorships, in which a U.S. donor makes regular payments to an impoverished Third World child, for example, while Africare House in Washington, DC, focuses on helping cooperatives improve food production and health care.

Nor is the booming field of microlending without its detractors—or its controversies. David Munro, an official with Techno-Serve of Norwalk, Connecticut, says he prefers to work on a larger scale: "I also don't see [microlending] as passing on much in the way of skills."

And officials at the U.S. Agency for International Development (AID), which finances a big chunk of many private groups' overseas operations, say they support the principle of expanding poverty lending but oppose congressional efforts to mandate minimum levels. AID has more than doubled its micro-enterprise budget, which includes microlending, training, and other activities, to an estimated $114 million this year from $58 million in 1988.

Source: Brent Bowers, *The Wall Street Journal*, June 7, 1991, p. B 2.

200-Year History of Sovereign Debt Defaults.   Investment banks are preparing a new generation of sovereign credits. Enthusiasm for emerging-market bonds is so great that one banker said "I honestly think that any sovereign can access the market." Evidence of the correctness of that banker is the many dubious credit-risk countries in or about to enter the market. Among them are Jordan, Lebanon, Morocco, Slovakia, Slovenia, and Tunisia.

Investors and investment bankers seem to have forgotten or are ignoring history, which is littered with sovereign defaults. Since 1800, Ecuador has been through periods of default and rescheduling totaling 113 years. Greece is not far behind with 87 years in three separate periods of default. Such prestigious names as the Netherlands, Austria, Japan, and China have all failed to meet their external obligations at some point during the last two centuries. Egypt, which defaulted on its external debt in 1876, had spent more of its borrowed money on ballet dancers and the like than on public works.[9]

Of course, investors and investment bankers do not have to look 200 years into history to find sovereign deadbeats. We have been discussing efforts of lenders, investors, and sovereign borrowers to work themselves out of the debt crises that broke upon the world in the 1980s.

Some Positive Developments.   In 1991, the Paris Club, which is a group of Western creditor governments, forgave half of Poland's debt. That is a reduction of some $17.5 billion. Also in 1991, the United States forgave the Egyptian debt as an expression of thanks for Egypt's support in the war against Iraq. And in 1991, Chile floated a $320 million Eurobond issue that was fully subscribed by 20 European, Japanese, and North American banks. This was the first time since the Latin American debt crisis began in 1982 that a country from that region has obtained credit not arising from the crisis.[10]

Longer-Term Solutions.   A number of cures have been suggested. We shall list a few.

1. Borrowing countries will have to pursue policies ensuring that new money they obtain is used for economic growth rather than for consumption, capital flight, or overambitious government schemes or armaments.

2. Borrowers should build up reserves in good years to enable them to withstand the fluctuations in commodity export prices that are inevitable even if no more oil price shocks occur.

3. The developed countries must strive for their own economic growth and open their markets to LDC exports even though that means competition with some DC industries.

4. The IMF and other creditors must not try to enforce too stringent austerity measures on debtors. Social unrest and trade contraction must be avoided or at least minimized.

5. The IMF, the World Bank, and other agencies that aid LDCs must be assured of sufficient funding so that they can take long-term views.

6. Parts of the huge LDC external debts must be changed in form to types of equity. These could be ownership interests in projects being developed or shares of export earnings. Other parts of the debts should be lengthened in maturity, with interest rate ceilings applied. A novel use for sovereign debt was arranged by the debtor country, Senegal, and a Dutch organization, the Netherlands UNICEF Committee. The Dutch organization bought $24 million of Sengalese foreign debt and converted it into projects for women and children in the African nation. Child immunization and education of the street children of Dakar are two of the projects. Since begun by Senegal, similar "debt for children" swaps have benefited children in Madagascar, Jamaica, and the Philippines.[11]

7. The LDCs must relax their restrictions on foreign investments and on repatriation of profits from existing investments. They must encourage new money from foreign private sources—nonbank sources—because the banks are now overcommitted with LDC loans and are not likely prospects for new, economic growth money.

8. Blame for the debt crises belongs to several parties. The LDCs borrowed more than they could productively invest, and much of the borrowed money was wasted at home or corruptly sent abroad for the personal accounts of political leaders. The lending banks were encouraged to lend by the governments of their countries because the governments were thus relieved to that extent of foreign aid demands by the LDCs. But the banks must also bear a share of the blame; they made limited inquiries regarding the uses of the borrowed money or the soundness of the projects in which the money would be invested. They failed to get collateral to secure the loans, and one reason they were so casual was that the loans were almost always to governments or guaranteed by governments. They seem to have forgotten how wrong the banker we mentioned above was when he said during the 1970s "countries don't go bust."

Do the Wrong Thing, Young Bankers.   That was the title of an article Alan Abelson wrote for *Barron's* several years ago, pointing out that bankers during the 1960s and 1970s made fortunes by shoveling out loans that exploded into the debt crises and problems of the 1980s and 1990s. And indeed, the 1990s American bankers seem to be following his advice.

The same American banks that were brought to their knees by the Third World debt crises in the 1980s are at it again: lending huge sums to developing countries. Worse, they are doing it largely undetected by regulators and investors.[12]

The Biggest "Debtor"? The United States

After 70 years as the world's leading creditor, the United States has become the world's biggest debtor, which causes some to forecast adverse effects for America. Before looking at some of those effects, we should define the debt, see how it differs from the LDC debts, and put its growth into perspective with the growth rates of the other G7 countries.

U.S. Debt Defined.   Conceptually, the U.S. foreign debt—what the Department of Commerce calls a **net negative international investment position**—is the difference between the value of overseas assets owned by Americans and the value of United States assets owned by foreigners. These assets consist of commercial bank deposits, foreign exchange holdings, corporate securities, real estate, physical plant, and other direct investments. The popular press calls the difference *debt*, but the Commerce phrase, *net negative investment position*, is more accurate. One reason is the differences between LDC and U.S. debt.

net negative international investment position
The U.S. Commerce Department's description of what is commonly called the U.S. international debt.

Differences between U.S. and LDC Debt.   First, over $300 billion of the U.S. foreign-owned assets are obligations of the U.S. Treasury or U.S. corporations that are traded daily in world financial markets. Their worth, unlike the face value of an LDC debt, is subject to constant change.

Second, U.S. foreign assets are often measured at book value, which results in an estimated undervaluation of up to $200 billion. Book value would be cost when bought, which may have been years ago, less depreciation. Inflation alone would result in prices much higher than book if the assets were sold today.

Third, U.S. assets abroad reportedly earn more in interest and dividend per dollar of investment than foreign holdings earn in America.

Fourth, although current U.S. net liabilities are immense in absolute terms, they are relatively small in terms of other economic indicators. Total

U.S. debt amounts to 6 percent of U.S. GNP—as compared to over 40 percent for Brazil, upward of 50 percent for Mexico, and over 60 percent for Venezuela. The annual service cost of the U.S. debt is less than 1 percent of U.S. exports of goods and services. The corresponding cost for the three developing countries mentioned above averages more than 32 percent. As pointed out previously, Mexico, in particular, and Venezuela are bringing their debt loads down.

Fifth, the most distinctive characteristic of the U.S. foreign debt is its denomination in US$s. In theory, at least, this implies that the United States could discharge its foreign obligations at any time by printing the needed number of US$s. The LDCs, whose debt is not denominated in their own currencies, do not have that power.

Adverse Effects on America.   Having made the distinctions and comparisons, it cannot be denied that continuing growth of the U.S. net negative investment position will damage America. Financially, the interest cost of foreign debts is a drag on the balance of payments. Foreign creditors and suppliers may become reluctant to accept US$s. An increasing volume of world trade denominated in other currencies would cause losses for American companies and banks.

Politically, pressures could build for protectionism, exchange controls, or restrictions on capital flows. A large debtor country could not remain a major reserve currency economic power for long, and America's power to affect world events would erode.

In sum, although the U.S. net foreign obligations may not create for the U.S. economy or policies the same problems that LDC debts present LDCs, these obligations are very real dangers for the American world position. It has been suggested that increasing the very low current rate of U.S. national savings would be an important step toward a solution. The U.S. savings rate is by far the lowest among the G7 countries.[13]

SUMMARY

1. **Realize that much money is made, and lost, in the foreign exchange (FX) markets.** The foreign exchange (FX) markets are worldwide and collectively involve more money than any other market. On most days you can trade moneys 24 hours somewhere in the world.

2. **Understand FX quotations, including cross-rates.** FX information can be found in financial publications such as *The Wall Street Journal* or the *Financial Times* and the financial section of major newspapers. *The Wall Street Journal* lists 43 currencies in terms of their trades with the US$. The spot rate (for delivery in two business days) is reported for all 43. For the more heavily traded currencies, 30-, 90-, and 180-day forward rates are reported.

3. **Recognize currency exchange risks.** A currency exchange risk is borne by whomever is to receive a foreign currency or is to pay a foreign currency in the future.

4. **Expect currency exchange controls.** Most countries have less hard, convertible currencies than they need. They therefore ration them. Anyone wanting them must apply to a government agency, specifying how much is wanted and the use to which it will be put.

5. **Anticipate financial forces such as balance of payments, tariffs, taxes, inflation, fiscal and monetary policies, and differing accounting practices that affect business.** Business managers must be prepared to react to financial forces that can affect the business. These include balance-of-payments deficits, tariffs and other taxes, inflation, and fiscal or monetary policies of the host government. Accounting policies and practices differ from country to country, so businesses must conform to host country rules and translate the resulting numbers for them to be understood by people in the home country.

6. **Understand sovereign debt, its causes and solutions.** Sovereign debt is the debt of a government. Commercial and investment banks are in the business of lending money or underwriting bonds through which governments borrow money. As governments receive the borrowed money, corruption and inefficiency can arise, so that a lot of the money does not benefit the country or its people. Some of the debt is repaid, but much is rescheduled or swapped for assets or other uses.

7. **Know that a Third World vegetable stand might be a better credit risk than a Third World government.** Some of the best credit risks in LDCs are the small-business entrepreneurs.

8. **Know that Third World governments are not the only ones in debt; the largest debt is that of the United States.** The United States is the world's biggest "debtor." The U.S. Department of Commerce calls it a *net negative international investment position*.

KEY WORDS

- vehicle currency   189
- intervention currency   189
- safe haven   189
- cross-rates   189
- spot rate   190
- forward rate   190
- trading at a discount   192

- trading at a premium   192
- currency exchange controls   194
- export incentives   195
- sovereign debt   202
- net negative international investment position   209

QUESTIONS

1. In an American financial paper, you see the quotation: "Norway (krone) . . . 1478." What does that mean?

2. What is the difference between spot and forward currency markets?

3. What does it mean when a currency is said to be trading at a premium to the US$ in the forward market? Why would this happen?

4. If you agree to pay a certain amount of foreign currency to someone in six months, which of you bears the currency fluctuation risk? Explain.

5. What are currency controls? Why are they imposed?

6. What is the importance of the state of the BOP to private companies?

7. What are some ways in which inflation affects business decisions?

8. What two numbers must you know to compute real interest rates?

9. What is the LDC debt market, and why did it develop?

10. Might the huge U.S. debt have adverse consequences for America? Explain.

MINICASE 6–1   Management Faces a BOP Deficit

You are the chief executive officer of a multinational's subsidiary in a developing host country. The sub has been in business for about eight years, making electric motors for the host country's domestic market with mediocre financial results. Before you left the home country a month ago, you were told to make the sub profitable or consider closing it.

After a month in the host country, you have discovered that it is running a worsening BOP deficit and that the government officials are very concerned about the situation. They are considering various measures to stanch or reverse the deficit flow.

What measures might be adopted? Can you think of some ways your company might profit from them, or at least minimize damage?

CHAPTER

7

Economic and Socioeconomic Forces

There is so much information—some of it quite meaningless—put out every day about every conceivable aspect of the U.S. economy that companies, banks, and individual investors can find reasons to justify almost any move they make.

Paul Fabra, leading French economist, Columbus Dispatch, *August 9, 1994, p. 1–D*

CONCEPT PREVIEWS

After reading this chapter, you should be able to:

1. **understand** the purpose of economic analyses

2. **recognize** the economic and socioeconomic dimensions of the economy

3. **observe** how a nation's consumption patterns change over time

4. **identify** what factors cause changes in hourly wage rates expressed in dollars

5. **understand** the significance for businesspeople of the large foreign debts of some nations

6. **ascertain** the reasons for the worldwide downward trend in birthrates and its implications for businesspeople

7. **understand** indicative plans and their importance for businesspeople

Economic Analysis—Why India Is a New Market

"India Gets Moving."[a] "India Is Opening for Business." These are some of the headlines that managers are seeing in their business magazines. With a population of 883.6 million, the sixth-largest economy in the world (based on PPP), and the second only to China's economy in the developing world, India is said to have a rapidly growing middle class estimated to be between 100 million and 300 million people.[b] The National Council of Applied Economic Research, an independent research organization in India, estimated in 1990 that there was an upper-middle class of about 100 million people (20.2 million households) with an annual household income of more than $1,400. The organization's director describes a lower-middle class of 200 million people with annual household incomes of $700 to $1,400. They buy more than 75 percent of radios and toilet soap, over 60 percent of detergents, and 33 to 50 percent of all TVs, soft drinks, and shampoo sold.[c] • Is that really a middle class? These incomes are not as small in India as they would be in the United States because Indian living costs are lower. The director of the research council says, "Income-distribution numbers in India simply don't make sense when converted into dollars. Consumption patterns are a much better indicator."[d] • Managers unfamiliar with international economic data might look at India's GNP/capita of $310 and its population of 883.6 million and conclude that India is no market for their company's line of luxury pleasure boats. Who can afford a boat on $310 a year? An international economist, however, would know that these data are by no means sufficient to make such a decision. • Because GNP/capita is an average, some people in India must earn more than $310 annually. Are there people with sufficient income to purchase boats? How can the analysts find out? • (1) First, they know that because India's living costs are lower than American costs, its average income translated to U.S. dollars represents more purchasing power than is evident from the $310 GNP/capita figure. To find out how much, analysts can go to World Bank data and discover that, based on a comparison of the purchasing power of the two currencies, the $310 in rupees is equivalent to US$1,210.[e] This is the purchasing power parity (PPP) that we examined in Chapter 3. • (2) Next, they want to know the purchasing power of the middle and upper classes. They first obtain the GNP in dollars of equivalent purchasing power by multiplying the dollar equivalent of India's GNP/capita by the population: $1,210 × 883.6 million = $1,069.16 billion. • (3) How much of the gross national product goes to the middle and upper classes? Table 7–2 provides the percentage share of per capita expenditure accruing to percentile groups ranked by per capita expenditure.[f] The values for India are as follows: lowest 20 percent, 8.8; second quintile, 12.5; third quintile, 16.2; fourth quintile, 21.3; fifth quintile, 41.3; and highest 10 percent, 27.1. Assume that the fourth quintile

Sources: [a] "India Gets Moving," *Fortune*, September 5, 1994, pp. 100–4; [b] "India at the Crossroads," *East-West Report* (Vienna: Bank Austria, February 1994), pp. 52–53; [c] "India Is Opening for Business," *Fortune*, November 16, 1992, pp. 128–30; [d] Ibid., p. 130; [e] World Bank, *World Development Report 1994* (New York: Oxford University Press, 1994), p. 220; [f] Ibid., p. 220; [g] "India Gets Moving," p. 104.

represents the upper-middle class and the fifth quintile represents the upper class. The upper-middle class has 21.3 percent of the consumer expenditures and the upper class has 41.3 percent. Assuming that the distribution of consumer expenditures represents the distribution of income, then the upper-middle class has 0.213 × \$1,069.16 billion = \$227.73 billion and the upper class has 0.413 × \$1,069.16 billion = \$441.56 billion. The income of the highest 10 percent is 0.271 × \$1,069.16 billion = \$289.74 billion. • (4) The next step is to determine the per capita income for specific class segments:

$$\text{Population per quintile} = \frac{883.6 \text{ million}}{5} = 176.72 \text{ million persons.}$$

$$\text{Upper-middle class per capita income} = \frac{\$227,730 \text{ million}}{176.72 \text{ million persons}} = \$1,289.$$

$$\text{Upper-class per capita income} = \frac{\$441,560 \text{ million}}{176.72 \text{ million persons}} = \$2,499.$$

$$\text{Per capita income of highest 10 percent} = \frac{\$289,740 \text{ million}}{88.36 \text{ million persons}} = \$3,279.$$

• (5) Then, using the five people per household figure of the research council, analysts can estimate the per capita income for each segment:

$$\text{Upper-middle class household} = 5 \times \$1,289 = \$6,445.$$
$$\text{Upper-class household} = 5 \times \$2,499 = \$12,495.$$
$$\text{Highest 10 percent} = 5 \times \$3,279 = \$16,395.$$

Add to this purchasing power another 20 to 50 percent coming from the underground economy, the result of India's high taxes that have made tax evasion the national pastime.[g] It appears that there is a sizable market in India for the firm's pleasure boats after all.

Among the most significant uncontrollable forces for businesses are the economic forces. How the scarce resources of land, labor, and capital are being allocated to the production and distribution of goods and services and the manner in which they are consumed are of paramount importance to managers. To keep abreast of the latest developments and also to plan for the future, firms for many years have been assessing and forecasting the economic conditions at the local, state, and national levels.

Even though the data published by governments and international organizations, such as the World Bank and the IMF, are not as timely or as accurate as business economists would like, these are what they have and they must work with them. However, economists do not work solely with government-published data. Private economic consulting specialists—such as Data Resources, Inc., Chase Econometric Associates, Business International, the Economist Intelligence Unit, and Wharton Economic Forecasting Associates—provide economic forecasts (some do industry forecasts as well) to which many multinationals subscribe. Other sources are various industry associations, which generally provide industry-specific forecasts to their members.

In addition, economists and marketers use certain economic indicators that they have found to predict trends in their industry. Pitney Bowes' Data Documents division, for example, uses changes in the growth of the U.S. GNP to predict the sales of its business forms because its sales have for years generally lagged changes in GNP growth by six months.[1] We shall discuss the use of market indicators in Chapter 14, Market Assessment and Analysis.

FIGURE 7–1 Impact of economic forecast on firm's functional areas

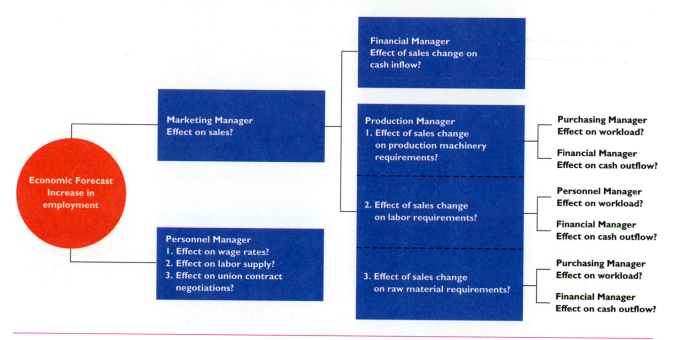

The purpose of economic analyses is, first, to appraise the overall outlook of the economy and then to assess the impact of economic changes on the firm. An examination of Figure 7–1 will illustrate how a change in just one factor of the economy can impact all the major functions of the company.

A forecast of an increase in employment would cause most marketing managers to revise upward their sales forecasts, which, in turn, would require production managers to augment production. This might be accomplished by adding another work shift, but if the plant is already operating 24 hours a day, new machinery will be needed. Either situation will require additional workers and raw materials, which will result in an extra workload for the personnel and purchasing managers. Should both the raw materials and labor markets be tight, the firm will probably have to pay prices and wage rates that are higher than normal. The financial manager may then have to negotiate with the banks for a loan to enable the firm to handle the greater cash outflow until additional revenue is received from increased sales.

Note that all of this occurs because of a change in only one factor. Actually, of course, many economic factors are involved, and their relationships are complex. By means of an economic analysis, an attempt is made to isolate and assess the impact of those factors believed to affect the firm's operations.

When the firm enters overseas markets, economic analyses become more complex because now managers must operate in two new environments: foreign and international. In the foreign environment, not only are there many economies instead of one, but they are also highly divergent. Because of these differences, policies designed for the economic conditions in one market may be totally unsuitable for the economic conditions in another market. For example, headquarters may have a policy requiring its subsidiaries to maintain the lowest inventories possible, and the chief financial officer may decree that they make only foreign currency-denominated loans because of more

INTERNATIONAL ECONOMIC ANALYSES

TABLE 7–1
Annual rates of inflation for
selected developing
countries

Country	1993
Brazil	2,038%
Zambia	289
Turkey	66
Uruguay	54
Peru	49
Kenya	46
Ecuador	45
Venezuela	38
Ghana	25
Jamaica	21

Source: *Monthly Bulletin of Statistics* (Washington, DC: United Nations, August 1994), pp. 186–92.

favorable interest rates. For nations whose annual inflation rates are low (0 to 15 percent), these policies usually work well. But what about for countries such as Brazil, with a 1993 inflation rate of 2,038 percent, or Zambia, with 289 percent? The last thing headquarters wants is for the subsidiaries in these countries to have cash or foreign currency–denominated loans, so the policy for markets with high inflation rates will be just the reverse of what it is for countries with low inflation rates. Table 7–1 illustrates that the chief financial officer has more than just Brazil and Zambia to be concerned about.

Besides monitoring the foreign environments, economists must also keep abreast of the actions taken by components of the international environment, such as regional groupings (EU, EFTA) and international organizations (UN, IMF, World Bank). American firms are very attentive to the EU's progress in reaching its goals and to the impact this will have on EU–U.S. trade relations. They are also following closely the UN's progress in developing world pollution standards, health standards, and so forth. Any of these actions can seriously affect firms.[2]

International economic analyses should provide economic data on both actual and prospective markets. Also, as part of the competitive forces assessment, many companies monitor the economic conditions of nations where their major competitors are located, because changing conditions may strengthen or weaken their competitors' ability to compete in world markets.

Because of the importance of economic information to the control and planning functions at headquarters, the collection of data and the preparation of reports must be the responsibility of the home office. However, foreign-based personnel (subsidiaries and field representatives) will be expected to contribute heavily to studies concerning their markets. Data from areas where the firm has no local representation can usually be somewhat less detailed and are generally available in publications from national and international agencies.[3] The reports from central or international banks are especially good sources for economic information on single countries. Other possible sources are the American chambers of commerce located in most of the world's capitals, the commercial officers in U.S. embassies, the United Nations, the World Bank, the International Monetary Fund, and the Organization for Economic Cooperation and Development.[4]

Dimensions of the Economy

To estimate market potentials as well as to provide input to the other functional areas of the firm, managers require data on the size and the rates of change of a number of economic and socioeconomic factors. For an area to be a potential market, it must have sufficient people with the means to buy a firm's products. Socioeconomic data provide information on the number of people, and the economic factors tell us if they have purchasing power.

Economic Dimensions.   Among the more important economic dimensions are GNP, distribution of income, personal consumption expenditures, personal ownership of goods, private investment, unit labor costs, exchange rates, inflation rates, and interest rates.

GNP.   Gross national product, the total of all final goods and services produced, and gross domestic product (GNP less net foreign factor incomes) are the values used to measure an economy's size. GNPs range from $5.9 trillion for the United States to $44 million for Sãotao Tomé and Príncipe (in the Gulf of Guinea off the coast of Gabon). What is the significance of GNP for the international businessperson? Is India, with a GNP of $272 billion, a more attractive market than Denmark, with $134 billion?

Imagine the reaction of managers who receive a report containing Figure 7–2, which shows a high *real* growth rate of **gross domestic product (GDP)** projected for Asia, at an annual rate of 6 percent. They will want to examine the data for individual countries in the area and compare growths with their subsidiaries' growths. The data might indicate that some markets where they have no operations need to be investigated. Of course, this is only the initial step. To compare the purchasing power of nations, managers also need to know among how many people this increase in GNP or GDP is divided.

> **gross domestic product (GDP)**
> *The total value of all goods and services produced domestically, not including (unlike GNP) net factor income from abroad*

GNP/Capita.   The not altogether satisfactory method of employing GNP/capita to compare purchasing power reveals that Denmark is far ahead of India, with $25,930 versus $310. In other words, although India's pie is twice as big as Denmark's, there are 170 times as many people to eat it.

What can we learn from GNP/capita? As we saw in Chapter 3, we can generally assume that the higher its value, the more advanced the economy. Generally, however, the rate of growth is more important to marketers because a high growth rate indicates a fast-growing market—for which they are always searching. Frequently, given the choice between investing in a nation with a higher GNP/capita but a low growth rate and a nation in which the conditions are reversed, management will choose the latter.

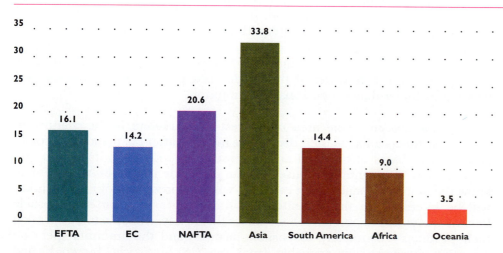

FIGURE 7–2

Five-year real projected growth in GDP (cumulative percentage change 1995–1999)*

*EFTA—European Free Trade Association; EC—European Community; NAFTA—North American Free Trade Agreement. Figure 7–2 serves only as an example.

Although differences in GNP/capita do tell us something about the relative wealth of a nation's inhabitants, the information is somewhat misleading because few of them have the equal share indicated by what is an arithmetic mean. This first crude estimate of purchasing power must be refined by incorporating data on how the national income is actually distributed.

income distribution
A measure of how a nation's income is apportioned among its people, commonly reported as the percentage of income received by population quintiles

Income Distribution.   Data on **income distribution** are gathered by the World Bank from a number of sources and published yearly in the *World Development Report*. Note that data in Table 7–2 refer to the distribution of the total income of the entire household rather than the per capita income except where noted. This distinction is important to market analysts because households with low per capita income are frequently large households with a high total income, while households with a lower total income are often smaller households with higher per capita income. Unfortunately, only a few countries gather data on the distribution of per capita income.

Despite the difficulties associated with income distribution studies, such as inconsistent measuring practices and wide variations in the representativeness of samples, the data provide some useful insights for businesspeople:

1. They confirm the belief that, generally, income is more evenly distributed in the advanced nations, although there are important variations among both developed and developing nations.

2. From comparisons over time (not shown), it appears that income redistribution proceeds very slowly, so that older data are still useful.

3. These same comparisons indicate that income inequality increases in the early stages of development, with a reversal of this tendency in the later stages. This is true for developed, developing, and socialist nations. The fact that the middle quintiles are growing at the expense of the top and bottom 20 percent signifies an increase in middle-income families, which are especially significant to marketers.

Contingent on the type of product and the total population, either situation (relatively even or uneven income distribution) may represent a viable market segment. For example, although Costa Rica's GNP is $6.2 billion, the fact that just 20 percent of the population receives over 50 percent of that income (10 percent gets 34.1 percent) indicates that there is a sizable group of people who are potential customers for low-volume, high-priced luxury products. On the other hand, the market is rather small (2.9 million population) for low-priced goods requiring a high sales volume.

This simple calculation based on GNP, total population, and income distribution may be all that is required to indicate that a particular country is not a good market; however, if the results look promising, the analyst will proceed to gather data on personal consumption.

discretionary income
The amount of income left after paying taxes and making essential purchases

Personal Consumption.   One area of interest to marketers is the manner in which consumers allocate their disposable income (after-tax personal income) between purchases of essential and nonessential goods. Manufacturers of a certain class of essentials—household durables, for instance—will want to know the amounts spent in that category, whereas producers of nonessentials will be interested in the magnitude of **discretionary income** (disposable income less essential purchases), for this is the money available to be spent on their products. Fortunately, disposable incomes and the amounts spent on essential purchases are available from the *UN Statistical Yearbook*, and discretionary income may be obtained by subtracting the total of these items

Country	Lowest 20 Percent	20–40 Percent	40–60 Percent	60–80 Percent	Highest 20 Percent	Highest 10 Percent
Australia (85)	4.4%	11.1%	17.5%	24.8%	42.2%	25.8%
Bangladesh (88–89)*	9.5	13.4	17.0	21.6	38.6	24.6
Belgium (78–79)	7.9	13.7	18.6	23.8	36.0	21.5
Botswana (85–86)	3.6	6.9	11.4	19.2	58.9	42.9
Brazil (89)†	2.1	4.9	8.9	16.8	67.5	51.3
Canada (87)	5.7	11.8	17.7	24.6	40.2	24.1
Chile (89)†	3.7	6.8	10.3	16.2	62.9	48.9
China (90)†	6.4	11.0	16.4	24.4	41.8	24.6
Colombia (91)†	3.6	7.6	12.6	20.4	55.8	39.5
Costa Rica (89)†	4.0	9.1	14.3	21.9	50.8	34.1
Denmark (81)	5.4	12.0	18.4	25.6	38.6	22.3
Finland (81)	6.3	12.1	18.4	25.5	37.6	21.7
France (89)	5.6	11.8	17.2	23.5	41.9	26.1
Germany (88)‡	7.0	11.8	17.1	23.9	40.3	24.4
Ghana (88–89)	7.0	11.3	15.8	21.8	44.1	29.0
Guatemala (89)†	2.1	5.8	10.5	18.6	63.0	46.6
Hong Kong (80)	5.4	10.8	15.2	21.6	47.0	31.3
Hungary (89)†	10.9	14.8	18.0	22.0	34.4	20.8
India (89–90)*	8.8	12.5	16.2	21.3	41.3	27.1
Indonesia (90)*	8.7	12.1	15.9	21.1	42.3	27.9
Israel (79)	6.0	12.1	17.8	24.5	39.6	23.5
Italy (86)	6.8	12.0	16.7	23.5	41.0	25.3
Ivory Coast (88)*	7.3	11.9	16.3	22.3	42.2	26.9
Jamaica (90)*	6.0	9.9	14.5	21.3	48.4	32.6
Japan (79)	8.7	13.2	17.5	23.1	37.5	22.4
Korea, Republic of (88)	7.4	12.3	16.3	21.8	42.2	27.6
Malaysia (89)†	4.6	8.3	13.0	20.4	53.7	37.9
Mexico (84)†	4.1	7.8	12.3	19.9	55.9	39.5
Morocco (90–91)*	6.6	10.5	15.0	21.7	46.3	30.5
Netherlands (88)	8.2	13.1	18.1	23.7	36.9	21.9
New Zealand (81–82)	5.1	10.8	16.2	23.2	44.7	28.7
Norway (79)	6.2	12.8	18.9	25.3	36.7	21.2
Pakistan (84–91)*	8.4	12.9	16.9	22.2	39.7	25.2
Peru (85–86)*	4.9	9.2	13.7	21.0	51.4	35.4
Philippines (88)*	6.5	10.1	14.4	21.2	47.8	32.1
Poland (89)*	9.2	13.8	17.9	23.0	36.1	21.6
Singapore (82–83)	5.1	9.9	14.6	21.4	48.9	33.5
Spain (88)	8.3	13.7	18.1	23.4	36.6	21.8
Sri Lanka (90)*	8.9	13.1	16.9	21.7	39.3	25.2
Sweden (81)	8.0	13.2	17.4	24.5	36.9	20.8
Switzerland (82)	5.2	11.7	16.4	22.1	44.6	29.8
United Kingdom (88)	4.6	10.0	16.8	24.3	44.3	27.8
United States (85)	4.7	11.0	17.4	25.0	41.9	25.0
Venezuela (89)†	4.8	9.5	14.4	21.9	49.5	33.2
Zimbabwe (90–91)*	4.0	6.3	10.0	17.4	62.3	46.9

TABLE 7–2

Percentage share of household incomes by percentile group of households

Note: Numbers in parentheses indicate year of study.
*Data refer to per capita expenditure.
†Data refer to per capita income.
‡Federal Republic of Germany before unification.

Source: *World Development Report,* 1994 (Washington, DC: World Bank, 1994), Table 30, pp. 220–21.

TABLE 7–3

Consumption patterns for selected countries, 1992 (1980)

	Private Consumption Expenditures/ Capita(US$)		Percentage of Private Consumption Expenditures					
Country			Food and Beverages		Clothing		Household Durables	
Switzerland	$20,391	($ 8,636)	23.7	(25.4)	4.1	(4.8)	3.3	(4.2)
Japan	16,833	(4,740)	18.9	(22.6)	6.4	(7.2)	6.8	(5.8)
United States	16,235	(6,438)	11.2	(14.5)	6.0	(6.7)	9.3	(9.6)
Sweden	15,241	(5,629)	18.2	(21.4)	6.4	(7.4)	8.4	(9.1)
Germany	14,941	(5,819)	19.7	(22.5)	8.0	(9.1)	9.3	(9.7)
Denmark	14,250	(6,283)	18.3	(21.6)	5.4	(5.9)	9.6	(9.2)
Norway	13,651	(5,264)	22.8	(24.7)	6.8	(8.8)	8.2	(12.5)
Italy	13,586	(2,937)	18.9	(26.7)	10.0	(11.4)	9.5	(9.5)
France	13,497	(5,568)	18.0	(20.2)	6.3	(7.3)	7.5	(6.7)
Belgium	12,960	(6,123)	17.0	(19.7)	6.2	(8.1)	9.6	(10.2)
Netherlands	12,724	(5,558)	13.8	(17.4)	6.9	(7.9)	5.4	(7.1)
Canada	12,688	(5,109)	13.5	(16.9)	5.3	(6.9)	13.3	(14.9)
Australia	10,269	(5,686)	19.0	(22.1)	5.6	(7.0)	6.4	(7.7)
Greece	5,427	(2,278)	32.7	(40.4)	9.0	(10.1)	4.8	(6.0)
South Korea	3,627	(1,404)	34.8	(45.0)	4.4	(8.6)	7.7	(2.9)
Mexico	2,536	(1,290)	32.8	(33.5)	7.3	(10.8)	9.5	(13.2)
Ecuador	804	(755)	36.3	(33.2)	10.4	(10.5)	2.7	(3.3)
Philippines	621	(464)	55.1	(57.2)	3.7	(3.7)	3.1	(3.4)
Sri Lanka	420	(212)	51.2	(54.7)	5.9	(6.0)	2.7	(2.3)
India	182	(148)	52.3	(56.0)	10.0	(11.4)	7.7	(7.4)

Source: "Indicators of Market Size for 115 Countries," *Crossborder Monitor*, August 31, 1994, pp. 1–12; and United Nations, *Yearbook of National Account Statistics, 1993*.

from disposable income. More detailed expenditure patterns can frequently be found in economic publications. Table 7–3, which reproduces data found in *Crossborder Monitor* and *Yearbook of National Account Statistics* is an example.

Note how the consumption patterns have changed in only 12 years. With the exception of Ecuador, consumers in all the countries shown have decreased the percentage spent on food as their total consumption expenditures have increased. This follows Engle's law (19th century German statistician) that says, holding demographic factors constant, as income increases, the percentage of income spent on food decreases.* Notice that no country in Table 7–3 experienced an increase in spending on clothing and 65 percent of them spent a lower percentage on consumer durables.

As you would expect, a significantly higher percentage goes for food in the poorer nations, and less is spent on consumer durables. Interestingly, the clothing percentages do not vary much among nations—although would you expect the percentage spent on clothing in Italy to be over 50 percent more than in France?

Don't underestimate the importance of the small percentage differences among nations. Marketers do not—each percentage point is worth a large sum of money. To appreciate its value, try multiplying the total per capita consumption expenditure by 0.01 by the population. If U.S. consumers had spent 1 percent more on clothing in 1992, for example, this would have amounted to $16,235 × 0.01 × 255.4 million, or $41 billion greater sales for the clothing industry.

---

*Consumer expenditures are used here as a proxy for family income.

If You Want to Get Ahead, Get a Telephone

What is the best gauge for measuring a country's level of development? Is it (1) per capita income, (2) state of the construction industry, (3) density of pollution, or (4) number of telephones? If you selected number four you are right, according to the International Telecommunications Union (ITU). In a recent report, the ITU observed that the total number of telephones installed in a country can often provide a better barometer of economic development than even per capita income.

The corollary is that nations with widespread and efficient telephone systems also have highly developed economies and large disposable incomes. Conversely, countries with poor telephone service are often plagued with underdeveloped economies and low-income levels.

In using the number-of-telephones principle to assess a country's fortunes, it is interesting to look at the United States. Recent statistics show that there are 95 telephones for every 100 households; and Beverly Hills, California, and Washington, DC, have more telephones than people.

In contrast, Asian Development Bank (ADB) data show that in Asian countries, the telephone density per 100 population is only 2 compared to 5.5 in Latin America and 0.8 in Africa. In Bangladesh and Nepal, there is less than one (0.1) telephone per 100 persons.

Most developing countries thus have a nagging

Telephone lines: An economic indicator? (per 1,000 people)

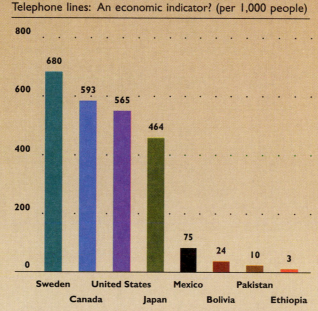

800

680
593
565
464

600

400

200

75
24
10
3

0

Sweden   United States   Mexico   Pakistan
Canada   Japan   Bolivia   Ethiopia

Jane Lewis/Tony Stone Images.

communications problem. For example, an ADB report points out that in Pakistan the telephone density is 0.5 per 100 population. But in rural areas, the situation is even worse, with as little as one telephone per 1,000 people. In fact, out of Pakistan's 45,000 villages, only about 1,900 have access to telephone services. One reason for this is that less than 15,000 villages have electricity.

Moreover, the demand for telephone service continues unabated in Pakistan, where people sometimes have to wait 10 years to obtain a telephone. The quality of service also leaves much to be desired. A sample survey revealed that only 25 percent of local and 15 percent of international call attempts were successful.

Poor telecommunications services take their developmental toll. According to Yoshiro Takano, a telecommunications specialist of the ADB, there is evidence of significant losses in efficiency incurred in agriculture, transportation, commerce, banking, government, tourism, and other sectors due to the lack or inadequacy of telecommunications services. Telecommunications also contribute to the quality of life by facilitating communication with kin and friends as well as access to emergency services.

Sources: Truman Becker, "If You Want to Get Ahead, Get a Telephone," *UN Development Forum,* November–December 1986, p. 7; and "Indicators of Market Size for 115 Countries," *Crossborder Monitor,* August 31, 1994, pp. 1–12.

TABLE 7–4 Per capita ownership or consumption of key goods and materials for selected countries

Country	1992 Private Consumption Expenditure ($/capita)	1992 Passenger Cars/000 Population	1992 Telephones/000 Population*	1993 TV Sets/000 Population	1992 Steel Consumed (kilos/capita)	1992 Trucks and Buses/000 Population	1992 Electricity (1,000 KWH/capita)
Europe							
France	$13,497	415	521	510	280	87	7.9
Germany	14,941	484	547	471	594	33	7.1
Italy	13,586	496	417	299	454	44	3.9
Sweden	15,241	416	680	431	351	37	16.8
Switzerland	20,391	466	606	333	294	46	8.1
United Kingdom	11,803	393	451	345	232	64	5.5
Middle East							
Egypt	549	21	39	91	91	7	0.8
Israel	7,712	166	355	288	213	34	4.5
Kuwait	4,300	259	173	400	111	66	12.8
Syria	1,823	7	42	54	14	10	0.8
Africa							
Ghana	363	6	3	16	n.a.	3	0.4
Kenya	222	5	8	10	8	6	0.1
Mauritius	1,727	48	73	143	n.a.	10	0.6
South Africa	1,794	87	88	87	110	34	3.7
Asia							
India	182	3	8	23	22	3	0.3
Japan	16,833	298	464	805	676	184	7.2
Pakistan	543	6	10	17	14	2	0.4
Philippines	621	7	10	109	42	2	0.4
South America							
Bolivia	589	34	24	64	7	7	0.3
Brazil	1,630	77	68	191	65	7	1.5
Colombia	880	21	84	165	28	20	1.1
Eastern Europe							
Romania	601	55	113	175	151	11	2.4
Hungary	2,369	196	125	414	149	22	3.0
Poland	919	137	103	260	150	27	3.5
North America							
Canada	12,668	477	593	635	373	137	18.3
Mexico	2,536	76	75	626	111	35	1.4
United States	16,235	561	565	843	392	178	12.0

n.a. = Not available.
*Telephone access lines.

Source: "Indicators of Market Size for 115 Countries," *Crossborder Monitor*, August 31, 1994, pp. 1–12.

Other indicators that add to our knowledge of personal consumption are those concerned with the ownership of goods. In addition, the per capita values for the consumption and production of strategic materials, such as steel and energy, serve as measures of a nation's affluence and level of development. As Table 7–4 illustrates, the more industrialized nations have considerably higher values for these indicators than do the developing nations. See the Worldview for one expert's opinion as to the most significant indicator.

TABLE 7–5 Average annual growth rate of consumption and investment for selected countries (percent)

Country	Government Consumption*		Private Consumption		Gross Domestic Investment†	
	1970–80	1980–92	1970–80	1980–92	1970–80	1980–92
Low-income countries						
Nigeria	11.4%	−3.4%	7.8%	−1.0%	11.4%	−6.6%
Burundi	3.5	4.5	4.5	4.2	16.3	3.0
India	4.1	6.8	2.8	5.1	4.5	5.3
Central African Republic	−2.4	−6.6	5.2	2.3	−9.7	2.5
Lower-middle-income countries						
Philippines	6.8	1.2	4.3	2.3	11.3	−0.6
Senegal	5.9	2.5	3.0	2.6	0.3	4.0
Chile	2.4	0.6	0.6	2.7	−2.1	9.2
Thailand	9.8	4.7	6.3	6.1	7.2	12.4
Upper-middle-income countries						
Korea, Republic of	7.4	6.9	7.4	8.3	14.2	12.7
Mexico	8.3	1.9	5.9	2.4	10.7	−0.8
Brazil	6.0	5.8	8.0	1.8	8.9	−0.3
Malaysia	9.3	3.5	7.5	5.3	10.8	5.5
Industrial market economies						
United Kingdom	2.4	1.2	1.8	3.6	0.2	4.5
Japan	4.9	2.3	4.7	3.6	2.5	5.8
United States	1.1	2.7	3.1	3.0	2.8	2.3
Germany‡	3.3	1.3	3.3	2.6	0.5	2.7

*Includes all levels of government and defense spending.
†Includes changes in inventory levels.
‡Data refer to Federal Republic of Germany before reunification.

Source: Adapted from *World Development Report, 1994* (Washington, DC: World Bank, 1994), pp. 176–77.

Private Investment. The amount of private investment (the part of national income allocated to increasing a nation's productive capacity) is another factor that contributes to the analysis of market size and growth. New investment brings about increases in GNP and the level of employment, which are signals of a growing market. A history of continual investment growth signifies, furthermore, that a propitious investment climate exists; that is, there are numerous profitable investment opportunities, and the government enjoys the confidence of the business community.

Table 7–5 shows the impact of the worldwide recession on the growth of investment. In the original table from which Table 7–5 was excerpted, 55 of the 88 countries suffered a smaller increase in private investment during the 1980–92 period than in the previous 1970–80 period. However, the increase was not evenly distributed over all nations—67 percent of the high-income nations experienced an increase during the 1980–92 period, but only 29 percent of the middle- and low-income nations did. Consumer spending also suffered from the recession, and only 17 nations had increases in private consumption in the 1980–92 period. The high-income nations in this group were Switzerland, Finland, the United Kingdom, Singapore, and New Zealand.

Similarly, the third area of expenditure, government spending, experienced global reduction. Governments of all nations in the original table reduced their rates of spending except 11, including the United States, Switzerland, India, Pakistan, and some developing nations of Africa. Notice the results of the austerity measures that Mexico had to take to service its huge foreign debt. In this environment, few investors were willing to put money in plants and inventories.

unit labor costs
Total direct labor costs divided by units produced

Unit Labor Costs. One factor that contributes to a favorable investment opportunity is the ability to obtain **unit labor costs** (total direct labor costs/units produced) lower than those currently available to the firm. Foreign trends in these costs are closely monitored because each country experiences a different rate of increase.

Countries with slower-rising unit labor costs attract management's attention for two reasons. First, they are investment prospects for companies striving to lower production costs, as discussed in Chapter 2; second, they may become sources of new competition in world markets if other firms in the same industry are already located there.

Changes in wage rates may also cause the multinational firm that obtains products or components from a number of subsidiaries to change its sources of supply.

> Zenith, the American TV and computer manufacturer, moved the production of its monochrome computer monitors from Taiwan to Mexico in 1992 because of the lower Mexican wage rates.

What are the reasons for the relative changes in labor costs? Three factors are responsible: (1) compensation, (2) productivity, and (3) exchange rates. Hourly compensation tends to vary more widely than wages because of the appreciable differences in the size of fringe benefits. Unit labor costs will not rise in unison with compensation rates if the gains in productivity outstrip the increases in hourly compensation. In fact, if productivity increases fast

TABLE 7–6 Labor compensation rates, 1989–1994*

| Country | Average Hourly Rate Including Fringe Benefits (US$) | | | | | | | | Relative Index (US = 100) | |
| | 1994 | | 1993 | | 1991 | | 1989 | | 1994 | 1989 |
	US$	Local	US$	Local	US$	Local	US$	Local		
Germany	$25.93	43.04	$25.56	42.30	$22.91	39.65	$17.75	33.39	150	124
Switzerland	23.00	34.27	22.66	33.49	21.69	31.14	16.73	27.38	133	117
Belgium	21.69	757.06	21.38	739.32	19.83	678.30	15.51	611.16	125	108
Norway	20.42	146.83	20.20	143.39	21.63	140.43	18.29	126.43	118	128
Japan	20.42	2084	19.20	2134	14.66	1974	12.53	1730	118	88
Austria	19.94	243.23	20.20	235.14	18.15	212.20	14.16	187.49	115	99
Netherlands	19.75	38.51	20.16	37.46	18.44	34.51	15.04	31.92	114	105
Denmark	19.55	127.47	19.12	124.00	18.26	116.97	14.49	106.11	113	101
Sweden	18.20	142.90	17.91	139.66	22.15	134.04	17.52	113.11	105	122
United States	17.30	—	16.79	—	15.58	—	14.32	—	100	100
Finland	17.25	95.58	16.56	94.82	21.25	86.11	16.85	72.39	100	125
France	16.53	93.89	16.31	92.41	15.26	86.17	12.54	80.02	96	88
Italy	15.79	25,719	15.97	25,116	18.60	23,081	14.41	19,770	91	101
United Kingdom	13.50	8.88	12.82	8.54	13.77	7.79	10.56	6.45	78	74
Ireland	12.10	8.29	11.80	8.03	12.08	7.48	9.66	6.81	70	67
Spain	11.14	1515	11.53	1470	12.20	1269	8.94	1059	64	62
Greece	6.92	1696	6.81	1559	6.82	1243	5.49	892	40	38
Portugal	4.19	782.9	4.60	741.4	4.24	614.6	2.97	467.4	24	21

*Dollar conversions are at average annual exchange rates.

Source: *Business Europe*, September 19–25, 1994, p. 2.

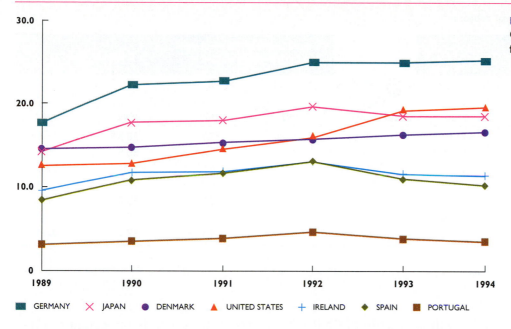

FIGURE 7–3
Comparison of labor costs for selected countries

enough, the unit costs of labor will decrease even though the firm is required to pay more to the workers.

Table 7–6 illustrates the rapidity with which labor compensation costs change. The United States had the highest hourly rate from 1982 until 1986, when it was surpassed by Switzerland, West Germany, and Norway. By 1989, it had dropped to 10th place behind Italy. In 1994, the United States was still in 10th place, but after Sweden. Italy had dropped to 13th in the rankings of international labor costs measured in U.S. dollars. See Figure 7–3 for a graphical presentation.

If you were to calculate the percentage changes in the hourly rates expressed in dollars and in the local currency, they would usually differ. The reason is that the change stated in dollars is the result of the real change in local currency plus that currency's appreciation or depreciation with respect to the dollar from one year to another. Let's make these calculations using the Finnish 1993 and 1994 hourly rates.

$$\frac{1994}{1993} \text{ hourly rate increase (\$)} = \frac{\$17.25}{16.56} = 1.042 \ (4.2\%).$$

$$\frac{1994}{1993} \text{ hourly rate increase (FM)} = \frac{95.58}{94.82} = 1.008 \ (0.8\%).$$

The rate increase in the Finnish markka (FM) is only 0.8 percent. Therefore, 81 percent [(4.2 − 0.8)/4.2] of the apparent increase in the dollar hourly cost is due to an increase in the dollar value of the FM from 1993 to 1994 and not to an increase in the hourly rate stated in Finnish currency.[5] If you wish to prepare a table of average wage costs for countries not included in Table 7–6, you will find a method for doing so in endnote 5 of this chapter.

Other Economic Dimensions.   We have mentioned only a few of the many economic indicators that economists study, and you learned about the importance to businesspeople of interest rates, balances of payments, and inflation rates in Chapter 6, Financial Forces. Which of the economic measures the analyst chooses to study will depend on the industry and the purpose of the study. Executives of an automobile manufacturer, for example, will want the economist's opinion as to where interest rates are headed and what is the rate

TABLE 7–7 Major international debtors

Country	Total Debt (\$ billions) 1992	External (\$ billions) 1980	Change in Debt since 1980 (percent)	Annual Interest Payments as a Percentage of Export Revenue 1992	1980	External Debt as a Percentage of GNP 1992	1980
Brazil	\$121.11	\$71.01	71%	9.2%	33.7%	28.5%	16.4%
Mexico	113.38	57.38	201	16.4	27.4	38.5	20.6
Indonesia	84.39	20.94	403	11.7	6.5	68.7	22.5
India	76.98	20.58	374	12.6	4.2	28.3	10.0
Argentina	67.57	27.16	249	18.7	20.8	33.7	7.2
China	69.32	4.50	1,540	4.2	1.5	15.7	n.a.
Turkey	54.77	19.12	286	13.3	14.9	47.9	22.4

n.a. = Not available.

Source: *World Development Report 1994*, pp. 200–1 and 206–7.

of growth of a nation's GNP. GNP, as you saw earlier, is important to other producers of industrial products, such as Pitney Bowes.

The large international debts of a number of middle- and low-income nations are causing multiple problems not only for their governments but also for multinational firms. Just look at the situation of the countries with the highest debts that are listed in Table 7–7. Note that there are no high-income nations, including the United States, with international debt.

Is this a problem for international bankers only, or should it concern multinational managements as well? Is it significant to global and multinational firms with subsidiaries in these countries that a high percentage of the countries' export earnings must go to service their foreign debts? Many analysts believe that annual interest payments greater than 10 percent of a nation's export revenue are a cause for concern.[6] If management agrees, then it will expect periodic reports on this situation from its economist. Let's examine the ramifications of these large foreign debts for an international firm.

If a large part of the foreign exchange a nation earns cannot be used to import components used in local products, then either local industries must manufacture them or the companies that import them must stop production. Either alternative can cause the multinational to lose sales if it has been selling the parts made in one of its home country plants to its subsidiary, a common occurrence because the home plant is usually more **vertically integrated** than its subsidiaries. A scarcity of foreign exchange can also make it difficult for the subsidiary to import raw materials and spare parts for its production equipment. If headquarters wants its affiliate to continue production, it may have to lend the foreign exchange and wait for repayment. Campbell Soup, Revlon, and Gerber closed their operations in Brazil because of this problem.[7] Other multinationals have resorted to barter or have begun to export their subsidiaries' products even though these actions have reduced exports or even local sales of their domestic plants.

Governments may impose price controls (which make it difficult for a subsidiary to earn a profit), cut government spending (which reduces company sales), and impose wage controls (which limit consumer purchasing power). The economic turmoil that follows can turn into a political crisis, such as occurred in Venezuela and Peru when rioting resulted after the presidents tried to impose austerity measures.

vertically integrated
Describes a firm that produces inputs for its subsequent manufacturing processes

An aspect of debt reduction that has interested some multinationals has been debt-for-equity swaps, which we discussed in Chapter 6. Argentina is one country that makes them. Foreigners have been able to buy Argentine dollar debt at a discount and convert it into Argentine currency at a rate closer to face value. They then invest the money in local firms. Campbell Soup took advantage of this situation to build a new meatpacking plant. The company purchased $60 million worth of Argentine foreign-debt paper in the world market at 17 percent of the par value. Argentina's central bank agreed to redeem the paper in Argentine currency at the equivalent of 30 cents on the dollar if the company used the money to build the plant. The debt-for-equity swap saved Campbell $8 million.[8] Grupo Visa, a Mexican conglomerate, reduced its foreign debt from $1.7 billion to $400 million with a private debt-for-equity swap. The company gave its foreign creditors a 40 percent share in the company in return for debt cancellation.[9]

Scarcity of foreign exchange can affect even those firms that merely export to nations with high foreign debt because the governments will surely impose import restrictions. When Latin American debt increased rapidly from 1981 to 1983, that region's share of U.S. exports dropped by one-third. To protect these export markets, firms had to extend long-term credit. From this you can see that managements will expect to receive information on the status of the foreign debt in nations where it is high in addition to the other economic data we have been examining. This is especially important now that the same American banks involved in the Third World debt crisis in the 1980s are once again lending huge sums to developing nations.[10]

Socioeconomic Dimensions.   A complete definition of market potential must also include detailed information about the population's physical attributes as measured by the socioeconomic dimensions. Just as we began with GNP in the study of purchasing power, we shall begin this section with an analysis of the total population.

Total Population.   Total population, the most general indicator of potential market size, is the first characteristic of the population that analysts will examine. They readily discover that there are immense differences in population sizes, which range from more than a billion inhabitants in China to less than 1 million each for 55 countries. The fact that many developed nations have less than 10 million inhabitants makes it apparent that population size alone is a poor indicator of economic strength and market potential. Switzerland, for example, with only 6.9 million people, is far more important economically than Bangladesh, with 114 million. Clearly, more information is needed; only for a few low-priced, mass-consumed products, such as soft drinks, cigarettes, and soap, does population size alone provide a basis for estimating consumption.

For products not in this category, large populations and populations that are increasing rapidly may not signify an immediate enlargement of the market; but if incomes grow over time, eventually at least a part of the population will become customers. Insight into the rapidity with which this is occurring may be obtained by comparing population and GNP growth rates (see Table 2–10, page 45). Where GNP increases faster than the population, there is probably an expanding market, whereas the converse situation not only indicates possible market contraction but may even point out a country as a potential area of political unrest. This possibility is strengthened if an analysis of the educational system discloses an accruement of technical and university graduates. These groups expect to be employed as and receive the wages of professionals, and when sufficient new jobs are not being created to absorb them, the government can be in serious trouble. Various developing nations already face this difficulty: Egypt and India are two notable examples.[11]

Age Distribution.   Because few products are purchased by everyone, marketers must identify the segments of the population that are more apt to buy their goods. For some firms, age is a salient determinant of market size; but unfortunately, the distribution of age groups within populations varies widely. Generally, because of higher birth and fertility rates, developing countries have more youthful populations than industrial countries. Figure 7–4 illustrates the tremendous difference in age distribution between developed and developing countries, which is the result of much higher birthrates in the developing nations. According to the World Bank, past and estimated average annual population percentage increases for nations grouped according to income are as shown in the table at the top of the next page.

FIGURE 7–4

Population by age and sex—1975 and 2000 (millions)

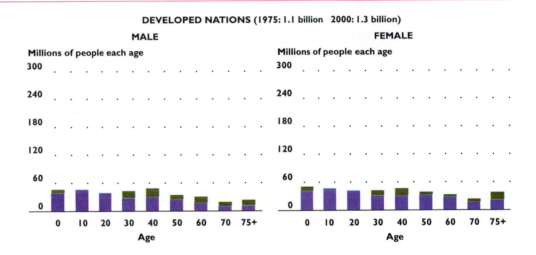

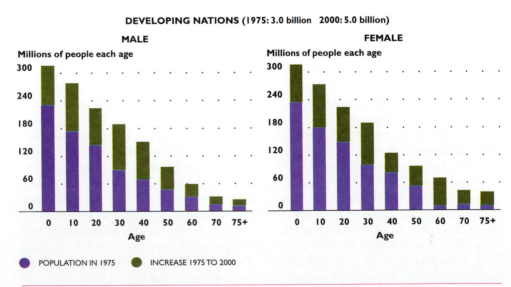

Source: Based on U.S. Bureau of Census projections.

	1970–80	1980–92	1992–2000
Low-income economies	2.2%	2.0%	1.7%
Middle-income economies	3.8	1.8	1.5
High-income economies	0.8	0.7	0.5

Source: *World Development Report, 1994* (Washington, DC: World Bank, 1994), pp. 210–11.

This situation is far from static, however, birthrates are decreasing worldwide. Of the 118 nations for which the United Nations provided information, only 9 countries from Africa experienced increases in their crude (born live) birthrates per thousand population over the 1970–92 period. Two were middle-income nations and seven were low-income nations.[12]

The population of developing countries, which now account for about 75 percent of the world's population, will rise to 80 percent by the year 2000. Figure 7–5 shows that of the 11 nations predicted to have over 100 million inhabitants by the year 2000, only 3 are industrialized; the rest are developing countries.

Significance for Businesspeople. What does this signify for businesspeople? In the developed nations, there will be a decrease in the demand for products used in schools and for products bought by and for children, a smaller market for furniture and clothing, but an increased demand for medical care and related products, tourism, and financial services. Firms confronted by a decreasing demand for their products will have to look for sales increases in the developing economies, where the age distribution is reversed. The high growth rates in the developing nations will provide markets for transportation systems, higher-yield food grains, fertilizers, agricultural tools, appliances, and so forth.

> Whirlpool, concerned about the decline in the number of householders aged 25 or less in the United States while noting the opportunities in overseas markets, acquired 53 percent of the Dutch electronics giant Philips' domestic appliance business in 1988. The acquisition enabled Whirlpool to become the world's largest major home appliance company, with manufacturing facilities in 11 countries and a distribution network covering 45 countries. In August 1991, Whirlpool bought the remaining 47 percent of the business from Philips.[13]

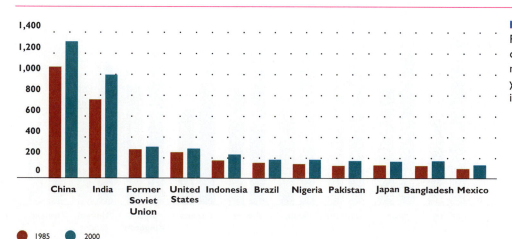

FIGURE 7–5

Population growth of countries with over 100 million inhabitants in the year 2000 (millions of inhabitants)

Many forces are responsible for reductions in birthrates. Governments are supporting family planning programs, to be sure, but there is ample evidence that improved levels in health and education along with an enhanced status for women, a more even distribution of income, and a greater degree of urbanization are all acting to reduce the traditional family size. In Mexico, for example, 71 percent of the women with seven or more years education practice contraception, but only 40 percent of those with no formal education do. In the Philippines, the percentages were 45 percent compared to 22 percent.[14] Experts claim that the combined effect of an effective family planning program and female education beyond the primary level is extremely powerful in reducing family size.[15]

While this is welcomed by governments in developing nations, declining birthrates are causing concern in the governments of industrialized nations. According to the World Bank's *World Development Report,* for over a decade (1980–92), the birthrates in developed nations have been considerably below the *replacement number* of 2.1 children. Of these countries, Australia's birthrate is the highest (1.4 percent). An increasing number of young Europeans are not getting married, and those who do are marrying later and having fewer children. By the year 2000, the present 9 percent unemployment rate in the European Union will be replaced by a shortage of workers. European governments will have to provide medical care and pensions for the 25 percent of their population that will be over 65 years old, and there will be fewer working taxpayers[16] (see Figure 7–6).

Japan's situation appears to be even more serious. Its fertility rate is only 1.57 per woman, well below the 2.1 population replacement value, and in the year 2025, Japan's population aged 65 and older will make up 25.7 percent of its population, whereas the same age group in the United States will amount to only 19.1 percent of the total population. The labor shortage has inflated wages to the point where the average manufacturing pay in Japan is $20.42 an hour as compared to $17.30 in the United States (see Table 7–6). By the year 2000, what had been the world's youngest industrial society will become the world's oldest.[17]

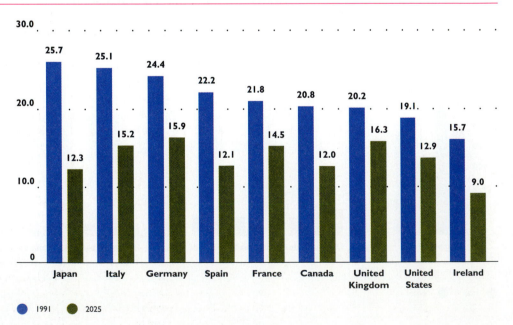

FIGURE 7–6
Percentages of elderly (over 65) in population

To counteract the shortage of workers, Japanese companies invested heavily in robots and raised their mandatory retirement ages to 60 from 55.[18] To attract younger employees, they reduced the large difference between the wages paid to the newly hired and the older workers and began to promote younger employees faster. They also were hiring more women.

However, the situation changed in the early 1990s. Slow growth in Japan coupled with similar conditions in its export markets resulted in factories with excessive capacity and too many employees. Instead of hiring, Japanese firms were laying off workers Japanese style: voluntary early retirement. In 1993, Japan Airlines, for example, offered retirement to employees only 35 years old.[19]

Early retirements and the fact that retirees are living longer are straining the social security systems of Japan and many other countries. In the industrialized nations, not only are social security system costs rising because of the growing number of retirees, but there are fewer people working and paying into the system to support them. However, in developing nations, just the opposite is occurring. The higher birthrates result in a younger population, as shown in Figure 7–4, and this reduces the dependency ratios and the costs to the workers supporting the sytem. Figure 7–7 shows the dependency ratios for selected industrialized and developing nations.[20]

Population Density and Distribution.   Other aspects of population that concern management are **population density** and **population distribution.** Densely populated countries tend to make product distribution and communications simpler and less costly than they are where population density is low; thus you might expect Pakistan, with 149 inhabitants per square kilometer, to be an easier market to serve than Canada (2.8 inhabitants/square kilometer) or Brazil (18.1 inhabitants/square kilometer).[21] The expectation,

population density
A measure of the number of inhabitants per area unit (inhabitants per square kilometer or square mile)

population distribution
A measure of how the inhabitants are distributed over a nation's area

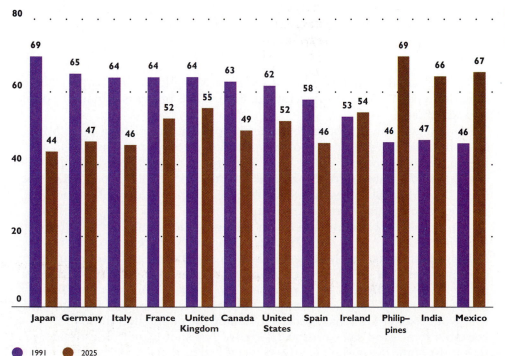

FIGURE 7–7
Dependency ratio per 100 people of working age

1991 ●   2025 ●

FIGURE 7–8 Population density

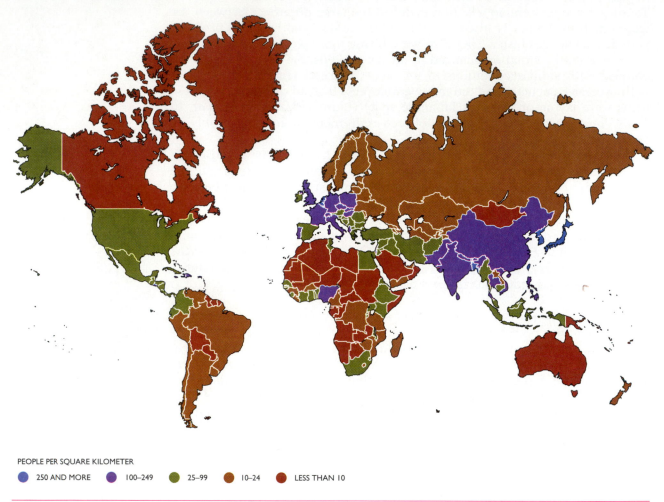

PEOPLE PER SQUARE KILOMETER

● 250 AND MORE   ● 100–249   ● 25–99   ● 10–24   ● LESS THAN 10

though, is another of those based on an arithmetic mean. We must know how these populations are distributed. Figure 7–8 presents a map of population densities.

One needs only to compare the urban percentages of total population to learn that Canada and Brazil possess population concentrations that facilitate the marketing process. While only 33 percent of Pakistan's population is urban, the percentages for Brazil and Canada are 77 and 78 percent, respectively. The physical forces, as we shall see in Chapter 8, contribute heavily to the formation of these concentrations.[22]

rural-to-urban shift
The movement of a nation's population from the rural areas to cities

An important phenomenon that is changing the population distribution is the **rural-to-urban shift**, which is occurring everywhere, especially in developing countries, as people move to cities in search of higher wages and more conveniences. This shift is significant to marketers because city dwellers, being less self-sufficient than persons living in rural areas, must enter the market economy. City governments also become customers for equipment that will expand municipal services to handle the population influx. Table 7–8 contains some good sales prospects. Figure 7–9 shows another estimate; note that most of the fast-growing cities projected to be megacities by the year 2000 are in developing nations.

1975		2000		**TABLE 7–8**
1. New York–Northeastern New Jersey	19.8	1. Mexico City	31.0	The most populous cities in the year 2000 (millions)
2. Tokyo–Yokohama	17.7	2. São Paulo	25.8	
3. Mexico City	11.9	3. Tokyo–Yokohama	24.2	
4. Shanghai	11.6	4. New York–Northeastern New Jersey	22.8	
5. Los Angeles–Long Beach	10.8	5. Shanghai	22.7	
6. São Paulo	10.7	6. Beijing	19.9	
7. London	10.4	7. Rio de Janeiro	19.0	
8. Greater Bombay	9.3	8. Greater Bombay	17.1	
9. Rhine–Ruhr	9.3	9. Calcutta	16.7	
10. Paris	9.2	10. Djakarta	16.6	

Note: Six of the largest urban centers will be in Asia, and none will be in Europe.

Source: United Nations.

An indicator of the extent of this movement is the change in the percentages of urban population. As Table 7–9 indicates, the greatest urban shifts are occurring in the low- and middle-income countries. In no country anywhere is there a net flow in the other direction.

Other Socioeconomic Dimensions.   Other socioeconomic dimensions can provide useful information to management. The increase in the number of working women, for example, is highly significant to marketers because it may result in larger family incomes, a greater market for convenience goods, and a need to alter the **promotional mix.** Personnel managers are interested in this increase because it results in a larger labor supply. It also signifies that changes may be required in production processes, employee facilities, and personnel management policies.

Data on the country's divorce rate, when available, will alert the marketer to the formation of single-parent families and single-person households, whose product needs and buying habits differ in many respects from those of a two-parent family (see Figure 7–10). In many countries, important ethnic groups require special consideration by both marketing and personnel managers.

> Canada, for example, has eight radio stations in five cities broadcasting 100 percent of the time to specific ethnic groups such as Italian, Ukrainian, German, Greek, and Chinese because more than 9 million of the country's 25 million people speak languages other than English and French. In addition, 8 television stations and 60 radio stations include some ethnic programs in their broadcast schedules.[23]

National Economic Plans

One other source of economic data that may prove useful to a firm, especially for its marketers, is the **national economic plans** that many countries publish. These range from the annual and five-year plans (in reality, budgets) used as production control instruments by the remaining communist nations, such as Cuba, Vietnam, and China, to the **indicative plans** of some free market economies. Instead of production targets, the five-year indicative plans contain the basic targets set by the government and some general policy statements on how the goals will be achieved. The government then attempts by means of the usual monetary and fiscal tools to create favorable conditions

promotional mix
A blend of the promotional methods a firm uses to sell its products

national economic plans
Plans prepared by governments stating their economic goals and means for reaching them, usually for periods of up to five years.

indicative plans
Forecasts made by governments with industry collaboration of the direction they expect the economy to take

FIGURE 7–9 25 megacities 1970–2000 (millions)

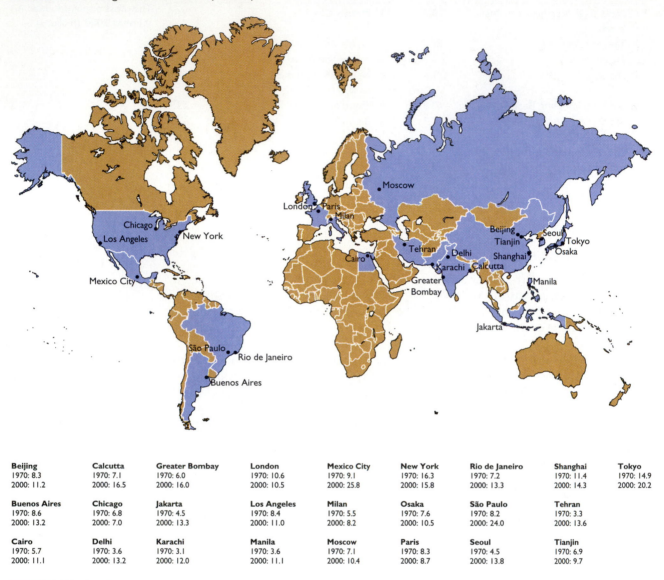

Beijing	Calcutta	Greater Bombay	London	Mexico City	New York	Rio de Janeiro	Shanghai	Tokyo
1970: 8.3	1970: 7.1	1970: 6.0	1970: 10.6	1970: 9.1	1970: 16.3	1970: 7.2	1970: 11.4	1970: 14.9
2000: 11.2	2000: 16.5	2000: 16.0	2000: 10.5	2000: 25.8	2000: 15.8	2000: 13.3	2000: 14.3	2000: 20.2

Buenos Aires	Chicago	Jakarta	Los Angeles	Milan	Osaka	São Paulo	Tehran	
1970: 8.6	1970: 6.8	1970: 4.5	1970: 8.4	1970: 5.5	1970: 7.6	1970: 8.2	1970: 3.3	
2000: 13.2	2000: 7.0	2000: 13.3	2000: 11.0	2000: 8.2	2000: 10.5	2000: 24.0	2000: 13.6	

Cairo	Delhi	Karachi	Manila	Moscow	Paris	Seoul	Tianjin	
1970: 5.7	1970: 3.6	1970: 3.1	1970: 3.6	1970: 7.1	1970: 8.3	1970: 4.5	1970: 6.9	
2000: 11.1	2000: 13.2	2000: 12.0	2000: 11.1	2000: 10.4	2000: 8.7	2000: 13.8	2000: 9.7	

Source: *Finance & Development*, December 1989.

for business so that the targets may be attained. This favoritism may be manifested in many ways, among which are special tax concessions to investors and foreign exchange allocations (when foreign exchange is controlled) to purchase imported capital equipment and raw materials.

TABLE 7–9
Rural-to-urban shift

	Percentages of Population in Urban Areas		
	1970	1992	Percentage Increase
Low-income countries	18%	27%	50%
Middle-income countries	46	62	35
High-income countries	74	78	5

Source: *World Development Report, 1994* (Washington, DC: World Bank, 1994), pp. 222–23.

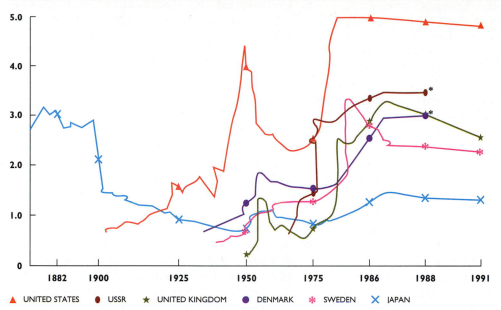

FIGURE 7-10
Changing divorce rates in selected countries

▲ UNITED STATES   ● USSR   ★ UNITED KINGDOM   ● DENMARK   ✱ SWEDEN   ✕ JAPAN

*Data not available after 1988.

Source: *U.N. Demographic Yearbook* 1992, pp. 318–320.

Information about national development plans and budgets is regularly reported in such publications as *Business International* and *Business America.* Commercial attachés in American embassies and the overseas American chambers of commerce are additional sources of information.

Industry Dimensions

Every firm is concerned about the general economic news because of its impact on consumer purchases, prices of raw materials, and investment decisions, but certain factors are more significant than others to a given industry or to a specific functional area of a firm. The size and growth trend of the automobile industry is of paramount importance to a tire manufacturer, for example, but is of no interest to an appliance manufacturer. Nor would the quantity of machine operators graduated by technical schools be useful to financial officers, although these data are of vital interest to human resources managers of manufacturing plants. Managers want data not only about the firm's industry but also about industries that supply and purchase from the company. The minicase at the end of this chapter illustrates the use of both macroeconomic and industry-specific data.

Industry studies are generally made by the firm's economists or its trade association, but they can also be purchased from independent research organizations, such as Fantus (New York) and The Economist Intelligence Unit (London). Government agencies, chambers of commerce, and trade publications such as *Advertising Age* publish them as well. Many international banks publish free newsletters containing useful economic data.

SUMMARY

1. **Understand the purpose of economic analyses.** To keep abreast of the latest economic developments and also to plan for the future, firms regularly assess and forecast economic conditions at the local, state, and national levels. When they enter international

operations, the economic analysis increases in complexity because managers are operating in two new environments: foreign and international. There are more economies to study, and these economies are frequently highly divergent.

2. **Recognize the economic and socioeconomic dimensions of the economy.** The various functional areas of a firm require data on the size and rates of change of a number of economic and socioeconomic factors. Among the more important economic dimensions are GNP, GNP/capita, distribution of income, personal consumption expenditures, private investment, unit labor costs, and financial data, such as exchange rates, inflation rates, interest rates, and the amount of a nation's foreign debt. The principal socioeconomic dimensions are total population, rates of growth, age distribution, population density, and population distribution.

3. **Observe how a nation's consumption patterns change over time.** Marketers must know how consumers allocate their discretionary incomes since this is the money being spent on their products. Because consumers' spending patterns change over time as their incomes increase, businesspeople must study their buying patterns.

4. **Identify what factors cause changes in hourly wage rates expressed in dollars.** Hourly labor rates, especially when stated in U.S. dollars, change rather rapidly. There are three factors responsible: (1) real changes in compensation, (2) changes in productivity, and (3) changes in exchange rates.

5. **Understand the significance for businesspeople of the large foreign debts of some nations.** Large foreign debts may indicate that the government will impose exchange controls on its country's businesses. If a large part of the country's export earnings go to service its external debt, there will be little remaining for use by firms in the country to pay for imports of raw materials, components used in their products, and production machinery. The government could impose price and wage controls. There is also the possibility that firms can buy some of the discounted debt to obtain local currency at a favorable exchange rate.

6. **Ascertain the reasons for the worldwide downward trend in birthrates and its implications for businesspeople.** Birthrates are declining in nearly all nations because (1) governments are providing family planning programs, (2) women are continuing their education and marrying later, and (3) a greater degree of urbanization is enabling women to become employed and self-supporting, which contributes to a delay of marriage.

7. **Understand indicative plans and their importance for businesspeople.** National economic plans, for which no American counterpart exists, provide an insight as to government expectations. In communist nations, national plans are often the equivalent of market studies. Many developed and developing nations use indicative plans to set out their goals and provide some general policy statements as to how they will be achieved.

KEY WORDS

- gross domestic product (GDP)   217
- income distribution   218
- discretionary income   218
- unit labor costs   224
- vertically integrated   226
- population density   231

- population distribution   231
- rural-to-urban shift   232
- promotional mix   233
- national economic plans   233
- indicative plans   233

QUESTIONS

1. Management learns from the economic analysis of Country A that wage rates are expected to increase by 10 percent next year. Which functional areas of the firm will be concerned? Why are they concerned?

2. Check the *World Development Report* in the library to learn which country in each income group (low-, medium-, and high-income economies) is the leader in the rate of GNP per capita growth over the last 15 to

20 years. In each case, is the rate of increase greater than the population growth? What can you deduce from that?

3. What common problem does the use of GNP per capita and population density values present?

4. Choose two poor nations from Table 7–2 that appear to be good candidates for high-priced luxury goods even though their GNP/capita ratios as shown in Table 2–10 are low. What is the approximate size of the population segment with the highest income? How can you use this information?

5. If the clothing industry association to which your firm's Swiss subsidiary belongs could mount a successful promotional program to cause the Swiss to increase their clothing expenditures by 1 percent annually, what would be the total increase in sales for the clothing industry?

6. In 1994, Switzerland had the second-highest average hourly compensation rate.
   a. What was the percentage increase in dollars?
   b. What was the percentage increase in the labor cost stated in Swiss francs?
   c. What percentage of the change when stated in dollars was due to changes in the franc–dollar exchange rate?

7. The staff economist has given to the chief financial officer a report on the foreign debt situation of Argentina, as shown in Table 7–7. What concerns might the chief financial officer have?

8. What would be the concerns of the chief financial officer if he or she were to receive the information on annual inflation rates from Table 7–1?

9. What problems is the reduction in birthrates causing for European governments.

10. Choose a country and a product, and estimate the market potential of the product based on the economic and socioeconomic dimensions. What other environmental forces should you investigate?

MINICASE 7–1   World Laboratories

World Laboratories (WL) is a large multinational pharmaceutical manufacturer specializing in the production of ethical pharmaceuticals (available to the public only by prescription). These products are characterized by a high degree of research, and because of the limited protection offered by patents, they have a relatively short product life. WL does make some over-the-counter products, but these comprise only about 20 percent of total company sales.

The South American division manager must make a sales forecast for ethical drugs, which he will use to set quotas for the six countries in his division that have manufacturing plants. These products produce about 75 percent of the total sales in each market. At present, WL's market share and sales by category of drug (pediatric, general, geriatric) in each country are as shown in table below.

Total health care has grown faster than world population and world income since 1970. A conservative average of the total amount per capita spent on health care, both private and public, for pharmaceuticals in South America is 20 percent. This is lower than in the United States and Europe; but in government clinics, medicine is generally offered without charge or at a substantial discount from the price charged in pharmacies. According to WL's subsidiaries the patients at clinics pay, on average, 40 percent of the drugs' listed price when those given at no charge are included. Obviously, private drugstores that get only 40 percent off list (60 percent of list price is their cost) cannot compete. WL, however, still earns a 12 percent profit based on its selling prices when it sells to governments at list less 50 percent because of the low marketing costs on such

	Market Share (percent)	Pediatric (0–14 years)	General (15–64 years)	Geriatric (65 and older)
Argentina	30%	32.0%	58.0%	10.0%
Brazil	24	29.3	65.7	5.0
Chile	55	32.1	62.8	5.1
Paraguay	65	41.2	55.4	3.4
Peru	45	42.0	56.5	1.5
Uruguay	38	27.0	63.9	9.1

	GNP (billions of dollars)			Foreign Debt (billions of dollars)			Percent Change from Previous Year		
	1986	1989	1992	1986	1989	1992	1986	1989	1992
Argentina	$ 73.1	$ 67.8	$200.3	$ 51.4	$ 64.7	$49.1	+4.5%	+9.8%	+4.0%
Brazil	249.8	375.1	425.4	111.0	111.3	99.2	+4.2	−2.4	+4.3
Chile	16.6	22.9	37.1	20.7	18.2	14.9	+4.7	−7.1	−1.3
Paraguay	3.6	4.3	6.0	1.9	2.5	1.5	+8.1	0	−16.6
Peru	21.4	23.0	21.3	14.5	19.9	15.6	+2.3	−7.0	+2.0
Uruguay	5.8	8.1	10.4	5.2	3.8	3.4	+4.6	0	−8.8

	Total Debt Service as Percentage of Export Receipts			Total Government Expenditures as Percentage of GNP			Percentage of Government Expenditures on Health Care		
	1986	1989	1992	1986	1989	1992	1986	1989	1992
Argentina	50.9%	36.1%	34.4%	12%	15.5%	13.1%*	1.3 %	2.0%	3.0%*
Brazil	41.4	31.3	23.1	9[†]	30.6	25.6	6.4	6.1	6.9
Chile	37.9	27.5	20.9	13	32.5	22.1	6.0	5.9	11.1
Paraguay	18.5	11.9	40.3	7	8.9	9.4	3.1	3.0	4.3
Peru	26.2	6.8	23.0	11	11.6	12.5	5.8[†]	5.5	5.6*
Uruguay	24.7	29.4	23.2	14	25.8	28.7	4.8	4.5	5.0

*1991.
[†]1988.

	Population per Physician*			Annual Inflation Rate			Population (millions)			Population Distribution 1991		
	1980	1984	1990	1986	1989	1992	1986	1989	1992	0–14 Years	15–64 years	65+ years
Argentina	430	370	n.a.	82%	3,072%	25%	31.0	31.9	33.1	29.4%	62.2%	8.4%
Brazil	1,200	1,080	n.a.	58	1,234	1,056	138.4	147.3	153.9	34.2	62.8	3.0
Chile	1,930	1,230	2,150	17	14	15	12.2	13.0	13.6	30.6	63.3	6.1
Paraguay	1,310	1,460	1,250	24	31	15	3.8	4.2	4.5	40.3	56.7	3.0
Peru	1,390	1,040	960	63	3,121	74	19.8	21.2	22.4	37.1	60.8	2.1
Uruguay	510	510	n.a.	76	73	68	3.0	3.1	3.1	25.4	63.3	11.3

n.a. = Not available.
*Latest estimate available from World Health Organization.

	Percentage of GNP for Private Consumption Expenditure		Percentage of Private Consumption Expenditure for Health Care (1889–1992)
	1989	1992	
Argentina	54.8%	79.3%	3%
Brazil	55.3	60.0	5
Chile	72.7	65.8	4
Paraguay	75.9	69.3	2
Peru	84.6	72.6	3
Uruguay	64.0	65.8	5

Sources: Various *World Development Reports* and Banco Nacional de Comercio Exterior, *Comercio Exterior,* February and March 1989 issues.

large volumes, as compared to an average 20 percent of selling price on sales to private pharmacies.

Here are the data that the staff economist has just given to the South American division manager. Help him do the forecast. If you have to make any assumptions, please make a note of them. If marketing costs for government sales average 6 percent of WL's selling price, while they average 11.5 percent to private pharmacies, should the division manager try to change the present government–private pharmacy sales ratio that now prevails in any of the six markets? Should he have any other concerns based on these data?

CHAPTER

8

Physical and Environmental Forces

If you do this . . .
Look at a map of the world, as large
a map as possible. At first sight, it
seems to be a maze of lines, colors,
and unfamiliar names. Go on
looking and studying until the mere
mention of a town, country, or river
enables it to be picked out
immediately on the map. Those who
are concerned with overseas
marketing must, as a basis, know
their export geography as well as the
streets around their home.
Henry Deschampneufs, Selling
Overseas
You won't be told this . . .
Middle East consultant, piqued by
his clients' ignorance of the region,
begins his briefings by saying, "Iraq
isn't the past tense of Iran."
The Wall Street Journal, *July 5,*
1985, p. 32.

CONCEPT PREVIEWS

After reading this chapter, you should be
able to:

1. **understand** the importance of a country's location in political and trade relationships

2. **understand** how surface features contribute to economic, cultural, political, and social differences among nations and among regions of a single country

3. **comprehend** the importance of inland waterways and outlets to the sea

4. **recognize** that climate exerts a broad influence on business

5. **understand** why managers must monitor changes in the discovery and the use of mineral resources and energy sources

6. **understand** why managers must be alert to changes in a nation's infrastructure

7. **appreciate** the impact of industrial disasters such as the Alaskan oil spill and the Bhopal accident on global and multinational firms

Why Switzerland Makes Watches

Watches, lace, carvings, chocolate, cheese, precision machinery, pharmaceuticals—what do they have in common? All are produced in Switzerland; all have a high value per kilo; the Swiss versions are known for their quality; and physical forces are primarily responsible for their being produced in Switzerland. • To appreciate why this is so, consider the following: (1) Switzerland is mostly mountainous, with little level land; (2) it is close to the heavily populated lowlands of Western Europe; (3) Transportation across the mountains to these markets is relatively expensive; and (4) Switzerland has practically no mineral resources. • One way to overcome the lack of local sources of raw materials and high transportation costs is to import small amounts of raw materials, add high value to them, and export a lightweight finished product. The Swiss have done precisely this with the manufacture of watches. They import small volumes of high-quality Swedish steel costing 40 cents per ounce that they then convert to watch movements selling for $60 per ounce. Because of their light weight, the cost of transporting these movements to market is minimal. Precision machinery and pharmaceuticals are other products that minimize the need for importing bulky raw materials. For all of these products, emphasis is placed on the value added by manufacturing, which is based on skill, care, and tradition. • Although the Swiss slopes do not support much agriculture, they are adequate for raising cattle and goats. Production of milk is no problem, but getting it to its major markets outside Switzerland is. Fluid milk is bulky in relation to its value and expensive to transport. The dairymen do to the milk what the watchmakers do to the steel—convert it to a concentrated, high-value product: cheese. Because Swiss cheesemakers have no advantage over their counterparts in the lowland dairying areas nearer to the important markets, they have to compete on the basis of high quality and reputation, which they have carefully promoted. • The plentiful supply of milk is responsible for another product: milk chocolate. The Swiss import the raw chocolate and convert the milk into another high-value-per-kilo product. Certainly the Swiss manufacturer pays higher transportation costs to bring sugar and chocolate in and ship the finished product out than does Hershey in Pennsylvania. Again, their product must be perceived to be superior so that it will bring a higher price to offset the greater costs. • What about the lace and carvings? Physical forces are responsible for these also. The heavy snowfall and cold temperatures of the Swiss winter leave the dairymen and their wives with little to do. About the only work necessary is feeding the animals with stored hay. To help pass the time and earn some money, Swiss women make lace and embroidery while the men carve figures and cuckoo clocks.

Source: Adapted from Rhoads Murphey, *The Scope of Geography*, 2nd ed. (Skokie, IL: Rand McNally, 1973), pp. 65–67.

The opening article illustrates what one writer meant when he wrote that "the physical character of a nation is perhaps the principal and broadest determinant of both the society found there and the means by which that society undertakes to supply its needs."[1]

Strictly speaking, the physical elements are not forces because, except for natural disasters (such as earthquakes, floods, and hurricanes), they are passive. However, there are similarities between them and the uncontrollable forces we describe in this section: their effects are not constant, and although they have a profound impact on the way people organize their activities, the physical forces are only one set of the many factors that influence humanity. In fact, cultural, political, and economic factors may be more important than the physical factors in determining land use and the nature of the economy. How else can you explain the great differences between southeast China and the U.S. Southeast? Their physical environments are very similar, but they support different people with wide divergencies in their cultures and land use.

Probably the most important reason for considering the physical elements as uncontrollable forces is that they have many aspects of the foreign environmental forces we discussed in Chapter 1. Also, as we shall illustrate, managers must adjust their strategies to compensate for differences among markets of the physical forces just as they do for the other uncontrollable forces.

Although the scope of geography is extremely broad, it is possible to select some elements that are particularly significant for the businessperson: (1) location, (2) topography, (3) climate, and (4) natural resources.

LOCATION

Where a country is located, who its neighbors are, and what its capital and major cities are should be part of the general knowledge of all international businesspeople. Location is important because it is a factor in explaining a number of a nation's political and trade relationships, many of which directly affect a company's operations.

Political Relationships

At the height of the cold war, the location of Austria enabled that country to be a political bridge between the noncommunist nations of the West and the communist nations of the East. It was bounded on the west by Germany, Italy, and Switzerland and on the east by Czechoslovakia, Hungary, and Yugoslavia. In addition, Austria's political neutrality made it a popular location for the offices of international firms servicing Eastern European operations. Vienna, Austria's capital, is only 40 kilometers from the Czech Republic and 60 kilometers from Hungary.

Because of the recent political and economic changes in both Western and Eastern Europe, Austria is taking advantage of its location to (1) increase trade with the East, (2) become the principal financial intermediary between the two regions, and (3) strengthen its role as the regional headquarters for international businesses operating in Eastern Europe.

The collapse of COMECON (the economic grouping of former communist satellite nations) forced Eastern enterprises to reorient their trade toward the West. Because of their location on the borders of former communist nations Czechoslovakia and Hungary, Austrian entrepreneurs have captured an important share of the Western nations' exports to the East. For example, after Germany, Austria is the second-largest exporter to Hungary. East–West traffic via Austria is projected to increase five- to sevenfold over the next 20 years. Because of low wage costs in the East and low transport costs due to Austria's proximity to its Eastern neighbors, Austrian producers send textiles, furniture, and machinery components to Eastern countries for further processing and assembly and then bring them back to Austria. Called **passive processing**, it is similar to what foreign firms do in the Mexican maquiladoras. This trade is seven times greater than what it was before the opening of the East.[2]

Austria's location enabled the country to develop close trading links with the European Union members, especially the two on its borders, Germany and Italy. As Austria's main trading partner, the EU supplies nearly 70 percent of its imports and takes 65 percent of its exports. In recent years, Austria has been fifth as a supplier to the EU and third, ahead of Japan and behind only the United States and Switzerland, as an export market for the EU. After many years of close association with the EU, Austria became a full member in 1995.[3]

Finland is another country whose location has shaped its political relationships. For years, Finland, which shared a 780-mile border with the Soviet Union, thrived on a balancing act it did between that country and Western Europe, while maintaining a policy of neutrality. It was the only nation in the world that was at the same time a member of the Soviet trading bloc, COMECON, and the European Free Trade Association (EFTA). However, Finland lost an important market with the Soviet collapse and turned toward the West. As a result of its active participation in the earlier EC/EFTA negotiations, Finland had already established a high level of integration with the EU. Finland became a full member of the EU on January 1, 1995.[4]

Trade Relationships

Geographical proximity is often the major reason for trade between nations. As you saw in Chapter 2, the largest and the third-largest trading partners of the United States—Canada and Mexico—lie on its borders. Deliveries are faster, freight costs are lower, and it is less expensive for sellers to service their clients. This is also one reason so many American firms have plants on the Mexican side of the common border. Geographic proximity has always been a major factor in the formation of trading groups, such as the EU, EFTA, and the North American Free Trade Agreement. The latter, which took effect on January 1, 1994, created a trading block of 362 million people and $6 trillion in GDP.

Nearness to the market is also why Japan's sales to the Association of Southeast Asian Nations (ASEAN)* are over twice those of either the United States or Europe.[5] Because it is closer to Japan, China has been able to take over part of the sales of soybeans and wheat formerly supplied by the United States.

Did you ever stop to think where the fresh grapes, peaches, and raspberries that you eat in the dead of winter come from? Probably not. But Chile's U.S. sales of such fruit, averaging nearly $1 billion annually, are possible because of its location in the southern hemisphere, where the growing seasons are the opposite from those of the United States.

Surface features such as mountains, plains, deserts, and bodies of water contribute to differences in economies, cultures, politics, and social structures, both among nations and among regions of a single country. Physical distribution is aided by some features but hindered by others. Differences in **topography** may require products to be altered. For example, the effects of altitude on food products begin to be seen at heights above 3,000 feet, so

passive processing
The finishing or refining in Eastern European countries of semifinished goods from the West; after finishing, the goods are returned to the West; similar to Mexican maquiladora operations

TOPOGRAPHY

topography
The surface features of a region

---

*ASEAN members are Indonesia, Malaysia, Philippines, Singapore, Thailand, and Brunei.

producers of cake mixes must change their baking instructions; and internal combustion engines begin to noticeably lose power at 5,000 feet, which may require the manufacturer of gasoline-powered machinery to use larger engines.

Let us examine some of the principal surface features to give you an idea of what businesspeople should look for.

Mountains and Plains

Mountains are barriers that tend to separate and impede exchange and interaction, whereas level areas (plains and plateaus) facilitate them. The extent to which mountains serve as barriers depends on their height, breadth, length, ruggedness of terrain, and whether there are any transecting valleys.

An example of such a barrier is the Himalaya Mountains. Travel across them is so difficult that transportation between India and China has been by air or sea rather than overland. The contrast between the cultures of the Indo-Malayan people living to the south of the mountains and the Chinese living to the north is evidence of the Himalayas' effectiveness as a barrier. In similar fashion, the Alps, Carpathians, Balkans, and Pyrenees have long separated the Mediterranean cultures from those of northern Europe.

Mountains Divide Markets.   A greater problem for businesspeople is posed by those nations divided by mountain ranges into smaller regional markets, each with its own distinctive industries, climate, culture, dialect, and sometimes even language. Such is the case of Spain, where there are five separate regions. The cultural differences of two of them, Catalonia and the Basque country, are so great that they have separate languages, not dialects, and each has a sizable minority that wishes to secede from Spain to form a separate nation. Although the Basques and the Catalans can speak Spanish, when they are among themselves they use their own languages, which are completely unintelligible to other Spaniards in both commerce and the home. This creates the same kind of problems found wherever there are language differences: Spanish-speaking managers do not attain the empathy with their local employees that they do in other parts of Spain, and sales representatives who speak the local language are more effective.[6] Moreover, the language differences increase promotional costs if, to be more effective, Spanish companies choose to prepare their material in Basque, Catalan, and Spanish.

Political unrest is prevalent among the Basques on the northern Spanish-French border and, to a lesser extent, among the Catalans on the southern Spanish-French border. Since 1968, an armed terrorist group called ETA has killed over 700 people, mostly soldiers and policemen, in their campaign for independence of the Basque country. They have financed their attacks by bullying local businesses into paying their "revolutionary tax" or by holding wealthy businesspeople for ransom. These actions have always outraged many Basques, but the kidnapping of a wealthy businessman in July 1993 brought forth an unprecedented, universal condemnation from all levels of Basque society. In September, over 50,000 people marched in San Sebastian, a Basque city on the Spanish-French border, to demand the businessman's freedom. In another Basque city, a number of businessmen received ransom demands for $23 million, but they did the unheard of—they refused to pay.

Most Basques do not want to secede from Spain. This region is one of the most industrialized in the country and would be more so if the violence were not frightening off many foreign and Spanish investors. In fact, in 1979 the majority of the Basque population voted for more autonomy, but not total separation. But this did not stop the extortion, threats, and violence of the

FIGURE 8–1 The cantons and major language areas of Switzerland

GERMAN   FRENCH   ITALIAN   ROMANSH

ETA. It appears, however, that the nonsepartists are finally defying the gunmen and winning.[7]

Switzerland is another country separated into distinctive cultural regions by mountains. In a country one-half the size of Maine, four different languages and 35 different dialects are spoken—Italian, French, German, and Romansh (see Figure 8–1). To the consternation of advertising managers attempting to reach all regions of the country, each of the three major language groups has its own radio and television network, and the fourth, Romansh (Latin), is also used by the German stations.

In China, dozens of dialects or languages were developed in villages segmented by mountains. This caused a communications problem that hindered economic development until the government decreed Mandarin to be the official language.

Colombia is similar to Switzerland in that mountains divide its markets. Three ranges of the Andes divide Colombia from north to south into four separate markets, each with its own culture and dialects (see Figure 8–2). Depending on the product, this could require marketers to create four distinctive promotional mixes.

Colombia differs from Switzerland, however, in that besides containing distinct cultures within its borders, it also experiences a range of distinct climates. Because of its location near the equator, Colombia has no seasons;

FIGURE 8–2
Map of Colombia

COLOMBIA
——— DEPARTMENT, INTENDENCIA AND COMISARÍA BOUNDARIES   ⬤ ELEVATIONS ABOVE 14,000 METERS

but the great differences in altitude throughout the country result in a variety of climates. These range from hot and humid at sea level (mean average temperature of 82 degrees in Barranquilla) to cold and dry in the 10,000-foot-high snow-capped mountains (57 degrees in Bogotá). Imagine the production and inventory problems that such differences occasion for the manufacturer that must produce a distinct product and package for each zone. A product with adequate cooling and lubrication for the temperate zone would function well in Bogotá, but might be woefully deficient in Barranquilla. Similarly, a machine powered with an internal combustion engine might perform well in barranquilla, but be severely underpowered in the 10,000-foot altitude of Bogotá.

Because these climatic conditions are not peculiar to Colombia, market analysts should examine topographical maps to see which tropical countries possess this combination of lowlands and mountains. If the firm's products will not function properly in such climatic extremes, either they must be redesigned or the company must bypass this market.

Population Concentration. Mountains also create concentrations of population either because the climate is more pleasant at higher altitudes or because they are barriers to population movement. For example, nearly 80 percent of Colombia's population is located in the western highlands (only one-third of the nation's area) because the climate there is moderate. Eighty percent of Brazil's 150 million people inhabit a 300-mile-wide coastal strip separated from the remainder of the country by a mountain range. Except in the tropics, the population density generally decreases as the elevation increases. If you were to place a population map over a topographic map, the blank areas on the population map would generally coincide with the areas of higher elevation. For example, 90 percent of Switzerland's population is located in a narrow belt at the base of the Alps. The reason for this is that dense population requires commerce, manufacturing, and agriculture, which all depend on the good transportation and ease of communication afforded by the plains.

Deserts and Tropical Forests

Deserts and tropical forests, like mountains, separate markets, increase the cost of transportation, and create concentrations of population.

Deserts. Over one-third of the earth's surface consists of arid and semiarid regions located either on the coasts where the winds blow away from the land or in the interior where mountains or long distances cause the winds to lose their moisture before reaching these regions. Every continent has them, and every west coast between 20 and 30 degrees north or south of the equator is dry. Since people, plants, and animals must have water to exist, the climatic and vegetational deserts are also the human deserts. Only where there is a major source of water, as in Egypt, is there a concentration of population.

Nowhere is the relationship between water supply and population concentration better illustrated than in Australia, a continent the size of the continental United States but with only 16 million inhabitants. Its surrounding coastline is humid and fertile, whereas the huge center of the country is mainly a desert closely resembling the Sahara (see Figure 8–3).

Because of its geography, Australia's population has tended to concentrate (1) along the coastal areas in and around the state capitals, which are also major seaports, and (2) in the southeastern fifth of the nation, where more than one-half of the population lives. This gives Australia one of the highest percentages of urban population in the world. The 85 percent of the total population living in cities is surpassed only by Belgium (96 percent), Israel (92 percent), Venezuela (91 percent), the Netherlands (89 percent), the United Kingdom (89 percent), and Germany (86 percent).[8]

The distances between these cities and the fact that they are seaports make coastal shipping preferred over road and rail transportation.[9] However, these long distances between major markets result in transportation account-

FIGURE 8–3
Map of Australia

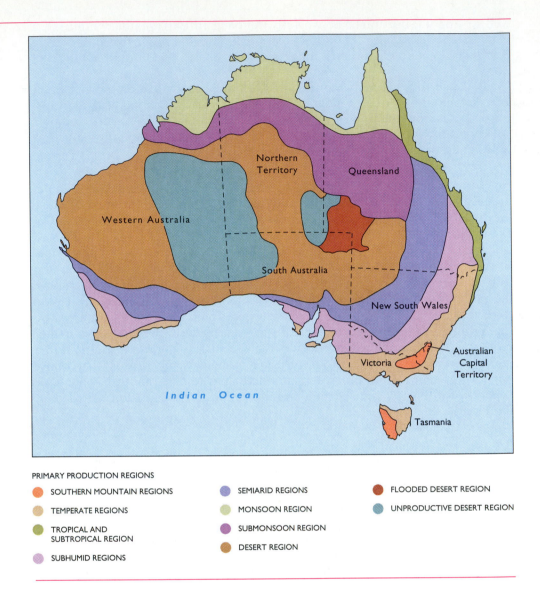

PRIMARY PRODUCTION REGIONS

- SOUTHERN MOUNTAIN REGIONS
- TEMPERATE REGIONS
- TROPICAL AND SUBTROPICAL REGION
- SUBHUMID REGIONS

- SEMIARID REGIONS
- MONSOON REGION
- SUBMONSOON REGION
- DESERT REGION

- FLOODED DESERT REGION
- UNPRODUCTIVE DESERT REGION

ing for as much as 30 percent of the final cost of the product, as compared with the more usual 10 percent in the United States and Europe.

The population distribution also has a profound impact on Australia's media. First of all, there are only three upper-socioeconomic-group newspapers and a few magazines that can be considered national media. All other media are concentrated in capital city areas. This requires advertisers to buy space or time on a state-by-state or city-by-city basis. Although most capital city areas have three commercial TV channels, there is little networking.

Even though 70 percent of the country is arid or semiarid, some areas in the northern rim receive up to 100 inches of rainfall annually, much like the monsoon areas of India. Thus firms entering the Australian market face the same extreme differences of temperature and humidity encountered in Colombia.

Were it not for the uniform topography of Australia, the temperature differences would be even greater, as they are in countries with large, hot desert areas and irregular surfaces. Iran is such a nation. In the summer, temperatures may reach 130°F, whereas winter temperatures in high altitudes may drop to –18°F. From December to March, it is possible to ski just an hour-and-a-half's drive from Teheran, the capital. Like Australia, Iran's population distribution is heavily influenced by climate and topography. More than 70 percent of the country—consisting mostly of mountains and deserts—is uninhabited, and one-half of the population lives in urban areas.

Tropical Rain Forests.   Vegetation can be an effective barrier to economic development and human settlement, especially when it is combined with harsh climate and poor soil. This occurs in the world's tropical rain forests located in the Amazon basin, Southeast Asia, and the Congo. Except in parts of West Africa and Java, they are thinly populated and little developed economically. For example, the greatest rain forest of them all—in the Brazilian Amazon—has been called one of the world's greatest deserts because of its low population density. Although it covers more than 1 million square miles (one-fourth of the U.S. land area) and occupies one-half of Brazil, it is inhabited by just 4 percent of the country's population. Only true deserts have a population density lower than the Amazon's one person per square mile.

Canadian Shield.   Although the **Canadian Shield** is neither a desert nor a tropical forest, this massive area of bedrock covering one-half of Canada's land mass has most of their characteristics—forbidding topography, poor soil, and harsh climate. The Shield is swept by polar air, which permits a frost-free growing season of only four months. During that time, residents are molested by swarms of black flies and mosquitoes. Like deserts and tropical forests, its population density is very low: only 10 percent of Canada's population inhabits the region.

Canadian Shield
A massive area of bedrock covering one half of Canada's land mass

Relevance for Businesspeople.   Managers know that in more densely populated nations, it costs less to market their products (population centers are closer and communication systems are better), more people are available for employment, and so forth. Therefore, when they compare population densities such as Canada's 2.8 inhabitants per square kilometer, Australia's 2.3, and Brazil's 18.1 with the Netherlands' 411 or Japan's 329, they may draw the wrong conclusions.[10] However, if they are aware that the population in each of the first three countries is highly concentrated in a relatively small area for the reasons we have been examining, then a very different situation prevails. Notice in the next section how bodies of water also are responsible for concentrations of population.

Bodies of Water

This surface feature, unlike mountains, deserts, and tropical forests, attracts people and facilitates transportation. A world population map clearly shows that bodies of water have attracted more people than have areas remote from water. Those densely populated regions that do not coincide with rivers or lakes are generally close to the sea. You would note from the map that populations cluster around the Amazon, the Congo, the Mississippi, the St. Lawrence, and the Great Lakes. In Europe, the plain of the Po (Italy) and the Rhine are easily recognizable. So are rivers that cross deserts, such as the Nile, the Indus (Pakistan), the Tigris-Euphrates (Iraq), and the Amu Darya (central Asia), although these are more important for the irrigation water and fertile soil they bring than for transportation.

Bodies of water that are significant because they provide inexpensive access to markets in the interior of various nations are the inland waterways.

Inland Waterways.   Before the construction of railways, water transport was the only economically practical carrier for bulk goods moving over long distances. Water transport increased even after the building of railroads, although its importance relative to railroads has diminished everywhere with one exception—the Rhine waterway, the world's most important inland waterway system.

Rhine waterway
A system of rivers and canals, the main transportation artery of Europe

Rhine Waterway. The **Rhine waterway**, the main transportation artery of Europe, carries a greater volume of goods than the combined railways that run parallel to it. As an illustration of the Rhine's significance, one-half of Switzerland's exports and nearly three-fourths of its imports pass through Basel, the Swiss inland port. This cargo is carried on the country's own 31-vessel oceangoing fleet via the Rhine waterway to Rotterdam, 500 miles to the north (see Figure 8–4).

For years, shipments have moved between the Netherlands, Belgium, Germany, France, Austria, and Switzerland by means of the Rhine and its connecting waterways; but the Rhine-Main-Danube canal completed in 1992 gives access to the Atlantic Ocean, 13 countries, and the Black Sea. From there, shipments can continue to Moscow over the interconnected system of the Volga and Don rivers. Not many ships undertake the entire 30-day voyage from Rotterdam to the Black Sea (3,500 kilometers), but it has stimulated shipping over shorter east-west routes, such as Nuremburg to Budapest or Vienna to Rotterdam. Increasingly, firms have been turning to the Rhine waterway as an environmentally friendly alternative to road transportation (see the Worldview on page 253).

Other Waterways. In every continent except Australia, which has no inland waterways, extensive use is made of water transportation. In South America, the Amazon and its tributaries offer some 57,000 kilometers of navigable waterways during the flood season. Oceangoing vessels can reach Manaus, Brazil (1,600 kilometers upstream), and smaller river steamers can go all the way to Iquitos, Peru (3,600 kilometers from the Atlantic).

Farther south, the governments of Argentina, Bolivia, Brazil, Paraguay, and Uruguay are working to develop the Paraná and Paraguay rivers as a

Cargo ships passing through Germany on Europe's main transportation artery, the Rhine waterway.

Hans Wolf/The Image Bank

FIGURE 8–4 Europe's major inland waterways

— CANALS

Source: Karte der WasserstraBen in Deutschland und Benelux

trade corridor connecting the vast landlocked interior of South America with seaports at the River Plate estuary near Montevideo (see Figure 8–5). Although, at present, the rivers are only partly navigable, Argentina uses river ports on the Paraná to handle 25 percent of its exports and Paraguay imports most of its fuel on the Paraguay river. A preliminary feasibility study of the waterway claims that some simple engineering projects costing only $240 million will convert the 3,400-kilometer river system into the main transportation artery for the southern part of the continent by the year 2000.[11]

In Asia, the major waterways are the Yangtze (China), the Ganges (India), and the Indus (Pakistan). Rivers are especially important in China because water is the least expensive, and often only, means of moving industrial raw materials to the manufacturing centers. Oceangoing vessels can travel up the Yangtze as far as Wuhan, 1,000 kilometers from the sea. This river and its tributaries form the densest waterway system in the world, with over 30,000 kilometers usable by steamships, launches, or junks.

Although the United States possesses extensive rail and highway systems, it also depends heavily on two waterways. One, the Great Lakes–St. Lawrence, enables ocean freighters to travel 3,700 kilometers inland, thus transforming lake ports into ocean ports. The other waterway, the Mississippi, connects the Great Lakes to the Gulf of Mexico and is especially important for carrying bulky commodities, such as wheat, cotton, coal, timber, and iron ore.

Outlets to the Sea.   Historically, navigable waterways with connections to the ocean have permitted the low-cost transportation of goods and people from a

FIGURE 8–5

Paraná-Paraguay rivers trade corridor

country's coast to its interior and even now are the only means of access from the coasts of numerous developing nations.

This has been a particularly troublesome problem for Africa, in which 14 of the world's 20 landlocked developing countries are located. Almost one-third of all sub-Saharan countries are landlocked, and some are more than 1,000 kilometers from the sea by the shortest land route. The implications for these poor nations are obvious: they must construct costly, long truck routes and extensive feeder networks for relatively low volumes of traffic. Further-more, governments in countries with coastlines through which the imports and exports of the landlocked nations must pass are in a position to exert considerable political influence. Small wonder that struggles for outlets to the sea still exist and are important political and economic factors.

One outstanding example is the century-long struggle by Bolivia to regain from Chile an outlet to the Pacific Ocean that it lost in an 1879 attack. These countries have held discussions for decades without reaching a workable agreement. Until Bolivia has its own coastline, it must use Arica, the free port in northern Chile, and inland waterways. Now, the governments of Peru, Bolivia, and Chile are meeting to prepare an economic accord that would include a bi-ocean corridor connecting Bolivia, Paraguay, and Brazil with northern Chile, especially Africa. Such an agreement would facilitate Bolivia's use of Chilean ports.[12]

This dispute affects business transactions between the two countries. One of the writers, representing a Chilean subsidiary of an American

WORLDVIEW

Helping the Environment while Saving Money

The management of Neckermann, a $2.4 billion German mail-order firm, wanted to help protect the environment so it formulated a policy directing its employees to work to this end. The logistics department, responsible for handling imports from European countries and Asia, proposed sending more imports to Rotterdam from where they would be forwarded in barges via the Rhine waterway to the firm's three warehouses in Frankfurt. Under the old arrangement, imports arriving in Hamburg were sent by rail or road to Frankfurt. The 120,000 tons of merchandise from European suppliers now comes by rail instead of truck as it formerly did. These changes have provided two benefits: less environmental damage and lower costs.

Based on estimates by the prestigious Planco Institute, the company calculates that the new environmentally friendly system of waterways and rail has reduced total costs to the environment (air, ground, water, and noise pollution) from $1.6 million under the old road-intensive arrangement to $722,000. In addition, the firm is saving $241,000 annually by shipping containers over the Rhine waterway from Rotterdam to Frankfurt instead of using rail from Hamburg to Frankfurt. It is now considering supplying its Mannheim warehouse by barge, and it may also use barges on the Rhine waterway to handle the 500 containers that come each year from Eastern Europe. This has been made possible by the new Main-Danube canal that extends the Rhine waterway all the way to the Black Sea.

Other firms, among them Ford and Unilever, had already changed to the more environmentally friendly river system. These companies predict that others will increase their use of waterways when, as expected, the European Union deregulates waterway rates.

Source: "Why Neckermann Chose the Rhine Option," *Business Europe*, January 24–30, 1994, p. 7.

multinational, called on a large government-owned mine in Bolivia to sell Chilean-made products. The purchasing agent asked how anyone could expect her, a Bolivian, to buy goods made in Chile. Although appreciating that the parent company was American, she said "The products are still made in Chile."

CLIMATE

climate
Meteorological conditions, including temperature, precipitation, and wind, that prevail in a region

Climate (temperature and precipitation) is probably the most important element of the physical forces because it, more than any other factor, sets the limits on what people can do both physically and economically. Where the climate is harsh, there are few human settlements, but where it is permissive, generally there are great clusters of population. However, climate is not deterministic—it allows certain developments to occur, but it does not cause them. Nonclimatic factors, such as mineral deposits, accessibility to an area, economic and political organizations, cultural tradition, availability of capital, and the growth of technology, are more important than climate in the development of trade and manufacturing.[13]

Similar climates occur in similar latitudes and continental positions, and the more water-dominated an area, the more moderate its climate. Thus, the northwest United States and northwest Europe, which are at similar latitudes and both influenced by the sea, have mild, moist climates. Southeast Australia, New Zealand, and part of South Africa are at the same latitude and close to the sea. They too have mild, moist climates. At the other extreme, Kansas and Central Asia, which are both far from the sea and at the same latitude, are dry and have cold winters and hot summers.

Climate and Development

For centuries, writers have used climatic differences to explain differences in human and economic development. They have suggested that the greatest economic and intellectual development has occurred in the temperate cli-

FIGURE 8–6 Impact of climate on economic development

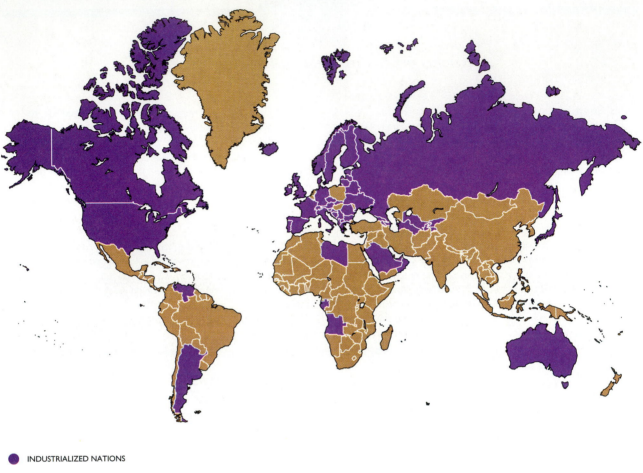

● INDUSTRIALIZED NATIONS

mates of northern Europe and the United States because the less temperate climates limit human energy and mental powers.[14] The map in Figure 8–6 seems to support this thesis. However, marketers must not be taken in by this ethnocentric reasoning, which fails to explain the difference in the level of technology employed in the 1600s by the inhabitants of northeastern North America and the inhabitants of northern Europe. Clearly there were other factors involved, such as the Industrial Revolution, population size, and location.

This is not to say that climate has not had some influence on economic development. Studies by the World Bank have shown that many of the factors responsible for the underdeveloped state of most tropical nations are present because of the tropical climate. Continuous heat and the lack of winter temperatures to constrain the reproduction and growth of weeds, insects, viruses, birds, and parasites result in destroyed crops, dead cattle, and people infected with debilitating diseases.[15]

As grim as this may sound, there is hope. The World Bank points out that techniques are becoming available to control pests and parasites. Once this is accomplished, the very characteristics that are now detrimental to tropical Africa will give it sizable advantages over the temperate zones in agriculture. The resulting income would create a market in tropical Africa that could easily surpass that of the Middle East at the time oil prices were at their highest.

Climatic Implications for Businesspeople

The differences in climatic conditions among a firm's markets can have a significant impact on its product mix. For example, internal combustion engines designed for temperate climates generally require extra cooling capacity and special lubrication to withstand the higher temperatures of the tropics. Goods that deteriorate in high humidity require special, more expensive packaging, machinery operating in dusty conditions needs special dust protection, and so forth.

When climatic extremes exist in a single market and the product is temperature- or humidity-sensitive, the company may have to produce and stock two distinct versions to satisfy the entire market. Severe winters, such as those in Canada, or the heavy monsoon rains that fall in northern Australia and India can impede distribution. This may require the firm to carry extraordinarily large inventories in its major markets to compensate for delays in delivery from the factory. All of these conditions, of course, have an adverse effect on profitability.

What are **natural resources**? There is no commonly accepted definition among the professionals who work with them. One well-known economic geographer, Joseph H. Butler, states, "To meet their economic needs—including the basic ecological requirements of water, food, clothing, and shelter—people undertake the production of goods and services by extracting *natural resources* from the environment." He adds that all three sectors of the natural environment provide raw materials: the solid portion of the earth, the water portion, and the atmosphere.[16] For our purposes, we can define natural resources as anything supplied by nature on which people depend.

During the Arab-Israeli war in 1973, Arab exporters of petroleum used an oil embargo on some nations and the threat of an embargo on others to obtain political support from Western Europe. Realizing that not only their industries but also their national defense depended on a substance other nations could use as a political force, the United States and other oil-importing nations initiated a worldwide campaign to conserve mineral fuels and to search for new energy sources. The 1990 Iraqi invasion of Kuwait, followed by Operation Desert Storm, reminded industry and government officials of the necessity to continue searching for alternative energy sources.

Alternative Energy Sources

Oil Sands and Shale.   One potential energy source is the tar sands of Athabasca, Canada, which contain bitumen, a tarlike crude. Instead of being pumped from wells, bitumen is strip-mined and sent to a separation plant, where it is converted into a higher-quality synthetic crude oil. At its current cost (including royalty and capital charges) of about US$18 a barrel, the cost of extracting bitumen from the tar sands is becoming competitive with that of conventional crude.[17] Presently, the two major tar sands plants, Syncrude and Suncor, are producing about 16 percent of Canada's crude oil (both natural and synthetic), but this is expected to rise as the production of conventional crude drops. Syncrude estimates that another 200 billion barrels of synthetic crude, more than the combined reserves of Saudi Arabia and its neighbors, can be recovered using present extraction technology.[18]

The United States has a vast amount of oil that is known to be recoverable from **shale** in Colorado, Utah, and Wyoming. However, the recovery process is also expensive, which makes the end product unable to compete with today's prices of conventional crude. In addition, there are environmental problems connected with the disposition of huge quantities of waste shale. So far, Union

NATURAL RESOURCES

natural resources
Anything supplied by nature on which people depend

shale
A fissile rock (capable of being split) composed of laminated layers of claylike, fine-grained sediment

Oil is the only company to have built a recovery plant, with a daily production of 6,000 barrels. The total U.S. shale oil reserves are estimated to be 600 billion barrels—more than all of OPEC's total proven reserves.

Crude from Coal.   A promising source of synthetic oil and gas is coal gasification. South Africa, concerned it might be shut off from oil imports for political reasons, has built three plants that supply a large portion of its oil and gas from low-grade coal, which is plentiful. In North Dakota, a coal gasification plant using the South African process produces methane gas and petrochemical by-products from lignite. Although the present cost of producing its synthetic gas is about 50 percent more than the market price of natural gas, the firm does make a profit from the sale of ammonia (fertilizer), xenon (aerospace and nuclear medicine), and other chemical products.[19] One other coal gasification plant in California supplies gas to a nearby public utility.

New Finds.   Spurred by the high oil prices of the 1970s, which required oil-importing nations to divert huge sums of foreign exchange to pay for their oil imports, many governments opened their countries to oil exploration by foreign firms. In only a few years, new oil finds were made in the Middle East, Africa, Asia, and Latin America. As a result, we learned in the 1980s that there is far more oil than we thought. The World Energy Council (WEC), an energy organization based in London, estimates that there is sufficient oil to last 60 years at today's rate of consumption plus another 170 years' supply of the more costly bitumen and oil-bearing shales that we discussed previously. However, it is not the size of the reserves that is the problem, but the massive investment needed to develop them.

Russia and China serve as good examples. China's reserves are believed to be huge; only Saudi Arabia's are larger. Although it lacks capital, the Chinese government has opened only a small part of its reserves to foreign investors. The former Soviet Union also has plenty of oil, but again the problem is to get it out.[20] In 1994, commercial production began in the rich fields north of the Arctic Circle. It was the first major Russian oil field to be developed by a U.S.-Russian joint venture. Conoco and its Russian partner estimate the initial development cost to be over $1 billion.[21] More recently, a consortium of Texaco, Exxon, Amoco, and Norsk Hydro appears to be ready to sign a $45 billion agreement with Russia for the rights to work in the same region where Conoco has its operation.[22]

Renewable Sources of Energy.   Most people in the energy industry believe that one day renewable energy sources will replace fossil fuels.[23] There are at least eight types: hydroelectric, solar, wind, geothermal, waves, tides, biomass, and ocean thermal energy conversion. None is universal, but all appear to have an application under appropriate conditions. Of the eight, hydroelectric has had an extensive application—5.7 percent of the total energy consumed in the world comes from hydroelectric installations.

Currently, the costs of generating electricity per kilowatt hour for various fuels in the United States are as follows:

Coal	4–5¢	Wind	5–9¢
Gas	4–5¢	Biomass	6–8¢
Hydro	4–7¢	Solar	10–12¢
Geothermal	5–8¢	Photovoltaic	30–40¢[24]

Figure 8–7 compares the percentages of each type of energy for American and world energy sources.

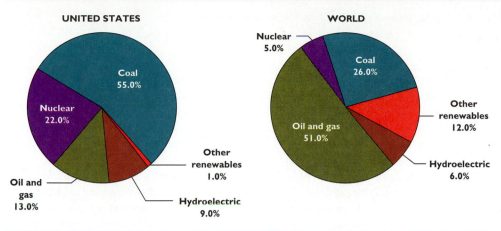

Sources: "The Sun Shines Brighter on Alternative Energy," *Business Week*, November 8, 1993, p. 94; and "The New Prize," *The Economist*, June 18, 1994, p. 9.

Improved technology has resulted in new support for solar, wind, and biomass energy (burning wood or other solid waste), in the United States. In August 1993, 68 utility companies agreed to buy $500 million worth of solar panels to generate electricity, and power companies in Vermont, Texas, and Maine have an agreement with the U.S. Department of Energy to test new, more efficient wind turbines. Already, California Edison gets 13 percent of its power from renewable sources.[25]

Nonfuel Minerals

Although much of the world's attention has centered on the discovery of new energy sources, Table 8–1 shows that there are also other mineral resources about which governments and industry are apprehensive. Nearly all of the world's chrome, manganese, platinum, and vanadium are produced by South Africa and the former Soviet Union. Chrome and manganese are indispensable for hardening steel; platinum is a vital catalytic agent in the oil-refining process and is used in automotive catalytic converters; and vanadium is used in forming aerospace titanium alloys and in producing sulphuric acid. The United States depends on South Africa to supply 79 percent of its platinum, 78 percent of its chromium, 41 percent of its manganese, and 20 percent of its vanadium. Although South Africa never threatened to stop the export of these strategic metals, government and industry leaders are well aware that if the South African source had been lost, the major industrial societies in the West would have been heavily dependent on their communist enemies for their supply, in both wartime and peacetime.

Bleak Situation?   The situation appears bleak, but remember that we are discussing known reserves. Do other sources exist? Consider this. Only relatively small areas, mostly in the traditional mining countries, have been adequately explored. For example, it is estimated that only 5 percent of the potential mineral-containing areas in Mexico and only 10 percent of those in Bolivia have been studied extensively.

Furthermore, a relatively new technology, satellite mapping, has enabled geologists to locate new sources. Prior to this discovery, geologists believed Brazil to have few minerals, but they now know that it possesses extensive deposits of chromium, nickel, copper, lead, zinc, and manganese.

TABLE 8–1 Major world sources of industrial minerals that the United States must import

Mineral	Percentage of Consumption Imported	Major Sources	Use
Columbian	100%	Brazil, Canada, Germany	Steelmaking, aerospace alloys
Graphite	100	Mexico, China, Brazil, Madagascar	Metallurgical processes
Manganese	100	South Africa, France, Gabon	Steelmaking
Mica (sheet)	100	India, Belgium, Brazil, Japan	Electronics and electrical equipment
Strontium	100	Mexico, Spain, Germany	TV picture tubes
Bauxite	100	Australia, Guinea, Jamaica, Brazil	Aluminum production
Diamonds (industrial)	98	Ireland, Zaire, U.K., South Africa	Machinery for grinding and cutting
Fluorspar	87	Mexico, South Africa, China, Canada	Metallurgical and chemical industries
Platinum group	94	South Africa, U.K., former Soviet Union	Electrical equipment, catalytic converters
Cobalt	76	Zaire, Zambia, Canada, Norway	Aerospace alloys, cutting tools, magnets
Tantalum	87	Germany, Thailand, Australia	Electronic components
Nickel	64	Canada, Norway, Australia, Dominican Republic	Stainless steel and other alloys
Chromium	74	South Africa, Turkey, Yugoslavia, Zimbabwe	Stainless steel
Tin	73	Brazil, Bolivia, China, Indonesia, Malaysia	Cans, electrical construction
Tungsten	85	China, Bolivia, Peru, Germany	Lamp filaments
Barite	53	China, India, Mexico, Morocco	Oil field fluids
Potash	67	Canada, Israel, Germany, former Soviet Union	Fertilizer

Source: *World Almanac, 1994* (New York: Newspaper. Enterprise Association, 1994), p. 181.

Seabed Mining—An Untapped Source.   The existence of metal deposits on the ocean floor was discovered in 1876, when a British explorer found a number of small, metal-containing nodules. Little attention was paid to them until the 1960s, when tests showed that these nodules were present in practically every sea and in some lakes, such as Lake Michigan. However, the nodules richest in metallic content are nearly all located on the ocean floor, at depths of from three to five miles. Although geologists are not sure how they are formed, they do know where they are most numerous and what their metallic content is. Analysis shows that all of the nodules contain some 30 metals but have an extremely high copper, nickel, manganese, and cobalt content. This last metal, all of which is now imported in the United States, is especially important, as it is widely used in military and vital civilian technologies. For example, 900 pounds of cobalt are needed to produce just one engine for the F16 fighter plane. Table 8–2 compares the metal content of seabed sources with that of land sources.

TABLE 8–2
Average metal content (percent)

Sources	Copper	Cobalt	Nickel	Manganese
North Pacific	1.16%	0.23%	1.28%	24.6%
North Atlantic	0.15	0.34	0.30	14.2
South Atlantic	0.15	0.31	0.48	18.0
Indian Ocean	0.19	0.28	0.50	14.7
Continental reserves				
Minimum	0.50	0.07	0.40	40.0
Maximum	0.50	0.10	1.00	50.0

Source: "In Search of Metals on the Seabed," *Kredietbank Weekly Bulletin* (Brussels), June 13, 1980, p. 1.

Vacuuming for Diamonds

De Beers, the South African group that dominates the world's diamond market, did not wait for LOST to go into effect before beginning to mine the seabed for diamonds off the coast of Namibia. In fact, in 1991 the firm first took samples of the seabed, which is the size of the Netherlands, to locate diamonds. It is now using the latest technology to recover thousands of small precious stones spread over this area. Experts believe the diamonds are 60 million years old and traveled a thousand miles down the Orange River in Namibia to the ocean.

De Beers has spent over $50 million to purchase and convert seven oil exploration ships into floating vacuum cleaners that suck up tons of material containing diamonds from the seabed. To avoid theft, the firm cans the material on a production line similar to that used to can fruit. Nearly every diamond found is of gem quality. Although it costs over $40 million to operate each ship, this is still less than the $500 million it would cost to open a diamond mine on land. To uncover the stones on the ocean floor, crews use either huge drills operated directly from the ships or truck-sized underwater robotic crawlers with hydraulic drills operated remotely.

In 1993, the second year of operation, the company obtained more than 300,000 carats of diamonds from the seabed, a 16 percent increase over 1992. The operation's general manager estimated the 1994 result would be even greater. Although De Beers is not saying what the diamonds are worth, the 1993 seabed mining production was one-third of Namibia's total output in weight and was thought to be more than one-third in value. The company is planning to expand its floating mines to the coasts of South Africa and Sierra Leone.

Source: "De Beers Sucks Up a Fortune in Gems from Its Floating Mine," *Financial Times*, August 29, 1994, p. 14.

Metal deposits are also found in the crust of chimneylike structures up to 100 feet in height that were formed when hot water rushed up from active volcano vents in the sea floor. The **polymetallic deposits** contain significant quantities of cobalt, manganese, nickel, and other metals.

Since 1974, UN members have been negotiating a treaty to put seabed mining under UN control. For years, the U.S. government refused to sign the Law of the Sea Treaty (LOST) because it created a huge UN bureaucracy consisting of the International Seabed Authority (ISA), which would regulate private mining, and the Enterprise, an international version of state-owned mining companies that would compete with private enterprise. It also required the three American consortia that already hold U.S. ocean mining licenses to transfer their seabed mining technology to the Enterprise.[26] After the technology transfer requirement was removed, the United States signed the treaty. The ISA is receiving $2.5 million in UN funds to finance its first year of operation.[27] For a report on a multinational that is not waiting for LOST before beginning seabed mining, see the Worldview, "Vacuuming for Diamonds."

polymetallic deposits
Those that contain a number of metals

Changes Make Monitoring Necessary

Mineral Resources. You saw how crude oil prices spurred the discovery of oil by non-OPEC members as they sought to lessen their dependence on imported oil. New land-based sources of strategic nonfuel minerals have also been discovered, and we have learned that the seabeds contain vast amounts of these minerals in the form of nodules and seafloor crusts.

Concomitantly, important discoveries are being made that could lessen our need for these minerals. For example, in 1984 the U.S. Air Force in conjunction with Pratt and Whitney announced the development of two new cobalt-free superalloys for possible application in a new generation of fighter jet engines.

A Gnat and the Elephant

A tiny, nine-person company, A-55 LP, has formed a joint venture with Caterpillar, a multinational with 50,000 employees. What's the attraction? A German inventor and owner of A-55 LP, Rudolf W. Gunnerman, claims he has invented a technology that enables internal combustion engines to burn a mixture of half fuel and half water. The mixture gets 40 percent more mileage with less pollution. He believes the water breaks down into oxygen and hydrogen, with the hydrogen supplying the energy.

Actually, the drivers do not simply mix water with gasoline; they have to buy a prepared mixture, 0.5 percent of which is an emulsifier that enables the water and fuel to mix. The inventor says the conversion of a gasoline motor to run on the mixture would cost less than $500. The city of Reno, Nevada, used the product to power a city bus for five months and experienced a 29 percent increase in miles per gallon of diesel fuel.

After 11,000 miles, the engine was removed and sent to Caterpillar for evaluation. Caterpillar was so interested that it has now formed a joint venture with the inventor's company to perfect and market the product. It is expected that the new product will find a global market.

Caterpillar's technical manager and acting general manager of the joint venture, called Advanced Fuels LLC, says "It's certainly a very exciting technology. But a lot of work still needs to be done, and a lot of surprises can crop up as you go to product development." How big is this new fuel? An expert who tracks emerging transportation technology claims that if it works as expected, the United States would no longer have to import crude oil.

Source: "Engines That Run on Water," *Business Week*, August 8, 1994, p. 47.

Probably the most fascinating discovery of all is a solar-powered technique to produce hydrogen from water. Instead of using gasoline for fuel, aircraft and automobiles might use hydrogen. In the 1950s, Lockheed flew a B-57 bomber that had one engine converted to burn hydrogen, and in 1988, a similarly converted Russian plane completed a test flight. Hydrogen can also be used in conventional gasoline engines. In 1990, Mercedes-Benz demonstrated several models fitted with engines that ran on hydrogen, but the company believes it will be another 10 years before costs will be low enough for the car to be marketable. The process of extracting hydrogen from water is still expensive and the heavy tank required for the flammable gas holds only enough to drive 75 miles before a refill.[28]

Relevance to Businesspeople.   Do these discoveries have any significance for businesspeople? Obviously, sellers of commodities and products that are being threatened by the discoveries must monitor them and prepare for new competition. More important, all firms supplying goods and services to nations that depend on the traditional minerals for foreign exchange to pay for those goods and services must be aware of developments that can destroy old markets and create new ones. Imagine the loss of purchasing power in the Middle Eastern countries if lower-cost hydrogen available from water takes the place of gasoline. We have already seen cutbacks in the purchases of these countries because of lower crude oil prices, but what if petroleum were needed only by the petrochemical industry and not for transportation?

Other Changing Physical Forces.   Mineral resources are not the only physical forces that change. Modifications of infrastructure, most of which are of great significance to businesspeople, are being made constantly. For example, new settlements and new industries are attracted to areas in which dams have been built to control flooding and to provide power and irrigation water. New highways and new railways reduce delivery times to present markets and thus enable firms to cut their distribution costs by reducing their inventories. For example, improved highways now permit regularly scheduled overland delivery service from London to cities as far east as Moscow. One Russian trucking firm now makes the London-Moscow run in just eight days, a trip that formerly took months by sea.

However, when the Brazilian government sought a World Bank loan to construct a paved highway to connect the mineral-rich but economically stagnant state of Acre to the rest of Brazil, American environmentalists complained, and the loan was postponed. The environmentalists' concern was that the road would destroy the Amazon tropical forest, which they say converts carbon dioxide to oxygen and absorbs heat, thus reducing the greenhouse effect. Nevertheless, Brazil's foreign minister said "Brazil isn't going to become the ecological reserve for the rest of the world. Our biggest commitment is with economic development."[29] Despite its cost, one of Latin America's major infrastructural achievements, the Trans-Andean Highway, has greatly increased trade and tourism between Argentina and Chile.

New infrastructure is responsible for economic development in developed nations also. The 31-mile Channel Tunnel, or Chunnel, connecting England and France, which began service in November 1994, has attracted heavy investment. The population of Calais, the city at the French end of the tunnel, is expected to double to 200,000, many of whom will be British citizens attracted by cheaper housing and the ability to live in France and commute daily to work in Great Britain. Distribution costs are expected to be significantly lower because the trip from London and Paris takes about three hours through the tunnel compared to the seven hours using ferries and trains. The trip from London to Brussels, Belgium, takes just three hours and 15 minutes.[30]

Another time-saver is the Seto Ohashi bridge in Japan, which links the island of Shikoku with the central island of Honshu. What used to be a two-hour ferry ride is now a 10-minute drive. The sharp reduction in travel time is having a profound impact on agriculture. Faster delivery times for produce are calculated to result in a $30 million increase in farmers' income.[31]

The Trans-Andean Highway.

Loren McIntyre

Destruction of Natural Resources

Historically, nations have paid relatively little attention to the contamination and destruction of the world's natural resources. Entire forests have been destroyed by people wanting to get firewood or to clear land and by contaminated air and water. Pollution control of air and water was considered a luxury that governments, anxious to attract new industry and to keep the industry they had, could ill afford to impose. As the secretary of mines and energy for the state of Bahia, Brazil, stated, "Brazil can't afford pollution control like Japan or the United States. It's cultural imperialism."

However, such tragedies as the Bhopal disaster and the horrendous Sandoz spill into the Rhine have forced officials to realize that the price for such negligence is too high.

The Bhopal Disaster.   What is described as the world's worst man-made industrial disaster killed at least 7,000 people. On December 4, 1984, the deadly gas methyl isocyanate, used in the production of insecticides, leaked from storage tanks at the Bhopal plant of Union Carbide (India), a joint venture of Union Carbide (50.9 percent) and Indian capital. Government financial institutions owned nearly 26 percent of the company. Although suits totaling $250 billion were filed on behalf of Bhopal victims, in 1989 the Indian supreme court reached an out-of-court settlement with Union Carbide (U.S.) for $470 million.[32] Ten years later, Indian courts have paid out only $20 million to settle 94,000 compensation claims, or $213 per claimant. A key issue of great interest to American multinationals was whether the lawsuits seeking damages should be tried in American or Indian courts. Attorneys for the victims fought to have the case tried in the United States, but an American judge ruled that it should be heard in India.[33]

The Rhine Spill.   On November 1, 1986, a fire broke out in the Sandoz warehouse in Basel, Switzerland, where pesticides were stored. The building had neither automatic alarms nor a sprinkler system. The drainage system could not handle all the water the fire brigades pumped into the flames and soon chemicals mixed with water flowed into the nearby Rhine. No one was harmed, and two days passed until dead fish appeared in the river. Cities turned off their river supplies of drinking water, and in one part of the upper Rhine, almost every creature died.

Critics of the manner in which the spill was handled compared the Swiss government's 24-hour delay in advising other governments to the Russian delay in informing the West about the Chernobyl disaster.[34] However, there is one noticeable difference between the two catastrophes: Russia refused to pay any part of the $121 million damages claimed by German farmers as a result of the Chernobyl nuclear power plant explosion, whereas Sandoz, the Swiss pharmaceutical and chemical products maker, immediately said it would honor claims for damages caused by the Rhine spill.[35]

Alaskan Oil Spill.   Called America's Chernobyl, the worst oil spill in this country's history occurred near Valdez, Alaska, in 1989, when an Exxon tanker hit a reef and spilled 10 million gallons of crude oil. Exxon's cleanup group involved more than 11,000 people, 1,200 vessels, and 80 aircraft.[36] The company spent over $2.5 billion for the cleanup and $1 billion to settle federal and state criminal charges. In addition, in 1994 Exxon was ordered by a federal jury in Alaska to pay $5 billion to fishermen and other Alaskans, the largest punitive award ever against a corporation. In an earlier phase of the trial, the jury awarded $287 million to 10,000 fishermen. Another group of 4,000 native Alaskans settled their claims for $20 million.[37]

Pitching in to help with the oil clean-up effort in Prince William Sound, Alaska

Alan Levenson/Tony Stone Images

Eco-Terrorism in the Gulf War.   An ecological disaster far worse than the Valdez oil spill was caused by the Iraqi army before its retreat from Kuwait. A total of 732 oil wells were either sabotaged by the army or were set fire during combat. Moreover, 75 million barrels of oil spilled out over the desert, forming lakes that birds mistakenly took for real ones, flying to their deaths.[38] Iraqi troops also let oil escape from Kuwait's Sea Island terminal, creating a spill 27 times larger than the Valdez disaster.

The estimated 42 billion gallons of oil that spread over the desert into the Persian Gulf, along with the oil well fires and the war damage, have resulted in an enormous ecological disaster. Years after the war, no one knows if the ecology suffered a crippling blow or if the damage can be absorbed. Although the oil made Kuwait's beaches look like an asphalt highway after the war, the Kuwaitis did little to clean it up.[39]

Spill in the Tundra.   The U.S. Department of Energy claims that an oil slick 7-miles long, 35-miles wide, and three-feet deep is oozing over the frozen tundra in northern Russia near the Arctic Circle. If true, it is the third-largest oil spill in history. More important, it is just part of the 30 to 50 millions of barrels of oil that leak annually onto the Russian tundra from pipelines owned by privatized Russian oil companies. No one knows what is required to clean up large oil spills in the Arctic, but research in Canada suggests that cleaning up small areas at northern military bases will cost hundreds of millions of dollars.[40]

Relevance to Businesspeople.   Antipollution activism, already a potent force in Europe and North America, is spreading to other parts of the world. Local citizen groups have increased their influence on government policies and have worked to delay the projects of multinationals in newly industrializing countries, such as Brazil, India, Malaysia, Mexico, and Thailand. The notion of economic growth at any cost is being challenged, and many nations, developing as well as developed, are now requiring environmental impact assessments before approving new industrial plants. Multinational producers of hazardous materials are finding that these changes are resulting in higher costs and are making the locating of overseas plants more difficult.

Multinationals in hazardous industries will resist the minority positions in joint ventures mandated by numerous governments when such positions cause them to lose control to the local majority on questions of equipment, plant safety, and environmental controls. Warren Anderson, chairman of Union Carbide at the time of the Bhopal disaster, voiced the concern of many multinational managements when he said "India sued us on the novel theory that any multinational engaged in hazardous operations is totally liable for any mishap, regardless of what share it may own. Is the insistence by Third World countries on local content in goods manufactured for local markets always realistic? It was, for example, at India's insistence that Carbide started making, instead of just mixing, agricultural chemicals in the Bhopal plant."[41]

SUMMARY

1. **Understand the importance of a country's location in political and trade relationships.** A nation's location is a significant factor in its political and trading relationships. Austria, for example, located on the borders of both Eastern and Western Europe, has become the financial intermediary between the two regions as well as regional headquarters for numerous international firms that have Eastern European operations. Two major trading partners of the United States, Canada and Mexico, are located on its borders.

2. **Understand how surface features contribute to economic, cultural, political, and social differences among nations and among regions of a single country.** Mountains divide nations into smaller regional markets that often have distinct cultures, industries, and climates. Sometimes even the languages are different. Deserts and tropical forests act as barriers to people, goods, and ideas.

3. **Comprehend the importance of inland waterways and outlets to the sea.** Bodies of water attract people and facilitate transportation. Water transportation has increased even after the building of railroads and highways. Various European firms are shipping goods in barges on the Rhine waterway instead of using highways.

4. **Recognize that climate exerts a broad influence on business.** The differences in climatic conditions among a firm's markets can significantly affect its marketing mix. A product sold for use in northern Canada may need protection against cold weather, while the same product used in the tropics might re-

quire extra cooling to resist the heat. Heavy seasonal rains can require the firm to carry large inventories because of the difficulty in replenishing stock in inclement weather.

5. **Understand why managers must monitor changes in the discovery and the use of mineral resources and energy sources.** The discovery of a new energy source or the reduction in the cost of producing an alternative source may offer a company an opportunity to economize on its use of energy. A new oil or mineral find might provide a country with new income, which in turn could make it a valuable customer for international firms, as occurred in the Middle East when crude oil prices tripled. On the other hand, imagine what would happen to the income of oil-producing nations if hydrogen would become an economical fuel.

6. **Understand why managers must be alert to changes in a nation's infrastructure.** New roads, bridges, and canals often open new markets in developed and developing countries.

7. **Appreciate the impact of industrial disasters such as the Alaskan oil spill and the Bhopal accident on global and multinational firms.** Industrial accidents such as the Bhopal disaster and the Rhine River spill have caused both developed and developing nations to be more concerned about the protection of natural resources. International chemical manufacturers are reassessing their positions concerning joint ventures when they cannot control the choice of equipment, plant safety, and maintenance.

KEY WORDS

- passive processing   243
- topography   243
- Canadian Shield   249
- Rhine waterway   250

- climate   253
- natural resources   255
- shale   255
- polymetallic deposits   259

QUESTIONS

1. Of the 25 nations listed by the UN as the least developed nations, 14 are landlocked. Is this a coincidence, or does the lack of a seacoast contribute to their slower development?

2. Analyze the potential of oil shale and oil sands as future energy sources. What problems are involved in using these natural resources?

3. Assume you are a member of your company's long-range planning committee. You have heard that experiments have been successful in separating hydrogen from water and that the hydrogen is then combined with carbon to form hydrocarbons. It is said that the product may cost 20 percent less than crude oil obtained from wells. Discuss with your colleagues how this development may affect your marketing plans in the Middle East and in the oil-poor developing countries.

4. *a.* Why do you suppose the blank areas on a population map generally coincide with the areas of higher elevation on a topographic map?

   b. Why are the tropics an exception to this rule?

5. International businesspeople, unless they are in the business of refining minerals or petroleum, have no need to concern themselves with world developments in natural resources. True or false? Explain.

6. Mountains, deserts, and tropical rain forests are generally culture barriers. Explain.

7. Explain how bodies of water are responsible for concentrations of population.

8. What will be the consequences for international firms of such disasters as the Rhine spill, Bhopal accident, and the Alaskan oil spill?

9. How can climatic differences affect a firm?

10. What is the relationship between Australia's water supply and its physical distribution costs?

MINICASE 8–1   Bhopal Fallout

Harry Johnson, CEO of International Chemical, called a meeting of the newly formed crisis management committee, which consists of the vice president of manufacturing; the vice president–legal; the vice president of health, safety, and environment; the chief financial officer; and the public relations officer. Johnson had formed the committee after Union Carbide's Bhopal disaster to examine International Chemical's contingency plans. Because the two companies have similar international organizations and produce similarly toxic products, he asked the members to review the information they had on the Bhopal disaster and make recommendations as to what each person's area would do should their company have a similar accident. Johnson also asked the vice president of health, safety, and environment to begin the meeting by giving the committee a synopsis of

the series of events that occurred during the first days after the disaster.

He begins, "As you know, on the night of December 2, a series of runaway chemical reactions heated the interior of a partially buried tank holding 10,000 gallons of methyl isocyanate (MIC) used in the manufacture of Sevin and other pesticides. An escape valve opened, which released a lethal cloud over Bhopal. No one knows how it happened, but Union Carbide investigators say that, by accident or through sabotage, a large quantity of water had been poured into the tank, which then reacted with the MIC to produce heat and open the valve. A refrigeration unit that could have kept the tank temperature at a manageable level had broken down five months previously and had not been repaired. A temperature alarm that would have alerted workers was not properly set. Last of all, a scrubber designed to neutralize toxic vapors was not turned on until the reaction was out of control.

"Union Carbide headquarters in Connecticut first heard of the accident at 3 A.M. on December 3, when employees from Union Carbide in Bhopal called Lutz (chairman of UC Eastern, the division responsible for Asian operations) at his home. By 6 A.M., Lutz, Oldfield (president of the agricultural products division, which markets the insecticides produced at Bhopal), Browning (director of health, safety, and environment), and Van Den Ameele (manager of press relations) met at headquarters. Although they were skeptical about the accuracy of the growing estimate of the numbers of dead and injured, they agreed that a swift response was needed and that top management would need to make some decisions. By midmorning, they called UC's president and went to a hastily called meeting of the senior management committee. When Carbide board chairman Warren Anderson, in bed with a bad cold, was informed by telephone of the problem, he organized a crisis committee of legal, finance, and public affairs people.

"Within 12 hours, the committee dispatched a medical and technical team to arrange relief for the victims, to investigate the incident, and to assist with the safe disposal of the remaining MIC supplies at the plant. They held a press conference even though they did not have all the answers for the press. The next day, as the death toll continued to mount, Anderson took the company jet to Bhopal. On arrival, he was arrested, held briefly, and then sent to New Delhi, the capital. There, Indian officials told him to leave for his own good. His offer of $1 million in aid and the use of the company guest house to shelter orphans of the victims was refused.

"Because Carbide managers did not know what had caused the leak, they stopped production of MIC in the United States and converted all of their stocks of MIC worldwide into pesticides. The crisis caused the price of Carbide stock to fall, so the team began to stress the company's financial soundness in press releases and briefings. To bolster employee morale, the UC president made a videotape for Carbide employees worldwide in which he assured them of the company's ability to handle any likely damage settlement. By the way, even though Carbide provided the specifications for the Indian plant, it was designed and built in India at the insistence of the Indian government, which has a 25 percent interest in the Indian company. Carbide has 50.9 percent, but it has been essentially an Indian operation. The other investors are Indian."

"Thanks for the rundown," says Johnson. "I don't need to tell you that managements of multinational producers all over the world are studying Union Carbide's situation very closely. I read that one executive said this accident could rewrite the whole book on how to operate in foreign countries and how one covers one's risks overseas. Who wants to start the discussion on (1) what we need to do now to avoid both an accident and risk to the company if there should be one and (2) what should our plan be in case—and I hope it never happens—we should have a similar accident?"

Sources: "Women Protest Decade after Anniversary of Deadly Disaster," *McAllen Monitor,* December 4, 1994, p. 2A; "Indian Gassing Victims Endure Another Disaster—No Aid," *San Antonio Express-News,* November 29, 1994, p. 4A; "Union Carbide: Coping with Catastrophe," *Fortune,* January 7, 1985, pp. 50–53; "Anderson Reflects on Managing Bhopal," *Industry Week,* October 13, 1986, p. 21; "For Multinationals It Will Never Be the Same," *Business Week,* December 24, 1984, p. 57; and "Bhopal Report," *C&EN,* February 11, 1985, pp. 14–52.

Sociocultural Forces

Speaking about cultural differences among Europeans . . . *It is no good focusing on similarities and common interests and hoping things will work out. We have to recognize the differences and work with them.*

Dr. Allan Hjorth, Copenhagen Business School, trainer in cross-cultural behavior

CONCEPT PREVIEWS

After reading this chapter, you should be able to:

1. **understand** the significance of culture for international business

2. **understand** the sociocultural components of culture

3. **appreciate** the significance of religion to businesspeople

4. **comprehend** the cultural aspects of technology

5. **discuss** the impact of the "brain drain" and the "reverse brain drain" on developed and developing nations

6. **appreciate** the importance of the ability to speak the local language

7. **recognize** the importance of the unspoken language in international business

8. **discuss** the two classes of relationships within a society

9. **discuss** Hofstede's four cultural value dimensions

Six Rules of Thumb for Doing Business in Another Culture

Knowing your customer is just as important anywhere in the world as it is at home, whether aiming to sell computers in Abidjan or soft drinks in Kuala Lumpur. Each culture has its logic, and within that logic are real, sensible reasons for the way foreigners do things. If the salesperson can figure out the basic pattern of the culture, he or she will be more effective interacting with foreign clients and colleagues. The following six rules of thumb are helpful. • (1) *Be prepared.* Whether traveling abroad or selling from home, no one should approach a foreign market without doing his or her homework. A mentor is most desirable, complemented with endless reading on social and business etiquette, history and folklore, current affairs (including current relations between your two countries), the culture's values, geography, sources of pride (artists, musicians, sports), religion, political structure, and practical matters such as currency and hours of business. Mimi Murphy, an exporter who trades primarily in Indonesia, says, "Whenever I travel, the first thing I do in any town is read the newspaper. Then when I meet my customer, I can talk about the sports or the news of the day. He knows that I am interested in the things he is interested in, and he will want to do business with me." • (2) *Slow down.* Americans are clock-watchers. Time is money. In many countries, we are seen to be in a rush, in other words, unfriendly, arrogant, and untrustworthy. Almost everywhere, we must learn to wait patiently. • (3) *Establish trust.* Often American-style crisp business relationships will get the sales representative nowhere. Product quality, pricing, and clear contracts are not as important as the personal *relationship and trust* that is developed carefully and sincerely over time. The marketer must be established as simpatico, worthy of the business, and dependable in the long run. • (4) *Understand importance of language.* Obviously, copy must be translated by a professional who speaks both languages fluently, with a vocabulary sensitive to nuance and connotation, as well as talent with idiom and imagery in each culture. An interpreter is often critical and may be helpful even where one of the parties speaks the other's language. • (5) *Respect the culture.* Manners are important. The traveling sales representative is a guest in the country and must respect the hosts' rules. As a Saudi Arabian official states in one of the *Going International* films, "Americans in foreign countries have a tendency to treat the natives as foreigners and they forget that actually it is *they* who are the foreigners themselves!" • (6) *Understand components of culture.* A region is a sort of cultural iceberg with two components: *surface culture* (fads, styles, food, etc.) and *deep culture* (attitudes, beliefs, values). Less than 15 percent of a region's culture is visible, and strangers to the culture must look below the surface. Consider the British habit of automatically lining up on the sidewalk when waiting for a bus. This surface cultural trait results from the deep cultural desire to lead neat and controlled lives.

Sources: "How to Negotiate European Style," *Journal of European Business,* July–August 1993, p. 46; and U.S. Department of Commerce, *Business America,* June 25, 1984, p. 7.

Did you see the quotation at the beginning of the chapter? It is from a cross-cultural expert who teaches businesspeople how to do business in the various European cultures. Incidentally, courses like the one taught by Dr. Hjorth are compulsory at many European business schools.[1] Notice, too, the opening section, which provides hints on doing business in unfamiliar cultures. Please remember that the national characteristics you encounter in this chapter and elsewhere are generalizations. They are broadly true, but there are always exceptions. Furthermore, characteristics change over time. The Scandinavians were considered by a 10th-century writer to be "the filthiest race God ever created" and a noted 18th-century writer was amazed at the lack of German military spirit and how easygoing they were compared to the French.[2] Before we examine the significance of culture for international businesspeople, let us first define culture.

WHAT IS CULTURE?

culture
Sum total of beliefs, rules, techniques, institutions, and artifacts that characterize human populations

Although there are almost as many definitions of culture as there are anthropologists, most anthropologists view **culture** as the *sum total of the beliefs, rules, techniques, institutions, and artifacts that characterize human populations.*[3] In other words, culture consists of the learned patterns of behavior common to members of a given society—the unique lifestyle of a particular group of people.[4] Most anthropologists also agree that

1. Culture is *learned*, not innate.
2. The various aspects of culture are *interrelated*.
3. Culture is *shared*.
4. Culture *defines the boundaries* of different groups.[5]

Because society is composed of people and their culture, it is virtually impossible to speak of one without relating to the other. Anthropologists often use the terms interchangeably or combine them into one word—*sociocultural*.[6] This is the term we shall use, because the variables in which businesspeople are interested are both social and cultural.

SIGNIFICANCE OF CULTURE FOR INTERNATIONAL BUSINESS

ethnocentricity
Belief in the superiority of one's own ethnic group

When people work in societies and cultures that differ from their own, the problems they encounter in dealing with a single set of cultures are multiplied by the number of cultural sets they find in each of their foreign markets.

All too often, unfortunately, people who are familiar with only one cultural pattern may believe they have an awareness of cultural differences elsewhere, when in reality they do not. Unless they have had occasion to make comparisons with other cultures, they are probably not even aware of the important features of their own. They are probably also oblivious to the fact that many societies consider their culture superior to all others (**ethnocentricity**) and that their attempts to introduce the "German way" or the "American way" may be met with stubborn resistance.

How do international businesspeople learn to live with other cultures? The first step is to realize that there are cultures different from their own. Then they must go on to learn the characteristics of those cultures so that they may adapt to them. E. T. Hall, a famous anthropologist, claims this can be accomplished in only two ways: (1) spend a lifetime in a country or (2) undergo an extensive, highly sophisticated training program that covers the main characteristics of culture, including the language. The program he mentions must be more than a briefing on a country's customs. It should be a study of what culture is and what it does, imparting some knowledge of the various ways in which human behavior has been institutionalized in a country.[7]

Culture Affects All Business Functions

Marketing.   In marketing, for example, the wide variation in attitudes and values prevents many firms from using the same marketing mix in all markets.

> In Japan, Procter & Gamble (P&G) used an advertisement for Camay soap in which a man meeting a woman for the first time compared her skin to that of a fine porcelain doll. Although the ad had worked well in South America and Europe, it insulted the Japanese. "For a Japanese man to say something like that to a Japanese woman means he's either unsophisticated or rude," said an advertising man who worked on the account. Interestingly, P&G used the ad despite the warning from the advertising agency.
>
> Another Camay ad that failed in Japan was one showing a Japanese woman bathing when her husband walks into the bathroom. She begins to tell him about her new beauty soap, but the husband, stroking her shoulder, hints that suds are not what is on his mind. Although it was well received in Europe, it failed badly in Japan where it is considered bad manners for a husband to intrude on his wife.
>
> P&G also erred because it lacked knowledge of the business culture. The company introduced Cheer detergent by discounting its price, but this lowered the soap's reputation. Said a competitor, "Unlike in Europe and the United States, once you discount your product here, it's hard to raise the price again." Wholesalers were alienated because they made less money due to lower margins. Moreover, apparently P&G didn't realize that Japanese housewives do not have a family car to carry groceries, so they shop in the neighborhood mom-and-pop stores close to home. These small retailers, who sell 30 percent of all the detergent sold in Japan, have limited shelf space and thus do not like to carry discounted products because of the lower profit earned.[8]

Unlike P&G, Disney seemed to have an ideal global product and global promotion. According to the *Tokyo Disneyland Guidebook,* the Tokyo theme park is the same as those in California and Florida. Euro Disney, now called Disneyland Paris, is also similar, although, because of the French insistence on protecting their language and culture, Mickey and Donald developed French accents and the Sleeping Beauty castle is called *Le Chateau de la Belle au Bois Dormant.*[9] The Worldview illustrates the problems a global firm can have when its management errs when making culturally sensitive decisions.

Human Resource Management.   The national culture is also a key determinant for the evaluation of managers. In the United States, results are generally the criteria for the selection and promotion of executives; but in Great Britain, an American general manager complained that people were promoted because of the school they attended and their family background but not for their accomplishments. School ties are important in France, too. IBM would hire an Italian who fits within the IBM way of doing things, but Olivetti, whose corporate culture is informal and nonstructured with little discipline, looks for strong personalities and not "too good grades."[10] You can get Olivetti's address from the nearest AT&T office.

Production and Finance.   Personnel problems can result from differences in attitudes toward authority, another sociocultural variable. Latin Americans have traditionally regarded the manager as the *patron* (master), an authoritarian figure responsible for their welfare. When American managers accustomed to a participative leadership style are transferred to Latin America, they must become more authoritarian, or their employees will consider them weak and incompetent and they will encounter serious difficulties in having their orders carried out.

WORLDVIEW

Cultural Success and Failure in Disneyland

Why is it that Disneyland Paris is having problems with falling attendance and losses while Tokyo Disneyland has a steadily increasing attendance and is the most profitable Disney park? The many experts who predicted that Tokyo Disneyland attendance would peak in the first year and then taper off were wrong; instead, it has increased steadily. Over 16 million people visited the park in 1993 and spent an average of $85. Visitors to Disneyland in Los Angeles and Disney World in Florida spend between $60 and $70, while those going to Disneyland Paris spend only $45 on average.

Unfortunately for Disney, Tokyo Disneyland is wholly owned by a Japanese firm, the Oriental Land Co., which licenses Disney characters and other copyrighted material from the American firm. The park owes some of its success to its location in a metropolitan area of 30 million people, but a cultural change is believed to be a major reason for its success. Some say that Walt Disney Productions has written a new chapter in Japanese social history by popularizing the idea that family outings can be fun. Families now account for half of the park's visitors. An executive of the park owners states, "Leisure was not always a part of the Japanese life-style. Fathers used to see family outings as a duty."

The staggering losses at Disneyland Paris stem from the high interest costs and high overheads, many of which were caused by cultural errors. To cover the project's $4 billion cost, Disney put up just $170 million for 49 percent of the operation and public shareholders paid $1 billion for the 51 percent they own. The $2.9 billion balance was borrowed at interest rates of up to 11 percent. Disney management expected to reduce the debt by selling the six big hotels it had built, but the $340 per night price it charged had kept them about half full. Moreover, the guests

Sichov/SIPA

have not been staying as long or spending as much as Disney had calculated.

Disney executives believed, incorrectly, that they could change the French attitude of not wanting to take their children from school during the school year as Americans do or to take more short breaks during the year instead of one long vacation during the month of August. This would have given Euro Disney steady, high attendance all year round rather than for just one month.

One reason the visitors haven't spent more has been the extremely high prices. Almost two years passed before Disney lowered them. Another reason the guests haven't spent more, even though in this case they want to, is also due to a cultural problem: the breakfast debacle. Apparently, a decision involving millions of dollars in revenue was not based on research but only on what someone told Disney. One executive said, "We were told that Europeans don't take breakfast, so we downsized the restaurants." However, when the park opened, everyone wanted breakfast and they wouldn't settle for just croissants and coffee; they wanted bacon and eggs. Disney tried to serve 2,500 breakfasts in hotel restaurants seating 350 people. The Disney solution for the French public, known worldwide as connoisseurs of good eating: prepackaged breakfasts delivered to hotel rooms.

As a French banker put it, "Euro Disney is a good theme park married to a bankrupt real estate company—and the two can't be divorced."

Sources: "Tokyo Disney Shifts Japanese Ideas on Leisure," *The Columbian,* May 1, 1994, p. F7; "Mickey n'est pas fini," *Forbes,* February 14, 1994, p. 42; "Euro Disney's Wish Comes True," *The Economist,* March 19, 1994, p. 83; "Mouse Trap," *The Wall Street Journal,* March 10, 1994, p. A1; and "Euro Disney to Cut Admission Price 22% for the Peak Season Beginning in April," *The Wall Street Journal,* December 15, 1994, p. A12.

A production manager who had been sent to Peru from the United States was convinced that he could motivate the workers to higher productivity by instituting a more democratic decision-making style. He brought in trainers from the home office to teach the supervisors how to solicit suggestions and feedback from the workers.

Shortly after the new management style was introduced, the workers began quitting their jobs. When asked why, they replied that the new production manager and his supervisors apparently didn't know what to do and were therefore asking the workers for advice. The workers thought the company wouldn't last long with that kind of management, and they wanted to quit before the collapse, because then everyone would be hunting for a job at the same time.

Production managers have found that attitudes toward change can seriously influence the acceptance of new production methods; even treasurers come to realize the strength of the sociocultural forces when, armed with excellent balance sheets, they approach local banks, only to find that the banks attach far more importance to who they are than to how strong their companies are.[11] One reason for Disney's financial problems in Paris has been the arrogant and insensitive attitude of Disney executives to European business culture. A top French banker involved in the negotiations to restructure the park's debt claimed, "The Walt Disney group is making a major error in thinking it can impose its will once more."[12] These are just a few examples to show sociocultural differences do affect all of the business functions. As we examine the components of the sociocultural forces, we shall mention others.

SOCIOCULTURAL COMPONENTS

From the foregoing, it should be apparent that to be successful in their relationships with people in other countries, international businesspeople must be students of culture. They must have factual knowledge, which is relatively easy to obtain, but they must also become sensitive to cultural differences, and this is more difficult. Hall, as we saw, recommended spending a lifetime in a country or, in lieu of this, undergoing an extensive program to study what the culture is and what it does. But most newcomers to international business do not even have the opportunity for area orientation. They can, however, take the important first step of realizing that there are other cultures. In this short chapter, we cannot do more than point out some of the important sociocultural differences as they concern businesspeople, in the hope that you will become more aware of the need to be culturally sensitive—to know that there are cultural differences for which you must look. Remember that the more you know about another's culture, the better will be your predictions of that person's behavior.

The concept of culture is so broad that even the ethnologists (cultural anthropologists) have to break it down into topics to facilitate its study. A listing of such topics will give us a better understanding of what culture is and may also serve as a guide to international managers when they are analyzing a particular problem from the sociocultural viewpoint.

As you can imagine, experts vary considerably as to the components of culture, but the following list is representative of their thinking:

1. Aesthetics.
2. Attitudes and beliefs.
3. Religion.
4. Material culture.
5. Education.
6. Language.
7. Societal organization.
8. Legal characteristics.
9. Political structures.[13]

We shall examine the first seven components in this chapter and leave the legal characteristics and political structures for later chapters.

Aesthetics

Aesthetics pertains to a culture's sense of beauty and good taste and is expressed in its art, drama, music, folklore, and dances.

Art. Of particular interest to international businesspeople are the formal aspects of art, color, and form, because of the symbolic meanings they convey. Colors, especially, can be deceptive because they mean different things to different cultures. The color of mourning is black in the United States and Mexico, black and white in the Far East, and purple in Brazil. Because green is a propitious color in the Islamic world, any ad or package featuring green is looked at favorably there. However, it is repugnant in parts of Asia, where it connotes the illness and death of the jungle. While in the United States mints are packaged in blue or green paper, in Africa the wrapper is red. These examples illustrate that marketers must be careful to check if colors have any special meanings before using them for products, packages, or advertisements.

Be careful of symbols, too. Seven signifies good luck in the United States but just the opposite in Singapore, Ghana, and Kenya. In Japan, the number four is unlucky. If you are giving your Japanese client golf balls, make sure there are more or less than four in the package. Also, in general, avoid using a nation's flag or any symbols connected with religion.

> The Yokohama Rubber Company had to recall tires with a tread pattern that Moslems claim resembles the Arabic word for Allah. A representative said the company had stopped producing the tires and was replacing them with new ones free of charge. He also said that the treads were designed by a computer and were not meant to blaspheme Allah.[14]

It is also important to learn whether there are local aesthetic preferences for form that could affect the design of the product, the package, or even the building in which the firm is located. The American style of steel and glass in the midst of oriental architecture will be a constant reminder to the local population of the outsider's presence.

Music and Folklore. Musical commercials are generally popular worldwide, but the marketer must know what kind of music each market prefers, because tastes vary. Thus, a commercial that used a ballad in the United States might be better received to the tune of a bolero in Mexico or a samba in Brazil. However, if the advertiser is looking to the youth market with a product patently American, then American music will help reinforce its image.

Those who wish to steep themselves in a culture find it useful to study its folklore, which can disclose much about a society's way of life. Although this is usually more than the foreign businessperson has time for, the incorrect use of folklore can sometimes cost the firm a share of the market. For example, associating a product with the cowboy would not obtain the same results in Chile or Argentina as it does in the United States, because in these countries the cowboy is a far less romantic figure—it's just a job. In another instance, a U.S. company may be paying handsome royalties to use American cartoon characters in its promotion, only to find they are considerably less important in foreign markets. In Mexico, songs of the "Singing Cricket" are known to all youngsters and their mothers, and a commercial tie-in with that character would be as advantageous to the firm as its use of Peanuts or Mickey Mouse. In many areas, especially where nationalistic feeling is strong, local firms have been able to compete successfully with foreign affiliates by making use of indigenous folklore in the form of slogans and proverbs. Tales of folklore are

A Cultural Difference in Sex Roles—Women's Credibility in Male Strongholds

Dorothy Irvine saw an opportunity to double her import-export company's annual $50,000 revenue when she learned that a small Japanese trading company was searching for an agent in the United States. She believed her firm, which was already trading with Japan, could handle the job. Irvine followed the Japanese custom of having a high-level Japanese executive introduce her to the owner of the trading company.

She made four special trips to Japan to meet with the owner. These cost her thousands of dollars in travel expense and three weeks of preparation time. However, the man never took her seriously. Irvine claims, "it is almost as if they were leading me along because I'd been introduced by somebody they respected." To corroborate her opinion, she asked an American businessman to accompany her to a meeting. They both agreed that because she was a woman, she wasn't making any progress. "I would loved to have had the business," said Irvine. "It was very frustrating."

Source: "Gender Gap," *The Wall Street Journal,* October 16, 1992, p. R20.

valuable in maintaining a sense of group unity.[15] Knowing them is an indication that one belongs to the group, which recognizes that the outsider is unfamiliar with its folklore.

Attitudes and Beliefs

Every culture has a set of attitudes and beliefs that influence nearly all aspects of human behavior and help bring order to a society and its individuals. The more managers can learn about certain key attitudes, the better prepared they will be to understand why people behave as they do, especially when their reactions differ from those that the managers have learned to expect in dealing with their own people.

Among the wide variety of subjects covered by attitudes and beliefs, some are of prime importance to the businessperson. These include attitudes toward time, toward achievement and work, and toward change.

Attitudes toward Time.   This cultural characteristic probably presents more adaptation problems for Americans overseas than any other. Time is important in the United States, and much emphasis is placed on it. If we must wait past the appointed hour to see an individual, we feel insulted. This person is not giving our meeting the importance it deserves. Yet the wait could mean just the opposite elsewhere. Latin American or Middle Eastern executives may be taking care of the minor details of their business so that they can attend their important visitor without interruption.

> An American who has worked in the Middle East for 20 years explains the Middle Eastern concept of time this way: "A lot of the misunderstandings between Middle Easterners and foreigners are due to their different concepts of time and space. At worst, there is no concept at all of time in the Middle East. At best, there is a sort of open-ended concept." The head of Egypt's Industrial Design Center, an Egyptian, states, "The simple wristwatch is, in some respects, much too sophisticated an instrument for the Middle East. One of the first things a foreigner should learn in Egypt is to ignore the second hand. The minute hand can also be an obstacle if he expects Egyptians to be as conscious as he of time ticking away.[16]

Probably even more critical than short-term patience is long-term patience. American preoccupation with monthly profit and loss statements is a formidable barrier to the establishment of successful business relationships with

Asian and Middle Eastern executives, especially during the development of joint ventures and other business relationships that have good potential in the long run—precisely the factors in which these people are most interested.[17]

Americans, Be Prompt.   Few cultures give the same importance to time that Americans and Europeans do. If any appointment is made with a group of Germans to see them at 12 noon, we can be sure they will be there; but to get the same response from a Brazilian, we must say noon English hour. If not, the Brazilian may show up anytime between noon and 2 o'clock. Compare this with Japan, where a description of an apartment in the rental contract includes the time in minutes required to walk to the nearest train station.

Should Americans follow the local custom or be prompt? It depends. In Spain, a general rule is to never be punctual. If you are, you will be considered early. However, in the Middle East, the American penchant for punctuality is well known, and lateness from Americans is considered impolite. The Arabian executives, nonetheless, will usually not arrive at the appointed hour; why should they change their lifetime habits just for a stranger?

Mañana.   Probably one of the most vexing problems for the newcomer to Latin America is the *mañana* attitude. Ask the maintenance man when the machine will be ready, and he responds *"mañana."* The American assumes this means "tomorrow," the literal translation, but the maintenance man means "some time in the near future," and if he is reprimanded for not having the machine ready the next day, he is angry and bewildered. He reasons that everyone knows mañana means "in the next few days."

This example illustrates that the ability to speak the local language is only half the task of communicating. A manager of an American subsidiary in Saudi Arabia says, "You can be talking the same language with someone, but are you talking on the same wavelength?" He states that he has met few Japanese or Koreans fluent in Arabic, yet they are able to understand and adapt to local conditions much better than Westerners can because they seem to be more sensitive to the Middle Easterner's mentality.[18]

Directness and Drive.   The American pride in directness and drive is interpreted by many foreigners as being brash and rude. Although we believe it expedient to get to the point in a discussion, this attitude often irritates others. Time-honored formalities are a vital part of doing business and help to establish amicable relations, considered by people in many countries to be a necessary prerequisite to business discussions. Any attempt to move the negotiations along by ignoring some of the accepted courtesies invites disaster.

Deadlines.   Our emphasis on speed and deadlines is often used against us in business dealings abroad. In Far Eastern countries such as Japan, an American may be asked how long he or she plans to stay at the first meeting. Then negotiations are purposely not finalized until a few hours before the American's departure, when the Japanese know they can wring extra concessions from the foreigner because of his or her haste to finish and return home on schedule.

> Three Americans, none of whom had ever been to Japan, went to sell tractors to Japanese buyers. They thought the discussions had gone well and prepared to wrap up the deal. However, there was no reaction from the Japanese. The silence became disquieting, and so the Americans lowered the price. Because there was still no reaction, they again lowered the price. This went on until their price was far lower than they had planned. What they didn't know was that the Japanese had become silent not to indicate

rejection of the proposition, but merely to think it over, a customary Japanese negotiating practice.[19]

Attitudes toward Achievement and Work.   "Germans put leisure first and work second," says a German-born woman now living in the United States. "In America, it's the other way around."

Angela Clark was born in Germany but now works for J.C. Penney as merchandising manager in Washington, DC. Andreas Drauschke has a comparable job for comparable pay in Berlin. There is no comparison, however, in the hours each works. Drauschke works a 37-hour week, with a six-week annual vacation. The store closes at 2:00 P.M. on Saturdays and opens again on Monday. It is open one night a week. Clark works a minimum of 44 hours a week, including evenings and often on Saturdays and Sundays. She brings work home and never takes more than one week's vacation at a time. "If I took any more, I'd feel like I was losing control," she says.

   In the United States, Germans are known for their industriousness, but a comparison of workloads shows that there is little basis now for that stereotype. The average workweek in U.S. manufacturing plants is 37.7 hours and is increasing, whereas, in Germany, it is 30 hours and has been falling over recent years. All German workers are guaranteed by law a minimum of five weeks' annual vacation.[20]

Like the Germans, the Mexicans say "Americans live to work, but we work to live." This is an example of the extreme contrasts among cultural attitudes toward work. Where work is considered necessary to obtain the essentials for survival, once these have been obtained, people may stop working. They do not make the accomplishment of a task an end in itself. This attitude is in sharp contrast to the belief in many industrial societies that work is a moral, and even a religious, virtue.

To the consternation of the production manager with a huge back order, the promise of overtime often fails to keep the workers on the job. In fact, raising employees' salaries frequently results in their working less (economists call this effect the backward-bending labor supply curve).

It is important, however, to note that an additional change has occurred repeatedly in many developing countries as more consumer goods have become available. The **demonstration effect** (seeing others with these goods) and improvements in infrastructure (roads to bring the products to them and electric power to operate them) cause workers to realize they can have greater prestige and pleasure by owning more goods. Thus, their attitude toward work changes, not because of any alteration of their moral or religious values, but because they now want what only money can buy.

demonstration effect
Result of having seen others with desirable goods

A Mexican distributor came to one of the writers to complain that a number of his salesmen were producing well for the first week or two of the month but were then slacking off. Investigation showed that the commissions plus salary earned during the periods of high production were about the same each time. It was apparent that the salesmen had earned what they required to live so that they could loaf the rest of the month. By instituting contests and informing the salesmen's wives about the prizes to be won, considerable improvement was obtained.

In the industrialized nations, the opposite trend is being observed. As noted, in Germany there is a tendency toward shorter workweeks and longer vacations. Even in Japan the 48-hour week has been reduced to 46 hours and is expected to be down to 40 hours by the mid-1990s. Japanese still take far fewer paid vacation days annually (9) than do workers in the United States (19), Great Britain (24), France (26), and Germany (29).[21]

"The Protestant work ethic isn't cutting it, so we're switching to Shinto."

Reprinted from *The Wall Street Journal:* permission of Cartoon Features Syndicate.

Prestigious Jobs.   Another aspect of the attitude toward work is the prestige associated with certain kinds of employment. In this country, some types of work are considered more prestigious than others, but there is nowhere near the disdain for physical labor here that there is in many developing countries. The result is an overabundance of attorneys and economists and a lack of toolmakers and welders even when the wages are higher for the latter. The distinction between blue-collar workers and office employees is especially great, as typified by the use of two words in Spanish for the worker—*obrero* (one who labors) signifies a blue-collar worker, whereas *empleado* (employee) signifies an office worker.[22]

Significance to Businesspeople.   The lesson to be learned from this discussion is that it is highly possible that managers will encounter sharp differences in the attitudes toward work and achievement in other cultures compared to their own when they go overseas. However, they must recruit subordinates with a need to progress, whatever the underlying motive. One good source for such people is among relatively well-educated members of the lower social class who view work as a route to the prestige and social acceptance that have been denied them because of their birth.

Attitudes toward Change.   The American firm, accustomed to the rapid acceptance by Americans of something new, is frequently surprised to find that new does not carry that kind of magic in markets where something tried and proven is preferred to the unknown. Europeans are fond of reminding Americans that they are a young nation lacking traditions. The near reverence for traditional methods makes it more difficult for a production manager to install a new process, a marketer to introduce a new product, or a treasurer to change an accounting system.

The New Idea.   Yet, undeniably, international firms are agents of change, and their personnel must be able to counter resistance to it. The new idea will be more readily acceptable the closer it can be related to the traditional one while at the same time being made to show its relative advantage. In other words, the more consistent a new idea is with a society's attitudes and experiences, the more quickly it will be adopted.

Economic Motivation. In these times of rising expectations, economic motives can be a strong influence for accepting change. Thus, if factory workers can be shown that their income will increase with a new machine or housewives can be convinced that a new frozen food will enable them to work and still provide satisfactory meals for their families, they can be persuaded by the gain in their economic welfare to accept ideas that they might otherwise oppose.

Religion

Religion, an important component of culture, is responsible for many of the attitudes and beliefs affecting human behavior. A knowledge of the basic tenets of some of the more popular religions will contribute to a better understanding of why people's attitudes vary so greatly from country to country. Figure 9–1 presents a map of the major religions of the world.

FIGURE 9–1 Major religions of the world

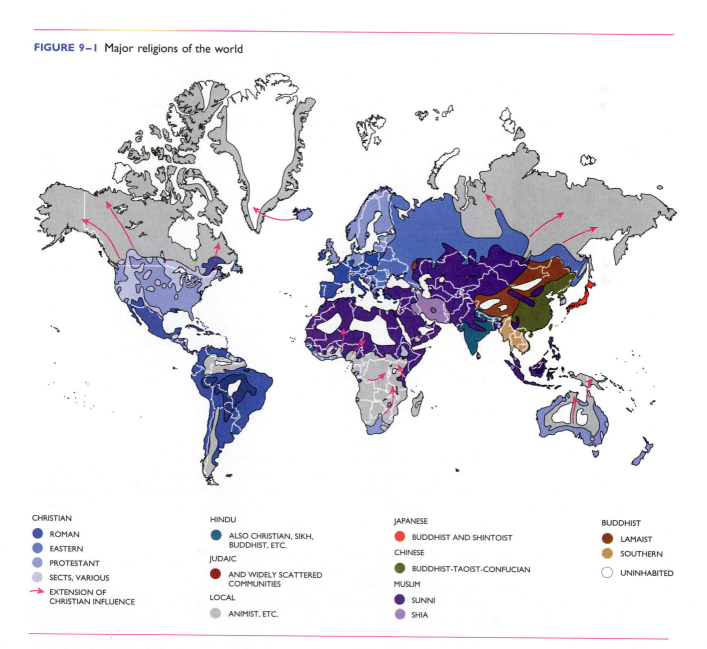

CHRISTIAN
- ROMAN
- EASTERN
- PROTESTANT
- SECTS, VARIOUS
- → EXTENSION OF CHRISTIAN INFLUENCE

HINDU
- ALSO CHRISTIAN, SIKH, BUDDHIST, ETC.

JUDAIC
- AND WIDELY SCATTERED COMMUNITIES

LOCAL
- ANIMIST, ETC.

JAPANESE
- BUDDHIST AND SHINTOIST

CHINESE
- BUDDHIST-TAOIST-CONFUCIAN

MUSLIM
- SUNNI
- SHIA

BUDDHIST
- LAMAIST
- SOUTHERN
- UNINHABITED

Work Ethics.   We have already mentioned the marked differences in the attitudes toward work and achievement. Europeans and Americans generally view work as a moral virtue and look unfavorably on the idle. This view stems in part from the **Protestant work ethic** as expressed by Luther and Calvin, who believed it was the duty of Christians to glorify God by hard work and the practice of thrift.

In Asian countries where Confucianism is strong, this same attitude toward work is called the **Confucian work ethic,** and in Japan, it's called the Shinto work ethic after the principal religion of that nation. Interestingly, because of other factors—such as a growing feeling of prosperity and a shift to a five-day workweek (with two days off, workers develop new interests)—Japanese employers are finding that younger workers no longer have the same dedication to their jobs that their predecessors had. Workers rarely show up early to warm the oil in their machines before their shifts start, and some management trainees are actually taking all of their 15 days' vacation time. A representative of the Employers Association states, "Our universities are leisure centers." A recent college graduate claims, "Students ski in the winter and play tennis in the summer. What the companies sometimes find out is that some new employees like skiing better than working."[23]

Asian Religions.   People from the Western world will encounter some very different notions about God, man, and reality in **Asian religions.** In the Judeo-Christian tradition, this world is real and significant because it was created by God. Human beings are likewise significant; so is time, because it began with God's creation and will end when His will has been fulfilled. Each human being has only one lifetime to heed God's word and achieve everlasting life.

In Asian religions, especially in the religions of India, the ideas of reality are different. There is a notion that this world is an illusion because nothing is permanent. Time is cyclical, so all living things, including humans, are in a constant process of birth, death, and reincarnation. The goal of salvation is to escape from the cycle and move into a state of eternal bliss *(nirvana).* The notion of *karma* (moral retribution) holds that evil committed in one lifetime will be punished in the next. Thus, karma is a powerful impetus to do good so as to achieve a higher spiritual status in the next life. Asians who hold these views cannot imagine that they have not had past lives when they may have been plants, animals, or human beings. Of the seven best-known religions that originated in Asia, four came from India (Hinduism, Buddhism, Jainism, and Sikhism), two from China (Confucianism and Taoism), and one from Japan (Shintoism).

Hinduism.   This is a conglomeration of religions, without a single founder or a central authority, that is practiced by more than 80 percent of India's population. Although there is great diversity among regions and social classes, Hinduism has certain characteristic features. Most Hindus believe that everything in the world is subject to an eternal process of death and rebirth *(samsura)* and that individual souls *(atmans)* migrate from one body to another. They believe one can be liberated from the samsura cycle and achieve that state of eternal bliss (nirvana) by (1) yoga (purification of mind and body), (2) devout worship of the gods, or (3) good works and obedience to the laws and customs *(dharmas)* of one's caste.

A knowledge of the **caste system** is important to managers because the castes are the basis of the social division of labor. The highest caste, the Brahmins or priesthood, is followed by the warriors (politicians, landowners), the merchants, the peasants, and the untouchables. An individual's position in

---

Protestant work ethic
Christian duty to glorify God by hard work and the practice of thrift

Confucian work ethic
Same as Protestant work ethic

Asian religions
The primary ones are Hinduism, Buddhism, Jainism, and Sikhism (India); Confucianism and Taoism (China); and Shintoism (Japan)

caste system
An aspect of Hinduism by which the entire society is divided into four groups (plus the outcasts) and each is assigned a certain class of work

a caste is inherited, as is that person's job within the caste, and movement to a higher caste can be made only in subsequent lives. Although the government of India has officially outlawed discrimination based on the caste system, and in fact has worked to improve the situation of those in the lower castes, such discrimination still exists. The manager who places a member of a lower caste in charge of a group of people from a higher one does so at a considerable risk of employee dissatisfaction.

Buddhism.   This religion began in India as a reform movement of Hinduism. At the age of 29, Prince Gautama rejected his wife, son, and wealth and set out to solve the mysteries of misery, old age, and death. After six years of experimenting with yoga, which brought no enlightenment, he suddenly understood how to break the laws of karma and the endless cycle of rebirth (samsura). Gautama emerged as the Buddha (the Enlightened One).

He renounced the austere self-discipline of the Hindus as well as the extremes of self-indulgence, both of which depended on a craving that locked people into the endless cycle of rebirth. Gautama taught that by extinguishing desire, his followers could attain enlightenment and escape the cycle of existence into nirvana. By opening his teaching to everyone, he opposed the caste system.

Because Buddhist monks are involved in politics in the areas where their religion is prevalent and because they are a mobilizing force for political and social action, managers working in these areas need to be aware of what these religious leaders are doing.

A Buddhist teaching is that if people have no desires, they will not suffer. This is important to marketers and production managers because if Buddhists and Hindus have no desires, they have little motive for achievement and for the acquisition of material goods.

Jainism.   This religion was founded by Mahavira, a contemporary of Buddha. The Jain doctrine teaches that there is no creator, no god, and no absolute principle. Through right faith, correct conduct, and right knowledge of the soul, Jains can purify themselves, become free of samsura, and achieve nirvana. Although relatively few in number, Jains are influential leaders in commerce and scholarship. Their greatest impact on Indian culture is manifested in the widespread acceptance of their nonviolence doctrine, which prohibits animal slaughter, war, and even violent thoughts.

Sikhism.   This is the religion of an Indian ethnic group, a military brotherhood,* and a political movement that was founded by Nanek, who sought a bridge between Hinduism and Islam. Sikhs believe there is a single god, but they also accept the Hindu concepts of samsura, karma, and spiritual liberation. The Sikh's holiest temple was partly destroyed by Indian troops who suppressed their movement for self-government. More than 80 percent of all Sikhs live in the Indian state of Punjab, which they hope to make an autonomous state.

Confucianism.   The name of Confucius is inseparable from Chinese culture and civilization, which were already well developed when he set out to master ancient traditions and transform them into a rational system capable of guiding his people's personal and social behavior. Confucianism may be considered a religion inasmuch as Confucius built a philosophy on the notion

---

*Baptism into the Sikh brotherhood requires all members to take Singh as a second name.

that all reality is subject to an eternal mandate from heaven; however, he refused to speculate on the existence of Chinese folk deities and was agnostic on the question of life after death.

Confucius taught that each person bears within himself the principle of unselfish love for others, *jen*, the cultivation of which is its own reward. A second principle, *li*, prescribes a gentle decorum in all actions and accounts for the Chinese emphasis on politeness, deference to elders, and ritual courtesies such as bowing.

Taoism. This is a mystical philosophy founded by Lao-tzu, a contemporary of Confucius. Taoism, which means "philosophy of the way," holds that each of us mirrors the same forces, the male and the female energies (yin and yang) that govern the cosmos. The aim of Taoist meditation and rituals is to free the self from distractions and become empty so as to allow the cosmic forces to act.

Fung Shui. This ancient custom, with roots in Taoism and nature worship, is based on a simple concept. If buildings, furniture, roads, and other man-made objects are placed in harmony with nature, they can bring good fortune. If not, they will cause a disaster. Although the Chinese government discourages *fung shui* in China, Chinese people around the world practice it, and foreigners living in cities such as Hong Kong and Singapore frequently find fung shui can impact their lives.[24]

> Shortly after arriving in Hong Kong, a Citibank vice president moved to a new office building. To please his staff, he called a fung shui man to analyze the omens of the office. The man examined the office with a compasslike instrument and then gave the vice president the bad news. He would be harmed seriously unless he installed an aquarium with six black fish and put his desk in an inconvenient spot near his office door. The executive ignored the warnings and within days developed a back problem, caused—he thought—by stretching exercises. A physician found two discs had slipped and said the vice president would be paralyzed for life if he didn't spend two weeks in traction. While he was in the hospital, his secretary installed the fish tank and rearranged the furniture. Today, he sits by the door, near the fish. He says his health is better than ever, and he is frightened of fung shui.[25]

Shintoism. This is the indigenous religion of Japan. It has no founder or bible. Shinto legends define the founding of the Japanese empire as a cosmic act, and the emperor was believed to have divine status. As a part of the World War II settlement, the emperor was forced to renounce such a claim. Shintoism has no elaborate theology or even an organized weekly worship. Its followers come to the thousands of Shinto shrines when they feel moved to do so.

Islam. About 950 million followers make this youngest universal faith the second largest after Christianity (which has 1.8 billion adherents). Islam means "to submit" in Arabic; and Muslim, meaning "submitting," is the present participle of the same verb. This faith accepts as God's eternal word the Koran, a collection of Allah's (God's) revelations to Muhammad, the founder of Islam. Unlike the founders of the other major religions, the prophet Muhammad was not only the spokesman of Allah but also the founder of what became a vast temporal and ecclesiastical empire; in other words, he was a head of state as well as a prophet of God. In Muslim nations, there is no separation of church and state.

The basic spiritual duties of all Muslims consist of the five pillars of faith: (1) accepting the confession of faith ("There is no God but God, and Muhammad is the Messenger of God"); (2) making the five daily prayers while

A Shinto priest beating a tiako at the Shogoin Temple in Kyoto, Japan.

Nicholas DeVore/Tony Stone Images

facing Mecca (Muhammad's birthplace, where he was inspired to preach God's word in the year A.D. 610); (3) giving charity; (4) fasting during the daylight hours of Ramadan, a 29- or 30-day month in Islam's lunar calendar; and (5) making a pilgrimage to Mecca at least once in their lifetime. Some Muslims claim there is a sixth duty, *jihad,* which refers to the various forms of striving for the faith, such as the inner struggle for purification. However, this term is often translated as "the holy war."

The split that occurred between the Sunnis and the Shiites over the succession to Muhammad's authority is as important as the division that took place in Christendom with the Reformation. Muhammad's survivors decided that his successors (called *caliphs*) should be elected by members of the Islamic community, and they were—four times. But after the fourth successor, Ali (Muhammad's cousin), was murdered, the caliphate passed to the monarchical house of Ummaya. Ali's son, Hussayn, claimed the caliphate was his, as Muhammad's heir, and he started a rebellion to confirm his claim. Hussayn was killed in a battle by a Sunni caliph.

This split the Muslim world between the Sunnis (followers of the Prophet's Path) and the Shiites (Party of Ali). After their defeat, the Shiites, feeling they had been wronged, became dissenters within the Arab empire who were given to violence against authority. Although the Shiites and the Sunnis agree on the fundamentals of Islam, they differ in other respects. The Sunnis are an austere sect that is less authoritarian and more pragmatic than the Shiites. In their view, as long as Muslims accept Allah, they are free to interpret their religion as they like. The Shiites, on the other hand, insist that those claiming to be Muslim must put themselves under the authority of a holy man (*ayatollah*).

This has created a clergy that wields enormous temporal and spiritual power, with the result that religious leaders impact business as well as religion. Consider two harmless consumer products, Coca-Cola and Pepsi-Cola. Both were banned from Iran for 15 years after the Islamic revolution in 1979, but returned in 1993 and are now extremely popular with Iranians. However, Iran's spiritual leader, Ayatollah Ali Khomenei, has ruled that Coca-Cola and Pepsi-Cola contribute to the enhancement of Zionism and therefore are forbidden.[26] Business leaders wonder what the Ayatollah will condemn next.

Salman Rushdie.   An example of the Shiite's political power occurred in early 1989, when a book, *The Satanic Verses*, precipitated what some Islamic experts regard as the most incendiary literary fight in Islamic history. Although Salman Rushdie, the author, denied that his novel was antireligious, nearly all Muslims considered it blasphemous. On February 14, Ayatollah Khomeini, Iran's late spiritual ruler, announced that the author must die for the sin of insulting Islam and promised martyrdom for anyone who killed him. Another cleric announced that a bounty of $2.6 million had been offered. The following day, the bounty was doubled.[27]

In November 1993, Rushdie met with President Clinton and the U.S. secretary of state, apparently to pressure the Iranian government to lift the death sentence. Although Rushdie has escaped harm, several of his translators and editors involved in the book's publication have been killed or seriously wounded.[28] Another author, Taslima Nasrin, has been living in Sweden since she fled from her home in Bangladesh, where she, like Rushdie, faces a death threat from Muslim fundamentalists who have denounced her writings as blasphemous.[29] At the same time in Egypt, Nobel Prize–winning author Naguib Mahfouz, also under a death sentence since 1989 from Islamic radicals for a book written in 1959, was stabbed several times in the neck but managed to live.[30]

Sunni-Shia Conflict.   Businesspeople doing business with Muslim countries should understand the Sunni-Shia conflict, because much of what occurs in these countries is the result of it. Although most Muslim countries are Sunni governed, many of them, such as Kuwait, the emirates, Bahrain, and other small states in the Gulf, have substantial Shia populations. Furthermore, small Shia minorities can cause trouble for the government. For example, Saudi Arabia's Shia population is very small—only 250,000—and is concentrated in the eastern oil fields. Iran's Shia government continually broadcasts appeals to the Saudi Shiites to overthrow the regime. In Iraq, the ruler Saddam Hussein and his army are Sunnis, but 52 percent of the population is Shiite. As you can imagine, this division has given rise to violent clashes between religious dissidents and government forces. On the other hand, Syria is predominantly Sunni, but its government is controlled by a Shia sect.[31]

Even where the Sunni-Shia conflict is not a problem, two of the five pillars of faith can be bothersome to Western managers. The dawn-to-dusk fasting during the month of Ramadan causes workers' output to drop sharply, and the requirement to pray five times daily also affects output, because when they hear the call to prayer, Muslim workers stop whatever they are doing to pray where they are.

> An American manager in Pakistan for the purpose of getting a new factory into production came to the plant the first day, saw that production had started as it should, and went into his office to do some work. Suddenly, all of the machinery stopped. He rushed out, expecting to find a power failure.

Instead, he found workers on their prayer rugs. The manager returned to his office and lowered his production estimates.

Animism.   In a number of African and Latin American countries, animism, a kind of spirit worship that includes magic and witchcraft, is a major religion. It is often combined with Catholicism to present a strange mixture of mysticism, taboos, and fatalism. Animists believe their dead relatives are ever present and will be pleased if the living act in the same way as their ancestors. The resultant strong tendency to perpetuate traditions makes it extremely difficult for marketers and production managers to initiate changes. To be accepted, these changes must relate to the animists' beliefs. The foreign manager must also be cognizant of the proper religious protocols in situations such as factory and store dedications. If the evil spirits are not properly exorcised, they will remain to cause all sorts of problems, such as worker injuries, machinery breakdowns, and defective products.

> Evil spirits wreaked havoc in an American-owned semiconductor factory in Kuala Lumpur, Malaysia. The plant consists of an enormous room filled with hundreds of women looking into microscopes and television monitors.
> One afternoon, a girl claimed she saw an ugly woman in her microscope. The operator was pulled screaming to the first-aid room. The manager admitted that was a mistake: "Before I knew it, we had girls all over being held down by supervisors. It was like a battlefield."
> The factory was evacuated, but when the night crew arrived, the spirit returned. "Word had gone out that evil spirits were loose in the factory because of a dance we had the previous weekend. At night, it was worse. All we could do was hold them down, carry them out to the buses, and send them home."
> The next morning, a licensed healer was brought in. His recommen- dation—sacrifice a goat. That afternoon, a goat was killed and its blood was sprinkled on the factory floor. It was cooked in the cafeteria and eaten by the workers.
> "Next morning, we started up, and everything was fine.[32]

Table 9–1 lists the religious populations of the world.

The Importance of Religion to Management.   You have seen that religions have a pervasive influence on business. How effective can offers to pay time and a half for overtime and bonuses based on productivity be in a company whose workers are mainly Buddhists or Hindus? Strict adherents to these religions attempt to rid themselves of desires, and thus they have little need for an income beyond that which permits them to attain the basic necessities of life. When their incomes begin to rise, they have a tendency to reduce their efforts so that personal incomes remain unchanged.

Religious holidays and rituals can affect employee performance and work scheduling. When members of different religious groups work together, there may even be strife, division, and instability within the work force. Managers must respect the religious beliefs of others and adapt business practices to the religious constraints present in other cultures. Of course, to be able to do this, they must first know what those beliefs and constraints are.

Material Culture

Material culture refers to all man-made objects and is concerned with *how* people make things (technology) and *who* makes *what* and *why* (economics).

material culture
All manmade objects; concerned with how *people make things (technology) and* who *makes* what *and* why *(economics)*

Technology.   The technology of a society is the mix of the usable knowledge that the society applies and directs toward the attainment of cultural and economic objectives; it exists in some form in every cultural organization. It is

TABLE 9–1 Estimated religious population of the world (in millions)

Religionists	Africa	Asia	Europe	Latin America	North America	Oceania	Former U.S.S.R	World	Percent
Christians	327.20	285.37	413.76	435.81	239.00	22.63	109.25	1,833.02	33.4%
Roman Catholics	122.91	123.60	262.64	405.62	97.02	8.21	5.59	1,025.59	18.7
Protestants	87.33	81.48	73.94	17.26	96.31	7.52	9.86	373.70	6.8
Orthodox	28.55	3.66	36.17	1.76	6.01	0.58	93.71	170.42	3.1
Anglicans	26.86	0.71	32.96	1.30	7.34	5.72	<	74.88	7.4
Other Christians	61.55	75.93	8.06	9.86	32.32	0.61	0.10	188.43	3.4
Muslims	278.25	636.98	12.57	1.35	2.85	0.10	39.23	971.33	17.7
Nonreligious	1.90	691.14	52.41	17.16	25.27	3.29	85.07	876.23	16.0
Hindus	1.48	728.12	0.70	0.88	1.27	0.36	<	732.81	13.4
Buddhists	0.02	313.11	0.27	0.54	0.56	0.03	0.41	314.94	5.7
Atheists	0.32	161.41	17.60	3.22	1.32	0.54	56.90	240.31	4.4
Chinese folk religionists	0.01	186.82	0.60	0.73	0.12	0.21	<	187.11	3.4
New religionists	0.02	141.38	0.50	1.42	1.42	0.10	<	143.42	2.6
Tribal religionists	70.59	24.95	<	0.94	0.41	0.67	<	96.58	1.8
Jews	0.34	5.59	1.47	1.09	7.00	2.24	2.24	17.82	0.3
Sikhs	0.03	18.27	0.23	<	0.25	<	<	18.80	0.3
Shamanists	<	10.23	<	<	<	<	0.25	10.49	0.2
Confucians	<	5.99	<	<	0.26	<	<	6.03	0.1
Baha'is	1.50	2.68	0.09	0.80	0.37	<	<	5.52	0.1
Jains	0.05	3.72	0.02	<	<	0.77	<	3.79	<0.1
Shintoists	<	3.22	<	<	<	<	<	3.22	<0.1
Other religionists	0.43	12.29	1.47	3.57	0.49	<	0.33	18.59	0.3
World population	682.13	3,231.27	500.71	465.99	279.99	27.23	292.69	5,480.01	100.0

Note: Totals not exact due to rounding. < = less than 10,000.
Source: *World Almanac 1994*, p. 727.

significant in the efforts of developing nations to improve their level of living and a vital factor in the competitive strategies of multinational firms.

Technological superiority is the goal of most companies, of course, but it is especially important to international companies because:

1. It enables a firm to be competitive or even attain leadership in world markets.

   At one time, Procter & Gamble and Unilever were competing worldwide for the laundry detergent market, but then P&G introduced Tide, a synthetic detergent with superior cleaning power. Its sales took off and left Unilever far behind. Finally, Unilever introduced its own synthetic detergent, but P&G had stolen the lead.

2. It can be sold (licensing or management contract), or it can be embodied in the company's products.

3. It can give a firm confidence to enter a foreign market even when other companies are already established there.

4. It can enable the firm to obtain better-than-usual conditions for a foreign market investment because the host government wants the technology that only the firm has (for example, permission for a wholly owned subsidiary in a country where the government normally insists on joint ventures with a local majority).

   IBM, confident of its superior technology, insisted on and obtained permission from the Mexican government to set up a wholly owned subsidiary when other computer manufacturers were forced to accept local partners.

5. It can enable a company with only a minority equity position to control a joint venture and preserve it as a captive market for semiprocessed inputs that it—but not the joint venture—produces.

6. It can change the international division of labor. Some firms that had moved production overseas where labor was cheaper have now returned to their home countries because production methods based on new technology have reduced the direct labor content of their products. With labor costs as low as 5 percent of the total cost in automated production systems, going overseas to save 30 to 40 percent in labor costs, for example, produces only about a 2 percent cost saving. This is more than offset by the transportation costs to bring the finished merchandise to the United States. Numerous electronics manufacturers such as Tandy, Compaq, and Xerox have brought production back to this country.

7. It is causing major firms to form competitive alliances in which each partner shares technology and the high costs of research and development.

When IBM realized that it needed liquid-crystal displays for portable computers, it formed a joint venture with Toshiba. IBM supplied the expertise in materials and Toshiba furnished superior manufacturing processes.[33]

Cultural Aspects of Technology.   Technology includes not only the application of science to production, but also skill in marketing, finance, and management. Its cultural aspects concern governments because their people may not be ready to accept the cultural changes a new technology may bring. Some say the shah of Iran's overthrow resulted in part from his trying to introduce new technology too rapidly.

Technology's cultural aspects are certainly important to international managers, because new production methods and new products often require people to change their beliefs and ways of living. The self-employed farmer frequently finds the discipline required to become a factory worker excessively demanding. If workers have been accustomed to the production conditions of cottage industries in which each individual performs all of the production operations, they find it difficult to adjust to the monotony of tightening a single bolt. The "throw away instead of repair" philosophy behind the design of so many new products necessitates a change in the use habits of people who have been accustomed to repairing something to keep it operating until it is thoroughly worn out. Generally, the greater the difference between the old and new method or product, the more difficult it is for the firm to institute a change.

High GNP—High Level of Technology.   The differences in levels of technology among nations are used as a basis for judging whether nations are developed or developing. Generally, a nation with a higher GNP per capita utilizes a higher level of technology than one whose per capita income is smaller. Because of **technological dualism,** however, analysts must not assume that since the general technological level in a market is low, the particular industry they are examining is employing a simple technology.

technological dualism
The side-by-side presence of technologically advanced and technologically primitive production systems

Technological Dualism.   Technological dualism is a prominent feature of many developing nations. In the same country, one industry sector may be technologically advanced, with high productivity, while the production techniques of another sector may be old and labor intensive. This condition may be the result of the host government's insistence that foreign investors import only the most modern machinery rather than used-but-serviceable equipment that would be less costly and could create more employment.

Sometimes the preferences are reversed. The host government, beset by high unemployment, may argue for labor-intensive processes, while the foreign firm prefers automated production, both because it is the kind the home office is most familiar with and because its use lessens the need for skilled labor, which is usually in short supply. To understand which policy the host government is following, management must study its laws and regulations and talk with host country officials.

appropriate technology
The technology (advanced, intermediate, or primitive) that most closely fits the society using it

Appropriate Technology. Rather than choosing between labor-intensive and capital-intensive processes, many experts in economic development are recommending **appropriate technology**, which can be labor intensive, intermediate, or capital intensive. The idea is to choose the technology that most closely fits the society using it. For example, in Africa, bricks are usually made in large-city factories using modern technology or locally in hand-poured, individual molds. In Botswana, an American group, AT International, designed an inexpensive small press with which four people can produce 1,500 bricks a day.[34] This is an intermediate technology that is also an appropriate technology.

In India, a small manufacturer, Patel, has taken three-fourths of the detergent market from Lever, the giant multinational, by using labor-intensive technology. Lever's Surf brand dominated the market until Patel, realizing that a high-quality, high-priced product was not appropriate for a poor country, set up a chain of shops in which people mixed the ingredients by hand. This primitive method is tailored to Indian conditions and now enables the company to outsell Lever on the basis of price. Its annual sales exceed $250 million.[35]

boomerang effect
When technology sold to companies in another nation is used to produce goods to compete with those of the seller of the technology

Boomerang Effect. One reason firms sometimes fear to sell their technology abroad is the **boomerang effect**. For example, Japanese firms have become less willing to sell their technology to NIEs, such as Korea. They fear that by giving Korea their technology today, they make Korea a tougher competitor tomorrow. As a result, Korea is turning more to the United States for technical assistance. This suggests why Korean-American ties of all kinds are strengthening. As an official from the Korean Ministry of Science and Technology said on a visit to the United States, "If America and Korea join together, we can overcome Japan."[36] Interestingly, fear of the boomerang effect has caused some American firms to restrict the sale of their technology to the Japanese.

Government Controls. The level of technology used by a foreign investor in a new manufacturing facility has a widespread impact. It affects the size of the investment, the quality and number of workers employed, the kinds and quality of production inputs, what the facility can produce, and even what the host country can export. If the product cannot compete in the world market because production costs are excessive, quality is inferior, or the design is obsolete, the host government will not obtain the foreign exchange it otherwise would have. For these reasons, plus what many governments consider abuses in the sale of technology, many developing countries enacted strong laws that control the purchase of technical assistance by, for example, limiting both royalties paid to and the requirements made by the multinationals. The latter could include requiring licensees to transfer to licensors any improvements they make in the technology, prohibiting licensees from exporting, and obliging licensees to purchase raw materials from the licensor. Recently, however, host governments have recognized that technology is probably the most powerful stimulus to economic growth there is, so many are loosening controls as they pursue policies to attract foreign investment.[37]

Economics.   The decision the global or multinational headquarters makes as to the kind of technology to be used by a subsidiary will, within any constraints imposed by the host government, depend on various measurements of the material culture. Economic yardsticks such as power generated per capita and number of high school graduates can uncover possible problems in the distribution and promotion of the product, help determine market size, and provide information on the availability of such resources as raw materials, skilled and unskilled labor, capital equipment, economic infrastructure (communications, financial system), and management talent. You studied these in Chapter 7.

Education

Although education in its widest sense can be thought of as any part of the learning process that equips an individual to take his or her place in the adult society, nearly everyone in the Euramerican culture equates education with formal schooling.

Education Yardsticks.   The firm contemplating foreign investment has no indicators of the educational level of a country's inhabitants except the usual yardsticks of formal education: literacy rate, kinds of schools, quantity of schools and their enrollments, and possibly the amount per capita spent on education. Such data underestimate the size of the vocationally trained group in the many developing countries where people learn a trade through apprenticeships starting at a very early age (12 to 13 years). Like other international statistics, the published literacy rate must be suspect. One definition of adult literacy used by UNESCO is "the proportion of the population over the age of 15 who can, with understanding, read and write a short, simple statement on their everyday life."[38] In some countries, the literacy census consists of asking respondents whether they can read and write, and the signing of their names is taken as proof of their literacy. Nevertheless, these data do provide some assistance. Marketers are interested in the literacy rate because it helps them decide what type of media to employ and at what level they should prepare advertisements, labels, point-of-purchase displays, and owner's manuals. The personnel manager will use the literacy rate as a guide in estimating what kinds of people will be available for staffing the operation.

As with most kinds of data, the trends in education should be studied. It is important to realize that the general level of education is rising throughout the world. Figure 9–2 illustrates the extent of this increase for higher education.

Note that in a little over 25 years, the percentage of adults aged 20 to 24 in post–high school education tripled in the low-income nations, increased by 11 times in the oil-exporting countries, and more than doubled in the high-income nations. The implication for international businesspeople is that they must prepare to meet the needs of more sophisticated and better-educated consumers. They also can expect a better-educated work force.

Although these data are indicative of the general level of education, unfortunately they tell us nothing about the quality of education, nor do they indicate how well the supply of graduates meets the demand.

Educational Mix.   Until the 1970s, management education in Europe lagged far behind what was available in the United States. There was a feeling that

FIGURE 9–2
Percentage of adults aged 20 to 24 in post–high school education

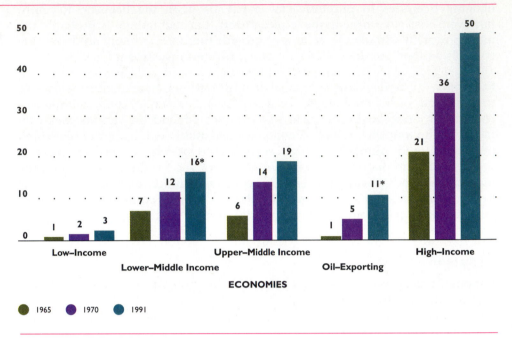

*1990.

Source: *World Development Report*, 1991, 1993, 1994 (New York: World Development Bank, 1991, 1993, 1994), pp. 260–61, 216–17, and 294–95.

managers were born, not made, and that they could be trained only on the job. Thus, there was little demand for formal business education.

However, a combination of factors has caused a proliferation of European business schools patterned on the American model:

1. Increased competition in the European Union, resulting in a demand for better-trained managers.
2. The return to Europe of American business school graduates.
3. The establishment of American-type schools with American faculty and frequently with the assistance of American universities.

This trend has been much slower in developing countries, where, historically, higher education has emphasized the study of the humanities, law, and medicine. Engineering has not been popular because, with the exception of architecture and civil engineering, there have been few engineering job opportunities in these preindustrial societies. Business education has been less popular than other fields because a business career lacked prestige.

> In Chile, one of the writers was asked to train an engineer to be a V-belt technician. Noticing that the engineer could not comprehend engineering terms, the writer asked him what kind of engineer he was. To the writer's surprise, the answer was *commercial engineer*. In a land of professional titles, apparently the government thought this was the best way to give professional recognition to business graduates. In Latin America, a person is commonly addressed by his professional title—*Ingeniero* Garcia (engineer) or *Licenciado* Lopez (economist or attorney). A similar practice is followed in Germany and in most central European countries.

As developing nations industrialize, there is a greater competition in the marketplace and the job opportunities for engineers and business school graduates increase. Not only do the multinationals recruit such personnel, but the local firms do too when they find that the new competition forces them to improve the efficiency of their operations.

Brain Drain.   Most developing nations are convinced that economic development is impossible without the development of human resources, and for the last two decades especially, governments have probably overinvested in higher education in relation to the demand for students. The result has been rising unemployment among the educated, which has led to a **brain drain**, the emigration of professionals to the industrialized nations. A study done by UNCTAD estimated that about 500,000 professionals had left Third World countries since World War II. However, the incidence of brain drain varied enormously because most come from a limited number of countries in Asia, such as India, Pakistan, Egypt, and Korea.[39]

brain drain
The emigration of highly educated professionals to another country

The prime minister of Jamaica made an interesting observation. During the 1977–80 period, over 8,000 top professionals, 50 percent of the country's most highly trained citizens, emigrated, primarily to the United States. He estimated that the education of these people cost his nation $168.5 million, or $20,000 per person. During the same period, U.S. aid to Jamaica totaled only $116.3 million.[40]

Brain drain facts:

1. Each year, 6,000 Taiwanese come to study in the United States, but only 20 percent return home.

2. There are 8,000 Israeli engineers in the United States, which Israel says has created a severe bottleneck in its own development of sophisticated industry.

3. About one-half of the 1,000 students who graduate annually from the 27 Philippine medical schools go abroad.

4. The United States alone has 4,000 Greek research scientists, compared with just 5,000 living in Greece. There are also 1,200 Greek business professors working in the United States, but there is no university M.B.A. program in Greece and there is an acute shortage of skilled managers.

5. In U.S. graduate schools of engineering, half of the assistant professors under age 35 are foreign.

6. At IBM's research headquarters, 27 percent of the researchers are foreign.[41]

7. Governments of industrialized nations fear that unemployed Soviet scientists will work for countries such as Iraq, Syria, and Libya on the development of nuclear, biological, and chemical weapons. To prevent this, other nations besides Israel are offering them employment. The South Koreans, for example, agreed in 1992 to hire 110 scientists to work at their research institutes.[42]

Government authorities are deeply concerned about the loss of skills and have come to realize that there must be faster new job creation, not only to stop the costly loss but also to avoid serious political repercussions. To provide more jobs, they are adopting developmental plans that encourage labor-intensive exports and discourage the introduction of labor-saving processes. The pressure of the unemployed educated is also forcing officials in many areas to soften the terms for foreign investment.

Reverse Brain Drain.   A **reverse brain drain** is preoccupying American educators and businesspeople. After suffering a severe brain drain for over 30 years, Korea and Taiwan are luring home those Korean and Taiwanese engineers and scientists with American doctorates and 10 or more years' experience in American high-tech firms. More money and the opportunity to start businesses in these industrializing countries are the attractions.[43] The returnees

reverse brain drain
The return of highly educated professionals to their home countries

are having a visible effect on their countries' competitiveness. The director of the science office at Sun Microsystems says, "Half the engineering vice presidents in Taiwan electronics companies went to school in the United States, worked at Sun, worked at Hewlett-Packard, and brought back cash to Taiwan to start companies."

In 1993, more than 48 percent of those who obtained engineering doctorates at American universities were citizens of other countries. Because, after graduation, many stay to work in Silicon Valley and top R&D centers such as AT&T Bell Laboratories, they provide a vast talent pool to meet the needs of American industry.[44] The director of the Commission on Professionals in Science and Technology said, "We've been counting on foreign graduates to stay here and fill our needs because we haven't been filling our own needs for a long time. There's nobody to replace them."[45]

Adult Literacy.   Many governments are also questioning the wisdom of spending funds to highly educate a few and are now giving priority to primary educators as a means of achieving universal literacy. The success of these programs is evidenced by the reduction of world adult illiteracy from 42 percent in 1960 to 35 percent in 1990.

However, the latest data show that the literacy rate was still below the world average in at least 70 nations. Only Norway claimed 100 percent adult literacy, and in Saudi Arabia and Togo, only the male literacy rate was mentioned. Figure 9–3 lists the nations with literacy rates of less than 30 percent.

Inasmuch as the results of an adult literacy program are immediate, whereas it takes 10 to 20 years for the primary school generation to be productive, more attention is being given to adult education, an important trend for international managements to note. For example, in only four years, Brazil was able to reduce the illiteracy rate for adult Brazilians by one-third, and the cost, allowing for dropouts, was only $11 per student. The program's

FIGURE 9–3 Nations whose adult literacy rate is less than 30 percent

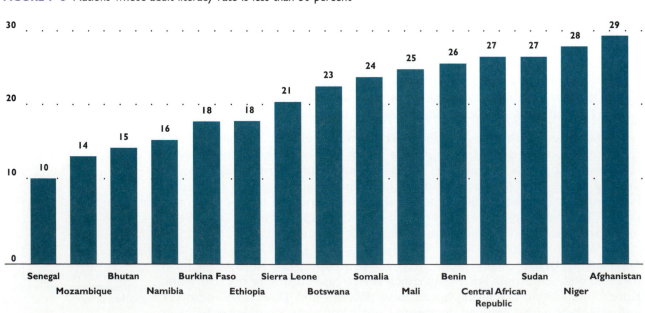

Source: *World Almanac, 1994,* p. 647–737.

Economies	Total			Female		
	1965	**1970**	**1991**	**1965**	**1970**	**1991**
Lower income	49%	55%	79%	37%	55%	79%
Lower-middle income	89	93	104*	81	83	97†
Upper-middle income	98	94	105	94	92	105
High-income	104	106	104	105	106	103
World	85	83	102	74	71	96

TABLE 9–2
Percentage of school-age population in primary schools

*Percentages may exceed 100 percent because some pupils are younger or older than the country's standard primary school age.
†1990.

Sources: *World Development Report, 1991* (New York: World Bank, 1991), pp. 260–61; and *World Development Report, 1994* (New York: World Bank, 1994), pp. 216–17.

annual budget was $26 million, which is less than New York City spends just to repair and maintain its school buildings.

Women's Education.   Another important trend is the fall in the illiteracy rate for women. The literacy differences between older and younger female age groups is striking. In Africa, which has the world's highest illiteracy rate, the percentage of women who could read and write grew from 18 percent in 1970 to 45 percent in 1990.

Nearly every government now has a goal, if not an actual policy, of providing free and compulsory education for both genders. Notice in Table 9–2 the improvement from 1965 to 1991.

Many more women are enrolling in universities worldwide. As you can see in Table 9–3, the percentage of women of university age attending universities in Africa and the Arab states has tripled in just 30 years.

These statistics are significant to businesspeople because in almost every country, educated women have fewer, healthier, and better-educated children than do uneducated women. They achieve higher labor force participation rates and higher earnings. Undoubtedly, this is leading to an increased role for women in the family's decision making, which will require marketers to redo their promotional programs to take advantage of this consequential trend.

Language

Probably the most apparent cultural distinction that the newcomer to international business perceives is in the means of communication. Differences in the spoken language are readily discernible, and after a short period in the new culture it becomes apparent that there are variations in the unspoken language (manners and customs) as well.

	1960	1990
World	39%	54%
Developed nations	65	79
Developing nations	29	48
Africa	14	38
North America	82	93
Arab states	16	50
Asia	33	48
Oceania	65	75

TABLE 9–3
Percentage of university-age women enrolled in universities

Source: *UNESCO Statistical Yearbook 1992* (New York), pp. 2–20, and 2–31.

Spoken Language.   Language is the key to culture, and without it, people find themselves locked out of all but a culture's perimeter. At the same time, in learning a language, people can't understand the nuances, double meanings of words, and slang unless they also learn the other aspects of the culture. Fortunately, the learning of both goes hand in hand; a certain feel for a people and their attitudes naturally develops with a growing mastery of their language.

Languages Delineate Cultures.   Spoken languages demarcate cultures, just as physical barriers do. In fact, nothing equals the spoken language for distinguishing one culture from another. If two languages are spoken in a country, there will be two separate cultures (Belgium); if four languages are spoken, there will be four cultures (Switzerland); and so forth.

A poll taken of the German-speaking and French-speaking cultures in Switzerland illustrates how deeply opinions on crucial issues diverge even in a small country.[46] For example, 83.3 percent of the German Swiss regard environmental protection as one of Switzerland's five major problems, compared to 45.1 percent of the French Swiss. Note in Figure 9–4 how each culture rates the importance of various domestic issues.

The results of a 1994 opinion poll "prove that there is no such thing as an average Swiss citizen. Each linguistic region attaches different importance to the particular problem. In German-speaking Switzerland, drugs head the list of worries. In French-speaking Switzerland and the Ticino (Italian-speaking), where jobless figures are higher, unemployment is seen as the number one problem by far, ahead even of drugs." The energy tax that receives only guarded support of the German-speaking Swiss is opposed by the majority of the French-speaking area and totally rejected in Ticino.[47]

What is occurring in Canada because of the sharp divisions between the English- and French-speaking regions is ample evidence of the force of languages in delineating cultures. The differences among the Basques, Catalans, and Spaniards and the differences between the French and Flemish of

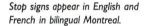

Stop signs appear in English and French in bilingual Montreal.

Walter Bibliow/The Image Bank

FIGURE 9–4 Differences in what's worrying the Swiss (percent)*

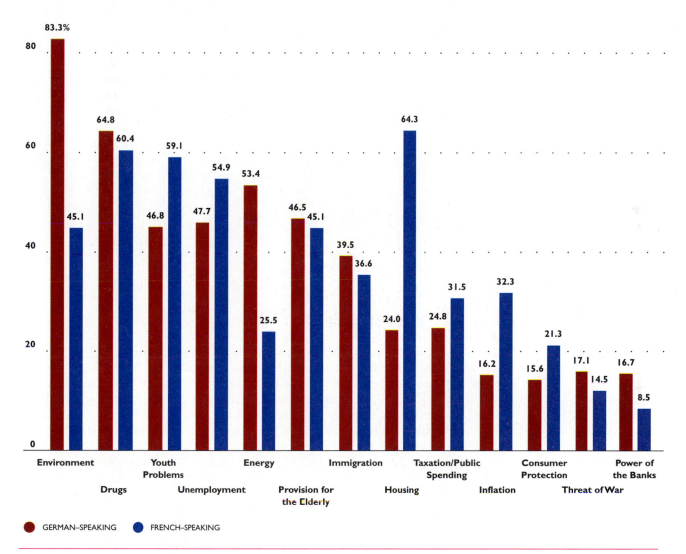

*Carried out by Isopublic on a representative sample of respondents from all sections of the population between May 4 and July 8, 1988.

Source: "What's Worrying the Swiss?" *Bulletin* (Zurich: Crédit Suisse, April 1988), p. 4.

Belgium (see Figure 9–5) are other notable examples of the sharp cultural and often political differences between language groups. However, it does not follow from this generalization that cultures are the same wherever the same language is spoken. As a result of Spain's colonization, Spanish is the principal language of 21 Latin American nations, but no one should believe that Chile and Mexico are culturally similar. Moreover, generally because of cultural differences, many words in both the written and spoken languages of these countries are completely different. Even within a country, words vary from one region to another, also due in part to cultural differences.

FIGURE 9–5
How language divides
Belgium

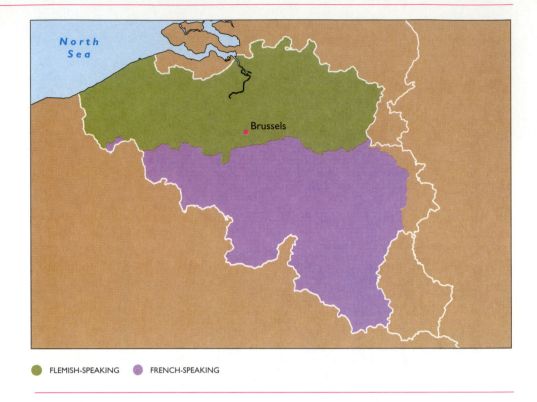

FLEMISH-SPEAKING   FRENCH-SPEAKING

Foreign Language.   Where many spoken languages exist in a single country (India and many African nations), one foreign language usually serves as the principal vehicle for communication across cultures. Nations that were formerly colonies generally use the language of their ex-rulers; thus French is the **lingua franca**, or "link" language, of the former French and Belgian colonies in Africa, English in India, and Portuguese in Angola.[48] Although they serve as a national language, these foreign substitutes are not the first language of anyone and, consequently, are less effective than the native tongues for reaching mass markets or for day-to-day conversations between managers and workers. Even in countries with only one principal language, such as Germany and France, there are problems of communication because of the large numbers of Greeks, Turks, Spaniards, and others who were recruited to ease labor shortages. A German supervisor may have workers from three or four countries and be unable to speak directly with any of them. To ameliorate this situation, managements try to separate the work force according to origin; for instance, all Turks are placed in the paint shop, all Greeks on the assembly line, and so on. But the preferred solution is to teach managers the language of their workers. Invariably, such training has resulted in an increase in production, fewer product defects, and higher worker morale.

> General Tire–Chile sponsored a reverse language training program in which every employee could take free English courses given on the premises after work. Not only managers but also supervisors and even workers attended classes. The program was an excellent morale builder.

English, the Link Language of Business.   When a Swedish businessperson talks with a Japanese businessperson, the conversation generally will be in English. The use of English as a business lingua franca is spreading in Europe so

lingua franca
A foreign language used to communicate among a nation's diverse cultures that have diverse languages

rapidly that it is replacing French and German as the most widely spoken language among Europeans. Satellite television is credited for bringing it to millions of homes where English was previously not spoken. Already 10 million homes receive English news broadcasts from the Super Channel in England, and this number is expected to rise to 45 million homes by 1996. In Norway, for example, learning English is compulsory; but even where it is not, young Europeans choose to study it as their second language. English is now spoken by 42 percent of the 15-to-25-year olds. This is double the number of people who have learned French and over four times as many who know German.[49] A number of European multinationals—such as Philips, the Dutch electronics manufacturer ($32 billion annual sales), and Olivetti, the Italian computer manufacturer ($6 billion annual sales)—have adopted English as their official language.[50] Similarly, some major Japanese firms, such as Matushita and Sony, use English as their international business language.

Must Speak the Local Language.   Even though more and more businesspeople are speaking English, when they buy, they insist on doing business in their own language. The seller who speaks it has a competitive edge. Moreover, knowing the language of the area indicates respect for its culture and the area's people. Figure 9–6 shows a map of major languages of the world.

In many countries, it is a social blunder to begin a business conversation by talking business. Most foreigners expect to establish a social relationship first, and the casual, exploratory conversation that precedes business talks may take from 15 minutes to several meetings, depending on the importance of the meetings. Obviously, people can establish a better rapport in a one-on-one conversation than through an interpreter. Look at the trouble this person would have avoided if he had spoken Spanish.

> A German engineer, in Colombia to work on a pipeline, arrived at a hotel in the interior, where he tried to explain to the desk clerk that he had a suitcase full of cash that he wanted the hotel to keep. Because he knew no Spanish, he was having difficulty making himself understood. During the conversation, the desk clerk opened the suitcase in front of everyone in the lobby. A week later, the engineer was kidnapped by a guerrilla group and held for a month.[51]

Translation.   The ability to speak the language well does not eliminate the need for translators. The smallest of markets requires technical manuals, catalogs, and good advertising ideas, and a lack of local talent to do the work does not mean that the organization must do without these valuable sales aids. The solution, even when the parent firm does not insist on international standardization, is to obtain this material from headquarters and have it translated if the costs are not prohibitive and suitable reproduction facilities are available locally. If the catalog or manual cannot be reproduced locally, the translation can be made and sent to the home office for reproduction. The home office already has the artwork, so the only additional cost is setting the type for the translations. Remember, though, a French or Spanish translation will be up to 25 percent longer.

Allowing headquarters to translate can be extremely risky because words from the same language frequently vary in meaning from one country to another or even from one region to another, as was mentioned earlier. A famous example that illustrated how only a single word incorrectly translated can ruin an otherwise good translation occurred in Mexico. The American headquarters of a deodorant manufacturer sent a Spanish translation of the manufacturer's international theme, "If you use our deodorant, you won't be embarrassed in public." Unfortunately, the translator used the word *em-*

FIGURE 9–6 Major languages of the world

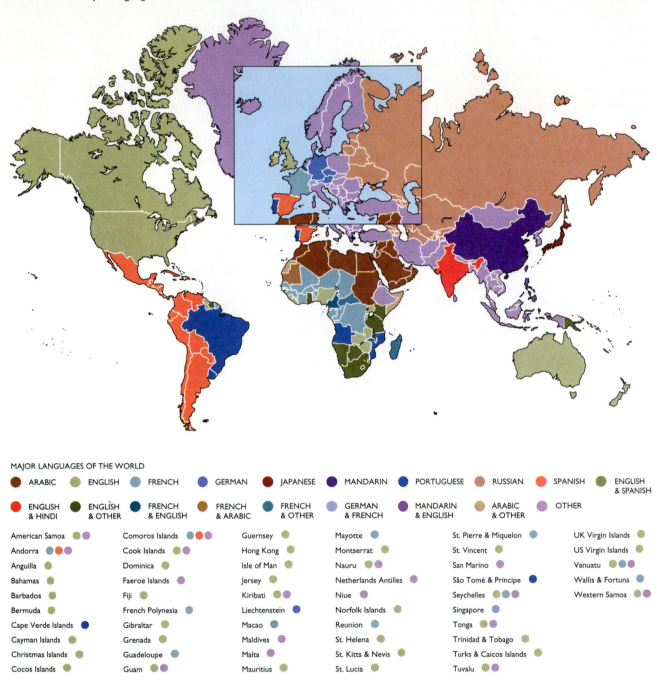

MAJOR LANGUAGES OF THE WORLD

ARABIC · ENGLISH · FRENCH · GERMAN · JAPANESE · MANDARIN · PORTUGUESE · RUSSIAN · SPANISH · ENGLISH & SPANISH

ENGLISH & HINDI · ENGLISH & OTHER · FRENCH & ENGLISH · FRENCH & ARABIC · FRENCH & OTHER · GERMAN & FRENCH · MANDARIN & ENGLISH · ARABIC & OTHER · OTHER

American Samoa · Andorra · Anguilla · Bahamas · Barbados · Bermuda · Cape Verde Islands · Cayman Islands · Christmas Islands · Cocos Islands

Comoros Islands · Cook Islands · Dominica · Faeroe Islands · Fiji · French Polynesia · Gibraltar · Grenada · Guadeloupe · Guam

Guernsey · Hong Kong · Isle of Man · Jersey · Kiribati · Liechtenstein · Macao · Maldives · Malta · Mauritius

Mayotte · Montserrat · Nauru · Netherlands Antilles · Niue · Norfolk Islands · Reunion · St. Helena · St. Kitts & Nevis · St. Lucia

St. Pierre & Miquelon · St. Vincent · San Marino · São Tomé & Príncipe · Seychelles · Singapore · Tonga · Trinidad & Tobago · Turks & Caicos Islands · Tuvalu

UK Virgin Islands · US Virgin Islands · Vanuatu · Wallis & Fortuna · Western Samoa

barazada for embarrassed, which in Mexican Spanish means pregnant. Imagine the time that the Mexican subsidiary had with that one.[52]

Use Two Translations.   To avoid translation errors, the experienced marketer will prefer what are really two translations. The first will be made by a bilingual native, whose work will then be translated back to a bilingual foreigner to see how it compares with the original. This work should preferably be done in the market where the material is to be used. No method is foolproof, but the double-translation approach is the safest way devised so far.

Some problems with translations:

1. Information about the air conditioner in a Japanese hotel—"Cooles and heates. If you want just condition of warm in your room, please control yourself."

2. A Hong Kong dentist advertises—"Teeth extracted by the latest Methodists."

3. The person that wrote this menu for a restaurant in Hong Kong got nothing right—"Rainbow troat, fillet streak, popotoes, chocolate mouse."

4. A sign at a German campsite—"It is strictly forbidden on our camp site that people of different sex, for instance men and women, live together in one tent, unless they are married with each other for that purpose."

5. A car rental agency in Tokyo suggests this to its customers—"When passenger of foot heave into sight, tootle the horn. Trumpet him melodiously at first but if he still obstacles your passage, then tootle him with vigor."[53]

Technical Words.   Typically, translators have a problem with technical terms that do not exist in a language and with common words that have a special meaning for a certain industry. Portuguese, for example, is rich in fishing and marine terms, a reflection of Portugal's material culture; but unlike English, it is exceedingly limited with respect to technical terms for the newer industries. The only solution is to employ the English word or fabricate a new word in Portuguese. Unless translators have a special knowledge of the industry, they will go to the dictionary for a literal translation that frequently makes no sense or is erroneous.

Resolving such problems by using English words may not be a satisfactory solution even if the public understands them, especially in France or Spain, which have national academies to keep the language "pure." The French, in their continuous effort to keep their language free of English words, passed a bill in 1994 prohibiting the use of foreign words and phrases in all business and government communications, radio and TV broadcasts, and advertising when there are suitable French equivalents. This was the second victory for the cultural ministry that is in charge of "protecting the language from corruption." Earlier in 1994, the National Assembly adopted a law requiring a minimum of 40 percent of the songs broadcast on radio to be in French. Although American English is not named as the enemy, the law is clearly aimed at words such as *le airbag* when there is a perfectly good French phrase, *coussin gonfiable de protection,* or *le cash flow* instead of *marge brute d'auto-financement.* Small wonder French businesspeople and researchers prefer to use English terms. After the bill's passage, the English Parliament discussed a bill that would outlaw the similar use of French in the United Kingdom.[54]

International businesspeople need to know that other governments have similar programs to keep the local culture pure. For example, Canada has a heritage minister whose job is to "safeguard Canadian culture," and Mexico, as Wal-Mart learned, has tough laws requiring labels in Spanish and metric measurements on imported goods.[55]

Wal-Mart has had language problems with the governments of both of America's NAFTA partners. Its New York stores broke the laws of Ontario by mailing circulars in English to residents of that French-speaking province;

then the company was criticized for sending memos in English ordering Canadian employees to work extra hours without extra pay. Two months later, Mexican trade inspectors closed Wal-Mart's first supercenter store in Mexico City, charging the company with violating import regulations by not putting Spanish-language labels on its merchandise.

More than pride is involved here. The president of the Association of French-Speaking Computer Specialists, a former air force general, says the foreign jargon makes work more difficult for French computer specialists who are not fluent in English and worse, it creates the impression among consumers that computing is a uniquely American science and that French computers are imitations that French buyers should avoid. The French culture minister says the time has come to head off an aggressive expansion of English in culture and trade: "A foreign language often becomes a tool of domination, uniformization, a factor of social exclusion, and, when used snobbishly, a language of contempt."[56]

Note the economic reason for keeping the language pure and separate from other languages. Those learning a foreign language are not only potential tourists but are likely to be empathetic toward anything that comes from that country. An Argentine engineer who reads French and not English will turn to French technical manuals and catalogs before specifying the machinery for the new power plant he is designing. However, if he constantly finds English technical terms in the French text, which forces him to consult his Spanish-English dictionary, he may decide to learn English and read American manuals and catalogs. Moreover, as the French general stated, if the French language doesn't have the technical terms and American English does, this indicates that the discovery and development of the industry has been occurring in the United States, not France, and that the Americans are the experts.

In Japan, the reverse situation exists, probably because for decades the country coveted foreign products while it struggled to overtake the more advanced West. Even now, most Japanese cars sold in the domestic market have almost nothing but English on them. A Nissan official explains that English is thought to be more attractive to the eye. Perhaps this is why people quench their thirst with a best-selling soft drink called "Pocari Sweat" and order from menus announcing "sand witches" and "miss Gorilla" (mixed grill). They also puff away on a cigarette called Hope.[57]

No Unpleasantness.   One last aspect of the spoken language worthy of mention is the reluctance in many areas to say anything disagreeable to the listener. The politeness of the Japanese and their consideration for others make *no* a little-used word even when there are disagreements. An American executive, pleased that her Japanese counterpart is nodding and saying yes to all of her proposals, may be shaken later to learn that all the time the listener was saying yes (I hear you) and not yes (I agree). Western managers who ask their Brazilian assistants whether something can be done may receive the answer *meio deficil* (somewhat difficult). If managers take this answer literally, they will probably tell the assistants to do it anyway. The assistants will then elaborate on the difficulties until, hopefully, it will finally dawn on the executives that what they ask is impossible, but the Brazilians just don't want to give them the bad news.

unspoken language
Nonverbal communication, such as gestures and body language

Unspoken Language.   Nonverbal communication, or the **unspoken language**, can often tell businesspeople something that the spoken language does not—if they understand it. Unfortunately, the differences in customs among cultures may cause misinterpretations of the communication.

"First, le coca cola. Now peanut butter. Who will save La Belle Langue Française?"

Source: Pearson, *Knickerbocker News*, Albany, New York.

Gestures.   Although gestures are a common form of cross-cultural communication, the language of gestures varies from one region to another. For instance, Americans and most Europeans understand the thumbs-up gesture to mean "all right," but in southern Italy and Greece, it transmits the message for which we reserve the middle finger. Making a circle with the thumb and the forefinger is friendly in the United States, but it means "you're worth zero" in France and Belgium and is a vulgar sexual invitation in Greece and Turkey.[58] The best advice for the foreign traveler is to leave gestures at home.

Department store greeter in Tokyo bows politely to a customer.

Charles Gupton/Stock Boston

Closed Doors.   Americans know that one of the perquisites of an important executive is a large office with a door that can be closed. Normally, the door is open as a signal that the occupant is ready to receive others, but when it is closed, something of importance is going on. Contrary to the American open-door policy, Germans regularly keep their doors closed. Hall, the noted anthropologist mentioned at the beginning of this chapter, says that the closed door does not mean that the person behind it wants no visitors but only that he or she considers open doors sloppy and disorderly.[59]

Office Size.   Although office size is an indicator of a person's importance, it means different things to different cultures. In the United States, the higher the status of the executive, the larger and more secluded the office; but in the Arab world, the president may be in what for us is a small, crowded office. In Japan, the top floor of a department store is reserved for the "bargain basement" (bargain penthouse?) and not for top management. The French prefer to locate important department heads in the center of activities, with their assistants located outward on radii from this center. To be safe, never gauge people's importance by the size and location of their offices.

Conversational Distance.   Anthropologists report that conversational distances are smaller in the Middle East and Latin America, though our personal experience in Latin America has not shown this to be the case.[60] Whether this generality is true or false, we must remember that generalities are like arithmetic means; perhaps more people do than do not act in a certain way in a culture, but the businessperson will be dealing with just a few nationals at a time. Luck may have it that he or she will meet exceptions to the stereotype.

The Language of Gift Giving.   Gift giving is an important aspect of every businessperson's life both here and overseas. Entertainment outside office hours and the exchange of gifts are part of the process of getting better acquainted. However, the etiquette or language of gift giving varies among cultures, just as the spoken language does, and although foreigners will usually be forgiven for not knowing the language, certainly they and their gifts will be better received if they follow local customs.

Acceptable Gifts.   In Japan, for example, one never gives an unwrapped gift or visits a Japanese home empty-handed. A gift is presented with the comment that it is only a trifle, which implies that the humble social position of the giver does not permit giving a gift in keeping with the high status of the recipient. He in turn will not open the gift in front of the giver because he knows better than to embarrass him by exposing the trifle in the giver's presence.

  The Japanese use gift giving to convey one's thoughtfulness and consideration for the receiver, who over time builds up trust and confidence in the giver. Japanese never give four of anything or an item with four in the name because the word sounds like the one for death. White and yellow flowers are not good choices for gifts because in many areas they connote death. In Germany, red roses to a woman indicate strong feelings for her, and if you give cutlery, always ask for a coin in payment so that the gift will not cut your friendship. Cutlery is a friendship cutter for the Russians and French also. Traditions vary greatly throughout the world, but generally safe gifts everywhere are chocolates, red roses, and a good Scotch whiskey (not in the Arab world, however—instead, bring a good book or something useful for the office).[61]

Gifts or Bribes?   The questionable payments scandals (called bribery scandals by the press) exposed the practice of giving very expensive gifts and money to well-placed government officials in return for special favors, large orders, and protection. Some payments were **bribes**; that is, payments were made to induce the payee to do something for the payer that is illegal. But others were **extortion** made to keep the payee from harming the payer in some way. Still others were tips to induce government officials to do their jobs.[62]

bribes
Gifts or payments to induce the receiver to do something illegal for the giver

extortion
Payments to keep the receiver from causing harm to the payer

All three are payments for services, and usually they are combinations of two or possibly all three types. To distinguish among them, look at this example. If you tip the headwaiter to get a good table, that is a bribe; but if you tip him because you know that without it, he'll put you near the kitchen, that's extortion. If you tip him for good service after eating, that is a tip. Part of the problem of adhering to American laws is the difficulty in making this distinction.

Although the media exposure about questionable payments is fairly recent, for a long time it has been common knowledge in the international business community that gifts or money payments are necessary to obtain favorable action from government officials, whether to obtain a large order, avoid having a plant shut down, or receive faster service from customs agents. Their pervasiveness worldwide is illustrated by the variety of names for bribes—*mordida* (bite in Latin America), *dash* (West Africa), *pot de vin* (jug of wine—France), *la bustarella* (envelope left on Italian bureaucrat's desk), or *grease* (United States). Even the Soviets were not exempt according to a *Business International* study of multinational managers, who declared that representatives of the Russian state trading organization permitted gifts to be deposited in their Swiss bank accounts.

Questionable Payments.   These come in all forms and sizes, from the petty "expediting" payments that have been necessary to get poorly paid government officials to do their normal duties to huge sums to win large orders.

> One of the writers was able to reduce by one-half the average age of receivables from a major Mexican governmental customer by the payment of $4 a month to a clerk whose sole job was to arrange suppliers' invoices according to their dates, so that the oldest were on top and would be paid first. His company's invoices were placed on top regardless of their date and were paid promptly.

Included by the Securities and Exchange Commission (SEC) as questionable payments are contributions to foreign political parties and the payment of agents' commissions, even when these actions are not illegal in the country where they are made.[63] By means of the Foreign Corrupt Practices Act,* the United States is, in effect, requiring American firms to operate elsewhere according to this country's laws, which frequently places these firms at a competitive disadvantage. Many managements have responded by issuing strict orders not to make any questionable payments, legal or illegal, and some have been surprised to find that their business has not fallen off as they expected. Their action has been reinforced by a number of governments that have either passed stricter laws or begun to enforce those they already have. Given the combination of low salaries of foreign officials and the intense competition for business, one should not be too sanguine about the prospects for completely eliminating this practice.

---

*The Foreign Corrupt Practices Act is discussed in Chapter 11.

There is, nevertheless, a new nongovernmental agency, Transparency International, founded in Berlin in May 1993 and modeled after Amnesty International, the human rights agency. The agency was founded by aid specialists, many with World Bank and other international agency experience, who are disgusted with greedy businesspeople and government officials from developing nations. Its mission is to upgrade business ethics in the developing world. Ecuador will be the test case in the new effort to fight the corruption that often occurs when the poorer, developing nations buy from industrialized countries. The country bought nine French locomotives that turned out to be too heavy for its track system. Because they were bought as a result of bribery, Ecuador's vice president asked Transparency International to devise a credible anticorruption regime for the country.

One of the first acts is to require the chairmen or presidents of foreign firms that do business with Ecuador and government buyers to sign statements promising there will be no bribes. One early task is to enforce tight rules when awarding contracts for a hydroelectric project costing several hundred million dollars. Some American firms are supportive, but Japanese companies have rebuffed the group as they are not eager to halt bribery. EU companies, for whom bribe payments are legitimate business deductions, also show little interest.[64]

Societal Organization

Every society has a structure or an organization that is the patterned arrangement of relationships defining and regulating the manner by which its members interface with one another. Anthropologists generally study this important aspect of culture by breaking down its parts into two classes of institutions: those based on *kinship* and those based on the *free association* of individuals.

Kinship.   The family is the basic unit of institutions based on kinship. Unlike the American family, which is generally composed of the parents and their children, families in many nations—especially in the developing ones—are extended to include all relatives by blood and by marriage.

extended family
Includes blood relatives and relatives by marriage

Extended Family.   For the foreign firm, the **extended family** is a source of employees and business connections. The trust that people place in their relatives, however distant, may motivate them to buy from a supplier owned by their cousin's cousin, even though the price is higher. Local personnel managers are prone to fill the best jobs with family members, regardless of their qualifications.

Member's Responsibility.   Although the extended family is large, each member's feeling of responsibility to it is strong. An individual's initiative to work is discouraged when he or she may be asked to share personal earnings with unemployed extended family members, no matter what the kinship is. Responsibility to the family is frequently a cause of high absenteeism in developing countries where the worker is called home to help with the harvest. Managements have spent large sums to provide comfortable housing for workers and their immediate families, only to find them living in crowded conditions when members of the extended family have moved in.

Pedro Diaz Marin.   In Latin America, where the extended family form is common, individuals use the maternal surname (Marin) as well as the paternal (Diaz) to indicate both branches of the family. It is a common sight to find two businesspeople or a businessperson and a government official, when meeting for the first time, exploring each other's family tree to see whether they have common relatives. If they find any kinship at all, the meeting goes much more smoothly—after all, they're relatives. Incidentally, the name appearing first in Korea is the paternal surname.

Associations. Social units not based on kinship, known as **associations** by anthropologists, may be formed by age, gender, or common interest.[65]

associations
Social units based on age, gender, or common interest, not on kinship

Age. Manufacturers of consumer goods are well aware of the importance of segmenting a market by age groups, which often cut across cultures. This fact has enabled marketers to succeed in selling such products as clothing and records to the youth market in both developed and developing nations. However, international marketers may go too far if they assume young people everywhere exert the same buying influence on their parents as they do here. Kellogg's attempt to sell cereals in Great Britain through children was not successful because English mothers are less influenced by their children with respect to product choice than are American mothers. Senior citizens form an important segment in the United States, where older people live apart from their children; but where the extended family concept is prevalent, older people continue to live with and exert a powerful influence on younger members of the family.

Gender. Generally, the less developed the country, the less equal are the genders with respect to job opportunities and education. Even today, the Chinese offer congratulations only on the birth of a son; the birth of a daughter draws condolences.

As nations industrialize, more women enter the job market and thus assume greater importance in the economy. This trend is receiving further impetus as the women's movement for equality of the sexes spreads to the traditionally male-dominated societies of less developed countries. Among the industrialized nations, the United States has the greatest percentage of women in upper management. Although women in Germany, Great Britain, Denmark, and France make up 40 percent of the work force, only 4 percent are in executive positions.[66] According to a United Nations report, women do two-thirds of the world's work, receive a tenth of its income, and own a hundredth of its property.[67]

A word of caution, however, must be given to those who, noting the apparently sequestered life of women in some areas, conclude that they have little voice in what the family buys or how it acts. Despite the outward appearance of male domination, women exert a far more powerful influence behind closed doors than the unknowing outsider might suspect.

Common Interest. Common interest groups are composed of people joined together by a common bond, which can be political, occupational, recreational, or religious. Even before entering a country, management should identify such groups and assess their political and economic power. As we will see in later chapters, consumer organizations have forced firms to change their product, promotion, and prices, and investments have been supported or opposed by labor unions, which are often a powerful political force.

Class Mobility. In most countries, the ease of moving from one social class to another lies on a continuum from the rigid caste system of India to the relatively flexible social structure of the United States. Less developed countries tend to be located nearer the position of India, whereas the industrial nations are closer to the U.S. position. As industrialization progresses, barriers to mobility weaken. Management must assess mobility between classes because interclass rigidity, especially when accompanied by low social status for business, can make it extremely difficult for the firm to obtain good management personnel locally.

UNDERSTANDING NATIONAL CULTURES

To help managers of IBM understand the many national cultures in which the company operates, Geert Hofstede, a Danish psychologist, interviewed thousands of employees in 67 countries. He found that the differences in their answers to 32 statements could be based on four value dimensions: (1) individualism versus collectivism, (2) large versus small power distance, (3) strong versus weak uncertainty avoidance, and (4) masculinity versus femininity."[68]

Individualism versus Collectivism

According to Hofstede, people in collectivistic cultures belong to groups that are supposed to look after them in exchange for loyalty, whereas people in individualistic cultures are only supposed to look after themselves and their immediate family.[69] Therefore, organizations operating in collectivistic cultures are more likely to rely on group decision making than those in individualistic cultures where the emphasis is on individual decision making.

Large versus Small Power Distance

Power distance is the extent to which members of a society accept the unequal distribution of power among individuals. In large power distance societies, employees believe their supervisors are right even when they are wrong, thus employees do not take any initiative in making nonroutine decisions. On the other hand, a participative management style of leadership is likely to be productive for an organization in a low power distance country.[70]

Strong versus Weak Uncertainty Avoidance

This is the degree to which members of a society feel threatened by ambiguity and are reluctant to take risks. Employees in high risk-avoidance cultures such as Japan, Greece, and Portugal tend to stay with their organizations for a long time. Those from low risk-avoidance nations such as the United States, Singapore, and Denmark, however, are much more mobile. It should be apparent that organizational change in high uncertainty-avoidance nations is likely to receive strong resistance from employees, which makes the implementation of change difficult to administer.[71]

Masculinity versus Femininity

This is the degree to which the dominant values in a society emphasize assertiveness, acquisition of money and status, and achievement of visible and symbolic organizational rewards (masculinity) as compared to the degree to which they emphasize people relationships, concern for others, and the overall quality of life (femininity).[72]

Scores for the Four Dimensions

Table 9–4 presents the scores for Hofstede's four dimensions.[73]

Plots of Dimensions and Management Implications

Figure 9–7 plots the scores for selected Anglo and Latin American (Hofstede's terms) nations on the power distance and uncertainty avoidance dimensions. The Latin American countries in the second quadrant scored relatively high on power distance and uncertainty avoidance. The lines of communication in

Country	Power Distance	Uncertainty Avoidance	Individualism	Masculinity
Mexico	81	82	30	69
Venezuela	81	76	12	73
Colombia	64	80	13	64
Peru	90	87	16	42
Chile	63	86	23	28
Portugal	63	104	27	31
United States	50	46	91	62
Australia	49	51	90	61
South Africa (SAF)	49	49	65	63
New Zealand	45	49	79	58
Canada	39	48	80	52
Great Britain	35	35	89	66
Ireland	28	35	70	68

TABLE 9–4

Scores for Hofstede's value dimensions

organizations in these countries are vertical, and employees know who reports to whom. By clearly defining roles and procedures, the organizations are very predictable. The Anglo nations in the fourth quadrant scored low on both dimensions. Organizations in these countries are characterized by less formal controls and fewer layers of management. More informal communication is used.[74]

The scores for individualism and power distance are plotted in Figure 9–8. The Latin countries (first quadrant) scored relatively high on power distance and low on individualism. Employees tend to expect their organizations to look after them and defend their interests. They expect close supervision and managers who act paternally. On the other hand, people in the Anglo countries (third quadrant), which scored low on power distance and high on individualism, prefer to do things for themselves and do not expect organizations to look after them.[75]

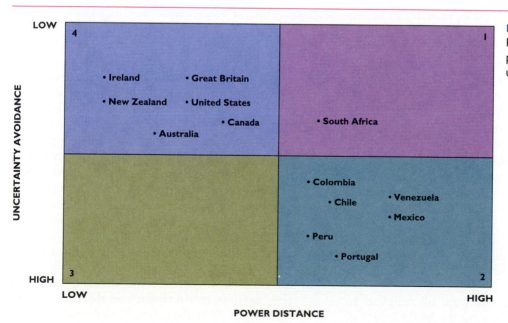

FIGURE 9–7

Plot of selected nations on power distance and uncertainty avoidance

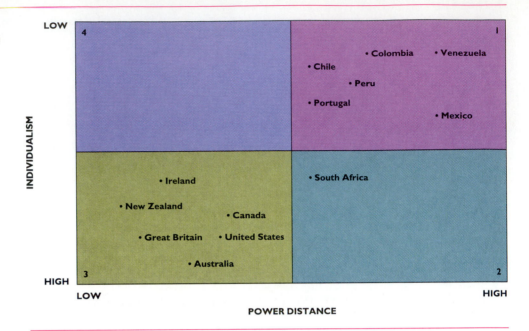

Hofstede's four dimensions have given managers a basis for understanding how cultural differences affect organizations and management methods. They assist in showing that management skills are culturally specific; that is, "a management technique or philosophy that is appropriate in one national culture is not necessarily appropriate in another." Clearly, managing in different Western countries requires different activities, thus generalizations are not justified. However, other researchers, using other data, have found the same or closely similar dimensions, leading Hofstede to conclude that "there is solid evidence that the four dimensions are, indeed, universal."[76]

SUMMARY

1. **Understand the significance of culture for international business.** To be successful in their relationships overseas, international businesspeople must be students of culture. They must not only have factual knowledge, but they must also become culturally sensitive. Culture affects all functional areas of the firm.

2. **Understand the sociocultural components of culture.** Although experts differ as to the components of culture, the following is representative of what numerous anthropologists believe to exist: (1) aesthetics, (2) attitudes and beliefs, (3) religion, (4) material culture, (5) education, (6) language, (7) societal organization, (8) legal characteristics, and (9) political structures.

3. **Appreciate the significance of religion to businesspeople.** Knowing the basic tenets of

other religions will contribute to a better understanding of their followers' attitudes. This may be a major factor in a given market.

4. **Comprehend the cultural aspects of technology.** Material culture, especially technology, is important to managements contemplating overseas investment. Foreign governments have become increasingly involved in the sale and control of technical assistance. Technology may enable a firm to enter a new market successfully even where competitors are already established. It often enables the firm to obtain superior conditions for an overseas investment because the host government wants the technology.

5. **Discuss the impact of the "brain drain" and the "reverse brain drain" on developed and developing nations.** Developed nations have

received thousands of scientists and highly-trained professionals from developing nations without contributing any part of the cost of their education. They also have lost hundreds of scientists who obtained industry experience in developed countries to recruiters from their countries of origin.

6. **Appreciate the importance of the ability to speak the local language.** Language is the key to culture. A feel for a people and their attitudes naturally develops with a growing mastery of their language.

7. **Recognize the importance of the unspoken language in international business.** Because the unspoken language can often tell business-people something that the spoken language does not, they should know something about this form of cross-cultural communication.

8. **Discuss the two classes of relationships within a society.** A knowledge of how a soci-ety is organized is useful because the arrangement of relationships within it defines and regulates the manner in which its members interface with one another. Anthropologists have broken down societal relationships into two classes: those based on kinship and those based on free association of individuals.

9. **Discuss Hofstede's four cultural value dimensions.** Geert Hofstede, a Danish psychologist, interviewed IBM employees in 67 countries and found that the differences in their answers to 32 statements could be based on four value dimensions: (1) individualism versus collectivism, (2) large versus small power distance, (3) strong versus weak uncertainty, (4) masculinity versus femininity. These dimensions assist managers to understand how cultural differences affect organizations and management methods.

KEY WORDS

- culture   270
- ethnocentricity   270
- aesthetics   274
- demonstration effect   277
- Protestant work ethic   280
- Confucian work ethic   280
- Asian religions   280
- caste system   280
- material culture   285
- technological dualism   287

- appropriate technology   288
- boomerang effect   288
- brain drain   291
- reverse brain drain   291
- lingua franca   296
- unspoken language   300
- bribes   303
- extortion   303
- extended family   304
- associations   305

QUESTIONS

1. Why is it helpful for international business-people to know that a national culture has two components?

2. A knowledge of culture has been responsible for Disney's success in Tokyo, and ignorance of culture has been responsible for the company's large losses in Paris. Discuss.

3. Why do international businesspersons need to consider aesthetics when making marketing decisions?

4. How can the demonstration effect be used to improve productivity? To improve sales?

5. Some societies view change differently than do Americans. What impact does this have on the way American marketers operate in those markets? The way American production people operate?

6. Why must international businesspeople be acquainted with the beliefs of the major religions in the areas in which they work?

7. What Buddhist belief would cause American marketing and production managers to think carefully before transferring their marketing plans or bonus plans to an area where Buddhists are present in large numbers?

8. Why is technological superiority especially significant for international firms?

9. What is the significance of the extended family for international managers?

10. Use Hofstede's four dimensions to analyze this situation: John Adams, with 20 years of experience as general foreman in the United States, is sent as production superintendent to his firm's new plant in Colombia. He was chosen because of his outstanding success in handling workers. Adams uses the participative management style. Can you foresee him having any problems on this new job?

| MINICASE 9–1 | Be Attuned to Business Etiquette |

The proverb "When in Rome, do as the Romans do" applies to business representatives as well as tourists. Being attuned to a country's business etiquette can make or break a sale, particularly in countries where 1,000-year-old traditions can dictate the rules for proper behavior. Anyone interested in being a successful marketer should be aware the following considerations:

- *Local customer, etiquette, and protocol.* An exporter's behavior in a foreign country can reflect favorably or unfavorably on the exporter, the company, and even the sales potential for the product.
- *Body language and facial expressions.* Often, actions do speak louder than words.
- *Expressions of appreciation.* Giving and receiving gifts can be a touchy subject in many countries. Doing it badly may be worse than not doing it at all.
- *Choices of words.* Knowing when and if to use slang, tell a joke, or just keep silent is important.

The following informal test will help exporters rate their business etiquette. See how many of the following you can answer correctly. (Answers follow the last question.)

1. You are in a business meeting in an Arabian Gulf country. You are offered a small cup of bitter cardamom coffee. After your cup has been refilled several times, you decide you would rather not have any more. How do you decline the next cup offered to you?
   a. Place your palm over the top of the cup when the coffee pot is passed.
   b. Turn your empty cup upside down on the table.
   c. Hold the cup and twist your wrist from side to side.

2. In which of the following countries are you expected to be punctual for business meetings?
   a. Peru.
   b. Hong Kong.
   c. Japan.
   d. China.
   e. Morocco.

3. Gift giving is prevalent in Japanese society. A business acquaintance presents you with a small wrapped package. Do you:
   a. Open the present immediately and thank the giver?
   b. Thank the giver and open the present later?
   c. Suggest that the giver open the present for you?

4. In which of the following countries is tipping considered an insult?
   a. Great Britain.
   b. Iceland.
   c. Canada.

5. What is the normal workweek in Saudi Arabia?
   a. Monday through Friday.
   b. Friday through Tuesday.
   c. Saturday through Wednesday.

6. You are in a business meeting in Seoul. Your Korean business associate hands you his calling card, which states his name in the traditional Korean order: Park Chul Su. How do you address him?
   a. Mr. Park.
   b. Mr. Chul.
   c. Mr. Su.

7. In general, which of the following would be good topics of conversation in Latin American countries?
   a. Sports.
   b. Religion.
   c. Local politics.
   d. The weather.
   e. Travel.

8. In many countries, visitors often are entertained in the homes of clients. Taking flowers as a gift to the hostess is usually a safe way to express thanks for the hospitality. However, both the type and color of the flower can have amorous, negative, or even ominous implications. Match the country where presenting them would be a social *faux pas.*
   a. Brazil.   1. Red roses.
   b. France.   2. Purple flowers.
   c. Switzerland.   3. Chrysanthemums.

9. In Middle Eastern countries, which hand does one use to accept or pass food?
   a. Right hand.
   b. Left hand.
   c. Either hand.

10. Body language is just as important as the spoken word in many countries. For example, in most countries, the thumbs-up sign means "OK." But in which of the following countries is the sign considered a rude gesture?
   a. Germany.
   b. Italy.
   c. Australia.

Answers: 1—*c*. It is also appropriate to leave the cup full. 2—*a, b, c, d,* and e. Even in countries where local custom does not stress promptness, overseas visitors should be prompt. 3—*b*. 4—*b*. 5—*c*. 6—*a*. The traditional Korean pattern is surname, followed by two given names. 7—*a, d,* and e. 8—*a* and 2. Purple flowers are a sign of death in Brazil, as are chrysanthemums in France (*b* and 3). In Switzerland (*c* and 1), as well as in many other north European countries, red roses suggest romantic intentions. 9—*a*. Using the left hand would be a social gaffe. 10—*b*.

How's Your Business Etiquette?

8–10   Congratulations, you have obviously done your homework when it comes to doing business overseas.

5–7   Although you have some sensitivity to the nuances of other cultures, you still might make some social errors that could cost you sales abroad.

1–4   Look out, you could be headed for trouble if you leave home without consulting the experts.

Where to Turn for Help

Whether you struck out completely in the business etiquette department or just want to polish your skills, there are several sources you can turn to for help.

- *Books.* Although two years ago business etiquette information may have been difficult to locate, most good bookstores today carry a variety of resource materials to help the traveling business representative.
- *Workshops and seminars.* Many private business organizations and universities sponsor training sessions for the exporter interested in unraveling the mysteries of doing business abroad.
- *State marketing specialists.* In some states, your first contact should be your state agriculture department, where international specialists there can pass on their expertise or put you in touch with someone who can.

Source: *Foreign Agriculture,* U.S. Department of Agriculture, February 1987, pp. 18–19.

10

Political Forces

> *Politics have no relation to morals.*
> Niccoló Machiavelli

CONCEPT PREVIEWS

After reading this chapter, you should be able to:

1. **identify** the ideological forces that affect business and understand the terminology used in discussing them

2. **understand** that although most governments own businesses, they are privatizing them in growing numbers

3. **explain** the changing sources and reasons for terrorism and the methods and growing power of terrorists

4. **explain** steps that traveling international business executives should take to protect themselves from terrorists

5. **understand** the importance to business of government stability and policy continuity

6. **discuss** the power sources of international organizations, labor unions, and international companies

7. **understand** country risk assessment by international business

I'm from the Government, and I'm Here to Help You

In 1991, John Much, a North Sea fisherman, bought the Pornstrom, a rotting prawn-fishing boat, not to go fishing in but for the fishing license that came with it. His accountant advised him to create a tax deduction by donating the boat to the national coastal parks as a tourist attraction. • The German environment ministry vetoed the gift because Much didn't have an official "gift contract." Clearing that hurdle took 10 months. Then objections came from the office for land and water industry, which wanted to know where the boat would be wintered, and from the harbor master, who refused to allow a crane on his jetty to haul the boat from the water. • Then the Tonning city planning office demanded planning permission, including regional permission from the interior ministry, which in turn required permission from the listed objects and monuments department. • The federal shipping and hydrographers' office demanded written confirmation that the boat was to be put on land. That confirmation was from the Tonning town council, but the construction office refused to build foundations for the boat, and a private firm had to be contracted to build it. • Finally, 18 months after Mr. Much offered the boat as a gift, it was lowered into place in the national park. Mr. Much was not present for the handing-over ceremony—he had gone fishing in frustration. • Today, few visitors will understand the purpose of the fishing boat in a field. The explanatory notices have been removed. There was no planning permission for them.

Source: Tony Paterson, "The Not So Everyday Tale of Fishing Folk," *The European*, February 4–7, 1993, p. 5.

Chapter 11 deals with the legal forces affecting international business. Of course, laws and their interpretation and enforcement reflect political ideologies and outlooks as well as government stability and continuity. Therefore, this chapter is intended as background for and a companion to Chapter 11.

In a number of ways, the political climate of the country in which a business operates is as important as the country's topography, its natural resources, and its meteorological climate. Indeed, we shall see examples in which a hospitable, stable government can encourage business investment and growth despite geographic or weather obstacles and scarcity of natural resources. The opposite is equally true. Some areas of the world that are relatively blessed with natural resources and manageable topography and weather have been very little developed because of government instability. Occasionally, a country's government is hostile to investment in its territory by foreign companies even though they might provide capital, technology, and training for development of the country's resources and people.

Many of the political forces with which business must cope have ideological sources, but there are a large number of other sources. These include nationalism, terrorism, traditional hostilities, unstable governments, international organizations, and government-owned business. Figure 10–1 presents a world map of freedom.

FIGURE 10–1 1994 map of freedom

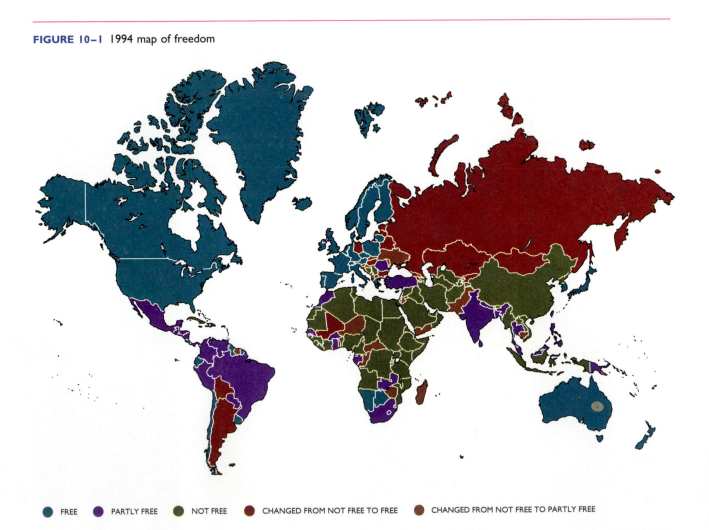

FREE   PARTLY FREE   NOT FREE   CHANGED FROM NOT FREE TO FREE   CHANGED FROM NOT FREE TO PARTLY FREE

It should be pointed out that the international company itself can be a political force. Some firms have budgets or sales larger than the GNP of some of the countries with which they negotiate. Although budgets and GNPs do not translate directly or necessarily into power, it should be clear that companies with bigger budgets and countries with bigger GNPs possess more assets and facilities with which to negotiate. Refer to Table 1–3 for some examples.

This chapter will provide an indication of the types of risks to private business posed by political forces. As we shall see, some of the risks can stem from more than one political force.

Such names as communism, socialism, capitalism, liberal, conservative, left wing, and right wing are used to describe governments, political parties, and people. These names indicate ideological beliefs.

IDEOLOGICAL FORCES

Communism

In communist countries, the government owns all the major factors of production. With minor exceptions, all production in these countries is by state-owned factories and farms. Labor unions are government controlled.

Communism as conceived by Karl Marx was a theory of social change directed to the ideal of a classless society. As developed by Lenin and others, communism typically involves the seizure of power by a conspiratorial political party, the maintenance of power by stern suppression of internal opposition, and commitment to the ultimate goal of a worldwide communist state.

communism
Marx's theory of a classless society, developed by his successors into control of society by the Communist party and the attempted worldwide spread of communism

Although private companies from noncommunist countries usually cannot own plants in a communist country, they can do business with it. We shall discuss how this is done in Chapter 17. But before we get there, we should point out that recent developments in the People's Republic of China, the former Soviet Union, and Eastern Europe are opening opportunities for foreign investment.

Communist Government Takeover of a Previously Noncommunist Country. This business risk is not dealt with in Chapter 17. Given one of communism's basic tenets—state ownership of all the productive factors—the government will take over private business. This occurred in Russia after the 1917 Bolshevik Revolution, and it has been repeated after each communist takeover of a country.

Compensation for Expropriated Property. To date, none of the new communist governments has compensated the foreign former owners directly. A few of the owners have gotten some reimbursement indirectly out of assets of the communist government seized abroad after the communist government confiscated foreign private property within its country. For example, the U.S. government seized assets of the Soviet Union in the United States after American property in the U.S.S.R. was confiscated. American firms or individuals whose property had been confiscated in the U.S.S.R. could file claims with a U.S. government agency, and if they could substantiate their loss, a percentage of it was paid.

expropriation
Government seizure of the property within its borders owned by foreigners, followed by prompt, adequate, and effective compensation paid to the former owners

Expropriation and Confiscation. The rules of traditional international law recognize a country's right to expropriate the property of foreigners within its jurisdiction. But those rules require the country to compensate the foreign owners, and *in the absence of compensation,* **expropriation** *becomes* **confiscation.**[1]

confiscation
Government seizure of the property within its borders owned by foreigners without payment to them

Communism Collapses.

We have insufficient space to detail the reasons for communism's failure as an economic and social system. We shall present a couple of basic reasons and a few anecdotes that illustrate the results. See the endnotes for more.

The U.S.S.R. concentrated its best scientists, engineers, managers, and raw materials in production for the military; it neglected production of consumer goods. Gross production was the goal, and managers would go to ridiculous extremes to report the production figures set by government central planners.

Since Soviet central planning allowed only one condom factory and birth control pills were very expensive under the communist regime, the two products were rarely available except to the privileged. As a result, abortion was by far the country's most common form of birth control. All these abortions were then counted as part of doctors' gross production and therefore swelled the reported national income.

Factories under construction got a certificate putting them into commission on the scheduled completion date even though they were almost never actually completed on schedule. Because of the certificate, the factory had to report production coming from it even though it had not yet produced anything.

The first deputy chairman of the U.S.S.R. Committee for National Control, with the splendidly appropriate name of A. Shitof, reported that at least half the enterprises lied to exaggerate their output. Some enterprises used other deceptions. For instance, a factory reaching only 50 percent of its targeted output could have made a small change in its next shipped machine and doubled the price, say from $10,000 to $20,000—presto, doubled output.[2]

Capitalism

capitalism
An economic system in which the means of production and distribution are for the most part privately owned and operated for private profit

The capitalist, free enterprise ideal is that all the factors of production should be privately owned. Under ideal **capitalism**, government would be restricted to those functions that the private sector cannot perform: national defense; police, fire, and other public services; and government-to-government international relations. No such government exists.

Reality in so-called capitalist countries is quite complex. The governments of such countries typically regulate privately owned businesses quite closely, and frequently these governments own businesses.

Regulations and Red Tape.

All businesses are subject to countless government laws, regulations, and red tape in their activities in the United States and all other capitalist countries. Special government approval is required to practice such professions as law or medicine. Tailored sets of laws and regulations govern banking, insurance, transportation, and utilities. States and local governments require business licenses and impose use restrictions on buildings and areas.

Complying with all the laws and regulations and coping with the red tape require expertise, time, and of course, expense. A business found in noncompliance may incur fines or even the imprisonment of its management. The true story at the beginning of this chapter—entitled "I'm from Government, and I'm Here to Help You"—is a ridiculous example of how bureaucracies can delay and sometimes prevent safe and sensible actions.

Socialism

socialism
Public, collective ownership of the basic means of production and distribution, operating for use rather than for profit

Socialism advocates government ownership or control of the basic means of production, distribution, and exchange. Profit is not an aim.

In practice, so-called socialist governments have frequently performed in ways not consistent with the doctrine. One of the most startling examples of this is Singapore, which professes to be a socialist state but in reality is aggressively capitalistic.[3]

European Socialism.   In Europe, socialist parties have been in power in several countries, including Great Britain, France, Spain, Greece, and Germany. In Britain, the Labour party—as the socialists there call their political party—has nationalized some basic industries, such as steel, shipbuilding, coal mining, and the railroads, but has not gone much further in that direction. A vocal left wing of the Labour party advocates nationalizing all major British business, banks, and insurance companies.

Social Democrats is the name the Germans use for their socialist political party. During the several years that this party was in power before it lost to the Christian Democrats in 1982, it nationalized nothing and, in action and word, seemed more capitalist than socialist. The socialist governments of France and Spain have embarked on programs to privatize government-owned businesses; such programs do not conform to pure socialist doctrine.

LDC Socialism.   The less developed countries (LDCs) often profess and practice some degree of socialism. The government typically owns and controls most of the factors of production. Shortages of capital, technology, and skilled management and labor are characteristic of an LDC, and DCs or international organizations often provide aid through the LDC government. Also, many of the educated citizens of an LDC tend to be in or connected with the government. It follows that the government would own or control major factories and farms.

Unless the LDC government is communist, it will make occasional exceptions and permit capital investment. This happens when the LDC perceives advantages that would not be possible without the private capital, such as more jobs for its people, new technology, skilled managers or technicians, and export opportunities.

Risks for Businesses Dealing with Socialist Countries.   The practices of the countries that profess socialism range widely. In Singapore, for example, business-people must be careful to comply with all the applicable laws and regulations, as in any capitalist country. At the other extreme, such as in an LDC, where most or all of the major production factors are government owned, they must do business much as in a communist country.

Conservative or Liberal

We should not leave the subject of ideology without mention of these words as they have come to be used in the mid- and late 20th century. Politically, in the United States, the word **conservative** connotes a person, group, or party that wishes to minimize government activity and maximize the activities of private businesses and individuals. Conservative is used to mean something similar to **right wing**, but in the United States and the United Kingdom, the latter is more extreme. For instance, the Conservative party, one of the major political parties in the United Kingdom, is said to have a right-wing minority.

In the United States there is at least one exception to the generalization that conservatives wish to minimize government activities: the antiabortion movement calling for governmental control of abortion decisions. Although not all antiabortionists are conservative, the media present their position as such.

conservative
A person who wishes to minimize government activities and maximize private ownership and business

right wing
A more extreme conservative position

Right and Left—What Do These Terms Mean?

After the French Revolution, an assembly was chosen, and it settled down to face the problems of reform. The radicals sat on the president's left and the conservatives on his right. This disposition provided thereafter—in other countries as well as France—a useful addition to the terminology of politics.

A former member of the British Parliament made some interesting points on this subject. He found the Far Left similar to the Far Right. The terms "Right" and "Left" are losing their purchase. Under conventions established earlier in our century, people on the Far Right are seen as "Fascists" and people on the Far Left as "Communists," so that on the Left-Right axis, the two are supposed to be opposites, or at least at opposite extremes as far away from each other as it is possible to get. But a majority of observers seem to agree that the kinds of society they establish when they get into power have fundamental features of a striking nature in common—and are a good deal more like each other than either of them is like Liberal Democracy, which is supposed to separate them in the middle, halfway between them.

Source: *Forbes*, May 23, 1983, p. 20.

Also, connotations of *conservative* can differ depending on the application. For example, as the People's Republic of China and countries of eastern Europe and the former Soviet Union move from centrally planned economies to market economies and from dictatorships toward democracies, the people and groups trying to impede, stop, or reverse such movements are called *conservatives*. These people, typically members of communist (usually renamed) parties, the KGB (secret police), or the armed forces, long for "the good old days" when the governments owned and ran everything. That is precisely opposite to the wishes of conservatives in the United States and the United Kingdom, who want the least possible government involvement.

liberal
In the 20th-century United States, a person who urges greater government involvement in most aspects of human activities

Politically, in the United States in the 20th century, the word **liberal** has come to mean the opposite of what it meant in the 19th century. It now connotes a person, group, or party that urges greater government participation in the economy and regulation or ownership of business. Liberal and **left wing** are similar, but the latter generally indicates more extreme positions closer to socialism or communism.

left wing
A more extreme liberal position

Unique to the United States.   This usage has not spread outside the United States.

> A conversation one of the authors had with an Italian lawyer at lunch in Rome turned to politics. The Italian identified himself as a liberal, and the author understood it in the American meaning. As the conversation proceeded, the author learned that he had been wrong. The lawyer meant it in the Italian sense; he was a member of the Liberal party, a political party near the right end of the Italian political spectrum.

There are other Liberal parties in Europe that are not liberal in the American sense.

We do not want to overemphasize the importance of the labels *conservative, liberal, right wing,* and *left wing.* For one thing, individuals and organizations may change over time or may change as they perceive shifts in the moods of voters. Some feel that these labels are too simplistic or even naive and that reality is more complex. Nevertheless, we wanted to bring them to your attention because they are much used in discussions of international events and because different political forces flow from, for example, a right-wing government than from a left-wing one. Businesspeople must do their best to influence those political forces and then forecast and react to them.

One might reasonably assume that government ownership of the factors of production is found only in communist or socialist countries, but that assumption is not correct. Large segments of business are owned by the governments of numerous countries that do not consider themselves either communist or socialist. From country to country, there are wide differences in the industries that are government owned and in the extent of government ownership.

GOVERNMENT OWNERSHIP OF BUSINESS

Why Firms Are Nationalized

There are a number of reasons, sometimes overlapping, why governments put their hands on firms. Some of them are (1) to extract more money from the firms—the government suspects that the firms are concealing profits; (2) an extension of the first reason—the government believes it could run the firms more efficiently and make more money; (3) ideological—when left-wing governments are elected, they sometimes nationalize industries, as has occurred in Britain, France, and Canada; (4) to catch votes as politicians save jobs by putting dying industries on life-support systems, which can be disconnected after the election; (5) because the government has pumped money into a firm or an industry, and control usually follows money; and (6) happenstance, as with the nationalization after World War II of German-owned firms in Europe.

All governments are in business to some degree, but outside the communist nations or LDCs, none is so far into business as Italy or France.

Italy.   The Italian government-owned Institute for Industrial Reconstruction (IRI) has been called an "industrial octopus."[4] In 1978, IRI was a leader in one category: it lost more money—$970 million—than any other company. The number two loser was another state-owned company, British Steel, which lost $798 million. The Italian government owns companies in many industries, including salt, tobacco, matches, mining, railways, airlines, auto manufacturing, steel, telephone, power plants, banking, restaurants, chocolate and ice cream production, radio and television stations, and refineries. IRI continued to grow, and by 1994 it controlled over 500 companies employing over 500,000 people.

IRI's losses also continued to grow, so that for 1993 it reported a $6.4 billion loss; nevertheless, it had been able to borrow money, and at the end of 1993 it had a debt of some $43 billion.[5] But IRI's operations may be turned around as one of the many results of a historic change in Italian politics. After hundreds of high-level politicians and business leaders were convicted of corruption, an entirely new group of individuals and political parties won 1994 elections and formed a new government, referred to as *conservative* or *right wing*. One thing it did was to convert IRI into a public stock company. In the beginning, the Italian government owned all the stock; it then began selling the stock of parts of IRI, including two big banks and its food processing subsidiary. The government also installed new management of IRI, a signal of its commitment to privatize as much of the company as possible.[6]

Having named British Steel as a loser, we should update that story: by 1991, it had become the world's most profitable integrated steel company and had been privatized. Privatization is discussed later in this chapter.

United States.   Historically, the United States has been opposed to nationalizing industries, but it took a large step in that direction when it set up the Consolidated Rail Corporation (Conrail) in 1976. Conrail took over six bankrupt railroads in the northeastern United States. Ten years later, the U.S. government was taking steps to sell Conrail; one proposal was to sell it to a private rail company, but this evoked opposition from Conrail's managers and employees as well as from competing railroads. Instead, its stock was sold publicly to private buyers, including many Conrail workers and managers. Since then, the United States has done little more to privatize government-owned businesses or operations.

France.   The French government has been in business for centuries. When Louis XIV began building the magnificent Versailles Palace, the plans included thousands of mirrors and crystal chandeliers. The Venetians were the dominant glassmakers of the world at that time, and Louis's finance minister, Colbert, did not like the thought of paying them for all of those mirrors and chandeliers. Colbert set up the company now known as Saint-Gobain, and Louis insisted on owning the company himself, rather than allowing idle nobles and courtiers to own it. Louis feared that if they owned the company, they would become rich and powerful and possible rivals to his rule.

From the time of Louis XIV until quite recently, the French government, for any of the reasons listed above, has collected businesses. By the early 1990s, state-owned businesses accounted for about one-third of the nation's GNP; government-owned manufacturers and banks employed more than a million people. Then attitudes toward government ownership of business changed in France and in most countries, as discussed later under Privatization.

Unfair Competition?

Where government-owned companies compete with privately owned companies, the private companies sometimes complain that the government companies have unfair advantages. Some of the complaints are (1) government-owned companies can cut prices unfairly because they do not have to make profits; (2) they get cheaper financing; (3) they get government contracts; (4) they get export assistance; and (5) they can hold down wages with government assistance.[7]

Another huge advantage state-owned companies have over privately owned business comes in the form of direct subsidies, payments by the government to their companies. The EU Commission is trying to discourage such subsidy payments. In 1991, it began requiring annual financial reports from state-controlled companies as part of a crackdown on the subsidies that can distort competition.[8]

Government-Private Collaboration Difficult

The objectives of private firms and those of government agencies and operations usually differ. Figure 10–2 illustrates some of the differences.

privatization
The transfer of public-sector assets to the private sector, the transfer of management of state activities through contracts and leases, and the contracting out of activities previously conducted by the state

PRIVATIZATION

Britain's former prime minister, Margaret Thatcher, was the acknowledged leader of the **privatization** movement. During her 11 years in office, Thatcher decreased state-owned companies from 10 percent of Britain's GNP to 3.9 percent. She sold over 30 companies, raising some $65 billion.[9] Thatcher pioneered in what has become a worldwide movement to privatize all sorts of government activities.

FIGURE 10–2
Planners and business investors—Why can't they collaborate?

Source: Robert P. Vichas and Kimon Consias, "Public Planners and Business Investors—Why Can't They Collaborate?" *Long Range Planning*, no. 3 (Pergamon Press, Ltd., 1981), p. 83.

Airports, Garbage, Postal Services, and?

The American Lockheed Company, after quietly and profitably running Burbank Airport in California for decades, is expanding abroad. As owner or manager, Lockheed is operating or bidding to operate airports in Canada, Russia, Turkmenistan, Australia, Turkey, Hungary, Argentina, and Venezuela. Hughes Aircraft Company is in the business with Trinidad and Tobago and has completed studies for the Ukraine on ways to upgrade that country's airports.[10]

One study found that it cost the New York Department of Sanitation $40, of which $32 was for labor, to deal with a ton of rubbish. It cost private collectors only $17, (of which $10 was for labor).[11]

Several countries are privatizing their postal services; the British are studying such a move and the Germans are moving. In Germany, the three operating divisions of the Federal Bundespost—postal services, telecommunications, and the postal bank—are being converted into three public companies, the stock of which can be sold to nongovernment owners.[12]

And the list of government-owned businesses and activities being sold to private owners or turned over to private companies to manage and operate goes on and on. The space available here is too limited to treat the subject thoroughly; instead, we refer you to the endnotes cited in this section and to articles on privatization that frequently appear in newspapers and periodicals.

Private Buyers Do Well, but an American Needs a Passport

Privatization is the sizzling political trend all over the world—that is everywhere except in the United States. From 1985 through 1993, $350 billion worth of public assets were privatized. Since 1980, the People's Republic of China has gone from nearly 80 percent to less than 50 percent state ownership. Chile has privatized 75 percent of its state-owned enterprises, and Mexico, about 33 percent. Now France, Germany, Italy, and other European countries are selling.

And the buyers are profiting. Financial analyst, John Duckett of Wheat First Securities, notes that the seven major privatizations during 1993 were on average up by more than one-third from the offering price in an otherwise stale market. Through March 1994, YPF (Argentina) was up from its offering price of $19 to $23.80, Argentaria (Spain) from $32.15 to $42.31, and CSN (Brazil) from $12.50 to $32.20.

These are not isolated examples. A study by Alliance Capital discovered that over the past five years, stocks of privatized companies have climbed by 174 percent versus an 85 percent rise in the S&P 500. But the privatization trend has not begun in the United States, by either the national or state governments. Fortunately, American investors can partake in the trend by buying mutual funds that do hold shares of the world's newly privatized companies.[13]

Privatization Anywhere and Any Way

As you can see from Figure 10–3, privatization is worldwide. It is an advertisement by a Japanese investment bank, Daiwa, bragging about its senior role in privatizations in Australia, Britain, Italy, Malaysia, Scotland, and Singapore.

It should be noted, however, that privatization does not always involve ownership transfer from government to private entities. Activities previously conducted by the state may be contracted out, as Indonesia has contracted a Swiss firm to run its customs administration, and Thailand has private companies operating some of the passenger trains of its state-owned railroad.

Governments may lease state-owned plants to private entities, as Togo has done. They may combine a joint venture with a management contract with a private group to run a previously government-operated business. Rwanda did this with its match factory.[14]

Figure 10–4 shows privatization by geographic region. The percentages in the figure total 100 without reference to the United States, which illustrates the previously made point that neither the U.S. government nor the individual state governments are participating in the privatization trend.

NATIONALISM

nationalism
A devotion to one's own nation, its political and economic interests or aspirations, and its social and cultural traditions

Nationalism has been called the "secular religion of our time." In most of the older countries, loyalty to one's country and pride in it were based on such shared common features as race, language, religion, or ideology. Many of the newer countries, notably in Africa, have accidental boundaries resulting from their colonial past, and within these countries, there are several tribes and languages. This has resulted in civil wars, as in Rwanda, Nigeria, and Angola, but it has not prevented these new countries from developing instant and fierce nationalism.

Nationalism is an emotion that can cloud or even prevent rational dealings with foreigners. For example, the chief of the joint staffs of the Peruvian military, when taking charge in Peru, blamed the ills of its society on foreign companies.

Some of the effects of nationalism on international companies are (1) requirements for minimum local ownership or local product assembly or manufacture; (2) reservation of certain industries for local companies; (3) preference of local suppliers for government contracts; (4) limitations on the number and types of foreign employees; (5) protectionism, using tariffs, quotas, or other devices; (6) seeking a "French solution"* instead of a foreign takeover of a local firm;[15] and (7) in the most extreme cases, expropriation or confiscation.

GOVERNMENT PROTECTION

A historical function of government, whatever its ideology, has been the protection of the economic activities—farming, mining, manufacturing, and so forth—within its geographic area of control. These must be protected from attacks and destruction or robbery by terrorists, bandits, revolutionaries, and foreign invaders. A war was required to free Kuwait and its oil wealth from Iraq.

---

*The French solution is to make every effort to find a French company rather than a foreign one to take over the French firm.

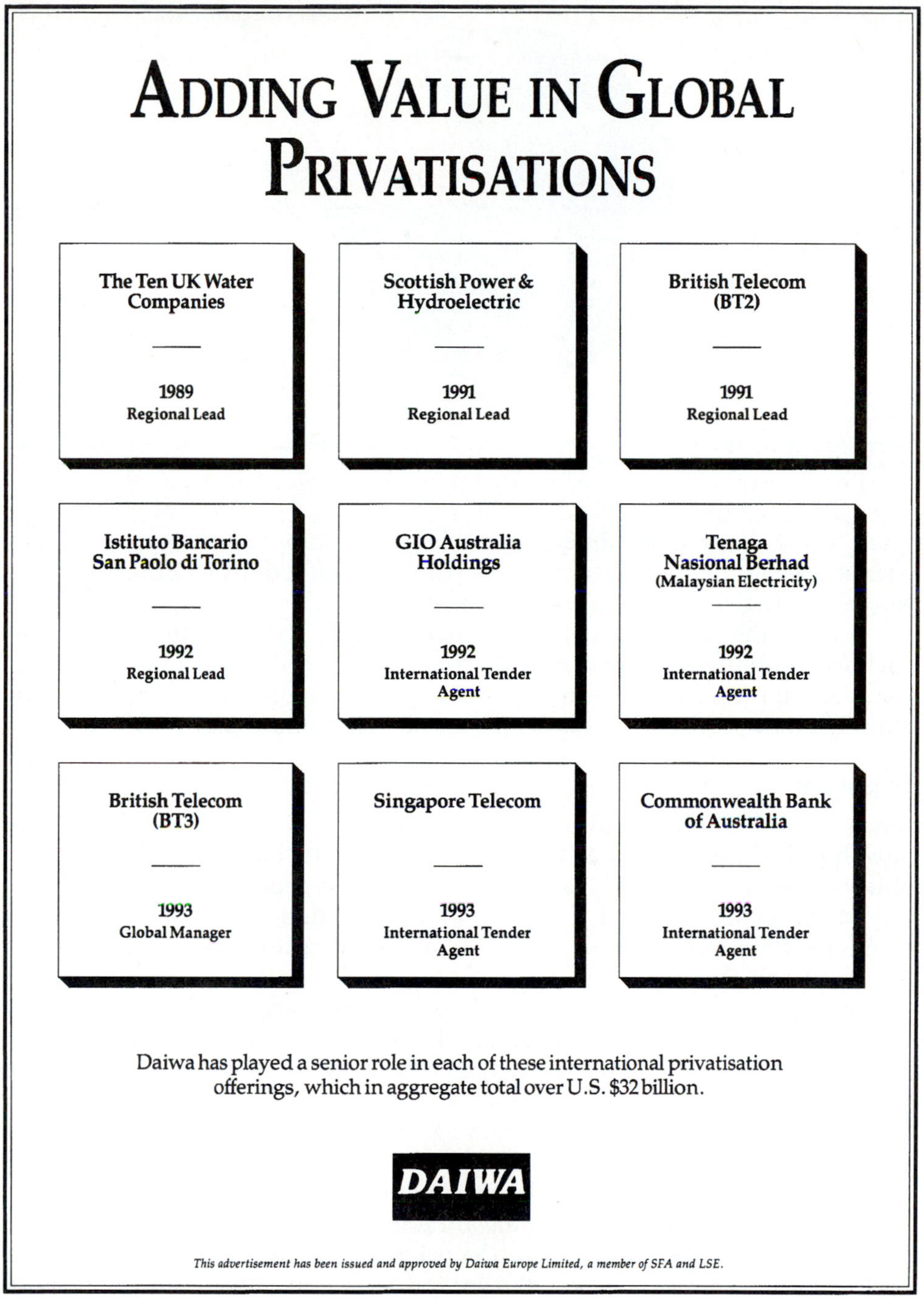

FIGURE 10–3
Advertisement of Daiwa's role in privatizations worldwide

Source: *Euromoney*, December 20, 1994, p. 92.

Iraq Grabs for Economic-Political Power

In 1990, the Iraqi armed forces moved massively into Kuwait, quickly overwhelming the defenders of that much smaller country. Although Kuwait is small, it is oil rich. If Iraq held Kuwait, the combined petroleum reserves of the two countries would make Iraq a major player in petroleum politics.

An even greater prize was lying next door: Saudi Arabia, with the world's largest proved petroleum reserves. With armed forces no match for those of Iraq, Saudi Arabia might even have followed Iraqi orders without an invasion.

FIGURE 10–4
Privatizations by region

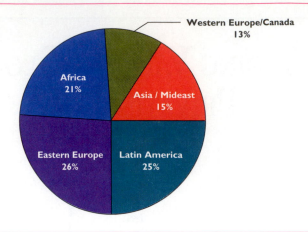

Source: "Privatization Worldwide Summary," prepared for the Transnational Corporations and Management Division of the United Nations. Used here by permission of the author, Michael S. Minor.

That would have made Iraq the world's mightiest petroleum power and permitted it to influence strongly the policies and actions of Europe, Japan, North America, and most of the rest of the world.

Led by the United States and sanctioned by the UN, an international coalition mobilized and transported armed forces to the Middle East. A short war, code-named, Desert Storm, in early 1991 forced Iraqi forces out of Kuwait, although they set fire to hundreds of Kuwaiti oil wells as they retreated.

Terrorism

terrorism
Unlawful acts of violence committed for a wide variety of reasons, including to overthrow a government, gain release of imprisoned colleagues, exact revenge for real or imagined wrongs, or punish nonbelievers of the terrorists' religion

Since the 1970s, the world has been plagued by **terrorism.** Various groups have hijacked airplanes, shot and kidnapped people, and bombed people and objects. A common denominator of these terrorist groups has been hatred of the social, economic, and political orders they find in the world. Another characteristic is their confusion as to what sort of order they would substitute if they had the chance.

During the 1970s and 1980s, Italy was particularly hard hit by terrorist violence directed against businesses and politicians. Between 1975 and 1982, terrorist groups almost shattered Italy's faith in its ability to govern itself without resorting to a communist or fascist police state. However, the democratic Italian government struck back successfully by creating a special, 25,000-strong antiterrorist squad. Once caught, terrorists were tried, convicted, and sentenced to prison by the Italian courts.

Coinciding with those events, the attraction of terrorist groups lessened for educated, idealistic young Italians, the original source of the groups' recruits. And with their charisma fading, the groups had many penitents and defectors. As these young Italians became disenchanted, terrorist leaders turned to more conventional crime. They began cooperating with the Mafia, which is growing and becoming more feared by Italian authorities. The Bank of Italy has warned that the Mafia threatens to contaminate Italy's financial system.[16]

Terrorism Worldwide.   Italy is by no means alone as a victim of terrorism. It exists worldwide. A few of the better known gangs are the Irish Republican Army (IRA), the Hamas and other radical Islamic fundamentalist groups, the Basque separatist movement (ETA), the Japanese Red Army, and the German Red Army Faction.

All of them and others had sanctuaries in the former East Germany, other former Eastern European Soviet satellites, and the Soviet Union itself. The

WORLDVIEW

British Gas Privatized

The following statement was issued by British Gas. It shows the sort of profitable expansion a privatized company can realize.

We've been helping to provide Britain with gas to meet its energy needs for many years now. And very successfully too. But success can't last unless you build on it. Which is why we've developed opportunities abroad.

In one sense, we've been fortunate. The increased concern over environmental issues has helped people to see the advantage of gas over other fossil fuels.

But think. How many companies could have capitalized on this development the way British Gas has?

Even a very quick summary of our major projects shows the scale of our growth worldwide. Our Exploration and Production business, for example, has invested over £1 billion in acquisitions over the past four years. Their entrepreneurial spirit has established British Gas across five continents.

Our Global Gas business has made a major investment in Consumers' Gas of Toronto, Canada. Which means there is now a British gas company with customers on both sides of the Atlantic. Us.

The changes in East/West relations also gave British Gas enormous opportunities. In the U.S.S.R., for example, we've agreed in principle to take a stake in the development of a major oil and gas field. And in what was formerly the German Democratic Republic, we now have a stake in two large gas distribution companies. Then there's the Gulf of Suez. Our oil discovery there is one of the largest in the area for more than a decade.

Does all this activity mean we are neglecting Britain? Not in the slightest. If we were, we wouldn't have signed up 270,000 new customers last year, or added half a million central heating systems to homes throughout the country. We wouldn't be selling gas to generate electricity. Also we wouldn't have succeeded in keeping gas prices amongst the lowest in Europe.

And with the world and its leaders coming closer together recently, there has never been a better time for British Gas to become a superpower in world energy.

The world is turning to British Gas.

Source: Advertisement for British Gas, 1991.

Kuwaiti exiles read the latest news on the fate of their Iraqi-occupied homeland during Desert Storm.

Reuters/Bettmann

East German secret police, the Stasi, and the Soviet secret police, the KGB, provided financing, training, and protection to terrorist groups.[17]

Government-Sponsored Terrorism: An Act of War. In addition to the Soviet Union and its European satellites, other countries financed, trained, and protected terrorists. They included Iran, Iraq, Libya, and Syria. In 1986, a British court convicted a Palestinian of trying to smuggle explosives (concealed in the baggage of his pregnant girlfriend) aboard an El Al Israel 747 aircraft. The flight from London to Tel Aviv would have been blown up over Austria. It was developed at the trial that the material for the explosives had been brought into London in Syrian diplomatic pouches aboard the Syrian government airline; the Syrian ambassador had sanctioned or even directed the operation. In international law, government action to damage or kill in another country is an act of war.

Kidnapping for Ransom. Kidnapping is another weapon used by terrorists. The victims are held for ransom, frequently very large amounts, which provides an important source of funds for the terrorists. Italian industry is not alone in being subjected to terrorism and kidnapping for ransom. For example, industry in Argentina has paid ransom of several hundred million dollars for the release of kidnapped business executives.[18]

By 1986, Colombia and Peru had become the most dangerous places for American executives, and a long stay by a high-ranking American executive in either country is risky. Brief visits are usually fairly safe because kidnappings take a while to plan, so top executives from the United States practice what is called commando management. They arrive in Bogota or Lima as secretly as possible, meet for a few days with local employees, and fly off before kidnappers learn of their presence.[19]

Countermeasures by Industry. Insurance to cover ransom payments, antiterrorist schools, and companies to handle negotiations with kidnappers have come into being.

A woman cries on the grave of her son, a Bosnian defender who was killed in the war.

Reuters/Bettmann

As kidnapping and extortion directed against businesses and governments have become common fund-raising and political techniques for terrorists, insurance against such acts has grown into a multimillion-dollar business. The world's largest kidnapping and extortion underwriting firm is located in London. The firm, Cassidy and Davis, underwriter for Lloyd's of London, says that it covers some 9,000 companies. Cassidy and Davis does not sit back and wait for claims to be filed. It runs antiterrorism training courses for executives, with subjects ranging from defensive driving techniques—escape tactics and battering through blockades—to crisis management. Country-by-country risk analyses are instantly available on international computer hookups.

Cassidy and Davis works closely with Control Risk, Ltd., a London-based security service company that advises firms or families in negotiations with kidnappers. Cassidy and Davis encourages its clients to use Control Risk services. The premiums for the insurance underwritten by Cassidy and Davis range from some $3,000 a year for $1.5 million of coverage in low-risk England to $60,000 a year for the same coverage in high-risk Peru.[20]

Figures 10–5 and 10–6 are checklists for executives traveling to and in countries where they are at risk of being kidnapped. Figure 10–5 indicates what should be done before leaving the home country; Figure 10–6 is about what to do once in the host country.

Before leaving the United States, travelers can get information about their destinations, including warnings about dangers there, from consular information sheets. With a computer and modem, you can log on to the Consular Affairs Bulletin Board [(202) 647-9225, no access charge]. A more cumbersome method is to phone the State Department's automated answering system [(202) 647-5225] to hear the sheets read aloud.

Terrorism Changes. On the positive side, terrorists have lost their havens, finance sources, and training bases in East Europe and the Soviet Union. There is better cooperation between antiterrorist officials in governments of Europe, Japan, and North America. New American laws give the United States powers to hunt down terrorists anywhere in the world. Since 1985, the United States has convicted more than 460 people on domestic terrorism charges and more than 60 on international charges.[21]

But there are negatives. A different kind of terrorism is breaking out in the post–Soviet empire period. This is ethnoterrorism, as various European racial groups fight to establish their own nations and for land for their people. The Croats, Serbs, and Slovenians of the former Yugoslavia are killing each other as are various racial groups in the splintered Soviet Union.

Germany has emerged as the weak link in the Western countries' antiterrorist chain. It has never had decisive success against the Red Army Faction, which continues its series of spectacular murders, including the 1989 killing of the Deutsche Bank head, Alfred Herrhausen.

The German mishandling of the investigation of the Pan Am Lockerbie bombing is emblematic of German security shortcomings. At one point, 16 terrorists were rounded up, but 14 were released almost immediately, enraging antiterrorist agents around the world.[22]

Nuclear Terrorism. Failing security standards at former Soviet nuclear installations are permitting uranium to be stolen, which is then smuggled for sale to unauthorized buyers such as terrorists. NATO describes this as the greatest threat to international security since the end of the Cold War.

Interpol, the international police agency, has set up a specialized group involving police forces in 24 European nations, but the smuggling continues.

FIGURE 10–5
Before leaving

- Your personal and legal affairs should be in order.
- Except on a need-to-know basis, tell no one of your travel plans. This is not hysterical paranoia; it's good discipline. A business executive on a fishing boat out of Miami who discusses an upcoming business trip to Central America in the presence of Cuban deckhands may find that future stay in Central America considerably longer than planned.
- Sanitize all documents and business identity. All company logos and identification should be removed from briefcases and luggage. A last name, or fictitious name you've created, is sufficient identification on these items. If you use business cards, acronyms such as CIA for certified internal auditor should be eliminated. Whatever documents you need to conduct your business can be mailed or wired ahead so that they are waiting for you. If the trip comes up very suddenly or there are no company offices to receive the documents, carry them in your luggage. Never carry any business identification or documents on your person. In addition to a passport with visas, a jewelry bracelet or pendant-type ID with name, Social Security number, and blood type is the only identification you would need while in transit.

- Check with your company and other companies to find someone who has conducted business in the country you are going to. Contact that person and ask questions about cultural mores and the political climate in that country. Then look in an encyclopedia or go to the library and read all you can on the subject.
- If your company doesn't already have an individual designated to coordinate and monitor foreign trips, contact the appropriate management and see that someone knows the where, when, and how of your trip. Your family should be given that person's name and phone numbers.
- The company should have an established code for use by all its personnel who are engaged in foreign business. If not, a simple code system should be devised so that communication can be made under extraordinary circumstances (like on a video made by terrorists who have kidnapped you). The code should be provided to the company and your family.
- Have your company acquire a telephone directory for the State Department from the Government Printing Office. It can be used to contact the appropriate departmental sections for pretrip inquiries (operational intelligence). And, in the unfortunate event of a company employee kidnapping, it would be an absolute necessity in crisis management.

Source: *The Internal Auditor*, October 1986, p. 25.

Interpol is treating 30 cases as extremely serious, but this could be just the tip of the iceberg. Some cases involve as much as 250 kilograms of weapons-grade uranium; others may involve more. It takes only 7 kilograms of such uranium to make a nuclear bomb.[23]

Islamic Fundamentalist Terrorism.   The German secret service identified two extremist Islamic fundamentalist groups as potential uranium customers. The bases for the threats posed by those groups are different and deserve some discussion.

Israel has made uneasy peace with Islamic countries and groups, first with Egypt, then in 1994 with the Palestine Liberation Organization and Jordan. By nonfundamentalist thinking, peace should reduce hostilities and tensions. For some fundamentalists, however, the opposite is true, and the more prominent such peace efforts appear, the more infuriated these groups become. Their hatred of Christians, Jews, secularists, democrats, and the West in general is unrelenting. To these radical groups, "peace" is nothing more than a continuation of the Zionist-infidel conspiracy waged against Islam since the Crusades. Nothing will satisfy them until the infidel—Zionists have been defeated.

- First, slow down. Leave yourself time to think and evaluate. You're not in America. The rush and rat-race pace of hyperactivity typical of American businesspeople will only get you in trouble here.
- Take nothing for granted. Locate where elevators and stairways are so you can find them, even in the dark.
- Learn your rooms. Locate windows and doors and check to see if they are locked or if they can be locked. If you are not satisfied with your room, either change rooms or change hotels. Remember, if you change hotels, let the company and your family know.
- Do not conduct any business in your room or over the phone. The reasons are obvious.
- Whenever possible, you schedule business meetings and the locations. If this is not possible, check with your contacts and determine whether the location of scheduled meetings is safe. Remember, it's not the people you're conducting business with that present the threat (unless you're a major corporate executive and that fact is well known in advance); the danger is in becoming an object of surveillance.
- You are most vulnerable when you're moving, particularly if that movement is predictable. Vary times and methods of movement. Whether you're using a company-provided car and driver or taxis, use different entrances and exits when you enter and leave the hotel. If you are using

company or rented transportation, change cars whenever the mood strikes you. Always follow your instincts.
- Always be aware of your surroundings and alert for surveillance. If terrorists are following you and they realize you recognize that fact, you've just made yourself a higher risk for them to consider. Terrorists will not just be lurking in the streets waiting for someone they can attack. They will spend many hours and much effort to observe potential targets. Then, they will select the target that's going to cost them the least. Being alert makes you a more difficult target and raises the possibility, from the terrorist's point of view, that you have or will notify the authorities.
- Avoid being photographed.
- Do not respond to telephone inquiries or apparent spontaneous interest by people you meet to know more about you, however innocent or sincere either may seem. Handle it diplomatically.
- Avoid night movements, but if you must, never walk. Not walking anywhere, anytime, is the best rule; but if it can't be avoided, be particularly sensitive to surveillance and try to stay in crowded areas.
- Read newspapers and stay in touch with your in-country contacts on a daily basis to stay informed on political climate indicators.
- Try to fit in with the native people as much as possible regarding dress and manners. This not only ingratiates you with the locals but also makes you more difficult to see.

FIGURE 10–6
After arriving

Source: *The Internal Auditor*, October 1986, p. 27.

Fundamentalist groups, including Hamas, Hezbollah, and Islamic Jihad, have established their own infrastructure throughout the West. Recent fatal bombings that have been claimed by or attributed to them include those of the New York World Trade Center, the Israeli embassy and a Jewish center in Buenos Aires, a Panamanian airplane, and the Israeli embassy in London.

As noted earlier, government-sponsored terrorism is an act of war, and analysts have determined that Iran is involved in at least some of the above mentioned blasts and many more. Iran is not the only power aiding and abetting Islamic fundamental terrorists. Syria has provided sanctuary for them and allowed the free passage of weapons and explosives from Iran through the Syrian capital, Damascus, to Lebanon and beyond.[24]

Government **stability** can be approached from two directions. One can speak of either a government's simple ability to maintain itself in power or the stability or permanence of a government's policies. It is safe to generalize that business (indeed almost all agricultural, commercial, and financial activities) prospers most when there is a stable government with permanent—or at most, gradually changing—policies.

stability
A government can be said to be stable if it maintains itself in power and when its fiscal, monetary, and political policies are predictable and not subject to sudden, radical changes

GOVERNMENT STABILITY

Stability and Instability: Examples and Results

Instability in Lebanon.   Here is a classic example of the impact of a change from order to chaos—from stability to **instability**—on the business and finances of a prosperous country. Until 1974, Lebanon prospered as the trading, banking, international company regional headquarters, business services (that is, accounting, legal, and financial services), transportation, and tourist center of the Middle East. The country achieved this prosperity with virtually no natural resources; its land is mostly arid desert or mountains. Its prosperity was the work of an industrious people given political stability.

Then civil war broke out in Lebanon. The details of that civil war are beyond the scope of this book, but its reasons included ideological and religious differences. The results were catastrophic. Homes, offices, banks, stores, transportation, communications, and hospitals were destroyed. The people fled the country or fought and survived as best they could. Almost all of the previous commercial activities ended.

Stability in Bolivia?   In 152 years of independence from Spain, Bolivia had 187 governments. Then, in 1972, a government seized power and by 1976 had established the durability record for any Bolivian government in the 20th century. The economic results were startling and encouraging.

Bolivia's GNP grew by 7.3 percent in 1975 and 7 percent in 1976, and its inflation rate was about 12 percent. At the same time, such neighbors as Argentina, Chile, and Peru were experiencing varying types of political unrest, were growing more slowly or not at all, and were suffering much higher rates of inflation.

Hector Ormachea, the Bolivian government official in charge of negotiating development loans abroad, spoke of "projects, not politics." And projects resulted—more than 300 by 1977. They ranged from roads into areas previously accessible only by air, to oil exploration, mining ventures, and agricultural and industrial development.

Unused Wealth.   Bolivia is potentially a rich country. Its resources include tin, zinc, antimony, copper, gold, tungsten, and bismuth, and it is more than self-sufficient in oil despite very little recent exploration or drilling.

The country's resources have scarcely been touched, at least in part because of Bolivia's previous political instability. Past governments had been quick to nationalize foreign mines. Given the mid-1970s stability, European, Japanese, and U.S. firms negotiated to explore for and extract the resources.[25]

Renewed Foreign Confidence.   Another sign of renewed foreign confidence in Bolivia was given in 1977. Underwriters led by the Arab Finance Corporation and Merrill Lynch International handled the sale in Europe of Bolivian debt securities. Although the amount was a relatively small $15 million, it was the first offering to foreign investors in about 50 years. Until Bolivia had achieved political stability, it would have been fruitless to try to borrow money abroad; no one would have lent it.[26]

Perils of Pauline.   By 1979, there was further political turmoil in Bolivia; between then and 1985, there were 12 Bolivian governments, most of them military. Inflation soared to about 25,000 percent in 1985, and in that year over half of Bolivia's export earnings—some $600 million—came from sales of cocaine; less than $500 million came from sales of minerals, oil, gas, and agricultural products. While the few cocaine traffickers got rich, the great bulk of the Bolivian population—growing at 2.6 percent a year—sank more deeply into poverty. Domestic investment declined and production collapsed.

instability
An unstable government is the opposite of a stable one; it cannot maintain itself in power or makes sudden, unpredictable, or radical policy changes

Arabs (Palestinian intifada) burn an Israeli flag.

A. Tannenbaum/SYGMA

Miracle of La Paz?* In 1985, a new Bolivian president, Victor Paz Estenssero, was democratically elected. Estenssero immediately froze salaries in the state sector (which accounted for roughly 40 percent of the economy), removed price controls, stopped subsidies, slashed many import tariffs, floated the currency (the boliviano), and liberalized labor laws to allow easy firing and hiring. He told state enterprises to cover their costs or close, put new taxes on cars and houses, and offered a back tax amnesty.

Inflation plunged to near zero, foreign development aid is being restored, local investments have been starting up, and an attack has begun on the big drug traffickers. In 1993, Gonzalo Sanchez de Lozada, the planning minister who masterminded Bolivia's anti-inflation program, was elected president. Bolivians are sensitive about privatization, particularly to foreigners, so the new government is achieving the desired results by a different route. First, the word *privatization* is not used; the program is called "Capitalization of Public Enterprises in Bolivia." Second, 50 percent of the stock of those enterprises is distributed, free of charge, to Bolivians of voting age. Third, the remaining 50 percent, together with management of the enterprises, can be bought by private foreign companies. The government expects to attract $8 billion in foreign investment by 1998 and forecasts a 7 to 8 percent rate of GDP growth by 1997.[27]

William Colby, former director of the American CIA and now an international investment advisor, recently wrote a report on Bolivia. In it he notes that Bolivia's 7.5 percent inflation rate is low compared to other South American countries and that YPFB, the state oil concern, is flush with money thanks to hefty exports to Chile and Argentina. YPFB is one of those state enterprises being "capitalized." Colby ends his report by writing, "I see real opportunity here."[28]

traditional hostilities
Long-standing enmities between tribes, races, religions, ideologies, or countries

We need mention only a few of the **traditional hostilities** to illustrate their powerful impact on business and trade.

TRADITIONAL HOSTILITIES

---

*La Paz is the capital of Bolivia.

Arab Countries–Israel

Israel is surrounded on three sides by Arab countries, but until the peace efforts initiated by the Egyptian Anwar Sadat, the Arab countries would not trade or have other peaceful dealings with it. Indeed, some Arab countries still boycott companies that trade with Israel, and because some of the Arab countries are extremely rich OPEC members, the boycott can be financially painful.*

The year 1994 saw further progress toward peace between Israel and its Arab neighbors, specifically the Palestine Liberation Organization and Jordan. While these developments may cut down incidents such as the pictured Palestinian intifada burning of Israeli flags, there is fervent opposition to those peace moves among Palestinians, other Arabs, and in powerful parts of the Islamic world.

We have brought to your attention the escalating force, fury, and destructiveness of certain Islamic fundamentalist groups around the world. As noted, their hate and violence are not limited to Israel and Jews; they strike also at Christians, secularists, democrats, and the West in general. And although they have support from Arab states such as Iraq, Libya, and Syria, their main support now appears to come from the non-Arabic but fundamental-Islamic Iran.

Hutus and Tutsis in Burundi and Rwanda

The majority Hutus and the Tutsis have been at each other's throats for many years. Burundi and Rwanda, where they constitute most of the population, were colonies of Belgium from the 19th century to after World War II. During that period, Hutu-Tutsi hostilities were kept at low levels, but they broke out in the 1990s, first in Burundi, where they were quelled, and then in 1993 and 1994 in Rwanda. The Hutus ran the government and army in Rwanda, and at least part of the army embarked on a campaign to exterminate the Tutsis. Some million people were massacred, and a Tutsi-led army coming in from Uganda retaliated. The Tutsi army defeated the Hutus, whose subsequent retreat led to the worst refugee situation in the world's history. Over a million Hutus swarmed and crammed into Zaire, where they were held in camps at the border. Cholera and dysentery took thousands of lives.

The Tutsis installed a new government in Rwanda and invited the Hutus to return. They did so slowly, but chances look slim for the cooperation between the Hutus and Tutsis that would be necessary to achieve conditions attractive to foreign investors.

Tamils and Sinhalese in Sri Lanka

The Tamils form a substantial minority of the Sri Lankan population. An armed group calling itself the Tamil Tigers has been fighting a bloody series of battles with the Sri Lankan army and has committed terrorist murders and bombings of the Sinhalese population.

The Tamils want a separate state, and a large Tamil population in India has given them support. The late Indian president Rajiv Ghandi sent troops to Sri Lanka in an attempt to suppress the Tamil uprising. They failed, and the troops were withdrawn, but Ghandi gained Tamil hatred for his attempt. His murder—by a bomb hidden in a flower arrangement offered him by a woman when he was campaigning for election in the Indian Tamil state in 1991—was blamed on the Tigers or their allies.

---

*See Chapter 11 for a discussion of U.S. law dealing with this boycott.

Croats, Bosnians, and Serbs in the Former Yugoslavia

This historical enmity was mentioned above, and they are killing each other despite UN efforts at peacemaking. There are ethnic and religious elements in these conflicts, and each group has engaged in rape, torture, and murder as it overran another group. The horrible term *ethnic cleansing* has been heard often. Many of the Bosnians are Muslims as a result of Turkey's dominance in this area for several hundred years, and their conflicts with their Christian neighbors adds bitterness to the situation. The Serbs are the best armed, having got most of the weapons of the former Yugoslav army.

South Africa

We should emphasize that the examples given above are, unfortunately, only a few of many racially based hostilities around the world. We presented another in the fifth edition of this book: the black-white strife of South African apartheid. Since that was written, South Africa has elected a new multirace government. The new president is Nelson Mandela, a black who spent several years in prison because of his opposition to apartheid.

Most of the world imposed sanctions against investing in, lending to, or trading with South Africa as protests against apartheid. Now that it is ended, the sanctions are off, and South Africa, rich in natural resources, may again become a prosperous place for business.

As discussed above, nationalism is a powerful political force that has grown greatly during the mid and late 20th century. There are also international political forces with which business must contend. Here we shall cover briefly the political impact of some of the international organizations introduced in Chapter 4.

INTERNATIONAL ORGANIZATIONS

United Nations (UN)

The UN is highly politicized. The member-countries vote as blocs formed because of ideology or perceived similar objectives.

UN personnel advise member-countries on such matters as tax, monetary, and fiscal policies. The UN is active in the harmonization of laws affecting international trade. It had a hand in drafting an international commercial arbitration convention. It has drafted a code of conduct for multinational business. Any of the political ideologies we have discussed can be reflected in the content and spirit of tax, trade, and arbitration laws; conduct codes; and fiscal or monetary policies.

The Transnational Corporations Division of the UN has had a change of attitude resulting from a change of political orientation. During the early UN years, the division tended to be hostile to private international companies, saying they cheated and victimized LDCs that needed UN protection. The new, changed attitude is that LDCs should encourage investment by those companies to obtain such things as capital, technology, and management skills.

UNCTAD is credited with having influenced the IMF to ease its restrictions on loans to LDCs. This is important to banks lending to and suppliers selling to LDCs.

Virtually all of the specialized UN agencies are now actively advising LDCs about what to buy for their agriculture, industry, airlines, health programs, weather stations, and so forth. These are huge markets for business.

In Chapter 4, we spoke of the many peace-making and peace-keeping operations of the UN around the world. Even if inadvertently, these military incursions have political results.

World Bank Group

One or another member of the World Bank Group finances large parts of the purchases made by LDCs. Although the Bank's charter bans political activity by its officers and employees, it is reported that its president was involved in campaign-planning strategy for one of the U.S. presidential candidates in 1980.[29]

IMF, GATT/WTO, and OPEC

The IMF can have great influence on the fiscal and monetary policies of the nations that it assists, and as reported in Chapter 4, many believe its power is growing.

Although GATT has in general strived to lower barriers to trade, it has condoned their erection by LDCs in some cases. Import barriers are, of course, an important political force affecting multinational business operations.

The political power of OPEC was discussed in Chapter 4. We mention it here again to remind you that petroleum is now as much a political force as it is a commodity.

EU

Slowly, the member-nations of the EU are surrendering parts of their sovereign powers to the Brussels headquarters. Mention of only a few areas will illustrate the extent of the EU's influence on business. Among other things, the EU is working to harmonize laws dealing with taxes, patents, labor conditions, competition, insurance, banking, and capital markets.

Harmonization of differing national laws is one matter, but the EU has now gone a step beyond that—to lawmaking. This is occurring in such fields as company law, antitrust, and consumer and environmental protection.[30] The objective of some Europeans is to create a political, as well as an economic, power to rival America and Japan.

Organization for Economic Cooperation and Development (OECD)

This 25-member organization of industrialized countries has issued "Guidelines for Multinational Enterprises." Although it has been said that OECD guidelines merely create a voluntary set of principles upon which to build sound international relations, they can have significant impact. For example, when Badger, Raytheon's subsidiary in Belgium, closed shop, it did not have enough money to meet its labor termination obligations under Belgian law. The Belgian government and labor unions used the pressure of the OECD "voluntary" guidelines to convince Raytheon to pay Badger's obligations.

LABOR

Workers and labor unions are the subject of Chapter 12, but we would be remiss if we did not mention them in connection with the political forces bearing on business. The European labor unions are ideologically oriented, usually toward the left. The American unions are said to be more pragmatic, but in practice they are extremely active politically. They supply large amounts of money and workers to support the political candidates they favor.

In Europe, the United States, and, increasingly, Japan, labor makes its political force felt not only at the polls but also in the legislatures. Unions lobby for or against laws as these are perceived to be for or against the interests of labor.

INTERNATIONAL COMPANIES (ICs)

International business is not merely a passive victim of political forces. It can be a powerful force in the world political arena.[31]

55 of World's 100 Biggest Economic Units Are Firms, Not Nations

An IC negotiating with a country may have annual sales bigger than the country's GNP. According to rankings in 1992, General Motors' sales of $132.8 billion made it the 22nd-largest economic unit. Its sales were larger than the $130.9 billion GNP of Iran. Sales of Exxon, Ford, and Royal Dutch Shell ranked 31st, 32nd, and 33rd, followed by the GNP of Hong Kong. Of course, the GNP of most other countries is even smaller; the total GNP of the countries with the 70 smallest GNPs is about equal to GM's sales.[32]

Large financial size carries power. However, an IC's power need not rest solely on size. It can come from the possession of scarce capital, technology, and management, plus the capability to deploy those resources around the world. An IC may have the processing, productive, distributive, and marketing abilities necessary for the successful exploitation of raw materials or for the manufacture, distribution, and marketing of certain products. Those abilities are frequently not available in LDCs. Recognition of the desirability of IC investments is growing.[33]

It is arbitrary to place this subject in a chapter on political forces because **country risk assessment (CRA)** involves many risks other than political risks. It is probably important enough to warrant a separate chapter, but one of our objectives was to avoid an overlong book. We shall introduce our readers to CRA here; there is a growing literature about it, and those who are interested can find much material.[34]

The political events of recent years have caused firms to concentrate much more on the CRA. Firms that had already done CRA updated and strengthened the function, and many other companies began the practice.

COUNTRY RISK ASSESSMENT (CRA)

country risk assessment (CRA)
A bank or business having an asset in or payable from a foreign country, or considering a loan or an investment there, evaluates that country's economic situation and policies and its politics to determine how much risk exists of losing the asset or not being paid

Types of Country Risks

Country risks are increasingly political in nature. There are wars, revolutions, and coups. Less dramatic, but nevertheless important for businesses, are government changes by election of a socialist or nationalist government, which may be hostile to private business and particularly to foreign-owned business.

The risks may be economic or financial. There may be persistent balance-of-payments deficits or high inflation rates. Repayment of loans may be questionable.

Labor conditions may cause investors to pause. Labor productivity may be low, or labor unions may be militant.

Laws may be changed about such subjects as taxes, currency convertibility, tariffs, quotas, or labor permits. The chances for a fair trial in local courts must be assessed.

Terrorism may be present. If it is, can the company protect its personnel and property?

Information Content for CRA

The types of information a firm will need to judge country risks will vary according to the nature of its business and the length of time required for the investment, loan, or other involvement to yield a satisfactory return.

Nature of Business. Consider, for example, the needs of a hotel company compared with those of heavy-equipment manufacturers or manufacturers of personal hygiene products or mining companies. Banks have their own sets of problems and information needs. Sometimes there are variations between firms in the same industry or on a project-to-project basis. The nationality—

home country—of the company may be a factor; does the host country bear a particular animus, or friendly attitude, toward the home country?

Length of Time Required. Export financing usually involves the shortest period of risk exposure. Typically, payments are made within 180 days—usually less—and exporters can get insurance or bank protection.

Bank loans can be short, medium, or long term. However, when the business includes host country assembly, mixing, manufacture, or extraction (oil or minerals), long-term commitments are necessary.

With long-term investment or loan commitments, there are inherent problems with risk analysis that cannot be resolved. Most such investment opportunities require 5, 10, or more years to pay off. But the utility of risk analyses of social, political, and economic factors decreases precipitously over longer time spans.

Who Does Country Risk Assessing?

General or specific analyses, macro or micro analyses, and political, social, and economic analyses have been conducted—perhaps under different names—for years. The Conference Board located bits and pieces of CRA being performed in various company departments—for example, the international division and public affairs, finance, legal, economics, planning, and product-producing departments. Sometimes the efforts were duplicative, and the people in one department were unaware that others in the company were similarly involved.

Efforts are now being made to concentrate CRA and to maximize its effectiveness for the company. These efforts include guidelines about the participation of top management.

Outside consulting and publishing firms are another source of country risk analysis. As CRA has mushroomed in perceived importance, a number of such firms have been formed or have expanded.

Instead of or in addition to the outside consultants, a number of firms have buttressed their internal risk analysis staffs by hiring such experts as international business or political science professors or retired State Department, CIA, or military people.

CRA Procedures

The Economist Intelligence Unit breaks its assessments down into three categories. First is medium-term lending risk, covering such factors as external debt and trends in the current account. Second is political and policy risk, including factors such as the consistency of government policy and the quality of economic management. Third is short-term trade risk, including foreign exchange reserves.[35]

The *International Country Risk Guide (ICRG)*, put out by a U.S. division of International Business Communications Ltd. of London, takes a somewhat different approach. It offers individual ratings for political, financial, and economic risk, plus a composite rating. The political variable includes factors such as government corruption and how economic expectations diverge from reality. The financial rating looks at such things as the likelihood of losses from exchange controls and loan defaults. Economic ratings take into account such factors as inflation and debt service costs.[36]

The *ICRG*, Crédit Suisse, and other organizations publish country risk rankings periodically. Another highly regarded publisher of rankings is

Euromoney. Table 10–1 shows *Euromoney*'s judgment of the 50 least risky and the 50 most risky countries in 1993. Observe the headings of the 10 columns to the right of each country name, and you will see the criteria used by *Euromoney* and the scores for each in arriving at its conclusions.

Lessons of the International Debt Crisis

There are at least five lessons that CRA analysts should have learned. First, many developing countries are vulnerable to external shocks. One thing that has become apparent is the importance of a country's export and import structure in weathering an external economic shock. For example, the newly industrialized countries of Asia with their diversified export structures have been in a much better position to deal with the collapse of commodity prices and the erection of protectionist barriers than have been other countries with a comparable level of development but lopsided export structures (such as Indonesia and Mexico).

Second, the development of the debt crisis has shown clearly that the economic policies of debtor countries have a decisive impact on default risk. The countries that have become most deeply mired in the crisis are the ones that adopted expansionary fiscal and monetary policies. The results were inflation, current account deficits, loss of international competitiveness, and capital flight. Such has been the fate of the Philippines and the high-debt countries of Latin America.

By contrast, those countries that allowed the altered world market prices and demand conditions to take effect on their economies and adapted their economic policies to accommodate changed conditions have fared much better. Restrictive fiscal and monetary policies damped inflation, while occasional devaluations of their currencies kept trade balances under control. South Korea withstood the debt crisis through skillful economic policies.

Third, sustained economic growth is a major requirement for high-debt countries to service their debt and reduce its burden. Austerity alone cannot be a solution, economically, politically, or socially.

Fourth, the social and potential political costs of overindebtedness combined with austerity are proving high. Social and political tensions have risen sharply and threaten the survival of several democratically elected governments. That, in turn, greatly increases the danger of a debt moratorium.

Figure 10–7 (page 342), presents two rankings by the Economist Intelligence Unit. One deals with developing or emerging countries, showing Iraq as the riskiest and Russia in second place. The other shows an assessment of Asian risk.

The fifth lesson from the debt crisis for CRA analysts is the global ripple effect of seemingly independent risks or economic shocks. For example, the oil price collapse at the beginning of 1986 jacked up oil-exporting countries' default risk while lessening that risk for oil importers, thus affecting international interest and exchange rates and triggering a whole series of fiscal and monetary policy responses. The tequila effect was the phrase applied to the global ripples caused by the financial crises in the Mexican economy at the end of 1994 and into 1995.

The 1987 stock market crash caused worldwide economic reverberations. Other events that would have global effects if they were to occur include sustained changes in world interest rates, recession in major market countries, creation of debtor-country cartels, or the banking system's loss of confidence in an entire region.

TABLE 10–1
Country risk rankings, 1993*

	Rank				Economic Performance (10)	Political Risk (20)
March 93	September 92	Country	Total Score			
1	1	Japan	99.44		9.44	20.00
2	6	United States	99.07		9.07	20.00
3	3	Switzerland	99.01		9.01	20.00
4	5	France	98.46		8.88	19.57
5	2	Netherlands	98.24		8.88	19.36
6	7	Austria	97.94		9.01	18.94
7	4	Germany	97.93		8.57	19.36
8	9	United Kingdom	97.77		8.20	19.57
9	8	Canada	97.77		9.01	19.15
10	10	Belgium	96.68		8.51	18.94
11	18	Luxembourg	95.79		8.57	19.15
12	12	Denmark	95.15		9.13	18.72
13	11	Norway	94.72		9.07	18.09
14	14	Singapore	92.54		10.00	18.51
15	15	Australia	92.54		8.14	17.87
16	13	Sweden	92.45		6.89	17.87
17	17	Spain	91.20		7.58	18.09
18	16	Finland	91.17		8.01	17.23
19	19	New Zealand	91.12		8.14	17.45
20	21	Ireland	90.46		7.89	16.81
21	24	Iceland	88.35		6.46	17.66
22	20	Taiwan	87.94		9.13	18.51
23	22	Italy	87.59		7.39	17.66
24	25	Hong Kong	85.65		9.07	16.81
25	27	United Arab Emirates	82.20		7.45	17.02
26	26	Saudi Arabia	79.38		7.02	17.02
27	30	Bahrain	78.53		7.02	16.17
28	23	Portugal	78.38		7.58	16.17
29	32	Israel	76.88		6.21	15.32
30	33	Kuwait	75.48		6.83	15.53
31	28	Greece	74.67		5.84	14.26
32	29	Korea, Republic of	73.96		8.57	17.23
33	31	Malaysia	73.01		8.57	16.81
34	36	Thailand	72.90		8.57	15.32
35	34	Brunei	72.59		8.57	16.17
36	38	Qatar	70.37		6.89	15.74
37	42	Oman	68.78		7.39	16.60
38	39	Malta	66.15		7.64	15.96
39	35	Chile	65.70		7.33	14.47
40	41	Cyprus	61.94		7.95	14.47
41	40	Indonesia	61.89		7.14	14.04
42	43	China	60.73		7.52	14.26
43	47	South Africa	59.04		5.40	12.98
44	37	Turkey	58.55		5.84	13.62
45	44	Bahamas	57.19		6.46	15.32
46	45	Mexico	55.11		6.46	13.19
47	46	Hungary	54.92		5.90	12.55
48	49	Czech Republic	54.89		7.08	10.85
49	48	Colombia	52.80		5.47	12.55
50	61	Barbados	51.83		4.72	12.77

*Numbers in parentheses under column headings indicate weighting.

Debt Indicators (10)	Access to Bank Lending (10)	Access to Short-Term Finance (10)	Access to Capital Markets (10)	Discount on Forfaiting (10)	Credit Ratings (10)	Debt in Default or Rescheduled (10)
10.00	10.00	10.00	10.00	10.00	10.00	10.00
10.00	10.00	10.00	10.00	10.00	10.00	10.00
10.00	10.00	10.00	10.00	10.00	10.00	10.00
10.00	10.00	10.00	10.00	10.00	10.00	10.00
10.00	10.00	10.00	10.00	10.00	10.00	10.00
10.00	10.00	10.00	10.00	10.00	10.00	10.00
10.00	10.00	10.00	10.00	10.00	10.00	10.00
10.00	10.00	10.00	10.00	10.00	10.00	10.00
10.00	10.00	10.00	10.00	10.00	10.00	10.00
10.00	10.00	10.00	10.00	10.00	9.62	10.00
10.00	10.00	10.00	10.00	10.00	9.23	10.00
10.00	10.00	10.00	10.00	8.07	10.00	10.00
10.00	10.00	10.00	10.00	8.07	9.23	10.00
10.00	10.00	10.00	10.00	7.95	9.62	10.00
10.00	10.00	7.50	10.00	8.07	8.46	10.00
10.00	10.00	10.00	10.00	8.07	8.46	10.00
10.00	10.00	10.00	10.00	8.07	9.62	10.00
10.00	10.00	10.00	9.00	8.07	8.46	10.00
10.00	10.00	10.00	9.00	8.07	8.85	10.00
10.00	10.00	10.00	10.00	7.84	7.69	10.00
10.00	10.00	10.00	10.00	8.07	7.69	10.00
10.00	10.00	10.00	10.00	8.07	6.15	10.00
10.00	10.00	5.00	8.00	8.07	9.23	10.00
10.00	10.00	10.00	6.00	8.07	8.46	10.00
10.00	10.00	6.00	8.00	10.00	5.77	10.00
10.00	10.00	10.00	10.00	7.73	0.00	10.00
10.00	10.00	7.50	10.00	7.84	0.00	10.00
10.00	10.00	7.50	10.00	7.84	0.00	10.00
9.20	0.43	10.00	10.00	8.07	6.92	10.00
10.00	10.00	8.00	7.00	7.27	3.08	10.00
10.00	10.00	7.50	8.00	7.61	0.00	10.00
10.00	8.00	10.00	5.00	7.73	3.85	10.00
9.74	1.76	5.00	7.00	7.73	6.92	10.00
9.43	2.37	5.00	7.00	8.07	5.77	10.00
9.42	5.98	3.00	7.00	7.84	5.77	10.00
0.00	10.00	10.00	10.00	7.85	0.00	10.00
10.00	10.00	0.00	10.00	7.73	0.00	10.00
9.57	0.00	7.50	10.00	7.73	0.00	10.00
9.87	0.00	10.00	5.00	7.84	0.00	9.84
8.76	4.57	6.00	7.00	7.61	3.85	6.12
9.27	0.00	7.50	3.00	5.91	3.85	10.00
8.71	4.46	3.00	6.00	5.45	3.08	10.00
8.95	0.00	2.50	6.00	7.27	4.23	10.00
9.70	5.00	4.50	6.00	5.45	0.00	10.00
8.96	0.42	5.00	5.00	6.25	3.46	10.00
0.00	10.00	5.50	4.00	5.91	0.00	10.00
9.07	0.92	5.50	7.00	7.27	1.92	3.77
8.62	0.00	5.00	6.00	4.55	2.31	10.00
9.57	0.00	6.00	5.00	4.09	2.31	9.99
8.92	1.07	5.50	4.00	5.45	0.00	9.84
9.39	0.00	5.50	4.00	5.45	0.00	10.00

Continued

TABLE 10–1
Country risk rankings, 1993
—concluded

Rank					
March 93	September 92	Country	Total Score	Economic Performance (10)	Political Risk (10)
120	145	Cape Verde	24.20	1.80	6.17
121	121	Central African Republic	24.00	1.55	2.98
122	130	Haiti	23.99	1.24	3.83
123	128	Vietnam	23.95	4.72	7.23
124	111	Mali	23.85	1.93	4.26
125	104	Angola	23.57	1.74	4.68
126	117	Estonia	23.35	2.92	7.66
127	157	Myanmar	23.24	1.37	4.26
128	139	Peru	22.90	3.42	4.68
129	97	Libya	22.76	4.04	8.72
130	137	Tanzania	22.68	2.24	5.32
131	141	Lebanon	22.50	3.42	5.74
132	125	Yugoslavia (Serbia, Montenegro)	21.96	1.61	0.43
133	123	Latvia	21.70	2.55	6.38
134	118	Lithuania	21.36	2.42	6.17
135	127	Uganda	21.06	0.99	4.26
136	126	Ethiopia	20.87	1.12	2.34
137	140	Mauritania	20.82	1.55	4.47
138	150	São Tome and Principe	20.65	1.18	7.02
139	131	Bosnia-Herzegovina	20.62	0.06	0.00
140	138	Guinea-Bissau	20.50	1.18	4.68
141	147	Zambia	20.29	1.93	4.04
142	146	Kyrgystan	19.91	2.61	5.53
143	159	Sierra Leone	19.71	1.37	4.47
144	149	Mongolia	19.20	2.17	7.02
145	122	Ukraine	19.17	2.30	5.11
146	136	Zaire	18.86	1.06	2.34
147	132	Belarus	18.75	2.30	4.68
148	134	Kazakhstan	18.55	2.73	4.04
149	129	Russia	18.13	2.17	4.68
150	142	Albania	17.77	1.49	1.28
151	167	Korea, North	16.73	1.18	2.55
152	144	Uzhbekistan	16.37	2.05	2.55
153	160	Guyana	15.71	2.42	5.11
154	151	Congo	15.70	1.93	2.98
155	148	Georgia	15.57	1.40	3.40
156	143	Turkmenistan	15.28	1.74	2.77
157	168	Iraq	14.41	1.06	0.85
158	162	Liberia	14.17	0.68	1.49
159	156	Moldova	14.05	1.37	1.91
160	152	Tajikistan	13.80	1.12	1.91
161	153	Azerbaijan	13.66	1.61	1.28
162	154	Armenia	13.58	1.30	1.28
163	166	Somalia	12.94	0.00	2.13
164	164	Mozambique	12.83	0.99	2.34
165	169	Cambodia	12.15	0.87	1.28
166	158	Afghanistan	12.08	0.81	1.28
167	163	Sudan	9.66	0.43	1.06
168	161	Nicaragua	7.37	1.18	3.62
169	165	Cuba	6.75	0.56	3.19

Debt Indicators (10)	Access to Bank Lending (10)	Access to Short-Term Finance (10)	Access to Capital Markets (10)	Discount on Forfaiting (10)	Credit Ratings (10)	Debt in Default or Rescheduled (10)
9.38	0.00	0.00	0.00	0.00	0.00	6.85
9.18	0.00	1.50	0.00	0.00	0.00	8.78
9.68	0.00	0.50	0.00	0.00	0.00	8.74
0.00	0.00	0.00	2.00	0.00	0.00	10.00
8.90	0.00	0.00	0.00	0.00	0.00	8.77
9.13	0.00	0.50	2.00	0.00	0.00	5.52
0.00	0.00	1.00	3.00	0.00	0.00	8.77
9.23	0.00	1.00	0.00	0.00	0.00	7.39
9.08	0.00	3.50	2.00	0.00	0.00	0.23
0.00	0.00	0.00	0.00	0.00	0.00	10.00
6.50	0.00	0.50	2.00	0.00	0.00	6.13
0.00	0.00	3.00	2.00	0.00	0.00	8.34
9.47	1.09	0.00	0.00	0.00	0.00	9.36
0.00	0.00	1.00	3.00	0.00	0.00	8.77
0.00	0.00	1.00	3.00	0.00	0.00	8.77
8.09	0.00	0.50	0.00	0.00	0.00	7.22
9.01	0.00	0.25	0.00	0.00	0.00	8.15
7.47	0.00	0.00	0.00	0.00	0.00	7.33
6.02	0.00	0.00	0.00	0.00	0.00	6.43
9.47	1.09	0.00	0.00	0.00	0.00	10.00
5.86	0.00	0.00	2.00	0.00	0.00	6.79
7.03	0.10	0.50	2.00	0.00	0.00	4.69
0.00	0.00	1.00	2.00	0.00	0.00	8.77
8.45	0.00	0.50	0.00	0.00	0.00	4.93
0.00	0.00	0.00	0.00	0.00	0.00	10.00
0.00	0.00	1.00	2.00	0.00	0.00	8.77
8.28	0.00	0.50	1.00	0.00	0.00	5.68
0.00	0.00	1.00	2.00	0.00	0.00	8.77
0.00	0.00	1.00	2.00	0.00	0.00	8.77
0.00	0.00	0.50	2.00	0.00	0.00	8.77
0.00	0.00	3.00	2.00	0.00	0.00	10.00
0.00	0.00	3.00	0.00	0.00	0.00	10.00
0.00	0.00	1.00	2.00	0.00	0.00	8.77
0.22	0.00	0.50	2.00	0.00	0.00	5.46
7.69	0.00	0.50	0.00	0.00	0.00	2.61
0.00	0.00	2.00	0.00	0.00	0.00	8.77
0.00	0.00	1.00	1.00	0.00	0.00	8.77
0.00	0.00	2.50	0.00	0.00	0.00	10.00
8.36	0.00	0.50	1.00	0.00	0.00	2.14
0.00	0.00	1.00	1.00	0.00	0.00	8.77
0.00	0.00	1.00	1.00	0.00	0.00	8.77
0.00	0.00	1.00	1.00	0.00	0.00	8.77
0.00	0.00	1.00	0.00	0.00	0.00	10.00
6.85	0.00	0.50	0.00	0.00	0.00	3.45
5.31	0.00	0.50	0.00	0.00	0.00	3.68
0.00	0.00	0.00	0.00	0.00	0.00	10.00
0.00	0.00	0.00	0.00	0.00	0.00	10.00
7.66	0.00	0.50	0.00	0.00	0.00	0.00
0.00	0.00	0.50	1.00	0.00	0.00	1.07
0.00	0.00	3.00	0.00	0.00	0.00	0.00

Source: *Euromoney*, March 1993, pp. 92–95.

FIGURE 10–7 Assessments of country risk

COUNTRY - RISK RATINGS

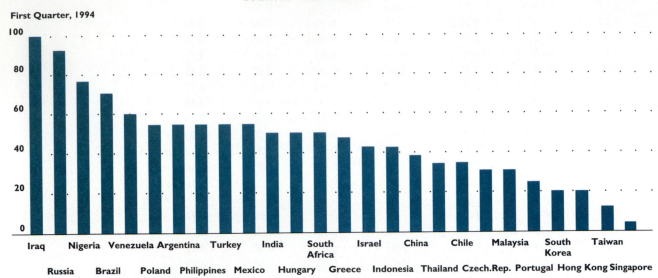

First Quarter, 1994

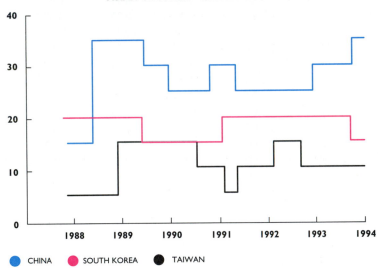

ASIAN COUNTRY - RISK RATINGS

● CHINA   ● SOUTH KOREA   ● TAIWAN

The chart shows the quarterly summary of national credit-risk ratings (based on economic and political factors) produced by the Economist Intelligence Unit (EIU), a sister company of *The Economist.* Iraq is still the riskiest country in the chart, with a maximum rating of 100. Russia remains the second riskiest; but the holding of elections there has improved its score from 95 points to 90. Stronger government in Poland has cut its rating from 60 to 55.

Asian economies are among the least risky in the developing world. But China's rating has been increasing: the EIU fears that the government will have to impose price and credit controls and bring growth to an abrupt halt.

Source: *The Economist,* May 21, 1994, p. 120.

SUMMARY

1. **Identify the ideological forces that affect business and understand the terminology used in discussing them.** We discussed capitalism, communism, socialism, conservative, liberal, right wing, and left wing.

2. **Understand that although most governments own businesses, they are privatizing them in growing numbers.** Even governments that consider themselves capitalist and conservative own some businesses. But almost all governments—with the United States lagging behind—are privatizing and getting out of businesses.

3. **Explain the changing sources and reasons for terrorism and the methods and growing power of terrorists.** The former Soviet Union and eastern European satellite countries no longer finance, train, and shelter terrorists, but they have been replaced by countries such as Iran, Iraq, Libya, North Korea, and Syria. Radical Islamic fundamentalists represent a growing threat with their hatred of Christians, Jews, secularists, democrats, and the West generally. They are infuriated by the peace moves between Israel and its Arab neighbors. Nuclear terrorism is a new fear, as security has failed at nuclear sites in the former Soviet Union and enriched uranium is being stolen and smuggled around the world.

4. **Explain steps that traveling international business executives should take to protect themselves from terrorists.** Before international business executives travel abroad and after they arrive in the host country, they should take steps to protect themselves from terrorists. See Figures 10–5 and 10–6.

5. **Understand the importance to business of government stability and policy continuity.** Business can rarely thrive in a country with an unstable government or rapid, drastic policy changes. See the story about Bolivia.

6. **Discuss the power sources of international organizations, labor unions, and international companies.** Large international businesses have political power, as do labor unions and international organizations such as the UN and the EU.

7. **Understand country risk assessment by international business.** Country risk assessment is now considered a necessity by most international businesses before they commit people, money, or technology to a foreign country. CRA involves evaluating a country's economic situation and policies as well as its politics.

KEY WORDS

- communism   315
- expropriation   315
- confiscation   315
- capitalism   316
- socialism   316
- conservative   317
- right wing   317
- liberal   318

- left wing   318
- privatization   320
- nationalism   322
- terrorism   324
- stability   329
- instability   330
- traditional hostilities   331
- country risk assessment (CRA)   335

QUESTIONS

1. *a.* What is ideology?
   b. Why is it important to international business?

2. *a.* What is the capitalist, free enterprise ideal?
   b. What is the actual situation in capitalist countries?

3. What impact can terrorism have on business?

4. Why does business fear sudden changes in government policies?

5. How can traditional hostilities affect business?

6. How can ICs use their strengths to influence government policies?

7. Is country risk assessment (CRA) an exact science? Explain.

8. *a.* In terms of exposure to political risk (for example, expropriation), which of the following businesses would you consider the most and least vulnerable?

banks	cosmetics
mines	manufacturers
oil fields	manufacturers of
oil refineries	personal hygiene
heavy-equipment	products
manufacturers	hotels
	automobile
	manufacturers

b. Are the most vulnerable businesses high profile or low profile? What are some ways to change the profile of a company in a foreign country?

9. Discuss the lessons CRA analysts should have learned from the world debt crisis.

10. Islamic fundamentalism is a growing terrorist threat. Why?

MINICASE 10–1　Company Privatization

You are the chief executive officer of a company that the government has just denationalized by selling the company's stock to the company's employees. In the past, any major decision about company policy required approval by a government agency, which was time consuming. Wages and salaries had been established by reference to civil service "equivalents," and incentive payments were unheard of.

Maintenance of the plant and equipment was lax, breakdowns were frequent and expensive, and utility expenses were high.

You want the newly privatized company to be a success. Suggest some programs that you would institute to improve its chances of success.

Legal Forces

Approximately 2,700 Americans are currently detained in foreign prison cells, usually under primitive conditions, and about 50 percent are charged with drug involvement. They think they are smarter than the customs officials, but the officials have seen it all. A growing number of countries have enacted stringent drug laws that impose mandatory prison sentences for very small amounts of marijuana or cocaine, and a score of young Americans are permanently camped in Thailand prisons, serving life sentences for their drug convictions. Some countries, including Malaysia, Saudi Arabia, Thailand, and Turkey, can now impose the death penalty upon drug offenders.

Gary Shaeffer,

U.S. Bureau of

Consumer Affairs

CONCEPT PREVIEWS

After reading this chapter, you should be able to:

1. **appreciate** the complexity of the legal forces that confront international business

2. **understand** that many taxes have purposes other than to raise revenue

3. **discuss** enforcement of antitrust laws

4. **recognize** the importance of tariffs, quotas, and other trade obstacles to international business

5. **appreciate** the risk of product liability legal actions, which can result in imprisonment for employees or fines for them and the company

6. **appreciate** the effects of price and wage controls, labor laws, and currency exchange

7. **recognize** the importance of being aware of peculiarities of local law

8. **understand** contract devices and institutions that assist in interpreting or enforcing international contracts

9. **anticipate** the need and methods to protect your intellectual properties

10. **recognize** how industrial espionage affects international business

11. **understand** the numerous difficulties and burdens placed by U.S. laws and practices on American ICs, which other countries do not impose on their ICs

Not Again!?

In the mid-1970s, Lockheed Corporation was among the companies tarred in a scandal about overseas bribes, and it eventually admitted to paying $38 million to win business from foreign governments. The highest-ranking foreign official charged—and then convicted by Japan—for accepting the bribes was the Japanese prime minister Kakeui Tanaka. The American law that Lockheed broke is the Foreign Corrupt Practices Act. • In 1994, a grand jury in Atlanta charged Lockheed and two of the company's former employees with violating the same law. They allegedly paid $1.8 million to Leila I. Takla, an Egyptian government official, for influencing Egypt to buy Lockheed C-130 Hercules aircraft. • To hide the payments, Takla set up an Egyptian company that was nominally run by her husband but actually under her control. The grand jury indictment also said that after U.S. investigators discovered improper payment, Takla sent a letter to Lockheed forfeiting the entire $1.8 million commission. Three months later, however, Lockheed began negotiating what the grand jury called a $1 million "termination fee" in lieu of her commission. • In 1995, Lockheed pled guilty and paid a $21.8 million criminal fine and a civil settlement of $3 million. This was by far the largest fine ever paid under the act.

Sources: Roy J. Harris, Jr., and Thomas E. Ricks, "Lockheed Faces Possible Suspension on Air Force Contracts after Indictment," *The Wall Street Journal,* June 24, 1994, p. A14; and James F. Peltz, "Lockheed Fine," *Los Angeles Times,* January 28, 1995, pp. 1 and 8.

Any attempt to teach a course on the legal forces that affect international business would be overwhelmed or bogged down by the immensity and variety of those forces. International business is affected by many thousands of laws and regulations on hundreds of subjects that have been issued by states, nations, and international organizations.

Nevertheless, this text, which is an introduction to international business, would be incomplete without some discussion of the many legal forces that affect international business. We shall first examine several national legal forces, with brief comments; we'll then discuss some international legal forces.

Although many U.S. laws and regulations affect the activities of international firms, there has been no successful effort to coordinate them. Some are at cross-purposes, and some diminish the ability of American business to compete with foreign companies. We shall close this chapter with a brief examination of some of these laws and regulations. The account about Lockheed's legal difficulties illustrates the application of one such law.

We shall now proceed to deal with specific legal forces. Some of them, such as taxation, concern every business and businessperson, whereas others, such as antitrust, involve fewer firms.

SOME SPECIFIC NATIONAL LEGAL FORCES

nonrevenue tax purposes
Include redistributing income, discouraging consumption of some product, such as tobacco or alcohol, or encouraging purchase of domestic rather than imported products.

Taxation

Purposes.   The primary purpose of certain taxes is not necessarily to raise revenue for the government, which may surprise those who have not studied taxation. Some of the many **nonrevenue tax purposes** are to redistribute income, to discourage consumption of such products as alcohol or tobacco, to encourage consumption of domestic rather than imported goods, to discourage investment abroad, to achieve equality of the tax amounts paid by taxpayers earning comparable amounts, and to grant reciprocity to resident foreigners under a tax treaty.

Even this short list of purposes suggests the economic and political pressures brought to bear on government officials responsible for tax legislation and collection. Powerful groups in every country push for tax policies that favor their interests. These groups and interests differ from country to country and frequently conflict, which accounts, in part, for the complexity of the tax practices that affect multinationals.

National Differences of Approach.   Among the many nations of the world, there are numerous differences in tax systems.

Tax Levels.   For one thing, tax levels range from relatively high in some Western European countries to zero in tax havens.* Some countries have capital gains taxes,† and some do not. Those that have them tax capital gains at different levels. Incidentally, the United States levies one of the highest long-term capital gains taxes. Capital gains tax rates of the world's major industrial nations are as shown in Table 11–1.

The rates given in the table are not exact since levels of exemption vary for small gains and treatment of gains differ because of inflation. For instance, the 40 percent U.K. rate is misleading because gains there are inflation-proofed, that is, not taxed if they are caused by inflation.

In the United States, the capital gains tax is controversial. Those defined in the previous chapter as "liberal" argue the tax rate should remain high because any reduction would reward the rich, the group having the most

---

*A tax haven is a country in which income of defined types incurs no tax liability.
†Capital gain is realized when an asset is sold for an amount greater than its cost.

Country	Period to Qualify for Long-Term Treatment	Maximum Long-Term Rate	Maximum Short-Term Rate
United States	None	33%	33%
United Kingdom	None	40	40
Sweden	One year	18	45
Canada	None	19.33	19.33
France	None	16	16
Germany	Six months	Exempt	56
Belgium		Exempt	Exempt
Italy		Exempt	Exempt
Japan	None	5	5
Netherlands		Exempt	Exempt
Hong Kong		Exempt	Exempt
Singapore		Exempt	Exempt
South Korea		Exempt	Exempt
Republic of China		Exempt	Exempt

TABLE 11–1

Capital gains tax rates in industrial countries

Source: *Financial Times*, July 21, 1994, p. 7.

assets that have increased in price. The "conservatives" argue that the capital gains tax locks in money that would be better invested elsewhere to create jobs and increase productivity. Some maintain that the United States should levy no capital gains tax,[1] following the example of many countries as shown in Table 11–1.

Tax Types. There are different types of taxes. We have just introduced one, the capital gains tax. Although the United States levies a relatively high capital gains tax, it relies for most of its revenue on the income tax. As indicated by the name, this tax is levied on the income of individuals and businesses. A generality, subject to exceptions, is that the higher the income, the higher the income tax. In the 1970s and 1980s, much discontent developed among Americans over the impact of the income and other taxes. Possibly as a result, there has been growing support for a *value-added tax (VAT)* in the U.S. Congress and Treasury.

Many suggest that the United States use a VAT similar to the VATs in effect in all European Union countries, where they are main sources of revenue. A simplified example of how a VAT works on a loaf of bread can be seen in Table 11–2. We shall assume a VAT of 10 percent. The wheat farmer sells to the miller for 30 cents the part of the wheat that eventually becomes the loaf. So far, the farmer has added 30 cents of value by planting, growing, and harvesting the wheat. The farmer sets aside 3 cents (10 percent of 30 cents) to pay the VAT. The miller makes loaves of bread out of the wheat and sells them to the wholesaler for 50 cents each. Thus, the miller has added 20 cents of value (50 cents – 30 cents) and must pay a VAT of 2 cents (10 percent of 20 cents). The wholesaler now advertises and distributes the loaves, selling them

Stage of Production	Selling Price	Value Added	VAT at 10 Percent	Cumulative VAT
Farmer	30¢	30¢	3¢	3¢
Miller	50¢	20¢	2¢	5¢
Wholesaler	70¢	20¢	2¢	7¢
Retailer	$1.10	40¢	4¢	11¢

TABLE 11–2

Value-added tax on a loaf of bread

to retailers for 70 cents. The wholesaler has added 20 cents of value and owes 2 cents VAT. Finally, the retailer adds 40 cents by its display, advertising, and sales efforts and owes 4 cents of VAT. The loaf of bread is sold for $1.10 retail and has borne a cumulative VAT of 11 cents, 10 percent of $1.10.

The VAT has proponents and opponents. In general, their arguments are as follows: The proponents say the VAT is relatively simple and can be raised or lowered easily to balance desired income with the burden. The opponents argue that it is a consumption-type tax that bears most heavily on the poor.

In addition, some U.S. VAT proponents argue that the present situation, in which the major European countries rely heavily on the value-added tax, is unfair to the United States because of WTO* regulations. WTO permits the rebate of VAT when a product is exported from a country but does not permit the rebate of income taxes. The rebates enable exporting countries to offer lower-priced, more competitive goods, and VAT proponents want the United States to inaugurate the VAT and lower income taxes to take advantage of those WTO rules.

Another form of tax on ICs has been a bone of contention for at least two decades. This is the unitary tax system that several U.S. states had imposed; most have since repealed those tax laws under threats of retaliation by foreign governments.

International tax treaties are almost universally built on the "arm's length" or "water's edge" principle: taxable profits for a subsidiary in a country will be assessed as though it were conducting its business independently. The unitary system, by contrast, calculates the worldwide income of the IC and then assesses the tax due in proportion to the percentage of the group's property, payroll, and sales in the state.

California was the last state to move away from the unitary principle. The 1986 and 1988 changes in California's tax laws did not eliminate the unitary approach but instead now permit ICs to choose either a water's edge or unitary system. A company's circumstances, for instance, the sources or types of income involved, would determine which would be more advantageous.[2]

Complexity of Tax Laws and Regulations.   From country to country, the complexity of tax systems differs. Many consider that of the United States to be the most complex; the Internal Revenue Code runs over 5,000 pages, and official interpretations add more than 10,000 to that number. In addition to the code and Treasury interpretations, there are many thousands of pages of judicial rulings.

Who Obeys the Law?   Compliance with tax laws and their enforcement vary widely. Some countries, such as Germany and the United States, are strict. Others, such as Italy and Spain, are relatively lax. The Italian practice allows the taxpayer to declare a very low taxable income to which the government counters with a very high amount. They then negotiate a compromise figure.[3]

> One of the authors remembers the shock and horror that greeted his suggestion to Italian tax advisors that a new Italian subsidiary of an American IC declare its true income to the Italian authorities. As the advisors forcefully pointed out, no one would believe us.

foreign tax credit
U.S. citizens who reside and pay income taxes in another country can credit those taxes against U.S. income tax

Other Differences.   There are many other differences, too numerous to list all here; but a few are tax incentives to invest in certain areas, exemptions, costs, depreciation allowances, **foreign tax credits,** timing, and double corporate

---

*See Chapter 4 for discussion of the World Trade Organization.

taxation—that is, taxation of the profits of a corporation and then of dividends paid to its stockholders.

Tax Conventions, or Treaties. Because of the innumerable differences between nations' tax practices, many of them have signed **tax treaties** with each other. Typically, tax treaties define such terms as income, source, residency, and what constitutes taxable activities in each country. They address how much each country can tax the income earned by a national of one country living or working in the other. All of these treaties contain provisions for the exchange of information between the tax authorities of the two countries.

The presence or absence of a tax treaty is often a factor in international business and investment location decisions. It is now fully accepted that treaties facilitate international flows of goods, capital, services, and technology.

However, countries sign treaties for different motives. Most OECD countries regard treaties as providing a standard framework for all countries in allocating taxing jurisdiction. Among emerging market countries treaties are viewed as a key tool in giving foreign investors confidence in their stability. See Figure 11–1 for the network of tax conventions between OECD countries.[4]

tax treaties
Treaties between countries that bind the governments to share information about taxpayers and to cooperate in tax law enforcement

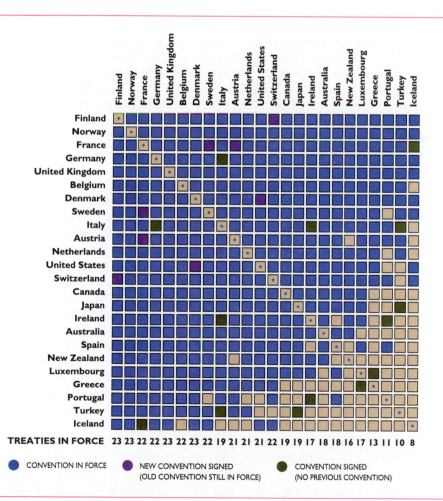

FIGURE 11–1

Network of tax conventions between OECD countries*

*As of February 28, 1994.

Source: Tax Information Exchange between OECD member countries, OECD, Paris, 1994.

Antitrust and Restrictive Trade Practices Legislation

In the tax area, it is the taxpayers (here, international business) against the tax collectors (the governments). Antitrust actions also involve business versus government, and occasionally, government versus government.

antitrust laws
American laws to prevent price-fixing, market sharing, and business monopolies

restrictive trade practices laws
The European phrase for what are called antitrust laws in the United States

U.S. Laws and Attitudes are Different.   The U.S. **antitrust laws** are stricter and more vigorously enforced than those of any other country. However, other countries, as well as the EU, are becoming more active in the antitrust field. In the EU, these laws are referred to as **restrictive trade practices laws.**

The German antitrust laws are the toughest after those of the United States, and, during 1986, the German Federal Cartel Office tightened its grip—literally, in some cases. Wolfgang Kartte, president of the Cartel Office, tells the story of a raid his investigators made on the office of a heating equipment supplier. One of the supplier's managers stuffed a memo in his mouth and tried to swallow it, but a quick-thinking investigator grabbed the man by the throat and forced him to spit out the memo. Half-chewed but still legible, it provided valuable evidence of illegal price-fixing.

In 1991, the European Court of Justice gave a major boost to EU efforts to inject competition into economic sectors still largely dominated by powerful state monopolies. The Court confirmed that the EU Commission can force EU member-governments to dismantle state monopolies that block progress toward an open, community-wide market.[5]

Article 85 of the Treaty of Rome outlaws any agreement or action to rig markets or distort competition. Under the authority of that article, the Commission fined the Dutch chemicals group, Akzo, ECU 7.5 million in 1991.[6] Later in 1991, empowered by Article 86, which bans abuse of dominant positions, the Commission imposed a record ECU 75 million fine on Tetra Pak, a Swiss-based liquid packaging group, for eliminating competitors in the European market.[7] That record was broken in 1994 as the EU Commission levied fines totaling $158.58 million on 19 carton-board producers. They had formed what the Commission described as Europe's "most pernicious" price-fixing cartel.[8]

Also in 1991, the Commission for the first time used its authority under a 1990 law to veto a major business transaction. Using its expanded power, it blocked the acquisition of Boeing's de Haviland subsidiary by a French-Italian consortium, Avions de Transport Regional (ATR). The Commission said the acquisition would have given ATR an unfair advantage that would allow it to crowd out competition.

A number of important differences in antitrust laws, regulations, and practices exist between the United States, other nations, and the EU. One difference is the effort of the United States to apply its laws extraterritorially (outside the United States). We deal with that later in this chapter. Another difference is the per se concept of the U.S. law. Under the U.S. laws, certain activities, such as price-fixing, are said to be illegal per se. This means that they are illegal even though no injury or damage results from them.

The Treaty of Rome articles dealing with restrictive trade practices do not contain the per se illegality concept of U.S. antitrust law. For example, a cartel that allows consumers a fair share of the benefits is legally acceptable in the EU. Also, the treaty is not violated by market dominance—only by misuse of that dominance to damage competitors or consumers.

The EU versus Hoffman-La Roche.   The EU Court of Justice upheld the Commission's decision that the giant Swiss drug company Hoffman-La Roche was guilty of abusing its dominant position. Hoffman was fined DM732,000.

There was at least one bizarre element in the Hoffman case. Stanley Adams, a British subject, was an employee at the company's head office in Basel, Switzerland. He took some confidential documents about Hoffman's pricing and marketing practices and made them available to the EU antitrust regulators, who were already investigating the company. The company and the Swiss government reacted furiously, and when Adams, who was in Italy when the loss of the documents was discovered, returned to Switzerland, he was arrested and convicted under Swiss laws against industrial espionage. He was sent to prison, and his wife committed suicide on being told that he would be there at least 20 years. Finally, the EU bailed him out of the Swiss prison and he left the country.

Although Adams had his freedom, his troubles were not over. He was unable to get credit or employment, and he lost a farm he tried to operate in Italy. He then moved to England and sued the EU Commission for £500,000 damages for revealing his identity to Hoffman and for not warning him of the dangers he faced if he returned to Switzerland. In 1985, Adams won his case in the European Court of Justice.[9]

The Swiss Government versus the EU.   The Hoffman-La Roche case caused government-versus-government friction. The EU complained to the Swiss that Adams should not be prosecuted under Swiss law, because all he had done was cooperate with the EU Commission's efforts to enforce the law. The Swiss prosecuted and convicted him, notwithstanding the EU's complaints, because he had violated Swiss law in Switzerland.

The U.S. Government versus other Governments.   More common examples of government-versus-government conflict occur when the U.S. government attempts to enforce its antitrust laws outside the U.S. borders. This is referred to as **extraterritorial application of laws.** In 1979, a grand jury in Washington, DC, indicted three foreign-owned ocean-shipping groups on charges of fixing prices without getting approval from the U.S. Federal Maritime Commission. The other governments, European and Japanese, protested bitterly, arguing (1) that shipping is international by definition, so the United States has no right to act unilaterally and (2) that the alleged offenses were both legal and ethical practices outside the United States.[10]

Sir Freddie Laker's airline, a low-price transatlantic service, ceased operations on February 5, 1982. Shortly thereafter, its liquidators commenced a private antitrust suit in an American court, alleging that British Airways (BA) had conspired to put Laker out of business. They asked over $1 billion in damages. Sir Freddie settled his personal suit for $10 million and retired to the Bahamas.

"Sue the Bastards."   That was the advice Sir Freddie gave Richard Branson, whose Virgin Atlantic Airways alleged "dirty tricks" by BA beginning in 1991. Virgin did file a libel action against BA. Although that action was settled, including an apology by BA's chairman, Virgin filed an antitrust suit against BA in U.S. courts in 1993. Virgin's case is that BA is dominant at London's Heathrow airport and uses its muscle to hurt Virgin on transatlantic services. The smaller British airlines such as Laker and Virgin turn to American courts with their grievances because the British government has given them little or no protection.[11]

The private suits irked the British government, but what disturbed it most was the U.S. Justice Department's move in spring of 1983 to begin a criminal grand jury investigation of essentially the same allegations. It was another example of the U.S. government's efforts to apply its law extraterritorially.

extraterritorial application of laws
When a country attempts to apply its laws to foreigners or nonresidents and to acts and activities that took place outside its borders

Other Governments versus the U.S. Government.   In 1977, the United States tried to force seven executives of the British company Rio Tinto-Zinc to testify in connection with an antitrust action in the United States. In that instance, Britain's highest court, the House of Lords, turned down the U.S. demands on the grounds that they infringed on British jurisdiction and sovereignty and that the United States was trying to investigate the activities of companies not subject to U.S. jurisdiction.[12]

A number of countries have passed statutes to prevent persons within their territories from cooperating with the United States and have established criminal sanctions for those who comply with U.S. law in violation of those statutes. Among these countries are Australia, Canada, Britain, the Netherlands, and Germany. Thus, persons or companies can find themselves in the position of being forced to break the law of either the United States or of a country with this type of statute.

In January 1991, Sir Leon Brittan, the EU Commission's vice president of competition policy, met with U.S. attorney general Dick Thornburgh in Washington, DC, to begin coordinating U.S. and European antitrust policy. Brittan's goal is some variety of formal agreement that will prevent Europe and the United States from colliding over mergers involving both.[13]

However, a change of U.S. policy in 1992 may cause collisions. The new policy is to enforce antitrust laws against foreign companies suspected of colluding to hurt U.S. exporters. Prior to the policy change, the Justice Department challenged anticompetitive activity by foreign companies only if direct harm to U.S. consumers resulted from the activity. Some 15 countries, including Canada, Japan, and some in Europe, urged the United States to be cautious in implementing the new policy.[14]

Japan's Toothless Tiger.   Japan's Fair Trade Commission (FTC), which is supposed to enforce antitrust laws, has been nicknamed the toothless tiger. It is viewed as one of the weakest bodies in government, easily bullied by the powerful ministries of finance and international trade and industry, both of which have vested interests in ensuring that Japan's cozy ways of doing business prevail. Most of FTC's victims are small and weak; when it has investigated powerful industries such as cars, car parts, construction, glass and paper, it punished them at worst with raps on the knuckles and "recommendations." They are all businesses from which foreigners complain they are excluded.

A major difference between American and Japanese trust-busting is that around 90 percent of the U.S. complaints are initiated by private parties, while in Japan a private antitrust action can be brought only if the FTC has investigated the case first. Because of Japan's arcane discovery laws, the only way the FTC can obtain information on a firm is to raid it. As a result, the FTC won't make a move unless it is sure the laws are being broken. Of course, it is almost impossible to be sure of that without information. Given all this, it is easy to understand why the FTC is considered to be a toothless tiger.[15]

Tariffs, Quotas, and Other Trade Obstacles

Although we introduced these subjects in Chapter 3, they are legal forces. For that reason, we mention them again here.

Every country has laws on one or more of these subjects. The purposes of tariffs are to raise revenue for the government and to protect domestic producers. Quotas, which limit the number or amount of imports, are for protection.

There are many other forms of protection or obstacles to trade in national laws. Some are health or packaging requirements. Others deal with language,

Abuse of a Dominant Position

The director-general for competition of the EU Commission wants small and medium-sized enterprises (SMEs) to be aware of protection available to them under Article 86 of the Treaty of Rome. Activities from which SMEs are protected are classified as (1) exploitive, (2) exclusionary, and (3) predatory.

Exploitive abuse arises where the dominant company unfairly takes advantage of its market power by charging excessive prices or "tying." Tying, or bundling, occurs when a customer buying the product or service for which the supplier has a dominant market position is also required by the supplier to purchase other products or services from it where active competition exists.

Exclusionary abuse occurs when a customer is required to buy all of what it needs to do business from the dominant firm. Predatory abuse occurs when a dominant firm attempts to drive a competitor out of business by selling below cost.

The Commission wants SMEs to bring complaints about any such activities by contacting DG IV Information Office at: European Commission, Rue de la Loi 200, B-1049, Brussels, Belgium.

Source: Claus Dieter Ehlermann, "Community Competition Policy and Small and Medium-Sized Companies," *Supplement—Frontier Free Europe*, no. 3, 1994.

Connie Coleman/Tony Stone Images

such as the mandatory use of French on labels and in advertising, manuals, warranties, and so forth for goods sold in France.

The following list is a sampling of U.S. export products, export destinations, and the trade barriers encountered at the destinations.

Product	Destination	Barrier
Carbon steel	EU	Imports limited to 8 percent of market
Pesticides	Canada	Residue standards bar some U.S. chemicals
Machine tools	Japan	Government subsidizes domestic industry
Machine tools	Argentina	Money from sales must remain in Argentina for months
Paperboard	Japan	Specifications require smoother board than is produced in the United States

In other countries, U.S. exports may encounter weak patent or trademark protection, very high tariffs, zero quotas, quarantine periods, or a variety of other obstacles.

Of course, the United States imposes barriers against the import of a number of products. It sometimes uses tariffs, sometimes quotas, and often a more modern form of quota called by some *"voluntary" restrain agreements* (VRAs) and by others *"voluntary" export restraints* (VERs). "Voluntary" is in quotes because these barriers are imposed by the U.S. government on the exporting countries. The inevitable result is higher costs to American consumers as exporters send only the higher-priced, top of their lines and importers charge more for scarcer products.[16]

One justification for protectionism is that it saves domestic jobs. The cost to the American consumer to save one job in the U.S. car industry was estimated to be $250,000.[17]

The United States is not the only country that imposes VRAs and VERs on its trading partners—far from it. Japan, Canada, the EU countries, and many others require countries exporting to them to "voluntarily" limit the number or value of goods exported.

In 1982, the French came up with a novel protectionist device. Japanese videotape recorders were one of the French imports causing a large balance-of-payments deficit with Japan. The recorders normally entered France through the major port of Le Havre, which had a large detachment of customs officers to process imports. Then the French government issued a decree requiring all of the recorders to enter France through Poitiers, which had a tiny customs post. The result was long delays that reduced the number of recorders entering France. Japan then "voluntarily" agreed to limit the number of recorders it exported to France.

Product Liability, Civil and Criminal*

Manufacturers' liability for faulty or dangerous products was a boom growth area for the American legal profession beginning in the 1960s and continuing into the 1990s. Liability insurance premiums have soared, and there are concerns that smaller, weaker manufacturing companies cannot survive.

product liability
Holding a company and its officers and directors liable and possibly subject to fines or imprisonment when their product causes death, injury, or damage

strict liability
Holds the designer/ manufacturer liable for damages caused by a product without the need for a plaintiff to prove negligence in the product's design or manufacturer

Now that boom may spread to Europe, where directives of the EU Commission are pushing new **product liability** laws that would standardize and toughen existing ones. A directive (O.J. No. L 210/229), was adopted in 1985 that was to be effective in 1988, imposed a system of **strict liability**.

There are several reasons to believe that the impact of strict liability upon product designers and manufacturers in Europe and Japan will not be as heavy or severe as it is in the United States. In Europe, the directive permits the EU member-countries to allow "state-of-the-art" or "developmental risks" defenses, which allow the designer/manufacturer to prove that at the time of design or manufacture, the most modern, latest-known technology was used. The countries are permitted also to cap damages at amounts not less than 70 million ECUs.[†] Damages awarded by American juries have been hundreds of millions of dollars.

Major differences in legal procedures in the United States as compared with those in Europe and Japan will limit or prevent product liability awards by European and Japanese courts. In the United States but not elsewhere, lawyers take many cases on a contingency fee basis whereby the lawyer charges the plaintiff no fee to begin representation and action in a product liability case. The lawyer is paid only when the defendant settles or loses in a trial; but then the fee is relatively large, running between one-third and one-half of the settlement or award. In addition, outside the United States, when the defendant wins a lawsuit, the plaintiff is called upon to pay all defendant's legal fees and other costs caused by the plaintiff's action.[18]

---

*Civil liability calls for payment of money damages. Criminal liability results in fines or imprisonment.
†At the exchange rate on April 11, 1995, ECU 70 million was equal to US$92 million.

"Excuse me, sir.... Want to sue a multinational?"

Source: © 1987, Cartoonists & Writers Syndicate.

In the United States, product liability cases are heard by juries that can award plaintiffs actual damages plus punitive damages. As the name indicates, punitive damages have the purpose of punishing the defendant, and if the plaintiff has been grievously injured or the jury's sympathy can be otherwise aroused, it may award millions of dollars to "teach the defendant a lesson." Outside the United States, product liability cases are heard by judges, not juries. Judges are less prone to emotional reactions than juries, and even if the judge were sympathetic with a plaintiff, punitive damages are not awarded by non–U.S. courts.[19]

As indicated at the beginning of this discussion of product liability, the EU (then the EC) adopted a directive in 1985, which was to be effective in 1988, imposing a system of strict liability. But, because the concept of strict liability is abhorrent to some cultures, the directive had not been implemented by France, Ireland, or Spain as late as 1994. In order to encourage them to pass implementing laws, the EU permits "state-of-the-art" defenses and caps on damage awards, both mentioned above.[20]

Buyer Beware in Japan.   The Japanese law on product liability is similar to that in the United States prior to 1963. The plaintiff must prove design or manufacturing negligence, which particularly with complex, high-tech devices is virtually impossible. The plaintiffs' difficulties are exacerbated by the failure of Japanese legal procedures to provide discovery, the process by which plaintiffs can seek defendants' documents relevant to their cases. Discovery is available to plaintiffs in U.S. courts but not in Europe.[21]

In a survey of more than 500 chief executives by the Conference Board, more than one-fifth believe strict American product liability laws have caused their companies to lose business to foreign competitors.[22] But, as foreign firms buy or build U.S. plants, they are being hit by the same liability and insurance problems long faced by American companies.[23]

"He's in jail. May I take a message?"

Reprinted from *The Wall Street Journal;* permission of Cartoon Features Syndicate.

Price and Wage Controls

Although some countries call their **price and wage controls** "voluntary," governments can apply pressure to companies or labor unions that raise prices or demand wage increases above established percentages. The U.S. government, for example, has withheld government business from companies that violate its guidelines. This has resulted in union lawsuits challenging the legality of such punishment.

Communist countries, of course, just set prices and wages. There are no significant free markets and no effective labor unions that are not government agencies. Most noncommunist countries also have some price and wage control laws. As inflation spreads and grows in the world, price and wage controls can be expected to become more widespread and more restrictive.

price and wage controls
Prohibitions or limits on upward movements of prices or wages imposed by a government to combat inflation when the government has been unable or unwilling to slow or halt it by fiscal or monetary measures

Labor Laws

Virtually every country has laws governing working conditions and wages for its labor force. Even though hourly wages may be low in a country, employers must beware, because fringe benefits can greatly increase labor costs. Fringe benefits can include profit sharing, health or dental benefits, retirement funds, and more. Some labor laws make the firing of a worker almost impossible or at least very expensive. This subject is considered more extensively in Chapter 12.

Currency Exchange Controls

Almost every country has currency exchange controls—laws dealing with the purchase and sale of foreign currencies. Most countries, including LDCs and communist countries, have too little hard foreign currency.* There is the rare country, such as Switzerland, that sometimes feels it has too much.

Exchange Control Generalities.   The law of each country must be examined, but some generalizations can be made. In countries where hard foreign currency is scarce, a government agency allocates it. Typically, an importer of productive capital equipment gets priority over an importer of luxury goods.

---

*A hard currency is readily exchangeable for any other currency in the world.

People entering such a country must declare how much currency of any kind they are bringing in. On departure, they must declare how much they are taking out. The intent is twofold: (1) to discourage travelers from bringing in the host country's national currency bought abroad at a better exchange rate than inside the country, and (2) to encourage them to bring in hard foreign currency.

Switzerland—A Special Case.   Switzerland is a special case because its government has imposed controls to keep foreign currencies out rather than in. Switzerland enjoyed relatively low inflation during the 1970s and into the 1990s, and its Swiss franc has remained one of the hardest of the hard currencies. As a result, people from all over the world have wanted to get their money into Switzerland, and the Swiss have felt the need to defend against being inundated with too much currency, which would escalate their inflation. They have used several devices to discourage the inflow of foreign money. Among these devices are low interest rates and even a negative interest rate on some kinds of deposits. Limitations have been placed on the sale to foreigners of bonds denominated in Swiss francs.

Miscellaneous Laws

Individuals working abroad must be alert to avoid falling afoul of local laws and of corrupt police, army, or government officials. Some examples make the point.

A Plessey employee, a British subject, is serving a life sentence in Libya for "jeopardizing the revolution by giving information to a foreign company." In the summer of 1986, two Australians were executed in Malaysia for possession of 15 grams or more of hard drugs. Saudi Arabia and other Muslim countries strictly enforce sanctions against importing or drinking alcohol or wearing revealing clothing. Foreigners in Japan who walk out of their homes without their alien registration cards can be arrested, as happened to one man while he was carrying out the garbage. In Thailand, people can be jailed for mutilating paper money or for damaging coins that bear the picture or image of the royal prince, as was one foreigner who stopped a rolling coin with his foot. Neither *Playboy* nor *Penthouse* can be brought into Singapore.

Travelers and vacationers can also run afoul of unexpected laws in different countries. In the People's Republic of China, unmarried couples—foreigners included—face a possible 10 days in jail if they stay overnight in the same room. In Greece, travelers who exceed their credit card limits may be sentenced to prison for as long as 12 years.

A Philadelphia law firm, International Legal Defense Counsel (ILDC), has made a reputation dealing with countries where American embassies and consulates are of little legal help and where prison conditions are so squalid that survival is the first concern. One of their cases involved a Virginia photographer named Conan Owen. He was duped into transporting a package of cocaine from Colombia to Spain, where he was arrested and slapped with a stiff prison sentence. The U.S. attorney general personally interceded with no success, and Owen languished in prison for nearly two years. Then ILDC sprang him by use of a bilateral prisoner transfer treaty that permits American inmates in foreign jails to do their time in a facility back home. Once in the United States, Owen was quickly freed.

Among ILDC publications that give travelers legal advice are *The Hassle of Your Life: A Handbook for Families of Americans Jailed Abroad* and *Know the Law: A Handbook for Hispanics Imprisoned in the United States.*[24]

INTERNATIONAL FORCES

Business Contracts

When contracting parties are residents of a single country, the laws of that country govern contract performance and any disputes that arise between the parties. That country's courts have jurisdiction over the parties, and the court's judgments are enforced in accordance with the country's procedures. When residents of two or more countries contract, those relatively easy solutions to disputes are not available.

United Nations Solutions.   When contract disputes arise between parties from two or more countries, which country's law is applicable? Many countries, including the United States, have ratified the UN Convention on Contracts for the International Sale of Goods (CISG) to solve such problems.

The CISG established uniform legal rules to govern the formation of international sales contracts and the rights and obligations of the buyer and seller. The CISG applies automatically to all contracts for the sale of goods between traders from different countries that have ratified the CISG. This automatic application will take place unless the parties to the contract expressly exclude—opt out of—the CISG.[25]

European Union Solutions.   The law applicable to contracts between EU residents is determined by an amendment to the Rome Convention, which came into effect in 1991. It established two principles. First, if the parties agree at the outset which country's law should apply, then that choice will be upheld. Second, if no such choice is made, the law of the country most closely connected with the contract will apply. A set of rules has been established to make this work in practice.[26]

arbitration
A process, agreed to by parties to a dispute in lieu of going to court, by which a neutral person or body makes a binding decision

Private Solutions, Arbitration.   Many parties either cannot or do not wish to accept UN or EU solutions. Instead of going to court in any country, they opt for **arbitration**. At least 30 organizations now administer international arbitrations, the best known of which is the International Court of Arbitration of the International Chamber of Commerce in Paris. More than 450 disputes were filed with that body during 1993, and the number is expected to increase 15 to 20 percent annually over the next several years.[27] People and businesses may prefer arbitration for several reasons. They may be suspicious of foreign courts, but regardless of that, arbitration is always faster than law courts, where cases are usually backlogged and procedures are formal. Arbitration procedures are informal. They can also be confidential, avoiding the perhaps unwelcome publicity accompanying an open court case.

Although London, New York, and Paris are traditional arbitration centers, Hong Kong is growing as one. This follows from the explosive growth of business and trade in the Pacific Rim countries and a 1991 cooperation agreement between the Hong Kong International Arbitration Center and its counterpart in the People's Republic of China.[28]

Enforcement of Foreign Arbitration Awards.   Enforcement can pose problems. One solution is the UN Convention on the Recognition and Enforcement of Foreign Arbitral Awards. The United States and most UN member-countries of industrial importance have ratified this convention. It binds ratifying countries to compel arbitration when the parties have so agreed in their contract and to enforce resulting awards.

In instances where the contract in dispute involves investment in a country from abroad, another arbitration tribunal is available. This is the International Center for Settlement of Investment Disputes, sponsored by the

World Bank. Investors were encouraged in 1986 when Indonesia proved willing to abide by a decision of the center even though an adverse opinion could have cost the country several million dollars.

Other organizations are working toward a worldwide business law. The Incoterms of the International Chamber of Commerce and its Uniform Rules and Practice on Documentary Credits now enjoy almost universal acceptance. The UN Commission on International Trade Law and the International Institute for the Unification of Private Law are doing much useful work. The Hague-Vishy Rules on Bills of Lading sponsored by the International Law Association have been adopted by a number of countries.[29]

Despite Legal Uncertainties, Trade Grows.   It is to the credit of international business that, with the exception of the recession years between 1980 and 1983, world trade has grown each year. That is evidence that despite legal uncertainties, most international contracts are performed fairly satisfactorily.

In 1993, the United States became the world's largest merchandise exporter by selling some $465 billion of its products to foreigners. Germany was second at $362 billion, followed closely by Japan at $360 billion.[30] Historically, trade contracts dealt mostly with merchandise trade, but in recent years, trade in services has grown rapidly, and of course, it is the subject of international contracts. Although the United States runs a persistent deficit in its merchandise trade, it enjoys a smaller but growing surplus in its services trade.[31]

Patents, Trademarks, Trade Names, Copyrights, and Trade Secrets— Intellectual Properties

A patent is a government grant giving the inventor of a product or process the exclusive right to manufacture, exploit, use, and sell that invention or process. Trademarks and trade names are designs and names, often officially registered, by which merchants or manufacturers designate and differentiate their products. Copyrights are exclusive legal rights of authors, composers, playwrights, artists, and publishers to publish and dispose of their works. Trade secrets are any information that a business wishes to hold confidential. All are referred to as **intellectual properties**.

Trade secrets can be of great value, but each country deals with and protects them in its own fashion. The duration of protection differs, as do the products that may or may not be protected. Some countries permit the production process to be protected but not the product. Therefore, international companies must study and comply with the laws of each country where they might want to manufacture, create, or sell products.

intellectual properties
Patents, trademarks, trade names, copyrights, and trade secrets, all of which result from the exercise of someone's intellect

Patents.   In the field of patents, some degree of standardization is provided by the International Convention for the Protection of Industrial Property, sometimes referred to as the Paris Union. Some 90 countries, including the major industrial nations, have adhered to this convention.

Most Latin American nations and the United States are members of the Inter-American Convention. The protection it provides is similar to that afforded by the Paris Union.

A major step toward the harmonization of patent treatment is the European Patent Organization (EPO). Members are the EU countries and Switzerland. Through EPO, an applicant for a patent need file only one application in English, French, or German to be granted patent protection in all member-countries. Prior to EPO, an applicant had to file in each country in the language of that country.

The World Intellectual Property Organization (WIPO) is a UN agency that administers 16 international intellectual property treaties. It is an open question whether WIPO will work with or compete with a new organization created in the Uruguay GATT negotiations, which is called TRIPS for "trade-related aspects of intellectual property." TRIPS will operate under the aegis of the World Trade Organization.

WIPO's activities are increasing, as nearly 29,000 international patent applications were filed in 1993 under the Patent Cooperation Treaty, which enables investors to apply for registration in several countries with a single application. This is five times the number in the mid-1980s, and the average number of designated countries per application has jumped from 10 to 31. In addition, WIPO advises developing countries on such matters as running patent offices or drafting intellectual property legislation. Interest in LDCs about intellectual property matters has been growing.[32]

At the UN, representatives of the developing nations have been mounting attacks on the exclusivity and length of patent protection. They want to shorten the protection periods from the current 15 to 20 years down to 5 years or even 30 months. But companies in industrialized countries that are responsible for the new technology eligible for patents are resisting the changes. They point out that the only incentives they have to spend the huge amounts required to develop the technology are periods of patent protection long enough to recoup their costs and make profits.

Trademarks.   Trademark protection varies from country to country, as does its duration, which may last from 10 to 20 years. Such protection is covered by the Madrid Agreement of 1891 for most of the world, though there is also the General American Convention for Trademark and Commercial Protection for the Western Hemisphere. In addition, protection may be provided on a bilateral basis in friendship, commerce, and navigation treaties.

An important step in harmonizing the rules on trademarks was taken in 1988 when regulations for a European Union trademark were drafted. A single European Trademark Office will be responsible for the recognition and protection of proprietary marks in all EU countries, including trademarks belonging to companies based in non-EU member-countries.

Trade Names.   Trade names are protected in all countries adhering to the Industrial Property Convention, which was mentioned above in connection with patents. Goods bearing illegal trademarks or trade names or false statements on their origin are subject to seizure at importation into these countries.

Copyrights.   Copyrights get protection under the Berne Convention of 1886, which is adhered to by 55 countries, and the Universal Copyright Convention of 1954, which has been adopted by some 50 countries. The United States did not ratify the Berne Convention until 1988, by which time it was driven to do so by the need for greater protection against pirating of computer software.

Trade Secrets.   Trade secrets are protected by laws in most nations. Employers everywhere use employee secrecy agreements, which in some countries are rigorously enforced.*

---

*Remember the unfortunate Mr. Adams, who was imprisoned by the Swiss for giving Hoffman-La Roche secrets to the EC, and the even more unfortunate Mrs. Adams, who committed suicide after being told that her husband would be in prison 20 years.

Industrial Espionage.   **Industrial espionage** among companies that develop and use high technology is not unusual, but 1983 saw the end of an extraordinary example of corporate warfare between two of the world's mightiest and most technologically advanced corporations. Hitachi tried to obtain trade secrets of IBM, and in June 1982, two Hitachi employees were arrested by the FBI. IBM and the FBI had cooperated in what *Fortune* called a "superbly executed sting." In February 1983, Hitachi and two of its employees pleaded guilty to an indictment of conspiring to transport stolen IBM property from the United States to Japan.

Malaysia and Thailand have accused other Japanese companies, including Mitsubishi, of being too slow to transfer intellectual properties and technology to them. But a Japanese diplomat in Bangkok says that is a myth. More telling is this Japanese businessman's perspective: "The Thais think they can sit behind their desks and the technology will fall on them from the sky. If they want the technology, they should have the guts to do what we did, which is to go out and steal it."[33]

Costly Intellectual Property Rip-Offs.   The U.S. International Trade Commission says unauthorized use abroad of American-owned intellectual property costs the United States more than $61 billion a year. That is the amount of lost exports, domestic sales, and royalties. But total extended losses are actually much higher since the $61 billion does not reflect related losses such as increased unemployment that stems from intellectual property piracy.[34]

U.S. industry and the government are trying to combat this. Among other means, several companies have gathered evidence of pirating in countries that have laws against such activities but whose police are unwilling or unable to actively enforce them. On being presented with evidence of illegal practices, they have no excuse not to do their duty.

The U.S. government is using bilateral aid and trade pressures to push other countries, including Japan, Taiwan, South Korea, Thailand, and Indonesia to pass and enforce intellectual property protection laws.

There has been flagrant piracy of foreign-owned intellectual property in the People's Republic of China. But in their battles against the copiers, owners found a powerful Chinese ally in 1994. Deng Rong is the daughter of China's paramount leader, Deng Xiaoping, and she wrote a biography of her father. She was furious when she learned that her work was being relentlessly copied by Chinese publishers, and the order went out to take a tough stand against such rogues. In 1994, police began to raid book and music stores and to confiscate pirated books and CDs.[35]

An American-PRC Trade War Because of Intellectual Property Rip-Offs?   At the beginning of 1995, the United States was threatening to slap 100 percent tariffs on Chinese exports to the United States, and the PRC was threatening to retaliate. In such a face off, the United States would be at an advantage based on the trade balance between the two countries. While U.S. exports to China rose from $3 billion to $8.8 billion a year from 1987 to 1994, China's exports to the United States rose from $3.1 billion to $38 billion. In a tariff battle, the PRC would have much more to lose than the United States, and war was averted at least temporarily by a PRC agreement to better protect intellectual property.

Several international standardizing forces have already been discussed. In the tax area, there are tax conventions, or treaties, among nations. Each country tries to make each such treaty as nearly as possible like the others, so that patterns and common provisions may be found among them.

industrial espionage
The effort of one company to steal another company's trade secrets by, for example, attempting to bribe an employee, eavesdropping electronically on internal communications, or hacking into the target company's computer data

INTERNATIONAL STANDARDIZING FORCES

In antitrust, the EU member-countries ope rate under Articles 85 and 86 of the Treaty of Rome. In an unusual bilateral move, Germany and the United States signed an executive agreement on antitrust cooperation. This was the first attempt by national governments to cooperate on antitrust matters concerning firms operating in both countries.

In the field of commercial contract arbitration, we mentioned the UN Convention. If the disputed contract involves investment from one country into another, it can be submitted for arbitration by the International Center for Settlement of Investment Disputes at the World Bank, and, in 1988, the UN Convention on the International Sale of Goods came into effect.

Several international patent and other agreements were pointed out. Chapter 4 covered a number of UN-related organizations and other worldwide associations. Each of them has some harmonizing or standardizing effect. The same can be said of the regional international groupings and organizations dealt with in Chapter 4.

Two standardizing organizations that American industry will ignore at its peril are the International Organization for Standardization (IOS) and the International Electrotechnical Commission (IEC). The IEC promotes standardization of measurement, materials, and equipment in almost every sphere of electrotechnology. The IOS recommends standards in other fields of technology. Most government and private procurement around the world demands products that meet IEC or IOS specifications, and therein lies the danger for American companies. All IEC and IOS measurements are in the metric system, which has not been adopted in the United States, thereby imposing an additional burden on American firms trying to export American-made products.

U.S. LAWS THAT AFFECT THE INTERNATIONAL BUSINESS OF U.S. FIRMS

Although every law relating to business arguably has some effect on international activities, some laws warrant special notice. We will look briefly at U.S. antitrust and taxation laws, the Foreign Corrupt Practices Act, and the antiboycott law.

Antitrust

Earlier in this chapter, we mentioned the hostility aroused among foreign governments by the aggressive enforcement abroad of U.S. antitrust laws.

The Laws Impede U.S. Exports.   The U.S. antitrust rules preventing American companies from teaming up to bid on major products abroad impede U.S. exports. For example, General Electric and Westinghouse had to compete against each other for pieces of the $450 million Brazilian Itaipu Dam generator and turbine contracts. The contracts went to a huge European group led by Siemens of Germany and Brown Boveri of Switzerland. The European governments actively supported their companies. The U.S. government, however, would not let GE and Westinghouse cooperate and did nothing to support their efforts.

Such restrictions on cooperation abroad were cited as the worst obstacle to exports caused by the U.S. antitrust regulations and enforcement procedures in a study by the National Association of Manufacturers (NAM). About 70 percent of the over 100 companies that responded to the NAM questionnaire said U.S. antitrust laws and practices caused a decline in their international competitiveness.

Export Trading Companies (ETCs).   In 1982, the Export Trading Company Act was signed into law. The centerpiece of the ETC act is its limitation of the applicability of antitrust law to foreign trade. There are many ambiguities in the act, but it does make some important changes in antitrust law.

Companies wishing to establish ETCs apply to the U.S. government for a certificate of antitrust immunity. The certificate safeguards the ETC from government prosecution—assuming the ETC performs as indicated in the certificate of application—but does not immunize it against private party antitrust suits. However, any damages awarded in such suits are limited to actual damages rather than the treble damages awarded in other such private actions.*

Despite passage of the ETC act, there is strong feeling both in and out of government that the antitrust laws constitute severe burdens on the ability of American companies to compete at home or abroad with foreign competitors. The late Malcolm Baldrige, secretary of commerce in the Reagan administration, made several points. The U.S. antitrust laws were largely written in the early 1900s, and they followed the economic theory of that time: "Big is bad; small is good." That theory was proper when other countries could not compete with America and U.S. companies did not need to export to grow. But now, more than 90 years later, U.S. goods face severe competition, and the range and variety of that competition are increasing. The world economy has changed, trade patterns have changed, but the antitrust laws have not.

Baldrige and others would like Congress to repeal Section 7 of the Clayton Act, which prohibits mergers and acquisitions that *may* reduce competition or *tend* to create a monopoly. Baldrige made this comment on the italicized words: "No one can live in an environment where the antitrust enforcers try to read your mind and then can arrest you for their idea of what you might be thinking."[36]

Taxation

As we have remarked, the U.S. tax system is considered by many to be the world's most complicated. That in itself makes doing business more complicated and, therefore, more expensive for a U.S. company than for companies based elsewhere. There is, however, one tax incentive for exports worthy of mention.

Export Incentive.   In 1971, the U.S. Congress amended the Internal Revenue Code (IRC) to permit the Domestic International Sales Corporation (DISC) as an encouragement for American companies to export. This gave a tax break to companies that exported products manufactured in the United States with American labor.

It worked. The U.S. Treasury estimated that in the fiscal year ended June 30, 1976, DISC operations boosted U.S. exports to some $2.9 billion higher than they would have been without DISC.[37] In spite of that and in the face of continuing and growing U.S. BOP deficits, the Carter administration recommended abolishing the DISC. U.S. labor unions also want its abolition, saying it favors big business even though exports mean jobs. Congress did not abolish the DISC, but it did cut back the tax benefit originally provided.

The Tax Reform Act of 1984 largely replaced the DISC with the new Foreign Sales Corporation (FSC). From the point of view of exporters, a major advantage of the FSC over the DISC is that the tax exemption is permanent— there is no recapture of the benefit in future years if dividends are paid or if the FSC no longer satisfies qualification requirements. Another break given exporters by the 1984 law is permanent forgiveness of taxes deferred under DISC provisions.

---

*The possibility of treble damages against British Airways is one of the worries of the U.K. government because of the private antitrust action being brought against BA and other airlines by the Laker Airways liquidator.

national tax jurisdiction
A tax system for expatriate citizens of a country whereby the country taxes them on the basis of nationality, even though they live and work abroad

Taxing Americans Who Work Abroad.   Observing a so-called **national tax jurisdiction**, rather than a **territorial tax jurisdiction**, the United States is almost alone among countries in taxing its people according to nationality rather than on the basis of where they live and work. As a result, Americans living or working in another country must pay taxes there and to the United States. In addition to higher tax payments, this requires the time and expense of completing two sets of complicated tax returns. In 1981, the sections of the IRC dealing with this subject were again amended. Although the burden of completing two tax returns was not lifted, the new law gave relief, starting in 1982, in the amount of American taxes to be paid by exempting the first $85,000 of earned income.* In 1986, this exemption was lowered to $70,000.

territorial tax jurisdiction
Expatriate citizens who neither live nor work in the country—and therefore receive none of the services for which taxes pay—are exempt from the country's taxes

When American Taxes Are Anti-American.   Suppose an American multinational wants to open a new factory, store, warehouse, or office building in the United States. That would create new jobs for Americans, along with all the benefits that flow from new jobs.

But when the company's executives look at the new U.S. tax law, they hesitate because of the section dealing with allocation of interest expense. When an American company with subsidiaries in many countries borrows money to finance a U.S. business, the interest is treated as if it were paid in part to finance foreign operations. That results in a partial loss of the tax deduction and, thus, higher after-tax interest cost.

Foreign companies—including foreign-based multinationals—have no such requirement and can deduct 100 percent of interest on borrowings to finance a U.S. operation. Therefore, they have lower after-tax interest costs and, to that extent, can be more competitive in the United States than many U.S. companies.[38]

There is much more to be said about how America's tax system burdens the competitiveness of U.S. business throughout the world. We lack space in this book for a comprehensive discussion but refer you to the endnotes cited in this section for more on the subject.

Foreign Corrupt Practices Act (FCPA)

questionable or dubious payments
Bribes paid to government officials by companies seeking purchase contracts from those governments

During the 1970s, revelations of **questionable or dubious payments** by American companies to foreign officials rocked governments in the Netherlands and Japan. Congress considered corporate bribery "bad business" and "unnecessary," and President Carter found it "ethically repugnant." As a result, the Foreign Corrupt Practices Act (FCPA) was passed and signed.

Uncertainties.   There were a number of uncertainties about terms used in the FCPA. An interesting one involves *grease*. According to the FCPA's drafters, the act does not outlaw grease, or facilitating payments made solely to expedite nondiscretionary official actions. Such actions as customs clearance or telephone calls have been cited. There is no clear distinction between supposedly legal grease payments and illegal bribes. To confuse matters further, U.S. Justice Department officials have suggested that they may prosecute some grease payments anyway under earlier antibribery laws written to get at corruption in the United States.[39]

Other doubts raised by the FCPA concerned the accounting standards it requires for compliance. That matter is connected to questions about how far management must go to learn whether any employees, subsidiaries, or agents

---

*Earned income includes salaries, bonuses, and commissions. Interest, dividend, and royalty income is called unearned income.

may have violated the act; even if management were unaware of an illegal payment, it could be in violation if it "had reason to know" that some portion of a payment abroad might be used as a bribe.[40]

Other Countries' Reactions to Bribes.*

Attitudes of business and government officials in Europe toward the FCPA range from amusement to incredulity, and no other government has taken a position similar to that represented by the FCPA—quite the opposite.[41] German tax collectors, for example, permit resident companies to deduct foreign bribes, which are called *sounderpesen*, or special expenses. In Britain, corrupt payments, even to British government officials, qualify for tax deductions.

Leading industrial nations such as Britain, France, Germany, and Japan cite many reasons for not adopting FCPA-type laws. They claim such laws might be seen as meddling in other countries' affairs, and unlike the Americans, they aren't eager to regulate their own citizens overseas, especially in business and tax matters. In response to suggestions that Japan enact an FCPA-type law, a foreign ministry official in Tokyo said "We cannot accept the idea of [foreign] recommendation somehow obliging Japan to change its criminal law system."

Of course, greed and distrust play their parts. Recessions at home have driven European and Japanese companies to compete much more vigorously for exports. Add to that the prevalence of bribery, and companies will not trust their competitors to play fair or obey an FCPA law if it existed.[42]

Just how pervasive these practices are was disclosed by Lloyd N. Cutler, a Washington attorney who did a study of the subject for the Northrop Corporation. Cutler said "Almost all European and Japanese export sales of the type that generate corrupt payments are arranged with government export financing or other government support."[43] So far, no other industrialized nation has a law resembling the FCPA, and an anticommercial bribery treaty proposed by the United States is languishing in an inactive committee of the United Nations.

In 1985, Dancare Corporation, a Danish company, got in trouble because of $730,000 in bribes it had paid to get a contract in Saudi Arabia. The trouble was not that it had paid the bribes, but that the bribes were not clearly indicated as such in the company's tax records. The Danish tax chief now advises Danish firms to book illicit payments openly under "bribes." Whether the bribes are in the form of cash, sexual favors, or luxury goods doesn't matter, as long as their value is noted on the tax records. Receipts are desirable but not essential.[44]

Bribes paid in Denmark are illegal; bribes paid abroad to secure export business are both legal and tax-deductible expenses. In the contest for the Saudi Arabian business, the Dancare Corporation bid was more than $730,000 above potential American competitors. Of course, they would have been in violation of the FCPA if they paid a bribe to get the contract and certainly would have been unable to deduct the payment from American taxes.

Is America Losing?

Is the FCPA causing American exporters to lose business? Yes, answer a number of companies, several of which are in the construction business. The United States, which in 1976 ranked first in the overseas

---

*Other words with similar connotations are *dash, squeeze, mordida, cumshaw,* and *baksheesh.* Bribes and questionable payments were mentioned in connection with sociocultural forces in Chapter 9.

construction market, dropped to fifth in 1987, falling behind Japan, Korea, West Germany, and Italy. As Daniel Tarullo, assistant secretary of state for economic and business affairs in the Clinton administration put it, "Companies which don't pay bribes because of legal restraints are unfairly disadvantaged." Mickey Kantor, the U.S. trade negotiator, says the U.S. policy puts its businesspeople in a difficult position regarding illicit payments.[45]

Billions Lost Overseas.   There are estimates of losses in the billions of dollars. Critics have cited the ambiguities in the FCPA as one of the possible causes of U.S. business foregoing legitimate overseas opportunities. It cannot operate comfortably in an environment in which management is unsure of the FCPA's interpretation and application.

In response to the negative feedback about the FCPA's effect, the General Accounting Office completed a survey in 1981. It randomly selected 250 companies from *Fortune*'s list of the 1,000 largest industrial firms. About one-third of the respondents stated they had lost overseas business as a result of the FCPA. Over 60 percent were of the opinion that, all things being equal, U.S. multinationals could not profitably compete against foreign companies that could legally bribe to make sales.[46]

Antiboycott Law

As a part of the hostility and wars between the Arab countries and Israel, several Arab countries boycott foreign companies that do business with Israel. They will not buy from such companies. Inasmuch as several Arab countries are extremely rich oil producers, they are very large potential markets from which sellers do not like to be excluded. In 1977, however, the United States passed an act forbidding American companies to comply with any Arab boycott law or regulation.

Contrast American and British Attitudes.   As in the case of the FCPA, few other countries have any such antiboycott law. A British House of Lords select committee studying similar legislation for Britain found 2.7 billion reasons to bury it in 1978. During 1977, British exports to Arab markets totaled £2.7 billion.[47]

Other Attitudes.   In the aftermath of the Iraq-Kuwait war, some other countries seemed to come around to the U.S. view. Belgium, Canada, France, Germany, Luxembourg, and the Netherlands now forbid their companies to comply with the boycott.

Changing Attitudes.   Although it has not yet occurred, problems with the antiboycott law may dissolve because of ongoing political developments in the Middle East. We refer, of course, to the peace agreements between Israel and Egypt, the Palestine Liberation Organization, and Jordan and Israeli negotiations with Syria. As of yet, however, the Arab League has not rescinded its declared boycott of companies that do business with Israel nor has the United States repealed its law forbidding American firms to comply with the boycott.

Action under the Antiboycott Law.   Not only is the antiboycott law not repealed, it is being enforced. In 1993, Baxter International, Inc., the world's largest hospital supply company, became the first firm to plead guilty to a felony charge of violating that law. Baxter had a plant in Israel and was blacklisted by the Arab League. Baxter wanted to do business in Arab countries, and then came under additional pressure from the Swiss company, Nestlé SA, which threatened to back out of a proposed clinical nutrition venture if Baxter failed to get off the blacklist.

The story is long and complex. We refer you to the article cited at the end of this paragraph to learn how a vengeful, fired employee nailed Baxter. And he nailed Baxter big time as the company agreed to pay $6.6 million in civil and criminal fines, by far the largest ever assessed under the antiboycott statute. Also under the agreement, Baxter is prohibited for two years from doing business in Syria and Saudi Arabia.[48]

Regulations in the antiboycott legislation also forbid response to any Arab question or questionnaire that deals with Israel. As a condition of bidding on a contract with an Arab country, a company may be asked whether any components to be supplied under the proposed contract will be sourced in Israel. Even though the company has no Israeli suppliers and no intentions of using any, it would be in violation of the antiboycott law and regulations to so inform the Arab country. In 1993, American Express Bank was fined $103,000 for providing Lebanon and Oman information about business relations with Israel.[49]

Are Export Contracts Being Lost?   Is the antiboycott law causing American exporters to lose business? Yes, according to Chase Manhattan Bank, especially in the relatively hard-line Arab countries, such as Iraq, Libya, and Syria. Even in Arab countries friendlier to the United States, the law causes difficulties and burdens not faced or borne by most non-American competitors.[50] Commenting on the law and the government's tough enforcement of it, Philip Hinson, Middle East affairs director of the U.S. Chamber of Commerce, says "They've had a randomly harmful effect on U.S. exports."

Another complaint by American companies about the law is the cost of compliance. Joseph Komalick, editor of the *Boycott Law Bulletin,* says that some U.S. multinationals have as many as 20 lawyers check the legality of Middle East contracts to make sure they don't violate the law.[51]

One argument against the boycott legislation is that it hurts American business but does no harm to the Arab countries. They can buy whatever they want—or adequate substitutes—from Europe or Japan.[52]

Some Laws and Agencies Aid U.S. Exports and Investment

We do not mean to give the impression that all U.S. laws and government agencies pose obstacles to the international business of U.S. companies. The U.S. Department of Commerce actively encourages exports by American companies. U.S. embassies and consular offices can be helpful with information and introductions for Americans who wish to export to or invest in foreign countries. The FSC provides some tax incentives for U.S. exporters.

COMMON LAW OR CIVIL LAW?

Historically, there has been a clear distinction between common law, which developed in England and spread to the English colonies, and civil law, which originated on the continent of Europe. Courts made common law as they decided individual cases; civil law was made by kings, princes, or legislatures issuing decrees or passing bills.

As time has passed, legislatures and government agencies in the United States have made more and more laws and regulations. The courts, in turn, have interpreted these laws and regulations as parties have argued about what they mean. That is the sort of procedure one finds in Europe, but vast differences in practices have developed that have less to do with the traditional common-civil law approaches than with historical government-citizen (or subject) relationships and attitudes.

WORLDVIEW

European Parliament, U.S. Congress Compared

Courtesy European Commission Delegation, Washington, DC

Doug Armand/Tony Stone Images

European Parliament

Legislative roles. Advisory, and may amend Commission proposals before their consideration by the council. Approves budget.

Relation to executive. Reacts to specific Commission proposals, but provides public forum for EU issues. Can remove entire Commission but not replace it. Can force some changes in budget. Questions Commissioners in plenary.

Election, chambers, sessions. Elected for five-year term by direct vote, but under national electoral laws. Single chamber meets one week in plenary, two weeks in committee, and one week in political groups each month.

Jurisdictions. Community laws, regulations, and budget (in part), which cover areas defined by the Treaty of Rome creating the EU. Defense excluded.

U.S. Congress

Legislative roles. Exclusive authority to introduce legislation. Two houses consider, amend, and move draft laws to the other for final vote: bills passed proceed to president for action.

Relation to executive. Legislative coresponsibility. Consents to treaties and appointments (Senate). Has own investigative and budget arms to check on executive. Committees both authorize and allow funds and oversee expenditure. Questions executive officials in committee.

Election, chambers, sessions. Two chambers: House elected for two years by equal population districts; Senate elected for six years by states; generally equal roles in legislation. House and Senate together set a calendar of sessions, which average 180–200 days a year.

Jurisdictions. Entire federal structure, which under the Constitution extends to almost every aspect of country except local and state taxing, police, and education functions.

European Practice

Europe has a history of thousands of years of tyranny, which recently has been covered with a veneer of democracy. People have greater reason to fear their governments in Europe than in the United States, and government service has more prestige. Before a new law is presented to the legislature (which, unlike legislatures in the United States, is always controlled by the same political party that controls the executive branch), consensus is achieved among most of the people, businesses, and government agencies that will be affected.

In contrast to American practices, European legislation is rarely amended, and regulations are rarely revised. Courts are not as often asked to give their

European Parliament

Staffs. Entrance exam into civil service for secretarial; free hire for political groups. Very small personal staff.

Committee structure. *Substantive* (12): Political Affairs; Agriculture; Economics & Monetary; Energy; Research & Technology; External Economic Relations; Social Affairs & Unemployment; Regional Policy & Planning; Transport; Environment, Public Health, & Consumer Protection; Youth, Culture, Education, Information, & Sport; Development & Cooperation. *Budgetary:* Budget; Budgetary Control. *Institutional:* Rules of Procedure & Petitions; Verification of Credentials; Institutional Affairs.

Leadership. President and 12 vice presidents represent national and party balance in plenary vote; they form Bureau for general direction of Parliament. Seven political group chairmen are added to form Enlarged Bureau, which handles most important matters involving political management. Five *questors* serve as ombudsmen for many administrative matters. *Rapporteurs,* selected by committee members, draft and defend reports. Committee chairmen function as leaders and coordinators of their committees.

Role of parties. Committee assignments, chairmenships, and interparliamentary delegations determined by relative size of each of seven political groups. Discipline varies depending on ideological breadth of groups, but generally is much greater than in U.S. Congress. Group chairmen elected for one-half of five-year term of Parliament but may be reelected. Parties tried to run Community-wide electoral campaigns in first direct election in 1979, with varying success. Most members elected on party-list system, which requires them to keep active role in national parties.

U.S. Congress

Staffs. Generally meritocratic entrance to committee staff. Political appointment for some housekeeping jobs. Large personal staffs.

Committee structure. *Substantive* (17): (House used as example, but Senate is similar): Agriculture; Armed Services; Banking, Finance, & Urban Affairs; Education & Labor; Energy & Commerce; Foreign Affairs; Intelligence; Interior & Insular Affairs; Judiciary; Merchant Marine & Fisheries; Post Office & Civil Service; Public Works & Transportation; Science & Technology; Small Business; Veterans; Ways & Means. *Budgetary:* Appropriations; Budget. *Institutional:* Administration; Rules; Standards of Conduct. *Investigative:* Government Operations.

Leadership. *House:* Speaker elected by majority party and speaks for it, but his function, partly, is to represent House in broad nonpartisan way; majority and minority parties each name leader and whip. These five form leadership for the management of 435-member House. *Senate:* Vice president is constitutionally presiding officer, but this is largely a ceremonial function; majority and minority leaders, and their whips, manage 100-member Senate on collegial basis. *Both:* Committee chairmen and (in last decade) subcommittee chairmen play major role in writing legislation and managing it on floor.

Role of parties. Only two major parties. Decisions taken by each house on organization generally follow party votes. Substantive issues bring more diversity, although speaker and president can have effects in organizing party positions. National parties weak and have little effect on Congress, which runs own campaign committees, by party, in each house. No effective means of disciplining errant members. Committee assignments and chairmanships depend on party caucus votes. Seniority plays presumptive role in these votes.

interpretations, and if they are, the decisions are rarely appealed. Once a consensus has been reached, it is considered very bad form to open the subject again, and those who do may find themselves left out of the consultations the next time around.

American Practice

In contrast to European custom, Americans have a weaker tradition of obeying their governments and have had very little fear of them. Americans are much more likely than Europeans to challenge laws in the courts, in the streets, or by disobedience. Legislation in America is a product of an ongoing adversarial proceeding, not of consensus; law is written by one independent branch of government for implementation by a second and for interpretation by yet a third. Different political parties or people with conflicting philosophies frequently control the three different branches of government.

Laws and regulations are constantly being amended or revised by the legislatures and the agencies. Courts interpret laws in ways that are sometimes surprising, the courts may strike laws down as being unconstitutional.

In the United States, the legislative body is now called Congress, and it convened as representatives of the several English colonies even before the United States become a country. In Europe, the legislative body of the European Union is called the European Parliament. It was brought into being by the Treaty of Rome, signed in 1957. The Worldview contains an interesting comparison of those two legislatures. Bear in mind that the European Parliament is gradually gaining power and can be expected to be a growing force in the EU.

SUMMARY

1. **Appreciate the complexity of the legal forces that confront international business.** International business is affected by many thousands of laws and regulations issued by states, nations, and international organizations. Some are at cross-purposes, and some diminish the ability of firms to compete with foreign companies.

2. **Understand that many taxes have purposes other than to raise revenue.** Certain taxes have purposes other than to raise revenues. For example, some aim to redistribute income, discourage consumption of certain products, encourage use of domestic goods, or discourage investment abroad. In addition, taxes differ from country to country. Tax treaties, or conventions, between countries can affect decisions on investment and location.

3. **Discuss enforcement of antitrust laws.** The United States, which has the toughest antitrust laws, tries to enforce them outside as well as inside the country, or extraterritorially. Although the EU does not attempt extraterritorial enforcement of its antitrust laws, they can have serious effects. In 1994, the EU levied a $158.58 million fine on a carton-board cartel. Japan's enforcement of its antitrust laws is weak to nonexistent.

4. **Recognize the importance of tariffs, quotas, and other trade obstacles to international business.** Tariffs are taxes on imports. Quotas limit the number or amount of a product that may be imported. Quotas are frequently called "voluntary" export restraints or "voluntary" restraint agreements.

5. **Appreciate the risk of product liability legal actions, which can result in impris-** onment for employees or fines for them and the company. Product liability refers to the civil or criminal liability of the designer or manufacturer of a product for injury or damages it causes. In several ways, product liability is treated differently in the U.S. legal system than in other countries. For example, only in the United States does one find lawyers' contingency fees, jury trials of these cases, and punitive damages. Although the principle of strict liability has been adopted in Europe, defendants are permitted to use state-of-the-art defenses and countries can put a cap on damages. Product liability is virtually unknown in Japan.

6. **Appreciate the effects of price and wage controls, labor laws, and currency exchange.** Price and wage controls, labor laws, and currency exchange controls must be observed in each country where you do business.

7. **Recognize the importance of being aware of peculiarities of local law.** Miscellaneous laws in host countries can trip up foreign businesspeople or tourists. Charges can range from simply not carrying an alien registration card to narcotics possession.

8. **Understand contract devices and institutions that assist in interpreting or enforcing international contracts.** International contracts should specify which country's law and courts should apply when disputes arise. The UN's CISG and the EU's Rome Convention have established rules for solving contract disputes. Arbitration is an increasingly popular solution.

9. **Anticipate the need and methods to protect your intellectual properties.** Patents,

trademarks, trade names, copyrights, and trade secrets are referred to as intellectual properties. Pirating of those properties is common and is expensive for their owners. The UN's World Intellectual Property Organization (WIPO) was created to administer international property treaties. But it is an open question whether the WIPO will cooperate or compete with TRIPS, a WTO agency with a similar purpose.

10. **Recognize how industrial espionage affects international business.** Industrial espionage is one company's attempt to steal

another company's trade secrets, a crime punishable in some countries by fines or imprisonment.

11. **Understand the numerous difficulties and burdens placed by U.S. laws and practices on American ICs, which other countries do not impose on their ICs.** The FCPA and Arab boycott legislation are unique to the U.S. and are costly obstacles to U.S. ICs. Although the common law and the civil law have different roots, the differences between them are gradually eroding.

KEY WORDS

- nonrevenue tax purposes   348
- foreign tax credit   350
- tax treaties   351
- antitrust laws   352
- restrictive trade practices laws   352
- extraterritorial application of laws   353
- product liability   356
- strict liability   356

- price and wage controls   358
- arbitration   360
- intellectual properties   361
- industrial espionage   363
- national tax jurisdiction   366
- territorial tax jurisdiction   366
- questionable or dubious payments   366

QUESTIONS

1. Explain some purposes of taxes other than to raise revenues.

2. Why do some people feel that a VAT should replace some or all of the U.S. income tax?

3. Why does a national tax system put citizens of that country at a disadvantage?

4. What objections have other countries to extraterritorial application by the United States of its antitrust laws?

5. When an American traveling abroad falls afoul of the criminal laws of a foreign country, are the U.S. embassy or the U.S. consulates likely to be of much help? Where else can the traveler look for aid?

6. What are some advantages that arbitrating contract disputes may have as compared to using the courts?

7. Are tariffs the only type of obstacle to international trade? If not, name some others.

8. Can product liability be criminal? If so, in what sorts of situations?

9. *a.* Does the Foreign Corrupt Practices Act forbid all bribes? Explain.

   b. Does the antiboycott law permit U.S. exporters to Arab countries to certify that the products are not of Israeli origin if that is true?

   c. Are attitudes and practices of Arab countries and the Arab League concerning the Israeli boycott changing? If so, to what extent?

10. *a.* Comparing the United States with Western Europe, what are the differences in practices as to making, amending, and interpreting laws?

    b. What are the reasons for those differences?

MINICASE 11-1   Italian Law

A California-based company is expanding very well and has just made its first export sale. All of its sales and procurement contracts up to now have contained a clause providing that if any disputes should arise under the contract, they would be settled under California law and that any litigation would be in California courts.

The new foreign customer, which is Italian, objects to these all-California solutions. It says it is buying and paying for the products, so the California company should compromise and allow Italian law and courts to govern and handle any disputes.

You are the CEO of the California company, and you very much want this order. You are pleased with the service your law firm has given, but you know it has no international experience. What sorts of solutions would you suggest that your lawyers research as possible compromises between your usual all-Californian clause and the customer's wish to go all-Italian?

Labor Forces

Moves of unions to join a board of directors offer little to American unions. We do not want to blur in any way the distinctions between the respective roles of management and labor in the plant. If unions were to become a partner in management, they would be most likely the junior partner in success and the senior partner in failure.

Thomas R. Donahue, executive assistant to the president, AFL–CIO

LEARNING OBJECTIVES

After reading this chapter, you should be able to:

1. **recognize** forces beyond management control that affect the availability of labor

2. **understand** the political and economic reasons that cause people to flee their home countries

3. **explain** why refugees are a source of labor but frequently a burden for the countries to which they flee

4. **discuss** guest workers and problems that may develop because of them

5. **explain** how the composition of a country's labor force affects productivity

6. **understand** women's positions in labor forces

7. **name** other forces that affect productivity

8. **discuss** differences in labor unions from country to country

9. **understand** how labor is getting a voice in management

Job Sharing, German Style

With EU-wide unemployment exceeding 10 percent, a top goal for governments across Europe and for employers is to preserve jobs. But for Germany's troubled and overmanned Volkswagen, the only way to become competitive appeared to be slashing the domestic work force from 100,000 to 70,000. • Instead, Volkswagen and Germany's largest labor union, IG Metall, agreed on a four-day workweek as an alternative to the work-force slash. The union got its long-sought goal of a 35-hour week, and VW got a wage cost savings of 10.75 percent. VW estimates its 1994 wage cost savings at nearly $1.3 billion, and no employees needed to be laid off.[a] • If the number of working hours were an important factor in employment, then America and Japan, where the working week is longer than in most of Europe, would have more unemployment. In fact they have less.[b]

Sources: [a]*Crossborder Monitor,* December 22, 1993, p. 21; [b]*The Economist,* August 6, 1994, p. 56.

The quality, quantity, and composition of the available labor force are considerations of great importance to an employer. This is particularly true if the employer is required to be efficient, competitive, and profitable. As we have indicated, there are government-owned plants whose objectives are to provide employment or essential services, with profitability and competitiveness being secondary.

labor quality
The skills, education, and attitudes of available employees

labor quantity
The number of available employees with the skills required to meet an employer's business needs

Labor quality refers to the attitudes, education, and skills of available employees. **Labor quantity** refers to the number of available employees with the skills and so forth required to meet an employer's business needs. Circumstances can arise in which there are too many available workers, which can be good or bad for the business.

If there are more qualified people than a company can economically employ, its bargaining position is strengthened and it can choose the best employees at relatively low wages. On the other hand, high unemployment can cause social and political unrest, which is usually not conducive to profitable business.

Many of the labor conditions in an area are determined by the social, cultural, religious, attitudinal, and other forces we have already discussed. Other determinants of labor conditions are political and legal forces, and here we shall enlarge somewhat on those which were introduced in Chapters 10 and 11.

We shall look at such subjects as labor availability, the reasons for its availability or scarcity, the types of labor likely to be available or scarce under different circumstances, productivity, and employer-employee relationships. These relationships are affected by employee organizations, such as labor unions. One cannot generalize about unions because they differ so greatly from country to country or even within one country.

Management of private business in capitalist societies has been thought of as representing the shareholders/owners and bondholders/lenders who put up the money that enabled the business to start and run. The shareholders and bondholders could call the tunes. But some new and different music is now being heard by management in several countries where labor is getting seats on boards of directors.

LABOR MOBILITY

labor mobility
The movement of people from country to country or area to area to get jobs

Classical economists assumed the immobility of labor, one of the factors of production. Undoubtedly, labor is imperfectly mobile; leaving aside political and economic obstacles, more complications are involved in moving people than in moving capital or most goods.

But however imperfect it may be, **labor mobility** does exist. At least 60 million people left Europe to work and live overseas between 1850 and 1970. Between the end of World War II and the mid-1970s, some 30 million workers from southern Europe and North Africa flowed into eight northern European countries where they were needed because of the economic boom enjoyed there. This movement is slowing or even reversing now.[1] We'll further discuss these "guest workers" later in this chapter.

Another huge worker migration began during the 1970s as the sparsely populated, and newly very rich, Arab OPEC countries needed labor not only in their oil fields but also for the explosion of construction projects they undertook and services they required. Countries supplying most of these workers were Egypt, Algeria, Morocco, Pakistan, and India.

There are probably 11 million Mexicans at work in the United States, most illegally, and the number is growing. In addition, there are many Cubans, Haitians, Central Americans, Southeast Asians, and others in the U.S. work force. The cause of such migrations is typically a combination of (1) problems, economic or political, at their sources and (2) perceived opportunities at their destinations.

Refugees: Political and Economic

Throughout history, there have been flights of people from oppression. During the 1960s and 1970s, millions fled from East to West Germany, from the People's Republic of China to Hong Kong and elsewhere, from North to South Vietnam and then as "boat people" from Vietnam to wherever they could land and hope to be accepted. In 1980, the flight of people from Cuba resumed. These people fled for political reasons. Those going from Mexico to the United States and from southern Europe to northern Europe go for primarily economic reasons: better jobs and pay.

Population Pressures.   One of the most important pressures creating both political and economic **refugees** is the booming population growth taking place primarily in the poor LDCs. Some 95 percent of the projected increase in the world's population from 5.7 billion in 1994 to over 10 billion by the year 2050 will be in those areas.[2]

refugees
People who flee one country for another for political or economic reasons

Women bear most of the burdens of the baby boom, graphically illustrated by the photograph of a pregnant woman carrying her still-infant last child in a back sling. The closely spaced pregnancies plus the constant child-care responsibilities are resulting in a growing number of female illiterates and the deterioration of female health.

These are human tragedies first and foremost. In terms of labor force efficiency and productivity, the women and children victims of these developments will be negative forces.

Millions Flee.   In 1970, there were 2.5 million refugees; in 1994, there were around 19 million plus 25 million "displaced persons."[3] Several million Afghan refugees in Pakistan and Iran are awaiting reestablishment of peace in their country now that the Soviet army has left. One of the worst refugee flows occurred in 1994 as members of the Rwandan Hutu and Tutsi tribes butchered and fled from each other. Oil-producing and industrializing Malaysia is estimated to have more than a million illegal aliens, most of whom are from overcrowded Indonesia. Figures 12–1 and 12–2 show maps of international immigration and emigration, respectively.

The Ex-Soviet Empire.   As the previous Soviet satellite countries of eastern Europe and the parts of the disintegrating Soviet Union struggle to change from centrally planned to market economies, unemployment and discontent are dangerously high. Their people can see and read about the wealth of western Europe.

The Iron Curtain was erected to keep those people from fleeing to the noncommunist West. Now that the Curtain has collapsed, watchtowers and armed guards have made a jarring reappearance—this time on the Western side of the border. The western European countries are trying to control and regulate a tide of migrants from Albania, Bulgaria, Hungary, Romania, and, it is feared, the ex-Soviet Union. An Austrian army major, Peter Logar, who helps coordinate the border patrol, says "There are 40 million Russians living below the poverty level, and they're hungry."[4]

Refugees Welcome?   Refugees are not welcome in most countries. As indicated in the previous section, western Europe is living in dread of a flood from the East. The few countries willing to accept some refugees will take only limited numbers. Their reasons differ. Countries near Vietnam and Cambodia, from which refugees came, are poor and have difficulty feeding their own people. Most of the richer countries, such as Japan and the countries of Western Europe, are not racially diverse and are reluctant to bring in large

FIGURE 12–1 International immigration

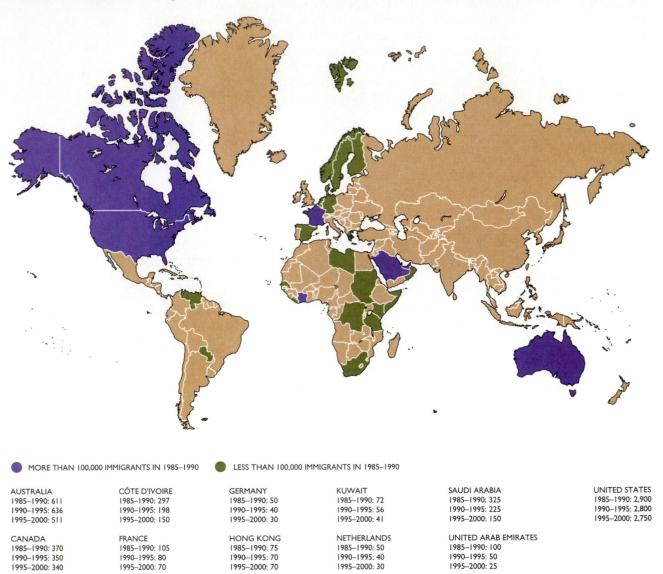

● MORE THAN 100,000 IMMIGRANTS IN 1985–1990   ● LESS THAN 100,000 IMMIGRANTS IN 1985–1990

AUSTRALIA	CÔTE D'IVOIRE	GERMANY	KUWAIT	SAUDI ARABIA	UNITED STATES
1985–1990: 611	1985–1990: 297	1985–1990: 50	1985–1990: 72	1985–1990: 325	1985–1990: 2,900
1990–1995: 636	1990–1995: 198	1990–1995: 40	1990–1995: 56	1990–1995: 225	1990–1995: 2,800
1995–2000: 511	1995–2000: 150	1995–2000: 30	1995–2000: 41	1995–2000: 150	1995–2000: 2,750

CANADA	FRANCE	HONG KONG	NETHERLANDS	UNITED ARAB EMIRATES
1985–1990: 370	1985–1990: 105	1985–1990: 75	1985–1990: 50	1985–1990: 100
1990–1995: 350	1990–1995: 80	1990–1995: 70	1990–1995: 40	1990–1995: 50
1995–2000: 340	1995–2000: 70	1995–2000: 70	1995–2000: 30	1995–2000: 25

Note: Numbers are in thousands.

numbers of alien races. European countries with guest workers are experiencing race relations problems. Even in such a relatively rich and racially diverse country as the United States, which is accepting—or getting—millions of refugees, there are difficulties. One of them is finding work for all of the new people; another is educating their children.

Packing Up.   When oil prices were high, the Middle East's fastest-growing export was labor. For such countries as Egypt, Jordan, Pakistan, and North and South Yemen, workers' remittances were bigger than total merchandise exports. As tumbling oil prices pushed the area's oil producers into recession, the expatriates who flocked to jobs there in the 1970s and early 1980s were packing their bags and going home. The home countries will sorely miss the income; and their already large unemployment rolls will swell.[5]

FIGURE 12–2 International emigration

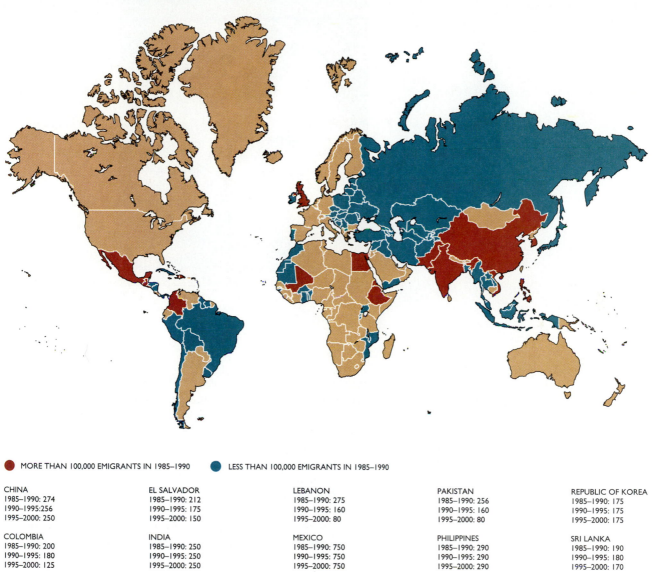

● MORE THAN 100,000 EMIGRANTS IN 1985–1990   ● LESS THAN 100,000 EMIGRANTS IN 1985–1990

CHINA	**EL SALVADOR**	**LEBANON**	**PAKISTAN**	**REPUBLIC OF KOREA**
1985–1990: 274	1985–1990: 212	1985–1990: 275	1985–1990: 256	1985–1990: 175
1990–1995:256	1990–1995: 175	1990–1995: 160	1990–1995: 160	1990–1995: 175
1995–2000: 250	1995–2000: 150	1995–2000: 80	1995–2000: 80	1995–2000: 175
COLOMBIA	**INDIA**	**MEXICO**	**PHILIPPINES**	**SRI LANKA**
1985–1990: 200	1985–1990: 250	1985–1990: 750	1985–1990: 290	1985–1990: 190
1990–1995: 180	1990–1995: 250	1990–1995: 750	1990–1995: 290	1990–1995: 180
1995–2000: 125	1995–2000: 250	1995–2000: 750	1995–2000: 290	1995–2000: 170

Note: Numbers are in thousands.

Countries that receive many refugees or have high birthrates may have too many people for the available jobs, but there are also countries that have too few people. France, Germany, the Scandinavian countries, and Switzerland, all of which have low birthrates, fall into the latter category. And to those countries have legally come the so-called **guest workers** to perform certain types of jobs, usually in service, factory, or construction work.

In 1994, there were 4.3 million immigrants in France who did not qualify for French nationality, including 3.4 million Arabs and 206,000 people from black Africa. Germany had 4.6 million foreigners, of whom 1.7 million are Turks. England, Switzerland, and the Scandinavian countries also had large numbers of foreign workers and their families. Most of the guest workers are from southern Europe, North Africa, and Turkey.

LABOR SHORTAGES AND GUEST WORKERS

guest workers
People who go to a foreign country legally to perform certain types of jobs

The burdens of women in poor countries: working while caring for two small children.

Penny Tweedie/Tony Stone Images

Guest Worker Problems

Economic.   Guest workers provide the labor host countries need, which is desirable as long as the economies are growing. But when the economies slow, as they did during the mid-1970s, 1980s, and 1990s, fewer workers are needed and problems appear. Unemployment increases among the native workers, who then want the jobs held by guest workers. It is conveniently forgotten that the guest workers took jobs the natives would not do when times were good. To appease their citizens, some countries refused to renew the guest workers' permits. In other countries, where the work was seasonal, the guest workers were deported at the end of the season instead of being permitted to stay and take other work. The French, for example, paid surplus foreign workers 10,000 francs (about $1,500) as a "go home" bonus; and Germany offered "repatriation assistance"—equivalent to about $4,000, plus a lesser amount per child—for certain unemployed foreign workers to leave.

Racial.   The introduction of large numbers of foreigners into host countries caused some racial frictions even while the economies were healthy. In France, for instance, French workers often refuse to share low-cost housing projects with outsiders, especially Arabs and Africans.

By 1991, the racial content of the anti–guest worker arguments in France had become loud and clear.

> During 1991, both authors attended conferences and conducted other research in France. The conferences were in Marseille. One author flew to Paris, the other to Nice; they then proceeded to Marseille, which has a high percentage of immigrant guest workers. People advised both authors not to go to dangerous Marseille, but if they were foolhardy enough to travel there, to be very careful. The warnings left no doubt that the dangers were due to the large numbers of Arabs and blacks in Marseille. In any event, the authors and their families had a delightful stay in Marseille, with none of them experiencing any difficulties.

But the point is that the French feelings against the immigrants has escalated and is based largely on race. French leaders of the left, right, and center are speaking out against more immigration. One leader denounced the "smell and the noise" of France's "scrounging" immigrant population. Carrying the immigrant debate still further, Edith Cresson, who became prime minister in 1991, spoke of how to organize the mass expulsion of immigrants.[6]

In Germany, there is concern about the foreigners—workers and their families—who show no signs of wanting to leave. The worst relations are with the Turks, who form the largest alien group.

The alien workers and their families are frequently crowded into older, substandard housing. They have created slum neighborhoods in the midst of wealthy Western Europe, and with higher birthrates they are growing in numbers more rapidly than the natives, whose birthrates are among the world's lowest.

Another country that is making a 180-degree turn in its attitude toward immigration is Italy. Traditional tolerance made Italy a haven for untold thousands of illegal immigrants, many of them from poor, black African states. More recently, Albanians and Yugoslavs have swelled their ranks.

Now sentiment toward immigrants has soured sharply as their numbers have increased and the economy has slowed. Violent racial incidents have become more commonplace. In 1991, Italy appointed a new immigration minister, Margherita Boniver. Her tasks are to keep racism under control while enforcing immigration limits on a country-by-country quota basis.[7]

New Guest Workers.   Trying to cut off its dependence on cheap Palestinian labor, Israel has launched a massive recruitment campaign that would bring some 18,000 East European guest workers to Israeli farms and construction sites. This comes after a series of terrorist attacks inside Israel committed by Palestinian extremists.

Despite a 10 percent jobless rate, few Israeli citizens, Jewish or Arab, are attracted to work in agriculture or construction. The reason for that is that wages in those sectors are only marginally higher than Israeli unemployment benefits.[8]

Political or Economic Refugees

When refugees flow into a country, the resulting growth of the labor force includes whatever ages, genders, and skills are able to get in. They are not coming for specific jobs; they are fleeing oppression or poverty. At the outset, they cause problems for the host country, which must try to feed, clothe, educate, and find work for the newcomers.

Some, for various reasons, remain burdens on the host country or on international refugee relief agencies. So it has been for many of the Palestinians who fled from Israel. This is not to suggest that the Palestinians are less intelligent or industrious than other groups. Their problems and difficulties have been tremendously increased by the wars and political upheavals in the Middle East.

Others find more peaceful surroundings, adapt relatively quickly, and become upwardly mobile in their new society. This holds true for many of the Cuban refugees in the United States. Many believe the rehabilitation and growth of downtown Miami owes much to the Cubans' influence and work.[9]

Quite different is the type of worker involved in the movement from southern to northern Europe. Specific types of workers and skills were needed

COMPOSITION OF THE LABOR FORCE

Guest Workers in Japan?

Japan does not have guest workers in the European sense, where they are legal. In Japan, they are illegal. Coming mostly from the Philippines, Bangladesh, and Pakistan, they commonly enter Japan with tourist visas, often on false passports, find jobs, and stay.

The law only prohibits migrant laborers from working in Japan; it does not prohibit employers from hiring them. So clandestine workers in Japan have no legal rights. They cannot force employers to pay fair wages or appeal to the police for help.

A Japan Labor Ministry survey showed that on average they earn less than half the wages of their Japanese co-workers. Firms save even more on labor costs because illegal workers do not receive the insurance or other benefits usually demanded by Japanese employees. These non-Japanese laborers work on average 60 to 70 hours a week in small factories, the fast-food industry, or construction.

Just as European contractors did in the 1970s, Japan's contractors and smaller manufacturers have begun to depend on cheap foreign labor to offset rising costs associated with the yen's appreciation. Even at much higher legal wages and benefits, there is a severe shortage of Japanese laborers who are willing to perform the dangerous or dirty work done by the illegals.

The situation is particularly dangerous for young women employed in the bars and massage parlors of Japan's ubiquitous "entertainment industry." As frequently happens, young women come to Japan expecting to work as waitresses or hotel clerks, but exploitive business owners take their passports away and force them to work as prostitutes.

Japan historically has relied heavily on foreign workers to fill labor shortages, but it is far from a melting pot. Thousands of Koreans and Chinese were forcibly recruited during World War II to work in factories and mines. Most of the 660,000 people of Korean and Chinese ancestry who remain in Japan are virtually indistinguishable from their Japanese neighbors. Nevertheless, they are still classified as "resident aliens" and must carry alien registration cards.

---

there, and only persons who fit the needs were given work permits. They often did not or could not bring their families. They tended to be immediate benefits rather than burdens to the host economy.

The status of many Mexicans in the United States falls between that of the guest worker and that of the political refugee. For one thing, most guest workers are legally in the host country; the opposite is true for many Mexicans in the United States. For the most part, the Mexicans are economic, not political, refugees, but they bring their families when possible, thus creating more social burdens than do guest workers. Although the Mexicans usually come to work, they do not necessarily come prepared for specific jobs that are available in the host country.

Labor Force Composition and Comparative Productivity

labor force composition
The mix of people available to work, in terms of age, skill, gender, race, and religion

Another change in **labor force composition** in the United States began in the mid-1970s. The percentage of adult women in the American labor force increased by some 10 percent during the 1970s. And the increase continued, reaching 73 percent in 1989, when it ended. One reason given for the end was disillusionment of many two-income couples with their stressful life-styles. When interest rates dropped in the early 1990s, many seized the opportunity to refinance their mortgages and used the extra cash to work less rather than to consume more.[10]

The size of the total U.S. labor force increased by 34.8 million workers between 1974 and 1994, a gain of over 32 percent. A unique feature of U.S. labor force growth—female and male—is that many of the new workers are

Reuters/Bettmann

Guantanamo Bay: a safe haven for these Cuban refugees trying to get to the United States.

political or economic refugees who speak little, if any, English in addition to being unskilled. This growth and heterogeneity of the American labor force made an increase of **labor productivity** difficult but not impossible.

Throughout the 1980s and into the 1990s, productivity growth in the manufacturing sector more than doubled to 3.3 percent a year from 1.4 percent a year in the 1950–1981 period. During that same time period, the annual growth in labor productivity increased to 3.8 percent from 2.3 percent.

Unit labor costs stopped their 17-year rise and declined. This did not result from reduced wages or employment but from increased productivity.[11]

Although productivity has grown in most OECD countries, U.S. productivity is nonetheless still well above the European and Japanese averages, even in manufacturing. U.S. labor costs in manufacturing are currently some 30 percent below foreign competitors.

Human capital has been a major contributor to economic growth in the United States. Up to a quarter of income growth per worker since World War II can be attributed to better education. Although other OECD countries have also made major gains, educational attainment as a whole in the United States remains higher than elsewhere.

On the negative side, for over a decade the U.S. system has not shown itself capable of boosting the skills of individuals who do not intend to go to college. They are found especially among inner-city "minorities."[12]

Statistics in a U.K. Treasury economic progress report show the relative productivity of the U.S. worker to be the highest among the industrial countries, per person, person employed, and hours worked (see Figure 12–3). The low ranking of Japan on the second and third bars of the figure is accounted for by the remarkable inefficiency of its workers in farming and distribution and by the fact that the Japanese work more hours than the others. They work 2,129 hours a year while the British work 1,511. At least one economist feels that productivity levels in all countries eventually will converge as capital and technology spread throughout the world.[13]

labor productivity
Measures how many acceptable units of a product are produced by a worker during a given time and the cost per unit

unit labor costs
The cost in labor to produce one unit of output

FIGURE 12–3 Relative productivity (whole economy 1986, Britain = 100)

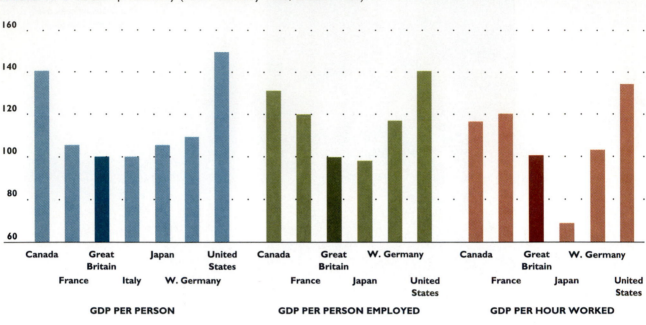

In addition to the relative skill of labor forces, there are other causes for rapidity or slowness of productivity growth. These causes are interlocking, and we shall look briefly at some of them.

Research and Development (R&D).   More efficient tools and machines result from more extensive and effective R&D. The R&D a company can do depends on its management policies but also on how many after-tax dollars are available and on whether R&D can be deducted as a pre-tax expense. Governments do a great deal of R&D, which can also boost productivity.

Tax Policies.   As indicated, a nation's tax policies can influence how much money is available to private business for R&D. They can also make immense differences in the amount available to private business to buy new plant, tools, and machines. They can do this through higher or lower tax rates.

Policies on depreciation are also important. Present U.S. tax policy permits depreciation only of the historic cost of plant, tools, and machines. With inflation, however, the replacement cost will be higher than the historic cost. If business could depreciate the current or replacement cost, the result would be lower taxes and more money left to the company for R&D, reinvestment, or other uses. See Chapter 6 for more on this.

Savings Rates.   If people save a large percentage of their income (as opposed to spending it on current consumption), there is a larger pool of money available with which to buy company stocks or lend to business. People save for such reasons as creating a nest egg against hard times and because they have confidence in their currencies. A number of countries give tax breaks to interest or dividends earned on savings, and some countries have involuntary savings plans. Most OECD countries have savings rates higher than those of the United States, which threatens to lead to higher economic and productivity growth rates.

The savings rates for the G7 countries in descending order from the biggest savers to the smallest are given below.

Countries	Savings as Percentages of After-Tax Income
Japan	18.1%
Germany	14.8
Britain	12.3
France	12.2
Italy	11.7
Canada	11.3
United States	4.1

As you see, the United States is at the bottom of the industrial country savings league. Thus, there is much less money available in the United States for R&D and other job- and efficiency-creating investment than in those other countries. And the trend does not encourage hope that the United States will move up the league. Japan's savings rate has climbed seven percentage points since the early 1980s, and the rate in Britain has jumped seven points since 1988. The rates in France and Germany have risen three points since the mid-1980s. The U.S. savings rate was close to 10 percent at the beginning of the 1975–80 economic upturn and 8 percent at the start of the 1982–90 expansion. As the table shows, it is now down to near 4 percent.[14]

A Walk on the Brighter Side. The United States came out of World War II with undamaged factories and a hoard of technology developed during the war. As a result, its productivity level was four to five times higher than the ravaged European and Japanese economies. A major American policy goal was the reconstruction of Europe and Japan. Reconstruction was successful, and the gap was narrowed. By the mid-1960s, European and Japanese growth slowed, and in the late 1970s, the German growth rate for manufacturing fell behind the American rate. It is still falling, and the Japanese rate since 1980 has been virtually identical to that of America. As of 1994, the American worker's productivity is 30 percent higher than the Japanese overall rate and 28 percent higher in manufacturing.

Social Status

There are societies in which a person's social status is established by the caste or social group into which he or she is born. India presents an extreme example of the caste system, and intercaste battles that cause fatalities and home burnings still occur between upper-caste Hindus and the untouchables, whom Mahatma Gandhi called *harijans,* the children of God.[15] Obviously, a would-be employer must tread carefully when both upper-caste Hindus and harijans are in the employee pool.

Some say that the class system in Great Britain is eroding, but people there are still classified by the accents they acquire at home and school. When Margaret Thatcher was elected prime minister, commentators saw fit to point out that she was "only" the daughter of a small-store owner even though her accent was "upper class," apparently acquired at Oxford University. Although class differences do not cause riots in Britain, as caste differences do in India, a foreign employer should, nevertheless, be conscious of the possibilities for friction arising from those differences.

In Japan, there remains an odd caste holdover from the 17th century, when the feudal Togugawa regime imposed a rigid social pecking order on the country. The warrior-administrator samurai were at the top. Below them were

SOCIAL STATUS, GENDER, RACE, TRADITIONAL SOCIETY, OR MINORITIES: CONSIDERATIONS IN EMPLOYMENT POLICIES

farmers and artisans, then merchants, and at the very bottom, those with occupations considered dirty and distasteful, such as slaughterers, butchers, and tanners.

As in India, where discrimination against untouchables is illegal, all natives of Japan who are of the Japanese race are legally equal. However, the descendants of the lowest Japanese class remain trapped in their ghettos, working in small family firms that produce knitted garments, bamboo wares, fur and leather goods, shoes, and sandals. They call themselves *burakumin* (ghetto people), and claim they number about 3 million people living in some 6,000 ghettos. Their average income is far below that of other Japanese.

Gender

Degrees of women's liberation and of women's acceptability in the work force range from fairly advanced in the United States and Western Europe to virtually nil in many countries. Even where women have made some strides out of their traditional roles, their progress is not necessarily secure, as witness the women's marches in Iran when the Islamic government that succeeded the shah ordered women back to their traditional dress and roles.

Employers must consider the sexist attitudes of the host society. In a country such as the United States, which has seen large strides in the status and acceptability of women in business and the professions, the hiring and promotion of women can be a business advantage. It can also be a legal advantage, because it complies with "affirmative action" laws and regulations of the U.S. and state governments. These laws encourage the hiring and promotion of women and minorities. But there are many countries in which customs, attitudes, or religion are hostile to women in the professions or business.

> Think like a man, act like a lady, work like a dog. That is the formula for the success of a woman working in the man's world of Japanese business.[16]

Women make up only 6.7 percent of the Japanese executive roster, far below the American or Swedish rates. Tradition, a burden for women executives in most countries, is one reason.

A second reason is after-hours drinking sessions, which are common in many countries but more prevalent in Japan. Much of Japanese consensus decision making is accomplished during such sessions. Female managers tend to consider these a waste of time and to be somewhat uncomfortable at the freewheeling exchanges among the men as inhibitions fall away. The drinking is often very heavy, and drunkenness is not a disgrace; overimbibers are delivered carefully home.

The discomfort goes both ways. One computer salesman, talking about after-hours drinking sessions with his female section chief, complained, "I don't know what to talk about with her. She's not married, so I must avoid any remarks with sexual connotations. With a man, I could have a drink and talk about anything."

Other Countries Hinder Women.   Japan is not the only country where women are encountering problems in making or retaining progress. We spoke of the setback for women in Iran, and women have been having troubles in other Moslem countries also.

One step forward in Pakistan has been accompanied by several steps backward. The forward step was a decision by the federal court that women could serve as judges. Two of the backward steps are a ban on women from taking part in public sporting events and a change in the law of evidence that makes the word of one male witness equal to that of two women. When women in Lahore protested against this devaluation of their legal personalities, police set upon them, injuring 13.

Other backward steps in Pakistan are proposals to deny women the vote, to deny them the right to drive a car (as in Saudi Arabia), to halve the blood money paid for a female victim as compared with a male victim, and to impose the death penalty for prostitution, but only for the woman and not her customer. Segregated schools for women are being established. Women cannot attend men's schools in Saudi Arabia, and that country, which gives much financial aid to Pakistan, is thought to be a strong influence on Pakistani policies. A pointer to what the segregated female schools may teach is provided by one college, which has banned women from physics and mathematics and channeled them instead into a new course called household accounts.

Women's Education Is Good for Us All.   Studies show persistent correlation between the length of women's schooling and birthrates, child survival, family health, and a nation's overall prosperity. One study ranked countries by the extent of schooling given their girls. At the top of the scale was France, where almost all girls attend secondary school and women average more than 11 years of education. At the bottom was the poverty-stricken Chad, an African country where women have on average less than one month of schooling.[17]

Very low levels of education are almost always present in societies where there are many cases of female genital mutilation, sometimes called female circumcision. The World Health Organization, a UN agency, says that people in those societies think they are doing the right thing for their daughters and do not see the link between genital mutilation of a child and the pain, infections, and ill health she may suffer as a woman.[18]

Are the UN and the EU Commission Good to Girls?   No. At the UN, sexism is blatant. Of 136 secretariat or agency heads since 1948, only one has been a woman. And the EU is also for the boys. The highest level of Eurocracy consists of 30 directors general; of these, just one is female. The influence brokers of the EU are the 17 *chefs de cabinet,* and Sue Binns, a former British career diplomat, is the sole woman among them. Although the EU Commission advertises itself as an equal opportunity employer, that appears not to be the case for positions higher than secretaries or executive assistants.[19]

At the other end of the scale is Scandinavia. A UN report ranked countries according to the quality of life for women in comparison to men. Factors included wage rates, adult literacy, life expectancy, job opportunities, and time in education. The best 12 in descending order were Finland, Sweden, Denmark, France, Norway, Australia, Austria, Czechoslovakia, the United States, Switzerland, Germany, and the United Kingdom.[20]

Race

Unfortunately, examples of racial conflicts and discrimination are found worldwide. There have been black-versus-white conflicts in such places as the United States, South Africa, and Great Britain, and Arab-, Indian-, or Pakistani-versus-black conflicts in Africa. Earlier in this chapter, we discussed racial friction caused by guest workers in Europe, and there has been bloody conflict in Sri Lanka between Tamils and Sinhalese. Some say the Chinese have an attitude of superiority toward blacks, and in 1988, antiblack riots erupted at several Chinese universities.[21]

In another part of the world, Japan has come under increasing criticism for its laws denying Japanese citizenship to anyone not of the Japanese race. The largest alien group affected is the Koreans, many of whom were brought to Japan as workers when Japan occupied Korea. Now the second- and third-generation descendants of those Koreans, all of whom were born in Japan, with Japanese as their native tongue, are still considered aliens and not

Sweden's Working Women Enjoy a Baby Boom

Sweden's birthrate is the fastest-growing in Western Europe. Swedish women are having 2.13 children each, surpassed in Western Europe only by Iceland (2.3) and Roman Catholic Ireland (2.17). It is Sweden's highest fertility rate since the early 1960s.

This is happening in a country where women can have free abortions on demand up to the 18th week of pregnancy and every form of birth control device is available at low cost. Sweden is overwhelmingly secular, and the nominally dominant Lutheran church holds no doctrinal objection to family planning.

Thus are confounded the innumerable gloomy critics who love to argue that the famed Swedish welfare state has undermined the traditional morality of the nation.

The two-child family is now the norm in Sweden. "Having several children may have acquired an increased prestige value as people's economic situation has improved," argues Mr. Jan Hoem at the demography department of Stockholm University.

The rising birthrate also suggests that the difficulties in the Swedish economy over the past two years have not discouraged Swedes from having babies.

At the same time there has been a rapid growth in the number of Swedish women at work. As many as 84.8 percent of women with children under the school-starting age of seven years were in the labor market last year, working an average of 26.5 hours a week, compared with 35.4 hours for men.

Sweden thus combines the highest employment activity rate in Western Europe with the highest growth in birthrate. Indeed, Swedish social policy has sought both to underpin families with children and enable women to play a full part in the labour market.

There appears to be a clear social pattern for Swedish women—they get educated, find a job, and then have their children without losing their job. As a result, the mean age of a woman having her first baby in Sweden is more than 28 years.

Mr. Hoem says "I know of no other country with a similar political system and at a comparable stage of industrial development that has so consistently tried to facilitate women's entry into the labour market and their continued attachment to it at a minimal cost to child-bearing and child-rearing."

Women benefit from the comprehensive and generous welfare benefit system that has evolved over the past 20 years and is designed to support the family structure.

In the current financial year an estimated Skr56 billion ($8.73 billion), around 13 percent of total budget expenditure, is being provided for families with children. It includes Skr13 billion in grants for child-care facilities.

This year the child allowance has been increased by Skr2,280 to Skr9,000 per child as part of a reform of the tax system. Families with more than two children receive a supplementary allowance.

On the top of this the state provides a parental leave benefit payable for 15 months for the birth or adoption of a child. For the first 360 days this means receiving payments up to 90 percent of previous income, with a ceiling of Skr241,500. These benefits can be utilized at any stage before the child reaches the age of 8. In the case of multiple births, there is an additional 180 days per child. The benefit is payable to either parent.

By extending the parental leave with other forms of leave, parents would still be eligible for the benefit for a second child without having to return to work. "With an eligibility as long as two years or more, many parents find it manageable to have two children sufficiently closely spaced to take advantage of the benefit," says Mr. Hoem.

On top of the family allowance and parental leave benefit there is also what is called the "occasional parental benefit" for the care of sick children amounting to 60—in certain cases, 120—days per child per year. The child has to be 12 years or less to receive this support. The entitlement amounts to 80 percent of income for the first 14 days per child per year. A father is allowed to have the benefit for 10 days per child around its birth or adoption.

It is estimated that around 60 percent of preschool children are in some form of child-care centre at a total cost to the state of Skr29.7 billion in the last financial year.

As Hoem argues, this all amounts to a "low-key and largely indirect pro-natalism."

Source: Robert Taylor, *Financial Times*, July 30, 1991, p. 2.

---

granted the rights and privileges of Japanese citizenship. The relatively few Vietnamese refugees permitted into Japan are beginning to feel the same racial discrimination.

In the interest of balance, it should be pointed out that blacks have been known to discriminate against other races. Probably the best-known instance occurred in Uganda when the black-run government seized the property, shops, and land of people of Indian or Pakistani heritage, drove them out, and turned the seized assets over to black Ugandan citizens.

Small Businesses and Jobs

Only 7 percent of the 14 million businesses in the EU have more than nine employees.

Small businesses are particularly important in Italy and Spain, where they form the backbone of those economies. At the European Council 1994 meeting in Corfu, the Commission was directed to take several steps to mobilize and assist small businesses in job creation.

One step is creation of the European Investment Fund to finance or guarantee job-creating projects. By 1997, about 4 billion ECUs are expected to be available. Another step is to encourage member-countries to simplify administrative formalities. They will also be encouraged to increase national or regional policies of support to small business. European tax systems generally penalize small businesses. In 1994, the Commission issued a legally binding recommendation to member-countries to end this tax discrimination.

In Latin America, millions of women have turned to self-employment to support themselves and their families. They work as vendors, seamstresses, food makers, microscale manufacturers, and service providers, and frequently expand to hire employees, subcontract, and grow to larger businesses. The Inter-American Development Bank's Microenterprise Division gives them access to credit on fair market terms and advice on managing their businesses and marketing their product. Loans can be in small amounts—as little as $50—to serve the needs of even the smallest-scale microentrepreneurs.

Men are not discriminated against and can get small-business loans, but lenders say women are a better investment. For one thing, women are more likely than men to pay back their loan on time and in full. They also have a solid track record of using their loans to expand their businesses, boost profits, and hire new workers.

The United States Peace Corps is seeking people to help countries around the world in small-business development. They want people with education or experience in all fields of business, including finance, marketing, accounting, international trade, management, retail operations, credit program, hotel management, tourism, agribusiness, and cost analysis.

The Peace Corps has people in Africa, Latin America, Central Europe, and the former Soviet republics. Some of the countries that are hosting Peace Corps workers in small business are in Africa (Togo, Tonga, and Zimbabwe), in Latin America (Chile, Nicaragua, and Uruguay), and in Central or Eastern Europe (Czech Republic, Poland, and the Slovak Republic). To discuss Peace Corps jobs, phone 1 (800) 424-8580 from anywhere in the United States.

Voice Processing Corp. (VPC), with 40 headquarters employees, has turned a potential Tower of Babel into a competitive advantage worldwide. Among the 40 are people representing 11 nationalities and most of the world's major religions. Combined, they speak 30 languages.

VPC makes speech-recognition software, and the diverse work force has been central to the successful foreign expansion of the company from its base in Cambridge, Massachusetts. The prediction is that overseas customers will account for half the company's projected fiscal 1995 revenue of over $10 million, up from 30 percent of the $5 million 1994 sales.

Employees sometimes take an intensely personal interest in expansion into their homelands. For example, senior software engineer Tonytip Ketudit says introducing VPC products to his native Thailand has become his pet project, and he has used a vacation there to contact a potential distributor.

Sources: "Survey Reveals Small-Scale EU," *Financial Times*, September 1, 1994, p. 3; "An Integrated Programme to Mobilize the Growth and Employment Potential of SMEs," *Frontier Free Europe*, European Commission, July–August 1994; "For Women: Big Gains from Micro-Business," *IDB Erta*, Inter-American Development Bank, 1994; and Michael Selz, "Small Company Goes Global with Diverse Work Force," *The Wall Street Journal*, October 12, 1994, p. B2.

Minorities

Traditional societies combined with racial attitudes sometimes present opportunities along with problems for employers. There are societies in which merchants, businesspeople, and bankers are looked down on, and the people prefer to follow political, religious, military, professional, or agricultural careers. In such societies, outsiders may dominate commercial and banking activities. Some examples are the Indians and Pakistanis in East Africa, the Chinese in southeast Asia, and the Greeks in Turkey.

An advantage for a foreign employer moving into these societies is that such **minorities** may be immediately available, bringing financial and managerial skills to the employer. They speak the local language and usually one or more others, and they are less nationalistic than the majority.

A disadvantage is that such people are often unpopular with the majority local population. The foreign employers can easily become too dependent on minority employees, thus becoming isolated and insulated from the real world of the majority.[22]

traditional societies
Tribal, nomadic states of people before they turn to organized agriculture or industry

minorities
Usually a relatively smaller number of people identified by race, religion, or national origin who live among a larger number of different people

EMPLOYER-EMPLOYEE RELATIONSHIPS

labor market
The pool of available potential employees with the necessary skills within commuting distance from an employer

When a foreign employer arrives in a **labor market,** it must take what it finds. Of course, a prudent company will study the labor market when considering whether to invest in a country. A company does not even have to travel to a prospective host country to gain information about its labor force. In addition to *Foreign Labor Trends* released by the Bureau of International Labor Affairs of the U.S. Department of Labor, two good information sources are the *Handbook of Labor Statistics* (available from the Bureau of Labor Statistics of the U.S. Department of Labor in Washington, DC) and the *Yearbook of Labor Statistics* (published by the United Nation's International Labor Office in Geneva, Switzerland).

These sources give information for most countries of the world on several subjects, including the number of labor strikes, or work stoppages, per year. The number of workers who went on strike is indicated, as is the number of working days lost. Last, but perhaps most informative, for each country the days lost per thousand employees in nonagricultural industries is reported.

The countries about which those labor figures are reported vary greatly in size, culture, labor laws, and militancy of labor unions. Thus, the days lost per thousand is the only direct comparison among the countries. But these statistics are all raw numbers, and potential employers should investigate more deeply when considering a labor market.

Here are some other questions that employers should look into: (1) Was the period abnormal for any of the countries? (2) Were the strikes peaceful, or were they accompanied by violence, destruction, or death? (3) Were the strikes industrywide, or were they only against selected employers? (4) Were the strikes wildcat (unannounced), or was there usually warning that they were coming? and (5) Do the unions and the workers abide by labor agreements, and if not, what can the employer do?

Companies planning to invest in the traditional-society LDCs will examine the cultural, religious, tribal, and other factors discussed elsewhere. Of course, religious, racial, and linguistic schisms are not confined to LDCs. Among the developed countries where such problems exist are Belgium, Canada, Ireland, and Spain; and the United States is not free of racial disturbances. In addition to these matters, would-be employers will study the organizations of laborers.

Labor Unions: European, American, and Japanese

labor unions
Organizations of workers

European **labor unions** are usually identified with political parties and socialist ideology. A sense of worker identity is common in these unions, probably because European labor gained freedom from feudalism as well as various rights and powers through collective action.

In the United States, on the other hand, laborers already possessed many civil rights, including the vote, by the time unions became important. As a result, unionism in the United States has been more pragmatic than political and more concerned with the immediate needs of the workers.[23]

Labor legislation in the United States mostly confined itself to the framework of collective bargaining. In Europe, government's role is more active, with wages and working conditions frequently legislated. Many Latin American governments are very active in employer-employee relationships, frequently because the unions are weak and the union leaders are inexperienced or uneducated.

In West Germany and France, the influences of law and government administrative actions are more extensive and evident. Labor negotiations are conducted on national or at least regional levels, and in France, government representatives take part.

Reuters/Bettmann

The strike—labor's weapon of last legal resort.

Membership Trends.   Japanese unions are enterprise-based rather than industrywide and, as a result, tend to identify strongly with the interests of the company. For example, if unions are convinced a high wage increase would hurt the company's competitiveness, they tend not to ask for much of a pay raise. But in at least one industry, that approach has backfired.

During the late 1980s, when the Japanese economy was growing strongly, unions, particularly in the motor sector, did not press for significant wage increases. Instead, they allowed management to channel excess funds into capital equipment to build more cars more efficiently.

Then when the economy slowed down, far from reaping the benefits of their hard work and modest demands during the good years, workers suffered the impact of excess capacity in their industries. With economic growth stalled and the resultant industrial restructuring, unionization has fallen steadily. After falling below 30 percent of the total work force in 1983, union membership declined to 24.2 percent in 1993.[24]

As you can see in Figure 12–4, the union membership trend in most industrialized countries is down. If this continues, we can expect to see declines in the economic and political powers of organized labor.

Multinational Labor Activities

The internationalization of business has been under way for many years, and international companies have expanded rapidly since the 1950s. National unions have begun to perceive opportunities for companies to escape the organizing reach of unions by the relatively simple step of transferring to or commencing production in another country. And the unions see such steps as dangers.

To combat those dangers, national unions have begun to (1) collect and disseminate information about companies, (2) consult with unions in other countries, (3) coordinate with those unions' policies and tactics in dealing with some specific companies, and (4) encourage international companies' codes of conduct. Such multinational labor activity is likely to increase, although unions are divided by ideological differences and are frequently strongly nationalistic. Vastly more effort and money have been spent on

FIGURE 12–4 Trade-Union Membership*

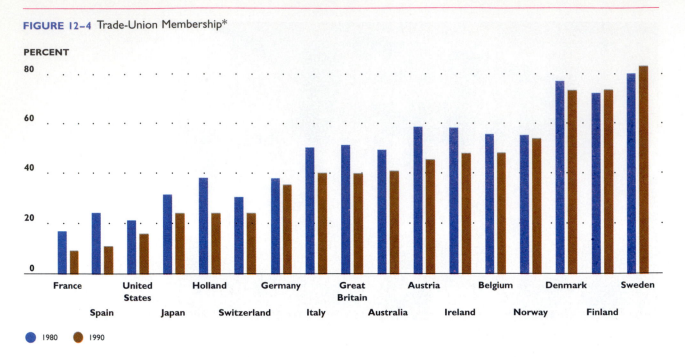

PERCENT

The influence of trade unions declined in most industrial countries during the 1980s, after rising in the previous decade. In 15 of the 17 OECD countries in the chart, union members made up a smaller share of the work force in 1990 than they had done 10 years before. Finland and Sweden were the two exceptions. Trade-union power suffered the biggest decline in Spain, where membership fell from 25 percent to 11 percent during the decade. Union membership was lowest in France: in 1990 only 10 percent of French workers belonged to a trade union. Swedish workers were the most likely to belong: 83 percent of them were union members in 1990. On average, trade-union membership in OECD countries fell by 6.4 percentage points during the period.

*As a percentage of wage-earners.

Source: *The Economist*, July 23, 1994, p. 102.

lobbying for protection of national industries than on cooperating with unions in other countries.

Some developments that occurred in 1980 demonstrate, however, that cooperation is possible. The Geneva-based International Union of Food and Allied Workers Association coordinated a boycott of Coca-Cola in Sweden, Spain, Mexico, and Finland. The cause of the boycott was alleged "antilabor practices" by the Coca-Cola franchise holder in Guatemala.

The International Metalworkers Federation asked West European governments to use their economic power against International Telephone & Telegraph Corporation (ITT) because it wanted changes in ITT's "personnel and social policies."

The first important arena in which successful multinational unionism may develop is the European Union. The EU member-countries are steadily eliminating or harmonizing their tariffs, taxes, monetary systems, laws, and much more. The resulting atmosphere will be more hospitable for the cooperation of national unions.

Also working in this area is the European Trade Union Confederation (ETUC), an umbrella organization of 15 pan-European industry committees representing 39 national union federations. One ETUC official is not very optimistic about the strength of the EU's social action program for labor, which he says is at best a "rubber sword."

However, some ETUC member-unions are doing very well on their own, cooperating across borders in pursuit of a common goal. For four months, the Federation of European Metalworkers (FEM) supported a strike against

British Aerospace (BAe) demanding a shorter workweek. BAe is part of the European Airbus consortium that supplies wings for the planes. The strike cost the consortium an estimated $200 million.

Settlement of the strike won a 37-hour workweek for the members of Amalgamated Engineering, a British union. Demonstrating cross-border union cooperation during the strike, the German engineering union, IG Metall, made financial donations to the British strikers. FEM's aim is for a standard workweek for its six million members in 16 European countries.[25]

The American union federation, the AFL–CIO, cooperates with LDC labor in three organizations: the African-American Labor Center; the American Institute for Free Labor Development for Latin America; and the Asian-American Free Labor Institute.

Codetermination

Europe, particularly Germany, is in the vanguard of another labor development, which, at first sight, horrified many business managers and owners. Laws were adopted that required employees to be given seats on the employer boards of directors.

It Began in Germany. Worker participation in management, frequently called **codetermination**, began in the German coal and steel industries in 1951. The law gave worker and shareholder representatives each 50 percent of the directorships. A neutral board member selected by both sides breaks any deadlocks, but that vote has rarely been needed, as labor and shareholder representatives usually resolve their differences.

codetermination
Participation by workers in a company's management

The 50-50 system was extended to all large German industry by a 1976 law that was challenged in court by German employers but upheld by the German high court.

It Has Spread. Other European countries and Japan either have or are seriously discussing codetermination-type legislation or practices. In the United States, neither business nor labor showed much enthusiasm for codetermination until the late 1970s. However, things are changing in the United States, where the terms *industrial democracy* and *worker participation* are sometimes used.

Developments in the United States. During the late 1970s and into the 1980s, the concept of industrial democracy spread in America. Both Chrysler Corporation and American Motors have had United Automobile Workers (UAW) officers as members of their boards of directors. Workers at General Motors get together in "quality circles" to help make decisions about their jobs and production quality. The Communications Workers of America signed a contract in August 1980 with American Telephone & Telegraph that included worker participation concepts. New labor contracts in the steel, rubber, oil, paper, glass, aerospace, food processing, and electrical products industries contain similar concepts. In addition, hundreds of large and small nonunion employers have adopted their own versions of industrial democracy; among these are IBM and Texas Instruments.[26]

Not everyone in the United States is pleased with worker participation (see the quotation at the beginning of this chapter). When Douglas Fraser, the UAW president, was elected to Chrysler's board in 1980, there were fears in labor and management that the conflicts between the two jobs were too great.

In his efforts to sell a new Chrysler contract to the UAW rank and file, Fraser reversed the typical charge of labor leaders—that management is bargaining in bad faith when it claims it cannot afford fatter wage and benefit offers. Fraser took just the opposite tack and chided the Chrysler chairman for painting too rosy a picture of Chrysler's finances. He even said that Chrysler's reported profits were based in part on financial "manipulations."

As a result, neither the UAW nor Chrysler management was happy with Fraser. Some union members felt he had not squeezed the company hard enough; management feared his talk of financial weakness and manipulation would hurt the company's reputation with its bankers and the investment community.[27]

Despite misgivings by both the UAW and Chrysler, Fraser was replaced on the carmaker's board by his successor as UAW president, Owen F. Bieber. Even though Bieber kept a lower profile than had Fraser, his board seat was one of five eliminated by Chrysler in 1991.

Joseph Blasi, who studies labor issues at Rutgers University, sums up American business and labor attitudes toward codetermination as follows: "American management seems to be very lukewarm about the idea, and American unions seem to be totally uninterested except when they own big portions of the company. So there is no one asking for it."[28]

Workers of the World

Some worldwide comparisons are interesting. How much does labor cost throughout the world and what percentage of the labor force is unemployed? Figure 12–5 shows labor costs in 19 countries, while Table 12–1 gives unemployment percentages by quarter from 1991.2 through 1994.1 for seven countries.

FIGURE 12–5 Labor Costs*

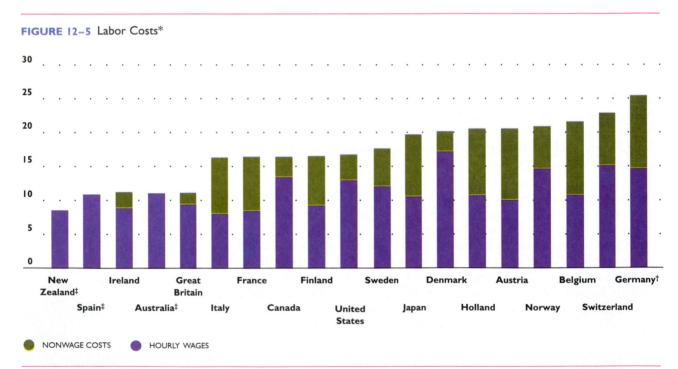

NONWAGE COSTS   HOURLY WAGES

Companies manufacturing in Western Germany have to bear higher hourly labor costs than in any other country, according to an international survey by the Swedish Employers' Confederation. In 1993, an average West German manufacturer paid total labor costs, including wages, holidays, benefits, and social-security contributions, of $25.59 an hour. New Zealand had the lowest costs of the 19 countries in the chart: an hour of manufacturing labor there cost only $8.01, less than one-third of the cost in Germany. Spain had the lowest labor costs of the 14 European countries, at $11.55 an hour. Nonwage costs made up the highest share of the total in Austria and Italy (50 percent), and the lowest share in Denmark (18 percent).

*Total labor costs in manufacturing for 1993: US$ per hour.
†Western.
‡Breakdown not available.

Source: *The Economist*, August 27, 1994, p. 98.

TABLE 12-1 Standardized unemployment rates (percent)*

	1991.2	1991.3	1991.4	1992.1	1992.2	1992.3	1992.4	1993.1	1993.2	1993.3	1993.4	1994.1
Canada	10.3	10.3	10.3	10.6	11.2	11.5	11.5	10.9	11.3	11.3	11.0	11.0
France	9.4	9.7	9.9	10.1	10.3	10.4	10.7	11.1	11.5	11.9	12.3	12.5
Germany	4.2	4.3	4.2	4.3	4.5	4.6	4.9	5.3	5.6	5.9	6.3	6.5
Italy	10.0	9.6	9.9	9.9	9.9	10.1	9.3	9.1	10.7	10.3	10.7	10.8
Japan	2.1	2.1	2.1	2.0	2.1	2.2	2.3	2.3	2.4	2.5	2.8	2.8
United Kingdom	8.6	9.1	9.3	9.5	9.7	10.1	10.4	10.5	10.3	10.4	10.0	9.9
United States	6.7	6.7	6.9	7.2	7.4	7.4	7.2	7.0	6.9	6.7	6.5	6.5

*The unemployment rates are reported by the governments of the countries after they are constructed from different definitions. In these standardized rates, however, the unemployed are all persons of working age who are without work, available for work, or seeking work either through registration at employment offices or other means. Total labor force is used as denominator.

Source: OECD, Main Economic Indicators.

SUMMARY

1. **Recognize forces beyond management control that affect the availability of labor.** Labor quality and labor quantity are beyond a company's control. There is a finite number of employees available in any labor pool with the skills required to meet an employer's needs.

2. **Understand the political and economic reasons that cause people to flee their home countries.** In many parts of the world, wars, revolutions, racial and ethnic battles, and political repression cause people to flee. They are political refugees. Others, known as economic refugees, go to other countries in hopes of better jobs and pay.

3. **Explain why refugees are a source of labor but frequently a burden for the countries to which they flee.** When refugees arrive, they usually need jobs but frequently lack the education, skills, strength, or health to perform available jobs, if any. They become education and welfare burdens.

4. **Discuss guest workers and problems that may develop because of them.** Guest workers are invited to a host country to perform specific types of jobs, usually in service, factory, or construction work. But when a country's economy slows, its native workers may want those jobs held by guest workers. In addition, racial friction has developed in some countries because of guest workers.

5. **Explain how the composition of a country's labor force affects productivity.** Workers come with all sorts of skills or abilities or without them. The better they are, the more productive they can be.

6. **Understand women's positions in labor forces.** From the mid-1970s, more and more women have entered the work force in most industrialized countries. Because of obstacles such as discrimination and changes in lifestyles, the growth of their numbers slowed in the 1990s. But acceptability of women in the work force is virtually nil in many other countries.

7. **Name other forces that affect productivity.** Productivity is affected by several forces other than workers' skills. Savings in a country can be invested in research and development, which results in better capital equipment for the workers. A country's tax policies can also influence how much money is available for R&D and other investments.

8. **Discuss differences in labor unions from country to country.** Labor unions tend to be more political in Europe and more pragmatic in the United States. They are losing membership in most of the industrial countries.

9. **Understand how labor is getting a voice in management.** Labor participation in management, called codetermination, has grown in Europe, Japan, and later, the United States. Industrial democracy and worker participation has recently spread in America. This has involved labor-management cooperation, in some instances including union officials as members of companies' boards of directors.

KEY WORDS

- labor quality   378
- labor quantity   378
- labor mobility   378
- refugees   379
- guest workers   381
- labor force composition   384
- labor productivity   385

- unit labor costs   385
- traditional societies   391
- minorities   391
- labor market   392
- labor unions   392
- codetermination   395

QUESTIONS

1. *a.* How could an excess of qualified employees be beneficial for an employer?
   b. How could it be detrimental?

2. Classical economists assumed the labor factor of production to be immobile. Is this assumption correct in the modern world? Explain.

3. What are some differences between labor that moves as do guest workers and labor that moves as do political or economic refugees?

4. What is the effect on productivity of the influx into the work force of inexperienced, unskilled workers?

5. What effects do the levels of a country's savings have on its relative competitiveness?

6. In several Southeast Asian and South Pacific countries, the Chinese minority is prominent in banking, finance, and business. What are the dangers for a foreign employer staffing the local company primarily with such a minority?

7. What is a major difference between European and American unions?

8. How do the Germans do job sharing? Is their method cutting down unemployment? Explain.

9. What are the prospects for effective multinational union collaboration? Discuss.

10. *a.* What is codetermination?
    b. Has codetermination worked well? Discuss.

MINICASE 12–1   Racism

Your company, an American IC, has decided to expand aggressively in Asia. It plans to source much of its raw materials, to subcontract, and to manufacture and market throughout Asia, from Japan in the north through New Zealand in the south.

You were appointed to organize and direct this major new effort and to determine where to locate the regional headquarters for the Asian Division. After considerable study, you selected the island nation of Luau.

Luau's advantages are several. It is about equidistant between New Zealand and Japan. It was a British colony, so the main language is English. It has a relatively efficient telephone and telegraph system and good air service to all the major Asian destinations in which you are interested and to the United States.

Not least important, the Luau government is delighted to have your company locate and invest there. It has made very attractive tax concessions to the company and to its personnel who will move there.

The company moves in, leases one large building, and puts out invitations to bid on the construction of a larger

building, which will be its permanent headquarters. Now, as you begin to work much more with the private banking and businesspeople of Luau and less with government officials, you begin to be more aware of a Luau characteristic about which you had not thought much previously. Almost all of the middle- and upper-management personnel in the business and finance sector are of Chinese extraction. The native population of Luau, which is the great majority, is a Micronesian race.

On inquiring why the Chinese are dominant in banking and business while the Micronesians stay with farming, fishing, government, and manual labor, you are told that this is the way it developed historically. The Chinese enjoy and are good at banking and business, while the native Luauans do not like those activities and have stayed with their traditional pastimes. The two groups buy and sell from and to each other, but there are almost no social relations and very little business or professional overlap between the groups. Occasionally, some of the Micronesians study abroad, and some work abroad for periods; when they return, they frequently go to work in a bank or business or take a government position.

You must staff your headquarters with middle- and lower-management people and with clerical help. You find that the only applicants for the jobs are Chinese, and you select the best available. They are quite satisfactory, and the operation gets off to a good start.

Then, as the months pass, you notice a gradual change of attitude toward you and the company among the government officials and among the people in general. They have become less friendly, more evasive, and less cooperative. You ask your Chinese staff about it, but they have noticed nothing unusual.

What could be happening? Why might the Chinese staff not notice it? What might you do to improve government and public relations?

CHAPTER

13

Competitive and Distributive Forces

> *If there is a single great fact of our era, it is the emergence of the first truly international marketplace and the struggle between the leading trading nations and blocs: the United States, Western Europe, Japan, Singapore–Taiwan–Hong Kong–Korea, Mexico–Brazil, and, potentially, China.*
>
> *Paraphrased from H. Lewis and D. Allison, The Real War: The Coming Battle for the New Global Economy and Why We Are in Danger of Losing*

CONCEPT PREVIEWS

After reading this chapter, you should be able to:

1. **explain** why international competition has increased among the United States, Japan, the EU, and Asian nations

2. **understand** the purpose of the keiretsu in Japanese industry

3. **appreciate** the importance of foreign direct investment on the American trade position

4. **describe** the responsibilities of government, management, labor, and consumers in maintaining the international competitiveness of the United States

5. **explain** the competitive environment in Japan, EU, and the developing nations, including the NIEs

6. **appreciate** the magnitude of product counterfeiting

7. **understand** the importance of industrial espionage

8. **describe** the sources of competitive information

9. **discuss** the channel members available to companies that export indirectly or directly or manufacture overseas

10. **explain** the structural trends in wholesaling and retailing

War and Corporate Sleuthing

THIS IS WAR! At least it is according to William Peacock, former assistant secretary of the U.S. Army and a colonel in the Marine Corps Reserve. He says that although society sets up rules to prevent unfair practices, and the objective is not to destroy your competitors, business and war have much in common. Executives should apply the nine principles of war (MOOSEMUSS) that have always brought victorious military campaigns: (1) *Mass*—concentrate your strength at the enemy's weak point. (2) *Objective*—be clear as to what you want to accomplish. (3) *Offense*—few competitions are won by passivity. (4) *Simplicity*—make your own strategy simple and clear for your employees. (5) *Economy of force*—the fewest resources possible to keep the operation functioning. (6) *Maneuver or strategy used*—frontal, flanking, or rear assault. (7) *Unity of command*—clear assignments of responsibility. (8) *Surprise*—timing of battle. (9) *Security*—keep your strategy secret. • It is apparent that many chief executives, a number of whom have military training, are following these concepts. Companies go to great lengths to keep their plans secret: IBM, for example, has a sign posted in its offices that shows two people at a lunch table and a warning, "Be careful in casual conversation. Keep security in mind." And, like the military, many have installed intelligence systems. Motorola, seeking a full-scale intelligence effort, hired a former CIA agent to organize its program. Its intelligence efforts paid off. • The company's top managers, in a meeting with the corporate intelligence people and European managers, raised the question, "Are you concerned about Japanese semiconductor makers?" One European manager said, "We see the Japanese—they have operations in Europe. But they're not aggressive." This prompted the intelligence staff to wonder why the Japanese weren't as aggressive with semiconductors as they were with VCRs and TVs. Motorola sent one of its intelligence staff, fluent in Japanese, to Tokyo. By visiting the U.S. embassy and various government offices, he learned that Japanese electronic manufacturers did plan within the next two years to double their capital investment in Europe for semiconductor plants, not for more VCR and TV plants. With this information, Motorola changed its strategy and began to work more closely with European manufacturers and customers and to compete vigorously with the Japanese for more partnerships in Europe. As a result, the company increased its market share even though the Japanese had begun their European assault.

Sources: "Motorola Illustrates How an Aged Giant Can Remain Vibrant," *The Wall Street Journal*, December 9, 1992, p. A1; William Peacock, *Corporate Combat* (Berkeley, CA: Berkeley Publishing, 1987), pp. 1–12; P. Kotler and G. Armstrong, *Principles of Marketing*, 4th ed. (Englewood Cliffs, NJ: Prentice-Hall, 1989), p. 93; "Competitive Intelligence Efforts on the Rise," *Marketing Communications*, January 20, 1987, p. 5; and "Corporate Spies Snoop to Conquer," *Fortune*, November 7, 1988, p. 76.

FIGURE 13-1
Intratriad trade, 1992
(billions of dollars)

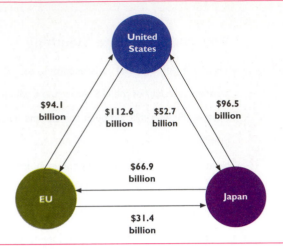

Source: *Basic Statistics of the Community* (Luxembourg: Eurostat, 1994), p. 310.

You may recall from Chapter 2 that developed nations account for three-fourths of (1) the world's international trade and (2) foreign direct investment. If so, you will understand why Kenichi Ohmae of the consulting firm McKinsey & Co. contends that for an international firm to compete in world markets, it must be present in at least two and preferably all three parts of a triad composed of the United States, Japan, and what is now the European Union.[1] Note that the triad includes nearly all of the world's developed countries, which are not only much larger markets (80 percent of the world's GNP) than are the developing nations, but also have business climates (political, financial, and legal forces) that are more favorable to business and are predictable. Figure 13–1 shows the trade patterns of the triad.

Recently, another group of countries has emerged to become a fourth important region, with a combined GDP of $1 billion. This group includes the newly industrialized economies (NIEs) in East Asia, consisting of the "Asian tigers" (South Korea, Taiwan, Hong Kong, and Singapore), and the two newly industrializing countries (NICs), Malaysia and Thailand.

Although it is true that Japan has invested heavily in the Asian Pacific nations and thus is well represented in that region, it is overly simplistic to think of Japan and the Asian NIEs as one trading bloc. In fact, our method of considering only two groups in the Pacific as being in competition is not completely adequate. Consider this. There are extremely strong trade flows (1) among the Asian NIEs themselves and (2) between these nations and members of the Association of South East Asian Nations (ASEAN).* For example, Asian NIEs export more to other Asian NIEs and ASEAN nations than they export to Japan. Firms from Asian NIEs are also important investors in ASEAN members.

In addition, a division of labor no longer exists just between Japan and the Asian countries or Japan and the ASEAN nations. Significant differences in labor costs have also developed among the Asian NICs and NIEs and between the Asian NIEs and the ASEAN nations. Rising labor costs in South Korea, for

---

*One of the Asian NIEs, Singapore, and the two emerging NICs, Malaysia and Thailand, are also members of ASEAN.

example, have forced some manufacturers to move to countries with lower labor costs, such as Indonesia.

> A South Korean company produces shoes under contract for Nike, L.A. Gear, and Reebok in its Indonesian plant. The owners used to make the shoes in Korea, but they moved the plant to Indonesia when Korean wages rose to $800 per month compared to the $40 per month being paid in China and Indonesia—about what the Koreans earned in the 1970s.
>
> Nike, which has no production facilities of its own, pays the manufacturer $5.60 per pair for the shoes that the company retails for prices ranging from $50 to $175. Indonesian factory workers receive 15 cents an hour. Interestingly, only New Balance, Saucony, and Van produce athletic shoes in the United States.[2]

These are some of the reasons we believe an examination of the uncontrollable competitive forces is more revealing if we study them using the four-entity format mentioned previously. Let us now examine the competition among the United States, the European Union, Japan, and the developing nations plus the NIEs.

In the 1980s, there was great concern in the United States and Europe over the ability of these nations to compete in world markets. Recently, the strong yen has caused the same uneasiness in Japan. Nations, of course, do not compete against each other; their companies do. However, because most economic and social conditions, as well as political actions, affect the ability of all of a nation's firms to compete in world markets, it is convenient to speak of **national (macro) competitiveness**.

COMPETITION AT THE MACRO LEVEL (NATIONAL COMPETITIVENESS)

national (macro) competitiveness
Ability of a nation's producers to compete successfully in world markets and with imports in their own domestic markets

United States

Although the lag in national competitiveness did not become apparent until the 1980s, it began in the 1970s. During that time, imports were getting a bigger share of the market, but they were offset by a growing share of the export market achieved with a dollar whose value was dropping relative to other major currencies at an average annual rate of 2.5 percent. However, when the dollar's value rose at the beginning of the 1980s, American unit labor costs mounted, causing imports to increase and U.S. exports to decrease; not until 1985—when the dollar's value again declined—did labor costs begin to fall and American exports become more price competitive.[3]

During these years, American firms first experienced growing competition in this country from European and Japanese firms that were buying U.S. firms because the cheap dollar made them inexpensive in those countries' currencies. Moreover, the size of the American market, the availability of raw materials, the developed capital markets, and the political stability combined to attract massive foreign investment, which created new competitors and strengthened old ones. From 1980 to 1984, foreign companies were acquiring 150 or fewer U.S. firms each year, at a maximum cost of $10 billion annually; but they bought 197 companies in 1985, 264 in 1986, 220 in 1987, and 307 in 1988. The dollar totals rose from $11 billion in 1985 to $55 billion in 1988.[4] Some of their more notable purchases are shown in Table 13–1.

As the value of the dollar rose and American firms experienced difficulty competing in both the U.S. and overseas markets, protectionist sentiment grew in this country, which provided additional impetus for foreign investors to set up U.S.-based operations. Figure 13–2 illustrates how U.S. firms lost domestic market share during the 1980s.

Target	Acquirer	Date	Value ($ billions)
Carnation	Nestlé (Swiss)	1984	$3.00
Chesebrough-Pond's	Unilever (U.K.-Dutch)	1986	3.10
Firestone	Bridgestone (Japan)	1987	2.65
Standard Oil	British Petroleum (U.K.)	1987	7.40
Celanese	Hoechst (Germany)	1987	2.72
Pillsbury	Grand Metropolitan (U.K.)	1988	5.76
Columbia Pictures	Sony Corp. (Japan)	1989	3.45
Holiday Inn	Bass (U.K.)	1989	2.00
MCA	Matushita Electric (Japan)	1990	6.60

Of course, when the dollar again fell in the late 1980s, foreign firms that were still supplying this market with exports found it difficult to compete pricewise with domestic products, and thus they too established production in the United States. Those that did not lost either sales or profits if they cut prices to remain competitive. Japanese exporters of high-technology items, including automobiles, electronics, and computers, lost over 40 percent of their profits as they tried to meet U.S. prices in face of a yen that rose from 260 per dollar to 123 in just two years.[5]

Although the overvalued dollar was one of the principal reasons for the decrease in American competitiveness, it was not the only one. A number of nonprice factors, such as quality, delivery time, after-sales service, reliability of supply, and trade barriers to U.S. exports, were also responsible. It was obvious that to increase American exports, corrective measures had to be taken by government, management, and labor.

Government.   One measure that U.S. government officials have taken is to threaten retaliation if other governments fail to remove trade barriers to American exports. Japan, which has had $50 billion annual trade surpluses with the United States for the last decade ($55 billion in 1994), is constantly being pressured by American trade officials to lower its nontariff barriers that prevent U.S. firms from doing business in that country.

> For years, the Japanese government had kept Motorola from having full access to Japan's cellular-telephone market, despite a U.S.-Japanese agreement that promises the company an open market. In February 1994, when U.S. trade representative Mickey Cantor discussed the case with the Japanese government without results, American officials said openly that the government would declare Japan in violation of the cellular trade deal, the first step in imposing trade sanctions.[6] Just one month later, Japan agreed to take measures to improve the company's access to the market. According to Motorola's Tokyo director of government relations, the personal involvement of the American ambassador to Japan, Walter Mondale, was critical in getting the agreement.[7]

The U.S. government has also used the threat of retaliation to try to eliminate another barrier to American exports in Asia—the competition from illegal copies of U.S. products. Various industry associations estimate that the rightful patent owners lose billions of dollars in sales every year. According to U.S. estimates, the cost of Chinese copyright violations of compact discs, software, and movies alone amounted to nearly $1 billion in 1993. Although China had enacted laws to protect U.S. copyrights, patents, and trademarks, it had not made any serious efforts to crack down on violators; hence, in December 1994 American officials suspended talks on the issue, and threatened to invoke Super 301, as discussed below. American and European

FIGURE 13–2 U.S. firms' share of U.S. market

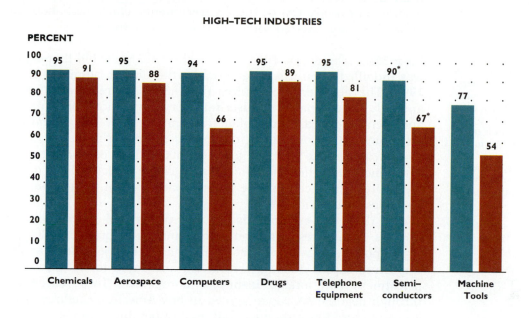

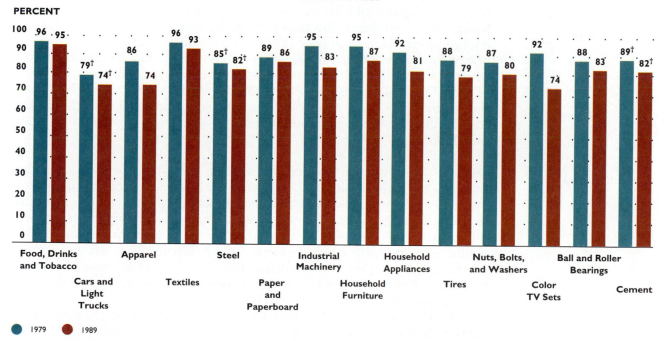

*Merchant producers only.
†Measured in units rather than dollars.

Source: *Fortune*, September 24, 1990, p. 64.

members of GATT had already rejected China's request to be admitted as a founding member of GATT's successor, the World Trade Organization, for the same reason.[8] In February, 1995, China agreed to shut down the sellers and manufacturers of pirated products, bar their export, prohibit the use of pirated products in government offices, and ensure a swift resolution of intellectual property court cases.[9]

The threat of retaliation against Taiwan and Korea has produced somewhat better results. Both have not only enacted laws to protect American patents, but unlike China, these governments, concerned about the effect of Super 301, have exerted some effort to enforce them.

Super 301
Section 301 of the U.S. 1988 Trade Act, renewed by the Clinton administration in March 1994; requires U.S. trade representative to prepare list of unfair trade practices of foreign countries; after one year of unsuccessful negotiation with offending country, the United States can impose punitive tariffs

Super 301.   The **Super 301** clause of the 1988 trade bill that expired in 1990 was modified when it was renewed by the Clinton administration in March 1994. The new version requires the U.S. trade representative to examine annually unreasonable or discriminatory restrictions on American exports and then prepare a list of unfair trade practices of foreign countries. Within six months, the government designates the worst practices on the list and begins to negotiate with the governments of these countries to change them. After one year, if the offending country has not rectified the unfair practice, the United States can impose punitive tariffs equal to the estimated value of lost sales by U.S. firms.[10]

In 1989, for example, Japan was designated specifically for resisting imports of satellites, supercomputers, and forest products; Brazil for requiring import licenses to protect local industry (90 percent of applications for importing capital goods are refused); and India for its barriers to foreign investment and foreign insurance companies. These cases were settled through negotiation. Japan agreed to buy American satellites, supercomputers, and more forest products but less timber, for instance.[11]

Since renewing Super 301, the United States has used it to threaten both China and Japan with little success. The Clinton administration threatened to invoke Super 301 during the 1994 talks with Japan, but at the last moment, it backed down, claiming to have reached a satisfactory agreement.[12] However, one of Japan's structural impediments to U.S. exports that has not been been resolved to the United States' satisfaction is the **keiretsu**. A keiretsu is a group of firms financially connected that tend to do business with themselves rather than with others. Both American businesspeople and trade officials contend the keiretsu system contributes greatly to the huge Japanese-U.S. trade imbalance.[13]

keiretsu
A group of financially connected Japanese firms that tend to do business among themselves

Keiretsu.   There are various forms of *keiretsu*, but two of the most important from the U.S. standpoint are (1) the vertically integrated production group as found in all the major Japanese automakers and (2) the horizontal group that is the present-day version of the pre-war *zaibatsu*. Although these family-owned conglomerates were broken up by the Allies after World War II, they continue to operate in much the same way because the Japanese government has never enforced the antimonopoly laws. This kind of keiretsu has a large bank at its core, and member-companies own minority interests in each other. Mitsui, Mitsubishi, Sumitomo, and Marubeni are examples.[14]

The U.S. government maintains that keiretsu groups construct informal barriers to the sale of foreign goods in Japan. A keiretsu such as the Toyota keiretsu can assemble an automobile from parts supplied only by keiretsu members, for example. This makes it nearly impossible for potential suppliers outside the keiretsu to obtain business from Toyota. Many fear that Japanese firms are using the keiretsu system in the United States. Ford's head of component operations complains that the Japanese still buy too many parts from Japanese suppliers that have set up operations in the United States and not enough parts from American firms.[15] Over 250 Japanese suppliers have set up U.S. plants to serve eight Japanese auto plants.[16]

Other efforts of the government to improve U.S. competitiveness include (1) stricter enforcement of dumping laws, (2) focusing on improvement of the nation's educational system, and (3) working to complete deregulation of industry (as an example from the trucking industry, a Dallas retailer pays less transportation costs to import a pair of jeans from Taiwan than it does to bring them in from Texas manufacturers in El Paso).

Government Must Do More.   Critics point out that more must be done. Some economists believe the most significant action the government can take to reduce the trade deficit is to lower the federal budget deficit, thereby decreasing the amount of savings consumed by the government. This would result in lower interest rates, which would enable American firms to pay less for loans to expand production facilities and purchase more technologically advanced equipment. But others claim that a trade deficit was created because the U.S. demand for imports when its economy was strong was greater than the volume of American exports that the less robust foreign economies could buy.

The Competitiveness Policy Council, a panel created by Congress as part of the Trade Act of 1988, says the government must reform its policies concerning taxes, technology, education, trade, and health care. The council recommends the federal government issue competitiveness impact statements for each bill it submits to Congress. The Trade Act mandated the competitiveness statements for a six-year trial period, but both the administration and Congress have ignored the requirement. The panel also recommends that American intelligence agencies be authorized to collect information on foreign competitors.[17]

Another measure suggested is to eliminate the double taxation of company profits. If shareholders' dividends aren't taxed, proponents say, more will be invested in America's industries. They want capital gains taxes brought back for the same reason. Some say the United States must have a national economic plan, but others compare this country's economic preference with that of countries having plans and say the less government involvement, the better. Legal experts recommend changes in U.S. antitrust laws to permit firms to finance, construct, and operate expensive high-tech production facilities jointly without fear of an antitrust suit. Such arrangements are becoming commonplace in Europe and Japan.

Research consortia are permitted in the United States, however, and in fact, the government is encouraging their formation. More than 100 research consortia have been formed by U.S. firms to foster development of products ranging from computers to light bulbs.[18]

Industrial Targeting.   The government can also do more to support American companies that face competition from targeted industries. **Industrial targeting,** the practice of government assisting selected industries to grow by a variety of means, is becoming common in Europe and Japan. France, for example, modernized its railroad construction industry by modernizing its rail system. Equipment contracts were given only to French suppliers. By building a strong home base first, French suppliers were ready for the export market. Increasingly, the U.S. mass transit market is being dominated by the French and Japanese, both of whose governments support target industries.

Another industry targeted by European nations is the production of commercial aircraft. Airbus Industrie, a consortium of French, German, British, and Spanish aircraft manufacturers, produce the parts that are then assembled in a giant hangar in Hamburg, Germany. Since the consortium began operations in 1970, it has received $13.5 billion in government aid. A Boeing official stated that the "Airbus was allowed to start a program without a sufficient order base and at production rates that would force a U.S. manufacturer to shut down."[19] In 1992, President Bush reached an agreement with the Europeans to limit their aid to loans of up to 33 percent of a plane's

industrial targeting
Government practice of assisting selected industries to grow

Succeeding in Japan against the Japanese

Applied Materials, one of the few manufacturers of computer-chip-making machinery left in the United States, has resisted Japanese competitors with a fortress strategy of defending its position in established markets while it moved into new ones. In 1980, the firm was small, with global sales of just $69 million, but by 1993, its sales had grown to $1.08 billion.

Beginning in the 1980s, Applied Materials built a fortress based on a market plan of three components: (1) management vision and its impact on the industry, the firms' customers, and its competitors; (2) thinking globally while acting locally; and (3) marketing strategies that enable the firm to maintain close contact with its customers.

Before formulating its vision, management looked backward to the 1970s to learn from the mistakes of the machine tools and consumer electronics industries that led to their being crushed by their Japanese competitors. Looking ahead, executives found that builders of chip-making machinery in the United States were predicted to fall from a dominant position in the market to less than 40 percent, while the Japanese market share would rise to 54 percent.

In preparing a new marketing strategy, management first studied the successes and failures of other firms in their industry that had tried to sell in the global market. From this, the company learned that it was essential to have direct access to the local distribution system and to establish close, continuing relationships with the company's customers. These two objectives were the driving force for the company's fortress strategy.

The company identified Japan as a growing but demanding market requiring special attention. In 1980, its CEO, Jim Morgan, established Applied Materials Japan with seven people in a small room near Tokyo. Most of the personnel were Japanese. His staff spent weeks with Japanese semiconductor manufacturers to learn how to make Allied's machines more suitable. Frequently, the company and its Japanese customer would jointly design a machine.

By 1990, one-third of the company's $567 million in sales were made to Japanese semiconductor manufacturers, compared to another 45 percent bought by American chip makers. The Japanese subsidiary grew to the point where it employs 700 people and has a research lab and a plant for final test and assembly.

How did the company penetrate the protectionist Japanese market? It followed its marketing strategy. Management had learned that the Japanese consider their suppliers as partners. As a result, Morgan would not allow Japanese partners to market his firm's products as his competitors were doing. The decision proved to be a good one; later, the competitors found their partners had dropped their products for Japanese products as soon as they became available. Technology developed by American manufacturers was copied and used by Japanese producers. However, its strategy of maintaining close, continuing relationships with its customers enabled Applied Materials to retain its Japanese customers.

Because of the similarities between the production techniques for making semiconductors and liquid-crystal display screens used in laptop computers, Allied's Japanese customers asked the company to enter this new field. Morgan expects the company will obtain 30 percent of its revenue from LCD equipment by the year 2000.

Sources: "Building a Fortress," *Sales & Marketing Management*, March 1994, pp. 45–46; "The Realist," *Forbes*, May 13, 1991, p. 116; and "U.S. Firm to Sell Gear to Make LCD Screens," *The Wall Street Journal*, September 12, 1991, p. B3.

---

development cost.[20] By 1994, Airbus had taken one-third of the commercial aircraft market and was earning a profit. Partly because of the huge developmental cost involved, Boeing is working on a project with the Airbus partners to design a superjumbo jet.[21]

The U.S. government has also targeted an industry for assistance: producers of flat-panel displays. Using techniques invented by Americans, Japanese industry dominates the manufacture of advanced flat screens used in notebook computers, video games, and control panels in jet aircraft. The Pentagon complains that it can't convince Japanese suppliers to tailor their screens for military equipment, and American computer manufacturers say that Japanese suppliers sometimes withhold their screens, leaving them at a disadvantage with Japanese computer makers.

By offering up to $120 million in matching R&D subsidies to companies that commit their own money for a production facility, the government hopes to persuade firms such as IBM, AT&T, and Xerox to begin flat-screen production. Many established companies say they will not make the private investment required to challenge the Japanese producers.[22] According to the Council on Competitiveness' latest report, displays are the only category of electronic components in which the United States is still losing badly and has made no real progress during the past five years.[23]

Impact of Foreign Direct Investment. It is important to understand the impact that foreign direct investment has on the U.S. trade position. Treasury officials, who in 1993 tried to reduce the American trade deficit by causing a decline in the value of the dollar, failed to understand that much of the trade imbalance is caused by intercompany shipments between overseas parent firms and their U.S. affiliates. It would require a massive devaluation of the dollar to stop such trade. Note the dramatic improvement in the American trade deficit in Table 13–2 when the trade deficit of U.S. affiliates of foreign companies is removed.

The 1992 benchmark survey of the Department of Commerce found that 66.6 percent of U.S. merchandise exports to Japan were made by American affiliates of Japanese firms. They also accounted for 77.4 percent of all U.S. imports from Japan.[24] The American affiliates exported merchandise valued at $41.5 billion to and imported $84.4 billion in goods from Japan, resulting in a U.S. trade deficit with Japan of $42.9 billion. The total trade deficit with Japan was only $47.3 billion. This confirms Professor Encarnation's research findings that ownership of companies in the United States *does* matter. Reich, Clinton's labor secretary, wrote, "It is a mistake to associate these foreign investments by American-owned companies with any result that improves the competitiveness of the United States."[25] Encarnation responded, "I point to the simple fact that so much U.S. trade depends directly on intracompany transactions between the U.S. parents and the majority subsidiaries of American multinationals."[26]

Complaints against the United States. The United States has come under attack from its trading partners for ignoring GATT rules while insisting that GATT's dispute procedure be strengthened. The EU, in its *1994 Report on United States Barriers to Trade and Investment,* complains about the unilateral elements in U.S. trade legislation that are contrary to GATT agreements. An example is the recent renewal of the Super 301 legislation, as discussed previously, after the United States had agreed to a multilateral dispute settlement mechanism during the GATT round in Uruguay. Besides unilater-

	U.S. Merchandise Trade Deficit	Trade Deficit of U.S. Affiliates of Foreign Companies	Trade Position of U.S. Firms	
1980	−$ 25.5	−$ 23.6	−$ 1.9	**TABLE 13–2**
1981	−28.0	−18.2	−9.8	Importance of company ownership on the U.S. merchandise trade deficit ($ billion)
1982	−36.5	−24.1	−12.4	
1983	−67.1	−27.6	−39.5	
1984	−112.5	−42.3	−70.2	
1985	−122.2	−56.9	−65.3	
1986	−145.1	−76.2	−68.9	
1987	−159.6	−95.4	−64.2	
1988	−127.0	−86.0	−41.0	
1989	−115.2	−85.5	−29.7	
1990	−109.0	−90.6	−18.4	
1991	−73.8	−81.3	7.5	
1992	−96.1	−81.0	−15.1	

Source: Joseph G. Carson, chief economist, Dean Witter, and *Survey of Current Business,* July 1994, p. 167.

alism, the EU also raises complaints about (1) the enforcement of U.S. legislation outside U.S. territory, (2) public procurement (buy American and small-business preference), (3) tariff barriers (large U.S. Customs user fees and high tariffs on numerous EU exports), (4) standards, and (5) patent protection laws.[27]

As you can see, the role of the government in improving the competitive position of American industry is significant; however, there is much that management, labor, and the consumers can do.

Management.   In the early 1980s, American managements, jolted by the rapid Japanese penetration of the U.S. market, began to make extensive changes in their firms' operations. The chairman of Chrysler says that when he returned to the United States in 1992 after working in Europe for four years, "the changes in productivity and altered attitude to product quality were just amazing."[28]

There is little question that American manufacturers have dramatically improved product quality and have continued to increase productivity. Although the U.S. growth in productivity over the last two decades is the lowest of the G7 nations, in 1993, it was third highest (1.5 percent) after the United Kingdom (3.2 percent) and Italy (1.9 percent). Japan's growth in 1993 was a *negative* 0.1 percent. In spite of a slower growth rate, the U.S. national productivity (GDP per total employed persons) remains considerably higher than that of all other G7 nations. In 1993, for example, the productivity of Italy and France was about 92 percent of the American level; Japan, at 73 percent, was still the lowest of all G7 countries. Figure 13–3 illustrates that although the U.S. productivity is the highest, its lead is narrowing.

Research.   One area where the U.S. industry lags is in spending on research. Observe in Figure 13–4 that, of the seven major industrialized nations, only the United Kingdom has had a lower growth rate. However, Figure 13–5 demonstrates that the United States spends 50 percent more than Japan on civilian R&D and over three times as much as the other G7 nations when purchasing power parities are considered.

FIGURE 13–3

National productivity (using purchasing power parities), 1973–1993

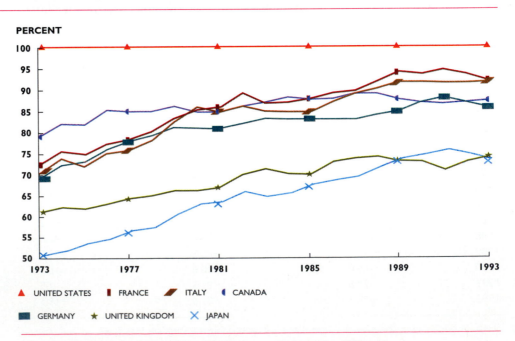

Source: *Competitiveness Index 1994* (Washington, DC: Council on Competitiveness, 1994), p. 16.

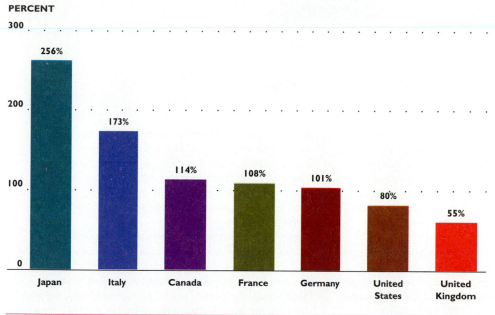

FIGURE 13–4
Growth in industry R&D
expenditures, 1971–1991

Source: *Competitiveness Index 1994* (Washington, DC: Council on Competitiveness, p. 19.

Investment in Plant and Equipment. This is another area where American industry's investment has been weaker than it has been in Japan for the last two decades (Figure 13–6). For example, since 1983, Japan's investment growth rate has increased by 22 percent to the United States' 12 percent. In 1993, though, U.S. investment grew by 11.8 percent while investment in all other G7 nations except Canada actually shrank during depressed economic conditions.[29] Various suggestions are offered for increasing investment in research and new equipment. Because U.S. capital recovery laws are harsher than the laws of most industrial nations, changing the country's tax laws to encourage

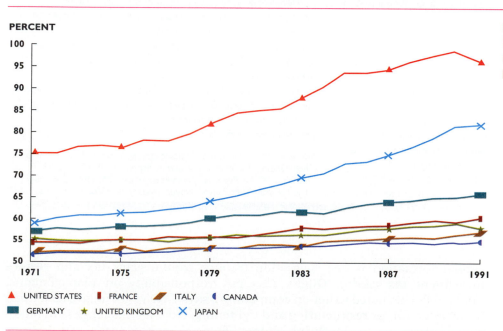

FIGURE 13–5
Investment in civilian R&D
(using purchasing power
parities), 1971–1991

Source: *Competitiveness Index 1994,* (Washington, DC: Council on Competitiveness, 1994), p. 20.

H-P to NEC, "Bonzai!"

In 1993, Hewlett-Packard (H-P), a major American multinational producer of computers, printers, and systems, was challenged by Japan's NEC. Japan's largest computer manufacturer was going to attack H-P's leadership in computer printers in the standard Japanese manner: undercut prices with a new, better product. This is the same strategy used by Japanese manufacturers years ago to take the market from H-P after it had introduced hand-held calculators.

This time the strategy failed. Months before NEC could launch its inexpensive monochrome inkjet printer, Hewlett-Packard had brought to market an improved color version and drastically cut the price by 40 percent of its best-selling black and white printer. NEC withdrew its printer, now overpriced and uncompetitive. The head of Canon's inkjet business explained H-P's success in this way: "H-P understood computers better, it understood American customers better. Japanese makers' culture hindered the kind of quick decision making needed in the fast-paced U.S. computer market."

When Hewlett-Packard marketers began to study the printer market, they knew the company would need a product more technologically advanced than the Oki and Seiko dot matrix printers dominating the printer market. A printer using the inkjet technology accidently discovered by an H-P scientist the year before was the answer. The inkjet printer was cheaper and more easily adaptable for color printing, and nobody else had perfected it.

The quality of the first inkjet H-P made was bad, but because the company believed PC users wanted better quality printouts of text and graphics, its engineers began a process of continual improvement to solve the inkjet's problems. When executives from Epson's U.S. company told their superiors in Japan that PC users would soon demand high-quality printers and that Epson should work on the inkjet technology, the response of Japanese executives was, "Who are these Americans to come over and tell us how to build our products?"

In 1988, H-P introduced the plain-paper inkjet printer, the Deskjet, that was expected to take market share from the Japanese. Instead of being positioned as competition for Japanese dot matrix printers, the Deskjet was competing with the more expensive H-P laser printers and sales were low. In the fall of 1988, H-P managers decided to meet dot matrix printers head

on. They did it with the obsessiveness of a Japanese company. Teams of H-P employees in "Beat Epson" sweatshirts studied Epson marketing practices, surveyed Epson customers, and dismantled Epson printers for engineering and design ideas. They discovered that Epson got a long life from a product by creating a broad product line made up of many variations of one basic printer.

By 1992, Japanese printer makers realized that dot matrix printers were being attacked by inkjets, whose sales were climbing while their sales fell. When they tried to enter the market with their own inkjets, they were stopped by H-P's lock on many important patents. When trying to develop print heads, engineers of the Citizen Watch Company found that H-P had filed so many patents that it was like being in a maze. "You go down this path and suddenly you're into an area that may infringe on their main patents and have to back up and start over," said a vice president of Citizen's U.S. unit.

H-P's economies of scale have allowed it to lower production costs and undercut any competitor's price. Its production experience enabled it to make continual improvements in the manufacturing process. Today's inkjet production costs are half what they were in 1988 when measured in constant dollars. These cost improvements have allowed H-P to carry out this competitive strategy: When a rival attacks, hit back fast and hard. When H-P learned that Canon was going to launch a color inkjet printer in 1993, it cut the price of its own version before the Canon version had come to market.

Hewlett-Packard has 55 percent of the world market for inkjet printers. The company's success with inkjets and laser printers has made it one of the fastest-growing American multinationals. The success of the printer division's mass market approach is causing other H-P divisions to try to make the lowest-cost personal and hand-held computers in the market.

H-P is just one of a number of American firms that are taking back American technologies such as cellular phones, disk drives, computer-chip-making machinery, and pagers that had been previously lost to the Japanese.

Sources: "How H-P Used Tactics of the Japanese to Beat Them at Their Game," *The Wall Street Journal,* September 8, 1994, p. A1; "Here's a PC for Peanuts," *Newsweek,* January 25, 1993, p. 63; and "The Invasion That Failed," *Forbes,* January 20, 1992, pp. 102–3.

---

capital formation is one suggestion (reduce capital gains tax and restore investment tax credit). Others also put responsibility on managements. Michael Porter, noted writer on competition, says, "We've got to give American industry credit for restructuring and tightening. Now the challenge is to build, grow, invest—not to cut, shrink, tighten."[30]

FIGURE 13–6 Investment in plant and equipment

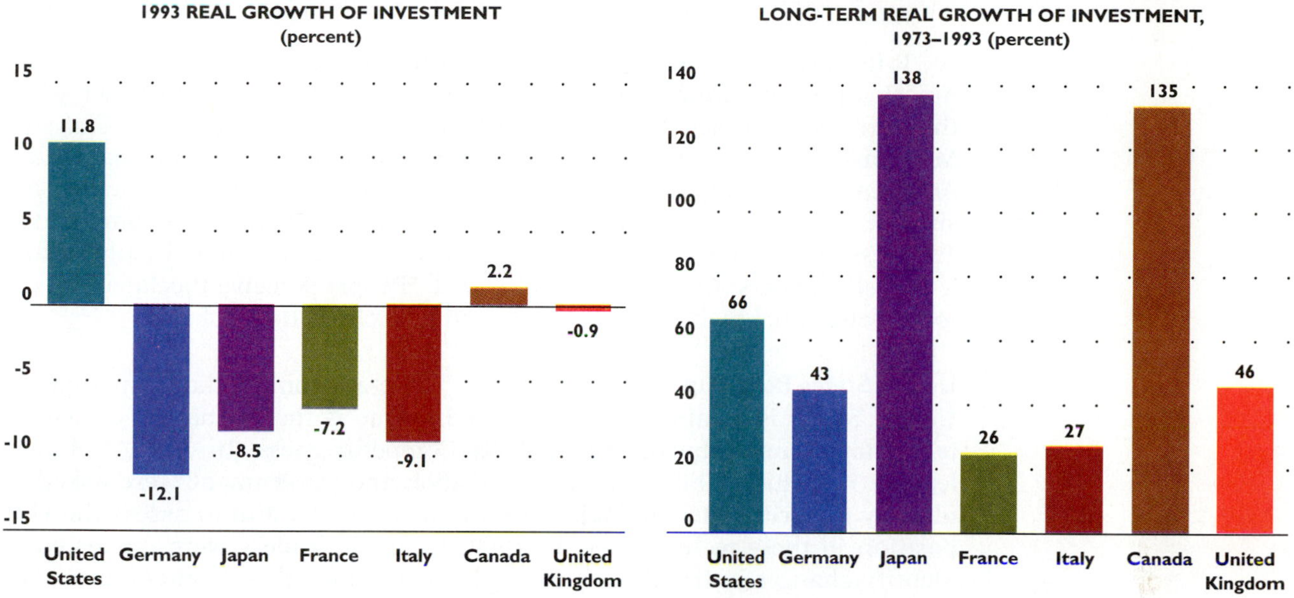

1993 REAL GROWTH OF INVESTMENT
(percent)

United States 11.8
Germany -12.1
Japan -8.5
France -7.2
Italy -9.1
Canada 2.2
United Kingdom -0.9

LONG-TERM REAL GROWTH OF INVESTMENT,
1973–1993 (percent)

United States 66
Germany 43
Japan 138
France 26
Italy 27
Canada 135
United Kingdom 46

Source: *Competitiveness Index 1994* (Washington, DC: Council on Competitiveness, 1994), p. 17.

Labor.　Labor must also take the long-term view, and unions have done so in recent years. There has been a marked increase in their willingness to work with management instead of maintaining the traditional adversarial role. An example is the looser work rules. Workers can be transferred to another workstation when needed and can perform a simple maintenance job instead of calling a maintenance worker to do it while they wait and do nothing. Managers' efforts to share profits and to involve workers in decision making by means of quality circles and shop floor meetings have contributed to this change in attitude.

One of the most important developments in U.S. labor relations is the acceptance by many unions of a more flexible participative approach to replace the traditional adversarial bargaining. An example is the union's agreement to self-managed workplace teams that have already made significant gains in production efficiency at companies such as Ford, Scott Paper, and Xerox.[31]

Consumers.　The U.S. consumer plays a very important part in American industry's drive to improve its competitiveness. Although American automobiles often have cost less than comparable foreign models, for years many American buyers have ignored the price advantage and purchased foreign autos. As a result, the market share of the American companies—General Motors, Ford, and Chrysler—declined to under 70 percent. Now, because of greatly improved quality, superior styling, and an average $3,000 price advantage over Japanese cars, the Big Three has increased its U.S. market share to over 77 percent.[32] Still, there are people who bought foreign products when there was more reason to do so and have continued to buy them even after the reasons no longer exist.

An economist at a Washington think tank, the Brookings Institution, remarked that it was a puzzle that our manufacturing industries need a cheap dollar to be able to sell competitively. "One reason," he said, "may be that some much-improved American products still have a bad reputation." Then, without thinking, the economist confirmed his own suspicion, "I bought a Citation in 1980, and it will be a long time before I buy another Chevy."[33]

It has been exceedingly frustrating to Chrysler dealers, for example, to see American buyers prefer the Mitsubishi Eclipse to the Plymouth Laser when they are identical sports coupes built by Diamondstar Motors, a Chrysler-Mitsubishi joint venture. A *Popular Mechanics* survey found that many Americans say they'd rather buy American rather than Japanese if the cars are similar. Yet, in a case where the cars are identical, not just similar, the Japanese outsells the American car. A dealer who owns both a Mitsubishi and a Chrysler dealership in the same city said, "People perceive the Japanese car to be better quality. It's a lot easier to sell an Eclipse than a Laser."[34]

United States Regaining Competitiveness.   There are some indications that the United States is regaining competitiveness. One is the evaluation of critical technologies made by the Council on Competitiveness. In 1991, technical leaders in industry, higher education, labor, and government were asked to identify the critical technologies driving the economy and to assess the U.S. position in these technologies. In 1994, technical leaders were requested to identify changes in the U.S. competitive position for these technologies. The 94 separate technologies identified were grouped into 26 categories (see Table 13–3) and graded as follows:

1. A (strong)—U.S. industry is in a leading world position, which it is not in danger of losing in the next five years.

2. B (competitive)—U.S. industry is roughly even with the best. This includes technologies in which the United States is leading, but it is uncertain whether leadership will be sustained over next five years.

3. C (weak)—U.S. is behind or likely to fall behind in next five years.

4. D (losing badly or lost)—U.S. industry is no longer a factor or is not likely to be a factor in the next five years. Considerable effort is required for U.S. to become competitive.[35]

Another indication that the United States has regained its competitiveness is the recognition given by the Swiss Business School, IMD, and the World Economic Forum, a Swiss research institute. Their annual *World Competitiveness Report* ranks 41 countries according to 381 criteria, including economic statistics and businesspeoples' opinions of their countries' strengths and weaknesses.[36] Japan, which had ranked first for the past eight years, dropped to third. The United States gained the top position followed by Singapore. The top-ranking countries in the 1994 report were:

1. United States	6. Switzerland
2. Singapore	7. Denmark
3. Japan	8. Netherlands
4. Hong Kong	9. New Zealand
5. Germany	10. Sweden

Finally, statistics on global sales and profits over the 1987–92 period demonstrate that American firms are the leaders or are highly competitive in nearly every major global industry. As Table 13–4 shows, American firms have obtained 37.4 percent of the sales and 47.7 percent of the profits in global markets.

Categories	1991	1994
1. Database systems	A	A
2. Drug discovery techniques and other biotechnologies	A	A
3. Jet and rocket propulsion	A	A
4. Magnetic information storage	A	A
5. Pollution and recycling	A	A
6. Software	A	A
7. Voice recognition and graphics	A	A
8. Computers	A	A
9. Design and engineering tools	B+	B+
10. Portable telecommunications equipment	B+	B+
11. Automotive power trains	B	B
12. Information networks and communications	B	B*
13. Joining and fastening technologies	B	B
14. Superconductors	B	B
15. Electronic controls	B−	B
16. Materials processing	B−	B
17. Microelectronics	B−	B+
18. Composite and advanced structural materials	C+	B
19. Commercialization and production systems	C+	B
20. High-speed and precision machining	C	C*
21. Printing, copying, and scanning equipment	C	C*
22. Optoelectronics (laser devices, photonics)	C	B
23. Chip-making equipment and robotics	D	C
24. Electronic ceramics and packaging material	D	C
25. Flat-panel displays	D	D
26. Optical information storage	D	C

TABLE 13–3
Graded report on U.S. competitiveness in critical technologies, 1991 and 1994

*American competitive position is beginning to improve, but has not moved to next letter grade.

Sources: "The New American Century," *Fortune,* Special Issue, Spring–Summer 1991, p. 22; and Council on Competitiveness, *Critical Technologies Update 1994* (Washington, DC: Council on Competitiveness, 1994), pp. 4–8.

European Union

With the formation of the European Community, one market was created out of six. Not only did the larger market attract new competitors from outside Europe, it also gave firms that had heretofore been selling in only one member-country an easy access to five additional countries. Competition increased with the admission of Greece in 1981 and was heightened when Spain and Portugal entered in 1986.

More Competition.   In addition, producers of industrial—not agricultural—products were confronted with competition from EFTA member-countries when the European Economic Zone was formed in 1984. In October 1991, a new agreement between the two groups was reached, which changed the European Economic Zone to the **European Economic Area (EEA).** However, after Switzerland's citizens voted against the EEA in December 1992, only six EFTA members remained in the organization. Under the agreement, capital, services, and most goods began to flow freely when the agreement went into effect on January 1, 1994. With the accession of former EFTA members, Austria, Sweden, and Finland, to the European Union on January 1, 1995, only three EEA members, Norway, Iceland, and Liechtenstein, are not part of the EU (see Figure 13–7).

European Economic Area
A free trade area for industrial products consisting of the 15 EU nations and 3 EFTA nations

TABLE 13–4
Shares of global corporate profits and sales, 1987–1992

Industry	United States		Japan		Europe	
	Profits	Sales	Profits	Sales	Profits	Sales
Energy equipment and services	99.6%	92.7%	0.8%	1.0%	−0.4%*	6.3%
Aerospace and military technology	81.6	75.8	0	0.4	18.4	23.8
Data processing and reproduction	65.1	73.2	10.7	22.2	24.2	4.6
Electronic components and instruments	65.0	61.8	30.5	35.8	4.5	2.4
Beverages and tobacco	63.0	63.4	3.6	16.4	33.4	20.2
Health and personal care	61.9	48.9	8.2	20.3	29.9	30.8
Leisure and tourism	60.3	45.7	7.4	16.3	32.3	38.1
Forest products and paper	59.7	51.0	7.0	17.4	33.3	31.6
Energy source	50.4	45.8	2.6	13.5	47.0	40.7
Metals—nonferrous	45.7	30.2	11.9	30.8	42.4	39.0
Recreation and other consumer goods	44.0	33.2	46.4	60.7	9.7	6.1
Food and household products	42.6	32.6	7.8	21.7	49.6	45.7
Electrical and electronics	41.1	21.4	25.7	50.7	33.2	27.9
Chemicals	41.0	28.2	13.3	30.3	45.7	41.5
Industrial components	38.2	24.5	32.5	44.7	29.3	30.8
Automobiles	23.6	37.0	31.0	35.3	45.5	27.6
Machinery and engineering	19.2	18.9	34.4	46.3	46.3	34.9
Appliances and household durables	16.5	7.6	74.4	66.6	9.1	25.7
Metals—steel	2.3	10.1	51.2	57.0	46.5	32.9
All industries	47.7%	37.4%	15.5%	31.5%	36.8%	31.1%

*Europe's businesses in this sector had a net loss.

Source: "The Other American Dream Team," *The Wall Street Journal*, February 15, 1994, p. A20.

Lomé Convention
An agreement between 69 African, Caribbean, and Pacific states (ACP) and the EC by which 99.2 percent of the ACP's exports are admitted duty free to the EC

Generalized System of Preferences (GSP)
An agreement under the auspices of GATT, under which many products of developing nations are provided duty-free access to most developed nations

A preferential arrangement, known as the **Lomé Convention,** was begun in 1975 and is a source of competition from developing nations for some European producers. This is an aid, trade, and investment treaty between 69 African, Caribbean, and Pacific states (ACP) and the EC that is renewed every five years. Virtually all ACP exports enter the EC duty free and are not subject to quotas (see Figure 13–8).[37]

Another preferential arrangement is the **Generalized System of Preferences (GSP).** Under the GSP, products from 140 developing nations not given preferential treatment under any other agreement such as the Lomé Convention are provided duty-free access to most developed nations, including EU members.

European Competitiveness.   It is difficult to compare the competitiveness of one country with that of 15, even though the 15 are members of a common market. However, there are some indications that the EU's competitiveness has declined. Its share of manufactured goods' exports has fallen by 14 percent in just 10 years (Table 13–5), and an EU study shows that the volume of EU high-tech exports to the rest of the world increased by 2 percent annually compared to a 7.7 percent annual growth in its high-tech imports.[38]

Improvement in productivity has been slow. Between 1979 and 1990, according to the Confederation of British Industry, value-added per worker in manufacturing rose by 4.6 percent in Japan, 3.5 percent in the United States, but only 2.5 percent in the European Union. EU labor costs, another factor affecting competitiveness, are higher than American costs, but lower than those of Japan when stated in U.S. dollars.[39] Table 13–6 shows the changes in ranking since 1985.

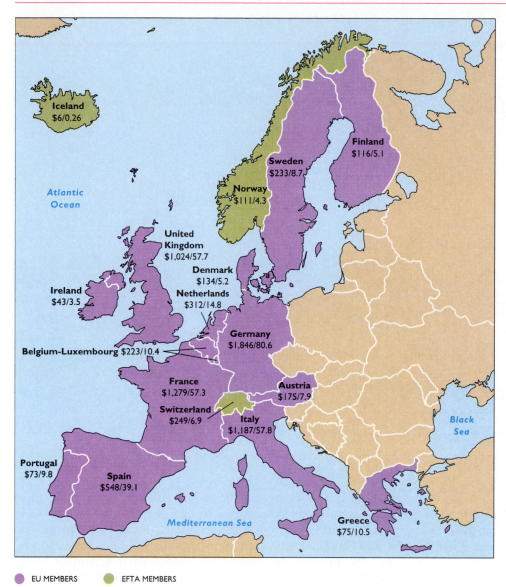

FIGURE 13–7
The European Economic Area (EU and EFTA) takes in some 380 million consumers*

● EU MEMBERS   ● EFTA MEMBERS

*$00 is GNP in billion dollars; 00.0 is population in millions.

Source: Data from *World Bank Atlas, 1994* (Washington, DC: World Bank, 1994), pp. 8, 9, 18, and 19.

The differences in costs measured in local currencies are larger, as Table 7–6 in Chapter 7 demonstrates. The United Kingdom's increase over the 1985–93 period was 76 percent, Italy's was 72 percent, and Germany's, 50 percent. In contrast, the U.S. and Japanese increases were 29 and 41 percent respectively.[40] A common complaint in Europe is that Europe's workers are overpaid, overprotected, and get too many holidays—43 days in Germany compared to 21 days in the United States and 22 days in Japan.[41]

In the opinion of many analysts, European managers have taken too long to adapt their operations to meet the fierce global services competition and to match agressive improvements of world-class manufacturers. In a survey of executives of 594 manufacturing firms in Europe, Japan, and the United States, respondents stated that Europe is still slow to develop new products and is poor at mixing products with services.[42]

FIGURE 13-8 Countries linked to the EU in the Lomé Convention Trade-and-Aid Treaty

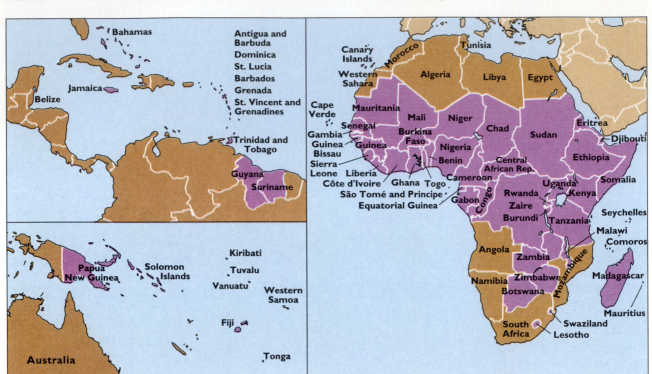

● COUNTRIES LINKED TO THE EC IN THE LOMÉ CONVENTION TRADE-AND-AID TREATY

However, one step many European firms are taking to improve their production efficiency is to close older plants to concentrate their production at their most efficient facilities. British Telecommunications, for example, has cut 170,000 jobs and invested $17 billion in new technology since it was privatized in 1984. The French steel company, Usinor-Sacilor, almost bankrupt in the early 1980s, has eliminated 50 percent of its work force and has invested in new technology to become the world's largest steel company after Japan's Nippon Steel.[43] Besides reducing the work-force size, managers are

TABLE 13-5

Area share of world trade in manufactured goods based on constant dollars (in percent)

	1986	1991	1993	1995
Share of exports				
Europe	54.1%	49.5%	47.0%	46.6%
Japan	13.8	11.7	11.0	10.0
United States	9.8	13.1	13.5	13.4
Asia*	11.5	15.2	17.5	19.0
Share of imports				
Europe	45.1	47.6	43.2	41.7
Japan	3.1	4.2	3.9	3.7
United States	17.7	15.1	17.3	18.0
Asia*	12.5	15.3	17.5	18.7

*Excluding Japan.

Source: *OECD Observer*, December 1993, p. 6.

	1985	1990	1991	1992	1993	1994
EU	$ 7.88	$17.19	$17.84	$19.49	$18.48	$19.09
United States	13.01	14.91	15.58	16.17	16.79	17.30
Japan	6.34	12.80	14.66	16.28	19.20	20.42
Asian NIEs	1.65	3.73	4.27	4.84	5.15	5.30*

TABLE 13–6
Average hourly compensation costs, including fringe benefits (U.S. dollars)

*Estimated.

Sources: *International Comparisons of Hourly Compensation Costs for Production Workers in Manufacturing, 1993* (Washington, DC: U.S. Department of Labor, 1994), p. 7; and "Comparative Labor Costs," *Business Europe,* September 19–25, 1994, p. 2.

giving workers more responsibility and more training as their global competitors from Japan and the United States do.[44]

European industry, like American industry, has been getting more competition from foreign-owned companies. For example, Europe's share of its own $250 billion information-technology market fell from a high of 43 percent in 1987 to 20 percent in 1991. Predictions are that European auto manufacturers will have only 55 percent of their home market by the end of the decade, down from 65 percent in 1992.[45]

Competition from Japan. During the early 1980s, Japanese firms were investing heavily in the United States, but another five years passed before they discovered Europe. Japanese managements had noted the experience of Japanese automakers who tried to supply the European market by exporting, much the same way they had supplied the United States. In countries with no quotas, such as Ireland, the Netherlands, and Germany, Japanese producers were formidable competitors, but in Italy, they were permitted just 1 percent of the market.[46] Fearing that when trade barriers were abolished among the EU countries after 1992, they would be replaced by new obstructions for nonmembers, Japanese firms, including Nissan, Toyota, and Honda, began to establish production plants within the EU.

Automobiles. In 1991, what was then the European Community (EC) negotiated with Japan to limit Japanese car imports. The agreement reached included the restriction suggested by the Association of European Car Makers, an industry association that included the European Ford and General Motors subsidiaries, but not the U.K. affiliates of Nissan and Toyota. The EC agreed to increase gradually in annual increments the share that the Japanese could have of the market from its 10.9 percent in 1991 to about 16 percent in 1990. The quota, similar to the American Voluntary Restraint Agreement, allows Japanese manufacturers to import 1.23 million cars annually (1991 level) from 1993 through 1999. Based on an assumed total market of 15.1 million cars and a maximum local production of 1.2 million, Japanese carmakers will be limited to 2.4 million sales (16 percent of total market) by 1999, compared with the 10.9 percent it had when the quota was established in 1991.

Actual production capacity of the three Japanese companies is far from the 1.2 million of the agreement for 1999. Forecast to reach 600,000 cars by 1995, they are producing just 400,000. Their market share was 11 percent in 1994, down from 12.5 percent in 1993, and none of the three firms is making money. The Toyota plant, established in 1992, is still losing money, producing 90,000 cars out of a planned 100,000, and the firm has abandoned its plan to double plant capacity. Productivity in the United Kingdom is 20 percent less than its productivity in Japan. Nissan's British plant, set up in 1986, is as efficient as its Japanese operation, but in 1994, British Nissan lost 10 million pounds ($15 million). Honda, the latest Japanese company to produce cars in Great Britain, assembled 50,000 in 1994, with plans for double that amount in

1995. Beginning in the year 2000, there will be no import restrictions, and most industry specialists believe the three Japanese transplants eventually will have a 20 to 35 percent market share.[47]

Not Only Automobiles.   Automobiles are only one facet of the Japanese on-slaught in Europe. As in the United States, Japanese imports have nearly eliminated the European motorcycle industry. Japanese cameras and watches are market leaders, and every small color TV tube used in Europe is made by Japanese electronic companies with local production facilities.

Japanese companies employ 40,000 workers in 150 plants located in the United Kingdom.[48] Because of investment in the United Kingdom by Japanese electronic products manufacturers, the country is an exporter of TVs, radios, and hi-fis.[49]

Japanese service companies have also invested in the European market and are competing with local firms in retailing, advertising, hotels, distribution, tourism, and insurance. Many have come because Japanese manufacturers frequently prefer to bring their service providers with them instead of having to use local suppliers. The president of a Japanese market research organization claims, "Toyota will bring every one of its subcontractors with it, all the way down to its construction firms and its insurance companies. Most of the service companies arriving in Europe have come to look after Japanese industry." The leading banks in Japan were among the first service companies to follow Japanese manufacturers to Europe. Advertising companies are now following the same pattern.

European manufacturers are concerned that Japanese manufacturers are buying local distributing companies. In Japan, large electronics producers do this to control marketing and pricing. Buying distributors in Europe permits them to maintain high prices and make it difficult for small competitors to get distribution. Barrie James, author of *The Trojan Horse*, a study of Japanese investment in Europe, says, "Over the long term, combining manufacturing with all the related services poses a greater risk for Europe than does a simple manufacturing penetration. Europe will end up facing the same oligopoly situation as Japan, under which prices rise and poorer European competitors increasingly get locked out of the market."[50]

Competition from the United States.
European firms face competition from American exports like they do from Japan, but, unlike Japan, U.S. companies have had European-based manufacturing facilities for a long time. European-produced GM and Ford cars compete in the automobile market; brands such as Heinz, Kodak, and Coca-Cola are household names (the English "hoover" their rugs instead of vacuuming them); and computer manufacturers IBM and Digital Equipment dominate the market. American firms supply two-thirds of Europe's software needs.[51] Probably because of the long-term political and cultural ties plus the fact that European multinationals have been free to invest in the United States with minimum hindrance, American companies have generally been well accepted in Europe. The occasional EC-U.S. "chicken," "pasta," and "citrus" wars have not had a serious impact on the European subsidiaries of American globals and multinationals.

Yet, European governments are working to help national companies to compete with American firms. They have helped Airbus in its battle against Boeing and have spent $7 billion during the 1990–94 period on research and development programs to support European industry. This is in addition to the amounts spent by the governments of countries where the firms in the Airbus consortium are located.

Programs the EU supports include *Espirit* for information technology, *Race* for communications technology, and *Brite/Euram* for new materials and manufacturing processes. It also contributes to the support of *Eureka*, an independent research program involving 20 nations, including EU members, and various firms that are involved in the research. Among Eureka's programs are *Eureka Audiovisual* (high-definition TV) and *Jessi* (semiconducter research). Although Jessi's purpose is to help European companies develop new microchip technology for competing against Japanese and American producers, IBM Europe is a member.[52]

The Last Barrier to the EU Market.   Some call the **ISO 9000** standards a management tool, while others look at them as barriers to trade. The set of five worldwide standards of the International Standards Organization establishing requirements for the management of quality has been adopted by over 60 countries, including all the industrialized nations. EU members have made ISO 9000 compliance part of their safety laws, and many EU companies require their suppliers to be certified as complying with the standards. Du Pont learned how important this is in Europe when it lost a large order for plastic film to an ISO-certified British company.[53] Although there is no law requiring ISO-certification to export to sell to Europe, if two firms are vying for an order, the one with the certification has a great competitive advantage.

The standards do not apply to products; rather they are an assurance through a system of internal and external audits that the certified firm has in place a quality system enabling it to meet its stated quality standards. Moreover, they apply to all service and manufacturing industries. The applicant for certification identifies and documents all the processes and elements that affect quality and installs mechanisms to make sure that employees are routinely following the procedures. When the applicant is ready, specially accredited independent auditors inspect the company to award a certificate of compliance.[54]

Competition from Asian Nations.   Companies from Asian nations that used to receive investment from Europeans taking advantage of lower labor costs are now investing in Europe because they find production costs cheaper there. In Great Britain, the largest recipient of direct Asian investment, Asian firms increased their investment from $230 million in 1989 to $1.25 billion in 1992. The Korean conglomerate Samsung (1993 sales—$51 billion) announced in 1994 that it would invest $700 million in Great Britain to build a plant capable of producing a broad line of electronic products ranging from microwave ovens to semiconductors. The reason given by the managing director of the Samsung U.K. subsidiary was that its $6 an hour labor costs are the same in Korea and Great Britain, and within two or three years, the Korean costs would be higher. He appeared to have no fear of European and Japanese competitors when he said, "We are increasingly confident that we can compete directly and win in the United Kingdom, Europe, or wherever."

The second of Korea's conglomerates, Daewoo (1993 sales—$31 billion) made a $200 million investment in France in 1989. It makes microwave ovens and color TVs in two plants and is constructing a third to produce picture tubes.[55] A smaller Korean conglomerate, Lucky Goldstar (1993 sales—$5 billion) is using expansion in Europe to grow. In 1994, the company announced an expansion of its plant producing television sets at labor costs similar to those of South Korea. The director of the U.K. subsidiary stated that "in Europe, many of the less competitive companies are fading away, including the Japanese. The South Korean companies are replacing them." Korean automakers, Kia and Hundai, also showed their confidence to sell in the European market when they began assembling cars in Germany. Daewoo Motor also expected to begin selling cars in Germany in 1995.[56]

ISO 9000
A group of five standards set by the International Standards Organization that are generic guidelines and models for ensuring the quality of a company's goods and services

There are now 35 Korean and 67 Taiwanese companies operating in Great Britain, where 16 Hong Kong manufacturers of textiles and electronics also have plants. One reason for EU investment given by numerous Asian companies is their perceived need to diversify to Europe and reduce their dependence on the United States and Asia. The marketing director of a Taiwanese manufacturer of electric motors explained that his company felt it had to enter Europe to reach its goal to be among the top five in its industry: "We can't ignore that market. We covered the rest of the world. Europe was next."[57]

Japan

For three straight years, the Japanese economy has been flat; and in 1994, unemployment reached a seven-year high with a possibility of going even higher.[58] Japanese industry is losing its competitiveness, and as a result, imports are growing and Japanese firms continue to move their production overseas as they have been doing for several years. "Why is this happening?" shocked Japanese are asking. Various factors are responsible, but the expensive yen, relatively high labor costs, and inefficient management practices are the primary reasons.[59] Look at some of the results of Japan's lack of competitiveness:

1. More than two-thirds of all audiovisual electronics are made abroad.
2. One-third of all electronic parts, such as semiconductor chips, lasers, and motors, for computers and consumer electronics are now made overseas. Electronics manufacturer, NEC (1993 sales—$33 billion) is farming out several millions of dollars of microchip production to factories in Tawain.
3. Thirty-one percent of all Japanese-brand cars and 39 percent of Japanese cameras are produced outside of Japan.
4. By 1994, Japan was importing almost as many color TVs as its domestic factories make.
5. Toyota, Nissan, and Honda are focusing the bulk of capital spending overseas. Although the domestic production of Toyota has fallen for three years, the company plans to increase U.S. output by 50 percent and double engine production by 1996.
6. Japanese electronics and chemical producers are the only ones that can remain profitable when the yen falls well below 100 yen per $1. Makers of cars, precision instruments, and cameras need a yen rate of at least 110 to a dollar. Other industries need 150 yen to the dollar to be competitive in the world market.

Japanese companies are attempting to improve their competitiveness by moving more production to Southeast Asia, where labor, land, and manufactured components are cheaper. This is the same strategy American companies followed in the 1980s.[60] Managers are recognizing that their inefficient office systems and management problems contribute as much to their lack of competitiveness as the expensive yen and flat economy. A Japanese management consulting firm estimates that Japan's large corporations have 12 percent too many managers, for example. The root cause for this and other management problems, such as slow response caused by consensus decision making and the many layers of managers, is lifetime employment. Few CEOs want to be the first to lay off workers, but a few hard-pressed large companies are doing so. Matushita, National, and Panasonic have eliminated a complete layer of senior management between the president's office and the product divisions.[61] Nippon Steel, largest nongovernment steelmaker in the world, announced a reorganization plan that cuts operating costs by $3 billion in three years by eliminating 40 percent of its 10,000 administrative employees and 15 percent of its factory work force.[62]

Competition from the United States.   Bargain hunting is in; high prices are out. The recession and high costs have motivated Japanese consumers and businesses to search for cheaper products and are creating new distribution channels for U.S. imports made cheaper by increased American competitiveness and the strong yen. Because of the economic slowdown, manufacturers have accumulated inventory that their conventional retailers cannot buy. Desperate to unload the merchandise, they have sought out the very discounters to whom they previously refused to sell.[63]

The Japanese recession has also weakened the strong arrangements between manufacturers and retailers under which the manufacturers' high suggested selling prices were considered inviolable. A discount cosmetics dealer won a court case in 1993 against Shiseido, Japan's largest cosmetics manufacturer, which had refused to sell to the discounter. Company officials said "they were shocked at the criticism they received as a result of the case because they have always refused to sell to retailers that don't comply with their standards."[64] On the other hand, Helene Curtis, the American cosmetics maker new to Japan, is eager to give discounters markdowns to increase its volume. In one year, its sales increased more than 20 percent.

Before the government made it easier for retailers to open new stores, a small convenience store could prevent the opening of a large store in its area for up to 10 years. Now local retailers must act on applications for stores larger than 5,400 square feet within one year. It was this revised law that enabled Toys "R" Us to open 16 toy superstores in just two years. By 1996, the company will have 32 stores, with 10 percent of the toy market.[65]

The advent of price-conscious consumers and the opening of the Japanese distribution system have attracted many U.S. companies who are enthusiastically attacking the Japanese market. Microsoft, Lotus, and Borland have taken more than half of the Japanese PC software market, causing some Japanese producers to complain about unfair competition. They say that "the Americans care more about market share than profits."[66] The strong yen and having PCs capable of running both English- and Japanese-language software enabled Compaq, Dell, Apple, and IBM to engage in a Japanese price war. Apple confidently announced publicly in 1992 that it would double annual sales in Japan to $1 billion by 1995. Its aggressive price-cutting program enabled it to reach $1.1 billion sales one year earlier, with a market share of 16 percent, up from 8.1 percent in 1992.[67] Compaq sold 45,000 PCs for 2 percent of the market, and Dell sold 20,000. NEC, the Japanese market leader for the last decade, saw its market share fall from 52 percent in 1992 to 49 percent in 1993, even though it cut its prices in half.[68]

The American automakers are also making inroads in the Japanese market. Exports of the Big Three rose 50 percent in 1994 to 68,000 cars. General Motors sold 39,500 Saabs, Opels, and American cars in 1994, and Ford doubled its sales to 47,000, of which 15,000 were imported and 32,000 were produced by Mazda with a Ford brand name.[69] Chrysler, which increased its sales 240 percent in 1994 (13,600 cars) over 1993 by selling mostly Jeeps, maintains the firm is too busy in other markets to launch a big sales campaign in costly Japan. Table 13–7 shows 1994 sales and sales projections for the year 2000.

Competition from Asian Nations.   Much of the competition in Japan from Asian countries is the result of Japanese firms moving their production to these countries to avoid high labor costs at home. Asia now accounts for 19

TABLE 13–7
1994 sales and 2000 sales projections of U.S. car brands in Japan in units

Companies	1994 Sales		2000 Sales Projections	
	Imports	Japanese-Made	Imports	Japanese-Made
General Motors	39,500	0	100,000	0
Ford	15,000	32,000	100,000	100,000
Chrysler	14,028*	0	100,000	0

*Includes 1,000 gray market cars, discussed later in chapter.

Source: Telephone conversations with Chrysler, General Motors, and Ford representatives

percent of Japan's foreign direct investment, compared with 12 percent in 1990. The country's Asian subsidiaries are the most profitable also. In 1992, they made a profit of $3.7 billion, whereas Japan's European earnings were just $50 million. Japanese companies in North America lost $1.6 billion.

Key industries, such as electronics manufacturers, are being accused of **hollowing out,** that is, closing their local production facilities and becoming marketing organizations for other, generally foreign producers. It is possible, for example, that soon VCRs will no longer be made in Japan. Mitsubishi already makes all its VCRs for export in Southeast Asia, and 61 percent of Matushita's foreign production, compared to 49 percent in 1985, is situated in Asia. Already, a tenth of the firm's Asian production is exported to Japan.[70] South Korea, which has long depended on Japan for investment and technology, is now successfully competing against it in the export of high-tech goods such as electronics, petrochemicals, machinery, and steel.[71]

> In Hong Kong, NEC is a company without a factory. The NEC subsidiary in Hong Kong supervises the production of PCs, printers, and disk drives, but manufactures nothing. Some factories in China make the printer parts and others assemble them. PC parts come from suppliers in Hong Kong and other parts of Asia and the disk drives from the Philippines. NEC has no investment in any of these companies producing NEC products, but maintains a team of 26 roving production specialists to see that quality control and product reliability meet NEC standards.[72]

This new Japanese strategy is creating regional groups capable of competing worldwide and also ties Asian nations to the Japanese economy. Firms, such as NEC, that formerly kept their technology and high-value-added production at home, are now sharing technology and supporting production networks. Instead of joint ventures, these new arrangements are bound together only with contracts that allow the partners to be flexible and autonomous. Although some of the Asian countries, especially Malaysia, welcome their ties with Japan, others remain concerned with being excessively dependent on the Japanese.[73]

Developing Nations and the NIEs

One factor that stands out in this analysis of competitive forces is that products made by Asian firms are competing strongly with the output of older, more experienced producers from the Europe, the United States, and Japan. Japanese companies that have been driven by the strong yen to build plants in East Asia are exporting their output back to Japan as you saw in the last section. Because of the recession, Japan's imports of less expensive TVs rose by 51 percent in 1994. In the 1980s, Japan made 95 percent of all VCRs in the world, but that figure has now dropped to 65 percent. The strong yen is driving the growing markets in Asian countries such as Malaysia, Indonesia, and Thailand to switch to the less expensive products from South Korea. This is causing prominent Japanese electronics makers to lose sales and earn less

hollowing out
Firms closing their production facilities and becoming marketing organizations for other, mostly foreign, producers

profits. Matushita, the world's largest appliance producer, reported its profits dropped 43 percent in 1994. Sony fared worse; its profits plunged 53 percent, while Korean electronics manufacturers reported a record 20 percent export sales growth.[74]

Korea Competes Worldwide. Korea's largest producers of appliances, consumer electronics, and microchips—**chaebol** Samsung, Goldstar, and Daewoo—are also successfully competing with their Japanese and European counterparts in many other markets. As a result of following a globalization strategy of locating production facilities in the EU, North America, and Asia, they now have a total of 31 foreign plants producing TVs, VCRs, and home appliances.

Samsung is also a world leader in the production of memory chips, with sales of $4.3 billion in 1994. As a measure of the firm's strength in the world market, last year about 95 percent of its semiconductor revenues came from foreign sales.[75] Samsung is now ranked seventh worldwide in semiconductor production. Referring to the strategy of using heavy capital investment and low pricing to gain market share, a Texas Instruments executive said, "The Koreans are doing to the Japanese exactly what the Japanese did to the Americans. They are pitiless."[76]

Not only have the NIEs greatly increased their merchandise exports, but certain developing nations have done so as well, as Table 13–8 illustrates. Although the export growth of the Asian NIEs should be no surprise (all but Hong Kong had growth in double figures), you might not be aware that Asian nations such as Thailand, China, Malaysia, and Pakistan also have made sizable gains. Colombia is the only Latin American country with over 10 percent growth. Note the impact of joining the EU on Portugal's export growth, the highest rate of any developed nation.

Counterfeiting. A special kind of competition confronting international companies in developed and developing nations is **counterfeiting**. The use of well-known manufacturers' names on products that are copies of the genuine article is estimated to cost the legitimate owners $200 billion annually worldwide.[77] Other kinds of counterfeiting include making (1) close copies

chaebol
Large South Korean conglomerates, mostly family-owned and directed, that have succeeded worldwide in such fields as microchips, electronics construction, shipbuilding, and steel

counterfeiting
Illegal use of a well-known manufacturer's brand name on copies of the firm's merchandise

	Average Annual Growth Rate*		Value in 1992
	1980–92	1970–80	
South Korea	11.9%	23.5%	$ 76.4
Taiwan	11.0	15.6	70.1
Singapore	9.9	4.2	63.4
Hong Kong	5.0	9.7	30.3
Thailand	14.7	10.3	32.5
China	11.9	8.7	84.9
Malaysia	11.3	4.8	40.7
Pakistan	11.1	0.7	7.3
Columbia	12.9	1.9	6.9
Portugal	11.6	1.2	18.5
Turkey	9.0	4.3	14.7
Germany	4.6	5.0	429.8
Japan	4.6	9.0	339.5
United States	3.8	6.5	420.8

TABLE 13–8
Average annual increases in merchandise exports for selected countries, 1970–1992 (dollars in billions)

*Service exports not included.

Source: *World Development Report, 1994* (Washington, DC: World Bank, 1994), Table 13, pp. 186–87.

Clone or Lotus 1-2-3? A pirated version, right, looks real.

Richard Howard

piracy
A kind of counterfeiting involving copying of trade-related intellectual property protected by patents, copyrights, and trademarks

with different names, (2) reproductions that are not exact copies, and (3) imitations that are cheap copies and fool no one. As discussed in Chapter 11, **piracy**, a kind of counterfeiting, is the copying of trade-related intellectual property protected by patents, copyrights, and trademarks. Computer software, semiconductors, videos, compact discs, and books are the kinds of products that are pirated.

Counterfeiting is extremely common in Asian nations such as South Korea, China, Hong Kong, Thailand, and Indonesia. Taiwan was, until recently, one of the major sources of counterfeit products, but under heavy pressure from the United States, the Taiwanese government passed strong copyright laws and banned the export of pirated products. Indonesia, which for years has been a major source of high-quality, inexpensive cassettes, also passed a stronger copyright law and banned the sale of pirated music tapes.[78] In Thailand, once ranked as worst in respecting intellectual property rights by the Asian Pacific Chambers of Commerce, counterfeit goods ranging from Levi's jeans and Rolex watches to pirated copies of *Pulp Fiction* videos are sold openly. However, Thailand's new laws to improve the protection of intellectual property went into effect in 1995.[79]

China, the Biggest Offender.   In 1995, the United States threatened to impose 100 percent import duties on over a billion dollars of Chinese exports to force the government to shut down 29 factories, many of them government-owned, that produced 75 million pirated compact discs and videodiscs in 1994. Besides CDs, the Chinese are producing knockoffs of Microsoft's software, fake cans of Coca-Cola, fake McDonald's hamburger retaurants, and even fake versions of a Jeep that Chrysler's joint venture manufactures in China.[80] For over two years, U.S. trade officials have been holding discussions with Chinese trade officials to convince them to improve protection of intellectual property rights, with few results.[81]

Counterfeit Products Can Be Dangerous.   Is your Polo shirt or Gucci handbag real? Easy-to-copy products with high markups, such as luxury goods (Gucci, Vuitton, and Cartier) have long been counterfeited, but products now routinely copied include pesticides, fertilizers, drugs, toys, car and airplane parts, and electronic items. Besides causing legitimate manufacturers to lose sales, these fakes sometimes bring tragedy to users when, as is frequent, they fail to perform as well as the original. Farmers in Zaire and Kenya bought what they thought was Chevron's top-quality pesticide, which turned out to be a fake made of chalk. The two countries lost two-thirds of their cash crops for that year.

In California, a major broker of aircraft parts admitted selling counterfeit parts made in Taiwan for a General Electric jet engine used on corporate jets. He told his customers they had been manufactured by GE or other approved firms. His firm also modified parts intended for military engines that it sold to nonmilitary customers with fraudulent documentation. The National Transportation Safety Board has identified at least 14 accidents or flight emergencies in which fake parts were involved.[82] In Mexico, officials confiscated 15,000 counterfeit burn remedies because many contained sawdust or dirt and caused raging infections. Nigerian pharmacists estimate that over a quarter of the 4,000 different medicines in that market are fake. In Europe, hospitals and pharmacies dispensed millions of counterfeit doses of a cardiac medicine, some at only half the labeled strength.[83]

Combating Imitations.   Levi Strauss has probably gone further than most firms to rid the market of imitations. The company has a corporate security organization with an annual million-dollar budget to stop this unfair competition. Levi Strauss was also instrumental in forming the International Anticounterfeiting Coalition (IAC), which now has 60 member-firms from 11 countries. Member-firms exchange information on problems they encounter in certain markets and how they handle them. The coalition lobbies in the United States and other countries to increase the penalties for commercial counterfeiting. Because of these efforts, U.S. Customs is now empowered to seize and destroy counterfeit goods discovered at a point of entry.

In addition to the IAC, other industry groups are working to stop product counterfeiting. One is the Intellectual Property Committee comprising 13 of the largest U.S. patent holders, such as IBM, General Electric, and Pfizer (the pharmaceutical industry is one of the biggest victims of international piracy). Another group, the International Intellectual Property Alliance, represents 1,600 firms in the software, motion picture, computer, and book and music publishing industries. A third, Business Software Alliance (BSA), estimates annual losses caused by pirated software reach $12 billion. The BSA president states the biggest software piracy is in Asia; over 90 percent of the software used in Japan, Thailand, and Taiwan is obtained illegally. In Spain, Italy, Mexico, Colombia, and Venezuela, at least 85 percent is illegal, compared with the 35 percent estimated to be pirated in the United States.[84]

Industrial Espionage.   Usually, a counterfeiter can copy a patent design by **reverse engineering**, that is, taking the finished article apart; but when that is not feasible, the copier might obtain blueprints or process information by means of **industrial espionage**.

For years, companies have been acquiring information about each other by hiring competitors' employees, talking to competitors' customers, and so forth. Recently, however, intensified competition has motivated firms to become more sophisticated in this endeavor, even to the point of committing illegal acts. Mitsubishi, for example, was indicted on charges of stealing

reverse engineering
Dismantling a competitor's product to learn everything possible about it

industrial espionage
Spying on a competitor to learn its trade and production secrets

industrial secrets from Celanese, and Hitachi pleaded guilty to conspiring to transport stolen IBM technical documents to Japan. General Motors accused Jose Lopez, its former head of global purchasing, of arranging an enormous act of industrial sabotage when he and some associates left the company to join Volkswagen. German prosecuters say the documents police obtained from one of the group's apartments contained detailed information about GM's future products and data on suppliers and parts costs. Such information could save Volkswagen billions of dollars and years of product development time.[85] A South Korean company paid Chien Ming Sung, a General Electric employee, $1 million annually for information about GE's industrial synthetic diamond production process. The information is said to be worth $500 million annually in future sales.[86] Apparently, these are not isolated incidents. A survey taken of 246 American companies in 1992 brought 32 replies from firms that claimed they had lost a total of $1.82 billion as a direct result of trade secrets and proprietary business information stolen from them.[87]

Foreign governments also engage in industrial espionage to aid their industries. The Soviet Union had a massive program to steal technology from American firms, especially those in the aircraft and computer industries. According to a story told in the Silicon Valley, there are so many Russian and Japanese agents traveling between there and Seattle, where Boeing is located, that they should have their own shuttle system.

There are many stories about the French government's participation in industrial espionage. European and American competitors suspect that some of the dramatic gains French companies are making in high-tech fields are due to stolen information. A secret French spy list of 49 targeted firms was recently published in American newspapers and authenticated by the CIA. On the list were 5 helicopter makers, 13 sensor makers, 10 producers of radar, 25 rocket and satellite manufacturers, and 2 commercial aircraft manufacturers, McDonnell-Douglas and Boeing.[88] American intelligence experts say that American businesspeople should not fly Air France because of possible bugged seats and French government spies posing as passengers and flight personnel. According to an executive of Pinkerton, a security agency, the French are very open about their industrial espionage. Government employees in France routinely enter the hotel rooms of visiting businesspeople to look through their briefcases.[89]

ANALYSIS OF THE COMPETITIVE FORCES

"The biggest single problem in international planning is the lack of efficient and good competitive information." This is the conclusion of *Business International's* study of 90 worldwide companies. The study also found that many companies have no organized approach to global competitive assessment; whatever is done is diffused among the various parts of the company. The Conference Board found, however, that more companies are establishing systematic methods for tracking competitive activity, and according to a recent Fortune 500 survey, 82 percent of the executives questioned considered a competitor analysis program to be very important.[90]

Is Competitor Assessment New?

Sales and marketing managers have always needed information about their competitors' products, prices, channels of distribution, and promotional strategies to plan their own marketing strategies. Sales representatives are expected to submit information on competitors' activities in their territories as part of their regular reports to headquarters. It also has been common practice to talk to competitors' customers and distributors, test competitors' products, and stop at competitors' exhibits at trade shows. Larger firms maintain company libraries whose librarians regularly scan publications and report their findings to the functional area they believe would have an interest in the information.

> One of the writers was working at Goodyear when a librarian reported reading about a patent application for vulcanizing hose that Dunlop, a competitor, had filed in South Africa. The process, although new, had already been patented elsewhere. She reasoned correctly that this new application in South Africa indicated Dunlop was preparing to use the process, which would enable it to produce a better-quality product at a lower price in its South African plant.
>
> Inasmuch as the Goodyear–South Africa facility had nothing to equal it, the process would give Dunlop a strong competitive advantage. Headquarters immediately notified the South African affiliate, which hurredly modernized its vulcanization process. By the time Dunlop installed its new process, the local Goodyear plant was ready. Thanks to an alert librarian, Dunlop failed to gain the competitive advantage it had expected.

Inasmuch as gathering information about the competition has been going on for so long, what is different about present-day **competitor analysis**? Essentially, the difference lies in top management's recognition that (1) increased competition has created a need for a broader and more in-depth knowledge of competitors' activities and (2) the firm should have a **competitor intelligence system (CIS)** for gathering, analyzing, and disseminating information to everyone in the firm who needs it. Moreover, many firms hire consultants or firms specializing in competitor analysis to provide information, and others send employees to seminars to learn how to do it themselves. Some even employ former CIA agents or investigators to handle data gathering and analysis.

competitor analysis
Principal competitors are identified, and their objectives, strengths, weaknesses, and product lines are assessed

competitor intelligence system (CIS)
Procedure for gathering, analyzing, and disseminating information about a firm's competitors

Sources of Information

There are five sources of information about the strengths, weaknesses, and threats of a firm's competitors: (1) within the firm, (2) published material, including computer databases, (3) customers, (4) competitors' employees, and (5) direct observations or analyzing physical evidence of competitors' activities. These sources are all used in the United States and other industrialized countries, but they can be especially helpful in developing nations, which usually have a paucity of published information.

Within the Firm.   As mentioned previously, a firm's sales representatives are the best source of this kind of information. Librarians, when firms have them, can also provide input to the CIS. Another source is the technical and R&D people, who, while attending professional meetings or reading their professional journals, frequently learn of developments before they are general knowledge. Incidentally, government intelligence agencies from all countries subscribe to and analyze other nations' technical journals.

Published Material.   In addition to technical journals, there are other types of published material that provide valuable information. Databases such as *Compuserve, Dialog, Dow Jones News/Retrieval,* and *NewsNet* enable analysts to obtain basic intelligence about sales, revenues, profits, markets, and other data needed to prepare detailed profiles of competitors. These services also enable users to create clipping folders based on search words such as the names of competitors, major customers, and suppliers or words describing a product's technology. England's Economist Intelligence Unit and the U.S.'s Predicast publish useful industry reports; and under the Freedom of Information Act, American firms and their foreign competitors can get information about companies from public documents. Aerial photographs of competitors' facilities are often available from the EPA or the U.S. Geological Survey if the company is near a waterway or has done an environmental impact study. The photos may reveal an expansion or the layout of the competitor's production facilities. Be careful not to take unauthorized aerial photographs—this is trespassing and is illegal.

Customers.   Companies frequently tell their customers in advance about new products to keep them from buying elsewhere, but often the customer passes this information on to competitors. For example, Gillette told a Canadian distributor when it planned to sell its new disposable razor in the United States. The distributor called BIC, who hurried its development and was able to begin selling its own razor shortly after Gillette did.[91]

A company's purchasing agent can ask its suppliers how much they are producing or what they are planning to produce in the way of new products. Because buyers know how much their company buys, any added capacity or new products may be for the firm's competitors. They can also allege that they are considering giving a supplier new business if the sales representative can prove the firm has the capacity to handle it. Salespeople often are so eager for the new business that they divulge their firm's total capacity and the competitor's purchases to prove they can handle the order.

Competitors' Employees.   Competitors' employees, actual or past, can provide information. Experienced human relations people pay special attention to job applicants, especially recent graduates, who reveal they have worked as interns or in summer jobs with competitors. They sometimes reveal proprietary information unknowingly. Companies also hire people away from competitors, and unscrupulous ones even advertise and hold interviews for jobs they don't have to get information from competitors' employees.

Direct Observation or Analyzing Physical Evidence.   Companies sometimes have their technical people join a competitor's plant tour to get details of the production processes. A crayon company sent employees to tour a competitor's plants under assumed names. Posing as potential customers, they easily gained access and obtained valuable information about the competitor's processes; admittedly, this was unethical, although standing outside a plant to count employees and learn the number of shifts a competitor is working is not considered unethical.

We have already mentioned the common practice of reverse engineering, which is an example of analyzing physical evidence, but intelligence analysts even buy competitors' garbage. It is illegal to enter a competitor's premises to collect it, but it is permissible to obtain refuse from a trash hauler once the material has left the competitor's premises. Another interesting analysis was done by a Japanese company that sent employees to measure the thickness of rust on train tracks leaving an American competitor's plant. They used the results to calculate the plant's output.[92]

We have pointed out when an act is legal or illegal, and we have also commented on whether, in our opinion, it was ethical. Certainly, businesspeople have a responsibility to use all ethical means to gather information about their competitors. The Japanese owe much of their rapid progress in high technology to their ability to gather information. Mitsubishi occupies two floors of a New York office building in which dozens of people screen technical journals and contact companies for brochures and other materials. Mitsubishi and other large Japanese firms do their own microfilming, which they send to their Tokyo headquarters for analysis.[93]

Benchmarking. This is an increasingly popular way for firms to measure themselves against world leaders. Whereas competitor analysis will help a firm spot differences between its performance in the market and that of its competitors, it does not provide a deep understanding of the processes that cause these differences.

Benchmarking involves several stages:

1. Management examines its firm for the aspects of the business that need improving.

2. It then looks for companies that are world leaders in performing similar processes.

3. The firm's representatives visit those companies, talk with managers and workers, and determine how they perform so well. Because the people who are going to use the newly acquired knowledge are line personnel, they, not staff people, should make these visits.

The problem, of course, is identifying which company to use as a benchmark. Some firms have been successful in choosing companies in their own industries, but often the ideal benchmark is in a completely different industry. When Nissan's Infiniti division wanted to change the negative view many people have of service in the car industry, it went to famous service companies for its role models. McDonald's taught the Infiniti team the value of a clean, attractive facility and teamwork. Nordstrom, the department store chain, taught Infiniti the importance of rewarding employees for providing outstanding service.[94] Xerox's investigation of leading Japanese manufacturers in a variety of industries has led to some basic changes in its relations with suppliers and how it develops products.[95]

Although sometimes a visit to another firm will provide an idea that can be used without change, generally some adaptation will be needed. The basic purpose of benchmarking is to make managers and workers less parochial by exposing them to different ways of doing things so as to encourage creativity.

Channels of distribution—systems of agencies through which a product and its title pass from the producer to the user—are both controllable and uncontrollable variables. We shall discuss the uncontrollable aspects in this section where we examine all the uncontrollable forces and then return to them in Chapter 15 when we consider them as controllable variables in the marketing mix.

How can a channel of distribution be both controllable and uncontrollable? It is controllable to the extent that the channel captain* is free to choose from available channel members those that will enable the firm to reach its target market, perform the functions it requires at a reasonable cost, and permit it the amount of control it desires. If the company considers that the established channels are inadequate, it may assemble a different network.

benchmarking
A technique for measuring a firm's performance against the performance of others that may be in the same or a completely different industry

DISTRIBUTIVE FORCES

---

*The *channel captain* is the dominant and controlling member of a channel of distribution.

Coca-Cola, dissatisfied with the complex Japanese system of distributing through layers of wholesalers, created its own system in which 17 bottlers sell directly to over 1 million retailers. The dramatic reduction in distributive costs coupled with the fact that each bottler was well versed in its own market enabled Coca-Cola to obtain 60 percent of the Japanese market. Note, however, that although a new system was created, new agencies were not.

The distributive *structure*, the agencies themselves, is generally beyond the marketer's control, so it must use those that are available. Yet new agencies are occasionally created when the established institutions do not fulfill the channel captain's requirements.

Compaq's Japanese subsidiary expected to sell its computers in Japan at prices well below those charged by Japanese PC makers. Part of its strategy in lowering prices was to sell directly to dealers, thus eliminating wholesalers. After the firm authorized dealers to buy directly from the factory, it learned that a number of them wanted to get part of their stock from wholesalers even though the price was higher. In this way, they could preserve old business and sometimes old school relationships. By agreeing to what was an odd arrangement for it, Compaq created a different type of retailer—one that bought the same product from both the factory and the wholesaler.[96]

INTERNATIONAL CHANNEL OF DISTRIBUTION MEMBERS

The selection of channel of distribution members to link the producer with the foreign user will depend first of all on the method of entry into the market. In Chapter 2, you learned that to supply a foreign market, a firm must either export to a foreign country or manufacture in it. If the decision is to export, the firm may do so *directly* or *indirectly*. Figure 13–9 shows that management has considerable latitude in forming the channels.

Indirect Exporting

For indirect exporting, a number of U.S.-based exporters (A) sell for the manufacturer, (B) buy for their overseas customers, (C) buy and sell for their own account, or (D) purchase on behalf of foreign middlemen or users. Although each type of exporter usually operates in the following manner, any given company may actually perform one or more of these functions.

A. Exporters that sell for the manufacturer.
   1. *Manufacturers' export agents* act as the international representatives for various noncompeting domestic manufacturers. They usually direct promotion, consummate sales, invoice, ship, and handle the financing. They are commonly paid a commission for carrying out these functions in the name of the manufacturer.
   2. *Export management companies* (EMCs), formerly known as combination export managers (CEMs), act as the export department for several noncompeting manufacturers. They will also transact business in the name of the manufacturer and handle the routine details of shipping and promotion. When the EMC works on a commission basis, the manufacturer invoices the customer directly and carries any financing required by the foreign buyer. However, most EMCs work on a buy-and-sell arrangement under which they pay the manufacturer, resell the product abroad, and invoice the customer directly. Depending on the arrangement, the EMC may act in the name of the firm it represents or in its own name.

FIGURE 13–9 International channels of distribution

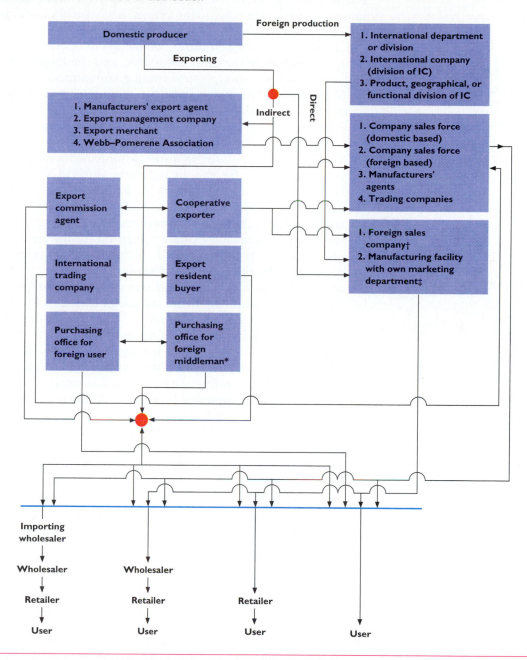

*There should be no direct connection between this category and the user. For simplification, a separate line to eliminate the user is not shown.
†Can be wholly owned or a joint venture. The foreign sales company may sell imports as well as local production from licensee, contract manufacturer, or joint venture.
‡Can be wholly owned, joint venture, or a licensee.

3. *International trading companies* are similar to EMCs in that they also act as agents for some companies and as merchant wholesalers for others. This, however, is only part of their activities. They frequently export as well as import, own their own transportation facilities, and provide financing. W. R. Grace

was at one time a major trading company that operated on the Pacific coast of South America. It owned sugar mills, large import houses, various manufacturing plants, a steamship company, and an airline. Although there have been a number of European and American international trading companies in operation for centuries, certainly the most diversified and the largest are the Japanese **sogo shosha** (general trading companies).

sogo shosha
The largest of the Japanese general trading companies

a. *Sogo shosha.* The general trading companies were originally established by the *zaibatsu*—centralized, family-dominated economic groups, such as Mitsui, Mitsubishi, and Sumitomo—to be the heart of their commercial operations. The head of Mitsui, for example, established a general trading company, Mitsui Bussan, at the same time (1870s) that he created the Mitsui Bank. Both institutions served as the nucleus for the rest of the Mitsui empire. The general trading companies obtained export markets, raw materials, and technical assistance for other companies of the zaibatsu and also imported goods for resale. Included in the zaibatsu in addition to banks and general trading companies were transportation, insurance, and real estate companies and various manufacturing firms. Although the zaibatsu were forced to dissolve after World War II, the companies that had been their major components survived.

The second largest general trading company is Mitsui & Co. This sogo shosha has $160 billion in sales and employs 12,000 persons throughout the world. It also has equity investments in more than 620 companies in Japan and 320 overseas.[97]

Although Mitsui & Co. is huge, it is only one company in the Mitsui Group (formerly the Mitsui zaibatsu), which consists of several hundred companies encompassing a wide range of businesses, including steelmaking, shipbuilding, banking, insurance, paper, electronics, petroleum, warehousing, tourism, and nuclear energy. The Mitsui Group is not a legal entity but exists as an informal organization of major enterprises that have related interests and related financial structures. They cooperate in promoting the economic interests of group members. To ensure cooperation, the top executives of the 68 major components of the former Mitsui zaibatsu meet for a weekly luncheon. Interestingly, the American subsidiaries of Mitsubishi and Mitsui together account for 10 percent of *all* U.S. exports.

b. *Korean general trading companies.* Similar in scope to the Japanese sogo shosha, these are owned by the huge Korean diversified conglomerates called *chaebol*. They are responsible for a major part of Korea's exports and are also the country's principal importers of key raw materials.

c. *Export trading companies.* You read in Chapter 11 that the Reagan administration, impressed by the success of the Japanese, Taiwanese, and Korean general trading companies, obtained passage of the Export Trading Company Act. The measure provides the mechanism for creating a new indirect export channel, the **export trading company (ETC).** For the first time in U.S. history, businesses were permitted to join together to export goods and services or offer export-

export trading company (ETC)
A firm established principally to export domestic goods and services and to assist unrelated companies to export their products

facilitating services without fear of violating antitrust legislation. Bank holding companies may also participate in ETCs. This not only increases the ability of trading companies to finance export transactions but also gives them access to the banks' extensive international information systems. Furthermore, because ETCs can import as well as export, they can engage in countertrade by selling their customers' products in other markets.

Any potential exporter may apply to the Department of Commerce for a *certificate of review*, a legal document that provides immunity from state and federal antitrust prosecution and significant protection from certain private antitrust lawsuits. The certificate allows firms and associations to engage in joint price setting and joint bidding and gives them the freedom to divide up export markets among companies and jointly own warranty, service, and training centers in various overseas markets. Note that the benefits of the ETC Act are available to *all exporters*, not just export trading companies.

The Commerce Department has issued over 100 certificates covering 4,400 companies. Most companies that have received certificates are export intermediaries for two or more firms from the same industry, although now the majority of the certificates are being issued to groups of companies. For example, the National Tooling and Machining Association, a national trade association with 3,150 members, received a certificate in 1988. The American Film Marketing Association (67 members) is another example.

B. Exporters that buy for their overseas customers.
   1. *Export commission agents* represent overseas purchasers, such as import firms and large industrial users. They are paid a commission by the purchaser for acting as resident buyers in industrialized nations.

C. Exporters that buy and sell for their own account.
   1. *Export merchants* purchase products directly from the manufacturer and then sell, invoice, and ship them in their own names so that foreign customers have no direct dealing with the manufacturer, as they do in the case of the export agent. If export merchants have an exclusive right to sell the manufacturer's products in an overseas territory, they are generally called *export distributors*. Some EMCs may actually be export distributors for a number of their clients.
   2. Sometimes called piggyback or mother hen exporters, **cooperative exporters** are established international manufacturers that sell the products of other companies in foreign markets along with their own. Carriers (exporters) may purchase and resell in their own name, or they may work on a commission basis. Carriers, like EMCs, serve as the export departments for the firms they represent. Large companies, such as General Electric and Borg-Warner, have been acting as piggyback exporters for years. A single carrier usually represents between 10 and 20 suppliers, though there is one large manufacturer of industrial machinery that has more than 1,000.

cooperative exporters
Established international manufacturers that export other manufacturers' goods as well as their own

3. *Webb-Pomerene Associations* are organizations of competing firms that have joined together for the sole purpose of export trade. The Export Trade Act of 1918 provides for the formulation of such groups and generally exempts them from antitrust laws. They are permitted to buy from the members and sell abroad, set export prices, or simply direct the promotional activities that are destined for overseas markets. At this time, there are only 30 associations, of which those in phosphate rock, wood pulp, movies, and sulfur are the most active. The Webb-Pomerene Associations failed to become an important export channel because (1) the antitrust exemption was very vague and (2) the exporting of services was not included. The intent of the Export Trading Act is to remedy these deficiencies.

D. Exporters that purchase for foreign users and middlemen.
   1. Large foreign users, such as mining, petroleum, and international construction companies, buy for their own use overseas. The purchasing departments of all the worldwide companies are continually buying for their foreign affiliates, and both foreign governments and foreign firms maintain purchasing offices in industrialized countries.
   2. *Export resident buyers* perform essentially the same functions as export commission agents. However, they are generally more closely associated with a foreign firm. They may be appointed as the official buying representatives and paid a retainer, or they may even be employees. This is in contrast to the export commission agent, who usually represents a number of overseas buyers and works on a transaction-by-transaction basis.

Direct Exporting

If the firm chooses to do its own exporting, it has four basic types of overseas middlemen from which to choose: (A) manufacturers' agents, (B) distributors, (C) retailers, and (D) trading companies. These may be serviced by sales personnel who either travel to the market or are based in it. If the sales volume is sufficient, a foreign sales company may be established to take the place of the wholesale importer. The manufacturing affiliates of most worldwide companies also import from home country plants or from other subsidiaries products that they themselves do not produce.

manufacturers' agents
Independent sales representatives of various noncompeting suppliers

A. *Manufacturers' agents* are residents of the country or region in which they are conducting business for the firm. They represent various noncompeting foreign suppliers, and they take orders in these firms' names. **Manufacturers' agents** usually work on a commission basis, pay their own expenses, and do not assume any financial responsibility. They often stock the products of some of their suppliers, thus combining the functions of agent and wholesale distributor.

distributors
Independent importers that buy for their own account for resale

B. *Distributors* or wholesale importers are independent merchants that buy for their own account. They import and stock for resale. **Distributors** are usually specialists in a particular field, such as farm equipment or pharmaceuticals. They may be given exclusive representation and, in return, agree not to handle competing brands. Distributors may buy through manufacturers' agents when the exporter employs them, or they may send their orders directly to the exporting firm. Instead of manufacturers' agents, exporters may employ their own salespeople to cover the territory and to assist the distributors. For years, worldwide companies such as Caterpillar, Goodyear, and Goodrich have utilized field representatives in export territories.

C. *Retailers*, especially of consumer products requiring little after-sales servicing, are frequently direct importers. Contact on behalf of the exporter is maintained either by a manufacturers' agent or by the exporter's sales representative based in the territory or traveling from the home office.

D. *Trading companies* are relatively unknown in the United States but are extremely important importers in other parts of the world. In a number of African nations, **trading companies** are not only the principal importers of goods ranging from consumer products to capital equipment, but they also export such raw materials as ore, palm oil, and coffee. In addition, they operate department stores, grocery stores, and agencies for automobiles and farm machinery. Although many trading companies are large, they are in no way comparable in either size or diversification (products and functions performed) to the sogo shosha.

trading companies
Firms that develop international trade and serve as intermediaries between foreign buyers and domestic sellers and vice versa

Trading companies in Brazil, Korea, Taiwan, and Malaysia are a recent development. They are of little use to exporters to these countries, inasmuch as their primary function is to promote their own country's exports. On the other hand, the English *importer/factor*, which performs some of the functions of a trading company, is of value to exporters. It will, on behalf of foreign manufacturers, warehouse goods, price them for the local market, deliver anywhere in the country, and factor (buy the seller's accounts receivable). The exporter must still develop the sales, however.

Another form of trading company is owned by the state. State trading companies handle all exports and imports in China, Vietnam, and Cuba; and in noncommunist nations where an industry is a government monopoly, such as petroleum in Mexico, exporters or their agents must deal with these government-owned entities.

Foreign Production

When the firm is selling products produced in the local market, whether they are manufactured by a wholly owned subsidiary, a joint venture, or a contract manufacturer, management is concerned only with the local channels of distribution. Generally, the same types of middlemen are available as in the home country, although the established channels and their manner of operating may differ appreciably from that to which management is accustomed. Differences between the foreign and domestic environmental forces are responsible.

Wholesale Institutions.
In other developed nations, as in the United States, the marketer will be able to select wholesalers that take title to the goods (merchant wholesalers, rack jobbers, drop shippers, cash-and-carry wholesalers, truck jobbers) and those that do not (agents, brokers). However, just as in the United States, as retailers have become larger, they have sought to bypass wholesalers to purchase directly from local manufacturers and foreign suppliers.

Japan. As you saw earlier, Japan's recession and improved communications with the United States have created value-conscious consumers and discount stores to attend them. Japanese tourists have seen lower-priced products in the United States, and Japanese entrepreneurs have gone there to study American retailing methods.[98] Moreover, the expensive yen has enabled discount retailers to import lower-priced products, thus undercutting traditional retailers and bypassing the intricate Japanese distribution system with its three levels of wholesalers. Although only 5 percent of what department stores sell is imported, from 15 to 30 percent of what the discounters sell is.[99]

Europe. Consumers and discount retailers in Europe are attacking high prices and high-cost, inefficient distribution channels much the way they do in Japan. Also, as in Japan, European legislators who have ignored consumers are beginning to understand that competition in retailing will reduce wholesale and retail prices, which in turn sharply reduces the high cost of living and creates more employment. By bypassing wholesalers and buying private-label goods directly from the manufacturers, discounters can offer the goods at lower prices to the consumer. Governments are passing laws to loosen the distribution systems and free up discounters.[100]

Diversity of Wholesaling Structures. Figure 13–10 gives you an idea of the diversity of the wholesaling and retailing structures among three developed nations. Generally, the structure varies with the stage of economic development. In less developed countries that depend on imports to supply the market, the importing wholesalers are large and few in number, and the channels are long. Historically, many of the importers were trading companies formed by international companies to import the machinery and supplies required by their local operation and to export raw materials for use in the home country plants. To obtain distributor prices, they were required by their suppliers to sell to other customers as well. Some of these operations became extremely diversified, owning automobile and industrial machinery agencies,

FIGURE 13–10

Retailers and wholesalers per 1,000 population

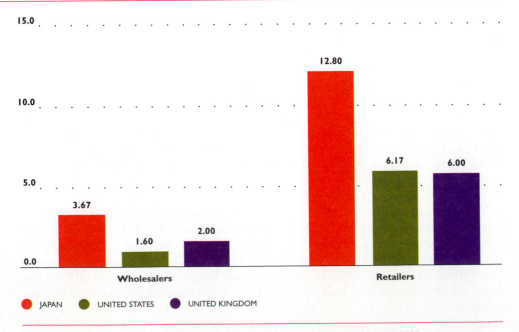

Source: *European Marketing Data and Statistics, 1994;* and *International Marketing Data and Statistics, 1994.*

grocery stores, and department stores. They literally could and did supply a complete city and an industry with all of its requirements.

As colonies became nations, the new governments began applying pressure to convert these trading companies to local ownership. Furthermore, these countries were industrializing, which meant more goods were being produced locally and fewer goods were being imported. Many of the local manufacturers were able to take control of the channels from the import jobber. To obtain more extensive market coverage, they canceled the importing wholesaler's exclusivity and gave their product lines to new wholesalers, many of which were formed by ex-employees of the importer. As economic development continued, markets broadened, permitting greater specialization by more and smaller wholesalers. El Salvador, not shown in Figure 13–10, has 0.08 wholesalers per 1,000 population, compared with 1.60 wholesalers in the United States. The 3.67 per 1,000 in Japan illustrates the complexity of that country's multilayered distribution system.

Japan's Multilayered System.   Characterized as a formidable trade barrier by foreign firms attempting to enter the market, the maze of wholesalers and retailers employed to reach the Japanese consumer has been severely criticized for its inefficiency. Figure 13–11 illustrates that channels for automobiles are certainly complex; but even simple products like soap may move through a "sales agent" (primary wholesaler) named by the manufacturer to sell to the rest of the wholesalers, two or three wholesalers, and a retailer in going from the manufacturer to the final consumer. Note the presence of the parallel importer.

Parallel Importers and Gray Market Goods.   **Parallel importers** are either wholesalers that import products independently of the manufacturer-authorized importer or that buy products for export and then sell them in the domestic market. Four transactions are possible:

parallel importers
Wholesalers that import products independently of manufacturer-authorized importers or buy goods for export and divert them to the domestic market

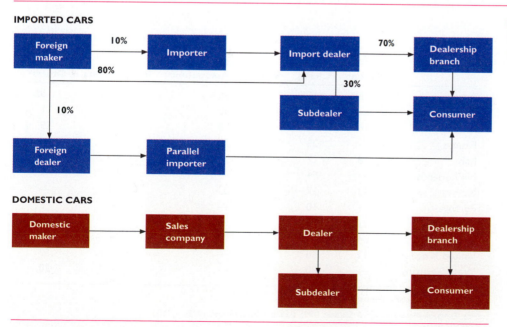

IMPORTED CARS

DOMESTIC CARS

FIGURE 13–11
Passenger car distribution channels in Japan

*A parallel importer acts independently of the foreign manufacturer and its authorized importer by obtaining the product from another source. It is a competitor of the authorized importer.

1. An importer buys from an overseas dealer in the home country. This occurs when authorized dealers in the importer's country charge more for the import than do the home country dealers.

2. An unauthorized dealer imports from the foreign subsidiary and competes in the home country against locally made products. Honda and other Japanese manufacturers are legitimately *reverse exporting*: exporting American-made products to Japan.

3. An unauthorized importer buys products overseas from the home office and competes with the local subsidiary. Most international companies can price lower for the export market than for the domestic market because they have less promotional expense. The subsidiary's price may be higher than the home office's price because of lower production volume, higher raw material costs, and so forth.

4. Goods are bought for export but are sold on the domestic market instead. This can occur when a manufacturer's export prices are lower than its domestic prices. For example, Quality King Distributors in New York annually sells millions of dollars' worth of Pampers, Tylenol, and Johnson & Johnson toothbrushes to dealers at prices 30 percent lower than domestic wholesalers can. The firm buys such products from exporters that sell to it rather than export them. A number of Japanese exports actually make a round trip from Japan to New York and back again. Unauthorized Japanese dealers can buy a Sony Walkman in New York for $90 and retail it in Tokyo for $165, the price that Japanese retailers normally ask.[101]

gray market
The sale of goods that are either legal-but-unauthorized imports bearing domestic manufacturers' trade names or exports that have been diverted to the domestic market

Although American manufacturers have gone to court trying to stop these **gray market** operations, they have had little success. U.S. gray market sales are estimated to total $10 billion annually.[102]

Retail Institutions.   The variation in size and number of retailers among countries is even greater than for wholesalers. Generally, *the less developed the country, the more numerous, more specialized, and smaller the retailers.* Exceptions to this generalization are France, Japan, and Italy, where the situation of

TABLE 13–9
European food distribution by type of organization (percent of market)

	Co-ops	Chains	Retailer-Controlled Voluntary Associations	Independents	Others*
Austria	15%	44%	36%	—	5%
Belgium	—	23	30	36%	11
Finland	16	—	50	5	29
France	—	25	27	18	29
Italy	8	12	25	45	—
Netherlands	—	54	—	39	7
Norway	23	37	33	7	—
Portugal	1	10	—	86	3
Sweden	21	8	44	—	27
Switzerland	34	—	14	34	18
United Kingdom	12	58	—	—	30
West Germany	—	80	—	—	20

*Other refers to specialty shops and department stores.

Source: *European Marketing Data & Statistics,* 1995 (London: Euromonitor, 1995), p. 317.

	1980	1988	1993
Austria	51	71	80[a]
Belgium	79	88	110[a]
Denmark	29	44	50[a]
Finland	27	44	97[b]
France	421	747	1,028
Greece	—	6[c]	—
Ireland	—	—	19
Italy	14	64	145
Luxembourg	3	5[c]	—
Netherlands	37	35	40[d]
Norway	67	80[c]	—
Portugal	—	—	23[d]
Spain	34	103	250
Sweden	65	108	121[e]
Switzerland	81	94	106[e]
United Kingdom	201	500	874
West Germany	813	1,583	1,973

TABLE 13–10
European hypermarkets and superstores (quantity)

[a] = 1990 [d] = 1992
[b] = 1991 [e] = 1989
[c] = 1986

Source: *European Marketing Data & Statistics, 1995* (London: Euromonitor, 1995), p. 321.

many small retailers has been maintained by stringent laws that have kept the expansion of supermarkets and mass merchandisers at a much lower rate than that of similarly developed countries. When retailing methods in the developing and developed nations are compared, the following generalizations are notable: *in going up the scale from developing to developed nations, one encounters more mass merchandising; more self-service, large-sized units; and a trend toward retailer concentration.*

Typical of this trend is the emergence of the European **hypermarket**—a huge combination supermarket/discount house with five or six acres of floor space where both soft goods and hard goods are sold. A similar type of outlet in Japan, the **superstore**, is a recent phenomenon that now accounts for over 10 percent of all retail sales. In Scandinavia and Switzerland, there is also a marked trend toward retailer concentration, but it is occurring for the most part through retailer-controlled voluntary chains and consumer cooperatives rather than through company-owned chains (see Tables 13–9 and 13–10).

hypermarkets
Huge combination supermarkets/discount stores where soft and hard goods are sold

superstores
Name given to hypermarkets in Japan, some parts of Europe, and the United States

SUMMARY

1. **Explain why international competition has increased among the United States, Japan, and EU, and Asian nations.** World competition has intensified, and there are four nations and groups of nations whose firms are in worldwide competition with each other—the United States, Japan, the EU, and the NIEs and other Asian nations. Nations do not compete with each other; their firms do—but most economic and social conditions, as well as political actions, affect the ability of all a nation's firms to compete. Using the term *national competitiveness* is a convenience.

2. **Understand the purpose of the keiretsu in Japanese industry.** A keiretsu is a group of financially connected Japanese firms that tend to do business among themselves. Two of the most important forms of keiretsu are the vertically integrated production group as found in all Japanese automakers and the horizontal group that is a family-owned conglomerate. American businesspeople and government trade officials claim that the keiretsu system acts as a barrier to American producers trying to sell to Japanese companies.

3. **Appreciate the importance of foreign direct investment on the American trade position.** Much of the American trade deficit is caused by intercompany shipments between foreign parent firms and their U.S. subsidiaries; only a massive decline in the value of the dollar would stop such trade. This confirms the assertion that ownership of companies in the United States does matter, contrary to what Secretary Reich alleged when he was a lecturer at Harvard.

4. **Describe the responsibilities of government, management, labor, and consumers in maintaining the international competitiveness of the United States.** Government must reduce the stifling government bureaucracy that hampers business, help improve the nation's education system, reduce the double taxation of dividends, and adopt a capital gains tax to encourage investment in modern technology. Management must take a long-term view in planning and should increase its investment in plant and equipment. Labor has contributed greatly by adopting a more flexible approach to bargaining with management. Consumers should investigate American-made products before making a purchase and not assume that American quality is the same as it was 15 years ago.

5. **Explain the competitive environment in Japan, EU, and the developing nations, including the NIEs.** It appears that both the Japanese and the EU countries are losing some of their competitiveness compared to the United States. Critics say Europe's competitiveness problems stem in part from the fact that European workers are overpaid, overprotected, and get too many holidays, all of which raise Europe's labor costs. The expensive yen, high labor costs, and inefficient management practices are causing Japanese industry to lose its competitiveness.

6. **Appreciate the magnitude of product counterfeiting.** Product counterfeiting is costing industry worldwide as much as $200 billion, some experts claim. It is especially common in Asia. American producers of software, compact discs, and videos allege they are losing millions of dollars in sales annually to pirated copies produced in China.

7. **Understand the importance of industrial espionage.** Industrial espionage is costing American firms billions annually in lost sales. General Motors accused its former global head of purchasing of sabotage when he and associates left the firm to join Volkswagen. He allegedly stole company secrets about a new small car that are said to be worth billions to Volkswagen in product development time saved. There are many reports of the French secret police spying on foreign industrialists. American and European competitors think that the gains the French are making in high-tech fields are due to information stolen by French industrial spies.

8. **Describe the sources of competitive information.** Sources of competitive information are from within the firm, published material, customers, competitors' employees, and direct observation.

9. **Discuss the channel members available to companies that export indirectly or directly or manufacture overseas.** Channel members available to those who (1) indirectly export are exporters that sell for manufacturers, (2) buy for their overseas customers, or (3) purchase for foreign users or middlemen. Direct exporters use manufacturers' agents, distributors, retailers, and trading companies. Firms manufacturing overseas generally have the same kinds of channel members they have in their domestic market, although their manner of operation may be different from what they are accustomed to.

10. **Explain the structural trends in wholesaling and retailing.** The retailing trend in Europe and Japan, as well as in many developing nations, is toward more discounters. Rigid, inefficient distribution systems depending on high prices are breaking up. Small retailers as well as large department stores are losing out to discounters. Wholesalers are being bypassed by retailers.

KEY WORDS

- national (macro) competitiveness   403
- Super 301   406
- keiretsu   406
- industrial targeting   407
- European Economic Area   415
- Lomé Convention   416
- Generalized System of Preferences (GSP)   416
- ISO 9000   421
- hollowing out   424
- chaebols   425
- counterfeiting   425
- piracy   426
- reverse engineering   427

- industrial espionage   427
- competitor analysis   429
- competitor intelligence system (CIS)   429
- benchmarking   431
- sogo shosha   434
- export trading company (ETC)   434
- cooperative exporters   435
- manufacturers' agents   436
- distributors   436
- trading companies   437
- parallel importers   439
- gray market   440
- hypermarkets   441
- superstores   441

QUESTIONS

1. If firms, not nations, compete worldwide, how can we speak of national competitiveness?

2. How can the U.S. government help American industry increase its competitiveness? What can industry and labor do? Do consumers have a role to play?

3. Why is it overly simplistic to consider Japan and the Asian countries as one trading bloc?

4. Why do some American managers claim that the Japanese keiretsu are restraints to trade and contribute importantly to the U.S. trade deficit with Japan?

5. What is industrial targeting? Does the United States engage in this practice?

6. Explain the significance of counterfeiting and piracy to American business.

7. What practice of Japanese manufacturers in Europe is causing concern in European companies?

8. What is occurring in Japan that is attracting the attention of American companies?

9. What are some information sources used in computer analysis? What are some ethical issues involved?

10. How do sogo shasha differ from their American counterparts?

MINICASE 13-1   America-Bashing—To Buy or Not to Buy American?

President Bush and a group of company CEOs went to Tokyo in January 1992 to explore, with the Japanese, ways to reduce the trade imbalance and increase Japan's imports of American cars. Three days of negotiations, in which the CEOs of the three American automobile manufacturers took part, produced few concrete agreements, although the Japanese did agree to buy an additional 19,000 automobiles, the equivalent of about four-days worth of Japanese shipments to the United States. Another agreement to buy more American auto parts was somewhat dubious. As one executive said, "I think you're going to see an awful lot of those parts being produced by Japanese companies in the United States."

Another factor that hardened the U.S.-Japanese relationship was a series of offending remarks made by prominent Japanese. In September 1986, Japan's prime minister Nakasone said that Japan has a high intelligence level, while on the average, the U.S. level is lower because of a considerable number of blacks, Puerto Ricans, and Mexicans. A book written in 1989 by Morita, the chairman of Sony, and Ishihara, a member of the Japanese parliament, was characterized by *U.S. News & World Report* as a "crash course in Japanese-style America-bashing." For example, Ishahara wrote that Japan can bring the United States to its knees by denying its technology to America: "If, for example, Japan sold computer chips to the Soviet Union and and stopped selling them to the United States, this would upset the entire military balance."

After the book, there was a lull in public utterances of this type until just after President Bush and his group returned from Japan. Then the speaker of the lower house of the Japanese parliament called American workers lazy and illiterate. Just as the foreign minister apologized for those remarks, Ishihara announced that American managers are inferior, which he thought was due to cultural differences. Only a week later, Japanese prime minister Miyazawa said American workers lack drive and a strong work ethic in a parliamentary discussion of the declining U.S. economy. There were some Japanese supporters of American workers—precisely those left out on a limb by those remarks. For example, the president of Toyota U.S.A. spoke out in favor of American workers on whom he depends for output in his factory.

Anger over this series of Japanese remarks and the massive trade deficit with Japan led to a ground swell of support for American products, especially American automobiles. Companies began offering their employees bonuses to buy American cars. Monsanto, for example, offers each of its 12,000 employees $1,000 for buying or leasing an American car. However, this brought up the questions: What is an American car or American anything? If a foreign-owned subsidiary located in the United States produces it, is it American? What about the product an American firm assembles in Mexico or Canada?

A. One company handles it this way. *First, buy from an American firm,* even if it assembles the product in Mexico or Singapore so as to be able to compete with foreign exports. Here are the reasons:

1. Being American, the firm will keep its profits in the United States; they will not be repatriated to some foreign country.

2. An American-owned company will give preference to American-made parts. We have all seen the high percentage of parts used in Japanese auto transplants that are manufactured in the United States by Japanese-owned parts manufacturers. They also purchase capital equipment from Japanese companies.

3. The top management is American, and the decisions it takes will generally benefit the United States, not another country.

4. You live in the United States, you work in the United States, so buy in the United States from American companies.

B. If there is more than one American company, buy from the one whose products are clearly marked as made in the United States.

There are people who do not agree with the idea of "Buy American." They say that the principles of free trade and freedom of choice are more important and that we should not let the heated rhetoric lead us to greater protectionism. On the other hand, one person said, "We Americans have it within our power to correct the trade deficit with Japan. If each one of us buys Ford, General Motors, or Chrysler, there will be no more deficit."

1. Should we give preference to buying American products? Is it in our interest to do so?

2. Does it make sense to distinguish between American-owned and foreign-owned companies in the United States? If it is made in the U.S.A., it's American. It does not make any difference where the owners live. Do you agree?

Sources: "Executives Divided on Bush Trade Trip," *The Wall Street Journal,* January 13, 1992, p. B1; "America-Bashing, Japanese Style," *U.S. News & World Report,* October 16, 1989, p. 45; "U.S.-Bashing by Japanese Turns Upward," *McAllen Monitor,* January 26, 1992, p. 1A; and "Anti-Japan Sentiments Called Counterproductive," *San Antonio Light,* January 24, 1992, p. F1.

Trading Attitudes

In Japan, a rice farmer pays $1,000 to have his crop harvested and then earns about that much from the sale of his crop. His labor, land costs, and other factors aren't taken into account. Despite the modernity that is characterized by Japan's cities, bullet trains, and prodigious manufacturing activity, traditional arts such as fan making still flourish.

These and other seemingly contradictory aspects of Japanese life, and more important, our inability to understand them, help form a central reason for our lack of balanced two-way trade with the Japanese.

The same phenomenon can be viewed in opposite ways by different parties. For example, the video "Trading Attitudes" mentions that in Japan even managers don't make decisions on their own, while in America the ability to make independent decisions is viewed as the hallmark of a good manager. Of course, the need to make lots of decisions and in a timely fashion can put stress on the individual manager. In the Japanese system, where decisions are made jointly, there is also more joint responsibility. Even understanding that difference, however, doesn't put everything into clear perspective. For instance, in the United States when mistakes are discovered we don't often expect high-ranking leaders to resign, while in Japan, the top leader may take personal responsibility and leave his post.

The video makes it clear that the Japanese are worried about the creativity of their people. This was mentioned by the schoolteacher, Mrs. Suzuki; the R&D manager for Star Micronics, Mr. Yoshio Mitsumori; and the housewife, Mrs. Shihoko Ozawa. This perceived lack of creativity on the part of the Japanese is blamed on various forces, such as rote learning in school and the emphasis on joint, rather than individual, decision making.

One reason for the possible lack of creativity that isn't developed in the video is the particular requirements of learning Japanese. The Japanese need to learn about 2,000 characters that Japan adopted from China (*kanji*) and two uniquely Japanese alphabets in addition (*hiragana* and *katakana*). The use of characters produces a visual effect that simply can't be achieved by an alphabetized language like English, and penmanship can truly be elevated to an art form. However, acquiring the basic tools needed for written communication takes longer than learning an alphabet and frankly requires considerable memorization. Further, all Japanese must take foreign language training, deflecting their attention away from other subjects, although it serves them well later in life. Most Japanese can at least read English; few Americans even recognize Japanese. The emphasis on memorization is mentioned specifically by Ozawa. Classes for young students are large (about twice as large as in the United States) and are closely regimented after the first few years. Students attend school five and one-half days a week and are in the classroom all year. Older students typically supplement public school with nighttime study at "cram schools" (*bushibans*). The more relaxed American style of learning promotes interaction and perhaps creativity, but it also has an ugly side. Japanese high schools simply do not need guards to patrol hallways,

Source: Written by Michael Minor, Associate Professor of International Business and Marketing, University of Texas—Pan American.

while guards are becoming common in the United States. The Japanese commentator also speculated that the emphasis on individual creativity in U.S. schools might widen the gap between brighter students and those less capable.

It is, of course, difficult to get good data on "creativity," but there is evidence that perhaps Japan isn't as far behind as everyone thinks. Perhaps we can assume that patents are a good indicator of relative creativity. If so, Japan leads. In 1988 there were 308,954 domestic applications for patents in Japan as compared to 75,632 in the United States, and more were granted in Japan to domestic parties (47,912) than in the United States (40,497).

Preferences and Markets

The logging example mentions that success in Japan depends on knowing just what the market is like. The president of the successful American firm, Vanport Manufacturing, Inc., built a Japanese-style house to acquaint his workers with how the products would be used in the Japanese construction industry. Vanport also had Japanese teach their workers how to grade lumber for its acceptability to Japanese tastes. Even the packaging is tailored: boards are bundled in groups of five, a perfect length and weight for the Japanese carpenter. Other mills, which have made less of an effort to adapt to market conditions, are often far less profitable.

Unlike American loggers, who appear to be gradually losing their jobs in the Pacific Northwest, Japanese loggers have plenty of work. But no one wants to do it. It is the type of work the Japanese characterize as the three K: *kitsui*, "difficult"; *kitanai*, "dirty"; and *kiken*, "dangerous." As we found in the chapter on labor forces, however, this phenomenon isn't limited to Japan: Germany brought many of its guest workers in to do the work that Germans weren't interested in doing anymore. Japan is now allowing more foreigners in than ever before (although still only a trickle by Western standards), so perhaps we might find that Japanese logging will eventually rely on foreign-born loggers.

The rice growers in America and Japan exhibit entirely different attitudes toward their product. In the United States, rice is usually treated as a vegetable, and the quantities we consume are fairly small. Americans haven't really developed a taste for rice, so we don't have sharply defined preferences. But in Japan rice is a daily staple and rice farming is a way of life. The author of this case lived a number of years in Asia, eating rice daily (often more than once a day), and developed clear taste preferences as a result. On trips to Japan he noticed that there is even a subtle difference between Chinese and Japanese rice, not to mention Japanese and American rice.

We might have a different attitude toward rice if the U.S. president planted rice in the fall and harvested it in the spring as a national ceremony, as is done by the Japanese emperor. In fact, American rice farmers might learn a lesson or two from the Vanport lumber company about the importance of customer preferences. American rice is long-grained and the grains don't stick together, but the Japanese want short grains that do stick together. None of the American farmers appeared to feel that they should actually plant rice the Japanese would like to eat or even displayed an interest in finding out what Japanese preferences for rice were. In fact, Japan began importing American rice due to a shortage in the early 1990s and it suffered in taste tests compared to Japanese and Thai rice.

Of course, Americans wouldn't buy Japanese cars if they weren't made to fit our own preferences. One quick example: In Japan the steering wheel is on the right, rather than the left side. Every car Japan makes for export to the United States has to have at least that modification.

Lifestyles of the Not-so-Rich and Not-so-Famous

Ron Bartel, a U.S. computer executive, is shown relaxing at both the office and home. His office appears to permit casual attire and workers have privacy. Mr. Mitsumori of Star Micronics works longer hours, 12 to 15 hours per day, six days a week. He also enjoys less privacy, since like most Japanese, he works in a large open area rather than having a private cubicle or office. In general, the average Japanese "salaryman" puts in over 225 hours more work per year than his American counterpart. This results in pressure from overwork that sometimes causes "salaryman sudden death syndrome," or *karoshi*. A high-ranking woman in Japan who requested two weeks' leave exhibited such unusual behavior for a Japanese that her superior asked her, in all seriousness, if she wanted to quit—no one in Japan ever asks for a long leave apparently. This obsession with work also leads to the "fallen leaves syndrome" later in life: work-obsessed husbands retire and, with no outside interests, cling to their wives (like wet leaves cling), so the divorce rate of Japanese couples in their 60s is comparatively high. Of course, this pressure is relative, since Germans industrial workers in 1993 worked 265 hours, or seven weeks, less than American industrial workers.

However, there is also the occasional story in the United States that matches the Japanese experience. The family of an attorney sued his law firm after he jumped to his death in 1992, claiming that the firm literally worked him to death.

The Next Chop-Stick Century?

Only a few years ago, American hackles were raised by the translation of a short book called *The Japan That Says No*, written by then Sony chairman and founder Akio Morita and a politician who was once considered seriously for the prime ministership, Shintaro Ishihara. The central message of this book was that Japan had paid too much attention to U.S. desires for too long and now needed to forge its own path without reference to American wishes.

But by the early 1990s Japan had changed, and so had Morita's attitude. In 1992 he wrote that Japanese management had to review their fundamental business practices, and Japanese businesses needed to institute rules of competition that were in line with American and European practice.

Somewhat later in the 1990s, a Japanese business professor, Seki Mitsuhiro, wrote that Japan now relied upon China and the countries of Southeast Asia for critical labor inputs and would have to reform business practices with those countries in mind. He points out that the three K (difficult, dirty, dangerous) apply to all jobs in basic industry, and Japanese are leaving them in droves, forcing businesses to either die off or switch to other fields. Japan, in other words, cannot continue to be successful without those developing nations that can supply workers willing to take jobs in basic industry.

Perhaps these two Japanese commentators are saying that our attitude toward Japan is based on the recent past, a relatively short period when Japanese industry was ideally suited to world conditions and Japanese exports entered the United States in seemingly unlimited quantities. Have these times been replaced by a new order, in which the Japanese must struggle to retain their present position? If so, perhaps we will finally gain a better understanding of Japan when its economy, like ours, doesn't always seem uniquely adaptable to the conditions dictating the winners and losers in international business.

1. We, and the Japanese, assume that creativity is a necessary attribute in business. What do the Japanese gain, and lose, as a result of their more regimented school system?

2. What managerial advice could a firm gain from examining the attitudes of American rice farmers toward the Japanese market?

3. The Japanese government has been trying for years to get more Japanese to take vacations. What are the long-term policy implications?

4. What events do you think changed Akio Morita's attitude about Japan between the 1980s and 1990s?

Sources: Masaaki Kotabe, "A Comparative Study of U.S. and Japanese Patent Systems," *Journal of International Business Studies*, First Quarter, 1992, pp. 147–68; Paul Herbig and Par Borstorff, "Karoshi: Salaryman Sudden Death Syndrome," in *Marketing: Satisfying a Diverse Customerplace*, ed. Tom K. Massey, Jr. (Kansas City: Southern Marketing Association, 1993); Adrian Furnham, "Journey into the Japanese Mind," *Financial Times*, January 23, 1995, p. 7; Richard Holman, "Postscripts," *The Wall Street Journal*, July 28, 1994, p. A10; Amy Stevens, "Suit over Suicide Raises Issue: Do Associates Work Too Hard?" *The Wall Street Journal*, April 15, 1994, p. B1; and Seki Mitsuhiro, *Beyond the Full-Set Industrial Structure: Japanese Industry in the New Age of East Asia* (Tokyo: LTCB International Library Foundation, 1994).

How Management Deals with Environmental Forces

Market Assessment and Analysis

The worst enemy of good research is the client who appears with a standard sampling technique and questionnaire and tells us to administer it across four or five countries. In some countries, high consumption of alcohol is seen as a macho attribute; but in others, where driving after only one drink can land you in jail, it is not surprising that people underclaim consumption.

Dawn Mitchell, managing director of RSL/Burke, English advertising research firm

CONCEPT PREVIEWS

After reading this chapter, you should be able to:

1. **discuss** environmental analysis and a modified version, market screening, used for market assessment and analysis

2. **explain** market indicators and market factors

3. **describe** the statistical techniques for estimating market demand and grouping similar markets

4. **appreciate** the value to businesspeople of trade missions and trade fairs

5. **discuss** some of the problems market researchers encounter in foreign markets

6. **understand** the purpose of an international management information system (IMIS)

7. **identify** the sources of information for the screening process

Grassroots Marketing Research

Entrepreneur Peter Johns, a 30-year veteran in international marketing, had the idea of distributing mail-order catalogs for upscale U.S. firms in Mexico. He felt that because of the improvement in the Mexican economy, the rich would want to buy foreign-made luxury goods. He also knew that the well-to-do Mexicans regularly make trips to the United States to load up on things they cannot get in their country. In fact, there is an axiom: the richer they are, the farther inland they go in the United States. However, when Johns went to confirm his beliefs with hard data, the market veteran found none to his liking. Government data were of no help. • The other alternative was personal observation, so Johns visited the affluent neighborhoods and shopping areas to see for himself. The satellite dishes and imported sports cars, along with other information he gathered, led him to the conclusion that his target market was about 300,000 families. • Johns formed a company to distribute the catalogs of 20 American firms, Choices Unlimited, in which Mexican investors owned 60 percent. But now he had a second problem. He needed mailing lists, but he couldn't find what he needed in Mexico. This time Johns went to the Mexican investors of his own company. They gave him memberships of the city's exclusive golf clubs. He also obtained directories of the parents of the students at some of the exclusive private schools. The information he gathered enabled him to make a flashy debut at a fancy members-only night club. After a fashion show followed by heavy food and drink, 800 people each put down $28 in pesos to become charter members. They'll get catalogs, promotional discounts, and more fashion-show invitations. Choices Unlimited has pledged to make deliveries from the United States in 15 days and has hired Federal Express to do it. Mexican Customs has also promised to give its packages fast service. • The entrepreneur rightly predicted that the North American Free Trade Agreement would give his business a big boost because it would eliminate or greatly reduce Mexico's 15 percent import duty on clothing and 20 percent duty on luxury goods. What he didn't count on, however, was Mexico's 40 percent devaluation of the peso, which raised the peso prices of imported products paid for in dollars over 60 percent. For example: (1) Before devaluation, Mexicans paid about 3.5 pesos (exchange rate varied) for a product priced at $1; (2) the peso's value dropped 40 percent, the 3.5 pesos were worth only $0.60; (3) At that rate, a dollar's worth of pesos is then worth $\frac{\$1.00}{0.60} = 1.67 \times 3.5$ pesos $= 5.8$ pesos; (4) Goods priced in dollars are about 65 percent $\left(\frac{5.8}{3.5}\right)$ more expensive since the devaluation for people paying in pesos or exchanging pesos for dollars to pay for them. • Johns and Mexicans involved in importing are confident that the $50 billion rescue package of the IMF, Bank for International Settlements, and the United States will stabilize the peso and that a cheaper peso will increase exports, thus strengthening the economy.

Sources: "The Egg on Zedillo's Face, *The Economist*, January 7, 1995, p. 31; "Putting Mexico Together Again," *The Economist*, pp. 65–67; and "Grass-Roots Marketing Yields Clients in Mexico City," *The Wall Street Journal*, October 24, 1991, p. B2.

This anecdote illustrates the difficulties that experienced marketers from industrialized nations have when they do market assessment and analysis in developing nations, even in one as advanced as Mexico. It also shows that experienced international marketers like Johns will not be stopped by lack of data but will use whatever methods are available to get what they need. Often these methods are quite ingenious. Note how Johns compiled his mailing list at no cost when he could not find what he needed. Later in this chapter, we shall look at other problems marketers have in doing research, especially in the developing nations.

The market research Johns did is the first step of the market screening process, determining the basic need potential. We shall describe this process fully in the next section. **Market screening** is a modified version of environmental scanning in which the firm identifies markets by using the environmental forces to eliminate the less desirable markets. **Environmental scanning,** from which market screening is derived, is a procedure in which a firm scans the world for changes in the environmental forces that might affect it.

For some time, environmental scanning has been used by management during the planning process to provide information about world threats and opportunities. Firms that scan have been shown to outperform those that do not. A study of Fortune 500 firms in 1993 found that 60 percent of the respondents had advanced scanning systems.[1] As you can imagine, the increased global competition from the enlarged EU, Japan, the Asian NIEs, and Asian developing nations, which we examined in Chapter 13, will motivate even more managements to scan the world for changes in the international business environment.

Market screening assists two different kinds of firms. One is selling exclusively in the domestic market but believes it might increase sales by expanding into overseas markets. The other is already a multinational but wants to be certain that changing conditions are not creating markets about which its management is unaware. In both situations, managers require an ordered, relatively fast method of analyzing and assessing the nearly 200 countries to pinpoint the most suitable prospects.

market screening
A version of environmental scanning in which the firm identifies desirable markets by using the environmental forces to eliminate the less desirable markets

environmental scanning
A procedure in which a firm scans the world for changes in the environmental forces that might affect it

MARKET SCREENING

Market screening is a method of market analysis and assessment that permits management to identify a small number of desirable markets by eliminating those judged to be less attractive. This is accomplished by subjecting the countries to a series of screenings based on the environmental forces examined in Section Three. Although these forces may be placed in any order, the arrangement suggested in Figure 14–1 is designed to progress from the least to the most difficult analysis based on the accessibility and subjectivity of the data. In this way, the least number of candidates is left for the final, most difficult screening.[2]

Initial Screening

Basic Need Potential. An initial screening based on the basic need potential is a logical first step, because if the need is lacking, no reasonable expenditure of effort and money will enable the firm to market its goods or services. For example, the basic need potential of certain goods is dependent on various physical forces, such as climate, topography, or natural resources. If the firm produces air conditioners, the analyst will look for countries with warm climates. Manufacturers of large farm tractors would not consider Switzerland a likely prospect, because of its mountainous terrain, and only countries known to possess gold deposits would be potential customers for gold-dredging equipment.

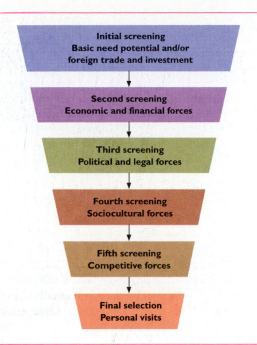

FIGURE 14–1
Selection of foreign markets

Generally, producers of specialized industrial materials or equipment experience little difficulty in assessing their basic need potential. The builder of cement kilns, for example, can obtain the names and addresses of cement plants worldwide merely by contacting the Portland Cement Association in Chicago. A list of firms in an industry, often on a worldwide basis, is available either from the industry association or from specialized trade journals.

This is certainly straightforward, but what about the less specialized products of more widespread consumption?

Foreign Trade and Investment.   If the nature of the good or service is such that a definite basic need potential cannot be readily established, analysts can learn from the United Nations' *International Trade Statistics Yearbook*, Volume II, which countries export and which import their firms' products and the dollar quantities. Furthermore, annual dollar values are given for the past five years, enabling analysts to establish trends for projecting future values. The *Yearbook* uses the United Nations Standard International Trade Classification system based on 1,312 subgroups identified by five-digit codes. These are combined progressively into 177 groups with three-digit codes, 56 divisions with two-digit codes, to 10 sections (one digit). Figure 14–2 reproduces a page from the *Yearbook* showing the motorcycles group, code 7851.

For those who want to know if American competitors are already exporting their firms's products and if so, where, analysts can use two U.S. Department of Commerce foreign trade sources. The *FT925*, you saw a page from the publication in Minicase 2–1, and the *U.S. Exports of Merchandise* that comes on a CD ROM from the Department of Commerce and replaces the publication *FT447*. The information on the CD ROM is especially helpful as it gives both units and dollar value, permitting the analyst to calculate the average price of the unit exported. It also lists more countries importing from and exporting to the United States than the old *FT447* did and in addition, how much of the amount exported to each destination passes through each U.S. Customs district. Both sources are available in the Government Documents section of university libraries and in Department of Commerce district offices.

FIGURE 14–2 Page from UN *International Trade Statistics Yearbook*

7851 MOTORCYCLES ETC											MOTO VELO MOTEUR AUXIL 7851

TRADE BY COMMODITY IN THOUSAND U.S. DOLLARS – COMMERCE PAR PRODUIT EN MILLIERS DE DOLLARS E.U

COUNTRIES–PAYS	IMPORTS – IMPORTATIONS					COUNTRIES–PAYS	EXPORTS – EXPORTATIONS				
	1988	1989	1990	1991	1992		1988	1989	1990	1991	1992
Total	3142253	3404317	3791805	4518690	5751507	Totale	3200382	3294453	3979105	4767128	6036074
Africa	x102405	x84383	x96151	x119159	x139356	Afrique	x1369	x1293	x2544	x1726	x1794
Northern Africa	28425	19935	20950	15761	x11087	Afrique du Nord	199	166	91	x141	x194
Americas	693995	707024	537436	744976	1149942	Amériques	244364	243999	351917	495689	x574180
LAIA	84890	67854	74195	161228	362338	ALAI	15027	30576	19822	16441	x59771
CACM	9037	6884	10170	10134	x15193	MCAC	x44	x105	x44	x65	x41
Asia	454751	x461494	599996	x809709	x1113215	Asie	2188197	2207553	2550258	3224706	4261643
Middle East	x36363	x19445	x39757	x94472	x85451	Moyen–Orient	3196	3093	x796	x966	x1619
Europe	1546041	1804655	2429640	2712248	3221575	Europe	581807	705398	966314	984989	1171547
EEC	1327388	1584909	2138703	2448723	2925713	CEE	532409	660580	904563	940169	1127247
EFTA	209622	212327	273131	246555	286440	AELE	44947	39363	52438	39849	37523
Oceania	x120426	x123909	x115345	x113093	x118280	Océanie	17770	x12586	x6958	x6776	x10294
Germany/Allemagne	318289	355483	454372	598124	854910	Japan/Japon	1973475	2027483	2266553	2841577	3637640
USA/Etats–Unis d' Amer	515172	546329	367190	492102	672529	USA/Etats–Unis d'Amer	207063	204119	325951	466332	503200
France, Monac	341459	386007	418746	491625	503771	Italy/Italie	227827	256255	331652	331043	358660
Italy/Italie	146519	204962	302274	380398	513728	Germany/Allemagne	116361	172918	218851	216601	214693
Spain/Espagne	126160	205319	298318	278653	279950	France, Monac	88358	131935	187584	193774	244706
United Kingdom	183776	201855	293851	229362	192157	Hong Kong	144026	72565	104863	225026	393887
Hong Kong	170618	90812	134067	283562	548330	Singapore/Singapour	24805	63258	117122	83898	100728
Netherlands/Pays–Bas	75929	75058	130399	167542	204541	Belgium–Luxembourg	24939	32460	65828	70333	65281
Switz. Liecht	109260	103946	148394	114652	143038	Czechoslavia	x59829	x51289	x58520	x22301	x15948
Singapore/Singpour	36024	77022	128991	91330	111054	United Kingdom	28343	22202	43263	58459	74020
Australia/Australie	90405	100817	90773	88899	97757	Spain/Espagne	29457	27612	35488	43002	137971
Japan/Japon	80919	83170	88807	103862	103451	Austria/Autriche	36015	27270	41989	29257	22141
Belgium–Luxembourg	47578	50337	79185	115979	119208	Former USSR/Anc. URSS	x15480	x27145	x26238	x30596	
Greece/Gréce	36961	55956	85228	74105	x96337	Former GDR	x91274	x44996	x16086		
Former USSR/Anc.URSS	x214111	x206908	x835	x5259		Korea Rupublic	13178	20275	20350	20038	24985
Canada	63572	62509	60855	61428	76885	Brazil/Brésil	12913	18968	17562	12132	46324
Portugal	32172	35196	55593	89562	135801	India/Inde	8839	x4743	22615	20685	x20962
Austria/Autriche	38366	41067	48439	60119	73121	Netherlands/Pays–Bas	10674	11452	13786	13971	15454
Sweden/Suéde	34446	36394	43540	42710	46404	Thailand/Thailande	7399	8006	7781	11933	x5439
Malaysia/Malaisie	17594	27959	31306	45151	x22946	Canada	21232	8161	5916	12527	10796
Sri Lanka	9057	24040	36036	41666	22022	Austrlia/Australie	16802	11633	5479	5770	8499
Mexico/Mexique	50406	36449	25936	30329	57388	Yugoslavia SFR	4389	5431	9282	x4750	
Argentina/Argentine	241	392	6515	79499	228356	Indonesia/Indonésie	10684	4036	3219	10377	44147
Pakistan	14738	22164	26463	31642	40364	Portugal	3038	2845	5601	7589	7354
Philippines	12442	x17847	33316	29045	45136	Norway, SVD, JM	4031	5864	2562	3777	4780
Viet Nam	x9920	x13778	x34476	x30229	x71608	Mexico/Mexique	1096	10042	473	1333	686
Colombia/Colombie	13488	21034	21426	22221	7598	Switz.Liecht	2750	3551	4549	3162	5803
China/Chine	36673	50830	9304	3963	8869	China/Chine	1224	1466	3073	5413	21989
Finland/Finlande	13449	19369	22785	18087	9631	Sweden/Suéde	2063	2619	3131	3298	4328
Iran(Islamic Rp. of)	x16746	x3755	x6691	x42674	x24953	Denmark/Danemark	3209	2675	2214	3499	6439
Turkey/Turquie	2285	2968	18748	29436	24276	Macau/Macao	939	1173	783	2896	3276
New Zealand	24116	17200	18100	15049	14200	Argentina/Argentine	833	1095	1235	2063	3067
Denmark/Danemark	16110	10772	14801	15106	18274	Malaysia/Malaisie	148	1283	2487	467	x1116
Burkina Faso	x13918	5460	6005	x22396	x29788	New Zealand	877	915	1426	988	1778
Bangladesh	x5934	x10013	x12183	x9983	x3637	Saudi Arabia	2293	1907	x135	x60	x26
Norway, SVD, JM	13635	11266	9678	10473	13820	Ireland/Irlande	160	179	259	1659	1600
So. African Customs Un	13989	8486	9647	x13225	x12480	Philippines	14	x4	256	1109	3716
Korea Rupublic	3829	10485	6077	9706	8948	Cyprus/Chypre	447	761	239	337	285
Yugoslavia SFR	5246	3497	11488	x8806		Cameroon/Cameroun	x160	441	x125	757	x2
Nigeria/Nigéria	x4702	x6091	x4373	x11058	x19120	Uruguay	46	313	443	450	79
Mauritius/Maurice	x1439	x2547	8394	9695	9637	Kenya	99		1179	x13	x6
Dominican Republic	x6450	x7224	x8151	x4482	x8171	So. Africa Customs Un	x411	x279	x396	x441	x481
Tunisia/Tunisie	7357	6339	9642	3496	1078	Panama	x683	x753	15	38	60
Ireland/Irlande	2435	3964	5937	8266	7035	Turkey/Turquie	276	171	181	284	93
Reunion/Réunion	5854	5022	5317	7569	7915	Finland/Finlande	78	59	176	353	470
Brazil/Brésil	489	809	7211	9219	8549	Nigeria/Nigéria	x161	x129	x266	x138	x105
Morocco/Maroc	4619	3537	5191	7795	6366	Sri Lanka	136	111	193	218	477
Israel/Israël	6374	4430	5070	6232	10367	Poland/Pologne	x107	x140	x80	x170	x340
Czechoslovakia	x1023	5415	8818	x1179	x2270	United Arab Emirates	x96	x72	x134	x175	x203
Loo People's Dem. Rp.	x7017	x2136	x4219	x8308	x6306	Greece/Gréce	43	48	38	239	x1069

(VALUES AS % OF TOTAL)(VALEUR EN % DU TOTAL)

	1983	1984	1985	1986	1987	1988	1989	1990	1991	1992		1983	1984	1985	1986	1987	1988	1989	1990	1991	1992
Africa	x5.6	x5.9	x3.7	x3.9	x3.3	3.2	x2.4	x2.6	x2.6	x2.4	Afrique	x0.1		x0.1	x0.0	x0.0	x0.0	x0.0	x0.1	x0.0	x0.0
Northern Africa	1.5	3.0	1.9	0.9	0.4	0.9	0.6	0.6	0.3	x0.2	Afrique du Nord	0.0	0.0	x0.0	x0.0	x0.0	x0.0	x0.0	x0.0	x0.0	x0.0
Americas	39.4	38.0	47.4	x40.0	x22.6	22.1	20.8	14.2	16.4	20.0	Amériques	x2.7	x3.0	3.0	x2.9	x4.6	7.6	7.4	8.8	10.4	x9.5
LAIA	1.3	1.0	0.7	x1.2	x1.5	2.7	2.0	2.0	3.6	6.3	ALAI	x0.0	0.1	0.3	0.1	0.1	0.5	0.9	0.5	0.3	x1.0
CACM	x0.1	0.1	0.2	x0.2	x0.3	0.3	0.2	0.3	0.2	x0.3	MCAC	x0.0	x0.0	x0.0	x0.0	x0.0	x0.0	x0.0	x0.0	x0.0	x0.0
Asia	11.7	12.6	x10.1	x7.8	x9.4	14.5	x13.6	15.8	x17.9	x19.4	Asie	84.0	83.3	83.9	80.2	69.2	68.4	67.0	64.1	67.6	70.6
Middle East	x1.8	x2.6	x1.7	x1.4	x0.7	x1.2	x0.6	x1.0	x0.1	x1.5	Moyen–Orient	x0.1	0.1	x0.1	x0.0	x0.0	0.1	0.1	x0.0	x0.0	x0.0
Europe	36.2	35.5	33.7	45.0	52.5	49.2	53.0	64.1	60.0	56.0	Europe	12.8	13.2	13.1	16.8	19.9	18.2	21.4	24.3	20.7	19.4
EEC	30.1	29.2	27.6	36.4	44.0	42.2	46.6	56.4	54.2	50.9	CEE	10.8	10.6	10.4	14.3	17.2	16.6	20.1	22.7	19.7	18.7
EFTA	6.1	6.2	6.0	8.4	8.3	6.7	6.2	7.2	5.5	5.0	AELE	1.9	2.1	2.6	2.3	2.5	1.4	1.2	1.3	0.8	0.6
Oceania	x4.0	x4.8	x5.2	x3.4	x3.5	3.8	x3.7	x3.1	2.5	x2.0	Océanie	x0.0		0.4	0.6	x0.4	x0.2	x0.1	x0.1	x0.0	x0.2
Germany/Allemagne	9.2	8.7	7.1	8.8	11.0	10.1	10.4	12.0	13.2	14.9	Japan/Japon	80.6	80.1	81.9	78.7	67.0	61.7	61.5	57.0	59.6	60.3
USA/Etats–Unis d' Amer	28.3	25.6	39.3	33.1	17.3	16.4	16.0	9.7	10.9	11.7	USA/Etats–Unis d'Amer	2.7	2.9	2.7	2.7	4.2	6.5	6.2	8.2	9.8	8.3
France, Monac	5.3	5.7	5.4	8.5	11.3	10.9	11.3	11.0	10.9	8.8	Italy/Italie	3.9	3.1	2.9	4.6	6.4	7.1	7.8	8.3	6.9	5.9
Italy/Italie	4.6	5.2	4.9	6.8	6.4	4.7	6.0	8.0	8.4	8.9	Germany/Allemagne	2.8	3.6	3.8	5.1	4.8	3.6	5.2	5.5	4.5	3.6
Spain/Espagne	0.7	0.7	0.9	1.8	3.0	4.0	6.0	7.9	6.2	4.9	France, Monac	1.8	1.7	1.6	1.9	2.4	2.8	4.0	4.7	4.1	4.1
United Kingdom	5.4	4.4	4.9	4.9	5.2	5.8	5.9	7.7	5.1	3.3	Hong Kong	2.8	2.6	1.4	0.8	1.1	4.5	2.2	2.6	4.7	6.5
Hong Kong	3.0	3.6	2.0	1.1	1.5	5.4	2.7	3.5	6.3	9.5	Singapore/Singapour	0.1	0.1	0.1	0.2	0.4	0.8	1.9	2.9	1.8	1.7
Netherlands/Pays–Bas	1.6	1.5	1.6	2.2	2.7	2.4	2.2	3.4	3.7	3.6	Belgium/Luxembourg	0.7	0.8	0.9	0.9	x0.9	1.0	1.7	1.5	1.1	
Switz.Leicht	2.8	3.1	3.3	5.1	4.7	3.5	3.1	3.9	2.5	2.5	Czechoslavakia					3.2	x1.9	x1.6	x1.5	x0.5	x0.3
Singapore/SIngapour	0.6	0.6	0.4	0.4	0.7	1.1	2.3	3.4	2.0	1.9	United Kingdom	1.0	0.8	0.6	1.0	1.2	0.9	0.7	1.1	1.2	1.2

x = Estimate.

Source: *International Trade Statistics Yearbook, 1992* (New York: United Nations, 1993).

To help in their search for markets, analysts can obtain from the nearest Department of Commerce field office numerous studies prepared by U.S. embassies. *Annual Worldwide Industry Reviews* and *International Market Research Reports* indicate major markets for many products. The *Country Market Surveys* indicate products for which there is a good market in a given country. We shall discuss these publications in greater detail in Chapter 16.

Other countries publish similar data. For example, the data office of the European Community, Eurostat, publishes an annual, *External Trade*. Additional information is available from *The Economist, Business International,* and other business publications listed in the appendix to this chapter. Many trade associations also publish export data.

Imports Don't Completely Measure Market Potential. Even when a basic need is clearly indicated, most experienced researchers will still investigate the trade flows to have an idea of the magnitude of present sales.

Management is aware, of course, that imports alone are rarely a measure of the full market potential. Myriad reasons are responsible, among which are lack of foreign exchange, high prices (duties and markups), and political pressures.

Moreover, import data indicate only that a country has been buying certain products from abroad and are no guarantee that it will continue to do so. Managements know that a competitor may decide to produce locally, which in many markets will cause imports to cease. Change in a country's political structure may stop imports also, as we saw in the case of Iran, where orders worth billions of dollars were suddenly canceled. Nevertheless, when there is no local production, import data do enable the firm to know how much is currently being purchased and provide management with an estimate, though conservative, of the immediate market potential at the going price. If local production is being considered and calculations show that goods produced in the country could be sold at a lower price, even without knowing the price elasticity of demand, the firm can reasonably expect to sell more than the quantity being imported.

Companies wanting to know about the amounts and geographic areas of U.S. foreign investment can obtain information at the industry level from certain issues of the *Survey of Current Business,* which also publishes similar information about foreign investors in the United States.

Second Screening—Financial and Economic Forces

After the initial screening, the analyst will have a much smaller list of prospects. This list may be further reduced by a second screening based on the financial and economic forces. Trends in the rates of inflation, exchange, and interest are among the major financial points of concern. The analyst should consider other financial factors such as credit availability, paying habits of customers, and rates of return on similar investments. It should be noted that this screening is not a complete financial analysis. This will come later if the market analysis and assessment disclose that a country has sufficient potential for capital investment.

Economic data may be employed in a number of ways, but two measures of market demand based on them are especially useful. These are *market indicators* and *market factors.* Other methods for estimating demand depending on economic data are *regression analysis, trend analysis,* and *cluster analysis.*

Market Indicators. **Market indicators** are economic data that serve as yardsticks for measuring the relative market strengths of various geographic areas. A well-known American example is the Buying Power Index published in the

market indicators
Economic data used to measure relative market strengths of countries or geographic areas

annual "Survey of Buying Power" by *Sales & Marketing Management*. The purpose of this index is to enable marketers to compare the relative buying power of countries and cities in the United States.

A somewhat similar index on a worldwide scale is published by *Crossborder Monitor* (formerly *Business International*). This index employs 40 indicators for 117 nations. The indicators include population, GDP, various categories of private consumption expenditures, and the production or consumption of steel, cement, electricity, and energy. These indicators are weighted and combined to form composite indexes of (1) market size, (2) market intensity, and (3) market growth.

1. *Market size* shows the relative size of each market as a percentage of the total world market. The percentages for each market are obtained by averaging data on population (given double weight), urban population, private consumption expenditures, steel consumption, cement and electricity production, and ownership of telephones, cars, and television sets.

   The market size index is a measurement of the potential market for goods and services. The index is the ratio, expressed in percent, of several consumption and production items for each country compared to the regional total for the same items.

$$\text{Market size index} = \frac{2(POP)+POPU+PCE+KWH+STL+CEM+TEL+CAR+TV}{2(POPR)+POPUR+PCER+KWHR+STLR+CEMR+TELR+CARR+TVR} \times 100,$$

where

POP = total population,

POPU = urban population,

PCE = private final consumption in $US,

KWH = electricity production,

STL = apparent crude steel consumption,

CEM = cement production,

TEL = telephones in use,

CAR = passenger cars in use, and

TV = television sets in use.

Variables ending in R are regional totals, and a 2 before a variable indicates double weighting.

2. *Market intensity* measures the degree of concentrated purchasing power the market represents as compared to the world intensity of 1.00. This is the richness of the market. To produce an index of relative buying power of the populations of the various markets, each country's share of the variables used in the market size index are put on a per capita basis. Car ownership, urban population, and private consumption are double weighted. The country's share is expressed as a ratio relative to the region total of the items with the region total set equal to one. Urban population is double weighted because much of the rural population does not participate in the money economy.

$$\text{Market intensity} = \frac{\dfrac{POP+2(POPU)+2(PCE)+KWH+STL+CEM+TEL+2(CAR)+TV}{POP}}{\dfrac{POPR+2(POPUR)+2(PCER)+KWHR+STLR+CEMR+TELR+2(CARR)+TVR}{POPR}}$$

3. *Market growth* is an average of the percentage growth of the following indicators over the past five years: population, steel consumption, electricity production, and ownership of cars, trucks, buses, and television sets.

An analysis of these three indexes will show the international sales manager which major regions and major markets were the fastest growing, what their growth rates were, and which have the highest degree of concentrated purchasing power. Table 14–1 presents these indexes, which show that from 1987 to 1992, all regions increased their market size measured as a percentage of the world market. However, of these areas, the market intensity indexes of the Middle East, Africa, Latin America, and Asia are below the world average. Of the 12 major markets, Russia, Brazil, Canada, and China failed to increase their market size. In addition, Russia, Brazil, China, and India failed to increase their market size. In addition, Russia, Brazil, China, and India failed to increase their market intensity. The percentage of five-year growth ranged from –9.29 percent for Russia to 94.71 percent for Mexico.

By comparing the values of the indexes with the sales results of the company's subsidiaries, management can quickly judge their performance.

	Market Size (percent of world market)		Market Intensity (world = 1.00)		Five-Year Market Growth (percent)
	1987	1992	1987	1992	1992
Major regions					
Western Europe	22.77	23.34	2.70	3.71	9.98
EC	18.69	20.06	2.97	4.10	10.60
EFTA	2.11	2.25	3.35	4.66	9.35
Eastern Europe	18.17	7.73	2.04	1.49	–8.10
Middle East	1.55	2.58	0.46	0.56	25.30
Africa	1.88	3.48	0.20	0.19	16.21
Asia	26.55	31.30	0.46	0.43	18.74
Oceania	1.15	1.17	3.11	3.68	1.68
North America	21.40	22.23	4.18	5.34	4.90
Latin America	6.52	8.18	0.81	0.93	17.79
LAIA*	6.00	7.50	0.87	1.01	19.73
World (total or average)	100.00	100.00	1.00	1.00	
Major markets					
United States	19.41	20.27	4.21	5.41	5.47
Russia	12.86	5.71	1.99	1.72	–9.29
Japan	8.07	10.04	3.17	5.30	21.02
Germany	4.21	4.86	3.56	5.04	9.43
United Kingdom	2.81	3.15	2.67	3.75	2.47
France	3.34	3.62	3.15	4.30	15.16
Italy	3.58	3.69	3.22	4.46	9.05
Brazil	3.00	2.56	1.01	0.85	–4.65
Canada	1.99	1.96	3.89	4.66	1.66
Mexico	1.49	2.47	0.80	1.44	94.71
China	12.24	9.98	0.48	0.26	22.73
India	2.31	4.91	0.13	0.13	29.83

TABLE 14–1
World market intensity index, 1987 versus 1992

*LAIA = Latin American Integration Association.

Source: "Indicators of Market Size for 115 Countries," *Crossborder Monitor*, August 31, 1994, p. 1, with the permission of the publisher, The Economist Intelligence Unit.

Other uses of the indexes are to set sales targets and to serve as a basis for allocating the promotional budget. Although Euromonitor does not calculate indexes, it does publish two annuals, *European Marketing Data & Statistics* and *International Data & Statistics*, which provide valuable data, some of which you saw in Chapter 13.

market factors
Economic data that correlate highly with market demand for a product

Market Factors.   **Market factors** are similar to market indicators, except they tend to correlate highly with the market demand for a given product. If the analyst of a foreign market has no factor for that market, he or she can usually use one from the domestic market to get a reasonable approximation. Moreover, an analyst who works for a multinational firm may be able to obtain market factors developed by comparable subsidiaries. To be able to transfer these relationships to the country under study, the analyst must assume that the underlying conditions affecting demands are similar in that market.

estimation by analogy
Using a market factor that is successful in one market to estimate demand in a similar market

The transfer process, **estimation by analogy,** works like this: (If car registration × 1.6 is used to estimate annual tire purchases in the United States, the forecaster who has no market factor for the country under study can use the same 1.6 for that market.) If the market analyst of a tire company knows that 0.9 replacement tires per car are sold annually in the United States, he or she might use the same market factor for a study of a new overseas market. If car registration is 4 million in the new market, then the analyst would forecast that 4 million × 0.9 = 3.6 million tires would be sold there. The constant in the country under study may be somewhat different (it usually is); but with this approach, the estimates will be in the right ballpark. Many such factors exist, and generally research personnel, either in the domestic operation or in foreign subsidiaries, are familiar with them.

regression analysis
Statistical technique utilizing a linear model to establish relationships between independent variables and the dependent variable

Regression Analysis.   In **regression analysis,** instead of using just one variable as in the case of market factors, the domestic division may be utilizing a linear model with several independent variables. For example, in estimating the market potential (MP) for household refrigerators, the marketing manager in the home country may have an equation such as: annual MP = 0.2 marriages + 0.3 divorces + 0.1 housing starts. If there are 500,000 marriages, 300,000 divorces, and 400,000 housing starts in one year, then according to the model, the increase in market potential that year is 0.2 × 500,000 + 0.3 × 300,000 + 0.1 × 400,000 = 230,000 refrigerators. The analyst, forecasting demand for a new market, may use the domestic model if there are no other data, or if sufficient historical data are obtainable locally, she or he may wish to construct a new one by means of regression analysis.[3]

trend analysis
Statistical technique by which successive observations of a variable at regular time intervals are analyzed to establish regular patterns that are used for establishing future values

Trend Analysis.   When the historic growth rates of either the pertinent economic variables or imports of a product are known, future growth can be forecast by means of **trend analysis.** A time series may be constructed similarly to the way a regression model is made, or the arithmetic mean of past growth rates may be applied to historical data. Caution is advised when using this second method because if the average annual growth rate is applied mechanically, in just a few years the dependent variable may reach an incredible size. For example, a 5 percent growth rate compounded annually will result in a doubling of the original value in only 15 years.

Inasmuch as trend analysis is based on the assumption that past conditions affecting the dependent variable will remain constant, the analyst will generally modify the outcome to take into account any changes that can be foreseen. Often there are obvious constraints that will limit upward growth, one of which is the near certainty that competitors will enter the market if large increases in demand continue for very long.

Cluster Analysis and Other Multivariate Techniques.   As multinationals extend their presence to more markets, managers in all functional areas are searching for ways to group countries and geographic regions by common characteristics to simplify their control. **Cluster analysis,** for which various computer programs are available, divides objects (market areas, individuals, customers, and other variables) into groups so that the variables within each group are similar. Marketers, for example, use cluster analysis to identify a group of markets where a single promotional approach can be employed; attorneys can use it to group nations according to similarities in certain types of laws; and so forth. Multidimensional scaling, factor analysis, and conjoint analysis are other techniques for examining differences and similarities among markets.[4]

cluster analysis
Statistical technique that divides objects into groups so that the objects within each group are similar

Periodic Updating.   If the estimates are altered appreciably in the periodic updatings that all long-term forecasts undergo, management may change the extent of the firm's involvement to be in line with the new estimates. Fortunately, the alternative forms of participation in a market permit the firm to become progressively more involved, with corresponding increases in investment. Most companies can enter a market in stages, perhaps in this sequence: exporting, establishment of a foreign sales company, local assembly, and finally, manufacturing. Even when the decision is whether to produce overseas, management may plan to assemble a combination of imported and domestically produced parts initially and then progressively to manufacture more components locally as demand rises. Automobile manufacturers have begun a number of foreign operations employing this strategy.

Third Screening—Political and Legal Forces

The elements of the political and legal forces that can eliminate a nation from further consideration are numerous.

Entry Barriers.   Import restrictions can be positive or negative, depending on whether management is considering exporting (can the firm's products enter the country?) or setting up a foreign plant (will competitive imports be kept out?). If one of management's objectives is 100 percent ownership, will the nation's laws permit it, or is some local participation required? Will the government accept a minority local ownership, or must a minimum of 51 percent of the subsidiary be in the hands of nationals? Are there laws that reserve certain industries for either the government or its citizens?[5] Is the host government demanding that the foreign owner turn over technology to its proposed affiliate that it wishes to keep at the home plant? Perhaps the host government has local content restrictions that the prospective investor considers excessive. There may be a government-owned company that would compete with the proposed plant. Depending on the circumstances and how strongly management wishes to enter the market, any one of these conditions may be sufficient cause for eliminating a nation from further consideration.

Profit Remittance Barriers.   When there are no objectionable requisites for entry, a nation may still be excluded if there are what management believes to be undue restrictions on the repatriation of earnings. Limits linked to the amount of foreign investment or other criteria may be set, or the nation may have a history of inability to provide foreign exchange for profit remittances.

> Decision 24 of the Andean Group has for years limited remittances to 14 percent of the foreign investment and automatic reinvestment of profits to 5 percent. Now these restraints have been loosened to 20 and 70 percent, respectively, in an effort to make foreign investment more attractive.

Other Factors.   Another factor of serious import to management studying the possibilities of investing in a country is the stability of government policy. Is there continuity in policy when a new president takes office, for example? What is the political climate? Is the government stable, or are there cases of infighting among government leaders? How about the public? Is there visible unrest? Have the armed forces a history of intervention when there are public disturbances? Russia and China are examples of countries with dubious political futures. Business can adapt to the form of government and thrive as long as the conditions are stable. Instability creates uncertainty, and this complicates planning. An often-heard complaint of businesspeople is that "they've changed the rules again."

Other concerns of management are tax laws, safety standards, price controls, and the many other factors we examined in the chapters on the political and legal forces. No matter how large a nation's potential market is, if its legal and political constraints are unacceptable to management, that nation must be eliminated from further consideration.

Some excellent sources of this kind of information may be found in *Financing Foreign Operations,* published by the Economist Intelligence Unit; *Overseas Business Reports,* obtainable from the U.S. Department of Commerce; the *Ernst & Young International Series;* and *Digest of Commercial Laws of the World,* published by Oceana.

Fourth Screening—Sociocultural Forces

A screening of the remaining candidates on the basis of sociocultural factors is arduous because these "facts" are highly subjective. The analyst, unless he or she is a specialist in the country, must rely on the opinions of others. It is possible to hire consultants, but they are expensive. U.S. Department of Commerce specialists can provide some assistance, and professional organizations and universities frequently hold seminars to explain the sociocultural aspects of doing business in a particular area or country. Reading *Overseas Business Reports* (U.S. Department of Commerce), international business publications (*Business International* and *The Economist*), and specialized books will augment the analyst's sociocultural knowledge. The use of a checklist of the principal sociocultural components as explained in Chapter 9 will serve as a reminder of the many factors the analyst must consider in this screening.

After the fourth screening, the analyst should have a list of countries for which an industry demand appears to exist. However, what management really wants to know is which of these countries seem to be the best prospects for the *firm's* products. A fifth screening based on the competitive forces will help to provide this information.

Fifth Screening—Competitive Forces

In this screening, the analyst examines markets on the basis of such elements of the competitive forces as:

1. The number, size, and financial strength of the competitors.
2. Their market shares.
3. Their apparent marketing strategies.
4. The apparent effectiveness of their promotional programs.
5. The quality levels of their product lines.
6. The source of their products—imported or locally produced.
7. Their pricing policies.
8. The levels of their after-sales service.

9. Their distribution channels.

10. Their coverage of the market. (Could market segmentation produce niches that are currently poorly attended?)

Countries in which management believes strong competitors make a profitable operation difficult to attain are eliminated unless management (1) is following a strategy of being present wherever its global competitors are or (2) believes entering a competitor's home market will distract the competitor's attention from its home market, a reason for foreign investment we discussed in Chapter 3 (cross investment).

Final Selection of New Markets

An executive of the firm should visit those countries that still appear to be good prospects. Before leaving, this person will review the data from the various screenings along with any new information that the researcher can supply. On the bases of this review and experience in making similar domestic decisions, the executive will prepare a list of points on which information must be obtained on arrival. Management will want the facts uncovered by the desk study (the five screenings) to be corroborated and will expect a firsthand report on the market, which will include information on competitive activity and appraisal of the suitability of the firm's present marketing mix and the availability of ancillary facilities (warehousing, service agencies, media, credit, and so forth).

Field Trip.   The field trip should not be hurried; as much time should be allotted to this part of the study as would be spent on a similar domestic field trip. Often time can be saved if the executive can join a government-sponsored trade mission or visit a trade fair, because such events attract the kinds of people this person will want to interview.

Government-Sponsored Trade Missions and Trade Fairs.   An important mission of foreign diplomatic ministries, such as the U.S. Department of State and the government department representing industry (the Department of Commerce in the United States), is to promote a nation's foreign trade. This is why commercial officers stationed in U.S. embassies report to both State and Commerce. One of the many means of assisting American firms is to sponsor a **trade mission**.

trade mission
A group of businesspeople and/or government officials (state or federal) that visits a market in search of business opportunities

When U.S. Department of Commerce trade specialists perceive an overseas market opportunity for an industry, they will organize a trade mission. The purpose is to send a group of executives from firms in the industry to a country or group of countries to learn firsthand about the market, meet important customers face to face, and make contacts with people interested in representing their products. Because of discounted air fares, hotels, and so forth, the cost to the firm is less than what it would pay if it went on its own. Moreover, the impact of a group visit is greater than it is for an individual. Before the mission's arrival, consulate or embassy officials will have publicized the visit and made contact with local companies they believe are interested. State governments, trade associations, chambers of commerce, and other export-oriented organizations also organize trade missions.

Probably every nation in the world holds a **trade fair** periodically. Usually, each nation has a specifically marked area where its exhibitors have their own booths staffed by company representatives. Although trade fairs are open to the general public, at certain hours (generally mornings), entrance is limited to businesspeople interested in doing business with the exhibitors.

trade fair
A large exhibition, generally held at the same place and same time periodically, at which companies maintain booths to promote the sale of their products

Trade Fairs Are for Small Firms Too

A two-year old firm, with only 24 employees, that produces color-verification equipment for magazines and newspapers showed its products at a German trade fair for the printing industry. As a result, the company received an order for a $125,000 unit and obtained six European distributors. The company now has 40 employees and has doubled its sales to over $2 million. A company executive says that 25 percent of the sales increase is due to overseas buyers at the Düsseldorf fair and that more sales are coming from four overseas original equipment manufacturers that intend to incorporate the firm's products in their own equipment.

One major difference between the attendees of European and American trade fairs is that nearly all Europeans go to buy, whereas only about 60 percent of the visitors at U.S. trade fairs expect to buy in the near future. Trade fairs in the United States are not the major marketing tool that they are for European and Asian companies.

Small firms without trade fair experience need to know that there are various types of trade shows. Two principal kinds are (1) horizontal trade shows, which exhibit a wide variety of consumer and industrial goods, and (2) vertical trade shows, which are product-specific, such as the Düsseldorf fair mentioned previously. In addition, the Department of Commerce has other low-cost programs that offer small firms good exposure in various countries for the purpose of making sales or obtaining overseas representation. Catalog or video catalog shows are especially helpful to small firms because a company representative does not need to be present. Commerce commercial officers will display a firm's catalogs and/or videos at American embassies and consulates to potential agents, distributors, and buyers invited to see them. The officers then give the exhibiting company the names and addresses of those who indicated they wanted to talk to company representatives.

"You have to take your product to the market where you want to sell," experienced trade fair promoters tell newcomers to international business, "because you can't bring the market to your product."

Sources: "Making the Most of Trade Fairs," *D & B Reports*, July–August 1993, p. 40; "Trade Fairs, Shows: Good Tools to Build International Markets," *Business America*, July 17, 1988, pp. 5–6; and "Sell Overseas at Trade Fairs," *Nation's Business*, March 1988, pp. 57–59.

Although showing products at trade fairs is an ancient sales promotion method, it continues to be effective. Although most trade fairs in developing nations are general, with displays of many kinds of products, those in Europe are specialized. Moreover, many of them do not admit the general public. Besides making contact with prospective buyers and agents, most exhibitors use them to learn more about the market. They not only receive feedback from visitors to their exhibits, but they have the opportunity to observe their competitors in action.[6]

Sometimes Local Research Is Required.   For many situations, the executive's report will be the final input to the information on which the decision is based. Occasionally, however, the proposed human and financial resource commitments are so great that management will insist on gathering data in the potential market rather than depending solely on the desk and field reports.[7] This would undoubtedly be the position of a consumer products manufacturer that envisions entering a large competitive market of an industrialized country. It might also be the recommendation of the executive making the field trip if he or she discovered that market conditions were substantially different from those to which the firm was accustomed. Often, in face-to-face interviews, information is revealed that would never be written. In these situations, research in the local market will not only supply information on market definition and projection but will also assist in the formulation of an effective marketing mix.

Research in the Local Market.   When a firm's research personnel have had no experience in the country, management should hire a local research group to do the work unless there is a subsidiary in a neighboring country from which a research team may be borrowed. Generally, home country research techniques may be used, though they may need to be adapted to local conditions.

A Japanese farming specialist takes a close look at grains of American rice displayed in an exhibit booth at a U.S. food fair in Tokyo.

Reuters/Bettmann

It is imperative, therefore, that the person in charge of the project have experience either in that country or in one that is culturally similar and preferably in the same geographic area.

Just as at home, the researchers will first try to obtain secondary data, but they frequently find that, except in developed nations, they either cannot find what they need or what they encounter is suspect. Fortunately, international agencies, such as the United Nations and the IMF, regularly hold seminars to train government officials in data collection, so that the recency and quality of secondary data in some countries are improving.

If secondary data are unavailable, the researchers must collect primary data, and here they face other complications caused by *cultural problems* and *technical difficulties.*

Cultural Problems. If the researchers are from one culture and are working in another, they may encounter some cultural problems. When they are not proficient in the local language or dialect, the research instrument or the respondents' answers must be translated. As we learned in the chapter on sociocultural forces, a number of languages may be spoken in a country, and even in countries where only one language is used, a word's meaning may change from one region to another.

Other cultural problems plague researchers as they try to collect data. The low level of literacy in many developing nations makes the use of mail questionnaires virtually impossible. If a housewife is interviewed in a country where the husband makes the buying decisions, the data obtained from her

Is This a Representative Sample?

Huge consumer surveys? Focus groups? How did Ford Europe decide what to include in its new minicar that will be coming on the market in 1996? Ford of Europe's Women's International Marketing Panel, a group of 20 Ford employees from 10 countries who range from entry-level secretaries to engineers, has been reminding the company's designers and engineers that women also drive cars and their needs are not the same as men's. For example, women want a car that is safe, reliable, easy to park, and inexpensive to operate. Yet they also want style and performance, according to Carol Giles, the panel co-chair and secretary to the vice president of sales.

How is this any different from what male buyers want? Giles says that according to the panel's studies, males are hung up on a car's prestige. "Women see prestige as a major and amusing male preoccupation—but it is irrelevant for women." She adds that women are also less interested in a car's technical specifications, wash it less often, and replace it less frequently than men.

Although they grow more attached to their cars than do men, women treat them more casually.

The reason Ford Europe did not form a women's advisory group until 1991 when the parent company has had one since the 1980s is that only 26 percent of the car buyers in Europe are women, compared with nearly 50 percent in the United States. However, over 50 percent of European small-car buyers are women, so they are having major input to every detail of the new supermini. "The involvement of women in determining what this car will be is unparalleled," says Matthew Taylor, manager of Ford's small-car marketing in Europe. And their input doesn't stop with the production of the car. Now Ford solicits the panel's comments on prospective ad campaigns.

Source: "Ford Cultivates Women's Advice on European Cars," *Advertising Age*, September 4, 1994, p. 27.

---

are worthless. Respondents sometimes refuse to answer questions because of their general distrust of strangers. In other instances, however, the custom of politeness toward everyone will cause respondents to give answers calculated to please the interviewer.

Often, people have practical reasons for not wanting to be interviewed. In some countries, income taxes are based on the apparent worth of individuals as measured by their tangible assets. In such countries, when asked if there is a stereo or TV in the household, the respondent may suspect the interviewer of being a tax assessor and refuse to answer. To overcome such a problem, experienced researchers often hire college students as interviewers because their manner of speech and dress correctly identify them for what they are.

Technical Difficulties.   As if the cultural problems were not enough, researchers may also encounter technical difficulties. First, up-to-date maps are often unavailable. Streets chosen to be sampled may have three or four different names along their length, and the houses may not be numbered. Telephone surveys can be a formidable undertaking, because in many countries, only the wealthy have telephones and the telephone directories are frequently out of date.

It is not only in developing nations that telephones are hard to get. In Belgium, a woman broke the Belgian national record when she applied for a telephone and received it in just two weeks. As the four millionth telephone subscriber, she was showered with gifts. While she celebrated 31,154 applicants were waiting to be connected. Delays of two years are common.[8]

In such countries as Brazil and Mexico, researchers often have problems in using their own phones because overloaded circuits make it next to impossible to get a line.[9] Mail surveys can be troublesome too, as mail deliveries within a city may take weeks or are sometimes not even made.

The postal service in Italy has been so slow (two weeks for a letter to go from Rome to Milan) that Italian firms have used private couriers to go to Switzerland to dispatch their foreign mail.

Mail questionnaires are not well received in Chile, where the recipient is required to pay the postman for each letter delivered. The response to a mail survey is often low by American standards in countries where the respondent must go to the post office to mail a letter—for example, Brazil. To increase returns, firms often offer such premiums as lottery tickets or product samples to persons who complete a mail questionnaire.

In some developing nations, researchers may have to obtain governmental permission to conduct interviews and, in some cases, submit questionnaires for prior approval. Some countries prohibit certain kinds of questions. For example, you cannot ask Egyptians about the ownership of consumer durables, and in Saudi Arabia, you are not permitted to ask questions about nationality.[10]

Research as Practiced.   The existence of hindrances to marketing research does not mean it is not carried out in foreign markets. As you might surmise from the discussion of the availability of secondary data, marketing research is highly developed in industrialized nations, where markets are large and incorrect decisions are costly. Problems like those we have mentioned are prevalent in the developing nations, but they are well known to those who live there. It does not take long for the newcomer to become aware of them either, because longtime residents are quick to point them out.

Analysts tend to do less research and use simpler techniques in these nations because often the firm is in a seller's market, which means everything produced can be sold with a minimum of effort. Moreover, competition is frequently less intense in developing nations because (1) there are fewer competitors and (2) managements are struggling with problems other than marketing, which keep them from devoting more time to the marketing function. Even now in Mexico, an important market for American firms, marketing research is unpopular. When it is done, the preferred method is house-to-house surveying.[11]

Although the situation is changing, the most common technique continues to be a combination of trend analysis and the querying of knowledgeable persons such as salespeople, channel members, and customers. Researchers then adjust the findings on the basis of subjective considerations.[12]

RECAPITULATION OF THE SCREENING PROCESS

Although the screening process we have described may appear time consuming, it does assure management that the principal factors have not been overlooked. Because most market-entry decisions can be implemented in stages, the firm can usually make adjustments in time to avoid significant losses when conditions change or if additional information indicates the initial decision was incorrect.

Where do you find this information? You may believe data are difficult to find, but the list in the appendix at the end of this chapter will show you there are many sources. The difficulty lies in converting all of these data into information that managers can utilize. For this, the firm needs an international management information system.

international management information system (IMIS) *Organized process of gathering, storing, processing, and disseminating information to managers to assist them in making business decisions*

INTERNATIONAL MANAGEMENT INFORMATION SYSTEM (IMIS)

The **international management information system (IMIS)** is an organized, continuous process of gathering, storing, processing, and disseminating information for the purpose of making business decisions. The system's size and complexity can range from a simple filing cabinet in a small firm to a system employing computers to process and store data, as is found in large firms. The means are less important than the end, which is to enable marketing and other managers to use all the sources of information at their disposal. These are:

1. *Internal sources*—market analyses, special research reports, and data from company sales, production, financial, and accounting records as reported by foreign subsidiaries, sales representatives, customers, and channel of distribution members.

2. *External sources*—reports from governments, trade associations, banks, consultants, customers, and data bases.

Both types of sources can provide data concerning the changes and trends in the uncontrollable environmental variables as well as feedback on the performance of the firm's controllable variables. There is a trend now toward decision support systems, which permit managers to make inquiries and receive specific answers not only from the firm's database, but from external, on-line databases as well.

SUMMARY

1. **Discuss environmental analysis and a modified version, market screening, used for market assessment and analysis.** A complete market analysis and assessment as described in this chapter would be made by a firm that either is contemplating entering the foreign market for the first time or is already a multinational but wants to monitor world markets systematically to avoid overlooking marketing opportunities and threats. Many of the data requirements for a foreign decision are the same as those required for a similar domestic decision, though it is likely that additional information about some of the international and foreign environmental forces will be needed.

   Essentially, the screening process consists of examining the various forces in succession and eliminating countries at each step. The sequence of screening based on (1) basic need potential, (2) financial and economic forces, (3) political and legal forces, (4) sociocultural forces, (5) competitive forces, and (6) personal visits is ordered so as to have a successively smaller number of prospects to consider at each of the succeedingly more difficult and expensive stages.

2. **Explain market indicators and market factors.** Market indicators are economic data used to measure relative market strengths of countries or geographic areas. Market factors are economic data that correlate highly with the market demand for a product.

3. **Describe the statistical techniques for estimating market demand and grouping simi-**lar markets. Some statistical techniques for estimating market demand and grouping similar markets are regression analysis, trend analysis, and cluster analysis.

4. **Appreciate the value to businesspeople of trade missions and trade fairs.** Trade missions and trade fairs enable businesspeople to visit a market inexpensively, make sales, obtain overseas representation, and observe competitors' activities.

5. **Discuss some of the problems market researchers encounter in foreign markets.** Cultural problems, such as a low level of literacy and distrust of strangers, complicate the data-gathering process, as do technical difficulties, such as a lack of maps, telephone directories, and adequate mail service. These hindrances to marketing research do not prevent the work from being done. There is a tendency in many markets, however, to do less research and use simpler techniques.

6. **Understanding the purpose of an international management information system (IMIS).** To provide continuing information on changes in the uncontrollable variables as well as feedback on the performance of the firm's controllable variables, many companies have set up international management information systems to gather, store, and use information in an organized manner.

7. **Identify the sources of information for the screening process.** The sources of information for the screening process are the environmental forces.

KEY WORDS

- market screening   454
- environmental scanning   454
- market indicators   457
- market factors   460
- estimation by analogy   460
- regression analysis   460

- trend analysis   460
- cluster analysis   461
- trade mission   463
- trade fair   463
- international management information system (IMIS)   467

QUESTIONS

1. Select a country and a product that you believe your firm can market there. Make a list of the sources of information you will use for each screening.

2. What is the basis for the order of screenings presented in the text?

3. If import data for a country are unobtainable, what readily available data might serve as a substitute?

4. Do a country's imports completely measure the market potential for a product? Why or why not?

5. What are some barriers related to the political and legal forces that may eliminate a country from further consideration?

6. What is the reason for making personal visits to markets that survive the first five screenings?

7. Why should a firm's management consider going on a trade mission or exhibiting in a trade fair?

8. What are the two principal kinds of complications that researchers face when they collect primary data in a foreign market? Give examples.

9. What do the market size index and the market intensity index tell you?

10. What is the purpose of an international management information system? What is the minimum recommended computer size?

MINICASE 14-1   Chromed Cycle Equipment Company

Jim Brown started Chromed Cycle Equipment Company (CCEC) three years ago. He makes chromed parts for motorcycles. Annual sales have reached $300,000 and now Brown is considering expanding his sales territory. He has heard accounts of the success that some small firms are having exporting and wonders if his firm might also increase sales that way. Brown is concerned, though, because his products are "low-tech" compared to those that most of the small companies are exporting.

To satisfy his curiosity, he calls a friend who is a professor of international business at the university and tells him he is interested in knowing in which countries there might be a market for his products. All countries importing motorcycles are possibilities, he thinks. He asks the professor if he can tell him:

1. Which countries import large amounts of motorcycles?

2. The rank of the top 5 import markets in order of their importance.

3. In which of these are the imports increasing over time?

4. From which countries will there probably be competition?

5. Brown calculates that the wholesale price of CCEC parts that each motorcycle can use is $126. He also estimates that the average wholesale export price for a motorcycle is $8,500. What is the possible market potential for each of the top 5 markets?

His friend tells him to meet him in the reference section of the library. When Brown arrives, the professor already has opened the U.N. *International Trade Statistics Yearbook* to the page showing the international trade in motorcycles (Figure 14–2 in text).

APPENDIX SOURCES OF INFORMATION USED IN SCREENINGS

I–II. First and second screening (basic need potential, economic and financial forces).
 A. GATT *Yearbook*.
 B. IMF *Direction of Trade, International Financial Statistics*
 C. OECD *Economic Outlook* and other publications.
 D. United Nations.
  1. *International Trade Statistics Yearbook*.
  2. *Statistical Yearbook*.
  3. *Demographic Yearbook*.
  4. Contact UN for catalog of publications.
 E. Eurostat publishes much data on EU trade. Ask EU office in New York City.
 F. World Bank (annual publications).
  1. *World Development Report* (also on computer disk).
  2. *Atlas*.
  3. *World Tables*.
  4. Ask for publications catalog.
 G. Asian Development Bank—*Annual Report* and newsletter.
 H. InterAmerican Development Bank—*Annual Report* and newsletter.
 I. Small Business Administration—*Export Information System Data Reports*.
 J. U.S. Department of Commerce.
  1. *FT925* and other foreign trade reports.
  2. *Foreign Trade Highlights*.
  3. *Annual Worldwide Industry Reviews*.
  4. *International Database* from Center for International Research, Department of Commerce.
  5. *Country Trade Statistics* and many others. See *A Basic Guide to Exporting* ($8.50 from the Government Printing Office) for a complete list or request information from nearest Department of Commerce field office. Additional Commerce publications are listed in Chapter 16.
  6. *National Trade Database*—CD-ROM from Department of Commerce; government documents section in university library should have it.
 K. *Crossborder Monitor* "Indicators of Market Size for 117 Countries" (annual).
 L. Monitor, London, England.
  1. *Europe Marketing Data & Statistics* (annual).
  2. *International Marketing Data & Statistics* (annual).
 M. *Worldcasts*—information access company.
 N. Commercial officers of foreign embassies in Washington, DC.
 O. Trade associations.
 P. Banks with international departments.
 Q. Chambers of commerce, such as the German-American Chamber of Commerce in New York City or the Mexican-American Chamber of Commerce in Mexico City.
 R. Databases such as Reuters' *Textline*, Dun & Bradstreet's *Datastream International*, Predicasts in Cleveland, Ohio, and The Economist Intelligence Unit in London, England.
 S. Many state governments have trade offices with country and market specialists and good libraries.

     T. Write to commercial officers in American embassies.
     U. Your company's suppliers and customers have data they might share.
     V. Big 8 accounting firms sell studies that they conduct, and some publish newsletters.

III. Political and legal forces.
     A. *Business International—Country Assessment Service.*
     B. *Business Environment Risk Index.*
     C. Frost and Sullivan—*Political Risk Country Reports.*
     D. European Union—*Europe.*
     E. Oceana Publishers, Dobbs Ferry, NY—publications on various law categories.
     F. International Chamber of Commerce—various publications.
     G. Association newsletters.
     H. Major city newspapers.
     I. Business magazines.

IV. Cultural forces.
     A. Brigham Young University—*Culturegrams.*
     B. Business magazines.
        1. *Business Week.*
        2. *The Economist.*
        3. *Fortune.*
        4. *Forbes.*
     C. Major city newspapers.

V. Competitive forces.
     A. Most of the sources listed in Part I.
     B. Talk with knowledgeable people, but be careful. You may be given misinformation on purpose.

Marketing Internationally

> We will market world brands that share global technology and common positioning, but with appropriate regional testing of product aesthetics and form, packaging materials, and market execution to best satisfy local customer demands for quality and value.
>
> Edwin L. Artzt, chairman and CEO, Procter & Gamble Company

CONCEPT PREVIEWS

After reading this chapter, you should be able to:

1. **understand** why at times there are differences between marketing domestically and internationally

2. **explain** why international marketing managers wish to standardize the marketing mix regionally or worldwide

3. **comprehend** why it is often impossible to standardize the marketing mix worldwide

4. **appreciate** the importance of distinguishing among the total product, the physical product, and the brand name

5. **explain** why consumer products generally require greater modification for international sales than industrial products or services

6. **understand** how the environmental forces affect the marketing mix

7. **discuss** the product strategies that can be formed from three product alternatives and three kinds of promotional messages

8. **explain** "glocal" advertising strategies

9. **understand** the intricacies of transfer pricing

10. **discuss** the distribution strategies of international marketers

11. **describe** the channel selection process of international marketers

Procter & Gamble, an Evolving Global Corporation

There have been some false starts and even some failures, but now Procter & Gamble's global marketing efforts are starting to bring results. The company, ranked 34 in *Fortune*'s "The World's Largest Corporations" and 12 in its "Largest U.S. Industrial Corporations," obtained $15.9 billion (52 percent of its total sales) from its non-U.S. operations. • This is all the more notable inasmuch as P&G faces more pressures in most foreign markets than it does in the United States. Many foreign countries have price controls, and there are more competitors in Europe because of the ease of shipping products across borders. For example, in France, P&G competes against Swedish, Danish, and Italian firms in many of its product categories. Commercial TV time, the most efficient way to introduce new products quickly, is limited, and in many countries, such as Belgium, Germany, Italy, and Japan, the use of premiums and gifts for promotion is either banned or severely restricted. • In the 1940s, P&G's strategy was to export its core products to build demand and then establish local sales companies or production facilities. Whether the products were exported or produced locally, they were marketed similarly everywhere. Although those products were not launched with global distribution in mind, new products are. According to Edwin Artzt, P&G's chairman, "If P&G were introducing Pampers today, it would plan to get the product into world markets in five years or less." It took the company 15 years to get them into 70 countries. Now the company tries to introduce products on a worldwide scale early in their development, not after they are established in one market, which gives competitors time to react in all other markets. • Sometimes P&G approaches foreign markets more as a regional market than as a global one; many of its products are changed to suit the local markets, for example. Camay's smell, Crest's flavor, and Head & Shoulders' formula vary from one region to another, as does the company's marketing strategy. "The idea of moving quickly by taking a piece of technology and implementing it to fit the habits of local markets has taken hold and is leading our operation," says Artzt. "[But] there is a reluctance to fix something that isn't broke—that is, alter a product or a marketing strategy that is successful in one market just because it doesn't fit the global pattern." • For many years, P&G had a philosophy of employing overseas the same policies and procedures that had been successful in the United States, but this practice sometimes gave the company problems. The company rolled out Vizir, based on Liquid Tide, in Europe in the 1980s. What the marketers failed to realize was the European washing machines were not equipped to accept liquid detergents. When Vizir was added to a powder dispenser, 20 percent was lost in the bottom of the washer. P&G developed a plastic dispenser that fit

Sources: "Taking Flak," *The Wall Street Journal*, April 10, 1993, p. A1; "P&G's Artzt on Ads: Crucial Investment," *Advertising Age*, October 28, 1991, p. 1; "Stodgy No More," *The Wall Street Journal*, March 5, 1991, p. A1; and "P&G Rushes On Global Diaper Rollout," *Advertising Age*, November 24, 1991, p. 6; "The Largest U.S. Industrial Corporations," *Fortune*, April 18, 1994, p. 220; and "Guide to the Global," *Fortune*, July 25, 1994, p. 164.

into powder dispensers and offered it free to consumers. One small problem—European washing machines are bolted to the wall. "When we called these women and said we wanted to mail you a liquid dispenser free, just tell us the washer model number, they said, 'I don't know, the washer is bolted to the wall and I can't see it,'" explained Artzt. The company finally solved the problem by inventing a reusable ball that sits on top of the clothes and dispenses the liquid. Vizir is now the third-largest-selling detergent in France and has been relaunched in other European countries. Artzt claims, "I think this will go down in history as one of the great all-time rescue jobs." • On the other hand, P&G recycled an ad campaign previously used in the United States when it relaunched Orange Crush in Peru. The TV spot showed a small boy who promises to save his soccer-playing brother's Orange Crush but then succumbs to temptation and drinks it himself. It is credited with playing an important part in a 60 percent sales increase. • To avoid a repetition of the washing machine problem, P&G's present strategy is to make global plans, then replan for each region and execute the plan locally. It uses autonomous "core teams" composed of representatives of each country in a region to plan a testing program or a development program for new products and product improvement. They recommend products and marketing strategies for the core products (product lines)—soap, toothpaste, diapers, and shampoo. P&G core teams are working on the smell and concentration levels of fabric softeners for different parts of the world, for example. • Even the core team concept is evolving; a new one for disposables and beverages has been organized globally rather than regionally, as the first four teams were.

The opening section illustrates how P&G has changed its marketing strategy from one of using the same procedures and policies overseas that have proven successful in the United States to one of making global plans, adjusting them for regions, and then adapting them to satisfy local demands.

Whether a policy or technique is first designed for global use and then adapted for local market differences or, as in the case of the Orange Crush advertisement, the idea comes first from the home country and then is used overseas, marketers must know where to look for possible differences between marketing domestically and marketing internationally. Sometimes, the differences are great; at other times, there are no differences.

Certainly there are some strong commonalities. Isn't it true that marketers everywhere must (1) know their markets, (2) develop products or services to satisfy customers' needs, (3) price the products or services so that they are readily acceptable in the market, (4) make them available to the buyers, and (5) inform potential customers and persuade them to buy?

ADDED COMPLEXITIES OF INTERNATIONAL MARKETING

Although the basic functions of domestic and international marketing are the same, the international markets served often differ widely because of the great variations in the uncontrollable environmental forces that we examined in Section Three. Moreover, even the forces we think of as controllable vary among wide limits: distribution channels to which the marketer is accustomed are unavailable, certain aspects of the product may be different, the promotional mixes are often dissimilar, and distinct cost structures may require different prices to be set.

The international marketing manager's task is complex. He or she frequently must plan and control a variety of marketing strategies rather than one and then coordinate and integrate those strategies into a single marketing program. Even the marketing managers of global firms such as P&G who utilize a single, worldwide strategy must know enough about the uncontrollable variables to be able to make changes in its implementation when necessary.

Both global and multinational marketing managers, like their domestic counterparts, must develop marketing strategies by assessing the firm's potential foreign markets and analyzing the many alternative marketing mixes. Their aim is to select target markets that the firm can serve at a profit and to formulate combinations of tactics for product, price, promotion, and distribution channels that will best serve those markets. In the previous chapter, we examined the market assessment and selection process; in this chapter, we shall study the formulation of the marketing mix.

As we indicated above, the marketing mix consists of a set of strategy decisions made in the areas of product, promotion, pricing, and distribution for the purpose of satisfying the customers in a target market. The number of variables included in these four areas is extremely large, making possible hundreds of combinations. Often the domestic operation has already established a successful marketing mix, and the temptation to follow the same procedures overseas is strong. Yet, as we have seen, important differences between the domestic and foreign environments may make a wholesale transfer of the mix impossible. The question that the international marketing manager must resolve is, "Can we standardize worldwide, must we make some changes, or must we formulate a completely different marketing mix?"

THE MARKETING MIX (WHAT AND HOW TO SELL)

Standardization, Adaptation, or Completely Different?

Management would prefer global standardization of the marketing mix—that is, it would prefer to employ the same marketing mix in all of the firm's operations because standardization can produce significant cost savings. If the product sold in the domestic market can be exported, there can be longer production runs, which lower manufacturing costs. Even when the standard product is manufactured overseas, production costs will be less because the extra research and design expense of either adapting domestic products or designing new ones for foreign sales will be avoided. Just the task of keeping many sets of specifications current requires additional, highly paid personnel in the home office.

> Generally, R&D is still highly concentrated in the home country, although some internationals have had overseas research facilities for years; recently, global firms have been locating R&D centers in foreign markets. When a firm's R&D is highly concentrated in the home county, the important product changes have to be made there. Foreign and domestic personnel compete for R&D time. Also, a product specification is rarely frozen (look at the minor changes in automobiles in a single model year). Notifying all of the production facilities worldwide about these modifications is difficult enough, but it is much more complex when the product is not internationally standardized.

For the many products, both consumer and industrial, that require spare parts for after-sales servicing, standardization greatly simplifies logistics and acquisition.

If advertising campaigns, promotional materials (catalogs, point-of-purchase displays), and sales training programs can be standardized, the expensive creative work and artwork need be done only once. Standardized pricing strategies for multinational firms that source markets from several different foreign subsidiaries avoid the embarrassment of having an important customer receive two distinct quotations for the same product. Although economies of scale are not as readily attainable for standardizing channels of distribution as for the other elements of the marketing mix, there is some gain in efficiency when the international marketing manager can use the same strategy in all markets. In summary, the benefits from standardization of the marketing mix are (1) lower costs, (2) easier control and coordination from headquarters, and (3) reduction of the time consumed in preparing the marketing plan.

In spite of the advantages of standardization, many firms find it necessary to either modify the present mix or develop a new one. The extent of the changes depends on the type of product (consumer or industrial), the environmental forces, and the degree of market penetration desired by management.

Product Strategies

The product is the central focus of the marketing mix. If it fails to satisfy the needs of consumers, no amount of promotion, price cutting, or distribution will persuade them to buy. Consumers will not repurchase a detergent if the clothes do not come out as clean as TV commercials say they will. They will not be deceived by advertisements announcing friendly service when experience demonstrates otherwise.

total product
What the customer buys, including the physical product, brand name, accessories, after-sales service, warranty, instructions for use, company image, and package

In formulating product strategies, international marketing managers must remember that the product is more than a physical object. The **total product,** which is what the customer buys, also includes the physical product, brand name, accessories, after-sales service, warranty, instructions for use, company image, and package (see Figure 15–1). The fact that the total product is purchased often makes it less expensive and easier for an international company to adapt the present product or even create a new one without altering its physical characteristics. Different package sizes and promotional messages, for example, can create a new total product for a distinct market. The relative ease of creating a new total product without changing the

---

FIGURE 15–1

Components of the total product

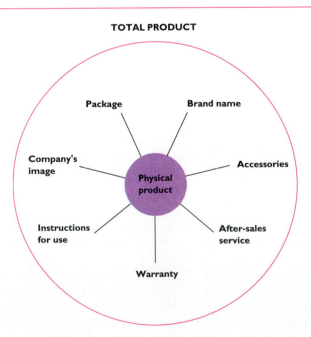

manufacturing process is an important reason there is more physical product standardization internationally than one might expect.

Total and Physical Product.   Much of the confusion in the ongoing discussion about whether a global firm can have global products results from the discussants not clarifying whether they are referring to the total product, the physical product, or the brand name. For example, Coca-Cola is always offered as an example of a global product, and it is true that the total product and the brand are global. However, the physical product is multinational; its sweetness varies according to local tastes, even in the United States.

Consider two products that Cadbury-Schweppes, the British-based food and soft drink multinational, produces: tonic water and chocolate. The tonic water is a global product physically, but as a total product, it is multinational because people buy it for different reasons. The French drink it straight, and the English mix it with alcohol. Chocolate is neither a global physical product nor a global total product; it is eaten as a snack in some places, put in sandwiches in some places, and eaten as a dessert in others. Because of strong local preferences, it also varies greatly in taste.[1] So does Nestlé instant coffee, which is produced in 200 different blends globally, all of which are sold under the brand name Nescafe, another example of brand name globalization.[2]

Type of Product.   One important factor that influences the amount of change to be made in a product is its classification as a consumer or industrial product or service. Generally, consumer products require greater adaptation than industrial products to meet the demands of the world market. If the consumer products are high style or the result of a fad, they are especially likely to require changes. We can think of these product types as being on a continuum ranging from insensitive to the foreign environment to highly sensitive, as shown in Figure 15–2.

Industrial Products.   As one would gather from Figure 15–2, many highly technical industrial products can be sold unchanged worldwide. Transistors, for example, are used wherever radios are manufactured. Timken advertises that its bearings are interchangeable no matter where produced (see Figure 15–3).

If product changes are required, they may be only cosmetic, such as converting gauges to read in the metric system by pasting a new face on a dial or printing instruction plates in another language. However, many overseas buyers of industrial products, Europeans especially, will not buy American machinery even with cosmetic changes such as dial conversion to metrics. They demand that the machine be made in the metric system to metric measurements. General Electric found out how serious this problem can be when its shipment of electrical goods was refused admission to Saudi Arabia because the electrical cords were six-feet long instead of the required metric standard of two meters (6.6 feet).[3]

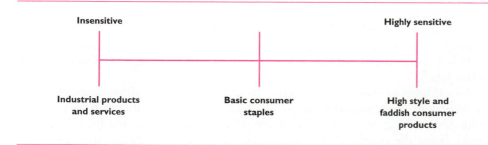

FIGURE 15–2

Continuum of sensitivity to the foreign environment

One of the authors arrived at the General Tire plant in Spain to install a V belt production department. When he told the company production managers he had a quotation for American machinery from a firm that supplied major V belt producers in the United States, they replied strongly they didn't want it. Since the machinery was of excellent quality, the writer asked why. They patiently explained that the mechanics had no wrenches to tighten bolts made in inches and if a simple nut or bolt had to be replaced, they would have to order it from the United States—they could not buy it from the local hardware store. We had the machinery built locally, and the American company lost a $100,000 order.

Relatively simple adaptations, such as lengthening pedals or changing seat positions, are frequently sufficient to compensate for the physical differences of foreign operators. However, somewhat more drastic modifications in the physical product may be necessary because of two problems that are especially prevalent in the developing countries—a tendency to *overload equipment* and to *slight maintenance*. These problems are comprehensible to anyone familiar with the cultural and economic forces in the foreign environment. Unlike American children, who grow up owning automobiles and working with tools, the mechanics and operators in many foreign countries rarely have such experience until they enter a training program, which is often on the job.[4]

A bulldozer operator learns that if he pulls a lever and steps on a pedal, his machine will push whatever is in front of it. It is not uncommon to see a bulldozer pushing on some immovable object until the engine fails or a part breaks from the overload. The extraordinary noise coming from the engine

On Global Marketing

"The globalization of markets is at hand. With that, the multinational commercial world nears its end and so does the multinational corporation. Different cultural preferences, national tastes and standards, and business institutions are vestiges of the past." So says Theodore Levitt, a Harvard business professor. The world has been homogenized, and the smart firms sell standardized products using standardized promotion methods. Levitt cites such examples as Coca-Cola, Pepsi-Cola, McDonald's, and Revlon.

But Coca-Cola's own advertising director replies, "What looks good as a generalization sometimes doesn't follow. The world is certainly becoming more globalized, but the global village is certainly not here, nor will it ever be." Coke's marketing manager noted that "Diet Coke clearly in many ways isn't appropriate for some undeveloped worlds." PepsiCo lets its overseas offices choose and reedit commercials it makes in the United States and makes local soft drinks like Shani, a currant-and-blackberry soda popular in the Mideast during Ramadan, the Moslem holy month. McDonald's, another company cited by Levitt, says it isn't an advocate of global marketing; it sells beer in Germany and in France, pot pies in Australia, and noodles in the Philippines. "We rely on the people native to the country to develop marketing programs," says the marketing vice president. Interestingly, McDonald's retains 74 different ad agencies in the United States to customize its promotion for local markets. Campbell Soup split the country into 22 different regions, each with different marketing strategies.

Is global marketing a nice fad, as a member of Booz, Allen & Hamilton, a well-known consulting firm, says it is? Is it a new idea? No, to both questions. Timken has made the same product and promoted it the same way for decades. Thirty years ago, Goodyear's Hi-Miler truck tire was being produced in Akron and its overseas plants and sold under translated names such as *Tragaleguas* (league-eater) for Spanish-speaking markets.

What is new is that companies are first studying their global markets and then, where possible, making a single product for all of them instead of making the product for the domestic market and adapting it to foreign markets. They search for global themes and adapt the promotion of them to fit the local markets. Products that are not culturally sensitive, such as nearly all industrial products and most consumer durables, clothing, and toilet articles, lend themselves to a single, worldwide theme and message; food products require much more adaptation to the local culture. For example, Colgate-Palmolive's Oral Care promotional program (for toothpaste) was successful worldwide.

To sum up, the success of global marketing depends on the kind of product and knowing when product or promotional adaptations are necessary.

Sources: Theodore Levitt, "The Globalization of Markets," *Harvard Business Review*, May–June 1983, pp. 92 and 96; and "Ad Fad," *The Wall Street Journal*, May 12, 1988, pp. 1 and 17.

---

makes no impression on the operator. Despite the careful instructions concerning cleanliness that ball-bearing manufacturers include in the package, one can find a mechanic removing the protective oiled paper to leave the bearing exposed to dust and grime before using it (he probably can't read). A very low-paid, uneducated man may be given the responsibility of lubricating equipment worth millions of dollars. He may overgrease or miss half of the fittings, and the equipment is destroyed.

To overcome these difficulties, such manufacturers as Caterpillar and Allis-Chalmers have established very thorough training programs wherever their products are sold. Many manufacturers have prepared simple instructions with plenty of pictures to get their message across to persons with limited reading ability. The other alternative is to modify the equipment, perhaps using a simpler bearing system that requires little maintenance. The machine may make more noise and be less efficient, but it runs longer with less maintenance.

Where the technology of even an adapted product is too advanced for their customers, manufacturers may market an entirely different product to accomplish the same purpose. A firm that produces electric cash registers in the United States, for example, may be able to earn good profits by marketing a hand-operated model in areas where electricity is unavailable. Products considered obsolete in advanced countries are frequently what developing countries need.[5] Also, foreign subsidiaries sometimes find market opportunities for product lines not manufactured by the parent company.

> Marketing managers in General Tire's affiliates saw the profit possibilities in selling fan and industrial V-belts in their markets. Although General Tire–USA did not produce them, management obtained the technology for their subsidiaries through licensing agreements with Gates Rubber, a renowned maker of V-belts, so that this totally new product was manufactured in a number of foreign plants.

Occasionally, adaptations are necessary to meet local legal requirements, such as those that govern noise, safety, or exhaust emissions. To avoid changing the product, some manufacturers design it to meet the most stringent laws even though it will be overdesigned for the rest of the markets. In some instances, governments have passed very strict laws to protect a local manufacturer from imports. When this occurs, the company may prefer to design the product to the next most stringent laws and stay out of the first market. Of course, this is what the government had in mind when it passed the laws. However, a word of caution for the company in this situation—test the local manufacturer's product before giving up on the market. On occasion, the local product also has failed to meet the specifications. When confronted with this evidence, the government has had to change the laws.

Consumer Products. Although consumer products generally require greater modification to meet local market requirements than do industrial products, some of them can be sold unchanged to certain market segments. Consumer products of this kind include a number of luxury items, such as large automobiles, sporting equipment, and perfumes. This is because every country in the world contains a market segment that is more similar to the same segment in other countries with respect to economic status, buyer behavior, tastes, and preferences than it is to the rest of the segments in the same country. This market segment includes the "jet set," foreign-educated and well-traveled citizens, and expatriates. Many products and services foreign to local tastes and preferences have been successfully introduced by first being marketed to this group. Gradually, members of other market segments have purchased these products and services until consumption has become widespread.

> Before McDonald's and other American fast-food franchisors went abroad, a common complaint among U.S. expatriates was that they couldn't get a good hamburger. A Brazilian returned from college in the United States and opened a drive-in similar to Dairy Queen in Rio de Janeiro. The first customers were Americans and members of the international set, but before long, word spread and Brazilians became customers. Thirty years ago, there was only one A&W root beer stand and one Dairy Queen in Mexico City. American expatriates and tourists were the principal customers. Today, many of the American fast-food franchisors are in such cities as Mexico City, Guadalajara, and Monterrey. When you arrive in Acapulco, the signs of Ponderosa, Kentucky Fried Chicken, and so forth make you think you never left home.

In introducing new products, especially when the goal is immediate market penetration, marketers must be aware that *generally, as they go down the economic and social strata in each country, they will tend to find greater dissimilarities among countries with respect to social and cultural values.* It follows from this that in general, the deeper the immediate market penetration desired, the greater must be the product modification. This does not necessarily mean the physical product must be changed. Perhaps a modifica-

Small Service Companies Go Overseas for High Profits

Small U.S. service companies are going overseas to look for business, and they're finding it. Last year, the city of Tokyo gave New York architect Rafael Vinoly a $50 million contract to build its $1 billion International Forum complex on a 6.7-acre site. According to the U.S. Department of Commerce, it was the largest such contract ever awarded to a foreign firm.

Another small service company, Macro Systems, is helping India's Steel Authority design and implement quality systems for its five steel plants; and ExecuTrain Corporation is signing its first master franchise for its computer-training business in Great Britain. Broadview Associates, a small firm specializing in mergers and acquisitions in the information-technology industry, claims its European office handled 15 deals last year that brought in nearly a third of the company's business. Smallness is an advantage, says a Broadview partner. Large investment bankers aren't interested in the smaller transactions generating fees of less than $1 million as is Broadview.

Japanese firms are going to great lengths to accommodate small American service companies. Soon after winning his Tokyo contract, Vinoly was given a $700,000 credit line by the Fuji Bank without being asked for collateral. Days later, a New York bank denied him a business loan even though he already had deposited in the bank an amount equal to that which he wanted to borrow. The city of Tokyo also agreed to pay Vinoly in six installments instead of once at the beginning and once at the end of the contract.

A small-business specialist with the International Trade Administration says that small companies are showing increasing interest in selling their services in foreign markets. She believes the GATT negotiations should establish a framework for trading in services that should make international trade more accessible to small service businesses. Already, many small U.S. companies are being approached by foreign concerns that see them as links to the large American market.

Sources: "Strategies for the New Export Boom," *Fortune*, August 22, 1994, pp. 124–30; and "Small Service Companies Find High Profits Overseas," *The Wall Street Journal*, March 29, 1991, p. B2.

---

tion of one of the other elements of the total product is sufficient—a different size or color of the package, a change in the brand name, or a new positioning if the product is consumed differently.

> Mars faced a drop in Bahrain's imports of candy when it was ready to launch M&Ms. Fortunately, its marketing research discovered that Bahrainis consider the peanut to be a health food, so Mars repositioned its peanut M&Ms. The company was able to turn the hot Gulf climate to its advantage by emphasizing its traditional slogan, "M&Ms melt in your mouth, not in your hand." As you will see later in this chapter, Mars followed promotional strategy number 2: same product—different message, although part of the message (slogan) remained the same.[6]

Detergent manufacturers were able to achieve deeper market penetration by offering consumers with limited purchasing power the small packages that we find only in American laundromats. In humid climates, cookies and crackers are packed in metal boxes to preserve both the package and the product.

Services. The marketing of services, sometimes called *intangibles*, is similar to the marketing of industrial products in that these products are generally easier to market globally than consumer products are. Andersen Consulting's 24,598 professionals offer worldwide in their 150 offices in 46 countries the same kinds of expertise in business strategy that they sell to American clients. Fifty-one percent of the firm's $2.88 billion revenues came from outside the United States in 1993.[7]

It is true that laws and customs sometimes force providers to alter their products. There are some markets that Manpower cannot operate in, for example, because in these countries, private employment agencies are against the law. Accounting laws vary substantially between nations, but Big Eight accounting firms operate globally. Price Waterhouse, for example, has over 400 offices in 118 nations, and its 7,200 professionals earned 55 percent of the firm's $1 billion in 1993 revenues outside the United States.[8] There are worldwide subscribers to Nexis, Mead Corporation's database, one aspect of the fast-growing international computer and data processing industry. Visa, MasterCard, and American Express, with combined billing of over $1 trillion in 1993, are examples of successful companies in the global credit card industry.[9] The physical product may vary slightly because of the local environmental forces, but the total product remains the same.

Foreign Environmental Forces. In Section Three, we examined the foreign environmental forces rather extensively, so here we will limit our discussion to a few concrete examples of how some of these forces affect product offerings.

Sociocultural Forces. Dissimilar cultural patterns generally necessitate changes in food and other consumer goods. The worldwide variation in the mundane chore of clothes washing certainly has caused problems for Procter & Gamble, as you read in the opening section, but it is also troublesome for European appliance makers. The French want top-loading washing machines, and the British want front-loading ones; the Germans insist on high-speed machines that remove most of the moisture in the spin-dry cycle, but the Italians prefer slower spin speeds because they let warm sun do the drying. Hence, Whirlpool must produce a variety of models, although after buying Philips appliance business in 1991, it has changed what was a collection of independent national companies into a Europe-wide organization that uses a few common platforms. This simplification allows the company to produce several models on the same chassis.

Competitors question Whirlpool's drive toward providing a common product mix for Europe. "Whirlpool sees Europe as a uniform market, but we also see the differences in customer demands and needs from country to country," says competitor Bosch-Siemens. However, Whirlpool's CEO argues the national differences are exaggerated;: "This business is the same all over the world. There is great opportunity to leverage that sameness."[10]

Although some multinational firms, such as Kodak and Campbell, have been extremely successful in employing the same brand name, label, and colors worldwide, other firms are sometimes surprised to learn they must change to other names, labels, or colors because of cultural differences. Green packages are taboo in the Far East because they remind the public of the dangers and illnesses of the jungle, but gold appears frequently on packages in Latin America because Latin Americans view it as a symbol of quality and prestige. In the Netherlands, blue is considered warm and feminine, but the Swedes consider it masculine and cold.

> Procter & Gamble found out that a gold package has value in Europe too after it launched its Crest Tarter Control Formula in the United Kingdom in a silver box, which was followed two months later by Colgate's equivalent in a gold box. Sheepish P&G officials, agreeing that Colgate's choice of gold was better than their silver, explained that silver was required because that was how the product was packaged in the United States.[11]

Even if the colors can remain the same, instructions on labels, of course, must be translated into the language of the market. Firms selling in areas where two or more languages are spoken, such as Canada or Switzerland, may need to use multilingual labels. Where instructions are not required, as in the case of some consumer or industrial products whose use is well known, there is an advantage to printing the label in the language of the country best known for the product. French labels on perfumes and English labels on industrial goods help to strengthen the product's image.

> A Mexican firm in which one of the writers had an interest copied an American brand of penetrating oil that was the best-selling import, even to the blue color. It put a label in English on the can. Then, to comply with the

law, a gummed sticker saying *Envasado en Mexico* (can filled in Mexico) was placed over part of the label. The Mexican product, unlike most locally made industrial products, had excellent acceptance from the start.

A perfectly good brand name may have to be scrapped because of its unfavorable connotations in another language. An American product failed to make it in Sweden because its name translated to "enema." In Latin America, a product had to be taken off the market when the manufacturer found that the name meant "jackass oil." Of course, this problem occurs in both directions, as a Belgian brewery found when it tried to introduce its Delerium Tremens lager to the U.S. market. American authorities told the company the name was an incitement to drinking. They also said that calling another beer Guillotine was like an American brewery calling its beer "electric chair."[12]

Sometimes a firm will not use a perfectly good name because someone has invented a story about its impropriety in foreign markets. This is what happened with the name Nova. As the story goes, Chevrolet couldn't sell Novas in (the storyteller picks a Spanish-speaking country) because Nova means *no va* (doesn't go) in Spanish. What the person doesn't realize is that the two are pronounced very differently—Nova has the accent over the first syllable, whereas the accent for *no va* falls on the *va*. Therefore, to someone speaking Spanish, the words have very different meanings. Most native Spanish-speaking people connect *nova* with star, which is probably what General Motors had in mind. You may be surprised to learn that Pemex, the government-owned oil monopoly that is the exclusive refiner and retailer of gasoline in Mexico, named its regular gasoline *Nova*.

Incidentally, an economic constraint to the international standardization of brand names is the refusal of some firms to let a subsidiary put their brand on a locally made product if it fails to meet their quality standards because of the inability to import the necessary raw materials or because the required production equipment is unavailable.

An important difference in the social forces to which American marketers are not accustomed is people's preference in other nations, both developed and developing, for making daily visits to the small neighborhood specialty shops and the large, open markets where they can socialize while shopping.

Pemex gasoline doesn't go.

Victoria Ball

There Still Is No European Consumer

Although casual observation seems to indicate that there is a convergence in shopping habits among Europeans, new comprehensive research reveals that national shopping and buying habits vary greatly.

A survey of 7,000 citizens of six EU countries—the United Kingdom, France, Germany, Italy, the Netherlands, and Spain—was conducted by a London-based research center. The results, published in *Frontiers: Planning for Customer Change in Europe,* show that in Italy, both rich and poor believe in paying high prices to get the best quality, whereas in Germany, even the rich shop for a bargain. Three-quarters of the Spaniards believe the most expensive wine is the finest, compared to only 5 percent of the French.

Only 30 percent of the British 25- to 44-year-olds know what they want to buy in a supermarket, compared to 47 percent of the same age group in the Netherlands. Still the ex-East Germans beat them—only 18 percent know what they want, but they are still recovering from the trauma of going to the store for decades without knowing what they would find. In comparison, 40 percent of the methodical West Germans have their shopping lists ready.

Even bread has national differences. The wide selection of German branded breads signifies that the Germans are spending more for special types, whereas the English regard bread as a commodity. Also types of bread that are common in one market are considered luxuries in other markets. French sophisticates form lines to buy sliced white bread, a common purchase in Great Britain, in the same way the English are buying French croissants.

Differences in consumer patterns are likely to be more cultural than economic and may be more pronounced within countries than between them. When considering such products as stereos and automobiles, London yuppies may have more in common with young, rich Parisians than with their own older countrymen. There are still some striking differences, however. While 60 percent of the British own a VCR, only 40 percent of the Germans do, and just 19 percent of the Italians. Unlike Americans, who prefer imported cars, the majority of the Italians would rather buy an Italian car even when it is clearly inferior to the same-priced foreign car. The Germans show above-average support for their domestic car industry also.

However, not all age groups are so different. According to a study by McCann-Erickson, the ad agency, European teenagers are a more homogeneous group now than ever. They are also more practical, materialistic, and hedonistic than their predecessors. As a result of being brought up in the market-led economies of the 1980s, they have become "expert consumers."

Sources: "The New European Consumer," *Eurobusiness,* July 1989, pp. 10–11; and "Revealed: How Shopping Habits Still Split Europe," *The European,* September 27–29, 1991, p. 17.

More frequent buying permits smaller packages, which is especially important to a shopper who has no automobile in which to carry purchases. However, this custom is changing in Europe, where a growing sophistication of consumption patterns is demanding the kinds of assortments that only a large store can offer. Shopping frequency is also slowing as European women, especially if employed, are finding that they have less free time than previously. As we mentioned in Chapter 13, the solution has been the huge combination supermarket–discount house (e.g., *hypermarché* in France) with ample parking and generally located in the suburbs.

A similar situation had been occurring in Mexico, especially after the signing of NAFTA and the lifting of many of the country's import restrictions. Enormous crowds, anxious to buy at lower prices, showed up at the Wal-Mart and Kmart stores when they first opened in 1993. So many people tried to enter the Monterrey Wal-Mart on opening day that store employees had to bar the doors to control the crowd.[13] Since the massive peso devaluation, the peso prices of imported American products, one of the store's attractions, have risen so high that store attendance has dropped precipitously. Mexicans, particularly those living in Monterrey or farther north, still come to shop in Texas border-city Wal-Marts where prices are lower, although as the peso's value continues to fall, this differential is evaporating.[14]

One can easily draw a parallel in this situation to that which began in the 1940s in the United States. The same conditions of rising incomes, a growing middle class, and an increasing number of working wives have combined to put a premium on the shopper's time, and just as occurred in the United States, supermarkets, mass merchandising, and catalog selling have moved in to fill this need.

Legal Forces. Legal forces can be a formidable constraint in the design of product strategies because if the firm fails to adhere to a country's laws governing the product, it will be unable to do business in that country. Laws concerning pollution, consumer protection, and operator safety are being enacted rapidly in many parts of the world and are severely affecting the marketer's freedom to standardize the product mix internationally. For example, American machinery manufacturers exporting to Sweden have found their operator safety requirements to be even stricter than those required by the Occupational Safety and Health Act (OSHA), so that if they wish to market in Sweden, they must produce a special model. We have previously mentioned that product standards set ostensibly to protect a nation's citizens can be very effective in protecting indigenous industry from foreign competitors.

Laws prohibiting certain classes of imports are extremely common in developing nations, as potential exporters learn when they research the world for markets. We know that products considered luxuries, as well as products already being manufactured, are among the first to be excluded from importation, but such laws also affect local production. As we saw in the previous section, prohibition of essential raw material imports can require a subsidiary to manufacture a product substantially different from what the parent company produces.

Foods and pharmaceuticals are especially influenced by laws concerning purity and labeling. Food products sold in Canada, whether imported or produced locally, are subject to strict rules that require both English and French on the labels as well as metric and inch-pound units. The law even dictates the space permitted between the number and the unit—16 oz. is correct, but 16oz. is not. The Venezuelan government, in an effort to protect consumers from being overcharged for pharmaceuticals, has decreed that the manufacturer or the importer must affix to the package the maximum retail price at which the product can be sold. Because of the Saudi Arabians' preoccupation with avoiding food containing pork, the label of any product containing animal fat or meat that is sold in Saudi Arabia must state the kind of animal used or that no swine products were used.

Legal forces may also prevent a worldwide firm from employing its brand name in all of its overseas markets. Managements accustomed to the American law, which establishes the right to a brand name by priority in use, are surprised to learn that in code law countries, a brand belongs to the person registering it first. Thus, the marketer may go into foreign markets expecting to use the company's long-established brand name only to find that someone else owns it. The name may have been registered by someone who is employing it legitimately for his own products, or it may have been pirated— that is, registered by someone who hopes to profit by selling the name back to the originating firm.

Both reasons stopped Ford from marketing its automobiles under established names in Mexico and Germany. In the case of Mexico, the reason was brand piracy. Ford refused to pay the high price the registrant wanted for the name, so for years the Falcon was known as the Ford 200. The use of the name Mustang by a bicycle manufacturer in Germany was legitimate. The firm was producing under that name when Ford entered the market.

To avoid Ford's predicament, the firm must register its brand names in every country where it wants to use them or where it might use them in the future. And this must be done rapidly. The Paris Convention grants a firm that has registered a name in one country only six months' priority in registering it elsewhere. To be certain that it has enough names for new products, Unilever, the English-Dutch manufacturer of personal care products, has over 100,000 trademarks registered throughout the world, most of which are not in use but are kept in reserve.

Economic Forces. The great disparity in income throughout the world is an important obstacle to worldwide product standardization. Many products from the industrialized countries are simply too expensive for consumers in the developing countries, so if the firm wishes to achieve market penetration, it must either simplify the product or produce a different, less costly one.

When Gillette discovered that only 8 percent of Mexican men used shaving cream (the rest use soapy water), it introduced a plastic tube of shaving cream at half the price of its aerosol can. Now more than twice that percentage use the less expensive package, and Gillette is selling the tube in other parts of Latin America. Because many Latin American customers can't afford to buy American-sized packages, the company sells packages of single razor blades and half-ounce packages of Silkience shampoo. Use of the plastic squeeze bottle, "the poor man's aerosol," is common where incomes are low.[15]

Similarly, Hoover saw an opportunity to sell a simple washing machine to Mexicans who could not afford the high-priced American-type machine. Although Hoover had no American model to simplify, it was able to copy its inexpensive British washer, which became an overnight success.

Economic forces affect product standardization in still another way. Poor economies signify poor infrastructure—bad roads, lack of sufficient electric power, and so on. Driving conditions in Mexico required Goodrich to design a tire for cut and bruise resistance rather than for high speed, as in the United States. The tire was so successful that residents in U.S. border towns preferred it to the U.S. product even though its price was higher.

The lack of a constant supply of electricity, another characteristic of many poorer countries, has compelled refrigerator manufacturers to supply a gasoline-driven product and office equipment firms to manufacture hand-operated machines. As one would expect, this condition has also provided the producers of small diesel standby generators with a ready market. Any users requiring a steady source of power, such as hospitals and theaters, are potential customers.

Market size influences the product mix, and, in the poorer countries, the populations are not only frequently smaller but also contain a large number of people who have no means to purchase anything but the bare necessities of life, thereby making the already small market even smaller. This means that normally the foreign subsidiary cannot afford to produce as complete a product mix as does the parent. Most automobile manufacturers assemble only the least expensive line and broaden the local product mix by importing, when permitted, the luxury cars. All international firms practice this marketing technique whenever possible because a captive foreign sales organization is available to promote the sales of the home organization's exports and because the revenue derived helps pay the subsidiary's overhead.

Boeing's 737 became the best-selling commercial jet in history partly because its engineers redesigned it for Third World aviation after its initial sales to developed nations dropped off. The runways in developing countries were too short for the original design and, being made of less expensive asphalt rather than concrete, were also too soft. By redesigning the wings to allow shorter takeoffs and landings and by selling 1 or 2 at a time instead of batches of 20 or 30, which airlines in the developed nations order, Boeing built a reputation with developing countries' airlines, which, as they grew, began to buy Boeing's larger planes.[16]

Physical Forces. Physical forces, such as climate and terrain, also mitigate against international product standardization. Where the heat is intense, gasoline-driven machinery and automobiles must be fitted with larger radiators for extra cooling capacity. Gasoline must have a higher flash point to prevent vapor locks and stalling.

The heat and high humidity in many parts of the tropics require electrical equipment to be built with extraheavy insulation. Consumer goods that are affected by moisture must be specially packaged to resist its penetration. Thus, one finds pills wrapped individually in foil and baked goods packaged in tin boxes to prevent their degradation by moisture.

High altitudes frequently require product alteration. Food manufacturers have found that they must change their cooking instructions for people who live at high altitudes because at such altitudes it takes much longer to cook and bake. The thinner atmosphere requires producers of cake mixes to include less yeast. Gasoline and diesel motors generate less power at high altitudes, so the manufacturer must often supply a larger engine.

Mountainous terrain implies high-cost highways, so in the poorer countries, roads of the quality we know are nonexistent. Trucks traveling poorer-quality roads need tires with thicker treads and heavy-duty suspensions. Because of the rough ride, packaging must be stronger than that used in the United States. From these examples, we can appreciate that even though an unchanged product may be culturally and economically acceptable in a market, the effect of the physical forces alone may be strong enough to require some product modification.

Due to space limitations, it is impossible to examine the influence of every environmental force on foreign product strategies. We believe sufficient practical examples have been offered so that these, together with the information contained in the chapters on these forces, will give the reader an idea of their pervasiveness not only in the formulation of the product strategies but also in the design of the entire marketing mix. In fact, as we will show at the end of this chapter, a useful guide in the marketing mix preparation is a matrix in which the marketing mix variables are tabulated against the environmental forces.

Promotional Strategies

Promotion, one of the basic elements of the marketing mix, is communication that secures understanding between a firm and its publics to bring about a favorable buying action and achieve a long-lasting confidence in the firm and the product or service it provides. Note that this definition employs the plural, publics, because the seller's promotional efforts must be directed to more than just the ultimate consumers and the channel of distribution members. Far too often, the other publics have been ignored by business not only in the United States but in other markets as well. Managements have awakened to the fact that the old advice of always maintaining a low profile in a foreign country is not necessarily the best course of action. Many companies have changed this strategy and are now making the general public, special interest groups, and governments aware of their public service activities.

Because promotion both influences and is influenced by the other marketing mix variables, it is possible to formulate nine distinct strategies by combining the three alternatives of (1) marketing the same physical product

promotion
All forms of communication between a firm and its publics

everywhere, (2) adapting the physical product for foreign markets, and (3) designing a different physical product with *(a)* the same, *(b)* adapted, or *(c)* different messages.[17] Let us examine the six strategies most commonly used.

1. *Same product—same message.* When marketers find that target markets vary little with respect to product use and consumer attitudes, they can offer the same product and use the same promotional appeals in all markets. Avon, Maidenform, and A.T. Cross follow this strategy.

2. *Same product—different message.* The same product may satisfy a different need or be used differently elsewhere. This means the product may be left unchanged, but a different message is required. Honda's campaign, "You meet the nicest people on a Honda," appeals to Americans who use their motorcycles as a pleasure vehicle; but in Brazil, Honda stresses economy as it tries to make its product a means of basic transportation.

3. *Product adaptation—same message.* In cases where the product serves the same function but must be adapted to different conditions, the same message is employed with a changed product. In Japan, Lever Brothers puts Lux soap in fancy boxes because much of it is sold for gifts.

4. *Product adaptation—message adaptation.* In some cases, both the product and the promotional message must be modified for foreign markets. In Latin America, Tang is especially sweetened, pre-mixed, and ready to drink in pouches. Unlike Americans, Latin Americans do not drink it for breakfast. There it is promoted as a drink for mealtime and for throughout the day, but not for breakfast.

5. *Different product—same message.* As we pointed out in our discussion of the economic forces' influence on product strategies, the potential customers in many markets cannot afford the product as manufactured in the firm's home country. The product may also be too technologically advanced to gain widespread acceptance. To overcome these obstacles, companies have frequently produced a very distinct product for these markets. The previously mentioned low-cost plastic squeeze bottle and inexpensive manually operated washing machines are two examples. The promotional message, however, can be very similar to what is used in the developed countries if the product performs the same functions.

6. *Different product for the same use—different message.* Frequently, the different product requires a different message as well. Welding torches rather than automatic welding machines would be sold on the basis of low acquisition cost rather than high output per labor-hour. LDC governments faced with high unemployment would be persuaded by a message emphasizing the job-creating possibilities of labor-intensive processes rather than the labor saving of highly automated machinery.

The tools for communicating these messages—the promotional mix—are advertising, personal selling, sales promotion, public relations, and publicity. No one of these tools is inherently superior to the others, though circumstances in a given situation may dictate that one of them should be emphasized more than the others. Just as in the determination of the product strategies, the composition of the promotional mix will depend on the type of product, the environmental forces, and the amount of market penetration desired.

Advertising.   Of all the promotional mix elements, **advertising** is the one with the greatest similarities worldwide. This is because most advertising everywhere is based on American practices. U.S. ad agencies have greatly aided the global propagation of American techniques as they have followed their domestic customers overseas. Today, the major American agencies are all global, with wholly owned subsidiaries, joint ventures, and working agreements with local agencies. In the latest annual worldwide ranking by income of the top 50 advertising agencies, 23 are American, 14 are Japanese, 4 are French, 3 are British, and 2 are Korean.[18] Table 15–1 lists the 15 largest agencies.

Global and Regional Brands.   Manufacturers are increasingly using global or regional brands for a number of reasons:

1. Cost is most often cited. By producing one TV commercial for use across a region, a firm can save up to 50 percent in the production cost.

2. There is a better chance of obtaining one regional source to do high-quality work than attempting to find sources in various countries that will work to the same high standard.

3. Some marketing managers believe their companies must have a single image throughout a region.

4. Companies are establishing regionalized organizations where many functions such as marketing are centralized.

5. Global and regional satellite and cable television are becoming available.[19]

Economies of scale are one reason some firms emphasize the regional or global standardization of advertising. Coca-Cola, for example, estimates that it saves over $8 million annually in the cost of thinking up new imagery by repeating the same theme everywhere. Texas Instruments, which used to have four different creative approaches in Scandinavia (one per country), now runs similar ads in all four countries at a savings of $30,000 per commercial.

advertising
Paid, nonpersonal presentation of ideas, goods, or services by an identified sponsor

Organization, Headquarters	Gross Income		Percent Change
	1992	**1991**	
1. WPP Group, London	2,813.5	2,661.8	5.7%
2. Interpublic Group, New York	1,989.2	1,835.9	8.4
3. Omnicom Group, New York	1,806.7	1,687.3	7.1
4. Saatchi & Saatchi, London	1,696.5	1,651.0	2.8
5. Dentsu, Tokyo	1,387.6	1,451.0	−4.4
6. Young & Rubicam, New York	1,072.3	1,057.1	1.4
7. Euro RSCG, Neuilly, France	951.2	999.0	−4.8
8. Grey Advertising, New York	735.4	673.2	9.2
9. Foote, Cone & Belding, Chicago	682.7	619.5	10.2
10. Hakuhodo Inc., Tokyo	661.1	655.6	0.8
11. Leo Burnett Co., Chicago	643.8	576.6	11.7
12. Publicis-FCB Communications, Paris	590.1	505.8	16.7
13. D'Arcy Masius Benton & Bowles, New York	558.4	534.6	4.5
14. BDDP Worldwide, Paris	293.0	277.0	5.8
15. Bozell, Jacobs, Kenyon & Eckhardt, New York	231.0	221.0	4.5

TABLE 15–1
World's top 15 advertising organizations (ranked by gross income in $ millions)

Source: "World's Top 50 Advertising Organizations," *Advertising Age,* January 3, 1994, p. 22.

All the advertising agencies listed in Table 15–1 are at least regional and many of them are global. McCann-Erickson Worldwide, part of the Interpublic Group, is the world's largest international agency. About 75 percent of its billings come from global marketers such as Coca-Cola, General Motors, Goodyear Tire, Exxon, McDonald's, and L'Oréal, and it handles more global accounts than any other—17 versus 6 for its nearest competitor.[20]

Pan-European accounts, helped by EC 1992, have been increasing and are estimated to reach $4 billion by 1996. Eurobrands for small cars, chocolates, instant coffee, and skin care products already outspend domestic competitors on national television. A good number of advertisers are switching from various domestic agencies to a single agency group for all Europe. Unisys, Dell Computer, Pirelli, and British American Tobacco are examples. Unilever, the British-Dutch personal care products giant, was producing its Snuggle fabric softener in 13 different formulas, 8 fragrances, and 12 colors just in Europe four years ago; it now has only 6 formulas, 2 fragrances, and 2 colors.[21] "International competition has forced companies to rationalize their brands," says the chairman of Grey Advertising.[22]

McCann-American saves money for its multinational clients in Latin America with regional advertisements. For example, one client, Coca-Cola, advertises its global brand in Latin America with commercials designed in one place, usually Venezuela, which are sent on film to local markets where they are reshot. The local Coca-Cola companies have the option to add music and indigenous voices. Another regional advertiser, Gillette, uses the same method.[23] With the advent of regional and global media, especially satellite and cable TV, global and regional advertising campaigns have become more feasible for those advertisers that want them. We have just seen how firms with global brands such as Coca-Cola and Gillette permit local affiliates to make changes to regional commercials in keeping with the slogan of many managements, "Think globally, act locally."

Availability of Media. Satellite TV broadcasters are making it possible for numerous programming networks to provide service to millions of households in dozens of countries. Star TV, TVB, and ABN broadcast programs in Chinese and English and also carry cable networks such as Turner, ESPN, HBO, and others with which they reach 3 billion people in Asia. A British satellite TV firm, Sky Broadcasting, transmits programs to European cable companies and directly to homes with satellite dishes. One of the major programming networks using satellite TV broadcasting is CNN, which reaches 78 million households in over 100 countries. MTV calculates its audience to be 210 million people in 78 countries. Its Asian subsidiary broadcasts in Mandarin and English; MTV Latino's programs are in Spanish. Fox, Discovery, ESPN, and HBO are other programmers that broadcast internationally and sell time to advertisers.[24] The Middle East Broadcast Center, started in 1992, is the only satellite TV network that broadcasts Western-style news, entertainment, and advertising to Muslim countries in Arabic. Although the owners are Saudis, the Arabic female newscasters are not required to wear head coverings.[25]

There are also more international print media available. *The European,* a daily newspaper; the international edition of *The Herald Tribune;* the Asian and European editions of *The Wall Street Journal;* and the international editions of the *Manchester Guardian* and *Financial Times* are some of the newspapers with wide circulation. The *Reader's Digest* has 39 foreign editions and *Elle* has 19. Because all editions of each magazine are written for readers with similar demographics, all editions attract similar advertisers.

Africa is marked by a scarcity of all media. Only 163 radio stations serve an area twice the size of the United States, and although there are 84 TV stations in all, one-third of them are located in just two countries (Nigeria, 18 and Ivory Coast, 10). Ten countries have no TV. Even these numbers are misleading, because in many countries the stations are government owned and noncommercial. Although there are 190 daily newspapers in the 53 African countries, 91 of them are located in only 6 countries. Four countries have no daily paper, and 19 have only one.[26] In this seller's market, an advertiser may find that the newspaper has accepted too many ads for the available space. Some newspapers' solution is a raffle to decide which ads will be published!

In Latin America and the Middle East, the opposite situation exists: there are too many newspapers and magazines. The problem in those regions is choosing the right ones for the firm's target market. In which of the 900 newspapers in Brazil or the 400 in Turkey should the ad be placed? Circulation figures are greatly exaggerated, and the advertisers must also be careful of the publication's political position to avoid associating their firms with the "wrong side"—the one contrary to what the majority of their potential customers believe in.

These problems and the high illiteracy rate in some nations have forced advertisers to go to other media to reach their markets. Cinema advertising is heavily used in many parts of the world, as are billboards. In the Middle East, where media options are limited, videotape ads are rapidly becoming an integral part of the media mix. Advertisers penetrate this lucrative market by buying spots on popular video tapes. Three or four breaks with six or seven spots each are created at the beginning, middle, and end of the film. Three-quarters of the households in the United Arab Emirates, Saudi Arabia, and Kuwait have videocassette recorders, and in the first three months after release, a well-received video tape can draw an audience of 1 million viewers in Saudi Arabia alone.[27] In a number of less developed countries, automobiles equipped with loudspeakers circulate through the cities announcing products, and street signs are furnished by advertisers that hang their messages on them. Homeowners can get a free coat of paint by permitting advertisers to put ads on their walls. Where mail delivery is reliable, direct mail is a powerful medium, as are trade fairs. Probably one of the most ingenious campaigns ever was that of a tea company that gave away thousands of printed prayers with a tea commercial on the other side to pilgrims bound for Mecca. Table 15–2 illustrates how the constraints we have discussed affect the distribution of advertising expenditures.

The point is that media of some kind are available in every country, and the local managers and ad agencies are familiar with the advantages of each kind. Media selection is extremely difficult for international advertising managers who try to standardize their media mix from the home office. We have mentioned only some of the problems, but from these you can appreciate that the variation in media availability is a strong reason for leaving this part of the advertising program to the local organization.

Type of Product.   Buyers of industrial goods and luxury products usually act on the same motives the world over; thus these products lend themselves to the standardized approach. This enables manufacturers of capital goods, such as General Electric and Caterpillar, to prepare international campaigns that require very little modification in the various markets. Certain consumer goods markets are similar too, as we saw in the previous section. However, another set of characteristics also permits firms to use the same appeals and sales arguments worldwide: when the product is low priced, is consumed in the same way, and is bought for the same reasons. Examples of such products are gasoline, soft drinks, detergents, cosmetics, and airline services. Firms such as Exxon (Esso overseas), Coca-Cola, Avon, and Levi Strauss have for

TABLE 15–2 Advertising expenditures in selected countries, 1992

| Rank | Country | Total Expenditures ($ millions) | Percent of Total | | | | | Advertising Expenditures as Percentage of GNP |
			Print	Cinema	Radio	TV	Outdoor/ Transit	
1	United States	$83,005	52.5%	neg.	10.9%	35.3%	1.3%	1.4%
2	Japan	43,901	38.5	neg.	5.7	40.1	15.6	1.3
3	Germany	17,275	76.3	0.9%	3.6	16.1	3.1	0.9
4	United Kingdom	13,728	62.2	0.6	2.0	31.7	3.6	1.3
5	France	9,112	51.2	0.6	6.6	29.5	12.0	0.7
6	Italy	8,227	40.9	0.2	3.5	49.5	5.9	0.7
7	Spain	7,868	55.2	0.7	10.5	26.8	4.6	1.4
8	Canada	6,140	50.2	neg.	11.8	26.7	11.3	1.1
9	South Korea	3,679	47.0	neg.	5.0	29.0	19.0	1.2
10	Australia	3,657	48.5	1.6	8.6	36.0	5.2	1.2
11	Netherlands	2,928	72.2	0.4	2.4	15.6	9.4	0.9
20	India	808	66.4	0.5	3.1	20.7	9.3	0.3
32	Brazil	n.a.	35.5	neg.	4.8	57.7	2.0	n.a.
32	Malaysia	435	22.7	0.2	9.4	66.2	1.5	0.8

Sources: *International Marketing Data & Statistics* (London: Euromonitor, 1995); and *European Marketing Data & Statistics* (London: Euromonitor, 1995).

years used the international approach successfully. Generally, the only changes they have made are a translation into the local language and the use of indigenous models.

Foreign Environmental Forces. Like variations in media availability, the foreign environmental forces act as deterrents to the international standardization of advertising, and, as you would expect, among the most influential of these forces are the *sociocultural* forces, which we examined in Chapter 9.

A basic cultural decision for the marketer is whether to position the product as foreign or local, and which way to go seems to depend on the country, the product type, and the target market. In Germany, for example, consumers are not at all impressed by the carmaker that announces it has American know-how. "After all," reason the Germans, "if so many Americans prefer BMWs and Mercedes over U.S. cars, why shouldn't we?" At the same time, such purely American products as bourbon, fast-food restaurants, and blue jeans have made tremendous inroads in Germany and the rest of Europe.

Similarly in Japan and other countries in the Far East, American identity of consumer products enhances their image. The young and the status conscious prefer the casual American look in clothing and seek the American label that identifies the wearer as belonging to the "in group." The influence of the American-style fast-food restaurants on Japanese youth was emphasized in a survey taken by the Japanese Ministry of Agriculture, which found that more than 50 percent of the country's teenagers would rather eat occidental foods than the traditional dishes. U.S.-based fast-food restaurants such as McDonald's (Japan's largest restaurant business), Dairy Queen, Mister Donut, and Kentucky Fried Chicken account for half this business. McDonald's alone is grossing over $2 billion annually, more than 10 percent of the company's global sales.[28]

The experience of the suppliers to the youth market already indicates that this too is essentially an international market segment, much like the market for luxury goods. The director of MTV Europe says, "18-year-olds in Paris have more in common with 18-year-olds in New York than with their own parents. They buy the same products, go to the same movies, listen to the same music, sip the same colas. Global advertising merely works on that premise." Almost all MTV Europe's 200 advertisers run unified English-language campaigns across its 28-nation broadcast area.[29] This means marketers can formulate global advertising campaigns for these consumers that will require little more than a translation into the local language. Before making the decision concerning local versus foreign identity, however, management should check with local personnel on a country-by-country basis.

Inasmuch as communication, the reason for advertising, is impossible if the language is not understood, translations must be made into the language of the consumers. Unfortunately for the advertiser, almost every language varies from one country to another. The same word may be perfectly apt in one country while signifying something completely different or even vulgar in another, as illustrated in Chapter 9. To avoid translation errors, the experienced advertising manager will use (1) a double translation and (2) plenty of illustrations with short copy.

Because a nation's laws generally reflect public opinion, closely allied to the cultural forces are the legal forces, which exert an extremely pervasive influence on advertising. We have seen how laws affect media availability, but they also restrict the kinds of products that can be advertised and even the copy employed in the advertisements.

American firms accustomed to using comparative advertising at home are surprised to find that legal restrictions on this technique still exist in some markets. Since the early 1990s, Pepsi-Cola has used comparative advertising to knock Coca-Cola, and wherever possible, Coke has used the courts to stop the ads. Although PepsiCo has won some victories in Japan, Mexico, Malaysia, and 10 countries in Europe, it now wants to use comparative advertising to break Coke's dominance of the international cola markets.

The company launched a series of TV commercials in 1995 aimed at testing the comparative advertising laws of 30 countries. The ads will present

Are these teens in Japan or the United States? Japan. But, like teens in the U.S., they wear Levi's and carry American skateboards.

Catherine Karnow/Woodfin Camp & Associates

the competitor's product in a way that is specifically prohibited in some countries as unfair advertising. "We intend to push the envelope on comparative advertising in markets across the world," says the marketing head for Pepsi-Cola International.[30] Germany's comparative advertising law is so strict that Goodyear couldn't even use its multinational tire campaign stating that nylon tire cord was stronger than steel. Incredibly, the steel wire manufacturers complained of "unfair competition."

Advertisers in the Islamic nations have had to be resourceful to avoid censorship. The use of women's photos in advertisements is forbidden unless the models are clearly Western—preferably blondes or redheads. "Erotic" sound effects are not permitted: a TV soft-drink commercial with a girl licking her lips to show she liked the taste was declared "obscene." In Pakistan, the government decreed that women models could advertise only women's products on TV. They cannot advertise cars or men's cologne, for example. Imagine Ford trying to sell its Mercury with a slinky male posed seductively behind the wheel, or how about an all-male Old Spice commercial?[31]

Globalization versus Localization.   With so many obstacles to international standardization, what should be the approach of the international advertising manager? The opinion of some experts seems to be that good ideas and good promotions can cross international borders. Robert Trebus, an ad agency executive, believes that far too often businesspeople ask how the product can be sold in Germany without first asking how the firm did it successfully in Sweden. Trebus stated back in the 1970s that "rarely will a campaign be a success in Sweden without having registered a like success in Greece." He believes too many managers are convinced that to be successful in different markets, they must approach each market differently.[32] However, the director of multinational accounts at McCann-Erickson claims that social classes across different countries have shared sensibilities: "A male middle executive in Italy has more in common with a male middle executive in the U.K. than with a farmer in Italy. It is those shared sensibilities that make global branding possible."[33]

This school of thought looks for similarities across segments and countries so as to capitalize on them by providing promotional themes with worldwide appeal, the strategy now followed by global corporations. A second school of thought believes that even though human nature is the same everywhere, it is also true that a Spaniard will remain a Spaniard and a Belgian a Belgian. Thus, it is preferable to develop separate appeals to take advantage of the differences among customers in different cultures and countries.

Neither Purely Global nor Purely Local.   You probably have already gathered from this discussion that for most firms neither a purely global nor a purely local campaign is the best way to handle international advertising. In fact, the president of a large international ad agency states, "About 15 percent of the multinational companies have global approaches, meaning campaigns will be roughly the same everywhere. Another 15 percent have strictly local approaches. But these two groups are rapidly disappearing into a group we call 'glocal,' meaning advertisers that have developed a common strategy for large regions."[34]

Gillette's Panregional Approach.   Gillette has its advertising organized in the following regional and cultural clusters: pan–Latin America, pan–Middle East, pan-Africa, and pan-Atlantic. The international advertising manager says the arrangement is based on the belief that the company can identify the same needs and buying motives among consumers in regions or countries linked by culture, consumers' habits, and level of market development for their products. Gillette might use the same European-style advertising for Australia and South Africa; but in Asia, it would link developing economies such as the Philippines, Indonesia, Thailand, and Malaysia. It will market the Asian tigers, Singapore, Hong Kong, and Taiwan, together, but handle Japan, China, and India separately.

Gillette, which sells 800 products in 200 countries, is trying to approximate a global marketing strategy with its panregional strategy, while allowing for regional and national differences. A vice president of Gillette's ad agency, who is also the firm's associate media director, explains Gillette's approach this way: "Our strategy is to develop the best media plans for each country, but then look for pangeographic opportunities to enhance the coverage."[35]

Programmed-Management Approach.   Another middle-ground advertising strategy is what some call the **programmed-management approach**, in which the home office and the foreign subsidiaries agree on marketing objectives, after which each puts together a tentative advertising campaign. This is submitted to the home office for review and suggestions. The campaign is then market tested locally, and the results are submitted to the home office, which reviews them and offers comments. The subsidiary then submits a complete campaign to the home office for review. When the home office is satisfied, the budget is approved and the subsidiary begins implementing the campaign. The result may be a highly standardized campaign for all markets or one that has been individualized to the extent necessary to cope with local market conditions. The programmed-management approach gives the home office a chance to standardize those parts of the campaign that may be standardized but still permits flexibility in responding to different marketing conditions.[36]

programmed-management approach
A middle-ground advertising strategy between globally standardized and entirely local programs.

Personal Selling.   Along with advertising, personal selling constitutes a principal component of the promotional mix. The importance of this promotional tool as compared to advertising depends to a great extent on the relative costs, the funds available, media availability, and the type of product sold.

Just as in the United States, manufacturers of industrial products rely more on personal selling than advertising to communicate with their overseas markets. However, producers of consumer products may also emphasize personal selling overseas, especially in the developing countries, because salespeople in these countries will often work for less compensation than would be demanded in the home country. A newcomer to marketing must be careful, nonetheless, to consider all of the expenses in maintaining a salesperson, as expense items like automobiles and their maintenance (rough treatment on bad roads) frequently may be three or four times the U.S. cost. Fringe benefits are commonly stipulated by law, and these too often comprise a higher percentage of the base wage in other countries.

Marketing managers will also give greater emphasis to personal selling where commercial TV and radio are unavailable or where the market is too small to support expensive TV advertising campaigns.

International Standardization.   By and large, the organization of an overseas sales force, sales presentation, and training methods are very similar to those employed in the home country.

Avon follows the same plan of person-to-person selling in Venezuela or the Far East as it does in this country and is extremely successful with it. When Avon entered Mexico, many of the local experts predicted that its plan would fail. The Mexican middle-class housewife would be out of the home shopping and playing bridge. The wall around the house would keep the Avon lady from reaching the front door, and when she rang the bell, the maid, as she did with all peddlers, would not let her in. Other American firms had used this approach and had failed for these reasons. However, Avon made small but important changes. For one thing, it mounted a massive advertising campaign to educate the Mexicans as to what they could expect from the visits before sending its salespeople out. Although the advertisements were the same as those in the United States, the advertising campaign was more extensive because the Mexican housewife had to be taught a new concept. This was not the common door-to-door salesperson whom she knew but a professional trained to help her look beautiful. Avon recruited educated middle-class women as representatives and trained them well. They were encouraged to visit their friends, much as Tupperware representatives do. What was essentially an American plan, with slight changes for cultural differences, made Avon's entry into the Mexican market an unqualified success. Since entering Mexico in 1990, Avon has built its sales force to 170,000, with sales of $370 million.[37]

Other firms also follow their home country approach. Missionary salespeople from pharmaceutical manufacturers, such as Pfizer and Upjohn, introduce their products to physicians, just as they do in the United States. Sales engineers from General Electric and Westinghouse supply their customers with the same kind of information required in this country. Salespeople calling on channel members perform the same tasks of informing middlemen, setting up point-of-purchase displays, and fighting for shelf space as do their American counterparts.

Because of the high costs of a sales call, many firms are using telemarketing and direct mail to qualify prospects and make appointments for the sales representatives. As you can imagine, European subsidiaries of American firms, such as Ford, Digital Equipment, and IBM, having learned the advantages of telemarketing from their American parents, are using the technique to increase sales. Barbie doll sends her French fans messages in special ink that they can read only under special lights in toy stores where the dolls are sold.

China has been identified as the number one growth opportunity for Avon ladies in the 1990s.

Courtesy Avon Products, Inc.

FIGURE 15–4 Cost of a Sales Call*

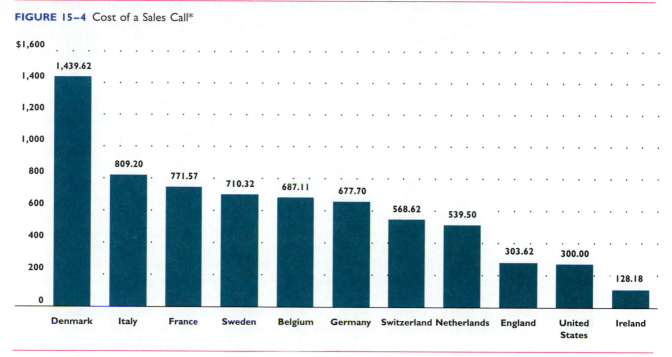

*Average cost of European call is $640.13.

Source: *Business Europe*, April 26, 1991, p. 3.

Dell Computer is selling computers in Japan and Europe by mail and telemarketing, although the company's vice president for international operations remembers, "In every country, they told us mail orders would not work." There was also a question about Dell's low price in Europe. Dell executives found that European buyers have a long-established prejudice: high price equals good quality, low price means shoddy quality. Yet Dell has surprised its competitors by its success in both markets. Starting in the last half of 1992, the firm's Japanese sales went from 2,000 to over 35,000 PCs in 1995. Dell's European sales are 10 times its sales in Japan.[38]

Computerized prospecting, or using computers to analyze customer call patterns to plan customer visits, is another American sales tool adopted by Europeans to reduce the cost of a sales call. Obviously, it's needed. According to a McGraw-Hill survey, the average cost of making a European sales call is $640 (see Figure 15–4) and it takes six calls before a sale is made.[39]

Recruitment. Recruiting salespeople in foreign countries is at times more difficult than recruiting them in the home country because sales managers frequently have to cope with the stigma attached to selling that exists in some areas (cultural forces). To help overcome this obstacle, salespeople are given titles that are essentially translations of American titles designed for the same purpose (territory or zone manager).

Another instance of the influence of cultural forces on recruiting is the need to hire salespeople who are culturally acceptable to customers and channel members. This can be difficult and costly in an already small market that is further subdivided into several distinct cultures with different customs and even languages, as we saw in the chapter on physical forces. If a cultural pocket will support a salesperson at all, the experienced sales manager will make every effort to recruit a person indigenous to the region.

American firms are aided in recruitment by their reputation for having excellent training programs. These generally come from the home office and are adapted, if necessary, to local conditions. When the product is highly technical, the new employees are often sent to the home office for training. Of course, the opportunity to take such a trip is also an effective recruiting tool.

sales promotion
Selling aids, including displays, premiums, contests, and gifts

Sales Promotion.   **Sales promotion** provides the selling aids for the marketing function and includes such activities as the preparation of point-of-purchase displays, contest, premiums, trade show exhibits, cents-off offers, and coupons. If no separate department exists for these activities, either the advertising or the sales department will perform them.

The international standardization of the sales promotion function is not difficult, because experience has shown that what is successful in the United States generally proves effective overseas. Couponing is a good example. Although the United States is the world's leader in couponing, several European markets and Canada are experiencing a rapid growth. A 1991 study reported that the consumers in the United Kingdom and Belgium are the most active EU coupon users. In 1990, an average of 17 coupons per household were redeemed in the United Kingdom and 18 per household in Belgium, compared to 77 in the United States and 26 in Canada. In Italy and Spain, only 3 coupons per household were redeemed. Although the number of coupons redeemed was much lower elsewhere, the growth in their use was much higher. In the United Kingdom, for example, there was a 21 percent increase in redemption from 1989 to 1990, the largest increase in the world.[40]

When marketers are considering transferring sales promotion techniques to other markets, they must consider some cultural and legal constraints.

Legal Constraints.   Laws concerning sales promotions tend to be more restrictive in other countries than they are in the United States or Great Britain. The Belgian, German, and Scandinavian governments are rather negative toward premiums, for example, believing that they detract consumers from considering just the merits of the product. Two-for-one offers are prohibited in Sweden and Norway, and although free samples are permitted everywhere, some governments limit their size. Mexico requires special offers and cents-off deals to be approved by a government agency before they can be used. Although these legal restrictions are bothersome, they have not stopped the use of sales promotions.

Sociocultural and Economic Constraints.   The cultural and economic constraints are more consequential than the legal constraints and do make some sales promotions difficult to use. If a premium is to fulfill the objective of being a sales aid for the product, it must be meaningful to the purchaser. A gadget to be used in the kitchen might be valued by an American but will not be particularly attractive to a Latin American with two maids to do the housework. Firms that attach premiums to the outside of packages in the less developed countries usually do so just once. Less than a week after the packages are on the shelf, the detached premiums are already being sold in the streets. Putting the prize inside the package is also no guarantee that it will be there when the purchaser takes the package home.

> While living in Mexico, one of the writers bought a product for the plastic toy it contained. When he opened the package at home, there was no toy for the children. Examining the package closely, he found that a small slot had been made in the top. Where labor costs and store revenues are low, the income from the sales of these premiums is extra profit for the retailer.

Contests, raffles, and games, however, have been extremely successful in countries where people love to play the odds. If Latin Americans or the Irish will buy a lottery ticket week after week, hoping to win the grand prize playing against the odds of 500,000 to 1, why shouldn't they participate in a contest that costs them nothing to enter? Point-of-purchase displays are well accepted by retailers, though many establishments are so small that there is simply no place to put all of the displays that are offered to them. Sales promotion is generally not as sophisticated overseas as it is in the United States, and our experience indicates that even American subsidiaries do not make sufficient use of the ideas coming from headquarters. The marketing manager who prepares a well-planned program after studying the constraints of the local markets can expect excellent results from the time and money invested.

Two Unsuccessful Sales Promotions.   In recent years there have been two famous, expensive examples of sales promotions that went wrong: Hoover in the United Kingdom and Pepsi-Cola in the Philippines.

Hoover in the U.K.   Hoover's promotional campaign is probably the most disastrous sales promotion in history. In the fall of 1992, the company offered two free air tickets to continental Europe or the United States to anyone spending at least £100 ($150) on Hoover products. Customers spending £300 would also receive free car rental and hotel rooms. Inasmuch as the cheapest pair of tickets costs £500, 200,000 customers rushed to buy inexpensive vacuum cleaners for £120. Hoover's mistake was to assume that most people would not collect their tickets after reading the offer's fine print that laid down the conditions about when the flight could be taken and which hotels could be used.

So many customers were infuriated about delays in obtaining tickets that Maytag, Hoover's owner, sent a team from the U.S. headquarters that fired the managing director and set up a task force of 250 people to issue the tickets. Maytag first announced it would take a $30 million charge against profits to pay for the ill-fated promotion but later said it would cost $72.6 million.[41]

Pepsi-Cola in the Philippines.   In February 1992, the Pepsi bottler in the Philippines (Pepsi owns 19 percent) began a promotion called "Number Fever," which would award cash prizes for winning numbers under bottle caps. When the company launched the promotion, it had only 16 percent of the market in which Coke had 78 percent. But by April, the promotion had been so successful (Pepsi's market share rose to 23 percent), the firm extended it to a second stage of an additional five weeks. On May 25, 1992, the winning number, 349, was drawn by computer and announced. Unfortunately, 349 had been printed on 900,000 caps, half of which carried a 1 million peso ($37,700) prize. A Pepsi employee discovered the error and tried to withdraw the number, but a news show had already announced it.

Because of the error, the company faced paying winners $18 billion dollars. It quickly suggested an offer of $19 to each person with a 349 cap. Since June 1992, the company has paid out $10 million, but still many people are not satisfied. PepsiCo, anxious to distance itself from the affair, says the promotion is a local problem. Pepsi's market share, which had gone from 19 percent to 25 percent, has plunged to 16 percent.[42]

Public Relations.   **Public relations** is the firm's communications and relationships with its various publics, including the governments where it operates, or as one writer has put it, "Public relations is the marketing of the firm." Although American internationals have had organized public relations programs for many years in the United States, they have paid much less attention to this important function elsewhere.

public relations
Various methods of communicating with the firm's publics to secure a favorable impression

Ironically, it is on the whole not true that they have neglected public-service activities through their foreign subsidiaries—only that they have failed to inform their publics of what they are doing. Exxon has for years sponsored the study of foreign art students in the United States, and the ITT International Fellowship Program, started in 1973, has already enabled more than 750 students from 54 countries to pursue advanced degrees in the United States and abroad.

Overseas subsidiaries of American firms support public-service activities locally. In Japan, Coca-Cola spends $5 million annually on good works such as programs for children and the handicapped. IBM Japan puts 1 percent of its profits into good works. In 1990, young ballerinas and basic-research scientists were among those receiving $14 million. Eastman Kodak sponsors soccer, and Du Pont, golf.[43]

The rising wave of nationalism and antimultinational feeling in many countries has made it imperative for companies with international operations to improve their communications to their nonbusiness publics with more effective public relations programs.

International pharmaceutical manufacturers are often viewed suspiciously by the public in developing nations. On one hand, they are in the business to alleviate suffering, but they are doing it to make it a profit at the poor people's expense. To improve its image, Warner-Lambert began a program in Africa called Tropicare that trains local health care providers in preventive medicine with audiovisual materials. In each country, the company has organized a commission of experts from national and international health organizations to ensure the quality of the educational material used in the program. The African program has been so successful that Warner-Lambert introduced it in Latin American in 1988.

Tropicare has provided many benefits for both the host countries and the company. It has helped Warner-Lambert to enter new markets, subdued criticism of the company's pricing and marketing practices in developing nations, and improved its image. The developing nations have benefited by having health providers who have received much-needed training.[44]

One of the most vexing problems for firms is how to deal with critics of their operations and motives. Some try to defuse criticism before it becomes a full-scale attack by holding regularly scheduled meetings at which topics of interest are debated. Others prefer to meet with critics privately, though they might find themselves caught in a never-ending relationship in which the critics continually escalate their demands. This is especially true of single-issue groups, whose existence depends on the continuance of the issue.

A successful strategy employed by some firms has been to address the issue without dealing directly with the critics. Instead, they work with international or governmental agencies. Another alternative is to do nothing. If the criticism receives no publicity, it may die from lack of interest. However, bad handling of a situation can have serious repercussions for a firm. Union Carbide's bungling of the Bhopal accident is an example. An example of a firm that uses public relations effectively is IBM. Its strong lobbying effort convinced EU commissioners that the highly regulated state-owned telephone and postal organizations are responsible for costly, inefficient phone systems. Partly because of IBM's efforts, one of the main EU objectives is to standardize and liberalize telecommunications.[45]

Pricing Strategies

Pricing, the third element of the marketing mix, is an important and complex consideration in formulating the marketing strategy. Pricing decisions affect other corporate functions, directly determine the firm's gross revenue, and are a major determinant of profits.

Pricing, a Controllable Variable.   Most marketers, especially Americans, are aware that effective price setting consists of more than mechanically adding a standard markup to a cost. To obtain the maximum benefits from pricing, management must regard it in the same manner as it does other controllable variables; that is, pricing is one of the marketing mix elements that can be varied to achieve the marketing objectives of the firm.

For instance, if the marketer wishes to position a product as a high-quality item, setting a relatively high price will reinforce promotion that emphasizes quality. However, combining a recognizably low price with a promotional emphasis on quality could result in an incongruous pairing that would adversely affect its credibility with the consumer—the low price might be interpreted as the correct price for an inferior product. Pricing can also be a determinant in the choice of middlemen, because if the firm requires a wholesaler to take title, stock, promote, and deliver the merchandise, it must give the wholesaler a much larger trade discount than would be demanded by a broker, whose services are much more limited.

These examples illustrate one of the reasons for the complexity of price setting: the interaction of pricing with the other elements of the marketing mix. In addition, two other sets of forces influence this variable: (1) interaction between marketing and the other functional areas of the firm and (2) environmental forces.

Interaction Between Marketing and the Other Functional Areas.   To illustrate this point, look at the following:

1. The finance people want prices that are both profitable and conducive to a steady cash flow.
2. Production supervisors want prices that create large sales volumes, which permit long production runs.
3. The legal department worries about possible antitrust violations when different prices are set according to type of customer.
4. The tax people are concerned with the effects of prices on tax loads.
5. The domestic sales manager wants export prices to be high enough to avoid having to compete with company products that are purchased for export and then diverted to the domestic market (one aspect of parallel importing).

The marketer must address all of these concerns and also consider the impact of the legal and other environmental forces that we examined in Section Three. Table 15–5 at the end of this chapter examines this aspect of pricing in greater detail.

International Standardization.   Companies that pursue a policy of unifying corporate pricing procedures worldwide know that pricing is acted on by the same forces that militate against the international standardization of the other marketing mix components. Pricing for the overseas markets is more complex because managements must be concerned with two kinds of pricing: (1) **foreign national pricing,** which is domestic pricing in another country, and (2) international pricing for exports.

foreign national pricing
Local pricing in another country

Foreign National Pricing.   Many foreign governments in their fight against inflation have instituted price controls, and the range of the products affected varies immensely from country to country. Some governments attempt to fix prices on just about everything, while others are concerned only with essential goods. Unfortunately, no agreement exists on what is essential, so in one market the prices of gasoline, food products, tires, and even wearing apparel may be controlled, while in another market only the prices of staple foods may be fixed. In nations with laws on unfair competition, the minimum sales price may be controlled rather than the maximum. The German law is so comprehensive that under certain conditions, even premiums and cents-off coupons may be prohibited because they are considered to violate the minimum price requirements. The international marketer must be watchful of a recent tendency of many nations, especially EU members, to open up their markets to price competition by weakening and even abolishing retail price maintenance laws.

Prices can vary because of appreciable cost differentials on opposite sides of a border. One government may levy higher import duties on imported raw materials or may subsidize public utilities, while another may not. Differences in labor legislation will cause labor costs to vary. Competition among local suppliers may be intense in one market, permitting the affiliate to buy inputs at better prices than those paid by an affiliate in another market, which must purchase raw materials from a single supplier, possibly a government monopoly.

Competition on the selling side is also diverse. Frequently, an affiliate in one market will face heavy local competition and be severely limited in the price it can charge, while in a neighboring market, a lack of competitors will allow another affiliate to charge a much higher price. As regional economic groupings reduce trade barriers among members, such opportunities are becoming fewer because firms must then meet regional as well as local competition.

One thing European firms cannot do is agree to fix prices in an effort to limit competition. The EU Commission recently imposed the largest fines ever under EU competition law—$116.7 million—on 16 European steel companies for price fixing and collaboration. The record fine on a single company is $93 million on Tetra Pak, a Swedish packaging firm, in 1991.[46]

Because a firm, for a number of reasons, does not introduce a new product simultaneously in all markets, the same product will not be in the same stage of the product life cycle everywhere. In markets where it is in the introductory stage, there is an opportunity to charge a high "skimming" price or a low "penetration" price, depending on such factors as market objectives, patent protection, price elasticity of demand, and competition. As the product reaches the maturity or decline stage, the price may be lowered, if doing so permits a satisfactory return. Because life cycles vary among markets, prices too will be different.

Table 15–3 illustrates how a product's price can vary in different cities in the world, differentials resulting from a combination of the reasons discussed above.

TABLE 15–3
Prices in major cities

	New York	London	Paris	Tokyo
Aspirin (100)	$ 0.99	$ 1.23	$ 7.07	$ 6.53
Compact disc	12.99	14.99	23.16	22.09
Levi's jeans	39.99	74.92	79.73	54.54
Ray-Ban sunglasses	45.00	88.50	81.23	134.49
Sony Walkman	59.95	74.98	86.00	211.34
Nike Air Jordans	125.00	134.99	157.71	172.91
Gucci loafers	275.00	292.50	271.99	605.19
Nikon camera	629.95	840.00	691.00	1,054.42

Source: "Tourists and Bargains Galore," *Fortune*, June 13, 1994, p. 12.

International Pricing. International pricing involves the setting of prices for goods produced in one country and sold in another. The pricing of exports to unrelated customers falls in this category and will be treated separately in the chapter on exporting. A special kind of exporting, *intracorporate sales*, is exceedingly common among worldwide companies as they attempt to rationalize production by requiring subsidiaries to specialize in the manufacture of some products while importing others. Their imports may consist of components that are assembled into the end product, such as engines made in one country that are mounted in car bodies built in another, or they may be finished products imported to complement the product mix of an affiliate. No matter what the end use is, problems exist in setting an intracorporate price, or **transfer price**.

transfer price
Intracorporate price, or the price of a good or service sold by one affiliate to another, the home office to an affiliate, or vice versa

Because it is possible for the firm as a whole to gain while both the buying and selling subsidiaries "lose" (receive prices that are lower than would be obtained through an outside transaction), the tendency is for transfer prices to be set at headquarters. The reason for this apparent anomaly is that the company obtains a profit from *both* the seller and the buyer.

The selling affiliate would like to charge other subsidiaries the same price it charges all customers, but, when combined with transportation costs and import duties, such a price may make it impossible for the importing subsidiary to compete in its market. If headquarters dictates that a lower-than-market transfer price be charged, the seller will be unhappy because its profit-and-loss statement suffers. This can be a very real headache to personnel whose promotion bonuses depend on the bottom line. In Chapter 18, we will see how home office management deals with this problem.

Both foreign governments and the U.S. government are also interested in profits and the part transfer prices play in their realization, because of the influence of profits on the amount of taxes paid. American and foreign tax agents have become very much aware that because of differences in tax structures, a firm can obtain meaningful profits by ordering a subsidiary in a country with high corporate taxes to sell at cost to a subsidiary in a country where corporate taxes are lower. The profit is earned where less income tax is paid, and the company clearly gains.

A recent study by professors at Florida International University found that false high invoice prices on American imports to avoid U.S. income taxes could have cost this country $28.7 billion in lost tax revenues. Fax machines from Japan billed at $25,000 each, French cordless phones at $4,233 each, and Spanish sand at $1,944 per ton are examples. Although the data did not identify the firms involved, the researchers found that the largest losses—$4 billion—involved imports from Japan.[47]

The manipulation of transfer prices for the reduction of income taxes and import duties or the avoidance of exchange controls has caused many governments to insist on arm's-length prices—the prices charged unrelated customers. Under Section 482 of the Internal Revenue Code, U.S. tax authorities are empowered to reconstruct an intracorporate transfer price and tax the calculated profits whenever there is reason to suspect that low prices were set for tax evasion.

U.S. tax officials are beginning to crack down on what they claim is rampant cross-border tax fraud by U.S. and Mexican companies. A nine-month study by an IRS team found tax fraud estimated to cost the U.S. government hundreds of millions of dollars annually. In one instance, they examined 1,174 tax returns filed by Mexican-controlled firms operating on the American side of the border and found that 70 percent claimed a loss in 1992. Overall, the companies showed a combined rate of return on their assets of negative 17 percent. "You can't stay in business very long losing 17 percent of

FIGURE 15–5
Hiding profits with transfer
pricing

GREAT BRITAIN

An item costs $100 to
produce. It is sold to a
Jamaican subsidiary for $100.

Tax rate: 52%
Tax paid: $0

JAMAICA

The Jamaican subsidiary
resells the item for $200 to
a U.S. subsidiary.

Tax rate: 5%
Tax paid: $5

UNITED STATES

The American subsidiary sells
item at cost for $200. No
profit earned. No tax paid.

Tax rate: 34%
Tax paid: $0

your assets every year," said the IRS official in charge of the investigation.[48]
Figure 15–5 shows how firms can hide profits with transfer pricing.

Distribution Strategies

The development of distribution strategies is difficult in the home country, but
it is even more so internationally, where marketing managers must concern
themselves with two functions rather than one: (1) getting the products *to*
foreign markets (exporting) and (2) distributing the products *within* each
market (foreign distribution). In this section, we will examine foreign distribution only, leaving the export channels for the next chapter.

Interdependence of Distribution Decisions.   When making decisions on distribution, care must be taken to analyze their interdependence with the other
marketing mix variables. For example, if the product requires considerable
after-sales servicing, the firm will want to sell through dealers that have the
facilities, personnel, and capital to purchase equipment and spare parts and to
train servicepeople. This will necessitate using a merchant wholesaler, which
will demand a larger trade discount than would an agent, because an agent
does not perform these functions. Channel decisions are critical because they
are long-term decisions; once established, they are far less easy to change than
those made for price, product, and promotion.

International Standardization.   Although management would prefer to standardize distribution patterns internationally, there are two fundamental constraints on its doing so: (1) the variation in the availability of channel
members among the firm's markets and (2) the inconsistency of the influence
of the environmental forces. Because of these constraints, international
managers have found it best to establish a basic but flexible overall policy. The
subsidiaries then implement this policy and design channel strategies to meet
local conditions.

Availability of Channel Members.   As a starting point in their channel design,
local managers have the successful distribution system used in the domestic
operation. Headquarters' support for a policy of employing the same channels
worldwide will be especially strong when the entire marketing mix has been
built around a particular channel type, such as direct sales force or franchised

Shoes	Percent of Total Sales	Toys	Percent of Total Sales	
Germany		Germany		**TABLE 15–4**
Organized independents (buying groups)	35%	Organized independent toy stores (buying groups)	37%	Percentage of total sales by type of outlet
Major shoe chains	29	Department stores	27	
Mail	7	Hypermarkets	15	
Department stores	6	Mail	8	
Hypermarkets	6	Independent toy stores	4	
Discount stores	6	Other retailers	9	
Independent shoe stores	4		———	
Other retailers	7		100%	
	———			
	100%			
France		France		
Independent shoe stores	56%	Hypermarkets/supermarkets	36%	
Direct sales	14	Toy stores	22	
Clothing stores	2	Department and variety stores	14	
Department stores	2	Mail	8	
Variety stores	1	Other retailers	20	
Other retailers	25		———	
	———		100%	
	100%			

Source: *Retail International* (London: Euromonitor, 1988), pp. 162, 171, 480, and 489.

operators. Avon, Encyclopedia Britannica, and McDonald's are examples of firms that consider their distribution systems inviolate, so locally there is little latitude in planning channel strategies. However, companies utilizing the more common types of middlemen are usually more inclined to grant the local organization greater freedom in channel member selection.

Although a general rule for any firm entering a foreign market is to adapt to the available channels rather than create new ones, a number of companies have successfully avoided the traditional channels because of their appalling inefficiencies. Coca-Cola did this in Japan, as we mentioned in Chapter 13.

Experienced marketers know they cannot get their products to the consumer by the same retail channel in every country, and even in Europe the differences are substantial. What is the best way to sell toys in France? A sure outlet is the hypermarket, which sells 36 percent of all toys purchased in France. In Germany, however, the hypermarket accounts for only 15 percent of toy sales (see Table 15–4). The most important kind of outlet for toys in Germany is independent retailers, which are organized into buying groups. Table 15–4 also indicates the differences in the way shoes are sold in these two neighboring countries.

Foreign Environmental Forces.   Environmental differences among markets add to the difficulty in standardizing distribution channels. Changes caused by the cultural forces generally occur over time, but those caused by the legal forces can be radical and quick and can dramatically slow trends responding to cultural demands.

To illustrate, hypermarkets, which are changing distribution patterns in Europe and particularly in France, a nation of small shopkeepers, numbered only 11 in that country in 1972. The combination of lower prices and one-stop shopping caught on with the French consumer, and 51 hypermarkets were opened in 1973. Manufacturers that saw a quick end to small shopkeepers failed to appreciate their political power. The Royer Law, passed in 1973, gave local urban commissions, often dominated by small merchants, the power to refuse construction permits for supermarkets and hypermarkets. After the law took effect, only 40 percent of the large-store applications were approved.

Although the trend toward more giant stores did not stop, the growth certainly slowed. There were only about 1,000 hypermarkets in 1993 when France's new prime minister announced a freeze on new construction. Both major hypermarket chains immediately complained about the order, even though France's retail sector is saturated and has little room for growth.[49]

Japan's Large Scale Retailers Law, very similar to the French law, had also slowed the opening of large retailers. However, because of pressure from Carla Hills, U.S. trade representative, and the trade talks called the Structural Impediments Initiative (SII), the Japanese Ministry of International Trade and Industry suddenly found it could reduce the period that small retailers could block the opening of new stores in their neighborhoods from an incredible 10 years to a maximum of 18 months. This was a breakthrough that foreign retailers needed.[50]

The first large U.S.-owned discount store to take advantage of the U.S. SII aimed at prying open new markets for American firms in Japan was Toys "R" Us. After three years of haggling with Japanese bureaucracy, local vested interests, and heavy, often hostile press coverage, the company opened its first store north of Tokyo. As you read in Chapter 13, because a revision of Japan's Large Scale Retailer's Law made store opening easier, Toys "R" Us had been able to open 16 superstores in only two years and expects to have 32 stores by 1996.

Another restriction of distribution has been tried in the EU. Manufacturers have attempted to prevent distributors from selling across national borders, but the Commission has prohibited them from doing so by invoking EU antitrust laws. Exclusive distributorships have been permitted, but every time the manufacturer has included a clause prohibiting the distributor from exporting to another EU country, the clause has been stricken from the contract. In effect, the firm that has two factories in the EU with different costs, and thus distinct prices, is practically powerless to prevent products from the lower-cost affiliate from competing with higher-cost products from the other affiliate.

Economic differences also make international standardization difficult, although marketers can adapt to economic changes. In 1960, very little frozen food was sold in France because of the consumer's preference for fresh food. However, tight economic conditions forced many housewives to seek employment, and with less time to spend preparing meals, they turned to frozen food. An added attraction of frozen food items was that their prices did not rise as fast as those of fresh foods. The result has been sales increases of 10 percent or more a year since 1973.

In Japan, high prices have also forced women to find jobs, and they no longer have time to shop and prepare the traditional Japanese foods. They fill their needs by purchasing more convenience foods advertised on TV with home delivery or by going to the more than 50 chains of convenience stores. The largest, 7-Eleven, has over 3,200 licensees, most of whom are former small shopkeepers. Its point-of-sale computer network is eliminating the need for small-scale wholesalers, whose number is already declining all over Japan.[51] Worldwide, marketers are seeing cultural barriers fall as economic conditions force housewives to obtain employment to supplement household income. The premium that outside employment places on their time is leading them to prefer one-stop shopping, labor-saving devices, and convenience foods. The result is an upheaval in the way goods are distributed, but American marketers that have U.S. experience as a guide are in a position to make inroads on their foreign competitors, for which this is a new phenomenon.

Can retailing be globalized? Retailers like France's Carrefour, with stores in France, Spain, Brazil, Argentina and the United States, think it can. So do Safeway, Gucci, Cartier, Benetton, and Toys "R" Us, which have made aggressive penetration in Canada, Europe, Hong Kong, and Singapore. Kaufhof, the German retailing giant, has 100 shoe stores located in Austria, France, Switzerland, and Germany and is also the leading mail-order shoe retailer in Europe. As Peter Drucker said in 1987, "To maintain a leadership position in any one developed country, a business—whether large or small—increasingly has to attain and hold leadership positions in all developed markets worldwide."[52]

Channel Selection

Direct or Indirect Marketing.
The first decision that management must make is whether to use middlemen, because it frequently has the option of marketing directly to the final user. Sales to original equipment manufacturers (OEMs)* and governments are, for the most part, made directly, as are the sales of high-priced industrial products like turbines and locomotives, because the firm is dealing with the relatively few customers and transactions but with large dollar value. Even in these cases, export sales may be consummated by local agents if (1) management believes this is politically expedient or (2) the country's laws demand it.

Other types of industrial products and consumer goods are marketed indirectly. The channel members are selected on the basis of their market coverage, their cost, and their susceptibility to company control. They must also, of course, perform the functions required by management.

Factors Influencing Channel Selection.
The factors that influence the selection of market channels may be classified as the characteristics of the market, the product, the company, and the middlemen.

Market Characteristics. Inasmuch as the reason for using channels is to enable the manufacturer to reach its target markets, the obvious place to start in channel selection is at those markets. Which of the available alternatives offer the most adequate coverage? Because of the variance in the target markets, the firm will most likely require multiple channels. Large retailers, governments, and OEMs may be handled by the company sales force or manufacturers' agents, whereas smaller retailers are supplied through wholesalers.

Product Characteristics. A low-cost product sold in small quantities per transaction generally requires long channels, but if the goods are perishable, short channels are preferable. If the product is highly technical, it may be impossible to obtain knowledgeable middlemen, and the manufacturer will be forced either to sell directly through company-owned distributors or to train independent middlemen. Caterpillar has enjoyed tremendous success in choosing this second alternative.

Company Characteristics. A firm that has adequate financial and managerial resources is in a much better position to employ its own sales force or agents than one that is lacking in these areas. A financially weak company must use

---

*Original equipment manufacturers buy components that are incorporated into the products they produce (for example, spark plugs to an automobile manufacturer).

middlemen that take title to and pay for the goods. If management is inexperienced in selling to certain markets, it must employ middlemen who have that experience.

Middlemen's Characteristics.   Most industrial equipment, large household appliances, and automobiles require considerable after-sales servicing, and much of the firm's success in marketing depends on it. If the firm is not prepared to provide this service, it cannot use agents. The same is true for warehousing and promotion to the final user. If the firm is unable to perform these functions or perceives a cost advantage in not performing them, then it must select middlemen that will service, warehouse, and promote its products.

It may be that no channel members are available to reach the firm's target markets and perform the desired functions. If there are none, management must decide to (1) desist from entering the market, (2) select other target markets, or (3) create a new channel. For example, if a frozen-food processor, after studying the available channels, finds that wholesale and retailer cold-storage facilities are nonexistent, it can either abandon the market or persuade middlemen to acquire the facilities. In a number of overseas markets, firms have purchased the equipment and either rented, leased, or sold it on easy terms to distributors and retailers.

> An Italian cheese producer in Brazil not only supplied cold-storage equipment but also established gathering facilities for the dairy farmers. The company provides veterinarians and dairy experts to teach the dairy farmers how to maintain their herds and increase output. Nestlé has similar programs in its developing country markets.

Legal Requirements.   Because the legal requirements for terminating middlemen vary from country to country, the time to think about how to terminate an agreement is before it is made. Although most countries have no special laws penalizing or precluding the termination of an agreement between the manufacturer and middlemen, some do. In Venezuela, for example, unjustly discharged agents may be entitled to the same severance benefits as discharged employees. In other countries, laws specify high termination compensation related to an agent's longevity, past earnings, goodwill, or "investment" in the product line. Countries with laws making it difficult to terminate agreements include Belgium, Costa Rica, the Netherlands, Norway, and Sweden. Evidently, before preparing a contract, management must consult local attorneys or local correspondents of international law firms.

Information Sources

Various sources will provide information about channels of distribution. The U.S. Department of Commerce, banks, credit agencies, and American chambers of commerce in foreign cities are all good. If the names of other companies whose products are being handled by prospective channel members are known, these companies should be contacted. We will discuss the information sources at greater length in the chapter on exporting (Chapter 16).

Foreign Environmental Forces and Marketing Mix Matrix

The matrix[53] shown in Table 15–5 summarizes many of the constraints on the internationalization of the marketing mix that have been discussed in this chapter and in Section Three. Table 15–5 will serve as a reminder of the many factors that marketing managers should consider when they are contemplating the standardization of marketing mix elements.

TABLE 15–5 Environmental constraints to international standardization of marketing mix

Factors Limiting Standardization	Product	Price	Distribution	Personal Selling	Promotion
1. Physical forces	1. Climatic conditions—special packaging, extra insulation, mildew protection, extra cooling capacity, special lubricants, dust protection, special instructions 2. Difficult terrain—stronger parts, larger engines, engines, stronger packing	1. Special product requirements add to costs 2. Difficult terrain—extra transportation costs, higher sales expense (car maintenance, longer travel time, more per diem expense)	1. Difficult terrain—less customer mobility, requiring more outlets, each with more stock 2. Varying climatic conditions—more stock needed when distinct products required for different climates	1. Buyers widely dispersed or concentrated—impacts on territory and sales force size 2. Difficult terrain—high travel expense, longer travel time, fewer daily sales calls 3. Separate cultures created by physical barriers—salespeople from each culture may be needed	1. Cultural pockets created by barriers—separate ads for languages, dialects, words, customs 2. Different climates—distinct advertising themes
2. Sociocultural forces	1. Consumer attitudes toward product 2. Colors of product and package—varying significance 3. Languages—labels, instructions 4. Religion—consumption patterns 5. Attitudes toward time—differences in acceptance of timesaving products 6. Attitudes toward change—acceptance of new products 7. Educational levels—ability to comprehend instructions, ability to use product 8. Tastes and customs—product use and consumption 9. Different buying habits—package size 10. Who is decision maker? 11. Rural-urban population mix	1. Cultural objections to product—lower prices to penetrate market 2. Lower educational level, lower income—lower prices for mass market 3. Attitudes toward bargaining—impacts list prices 4. Customers' attitude toward price	1. More and perhaps specialized outlets to market to various subcultures 2. Buyers accustomed to bargaining—requires small retailers 3. Attitudes toward change—varying acceptance of new kinds of outlets 4. Different buying habits—different types of outlets	1. Separate cultures—separate salespeople 2. Varying attitudes toward work, time, achievement, and wealth among cultures—difficult to motivate and control sales force 3. Different buying behavior—different kinds of sales forces 4. Cultural stigma attached to selling?	1. Language, different or same but with words having different connotations—advertisements, labels, instructions 2. Literacy, low—simple labels, instructions, ads with plenty of graphics 3. Symbolism—responses differ 4. Colors—significances differ 5. Attitudes toward advertising 6. Buying influence—gender, committee, family 7. Cultural pockets—different promotions 8. Religion—taboos and restrictions vary 9. Attitudes toward foreign products and firms

continued

Factors Limiting Standardization	Product	Price	Distribution	Personal Selling	Promotion
3. Legal-political forces	1. Some products prohibited 2. Certain features required or prohibited 3. Label and packaging requirements 4. Varying product standards 5. Varying patent, copyright, and trademark laws 6. Varying import duties 7. Varying import restriction 8. Local production required of all or part of product 9. Requirements to use local inputs that are different from home country inputs 10. Cultural stigma attached to brand name or artwork?	1. Varying retail price maintenance laws 2. Government-controlled prices or markups 3. Antitrust laws 4. Import duties 5. Tax laws 6. Transfer pricing controls.	1. Some kinds of channel members outlawed 2. Markups government-controlled 3. Retail price maintenance 4. Turnover taxes 5. Only government-owned channels permitted for some products 6. Restrictions on channel members—number, lines handled, licenses for each line 7. Laws on canceling contracts of channel members	1. Laws governing discharge of salespeople 2. Laws requiring compensation on discharging salespeople 3. Laws requiring profit sharing, overtime, working conditions 4. Restrictions on channel members	1. Use of languages 2. Legal limits to expenditures 3. Taxes on advertising 4. Prohibition of promotion for some products 5. Special legal requirements for some products (cigarettes, pharmaceuticals) 6. Media availability 7. Trademark laws 8. Taxes that discriminate against some kinds of promotion 9. Controls on language or claims used in ads for some products
4. Economic forces	1. Purchasing power—package size, product sophistication, quality level 2. Wages—varying requirements for labor-saving products 3. Condition of infrastructure—heavier products, hand instead of power-operated 4. Market size—varying width of product mix	1. Different prices 2. Price elasticity of demand	1. Availability of outlets 2. Size of inventory 3. Size of outlets 4. Dispersion of outlets 5. Extent of self-service 6. Types of outlets 7. Length of channels	1. Sales force expense 2. Availability of employees in labor market	1. Media availability 2. Funds available 3. Emphasis on saving time 4. Experience with products 5. TV, radio ownership 6. Print media readership 7. Quality of media 8. Excessive costs to reach certain market segments

Factors Limiting Standardization	Product	Price	Distribution	Personal Selling	Promotion
5. Competitive forces	1. Rate of new product introduction 2. Rate of product improvement 3. Quality levels 4. Package size 5. Strength in market	1. Competitors' prices 2. Number of competitors 3. Importance of price in competitors' marketing mix	1. Competitors' control of channel members 2. Competitors' margins to channel members 3. Competitors' choice of channel members	1. Competitors' sales force-number and ability 2. Competitors' emphasis on personal selling in promotional mix 3. Competitors' rates and methods of compensation	1. Competitors' promotional expenditures 2. Competitors' promotional mix 3. Competitors' choice of media
6. Distributive forces	1. Product servicing requirements 2. Package size 3. Branding— dealers' brands	1. Margins required by channel members 2. Special payments required— stocking, promotional	1. Availability of channel members 2. Number of company distribution centers 3. Market coverage by channel members 4. Demands of channel members	1. Size of sales force 2. Kind and quality of sales force	1. Kinds of promotion 2. Amounts of promotion

SUMMARY

1. **Understand why at times there are differences between marketing domestically and internationally.** Whether a policy or a technique is designed for global use or is first used in the home market and then used overseas, marketers must know where to look for possible differences between marketing domestically and marketing internationally. Sometimes there are great differences; sometimes there are none. Although the basic functions of marketing are the same for all markets, international markets can differ greatly because of the variations in the uncontrollable environmental forces. The marketing manager must decide if the marketing program can be standardized worldwide, if some changes must be made, or if a completely different marketing mix must be prepared.

2. **Explain why international marketing managers wish to standardize the marketing mix regionally or worldwide.** International marketing managers prefer to standardize the marketing mix regionally or worldwide because there can be considerable cost savings from marketing the same product, using the same promotional material and the same advertising. A standardized marketing mix is easier to control and less time is consumed preparing the marketing plan.

3. **Comprehend why it is often impossible to standardize the marketing mix worldwide.** A manager may not be able to standardize the marketing mix worldwide because of differences in the environmental forces. The amount of change depends considerably on the product type and the degree of market penetration desired by the manager.

4. **Appreciate the importance of distinguishing among the total product, the physical product, and the brand name.** Much of the confusion about whether a global firm can have global products is because the discussants do not differentiate between the physical and total products. A total product is

easier than a physical product to standardize. A brand name or a product concept may be standardized although the physical product varies among markets. Also, a firm may have to use a different brand name in a market because its present one has a bad connotation or because it may already be copyrighted by someone else.

5. **Explain why consumer products generally require greater modification for international sales than industrial products or services.** Industrial products and services generally can be marketed globally with less change than consumer products because they are less sensitive to the foreign environment, as Figure 15–2 indicates.

6. **Understand how the environmental forces affect the marketing mix.** Sociocultural forces such as worldwide differences in language and connotations of colors or words and variations in household tasks and shopping habits can require firms to rethink names, designs, and packaging of consumer goods.

   Legal forces can also constrain standardization of products. These include worldwide differences in laws concerning consumer protection, operator safety, and product labeling.

   Primary economic forces affecting standardization are the worldwide disparity in income and variations in infrastructures. Physical forces, such as climate and terrain, are also factors.

7. **Discuss the product strategies that can be formed from three product alternatives and three kinds of promotional messages.** Six commonly used promotional strategies can be formulated by combining the three alternatives of marketing the same product everywhere, adapting it, or designing a new product with the same, adapted, or different message.

8. **Explain "glocal" advertising strategies.** International advertising agencies will design an international program for an advertiser and then make local adjustments that local managers deem necessary. The programmed-management approach is an advertising strategy for combining inputs from global advertising advocates of the home office with opinions of local managers.

9. **Understand the intricacies of transfer pricing.** Transfer prices, the prices of goods involved in intracorporate sales, are subject to different conditions than are arm's-length prices (prices charged unrelated customers). An international firm may order an affiliate in a high-tax country to book all the profit where the income tax is lower, for example. One affiliate may be told to lower its prices to an affiliate in another market if this will enable the second to be competitive in its own market.

10. **Discuss the distribution strategies of international marketers.** Although an international firm would prefer to standardize its distribution patterns internationally, the facts that the same kinds of channel members are not available everywhere and that environmental forces vary among markets make standardization difficult or impossible at times.

11. **Describe the channel selection process of international marketers.** Factors influencing the channel selection process are characteristics of the (1) market, (2) product, (3) company, and (4) middlemen.

KEY WORDS

- total product   476
- promotion   487
- advertising   489
- programmed-management approach   495

- sales promotion   498
- public relations   499
- foreign national pricing   501
- transfer price   503

QUESTIONS

1. "Consumers are not standardized globally; therefore, with global brands, you either get lowest common denominator advertising or you get advertising that's right somewhere, but wrong elsewhere." This is an actual statement of a CEO of an international advertising agency. What's your opinion?

2. What future do you see for global advertising?

3. Are there any advantages to standardizing the marketing mix worldwide?

4. Why are manufacturers increasing their use of global and regional brands?

5. What is the basis for Gillette's taking its panregional approach?

6. What is a generality about similarities of social and cultural values in a country?

7. Why is food retailing changing in Europe and Japan?

8. Why must a marketer consider the economic forces when formulating a product strategy? Give some examples.

9. If manipulation of transfer pricing is so advantageous, why do so many companies use the market price as the transfer price?

10. Compare the amount of tax paid in the transactions showed in Figure 15–5 with a straight sale by the British subsidiary for $100 to the U.S. subsidiary, which then sells the item for $200.

MINICASE 15–1   U.S. Pharmaceutical of Korea*

U.S. Pharmaceutical of Korea (USPK) was formed in 1969. Its one manufacturing plant is located just outside Seoul, the capital. Although the company distributes its products throughout South Korea, 40 percent of its total sales of $5 million were made in the capital last year.

There are no governmental restrictions on whom the company can sell to. The only requirement is that the wholesaler, retailer, or end user have a business license and a taxation number. Of the 400 wholesalers in the country, 130 are customers of USPK, accounting for 46 percent of the company's total sales. The company also sells directly to 2,100 of the country's 10,000 retailers; these account for 45 percent of total sales. The remaining sales are made directly to high-volume end users, such as hospitals and clinics.

Tom Sloane, marketing manager of USPK, would prefer to make about 90 percent of the company's sales directly to retailers and the remaining 10 percent directly to high-volume users. He believes, however, that this strategy is not possible because there are so many small retailers. Not only is the sales volume per retailer small, but there is also a risk involved in extending them credit. USPK tends to deal directly with large urban retailers and leaves most of the nonurban retailers to the wholesalers.

However, the use of wholesalers bothers Sloane for two reasons: (1) he has to give them larger discounts than he gives retailers that buy directly from the firm and (2) because of the intense competition (300 pharmaceutical manufacturers in Korea), his wholesalers frequently demand larger discounts as the price for remaining loyal to USPK.

This intense competition affects another aspect of USPK's operations—collecting receivables. USPK has found that many wholesalers collect quickly from retailers but delay paying it. Instead, they invest in ventures that offer high short-term returns. For example, lending to individuals can bring them interest rates of up to 3 percent a month. The company's receivables, meanwhile, range from 75 to 130 days. Wholesalers are also the cause of another problem. Many are understaffed and have to rely on "drug peddlers" for sales. The drug peddler (there are perhaps 4,000 just in Seoul) make most of their money either by cutting the wholesalers' margins (selling at lower than recommended prices) or by bartering USPK's products for other pharmaceuticals. They do this by finding retail outlets where products are sold for less than the printed price. They exchange USPK's products at a discount for other drugs, which they sell to other retail outlets at a profit. As a result, USPK's products end up on retailers' shelves at prices lower than those that the company and its reputable wholesalers are selling them for.

The pharmaceutical industry has made some progress in persuading wholesalers and retailers to adhere to company price lists, but nonadherence is still a serious problem. One issue that manufacturers have not been able to resolve as yet is the manner in which demands from hospitals and physicians for gifts should be handled.

Sloane believes the industry can do much to solve these problems, although intense competition has thus far kept the pharmaceutical manufacturers from joining together to map out a solution.

1. What should Tom Sloane and U.S. Pharmaceutical of Korea do to improve collections from wholesalers?

2. How would you handle the distribution problem?

3. Can anything be done through firms in the industry to improve the situation?

4. How would you handle the demands for gifts?

*Based on an actual situation in Korea.

MINICASE 15-2   An Ethical Situation*

The Swiss pharmaceutical global corporation Hoffman-La Roche has made a major breakthrough in the relief of a serious disabling disease that affects 3 percent of the world's population. Their new product, Tigason, is the first product that effectively controls severe cases of psoriasis and dyskeratoses, skin disorders that cause severe flaking of the skin. Sufferers from this disease frequently retreat from society because of fear of rejection, thus losing their families and jobs. Tigason does not cure the disease, but it causes the symptoms to disappear.

*This is an actual situation.

There is one potential problem. Because of the risk of damage to unborn babies, women should not take the drug for one year before conception or during pregnancy. Hoffman-La Roche is well aware of the potential for harm to the company if the product is misused. It has seen the problems of another Swiss firm, Nestlé. After much discussion, the company has decided the product is too important to keep off the market. It is, after all, the product that gives the greatest relief to sufferers.

The marketing department is asked to formulate a strategy for disseminating product information and controlling Tigason's use.

As marketing manager, what do you recommend?

Export and Import Practices and Procedures

Speaking on why so many American firms don't do business outside the United States:

The biggest nontariff barrier for Americans in the world is the attitude of the CEO.

Kenneth Butterworth, CEO of Loctite (80 percent of profits and 60 percent of sales from overseas)

CONCEPT PREVIEWS

After reading this chapter, you should be able to:

1. **explain** why firms export

2. **describe** the three problem areas of exporting

3. **identify** the sources of export counseling

4. **describe** the main elements of the export sales assistance program of the U.S. Department of Commerce

5. **discuss** the meaning of the various terms of sale

6. **identify** some sources of export financing

7. **describe** the activities of a foreign freight forwarder

8. **understand** the kinds of export documents required

9. **discuss** some innovations in materials handling in sea and air transport

10. **identify** import sources

11. **describe** the activities of a custom-house broker

12. **explain** the Harmonized Tariff Schedule of the United States (HTSUSA)

Global Corporations and Small Companies Export

Du Pont, the twelfth largest U.S. exporter, has been able to remain a competitor in the tough chemical export market because it began to pay serious attention to exports back in 1978, when the dollar's value fell sharply. "We recognized that our business was changing from national to regional or global, so you didn't have a lot of options," says P. J. Roessel, Du Pont's director of international planning. "If you didn't participate in those foreign markets, your competitors would gradually get stronger and come and eat your lunch in the U.S." • Du Pont's marketing strategy is to promote the sale of U.S. exports by its overseas manufacturing subsidiaries. "We have plotted back for 25 years and have found that as we have invested and built abroad, exports have gone up in complete tandem," says Roessel. "Such subsidiaries are able to 'pull' products from the parent company to achieve real market synergy." A Japanese Du Pont subsidiary, for example, makes engineering plastics for autos and has developed markets for polyester and acetyl products made by Du Pont in the United States. • DataChem of Indianapolis, maker of hospital blood warmers and blood analyzers for physicians' offices, doesn't even have an export department, yet it exports 50 percent of its production overseas. Ramesh Shah, the company's CEO, and Dave Hepler, its director of sales and marketing, handle most of the export business. "Exporting doesn't take too much of our time—we use the fax, the telephone, and regular mail," explains Shah. • DataChem made its first sale, an $800 blood warmer, to Taiwan shortly after it started business. Now the firm, which has only 20 employees, exports products worth $400,000 to a number of countries. Last year, DataChem formed a joint venture in India that presently markets products made in Indianapolis, but next year it will open an assembly plant in India. Since January, the company also has had an agent/distributor in Saudi Arabia that handles sales to several Middle Eastern countries.

Sources: "Top 50 U.S. Industrial Exporters," *Fortune*, August 22, 1994, p. 132; "Exporting Pays Off," *Business America*, November 5, 1990, p. 9; and "Smoother Sailing Overseas," *Business Week*, April 18, 1986, p. 289.

WHO EXPORTS?

Many people believe that only large multinational firms like Du Pont export; others think that a firm can export only if it produces a product no one else has ever made, at least in the market where it wants to sell (see Table 16–1). However, the Small Business Administration (SBA) states that although many large multinational firms are major exporters, companies with less than $100,000 in annual sales also export. Of the nearly 100,000 firms exporting manufactured goods, 25 percent of them have less than 100 employees.[1]

The SBA also reports that many owners of small businesses believe that only the producers of exotic, high-tech products can export. Although it is true that these firms generally do well with exports, they are in the minority among exporters. Almost three times as many firms sell metal-working machinery overseas as sell computers and office machines.[2] A 1990 SBA survey found that 41 percent of the small firms that export had an export sales growth higher than their domestic sales growth and 23 percent had increased their export sales by between 20 percent and 49 percent over the previous year.[3]

In Chapter 2, when we examined why companies go overseas, we did not distinguish between reasons for exporting and foreign manufacturing. Let's look at some specific reasons for exporting.

WHY EXPORT?

With all the problems of doing business overseas, why do companies become involved in exporting instead of staying in their home country? There are a number of reasons, all of which are linked to the (1) desire to either increase profits and sales or (2) protect them from being eroded. Any of the following reasons for exporting, depending on the firm's situation, may achieve either goal.

TABLE 16–1
The 20 largest U.S. exporters

Company	Products	Exports ($ millions)	Total Sales ($ millions)	Exports as Percent of Sales
General Motors	Autos, locomotives	$14,913	$133,622	11.2%
Boeing	Aircraft	14,616	25,285	57.8
Ford	Autos and parts	9,483	108,521	8.7
General Electric	Aircraft engines, locomotives	8,498	60,823	14.0
Chrysler	Autos and parts	8,397	43,600	19.3
IBM	Information systems	7,297	62,716	11.6
Motorola	Semiconductors, radio equipment	4,990	16,963	29.4
Hewlett-Packard	Computers	4,738	20,317	23.3
Philip Morris	Tobacco, food	4,105	50,621	8.1
Caterpillar	Construction equipment	3,743	11,615	32.2
United Technologies	Aircraft engines, helicopters	3,503	20,736	16.9
Du Pont	Chemicals, fibers, plastics	3,500	32,621	10.7
Intel	Microchips, components	3,406	8,782	38.8
McDonnell Douglas	Aircraft, missiles	3,405	14,487	23.5
Archer Daniels Midland	Flour, oils, grains	2,900	9,811	29.6
Eastman Kodak	Photographic equipment	2,242	20,059	11.2
Raytheon	Electronic systems	2,063	9,201	22.4
Compaq Computer	Computers	1,922	7,191	26.7
Digital Equipment	Computers	1,800	14,371	12.5
Lockheed	Aerospace products	1,743	13,071	13.3

Source: "Top 50 U.S. Industrial Exporters," *Fortune*, August 22, 1994, p. 132.

- To serve markets where (1) the firm has no production facilities or (2) the local plant does not produce the firm's complete product mix—Many large multinationals like Du Pont, supply numerous foreign markets by exports because no firm, no matter how large, can afford to manufacture in every country where its goods are sold. Markets without factories are supplied from exports either from the home country or from a foreign affiliate. In markets of sufficient size to justify the production of some, but not all, of the product mix, the affiliate will supplement sales of local production with imports. A car plant in a developing nation may produce the least expensive cars and import luxury models if the law permits. Also, the more vertically integrated home plants (discussed in Chapter 2) export semifinished products that are inputs for the less integrated subsidiaries.

- To satisfy a host government's requirement that the local subsidiary exports—Developing governments often require the local affiliate to export, and some require that it earns sufficient foreign exchange to cover the cost of its imports. This is why Ford located a radio plant in Brazil that exports to Ford's European assembly plants.[4]

- To remain competitive in the home market—Many firms import labor-intensive components produced in their foreign affiliates or export components for assembly in countries where labor is less expensive and import the finished product. The Mexican in-bond plants discussed in Chapter 2 are based on this concept.

- To test foreign markets and foreign competition inexpensively—This is a common strategy used by firms that want to test a product's acceptance before investing in local production facilities. Exports also enable firms to test marketing strategies and make adjustments with less risk in a smaller market. If the strategy or product fails, the firm can withdraw without having a costly and sometimes damaging failure to the entire firm.

- To meet actual or prospective customers' requests for the firm to export—This type of *accidental exporting* is fairly common. A foreign buyer often will search for something it cannot find locally by consulting the *Thomas Register*, a publication listing American producers for hundreds of products. Every American consulate and local American chamber of commerce (French-American, Mexican-American, and so forth) has a copy.

- To offset cyclical sales of the domestic market.

- To achieve additional sales, which allow the firm to use its excess production capacity to lower unit fixed costs.

- To extend a product's life cycle by exporting to countries where technology is less advanced.

- To distract foreign competitors that are in the firm's home market by entering their home markets.

- To partake in the kind of success that the firm's management has seen others achieve by exporting.

WHY DON'T THEY EXPORT?

The two major reasons U.S. firms give for not exporting are (1) preoccupation with the vast American market and (2) a reluctance to become involved in a new and unknown operation. When nonexporting firms are asked why they are not active in international markets, they generally mention the following as problem areas: (1) locating foreign markets, (2) payment and financing

The 12 Most Common Mistakes and Pitfalls Awaiting New Exporters

The following may be considered the 12 most common mistakes and pitfalls made by new exporters.

1. **Failure to obtain qualified export counseling and to develop a master international marketing plan before starting an export business.** To be successful, a firm must first clearly define goals, objectives, and the problems encountered. Second, it must develop a definitive plan to accomplish an objective despite the problems involved. Unless the firm is fortunate enough to possess a staff with considerable export expertise, it may not be able to take this crucial first step without qualified outside guidance.

2. **Insufficient commitment by top management to overcome the initial difficulties and financial requirements of exporting.** It may take more time and effort to establish a firm in a foreign market than in domestic ones. Although the early delays and costs involved in exporting may seem difficult to justify when compared to established domestic trade, the exporter should take a long-range view of this process and carefully monitor international marketing efforts through these early difficulties. If a good foundation is laid for export business, the benefits derived should eventually outweigh the investment.

3. **Insufficient care in selecting overseas distributors.** The selection of each foreign distributor is crucial. The complications involved in overseas communications and transportation require international distributors to act with greater independence than their domestic counterparts. Also, since a new exporter's history, trademarks, and reputation are usually unknown in the foreign market, foreign customers may buy on the strength of a distributor's reputation. A firm should therefore conduct a personal evaluation of the personnel handling its account, the distributor's facilities, and the management methods employed.

4. **Chasing orders from around the world instead of establishing a basis for profitable operations and orderly growth.** If exporters expect distributors to actively promote their accounts, the distributors must be trained and assisted and their performance must be continually monitored. This requires a company marketing executive permanently located in the distributor's geographical region. New exporters should concentrate their efforts in one or two geographical areas until there is sufficient business to support a company representative. Then, while this initial core area is expanded, the exporter can move into the next selected geographical area.

5. **Neglecting export business when the U.S. market booms.** Too many companies turn to exporting when business falls off in the United States. When domestic business starts to boom again, they neglect their export trade or relegate it to a secondary place. Such neglect can seriously harm the business and motivation of their overseas representatives, strangle the U.S. company's own export trade, and leave the firm without recourse when domestic business falls off once more. Even if domestic

procedures, and (3) export procedures. A group of small businesses gave somewhat different but related reasons. Ninety percent of the respondents to a survey of the National Small Business United, a 60,000-member advocacy group, stated they do not export; the majority said the reasons are that they do not know where to start (locating foreign markets), fear the complexity (payment, financing, and export procedures), or do not know that information and federal support are readily available.[5]

Although considerable assistance is available from the federal and state departments of commerce, banks, the Small Business Administration, Small Business Development Centers (does your school have one?), private consultants (your international business professor may consult), and numerous other sources, some of which we mentioned in Chapter 14, too few managers are taking advantage of this assistance. Let us examine the three problem areas.

business remains strong, the company may eventually realize that it has only succeeded in shutting off a valuable source of additional profits.

6. **Failure to treat international distributors on an equal basis with domestic counterparts.** Often, companies carry out institutional advertising campaigns, special discount offers, sales incentive programs, special credit term programs, warranty offers, and so forth in the U.S. market but fail to make similar assistance available to their international distributors. This is a mistake that can destroy the vitality of overseas marketing efforts.

7. **Assuming that a given market technique and product will automatically be successful in all countries.** What works in one market may not work in others. Each market has to be treated separately to ensure maximum success.

8. **Unwillingness to modify products to meet regulations or cultural preferences of other countries.** Local safety and security codes, as well as import restrictions, cannot be ignored by foreign distributors. If necessary modifications are not made at the factory, the distributor must do them—usually at greater cost and, perhaps, not as well. It should also be noted that the resulting smaller profit margin makes the account less attractive.

9. **Failure to print service, sale, and warranty messages in locally understood languages.** Although

a distributor's top management may speak English, it is unlikely that all sales personnel (let alone service personnel) have this capability. Without a clear understanding of sales messages or service instructions, these persons may be less effective in performing their functions.

10. **Failure to consider use of an export management company.** If a firm decides it cannot afford its own export department (or has tried one unsuccessfully), it should consider the possibility of appointing an appropriate export management company (EMC).

11. **Failure to consider licensing or joint venture agreements.** Import restrictions in some countries, insufficient personnel/financial resources, or a too limited product line cause many companies to dismiss international marketing as unfeasible. Yet, many products that can compete on a national basis in the United States can be successfully marketed in most markets of the world. A licensing or joint venture arrangement may be the simple, profitable answer to any reservations. In general, all that is needed for success is flexibility in using the proper combination of marketing techniques.

12. **Failure to provide readily available servicing for the product.** A product without the necessary service support can acquire a bad reputation in a short period, potentially preventing further sales.

Source: *Business America*, December 7, 1987, pp. 14–15.

The first step in locating foreign markets, whether for export or foreign manufacturing, is to determine whether a market exists for the firm's products. The initial screening step described in Chapter 14 indicated a procedure to follow that will pose no problem for the experienced market analyst who is well acquainted with the available sources of information and assistance. However, newcomers to exporting, especially the smaller firms, may still be at a loss as to how to begin; for them, there are a number of export assistance programs available.

LOCATING FOREIGN MARKETS

Sources of Export Counseling

Trade Information Center. Individuals and firms new to exporting can begin their search for export counseling by first calling the Trade Information Center at 1(800)USA-TRADE. The Center is a one-stop source of information on federal export assistance programs offered by 19 federal agencies. International trade specialists advise businesses on issues ranging from how to begin exporting to specific tariff rates in a particular nation. They also assist callers to find export assistance offered by others. The Center maintains files on the various state and local organizations that help exporters such as state export assistance offices, World Trade Centers, small business development agencies, chambers of commerce, and other groups involved in international trade.

Firms that are already exporting and desire to expand their overseas business may bypass the Trade Information Center and go directly to the nearest district office of the Commerce Department's International Trade Administration (ITA). The ITA is the primary U.S. government agency responsible for assisting firms already exporting.

International Trade Administration.   The ITA offers a wide range of export promotion activities that include export counseling, analysis of foreign markets, assessment of industry competitiveness, and development of market opportunities and sales representation through export promotion events. Three units of ITA work together to provide these services:

1. *International Economic Policy*—Country desk officers in this unit are specialists in specific countries. They keep current on the economic and commercial conditions of their assigned countries so that they can offer information on trade and investment potential to firms wishing to sell to them.

2. *Trade Development*—This unit promotes the trade interests of American industries and offers information on markets and trade practices worldwide. It is divided into seven sectors: aerospace, automotive affairs and consumer goods, basic industries, capital goods and international construction, science and electronics, services, and textiles and apparel. Industry desk officers work with manufacturing and service industry representatives and associations to identify trade opportunities by product or service, industry sector, and market. They also develop export marketing plans and programs. Besides counseling American businesses in exporting, the unit's industry experts conduct executive trade missions, trade fairs, and marketing seminars.

3. *U.S. and Foreign Commercial Service (US&FCS)*—There are 67 district and branch offices throughout the United States and Puerto Rico that have trade specialists to help firms assess their export potential, select markets, locate overseas representatives, and obtain information on the various steps in exporting. Through a district office, a firm has access to all the assistance available in the Commerce Department. For example, the ITA's U.S. and Foreign Commercial Service has commercial officers working in 67 countries who can provide background information on foreign companies and assist in finding foreign representatives, conducting market research, and identifying trade and investment opportunities for American firms. The district offices also conduct export workshops and keep businesspeople informed about domestic and overseas trade events that offer potential for promoting American products.

Small Business Administration.   The Office of International Trade of the Small Business Administration (SBA) offers assistance through SBA district offices. The Office of International Trade also works through:

1. SCORE/ACE programs—Experienced executives offer free one-on-one counseling to small firms.

   2. SBDC/SBI programs—Small Business Development Centers (SBDCs) in many universities and colleges give export counseling, especially to inexperienced newcomers. Business students in Small Business Institutes (SBIs) provide in-depth, long-term counseling under faculty supervision.

Department of Agriculture.   Like the Department of Commerce, the Department of Agriculture has a single contact point, the Trade Assistance and Planning Office (TAPO) within it Foreign Agriculture Service (FAS) for agricultural exporters seeking market information. Commerce and Agriculture export assistance programs are similar in many ways.

Department of Commerce Export Assistance Program

Foreign Market Research.   After learning about the company and its products, the international trade specialist might advise the potential exporter to consult the National Trade Data Bank (NTDB), a service that selects the most recent trade promotions, "how to" publications, and international trade and economic data from 15 federal agencies and puts them on one CD-ROM that is updated monthly. The NTDB provides (1) a comprehensive guide for new exporters and (2) a source of specific product and regional information for experienced exporters searching for new markets. It also contains the Foreign Traders Index—a list of foreign importers, with descriptions of each and the products they wish to import.[6] From this list, the exporter can prepare a mailing list of those interested in its products and then make a bulk mailing. The NTDB is usually available in university SBDCs offering export assistance and in the government documents sections of university libraries. A business can also subscribe to the service for $360 annually.

   The trade specialist might also suggest signing up for the Trade Opportunities Program, which provides subscribers with current sales leads from overseas firms wanting to buy or represent their products or services. Another possibility is advertising in *Commercial News USA,* a monthly magazine that promotes the products and services of American firms to over 100,000 overseas agents, distributors, and government officials.

Smaller Number of Potential Markets.   When the research has identified a small number of potential markets, the firm may wish to use the Department of Commerce's Comparison Shopping Service. For $500 per market, the customer will receive a custom-tailored market research survey on a specific product of its choice. This service provides information on marketability, names of competitors, comparative prices, distribution channels, and names of potential sales representatives. Each study is conducted on-site by a U.S. commercial officer. For markets not included in the service, a Department of Commerce specialist may recommend such publications as *Country Market Surveys, Competitive Assessments,* and *Annual Worldwide Industry Reviews,* all of which are available on an industry basis.

   There are still other helpful publications and services. *Foreign Economic Trends Reports* summarize the economic and commercial trends in a country and are a good source of information as to which American products are most in demand. A series of reports, *Overseas Business Reports (OBR),* provide basic background data on specific countries. Each *OBR* discusses separate topics on a single country, such as basic economic data, foreign trade regulations, market factors, and trade with the United States. The firm may subscribe to *Business America,* a biweekly magazine, whose "International Commerce" section contains announcements about (1) U.S. promotions abroad in which the firm can participate; (2) foreign concerns looking for licensors, joint venture partners, or distributorships; and (3) opportunities to make direct sales.

Direct or Indirect Exporting.   When it has been established that there is an existing or potential market for its goods, the firm must choose between exporting indirectly through U.S.-based exporters or exporting directly using its own staff. If it opts for indirect exporting as a way to test the market, the trade specialist can provide assistance in locating one of the types of exporters listed in Chapter 13. However, should the firm prefer to set up its own export operation, it must then obtain overseas distribution.

The exporter may, as we mentioned previously, try a broad-based mailing to solicit representatives or use the Department of Commerce Agent/ Distributor Search service. Commercial officers of American embassies or consulates will, within 90 days, personally interview and identify up to six local prospects who have seen the company literature and expressed an interest in representation. The exporters may then obtain information covering their commercial activities and competence by asking the Department of Commerce to supply a *World Traders Data Report*. Credit reporting agencies, such as Dun & Bradstreet, FCIB (Finance, Credit, and International Business Association), and the exporter's bank, will also supply credit information.

The Foreign Agricultural Service of the U.S. Department of Agriculture offers similar services to potential exporters of agricultural products.

Show and Sell.   The Department of Commerce also organizes trade events that are helpful in both locating foreign representatives and making sales.[7] There are four kinds:

1. *Trade fairs.* Commerce organizes exhibitions or American pavilions at international trade fairs, which are held regularly in major cities worldwide. At one time, the U.S. government owned 15 trade centers in which American industry periodically held exhibitions, but for budgetary reasons, these have been reduced to 4 (London, Mexico City, Seoul, and Tokyo).

2. *Matchmaker program and trade missions.* Commerce representatives accompany groups of American businesspeople overseas to meet with qualified agents, distributors, and customers. Prior to their arrival, overseas consular officials make appointments with qualified agents, distributors, and customers. The Department of Commerce also sponsors state- and industry-organized trade missions.

3. *Foreign buyer program.* The Commerce Department annually sponsors about 20 domestic trade shows, which bring foreign buyers and U.S. manufacturers together. American consular officers promote these trade shows in over 60 countries to attract foreign business representatives.

4. *Catalog and video shows.* American manufacturers can gain market visibility without going overseas by participating in a catalog and video show. They merely give their literature and promotional videos to Commerce, which displays them for select audiences in several foreign countries.

Other Sources of Assistance

Other sources of assistance available to the exporter include the following:

World Trade Centers Association.   The World Trade Centers Association, another aid to marketing for the new exporter, was founded by the New York–New Jersey Port Authority, which has licensed over 60 centers world-

Various Types of Experts Help Small Firms Export

David Kratka, president of MMO Music Group, a small producer of sing-along tapes for karaoke machines in Elmsford, New York, didn't have to search for foreign business; foreign customers came to him. Although this seems like an enviable situation, in reality, Kratka figures the company probably lost foreign sales in the 1980s because he was too busy attending to the domestic market. He didn't have time to answer faxes and telephone calls from Asia and Europe.

Last year, after Kratka finally decided he could no longer handle the foreign inquiries alone, he hired an international sales director. Now foreign sales constitute about 15 percent of the firm's total $8 million sales. This is up from the 5 percent before he was hired.

Other companies find it easier and more economical to get exporting help from an outsider. A consulting firm, Export Resource Associates, is teaching exporting techniques to

CoBatCo, a waffle griddle maker in Illinois with 21 employees. Exports amounted to 13 percent of total sales last year compared to no foreign sales in 1990. "I think to some extent there were some opportunities in the late 80s that could have been pursued if we had the background to pursue them," said the president. "We didn't have knowledge of what a letter of credit even was."

Other small-firm managers without the time or international expertise to handle foreign sales turn to export management companies (EMCs) that typically handle everything from sales and distribution to credit and shipping. They usually charge a fee of between 10 and 15 percent of the shipment's value. The advantage of this approach is that experts handle the export function. The disadvantage, however, is that the control of the company's export business lies in the hands of outsiders.

Source: "Small Companies Look to Cultivate Foreign Business," *The Wall Street Journal*, July 7, 1994, p. B2.

wide. Through membership, exporters and importers have access to an online trading system called NETWORK. Exporters need only a computer and a modem to put offers to sell in an electronic database, and importers anywhere can send messages to the exporters' mailboxes accepting advertised prices or initiating electronic negotiations. Access can be gained with a local telephone in 800 cities in 64 countries.

The Trade Point Global Network.   The United Nations Conference on Trade and Development (UNCTAD) began a program in 1992 designed to lower the costs of conducting international trade. The program is based on the transmission of information in electronic form, including the Electronic Data Interchange (EDI), and establishes a network of "Trade Points" throughout the world. Each Trade Point is a trade facilitation center where all participants in international trade transactions, such as Customs, foreign freight forwarders, insurance firms, banks, transport companies, and so on, are under a single physical or virtual roof. The Trade Points are interconnected in a world electronic network that makes business opportunities and statistical data available to all members.

Presently, there are about 50 locations, all of which are self-financing. The only Trade Point presently located in North America is in Columbus, Ohio, although more are expected to be formed later. Because of the similarities between the two, the World Trade Center Association is cooperating with the Trade Point Global Network.[8]

District Export Councils.   The Department of Commerce has 51 district export councils composed of volunteer business and trade experts who assist in workshops and also arrange for consultation between experienced and prospective exporters.

State Governments.   All states have export development programs that offer assistance to exporters by providing sales leads, locating overseas representatives, and counseling. Twenty-two states also have export-financing programs, and more are setting them up.[9]

Export Marketing Plan

As soon as possible, an export marketing plan must be drawn up. An experienced firm will already have a plan in operation, but newcomers will usually need to wait until they have accumulated at least some information from foreign market research.

Same as Domestic Marketing Plan.

Essentially, the export marketing plan is the same as the domestic marketing plan. It should be specific about (1) the markets to be developed, (2) the marketing strategy for serving them, and (3) the tactics required to make the strategy operational. Sales forecasts and budgets, pricing policies, product characteristics, promotional plans, and details on the arrangements with foreign representatives are required. In other words, the export marketing plan will spell out what must be done and when, who should do it, and how much money will be spent. An outline for an export marketing plan appears in the Appendix at the end of this chapter.

Marketing Mix.

Because the comments in Chapter 15 concerning the marketing mix are valid for exporters, there is no need for a detailed discussion here. Two aspects that do require some explanation, however, are *export pricing* and *sales agreements for foreign representatives.*

Pricing Policies.

Pricing is a problem even for experienced exporters. Noncompetitive prices cause sales to be lost to foreign competitors, but incorrect pricing can also cause the exporter to lose money on a sale.

One new area of concern for many firms beginning to export is the necessity to quote **terms of sale** that differ from those normally used. For domestic sales, the company may be quoting FOB factory, which means all costs and risks from that point on are borne by the buyer. Foreign customers, however, may insist on one of the following terms of sale:[10]

terms of sale
Conditions of a sale that stipulate the point where all costs and risks are borne by buyer

1. *FAS (free alongside ship), port of exit.* The seller pays all of the transportation and delivery expense up to the ship's side. The buyer is responsible for any loss or damage to the shipment from that point on.

2. *CIF (cost, insurance, freight), foreign port.* The seller quotes a price that includes the cost of the goods, insurance, and all transportation and miscellaneous charges to the named foreign port in the country of final destination.

3. *CFR (cost, freight).* This is similar to CIF except the buyer purchases the insurance, either because it can obtain it at a lower cost or because its government, to save foreign exchange, insists that it use a local insurance company.

4. *FOB (free on board), at a named border crossing.* This is a common term used by exporters to Canada and Mexico. The seller quotes a price that covers all costs up to the border where the shipment is delivered to the buyer's representative.

CIF and CFR terms of sale are more convenient for foreign buyers because, to establish their cost, they merely have to add the import duties, landing charges, and freight from the port of arrival to their warehouse.

However, these terms can present a problem for new exporters if they forget the miscellaneous costs—wharf storage and handling charges, freight forwarder's charges, and consular fees—incurred in making a CIF shipment and simply add freight, insurance, and export packing costs to the domestic selling price. The resulting price may be too low, but more often it will be too high, because the domestic marketing and general administrative costs included in the domestic selling price are frequently greater than the actual cost of making the export sale.

The preferred pricing method is the use of the *factory door cost* (production cost without domestic marketing and general administrative costs), to which are added the direct cost of making the export sale and a percentage of the general administrative overhead. This percentage can be derived from managers' estimates of the part of their total time spent on export matters. The minimum FOB price will be the sum of these costs plus the required profit. If research in a market has shown either that there is little competition or that competitive prices are higher, then, of course, the exporter is free to charge a high price in that market (price skim) or to set a low price to gain a larger percentage of the market (penetration pricing). The course of action taken will depend on the firm's sales objectives, just as it does in the domestic market.

Sales Agreement. The sales agreement should specify as simply as possible the duties of the representative and the firm. Most of what is contained in the contract for a domestic representative can be used in export also, but special attention must be given to two points: (1) designation of the responsibilities for patent and trademark registration and (2) designation of the country and state, if applicable, whose laws will govern a contractual dispute. To be absolutely safe, the firm should register all patents and trademarks. Policing them may be left to the local representative if management so chooses. However, the firm should have the help of an experienced international attorney when drawing up an agreement.

U.S. exporters would prefer to stipulate the laws of the United States and their home state, but many nations, especially those of Latin America, will not permit this (Calvo Doctrine). The Calvo Doctrine, promulgated by Calvo, an Argentine jurist, holds that trying cases locally under foreign laws should not be permitted because it gives the foreign company an advantage over local firms, which must be tried under local laws. If an American state can be designated, its laws may be followed even though the dispute is adjudicated in a foreign country. The presiding judge will have the pertinent parts of the law translated or will call on witnesses who are known experts in the area of law involved.

The second major problem area concerns payment and financing procedures.

PAYMENT AND FINANCING PROCEDURES

Export Payment Terms

Payment terms, as every marketer knows, are often a decisive factor in obtaining an order. As a sales official of an international grain exporter put it, "If you give credit to a guy who is broke, he'll pay any price for your product." This is somewhat exaggerated, but customers will often pay higher prices when terms are more lenient. This is especially significant in countries where capital is scarce and interest rates are high. The kinds of payment terms offered by exporters to foreign buyers are (1) cash in advance, (2) open account, (3) consignment, (4) letters of credit, and (5) documentary drafts.

Cash in Advance. When the credit standing of the buyer is not known or is uncertain, cash in advance is desirable. However, very few buyers will accept these terms, because part of their working capital is tied up until the merchandise has been received and sold. Furthermore, they have no guarantee that they will receive what they ordered. As a result, few customers will pay cash in advance unless the order is either small or for a product of special manufacture.

Open Account.   When a sale is made on open account, the seller assumes all of the risk, and therefore these terms should be offered only to reliable customers in economically stable countries. The exporter's capital, of course, is tied up until payment has been received.

Consignment.   This follows the procedure well known in the United States by which goods are shipped to the buyer and payment is not made until they have been sold. All of the risk is assumed by the seller, and such terms should not be offered without making the same extensive investigation of the buyer and country that is recommended for open account terms. Multinationals frequently sell goods to their subsidiaries on this basis.

letter of credit (L/C)
Document issued by the buyer's bank in which the bank promises to pay the seller a specified amount under specified conditions

Letters of Credit.   Only cash in advance offers more protection to the seller than an export **letter of credit (L/C).** This document is issued by the buyer's bank, which promises to pay the seller a specified amount when the bank has received certain documents stipulated in the letter of credit by a specified time.

confirmed
Act of a correspondent bank in the seller's country by which it agrees to honor the issuing bank's letter of credit.

irrevocable
A stipulation that a letter of credit cannot be canceled

Confirmed and Irrevocable.   Generally, the seller will request that the letter of credit be **confirmed** and **irrevocable.** Irrevocable means that once the seller has accepted the credit, the customer cannot alter or cancel it without the seller's consent. Figure 16–1 is an example of a bank's confirmation of an irrevocable letter of credit. If the letter of credit is *not* confirmed, the correspondent bank (Merchants National Bank of Mobile) has no obligation to pay the seller (Smith & Co.) when it receives the documents listed in the letter of credit. Only the issuing bank (Banco Americano in Bogota) is responsible. If the seller (Smith & Co.) wishes to be able to collect from an American bank, it will insist that the credit be confirmed by such a bank. This is generally done by the correspondent bank, as it was in Figure 16–1. In this case, when the Merchants National Bank of Mobile confirmed the credit, it undertook an obligation to pay Smith & Co. if all of the documents listed in the letter were presented on or before the stipulated date.

air waybill
A bill of lading issued by an air carrier

Note that nothing is mentioned about the goods themselves; the buyer has stipulated only that an **air waybill** issued by the carrier be presented as proof that shipment has been made. Even if bank officials knew that the plane had crashed after the takeoff, they would still have to pay Smith & Co. *Banks are concerned with documents, not merchandise.*

pro forma invoice
Exporter's formal quotation containing a description of the merchandise, price, delivery time, method of shipping, terms of sale, and points of exit and entry

Prior to opening a letter of credit, a buyer frequently requests a **pro forma invoice.** This is the exporter's formal quotation containing a description of the merchandise, price, delivery time, proposed method of shipment, ports of exit and entry, and terms of sale. It is more than a quotation, however. Generally, the bank will use it when opening a letter of credit, and in countries requiring import licenses or permits to purchase foreign exchange, government officials will insist on receiving copies.

Letter of Credit Transactions.   Figure 16–2 illustrates the routes taken by the merchandise, letter of credit, and documents in a letter of credit transaction.

When a German buyer accepts the terms of sale that provide for a confirmed and irrevocable letter of credit, it goes to its bank to arrange for opening the required letter. The buyer will furnish the bank with the information contained in the pro forma invoice, specify the documents that the exporter must present to obtain payment, and set the expiration date for the credit.

The German bank then instructs its correspondent bank in the United States to confirm the credit and inform the seller that it has been established. The seller prepares the merchandise for shipment and notifies the freight

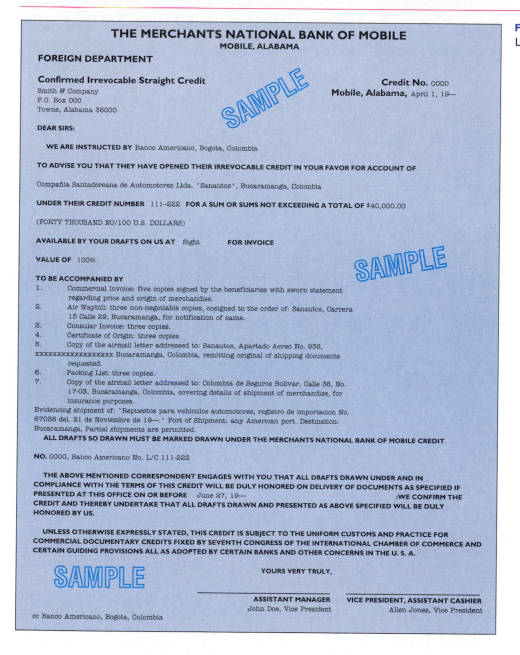

FIGURE 16–1
Letter of credit

forwarder, which books space on a ship, prepares the export documents, and arranges to have the merchandise delivered to the port. The documents, together with a sight or time draft drawn by the seller, are presented to the U.S. bank, which pays the seller and forwards the documents for collection to the German bank.

To obtain the documents that give title to the shipment, the buyer in Germany must either pay the *sight draft* or accept a *time draft*. Having done so, the buyer receives the documents, which are then given to the customhouse broker. The customhouse broker acts as the buyer's agent in receiving the goods from the steamship line and clearing them through German customs.

Documentary Drafts. When the exporter believes the political and commercial risks are not sufficient to require a letter of credit, the exporter may agree to payment on a documentary draft basis, which is less costly to the buyer.

FIGURE 16–2
Letter of credit transaction

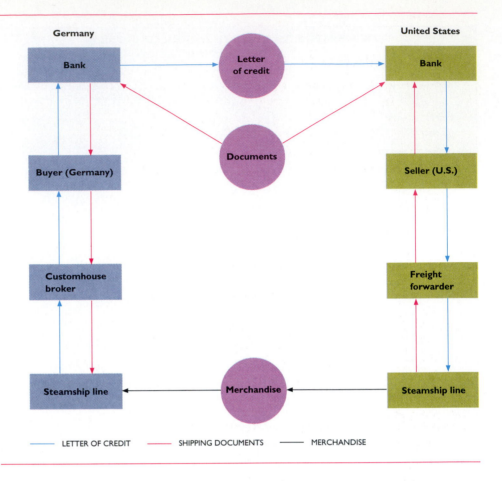

export draft
*An unconditional order that is drawn by the seller on the buyer to pay the draft's amount on presentation (**sight draft**) or at an agreed future date (**time draft**) and that must be paid before the buyer receives shipping documents*

An **export draft,** shown in Figure 16–3, is an unconditional order drawn by the seller on the buyer instructing the buyer to pay the amount of the order on presentation (**sight draft**) or at an agreed future date (**time draft**). Generally, the seller will request its bank to send the draft and documents to a bank in the buyer's country, which will proceed with the collection as described in the letter of credit transaction.

Although documentary draft and letter of credit terms are similar, there is one important difference. A confirmed letter of credit guarantees payment to the seller if the seller conforms to its requirements, but there is no such

FIGURE 16–3
Sight draft

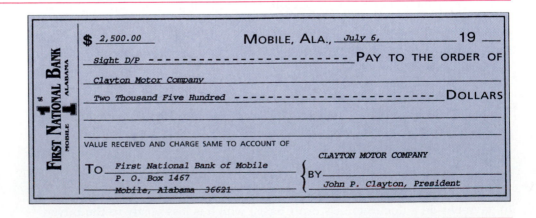

guarantee with documentary drafts. An unscrupulous buyer can refuse to pay the drafts when presented and then attempt to bargain with the seller for a lower price. The seller must then acquiesce, try to find another buyer, pay a large freight bill to bring back the goods, or abandon them. If the seller chooses the last alternative, customs will auction off the goods, and chances are the original buyer will be able to acquire them at a bargain price. The seller, of course, receives nothing.

Export Financing

Although exporters would prefer to sell on the almost riskless letter of credit terms, increased foreign competition and the universally tight money situation are forcing them to offer credit. To do so, they must be familiar with the available sources and kinds of export financing, both private and public.

Private Source.   Commercial banks have always been a source of export financing through loans for working capital and the discounting of time drafts. A bank may discount an export time draft, pay the seller and keep it until maturity, or, if it is the bank on which the draft is drawn, "accept" it. By accepting a time draft, a bank assumes the responsibility for making payment at maturity of the draft. The accepting bank may or may not purchase (at a discount) the draft. If it does not, the exporter can sell a **banker's acceptance** readily in the open market. In recent years, new types of financing have been developed: factoring and forfaiting.

Factoring.   This financing technique permits the exporter to be more competitive by selling on open account rather than by means of the more costly letter of credit method. **Factoring,** which has long been used in the United States to provide working capital to manufacturers short of cash, is now being employed in international trade. Factoring is essentially discounting *without* recourse because it is the sale of export accounts receivable to a third party, which assumes the credit risk. A factor may be a factoring house or a special department in a commercial bank.

Under the export factoring arrangement, the seller passes its order to the factor for approval of the credit risk. Once the order has been approved, the exporter has complete protection against bad debts and political risk. The customer pays the factor, which in effect, acts as the exporter's credit and collection department. The period of settlement generally does not exceed 180 days.

Forfaiting.   **Forfaiting** denotes the purchase of obligations that arise from the sale of goods and services and fall due at some date beyond the 90 to 180 days that are customary for factoring. These receivables are usually in the form of trade drafts or promissory notes with maturities ranging from six months to five years.

Because it is sold without recourse, forfaited debt is nearly always accompanied by bank security in the form of a guarantee or aval. Whereas the guarantee is a separate document, the aval is a promise to pay written directly in the document ("per aval" and the signature).

The forfaiter purchases the bill and discounts it for the entire credit period. Thus, the exporter, through forfaiting, has converted its credit-based sale into a cash transaction.

Although banks have traditionally concentrated on short-term financing, they have become involved in medium- and even long-term financing because numerous government and government-assisted organizations are offering export credit guarantees and insurance against commercial (customer goes

banker's acceptance
A time draft with maturity of less than 270 days that has been accepted by the bank on which the draft was drawn, thus becoming the accepting bank's obligation; may be bought and sold at a discount in the financial markets like other commercial paper

factoring
Discounting without recourse an account receivable

forfaiting
Purchasing without recourse an account receivable whose credit terms are longer than the 90 to 180 days usual in factoring; unlike factoring, political and transfer risks are borne by the forfaiter

bankrupt and can't pay) and political risks (government overthrown and foreign exchange unavailable to customer).[11]

Eximbank
Principal federal government agency that aids American exporters by means of loans, guarantees, and insurance programs

Export-Import Bank.   The U.S. Export-Import Bank (**Eximbank**) is the principal government agency responsible for aiding the export of American goods and services through a variety of loan, guarantee, and insurance programs.[12] Generally, its programs are available to any American export firm regardless of size.

Direct and Intermediary Loans.   The Eximbank provides two types of loans: (1) direct loans to foreign buyers of American exports and (2) intermediary loans to responsible parties, such as a foreign government lending agency that relends to foreign buyers of capital goods and related services (for example, a maintenance contract for a jet passenger plane). Both programs cover up to 85 percent of the value of the exported goods and services, with repayment terms of one year or more.

Working Capital Guarantee.   This program helps small businesses obtain working capital to cover their export sales. It guarantees working capital loans extended by banks to eligible exporters with exportable inventory or export receivables as collateral.

Guarantees.   Eximbank's guarantee provides repayment protection for private-sector loans to buyers of U.S. capital equipment and related services. The guarantee is available alone or may be combined with an Eximbank direct or intermediary loan.

Export Credit Insurance.   An exporter may reduce its financing risks by purchasing export credit insurance against payment default. The Eximbank has several policies for export sales, leasing of equipment, and consignments in foreign markets. The coverage may be comprehensive or limited to political risk only.

Since its inception in 1934, the Eximbank has supported over $200 billion in U.S. exports. Every industrialized nation and many that are industrializing have similar banks. Another government agency, the Small Business Administration, operates loan guarantee and direct loan programs to assist small-business exporters.

OTHER GOVERNMENT INCENTIVES

Overseas Private Investment Corporation (OPIC)
Government corporation that offers American investors in developing countries insurance against expropriation, currency inconvertibility, and damages from wars and revolutions.

Foreign Sales Corporation (FSC)
Special corporate form authorized by the federal government that provides tax advantages for exporting firms

Other government incentives for trade, although not strictly a part of export financing, are certainly closely related to it. These are the Overseas Private Investment Corporation (OPIC), the Foreign Sales Corporation (FSC), and the foreign trade zone (FTZ).

Overseas Private Investment Corporation (OPIC)

The **Overseas Private Investment Corporation (OPIC)** is a government corporation formed to stimulate private investment in developing countries. It offers investors insurance against expropriation, currency inconvertibility, and damages from wars or revolutions. OPIC also offers specialized insurance for American service contractors and exporters operating in foreign countries. Exports of capital equipment and semiprocessed raw materials generally follow these investments.

Foreign Sales Corporation (FSC)

The **Foreign Sales Corporation (FSC)** was authorized by the Tax Reform Act of 1984. It replaced the Domestic International Sales Corporation (DISC), which U.S. trading partners complained violated the General Agreement on Tariffs and Trade.

Unlike its DISC predecessor, an FSC must be located either in a U.S. possession other than Puerto Rico or in a foreign country that has an information exchange agreement with the United States. The FSC's shareholders' and directors' meetings must be held outside the United States, and its principal bank account must be maintained outside the United States.

The portion of the FSC's income that is exempt from U.S. corporate taxation is 32 percent if the FSC buys from independent suppliers or uses the Section 482* arm's-length pricing rule with related suppliers.[13]

Foreign Trade Zones

For centuries, various forms of duty-free areas have existed in many parts of the world to facilitate trade by lessening the effect of customs restrictions. These customs-privileged areas may be free ports, transit zones, free perimeters, export processing zones, or free trade zones. In each instance, a specific and limited area is involved, into which imported goods may be brought without the payment of import duties. There are hundreds of these areas in 72 countries. Of the five types, the free trade zone is the most common.

The **free trade zone** is an enclosed area considered to be outside the customs territory of the country in which it is located. Goods of foreign origin may be brought into the zone pending eventual transshipment, reexportation, or importation into the country. While the goods are in the zone, no import duties need to be paid.

free trade zone
An area designated by the government of a country for duty-free entry of any nonprohibited good

The American version, called the **foreign trade zone (FTZ),** has been growing in popularity, and there are now more than 400 of these zones in operation.† Many are situated at seaports, but some are located at inland distribution points.

foreign trade zone (FTZ)
American version of a free trade zone

Goods brought into the FTZ may be stored, inspected, repackaged, or combined with American components. Because of differences in the import tariff schedule, the finished product often pays less duty than what would be charged for the disassembled parts. Bicycles have been assembled in the Kansas City FTZ for that reason. Importers of machinery and automobiles improve their cash flow by storing spare parts in an FTZ, because duty is not paid until they are withdrawn.

Although the advantages of the FTZ to importers are well known, its benefits to exporters appear to have been overlooked. Foreign trade zones can provide accelerated export status for purposes of excise tax rebates and customs drawbacks. Manufacturers of such items as tires, trucks, and tobacco products are required to pay federal excise taxes when these items are produced, but the taxes are rebated if the items are exported. Firms including imported parts in their finished product must pay duty on the imports, but this duty is returned when the product is exported (customs drawback). The recovery of this money takes time, however, and meanwhile the exporter can have considerable capital tied up in excise taxes and import duties. Because a product is considered exported as soon as it enters an FTZ, the exporter can immediately apply for a rebate or a drawback while waiting to make an export sale. Although U.S. Customs has had the duty-drawback program in place for 200 years, many firms do not claim the money they're owed. As a result, each year a billion dollars in customs-duty refunds go unclaimed.[14]

If assembly or manufacturing is done in the FTZ using imported components, no duties need ever be paid when the finished product is exported. This

---

*See Chapter 15 for details on Section 482.
†Includes subzones for individual plants.

is also the purpose of the previously mentioned export processing zones in which firms use cheap local labor for assembly. There are various such zones in China, for example.

EXPORT PROCEDURES

When nonexporters complain about the complexity of export procedures, they are generally referring to documentation. Instead of the two documents (the freight bill and the bill of lading) to which they are accustomed when shipping domestically, they are suddenly confronted by five to six times as many documents for a foreign shipment. According to an OECD study, the average overseas transaction needs 35 documents with a total of 360 copies. The study states that the "paper costs" of international trade come to between 1.4 percent and 5.7 percent of the value of the trade. "Exports move on a sea of documents" is a popular saying in the industry. Although the extra burden may be handled by the traffic department, many firms give all or at least part of the work to a foreign freight forwarder.

Foreign Freight Forwarders

foreign freight forwarders
Independent businesses that handle export shipments for compensation

Foreign freight forwarders act as agents for exporters. They prepare documents, book space with a carrier, and in general act as the firm's export traffic department. If asked, they will offer advice about markets, import and export regulations, the best mode of transport, and export packing, and they will supply cargo insurance. After shipment, they forward all documents to the importer or to the paying bank, according to the exporter's requirements.

Export Documents

Correct documentation is vital to the success of any export shipment. For discussion purposes, we shall divide export documents into two categories: (1) shipping documents and (2) collection documents.

Shipping Documents.   Shipping documents are prepared by exporters or their freight forwarders so that the shipment may pass through U.S. Customs, be loaded on the carrier, and sent to its destination. They include the domestic bill of lading, export packing list, export licenses, export bill of lading, and insurance certificate. Inasmuch as the first two documents are nearly the same as those used in domestic traffic, we shall limit our discussion to the export licenses, the insurance certificate, and the export bill of lading. Note, however, that a domestic bill of lading for goods to be exported must contain a statement by the seller that these goods will not be diverted to another destination. Export package marks and the latest allowable arrival date in the port of export should be noted. The export packing list differs from the domestic list in that it is much more detailed with respect to the weights and measurements of each package. The material in each package must be itemized.

general export license
Any export license covering export commodities for which a validated license is not required; no formal application required

validated export license
A required document issued by the U.S. government authorizing the export of specified commodities

Export Licenses.   All exported goods with the exception of those going to U.S. possessions or Canada (with a few exceptions) require export licenses—either a *general license* or a *validated export license*.

Most products can be exported under a **general export license,** for which no special authorization is necessary. The correct general license symbol, which is obtainable from the Department of Commerce district office, is merely written in the *shipper's export declaration*. This document, which must be filed with U.S. Customs, indicates that there is an authorization to export and also provides the statistical information for The Bureau of Census. For strategic materials and all shipments to unfriendly countries, a **validated export license** is mandatory. This is a special authorization for a specific shipment and is issued only on formal application to the Department of Commerce's Office of Export Administration for scarce materials, strategic goods, and technology or to the Department of State for war materials.

Export Bill of Lading. The **export bill of lading (B/L)** serves three purposes: it is (1) a contract for carriage between the shipper and the carrier, (2) a receipt from the carrier for the goods shipped, and (3) a certificate of ownership. Bills of lading for foreign shipments called *air waybills* (air shipments) or *ocean bills of lading* (steamships) are issued when the shipments are made.

export bill of lading (B/L)
Contract of carriage between shipper and carrier: straight bill of lading is nonnegotiable; endorsed "to order" bill gives holder claim on merchandise

Ocean bills of lading may be either "straight" or "to order," but air waybills are always straight. A straight bill of lading is nonnegotiable, and only the person stipulated in it may obtain the merchandise on arrival. An order bill of lading, however, is negotiable. It can be endorsed like a check or left blank. In this case, the holder of the original bill of lading is the owner of the merchandise. Sight draft or letter of credit shipments require "to order" bills marked "Clean on Board" by the steamship company, which means there is no apparent damage to the shipment and it has actually been loaded onto the vessel.

Insurance Certificate. The insurance certificate is evidence that the shipment is insured against loss or damage while in transit. Unlike domestic carriers, oceangoing steamship companies assume no responsibility for the merchandise they carry unless the loss is caused by their negligence.

Marine insurance on an international transaction may be arranged by either the exporter or the importer, depending on the terms of sale. The laws of a country often require the importer to buy such insurance, thus protecting the local insurance industry and saving foreign exchange. If the exporter has sold on sight draft terms, it is at risk while the goods are in transit. In this case, the firm should buy contingent interest insurance to protect it in the event that the shipment is lost or damaged and it is unable to collect from the buyer. We believe that the exporter selling on CFR terms (the buyer purchases the insurance) should also buy contingent interest insurance to protect itself in case the buyer's insurance does not cover all risks. The premiums are low because damages are paid only on what is not covered by the buyer's policy.

Broadly speaking, there are three kinds of marine insurance policies: basic named perils, broad named perils, and all risks.

1. *Basic named perils* includes perils of the sea, fires, jettisons, explosions, and hurricanes.

2. *Broad named perils* includes theft, pilferage, nondelivery, breakage, and leakage in addition to the basic perils. Both policies contain a clause that determines the extent to which losses caused by an insured peril will be paid. The purchaser of the insurance may request either *(a)* free of particular average (excluding partial loss) or *(b)* with particular average (covering partial loss). Obviously, the rates differ.

3. *All risks* covers all physical loss or damage from any external cause and is more expensive than the policies previously mentioned. War risks are covered under a separate contract.

For the sake of convenience, the occasional exporter will ask the forwarder to arrange for insurance, but when shipments begin on a regular basis, the shipper can economize by going directly to a marine insurance broker. The broker, acting as the shipper's agent, will draw up a contract to fit the shipper's needs by choosing appropriate clauses from among the hundreds that are available.

The premiums charged depend on a number of factors, among which are the goods insured, the destination, the age of the ship, whether the goods are stowed on deck or under deck, the volume of business (there are volume discounts), how the goods are packed, and the number of claims the shipper has filed. Brokers will sometimes admit that in the long run it is preferable not to file numerous small claims, even if justified, because the higher premiums charged for future shipments will be greater than the money recovered.

Because neither the policies nor the premiums are standard, it is highly recommended that the exporter obtain various quotations.

Collection Documents.   The seller is required to provide the buyer with these documents to receive payment. For a letter of credit transaction, the collection documents must be submitted to a bank, but to collect against documentary drafts, anyone may be designated to act on the seller's behalf. A few exporters send their drafts overseas to a representative or bank for collection, but it is preferable to have a bank in the exporter's country forward them to its correspondent bank in the city of destination.

First of all, the collection costs are usually less, because the correspondent bank charges the exporter's bank less than it would charge the exporter. Second, because of the correspondent relationship between the banks, the foreign bank will generally exert a greater effort to collect the money on time. Should the exporter wish to change instructions to the foreign bank, the private cable codes and tests of banks permit new instructions to be authenticated and acted on quickly, whereas a cable from the exporter to a foreign bank would probably be ignored until it had been confirmed by a letter with a signature that could be checked for authenticity.

The documents required for collection vary among countries and among customers, but some of the most common are (1) commercial invoices, (2) consular invoices, (3) certificates of origin, and (4) inspection certificates.

Commercial Invoices.   Commercial invoices for export orders are similar to domestic invoices but include additional information, such as the origin of the goods, export packing marks, and a clause stating that the goods will not be diverted to another country. Invoices for letter of credit sales will name the bank and the credit numbers. Some importing countries require the commercial invoice to be in their language and to be visaed by their local consul.

Consular Invoices.   A few countries require both the commercial invoice and a special form called the *consular invoice*. These forms are purchased from the consul, prepared in the language of the country, and then visaed by the consul.

Certificates of Origin.   Although the commercial invoice carries a statement regarding the origin of the merchandise, a number of foreign governments require a separate certificate of origin. This document is commonly issued by the local chamber of commerce and visaed by the consul.

Inspection Certificates.   Inspection certificates are frequently required by buyers of grain, foodstuffs, and live animals. These are issued by the Department of Agriculture in the United States. Purchasers of machinery or products containing a specified combination of ingredients may insist that an American engineering firm or laboratory inspect and certify that the merchandise is exactly as ordered.

Courtesy European Commission Delegation, Washington, D.C.

Should you export using ocean freight or air freight? Many people are surprised to learn that in addition to being quicker, air freight is often cheaper than ocean freight.

Most newcomers are so preoccupied with making a sale and handling the extra paperwork needed when exporting that they fail to be concerned about the physical movement of their goods. Yet, if they knew about the advances in material-handling techniques, they might not only save money but also reach markets they previously could not serve.

For example, do you want to reduce handling costs? Do you want to reduce pilferage, always a problem in both the port of exit and the port of entry?

> One of the writers, a crew member of a merchant ship docked in an American port to discharge cargo, was leaving the ship when he heard a tremendous thump. The stevedores who were unloading the ship were picking up a large crate with the ship's winch and dropping it on the ground to break it open. Obviously, they suspected that it contained valuable merchandise. Within a few hours of a ship's arrival to unload, you can see peddlers in the street offering merchandise that arrived on the ship. You can purchase bananas, for example, outside the dock area soon after their arrival.

One means of drastically reducing both theft and handling costs is to use containers.

EXPORT SHIPMENTS

Containers

Containers are large boxes—8 by 8 feet in cross-section by either 10, 20, or 40 feet in length—that the seller fills with the shipment in its own warehouse. Airlines also provide smaller containers with rounded cross-sections for a better fit in the fuselage. The containers are then sealed and opened only when the goods arrive at their final destination. Containers will be picked up by a tractor-trailer or a railroad for delivery to shipside, where they will be loaded aboard ship. From the port of entry, railroads or trucks will deliver them, often unopened even for customs inspection, to the buyer's warehouse. In most countries, customs officials will go to the warehouse to examine the shipment. This not only reduces handling time, but it also minimizes the risks of damage and theft because the buyer's own employees unload the containers. If the importer or exporter has a warehouse on a river too shallow for ocean vessels, it can save time and expense by loading containers on barges, which are towed to the harbor where a LASH vessel is anchored.

LASH

LASH (lighter aboard ship) vessels give exporters and importers direct access to ocean freight service even though they are located on shallow inland waterways. Sixty-foot-long barges are towed to inland locations, loaded, and towed back to deep water where they are loaded aboard anchored LASH ships. Exporters that are not located in deep-water ports should check to see if this service is available. Not only will they decrease their risks, but they may gain from their competitors those customers facing the same problems because they too are located far from seaports. This is especially true in LDCs, where oceangoing vessels may wait in anchor a month or more for docking space. Not only do customers have to wait for the merchandise, but freight charges will be higher because the ship has a long, unproductive wait. All the expenses of operating the vessel, which can amount to thousands of dollars daily, are included in a demurrage charge added to the exporter's or importer's normal freight charge.

RO-RO

Another innovation in cargo handling is the RO-RO (roll on–roll off) ship, which permits loaded trailers and any equipment on wheels to be driven onto this specially designed vessel. RO-RO service has brought the benefits of containerization that we discussed to ports that have been unable to invest in the expensive lifting equipment required for containers. Innovative exporters might be able to combine their container shipments with other exporters' shipments of rolling stock. Of course, they must first know that RO-RO vessels exist.

Air Freight

Air freight has had a profound effect on international business because it permits shipments that once required 30 days to arrive in 1 day. Huge freight planes carry payloads of 200,000 pounds, most of which goes either in containers or on pallets. Airlines guarantee overnight delivery from New York to many European airports and claim that their planes can be completely loaded or unloaded within 45 minutes.

Many newcomers to exporting use ocean freight rather than air freight because ocean freight is so much cheaper. But if they compare the total costs of each mode, they frequently find that air freight is less costly. Total cost components that may be lower for air freight include the following:

1. *Insurance rates*—less chance of damage.
2. *Packing*—can go in domestic packaging instead of the heavier, more costly export packing, which the exporter may have to pay to have done by an outside firm.
3. *Customs duties*—when calculated on gross weights.
4. *Replacement costs for damaged goods*—less chance of damaging shipment. Mercedes ships many of its automobiles to the United States by air freight.
5. *Inventory costs*—rapid delivery by air freight often obviates the need for expensive warehouses.

In addition, customers will be more satisfied when they receive shipments sooner. There is less chance of dissatisfaction caused by damage in transit or a delay while a damaged shipment is repaired or replaced. Machinery shipped by air does not require a heavy coat of grease to protect it from the elements as does machinery sent by ship. The protective coating is extremely difficult to remove. Table 16–2 illustrates how the total cost of air freight may be lower than ocean freight.

	Ocean Freight (with warehousing)	Air Freight (no warehousing)
Warehouse administrative costs	$ 850	—
Warehouse rent	1,400	—
Inventory costs		
Taxes and insurance	630	$ 330
Inventory financing	240	160
Inventory obsolescence	1,500	0*
Seller's warehouse and handling costs	1,550	950
Transportation	350	2,000
Packaging and handling	250	100
Cargo insurance	60	30
Customs duties	110	107
Total	$6,940	$3,677

TABLE 16–2
Sea-air total cost comparison (shipment of spare parts)

*Minimal.

Even when the total costs based on these items are higher for air freight, it may still be advantageous to ship by air when factors other than the conventional expense, inventory, and capital are considered:

1. *Production and opportunity costs,* although somewhat more difficult to calculate, are properly a part of the total cost. Getting the product to the buyer more quickly results in faster payment, which speeds up the return on investment and improves cash flow. The firm's capital is released more quickly and can be invested in other profit-making ventures or can be used to repay borrowed capital, thus reducing interest payments. Production equipment may be assembled and sent by air so that it goes into production sooner without the transit and setup delays associated with ocean shipments, a strong sales argument.

2. *The firm may be air dependent;* that is, the exporter is in business only because of air freight. Suppliers of perishable food products to Europe, Japan, and the Middle East are in this category, as are suppliers of live animals (newly hatched poultry and prize bulls) and fresh flowers, a big, legal Colombian export. *Without air freight, these firms would be out of business.*

3. *The products may be air dependent* because the market itself is perishable. Consumer products with extremely short life cycles (high-fashion and fad items) are examples, but many industrial products also fit into this category. A computer, for example, is perishable to the extent that the time it loses between the final assembly and the installation at the customer's location is time in which it is not earning income (the leasing fee).

4. The sales argument that *spare parts and factory technical personnel are available within a few hours* is a strong one for the exporting firm that has to compete with overseas manufacturers.

IMPORTING

In one sense, importers are the reverse of exporters; they sell domestically and buy in foreign markets. However, many of their concerns are similar. As in the case of exporters, there are small firms whose only business is to import, and there are global corporations for whom the importing of millions of dollars of components and raw materials every year is just one of their functions.

Another class of importers, the nine Japanese sogo shosha we discussed in Chapter 13, imported $132 billion in 1993.[15]

How does the prospective importer identify import sources? In a number of ways:

1. If similar imported products are already in the market, go to a retailer that sells them and examine the product label to see where it is made. U.S. law requires the country of origin to be clearly marked on each product or on its container if product marking is not feasible (individual cigarettes, for example).

    Once you know where the product is produced, call the nearest consul or embassy of that country and request the names of manufacturers. One of the principal duties of all foreign government representatives is to promote exports. Some countries publish newsletters in which products are offered for export. Ask to be on their mailing lists. You can also call foreign chambers of commerce in your country (the German-American Chamber of Commerce in New York City is an example). The Japan External Trade Organization (JETRO), which provides information on Japanese exporters, has a number of offices in the United States and other countries. Foreign governments sponsor trade shows in many countries, as we mentioned in our discussion of how the U.S. Department of Commerce assists exporters. Visit these as well as industry shows in your home country. Once you have names and addresses of foreign manufacturers, you can write to them for quotations.

2. If the product is not being imported, you should contact all the sources listed in item 1. The only difference is that you will have to contact more countries. Banks, especially those with strong international departments, may publish newsletters with offers to buy and sell from overseas firms.

3. You can use the electronic bulletin boards of the World Trade Centers and the Trade Points. For a fee, you can put your name and what you wish to buy in their computerized data banks that will be seen around the world.

4. Accidental importing also takes place. When you visit a foreign country, look for products that may have a market at home. Finding one could put you into a new business, one that makes foreign traveling tax deductible.

Let's look at some of the technical aspects of importing for which customhouse brokers can provide assistance.

Customhouse Brokers

customhouse brokers
Independent businesses that handle import shipments for compensation

In every nation, there are **customhouse brokers** just as there are foreign freight forwarders; but instead of helping exporters to export (the function of foreign freight forwarders), they help importers to import. The functions of the two are very similar; in fact, a number of firms provide both services. In the United States, both are licensed: customhouse brokers are licensed by U.S. Customs after passing an extensive examination, and foreign freight forwarders are licensed by the U.S. Maritime Administration after passing an examination.

Principal Activity.   Acting as the agent for the importer, customhouse brokers bring the imported goods through customs, which requires them to know well the many import regulations and the extensive Tariff Schedule mentioned in Chapter 2. If a customs official places the import in a category requiring higher import duties than the importer had planned on paying, the importing firm may not be able to compete pricewise and still make a profit. Generally, customs evaluators everywhere use units for products that carry specific duties and the invoice price as the basis for ad valorem duties. As we explained in Chapter 2, there are some exceptions.

The practice of U.S. Customs is to use the transaction price, which appears on the commercial invoice accompanying the shipment, plus any other charges not included in the transaction price. These may be royalty or license fees, packing, or any assists. *Assist* is the U.S. Customs term applied to any item that the buyer provides free or at reduced cost for use in the production or sale of merchandise for export to this country. Examples are molds and dies sent overseas to produce a specific product, a common practice of importers that want the goods produced using their design, and components and parts that the buyer provides for incorporation in the finished article.

American-made goods can be returned to this country duty free; if they have been improved in any way, however, the importers must pay import duties. Mexico's twin-plant concept would not exist if Congress had not passed a law exempting American firms from paying import duties on the American components in finished products that are assembled in Mexico and exported to the United States.

Other Activities.   Customhouse brokers can also provide other services, such as arranging transportation for the goods after they have left Customs or even transportation for the goods from a foreign country if the exporter has not done so. Another important function is to know when imports are subject to import quotas and how much of the quota has been filled at the time of the import. No matter at which port the goods arrive, U.S. Customs, aided by a computer network to all American ports, knows immediately the quantity that has been imported. Merchandise subject to import quotas can be on the dock of an American port awaiting clearance through Customs; if the quota fills anywhere meanwhile, those goods cannot be imported for the rest of the fiscal year. The would-be importer must either (1) put them in a **bonded warehouse** or a foreign trade zone, where merchandise can be stored without paying duty and wait for the rest of the year, (2) abandon them, or (3) send them to another country. Importers of high-fashion clothing have lost millions of dollars because the quotas were filled and they could not sell the clothing until the following year—by then, it was out of fashion.

bonded warehouse
Authorized by customs authorities for storage of goods on which payment of import duties is deferred until the goods are removed

Import Duties

Every importer should know (1) how U.S. Customs calculates import duties and (2) the importance of the product classification. This requires knowing the Harmonized Tariff Schedule of the United States (HTSUSA), the American version of the global tariff code, the Harmonized System.

Harmonized System.   The Harmonized System consists of 5,019 six-digit headings and subheadings that all developed nations must use. The United States further subdivides the six-digit headings into 8,800 eight-digit classification lines and 12,000 ten-digit statistical reporting numbers. There are interpretative notes that must be followed in determining how goods are to be classified in the system. An importing firm that feels it is paying excessive import duties because its product has been incorrectly classified by customs officials can take the matter to court if it cannot reach an agreement with the officials. Similarly, an exporter can also have its agent in the importing country take the case before that country's courts. Any controversy can be brought before the Customs Cooperation Committee where contracting countries to the Harmonized System can present written views, make oral arguments, and then vote on the goods' classification.[16]

HTSUSA.   Each product has its own unique HTSUSA number. Figure 16–4 presents a page from the HTSUSA. All member-countries use the same system so it is possible to describe the product in any language by using the first six digits. The other four digits are for use just in this country. The HTSUSA also shows the *reporting units,* which Customs uses in its paperwork. The last three columns have to do with the rate of duty.

The percentages in the General column are the rates the United States charges for products coming from GATT members, the most favored nations. The Special column is for nations that receive preferential treatment; the rates are even lower than those for the most favored nation. The abbreviations indicate which nations they are:

1. A: a GSP beneficiary country (developing nation).
2. E: Caribbean Basic Economic Recovery Act (concessions providing for no or low duty for participating Caribbean Basin nations).
3. CA: Canada (NAFTA).
4. IL: Israel (FTA).
5. J: Andean Trade Preference Act (Colombia, Ecuador, Bolivia, Peru, and Venezuela).
6. MX: Mexico (NAFTA).

Finally, column 2 lists rates for nations that are not friends of the United States: Cuba, Vietnam, Afghanistan, Laos, North Korea, Kampuchea, and Azerbaijan. Note that these duty rates are considerably higher. Small wonder that China is fighting to remain a most favored nation.

A prospective importer should follow these rules:

1. Disclose fully to the U.S. Customs Service all foreign and financial arrangements before passing the goods through Customs. The penalties for fraud are high.
2. Ask the advice of a customhouse broker *before* making the transaction. Frequently, a simple change in the product can result in much lower import duties. For example, if you are an importer of jeans, you will pay higher duties if the label is outside the back pocket instead of under the belt. If the words on the label are stylized, duties are more than if they are in simple block letters. Any clothing that is ornamented pays more duty. This is why one importer brings in plain sports shirts and sews on an animal figure after they are in the United States.
3. Calculate carefully the landed price in advance. If there is a doubt about the import category, the importer can ask Customs to determine the category in advance and to put it in writing—just as you can obtain advanced rulings from the Internal Revenue Service. At the time of importation, customs inspectors must respect this determination. Many customs procedures are like those of the IRS. Both have similar procedures for appealing their decisions, for example. This is no coincidence—both are under the secretary of the Treasury.[17]

FIGURE 16–4
Page from the HTSUSA

HARMONIZED TARIFF SCHEDULE of the UNITED STATES (1995)
Annotated for Statistical Reporting Purposes

XVI
84–62

Heading/ Subheading	Stat. Suf– fix	Article Description	Units of Quantity	Rates of Duty General	Rates of Duty Special	2
8461		Machine tools for planing, shaping, slotting, broaching, gear cutting, gear grinding or gear finishing, sawing, cutting-off and other machine tools working by removing metal, sintered metal carbides or cerments, not elsewhere specified or included:				
8461.10		Planing machines:				
8461.10.40		Numerically controlled	....	4.4%	Free (A,CA,E,IL,J, MX)	30%
	20	Used or rebuilt	No.			
	60	Other	No.			
8461.10.80		Other	....	4.4%	Free (A,CA,E,IL,J, MX)	30%
	20	Used or rebuilt	No.			
	40	Other, valued under $3,025 each ...	No.			
	80	Other	No.			
8461.20		Shaping or slotting machines:				
8461.20.40	00	Numerically controlled	No....	4.4%	Free (A,CA,E,IL,J, MX)	30%
8461.20.80		Other	....	4.4%	Free (A,CA,E,IL,J, MX)	30%
	30	Used or rebuilt	No.			
	70	Other, valued under $3,025 each ...	No.			
	90	Other	No.			
8461.30		Broaching machines:				
8461.30.40		Numerically controlled	....	4.4%	Free (A,CA,E,IL,J, MX)	30%
	20	Used or rebuilt	No.			
	60	Other	No.			
8461.30.80		Other	....	4.4%	Free (A,CA,E,IL,J, MX)	30%
	20	Used or rebuilt	No.			
	40	Other, valued under $3,025 each ..	No.			
	80	Other	No.			
8461.40		Gear cutting, gear grinding or gear finishing machines:				
8461.40.10		Gear cutting machines	....	5.8%	Free (A,CA,E,IL,J, MX)	40%
	10	Used or rebuilt	No.			
		Other:				
	20	For bevel gears	No.			
		Other:				
	30	Gear hobbers	No.			
	40	Gear shapers	No.			
	60	Other	No.			
8461.40.50		Gear grinding or finishing machines	....	4.4%	Free (A,CA,E,IL,J, MX)	30%
	20	Used or rebuilt	No.			
	40	Other, valued under $3,025 each ..	No.			
		Other:				
	50	For bevel gears	No.			
	70	Other	No.			
8461.50		Sawing or cutting-off machines:				
8461.50.40		Numerically controlled	....	4.4%	Free (A,CA,E,IL,J, MX)	30%
	10	Used or rebuilt	No.			
	50	Other	No.			
8461.50.80		Other	....	4.4%	Free (A,CA,E,IL,J, MX)	30%
	10	Used or rebuilt	No.			
	20	Other, valued under $3,025 each ..	No.			
	90	Other	No.			
8461.90		Other:				
8461.90.40		Numerically controlled	....	4.4%	Free (A,CA,E,IL,J, MX)	30%
	10	Used or rebuilt	No.			
	40	Other	No.			
8461.90.80		Other	....	4.4%	Free (A,CA,E,IL,J, MX)	30%
	10	Used or rebuilt	No.			
	20	Other, valued under $3,025 each ..	No.			
	80	Other	No.			

Source: Harmonized Tariff Schedule of the United States. (Washington, DC: U.S. Government Printing Office, 1995), p. 84–62.

SUMMARY

1. **Explain why firms export.** Smaller firms, like the larger ones, export to increase sales. Some begin to export accidently, while others seek out foreign customers. Large multinationals export to serve markets where they have no manufacturing plants or the local plant does not produce all the product mix. Some host governments require an affiliate to export, and many firms export to remain competitive in the home market. Exporting is also an inexpensive way to test foreign markets. A product's life can be extended by exporting the product to markets with less advanced technology.

2. **Describe the three problem areas of exporting.** The three problem areas of exporting are (1) locating foreign markets, (2) payment and financing procedures, and (3) export procedures.

3. **Identify the sources of export counseling.** The Trade Information Center, Small Business Administration, Small Business Development Centers in universities, Department of Agriculture, state offices for export assistance, World Trade Centers Association, and the Trade Point Global Network are some sources of export counseling.

4. **Describe the main elements of the export sales assistance program of the U.S. Department of Commerce.** The Department of Commerce, the federal department in charge of export assistance, offers many programs covering all aspects of exporting. These include services that aid in conducting market research, such as the National Trade Data Bank, the Comparison Shopping Service, and various Commerce publications. Commerce can also assist in locating Foreign representatives and making sales through trade fairs, matchmaker programs, and catalog and video shows.

5. **Discuss the meaning of the various terms of sale.** Various terms of sales are possible in exporting. FAS (free alongside ship) means the seller pays all transportation expenses to ship's side; the buyer is responsible for loss or damages from that point on. CIF (cost, insurance, freight) means the seller quotes a price including cost of goods, insurance, and transportation to a specified destination. CFR (cost, freight) is like CIF, except the buyer pays insurance costs. FOB (free on board) means the seller charges for all costs up to a specified point at which the buyer becomes responsible.

6. **Identify some sources of export financing.** Some sources of export financing are commercial banks, factors, forfaiting, the Export-Import Bank (Eximbank), and the Small Business Administration.

7. **Describe the activities of a foreign freight forwarder.** Foreign freight forwarders act as agents for exporters. They prepare documents, book space on carriers, and function as a firm's export traffic department.

8. **Understand the kinds of export documents required.** Correct documentation is vital to the success of any export shipment. Shipping documents include export packing list, export licenses, export bills of lading, and insurance certificates. Collection documents include commercial invoices, consular invoices, certificates of origin, and inspection certificates.

9. **Discuss some innovations in materials handling in sea and air transport.** Innovations in transportation and materials handling enable exporters to reach new markets and reduce theft and cost. These include the use of containers and LASH and RO-RO vessels.

10. **Identify import sources.** Prospective importers can identify sources in a number of ways. They can examine the product label to see where it is made and then contact the nearest embassy of that country to request the name of the manufacturer. Foreign chambers of commerce and trade organizations provide information on their countries' exporters. Electronic bulletin boards and data banks are also useful.

11. **Describe the activities of a customhouse broker.** Customhouse brokers help importers to import. The functions of foreign freight forwarders and customhouse brokers are similar. An important function is to represent the importer in dealing with customs officials.

12. **Explain the Harmonized Tariff Schedule of the United States (HTSUSA).** The HTSUSA is the American version of the Harmonized System used by nations worldwide for classifying imported products. There is a sample page from the HTSUSA in the text.

KEY WORDS

- terms of sale   526
- letter of credit (L/C)   528
- confirmed   528
- irrevocable   528
- air waybill   528
- pro forma invoice   528
- export, sight, and time drafts   530
- banker's acceptance   531
- factoring   531
- forfaiting   531
- Eximbank   532
- Overseas Private Investment Corporation (OPIC)   532
- Foreign Sales Corporation (FSC)   532
- free trade zone   533
- foreign trade zone (FTZ)   533
- foreign freight forwarders   534
- general export license   534
- validated export license   534
- export bill of lading (B/L)   535
- customhouse brokers   540
- bonded warehouse   541

QUESTIONS

1. What are the common terms of sale quoted by exporters? For each, explain to what point the seller must pay all transportation and delivery costs. Where does the responsibility for loss or damage pass to the buyer?

2. *a.* Explain the various export payment terms that are available.
   b. Which two offer the most protection to the seller?

3. What is the procedure for a letter of credit transaction?

4. The manager of the international department of the McAllen Bank learns on the way to work that the ship on which a local exporter shipped some goods has sunk. The manager has received all of the documents required in the letter of credit and is ready to pay the exporter for the shipment. In view of the news about the ship, the manager now knows that the foreign customer will never receive the goods. Should the manager pay the exporter, or should he withhold payment and notify the overseas customer?

5. What is a foreign trade zone? Check with a customhouse broker or a U.S. Customs official or do some research in the library to find out the advantages of a foreign trade zone over a bonded warehouse.

6. What are the purposes of an export bill of lading?

7. An importer brings plain sports shirts to this country because the import duty is lower than it is for shirts with adornments. It then sews on a figure of a fox in this country. Should the importer do this operation in a foreign trade zone?

8. How would you find sources for a product that you want to import?

9. What does a customhouse broker do?

10. An importer in Vancouver, Washington, has the following dollar quotations from three manufacturers of gear-cutting machines. All prices are FOB border of each exporter's country. Disregarding transportation costs, which is the least expensive after paying import duty? See Figure 16–4 for appropriate import duties.
    a. $5,000 from Germany.
    b. $5,500 from Canada.
    c. $4,000 from Azerbaijan.

MINICASE 16–1   State Manufacturing Export Sales Price

State Manufacturing Company, a producer of farm equipment, had just received an inquiry from a large distributor in Italy. The quantity on which the distributor wanted a price was sufficiently large that Jim Mason, the sales manager, felt he had to respond. He knew the inquiry was genuine, because he had called two of the companies that the distributor said he represented, and both had assured him that the Italian firm was a serious one. It paid its bills regularly with no problems. Both companies were selling to the firm on open account terms.

Mason's problem was that he had never quoted on a sale for export before. His first impulse was to take the regular FOB factory price and add the cost of the extra-heavy export packing plus the inland freight cost to the nearest U.S. port. This price should enable the company to make money if he quoted the price FAS port of exit.

However, the terms of sale were bothering him. The traffic manager had called a foreign freight forwarder to learn about the frequency of sailings to Italy, and during the conversation she had suggested to the traffic manager that she might be able to help Mason. When Mason called her, he learned that because of competition, many firms like State Manufacturing were quoting CIF foreign port as a convenience to the importer. She asked him what payment terms he would quote, and he replied that his credit manager had suggested an irrevocable, confirmed letter of credit so as to be sure of receiving payment for the sale. He admitted that the distributor, however, had asked for payment against a 90-day time draft.

The foreign freight forwarder urged Mason to consider quoting CIF port of entry in Italy with payment as requested by the distributor to be more competitive. She informed him that he could get insurance to protect the company against commercial risk. To help him calculate a CIF price, she offered to give him the various charges if he would tell her the weight and value of his shipment FOB factory. He replied that the total price was $21,500 and

that the gross weight, including the container, was 3,629 kilos.

Two hours later, she called to give him the following charges:

1.	Containerization	$ 200.00
2.	Inland freight less handling	798.00
3.	Forwarding and documentation	90.00
4.	Ocean freight	2,633.00
5.	Commercial risk insurance	105.00
6.	Marine insurance—total of items	167.15
	1–5 × 1.1 = $27,858.60 at 60¢/$100*	

*Total coverage of marine insurance is commonly calculated on the basis of the total price plus 10 percent.

During that time, Mason had been thinking about the competition. Could he lower the FOB price for an export sale? He looked at the cost figures. Sales expense amounted to 20 percent of the sales price. Couldn't this be deducted on a foreign order? Research and development amounted to 10 percent. Should this be charged? Advertising and promotional expense amounted to another 10 percent. What about that? Because this was an unsolicited inquiry, there was no selling expense for this sale except for his and the secretary's time. Mason felt that it wasn't worth calculating this time.

If you were Jim Mason, how would you calculate the CIF port of entry price?

MINICASE 16–2 Morgan Guaranty Trust Company Confirmation Letter

MORGAN GUARANTY TRUST COMPANY
OF NEW YORK
INTERNATIONAL BANKING DIVISION
23 WALL STREET, NEW YORK, N.Y. 10015   March 5, 19*

Smith Tool Co. Inc.
29 Bleecker Street
New York, N.Y. 10012

> On all communications please refer to
>
> **NUMBER IC — 152647**

Dear Sirs:

   We are instructed to advise you of the establishment by
. Bank of South America, Puerto Cabello, Venezuela . . . .
of their IRREVOCABLE Credit No. 19845 . . . .
in your favor, for the account of John Doe, Puerto Cabello, Venezuela . . . .
for U. S. $3,000.00 (THREE THOUSAND U. S. DOLLARS) . . . .
available upon presentation to us of your drafts at sight on us, accompanied by:
Commercial Invoice in triplicate, describing the merchandise as indicated below

Consular Invoice in triplicate, all signed and stamped by the Consul of Venezuela

Negotiable Insurance Policy and/or Underwriter's Certificate, endorsed in blank, covering
marine and war risks

Full set of straight ocean steamer Bills of Lading, showing consignment to the Bank of
South America, Puerto Cabello, stamped by Venezuelan Consul and marked "Freight Prepaid",

evidencing shipment of UNA MAQUINA DE SELLAR LATAS, C.I.F. Puerto Cabello, from United
States Port to Puerto Cabello, Venezuela

Except as otherwise expressly stated herein, this credit is subject to the Uniform Customs and Practice
for Documentary Credits (1974 revision), International Chamber of Commerce Publication No. 290.

The above bank engages with you that all drafts drawn under and in compliance with
the terms of this advice will be duly honored if presented to our Commercial Credits
Department, 15 Broad Street, New York, N. Y. 10015, on or before March 31, 19* on which
date this credit expires.

   We confirm the foregoing and undertake that all drafts drawn and presented in
accordance with its terms will be duly honored.
                              Yours very truly,

                              Authorized Signature
   Immediately upon receipt, please examine this instrument and if its terms are not clear to
you or if you need any assistance in respect to your availment of it, we would welcome your
communicating with us. Documents should be presented promptly and not later than 3 P.M.

1. Who issued the letter of credit?

2. Is it irrevocable?

3. Has it been confirmed?

4. If so, by whom?

5. Who is the buyer?

6. Who is the seller?

7. What kind of draft is to be presented?

8. What documents are required?

9. What are the terms of sale?

10. When does the letter of credit expire?

11. Where does the seller go for payment?

12. Who pays the freight?

13. Who pays the marine insurance?

14. Must the steamship company attest that the merchandise has been loaded on ship?

15. What is the reason for your answer to question 14?

I. Purpose—Why has the plan been written?

II. Table of contents—Include a list of any appendixes.

III. Executive summary—This is short and concise (not over two pages) and covers the principal points of the report. It is prepared after the plan has been written.

IV. Introduction—Explains why the firm will export.

V. Situation analysis
   A. Description of the firm and products to be exported.
   B. Company resources to be used for the export business.
   C. Competitive situation in the industry.
      1. Product comparisons.
      2. Market coverage.
      3. Market share.
   D. Export organization—personnel and structure.

VI. Export marketing plan.
   A. Long- and short-term goals.
      1. Total sales in units.
      2. Total sales in dollars.
      3. Sales by product lines.
      4. Market share.
      5. Profit and loss forecasts.
   B. Characteristics of ideal target markets.
      1. GNP/capita.
      2. GNP/capita growth rate.
      3. Size of target market.
   C. Identify, assess, and select target markets.
      1. Market contact programs.
         a. U.S. Department of Commerce.
         b. World Trade Centers.
         c. Chamber of Commerce.
         d. Company's bank.
         e. State's export assistance program.
         f. Small Business Administration.
         g. Small Business Development Center in local university.
         h. Export hotline directory.
      2. Market screening.
         a. First screening—basic need potential.
         b. Second screening—financial and economic forces.
            (1) GNP/capita growth rate.
            (2) Size of target market.
            (3) Growth rate of target market.
            (4) Exchange rate trends.
            (5) Trends in inflation and interest rates.
         c. Third screening—Political and legal forces.
            (1) Import restrictions.
            (2) Product standards.
            (3) Price controls.
            (4) Government and public attitude toward buying American products.
         d. Fourth screening—Sociocultural forces.
            (1) Attitudes and beliefs.
            (2) Education.

    (3) Material culture.

    (4) Languages.

   e. Fifth screening—Competitive forces.

    (1) Size, number, and financial strength of competitors.

    (2) Competitors' market shares.

    (3) Effectiveness of competitors' marketing mixes.

    (4) Levels of after-sales service.

    (5) Competitors' market coverage—Can market segmentation produce niches that are now poorly attended?

   f. Field trips to best prospects.

    (1) Department of Commerce' trade mission.

    (2) Trade missions organized by state or trade association.

  D. Export marketing strategies.

   1. Product lines to export.

   2. Export pricing methods.

   3. Channels of distribution.

    a. Direct exporting.

    b. Indirect exporting.

   4. Promotion methods.

   5. After-sales and warranty policies.

   6. Buyer financing methods.

   7. Methods for ongoing competitor analysis.

   8. Sales forecast.

VII. Export financial plan.

  A. Pro forma profit and loss statement.

  B. Pro forma cash flow analysis.

  C. Break-even analysis.

VIII. Export performance evaluation.

  A. Frequency.

   1. Markets.

   2. Product lines.

   3. Export personnel.

  B. Variables to be measured.

   1. Sales by units and dollar volume in each market.

   2. Sales growth rates in each market.

   3. Product line profitability.

   4. Market share.

   5. Competitors' efforts in each market.

   6. Actual results compared to budgeted results.

Evolution of Centrally Planned Economies

If wealthy former West Germany finds it more and more difficult to get the former German Democratic Republic (which was an economic front-runner among the East European countries) back on its feet, one can imagine the difficulty of achieving this goal with the rest of Eastern Europe—including the parts of what used to be the U.S.S.R. In 1991 alone, $100 billion was spent by Bonn on its new eastern states, and an estimated $65 billion will be needed annually until the year 2000. It is doubtful that much can be achieved with the $40 billion from the European Bank for Reconstruction and Development.

Europe 92, September 1991

CONCEPT PREVIEWS

After reading this chapter, you should be able to:

1. **explain** the meaning of "centrally planned economies" and "market economies"

2. **understand** what the formerly communist countries are trying to achieve and how and why the industrial democracies should assist them

3. **realize** that Russia is still a mighty military power even though its forces have been removed from Eastern Europe where they left tremendous pollution

4. **identify** tensions in the Peoples' Republic of China (PRC) between capitalist-type economic developments and the rigid communist bureaucracy in Beijing

5. **realize** that even though the Soviet Union and the Warsaw Pact have collapsed, there remain dangerous countries and forces in the world

6. **relate** the different economic growth rates in the PRC and the states of the former Soviet Union to the different periods they were under communist governments

7. **explain** how companies from the industrial democracies do business in the former communist countries despite debt and quality difficulties

Export Experts

While U.S. policy makers debate the best ways to help economies in Eastern Europe, the former Soviet Union, and the PRC, the International Executive Service Corps (IESC) is busily doing it. The IESC, based in Stamford, Connecticut, is a nonprofit organization that hooks up experienced U.S. executives with struggling entrepreneurs around the globe. Most of the executives are retired, but a growing number are younger businesspeople and academics, and most are men, but there is a growing number of women as they climb the business and academic ladders. • In 1992, Richard Moore, a retired manager of export sales and marketing for Chrysler Corporation, was sent to Tallinn, Estonia, to work with an Estonian car dealer, Max Strasch. Strasch had been assembling, selling, and servicing Russian cars for 20 years and wanted an opportunity to deal in American autos. • Moore scrutinized the Estonian car dealer's business, formerly a state-owned enterprise, and gathered the necessary financial and other information to enable Strasch to apply to Chrysler for a dealership. Strasch's company was then called the Baltic American Car Company. • Chrysler was exploring other Estonian outlets and was at first cool to Baltic's overtures. Moore then stepped in on Baltic's behalf, pointing out to Chrysler that Strasch had extensively upgraded his facilities and that if Chrysler wouldn't deal with him, Moore would introduce him to a former Moore colleague who was now head of Mitsubishi's U.K. operations. • Chrysler saw the light and signed a contract with Baltic American. By mid-1994, Baltic forecasts sales of $8 million of Chryslers and Jeeps.

Source: Gregory Sandler, "Where Experts Are the Exports," *Journal of European Business*, September–October 1993, pp. 12–13.

"East is east and west is west and never the twain shall meet" was not accurate when Rudyard Kipling wrote it, and it is even less correct today. The former East European satellite countries of the Soviet Union and its three now independent Baltic states are moving toward the West as fast as they can. East and West Germany are no more, having united as Germany.

The Soviet Union has broken up, but most of its previous states may form a common economic market. The Russians have ended economic and military aid to countries such as Cuba, Afghanistan, and Angola, which will turn to the West for aid or trade.

The so-far implacably communist North Korea has begun talking with capitalist South Korea, and Vietnam is now seeking investments from the West.

Politically, the great communist iceberg, the Peoples' Republic of China, has barely begun to melt, but economically, the thaw is fairly well advanced from strict communism, and that is continuing. How the resulting tensions and contradictions will be resolved remains to be seen.

As the Soviet Union has dissolved and Russia's power and influence over Eastern Europe and its states wane, historical ethnic hostilities are bubbling up. There has been fighting, death, and damage in many places, including Yugoslavia and Georgia, and it is feared there will be more. Aside from the human toll it takes, fighting will impede the peoples' abilities to produce, buy, and sell. And, of course, investment, not to mention tourism, which brought much income to several of the affected areas, will dry up. These are developments international business managers must watch carefully.

Although momentous changes are taking place in the Eastern countries, it will be useful to identify them and thus distinguish them from the Western countries.

THE EAST COUNTRIES

East, as used in this chapter, includes the centrally planned economies of the former Union of Soviet Socialist Republics (U.S.S.R.), its East European satellites (Poland, East Germany, Czechoslovakia, Hungary, Romania, and Bulgaria), and its other satellites, such as Cuba, Ethiopia, South Yemen, and Vietnam. It also includes Yugoslavia and the People's Republic of China (PRC), which occupies mainland China and is to be differentiated from the Republic of China, which occupies Taiwan.

In the preceding paragraph, we spoke of **centrally planned economies**. In countries with such economies, the central, national government decides how much of what product will be made during each year or other planning period, such as a five-year plan. Historically in centrally planned economies, the governments have owned and controlled all major factors of production. They have also controlled labor, as the unions are or were essentially government agencies and workers must obtain government approval to move from one area or job to another.

centrally planned economies
The government owns all the important factors of production and dictates how much of each product will be made

In this chapter, we examine the evolution of the centrally planned economies away from domination by communist, government bureaucrats, toward freedom, with economic decisions increasingly governed by market forces. The evolution is coming in differing forms and at different speeds. The International Monetary Fund (IMF) refers to the countries of Central and Eastern Europe and Russia as "countries in transition."

THE WEST COUNTRIES

West, as used here, includes the industrial countries of Western Europe and North America plus Japan and such other countries as Australia and New Zealand. For practical purposes, the Western countries are members of the Organization for Economic Cooperation and Development (OECD).

All the OECD countries have **market economies** to one degree or another; that is to say, market forces, although government regulated, are permitted to operate. The governments do not own or control all farms, factories, mines, and labor unions. Supply and demand are important forces in establishing market prices, and sooner or later, privately owned businesses must make profits to survive.

market economies
Most factors of production are privately owned, and markets, prices, and profits determine how much of which products will be made

SOVIET DOMINANCE—COMECON

The East countries, identified above, were dominated by the communist U.S.S.R., which wanted to isolate them politically from the democratic West. Toward that end, the U.S.S.R. forbade them to participate in the Marshall Plan and to join the organization that is now the EU. The U.S.S.R. believed that trade with the West would carry with it democratic political pollution, and to prevent that, it created a trade organization called the Council for Mutual Economic Assistance (COMECON).

The purpose of COMECON was to maximize trade among the East countries and to discourage contacts with the West. Founded by Stalin in 1949, the Council for Mutual Economic Assistance proved to be neither mutual nor economic, and it finally failed in its political objectives. In theory, COMECON should have created a dynamic, expanding market for its members, but its isolation from the world outside deprived it of the discipline of international competition and cost-based pricing. This isolation, together with the rigidities and other flaws of centrally planned economies, brought about their collapse along with that of COMECON in 1991.

Aftermath of Collapse

The newly liberated nations of Eastern and Central Europe, after four decades of Soviet domination, tried to turn abruptly to the West, but old trade habits die hard, and a zero-sum game with no winners developed. Trade among the former COMECON members fell to just 10 percent of the volume of 1990, the last year of COMECON's existence, causing shortages in all the economies.

COMECON locked its members into a rigid and technologically inhibiting relationship. They now realize that as much as they would like economic integration with the West, they still need each other, although the degree of need varies from country to country. Although Poland and Hungary are having some success exporting to the West, Bulgaria, the Czech Republic, Slovakia, and Romania still depend heavily on the old COMECON area.

THE NEW EAST: EMERGING MARKET ECONOMIES

In this section, we exclude the PRC from the East countries. The situation and developments in the PRC differ so much from those in the former COMECON countries that we deal with it separately later in this chapter.

The Former Soviet Union: Current Developments

In the former Soviet Union, the command economy is dead, but the market is slow to develop. This prompts a disturbing question: Just how far can the economy fall? Industrial and agricultural output are down, and forecasts are gloomy. Hyperinflation is being pushed by round-the-clock running of two ruble printing presses and the two state mints pumping new but potentially useless currency into the economy.

The output of oil, which has been the country's main foreign exchange earner, fell from 11.4 million barrels a day in 1987 to an estimated 6.8 million barrels a day in 1993. It is feared there soon may not be enough to export.[1]

The Russian government still has the right to determine how 80 percent of the oil output is distributed. The main tools the government uses are quotas, which dictate how much oil each Russian oil company must deliver to the central government, how much to the regions, and most important, how much can be exported. Inevitably, allowing bureaucrats to decide how to allocate the commodity that produced 68 percent of Russia's foreign exchange earnings in 1993 gives rise to corruption.

Early in 1994, President Boris Yeltsin signed a decree saying that oil export quotas were to be abolished from July 1, 1994. That day came and nothing happened. A few days later, the president issued another decree, announcing that he had changed his mind and that quotas would stay at least until the end of the year.

This was a lobbying victory for the bureaucrats at the Ministry of Foreign Economic Relations who administered the quotas. They want to strengthen their hold on oil marketing, and a model for such a marketing monopoly is Gazprom, which exports all of Russia's gas. They may get their way, because the man who persuaded Yeltsin to change his mind was the prime minister, Victor Chernomyrdin. Chernomyrdin's job before he became prime minister was head of Gazprom.[2]

Russia's foreign debt increased from $65 billion in 1991 to as much as $84 billion in 1994. Its debt negotiators continue to hold up a restructuring package by arguing for sovereign immunity that would exempt Russia from being sued in case of debt nonpayment.

The 1986 economic Nobel laureate, James Buchanan, advises Russia to ask for deep discounts on its "old" (pre-1991) debt. He argues that Russian taxpayers should not be asked to repay loans made by undisciplined creditor banks to the Soviet Union.[3]

Buy a Dollar for 28 Cents.   From January to September in 1994, the price of Russian debt on the secondary debt market halved to 28 cents on the dollar. One trader claims that most of the buyers are Russian who could be acting on behalf of the Russian government. Buying back its loans for less than one-third of their face value is more cost effective than striking a rescheduling deal that would boost secondary market prices.[4]

What to Do?   Dr. James R. Wilburn, an economic advisor to officials of the Russian Federation, lists the country's needs.

- Overhaul the physical infrastructure, which is currently sadly deficient. This includes telecommunications, highways, and railroads. While it is nearly two and one-half times as large as the United States, the Soviet Union has only about one-fourth as many roads, and one-fourth of those are unpaved and subject to disappearing when the spring thaw turns dirt tracks into unpassable quagmires. Entire trains disappear, sometimes to be found months later, their cargoes stolen.
- Overhaul the economic infrastructure. Create modern systems of banking, finance, distribution, and wholesale trade.
- Revamp the legal system. Clarify legal rights affecting private property ownership and basic business dealings.
- Make money meaningful. The ruble is discredited, but a convertible currency is necessary whether it is called a ruble or something else.
- Create capitalists. Give people the incentives and skills to produce more, better, and faster.
- Persuade the West to help. The West should provide know-how, technology, and investment.

Wilburn comments, "There's no painless way to make the transition from communism to free enterprise."[5]

The Harvard Plan. Prior to the August 1991 coup attempt to overthrow Mikhail Gorbachev, he had rejected a plan for the Soviet Union put forward by a group of Harvard professors and Soviet economists. However, Boris Yeltsin embraced the plan, and he became much more powerful after the coup. The Harvard plan is similar to the one outlined above. One addition is that the Harvard plan would accord IMF and World Bank membership to the government(s) that succeed the Soviet Union.[6] In October 1991, the Soviet Union was granted associate IMF membership, but by 1992 there was no longer a Soviet Union, and Russia was granted the Soviet membership.

Joint Ventures (JVs) and Cooperatives. In 1988 and 1989, JVs were so hot that foreigners in Moscow joked about the new form of Russian greeting—"Hello! my name is Ivan. Would you like to start a joint venture with me?" But the mood has changed. "In my opinion," says Gerald A. Manassov, a former official of the Soviet State Statistics Committee, "everyone is disappointed with joint ventures."

Probably the most famous JV is the McDonald's on Pushkin Square in Moscow. But it took 14 years to work out, and the Canadian partners finally decided that they could only solve the problem of undependable Soviet supplies by setting up their own farm and bakery. The Soviet magazine, *New Times,* told of a hapless JV that had to fight the bureaucracy for a year to get a rubber stamp needed for most official documents.[7]

According to one study, less than 20 percent of the JVs that are officially registered actually start operation, and many JVs that do begin operation fail in the first year. This study makes the following recommendations for JVs' success in Russia.

- *Design characteristics:*
  Produce quality goods.

  Spend adequately on advertising.

  Ensure a good horizontal flow of information in the organization.

  Do good and adequate planning.

  Have at least one foreign worker at the JV to facilitate cross-cultural learning.
- *Employees:*
  Explain to all employees the JV's goals.

  Compensate workers with salaries plus incentives such as profit sharing.
- *JV partners' relations:*
  Select partner carefully.

  Maintain oversight but allow the JV autonomy.

  Communicate with the JV and partner at least once a week.

  Provide the JV adequate capital.

  Recognize cultural differences and that the Russian approach may be better.

  Understand the importance of partners' trust in each other.[8]

Small Free Markets. A Russian widow asked for a death certificate after her husband's funeral, but authorities first demanded back his tobacco ration coupons. "Tobacco is for the living," officials in the Lipetsk region south of Moscow told the woman.

In 1991, a Soviet newspaper reported a lucrative black market trade in death certificates in a Siberian town because they give bereaved families the right to a new suit to bury male relatives. Of course many survivors buried dead relatives in old suits, keeping the new ones for themselves.[9]

Russian Trade Turns Westward.   By 1994, Russia was trading more with developed countries, especially with Western Europe, than with the former Soviet states—a dramatic change in trading patterns since 1991. During the first two quarters of 1994, Russia's trade volume with the members of the EU stood at $16.8 billion ($9.9 billion exports and $6.9 billion imports), 37 percent of its total trade. This compared with $10.8 billion trade turnover with the other Commonwealth of Independent States (CIS)* member-states ($6.2 billion exports and $4.6 billion imports), 24 percent of its total trade. Trade with the former partners in COMECON had fallen even faster. Trade between them and Russia during the first half of 1994 was only $5.7 billion ($3.7 billion Russian exports and $2 billion imports).

By far, the largest part of Russian exports is raw materials, especially energy. The structure of Russian imports has switched massively from capital goods and equipment to consumer goods, mostly food.

Germany is the most important Russian trading partner, and for the foreseeable future the EU is forecast to be Russia's major market. Their geographical proximity will facilitate trade expansion. The EU also plays a dominant role in the formation of joint ventures, with over 90 percent of total JVs in Russia being between a company from one of the EU states and a Russian enterprise.[10]

Privatization Lures Cash to Russia.   Emerging market funds, hedge funds, and even pension funds have contributed to a record flow of financial investment into Russia, estimated at $500 million a month. Nancy Curtin, head of emerging European markets at Baring Asset Management, says, "It is very, very risky, but the value is unparalleled in terms of what you see in other emerging markets."

Besides Baring, other investment bankers sponsoring funds for investment in Russia and Eastern Europe include Pictet, the Swiss private bank; Cazenove; and Invesco. The funds can be bought on markets in Dublin, London, and Luxembourg. We have mentioned Gazprom, Russia's main gas producer and marketer. It has hired Kleinwort Benson of the United Kingdom to sell a 9 percent share-holding internationally.[11]

The Former Soviet Union: Problems Ahead

The choice is stark: some kind of Commonwealth of Independent States or a breakup, and there is the probability of civil wars. On the positive side, it was the power of the people that frustrated the August 1991 coup attempt. There were crowds, not mobs; protests, not looting; clarity of purpose, not confusion. The people have won the respect of the rulers who will now be wary of abusing their power.

One result has been that, under duress, Mikhail Gorbachev dissolved the Communist party. The party insisted on the loyalty of the bureaucracy, police, and armed services. It watched over all education. It published a newspaper called *Truth (Pravda)*, which was full of lies. The party was not just a political poison; it dominated and deadened the whole economy too.

Who Owns What Land?   Fifteen republics were caged inside the Soviet Union for most of the 20th century, and in different degrees they all longed to get out. It could be a messy, even bloody, process.

---

*The CIS consists of most, but not all, states of the former Soviet Union.

Pointing Way to Prosperity for East Europe Countries

As we approach the second anniversary of the revolutions in Eastern Europe, it becomes clear that none of the countries has found an open road to prosperity. Their experience is mixed, but some general lessons can be learned.

First, no one knows how to plan the transformation of a command economy into a market economy. Thick plans that lay out a sequence of steps to be taken are worthless. The best course is to scrap the old system as quickly as possible. Delay doesn't make change easier; it helps the old guard to grab the best properties for themselves.

Second, inflation is a serious risk. The risk is realized if the governments maintain the many subsidies to consumers and state enterprises and finance them by printing money. When prices are freed from controls, subsidies must be ended; the government must be willing to let living standards drop, and enterprises must get rid of their excess labor to control costs. If enterprises match the increase in prices with increased wages, their costs will rise and they will demand more subsidies. If they get them, inflation is almost certain to soar.

Third, markets are uncommon and competition is unknown. Even when companies are sold, they face little or no internal competition. To get more competition quickly, Eastern European economies must let world exports enter. This forces a wrenching adjustment as local products are forced to compete with foreign products at home and abroad.

Fourth, property rights are essential for efficiency, competition, and a well-functioning market system, but property rights are badly defined in these countries. All of them have been slow to privatize large state enterprises, but several countries have sold off many of the retail stores and service businesses.

Fifth, statistics are unreliable, so they cannot be used to guide decisions. In Poland and probably elsewhere, the measurement of production reports what is happening in the state industries. Private production and the output of new enterprises is estimated at 20 percent of the total but is not recorded in official statistics. Reported declines in output overstate the drop in production and living standards. Markets are growing in many of these countries, but market transactions are not recorded.

Sixth, several Eastern European countries agreed to make restitution of the property claims of former owners. Adjudication of claims takes time and delays the sale and revitalization of factories, businesses, and housing. This, in turn, delays the recovery. Payment of compensation to prior owners, instead of restitution of property, allows the transformation to proceed.

Seventh, the breakdown of COMECON—the communists' block trading arrangement—and the collapse of the Soviet economy have been hard blows for Eastern Europe. These countries now demand hard-currency payment and must pay hard currency for oil from the Soviet Union. Trade has slowed as a result, causing large losses of output and employment.

Eighth, setting the wrong exchange magnifies the cost of adjustment. Germany and Poland are opposite examples. The prosperous West Germans "helped" their East German cousins by exchanging East German marks at an effective rate of 1.8 to 1. This gave the East Germans a big boost in purchasing power that many used to buy Western goods. But, after the exchange, costs of products in East Germany were far above costs in competing countries. Many factories became uncompetitive and were forced to close. Poland took the opposite course. The Poles stabilized the currency at an exchange rate that favored exports in the first year of readjustment. Their pains were severe but less than in eastern Germany, where unemployment rates may reach 40 percent to 50 percent by year's end.

Achievements and commitment to reform differ from country to country, but there are some common features.

Poland, Hungary, and Czechoslovakia have made the most dramatic changes. All have made major transformations to establish democratic political systems and market economies. Currencies are convertible. Western goods are available and prices are decontrolled. Each has developed its own way of privatizing state enterprises.

Romania, Bulgaria, Albania, and Yugoslavia have not freed themselves fully from communist rule, and they have not established stable, democratic political systems and other requisites for a market system. The evolution of these countries is uncertain. At best, they will drift downward.

The former East Germany is in a different position than the others. As part of Germany, it is able to export to members of the European Community. Once the union was complete, eastern Germany had established legal, accounting, financial, and tax systems and developed social benefits and transfers. Yet, despite these advantages, the transition has been one of the most difficult.

Why? There is no single answer. German law imposes high costs for social benefits and pollution control. Also important is the assistance eastern Germans get from western Germans. Eastern Germans know they don't have to make the hard choices that the Poles and Czechoslovaks have made, so they are slow to adjust, demand wage increases up to 60 percent, and collect transfers when they are unemployed.

There is a lesson there about aid to Eastern Europe. The West should help by opening markets, not by offering financial assistance and loans to central governments.

Reprinted by permission of Allan H. Meltzer, University Professor of Economics and Visiting Scholar, American Enterprise Institute.

The internal borders of the Soviet Union were changed 90 times between 1921 and 1991, and someone resented each change. Of the 23 borders between the republics, 20 are disputed. Boris Yeltsin, president of the huge Russian republic, talks of taking pieces of adjacent republics into Russia, which has raised his neighbors' fears of a new imperialism.

What People Are Where?   Not only land borders were moved; the Soviet schemers and planners also moved people, mostly Russians, around. Some 25 million Russians now live outside Russia. In Kazakhstan and Kirghizia, the natives barely make a majority; so when they start taunting the Soviet old guard, they will also be taunting, and perhaps attacking, their neighbors down the street. Thus, ethnic battles could arise within as well as between the republics.

The world has had a foretaste of that kind of civil war in Yugoslavia. A miniversion of the Soviet Union once held together by Marx and machine guns, Yugoslavia is now splitting apart as republics want out and tribe turns on tribe. Multiply the Yugoslav population by 12, the land area by 100; throw in 30,000 nuclear warheads and an equally tangled history. Welcome to the disintegrating Soviet Union, and stand by for big trouble.

First, the Bad News.   Russia has sold missiles to India and submarines to Iran. Russian troops interfere in Georgia and Kirghizia. The American CIA employee, Ames, who spied for the Soviet Union, continued on the Russian payroll. The Bosnian Serbs' chestnuts were pulled from NATO fire by a Russian ultimatum.

In December 1993 Russian elections, a charismatic demagogue named Vladimir Zhirinovsky won over a third of the votes to become a power. Although some call him a clown, a buffoon, and a nut, others feel Zhirinovsky must be taken seriously. He is extremely racist in his attitudes about blacks, the Turko-Mongols, and other races in central Asia, the Caucasus, and beyond. He advocates a "Greater Russia" and a world parceled neatly among the "great powers."

"Greater Russia" in Zhirinovsky's view would include all the states of the former Soviet Union. It would dominate the vast region from Karachi to Istanbul, which would include Pakistan west of the Indus River, Afghanistan, Iran, and Turkey east of the Bosporus. He recognizes that achievement of his vision would require military action, but he points out that Russia is still a mighty military power and that such an undertaking would give the Russian army a purpose, which it lacks in 1995.[12]

A lack of purpose may be contributing to a booming death rate among Russian men. The causes include infectious disease, murder, suicide, and cardiovascular disease (see Table 17–1). As a result of a collapsing health system, people often die after a relatively mild heart attack.[13]

Then, Some Good News.   We saw above that Russian trade is turning rapidly to the West and that joint ventures are mostly with western Europeans. It is to the West that Russia must turn for technology and capital, and we saw also that investment funds have begun to put money into Russia and eastern Europe.

William Colby, former CIA director, now publishes reports for investors, and his outlook for the long term is positive. He states that real reform is taking hold in Russia, including privatization in the retail and production sectors, halving of inflation, and decollectivization of agriculture.

Colby recognizes obstacles, saying money and banking are antediluvian, the legal system offers few guarantees or real protection, and distribution,

	QI 1993	QI 1994	Increase	
Diseases				**TABLE 17–1**
Cardiovascular	288.7	331.6	15.0%	Causes of death in Russia*
Cancer	75.2	75.9	1.1	
Respiratory	30.4	34.3	12.8	
Digestive organs	13.7	14.7	7.5	
Infectious	5.9	7.0	17.9	
External causes				
Alcohol poisoning	11.0	13.2	20.0	
Suicide	12.1	13.1	9.0	
Murder	10.7	11.4	6.2	
Other	80.8	90.6	10.8	
Total	528.5	591.8	12.1	

*In thousands

Source: *The Economist,* July 9, 1994, p. 50.

shipping and other infrastructure are totally inadequate. In addition, crime and the Russian mafia have become major threats. Nevertheless, he feels "the potential payoff is huge for those willing to wait." The length of the wait depends on how fast and effectively Western financial and economic assistance is forthcoming.[14]

A source in the United States of information about Russia is the Russian Information Center at 731 Eighth Street, S.E., Washington, DC 20003. Their telephone is (202) 547-3800.

East Europe

The Worldview, "Pointing Way to Prosperity for East Europe Countries," presents an excellent overview of the East European situation and some country-to-country differences. Supplementing that, we discuss some difficulties and hopes for the region.

Realities Chill Investment Climate.   The parting of the Iron Curtain was accompanied by euphoria of would-be Western investors as they thought of a 130-million-person market. A cold dose of reality followed close behind. Blaming everything from state bureaucracy, regional politics, and the recession in the West to radical environmentalists and demands for bribes from entrenched communists, countless Western investors have aborted, delayed, or scaled back their entry into Eastern Europe. By one estimate, 90 percent of the Western businesspeople who investigate investments in Eastern Europe go home without opening their purses or wallets.[15]

Some specific disincentives were:

- A Polish steelmaker, offering itself for sale, claimed to be earning generous profits. But the deal fell through when the Western investors learned the company had been getting its iron ore "free" from the state.

- An equipment contract was not entered after a Polish bureaucrat grilled a California businessman seeking a license: "Are you a Jew? You look like a Jew to me."

- A big U.S. motel chain was scared out of Czechoslovakia by the demand of a communist bureaucrat for a "fee to facilitate" the investment. Such a payment would be illegal under American law.

■ A New Hampshire resort developer proposed a major ski complex in Czech Republic's Tatras Mountains but was driven out by the environmentalist Green party.[16]

Germany.   Given their common language, currency, culture, and history—except for 45 years of communist rule in East Germany—one would think investors from the former West Germany would have smooth sailing into the East. It ain't necessarily so; those 45 years loom large. BASF, the German chemical giant, was one of the first investors in the former East Germany, buying a chemical company there. The litany of problems it experienced—some of which follow—won't encourage many other investors.

■ BASF had difficulty purging from the staff former communist apparatchiks unwilling to cooperate with plant modernization.

■ It had to rewire the old telephone network, which was bugged.

■ When drawing up the Eastern company's first real set of accounts, BASF found that some 20 percent of total costs went for the factory's outdoor heated swimming pool, a hospital, and an abattoir.

■ The factory buses that carry employees to and from their residential neighborhoods leave before the end of the workday, and therefore, so do the employees.

■ About 40 percent of the eastern firm's output went to Eastern Europe, mostly Russia, and another 40 percent went to East German customers. Those sales have fallen by three-quarters. The Russians still place orders but cannot pay for them.

Nevertheless, BASF insists that eventually its eastern investment will pay off, and it is investing another DM500 million for further expansion. The majority of the eastern employees know that most of Eastern Germany's chemical industry is being shut down, and they are willing to cooperate with BASF's radical reshaping of the plant. The eastern labor force is still relatively cheap, about half the cost of western equivalents. But BASF says it is unlikely ever to buy another East German chemical plant.[17]

Other Investments in Eastern Europe.   One American firm that appears on the way to a successful Eastern European investment is Levi Strauss. Thanks in part to the eagerness and cooperation of the people and government of the Polish town of Plock (pronounced Pwotsk), the Levi's producer has been able to cut through red tape and other obstacles to set up production in the town.[18]

Some other U.S. companies invested in Eastern Europe are shown in Table 17–2. The table details the country, amount invested, and the type of project.

The EU and the East.   The trade and industrial policies of the European Union were singled out in a 1994 report by the European Bank for Reconstruction and Development (EBRD) as the main threats to Eastern European exports and investment. So-called voluntary export restraints imposed by the EU on the former communist states "can strengthen bureaucracies and existing exporters at the expense of new entrants," says the EBRD.

At mid-1994, some 19 antidumping measures imposed by the EU were in force along with 12 other trade restrictive measures. The mere threat of limited market access generates sufficient uncertainty so as to reduce investment in Eastern Europe.[19]

Progress Despite the EU.   Despite the hurdles that the EU continues to place in front of the economies in transition, they have made progress over the previous five years, as the EBRD report shows. The private sector accounted for more

TABLE 17–2 U.S. companies in Eastern Europe

Although American firms have been slower than those in other nations to invest in the rebuilding of Eastern Europe, the list of U.S. projects is growing. Here are examples of large-scale U.S. corporate investment in manufacturing and commerce in the region. Some dollar figures are estimates.

Company	Country	Amount (millions)	Type of Project
General Motors	Eastern Germany	$630	Car assembly
	Hungary	$200	Car assembly, engine production
Coca-Cola	Eastern Germany	$450	Soft drink plants, distribution network in 12 cities
	Hungary	$14	Bought control of two bottling plants
	Poland	$110	11 new bottling plants
General Electric	Hungary	$197	Bought 75% of lighting manufacturer Tungsram
Guardian Industries	Hungary	$120	Bought 80% of Hungarian Glass Works
Golub & Co. and A. Epstein & Sons	Poland	$100	Office complex
Ford	Hungary	$80	Fuel pump, ignition coil production
Sara Lee	Hungary	$50–60	Bought control of food firm Compack
Schwinn	Hungary	n.a.	Bought control of bike maker Csepel
U.S. West and Bell Atlantic	Czechoslovakia	$50	Cellular phones
Marriott	Poland	$20–40	Hotel
U.S. West	Hungary	$11	Cellular phones
United Technologies	Hungary	$10	Auto wiring harness production

Note: n.a. = Not available

Source: *Los Angeles Times*, July 9, 1991, p. A6.

than half of all economic activity in 9 of the 25 countries surveyed, and with the exception of Ukraine, most have managed to avoid hyperinflation.

Unemployment, whose rise over the five years after 1989 has been one of the clearest indicators of the shakeout from the Soviet-style heavy industries and arms plants that littered the region, started to ease in the fast-track reforming states. The EBRD report reveals a growing split between the group of central European countries closest to Western European markets and quickest to adopt macro-economic stabilization and micro-adjustment policies, and the slower, more distant parts of the former Soviet empire where reform started later from a less culturally prepared base.[20]

Table 17–3 shows changes in unemployment and inflation from 1993 to 1995.

Pollution. An immense problem for East Europe is pollution. As Soviet troops pulled out of the occupied countries, they left a legacy of pollution. One writer reports that "after 40 years, once victorious soldiers will be remembered for creating a trail of disaster."[21] Soviet soldiers were not the only polluters. The Eastern countries' industries polluted themselves, their neighbors, and nearby waterways. Figure 17–1 gives an indication of the extent and types of pollution.

After the communist armies forced the nationalist forces off mainland China to Taiwan in 1949, American contacts with the mainland were almost nonexistent until 1970. By then the PRC leadership had apparently embarked on a fundamental reappraisal of policies that included a new perception of the military threat posed by the Soviet Union.

During the early 1970s, the United States was winding down its Vietnam involvement while observing the U.S.S.R.'s growing military might. Both the PRC and the United States perceived each other as counterweights against the U.S.S.R., and they began political and trade relations based on mutual political advantage. In the matter of trade, the success of the changed

THE PEOPLE'S REPUBLIC OF CHINA (PRC)

TABLE 17–3

Trends in unemployment and inflation

	Unemployment		Inflation in Consumer Prices	
	1993*	1995†	1993*	1995†
Albania	17.5%	15.8%	85 %	16.0%
Bulgaria	16.4	16.4	73	44.1
Czech Republic	3.5	5.7	20.8	8.8
Estonia	2.6	8.0	89.8	15.0
Hungary	12.1	11.3	22.5	16.9
Latvia	5.3	13.0	109	15.0
Lithuania	1.4	9.0	390	30.0
Poland	15.7	16.8	35.3	22.7
Romania	10.2	15.1	256.1	58.6
Slovak Republic	14.4	14.9	23.2	12.5
Slovenia	14.5	13.0	32.3	14.0
Russia	1.1	6.5	896	198
Ukraine	0.4	12.5	4,735	338

*Estimate
†Average forecast

Source: *Financial Times*, October 20, 1994, p. 3.

relationship can be seen by comparing the U.S.–PRC trade figure of 1971, which was $4.9 million, to that of 1994, when it surged to some $29.5 billion. The PRC has run a persistent and growing trade surplus in its U.S. trade; the surplus of about $2.5 billion in 1988 had leaped to the neighborhood of $22 billion by 1993.[22]

The trade imbalance led to U.S. complaints about Chinese import barriers. In addition, the United States accused the PRC of exporting prison-made goods, falsely labeling them as made in nonprison factories. Another major U.S. complaint was PRC abuse of intellectual property rights such as patents and copyrights.[23]

A Capitalist People's Republic of China?

Although the PRC bureaucratic maze is probably second to none, some developments are now under way that would have shocked Chairman Mao.* The PRC is admitting foreign, private ownership of production facilities within the country, flirting with corporate stock issues, and investing abroad.

joint venture
As used in this chapter, a West firm operating in an East country in some form of cooperation with an agency of the East country government or with one of the new private organizations that are springing up

Joint Ventures (JVs).   In 1979, the PRC published a **joint venture** law, and companies came from America, Europe, Japan, and elsewhere to try the Chinese market. At first, the influx was slow due to vagaries in the law, so the Chinese released an implementing act in 1983 to clarify the law, and more foreign firms moved in.

JV Difficulties in the PRC.   Although some 666 joint ventures were in place by 1986, the difficulties for foreigners operating in the PRC caused some failures, losses, and low-profit or low-quality products. As a result, the first nine months of 1986 saw a 40 percent decline in foreign investments. This so concerned the government that it began giving seminars featuring representatives from successful joint ventures. The profitable foreign venturers told others how they had done it. Some of the keys are:

---

*Mao Tse-tung was the absolute dictator of the PRC until his death in 1976.

FIGURE 17–1 Polluted Eastern Europe

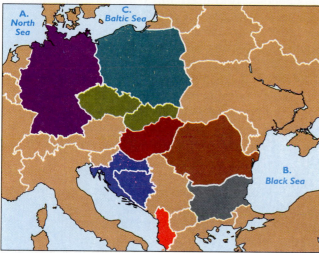

The nations of Eastern Europe and the region's seas all have severe environmental problems. Some of the worst are listed below:

A. NORTH SEA
Heavy-metals pollution: mercury, cadmium, lead.

B. BLACK SEA
90% biologically dead from pollutants.
Beaches periodically closed because of bacterial pollution.

C. BALTIC SEA
Much of the sea floor lifeless due to nitrogen compounds and organic wastes.
Beaches periodically closed because of pollution.

● POLAND
Little or no air pollution control.
Half the cities and 35% of industry do not treat waste.
Children have five times the lead of Danish children.
Air pollution damage to 82% of forests.

● GERMANY
A third of rivers and 9,000 lakes biologically dead.
Air pollution damage to 57% of forests.
15,000 unmonitored hazardous waste dumps.

● CZECH REPUBLIC, SLOVAKIA
Heavy air pollution.
70% of rivers badly polluted; 50% of drinking water below national standards.
30% of children have allergies.

● HUNGARY
1 of every 17 deaths blamed on air pollution.
44% of plants only do crude treatment of sewage.
700 of the country's 3,000 urban wells contaminated.
750 plant and animal species declared endangered or rare.

● ROMANIA
80% of river water unpotable.
Improperly stored radioactive waste.
Massive over-logging of forests.

● BULGARIA
Some children have extremely high lead levels.
Erosion damage to 80% of agricultural land.
Air pollution damage to 78% of forests.

● ZAGREB, CROATIA, BOSNIA
Sava River watershed heavily polluted.
Adriatic Sea coastline polluted by sewage, toxics.
Air pollution from coal burning, lead gasoline.
17,500 acres of agricultural land lost annually to urban sprawl, soil erosion, acid rain.

● ALBANIA
Air and rivers polluted.
10% of land drained, destroying wetlands.
Tirana, the capital city, does not treat its sewage.

Based on information from the *Los Angeles Times*, July 12, 1991, p. A17.

Insist on the right to hire and fire employees and to reward good workers with bonuses or otherwise.

Establish good training programs.

Choose the right location even if the costs are higher.

Obtain the support of local as well as Beijing authorities.

Be prepared to invest in infrastructure, such as power cables and water pipes.

Keep quality standards high.

Establish reliable foreign suppliers, because PRC sources may be unreliable.

The best technology isn't necessarily the most advanced; the technology should be easy to learn and maintain.

Specific difficulties for the foreign firm in a PRC JV include getting out profits or interest in convertible currency, finding qualified employees, and, even more difficult, firing employees. Both types of problems can be ameliorated by making clear, detailed agreements with the Chinese JV partner before investing. It is extremely important for these agreements to be approved by the highest appropriate PRC government agency; the Chinese partner or local bureaucrats may have inflated notions of their own power and fail to consult their superiors.

The perils of trying to open and operate a successful JV in China are legion. Start-up costs are high and rising fast. Once the JV begins work, it may encounter hidden political agendas, promised infrastructure that fails to appear, phantom night-shifts making batches of products the foreign partner never sees, and corruption often reaching up to the most senior officials. Government regulations change like shifting sand, and many Chinese officials still seem hostile to the whole idea of foreign firms making money.

The risks of these attitudes and practices are that they could drive potential foreign investors to other booming Asian countries, and in the first five months of 1994, the number of new joint venture projects approved fell by a third compared with the same 1993 period. Still, fearful of missing out on a huge market, foreign investors come "like moths to a flame," as one investor put it.[24]

Corporate Stock.   In 1983, the PRC authorized three enterprises to raise money by selling stock to private buyers. Many residents of the country, plus overseas Chinese and others, are potential buyers, but there are obstacles to the widespread, successful use of stock sales to raise capital for Chinese companies. Diehard communist cadres have to be convinced that stock issues are just a means of raising money and do not mean the PRC is giving up communism. Managers have to learn to report to a board of directors and be answerable to shareholders. The legal status of stock companies needs to be established in the PRC, and the mechanics of issuing and trading securities must be learned. Officials at the Bank of China's overseas branches and its 12 affiliates are probably ready to assist with the procedural problems.

Until September 1986, there was no formal, legal method to trade the securities. Then, for the first time since the communists came to power in 1949, the government authorized the establishment of a stock and bond exchange, in Shanghai. Public interest and trading are growing, but there is opposition. A number of Communist party faithful complain that a stock exchange is capitalist. The banks complain that people withdraw their deposits to buy securities.[25]

It must be recognized that the PRC is engaged in a unique historic experiment. It is attempting to liberalize toward a free market economy with private ownership of securities and private operation of farms and factories, while maintaining rigid Communist party control of the government and large parts of industry. Tensions grew and finally snapped at Beijing's Tiananmen Square in June 1989.

Political Backlashes.   The liberalization movement has been led by Deng Xiaoping, who was 85 years old in 1989, and many wondered whether his moderate, pragmatic policies would continue after his death or retirement. The American State Department felt there were enough like-minded leaders behind Deng to prevent reversal of his policies. However, others remember the "let a thousand flowers bloom" era under Mao Tse-tung. Mao encouraged playwrights, poets, and writers to speak out without fear of government reprisal. Quite a number of people took him at his word, and there was an outpouring of works that could not have been published previously. Suddenly, Mao changed his mind and his policy. The people who had spoken out were imprisoned, sent to labor gangs, or otherwise punished.

During 1986, Chinese students from a dozen campuses marched and demonstrated for political democracy, anathema to a communist government. After some hesitation, the government began to suppress the students, who then returned to campus. As a result, the Communist party chief, Hu Yaobang, was forced to resign because of accusations that he encouraged the students' demands for democratization.

A group of journalists joins the students' pro-democracy demonstration in Tiananmen Square.

Hu's downfall began a six-month campaign against "bourgeois liberalism," and in March 1989, a reporter for the *Financial Times* stated, "The halcyon days of China's economic and political liberalism appear to be over." Xinhua, the official Chinese news agency, made an unusually strident attack on Western influence, stating, "The Chinese people suffered enough from foreign invasions. . . . The Chinese people have become masters of themselves. . . . Copying foreign political systems and experiences will not save China."[26]

Hu's death in April 1989 triggered an outpouring of student sympathy and renewed demands for political democracy. Despite government crackdown threats, the student marches and calls for "democracy" spread from campus to campus.

As the students' demonstrations continued and grew while the government refused to talk with their representatives and failed to use force to disperse them, the students were joined by workers and others. Although demonstrations and marches occurred in many parts of the country, the ones that received the most attention were held in Tiananmen Square in the capital, Beijing. The demonstrators, unarmed and peaceful, were requesting political freedoms to accompany the new freedoms being applied to the economy. The demonstrations and marches went on through May until the night of June 3, 1989.

Deng had encouraged economic liberalizations but would have no part of political freedom for China. Zhao Ziyang, the party general secretary, was the highest-ranking supporter of the students' goals and was ousted from power in May. Then, supported by other hardliners such as Li Peng, Deng ordered the People's Liberation Army to open fire and to use its tanks to crush, sometimes literally, the demonstrations and the demonstrators.

The army moved in during the nights of June 3 and 4, and according to both Chinese and foreign observers, thousands of demonstrators were killed. This action was followed by months of arrests of people who had been involved, many of whom were summarily executed.

The Chinese government dismissed the Tiananmen massacre, saying that because the demonstrators had attacked and killed many of the soldiers, the square had to be cleared and the demonstrators dispersed. The government invited foreign businesspeople, most of whom had fled the country, to return and resume business as usual. Those people and their companies had to make decisions involving safety, ethics, and finance.

Ethically, do foreign companies want to do business with a government that ruthlessly butchers its own people? The fact is the PRC's civil rights record has been dreadful for years, yet foreign governments and firms have chosen to look the other way. Recently, it seemed possible that civil rights might improve, particularly if Zhao took power when Deng retired or died. But, beginning on June 3, 1989, when the government's brutal suppression was televised for several days before the foreign media were evicted, the probability of a more humane PRC seemed far less likely.

With regard to financial considerations, because China is a huge potential market just beginning to open, a firm would not want to be beaten out by its competitors. Because change is constant in China, there is the possibility that Zhao or other like-thinkers could return to power, creating even greater business opportunities for foreign firms.

Post-Tiananmen PRC.   What happened to the spirit of Tiananmen Square? Even asking that question in China now invites an early end to a conversation. Most of those who participated in the 1989 protests have since "jumped into the sea" (gone into business) and heeded Deng Xiaoping's call to get rich.

Today's students have turned from the Tiananmen theme music to nihilistic Chinese heavy metal, and the underground publishing industry is cashing in on pornography. The Communist party sells ads in its newspaper, and the People's Liberation Army makes and sells herbal medicine.[27]

Deng Xiaoping.   It is difficult to overestimate the influence of Deng in recent Chinese history. The economic reforms he had inaugurated beginning in 1979 led to the expectations that brought the students, workers, and others to Tiananmen Square requesting political reforms. However, to save the Chinese Communist party from the fate the party suffered in Russia and Eastern Europe, he ordered the army to clear Tiananmen Square, which it did in brutal fashion. That brought denunciation from abroad and created sullen hostility within China.

To divert the attention of the Chinese from the Tiananmen tragedy, in 1992 Deng made a highly publicized tour of southern China embracing the most radical—for China—experiments in economic reform. The eventual reforms unleashed an economic explosion that is, so far, keeping the hard-line communists in Beijing at bay. It all started in 1979.

The economic reforms had two main themes. The first, applied throughout rural PRC (where four-fifths of Chinese still live), was to restore family farms and let the market set most farm prices. Rural incomes doubled in six years, creating two things still sorely lacking in the republics of the former Soviet Union: a constituency for reform and a solid base for further growth.

The second vital part of Deng's reforms, which also distinguished the PRC from other would-be reformers like the Soviets and India, was the "open door," a cautious welcome for foreign firms and somewhat free trade. The provinces along PRC's coast were set free first; 14 cities were given the status of "coastal open cities" with freedoms and tax breaks for foreign trade and investment. Also created were five "special economic zones" (SEZs) with greater privileges still.

The results were explosive. Shenzhen, one of the SEZs, is an example. In 1979, Shenzhen had 100,000 inhabitants, mostly poor farmers and fishermen. Today there are more than 2 million people, glossy high rises, a limitless supply of prostitutes, traffic jams, and a GDP per capita close to $2,000 per year.[28]

Look out, Western Europe. The PRC will catch you unless ideology interrupts.

Two Chinas. There are two Chinas. Not the old two Chinas of communist Beijing and nationalist Taipei, but the political fiction as concocted in Beijing and the life as lived by the Chinese people. When these two Chinas mix in any room, there are embarrassing, awkward silences.

After Tiananmen, the Communist party reverted to heavy ideological propaganda that had nothing to do with the reality of PRC life. As a result, an experienced Hong Kong businessman stated, "I think it is no longer possible for them to make a quiet transition away from communism."

The failure of the hard-liners' coup in the Soviet Union served to heighten the post-Tiananmen paranoia of PRC leaders. After all, the Soviet plotters had all been handpicked by President Gorbachev. Whom could you trust?

The PRC leaders launched a campaign to test the loyalty of senior cadres. When asked to describe the test, a party historian said, "They're being told to point at a deer and call it a horse."[29]

In closed crisis meetings held in late 1991, the PRC Communist party failed to agree about who should own the means of production. Party pragmatists argued that the inefficient state-owned factories should be made more responsive to the market while nonstate industry should be allowed to flourish. But party ideologues were in favor of pumping more funds into state factories and increasing state control over the thriving nonstate sector.[30]

The contrast between the success of the PRC's private-sector business and the failure of its state-owned firms is stark. But ideology dies hard, and the ideologues control the army and police—at least they controlled enough of them in 1989 to crush the students and workers calling for democracy in Tiananmen Square.

One consideration that may influence the ideologues to moderate their stance is the PRC's successful foreign investment progress, as indicated by investments in private business outside the PRC.

Investments Abroad. Since 1979, the PRC has invested in over 700 joint ventures outside China. The first of these ventures were in trading houses, department stores, and servicing agencies, but in 1983, the emphasis changed to focus on manufacturing companies. The PRC wants overseas stakes in iron ore, aluminum, paper pulp, fertilizer, and fisheries projects and also wants to acquire technology and management skills.

Raising Capital Abroad. Early in 1994, approval was granted for 22 Chinese companies to list their securities on foreign stock exchanges. To appreciate how far down the road the country's economic reforms have come, consider that only recently, releasing commercial information to foreigners would have landed directors of PRC companies in jail; but at least 4 of the 22 were aiming for Wall Street, where disclosure requirements are far greater than in Hong Kong. For evident reasons, the Hong Kong stock market has been the first place PRC companies listed their securities; Hong Kong is geographically adjacent to the PRC, which is taking over full control of Hong Kong in 1997.

But, New York is more attractive than Hong Kong for three reasons. First, price/earnings ratios are greater so companies can raise more cash. Second, there are fewer Chinese companies listed in New York and thus, less competition. Third, and not at all least important in Chinese eyes, New York is perceived as carrying higher prestige.[31]

But How About China's Debts? Chinese state firms have been converting domestic assets into foreign ones and using them to play financial markets abroad. They have not been successful.

Even though Standard and Poor's, the rating agency, assigns the junk grade to China's debt, banks and other financial houses in America, Europe, and Japan have traded with and lent money to agencies of the Chinese state, a.k.a. the Communist party. By 1994, the results were hurting. In October 1994, 31 foreign banks, 26 of them Japanese, wrote to the Chinese central banker, Zhu Rongil, for help collecting $600 million from state enterprises.

In November 1994, Lehman Brothers, an American investment bank, filed writs in a New York court against three Chinese trading companies that it claims have defaulted upon $100 million in foreign exchange and swap contracts. In London, Merrill Lynch and Crédit Lyonais have been trying to collect $40 million from Citic, the overseas investment vehicle of the Chinese state.

In 1994, China's foreign debt was approaching $100 billion, and some say foreign bankers and dealers took inadvisable risks to drum up business with China. As one American investment banker said, "When you start talking about debts in the tens of millions, that rings alarm bells. I don't want to say the bankers deserve it, but Chinese companies should never be getting credit lines of this size."[32]

Don't Forget the Bureaucratic Maze.   The red tape is unbelievably costly and time consuming. It takes at least two years to start a business. In Shanghai, over 60 "chops" are required to get government approval of a project (chops are authorization stamps from various government bureaus—they even have a bureau governing the giving of prizes at parties). The bureaucracy created such obstacles that the mayor of Shanghai set up a new office—called the "one chop shoppe"—in an attempt to consolidate the bureaucratic maze.

Bribery of government officials is essential to get anything done. Even after government approval, there is a two-year wait to get a telephone, after which only 30 percent of local calls and 20 percent of long-distance calls make it through.[33]

The bureaucrats were too much for one poor Western businessman. He was French and had been negotiating with Chinese officials over a problem for a year and a half. When he believed he had finally resolved the matter and was preparing to board his aircraft for home, the officials came to him at the airport, saying another organization had not agreed to the terms. Problems remained. This was too much for the Frenchman, who was subsequently found running naked around Tiananmen Square and taken out of China in a straitjacket.[34]

Weaknesses in the PRC Economic Boom.   China's economic boom is exerting huge pressures on the country's crumbling infrastructure. For example, China's roads, railways, ports, and airports are proving inadequate; construction of low-cost housing lags far behind demand; and power shortages and blackouts are common.[35]

Compared with East Asia's miracle economies, the PRC suffers several disadvantages.

- Its arable land per farm worker is lower, and rapid growth in China's farm output has come to an end earlier in the country's development than was the case elsewhere in East Asia.
- The PRC's state-owned enterprises still get huge subsidies.
- The PRC's exporters of manufactured products are much more dependent on foreign capital than their counterparts in other East Asia economies.
- The PRC, with its communist government, has greater inequality of income than the Republic of China, Taiwan, or South Korea.[36]

Foreign companies must pay dearly to lure executives to live and work in China. Expatriates can cost foreign companies as much as 10 to 15 times more than indigenous workers. But, it is frequently necessary to have an expatriate because although technical skills are quite easy to find in the PRC, management skills are scarce.[37]

Risks of Incarceration for Foreign Businesspeople. It's not only political dissidents who are imprisoned in the PRC; businesspeople must tread lightly, as the following items show.

■ Australian entrepreneur James D. Peng's company in Shenzhen was accused of financial impropriety, and Peng returned to his home in Hong Kong, frightened to be in the PRC. He did, however, travel on business to Macao, a Portuguese territory, in October 1993, where around midnight one night the Macao police entered his hotel room, arrested him, and turned him over to the PRC police. By December 1994, he was still being held in a PRC prison without being charged of any crime.

■ In March 1994, an American, Philip Cheng, returned to Hong Kong after being held without charge in a PRC jail for seven months because a deal for an investment in Cheng's helmet factory went sour.

■ In the summer of 1993, Hong Kong businessman Choi Chee-ming, was released after being detained four years on gold-smuggling charges which were later dismissed.

■ In January 1994, another Hong Kong businessman, Chong Kwee-sung, was released after two and a half years in a PRC prison.

Central police authorities in Beijing admit that local police have detained and even kidnapped businesspeople to resolve economic disputes.[38]

Advice Is Available. Despite the dangers and difficulties, the PRC cannot be ignored economically. Figure 17–2 is a UN advertisement for a guidebook on trading with the PRC. It can be bought from United Nations Publications. Figure 17–3, is an advertisement of a conference entitled "China Financing for Growth." It is sponsored by the Bank of China, *Euromoney*, the Shanghai stock exchange, and several financial houses whose names appear in the ad.

EAST-WEST TRADE PROBLEMS

Getting paid for goods sold to the East is not easy. The Eastern nations' demand for Western goods and technology has been far greater than Western demand for Eastern exports. Therefore, the Eastern countries have not been able to pay for their imports with their exports.

The East Owes the West a Lot of Money

The IMF refers to the countries of Central and Eastern Europe and Russia as "countries in transition," and to finance their trade gaps with Western countries, they have borrowed heavily from Western governments and banks, international institutions, and suppliers. The total external debt of the transition countries in 1994 was $215.5 billion, up from $204.1 billion in 1993 and $124.5 billion in 1986.[39]

The Russian part of that debt was some $80 billion. Alexander Shokhin, Russia's economics minister, said the problem was not the size of the repayments, but the short period into which they were compressed. A part of Russia's problem, according to Shokhin, is the slow repayment to Russia of $147 billion owned by client countries of the former Soviet Union. They are paying only $2 billion a year instead of the $6 to 7 billion they were scheduled to pay.[40]

The reasons for the East's trade deficits and resulting large debts are easily stated. The manufactured products of the East European countries have not

FIGURE 17–2
Advertisement for UN
guidebook on trading with
China

Guidebook on Trading with The People's Republic of China

(4th edition)

The "How To" Guide on doing successful business with China

The scope and the depth of coverage in the "Guidebook on Trading with the People's Republic of China" make it the main source of information for businesses, consultants and others in the private sector, lawyers, legal aids and arbitrators among others. The extensive coverage includes substantial and vital information on:

● China's growing economy
● How to establish a business in China
● The rules, procedures and opportunities of selling to and buying from China
● How to apply for trademarks and file patents
● How to use their classification system of hundreds of goods and services
● All the modes of transportation available
● Customs, insurance and inspection regulations
● The potential market place of 30 cities and provinces including the major export markets
● How to establish joint ventures
● Drawing up contracts

With 584 pages of valuable information, over 175 statistical tables and annexes, names, addresses and telephone numbers of overseas representative offices, government, civil, economic and trade organizations, and national import and export corporations in China, this Guidebook is your ultimate source of information.
E.94.II.F.9   92-1-119641-3   584pp $75.00

Send orders to:

United Nations Publications, Sales Section
Room DC2-0853 **Dept.157A**, New York, N.Y. 10017.
Tel. (800) 253-9646, (212) 963-8302, Fax (212) 963-3489
VISA, MC and AMEX accepted. Please add 5% to gross
with a minimum fee of $3.50 for shipping & handling.

United Nations Publications

Source: *The Economist*, October 22, 1994, p. 39.

been of sufficient quality to compete in markets of the West against Western products. They do not export enough raw materials to pay for the imports they desire. In lower-technology or labor-intensive products in which their quality is competitive, they encounter protectionism due to pressure from labor unions in the Western countries.

East European Quality Improving.   The reasons for the East's trade deficit may be ending as changes in work habits yield exportable goods while costs remain low. More and more companies in Eastern Europe are rapidly raising the quality of their products to Western standards. Their success suggests that

FIGURE 17–3 Advertisement for conference on China financing

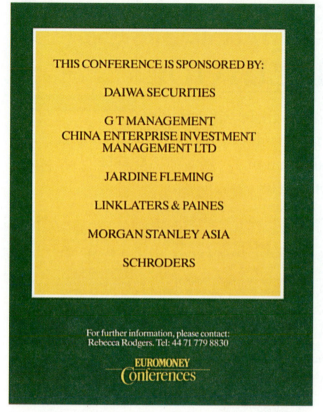

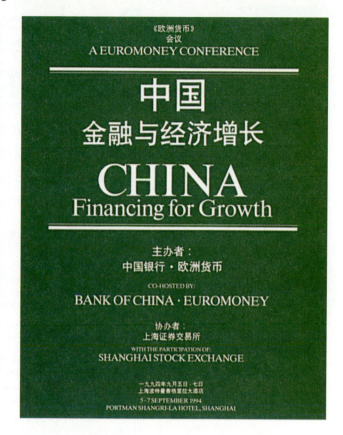

Source: *Euromoney*, August 1994, pp. 76–77.

these companies, especially in Poland, Hungary, and the Czech Republic, are rejoining the West more quickly than many people expected.

They are combining their continuing lower labor cost advantage with improving product quality to pose serious export threats. The Czech Republic, for example, has increased exports to the West to 70 percent of total exports from 31 percent in 1989.[41]

There are numerous sources of information about how to do business in Eastern Europe. One is provided by the Economist Intelligence Unit. You can see an advertisement for "Business Eastern Europe" in Figure 17–4.

Western Strategic Technology for Hostile Countries?

Because of long-standing East-West hostilities—the Warsaw Pact countries versus NATO; the cold war, or communism versus capitalism—the Western countries have limited the strategically useful technology they would sell to the East. To be sure, the countries have applied the limits with varying degrees of rigor; German and Japanese limits have probably been the leakiest, but there have been leaks from all Western countries. And successful Eastern espionage has stolen vast amounts of Western "secrets."

The Western agency charged with enforcing the limits was the Coordinating Committee on Multilateral Export Controls (CoCom), whose members are the NATO countries plus Japan and minus Iceland. Each member-country is responsible for enforcing the technology export limitations, and despite leaks and espionage, the consensus is that CoCom has prevented or at least delayed Eastern countries' receipt of militarily useful technology.

Source: *The Economist*, May 27, 1994, p. 49.

This situation is changing. CoCom restrictions on sales to China were relaxed as the perceived strategic threat has abated. The Warsaw Pact has dissolved, and CoCom went out of existence in 1994.

Although the Warsaw Pact no longer exists and the Soviet Union has fallen apart, Russia remains a mighty military power with nuclear and other weapons of mass destruction. The PRC is building its air force, army, navy, and nuclear arsenal. In addition, there are the so-called rogue countries such as Iran, Iraq, Libya, North Korea, and Syria, which are or have recently been aggressive as supporters of and havens for terrorists. Intelligence reports state that North Korea has nuclear weapons, and after the Gulf War, it was discovered that Iraq had almost developed them. Of course, the Gulf War resulted from Iraq's invasion of Kuwait, and it had invaded Iran a few years before that.

So, should a new CoCom or a similar organization be put into place in an attempt to at least hinder their access to potentially deadly technology and weapons? At the least, Western governments providing peacekeepers for trouble spots need to ensure that their soldiers do not have their own smart weapons turned against them.

In theory, members of such a new organization should subscribe to the nuclear Nonproliferation Treaty, the Australia Group (on chemical weapons), the Missile Technology Control Regime, and the Nuclear Suppliers Group. None of these have CoCom's enforcement mechanism, its rule of unanimity under which any member could veto export of listed goods or technology by any other member.

Yet, weaponry is spreading; goodwill is not. With the death of CoCom, Western governments may feel they need to do a better job of reinventing it.[42]

Nevertheless, West Trades with East

So, as we see, the East has not been able to sell enough to the West to make the money to pay for what it wants to buy from the West. Nevertheless, there has been a large volume of trade between the West and the Soviet-dominated East, with the U.S. share shrinking after 1979. As the immense debts of the Soviet bloc to the West illustrate, a lot of that trade has been financed by credits from Western banks, suppliers, and governments. One method that the East favors to obtain goods and technology is **countertrade**. There are many varieties of countertrade, all of which involve the Western seller taking all or part of its payment in Eastern goods or services rather than in money. Still another device is industrial cooperation between Western suppliers and Eastern factories through subcontracting, joint ventures, licensing, or other schemes to minimize the need for hard-currency payments East to West.

countertrade
Payment for imports at least in part with something other than money

Both countertrade and industrial cooperation are important and growing means for maintaining trade between the industrial West and countries that are short of hard, convertible currency. Such countries include not only the East but also the many noncommunist developing countries, frequently called less developed countries or LDCs.

Inasmuch as countertrade and industrial cooperation are as much applicable to West-LDC trade as they are to West-East trade, we shall discuss those subjects in more detail in Chapter 20. There we deal with finance, and both countertrade and industrial cooperation are used as substitutes for money.

Western resistance to countertrade and industrial cooperation has developed. Some of that resistance is directed particularly at the East, which we shall discuss here.

Opposition to Countertrade and Industrial Cooperation

Resistance to Eastern goods is sometimes based on (1) the inferior quality of the goods and of Eastern technology, (2) damage to competing Western companies and their workers, or (3) damage to producers and their workers in friendly countries with which the West has trade agreements.

As to quality and technology, these may not be enduring problems. One need only remember the Japanese example. After World War II, Japanese products were dismissed as inferior. Within 20 years, Japan was a world leader in technology and exports. Furthermore, it has been estimated that as many as 25 percent of all the scientists in the world are now employed in what was the U.S.S.R. There are technical areas in which the ex-U.S.S.R. leads the

United States, and there has been an increase of their patent registrations in the United States.

We mentioned above the rapid restoration of quality to products produced in the Czech Republic, Hungary, and Poland. They are becoming competitive, and a large majority of Czech trade is now with the West. A growing amount of Russian trade is also going that direction.

Dumping.   Resistance to Eastern goods being imported into Western countries is sometimes based on damage to competing Western companies and their workers. Western companies and unions have begun to complain that Eastern products are being dumped in Western markets.

dumping
The selling abroad of products at prices lower than those charged in the producing country or in other national markets

Dumping is selling in one export market at a price lower than prices charged in the domestic market or in third-country export markets. The sales prices may be lower than the production costs. *Predatory dumping* is dumping whose objective is to damage or destroy competitors in the country where the goods are dumped.

EU makers of steel, cars, chemicals, shoes, textiles, clothing, and electric motors are complaining loudly about unfair Eastern competition. Some of those EU producers, and related labor unions, are already getting protection from EU antidumping action, and others want more protection.

In 1989, a complaint was lodged against the Soviet Union for allegedly dumping the chemical potassium permanganate into the EU market. The complaint was on behalf of a Spanish company, Industrial Quimica de Nalon, which warned that its survival was threatened. It is the EU's only producer of this chemical.[43]

Attitude of American Labor.   One American labor union official said building factories for Eastern-bloc countries (industrial cooperation) was fine if production was for their home markets. But he pointed out that if an Eastern factory exported its products to the West in payment for the factory, it would be difficult for noncommunist trade unionists—"who have the right to bargain collectively and to strike"—to compete with the controlled and subservient labor of the East.[44]

The union official was talking about the cost of the labor, one determinant of the price of goods produced. He was complaining that the East had an unfair cost advantage because it had the power to keep labor under its thumb.

Now that communism is fading in most of Eastern Europe and the Soviet republics, it remains to be seen whether free and strong labor unions will come into being. If they do, presumably the attitudes of Western labor leaders will change.

In this regard, labor is freeing itself more quickly in Eastern Europe and Russia than in the PRC. In fact, it is an ongoing complaint of the United States that much PRC production is by prison labor.

Competition with Traditional Suppliers and Allies.   As to damage to suppliers and workers in friendly countries, it is clear that many Eastern exports will compete with products from other countries, particularly LDCs. The U.S. market has traditional suppliers and allies such as the Philippines and Caribbean and Central and South American countries. The EU countries have their ex-colonies in Africa and Asia, with which they maintain relatively close economic ties.

Some of these U.S. trading partners may exert behind-the-scenes pressures to protect their American markets. The countries mentioned above—the Philippines and so forth—all have embassies or representatives in the United States and friends in Congress and the executive branch. These can be expected to lobby for protection of their U.S. markets from the competition of Eastern countries.

PRC and Soviet Reforms Compared

Just as seemingly deep-seated forces are causing changes in the PRC, so also have changes in the former U.S.S.R. moved it away from the rigid, centralized, communist-state condition that characterized it for more than 70 years.

Differences.   Start with agriculture. Soviet agriculture has never recovered from the dual blow of the Bolshevik Revolution and Joseph Stalin's war against the kulaks, as Russia's farmers were called. Stalin forced the creation of huge state farms and starved, murdered, or deported the kulaks. The communist Soviet Union was a predominantly urban economy, and the people who worked on the collectivized farms were nothing but hired hands with little interest in the output of the farms or the maintenance of their equipment. The tradition of an independent, self-employed farmer hardly survived, even as a folk memory, 60 years after eradication of the kulaks.

Thus Gorbachev's offer to lease land to the hired hands fell on uncomprehending and unenthusiastic ears. The farm workers were making low but living wages. Why give that up and take chances with their own plot of farmland?

By contrast, China at the end of the 1970s was still an overwhelmingly agrarian economy, and the experience of farm collectivization was only a decade-and-a-half old. It was already breaking down at the roots before Deng proclaimed reform from the top. The results were startling as the Chinese farmers were given the freedom to grow and sell their own crops at market prices. Production soared, and many farmers became prosperous.

Not all Russian farmland was collectivized. Currently some 1.6 percent of its arable land is farmed by private farmers who can sell at market prices. That 1.6 percent of the land produces 30 percent of the food. About one-third of the state farm crops never reach the consumer because of poor storage, poor transportation, poor roads, and poor refrigeration, but pests aplenty.

So, cooperation and participation by the people who must make it work are the major reasons the Chinese agricultural reforms were much more successful than those of the Soviet Union.

The same seems to have occurred with industrial reforms. As with agriculture, the reforms began sooner in the PRC than they did in the U.S.S.R. Probably more important, the communist system was not imposed in China until after the communists won their civil war in 1949. The system was put in place in the Soviet Union after the 1917 revolution. Many Chinese had experienced private business and farming and noncommunist governments; not so for the people of the U.S.S.R.

Intellectuals in the former U.S.S.R. are delighted at the prospects of reform. They want to be free to research, write, compose, publish, and travel. However, as Gorbachev has said, the reform will "bog down if we fail to rally the people to its cause." That is not proving easy.

Workers are willing to recognize that the number one problem is productivity, but the overwhelming majority tend to lay blame on almost anyone but themselves. Notably absent are references to the alcoholism, absenteeism, and general lethargy that continue to cripple production.

All this is scarcely surprising. Today's work force in what was the Soviet Union comes from a system that for generations treated the individual as little more than a meaningless cog in the wheel of production. The centralization of political and economic power has at best discouraged and at worst viciously punished individual innovation and initiative. Having endured decades of

The decapitated head of the Lenin statue is carted off in Berlin.

Reuters/Battmann

powerlessness and alienation from the basic decisions that affect their lives, the Soviet people seem numb.

Selling to the East Is Changing

Selling to the East has never been easy. The centrally planned economies those countries had made their institutions, trading techniques, and behavior quite different from those of the West.

In past editions of this book, we presented East countries' purchasing procedures in terms of Soviet practices, to which other East countries were similar. Those practices included 11 steps, from the decision that new equipment was needed to the point the foreign supplier was paid. It was a cumbersome, highly bureaucratic procedure, and suppliers grumbled about it.

Then, in 1986, Mikhail Gorbachev began making changes in the Soviet trade bureaucracies. Some of them lost their monopoly powers, and some individual enterprises were given the right to deal directly with foreigners. In 1988, the government abolished the all-powerful Ministry of Foreign Trade, a move heralded as the cornerstone of reform.

The result was confusion instead of simplification. The enterprise managers were not prepared for their new responsibilities, and, partly as a result, government ministries continued to impose binding instructions in the form of state orders covering up to, and sometimes more than, 100 percent of factories' output.[45]

The confusion was not only on the Soviets' side. Byzantine as it was, the pre-Gorbachev system of Soviet procurement had been learned by foreigners selling to the U.S.S.R., and the foreign suppliers had come to know the Soviet bureaucrats who ran the system. Now the suppliers have to learn a new system and deal with different people.

To bridge this confusion gap, a growing number of firms are offering to act as go-betweens. (See the advertisement for one such firm in Figure 17–5.) These are Western companies that have traded in the U.S.S.R., and there is at least one Russian private consulting company, FAKT, offering its services. A German company, Varioline, and the accounting firm Ernst & Young linked

FIGURE 17–5
East-West broker

Source: Courtesy of Creditanstalt

up with a Russian-Finnish company to get into the business. One rather unique entry in the field is Aldriedge & Miller, Inc., a company formed by two American women with long experience working in the U.S.S.R.[46]

How Western Companies Sell to the East

Selling to the East is usually extremely time consuming and complex. How do Western companies sell in the East? A minority of Western companies open and maintain representative offices in Moscow or some other city. Most Western companies utilize the services of companies that specialize in dealing with the East, such as Satra Corporation or Tower International, Inc. These companies have dealt in many sorts of products and services, including chrome, steel, grain, shoes, hotels, and soybean mills. Their clients have included such major firms as IBM, Borg-Warner, Caterpillar Tractor, and USX.

There are at least two other methods of selling to the East: trade fairs and personal visits.

Trade Fairs. Exhibits at fairs are important ways for Western companies to reach potential customers in both Eastern Europe and the People's Republic of China. Attendance at the Chinese fairs is by invitation, and if you are not invited, it is unlikely that you can sell your product to the PRC. However, when a new exhibition is planned, it may be advertised with invitations issued to qualified exhibitors. Figure 17–6 is an example of one of these. Note that the United Nations Industrial Development Organization is a cosponsor of this one.

FIGURE 17–6
Trade fair invitation

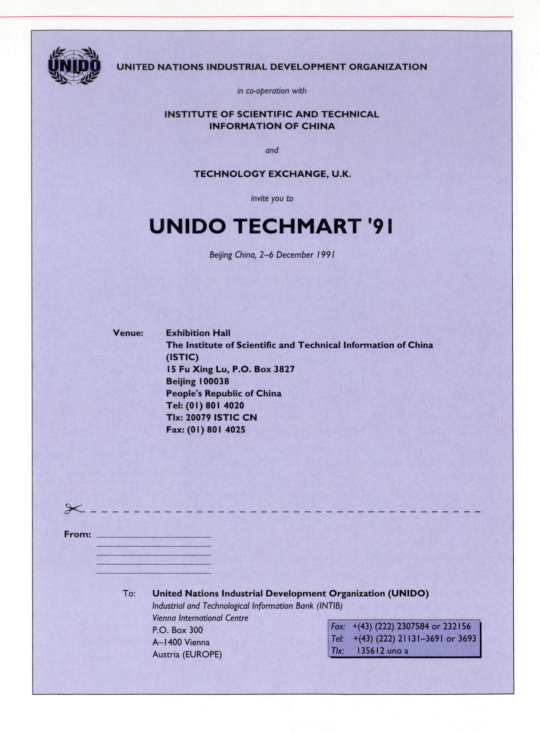

Common sense should probably indicate what to do and what not to do when your company has a stand at a trade fair. However, there have apparently been some unfortunate departures from common sense, so two UN officials have drawn up a checklist for "Manning a Trade Fair Stand." It is reproduced as Figure 17–7.

Personal Visits.   Personal contacts are important, and when you are trying to sell products to Eastern customers, you should not rely too much on correspondence. Personal business visits to Moscow or other capitals, as appropri-

1. Company representatives should be knowledgeable about the company and its products, empowered to conduct business negotiations, and clear on its objectives in exhibiting.
2. Never ignore a visitor to your stand.
3. Approach visitors who seem interested in your display; do not wait for them to approach you.
4. Look interested. Do not sit about chatting with your colleagues. Do not position yourself so as to hide your products or to block access to them.
5. Start the conversation with a positive remark about your product or a question that will generate a discussion.
6. Identify as quickly as possible the visitor's business and specific interest and his importance as a prospect. Always keep your objective in mind.
7. Answer all questions as forthrightly and factually as possible.
8. Remember to sell your company as well as your products, and relate your remarks to the visitor's interests.
9. Use the conversation to elicit information about the market and reactions to your products.
10. Carry negotiations as far forward as you are empowered to, if you are convinced the visitor represents a solid prospect.
11. Use inquiry forms and supplementary notes to record details about the visitor's company, his interests, and follow-up action to be taken.
12. Allow time after the fair closes to continue important discussions.
13. Provide promised information as soon as possible.
14. Observe fair hours, and never leave your exhibit unattended.
15. Use slack periods to make contacts at other stands, provided your own is manned.

FIGURE 17–7
Manning a trade fair stand

Source: Umphon Phanachet and Zhang Huixiang, *Guidebook on Trading with the People's Republic of China* (Trade Promotion Centre of ESCAP, 1982), p. 33.

ate, are almost always necessary if you hope to make sales. However, travel in those areas is expensive and not many sales are made, so a trip should not be made without some combination of the following conditions: (1) company personnel can meet key government officials; (2) the company is contemplating a long-term sales campaign or is at a crucial negotiating point near the end of a campaign; or (3) the volume and profitability of a potential sale warrants the trip.

The Chinese customer wants to scrutinize the Western executives personally and make assessments of their trustworthiness and goodwill. The Chinese want to feel they are dealing with a friend who will play fair and make possible a comfortable, long-term relationship.

> Hugh P. Donaghue, vice president of Control Data Corporation, visited China carrying three large boxes stuffed with product brochures and other literature, which he expected to hand to his Chinese hosts at the first meeting. It didn't work that way. They first asked him about his philosophy of life and then about Control Data's business philosophy. For 10 days, they talked about all sorts of subjects except Control Data products. Finally, as Donaghue was about ready to carry the three boxes home still full, the Chinese finally asked him what he had to sell. Control Data made sales and has been doing increased business with China.

As foreign companies have sold or tried to sell to the PRC over recent years, much experience has been acquired, and some checklists have been developed. One list is suggested by Ronald Wombolt, vice president and director of international operations of John Fluke Manufacturing Company, an American producer of electronic test and measurement instrumentation. Wombolt's checklist is:

FIGURE 17–8
The Republic of Kazakhstan and The Chase Manhattan Bank announcement

This announcement appears as a matter of record only.

The Republic of Kazakhstan

and

The Chase Manhattan Bank, N.A.

have established the

Kazakhstan International Bank (KIB)

a joint venture international investment bank,
head office in Almaty, Republic of Kazakhstan.

The Mercator Corporation acted as advisor in this transaction.

January 1994

Source: *Euromoney,* September 1994, p. 110.

Do not always offer your most favorable price up front. The Chinese want to bargain and negotiate.

Do not, without good cause, insist on selling on letter-of-credit terms. The Chinese are usually prompt payers.

Do not make any statement you can't back up, because the Chinese record everything you say in negotiating sessions.

Do not offer or accept any terms or conditions that you will not want in future transactions. Although the Chinese will constantly ask for something "this time only," it means every time.

Offer training in China and abroad.

Maintain a consistent pricing policy.

To follow the rules listed above, have the same group in your company deal with the Chinese over time, at least one of whom understands the language.[47]

Information about East-West Business. The U.S. Commercial Office in Moscow is available to U.S. companies wishing to do business there. Interested firms can contact the Trade Promotion Division, Bureau of East-West Trade, U.S. Department of Commerce, Washington, DC 20230, or the U.S. Commercial Office, U.S. Department of State–Moscow, Washington, DC 20520.

In recognition of the bureaucratic, linguistic, and cultural difficulties for Americans attempting to sell in the PRC market, the Chinese government set up its first U.S. trade promotion office in Los Angeles in 1986. It is called the China–U.S. Trading Corporation, and it is operated by the Foreign Enterprises Services Corporation (FESCO), a government agency.[48]

Other Help. Banks and others advertise their services for Westerners wishing to do Eastern business. Kazakhstan has attracted some of the largest foreign investments in the former USSR, and Figure 17–8 is one such advertisement.

The UN Economic and Social Commission for Asia and the Pacific publishes a "Guidebook on Trading with the People's Republic of China." Copies can be obtained from the UN at United Nations Plaza, New York, NY, 10017, U.S.A.

Help is also available for people in the East who are looking to the West. In Chapter 4, we mentioned classes and seminars given by the Bank for International Settlements for Eastern European private and central bankers.

SUMMARY

1. **Explain the meaning of "centrally planned economies" and "market economies."** The countries with centrally planned economies, sometimes called the East countries, were the now dissolved Soviet Union and its satellite countries in Central and Eastern Europe, plus Cuba, Ethiopia, North Korea, and others. Centrally planned economies were also found in the Peoples' Republic of China (PRC), Yugoslavia, and elsewhere. All those countries had, and some still have, communist governments. The countries with market economies, sometimes called the West countries, are found in Western Europe and North America, plus Japan, Australia, New Zealand, and others. They are members of the Organization for Economic Cooperation and Development (OECD) and are political democracies.

2. **Understand what the formerly communist countries are trying to achieve and how and why the industrial democracies should assist them.** Most of the formerly communist, centrally planned economies are trying to develop market economies and democratic governments. The West can help the emerging market economies by providing technology, management expertise, and trade opportunities. The joint venture (JV) is a favorite method for foreign companies to cooperate with companies or agencies in the East countries. Trade of Russia, Eastern European countries, and the PRC is increasingly with the West.

3. **Realize that Russia is still a mighty military power even though its forces have been removed from eastern Europe where they left tremendous pollution.** Russia, still a mighty military power, has some leaders with strongly nationalist leanings who would like to recreate and enlarge the Soviet Union. One legacy of communism to Eastern Europe and Russia is pollution.

4. **Identify tensions in the Peoples' Republic of China (PRC) between capitalist-type economic developments and the rigid communist bureaucracy in Beijing.** The PRC has developed capitalist institutions such as stock exchanges, and the economic zones along its coast are rapidly growing and privately owned. Some PRC companies' stock is listed on stock exchanges in Hong Kong and New York. The PRC government is still rigidly communist. It owns very large production facilities, most of which are money losers. It sometimes lashes out violently against would-be democratic demonstrators, as occurred at Tiananmen Square in Beijing in 1989. Deng Xiaoping was a towering figure in PRC devel-

opment, beginning the liberation of the economy in 1979, then ordering the army to crush the Tiananmen demonstrators, and finally encouraging the economic liberalization that permitted Chinese to get rich. PRC has a weak infrastructure with inadequate roads, railways, ports, airports, and communications.

5. **Realize that even though the Soviet Union and the Warsaw Pact have collapsed, there remain dangerous countries and forces in the world.** The CoCom, which attempted to limit East countries' access to West technology, ended its existence. There are still hostile and potentially hostile and dangerous countries, and the Western countries are discussing how to limit their access to dangerous weapons and technology.

6. **Relate the different economic growth rates in the PRC and the states of the former Soviet Union to the different periods they were under communist governments.** Communism took over in Russia in 1917, but not until 1949 in the PRC. That is a major reason market economies are growing much more rapidly in the PRC than in Russia.

7. **Explain how companies from the industrial democracies do business in the former communist countries despite debt and quality difficulties.** The PRC and the countries in transition, as the IMF calls Russia and the Eastern European countries, owe huge amounts of money to the West. The East countries are short of hard, convertible currency and try to trade goods instead of money for their purchases from the West. That is called countertrade. East countries are accused of dumping products in Western markets. Dumping is selling a product at a price lower than that charged in the country of origin or in third-country markets. Selling to the East requires patience, the personal touch, and usually, expert assistance.

KEY WORDS

- centrally planned economies   552
- market economies   553
- joint venture   562
- countertrade   573
- dumping   574

QUESTIONS

1. *a.* When East-West is spoken of, what countries are included in "East"?
   b. "West"?

2. What is a centrally planned economy?

3. What is a market economy?

4. *a.* What does the East want most from the West?
   b. What are the major obstacles to the East getting what it wants?

5. How is the East getting—and trying to get means to pay for—imports from the West?

6. What caused COMECON's demise?

7. *a.* What should Eastern countries do to achieve market economies with democracy?
   b. Should the West help them? Why?
   c. If yes, how?

8. Explain tensions in the PRC between its political and private economic sectors.

9. What are the results of the fact that communism was in power much longer in the U.S.S.R. than in the PRC?

10. How do Western companies do business in and with the East, and what sorts of assistance can they find?

MINICASE 17-1   Joint Venturing in Eastern Europe

You are the vice president for planning of an American manufacturer of machine tools. You report to the president, and he calls you to his office one day.

When you get there, he starts talking about how tough it is to get new business and about how well the company's European and Japanese competitors have been doing in the

American market. He then points out that the company has never made a sale in Eastern Europe, and he asks you why that is.

You reply that business has been good enough in the United States and in the several Latin American markets where the company's products are sold, so no sales efforts have been made in Eastern Europe. You can anticipate the president's next words, and they are not long in coming.

"Latin America has gone to hell in a handbasket! They are spending all their money paying back the greedy banks that lent them too much money, and they're broke when it comes to buying our stuff. We need new markets! Get out of here and see how we can get into Eastern Europe."

What steps are you going to take to try to get into those markets? To whom should you talk? Where can you turn for information? Should you make a trip to the area? If so, when? If not, why not?

Human Resource Management

> *How does it work out when there is*
> *a woman manager in the family?*
> *There is no solution because there is*
> *no problem in Japan. Management*
> *is for men only.*
> *William A. Cohen, in a review of*
> *Mitsuyuki Masatsager*

CONCEPT PREVIEWS

After reading this chapter, you should be able to:

1. **remember** some of the regional or cultural differences in labor conditions we shall present

2. **understand** why some economies are better at job creation than others and the differing unemployment rates

3. **understand** the difficulties of finding qualified executives for international companies (ICs) and the importance of foreign language knowledge

4. **compare** home country, host country, and third country nationals as IC executives

5. **realize** the growing role of women in international business

6. **remember** some of the complications of compensation packages for expatriate executives

You Want Me to Buy? Speak My Language

Michael Thomas's foreign language centers in Beverly Hills and New York charge pupils up to $14,000 for 10 days of intensive instruction in Chinese, French, German, or Spanish. Until recently, his star students were show business celebrities such as Woody Allen, Ann Margaret, and Donald Sutherland. Today, his best customers are executives from Boeing, Chase Manhattan, General Electric, Westinghouse, and the like.

Why the boom? "The answer's simple," says Thomas. "You are much more likely to make a sale if you can speak the customer's language."[a] • Among businesspeople, Spanish remains the hot language in 1995. Berlitz International, Inc., says Spanish makes up 37 percent of its classes, up from 25 percent in 1991. Other areas of growth are Mandarin and Brazilian Portuguese, demand for which doubled in 1994 at one New York office. • "There's certainly a use for languages associated with emerging markets, the biggest growth area in investment banking right now," says George Peng, an analyst with NatWest Securities Corp. High on his list are Spanish, Chinese, and Russian.[b]

Sources: [a]"Speak to me," *The Economist*, November 19, 1994, p. 44; and [b]Lee Valeriano, "Business Bulletin," *The Wall Street Journal*, December 29, 1994, p. A1.

In Chapter 12, we discussed some of the labor forces that international business management faces from country to country. Are there enough bodies present? Do the persons in the bodies possess the skills your operation needs? Even if there are sufficient bodies and skills, will they work for your operation? If there are insufficient bodies, skills, or willingness to work, can you find and train other labor?

The effectiveness of every organization depends to a great extent on how well its human resources are utilized. Their effective use depends on management's policies and practices. Management of a company's human resources is a shared responsibility. The day-to-day supervision of people on the job is the duty of the operating managers, who must integrate the human, financial, and physical resources into an efficient production system. However, the formulation of policies and procedures for (1) estimation of work force needs, (2) recruitment and selection, (3) training and development, (4) motivation, (5) compensation, (6) discipline, and (7) employment termination is generally the responsibility of personnel managers working in cooperation with executives from marketing, production, and finance as well as the firm's lawyers.

REGIONAL OR CULTURAL DIFFERENCES IN LABOR CONDITIONS

Japan's jobs-for-life culture
Particularly in large Japanese companies, the practice developed that once hired, an employee had a job for life

Japan's Jobs-for-Life Culture Disappearing

The prestigious Toyota Motor Corp. has begun hiring experienced automotive designers on a contract basis. These new employees, who may be of any age or nationality, will be hired on the basis of experience and offered merit-based rather than seniority-based pay increases. For Toyota to take these steps makes it easier for other companies to follow suit. A couple that have done so are Honda and Fujitsu.[1]

Pink Slip in Japan—A Psychological Abyss. In a land accustomed to lifetime job security, being laid off is particularly devastating. Middle-aged men suffer most. One says, "In the daytime I try to hide in the house. Only on weekends am I free to go outside. It's better not to tell people that I'm jobless. It gives the impression that I did something wrong, or that I'm not capable of keeping my job." Another says, "It's not good for a husband and wife to be together all the time," when asked how his wife coped with having him around so much. "For our health, it's better for me to work, but nothing's available."[2]

Adding to the pink-slip numbers is the growing trend of Japanese to move production overseas. There are two reasons for this. First, wages in most countries are now lower than in Japan. Second, Japan is being forced to export to the dollar-linked economies of its Asian neighbors, and as the yen rose in value in terms of the dollar, products priced in yen became less and less competitive.[3]

The Huge German-Polish Wage Gap

The Oder River is the border between Germany and Poland at the German town, Frankfurt an der Oder. At most places the river is not wide, but the gap between wages paid on the two sides is huge. In Poland, wages can be as low as 150 to 200 deutsche marks (DM) a month. This compares with DM1,500 to DM2,500 in Germany.

Of course, such a gap draws Polish workers to work legally or illegally in Germany. It is an open secret that on German building sites, contractors pay casual (illegal) laborers as little as DM2 an hour; a German laborer would cost DM15. But even at that, Polish workers earn more than they would in Poland.[4]

Wage Gaps Will Narrow. As the EU expands and workers can move freely from Poland and elsewhere in central and eastern Europe into Germany and other EU countries, the wage gaps will narrow. Time will tell whether wages across the EU reach common, universal levels.

100 to 200 Million Tiny Hands

According to a study released in mid-1994 by the Brussels-based International Federation of Free Trade Unions, which is the world's largest such group, 100 to 200 million children, ages 4 to 15, work in streets, factories, mines, and rock quarries. Often, they work and live in dangerous or filthy conditions for miserable wages or no compensation at all. Some of the countries mentioned in the report are Brazil, India, Mexico, Nepal, and the Philippines.

Sumptuous, high-pile, hand-knotted carpet, produced in Nepal by such children accounted for 60 percent of the country's export income in 1993. Nepal is one of the world's poorest countries, and it, along with other countries where **child labor** is prevalent, resents criticism from sources such as the Unions Federation.

They are suspicious of campaigns such as those by the Federation and others to eradicate countries' child labor and improve the lot of their work force. They consider these to be masked attempts to wipe out one of the few advantages they enjoy in the world economy: low wages. They point out also that in the poorest countries, most children have no other opportunities. School exists for only the wealthy, a tiny group. The owner of one Nepalese carpet factory says, "If a child is not employed, it will beg or lie in the street, or use drugs."[5]

child labor
Children below 16 years of age are forced to work in production and usually are given little or no formal education

PRC Workers' Paradise? Or Nightmare?

China's rulers say it is the former. Most labor union bodies outside China say it's the latter. They point to low wages, bad workplace conditions, widespread child and prison labor, and a spate of fatal industrial accidents.

China's only legal union, the All-China Federation of Trade Unions (ACFTU), is controlled by the Communist party, which bans all independent organizing. Many worker activists are in prison.

Labor leaders outside China who would like to improve the lot of Chinese workers fall into two camps. The isolate or anticontact lobby asserts that establishing ties with China and its ACFTU would legitimize Beijing's dismal human rights record. Those in favor of engagement believe it enables international unions to exert pressure for change within China.

Leaders in the isolate lobby include Chinese labor activists—those not in prison—whose efforts to liberalize Chinese labor relations were crushed in the 1989 Tiananmen Square massacre. They argue that human and trade-union rights have not improved since 1989 and say it's impossible to reform the ACFTU through dialogue. According to them, the ACFTU will change only when the PRC government changes.

Their stand is supported by labor leaders from Hong Kong, several EU countries, and the United States. However the American unions' position has splintered, and the head of the AFL–CIO's Asian arm acknowledges that over 100 U.S. local branches have contacts with the ACFTU, and several have visited China.

On the engagement side are representatives from Japan, Germany, Italy, and Singapore. The Japanese cite their "special historical and cultural links" with China. The Singapore union is investing in China. The Germans' and Italians' position is, in effect, "we can't stand by and do nothing."[6]

Children and Chickens

Labor trainers for ICs in developing nations have found that the people learn industrial skills rapidly. More difficult is teaching new workers who come from farms and villages how to adjust socially and psychologically to factory life. Some of these workers must be taught not only job skills but also the concept of time. They are not accustomed to reporting to work at the same time and place each workday or to meeting production schedules. They must be introduced to factory teamwork and to an industrial hierarchy. Frequently, the company must compromise and not attempt to change customary farm and village practices too quickly and completely.

A Spanish company opened a factory in Guatemala, hired local people, and tried to operate as if it were in Europe. The Spanish management installed work hours and production routines and schedules that had worked efficiently in Spain. But in Guatemala, in its early stage of economic development, the procedures were nearly disastrous.

The people refused to work and became hostile. Guatemalan troops were necessary to protect the factory. Management at last considered local needs and compromised, and mutually satisfactory solutions were found.

The solutions included four-hour breaks between two daily work periods. During the breaks, the male employees took care of their farms and gardens and the female employees attended to household needs and cared for their children. As another part of the solution, the employees were willing to work Saturdays to make up production lost during the breaks.[7]

Through compromise and patience, European management, operating in a preindustrial setting, was able to achieve satisfactory production. It studied, negotiated, and adapted to local needs. The alternatives were low production or perhaps even a destroyed factory.

JOB CREATION

Differing Unemployment Rates

In 1994, the OECD published a "Jobs Study" and, later in the year, a 500-page background analysis that offer excellent summaries of the ways in which employment in western Europe has been affected by competition from low-wage countries and technological change. The OECD concludes that European labor market rigidities have kept unemployment high, blaming minimum wages, generous unemployment benefits, and restrictive employment protection laws.

A later report by McKinsey, a management consultancy, contends that by focusing only on the labor market, the OECD study misses half the story. The McKinsey report's position is that product market barriers may be even more important than labor market rigidities in explaining why western Europe has high unemployment.

During the 1980s, America created many more jobs in services than western Europe did. For every 1,000 people of working age, America created 51 jobs (net of job losses) in private services, three times more than did France or Germany.

So Who Wants to Flip Hamburger?   Contrary to popular belief, the new American jobs were not mainly low-paying jobs of the hamburger-flipping variety. America created proportionately twice as many high-skilled jobs as did France and Germany. Indeed, four-fifths of all new jobs created in America were in professional, technical, administrative, or management categories.

Replacing Disappearing Jobs.   In a healthy economy, that is, free of government interference, the structure of jobs is constantly evolving; declining in some industries, expanding in others. If the economy works efficiently, new job creation should offset job losses.

But government interference, whether in the labor market, the capital market, or the product market, will block the expansion of jobs in new industries or products. McKinsey concludes that restrictive government regulations in product markets are often more important than those in the labor markets in explaining differences between Europe and America in job creation. Capital market barriers bear the least blame.

Ugly Heads of Government Interference.   Western Europe is riddled with product market barriers supposedly designed to preserve existing jobs or to protect the environment. Take retailing, which accounts for an average of 10 percent of all jobs in rich economies. In America, this has been a huge job creator; by contrast, employment in French retailing has shrunk.

Zoning regulations, restrictions on operating hours, and other anticompetitive practices have stunted the growth of retailing across western Europe. One egregious example is France's *loi Royer,* which gives committees of local politicians and shop owners power to block opening of new, large stores. Germany and Italy also have strict zoning laws that are used to keep out new entrants. Restrictions on opening hours are another ploy to protect small retailers. In Germany, Sunday trading is banned, and on all but one Saturday each month, shops must close at 2 P.M.

Or look at banking. Increased competition in America in the 1980s eliminated many jobs in traditional banking, but it also spurred the creation of an even larger number of jobs in areas such as securities and mortgages. In the less competitive environment of western Europe, fewer jobs were lost, but net job creation was smaller than in America.

McKinsey and the OECD agree that wage inflexibility has played a big role in retailing and other businesses. Generous minimum wages and jobless benefits keep wages too high at the lower end of the pay spectrum, preventing the growth of lower-skilled jobs.[8]

Japan's Job Creation Record.   According to the McKinsey study, Japan's job creation also lagged behind the American performance, but by a smaller margin. Although the American service industries outshone Japan's, the study found Japan's manufacturing did well. But much of that was attributable to new plant and equipment investment, which has slowed. See the material presented earlier in this chapter about the demise of Japan's lifetime job culture.[9]

OECD's Job Creation Strategies.   The OECD came up with a 60-point strategy for putting people back to work. The eight broad headings are:

- To enhance the creation and diffusion of technological know-how.
- To increase working time flexibility.
- To nurture an entrepreneurial climate.
- To increase wage and labor cost flexibility.
- To reform employment security provisions.
- To expand and enhance active labor market policies.
- To improve labor force skills.
- To reform unemployment and related benefit systems.[10]

Unemployment rates as percentages of total labor forces in various countries are shown in Figure 18–1.

STAFFING

Finding the right people to manage an organization can be difficult under any circumstances, but it is especially difficult to find good managers of overseas operations. Such positions require more and different skills than do purely domestic executive jobs. The right persons need to be bicultural, with

FIGURE 18–1 Worldwide unemployment rates*

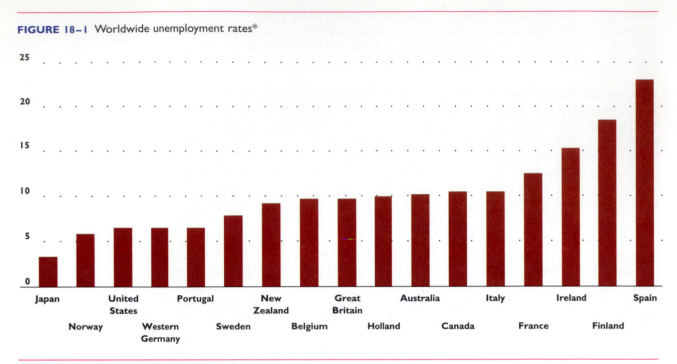

Because official definitions of unemployment differ from one country to another, national statistics on unemployment are not always comparable. However, the OECD estimates 17 of its members' unemployment rates by making use of a standardized definition. For most countries in the chart, these standardized figures do not differ significantly from the official national ones: the exceptions, however, are Belgium (where the OECD estimate is 9.7 percent compared with the official jobless rate of 13.5 percent for the same month), Western Germany (6.5 percent and 8.2 percent respectively) and Holland (9.9 percent and 7.5 percent). Spain, which has the highest jobless rate, has seen unemployment rise dramatically in recent years, from 16.0 percent to 23.4 percent since 1991.

*As percentage of total labor force.

Source: *The Economist,* May 7, 1994, p. 116.

knowledge of the business practices in the home country plus understanding of business practices and customs in the host country. And to truly understand a culture, any culture, it is necessary to speak the language of its people. Only with a good grasp of the language can one understand the subtleties and humor and know what is really going on in the host country.

The successful manager of a foreign affiliate must be able to operate efficiently in one culture and to explain operations in that culture to executives in another culture. Such managers exist, and they may be found in (1) the home country, (2) the host country, or (3) a third country.

Sources of Managers

Home Country.   Most ICs utilize citizens of their own countries, called **home country nationals,** in many foreign management and technical positions even though at first such personnel are usually not knowledgeable about the host country culture and language. Many such expatriates have adapted, learned the language, and become thoroughly accepted in the host country. Of course, it would not be necessary for a host country citizen to adapt, but for a variety of reasons, IC headquarters frequently needs or wants its own nationals in executive or technical positions abroad.

home country nationals
The country in which an IC has its worldwide headquarters is called the home country. Employees who are citizens of the home country are called home country nationals

Host Country Nationals Unavailable.   A foreign subsidiary often cannot find suitable host country personnel for management jobs, and in such instances, parent headquarters will send out its people to manage until local personnel can be found and trained. Those are full-time jobs, but other circumstances call for temporary help from headquarters. Labor negotiators and other specialists may be sent to troubleshoot such problems as product warranty, international contracts, taxes, accounting, or reporting. Teams may be sent from the home country to assist with new plant start-up, and they would probably stay until subsidiary personnel were trained to run and maintain the new facilities.

Training for Headquarters. Another reason for using home country citizens abroad is to broaden their experience in preparation for becoming high-level managers at headquarters. Firms with large parts of their earnings from international sources require top executives who have a worldwide perspective, business and political. It is difficult to impossible to acquire that sort of perspective without living and working abroad for a substantial time.

Headquarters' Representatives. Some firms, although their policy is to employ host country nationals in most positions, want at least one home country manager (commonly the general manager or the finance officer) in their foreign subsidiaries. If new technology for the subsidiary is involved, the parent company will probably station at least one of its technologically qualified experts at the subsidiary until its local personnel learn the technology. In this way, the home office can be confident that someone is immediately available to explain headquarters' policies and procedures, see that they are observed, and interpret what is happening locally to the IC's management. Positions that an IC must take or demands that it must make are sometimes not popular with a host government. It can seem unpatriotic for a host country national to do such things, whereas the host government can understand, and sometimes accept, such positions or demands from a foreigner.

> One of the authors remembers the relief expressed by the Argentinean executives of an Argentine subsidiary of an American IC because an American manager was present to press the Argentine government for what seemed to be unusually extensive payment guarantees. The contract was for a product partly manufactured and assembled in Argentina but mostly manufactured in the United States and imported into Argentina from the United States. The Argentinean executives feared that the very specific and high-level payment guarantees would antagonize government officials. The subsidiary was an Argentine company, subject to that country's laws and dependent in part on business from government departments and government-owned companies. Its managers were residents and would stay in Argentina, while the American was there only until the signing of this contract and the guarantees. After he flew away, the local people could blame him and the American parent IC, thus deflecting anger and resentment from themselves.

Host Country. When **host country nationals** are employed, there is no problem of their being unfamiliar with local customs, culture, and language. Furthermore, the first costs of employing them are generally lower (as compared to the costs of employing home country nationals), although considerable training costs are sometimes necessary. If there is a strong feeling of nationalism in the host country, having nationals as managers can make the subsidiary seem less foreign.

The government development plans and laws of some countries demand that employment in all sectors and at all levels reflects the racial composition of the society. In other words, more skilled and managerial slots must be given to the local people. If foreign-owned firms in Indonesia fail to hire enough *pribumi* (indigenous Indonesians), the firms are likely to encounter difficulties

host country nationals
Subsidiaries within the IC family of companies often are located in countries other than the home country. They are called host countries, and employee citizens of the host countries are called host country nationals

with reentry permits for foreign employees as well as with other government licenses and permits that they need. Bribery requests have been known to increase until more pribumi were hired and promoted. Malaysia threatens to revoke the operating licenses of foreign-owned firms that fail to have a satisfactory number of *bumiputra* (indigenous Malays) in sufficiently elevated jobs.[11]

A disadvantage of hiring local managers is that they are often unfamiliar with the home country of the IC and with its policies and practices. Differences in attitudes and values, as discussed in Chapter 9, can cause them to act in ways that surprise or displease headquarters. Also, local managers may create their own upward immobility if, because of strong cultural or family ties, they are reluctant to accept promotions that would require them to leave the country to work at parent headquarters or at another subsidiary.

A new problem has developed for foreign-owned companies that hire and train local, host country people. The best of these people may be pirated away by local firms or other IC subsidiaries, as local executive recruiters are constantly on the lookout to make raids.[12]

Finally, there can be a conflict of loyalty between the host country and the employer. For example, the host country national may give preference to a local supplier even though imported products may be less expensive or of better quality. Local managers might oppose headquarters' requests to set low transfer prices in order to lower taxes payable to the host government.

third country nationals
An employee who is a citizen of neither the home nor host country

Third Country.   The disadvantages often encountered when using employees from the home or host countries can sometimes be avoided by sending **third country nationals** to fill management posts. A Chilean going to Argentina would have little cultural or language difficulty, but IC headquarters should be careful not to rely too heavily on similarities in language as a guide to similarities in other aspects of the cultures. Mexicans, for example, would have to make considerable adjustments if they were transferred to Argentina, and they would find a move to Spain even more difficult. This is because the Mexican culture is far less European than that of either Argentina or Chile. Although the latter two cultures are certainly not identical, they do have many similarities. A fair generalization is that after an executive has adapted once to a new culture and language, a second or succeeding adaptation is easier.

An employer should not count on cost savings in using third country nationals. Although they may come from countries where salary scales are lower, in such countries as Brazil and most of the nations of northwestern Europe, salaries may be higher than American companies are paying at comparable position levels. Furthermore, many multinationals give international status* to both home country nationals and third country nationals, who then receive the same perquisites and compensation packages for the same job.

Selection and Training

The selection and training of managers varies somewhat, depending on whether the candidate is from the home country, the host country, or a third country.

Home Country.   Relatively few recent college graduates are hired for the express purpose of being sent overseas. Usually they spend a number of years in the domestic (parent) company, and they may get into the company's

---

*International status is discussed later in this chapter.

international operations by design and persistence, by luck, or by a combination of those elements. They may first be assigned to the international division at the firm's headquarters, where they handle problems submitted by foreign affiliates and meet visiting overseas personnel.

If the company feels that it will likely send home country employees abroad, it will frequently encourage them to study the language and culture of the country to which they are going. Such employees will probably be sent on short trips abroad to handle special assignments and to be exposed to foreign surroundings. Newly hired home country nationals with prior overseas experience may undergo similar but shorter training periods.[13]

It is increasingly possible for American ICs to supplement their in-house training for overseas work with courses in American business schools. In recognition of the growing importance of international business, those schools are expanding the number and scope of international business courses they offer. In addition, a number of university-level business schools are now operating in other countries.[14]

One large problem that has plagued employers is caused by the families of executives transferred overseas. Even though the employee may adapt to and enjoy the foreign experience, the family may not, and an unhappy family may sour the employee on the job or split up the marriage. In either event, the company may have to ship the family back home at great expense—seldom less than $25,000. Consequently, many companies try to assess whether the executive's family can adapt to the foreign ambience before assigning the executive abroad.

Host Country. The same general criteria for selecting home country employees apply to host country nationals. Usually, however, the training of host country nationals will differ from that of home country nationals in that host country nationals are more likely to lack knowledge of advanced business techniques and of the company.

Host Country Nationals Hired in the Home Country. Many multinationals try to solve the business technique problem by hiring host country students on their graduation from home country business schools. After being hired, these new employees are usually sent to IC headquarters to receive indoctrination in the firm's policies and procedures as well as on-the-job training in a specific function, such as finance, marketing, or production.

Host Country Nationals Hired in the Host Country. Because the number of host country citizens graduating from home country universities is limited, multinationals must also recruit locally for their management positions. To impart knowledge of business techniques, the company may do one or more things. It may set up in-house training programs in the host country subsidiary, or it may utilize business courses in the host country's universities. The IC may also send new employees to home country business schools or to parent company training programs. In addition, employees who show promise will be sent repeatedly to the parent company headquarters, divisions, and other subsidiaries to observe the various enterprise operations and meet the other executives with whom they will be communicating during their careers. Such visits are also learning experiences for the home office and the other subsidiaries.

Third Country. Hiring personnel who are citizens of neither the home country nor the host country is often advantageous. Third country nationals may accept lower wages and benefits than will employees from the home country, and they may come from a culture similar to that of the host country. In addition, they may have worked for another unit of the IC and thus be familiar with its policies, procedures, and people.

The use of third country nationals has become particularly prevalent in the LDCs because of shortages of literate, not to mention skilled, locals. It can be an advantage to get someone already residing in the country who has necessary work permits and knowledge of local languages and customs.

Host Country Attitudes. If the host government emphasizes employment of its own citizens, third country nationals will be no more welcome than home country people. Actually, third country nationals could face an additional obstacle in obtaining necessary work permits. For example, the host government can understand that the German parent company of a subsidiary would want some German executives to look after its interest in the host country. It may be harder to convince the government that a third country native is any better for the parent than a local executive would be.

Generalizations Difficult. We must be careful with generalizations about third country personnel, partly because people achieve that status in different ways. They may be foreigners hired in the home country and sent to a host country subsidiary either because they have had previous experience there or because that country's culture is similar to their own. Third country nationals may have originally been home country personnel who were sent abroad and became dissatisfied with the job but not with the host country. After leaving the firm that sent them abroad, they take positions with subsidiaries of multinationals from different home countries. Another way in which third country nationals can be created is by promotion within an IC. For instance, if a Spanish executive of the Spanish subsidiary of an Italian multinational is promoted to be general manager of the Italian firm's Colombian subsidiary, the Spanish executive is then a third country national.

geocentric
As used here, related to hiring and promoting employees on the basis of ability and experience without considering race or citizenship

As multinationals increasingly take the **geocentric** view toward promoting (according to ability and not nationality), we can be certain to see greater use of third country nationals. This development will be accelerated as more and more executives of all nationalities gain experience outside their native lands. Another, and growing, source for third country nationals is the heterogeneous body of international agencies. As indicated in Chapter 4, these agencies deal with virtually every field of human endeavor, and all member-countries send their nationals as representatives to the headquarters and branch office cities all over the world. Many of those people become available to, or can be hired away by, international companies.

Language Training. As stated at the beginning of this chapter, American companies are taking more seriously the language abilities of their employees. But neither they nor most Australian, British, Canadian, and New Zealand firms are sufficiently serious. The English speakers are stuck in a **language trap**.

language trap
A situation in which a person doing international business can speak only his or her home language

The English language has become the *lingua franca* of the world; it is everybody's second language. The high ground in the modern world is held by people who speak an international language well and have an impenetrable language of their own. Hungary went its own way within the Soviet empire since few Russians had a clue what the Hungarian dissidents were saying. Israel knows what the Arabs are planning in Arabic; most Arabs are flummoxed by Hebrew. The Japanese are wonderfully protected by their language as they move abroad selling and investing with particular gusto in the English-speaking world.

The French have at long last got the message. Suddenly, waiters in obscure bistros insist on speaking English. They are taking the battle to the enemy. Success is not persuading others to speak your language; it is persuading them that it is quite unnecessary to try.

When trying to sell to potential customers, it is much better to speak their language. As English speakers try to sell abroad, it is far more likely their customers will speak English than that the English speakers will be able speak the customers' language. Customers can then hide behind their language during negotiations.

Women

The subject of staffing the executive offices of modern companies is not completely covered without a look at the growing role of women. About half of the students in American business schools are now women; they have moved into the managements of banks, businesses, and government agencies and have been at least as successful as their male counterparts. Old-girl networks are now in place alongside the old-boy networks, providing role models and helping younger female managers.[15]

Some assistance is available for women in international business. During 1994, a conference was held in San Antonio, Texas, entitled "U.S.–Latin American Trade and Women: Breaking Trade and Gender Barriers." It was sponsored by Women in International Trade (WIT), a Washington-based organization with 3,000 members and 18 chapters nationally.

Adrienne Braumiller, a customs lawyer in Dallas and a member of WIT, says it is still difficult for Latin American businessmen to deal with women in positions of authority or responsibility. She says they "are very uncomfortable with us."[16]

That sort of attitude may be part of the reason that the percentage of women in their prime childbearing years who are in the labor force topped out in 1989, ending—for now anyway—a rapid quarter-century rise. Another part of the reason, according to Williams College economist Diane Macunovich, is that men now in their twenties are part of a small generation and enjoy a scarcity

Female executives are accepting foreign positions more frequently.

Women and Foreign Postings

When Carla Hills was first nominated for her job as U.S. trade representative, some people had doubts.

Philip Grub, a George Washington University professor of multinational management, told a conference that among concerns about Hills herself, he questioned the cultural sensitivity of sending a woman to negotiate with the Japanese. Senator Steven Symms wondered whether she would appear as rigorous as the "tough men, warriors" who preceded her.

Such anxieties go to the heart of the debate over who should be doing America's business overseas. In choosing their emissaries, companies are often daunted by stories of submissive Asian wives, racist remarks by Japanese leaders, and laws barring Saudi women from driving. The result is that women and minorities, although making small gains, are even rarer among managers abroad than they are at home.

But the few women and minority executives who have worked overseas say many companies are clinging to false notions about other cultures. Although the executives acknowledge that hurdles exist, they say misguided attitudes leave companies unreasonably pessimistic about overcoming them.

"It's a classic case of projection," says Lennie Copeland, a producer at Copeland Griggs Productions, Inc., in San Francisco, which makes films on cultural issues in business. "The American company has a problem accepting women, so they assume it's going to be worse overseas."

Women account for only 5 percent of American expatriate managers, although many more are sent on brief assignments, according to a survey by Moran, Stahl & Boyer, Inc., a New York consulting firm. Of the companies polled, 80 percent said there were disadvantages to sending women overseas.

"Clients refuse to do business with female representatives," one company told Moran. Another explained: "The desired expatriate is a 30-ish married man with preschool-age children. This is to project our image as a conservative institution with

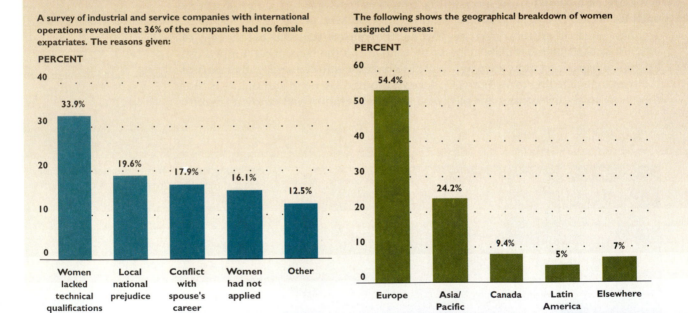

A survey of industrial and service companies with international operations revealed that 36% of the companies had no female expatriates. The reasons given:

PERCENT: Women lacked technical qualifications 33.9%, Local national prejudice 19.6%, Conflict with spouse's career 17.9%, Women had not applied 16.1%, Other 12.5%

The following shows the geographical breakdown of women assigned overseas:

PERCENT: Europe 54.4%, Asia/Pacific 24.2%, Canada 9.4%, Latin America 5%, Elsewhere 7%

glass ceiling
An unwritten and therefore invisible, but nevertheless real, ceiling in an organization's executive hierarchy above which females are rarely promoted.

premium in the job market. Hence, their wages have been rising so that a wife's income is no longer needed to achieve their desired standard of living.[17]

Still another reason for women to opt out of the executive rat race is referred to as the **glass ceiling**. Organizations could incur serious legal and public relations difficulties if they wrote or otherwise expressed levels in their executive hierarchy above which women would not be promoted. Nevertheless, very small percentages of women rise to CEO levels or even close to them.

good moral fiber. . . . Many of our potential female expatriates are single, and a swinging single is not the right image."

Even some executives with international experience agree that there are practical limits. They cite Saudi Arabia and Pakistan, for example, as places where it doesn't make sense to send a woman.

But Stephen J. Kobrin, a professor of international management at the University of Pennsylvania's Wharton School, contends that many cautionary arguments echo those once made by corporations against hiring women at home. "If you follow this to its logical conclusion," he says, "you're back in 1954."

Women executives who have worked abroad also complain that companies often fail to differentiate among nations in given parts of the world—ruling out, say, all of Asia for women. "People lump all those countries together," says Anna Ball, president of Ball Seed Company in West Chicago, Illinois. Ball adds that while she works comfortably in Japan, she finds South Korea and especially Taiwan much more accepting of businesswomen.

Conversely, many Americans assume England is the closest thing to home outside North America (the Moran survey showed that almost 24 percent of the female expatriates were posted there). But Americans find that many British men are uncomfortable with female managers.

Robert Petzinger, managing director of AT&T's international communications services in London, recently chose an American woman to head a sales force there. He says five of the men she will manage immediately let him know they thought he had "made the wrong choice." Petzinger adds that he has told the woman she faces a challenge.

Even where a culture puts several restraints on its own women, outsiders may be treated differently, notes Nancy Adler, associate professor at McGill University in Montreal. "You are seen as a foreigner first and then as a woman," she says. "The best predictor of success isn't how they treat their own women, but how they treat other Americans."

Pat Burns, director of industrial development for Madison Public Relations Group, Inc., in Washington, DC, has been doing business in northern Africa and the Mideast since the mid-1970s. On one occasion in Sudan, she was invited into the home of a businessman, who brought her a cushion, served her food, and washed her arms with rose water after the meal—all things a man normally would never do for a woman. After the meeting, Burns asked her local agent how the man could have violated accepted rules of conduct. "Oh, it's no problem," she recalls being told. "Women do not do business, therefore, you are not a woman."

Ironically, many women feel they have an advantage in business overseas for the same reason they have trouble in business at home: their different upbringing. Consultants say women are generally more patient than men and more interested in creating harmony and consensus.

"That's considered wimpy here," says Marlene L. Rossman, a New York marketing consultant, "and considered very appropriate overseas."

As companies address the "glass ceiling" problem at home, more are pushing the boundaries abroad as well. AT&T, for example, last year commissioned a 22-country study by Moran to evaluate how women are received in various places and what barriers they might face. A few of the findings are illustrative: Chinese businessmen seem less threatened by American women than by American men; there is less *machismo* in Argentina than in other Latin countries.

Daniel McCabe, manager of human resources for AT&T's international communications services, says he wanted to have a "defensible study behind us" when encouraging managers to send women farther afield.

Amid such efforts, though, one of the hardest parts of an overseas assignment for women remains: in showing respect and understanding for the local culture, they may have to tolerate attitudes they wouldn't brook at home. Burns says she has gone out of her way in the Mideast to express respect for a business partner's wife or daughter, or to praise women executives and officials. Still, she says, when a Saudi general recently invited her to visit and asked whether she minded using the women's entrance, she replied, "Not at all."

Source: Jolie Solomon, *The Wall Street Journal*, June 2, 1989, p. B1.

The reason for that, it is alleged, is that many organizations put a real but invisible—therefore "glass"—ceiling, on how high females can be promoted.

The women remaining in management are being transferred by their employers more often, and their husbands are more frequently the trailing spouses who move with their wives. In 1994, the percentage of male trailing spouses was 15.7 percent, up from 10.9 percent in 1993. More women also are being transferred abroad. Ten percent of foreign assignments were taken by women in 1993, up from 5 percent the year before.[18]

As was indicated in Chapter 12, attitudes toward and treatment of women differ vastly from one culture or religion to another. A review of that material in Chapter 12 could be helpful at this point.

Résumés Can Mislead

The résumés of most job applicants are probably reasonably accurate, although people are taught how to put their best foot forward and present themselves in the best light. Sometimes that light distorts reality.

The case of Friedrich von Braun is a good example. He was the managing director of Commodity Fundsters, a British company that was in financial difficulty.

Von Braun said that his claim to being the third son of a German baron was based on tales his mother had told him. He could not explain why he was brought up in Warrington, England, and was known to the locals as Fred.

His claim to have been educated at Eton was based on a one-day trip to Windsor in the summer of 1955; he said he had learned a lot about history at that time. He did spend two weeks at Oxford—in a squat on the Iffley Road.

As for his listed hobbies (opera and observing art), he admitted that his work had allowed him no time for either in the past 18 years.

He worked not for the famous banking firm Morgan Stanley, as listed in his résumé, but for Stanley Morgan, a Welsh farmer. His "brilliant" banking career was not with the American bank First Interstate but with a Panamanian financial company known to its liquidators as First Into Straits.

Von Braun said that his career details were misleading because of some "insignificant" typographical errors. He maintained that the mistakes were irrelevant to his ability to look after the interests of "wise" investors who entrusted their money to him.

People's Republic of China Different

An American banker sitting in his cramped hotel office in Beijing said, "Foreigners coming to China had better be prepared for the bleakness of Chinese life." China is an especially tough assignment for Western managers; for one thing, Western-style housing is unavailable, so most Western managers must spend their entire stays in a hotel room.

A study was made of the assets that a Westerner needed to succeed in China. Knowledge of Chinese business customs, negotiating style, and social practices ranked as most important, but not much more so than Chinese language, politics, and culture.

One manager quoted in the study remarked on "a general sense of uncertainty" in his business dealings. He noted the "vagueness of the Chinese system. You think something will be a problem, and it's not, and vice versa." Another stressed that Westerners in China should understand that despite the recent economic reforms, "communism and the bureaucratic system are number one."[19]

Selection Dos and Don'ts

Executives who should know better sometimes assume that all nationalities work within a framework of common cultures and business practices. Instant communication of information, supersonic travel, and the emergence of international financial institutions have created a global economy.

Yet, this economic interdependence does not translate into a common "business culture." Business standards and practices reflect the cultures in which they are rooted. Their nuances vary widely by continent, by country, and even by region.

An executive with no cross-cultural experience can, regardless of other professional credentials, unwittingly wreak havoc with corporate plans abroad. The ability of a company to succeed in another country rests heavily on the managers' abilities to function in that country's culture. An executive search firm has drawn up a checklist of dos and don'ts in selecting executives for foreign operations.

- Do promote from within. All things being equal, selecting a known employee reduces risk. The employee knows the company and the company knows the employee's strengths and weaknesses. The weaknesses of a new person may not be evident at first.

- Don't promote an insider if the outsider is clearly better qualified. "John's been doing a good job in New York, and he's always liked London" is not good enough. It can be a costly approach.

- Don't be blinded by language fluency. Just because a candidate is fluent in the host country's language does not mean he or she is the best person for the job. Unless your business is the local Berlitz franchise, the candidate must have the requisite technical and managerial skills.

- Do assess the total person. Functional skills, language proficiency, and knowledge of the international business environment are all important. With regard to international business savvy, third-country nationals are sometimes better qualified than people born in the host country who have not lived and worked abroad. It has been noted that Scandinavians, Dutch, and Swiss are disproportionately represented in international business management positions. They come from small countries with limited markets, so their education and business experience have been geared to the outside world. As a group, these executives have an outlook that is more cosmopolitan than nationalistic.[20]

Although there is no denying fundamental differences in cultures, some say good managers share the same skills worldwide. "The skills are the same," says Jane Wilson of Clark Wilson Publishing, which publishes materials that help companies rate managers' skills in clarifying and communicating goals, planning, problem solving, giving feedback, and tending to details. The 3M Company agrees. It rates its managers around the world on a single scale that seeks to gauge what level of responsibility they can handle. They can then be assigned where needed without regard to nationality. For example, in 1991, two of 3M's managers who are Italian were tapped to fill senior slots, one in the United States and the other in Japan.[21]

COMPENSATION

Establishing a compensation plan that is equitable, consistent, and yet does not overcompensate the overseas executive is a challenging, complex task. The method favored by the majority of American ICs has been to pay a base salary equal to that paid to a domestic counterpart and then, in the belief that no one should be worse off for accepting foreign employment, to add a variety of allowances and bonuses.

Salaries

The practice of paying home country nationals the same salaries as their domestic counterparts permits worldwide consistency for this part of the compensation package. Because of the increasing use of third country nationals, those personnel are generally treated in the same way.

Some firms carry the equal-pay-for-equal-work concept one step further and pay the same base salaries to host country nationals. In countries that legislate yearly bonuses and family allowances for their citizens, a local national may receive what appears to be a higher salary than is paid the **expatriate,** although companies usually make extra payments to prevent expatriates from falling behind in this regard. In Great Britain, it is the practice to pay executives relatively lower salaries and to provide them with expensive perquisites, such as chauffeured automobiles, housing, or club memberships. A number of American companies follow British practices in compensating their executives working in Britain.

expatriate
A person living outside of his or her country of citizenship

Allowances

Allowances are payments made to compensate expatriates for the extra costs they must incur to live as well abroad as they did in the home country. The most common allowances are for housing, cost of living, tax differentials, education, and moving.

allowances
Employee compensation payments added to base salaries because of higher expenses encountered when living abroad

Housing Allowances.   Housing allowances are designed to permit executives to live in houses as good as those they had at home. Typically, the firm will pay all of the rent that is in excess of 15 percent of the executive's salary.

Cost-of-Living Allowances.   Cost-of-living allowances are based on the differences in the prices paid for food, utilities, transportation, entertainment, clothing, personal services, and medical expenses overseas as compared to the prices paid for these items in the headquarters' city. Many ICs use the U.S. Department of State index, which is based on the cost of these items in Washington, DC, but have found it is not altogether satisfactory. For one thing, critics claim this index is not adjusted often enough to account for either the rapid inflation in some countries or the changes in relative currency values. Another objection is that the index does not include many cities in which the firm operates. As a result, many companies take their own surveys or use data from the United Nations, the World Bank, the International Monetary Fund, or private consulting firms. Figures and comparisons on costs of living, prices, and wages can also be found in private publications (see Figure 18–2).

Allowances for Tax Differentials.   ICs pay tax differentials when the host country taxes are higher than the taxes that the expatriates would pay on the same compensation and consumption at home. The objective is to ensure that expatriates will not have less after-tax take-home pay in the host country than they would at home. This can create a considerable extra financial burden on an American parent company because, among other things, the U.S. Internal Revenue Code treats tax allowances as additional taxable income. There are other tax disincentives for Americans to work abroad.*

Education Allowances.   Expatriates are naturally concerned that their children receive educations at least equal to those they would get in their home countries, and many want their children taught in their native language. Primary and secondary schools with teachers from most industrialized home

---

*For more on this subject and other effects of U.S. laws on American ICs, see the taxation section of Chapter 11.

FIGURE 18–2 Worldwide cost-of-living levels*

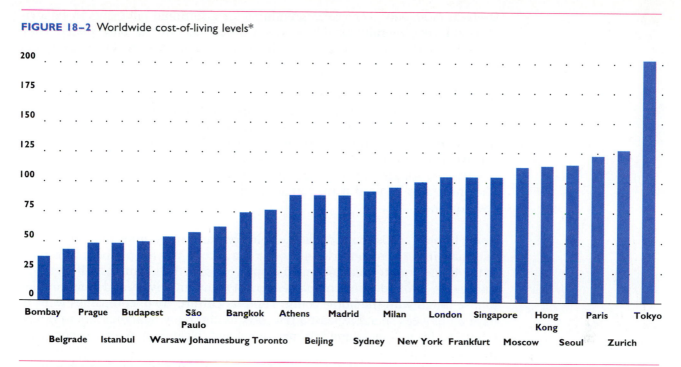

The chart summarizes the latest survey of the cost of living in the world's biggest cities by the Economist Intelligence Unit (EIU). Tokyo is the most expensive place for expatriates to live. Prices in the Japanese capital are more than double those in New York. Western Europe is also relatively pricey—lunch in Zurich or Paris will cost over 20 percent more than in New York. Moscow is becoming an ever more expensive place to live: last year the Russian capital was already 4 percent more expensive than New York; this year the difference is 10 percent. Moscow is now about as expensive as Hong Kong. The cost-conscious would do well to stay in Central Europe: life in Prague is half as expensive as in New York.

*Spring 1994; New York = 100.

Source: *The Economist,* June 25, 1994, p. 108.

countries are available in many cities around the world, but these are private schools and therefore charge tuition. ICs either pay the tuition or, if there are enough expatriate children, will operate their own schools. For decades, petroleum companies in the Mideast and Venezuela have maintained schools for their employees' children.

Moving and Orientation Allowances.   Companies generally pay the total costs of transferring their employees overseas. These include transporting the family, moving household effects, and maintaining the family in a hotel on a full expense account until the household effects arrive. Some firms find it less expensive to send the household effects by air rather than by ship because the reduction in hotel expenses more than compensates for the higher cost of airfreight. It has also been found that moving into a house sooner raises the employee's morale.

Companies may also pay for some orientation of the employees and their families. Companies frequently pay for language instruction, and some will provide the family with guidance on the intricacies of everyday living, such as shopping, hiring domestic help, and sending children to school.

Bonuses

Bonuses (or premiums), unlike allowances, are paid by firms in recognition that expatriates and their families undergo some hardships and inconveniences and make sacrifices while living abroad. Bonuses include overseas premiums, contract termination payments, and home leave reimbursement.

bonuses
Expatriate employee compensation payments in addition to base salaries and allowances because of hardship, inconvenience, or danger

Overseas Premiums.   Overseas premiums are additional payments to expatriates and are generally established as a percentage of the base salary. They range from 10 to 25 percent. If the living conditions are extremely disagreeable, the company may pay larger premiums for hardship posts.

Contract Termination Payments.   These payments are made as inducements for employees to stay on their jobs and work out the periods of their overseas contracts. The payments are made at the end of the contract periods only if the employees have worked out their contracts. Such bonuses are used in the construction and petroleum industries or by other firms that have contracts requiring work abroad for a specific period of time or for a specific project. They may also be used if the foreign post is a hardship or not a particularly desirable one.

Home Leave.[22]   ICs that post home country—and sometimes third country—nationals in foreign countries make it a practice to pay for periodic trips back to the home country made by such employees and their families. The reasons for this are twofold. One, companies do not want employees and their families to lose touch with the home country and its culture. Two, companies want to have employees spend at least a few days at company headquarters to renew relationships with headquarters' personnel and to catch up with new company policies and practices.

Some firms grant three-month home leaves after an employee has been abroad about three years, but it is a more common practice to give two to four weeks' leave each year. All transportation costs are paid to and from the executive's hometown, and all expenses are paid during the executive's stay at company headquarters.

Compensation Packages Can Be Complicated

compensation packages
For expatriate employees: can incorporate many types of payments or reimbursements and must take into consideration exchange rates and inflation

One might think from the discussion to this point that **compensation packages,** while costly—the extras may total 50 percent or more of the base salary—are fairly straightforward in their calculation. Nothing could be further from the truth.

What Percentage?   All allowances and a percentage of the base salary are usually paid in the host country currency. What should this percentage be? In practice, it varies from 65 to 75 percent, with the remainder being banked wherever the employee wishes. One reason for these practices is to decrease the local portion of the salary, thereby lowering host country income taxes and giving the appearance to government authorities and local employees that there is less difference between the salaries of local and foreign employees than is actually the case. Another reason is that expatriate employees have various expenses that must be paid in home country currency. Such expenses include professional society memberships, purchases during home leave, or tuition and other costs for children in home country universities.

What Exchange Rate?   Inasmuch as most of the expatriate's compensation is usually denominated in the host country currency but established in terms of the home country currency to achieve comparable compensation throughout the enterprise, a currency exchange rate must be chosen. In countries whose currencies are freely convertible into other currencies, this presents no serious problem, although the experienced expatriate will argue that an exchange rate covers only international transactions and may not present a true purchasing power parity between the local and home country currencies. For instance, such items as bread and milk are rarely traded internationally, and living costs and inflation rates may be much higher in the host country than in the home country. Multinationals attempt to compensate for such differences in the cost-of-living allowances.

More difficult problems must be solved in countries that have exchange controls and nonconvertible currencies. Without exception, those currencies are overvalued at the official rate, and if the firm uses that rate, its expatriate employees are certain to be shortchanged. Reference may be made to the free market rate for the host country currency in free currency markets in, for example, the United States or Switzerland, or to the black market rate in the host country; but these do not give the final answers. In the end, all companies must pay their expatriate employees enough to enable them to live as well as others who have similar positions in other firms, regardless of how the amount is calculated.

A common compensation component at many American companies is a stock plan that provides employees opportunities to acquire the company's stock on favorable terms. Such programs are designed to increase loyalty and productivity, but they sometimes run into problems outside the United States.

Share ownership is unknown or restricted in numerous countries. Pepsi-Co's vice president of compensation and benefits says, "We had to develop a customized approach in every country we operate in." Du Pont discovered it could not give stock options in 25 of 53 nations, primarily because those countries' laws ban or limit ownership of foreign shares. Reader's Digest Association and Colgate-Palmolive are designing global stock programs country by country.[23]

Compensation of Third Country Nationals

Although some companies have different compensation plans for third country nationals, there is a trend toward treating them the same as home country expatriates. In either event, there are areas in which problems can arise. One of these areas is the calculation of income tax differentials when an American expatriate is compared with an expatriate from another country. This results from the unique American government practices of taxing U.S. citizens even though they live and work abroad and of treating tax differential payments made to those citizens as additional taxable income. No other major country taxes its nationals in those ways.

Another possible problem area is the home leave bonus. The two purposes of home leave are to prevent expatriates from losing touch with their native cultures and to have them visit IC headquarters. A third country national must visit two countries instead of only one to achieve both purposes, and the additional costs can be substantial. Compare the cost of sending an Australian employee home from Mexico with that required to send an American from Mexico to Dallas.

Regardless of problems, the use of third country nationals is growing in popularity. As businesses race to enlarge their ranks of qualified international managers, third country nationals are in greater demand. They often win jobs because they speak several languages and know an industry or country well.

The numbers of third country nationals employed as executives by ICs continue to grow, and the possible combinations of nationalities and host countries are virtually limitless. For example, the head of Raychem's Italian subsidiary is French, the sales manager in France is Belgian, and the head of the Spanish unit is Cuban.[24]

International Status

In all of this discussion, we have been describing compensation for expatriates who have been granted **international status.** Merely being from another

international status
Entitles the expatriate employee to all the allowances and bonuses applicable to the place of residence and employment

Courtesy of Daily & Associates

country does not automatically qualify an employee for all of the benefits we have mentioned. A subsidiary may hire home country nationals or third country nationals and pay them the same as it pays host country employees. However, managements have found that although an American, for example, may agree initially to take a job and be paid on the local scale, sooner or later bad feeling and friction will develop as that person sees fellow Americans enjoying international status perquisites to which he or she is not entitled.

Sometimes, firms promote host country employees to international status even without transferring them abroad. This is a means of rewarding valuable people and of preventing them from leaving the company for better jobs elsewhere.

So international status means being paid some or all the allowances and bonuses we have discussed, and there can be other sorts of payments as individual circumstances and people's imaginations combine to create them. The Philippine Airlines ad shows two sleeping men. The one in the bottom picture is clearly the one with international status. The executives' compensation package is sufficiently important and complicated to have become a specialization in the personnel management field; at one firm, the title is "International Employee Benefits Consultant."[25]

Help is available from outside the IC. For one example, Ernst & Young publishes an International Series, pamphlets advising about transfer to spec-

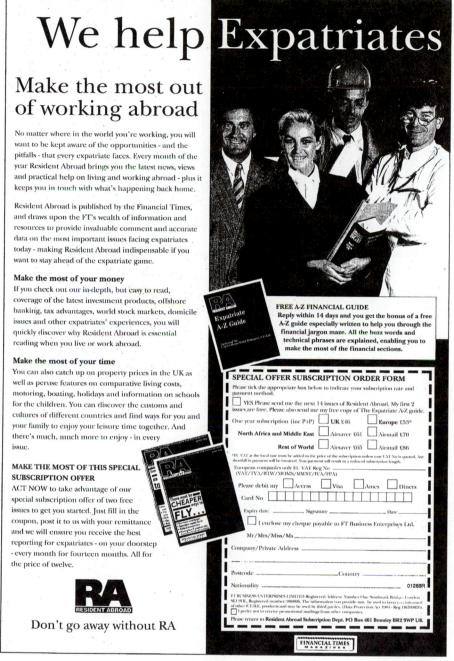

Source: *Financial Times*, August 20–21, 1994, p. 4.

ific countries.[26] Another sort of help is illustrated by the advertisement "We Help Expatriates" shown in Figure 18–3.

Comparisons of net and gross pay for hourly wage earners in several countries can be seen in Figure 18–4. Figure 18–5 shows the numbers for chief executive officers (CEOs) of companies based in 12 countries. Note that the CEOs of U.S.-based companies do far better than those of companies based in other industrial countries. But surprisingly, America's lead was limited to CEO pay. The pay of other American company managers was comparable to that of most others.

FIGURE 18–3
Assistance for executives abroad

FIGURE 18–4

Comparison in international hourly earnings (taxes and Social Security in percent of gross income)*

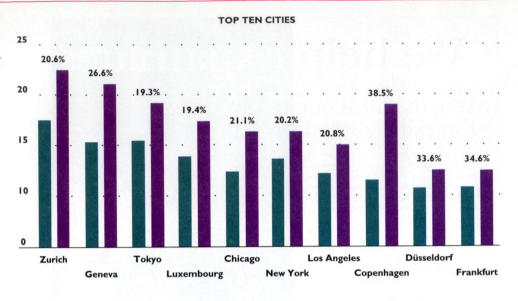

NET INCOME (U.S. $)   GROSS INCOME (U.S. $)

*Actual hourly wages in 12 occupations after taking into account working time, holidays, and vacations. Weighted by occupation.

Source: Richard Donkin, "Comparison in International Earnings," *Financial Times*, September 16, 1994, p. 1.

Perks

These originated in the perquisites of the medieval lords of the manor, whose workers paid parts of their profits or produce to the lords to be allowed to continue working. Today, perks are symbols of rank in the corporate hierarchy and are used to compensate executives while minimizing taxes. Among the most common perks are

Cars, which higher up the organization ladder come with chauffeurs.

Private pension plan.

Retirement payment.

Life insurance.

FIGURE 18–5 CEO total remuneration*

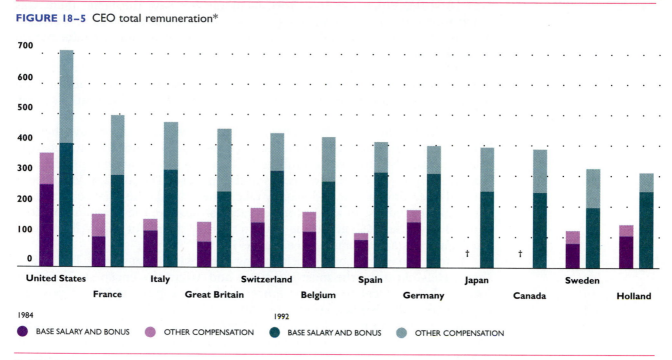

*In 1990 US$000s.
†Not available.

Source: "Nice Work." *The Economist,* December 10, 1994, p. 67.

Health insurance.

Company house or apartment.

Directorship of a foreign subsidiary.

Seminar holiday travel.

Club memberships.

Hidden slush fund (such funds are illegal, but some corporations are said to have them).

What's Important to You?

While working abroad as an executive of an American multinational, one of the authors had a colleague who was an American expatriate married to a French woman. They had raised a family in several countries where they had been assigned by the company. Together with some other cosmopolites, they devised a table of items deemed important to at least one of them in choosing a city for location of a company facility that employs foreigners.

The list included the usual items, such as cost of living, safety of personnel, medical facilities, housing, and schools. It also included such other items as availability of good wine at reasonable prices, quality of theater and whether it was live or cinema, number and type of one-star or better (*Michelin Guide*)* restaurants, type and accessibility of sports facilities for both participants and viewers, and shopping facilities for fashionable clothes.

The table of items was circulated informally throughout the firm's many locations, and many cities in its network were graded as to each item on a

---

*The *Michelin Guide* rates restaurants and hotels in France and neighboring countries.

1-to-10 scale. When the New York headquarters saw the table, there was much mirth and merriment; suggestions—perhaps not all of them serious—were made as to additional items about which they would like information when they visited the cities.

However, the mirth and merriment subsided as more and more executives being assigned or reassigned abroad used the table to demand better compensation packages. Some even refused transfers because of the ratings given a city.

Also important to employees may be the number of vacation days they are likely to get from country to country and comparisons of how much it costs to celebrate and then to treat a resulting hangover. As to vacation days, Europeans are well ahead of the Americans and Japanese. The average Japanese is entitled to 15 days a year and usually takes fewer, while the average American takes about 20 days. In the European vacation league, the Germans are tops with 40 days; the Irish are at the bottom with 27 days, but still well ahead of the Americans and Japanese (see Figure 18–6).

As to comparative costs of celebrating and treating hangovers, Table 18–1 shows Helsinki to be the most expensive and Milan the cheapest. The study gave a choice of celebratory beverages—scotch or gin—and three possible treatments—Alka-Seltzer, aspirin, or coffee.

Also of importance in decisions of where to locate an office are office rents and prices of items that employees might want to buy. Figure 18–7 gives office rents in 16 cities, while Table 18–2 compares prices of various items in 5 cities.

FIGURE 18–6 European holidays

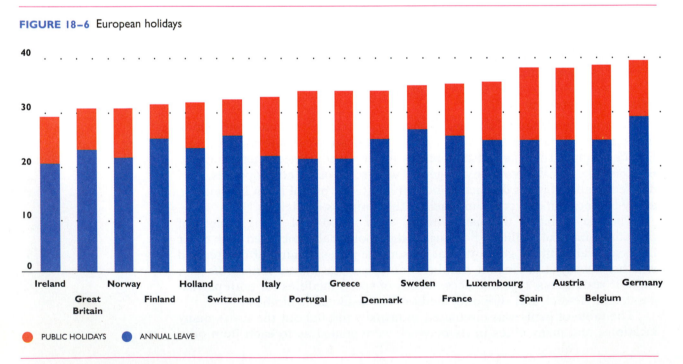

● PUBLIC HOLIDAYS   ● ANNUAL LEAVE

Source: *The Economist,* June 1, 1991, p. 97.

TABLE 18–1 The price of overindulgence around the world (in pounds sterling)

	75 cl. Scotch	75 cl. Gin	Average Indulgence Cost	12 Alka-Seltzers	100 Aspirins	16 oz. Coffee	Average Treatment Cost	Average Full Cost
Helsinki	30.83£	25.12£	27.98£	1.00£	3.66£	2.12£	2.26£	30.24£
Stockholm	30.09	22.47	26.28	0.77	2.99	2.07	1.94	28.22
Copenhagen	27.53	15.58	21.56	0.72	5.37	2.72	2.94	24.50
Singapore	22.87	18.89	20.88	1.20	4.62	2.60	2.81	23.69
Tokyo	18.51	11.65	15.08	—	9.71	6.04	7.88	22.96
Moscow	23.42	7.88	15.65	1.35	6.15	4.95	4.15	19.80
Sydney	17.11	10.14	13.63	1.22	3.21	3.37	2.60	16.23
Vienna	15.25	8.25	11.75	1.61	4.60	2.96	3.06	14.81
London	14.78	9.97	12.38	1.41	2.92	2.43	2.25	14.63
Cairo	14.25	10.90	12.58	0.23	1.96	3.56	1.92	14.50
Hong Kong	12.60	10.12	11.36	1.10	3.80	3.28	2.73	14.09
Amsterdam	11.97	9.02	10.50	1.36	7.42	1.69	3.49	13.99
Frankfurt	11.03	7.53	9.28	1.85	6.83	2.54	3.74	13.02
New York	11.22	9.83	10.53	1.03	3.42	2.32	2.26	12.79
Toronto	12.11	9.77	10.94	1.03	2.12	2.17	1.77	12.71
Brussels	12.54	8.79	10.67	1.07	3.04	1.91	2.01	12.68
Madrid	11.92	6.63	9.28	1.82	5.17	2.04	3.01	12.29
Paris	12.02	8.58	10.30	1.02	3.39	1.21	1.87	12.17
Milan	8.53	5.21	6.87	1.63	8.09	3.04	4.25	11.12

Source: *Financial Times,* December 20, 1991, p. 25.

FIGURE 18–7 Worldwide cost of office rents*

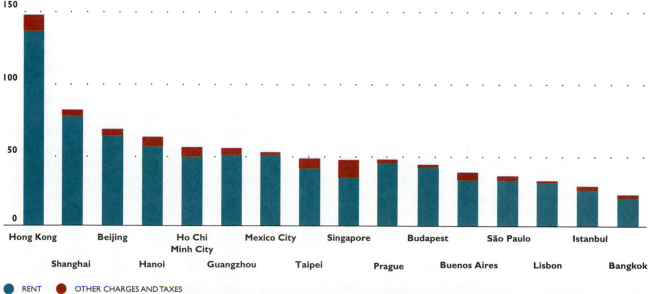

*US$s per square foot per year, June 1994.

Source: *The Economist,* August 6, 1994, p. 84.

TABLE 18–2

Shopper's guide for selected items in five cities

	New York	London	Paris	Tokyo	Mexico City
Aspirin (100 tablets)	$ 0.99	$ 1.23	$ 7.07	$ 6.53	$ 1.78
Cup of coffee	1.25	1.50	2.10	2.80	0.91
Movie	7.50	10.50	7.89	17.29	4.55
Compact disk	12.99	14.99	23.16	22.09	13.91
Levi's 501 jeans	39.99	74.92	75.40	79.73	54.54
Ray-Ban sunglasses	45.00	88.50	81.23	134.49	89.39
Sony Walkman (mid-range)	59.95	74.98	86.00	211.34	110.00
Nike Air Jordans	125.00	134.99	157.71	172.91	154.24
Gucci men's loafers	275.00	292.50	271.99	605.19	157.27
Nikon camera	629.95	840.00	691.00	768.49	1,054.42

Source: *Fortune*, June 13, 1994, p. 12.

SUMMARY

1. **Remember some of the regional or cultural differences in labor conditions we shall present.**
   a. The Japanese job-for-life culture is changing.
   b. There is still a huge wage gap between the neighboring countries, Germany and Poland.
   c. The International Federation of Free Trade Unions estimates there are from 100 to 200 million child (between 4 and 15 years old) laborers, mostly in the developing countries.
   d. Labor conditions in the PRC are reportedly very bad.
   e. ICs from developed countries must adjust their labor practices to succeed in developing countries.
2. **Understand why some economies are better at job creation than others and the differing unemployment rates.** The United States has created many more new jobs than has Western Europe and some more than Japan since 1980. Europe's sluggish job creation is blamed by the OECD and McKinsey Management Consultancy on high minimum wages, generous unemployment benefits, restrictive employment protection laws, and product market barriers.

3. **Understand the difficulties of finding qualified executives for international companies (ICs) and the importance of foreign language knowledge.** Knowledge of a people's language is essential to understand their culture and to know what's going on as every effective manager must.
4. **Compare home country, host country, and third country nationals as IC executives.** Sources of IC executives may be home country, host countries, or third countries, and their differing culture, language, ability, and experience can strengthen IC management.
5. **Realize the growing role of women in international business.** Women are increasingly important as IC executives and are being transferred, with trailing spouses, by their employers both domestically and internationally.
6. **Remember some of the complications of compensation packages for expatriate executives.** Expatriate manager compensation packages can be extremely complicated. Among other sources of complication are fluctuating currency exchange rates and differing inflation rates. Basic elements of those packages are salaries, allowances, and bonuses.

KEY WORDS

- Japan's jobs-for-life culture   586
- child labor   587
- home country nationals   590
- host country nationals   591
- third country nationals   592
- geocentric   594

QUESTIONS ■

1. Analyze arguments made by representatives of Nepal and other poor countries in justifying the child labor they utilize.

2. What adjustments in personnel practices did the discussed Spanish company's Guatamalan subsidiary make? Why?

3. Discuss recommendations made by the OECD and McKinsey Consultancy to Western Europe for the purpose of creating jobs.

4. Many laborers in the PRC work under bad and frequently dangerous conditions. Outsiders fall into two camps as to approaches to improve those conditions. Identify the two approaches and discuss the likely effectiveness of each.

5. When staffing a multinational organization for service outside the IC home country, what are some advantages and disadvantages of hiring home country personnel?

6. What is the English language trap?

7. Why has there been an increasing use of third country nationals in the foreign operations of ICs?

8. Why are expatriate employees frequently paid more than their colleagues at equivalent job levels in the home office?

9. Why are compensation packages for expatriates more complicated than those for domestic employees?

10. Women executives face obstacles to assignment and promotion both in the home country and in host countries. What additional obstacle applies to the latter?

MINICASE 18–1   Female Executives in International Business

For a number of reasons, women are being hired and promoted as executives by American business. The United States is almost alone in this development. Some Western European countries are moving slowly toward more female executive development, but elsewhere in the world, notably Latin American, Africa, Asia, and Eastern Europe, women are given very few executive opportunities.

Suppose you are the chief executive officer (CEO) of an American multinational. On your staff and in the U.S. operating divisions of your company are several bright, able, dedicated female executives. They are also ambitious, and in your company, international experience is a must before an executive can hope to get into top management.

An opening comes up for the position of executive vice president in the company's Mexican subsidiary. One of the women on your staff applies for the position, and she is well qualified for the job, better than anyone else in the company. Would you give her the position? What are the arguments pro and con?

Another position becomes available, this one as treasurer of the Japanese subsidiary. The chief financial officer of the company's California division applies for this job. She has performed to everyone's satisfaction, and she seems thoroughly qualified to become the treasurer in Japan. In addition, she speaks and writes Japanese. She is the daughter of a Japanese mother and an American father, and they encouraged her to become fluent in both English and Japanese.

Would you give her the job? Why or why not?

CHAPTER

19

Global Operations Management

There is a significant difference between the American and European philosophy of production and the Japanese philosophy of production. The Americans think stock is a necessary evil for smooth-running production, but the Japanese believe stock is an absolute evil.

Shigeo Shingo, dean of Japanese productivity and quality consultants

CONCEPT PREVIEWS

After reading this chapter, you should be able to:

1. **describe** the five global sourcing arrangements

2. **appreciate** the importance of the added costs of global sourcing

3. **understand** the Japanese efforts to improve quality and lower costs

4. **know** the just-in-time (JIT) production system

5. **comprehend** the problems with JIT

6. **understand** synchronous production

7. **understand** the objectives of the Malcolm Baldrige Award

8. **identify** the impediments to global standardization of production processes and procedures

9. **understand** the importance of intermediate and appropriate technology

10. **know** the two general classes of activities, productive and supportive, that must be performed in all production systems

Allen-Bradley and EMS1

Allen-Bradley (A-B), a Rockwell Automation business, has one of the most advanced electronics manufacturing operations in the world. This factory-within-a-factory is helping Allen-Bradley rapidly design and build circuit boards for its industrial automation controls and systems—products that are competitive worldwide. • At the facility, through the use of sophisticated software and extensive computer integration, circuit boards for Allen-Bradley products such as electronic motor starters, small programmable controllers, and machine vision systems are being designed, manufactured, and shipped to customers in as little as five months, an 85 percent improvement in a process that had taken as long as three years. • It is called EMS1, as the first such facility built according to the company's Electronic Manufacturing Strategy that shaped its creation. A-B developed that strategy in the mid-1980s to provide its operations with critically needed capacity for high-technology solid-state products. • EMS1 can manufacture a wide variety of circuit boards in lot sizes as small as one on a continuous flow assembly line. It does so through computerized control, bar-code part identification, and an ingenious conveyor system that integrates with 16 machines for assembly, test, or process. The conveyor system carries panels containing as few as one or as many as 84 individual circuit boards to each required assembly operation. The conveyor automatically directs the panels to the proper machines or lifts the panels up, over, and around processes that aren't required. The panels travel through EMS1 much as water flows through a stream—in the most direct route, in the shortest possible time—and they do so automatically. • Since completion of the EMS1 facility in 1992 in Milwaukee, five additional facilities were built and one more will be completed in 1996.

Source: Allen-Bradley.

As firms continue to enter global markets, global competition increases. This forces managements of both international and domestic companies to search for ways to lower costs and improve their products in order to remain competitive. Often the solution is *outsourcing;* that is, buying instead of making. For example, Allen-Bradley, the company in the opening section, is a significant outsource for manufacturers of electric motors globally.

SOURCING GLOBALLY

Reasons for Sourcing Globally

Although the primary reason for sourcing globally is to obtain lower prices, there are others. Perhaps certain products the company requires may not be available locally and must be imported. Another possibility is that the firm's foreign competitors are using components of better quality or design than those available in the home country.[1] To be competitive, the company may also have to source these components or production machinery in foreign countries. Table 19–1 presents the five most important reasons given and the percentages of respondents for each reason in a survey of 149 American companies that do foreign sourcing.

Note that although the primary reason for global sourcing given by American manufacturers is to obtain lower prices, half of the respondents believed that foreign suppliers had products not available locally and about one-fourth felt that they could buy higher-tech and better-quality products overseas.

Global Sourcing Arrangements

Any of the following arrangements can provide a firm with foreign products:

1. *Wholly owned subsidiary*—May be established in a country with low-cost labor to supply components to the home country plant; or the subsidiary may produce a product not made in home country.
2. *Overseas joint venture*—Established where labor costs are lower than in the home country to supply components to the home country.
3. *In-bond plant contractor*—Home country plant sends components to be machined and assembled or only assembled by an independent contractor in an in-bond plant.
4. *Overseas independent contractor*—Common in the clothing industry, in which firms with no production facilities such as DKNY, Nike, and Liz Claiborne contract foreign manufacturers to make clothing to their specifications with their label.
5. *Independent overseas manufacturer.*

TABLE 19–1
Five most important reasons for sourcing globally

Reason	Percentage of Respondents
1. Lower price available from foreign sources	74%
2. Availability of foreign products not available locally	49
3. Firm's worldwide operation and attitude	28
4. Advanced technology available from foreign sources	28
5. Higher-quality products available from foreign sources	25

Source: Laura M. Birou and Stanley E. Fawcett, "International Purchasing: Benefits, Requirements, and Challenges," *International Journal of Purchasing and Materials Management*, Spring 1993, p. 34.

Importance of Global Sourcing

As discussed in Chapter 13, there is a strong relationship between global sourcing and ownership of the foreign sources. Here are some additional data about American industry. In 1992, U.S. parent companies imported $104.1 billion (20 percent of all American imports) from their overseas subsidiaries.[2] In the same year, foreign firms imported from their U.S. affiliates $100.6 billion (22 percent of total American exports).[3] Note that the two values are nearly equal.

Finding Global Sources

The import sources discussed in Chapter 16 are the ones a professional purchasing agent would contact to learn about independent foreign sources. Foreign consulates and embassies are especially useful in furnishing the names of national firms searching for foreign customers. Many countries have programs to promote their industries similar to those of the U.S. Department of Commerce. As part of their sales promotional programs, local branches of foreign banks will generally assist in locating sources in their home countries when requested. Some even have newsletters with offers from firms in the home country to sell as well as buy.

Problems with Global Sourcing

Although global sourcing is a standard procedure for half of the U.S. firms with sales over $10 million, it does have some disadvantages.[4] Inasmuch as lower price is the primary reason companies make foreign purchases, they may be surprised that what appeared to be a lower price is not when all of the costs connected to the purchase are considered.

Added Costs.   The buyer must understand the terms of sale discussed in Chapter 16 because international freight, insurance, and packing can add as much as 10 to 12 percent to the quoted price, depending on the sales term used. The following is a list of the costs of importing, with an estimate of the percentage of the quoted price that each adds:

1. International freight, insurance, and packing (10–12%).
2. Import duties (0–50%).
3. Customhouse broker's fees (3–5%).
4. Inventory in the pipeline (5–15%).
5. Cost of letter of credit (1%).
6. International travel and communication costs (2–8%).
7. Company import specialists (5%).
8. Rework of products out of specification (0–15%).

Explanation of Added Costs.   To be certain of the cost of freight, insurance, and packing, the prospective importer should request a quotation with sales terms of CIF port of entry and stipulate that the merchandise be packed for export unless all shipments will be air freight. As discussed in Chapter 16, import duties can be extremely high if the exporting country is in column 2 of the HTSUSA (see Figure 16–4). Unless the goods enter duty-free, the duty must be added as part of the landed cost. To estimate the import duty, the importer should ask the customhouse broker for assistance. Brokers have experience in customs classification and can usually get nonbinding opinions from the Customs inspectors with whom they work. If the product will be imported regularly, the importer should request Customs to provide a binding tariff classification. This will be made in writing and must be honored by Customs officials.

Costs for inventory in the pipeline will vary according to the exporter's delivery promise. If it can ship from stock and air freight is a viable means, the importer may be able to work with only two weeks' inventory. If, however, the exporter must produce to fill the order and ship by ocean freight, it may need two months' inventory. Carrying costs include the opportunity cost of capital, cost of storage facilities, insurance, pilferage, depreciation, taxes, and handling.

If there is considerable import activity, the importer may want to set up an import group of employees to be in charge of the operation. One other item that requires explanation is the rework expense and scrap charges. Sometimes a foreign exporter will submit a sample of the article it is quoting that is perfect in every respect. Yet, the actual shipment may include various pieces out of specification. If the importer has not made arrangements in the purchasing contract for rebates or replacement, the costs can escalate severely.

> Boeing had such a problem with a Japanese firm. After purchasing a particular subassembly domestically for years with no problems, Boeing decided to buy the part from a Japanese manufacturer. It soon found that the Japanese firm's quality and delivery performance were poor. Boeing's engineers wished they had stayed with the American supplier.[5]

Other Disadvantages.   One disadvantage an importer should not have to face is an increase in price because the home currency has lost value as a result of exchange rate fluctuation. For example, if an American importer requires the exporter to quote dollar prices, the importer has no exchange rate risk. However, if the firm has a large volume of imports and the dollar is unstable, management may want a quotation in foreign currency. In that case, the chief financial officer of the importing company probably will protect the company from exchange rate risk using one of the hedging techniques discussed in the next chapter.

U.S. Firms that Have Returned

Many American firms have brought their overseas manufacturing facilities back to the United States. "We had our heads handed to us in Mexico," says the president of Invalco, which makes industrial flow meters and oil field valves. His firm's problem was the difficulties in crossing the Mexican-American border with goods going between the plant in Kansas and the in-bond operations in Mexico. His solution was to set up an electronic assembly and light machining operation with 10 Americans in Kansas to do the work previously performed by 30 Mexicans. The Kansans' pay is four times as high, but their productivity with less need for rework enables the company to do the job for less in the United States.

GE Fanuc, producer of robots, took over the production of a programmable logic controller from a manufacturer in Japan. Says the president, "We've exploded the myth that you can't produce competitively in the U.S. and with better quality. Even if the dollar's value against the yen doubled, the firm would continue to make them in the United States. The labor content is down to 5 percent, and these days it's important to look not only at labor and material costs, but also at the total cost of getting a product to a customer, including the time value of fast service." Made-to-order controllers can be delivered within two weeks.[6]

Du Pont formed a new subsidiary, Initiatives, in San Antonio to design and produce women's sportswear. The company designs clothing to be sold under a store's private label and produces it in Mexico using contract in-bond plants. The finished garments are shipped from the warehouse in San Antonio, and fabrics and components are collected there to be sent on to the Mexican manufacturers. The industry trend that makes San Antonio and the Mexican border important is the need to get the clothing into stores quickly before fashions change. This is easier when the goods are made in Mexico instead of Hong Kong or Taiwan. "Cutting delivery time is extremely appealing to retailers," said a Du Pont executive.[7]

Inasmuch as international firms maintain production facilities in countries at various levels of development—facilities utilizing factors of production that vary considerably in cost and quality from one country to another—it is understandable that production systems will also vary considerably even within the same company. Therefore, a single company may have a combination of plants that range from those with the most advanced production technology, such as found in Japan and the United States, to the less advanced technology of most developing nations.*

PRODUCTION SYSTEMS

Advanced Production Technology—Japan

The quotation at the beginning of the chapter states what had been a long-standing difference between the production philosophies of Japan and those of other industrialized nations. There are a number of reasons for this difference.

Immediately after World War II, General Douglas MacArthur, the supreme commander of the Allied powers in Japan, wanted reliable radios so the Japanese could hear the broadcasts of the occupation forces' order and propaganda programs. However, the Japanese radio vacuum tubes had a 90 percent failure rate. Because the local manufacturers could not give him the reliable radios he wanted, MacArthur sent for two American engineers, who prepared a two-month seminar on mass production as a system in which quality inspection is expensive and wasteful. They taught that statistics can be used to analyze what the system is doing and to get it under control to produce quality products. MacArthur ordered senior executives of the major Japanese firms to attend.

The final phase of the training was a course in the statistical control of quality. Because the man the engineers wanted to teach the course was not available, they turned to W. Edwards Deming, a statistician who had taught thousands of American industrial engineers how to use statistics in manufacturing during the war. In less than five years after the end of World War II, which destroyed Japan's production capability, Americans were teaching statistical quality control to Japan's engineers and the importance of quality to Japan's senior industrialists.[8] In appreciation of Deming's assistance, for 40 years Japan has awarded the prestigious Deming Prize annually to companies that meet a standard based on an evaluation process.[9] Florida Light & Power, which won the award in 1989, was the first non-Japanese company to do so.

What did Japan have to do to compete internationally? Japanese manufacturers realized that because of the limited size of the country's economy, they would have to export to grow. They were also aware that, because of the country's lack of natural resources, they would have to earn foreign exchange from exports to pay for the importation of petroleum, coal, and raw materials.

To be competitive in world markets, Japanese companies would have to provide high-quality products at low prices. But "Made in Japan" meant poor quality and shoddy manufacture to the rest of the world. For example,

---

*There are always exceptions to this generalization.

Toyota's first export, the Toyopet, was a disaster, and the company withdrew from the U.S. market. In the 1950s, the Japanese brought in various American experts, such as Juran, Feigenbaum, Deming, and others, who were largely ignored by American manufacturers. There are too many reasons for the Americans' attitudes to describe here, but essentially American firms were very successful at that time concentrating on producing quantity. They were selling everything they could make.[10]

Japanese Efforts to Lower Costs and Improve Quality

Lower Costs.   In examining the components of their costs, Japanese managers realized what all firms know: inventory costs are a major factor. Getting rid of inventory lowers labor cost by 40 percent, for example.[11] To operate without inventory, however, certain requirements would have to be met:

1. Components, whether purchased from outside suppliers or made in the same plant, had to be defect free, or else the production line would be shut down while the workers in all successive operations waited for usable inputs.

2. Parts and components had to be delivered to each point in the production process at the time they were needed; hence the name **just-in-time (JIT)**. Henry Ford incorporated elements of JIT in his moving assembly lines in the early 1900s.[12]

just-in-time (JIT)
A balanced system in which there is little or no delay time and idle in-process and finished goods inventory.

3. Customers everywhere want delivery when they make the purchase, so sellers maintain inventories of finished products. Sales often are made because one firm can supply the product from stock but a competitor cannot. How long do you want to wait for delivery of your car after you buy it?

   To eliminate inventories of finished goods and still respond quickly to customers' orders required manufacturers to set up flexible production units, which necessitated rapid setup times. Toyota, for example, learned to change a punch press die in 12 minutes; the same operation required three to six hours at General Motors.

4. It was also necessary to reduce process time. One way is to lower the time to transport work in progress from one operation to the next. American and European preoccupation with economic order lots resulted in their grouping machines by function (all drill presses together, punch presses together, and so forth), but transporting the machines' output to the next functional area takes time and costs money. Japanese firms grouped machines according to the workflow of a single product (an American invention—a separate production line for each product), which virtually eliminated transport cost. Also, because parts were arriving immediately from one operation to the next, when the output of the preceding operation was defective, that operation could be stopped until the cause was rectified. This too lowered production costs because fewer defective parts were produced.

5. Flexible manufacturing enables product changes to be made rapidly, but each change in the production line still costs money. So, the manufacturers simplified product lines and designed the products to use as many of the same parts as possible. This also contributed to the company suppliers' acceptance of the JIT concept because they received fewer but larger orders, which permitted longer, less costly (fewer production changeovers) production runs.

6. For just-in-time to be successful, manufacturers had to have the cooperation of their suppliers. They could not follow the common American practice of having numerous vendors, which buyers often play against one another to get the best price. Japanese firms used fewer vendors and sought to establish close relationships with them, including calling them in during the design of the product.

7. To lower costs, improve quality, and lower production times, Japanese managements required product designers, production managers, purchasing people, and marketers to work as a team. They realized that something better than the American and European "bucket brigade" was needed. That term stems from an analogy between the ancient method of putting out fires and the process by which an idea becomes a product in many firms.

> The research laboratory gets an idea. It passes the idea to the engineering department, which converts it to a design with all parts specified. Manufacturing gets the specifications from engineering and figures out how to make the product. Responsibility for selling it is "dumped" on marketing.

8. Getting these people together enabled suppliers to suggest using the lower-cost standard parts they regularly produce, manufacturing to indicate when a design change could simplify the production process, and marketing to contribute the customer's viewpoint, *all before the first product was produced.*[13]

Improve Quality. To improve quality, Japanese managers had to use a different human relations approach than the one common in the United States and Europe. Everyone—from top management to workers—had to be committed to quality. Getting worker involvement was not especially difficult, thanks to the Japanese practice of lifetime employment and the social benefits that Japanese companies offer their employees.

The concept they adopted originated, like so many others, in the United States. **Total quality management (TQM),** a companywide management approach to ensure quality throughout the organization, was invented in the Bell Laboratories in the 1920s. After World War II, as you saw earlier in the chapter, occupying Americans taught it to the Japanese, who in the 1970s retaught it to their teachers.[14]

Teams are necessary in the implementation of TQM, and one useful kind of team is the **quality circle,** an idea of Ishikawa, a Japanese quality expert. Look at how the president of Komatsu, Caterpillar's Japanese competitor, describes the use of quality circles in his company.

> The objective of the quality circle is to take part of the responsibility for the quality goal of each section. "Quality circle members are aware of the extent to which their achievement of their objectives will contribute to the results of their department, and also to the business of the company as a whole."
> A small group of employees, led by a foreman who has previously received quality control education, independently undertakes quality control activities. The circle's activities are divided among subdivisions of the circle led by a person junior to the foreman. Here is an example to illustrate that quality circles are used in all functional areas, not just in manufacturing.
> One day, telephone operators received complaints from outside callers regarding delays in answering telephones, so they surveyed company employees, who confirmed that the complaint was valid. They then studied the average time they were taking to answer a call and found that it was 7.4 seconds. They called the telephone company, who informed them that its standard was three seconds. The quality circle then discussed how to reach the three-second standard.[15]

total quality management (TQM)
Managing the entire organization so that it excels on all dimensions of product and services that are important to the customer

quality circle (quality control circle)
Small work groups that meet periodically to discuss ways to improve their functional areas and the quality of the product

Problems with Implementating the Japanese JIT System.   Many American manufacturers rushed to Japan to study the just-in-time "miracle" and mistakenly copied just one part of it: the narrow focus on scheduling goods inventories, called by some "little JIT." They failed to realize that what is important is "big JIT," a *total system* covering the management of people, materials, and relations with suppliers (also called *lean* production).[16] Moreover, many did not understand that JIT includes TQM, of which continuous improvement is an integral part.

Another difficulty was the difference in attitudes (a cultural force) between Japanese and Western managers. American managers and unions still valued highly the specialization of worker functions based on **Taylor's scientific management system**. This system contradicts the principles of quality circles: (1) participative decision making and (2) problem-solving capabilities of workers. Americans, pressured for quick results, were disappointed when quality circles didn't offer immediate solutions for improvement. The practice of not guaranteeing long-term employment also made it more difficult to attain the company loyalty for JIT.[17]

Advanced Production Technology—United States

Problems with JIT.   American production experts also realized that there were problems with JIT itself:

1. JIT is restricted to operations that produce the same parts repeatedly because it is a *balanced* system; that is, all operations are designed to produce the same quantity of parts. Yet, as Westinghouse saw when visiting Mitsubishi, repetitive operations may appear only in parts of the manufacturing process. It is far less useful for job shops (firms, or departments within larger firms, that specialize in producing small numbers of custom-designed products).*

2. Because JIT is a balanced system, if one operation stops, the entire production line stops—there is no inventory to keep succeeding operations working.

3. Achieving a balanced system is difficult because production capacities differ among the various classes of machines. It might require five lathes to keep one punch press busy, for example, and it takes dozens of tire-building machines to use the output of just one calender, a huge machine (similar in size to a newspaper printing press) that rubberizes the fabric used in making tires. This problem is less severe for large production units, of course.

4. JIT makes no allowances for contingencies, so every piece must be defect free when it is received, and delivery promises must be kept. **Preventive (planned) maintenance** is crucial. A sudden machine breakdown will stop the entire production process.

5. Much trial and error is required to put the system into effect.[18]

Synchronous Production.   The problems with JIT, especially the long time required for its installation in a production system, caused some American firms to realize that something else was needed if they were to regain market share lost to the Japanese. Some turned to **synchronous production,** also called synchronized manufacturing or optimized production technology. It is

---

Taylor's scientific management system
A system based on scientific measurements that prescribes a division of work whereby planning is done by managers and plan execution is left to supervisors and workers

preventive (planned) maintenance)
Maintenance done according to plan, not when machines break down

synchronous production
An entire manufacturing process with unbalanced operations that emphasizes total system performance

---

*Job shop also refers to a production system in which departments are organized around specific operations (grinding, drilling, and so forth).

a production system whose output is set at the output of the operation (**bottleneck**) that is working at full capacity.[19] Software was available that took into account such constraints as limited facilities, personnel, and machines when developing production schedules. This made installation much faster because production schedules and simulation could be done on a computer instead of having to arrive at solutions by trial and error, as is necessary with JIT.[20]

bottleneck
Operation in a production system whose output sets the limit for the entire system's output

Instead of attempting to achieve a balanced system like JIT, in which the capacities of all operations are equal, synchronous production aims to balance the *product flow* through the system, which leaves output levels of the various operations *unbalanced*.[21] For example, with the bottleneck operation producing at full capacity, perhaps only 60 percent capacity is needed at another operation. Because there is no reason for this operation to produce over 60 percent of its capacity, it is stopped at that point; anything more would be unwanted inventory. Inasmuch as work is assigned to each operation rather than to the entire system, as in JIT, there is no need for more work in process than that which is actually being worked on. Inventory may also be placed near the bottleneck to avoid any shutdown in this crucial operation, and sometimes, unlike JIT, there may even be a quality control inspector to check the bottleneck operation's input.

Notice that management's attention is focused on the bottleneck rather than on the other operations, because a production increase at the bottleneck means an increase for the entire production system; an increase in a non-bottleneck operation only adds to that machine's idle time.

Note another important difference between JIT and synchronous production: a defective part or component at any point of the production process can shut down a JIT system. But because a synchronous production system has

Allen-Bradley uses a screen printer to deposit solder paste onto panelized circuit boards. After this step, boards can be routed through any of five different assembly processes. A unique in-line conveyor can carry boards through each operation or, if necessary, bypass it entirely using an overhead loop.

A unique overhead conveyor routes panels past operations not required for that particular product. In the background, EMS1 manager Vince Shiely and EMS1 team member Larry Hanson discuss the results of an in-line, in-circuit test operation.

Courtesy Allen-Bradley, a Rockwell Automation business.

Robots Help Small Firms Become Competitive in World High-Tech Markets

Robots once were for large corporations such as manufacturers of automobiles and steel. Now they are making their way into small firms such as Engineering Concepts Unlimited (ECU), which makes small controllers to stop and start electric motors. The owner, Adam Suchko, says, "When we started building these, you put the parts in holes, you put the boards in a rack, flipped them over, and soldered the connections, one every three or four seconds." In 1989, he bought his first robot, a used automated soldering machine, at an auction for $350. After spending two months rebuilding it, he put it to work. The machine soldered hundreds of connections a second, and output increased 10 times what it was before the robot.

Now ECU has four robots, all rebuilt or used, and the company can build its controllers with no one in the building. The firm's longest production run *without people* is 50 hours. According to Suchko, the robots are survival tools that allow him to keep costs down: "If I shut the machines off, I'd have to hire another 10 people." With the robots, ECU builds controllers at a price and quality that enable them to be sold worldwide.

Although the United States has only 45,000 robots working on assembly lines, Japan has 400,000. This year, manufacturers are putting another 6,000 to 7,000 robots in service, and experts believe small businesses are ordering three or four times as many robots as they did five years ago. According to the CEO of the only American-owned robotics firm, Adept Technology ($50 million sales), there is no manufacturing capacity to make a VCR with 2,000 parts and sell it to Sears for $100. He points to a small display of products such as VCRs, camcorders, disk drives, and portable audio devices that have collective sales of $36 billion. "With robots," he says, "they could be made in the United States at competitive prices."

Source: "Look, World, No Hands," *Nation's Business*, June 1984, p. 41.

excess capacity in all operations except at the bottleneck, any defective part produced before the bottleneck can be remade, and thus the entire system is not stopped.

Incidentally, as firms adopt new manufacturing techniques such as synchronous production, they find that traditional accounting methods are inadequate to measure the costs of overhead. Managements are turning to *activity-based costing* to allocate the overhead burden according to its components, which vary among products.

Soft Manufacturing. In the new American factory, software and labor have become more important than production machines. Robots, if present, play only a supporting role. An IBM manufacturing executive explains, "We're not as enamored with automation as we were in the early 1980s." The firm found after research that it is more cost efficient to use hand labor with software networks than to use robots.

Soft manufacturing has made plants extremely agile. A firm can customize products one at a time while producing them at mass-production speeds. For example, the Motorola factory for pagers in Florida receives orders from dealers and Motorola sales representatives by E-mail or an 800 line. The data are digitalized and flow to the assembly line where robots select the components for humans to assemble. Orders are often completed in 80 minutes, permitting customers to receive them the same day they ordered them.

Soft manufacturing has enabled the United States to regain the lead in manufactured exports from Japan and Germany for the first time in a decade. In industries as diverse as computers, pagers, and construction equipment, Japanese and European manufacturers are rushing to copy American techniques.[22]

European Production Technology. According to knowledgeable sources, European manufacturers are about two years behind their American counterparts.[23] However, increasingly they are recognizing they must make substantial, rather than incremental, changes in processes and organizations to reach the high-performance levels of American and Japanese companies. In Germany, for example, the economic crisis caused by high wages, short working hours, and a strong mark forced managements into **reengineering, delayering,** and outsourcing to regain global competitiveness.[24] Note that reengineering calls for discontinuous thinking and is imposed from the top down, totally the opposite from continuous improvement associated with TQM.

The Single Market Program that lowered internal trade barriers among EU members has enabled European manufacturers to consolidate their operations to reduce costs. Because of the improvements in European distribution services, firms can supply all Europe from a single European manufacturing facility. As they close national plants, manufacturers are eliminating national distribution centers and factories. What were formerly national functions, such as purchasing, inventory management, and logistics management, are becoming pan-European functions.[25] IBM Europe, for example, has located all its PC production in Scotland. Its factory in France produces all of the mainframes for the European market and is one of only three IBM plants in the world making them (the U.S. and the Japanese plants are the other two).[26] See the Worldview for a description of the computer-integrated manufacturing system in the French plant.

reengineering
A radical redesign of business processes to achieve dramatic improvements in critical measures of performance, such as cost, quality, service, and speed

delayering
Removing levels of middle management

Comparisons of Productivity and Labor Costs

With advanced production technology available to firms in Japan, the United States, and Europe, there should be little differences in labor productivity among firms in the three areas. Figure 19–1 compares the labor productivity of Japan, the United States, and Germany for nine industry sectors.

A country's manufacturing productivity growth rates indicate the extent to which its industries are adopting advanced production technologies. According to the data in Figure 19–1—from a study by the McKinsey Global Research Institute, a subsidiary of the prestigious consulting firm, McKinsey & Company—the manufacturing productivity of the United States was behind

---

FIGURE 19–1 Labor productivity of Japan and Germany relative to the United States, 1990

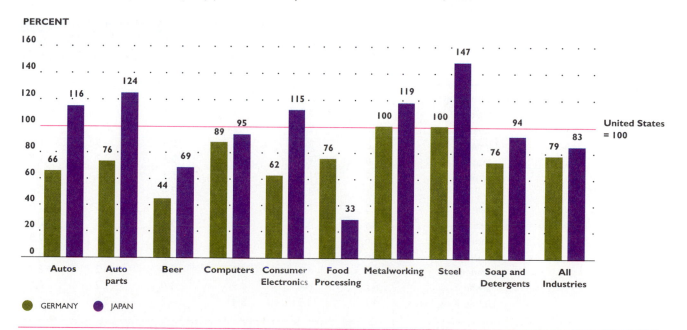

Source: "The Secret to Competitiveness," *The McKinsey Quarterly* no. 4 (1993), pp. 29–43.

that of Japan in consumer electronics, autos, auto parts, metal working, and steel in 1990. However, contrary to what the media report, the United States remains first in overall manufacturing productivity. In 1990, Japanese workers were only 83 percent as productive as American workers. German workers were 79 percent as productive. In none of the nine industries are German workers more productive than American workers.

Table 19–2 presents the rates of change of manufacturing productivity for 14 industrialized nations over the 1979–93 period.

Seven of the 12 nations for which we have data concerning the hourly productivity increases exceeded the U.S. increase for the 1979–93 period. Productivity increases were the largest in Japan, Belgium, Italy, and the United Kingdom, between 4.5 and 4 percent. However, for the 1990–93 period, only five nations had increases larger than the U.S. increase. Italy, Sweden, and the United Kingdom raised their productivity growth rates to between 4 and 4.5 percent annually. Japan and France suffered the most severe declines compared with the previous period.

Japan and the Netherlands had the best labor cost performances between 1979 and 1993. Unit labor costs in Belgium rose 1.5 percent annually, and the next lowest rate of increase was in the United States, with less than 3 percent annually. The remaining countries obtained increases of about 4 to 5 percent. Increases in Italy amounted to nearly 7 percent, and Korea's increase amounted to 7.5 percent annually.

A better indicator of changes in the competitiveness of a nation's goods in international markets is the unit labor costs measured in U.S. dollars. Exchange rate movements were the major factor in the changes in unit labor costs during the 1979–93 period. During that period, five nations had higher annual increases than the United States. Although the U.S. unit labor costs increased only 1.7 percent annually during the 1990–93 period, dollar-based unit labor costs declined in six countries, remained virtually unchanged in Korea, and rose about 1 percent in Belgium and France. The rate increased 12 percent in Japan primarily because of the 14 percent appreciation of the yen against the dollar.

TABLE 19–2

Annual changes in manufacturing productivity and unit labor costs for 14 countries (in percentages)

	Output per Hour		National Currency		U.S. Dollars	
	1979–93	1990–93	1979–93	1990–93	1979–93	1990–93
United States	2.4	2.5	2.8	1.7	2.8	1.7
Belgium	4.3	3.0	1.5	2.1	0.3	0.9
Canada	1.7	2.4	4.2	1.2	3.5	−2.1
Denmark	1.5	2.6	4.5	0.5	2.9	−1.1
France	2.8	1.2	4.9	2.5	2.7	1.1
Germany	1.9	1.2	3.7	5.1	4.5	4.3
Italy	4.1	4.6	6.9	3.4	2.1	−5.6
Japan	4.3	1.8	0.3	2.5	5.3	12.0
Korea	n.a.	n.a.	7.5	4.6	3.6	0.3
Netherlands	2.6	0.9	1.1	3.5	1.6	2.8
Norway	2.4	1.5	5.2	1.3	−2.4	−4.1
Sweden	2.9	4.2	4.9	−0.3	−4.2	−8.7
Taiwan	n.a.	n.a.	4.9	3.0	2.2	0.6
United Kingdom	4.1	4.5	5.4	4.7	2.8	−1.2

Unit Labor Costs (spanning National Currency and U.S. Dollars columns)

Note: n.a. = Not available.

Source: "Comparative Manufacturing Productivity and Unit Labor Costs," *Monthly Labor Review*, February 1995, p. 30.

WORLDVIEW

IBM Uses Computers to Build Computers

To protect its lucrative mainframe market from other manufacturers, especially Japanese, and competing systems such as networked PCs, IBM has installed its version of electronic ordering, JIT assembly, and computer-integrated manufacturing (CIM) in a plant located in Montpellier, France. The firm expects that these technologies will improve the quality and cost of the ES/9000 mainframes assembled there and increase its responsiveness to customer requirements. Over 90 percent are exported. Georges Foujols, responsible for implementing the plant's production strategy, says the real target is to be competitive with the outside world. "We don't want to implement CIM just because everybody else does it." The company boasts about its 100 percent implementation of CIM: all PCs are connected by computer networks and none stand alone.

Foujols found that the plant's processes were driven by the planning system, which calculated the supplies needed to produce the planned number of mainframes. This determined when the company ordered stock as well as what the plant produced and when. When the operators on the shop floor ran out of parts, they would call the parts supply department. Because often there were too few or too many parts, Foujols decided to use the operator's expertise to start the movement of products and parts.

The operators are now able to order parts electronically from the supplier, using a two-bin system. When one bin is empty, the operator notes the bar code electronically and the information is sent by IBM's main computer to the supplier as an order. The vendors participating in the electronic order process have had to learn about IBM's quality control system. Suppliers are fully accountable for the quality of their parts.

Although there is still a question about whether IBM's French factory is going to be able to compete in price and quality with its American and Japanese competitors into the 21st century, it does seem to be competing well with the company's U.S. and Japanese plants. Each month the three plants exchange data on cost, quality, and turnaround time, and according to the management in France, the quality of computers they deliver is better than that of either of the other two subsidiaries.

Source: "An Eastern Breeze in the Med," *Financial Times*, June 25, 1991, p. 18.

International Effort to Improve Quality and Lower Costs

Many companies, such as Allen-Bradley in the opening section, have successfully put into place JIT systems or have highly synchronized their production systems. Moreover, they have installed computer-integrated manufacturing (CIM), utilizing computers and robots to further improve productivity and quality. The Worldview describes IBM France's CIM system.

Western Firms That Are Succeeding.   General Motors, General Electric, Ford, IBM, Motorola—the list is long of American firms that have a synchronous production and a TQM system. Many have also reengineered and downsized to improve their global competitiveness.

In 1988, Corning, the glass manufacturer, copied Japan's extensive automation because, as the firm's executive president says, "The Japanese were better than us in manufacturing." However, management soon found that heavy automation undermined employee motivation. To involve workers, Corning let any worker sign a purchase order up to $500 without authorization, eliminated time clocks, created just one job classification, with one manager for 60 employees, and trained each employee to handle as many as 15 different jobs. Management also sought employee involvement when selecting manufacturing technology. "There were places where we could have robotized, but we decided against it. Even in boring and repetitive jobs, we have moved away from automation because humans adapt and robots don't," says the plant manager.

The plant has increased its productivity at a rate of 25 percent annually, and its integration of employees and technology has attracted so many

American, Japanese, and European companies that every month it conducts a tour—for a fee. Representatives from production, design, marketing, and suppliers work jointly on new products, a technique called *concurrent engineering*. As a result, new-product introduction, which used to take three years, now is done in one.[27]

Chrysler obtains similar benefits from concurrent engineering by bringing together under one roof representatives of product design, engineering, manufacturing, procurement, marketing, and suppliers. These groups, called *platform teams*, enabled the firm to design its "cab forward" design in only three years, with just one-third of the engineers it used for the previous group of cars. The platform team that designed the Neon made innovations that brought words of admiration from Toyota and Nissan. After Toyota's engineers broke down the car to its smallest part in Tokyo, a leaked copy of their report stated that the Neon incorporated "designed-in cost savings unprecedented in an American car." The president of Nissan, which also did an autopsy of the Neon, admitted it was an impressive product: "Where we would have used five parts to make up a component, the Neon has three. Where we would use five bolts, the Neon body-side was designed so cleverly it needs only three bolts."[28]

Service organizations are also applying many of the principles of synchronous production. American Financial Services, an international consumer finance and insurance company with $7 billion sales, asked its U.S. companies and subsidiaries in Canada, the United Kingdom, and Australia to develop their own programs. In only two years, the Canadian affiliate alone doubled its profits and saved $2 million. Management, recognizing that total decentralization was not the best way to manage the process globally, appointed a person to oversee its global operation and also appointed an international excellence steering committee.[29]

Examples of European worldwide firms using synchronous production systems are Electrolux (Swedish), Volkswagen (German), and Rover (English).[30] Fiat recently opened a $3 billion plant in southern Italy in an effort to instill different work practices. The company spent $64 million training workers and engineers to work in independent, multiskilled teams. Fiat's personnel chief says, "Top-down decision making is dead. Problems are solved by teams actually working on production."[31]

In France, Pechiney, the global aluminum producer, has 250 quality circles in 10 of its companies and 40 plants.[32] In a 1986 survey, the Australian Federation of Automotive Product Manufacturers found that 34 of 48 respondents were operating a full or pilot JIT system, and 8 more were planning to introduce it in 1987. Obviously, the fact that the local automakers were already using synchronous production influenced their decisions.[33]

The Malcolm Baldrige National Quality Award. In 1987, the U.S. government established the Malcolm Baldrige Quality Award to be given annually to a maximum of two firms in each of the following categories: manufacturing, service, and small business.

Objectives of the Award. The objectives of the award are to encourage American firms to improve quality and productivity while decreasing costs, to establish guidelines businesses and other organizations can use to evaluate their efforts to improve quality, and to recognize the firms that have improved the quality of their products and services.[34] The Secretary of Commerce and the National Institute of Standards and Technology are responsible for developing and administering the awards, with cooperation and financial support from the private sector.

Award Winners. Winners of the Baldrige Award are producing products or services as good as any in the world. Although as many as 6 firms can win the award every year, there has been a total of 19 from 1988 to 1993:

Year	Manufacturing	Service	Small Business
1988	Motorola Westinghouse Commercial Nuclear Fuel Division	—	Globe Metallurgical
1989	Millikin & Co. Xerox Business Products	—	—
1990	Cadillac IBM Rochester	Federal Express	Wallace Co.
1991	Solectron Zytec Corp.	—	Marlow Industries
1992	AT&T Network Systems Group Transmissions Systems Business Unit	AT&T Universal Card services	Granite Rock Co.
	Texas Instruments Defense Systems and Electronics Group	Ritz-Carlton Hotel Co.	
1993	Eastman Chemical Co.	—	Ames Rubber Co.

Many firms are using the Baldrige guidelines to help them set up their quality programs. Motorola, one of the first-year winners, believes so strongly in the program that it has told all of its suppliers to apply for the Baldrige award as evidence of their commitment to total quality management or lose Motorola's business.[35] Motorola executives carry the card shown on page 628 in their shirt pockets as a reminder of the company's beliefs, goals, and initiatives.

Reasons for Global Standardization of Production Systems

The advantages of synchronous production and TQM are compelling reasons numerous global and multinational corporations are installing them worldwide. Certainly, customers everywhere want quality products at low prices. Firms from industrialized nations commonly copy home production systems in their subsidiaries in other industrialized nations. For example, tire plants and car factories in the United Kingdom are very similar to the home country plants in the United States. In addition to those just mentioned, there are other important, although perhaps less obvious, reasons for global standardization.

Organization and Staffing.
Some of the reasons for the global standardization of a firm's production systems are the effects on organization and staffing.

Simpler and Less Costly when Standardized. The standardization of production processes and procedures simplifies the production organization at headquarters because their replication enables the work to be accomplished with a smaller staff of support personnel. Fewer labor-hours in plant design are involved because each new plant is essentially a scaled-up or scaled-down version of an existing one. The permanent group of experts that international companies maintain to give technical assistance to overseas plants can be smaller. Extra technicians accustomed to working with the same machinery can be borrowed from the domestic operation as needed.

Worldwide uniformity in production methods also increases headquarters' effectiveness in keeping the production specifications current. Every firm has hundreds of specifications, and these are constantly being changed

Malcolm Baldrige Quality Award.

Photograph courtesy of the National Institute of Standards and Technology, Office of Quality Programs, Gaithersburg, Maryland, 20899. Photograph by Steuben Glass.

OUR FUNDAMENTAL OBJECTIVE
(Everyone's Overriding Responsibility)

Total Customer Satisfaction

 MOTOROLA INC.

KEY BELIEFS—*how we will always act*
- Constant Respect for People
- Uncompromising Integrity

KEY GOALS—*what we must accomplish*
- Increased Global Market Share
- Best in Class
  —*People*
  —*Marketing*
  —*Technology*
  —*Product*
  —*Manufacturing*
  —*Service*
- Superior Financial Results

KEY INITIATIVES—*how we will do it*
- Six Sigma Quality
- Total Cycle Time Reduction
- Product and Manufacturing Leadership
- Profit Improvement
- Participative Management Within, and Cooperation Between Organizations

Courtesy of Motorola

because of new raw materials or manufacturing procedures. If all plants, domestic and foreign, possess the same equipment, notice of a change can be given with one indiscriminate mailing; there is no need for highly paid engineers to check each affiliate's list of equipment to see which ones are affected. Companies whose production processes are not unified have found that maintaining a current separate set of specifications for each of 15 or 20 affiliates is both more costly (larger staff) and more error prone.

Logistics of Supply.   Management has become increasingly aware that greater profits may be obtained by organizing all of its companies' production facilities into one logistical supply system that includes all of the activities required to move raw materials, parts, and finished inventory from vendors, between enterprise facilities, and to customers. The standardization of processes and machinery provides a reasonable guarantee that parts manufactured in the firm's various plants will be interchangeable. This assurance of interchangeability enables management to divide the production of components among a number of subsidiaries to achieve greater economies of scale and to take advantage of the lower production costs in some countries.

Rationalization.   **Manufacturing rationalization,** as this production strategy is called, involves a change from manufacturing by a subsidiary only for its own national market to producing a limited number of components for use by all subsidiaries. The Ford Escort car, for example, is sourced from a number of Ford factories. Figure 19–2 illustrates that the global car receives components from 15 nations.

manufacturing rationalization
Division of production among a number of production units, thus enabling each to produce only a limited number of components for all of a firm's assembly plants

SKF, a major bearing manufacturer with headquarters in Sweden, was able to reduce the types of ball bearings produced in five major overseas subsidiaries years ago from 50,000 to 20,000. Of the 20,000 remaining types, 7,000 have been rationalized among the five plants, and the other 13,000 are produced solely by one or another subsidiary for its local customers.[36]

These examples illustrate that for production rationalization to be possible, the product mix must first be rationalized; that is, the firm must elect to produce products that are identical worldwide or regionwide. Once this has been done, each subsidiary can be assigned to produce certain components for other foreign plants, thus attaining a higher volume with a lower production cost than would be possible if it manufactured the complete product for its national market only. Obviously, this strategy is not viable when consumers' tastes and preferences differ markedly among markets. For less differentiated products, however, manufacturing rationalization permits economies of scale in production and engineering that would otherwise be impossible. Nissan Motors has been able to employ the most modern methods, including CAM,* in its Mexican motor plant because of the high input it obtains through exports (80 percent of the total) to Tennessee, Japan, and Latin America. And Ford, as you read in Chapter 16, supplies engines for all Ford-Europe from one plant in England.[37]

Purchasing.   When foreign subsidiaries are unable to purchase raw materials and machinery locally, they generally look for assistance from the purchasing department at headquarters. Because unified processes require the same materials everywhere, buyers can handle foreign requirements by simply increasing their regular orders to their usual suppliers and passing on the volume discounts to the subsidiaries. However, when special materials are required, purchasing agents must search out new vendors and place smaller orders, often at higher prices.

Control.   All the advantages of global standardization cited thus far also pertain to the other functions of management. Three aspects of control—quality, production, and maintenance—merit additional discussion.

---

*CAM—computer-assisted manufacturing—generally includes automated materials handling and programmable robots.

FIGURE 19–2 Global manufacturing: the component network for the Ford Escort in Europe

UNITED KINGDOM
Carburetor, rocker arm, clutch, ignition, exhaust, oil pump, distributor, cylinder bolt, cylinder head, flywheel ring gear, heater, speedometer, battery, rear wheel spindle, intake manifold, fuel tank, switches, lamps, front disc steering wheel, steering column, glass, weatherstrips, locks, mirrors, starter, alternator

FRANCE
Cylinder head, master cylinder, brakes, underbody coating, weatherstrips, clutch release bearings, seat pads and frames, transmission cases, clutch cases, tires, suspension bushes, ventilation units, heater, hose clamps, sealers, hardware

CANADA
Glass, radio

UNITED STATES
EGR valves, hydraulic tappet, glass

ITALY
Carburetor, lamps, defroster grills

SWEDEN
Hose clamps, cylinder bolt, exhaust down pipes, pressings, hardware

NETHERLANDS
Tires, paints, hardware

BELGIUM
Tires, tubes, seat pads, brakes, trim

SPAIN
Wiring harness, radiator and heater hoses, fork clutch release, air filter, battery, mirrors

SWITZERLAND
Underbody coating, speedometer gears

GERMANY
Locks, pistons, exhaust, ignition, switches, front disc, distributer, weatherstrips, rocker arm, speedometer, fuel tank, cylinder bolt, cylinder head gasket, front wheel knuckles, rear wheel spindle, transmission cases, clutch cases, clutch, steering column, glass, mirrors, starter, alternator

NORWAY
Exhaust flanges, tires

DENMARK
Fan belt

AUSTRIA
Tires, radiator and heater hoses

JAPAN
Starter, alternator, cone and roller bearings, windscreen washer pump

Note: Final assembly takes place in Halewood, United Kingdom, and Saarlouis, Federal Republic of Germany.

Source: Based on information from Ford representative, June 19, 1989.

Quality Control. When production equipment is similar, home office control of quality in foreign affiliates is less difficult because management can expect all plants to adhere to the same standard. The home office can compare the periodic reports that all affiliates submit and quickly spot deviations from the norm that require remedial action, such as a large number of product rejects. Separate standards for each plant because of equipment differences are unnecessary.

Production and Maintenance Control.   A single standard also lessens the task of maintenance and production control. The same machinery should produce at the same rate of output and have the same frequency of maintenance no matter where it is located. In practice, there will be deviations because of the human and physical factors (dust, humidity, temperature), but at least similar machinery permits the home office to establish standards by which to determine the effectiveness of local managements. Furthermore, the maintenance experience of other production units as to the frequency of overhauls and the stock of spare parts needed will help plants avoid costly, unforeseen stoppages from sudden breakdowns.

Planning.   When a new plant can be built that is a duplicate of others already functioning, the planning and design will be both simpler and quicker because it is essentially a repetition of work already done:

1. Design engineers need only copy the drawings and lists of materials that they have in their files.
2. Vendors will be requested to furnish equipment that they have supplied previously.
3. The technical department can send the current manufacturing specifications without alteration.
4. Labor trainers experienced in the operation of the machinery can be sent to the new location without undergoing special training on new equipment.
5. Reasonably accurate forecasts of plant erection time and output can be made based on the experience with existing facilities.

In other words, the duplication of existing plants greatly reduces the engineering time required in planning and designing the new facilities and eliminates many of the start-up difficulties inherent in any new operation. To be sure, a newly designed plant causes problems when it is erected domestically, but those problems are greater when the plant is located in a different environment at a great distance from headquarters. Just how important the savings from plant duplication are was emphasized in a study of the chemical and refining industries that indicated the cost of technology transfer was lowered by 34 and 19 percent for the second and third start-ups.[38]

Since the case for global standardization of production is so strong, why do differences among plants in the same company persist?

Impediments to Globalization of Production Facilities

Generally, it is easier for international corporations to standardize the concepts of total quality management and synchronous production in their overseas affiliates than it is to standardize the actual production facilities. Units of an international multiplant operation differ in size, machinery, and procedures because of the intervention of the foreign environmental forces, especially the economic, cultural, and political forces.

Environmental Forces.   Let us examine the impact of the three kinds of forces just mentioned.

Economic Forces.   The most important element of the economic forces that impedes production standardization is the wide range of market sizes, discussed in Chapter 14.

A number of studies confirmed by personal experience have shown that the foremost criterion for plant design is the output desired. Once this is known, the engineering department of a multiplant operation will check to see whether a factory already has been built with a capacity similar to the output specified. If so, this facility will serve as a design standard for the new plant, though modifications may be made to eliminate any problems encountered in the original design. Many large multiplant firms actually have standard designs for large, medium, and small production outputs.

To cope with the great variety of production requirements, the designer generally has the option of selecting either a *capital-intensive process* incorporating automated, high-output machinery or a *labor-intensive process* employing more people and semimanual general-purpose equipment with lower productive capacity. The automated machinery is severely limited in flexibility (variety of products and range of sizes), but once set up, it will turn out in a few days what may be a year's supply for some markets.[39] For many processes, this problem may be resolved by installing one machine of the type used by the hundreds in the larger home plant. However, sometimes this option is not available; some processes use only one or two large machines, even in production facilities with large output—as we mentioned in the discussion of standardized manufacturing. Until recently, when the option was not available, plant designers had to choose between the high-output specialized machinery and the lower-output general-purpose machines mentioned earlier.

A third alternative is available: computer-integrated manufacturing, which IBM France is using. However, its high cost and high technological content generally limit its application to the industrialized nations and the more advanced developing nations. CIM systems enable a machine to make one part as easily as another in random order on an instruction from a bar code reader of the kind used in supermarkets. This reduces to one the economic batch quantity—the minimum number of a part that can be made economically by a factory. There is a limit, nevertheless, to the variety of shapes, sizes, and materials that can be accommodated.

Another economic factor that influences the designer's selection of processes is the *cost of production*. Automation tends to increase the productivity per worker because it requires less labor and results in higher output per machine. But, if the desired output requires the machines to be operated only a fraction of the time, the high capital costs of automated equipment may result in excessive production costs even though labor costs are low. In situations where production costs favor semimanual equipment, the designer may be compelled to install high-capacity machines instead because of a lack of floor space. Generally, the space occupied by a few high-capacity machines is less than that required for the greater number of semimanual machines to produce the same output. On the other hand, because the correct type and quality of process materials are indispensable for specialized machinery, the engineers could not recommend this equipment if such materials are unobtainable either locally or through importation. Occasionally, management will bypass this obstacle by **backward vertical integration**; that is, manufacturing capacity to produce essential inputs will be included in the plant design even though it would be preferable from an economic standpoint to purchase these materials from outside vendors. For example, a textile factory might include a facility for producing nylon fibers.

The economic forces we have described are fundamental considerations in plant design, yet elements of the cultural and political forces may be sufficiently significant to override decisions based on purely economic reasoning.

Cultural Forces.   When a factory is to be built in an industrialized nation where there is a sizable market and high labor costs, capital-intensive processes will undoubtedly be employed. However, such processes may also be employed in

backward vertical integration
Establishing facilities to manufacture inputs used in the production of a firm's final products

developing countries, which commonly lack skilled workers despite their abundant supply of labor. This situation favors the use of specialized machines because, although a few highly skilled persons are needed for maintenance and setup, the job of *attending* these machines (starting, feeding stock) can be performed by unskilled workers after a short training period. In contrast, general-purpose machinery requires many more skilled operators.[40]

These operators could be trained in technical schools, but the low prestige of such employment, a cultural characteristic, affects both the demand for and the supply of vocational education. Students do not demand it, and the traditional elitist attitude of the educational administrators in many developing nations causes resources to be directed to professional education instead of to the trades where they are needed.

Firms that attempt to reduce their requirements for skilled workers by installing automatic machinery are, of course, left vulnerable to another cultural characteristic of the less developed countries: absenteeism. If the setup and maintenance crews fail to report to work, the entire production line may be shut down. Some managers resolve this difficulty by training a few extra people as backups. Having extra personnel is viewed as production insurance necessary to keep the plant in operation. This extra expense may be far less than the expense of handling the greater number of labor-management problems resulting from larger work force in a nonautomated factory of similar capacity.

These economic and cultural variables, important as they are, are not the only considerations of management; the requirements of the host government must be met if the proposed plant is to become a reality.

Political Forces.　When planning a new production facility in a developing country, management is frequently confronted by an intriguing paradox. Although the country desperately needs new job creation, which favors labor-intensive processes, government officials often insist on the most modern equipment. Local pride may be the cause, or it may be that these officials, wishing to see the new firm export, believe only a factory with advanced technology can compete in world markets. They not only may be reluctant to take chances on "inferior" or untried alternatives, they may also feel that low-productivity technology will keep the country dependent on the industrialized countries. In some developing countries, this fear has been formalized by laws prohibiting the importation of used machinery.

Some Design Solutions.　More often than not, after consideration of the environmental variables, the resultant plant design will be a hybrid or one using intermediate technology.

Hybrid Design.　Commonly, in designing plants for developing countries, engineers will use a hybrid of capital-intensive processes when they are considered essential to ensure product quality and labor-intensive processes to take advantage of the abundance of unskilled labor. For example, they may stipulate machine welding rather than hand welding, but then use semimanual equipment for the painting, packaging, and materials handling.

Intermediate technology.　In recent years, the press of a growing population and the rise in capital costs have forced governments of developing nations to search for something less than highly automated processes. They are becoming convinced that there should be something midway between the capital- and labor-intensive processes that will create more jobs, require less capital, but still produce the desired product quality. Governments are urging inves-

intermediate technology
Production methods between capital- and labor-intensive methods

tors to consider an **intermediate technology,** which, unfortunately, is not readily available in the industrialized nations. This means that the ICs cannot transfer the technology with which they are familiar but must develop new and different manufacturing methods. It is also possible that the savings in reduced capital costs of the intermediate technology may be nullified by higher start-up costs and the greater expense of its transfer.

Appropriate Technology.   One global corporation, Philips in the Netherlands, has worked systematically to match a country's markets with its resources and ability to produce certain components to obtain an optimal technological mix. A pilot plant devises commercially viable production patterns based on the factors that enable foreign subsidiaries to manufacture small volumes with processes less automated than those of the home plant.

appropriate technology
Production methods— intermediate, capital-, or labor-intensive (or a mixture)—considered most suitable for an area according to its cultural, political, and economic situation

Rather than search for an intermediate technology, the emphasis of Philips and others is on employing the **appropriate technology,** which can range from the most advanced to the most primitive, depending on the economic, sociocultural, and political variables. For some products, the superiority in productivity and product quality of the modern process is so marked that it makes the labor-intensive method totally inappropriate. Compare resource mapping by satellites with geologists on horseback, for example. Yet in the case of sugar refining, it was found in India that for the same amount of capital, either a large plant capable of producing 12,000 tons of sugar annually with 900 employees or 47 small plants with an output of 30,000 tons employing 10,000 workers could be built.[41]

Table 19–3 compares appropriate technology and capital-intensive technology with respect to cost, number of workers, and cost per job for various industries. Note that the differences are significant.

Does this mean that the government of a developing nation should urge a company to adopt a less capital-intensive process? It depends. It is possible that the cost per unit produced will be higher with this process. In this case, government administration must choose between (1) the use of the less capital-intensive technology to save scarce capital and create more jobs and (2) the more capital-intensive processes that will provide a less expensive product for its citizens. The choice obviously depends on government priorities.

TABLE 19–3

Comparison of appropriate technology (AT) and capital intensive technology (CIT)

Industry	Annual Output of Plant	Ratios		
		Cost, AT Plant/Cost, CIT Plant	No. Workers, AT Plant/No. Workers, CIT Plant	Cost per Job, AT Plant/Cost per Job, CIT Plan
Brick making	16 million bricks	.2	3.2	.1
Cotton spinning	2,000 tons	.3	2.5	.1
Sugar processing	50,000 tons	.6	4.8	.1
Cotton weaving	40 million square yards	.5	2.1	.2
Corn milling	36,000 tons	.4	1.5	.3
Shoes	300,000 pairs	.5	1.4	.4
Leather processing	600,000 hides	.7	1.7	.6
Beer brewing	200,000 hectoliters	.6	0.9	.7
Fertilizer	528,000 tons of urea	.9	1.0	.9

Source: Calculated from Tables 2 and 3, Howard Pack, *Macroeconomic Implications of Factor Substitution in Industrial Processes,* World Bank Staff Working Paper No. 377 (March 1980).

These examples help substantiate a growing belief that there is no universally appropriate technology. In fact, proponents of this concept state that what may be suitable for the cultural, political, and economic situation in one region is not necessarily applicable even in another area of the same country. The concept's effect on attempts to standardize production facilities worldwide is obvious.

Local Production System

Basis for Organization.   Except for plants in large industrialized nations, the local production organization is commonly a scaled-down version of that found in the parent company. If at home the firm is organized by product companies or divisions (tires, industrial products, chemicals), the subsidiary will be divided into product departments. Manufacturing firms that use process organizations (departmentalized according to production processes) in the domestic operation will set up a similar structure in their foreign affiliates. In a paper-box factory, separate departments will cut the logs, produce the paper, and assemble the boxes. The only noticeable difference between the foreign and domestic operations is that in the foreign plant, all of these processes are more likely to be at one location because of the smaller size of each department.

Horizontal and Vertical Integration.   The local production organization is rarely integrated either vertically or horizontally to the extent the parent is. Some vertical integration is traditional, as in the case of the paper-box factory, and some will occur if it is necessary to assure a supply of raw materials. In this situation, the subsidiary might be more vertically integrated than the parent, which depends on outside sources for much of its inputs. However, the additional investment is a deterrent to vertical integration, as are the extra profits gained by supplying inputs to these captive customers from the home plants. Some countries prohibit vertical integration for certain industries. Mexico, for example, does not allow automobile manufacturers to own parts suppliers. Laws in Mexico, Brazil, and numerous other nations require a percentage of local content in finished products. When the subsidiary cannot meet the requirement by local outside sourcing, it may be forced to produce components that its parent does not.

Horizontal integration is much less prevalent in the foreign subsidiaries, although restaurant chains, banks, food-processing plants, and other industries characterized by small production units will, of course, integrate horizontally in the manner of the domestic company. Overseas affiliates themselves become conglomerates when the parent acquires a multinational. The many mergers and acquisitions of the late 1980s turned various affiliates into conglomerates.

> European ITT affiliates found themselves in hotels (Sheraton), car rental (Avis), and electrical connectors (Cannon Electric) when these multinationals were bought by the parent. The affiliates themselves acquired insurance companies, schools, and manufacturers of auto parts, cosmetics, and food products. At one time, ITT Europe ranked 25th in sales among European firms.

Design of the Production System.   A *production system* is essentially a functionally related group of activities for creating value. Although the production system as described below is basically one for producing tangible goods, nearly everything that is said applies equally to the production of services. Factors involved in the efficient operation of a production system include:

1. Plant location.
2. Plant layout.
3. Materials handling.
4. Human element.

Plant Location.   Plant location is significant because of its effect on both production and distribution costs, which are frequently in conflict. The gain in government incentives and in the lower land and labor costs obtained by locating away from major cities may be offset by the increased expense of warehousing and transportation to serve these markets. Management will, after ascertaining that adequate labor, raw materials, water, and power are available, seek the least-cost location, or the one for which the sum of production and transfer costs is minimized. Management's first choice may then be modified by market requirements, the influence of competitors' locations, employee preference (climate, recreational facilities), and conditions imposed by the local authorities.

Governments that are anxious to limit the congestion of large urban areas may either prohibit firms from locating in the major cities or offer them important financial inducement to locate elsewhere.

> Businesses that establish plants in the Mezzogiorno (southern Italy) can obtain soft loans, tax exemptions, and outright grants of up to 40 percent of the fixed investment. Nearly all of the European nations and some nations in Latin America offer similar advantages. For example, since 1989, a foreign firm that wants a wholly owned subsidiary in Mexico must locate outside Mexico City, Monterrey, and Guadalajara, which, in the government's opinion, are already overcrowded.

Firms that have come to a country to take advantage of low labor costs and export their production have a limited selection of plant locations. They must locate in **export processing zones,** such as Mexico's in-bond manufacturing zones, most of which are on the Mexican-American border. Similar zones exist in South Korea, Taiwan, Singapore, and some 50 other nations.[42]

export processing zones
Specific and limited areas into which imported components may be brought for further processing; the finished product must be reexported to avoid payment of import duties

Plant Layout.   Modern practice dictates that the arrangement of machinery, personnel, and service facilities should be made prior to the erection of the building. In this way, the building is accommodated to the layout that is judged most capable of obtaining a smoothly functioning production system.

The designer must attempt to obtain the maximum utility from costly building space while providing room for the future expansion of each department. Space can become critical very quickly if forecasts, especially for new products, prove to have been unduly pessimistic. Managements of plants located in developing countries may attempt to stint on space for employees' facilities, reasoning that the workers' standard of living in these countries is lower and that they will accept less just to have employment. Often, however, foreign labor laws are more demanding than those of the home country.

Materials Handling.   Considerable savings in production costs can be achieved by a careful planning of materials handling, which, as you have seen, is a major consideration in synchronous production. Production managers have often failed to appreciate that inefficient handling of materials may cause excessive inventories of partly finished parts to accumulate at some workstations, while at others, expensive machinery was idle for lack of work (bottleneck). This concerned marketers too, because poor materials handling can result in late deliveries and damaged goods, which in turn lead to order cancellation and a loss of customers. Therefore, marketers must also be included in the total quality control approach that we discussed earlier in this chapter.

Human Element.   The effectiveness of the production system depends on people, who are in turn affected by the system. Productivity suffers when there is extreme heat or cold, excessive noise, or faulty illumination. Colors also influence human behavior—pale colors are restful and unobtrusive, whereas bright colors attract attention. Plant designers take advantage of this fact by painting the walls of the working areas pale blue and green but marking exits with a bright yellow and painting safety equipment red. This practice is accepted nearly everywhere, although, as we indicated in the sociocultural chapter, color connotations vary among cultures.

For safety and ease of operation, controls of imported machinery must frequently be altered to accommodate smaller workers. Extra lifting devices, unnecessary in the home country, may be required. Where illiteracy is a problem, safety signs must include pictures. For example, a picture of a burning cigarette with a red line through it may substitute for a "no smoking" sign. Plants in multilingual nations and plants that employ large numbers of foreign workers will require warnings in more than one language.

Because of the prohibitive cost of automobiles in many developing nations, employees ride bicycles to work, so bicycle stands must be provided in parking lots. Special dietary kitchens are necessary when workers from more than one culture work together. These and other special conditions caused by environmental differences must be reckoned with in the design of the production system.

Operation of the Production System.   Once the production system has been put into operation, two general classes of activities, *productive* and *supportive*, must be performed.

Productive Activities.   After the initial trial period, during which workers become familiar with the production processes, management will expect the system to produce at a rate sufficient to satisfy market demand. It is the function of the line organization—from production manager to first-level supervisor—to work with labor, raw materials, and machinery to produce on time the required amount of product with the desired quality at the budgeted cost.

Obstacles to Meeting Production Standards.   Management must be prepared to deal with any obstacle to meeting the production standards. Among these obstacles are (1) low output, (2) inferior quality, and (3) excessive manufacturing costs.

   Low Output.   Any number of factors may be responsible for the system's failure to meet the design standards for output.

1. Raw materials suppliers may fail to meet delivery dates or may furnish material out of specification. This is a common occurrence in the sellers' markets of developing countries, but it is also occasionally a problem in the industrialized countries. The purchasing department must attempt to educate the vendor as to the importance of delivery dates and specifications, although the effectiveness of this strategy is limited when, as is often the case in developing nations, there is only one supplier. Increasing the price paid and sending technicians to assist the vendor generally improve this situation.

When the automobile plants in Mexico were required to incorporate locally made parts into the product, they not only provided their own technical assistance to vendors but also arranged for licensing agreements from U.S. suppliers and even guaranteed bank loans enabling the vendors to buy production machinery. This tremendous assistance program, literally dumped in the laps of small local manufacturers, was a leading factor in creating the Mexican parts industry.

2. Poor coordination of production scheduling slows the delivery of finished products when, for example, completely assembled automobiles wait for bumpers. Scheduling personnel may require additional training or closer supervision. Often, scheduling personnel—or any production workers, for that matter—are unaware of the importance of their jobs because they have not been shown "the big picture." Firms find that teaching employees why they do what they do, as well as how, pays off in creating a better attitude, which results in higher productivity. This has become crucial as firms strive for participative management, which is essential to synchronous production.

    Remember from page 272, Chapter 9 the experience of the American manager who tried to introduce participative management in Peru? The cultural forces of attitude toward authority and great difference between the educational levels, common in many countries, establishes a gulf between managers and workers. In fact, this is one of the reasons Japanese affiliates have had trouble introducing their production methods in the United States, where distances between managers and workers are much smaller than they are in most developing nations. Getting the participative management necessary for JIT and synchronous production will necessitate workers making sizable cultural changes, which, in our opinion, will require many years to attain.

    Another cultural problem is the desire to please everyone and the aversion to long-range planning. You have seen the importance of planning for the success of JIT, and you also learned that firm production schedules at least a month long are requisite. The desire to please everyone prevalent in some cultures tends to cause neglect of the schedule while production stops to attend the latest request from a customer. Moreover, because the markets are smaller in developing countries than in industrialized nations, product variations will have to be pared even more, and production systems will have to be even more flexible, if possible.

3. *Absenteeism*, always a problem for production managers everywhere in meeting production standards, has become even more significant in a bottleneck operation of a synchronous production system. Imagine the problems that occur when an entire department is idled because workers are at home helping the extended family with the harvest. When poor transportation systems make getting to work difficult, companies frequently provide transportation. To counteract absences due to illness and injury, they subsidize workers' lunches—prepared by trained nutritionists—and provide special shoes and protective clothing. Of course, management has the problem of educating workers not to remove the restraining apparel that they have never used before.

    Low morale conducive to high absenteeism will result if foreign managers trying to introduce the participative management necessary for synchronous production fail to assume the role of *patron* that most workers in developing countries expect. When employees have personal problems, they presume that the boss, not the personnel office, will find a solution. Personal debts, marital problems, and difficulties with the police are all part of manager-employee relations.

All too often, expatriate managers accept high absenteeism and low productivity as the norm instead of attempting to correct them. Yet those who apply all of the corrective means used at home, making adjustments for the foreign environment when necessary, do achieve notable success. One corrective measure, the discharge of unsatisfactory workers, is frequently impossible to apply because of legal constraints; but a consistent, energetic program of employee training, good union and labor relations, and the use of such morale builders as employee recognition, company reunions, sponsorship of team sports, and even suggestion boxes with rewards can be as successful in a foreign location as in the domestic operation.

Inferior Product Quality. Good quality is relative. What passes for good quality in the industrialized nations may actually be poor quality where a lack of maintenance and operating skills requires looser bearing fits and strong but more unwieldy parts. If the product or service satisfies the purpose for which it is purchased, the buyer considers it to be of good quality.

In World War II, the American military found that the Japanese submachine gun, poorly finished except at the working surfaces, was as effective a weapon as the American Thompson, which was finely finished all over. A gun collector would consider the American weapon to be of higher quality, but was it of higher quality from the Japanese standpoint?

Production quality standards are not set arbitrarily. It is the responsibility of the marketers, after studying their target market, to choose the price-quality combination they believe is most apt to satisfy that market. On the basis of this information, the quality standards for incoming materials, in-process items, and finished products should be established.

When the headquarters of global corporations insist that all foreign subsidiaries maintain the high-quality standards of the domestic plants, a number of problems can occur. Production may have to accept inputs of poorer quality when there is no alternative source of supply and then rework them. As we have pointed out, quality tolerances are especially tight for automated machinery. Finished-product standards set by a home office concerned about maintaining its global reputation can cause a product to be too costly for the local market. Many globals resolve this problem by permitting the subsidiary to manufacture products of lower quality under different brand names. If they wish the local plant to be a part of a worldwide logistic system, they may require a special quality to be produced for export. In some areas, "export quality" still denotes a superior product. Quality control, by the way, is not left exclusively in the hands of the subsidiary. Nearly all worldwide corporations require their foreign plants to submit samples of the finished product for testing on a regular basis.

Excessive Manufacturing Costs. Any manufacturing cost that exceeds the budgeted cost is excessive and naturally is of concern to the marketing and financial manager as well as to production personnel. Low output for any of the reasons we have discussed may be the cause, but the fault may also lie with the assumptions underlying the budget. Overoptimistic sales forecasts, the failure of suppliers to meet delivery dates, the failure of the government to issue import permits for essential raw materials in time, and unforeseen water or power failure are a few of the reasons output may be lower than expected.

Managements have always tried to limit inventories of raw materials, spare parts for plant machinery, and finished products, and those managements with synchronous production systems have a goal of almost complete elimination. But when there is an uncertainty of supply, as in most developing nations, stocks of these items can quickly get out of control. Production tends to overstock inputs to avoid the expense of changing production schedules when a given raw material has been exhausted. Maintenance personnel lay in an excessive stock of spare parts because they worry about not having something when they need it. Marketers, fearful of the frequent delays in production, overreact by building up finished goods inventories to avoid lost sales. When sales decrease, production may continue to produce finished products rather than lay off workers because the labor laws in many countries, unlike American labor laws, make employee layoffs both difficult and costly. In countries where skilled workers are in short supply, management does not dare to lay them off even if the law permits because these people will obtain employment elsewhere. The only alternative in the short run is to keep the factory running.

Finance, the one headquarters department that would ordinarily act to limit inventory building, will not move aggressively to stop this practice in countries afflicted with hyperinflation. It knows that under this condition, sizable profits can be made by being short in cash and long in inventory.

Supportive Activities.   Every production system requires staff units to provide the *supportive activities* essential to its operation. Two of these, quality control and inventory control, were examined in the previous section. Let us look now at the purchasing, maintenance, and technical functions.

Purchasing.   Production depends on the purchasing department to procure the raw materials, component parts, supplies, and machinery it requires to produce the finished product. The inability to obtain these materials when needed can result in costly shutdowns and lost sales. If the buyers agree to prices higher than what competitors are paying, the firm must either sell the finished product at higher prices or price competitively and earn less profit. The quality of the finished product may suffer if the quality of the purchased materials is inadequate.

Even in the industrialized countries before JIT was introduced, purchasing agents rarely could satisfy all of their companies' needs by waiting for the suppliers' representatives to come to them. They had to seek out and develop suppliers by visiting their plants and arranging for their companies' production and technical personnel to discuss matériel problems with the vendors' counterparts. In the developing countries, where many suppliers do not retain a sales force because they can sell everything they produce, supplier development assumes greater importance. The ability to locate vendors can easily compensate for a lack of other skills that management would require of a buyer at home.

When the firm depends heavily on imported materials, the prime criterion for hiring will be the purchasing agents' knowledge of import procedures and their connections with key government officials. The purchasing agents must constantly monitor government actions that can affect the availability of foreign exchange. They will often buy as much as possible of regularly consumed materials because they know they can always sell the excess to others, possibly at a profit. Interestingly, a study has found that the use of locally available raw materials varies according to the company's ownership. Those owned by parents from other developing nations imported 39 percent of their raw materials, locally owned plants imported 65 percent, and factories owned by multinationals or globals imported 76 percent.[43]

Whether to fill the critical position of purchasing agent with a local citizen or with someone from the home office is often the subject of considerable debate at headquarters. A native has the advantage of being better acquainted with the local supply sources and government officials, but he or she might suffer from such cultural disadvantages as a tendency to favor members of the extended family or to accept as a normal business practice the giving (scarce supply) or receiving (plentiful supply) of bribes. The employee from the home office, on the other hand, will be experienced in company purchasing procedures and should be free of these cultural disadvantages. Managers are not so naive as to believe that belonging to a certain culture guarantees an individual will or will not engage in unethical activities. However, the tendency to commit these acts may be greater when there are no cultural constraints.

Maintenance. A second function supporting production is the maintenance of buildings and equipment. The aim of the maintenance department is to prevent the occurrence of unscheduled work stoppages caused by equipment failures. Because of difficulty in obtaining imported spare parts and machinery, the machine shops of many maintenance departments actually manufacture these items.

> General Tire–Spain began building tire molds for its own use but became so proficient that it was soon selling them to other affiliates. General Motors subsidiaries are regularly supplied with tools and dies made by GM in Mexico.

It is common practice in industrialized countries to establish preventive maintenance programs in which machinery is shut down according to plan and worn parts are replaced. Such programs are especially important for a synchronous production system, as you know. With advance notice of a shutdown, the production department can schedule around the machine, or by working the machine overtime, the department can temporarily build up inventories, permitting the production process to continue during its overhaul.

This concept is not widely accepted in developing countries, where firms seem to take a fatalistic attitude toward equipment: "If it breaks down, we'll repair it." Furthermore, in a seller's market, maintenance personnel are pressured by production and marketing managers to keep machinery running. This short-term view allows no time for scheduled shutdowns. Subsidiaries that do practice preventive maintenance with overhaul periods based on headquarters' standards frequently find these standards inadequate because of local operating conditions (humidity, dust, and temperature) and the manner in which the operators handle the machinery. When the amount of spare parts ordered with the machinery is based on domestic experience, it is often insufficient.

In one sense, proper maintenance is more critical than 100 percent attendance of workers. The absence of one worker from a group of six usually will not halt production, but if a key machine suddenly breaks down, the entire plant can be idled.

Technical Function. The function of the technical department is to provide production with manufacturing specifications. Usually, technical personnel are also responsible for checking the quality of inputs and the finished product. The task of the technical department in a foreign subsidiary is not simply one of maintaining a file of specifications sent by the home office, because difficulty in obtaining the same kinds of raw materials as those used by the home plants may require substitutions that necessitate the complete rewriting of specifications.

> When a synthetic rubber plant was established in Mexico to produce some kinds of synthetic rubber, the government banned imports of all synthetic rubbers. Technical departments worked day and night to produce specifications that enabled the tire companies to substitute the few types available locally for the many kinds formerly imported.

The affiliate's technical manager is a key figure in the maintenance of product quality and thus is extremely influential in selecting sources of supply. Global and multinational companies go to great lengths in persuading host governments and joint venture partners of the need to place one of their people in this position. In this way, they are certain to keep the affiliate as a captive customer purchasing all of the inputs that the more highly integrated parent manufactures.

SUMMARY

1. **Describe the five global sourcing arrangements.** A firm may establish a wholly owned subsidiary in a low-labor-cost country to supply components to the home country plant or to supply a product not produced in the home country. An overseas joint venture may be established in a country where labor costs are lower to supply components to the home country. The firm may send components to be machined and assembled by an independent contractor in an in-bond plant. The firm may contract with an independent contractor overseas to manufacture products to its specifications. The firm may buy from an independent overseas manufacturer.

2. **Appreciate the importance of the added costs of global sourcing.** International freight, insurance, and packing may add 10 to 12 percent to the quoted price, depending on the sales term used. Import duties, customhouse broker's fees, cost of letter of credit, cost of inventory in the pipeline, and international travel are some of the other added costs.

3. **Understand the Japanese efforts to improve quality and lower costs.** Japanese manufacturers realized that because of the limited size of Japan's economy and its lack of natural resources, they would have to export to grow. To do so, they would have to be competitive with other nations, which meant improving their product quality and lowering their costs. To achieve these goals, they created a production system, just-in-time, based primarily on American production concepts.

4. **Know the just-in-time (JIT) production system.** JIT requires coordinated management of materials, people, and suppliers. JIT's goal is to eliminate inventories, reduce process and setup times, and use participative management to ensure worker input and loyalty to the firm. JIT includes total quality management (TQM), of which continuous improvement is an integral part.

5. **Comprehend the problems with JIT.** JIT is restricted to repetitive operations. It is a balanced system, so if one operation stops, the whole production line stops. But it is difficult to achieve a balanced system. In addition, JIT makes no allowances for contingencies. A sudden breakdown will stop the entire production system. Finally, it is a slow process to put JIT into effect.

6. **Understand synchronous production.** The goal of synchronous production is unbalanced production scheduling rather than the balanced scheduling of JIT; attention is focused on the bottleneck of the production system, and scheduling for the entire operation is controlled by the output of the bottleneck operation.

7. **Understand the objectives of the Malcolm Baldrige Award.** The Baldrige Award is intended to encourage American firms to improve quality and productivity and decrease costs. The award process establishes guidelines that businesses can use to evaluate their efforts to improve their quality. It also provides national recognition for firms that have met the award's standards.

8. **Identify the impediments to global standardization of production processes and procedures.** Differences in the foreign environmental forces, especially the economic, cultural, and political forces, cause units of an international multiplant operation to differ in size, machinery, and procedures.

9. **Understand the importance of intermediate and appropriate technology.** Governments of developing nations, preoccupied with high unemployment and rising capital costs, are urging investors to consider an intermediate technology rather than the highly automated processes of the industrialized nations. The multinationals' response,

in some instances, has been to search for an appropriate technology, which matches a country's market with its resources. Under this concept, the production processes used may vary from the most advanced to the most primitive, depending on the influence of the economic, sociocultural, and political variables.

10. **Know the two general classes of activities, productive and supportive, that must be performed in all production systems.** A production system is essentially a functionally related group of activities for creating value. After the system is operable, two general classes of activities, productive and supportive, must be performed. Productive activities are all those functions that are part of the production process. Among the important supportive activities are purchasing, maintenance, and the technical function.

KEY WORDS

- just-in-time (JIT)   618
- total quality management (TQM)   619
- quality circle   619
- Taylor's scientific management system   620
- preventive (planned) maintenance   620
- synchronous production   620
- bottleneck   621
- reengineering   623
- delayering   623
- manufacturing rationalization   629
- backward vertical integration   632
- intermediate technology   634
- appropriate technology   634
- export processing zones   636

QUESTIONS

1. What are the trade-offs for a firm that uses a just-in-time production system?

2. What advantages does synchronous production have over JIT?

3. What does quality in a pickup truck mean to you? To a farmer in Africa?

4. What difficulties do you see for global firms when they implement synchronous production in their plants located in developing countries? Are there any advantages that are more valuable to them than to plants in industrialized nations?

5. What is the connection between manufacturers' insistence on receiving components with zero defects from outside suppliers and JIT?

6. What are the advantages to a worldwide firm of global standardization of its production facilities?

7. Discuss the influence of the uncontrollable environmental forces in global standardization of a firm's production facilities.

8. Why might production costs be excessive?

9. Who should be in charge of the purchasing function of an overseas affiliate, a local person or someone from the home office? Why?

10. What is the importance of preventive maintenance? Why might it be difficult to establish a preventive program in an overseas plant?

MINICASE 19–1   Maquinas para el Hogar Penwick

Maquinas para el Hogar Penwick is a manufacturing subsidiary of Penwick Home Appliances in Boston. It is located in El Pais, a nation with 25 million inhabitants whose GNP per capita is $1,480. The country's annual inflation rate is about 30 percent, but the local company makes a good profit, in part because it keeps large stocks of components and raw materials purchased as much as 12 months before they are needed for production. The finished products are sold at prices set as if the raw materials and components had been purchased recently; hence the high profits. Penwick's competitors use the same strategy.

Penwick–El Pais has three competitors, none of which produces as complete a product mix or as many variations in each of the product lines of refrigerators, kitchen stoves and washing machines as does the local Penwick plant. José Garcia, the local marketing manager, is proud that Penwick–El Pais makes as many kinds of products and variations of products as the much larger home plant, and he has told the managing director of the local company that it is the wide product mix that maintains Penwick–El Pais's number-one position in sales. It is true that Manuel Cardenas, the local production manager, and Garcia frequently have heated discussions because Cardenas wants to make fewer product variations. Garcia accuses him of wanting to make black stoves like Henry Ford made black cars, but Cardenas claims he could double his production if he could make fewer kinds of products and less variations. Cardenas knows the value of long production runs and tries to get them. Garcia retorts that if Cardenas would pay attention to what he wants instead of making what Cardenas wants to make, he could sell more.

This is a sore spot with Cardenas because he tries hard to produce a new product according to Garcia's written request. If Garcia's memo says he wants a new size refrigerator in three colors to be available with or without beverage coolers or ice cube makers, these are the models Cardenas asks the product design department to design and make production specifications for. True, Garcia at one time or other has asked to attend meetings with Cardenas and his staff, but Cardenas considers this a waste of time. After all, he doesn't waste the design department's time by asking to attend their meetings; why should a salesperson attend his meetings? He has enough problems with the high prices for parts that the purchasing department gives him.

When he complains, they tell him that everything he orders is special manufacture for the vendors. Cardenas says that's their problem; this is what the design department specifies, and this is what he has to use to build the product.

Cardenas has more pressing problems. Headquarters has adopted a new production system, synchronous production, and now wants him to do the same. In fact, he had to send his assistant manager to Boston for a month's training. Now she and the design manager, who also went, are back, and they brought one of the home office experts with them. They're all going to have a long meeting with him this afternoon. Cardenas has read about synchronous production in technical journals and feels it does seem to have some advantages. But all of them have been in highly industrialized nations, and there are a lot of cultural and economic differences between El Pais and those countries.

You might role-play this case. Imagine you are one of the group of three that has come from Boston. Even though you know the local plant has orders to convert to synchronous production, you still have to win over the local personnel.

1. What will you say?

2. Can you think of any advantages that might be even more important for the local plant than they are for the larger home plant?

3. What problems do you foresee in putting synchronous production in place?

Financial Management

Ten minutes is a long-term outlook. Foreign currency dealers, Manufacturers Hanover Trust Company

CONCEPT PREVIEWS

After reading this chapter, you should be able to:

1. **realize** that the currencies of countries change in value in terms of each other

2. **understand** how currency value changes affect international business transactions

3. **recognize** the tremendous importance of financial management to an international company (IC)

4. **know** about financial management tools

5. **understand** why exporters sometimes accept payment in forms other than money

6. **differentiate** between hard, convertible currencies and soft, nonconvertible ones

7. **explain** the growing importance of international finance centers to ICs

8. **understand** *zaiteku*, or financial engineering

The "Achete" Incident

David Edwards was born in Wichita Falls, Texas, but was intrigued by international business and finance. He worked his way up the ladder of Citibank's international operation, where he moved into a senior slot in Paris as head of *les cambistes,* as the fast-and-furious currency exchange traders are called. His boldness and quick mind equipped him well for this high-pressure operation, and he did very well for his employer and for himself. Occasionally, however, his Wichita Falls French got him in trouble. He tells of one occasion when Citibank's currency trader at the Bourse,* who was a Frenchman, phoned him and reported that the U.S. dollar bids were going down fast. Edwards shouted into the telephone, "Aw, shit!" and slammed down the receiver. A few seconds later, the trader called Edwards on another phone and reported proudly that he had bought a large block of U.S. dollars. "You did what?" Edwards yelled, to which the startled trader protested, "But you said, *'achete.'* "[†] That evening, Edwards walked into his boss's office and said, "I've got a funny story to tell you, but it's going to cost you a quarter of a million dollars to hear it."

*Bourse *is the French word for stock and currency markets.*
[†]*Achete* means *buy* in French.
Source: Roy Rowan, *Fortune,* January 10, 1983, p. 46.

Currency futures market.

Courtesy of Chicago Mercantile Exchange

In Chapter 6, we spoke of some of the financial forces with which IC management is confronted and of the financial problems it must try to solve. In this chapter, we shall examine some of the tools and methods that financial management uses to solve those problems. The forces or problems we identified were fluctuating currency exchange rates, currency exchange controls, tariffs, taxes, inflation, and accounting practices.

One problem faced by the financial management of an IC that can be turned into an opportunity is the question of in what currency to raise capital. The company may need or be able to use two or more currencies. If so, its financial management can shop the many financial centers around the world to raise the currency it can use at the lowest cost.

A related problem results from payment for products sold internationally. The buyer may pay the seller in the seller's currency, which is the same as a domestic sale. But payment may be made in another currency. If it is a convertible currency, the seller can convert it to his or her currency, though there may be a currency exchange rate risk if payment is delayed—for example, if the seller extends credit to the buyer.

If the buyer has too little convertible currency, the seller may accept goods or services instead of money. Financial management must convert the goods or services to money, a growing phenomenon as international competition grows keener.

Elsewhere in the book, we deal with market assessment and analysis and with production planning. Early in their assessment, analysis, and planning, marketing and production management should bring in financial management to coordinate capital needs with capital availability.

The financial managers must examine the alternative ways of financing the marketing and production plans. How much capital of what sorts will be needed, and when? What are the best sources of this capital, and how long can the new operations be expected to need support before they are financially self-sufficient?

Wherever an IC does business, its financial manager must consider **fluctuating exchange rates**—the fluctuating values of currencies in terms of each other. Also to be considered is the value of each of those currencies in terms of the currency of the IC's home, or financial and tax-reporting, country.

The fluctuations create currency value risks. These may be categorized as (1) transaction risks and (2) translation risks.

Transaction Risks

Transaction risks usually involve a receivable or a payable denominated in a foreign currency. These risks arise from transactions, such as a purchase from a foreign supplier or a sale to a foreign customer. There are several methods by which the financial manager can buy protection against these risks.[1] The company can engage in several types of **hedging**, or if it is a buyer or a borrower, it may be able to accelerate or delay payments or provisions for payments. Within limits, price increases may be used.

Forward Hedge.   This is accomplished in the foreign exchange market and involves a contract. The IC contracts with another party to deliver to that party at an agreed future date a fixed amount of one currency in return for a fixed amount of another currency. Contracts in the major trading country currencies are generally available for 30-, 60-, 90-, or 180-day deliveries. Longer-term contracts can sometimes be negotiated, as can contracts with other than 30-, 60-, 90-, or 180-day maturities.

5 Norwegian Krone = 1 U.S. Dollar.   An example could work as follows. An American exporter sells $1 million of goods to a Norwegian importer. The rate of exchange on the date of sale is 5 Norwegian krone to 1 U.S. dollar (NK5 = US$1) and therefore involves NK5 million. The agreement is that the importer will pay the exporter NK5 million in 180 days.

The risk of any change in the US$–NK exchange rate is now on the American exporter. If the NK loses value, say, to NK7 = US$1, during the 180 days, the NK5 million will buy only US$714,285.71 when received. But the American exporter's expectation was to receive US$1 million, and the exchange rate change causes a loss of more than $285,000.

The Hedge Involves a Contract.   The U.S. exporter could use a forward hedge to protect against such a loss by contracting to deliver NK5 million to the buyer (the other party to the hedge contract) in 180 days in return for US$1 million, which the buyer agrees to deliver to the exporter at the same time. The actual amount the exporter receives will be less than $1 million because the buyer will want compensation for the risk of a drop in the value of the NK during the 180 days. Assume the buyer wants 1 percent and the exporter agrees. One percent would be $10,000, and the buyer would deliver $990,000 in exchange for NK5 million.[2]

The $10,000 can be regarded as a sort of insurance premium that the exporter pays to be certain how much in US$s it will receive in 180 days. Of

---

FLUCTUATING CURRENCY EXCHANGE RATES

fluctuating exchange rates
Currencies of different countries go up and down in value in terms of each other

transaction risks
In import/export transactions, the party that must pay or receive a foreign currency in the future takes the risk that the currency value will change to its disadvantage

hedging
Trying to protect yourself against losses due to currency exchange rate fluctuations

TABLE 20–1
Currencies traded on the
International monetary
market

Traded Currency	Ticker Code
British pound	BP
Canadian dollar	CD
Deutsche mark	DM
Dutch guilder	DG
French franc	FF
Japanese yen	JY
Mexican peso	MP
Swiss franc	SF

course, it must have made the business decision that $990,000 is an acceptable amount for the goods it is selling.

As with other prices in a free market society, there is no law or regulation that mandates 1 percent, or $10,000, as the cost for a $1 million hedge. In our example, the good financial manager for the exporter will shop around among banks and will find some prices lower than others. The NK is not traded on the International Monetary Market (IMM) at the Chicago Mercantile Exchange. If the currency of payment were one of the eight traded there, the financial manager should also get a quote for an IMM contract. The traded currencies are shown in Table 20–1.

The IMM Contract is a Futures Hedge.   If the financial manager uses IMM contracts, the hedge is with a futures, not a forward, contract. At the IMM, the traded currencies are treated as commodities (wheat, soybeans, sow bellies, and so forth) and traded as futures contracts. Futures contracts are traded by brokers, and the exporter must have a margin account with a broker. Futures contracts come in fixed amounts, such as BP25,000, and standardized delivery dates are used.

Currency Options.   At the end of 1982, the Philadelphia Stock Exchange began dealing in options to buy or sell currencies. That offered another hedge opportunity, which has been expanded since then in at least two ways. First, other exchanges have begun dealing in currency options in London, Chicago, Amsterdam, New York, and other cities. Second, there now exists an over-the-counter currency option market involving banks, multinationals, and brokers. Figure 20–1 is an advertisement for foreign currency trading.

Intra-IC Hedge.   A rapidly growing practice is for international companies to seek an internal hedge within their own network of parent, subsidiary, and affiliated companies. Suppose that in our NK–US$ case, the financial manager found that one of the IC's companies owed about NK5 million, payable about the same time as the NK5 million was receivable under the export contract. The NK payable by one unit of the IC could then be hedged (netted) against the NK receivable carried by the other IC unit. Thus, two hedges are achieved at no outside cost, and the bank, option, or IMM fees are avoided.

A Covered Position.   Even though the exporter in the above forward hedge example does not have any NKs at the time it enters the hedge contract, it does have the Norwegian importer's obligation to pay the NK5 million, which can be delivered to the other party to the hedge contract. If you either have the funds (NK5 million) when you enter the hedge contract or they are due from

FIGURE 20–1
Foreign currency trading

Source: Courtesy Chicago Mercantile Exchange

another business transaction on or before the due date under your hedge contract (as here), you are in a "covered" position.[3]

An Uncovered Position. A financial manager can also use the foreign exchange market to take advantage of an expected rise or fall in the relative value of currency. There will then be created an "uncovered" long or short position. For example, if the financial manager of an American company believes the NK will appreciate in value in the next few months, the procedure would be to go long on the NK at the spot rate, NK5 = US$1. This is a contract whereby the company buys, say, NK5 million for US$1 million, both currencies to be delivered at a future date. If the NK appreciates to NK4 = US$1, the financial manager was correct, and the NK5 million received by the company is worth $1,250,000. The company pays, as agreed, $1 million. If the financial manager believes the NK will depreciate in the next few months, the procedure would be to short NKs at the spot rate. An uncovered short position results when you sell the money or any other commodity without having it either on hand or due you under another business transaction.

Using the same rate (NK5 = US$1), and the same amount (NK5 million), the company agrees to deliver NK5 million at a future date in return for US$1 million. If, in fact, the NK depreciates to NK6 = US$1, the financial manager was again correct. The company can buy the NK5 million for approximately $830,000. The company will be paid, as agreed, $1 million.

Both of the above stories had happy endings for the company, but it exposed itself to risk. Short-term currency value movements are extremely uncertain in both direction and amount, and those company stories (and perhaps the financial manager) could have had sad endings if the currencies had moved in the other directions. People who study currency markets and deal in them daily tend to be modest in their forecasts of short-term movements.

We have interviewed and talked at length with foreign exchange market officers, bank traders, and bank economists in America, Asia, and Europe. Almost all of them expressed definite views, opinions, and forecasts about long-term currency value changes. Not one of them would hazard more than a guess about tomorrow's prices.

Credit or Money Market Hedge.   As indicated by its name, the credit or money market hedge involves credit—borrowing money. The company desiring a hedge is the borrower. The credit or money market hedge may be illustrated by the same transaction used above to discuss the forward exchange market hedge.

The Norwegian importer will pay NK5 million to the American exporter for the goods in 180 days. With the money market hedge, the exporter will borrow NK5 million from an Oslo bank on the day of the sale to the Norwegian importer.* The exporter will immediately convert to US$s at the current NK5 = US$1 rate, giving it the $1 million selling price; but it owes NK5 million to the Norwegian bank, due in 180 days. That will be repaid with the Norwegian importer's NK5 million payment.

The exporter has a variety of options for use of the $1 million. It can lend it, put it in certificates of deposit, use it in a swap (see below), or use it as internal operating capital. The financial manager will study all of the options to find which will be most beneficial.

Before a money market hedge is used, the exporter must compare the interest rates in its and the importer's countries. If the interest on the exporter's borrowing in the importer's country is significantly higher than the amount the exporter can earn on the money in its country, the cost of this type of hedge may be too great.

Other comparisons and checks should be made before borrowing the NK from an Oslo bank. Even though the NK is not one of the most widely traded

---

*Actually, the amount borrowed will usually be less than NK5 million. It will be an amount that, plus interest for 180 days, will total NK5 million at the end of that period. Thus, the NK5 million payment from the importer will exactly repay the loan, with no odd amounts plus or minus.

currencies, the financial manager should inquire of banks in major Eurocurrency centers (such as London, Paris, Zurich, and Frankfurt) to ascertain whether NKs could be borrowed at a lower interest cost. And in the case of NKs, other Scandinavian financial centers—Copenhagen, Helsinki, and Stockholm—should be checked for competitive bids.

Just as in the foreign exchange market hedge situation, an IC should check its company units to learn whether any of them have an NK balance that could be lent internally, that is, from the unit with the balance to the unit with the NK foreign exchange exposure. Thus, interest payments to banks outside the IC could be avoided.

Acceleration or Delay of Payment.

If an importer expects the currency in its country to depreciate in terms of the currency of its foreign supplier, it would likely be motivated to buy the necessary foreign currency as soon as it could. This assumes the importer must pay in the currency of the exporter, the opposite of our assumption in the hedging discussions.

Which Way Will the Exchange Rates Go? If the importer agreed to pay $1 million when the exchange rate was NK5 = US$1, its cost at that time would be NK5 million. If, before payment is due, the rate drops to NK6 = US$1, the cost will be NK6 million. The importer, then, would be tempted to pay early or, if possible, to make the currency exchange at once and use the foreign currency until the payment due date.

Of course, the opposite would be the case if the importer expects the NK to strengthen from the NK5 = US$1 rate at the time of the purchase contract. It would be motivated to delay payment and to delay conversion from NKs to US$s. For example, if the rate goes to NK4 = US$1, the necessary $1 million will cost only NK4 million. Payment accelerations or delays are frequently called **leads** or **lags**.

Unrelated Companies. Although independent, unrelated companies use acceleration or delay on each other, one may be doing so at the expense of the other. Usually, however, the exporter is indifferent as to the method used by the importer to protect itself against currency risk as long as payment is received on time in the agreed currency. The IC, on the other hand, may be able to realize enterprise-wide benefit using payment leads and lags.

Within an IC. For purposes of examining potential payment accelerations or delays between different country operations of one IC, we should differentiate two types of ICs. At one extreme is the IC that operates a coordinated, integrated worldwide business with the objective of the greatest profit for the total enterprise. At the other extreme is the independent operation of each part of the IC as its own separate profit center.

As pointed out above, international payment leads and lags between independent companies are usually of no concern to the exporter as long as it receives payment as agreed. The same would be true of IC units that operate autonomously. But an integrated, coordinated IC can benefit the enterprise as a whole by cooperating in payment leads or lags. The overall IC objective is to get its money out of weak currencies and into strong currencies as quickly as reasonably possible.

Thus, instead of incurring the hedging costs incurred by independent companies while awaiting the future day of payment, IC units can make payment immediately if trading out of a weak currency or delay payment until the payment date if trading out of a strong currency. If the profit of the unit paying immediately suffers from loss of interest on the money or shortage of

leads
Immediate purchases of a foreign currency to satisfy a future need because the buyer believes it will strengthen vis-à-vis the home currency

lags
Delayed purchases of a foreign currency to satisfy a future need because the buyer believes it will weaken vis-à-vis the home currency

operating capital (manager compensation and promotion frequently depend on profit), adjustment can be made to recognize that the IC gained as a result of the cooperation of that management's IC unit.

Effects of Leads and Lags on Foreign Exchange Markets.   When an importer in a weak currency country buys from an exporter in a strong currency country with payment in the future, the usual practice is to convert or hedge immediately. And by selling the currency expected to go down in value and buying the one expected to go up, the importer helps realize those expectations; the prophecies are self-fulfilling.

The opposite is done when the importer in a country with a strong currency buys from a country with a weak currency. Now the importer will hold onto its perceived strong currency until the last moment and not buy the weak currency till then. Again, this strengthens the perceived strong currency and weakens the other.

Objectives of Intra-IC Payments.   Within the strictures of applicable laws and the minimum working capital requirements of the parent and affiliates,[4] ICs can maximize their currency strengths and minimize their currency weaknesses.[5] Their objectives are to:

1. Keep as much money as is reasonably possible in countries with high interest rates. This is done to avoid borrowing at high rates or perhaps to have capital to lend at those rates.

2. Keep as much money as is reasonably possible in countries where credit is difficult to obtain. If the IC unit in such a country needs capital, it may be able to generate it internally.

3. Maximize holdings of hard, strong currencies, which may appreciate in value in terms of soft, weak currencies. Minimize, as much as reasonably possible, holdings of the latter. This objective may conflict with the first objective because strong currencies are usually available at lower interest rates than are weak ones. Financial management must consider all of the conditions, needs, and expectations and make a balanced judgment.

4. Minimize holdings of currencies that either are subject to currency exchange controls or can be expected to be subject to them during the period in which the company will hold those currencies.

exposure netting
Taking open positions in two currencies that are expected to balance each other

Exposure Netting.   **Exposure netting** is the acceptance of open positions* in two or more currencies that are considered to balance one another and therefore require no further internal or external hedging. Basically, there are two ways to accomplish this: (1) currency groups and (2) a combination of a strong currency and a weak currency.

Currency Groups.   Some groups of currencies tend to move in close conjunction with one another even during floating rate periods.[6] For example, some LDC currencies are pegged to the currency of their most important DC trading partner; and among European DCs, the European Monetary System (EMS) is an effort to coordinate movements of the participating governments' currencies vis-à-vis other currencies. In this situation, exposure netting could involve

---

*An *open* position exists when the company has greater assets than liabilities (or greater liabilities than assets) in one currency. A *closed,* or *covered,* position exists when assets and liabilities in a currency are equal.

the simultaneous long and short of, say, the Belgian franc and the Dutch guilder; the financial manager would have a franc receivable and a guilder payable and would feel that they cover each other.[7]

A caveat is in order here. The EMS was badly dented if not broken during the early 1990s as obstacles were encountered in efforts to enforce provisions of the Maastricht Treaty calling for economic and monetary union (EMU) within the EU. In 1995, strenuous efforts were underway to bring EMU into being, and the consensus was that a tight grouping of European currencies would be one result. It is suggested that you reread the material about this in Chapter 4.

A Strong Currency and a Weak Currency. A second exposure netting possibility involves two payables (or two receivables), one in a currently strong currency, such as the deutsche mark, and the other in a weaker one, such as the Canadian dollar. The hope is that weakness in one will offset the strength of the other.[8] This is not to infer that the deutsche mark is always strong and the Canadian dollar always weak. At any given time it could be just the opposite, or both strong, or both weak.

An advantage of exposure netting is that it avoids the costs of hedging. It is also more risky; the currencies may not behave as expected during the periods of the open receivables or payables.

Price Adjustments. Sales management often desires to make sales in a country whose currency is expected to be devalued. In such a situation, financial management finds that neither hedging nor exposure netting is possible or economic. Within the limitations of competition and the customer's budget, it may be possible to make price adjustments—to raise the selling price in the customer's currency. The hope is that the additional amount will compensate for the expected drop in value of the customer's currency.

Price Adjustments within an IC Group. If an IC is of the coordinated, integrated type, there is much opportunity to adjust selling prices in intraenterprise transactions between the parent and its affiliated companies or between affiliates. The selling prices are raised or lowered in anticipation of currency exchange rate changes, thereby maximizing gains and minimizing losses.

Government Reactions to Intraenterprise Price Adjustments. Such intraenterprise pricing practices are often used for purposes of (1) realizing higher profits in countries with lower tax rates and harder currencies and (2) decreasing import duties. Tax and customs officials have become more knowledgeable about such practices and now have the power to disregard prices that they consider unreasonably low or high. They then levy taxes or tariffs on what they determine to be reasonable profits or prices. Therefore, companies must use such practices carefully and with discretion; financial management should be able to substantiate its prices with convincing cost data. Some writers do not recommend aggressive use of transfer pricing* for foreign exchange management.[9]

The alternatives the financial manager for an American exporter should consider to reduce the risk of exchange losses are shown in Figure 20–2. We use the transaction discussed above, in which an American exporter sold $1 million of goods to a Norwegian importer. At the time of sale, the exchange

---

*Transfer pricing is a term for the pricing involved when one unit of an IC buys from another. See discussion of transfer pricing in Chapter 15.

FIGURE 20–2 Hedging currency risks

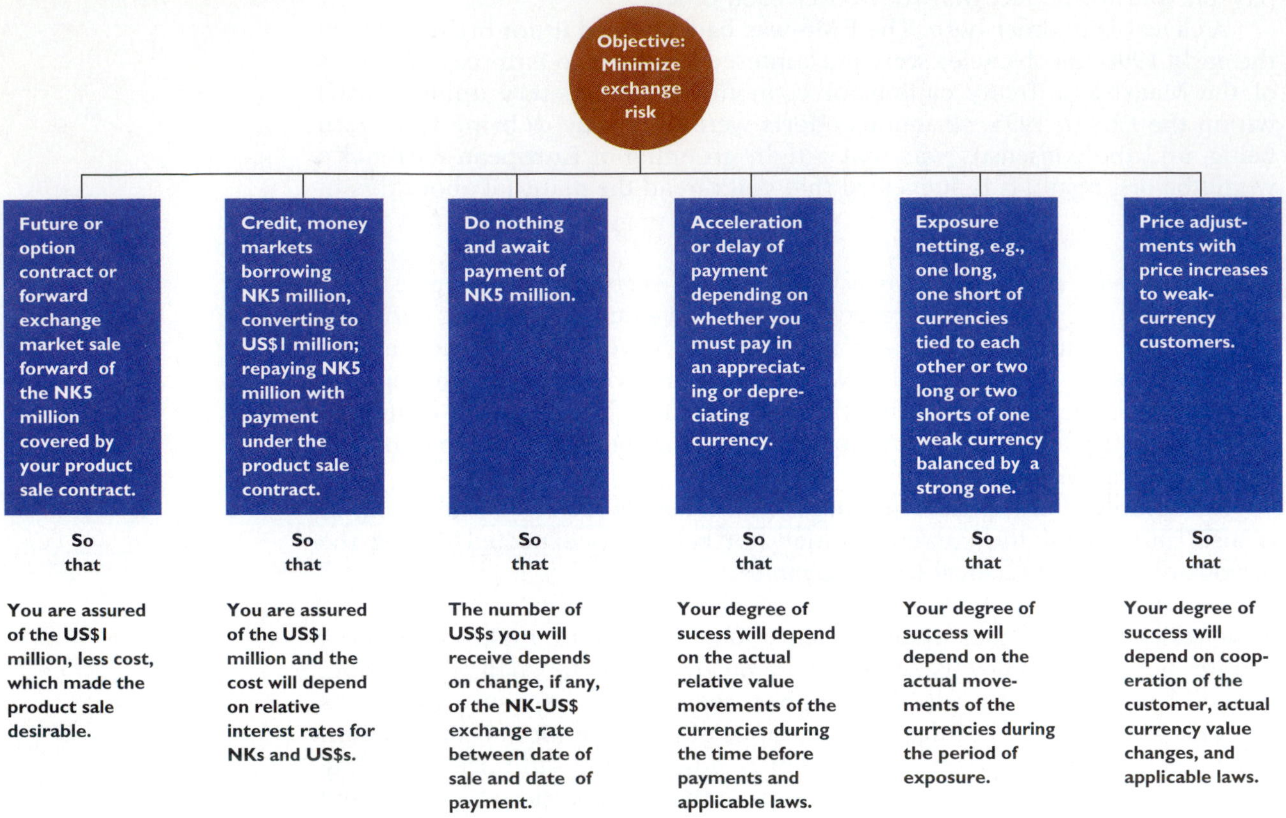

Objective: Minimize exchange risk

Future or option contract or forward exchange market sale forward of the NK5 million covered by your product sale contract.	Credit, money markets borrowing NK5 million, converting to US$1 million; repaying NK5 million with payment under the product sale contract.	Do nothing and await payment of NK5 million.	Acceleration or delay of payment depending on whether you must pay in an appreciating or depreciating currency.	Exposure netting, e.g., one long, one short of currencies tied to each other or two long or two shorts of one weak currency balanced by a strong one.	Price adjustments with price increases to weak-currency customers.
So that	**So that**	**So that**	**So that**	**So that**	**So that**
You are assured of the US$1 million, less cost, which made the product sale desirable.	You are assured of the US$1 million and the cost will depend on relative interest rates for NKs and US$s.	The number of US$s you will receive depends on change, if any, of the NK-US$ exchange rate between date of sale and date of payment.	Your degree of success will depend on the actual relative value movements of the currencies during the time before payments and applicable laws.	Your degree of success will depend on the actual movements of the currencies during the period of exposure.	Your degree of success will depend on cooperation of the customer, actual currency value changes, and applicable laws.

rate was $1 = 5 Norwegian krone. The sales contract called for the Norwegian importer to pay the American exporter NK5 million in six months, which placed the currency exchange risk on the exporter.

Only for Big Business?

Generally, only larger companies can afford the expertise and deal in big enough amounts to make currency risk hedging practical. However, in 1990 a new development brought some hedging possibilities within reach of medium and small businesses.

In January 1990, the U.S. Federal Reserve allowed American banks to hold foreign currency deposits in the United States. It is difficult or even impossible for a smaller firm to open a modest account at a foreign bank, but it is much less intimidating to deal with the firm's regular, local bank.

Now, to protect against a drop in the US$'s value, an importer from France can buy the number of French francs that will be needed to pay the French exporter. They can be held in its local account, earning interest until needed.

Translation Risks

We have just examined the risks that an international business incurs when it buys and sells between two or more countries and agrees to either make or receive a future payment in a foreign currency. The purchase or sale is a transaction, and the currency value change risk is called a transaction risk.

Financial statements of ICs must be stated in one currency, just as are the statements of any domestic business. The IC may have businesses and assets in several currencies, such as German marks, French francs, and Japanese yen, but its financial statements would be meaningless for most people if all of those currencies were used. One must be chosen, and the values of the others must be translated to the chosen currency.

Sooner or later, companies with international operations will have assets, liabilities, revenues, and expenses in more than one currency. The financial statements of an American IC must translate assets and so forth from the currencies of their locations into US$s.

The **translation risks** can be illustrated by assuming an American opens a Canadian dollar (C$) bank account of C$1 million at a time when the exchange rate is C$1 = US$1. If, one year later, the exchange rate has changed to C$1.10 = US$1 and the bank balance is still C$1 million, the American IC still has its C$1 million. However, the company must report financially in US$s, and the Canadian bank account is now worth only about US$909,090.

It does not follow from the drop in the relative value of the Canadian dollar in this example that the investment in Canada was unwise. It may be profitable, growing, and gaining market share. The American may be very pleased with the Canadian investment and have no intention of liquidating it, or may even be considering adding to it. After all, Canadian assets are now less expensive in US$ terms than they were at the time of the original investment.

Realistic Information. Ongoing translating and reporting bring up to date the values in US$s of previously reported assets and so forth. Management must base important decisions, such as dividends, pricing, new investment, and asset location, on the updating of all such asset and earnings values. It is unrealistic for management to base key decisions on the assumption that exchange rates have not changed and will not change.

Management Fears. Managers fear that shareholders and analysts will regard translated and reported foreign exchange losses as speculation, or worse, bad management. It is difficult to explain that reported losses are irrelevant or should be ignored. Even though reserves are not permitted under present U.S. accounting practices, many managers are attempting to insulate financial statements from foreign exchange market fluctuations by other means.

Some of these means are the same as those discussed above in connection with transaction risks. Management can hedge currencies, accelerate or delay payments, net exposures, or adjust prices. There are other means that can be used against transaction risks, but these are more often used in transaction situations. Management can neutralize the company's balance sheet through the use of swaps.

Neutralizing the Balance Sheet. **Neutralizing the balance sheet** means to endeavor to have monetary assets in a given currency approximate monetary liabilities in that currency. In that condition, a fall in the currency value of assets will be matched by the fall in payment obligations; thus, the translation risk is avoided.

However, before financial management neutralizes its balance sheet to avoid translation risk, it must look to the business needs of the parent and subsidiary companies. The ongoing business flow of and need for capital, the cost of capital from country to country, payrolls, payables and receivables, optimum location for new investment, and dozens of other business considerations must be factored in before an attempt is made to neutralize the balance sheets of all subsidiaries. In other words, maximizing the profit of the enterprise should be more important than avoiding translation risk where they conflict.

---

translation risks
The losses or gains that can result from restating the values of the assets and liabilities/payables and receivables arising from investments abroad from one currency to another

neutralizing the balance sheet
Having monetary assets in amounts approximately equal to monetary liabilities

Swaps

swaps
Trades of assets and liabilities in different currencies or interest rate structures to lessen risks or lower costs

Swaps may be used to protect against transaction risks, are more likely to be used against translation risks, but are most likely to be used to raise or transfer capital. Therefore, we shall treat swaps separately and examine several types: (1) spot and forward market swaps, (2) parallel loans, and (3) bank swaps. Interest rate swaps are dealt with below in the "Capital Raising and Investing" section.

Spot and Forward Market Swaps. Suppose an American parent wants to lend Italian lira (IL) to its Italian subsidiary and to avoid currency exchange risk. The parent will buy IL in the spot market and lend them to the subsidiary. At the same time, the parent will short the same amount of IL (buying US$s for forward delivery) for the period of the loan. The short lira position is covered with the lira repaid by the subsidiary, and the parent receives the dollars. The cost will depend on the discount rate in the forward market as compared to the spot market rate.

Parallel Loans. Keeping the American parent and its Italian subsidiary of the previous example, let's add an Italian parent company and its American subsidiary. Assume each parent wants to lend to its subsidiary in the subsidiary's currency. This can be accomplished without using the foreign exchange market. The Italian parent lends the agreed amount in lira to the Italian subsidiary of the American parent. At the same time and the same loan maturity, the American parent lends the same amount (at the spot IL-US$ rate) in US$s to the American subsidiary of the Italian parent. Figure 20–3 illustrates this.

As you see, each loan is made and repaid in one currency, thus avoiding foreign exchange risk. Each loan should have the right of offset, which means that if either subsidiary defaults on its repayment, the other subsidiary can withhold its repayment. This avoids the need for parent company guarantees.

This sort of parallel loan swap can be adapted to many circumstances and can involve more than two countries or companies. If a subsidiary in a blocked-currency country has a surplus of that currency in its local operation, perhaps the local subsidiary of another IC needs capital.[10] The other IC would like to provide that capital but would not like to convert more of its hard

---

FIGURE 20–3

Parallel loans by two parent companies (each to the subsidiary of the other)

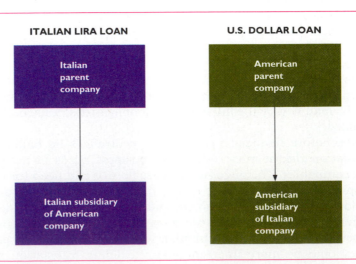

ITALIAN LIRA LOAN

Italian parent company

Italian subsidiary of American company

U.S. DOLLAR LOAN

American parent company

American subsidiary of Italian company

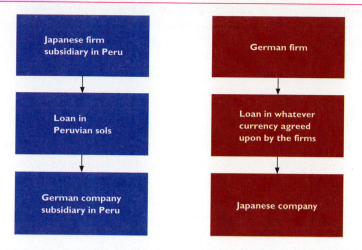

FIGURE 20–4
Parallel swap (where a soft currency is involved)

currency into a soft currency. The subsidiary of the first IC lends its surplus currency to the subsidiary of the second IC. The parent company of the second IC lends the parent company of the first IC an equivalent amount in some other currency that it can use. Figure 20–4 illustrates this.[11]

Interest may or may not be charged on swaps. That usually depends on whether interest rates in the two countries are at similar rates or widely different. In the latter situation, the borrower getting the higher-cost currency might pay an equivalently higher interest on repayment.

You may have observed that we have not mentioned banks in our discussion of swaps. These company-to-company loans are competition for commercial banks, but some banks will facilitate negotiations or act as a broker between clients in arranging swaps. Investment banks and other money brokers sometimes facilitate or even instigate swaps as a service to clients.

Bank Swaps.   Historically, swaps of this kind have been between banks (commercial or central) of two or more countries for the purpose of acquiring temporarily needed foreign exchange; but in recent years, companies have entered the field. A typical use of a bank swap is to finance expansion of an IC subsidiary in an LDC whose currency is soft and nonconvertible or blocked.

The mechanics are simple. Assume a Swiss IC wishes to expand a subsidiary's plant in Indonesia and, in doing so, to minimize foreign exchange risks and to avoid exchanging any more hard convertible Swiss francs (SFs) for soft Indonesian rupiahs (IRs).

The Swiss parent company may deal either with a commercial bank in Indonesia or with the Indonesian central bank. In either event, the Swiss IC deposits SFs in a Swiss bank to the credit of the Indonesian bank. In turn, the Indonesian bank lends IRs to the Indonesian subsidiary. At an agreed future date, the Indonesian bank repays the SFs and the subsidiary repays the IRs.

You may have observed that in this example the Indonesian rupiahs are lent and repaid in Indonesia and the Swiss francs are lent and repaid in Switzerland, which eliminates the need to use the foreign exchange markets. Thus, exchange market costs are avoided while both parties obtain a foreign currency for which they have a use.

We have spoken of swaps as methods to lessen translation risks and raise capital. There are also more common ways to raise capital.

CAPITAL RAISING AND INVESTING

When a company wishes to raise capital, its financial management must make a number of decisions. To cut the costs of capital, financial managers are increasingly exploring the uses of interest rate swaps and currency swaps. As these are relatively new and growing in popularity, we shall treat them separately.

Decisions

1. The currency in which the capital will be raised.
2. Long-term estimate of the strength or weakness of that currency.
3. How much of the money raised should be **equity capital** and how much should be **debt capital**.[12]
4. Whether the money should be borrowed from (a) a commercial bank by an ordinary loan; (b) a bank as part of a swap, discussed above; (c) another company as part of a swap or otherwise; (d) another part of the IC; or (e) a public offering in one of the world's capital markets, for example, in the New York or Eurobond markets.
5. If the decision is made to use one of the world's capital markets, management must then decide in which of those markets it can achieve its objectives at lowest cost. The IC can shop among the national markets in such diverse centers as New York, London, Paris, Zurich, Bahrain, Singapore, Tokyo, and the Cayman Islands. Or it can try the international, or Eurobond, Eurocurrency-type, markets in the above-named centers and elsewhere.[13]
6. How much money the company needs and for how long. For instance, if the company is moving into a new market or product, there will probably be a period during product introduction, plant construction, or whatever when the new venture will need more capital than it can generate.
7. Whether other sources of money are available. For example, if the company is forming or expanding a joint venture operation, the joint venturer may be a good source of money. Or if the move is into a country or area that wants the IC's technology or management or the jobs that will be created, the government may be a source of low-cost funds. Under such circumstances, the company may also be able to negotiate tax reductions or holidays.*

To optimize the decision results, the company needs up-to-date, accurate information. It should also have good, ongoing relationships with international bank officers and with financial management at other firms.

We have been dealing with external sources of capital, that is, sources outside the company's operations. Of course, a successful company generates its own capital internally, but that subject is not included here.

Interest Rate Swaps

Interest rate swaps are a product of the advent and evolution of currency swaps, which were intended as an arbitrage between currency markets. Interest rate swaps are themselves a form of arbitrage but are between the fixed-rate and the floating-rate interest markets. An interest rate swap, in its most basic form, is nothing more than an exchange by two parties of interest

equity capital
Capital raised by selling common stock representing ownership of the company

debt capital
Capital raised by selling bonds representing debt of the company

---

*A tax holiday is a period after an investment is made during which the government agrees not to tax the company's operations, profits, or executives.

"We need two hundred million bucks by Friday — any ideas?"

Reprinted from *The Wall Street Journal:* Permission Cartoon Features Syndicate.

rate flows on borrowings made in these two markets—fixed for floating and floating for fixed. As a result, each party obtains the type of liability it prefers and at a more attractive rate.

Bank-Intermediated "Plain Vanilla" Swaps. In a typical plain vanilla swap, a BBB-rated U.S. corporation is paired with an AAA-rated foreign bank. The BBB corporation wants to borrow at fixed rates but is discouraged from doing so by the high rates attached to its low rating. The company can borrow in the floating-rate market, however. The AAA foreign bank wants to borrow at floating rates, as its assets are tied to the London Interbank Offer Rate (LIBOR). The bank normally pays at LIBOR to obtain lendable funds. It is able to borrow at fixed rates, which are better than those the corporation could get.

When the swap is planned, the bank borrows at fixed rates in the Eurobond market, and the BBB corporation borrows at floating rates. With this done, the two then swap rates on their respective loans. The corporation entices the bank into doing this by discounting the floating rate to the bank by LIBOR minus 0.25 percent. In return, the bank gives the BBB corporation a fixed rate that is better than the one the corporation could acquire on its own. A hypothetical numerical example is shown below.

Assume the BBB firm can borrow at a fixed rate of 12.5 percent.

1. AAA bank issues 11 percent fixed-rate debt.
2. BBB firm taps floating-rate market at LIBOR plus 0.5 percent.
3. BBB firm swaps its floating rate to bank at LIBOR minus 0.25 percent.
4. AAA bank swaps its 11 percent fixed rate to BBB firm.

The net result is the BBB firm saves 150 basis points and passes 75 of them on to the AAA bank; the bank saves 25 basis points on the normal floating rate.

There are nine basic advantages to interest rate swaps. (1) Swaps give the corporation the flexibility to transform floating-rate debt to fixed-rate, and vice versa. (2) There are potential rate savings, as illustrated previously. (3) Swaps may be based on outstanding debt and may thus avoid increasing liabilities. (4) Swaps provide alternative sources of financing. (5) Swaps are private transactions. (6) There are no SEC reporting or registration requirements, as yet. (7) The swap contract is simple and straightforward. (8) Rating agencies, such as Moody's and S&P, take a neutral to positive position on corporate swaps. (9) Tax treatment on swaps is uncomplicated, as there are no withholding taxes levied on interest payments to overseas swap partners, and the interest expense of the fixed-rate payer is treated as though it were on a fixed-rate obligation.

The only drawback to swaps is the risk that one swap partner may fail to make the agreed payments to the other swap partner.

The impact of swaps on financial management practices is predicted to be great. It is foreseeable that corporations will use swaps to match assets to liabilities and to protect investments in capital assets, such as plant and equipment, from floating-rate interest fluctuations. Financial institutions also see swaps as a way to match receivables (loans made) to liabilities (investors' deposits). For example, to match a fixed-rate loan, the financial institution would sell a floating-rate CD and then swap it for a fixed-rate liability.

Many corporations and financial institutions have engaged in swaps. The Greyhound Corporation, for example, was involved in $80 million of swaps with Bank of America (three times) and Goldman Sachs (once). Transamerica, ITT Financial, Great Western Financial Corporation, and Consumer Power Company have also been involved in swaps.

Currency Swaps

Companies use currency swap markets when they need to raise money in a currency issued by a country in which they are not well known and must therefore pay a higher interest rate than would be available to a local or better-known borrower. For example, a medium-sized American company may have need of Swiss francs (SFs), but even though it is a sound credit risk, it may be relatively unknown in Switzerland.

If it can find, or if a bank or broker can pair it with, a Swiss company that wants US$s, the swap would work as follows. The American company would borrow US$s in the United States, where it is well known and can get a low interest rate; the Swiss company would borrow SFs in Switzerland for the same reason. They would then swap the currencies and service each other's loans; that is, the Swiss company would repay the US$ loan, while the American company would repay the SF loan.

Hedges and Swaps as "Derivatives"

derivatives
Financial instruments, such as futures, options, and swaps, the values of which are tied to price movements of underlying commodities or other instruments.

Currency value changes are not the only risks against which international businesses use hedges and swaps, sometimes referred to as **derivatives,** to protect themselves from changes in currency values. But if used unwisely, they can be as dangerous as the risks against which they are supposed to protect. A derivative is a contract, the value of which changes in concert with the price movements in a related or underlying commodity or financial instrument. The term covers standardized, exchange-traded futures and options, as well as over-the-counter swaps, options, and other customized instruments.[14]

In 1994, the vast German conglomerate, Metallgesellschaft, came close to collapse as a result of having used derivatives (options, forward agreements, and the like) wrongly in hedging itself against changes in oil prices. Later in that year, Orange County, California, lost some $2 billion by betting wrongly on the direction of interest rates—it bet they would go down; they went up.

Are Derivatives Safe?   That is a badly formulated question. Clearly, organizations can misuse these instruments, some of which are at the forefront of financial engineering and demand complex mathematics. To concentrate on the instruments themselves is to miss the woods for the trees. Derivatives are nothing more than risk-management tools. Used properly, they can be remarkably effective; firms and institutions of all sorts use them to take or limit risks in ways that were not possible until recently. But proper risk management is a tricky, three-stage process.

- Identify where the risks lie.
- Design an appropriate strategy for managing them.
- Select the right tools to execute the strategy.

All this has become too complicated for many managers. Just as it is uneconomic for the executives of most firms to identify and solve all their legal problems, it may be that they need outsiders' help in devising and executing risk-management strategies. So long as the firms' managers keep control of basic decisions, it may be more efficient to leave the execution of strategy and the final choice of instruments to outside experts.[15]

There are derivative exchanges around the world. Table 20–2 shows the location of the 10 top exchanges ranked by futures and option contract volume and the growth from 1993 to 1994.

SALES WITHOUT MONEY

A number of countries desire goods and products for which they do not have the convertible currency to pay. That has not prevented efforts by many suppliers to sell to them anyway. Such countries are usually less developed and poor. There are two main nonmonetary trade themes, countertrade and industrial cooperation.

Countertrade

Countertrade usually involves two or more contracts, one for the purchase of DC products or services and one or more for the purchase of LDC products or services. A Mitsui study speaks of six varieties of countertrade.[16] They are called (1) counterpurchase, (2) compensation, (3) barter, (4) switch, (5) offset, and (6) clearing account arrangements. All involve to a greater or lesser degree the substitution of LDC goods, products, or services for scarce DC money. They may be relatively simple, involving only two countries or companies, or quite complex, calling for a number of countries, companies, currencies, and contracts.

countertrade
International trade in which at least part of the payment is in some form other than hard, convertible currency

Counterpurchase. In counterpurchase situations, the goods supplied by the LDC are not produced by or out of the goods or products imported from the

Rank	Exchange	January–September 1994	January–September 1993	Percent Change
1	CBOT (Chicago)	171.1m	131.2m	30%
2	CME (Chicago)	153.0	110.3	38
3	Liffe (London)	118.3	68.8	72
4	CBOE (Chicago)	82.6	61.7	34
5	Matif (Paris)	76.3	53.6	42
6	BM&F (Brazil)	70.6	39.1	80
7	Nymex (New York)†	60.2	54.8	10
8	DTB (Germany)	39.3	22.6	74
9	LME (London)	34.2	25.3	35
10	Tiffe (Tokyo)	29.6	16.7	77

TABLE 20–2
Top 10 derivatives exchanges*
(ranked by futures and options contract volume)

*Ranked by futures and options contract volume; volume of options traded on individual securities not included.
†Nymex volumes are Nymex and Comex combined, for both years.

Source: Laurie Morse, "The Future of Futures Trading," *Financial Times*, November 16, 1994, p. II.

Courtesy Ryder System, Inc.

DC. An example of counterpurchase is PepsiCo's arrangement with Russia, to which PepsiCo sells the concentrate for the drink, which is then bottled and sold in that country. In exchange, PepsiCo has exclusive rights to export Russian vodka for sale in the West. In 1990, the two parties renewed and expanded the agreement, increasing the amounts of Pepsi-Cola and vodka to be sold and adding a new element. PepsiCo committed itself to buying at least 10 Russian-built freighters and tankers. PepsiCo intends to lease them on the world market through a Norwegian partner.[17]

In 1992, PepsiCo made a similar deal with Ukraine to sell $1 billion of Ukraine-built ships and to use part of the proceeds to buy soft-drink equipment and to build five Pepsi bottling plants in Ukraine. A difference between the Ukrainian and the Russian deals is that another part of the Ukrainian ships sale proceeds will finance the opening of 100 Pepsi-owned Pizza Hut restaurants in that republic.[18]

Uganda wanted 18 helicopters to help stamp out elephant and rhino poaching, but didn't have the $25 million to pay for them. The problem was solved by Gary Pacific, head of countertrade for McDonnell Douglas Helicopter. Pacific helped set up several local projects that generate hard currency, including a plant that will process Nile perch, a factory to turn pineapple and passion fruit into concentrate. He then found buyers of those products in Europe, and delivery of the helicopters began in 1994.[19]

Compensation.   Such transactions call for payment by the LDC in products produced by DC equipment. The products made in the LDC by the DC equipment are shipped to the DC in payment for the equipment. Dresser Industries has a compensation agreement with Poland for tractors. Poland is paying with tractors and other machines that Dresser then markets.

Barter.   Barter is an ancient form of commerce and the simplest sort of countertrade. The LDC sends products to the DC that are equal in value to the products delivered by the DC to the LDC.

Switch.   Frequently, the goods delivered by the LDC are not easily usable or salable. Then a third party is brought in to dispose of them. This process is called *switch trading*.

Offset.   The offset form occurs when the importing nation requires a portion of the materials, components, or subassemblies of a product to be procured in the local (importer's) market. The exporter may set up or cooperate in setting up a parts manufacturing and assembly facility in the importing country.

Clearing Account Arrangements.   These are used to facilitate the exchange of products over a specified time period. When the period ends, any balance outstanding must be cleared by the purchase of additional goods or settled by a cash payment. The bank or broker acts as an intermediary to facilitate settlement of the clearing accounts by finding markets for counterpurchased goods or by converting goods or cash payments into products desired by the country with a surplus.

How Important Is Countertrade?   Frequently, countertrade agreements and their executions are not reported publicly. Indeed, the parties often prefer privacy and confidentiality for competitive reasons and to not set precedents for future deals. Therefore, estimates of the extent of countertrade vary widely. The U.S. Commerce Department estimates that between 20 and 30 percent of world trade is now subject to some form of countertrade and that the proportion could reach 50 percent in 15 years.

Major U.S. firms report transactions involving some form of countertrade. *Business Week* and General Electric each independently estimate the volume at 30 percent of world trade. By far the lowest estimate, 8 percent, was made by the General Agreement on Tariffs and Trade.

Regardless of which estimate is nearest the truth, the value of countertrade is very large. Apply any of the estimates to the over $3.53 trillion volume of world trade and the result is big.[20]

An indication of the growing importance of countertrade is the growth of the American Countertrade Association (ACA), most of whose members are Fortune 500 heavyweights, including America's top exporters. But more and more smaller companies are joining, including many that had not previously thought much about countertrade or even exporting. Figure 20–5 shows ACA membership percentages by industry.

U.S. Government's Positions on Countertrade.   We say "positions" because different agencies contradict each other, and Congress contradicts itself. The Treasury Department is flatly opposed to countertrade, the Commerce Department helps companies engage in it, and the Export-Import Bank has no policy for dealing with it. In Congress, legislation has been introduced both to curtail countertrade and to encourage countertrade of U.S. surplus agricultural commodities.[21]

Other Governments' Positions on Countertrade.   The governments of most LDCs either encourage or require countertrade, but so also do such industrialized countries as Australia and New Zealand. No country forbids countertrade.

Twin Problems.   The age-old twin problems with goods coming from the LDC side of countertrade transactions are product quality and delivery reliability. In general, there are two ways the DC side is coping with those problems.

FIGURE 20–5
American Countertrade
Association membership by
industry

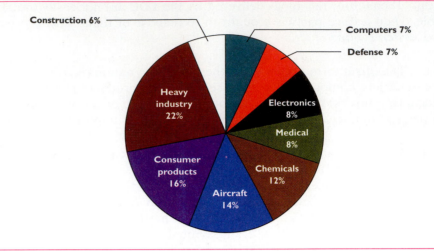

Source: Shelley Neumeier, "Why Countertrade Is Getting Hot," *Fortune*, June 29, 1992, p. 25.

One solution is inspection of the goods before they leave the LDC plant by a reliable, third-party organization. Two such organizations are the Paris-based Bureau Veritas, and the Societé Generale de Surveillance, whose main office is in Geneva.

Roger Gyarmaty of Veritas says, "We go back to the production process to see if the goods are being made to specifications. We see to it that delivery times and terms are being met. And we check the packaging and loading to be sure the goods are not damaged at those points. Companies can save up to two or three times the cost of our services just through fewer headaches when they receive the goods."[22]

A second solution is growing in popularity. The eastern European banking structure is developing, and the DC countertrade party is increasingly getting a guarantee of quality and delivery from a bank in the LDC country. When such a guarantee has been given, the bank takes a stern interest in the product's production line to avoid having to come up with precious foreign exchange in the event of quality or delivery that is not in accordance with the contract.[23]

New Directions. Not all countertrade is between DCs and LDCs. There is trade of Angolan coffee for Russian equipment, and developing countries frequently have agreements encouraging trade with each other, such as those between Argentina and Brazil and among the ASEAN member-countries.

Alan Linger, Lloyds Bank countertrade manager, believes such business could become triangular by including DCs. For example, DC goods would be exported to an Eastern European country, products of which would go to an LDC, which would then complete the triangle by shipping its commodities to the DC.[24]

Industrial Cooperation

industrial cooperation
Long-term relationships between DC companies and LDC plants in which some or all production is done in the LDC plant

Industrial cooperation, which LDCs favor, requires long-term relationships, with part or all of the production being done in the LDC involved. Part of the resulting products are sold in the DCs or the Third World.

One writer, Ronald E. Hayt, speaks of five different industrial cooperation methods.[25]

1. *Joint venture.* Two or more companies or state agencies combine assets to form a new and distinct economic entity, and they share management, profits, and losses.

2. *Coproduction and specialization.* The factory in the LDC produces certain agreed components of a product, while a company in the DC produces the other components. The product is then assembled at both locations for their respective markets.

3. *Subcontracting.* The LDC factory manufactures a product according to specifications of the DC company and delivers the product to the DC company, which then markets it.

4. *Licensing.* The LDC and DC parties enter into a license agreement whereby the LDC enterprise uses DC technology to manufacture a product. The DC company is paid a license royalty fee in money or in product. The latter method is preferred by the LDC.

5. *Turnkey plants.* The DC party is responsible for building the entire plant, starting it, training LDC personnel, and turning over the keys to the LDC party. Of course, the LDC wants to pay in products of the new plant.

Two threads run through countertrade and industrial cooperation. The first is that the LDC does not have enough hard, convertible currency to buy what it wants from the DC. That leads to the second, which is the effort of the LDC to substitute goods for currency.

INTERNATIONAL FINANCE CENTER

A number of new developments are forcing international companies to pay more attention to financial management. International financial management has become more and more different from domestic financial management, and in several such companies, the finance operation has become a profit center and is no longer merely a service. Some of the new developments are (1) floating exchange rates, whose fluctuations are sometimes volatile; (2) growth in the number of capital and foreign exchange markets where an IC can shop for lower interest costs and better currency rates; (3) different and changing inflation rates from country to country; (4) advances in electronic cash management systems; (5) realization by financial managers that through innovative management of temporarily idle cash balances of the IC units, they can increase yields and the enterprise's profit; and (6) the explosive growth of the use of derivatives to protect against commodity, currency, interest rate, and other risks. As a result, many ICs have established **international finance centers.**

international finance centers
Handle most or all international financial transactions for all units of an IC

Volatile, Floating Currency Exchange Rates

An international finance center can take advantage of volatile, floating currency exchange rates to make money for the IC in several ways. It would be aware of which currencies are most susceptible to sudden weakness, avoid borrowing in undervalued currencies, and maximize short-term assets in strong currencies. This is currency exposure management.

Capital and Exchange Markets

Like any company, an IC needs to raise capital from time to time. Unlike most domestic companies, it needs to exchange currencies. Given the proliferation of capital and exchange markets, the international finance center should advise and direct the parent and affiliates where to raise and exchange money at the lowest costs.

Inflation Rates

Inflation goes up and inflation goes down, and while it's going up in one country, it's going down in another. The international finance center should be aware of all those trends and advise and direct the IC system how to protect assets and profits from monetary erosion and other economic and political risks.

Electronic Cash Management

Currency exposure management is being simplified. New technology is permitting the creation of worldwide networks that enable firms to transfer funds electronically. The international finance center should evaluate and use the best of those developing systems. Some of them are Electronic Funds Transfer Network, Society for Worldwide Interbank Financial Telecommunications, Clearing House Automated Payment System, and Clearing House Interbank Payments Transfer.

Using Derivatives Correctly

As indicated earlier in this chapter, the use of derivatives has multiplied rapidly in the 1990s. They can be used to protect against, among other things, commodity price changes, currency exchange rate fluctuations, or interest rate changes. But they can be complex and can cause losses rather than provide protection. ICs or other organizations that want derivative protection should hire experts.

Other Uses of the International Finance Center

Mentioned above are only a few of the possible functions of an international finance center. Here are some others:

1. *Handle internal and external invoicing.* The center can make complex decisions about financing international trade among the IC units and between them and outside suppliers and customers. All data on imports and exports can be channeled through the center, which can determine which currencies will be used and how the trades will be financed.

2. *Help weak currency affiliate.* An affiliate with a weak currency could have difficulty obtaining needed imports. By placing itself in the trade chain, the center can arrange the financing needed by such an affiliate.

3. *Strengthen affiliate evaluation and reporting systems.* The center is in a unique position to understand and interpret the performance of affiliates in countries around the world. Inherent differences are exacerbated by volatile exchange rates, different inflation rates, varying tax laws and accounting rules, transfer price policies, and a host of environmental factors. IC decisions about transfer pricing, choosing one subsidiary over another to compete for a contract, or adding capital to one subsidiary rather than another also complicate performance evaluations, with which the international finance center can assist.

A Racy Convertible from Toyota

Although Toyota, Japan's biggest automaker, was flush with cash during 1986, in that year it floated the biggest convertible yen bond that had ever been seen in Japan. In one go, it raised ¥200 billion (about $1.23 billion), twice as much as any other Japanese company had ever raised in this way. Why?

As the bluest of Japanese blue chips, Toyota commanded the finest of fine terms, and those convertibles carried a coupon of only 1.7 percent. The normal interest for other companies was around 2.5 percent.

Toyota reinvested the ¥200 billion in financial instruments on better terms than it paid and thus made more than it could have made from building and selling automobiles. In Japan, this practice is called *zaiteku*, or "financial engineering," and numerous companies have been doing it.

For the 10 biggest earners from *zaiteku*, it accounted for at least a third of their pre-tax profits in the first half of 1986. For Nissan, *zaiteku* made the difference between a profit and a loss. But not all *zaiteku* practitioners were as skilled as Nissan—some lost money at it.[26]

SUMMARY

1. **Realize that the currencies of countries change in value in terms of each other.** Currency exchange rates, the cost of one currency in terms of others, fluctuate constantly.
2. **Understand how currency value changes affect international business transactions.** Anyone who has the obligation to pay or the right to receive a foreign currency in the future has a currency exchange risk. The risk may arise out of transactions (e.g., export or import contracts, in which case it is called a transaction risk). Or it may arise out of longer-term investments that are the subjects of financial statements, in which case it is called a translation risk.
3. **Recognize the tremendous importance of financial management to an international company (IC).** Financial management is vital to the success of ICs and has moved from being merely a service to being a profit center.
4. **Know about financial management tools.** Financial management tools include derivatives, hedges, payment timing, exposure netting, price adjustments, balance sheet neutralizing, and swaps.

5. **Understand why exporters sometimes accept payment in forms other than money.** Buyers frequently don't have or don't want to use hard, convertible currency and wish to pay in goods or services instead of money. The generic term for this is countertrade.
6. **Differentiate between hard, convertible currencies and soft, nonconvertible ones.** Hard, convertible currencies are accepted all around the world at uniform exchange rates. Soft, nonconvertible currencies are rarely of any use outside the country of issue.
7. **Explain the growing importance of international finance centers to ICs.** An IC's international finance center accumulates the expertise and information to transact all international financial dealings of all the IC's units most profitably and at lowest cost.
8. **Understand *zaiteku*, or financial engineering.** *Zaiteku*, or financial engineering, is used by companies with the highest credit ratings to borrow at lowest interest rates and make money by lending to companies with lower credit ratings.

KEY WORDS

QUESTIONS

1. Why is an exporter that is to be paid in six months in a foreign currency worried about fluctuating foreign exchange rates?
2. Are there ways that this exporter can protect itself? If so, what are they?

3. How does the credit or money market hedge work?

4. Why is acceleration or delay of payments more useful to an IC than to smaller, separate companies?

5. How would you accomplish exposure netting with currencies of two countries that tend to go up and down together in value?

6. Why is the price adjustment device more useful to an IC than to smaller, separate companies?

7. Some argue that translation gains or losses are not important so long as they have not been realized and are only accounting entries. What is the other side of that argument?

8. Is the parallel loan a sort of swap? How does it work?

9. How and why would a seller make a sale to a buyer that has no money the seller can use?

10. DC partners in countertrade contracts have had problems with quality and timely delivery of goods from the LDC partners. How are they trying to deal with those problems?

MINICASE 21 - 1   Dealing with the Transaction Risk Caused by Fluctuations of Relative Currency Values

You are the finance manager of an American multinational. Your company has sold US$1 million of its product to a French importer. The rate of exchange on the day of sale is US$1 = FF5, so on that day the 1 million U.S. dollars equals 5 million French francs.

The contract calls for the French importer to pay your company FF5 million six months from the date of sale. Therefore, your company bears the transaction risk of a change in the currency exchange rates between the US$ and the FF.

Assume your company has no need for French francs and will want U.S. dollars no later than the payment date. Assume further that you do not wish to carry the transaction risk. Give two methods by which you might protect your company from that risk.

Strategic Planning and Organizational Design

> Running a business without planning can be compared to driving a car while looking only at the rearview mirror. You can tell where you've been, but heaven help the occupants during a trip on winding or congested roads.
>
> Arthur Andersen & Co., Strategic Planning: A Fitness Program for Wholesaler-Distributors

CONCEPT PREVIEWS

After reading this chapter, you should be able to:

1. **understand** the benefits of global strategic planning

2. **describe** the steps in the global strategic planning process

3. **know** what a planning staff does

4. **understand** the purpose of corporate mission statements, objectives, quantified goals, and strategies

5. **state** which management tools are actually used by management

6. **describe** the new directions in strategic planning

7. **discuss** the various organizational forms

8. **describe** the current organizational trends and appreciate why CEOs are changing the organizational forms of the companies.

9. **understand** the concept of the virtual corporation

A Global Strategic Planner

Minnesota Mining & Manufacturing (3M), known as one of the best managed and most innovative American international companies, was founded in 1902. However, it was in business for nearly 50 years before it established an international division and began to export. Yet, by 1993, 49.2 percent of its total sales ($14.02 billion) were coming from foreign markets; $1.49 billion were from U.S. exports. Managers of its overseas subsidiaries operate with a high degree of autonomy and finance their own expansion. But corporate culture is worldwide; in fact, many managers are third country nationals (citizens of neither the home nor the host country who work in a host country affiliate). • Structured strategic planning was not adopted until 1981, after a new CEO joined the firm. He felt that although cross-functional teams at the product level were doing a good job of decision making, they weren't steering the company. Despite the long-term nature of many of its product developments, the company's planning was essentially short term. The president recognized that 3M could continue to innovate on a large scale only if its technological resources were shared among its units, and he wanted to operate on a planned global strategic basis without losing the autonomous, entrepreneurial ability of the product divisions. The result was a reorganization of the company's 200 organizational units worldwide into 23 strategic business centers (SBCs). • Within each SBC, planning starts with the operating managers of the various subsidiaries, who analyze internal strengths and weaknesses and external forces, such as new technology and government regulatory changes; make a competitor analysis; and determine the company resources they will need to achieve their objectives. Their plans go to the SBCs for review and consultation. SBC plans then go to a strategic planning committee consisting of vice presidents at headquarters who represent the four sectors into which the 23 SBCs are divided. The plans are reviewed with at least two members of the strategic planning committee present, and results of this review are discussed with SBC managements. Any differences between SBC managements and sector management are reconciled. • Two months later (July), the corporate headquarters' 34-person management committee, to which the 12 strategic planning committee members belong, reviews the plans and votes on spending priorities. Feedback and direction are given to the operating units, who then prepare operating plans and budgets by December and submit them to headquarters. There, they are finalized jointly with corporate worldwide plans. • A few days before the December operating reviews, the management committee holds brainstorming sessions to discuss trends and developments over the coming 15 years. The general manager of each business unit presents the best picture possible for that industry for the period. The outcome of this meeting is a broad guide for strategic planning. The

Sources: "The Mass Production of Ideas, and Other Impossibilities," *The Economist,* March 8, 1995, p. 72; "Top 50 U.S. Industrial Exporters," *Fortune,* August 22, 1994, p. 132; and Carol Kennedy, "Planning Global Strategies for 3M," *Long-Range Planning,* August 1988, p. 63.

FIGURE 21–1
3M strategic planning cycle

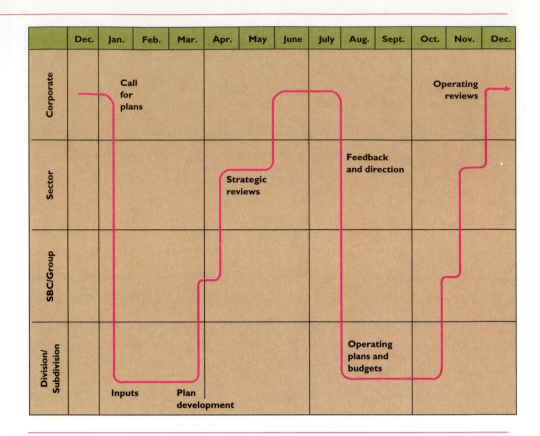

Source: "Planning Global Strategies for 3M," *Long-Range Planning*, February 1988, p. 15.

company's strategic planning cycle is diagrammed in Figure 21–1. • Although planning is done by operating managers, the director and staff of a planning services and development unit provide an analysis of 3M's 20 principal competitors worldwide and any other information the units require. They also try to identify opportunities and new products. • Under the guidance of Livio Simone, CEO, over $1 billion of 3M's 1994 revenues came from products launched during that year. The company registered 543 patents in 1994, 40 percent more than in 1991, the year Simone became CEO.

GLOBAL STRATEGIC PLANNING

Why Plan Globally?

Numerous international firms such as 3M have found it necessary to institute formal global strategic planning to provide a means for top management to identify opportunities and threats from all over the world, formulate strategies to handle them, and stipulate how to finance the strategies' implementation. Global strategic plans not only provide for consistency of action among the firm's managers worldwide but also require the participants to consider the ramifications of their actions on the other geographical and functional areas of the firm.

Standardization and Planning

Historically, more aspects of production than of marketing have been standardized and coordinated worldwide. Many top executives believe marketing strategies are best determined locally because of differences among the various foreign environments. Yet, there is a growing tendency to standardize not only marketing strategies but also the total product, which leads to their inclusion in the global strategic planning process. Of course, their standardization can also be the *result* of strategic planning as managements search for ways to lower costs and present a uniform company image as global producers of quality products. Let us look at the planning process.

Global Strategic Planning Process

Global strategic planning is the primary function of managers, and the manager of strategic planning and strategy making is the firm's chief executive officer. The process of strategic planning provides a formal structure in which managers (1) analyze the company's external environments, (2) analyze the company's internal environment, (3) define the company's business and mission, (4) set corporate objectives, (5) quantify goals, (6) formulate strategies, and (7) make tactical plans. For ease of understanding, we present this as a linear process; but in actuality, there is considerable flexibility in the order in which firms take up these items.

> In company planning meetings that one of the writers attended, the procedure was iterative; that is, during the analysis of the environments, committee members could skip to a later step in the planning process to discuss the impact of a new development on a present corporate objective. They then often moved backward in the process to discuss the availability of the firm's assets to take advantage of the environmental change.

Global and Domestic Planning Processes Similar.
You will note that the global planning process, illustrated in Figure 21–2, has the same format as the planning process for a purely domestic firm. As you know by now, most activities of the two kinds of operations are that way. It's the variations in values of uncontrollable forces that make the activities in a worldwide corporation more complex than they are in a purely domestic firm.

Analyze Domestic, International, and Foreign Environments.
Because a firm has little opportunity to control these forces, its managers must know not only what the present values of the forces are but also where the forces appear to be headed. An environmental scanning process similar to the market screening process described in Chapter 14 can be used for a continuous gathering of information.

Is There a Planning Staff?
If the firm has a planning staff, as 3M does, it will have the prime responsibility for this step of the process and will also be the repository for information sent from the various functional areas of the firm. It probably will have an environmental database. Planning personnel may also do the competitor analysis with input from R&D, marketing, and perhaps other departments, or they may gather information from the competitor intelligence system (if there is one) for integration into their analysis. They probably will subscribe to services that specialize in political risk assessment, such as *Business Risk Index,* The Economist Intelligence Unit's *Country Ratings,* and Frost & Sullivan's *World Summary* and *60 Country Reports.* We discussed country risk assessment in Chapter 10, Political Forces, and mentioned several sources of information in Chapter 14.

The planning staff may use global **watch lists**, which contain items pertinent to certain aspects of the uncontrollable environmental variables that top management has indicated are of special interest to the firm. Petroleum refiners are interested in anything having to do with oil spills and the use of methanol in automobiles, for example. Information for the global watch lists

watch list
List containing items of interest concerning the uncontrollable variables that are of special interest to the firm

FIGURE 21–2
The global strategic planning
process

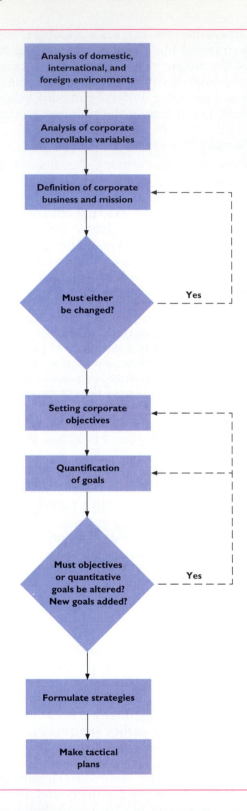

of international construction firms will come from the lists of loans made by the World Bank and other international lending agencies.

Analyze Corporate Controllable Variables.   An analysis of the forces controlled by the firm will also include a situational analysis and a forecast. The managers of the various functional areas will either personally submit reports on their units or will provide input to the planning staff (if there is one), who will in turn prepare a report for the strategy planning committee.

Often management will analyze the firm's activities from the time raw materials enter the plant until the end product reaches the final user with the aim of finding ways to perform them better or less expensively than its competitors.

> Although this has been credited to Porter (value chain), the concept has been around for decades. Marketers will remember that Wroe Alderson made the same analysis in the 1960s using a unit of analysis he called *transvection*. Transvection is a series of sorts and transformations beginning with raw materials entering the factory and terminating when the finished product is in the hands of the final consumer.[1]

After the analysis of corporate controllable variables, the planning committee must answer questions such as the following: What are our strengths and weaknesses? What are our human and financial resources? Where are we with respect to our present objectives? Have we uncovered any facts that require us to delete goals, alter them, or add new ones? After completing this internal audit, the committee is ready to examine its business, vision, and **mission statements**.

> **mission statement**
> *A broad statement that defines the organization's scope*

Define the Corporate Business, Vision, and Mission Statements. These broad statements communicate to the corporation's stakeholders (employees, stockholders, governments, suppliers, and customers) what the company is and where it is going. Some firms combine two or all three, whereas others have separate statements. The director of planning at 3M believes "the mission statement typically defines the scope of what you do, while the vision should be a vibrant and compelling image of the organization's purpose."[2] In any case, the planning committee must evaluate these statements against the changing realities uncovered in the external and internal analyses and then alter them when necessary.

Some Examples. Pfizer combines its business and mission statements into what it calls a *corporate description:*

> Pfizer Inc. is a research-based global health care company. Our mission is to discover and develop innovative, value-added products that improve the quality of life of people around the world and help them enjoy longer, healthier, and more productive lives. The Company has four business segments: health care, consumer health care, food science, and animal health. We manufacture in 31 countries and our products are available worldwide.[3]

Du Pont has statements defining the company and its vision, but no mission statement:

> Du Pont is a technology-based global company with more than 225 manufacturing and processing facilities on five continents and 125,000 employees worldwide. Our principal businesses are chemicals, fibers, polymers, petroleum, and diversified businesses (agricultural products, electronics, imaging systems, and medical products).
>   Du Pont is in the midst of a transformation. By 2002, we expect to be a different company, combining our mature experience with dynamic new vigor and capitalizing on our diversity of people, geographical locations, and products.[4]

Grand Metropolitan, the British conglomerate and owner of such American brands as Burger King, Pearle Vision, and Pillsbury, defines itself as "one of the world's leading consumer goods companies, specializing in branded food and drinks businesses." Its mission is "to be a major participant in every market in which it has a presence."[5] After defining any or all of the three statements, management must then set corporate objectives.

Set Corporate Objectives.   Objectives direct the firm's course of action, maintain it within the boundaries of the stated mission, and ensure its continuing existence. Goodyear Tire and Rubber Co. announced the following objectives "to strengthen its focus as a growth company capable of consistent earnings improvement":

1. Greater commitment to geographical diversity through global expansion.
2. Reduce company debt.
3. Increase operating margins.
4. Capital spending to increase productivity and production capacity.
5. Introduction of new products.[6]

How does Goodyear know if it achieves these objectives? How much does the company expect to reduce company debt, for example?

Quantify the Objectives.   When objectives can be quantified, they should be. The Goodyear CEO tells us that management's goal is to reduce debt to debt plus equity ratio to below 30 percent. He also wants to increase operating margins to 12 percent and maintain capital spending between $500 and $700 million annually. However, he does not attempt to quantify the number of products introduced nor does he set a goal for the amount of geographical diversity. Interestingly, the variables used to measure this last objective are the percentages of total unit sales and sales revenue made outside the U.S. In 1994, they were more than 40 percent of revenue and 45 percent of unit sales.[7]

This illustrates that despite the strong preference of most top managers for verifiable objectives, they frequently do have nonquantifiable or directional goals. One of PepsiCo's objectives, for example, is to accelerate profitable growth. Although this goal is not quantified, it does set the direction for managers and requires them to formulate more specific strategies to attain it. Incidentally, objectives do tend to be more quantified as they progress down the organization to the operational level, because, for the most part, strategies at one level become the objectives for the succeeding level. Up to this point, only *what, how much,* and *when* have been stipulated. *How* these objectives are to be achieved will be determined in the formulation of strategies.

corporate strategies
Action plans to enable organizations to reach their objectives

Formulate the Corporate Strategies.   Generally, participants in the strategic planning process will formulate alternate **corporate strategies,** or action plans, that seem plausible considering the directions the external environmental forces are taking and corporation's strengths and weaknesses. Suppose (1) their analysis of the external environment convinces them that the Japanese government is making it easier for foreign firms to enter the market and (2) the competitor analysis reveals that a Japanese competitor is preparing to enter the United States (or wherever the home market is). Should the firm adopt a defensive strategy of defending the home market by lowering its price there, or should it attack the competitor in its home market by establishing a subsidiary in Japan? Management may decide to pursue either strategy or both, depending on its interpretation of the situation.

When choosing among strategies, management must consider corporate culture.[8] If it decides to put into effect a quality control system that includes quality circles and heretofore there has been little employee participation in decision making, the strategy will have to include the cost of and time for training the employees to accept this cultural change.

Strategies May Also Be General. At the corporate level, strategies, like objectives, may be rather general. PepsiCo states that to achieve its objective of accelerating growth it is "executing these strategies of (1) segmenting the market to reach more people with more products, (2) expanding through existing and new distribution channels, (3) staying contemporary to attract new generations of customers, and (4) strengthening and expanding our infrastructure to make us more competitive in existing markets and to reach new markets."[9] You can be sure that the marketing function, which receives these strategies as its objectives, will be required to quantify as many as possible.

Scenarios. Because of the rapidity of changes in the uncontrollable variables, many managers have become dissatisfied with planning for a single set of events and have turned to **scenarios**, descriptions of future states basically different from the firm's present state.[10] Commonly, scenarios are made for the worst-case, most likely, and best-case situations, although planners are increasingly employing them when considering the firm's future they wish to create.[11]

scenarios
Descriptions of future states basically different from the firm's present state

Often, the "what if" questions raised reveal weaknesses in present strategies. Some of the common kinds of subjects for scenarios are large and sudden changes in sales (up or down), sudden increases in raw material prices, sudden tax increases, and a change in the political party in power. Frequently, scenarios are used as a learning tool for preparing standby or contingency plans.

Contingency Plans. Most managements prepare **contingency plans** for worst- and best-case scenarios and for critical events as well. Every operator of a nuclear plant has contingency plans, as do most producers of petroleum and hazardous chemicals since such ecological disasters as the Valdez oil spill and the tragic Bhopal gas leak occurred.

contingency plans
Plans for the best- or worst-case scenarios or for critical events that could have a severe impact on the firm

Prepare Tactical Plans. Because strategic plans are fairly broad, tactical (also called operational) plans are a requisite for spelling out in detail how the objectives will be reached. In other words, very specific, short-term means for achieving the goals are the object of tactical planning. For instance, if the British subsidiary of an American producer of prepared foods has as a quantitative goal a 20 percent increase in sales, its strategy might be to sell 30 percent more to institutional users. The tactical plan could include such points as hiring three new specialized sales representatives, attending four trade shows, and advertising in two industry periodicals every other month next year. This is the kind of specificity found in the tactical plan.

Management Tools

Generally, the adoption and use of management tools is discussed in planning meetings because some are useful in improving a firm's performance in critical areas. According to a survey taken of 9,000 American managers, tool usage is high and growing. The most commonly used tool (90 percent of the respondents) was the mission statement, followed by the customer satisfaction survey (90 percent). Next were total quality management (76 percent) and competitor profiling (74 percent).

Managers responded that the least used tools were value chain analysis (27 percent), five forces analysis (24 percent),* mass customization (20

---

*Michael Porter's five forces analysis consists of using (1 and 2) bargaining power of buyers and suppliers, (3 and 4) threats of substitute products and new entrants, and (5) rivalry of firms to attempt to measure industry competitiveness. See any principles of management text.

percent), and dynamic simulations (20 percent). According to the author, "Mass Customization and Dynamic Simulation may have low trial rates because they are relatively new, but Porter's Value Chain Analysis and Five Forces Framework have been around for at least 15 years."[12]

Strategic Plan Features and Implementation Facilitators

Sales Forecasts and Budgets.   Two prominent features of the strategic plan are *sales forecasts* and *budgets*. The sales forecast not only provides management with an estimate of the revenue to be received and the units to be sold but also serves as the basis for planning in the other functional areas. Without this information, management cannot formulate the production, financial, and procurement plans. Budgets, like sales forecasts, are both a planning and a control technique. During planning, they coordinate all of the functions within the firm and provide management with a detailed statement of future operating results.

Plan Implementation Facilitators.   Once the plan has been prepared, it must be implemented. Two of the most important plan implementation facilitators that management employs are policies and procedures.

Policies.   Policies are broad guidelines issued by upper management for the purpose of assisting lower-level managers in handling recurring problems. Because policies are broad, they permit discretionary action and interpretation. The object of a policy is to economize managerial time and promote consistency among the various operating units. If the distribution policy states that the firm's policy is to sell through wholesalers, marketing managers throughout the world know that they should normally use wholesalers and avoid selling directly to retailers. The disclosure of the widespread occurrence of bribery prompted company presidents to issue policy statements condemning this practice. Managers were put on notice by these statements that they were not to offer bribes.

Procedures.   Procedures prescribe how certain activities will be carried out, thereby ensuring uniform action on the part of all corporate members. For instance, most international corporate headquarters issue procedures for their subsidiaries to follow in preparing annual reports and budgets. This assures corporate management that, whether the budgets originate in Thailand or Brazil, they will be prepared using the same format, which facilitates comparison.

Kinds of Strategic Plans

Time Horizon.   Although strategic plans may be classified as short, medium, or long term, there is little agreement as to the length of these periods. For some, long-range planning may be for a five-year period. For others, this would be the length of a medium-term plan; their long range might cover 15 years or more. Short-range plans are usually for one to three years; however, even long-term plans are subject to review annually or more frequently if a situation requires it. Furthermore, the time horizon will vary according to the age of the firm and the stability of its market. A new venture is extremely difficult to plan for more than three years in advance, but a five- or six-year horizon is probably sufficient for a mature company in a steady market.

Level in the Organization.   If the corporation has three organizational levels, as 3M does, there will be three levels of plans, each of which will generally be more specific and for a shorter time frame than it is at the level above. In addition, the functional areas at each level will have plans and sometimes will be subject to the same hierarchy, depending mainly on how the company is organized.

Methods of Planning

Top-Down Planning.   In **top-down planning**, corporate headquarters develops and provides guidelines that include the definition of the business, the mission statement, company objectives, financial assumptions, the content of the plan, and special issues. If there is an international division, its management may be told that this division is expected to contribute $5 million in profits, for example. The division, in turn, would break this total down among the affiliates under its control. The managing director in Germany would be informed that the German operation is expected to contribute $1 million; Brazil, $300,000; and so on.

> **top-down planning**
> *Planning process that begins at the highest level in the organization and continues downward*

Disadvantages of top-down planning are that it restricts initiative at the lower levels and shows some insensitivity to local conditions. Furthermore, especially in an international company, there are so many interrelationships that consultation is necessary. Can top management, for example, decide on rationalization of manufacturing without obtaining the opinions of the local units as to its feasibility?

The advantage of top-down planning is that the home office with its global perspective should be able to formulate plans that ensure the optimal corporatewide use of the firm's scarce resources.

Bottom-Up Planning.   **Bottom-up planning** operates in the opposite manner. The lowest operating levels inform top management of what they expect to do, and the total becomes the firm's goals. The advantage of bottom-up planning is that the people responsible for attaining the goals are formulating them. Who knows better than the subsidiaries' directors what and how much the subsidiaries can sell? Because the subsidiaries' directors set the goals with no coercion from top management, they feel obligated to make their word good. However, there is also a disadvantage. Each affiliate is free to some extent to pursue the goals it wishes to pursue, and so there is no guarantee that the sum total of all the affiliates' goals will coincide with those of headquarters. When discrepancies occur, extra time must be taken at headquarters to eliminate them.[13] Japanese managements almost invariably use bottom-up planning because they strive for a consensus at every level.

> **bottom-up planning**
> *Planning process that begins at the lowest level in the organization and continues upward*

Iterative Planning.   It appears that **iterative planning**, which 3M practices, is becoming more popular, especially in global companies that seek to have a single global plan while operating in many diverse foreign environments. Iterative planning combines aspects of both top-down and bottom-up planning.

> **iterative planning**
> *Repetition of the bottom-up or top-down planning process until all differences are reconciled*

New Directions in Planning

Planning during the 1960s and early 70s commonly consisted of a company's CEO and the head of planning getting together to devise a corporate plan, which would then be handed to the operating people for execution. Changes in the business environment, however, caused changes to be made in three areas: (1) who does the planning, (2) how it is done, and (3) the contents of the plan.

Who Does It.   By the mid-70s, strategic planners had become dominant figures in their companies. They were accustomed to writing a blueprint for each subsidiary, which they would then present to the management of each operating unit. The planners' power grew and the operating managers' influence waned, and of course there was hostility between the two groups. Roger Smith, former chairman of GM, says, "We got those great plans together, put them on a shelf, and marched off to do what we would be doing anyway."[14]

But a number of factors were acting to upset this pattern. It became clear that world uncertainty made long-range planning in detail impossible, so corporate plans had to be short and simple. With huge, detailed plans no longer as useful as they had been, there was less need for professional planners. Stronger competition made a practical knowledge of the company and the industry an essential input to strategic planning. This brought senior operating managers into the planning process, enabling firms to change the role and reduce the size of their planning staffs. General Electric, for example, reduced its corporate planning group from 58 to 33, and GM decreed that "planning is the responsibility of every line manager. The role of the planner is to be the catalyst for change—not to do the planning for each business unit."[15]

How It Is Done.   By the 1980s, firms were using computer models and sophisticated forecasting methods to help produce the voluminous plans we mentioned above. These plans were not only huge but also very detailed. As a Texas Instruments executive put it, "The company let its management system, which can track the eye of every sparrow, creep into the planning process, so we were making more and more detailed plans. It became a morale problem because managers knew they couldn't project numbers out five years to two decimal points."[16]

The heavy emphasis on these methods tended to result in a concentration on factors that could be quantified easily. However, the less quantifiable factors relating to sociopolitical developments were becoming increasingly important. Also, the rapid rise in the levels of uncertainty made it clear to top managers that there was no point in using advanced techniques to make detailed five-year forecasts when various crises were exposing the nonsense of many previous forecasts. Prior to 1973, for example, there had been a great discussion as to whether the price of crude oil would ever go above $2 per barrel.

Because of these problems, many firms have moved toward less structured formats and much shorter documents. General Electric chairman J. F. Welch says, "A strategy can be summarized in a page or two."[17]

Contents of the Plan.   The contents of the plan are also different. Managements of many companies say they are much more concerned now with issues, strategies, and implementation. The planning director of Shell Oil, the British-Dutch transnational, says,

> The Shell approach has swung increasingly away from a mechanistic methodology and centrally set forecasts toward a more conceptual or qualitative analysis of the forces and pressures impinging on the industry. What Shell planners try to do is identify the key elements pertaining to a particular area of decision making—the different competitive, political, economic, social, and technical forces that are likely to have the greatest influence on the overall situation. In a global organization, the higher level of management is likely to be most interested in global scenarios—looking at worldwide developments—while the focus becomes narrower as one proceeds into the more specialized functions, divisions, and business sectors of individual companies.[18]

Summary of the Planning Process

Perhaps a good way to summarize the new direction in planning is to quote Frederick W. Gluck, a director of the multinational management consulting firm McKinsey & Co. and a principal architect of its strategic management practice. Gluck says that if major corporations are to develop the flexibility to compete, they must make the following major changes in the way they plan:

1. Top management must assume a more explicit strategic decision-making role, dedicating a large amount of time to deciding how things ought to be instead of listening to analyses of how they are.

2. The nature of planning must undergo a fundamental change from an exercise in forecasting to an exercise in creativity.

3. Planning processes and tools that assume a future much like the past must be replaced by a mind-set that is obsessed with being first to recognize change and turn it into a competitive advantage.

4. The role of the planner must change from being a purveyor of incrementalism to that of a crusader for action and an alter ego to line management.

5. Strategic planning must be restored to the core of line management responsibilities.[19]

ORGANIZATIONAL DESIGN

Organizing normally follows planning because the organization must implement the strategic plan. The planning process itself, because it encompasses an analysis of all the firm's activities, often discloses a need to alter the organization. Changes in strategy may require changes in the organization, but the reverse is also true. For instance, a new CEO may join the firm, or an important customer may change its method of operating, perhaps adopting a synchronous production process. Planning and organizing are so closely related that normally the structure of the organization is treated by management as an integral part of the planning process.

In designing the organizational structure, management is faced with two concerns: (1) finding the most effective way to departmentalize to take advantage of the efficiencies gained from the specialization of labor and (2) coordinating the firm's activities to enable it to meet its overall objectives. As all managers know, these two concerns run counter to each other; that is, the gain from the increased specialization of labor may sometimes be nullified by the increased costs of greater coordination. It is the constant search for an optimum balance between them that causes firms to make frequent changes in their organizational structures. However, as one critic of this frantic search for the suitable organization points out, "The companies I studied have *not* continually reorganized their operations. Each has retained for years a simple structure built around an **international division**—a form of organization that many management theorists regard as embryonic, appropriate only for companies in the earliest stages of worldwide growth."[20] IBM and Ford are two global firms that had international divisions for years after most had abandoned the international structure. New CEOs, however, have reorganized their companies, eliminating the international division. IBM created a single, worldwide sales and services organization and organized it by industry and technology specifications. Ford has begun a major realignment that will result in a single set of global processes and systems in product development, manufacturing, supply, and sales activities.[21]

international division
A division in the organization that is at the same level as the domestic division and is responsible for all non–home country activities

Evolution of the Global Company

As discussed in Chapter 2, companies often enter foreign markets first by exporting and then, as sales increase, forming overseas sales companies and eventually setting up production facilities. As the firm's foreign involvement changed, its organization frequently changed. It might first have had *no one* responsible for international business; each domestic product division may

FIGURE 21–3 International division

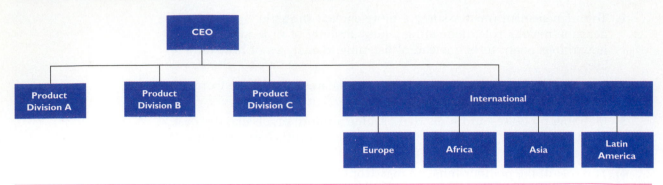

have been responsible for filling export orders. Next, an export department might have been created, and when the company began to invest in various overseas locations, it might have formed an international division to take charge of all overseas involvement. Larger firms may organize their international divisions on a regional, or geographical, basis, as did Ford and IBM (Figure 21–3).

As their overseas operations increased in importance and scope, most managements, with some exceptions, felt the need to eliminate international divisions and establish worldwide organizations based on *product, region,* or *function.* In rarer instances, customer classes are also a top-level dimension. Some service companies and financial institutions are organized this way. At secondary, tertiary, and still lower levels, these four dimensions—plus (1) process, (2) national subsidiary, and (3) international or domestic—provide the basis for subdivisions.

Managements who changed to these types of organizations felt they would (1) be more capable of developing competitive strategies to confront the new global competition, (2) obtain lower production costs by promoting worldwide product standardization and manufacturing rationalization, and (3) enhance technology transfer and the allocation of company resources.

Global Corporate Form—Product.   Frequently, this structure is a return to preexport department times in that the domestic product division has been given responsibility for global line and staff operations. In the present-day global form, product divisions are responsible for the worldwide operations

FIGURE 21–4 Global corporate form—product

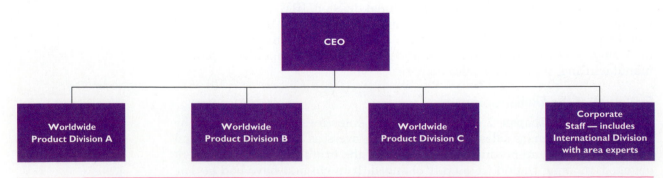

Japanese Firms Formulate Global Strategies

Many Japanese firms are striving to become global companies. Although they have had foreign factories and sales offices for decades, their product development, marketing, financing, and investment plans have been directed from Japan; they are Japanese multinationals whose management philosophy is decidedly ethnocentric (home country does it better). Why should long-established firms like Toyota, Matsushita, and Hitachi, all of which are convinced of the superiority of the "Japanese way," change their methods of operating which have been so profitable for so long?

The main reason is that their overseas manufacturing operations are becoming so large and diversified that they are beyond effective centralized control from the home offices. Governments, especially those of EU members, are enacting stricter local-content laws requiring local manufacture, not just assembly. NEC, for example, has formulated a new global strategy of manufacturing in "optimum locations." A network of regional manufacturing operations now does work for each other, with or without support from NEC plants in Japan. Matsushita is rearranging its 69 overseas plants in a "global localization" plan to supply four "major poles"—North America, Europe, Japan, and the rest of Asia. It now has regional headquarters for each area. To get the latest technology needed to remain competitive worldwide, Japanese companies have established research centers in the United States and Europe. These too are becoming difficult to manage from Japan.

For many Japanese companies accustomed to strict control from headquarters, it is going to be difficult to give responsibility and authority to distant operations and leave it to their local managers to adjust to the cultures, tastes, and business practices of their markets. Also, they are not particularly skilled in dealing with minorities (which they don't have at home), as their records in the United States and other countries show. They have the same problem with unions as well.

The role model for many of the Japanese companies trying to become global is IBM. They are impressed by the more than 30 research facilities IBM has around the world. Of course, IBM's global success is not due solely to a worldwide network of research centers; one of the ingredients of its success is that IBM-Germany is a true German company, as IBM-Japan is a Japanese company. An executive of a large Japanese publisher, when asked which firm had written the software his firm uses for computer translation, said it could only have been a Japanese company—IBM.

Source: "The Multinational, Eastern Style," *The Economist*, June 24, 1989, pp. 63–64.

---

such as marketing and production of products under their control. Each division generally has regional experts; so while this organizational form avoids the duplication of product experts common in the company with an international division, it creates a duplication of area experts. Occasionally, to eliminate placing regional specialists in each product division, management will have a group of managerial specialists in an international division who advise the product divisions but have no authority over them (see Figure 21–4).

Although organization by products is most favored by global companies, having that type of organization alone does not guarantee that a firm is global. The Worldview above describes the attempt of Japanese companies organized by products to change from multinational to global companies.

Global Corporate Form—Geographical Regions. Firms in which geographic regions are the primary basis for division put the responsibility for all activities under area managers who report directly to the chief executive officer. This kind of organization simplifies the task of directing worldwide operations, because every country in the world is clearly under the control of someone who is in contact with headquarters (see Figure 21–5).

Of course, this organizational type is used for both multinational (multidomestic) and global companies. Global companies that use it consider the division in which the home country is located as just another division for

FIGURE 21-5 Global corporate form—geographic regions

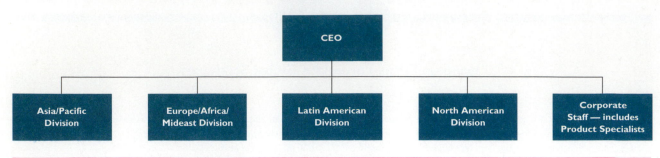

purposes of resource allocation and a source of management personnel. Some U.S. global companies have created a North American division that includes Canada, Mexico, and Central American countries in addition to the United States, possibly in part to emphasize that the home country is given no preference.

The regionalized organization appears to be popular with companies that manufacture products with a rather low, or at least stable, technological content that require strong marketing ability. It is also favored by firms with diverse products, each having different product requirements, competitive environments, and political risks. Producers of consumer products, such as prepared foods, pharmaceuticals, and household products, employ this type of organization. The disadvantage of an organization divided into geographic regions is that each region must have its own product and functional specialists so that although the duplication of area specialists found in product divisions is eliminated, a duplication of product and functional specialists is necessary.

Production coordination across regions presents difficult problems, as does global product planning. To alleviate these problems managements often place specialized product managers on the headquarters staff. Although these managers have no line authority, they do provide input to corporate decisions concerning products.

Global Corporate Form—Function. Few firms are organized by function at the top level. Those that are obviously believe worldwide functional expertise is more significant to the firm than product or area knowledge. In this type of organization, those reporting to the CEO might be the senior executives responsible for each functional area (marketing, production, finance, and so on), as in Figure 21–6. The commonality among the users of the functional form is a narrow and highly integrated product mix, such as that of aircraft manufacturers or oil refining companies. For example, Sun Co., a petroleum company that also mines coal, has three group heads reporting to the CEO: (1) refining and marketing, (2) exploration and production, and (3) energy minerals. Because of the presence of the last group, Sun really has a mixed, or hybrid, organization.

hybrid organization
Structure organized by more than one dimension at the top level

Hybrid Forms. In a **hybrid organization,** a mixture of the organizational forms is used at the top level and may or not be present at the lower levels. Figure 21–7 illustrates a simple hybrid form.

Such combinations are often the result of a regionally organized company having introduced a new and different product line that management believes can best be handled by a worldwide product division. An acquired company

FIGURE 21–6 Global corporate form—function

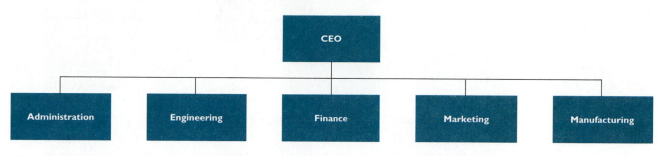

with distinct products and a functioning marketing network may be incorporated as a product division even though the rest of the firm is organized on a regional basis. Later, after corporate management becomes familiar with the operation, it may be regionalized.

A mixed structure may also result from the firm's selling to a sizable, homogeneous class of customers. Special divisions for handling sales to the military or to original equipment manufacturers are often established at the same level as regional or product divisions.

Matrix Organizations.   The **matrix organization** has evolved from management's attempt to mesh product, regional, and functional expertise while still maintaining clear lines of authority. It is called a matrix because it superimposes an organization based on one dimension on an organization based on another dimension. In such an organization, both the area and product managers will be at the same level and their responsibilities will overlap. An individual manager—say, a marketing manager in Germany—will have a multiple reporting relationship, being responsible to the area manager and, in some instances, to an international or worldwide marketing manager at headquarters. Figure 21–8 illustrates an extremely simple matrix organization based on two organizational dimensions. Note that the country managers are responsible to both the area and the product line managers.

matrix organization
An organizational structure composed of one or more superimposed organizational structures in an attempt to mesh product, regional, functional, and other expertise

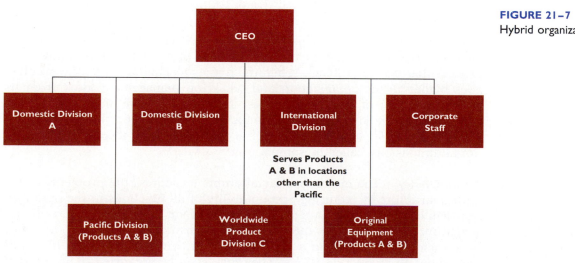

FIGURE 21–7
Hybrid organizational form

FIGURE 21–8
Regional-product matrix

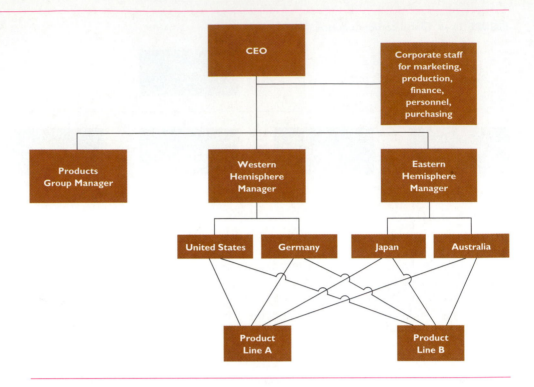

Ciba-Geigy, the Swiss chemical and pharmaceutical multinational, has an organizational structure based on a matrix of three dimensions: (1) product, (2) function, and (3) geographic region. Lines of communication flow both horizontally and vertically across these main dimensions. However, final authority rests with the executive committee, which is the highest executive body in the parent company. The task of this committee is to maintain two-way communication between the home office and the lower units. Committee members are not supermanagers of the divisions.

Problems with the Matrix.   Although at one time it seemed that the matrix organizational form would enable firms to have the advantages of the product, regional, and functional forms, the disadvantages of the matrix form have kept most worldwide companies from adopting it. One problem with the matrix is that the two or three managers (if it is a three-dimensional matrix) must agree on a decision. This can lead to less-than-optimum compromises, delayed responses, and power politics where more attention is paid to the process than to the problem. When the managers cannot agree, the problem goes higher in the organization and takes top management away from its duties. Because of these difficulties, many firms have maintained their original organizations based on product, function, region, or international division and built into the structure accountability for the other organizational dimensions, called by some a **matrix overlay**

Matrix Overlay.   The matrix overlay attempts to address the problems of the matrix structure by requiring accountability of all functions in the organization while avoiding the burdensome management stresses of a pure matrix structure. We have already mentioned how a firm organized by product may have regional specialists in a staff function with the requirement that they have input to product decisions. They may even be organized in an international division, as mentioned previously. Conversely, a regional organization

matrix overlay
An organization in which top-level divisions are required to heed input from a staff composed of experts of another organizational dimension in an attempt to avoid the double-reporting difficulty of a matrix organization but still mesh two or more dimensions

would have product managers on its staff who provide input to regional decisions.[22]

Strategic Business Units.   **Strategic business units (SBUs)**, which originated with General Electric, are a relatively new organizational form in which product divisions have been redefined as though they were distinct, independent businesses. An SBU is commonly defined as a business entity with a clearly defined market, specific competitors, the ability to carry out its business mission, and a size appropriate for control by a single manager. Most SBUs are based on product lines, and if a product must be modified to suit different markets, a worldwide product SBU may be divided into a few product/market SBUs serving various countries or groups of countries. Strategic business units do not determine how a company as a whole will organize its internal operations.

strategic business unit (SBU)
Business entity with a clearly defined market, specific competitors, the ability to carry out its business mission, and a size appropriate for control by a single manager

Changes in Organizational Forms

The rapidly changing business environment caused by increased global competition, customer preference for custom-made, not mass-produced, products, and faster technological change is pressuring managements to step up their search for organizational forms that will enable their firms to act more quickly, reduce costs, and improve the quality of product offerings. Not only are they mixing older, established forms, but they are also changing to different forms, many of which are modified versions of long-established forms with new names.

What is new is the acceptance by many managements of the need for frequent reorganization. Present in these reorganizations, called *reengineering* by many, is a significant reduction in the levels of middle management, restructuring of work processes to reduce the fragmenting of the process across functional departments, empowerment of employees, and the use of computers for instant communication and swift transmittal of information. CEOs are striving to make their organizations lean, flat, fast-to-respond, and innovative.[23]

Royal Dutch Shell, in one of the largest corporate restructurings ever attempted, announced it is dismantling its three-dimensional matrix organization of regional units, business sectors, and business functions (marketing, production, and so forth) and is changing to a "weakened matrix." The company will be organized at headquarters into five business organizations representing Shell's main activities: exploration and production, oil products (refining and marketing), chemicals, gas, and coal. The national operating companies will have a "dotted-line relationship" with the corporate center just described, but will report directly to an *international business division*, an organizational form largely discarded by experts in the organizational design of global firms.[24]

Current Organizational Trends

Two organizational forms are now receiving the attention of many CEOs: the virtual corporation and the horizontal corporation.

Virtual Corporation.   A **virtual corporation**, also called a *network organization*, enables companies to come together quickly to take advantage of a specific marketing opportunity. These alliances or outsourcing agreements enable each member to concentrate on what it does best, its core competency. Thus, a virtual corporation can have capabilities superior to those of any one member. Once the opportunity ends, the virtual corporation normally will disband.[25]

virtual corporation
A temporary group of independent companies, including manufacturers, marketers, suppliers, customers, and competitors, connected by a computer network for the purpose of designing, manufacturing, and marketing a product

The Virtual Company in Small Business

In today's global markets, companies must move fast to take advantage of opportunities, and often they lack the expertise to bring new products quickly to market. More firms are turning to virtual corporations (previously known as *consortia*), which are a temporary group of independent companies formed to exploit a specific opportunity. They may be suppliers, manufacturers, marketers, customers, and even competitors. Each member contributes its expertise. There is no central office or hierarchy. Once the job is finished, the group will generally disband.

Two years ago, Ron Oklewicz, formerly of Xerox and Apple Computer, had an idea for producing a handheld, pen-based computer. He started TelePad with a few engineers, limited designing skills, and no manufacturing plant. A prominent industrial design firm helped design and develop it. Intel, the computer chip

manufacturer, sent a team to assist with some engineering problems. A battery maker is working with TelePad to design a portable power supply. The computer is being produced using spare capacity at an IBM plant. Even an outside firm issues the paychecks for the company's 14 employees.

The virtual corporation enables TelePad to avoid the inefficiencies of vertical integration and takes advantage of world-class partners to bring its product to market faster. The president says he is leveraging his 14 employees into over a thousand highly trained experts in design, production, and marketing.

Source: "The Corporation," *Business Week*, February 8, 1993, pp. 98–103.

Although the name is new, the virtual corporation concept has existed for decades. It has been extremely common for a group of construction firms, each with a special area of expertise, to form a consortium to bid on a contract for constructing a road or an airfield, for example. After finishing the job, the consortium would disband. Other examples of network organizations are the various clothing and athletic shoe marketers such as DKNY, Nike, and Reebok. These latter are also called *modular corporations*.

horizontal corporation
A form of organization characterized by lateral decision processes, horizontal networks, and a strong corporatewide business philosophy

Horizontal Corporation. Another organization, the **horizontal corporation**, has been adopted by some large technology-oriented global firms in highly competitive industries such as electronics and computers. Firms such as AT&T, General Electric, and Du Pont have chosen this organizational form to give them the flexibility to respond quickly to advances in technology and be product innovators.[26] In many companies, teams are drawn from different departments to solve a problem or deliver a product.

This organization has been characterized as "anti-organization" because its designers are seeking to remove the constraints imposed by the conventional organizational structures. In a horizontal corporation, employees worldwide create, build, and market the company's products through a carefully cultivated system of interrelationships. Marketers in Great Britain speak directly to production people in Brazil without having to go through the home office in Germany, for example. Proponents of the horizontal organization claim lateral relationships incite innovation and new product development. They also state that the organization "puts greater decision-making responsibility in the hands of middle managers, who are not required to clear every detail and event with higher-ups. The idea is to substitute cooperation and coordination, which are in everyone's interests, for strict control and supervision."[27]

Corporate Survival into the 21st Century

Managers will make greater use of the *dynamic network structure* that breaks down the major functions of the firm into small companies coordinated by a small-sized headquarters organization. Business functions such as marketing or accounting may be provided by separate organizations connected by computers to a central office.[28] To attain the optimum level of vertical integration, a firm must focus on its core business. Anything not essential to the business can be done cheaper and faster by outside suppliers.[29]

As American companies prepare for the global battles of the 21st century, we must remember that organizations, like people, have life cycles. In their youth, they're small and fast-growing, but as they age, they often become big, complex, and out of touch with their markets. The firms of tomorrow must learn how to be large and entrepreneurial. As one CEO put it, "Small is not better; focused is better."[30]

SUMMARY

1. **Understand the benefits of global strategic planning.** Many global companies have instituted formal worldwide strategic planning to identify opportunities and threats, formulate strategies to handle them, and stipulate the means to finance those strategies.

2. **Describe the steps in the global strategic planning process.** Global strategic planning provides a formal structure in which managers (1) analyze the company's external environment, (2) analyze the company's internal environment, (3) define the company's business and mission, (4) set corporate objectives, (5) quantify goals, (6) formulate strategies, and (7) make tactical plans.

3. **Know what a planning staff does.** The planning staff assists the operating managers by providing information on the environments.

4. **Understand the purpose of corporate mission statements, objectives, quantified goals, and strategies.** Statements of the corporate business, vision, and mission communicate to the firm's stakeholders what the company is and where it is going. A firm's objectives direct its course of action, and its strategies enable management to reach its objectives.

5. **State which management tools are actually used by management.** According to a survey of 9,000 managers, the most commonly used tool is the mission statement, followed by the customer satisfaction survey. TQM was next, followed by competitor profiling. Least used were Porter's value chain analysis and five forces analysis, followed by mass customization and dynamic simulation.

6. **Describe the new directions in strategic planning.** Operating managers, not planners, now do the planning. Firms use less structured formats and much shorter documents.

Managers are more concerned with issues, strategies, and implementation.

7. **Discuss the various organizational forms.** Companies may (1) have an international division, (2) be organized by product, function, or region, or (3) have a mixture of them (hybrid form). To attain a balance between product and regional expertise, some managements have tried a matrix form of organization. Its disadvantages, however, have caused many managements to put a matrix overlay over the traditional product, regional, or functional form instead of using the matrix.

8. **Describe the current organizational trends and appreciate why CEOs are changing the organizational forms of their companies.** CEOs are examining horizontal and virtual corporations. A horizontal corporation is characterized by lateral decision processes, horizontal networks, and a strong corporate-wide business philosophy. A virtual corporation is a temporary group of independent companies, including manufacturers, marketers, suppliers, customers, and competitors, connected by a computer network for the purpose of designing, manufacturing, and marketing a product. CEOs are also changing the organizational forms of their companies so that their firms will act more quickly, reduce costs, and improve the quality of product offerings.

9. **Understand the concept of the virtual corporation.** A virtual corporation enables companies to come together quickly to take advantage of a specific marketing opportunity. Because each member concentrates on what it does best, a virtual corporation can have capabilities superior to those of any member. Once the opportunity ends, the virtual corporation normally will disband.

KEY WORDS

- watch list   675
- mission statement   677
- corporate strategies   678
- scenarios   679
- contingency plans   679
- top-down planning   681
- bottom-up planning   681
- iterative planning   681

- international division   683
- hybrid organization   686
- matrix organization   687
- matrix overlay   688
- strategic business unit (SBU)   689
- virtual corporation   689
- horizontal corporation   690

QUESTIONS

1. Why have many worldwide firms found it necessary to institute global strategic planning?

2. Prepare a watch list for Exxon.

3. Suppose the competitor analysis reveals that the American subsidiary of your firm's German competitor is about to broaden its product mix in the American market by introducing a new line against which your company has not previously had to compete in the home market. The environmental analysis shows that the dollar–mark exchange rate is going to continue to make American exports expensive in Germany. Do you recommend a defensive strategy, or do you attack your competitor in its home market? How will you implement your strategy?

4. You have been employed by the Brazilian subsidiary of an American multinational corporation whose primary interest is in the financial performance of its subsidiaries. A Japanese firm is setting up a Brazilian subsidiary and has offered you a salary that you cannot refuse. What cultural adjustments will you probably have to make in your new job?

5. You are the CEO of the Jones Petrochemical company and have just finished studying next year's plans of your foreign subsidiaries. You are pleased that the Israeli plan is so optimistic because that subsidiary contributes heavily to your company's income. But OPEC is meeting next month. Should you ask your planning committee, which meets tomorrow, to construct some scenarios? If so, about what?

6. The planning perspective should be benefit oriented rather than solution oriented. Please explain the meaning of this statement.

7. Your firm has used bottom-up planning for years, but the subsidiaries' plans differ with respect to approaches to goals and assumptions—even the time frames are different. How can you, the CEO, get them to agree on these points and still get their individual input?

8. Your matrix organization isn't working; decisions are taking too long, and it seems to you that, instead of best solutions, you're getting compromises. What can you, the CEO, do?

9. You are the CEO of Mancon Incorporated, and you have just acquired Pozoli, the Italian small-appliance maker (electric shavers, small household and personal care appliances). It has been in business 30 years and has manufacturing plants in Italy, Mexico, Ireland, and Spain. Its output is sold in more than 100 markets worldwide, including the United States. Your company is now organized into two product groups—shaving, personal care, and an international division at the top level. How are you going to include Pozoli in your organization?

10. It is obvious that in formulating new strategies, management may uncover a need to change its organization. Can you give some situations where the reverse may be true?

MINICASE 21–1   Electrex, Incorporated—Must It Reorganize?

Electrex, Inc. manufactures electronic and electrical connectors used on such diverse products as computers, home appliances, telecommunications, and the air bag and antiskid systems of American cars. The company has been in business since 1965. The table provides the important financial information for the last five years.

For some time, Electrex had been exporting to the Far East, where its major markets are Japan, Singapore, and Taiwan. When its foreign sales were confined to exports, the company functioned well with an export department whose manager reported to the company's marketing manager. In 1990, however, other American firms tried to enter the market, and there were rumors that a Japanese firm was searching for a licensor in the United States to supply it with manufacturing technology. Electrex decided to set up its first foreign plant in Japan. When it did, it hired financial and marketing people with Japanese experience and established an international division at headquarters to oversee the Japanese operation. The president felt that the situation would be repeated in Taiwan, Singapore, and Thailand. These were all good export markets at that time, but it was reasonable to suppose that some competitor would soon set up manufacturing facilities in one or more of them. Having a small international division with some Far East expertise that is responsible for monitoring these markets would help the firm avoid being surprised by a competitor's move.

After the Japanese Electrex plant was in production, more Japanese firms were willing to do business with the company than when it served the market by exports. In fact, the major portion of the 1994 sales increase was due to improved sales to the Japanese. However, the new customers also brought the company into a new, higher level of competition than it had known before. The Japanese competitors were bringing out new products at a considerably faster rate than Electrex. The president wondered if horizontal linkages across functions, such as the automakers have used to reduce their design time, might help his firm. Also, on his trips to Japan, the marketing people told him things about the market and the competitors that were not being sent to the Electrex home office.

It was obvious to the president that overseas production and growth in overseas sales demanded a reorganization of the firm. Even though the company had only one plant in Japan now, the president was confident that other plants would soon be needed. How should the company be organized to handle the new foreign production facilities? How can Electrex reduce the time needed to bring new designs to market?

Five-Year Financial Highlight Summary (in $ millions)

	1994	1993	1992	1991	1990
Net sales	$353.0	$298.2	$271.9	$257.4	$231.1
Gross profit	134.1	116.3	110.3	106.7	94.9
Selling, general, and administrative expense	70.5	61.2	55.8	51.8	45.1
Income from operations	63.6	55.1	54.5	54.9	49.8
Income taxes	23.9	20.9	20.9	21.8	20.9
Effective tax rate (%)	37.6	37.9	38.3	39.7	42.0
Net income	39.7	34.2	33.6	33.1	28.9

22

Control and Technology-Driven Changes

> *Successful leaders will have to relinquish control.*
>
> Kevin Kelly, executive editor of
> Wired

CONCEPT PREVIEWS

After reading this chapter, you should be able to:

1. **explain** why decisions are made where they are among parent and subsidiary units of an international company (IC)

2. **understand** how an IC can maintain control of a joint venture or of a company in which the IC owns less than 50 percent of the voting stock

3. **list** the types of information an IC needs to have reported to it by its units around the world

4. **explain** how the high-performance workplace era is being implemented in different countries

5. **understand** de-jobbing and how it is affecting workers' activities and traditional workplace hierarchy

6. **describe** the third industrial revolution

7. **understand** the arguments of those who hold that new technology will de-job workers and those who maintain that new technology will create more jobs than it destroys, as history has shown

8. **explain** digital or soft factories

9. **explain** why successful managers must sometimes relinquish control in a world out of control, as exemplified by Internet

The Biggest Breakthrough since the Lathe

The most spectacular computer-controlled tools are hexapods. These machines represent the biggest advance in machine tools since Henry Mandslay perfected the industrial lathe in 1880. • Hexapods are capable of handling unprecedentedly complex machining tasks. Embodying the same mechanical principles as a flight training simulator, a hexapod has six legs with computer-controlled motors that enable the machine's spindle platform to bring tools to bear from any angle in three-dimensional space. Unlike conventional machinery in which the spindle follows the path of a mechanical guideway, the spindle in a hexapod maneuvers through the air as prescribed by software. • These machines will bring great flexibility and mobility to manufacturing. A hexapod can weigh one-tenth as much as a conventional machine tool of comparable power and, unlike the standard tool, incorporates its own frame and needs no special foundation or external support. It can be moved easily and rapidly in a truck and can work anywhere parts need to be made.

"The Digital Factory," *Fortune*, November 14, 1994, p. 93.

The planning that is the necessary foundation for all aspects of any successful business was dealt with in Chapter 21. The control activities of which we shall speak here are the efforts to (1) put the plans into effect, (2) learn whether the plans are working as intended (they rarely do), and (3) make whatever corrections seem called for and practicable.

Control and many other aspects of the business world are being affected and altered by oncoming technology. An example is the hexapod, referred to above as the biggest advance in machine tools since perfection of the industrial lathe. The personnel structure of production organizations is changing as traditional jobs evolve into tasks performed by changing teams of workers. Hierarchy disappears as workers move from team to team. Successful leaders must encourage innovation and experimentation, and control is replaced by encouragement and incentives.

Soft or digital factories bring suppliers, producers, and customers together as companies can customize products literally in quantities of one, while turning them out at mass production speed. A product can be produced as the customer describes the desired features.

There is disagreement whether new technology will destroy jobs. Historically, it has created more that it destroyed.

CONTROL

subsidiaries
Companies controlled by other companies through ownership of enough voting stock to elect board of directors majorities

affiliates
Sometimes used interchangeably with "subsidiaries," but more forms exist than just stock ownership

Every successful company uses controls to put its plans into effect, evaluate their effectiveness, make desirable corrections, and evaluate and reward or correct executive performance. Matters are more complicated for an international company than for a one-country operation. In earlier chapters, we have brought out the complicating causes. They include different languages, cultures, and attitudes; different taxes and accounting methods; different currencies, labor costs, and market sizes,; different degrees of political stability and security for personnel and property; and many more. For these reasons, international companies need controls even more than do domestic ones.

Subsidiaries, 100 Percent Owned

The words subsidiaries and affiliates sometimes are used interchangeably, and we shall examine first the control of those in which the parent has 100 percent ownership. This avoids for now the additional complications of joint ventures or subsidiaries in which the parent has less than 100 percent ownership. We shall deal with those later in the chapter.

Where Are Decisions Made?

There are three possibilities. Two of them are that all decisions are made at either the IC headquarters or at the subsidiary level. Theoretically, all decisions could be made at one or the other location. As common sense would indicate, they are not; instead, some decisions are made at one place, some are made at the other place, and some are made cooperatively.[1] Many variables determine which decision is made where. Some of the more significant variables are (1) product and equipment, (2) the competence of subsidiary management and reliance on that management by the IC headquarters, (3) the size of the IC and how long it has been one, (4) the detriment of a subsidiary for the benefit of the enterprise, and (5) subsidiary frustration.

Product and Equipment.   As to decision location, questions of standardization of product and equipment and second markets can be important.

Standardize?   An easily made argument is that the product and the equipment with which to make it should be tailored to fit each national market. The other side is that overall enterprise gains from worldwide uniformity may more than compensate for individual country losses. Standardization of equipment may result in lower purchasing costs of the equipment as well as savings in equipment operation training, maintenance, and spare parts.

As to the product, uniformity gives greater flexibility in its sourcing. For example, if the product is made in two or more countries and such difficulties as strikes, natural disasters, political upheavals, or currency problems affect one country, the product can be delivered from the other.

In determining whether equipment and product should be standardized worldwide or tailored to different national markets, a company should gather opinions from each affected subsidiary. If any subsidiary can demonstrate that the profit potential that can be realized from tailoring to its own market is greater than the profit potential the enterprise will realize from standardization, the subsidiary should be permitted to proceed. Elements of profit potential would include the size of the subsidiary's market, the competition there, and the possibilities for exporting to areas with similar characteristics. Of course, the decision in such a case is cooperative in that the parent has the power to veto or override its subsidiary's decisions.

Second Markets.   The parent company may introduce a product in its largest market; by the time that product is offered in smaller markets, the company may have adapted it to eliminate "bugs" or improve performance. The parent would want to ensure that the mistakes already discovered and corrected would not be repeated in later markets. Even though some subsidiaries may wish to alter the product, second-market situations would indicate IC central decision making. Such decision making would be necessary to ensure uniformity of quality and performance as well as market timing and product improvement.

Competence of Subsidiary Management and Headquarters' Reliance on It.   Reliance on subsidiary management can depend on how well the executives know one another and how well they know company policies, on whether headquarters management feels that it understands host country conditions, on the distances between the home country and the host countries, and on how big and old the parent company is.

Moving Executives Around.   Some ICs have a policy of transferring promising management personnel between parent headquarters and subsidiaries and among subsidiaries. Thus, the manager learns firsthand the policies of headquarters and the problems of putting those policies into effect at subsidiary levels.

A result of such transfers, which is difficult to measure but nevertheless important, is a network of intra-IC personal relationships. This tends to increase the confidence of executives in one another and to make communication among executives easier and less subject to error.

Another development is that some ICs have moved their regional executives into headquarters to improve communications and reduce cost.

Understanding Host Country Conditions.   One element in the degree of headquarters' reliance on subsidiary management is the familiarity of headquarters with conditions in the subsidiary's host country. The less familiar or the more different conditions in the host country are perceived to be, the more likely headquarters is to rely on subsidiary management.

How Far Away is the Host Country?   Another element in the degree of headquarters' reliance on subsidiary management is the distance of the host country from home headquarters. Thus, an American parent is likely to place more reliance on the management of an Indonesian subsidiary than on the management of a Canadian subsidiary. This would be for two reasons: American management would perceive management conditions in Canada to be more easily understood than conditions in Indonesia, and Indonesia is much farther from the United States than Canada is.

Size and Age of the IC.   As a rule, a large company can afford to hire more specialists, experts, and experienced executives than can a smaller one. The longer a company has been an IC, the more likely it is to have a number of experienced executives who know company policies and who have worked at headquarters and in the field. Successful experience builds confidence.

In most ICs, the top positions are at headquarters, and the ablest and most persistent executives get there in time. Thus, over time, headquarters of a successful company is run by experienced executives who are confident of their knowledge of the business in the home and host countries and in combinations thereof.

It follows that in larger, older organizations, more decisions are made at headquarters and fewer are delegated to subsidiaries. Smaller companies, in business for shorter periods of time, tend to be able to afford fewer internationally experienced executives and will not have had time to develop them internally. Smaller, newer companies have no choice but to delegate decisions to subsidiary managements. During the 1980s and early 1990s, it became something of a management fad among larger ICs also to empower subsidiary managers and decentralize. As do most fads, however, this practice faded by the mid-1990s, and ICs began to shift power to the parent in the home country.[2]

Benefiting the Enterprise to the Detriment of a Subsidiary.   An IC has opportunities to source raw materials and components, locate factories, allocate orders, and govern intraenterprise pricing that are not available to a non-IC. Such activities may be beneficial to the enterprise yet result in a **subsidiary detriment**.

subsidiary detriment
A small loss for a subsidiary results in a greater gain for the total IC

Moving Production Factors.   For any number of reasons, an IC may decide to move factors of production from one country to another or to expand in one country in preference to another. Tax, labor, market, currency, or political stability are a few possible reasons.

The subsidiary from which factors are being taken would be unenthusiastic. Its management would be slow, at best, to cut the company's capacity. Headquarters would make such decisions.

Which Subsidiary Gets the Order?   Similarly, if an order—say, from an Argentine customer—could be filled from a subsidiary in France or another in South Africa or a third in Brazil, parent headquarters might decide which subsidiary gets the business. Among the considerations in the decision would be transportation costs, production costs, comparative tariff rates, customers' currency restrictions, comparative order backlogs, and taxes. Having such a decision made by IC headquarters avoids price competition among members of the same IC group.

Multicountry Production.   Frequently, the size of the market in a single country is too small to permit economies of scale in manufacturing an entire industrial product for that one market. An example is Ford's production of a light vehicle for the Asian market.

In that situation, Ford negotiated with several countries to the end that one country would make one component of the vehicle for all of the countries involved. Thus, one country makes the engine, a second country has the body-stamping plant, a third makes the transmission, and so forth. In this fashion, each operation achieves the efficiency and cost savings of economies of scale. Of course, this kind of multinational production demands a high degree of IC headquarters' control and coordination.

Which Subsidiary Books the Profit?   In certain circumstances, an IC may have some choice of two or more countries in which to declare profits. Such circumstances may arise where two or more units of the IC cooperate in supplying components or services under a contract with a customer unrelated to any part of the IC. Under these conditions, there may be opportunities to allocate higher prices to one unit or subsidiary and lower prices to another within the global price to the customer.

If the host country of one of the subsidiaries has lower taxes than the other host countries, it would be natural to try to maximize profits in the lower-tax country and minimize them in the higher-tax country. Other differences between host countries could dictate the allocation of profit to or from the subsidiaries located there. Such differences could include currency controls, labor relations, political climate, or social unrest. It is sensible to direct or allocate as much profit as reasonably possible to subsidiaries in countries with the least currency controls, the best labor relations and political climate, and the least social unrest.

The intraenterprise transaction may also give a company choices of profit location. Pricing between members of the same enterprise is referred to as *transfer pricing,* and while IC headquarters could permit undirected, arm's-length negotiations between itself and its subsidiaries, that might not yield the most advantageous results for the enterprise as a whole.

Price and profit allocation decisions like these are usually best made at parent company headquarters, which is supposed to maintain the overall view, looking out for the best interests of the enterprise. Naturally, subsidiary management does not gladly make decisions to accept lower profits, largely because its evaluation may suffer.

The following two tables illustrate how the total IC enterprise might profit even though one subsidiary makes less. Assume a cooperative contract by which two subsidiaries are selling products and services to an outside customer for a price of $100 million. The host country of IC Alpha levies company income taxes at the rate of 50 percent, whereas IC Beta's host country taxes its income at 20 percent. The customer is in a third country, has agreed to pay $100 million, and is indifferent to how Alpha and Beta share the money. The first table below shows the enterprise's after-tax income if Alpha is paid $60 million and Beta, $40 million.

	Receives (in $ millions)	Tax (in $ millions)	After Tax (in $ millions)
Alpha	$60	$30	$30
Beta	40	8	32
			$62

Thus, after tax, the enterprise realizes $62 million.

The second table shows the after-tax income if Alpha is paid $40 million and Beta, $60 million.

	Receives (in $ millions)	Tax (in $ millions)	After Tax (in $ millions)
Alpha	$40	$20	$20
Beta	60	12	48
			$68

Thus, after tax, the enterprise realizes $68 million.

These simple examples illustrate that the IC would be $6 million better off if it could shift $20 million of the payment from Alpha to Beta, while the customer is no worse off, as it pays $100 million in either case. Alpha, having received $20 million less payment, is $10 million worse off after taxes, but Beta is $16 million better off and the enterprise if $6 million ahead on the same contract. Given the number of countries and tax laws in the world, there are countless combinations of how such savings can be accomplished. Financial management awareness and control are the keys.

We do not mean to leave the impression that the host or home governments are unaware of or indifferent to transfer pricing and profit allocating by ICs operating within their borders. The companies must expect questioning by host and home governments and must be prepared to demonstrate that prices or allocations are reasonable. This may be done by showing that other companies charge comparable prices for the same or similar items or, if there are no similar items, by showing that costs plus profit have been used reasonably to arrive at the price. As to allocation of profits, the IC in our example would try to prove that the volume or importance of the work done by Beta or the responsibilities assumed by Beta, such as financing, after-sales service, or warranty obligations, justify the higher amount being paid to Beta. Of course, the questioning in this instance would come from the host government of Alpha if it got wind of the possibility of more taxable income for Beta and less for itself.[3]

Subsidiary Frustration.   An extremely important consideration for parent company management is that the management of its subsidiaries be motivated and loyal. If all the big decisions are made, or are perceived to be made, at the IC headquarters, the managers of subsidiaries could lose incentive and prestige or face with their employees and the community. They may grow hostile and disloyal.

Therefore, even though there may be reasons for headquarters to make decisions, it should delegate as much as is reasonably possible. Management of each subsidiary should be kept thoroughly informed and be consulted seriously about decisions, negotiations, and developments in its geographic area. The mid-1990s trend for ICs to shift power away from subsidiaries toward the parent has caused the forecastable frustration to subsidiary management, followed by resignations. Some companies reporting this development were IBM, European International, and CS First Boston.[4]

Joint Ventures and Subsidiaries Less than 100 Percent Owned

A joint venture may be, as defined in Chapter 2, a corporate entity between an IC and local owners or a corporate entity between two or more companies that are foreign to the area where the joint venture is located, or it may involve one company working on a project of limited duration (constructing a dam, for example) in cooperation with one or more other companies. The other companies may be subsidiaries or affiliates, but they may also be entirely independent entities.

All the reasons for making decisions at IC headquarters, at subsidiary headquarters, or cooperatively apply equally in joint venture situations. However, headquarters will almost never have as much freedom of action and flexibility in a joint venture as it has with subsidiaries that are 100 percent owned.

Loss of Freedom and Flexibility.   The reasons for that loss of freedom and flexibility are easy to see. If shareholders outside the IC own control of the affiliate, they can block efforts of IC headquarters to move production factors away, to fill an export order from another affiliate or subsidiary, and so forth. Even if outside shareholders are a minority and cannot directly control the affiliate, they can bring legal or political pressures on the IC to prevent it from diminishing the affiliate's profitability for the enterprise's benefit. Likewise, the local partner in a joint venture is highly unlikely to agree with measures that penalize the joint venture for the IC's benefit.

Control Can Be Had.   With less than 50 percent of the voting stock and even with no voting stock, an IC can have control. Some methods to maintain control are:

- A management contract.
- Control of the finances.
- Control of the technology.
- Putting people from the IC in important executive positions.

As might be expected, ICs have encountered resistance to putting IC personnel in the important executive positions from their joint venture partners or from host governments. The natural desire of these partners and governments is that their own nationals have at least equality in the important positions and that they get training and experience in the technology and management.[5]

Reporting

For controls to be effective, all operating units of an IC must provide headquarters with timely, accurate, and complete reports. There are many uses for the information reported. Among the types of reporting required are (1) financial, (2) technological, (3) market opportunity, and (4) political and economic.

Financial.   A surplus of funds in one subsidiary should perhaps be retained there for investment or contingencies. On the other hand, such a surplus might be more useful at the parent company, in which case payment of a dividend is indicated. Or perhaps another subsidiary or affiliate needs capital, and the surplus could be lent or invested there. Obviously, parent headquarters must know the existence and size of a surplus to determine its best use.

Technological.   New technology should be reported. New technology is constantly being developed in different countries, and the subsidiary or affiliated company operating in such a country is likely to learn about it before IC headquarters hundreds or thousands of miles away. If headquarters finds the new technology potentially valuable, it could gain competitive advantage by being the first to contact the developer for a license to use it.

Market Opportunities.   The affiliates in various countries may spot new or growing markets for some product of the enterprise. This could be profitable all around, as the IC sells more of the product while the affiliate earns sales commissions. Of course, if the new market is sufficiently large, the affiliate may begin to assemble or produce the product under license from the parent company or from another affiliate.

Other market-related information that should be reported to IC headquarters includes competitors' activities, price developments, and new products of potential interest to the IC group. Also of importance is information on the subsidiary's market share and whether it is growing or shrinking, together with explanations.

Political and Economic.   Not surprisingly, reports on political and economic conditions have multiplied mightily in number and importance over the past 15 or so years as revolutions—some bloody—have toppled and changed governments.[6] Democracies have replaced dictatorships, one dictator has replaced another, countries have broken apart or reunited—changes have been occurring on almost every continent.

One early example of how accurate reporting saved an American company a lot of money involved Citibank in Iran, where the bank had a representative office during the 1970s. Even though some government intelligence services were said to have been surprised when the Ayatollah Khomeini threw out the shah of Iran in 1979, the Citibank Tehran office had become aware of potential danger as early as the summer of 1978. The office first lowered the ceiling on Iranian loans and then froze any new business, even to existing customers, in the autumn of 1978.[7]

TECHNOLOGY-DRIVEN CHANGES

As the second half of the 18th century saw the birth of the age of industry, the end of the 20th sees the dawn of a less euphonious era, the age of the high-performance workplace. As mass production jobs migrate to developing countries, rich-world firms are being forced to compete on quality rather than price, variety rather than volume, and after-sales service rather than quantity.

The basic aims of the high-performance workplace—to move away from mass production by improving efficiency and service—are broad enough for the phrase to mean different things to different managers around the world.

Companies in Japan, led by automakers such as Toyota, reduced production to whittle down inventories and used teams of workers to eliminate bottlenecks, guarantee quality, and institutionalize improvement. The result was a dramatic fall in how long it took to make things.

Flexible specialization is the approach used in northern Italy. Companies turn to industrial networks to combine the virtues of small firms (timeliness, customization) with the advantages of big organizations (economics of scale, global reach). For example, Benetton, a clothing firm, uses its fluid relationship with a myriad of suppliers, some specializing in design, others in manufacturing, to pander to the public's whims.

The specialty in Germany is *diversified quality*, which involves producing short batches of luxury goods such as cars or machine tools. German managers say that their traditional advantage in this area—their highly skilled workforce—is being reinforced by information technology that makes it easier to combine the virtues of craft and mass production.

The approach in Sweden centers on autonomous teams of highly skilled craftsmen. In Volvo's Uddevalla plant, for example, teams were responsible for assembling entire cars and had direct contact with customers.

Among American companies, one can find variations of all the high-performance workplace practices discussed above. Indeed, some of the practices the Americans are said to have learned from abroad originated in the United States. For example, lean production and total quality management were invented in the Bell Labs in the 1920s and became central to American war production. The occupying Americans taught them to the Japanese, who then retaught them to their teachers in the 1970s.

Is Nothing New?

Many managers are revamping mass production, cutting labor costs, contracting out, and using computers to customize products. Indeed, many of the trendiest workplaces are old-fashioned factories in disguises. Italian clothing firms rely on cheap part-timers in southern Italy and Turkey. Many managers struggling to cut costs are turning to flexible mass production to achieve a high-performance workplace.[8]

"De-jobbing"

The conditions that created jobs 200 years ago—mass production and large organizations—are disappearing. Technology enables companies to automate production lines where many job holders used to do repetitive tasks. Instead of long production runs where the same thing has to be done again and again, firms are increasingly customizing production. Big firms, where most of the good jobs used to be, are unbundling activities and farming them out to little firms. New computer and communication technologies are "de-jobbing" the workplace, changing from the traditional, fixed-jobs approach to one in which teams perform tasks. And the composition of these teams changes as the tasks evolve.

de-jobbing
Replacing fixed jobs with tasks performed by evolving teams

Today's organization is rapidly being transformed from a structure built out of jobs into a field of work needing to be done. A fast-moving organization, such as Intel, will hire a person to be part of a specific project. The project will change over time, and the person's responsibilities and tasks change with it. Then the person is assigned to another project, probably before the first is finished, and then maybe to a third. As projects evolve and change, the person will work with several team leaders, keeping different schedules, being in various places, and performing a number of different tasks.

Hierarchy Implodes. Under these conditions, **hierarchy** cannot be maintained; people no longer take their cues from a job description or a supervisor's instructions. Signals come from the changing demands of the project. Workers focus their efforts and collective resources on work that needs doing, changing as that changes.

hierarchy
A body of persons organized or classified according to rank or authority

Traits of Companies with De-Jobbed Workers. They share four:

- They encourage employees to make the kinds of operating decisions that used to be reserved for managers.
- They give employees the information they need to make such decisions.
- They give employees lots of training to create the kind of understanding of business and financial issues that used to concern only an owner or executive.
- They give employees a stake in the fruits of their labor—a share of profits.[9]

Third Industrial Revolution. In the first industrial revolution, machines replaced human labor. In the second, production lines permitted mass production. In the **third industrial revolution,** new computer and communication technologies are making their impact on the workplace and the economy. In the agricultural, manufacturing, and service sectors, machines are replacing human labor and promise (threaten?) an economy of near-automated production by the mid-decades of the 21st century.

third industrial revolution
Changes in the modern workplace created by new computer and communication technologies, which some argue are replacing human labor

As a result, one author predicts that the global labor market will polarize into two parts. There will be a new cosmopolitan elite of "symbolic analysts" who control the technologies and the forces of production. At the other pole will be a growing number of permanently displaced workers. He forecasts that blue-collar workers will pass from the workplace.

He also believes destructive conflict between the two diverse forces can be avoided. Almost by definition, according to him, they won't be able to work together in business or government because there will be little or nothing for former blue-collar workers to do. He sees hope for future job prospects in the expansion of voluntary, nongovernmental organizations that will bring about "a rebirth of the human spirit."[10]

But, Remember the First Industrial Revolution.   Since the early 19th century, people have predicted that machines would destroy jobs, and at that time, the Luddites responded by destroying the looms and jennies that they feared threatened their jobs. Karl Marx said that by investing in machinery, factory owners would create a vast army of unemployed. But the world's experience has been that new technology has created more jobs than it has destroyed, and there is respectable opinion that it will do so again.

For example, the American Bureau of Labor Standards points out that in the 10 years since 1985, employment in the computer software industry has almost trebled; moreover, the Bureau forecasts that between 1995 and 2005, the number of jobs for computer systems analysts and programmers will more than double and be the fastest-growing occupations after health care workers. Technological changes cause need for teachers and trainers. Virtual reality experiences, such as pretending to be a jet pilot in a simulator session, could become as popular as going to the cinema, which would create many jobs.

The OECD finds little support for the view that technological change is to blame for high unemployment. To the contrary, the countries that have been most successful in creating jobs—the United States and Japan—have also seen the fastest shift in their industrial structure towards a high-tech, knowledge-based economy.[11]

Digital or Soft Factories Putting People to Work.   Software and computer networks have emerged as more important than production machines, and human workers are back in unexpected force. **Digital or soft factories** bring agility to the plant; companies can customize products literally in quantities of one, while turning them out at mass production speeds. Soft manufacturing also blurs traditional boundaries by tying production to both suppliers and customers. Some examples will illustrate that process.

digital or soft factories
Facilities in which software and computer networks have emerged as more important than machines; they bring human workers back into faster and more agile production and tie production to both suppliers and customers

- By 800 lines or E-mail, orders for a variety of pagers stream into Motorola's salespeople. As they take the orders, they digitize the data that flows to the assembly line. There, pick-and-place robots select the proper components, which are assembled by humans. Often the order is complete within 80 minutes, and depending on the customer's location, it can be delivered the same or next day. Sherita Ceasar, director of manufacturing, says, "Our vision is simultaneous manufacturing, to make the pager even as the customer talks. We're getting close."

- IBM applies similar procedures in filling orders for the several models of its PCs. They take some 5,000 customer calls a day and are able to make next-day delivery by Airborne Express.

- General Electric has tripled its locomotive output since 1992 while customizing cabs, propulsion motors, and paint schemes. Through improved software use, the company has cut the time it needs to complete a locomotive for delivery from two years to six months.

- The U.S. Labor department has recorded a gain of some 214,000 workers in soft manufacturing in the 12 months to the end of 1994. Each new high-paying manufacturing job creates 4.5 additional jobs in the economy.[12]

Managing in a World out of Control

The Internet may be the closest thing to a working anarchy the world has ever seen. Nobody owns it, nobody runs it, and most of its 30 million or so citizens get along by dint of on-line etiquette, not rules and regulations. Etiquette, however, has not prevented some users from copping names generally associated with others.* The coppers may be pretenders, competitors, speculators hoping that the name might one day be worth something, or just pranksters. Some legal battles for names involve Kaplan Educational Center, which found its name had been taken by its chief competitor, Princeton Review; MCI, whose name was registered by its rival, Sprint; and MTV, which was beaten to that name registration by a former employee.[13]

Internet has been built up without any central control because the U.S. Defense Department wanted to ensure it could survive a nuclear attack. The Net has proven a paragon of hothouse expansion and constant evolution. Though it may be messier and less efficient than a similar system designed and run by an agency or company, this organically grown network is also more adaptable and less susceptible to a systemwide crash.

The consequences for management in a world out of control, such as Internet, are discussed in a book by Kevin Kelly titled *Out of Control: The Rise of Neo-Biological Civilization*. Among the points made in a review of the book is a recipe developed at MIT for devising a system of distributed control: (1) do simple things first, (2) learn to do them flawlessly, (3) add new layers of activity over the results of the simple task, (4) don't change the simple things, (5) make the new layer work as flawlessly as the simple, and (6) repeat ad infinitum. Many organizations would benefit by adopting organizing principles as deceptively simple as these.

Increasingly, the most successful companies, like the machines and programs so many of them now make, and the networks on which they all will rely will advance only by evolving and adapting in this organic, bottom-up way. Successful leaders will have to relinquish control. They will have to honor error because a breakthrough may at first be indistinguishable from a mistake. They must constantly seek disequilibrium.[14]

CONTROL: YES AND NO

We have spoken of control within the IC family of parent, subsidiaries, affiliates, and joint ventures. This deals with where decisions are made on a variety of subjects under different circumstances. Timely and accurate reporting to the parent is necessary for success of the IC family. The trend in this area of control is toward centralized decision making, with more being done by the parent.

The other control of which we have spoken involves the design, production, and order-filling functions of companies. Here, the explosion of software, computer networks, and information technology, including Internet, have tended to decentralize and de-job organizations. More and more, workers do evolving tasks with changing teams of other workers. Hierarchies dissolve and successful leaders relinquish control as workers are trained and encouraged to cope with evolving tasks and rewarded for coping well.

---

*The U.S. government pays Network Solutions, a Virginia-based company, to run InteNIC, which registers Internet "domain" names—the on-line monikers such as microsoft.com—that companies reserve for themselves so that customers and clients can find them on line.

SUMMARY

1. **Explain why decisions are made where they are among parent and subsidiary units of an international company (IC).** Several considerations govern where decisions are made in an IC family of organizations. They include desirability to standardize products as opposed to differentiating them for different markets, the competence of organization managements, the size and age of the IC, the benefit of one part of the family to the detriment of another, and building confidence or avoiding frustration of management.

2. **Understand how an IC can maintain control of a joint venture or of a company in which the IC owns less than 50 percent of the voting stock.** Control can be maintained over a joint venture or a company in which the IC owns less than 50 percent of the voting stock by several devices, including a management contract, control of the finances, control of the technology, or putting people from the IC in key executive positions.

3. **List the types of information an IC needs to have reported to it by its units around the world.** Subsidiaries should report to the IC information about financial conditions, technological developments, market opportunities and developments, and economic and political conditions.

4. **Explain how the high-performance workplace era is being implemented in different countries.** The high-performance workplace is being implemented differently from country to country. The Japanese used lean production; the northern Italians, flexible specialization; the Germans, diversified quality; the Swedes, autonomous teams; and the Americans, a combination.

5. **Understand de-jobbing and how it is affecting workers' activities and traditional workplace hierarchy.** Some maintain that new technology is de-jobbing the workplace, replacing fixed jobs with tasks performed by evolving teams, so that traditional hierarchy of the workplace disappears.

6. **Describe the third industrial revolution.** The first industrial revolution occurred in England as jennies and looms replaced human labor in the textile mills. The second saw production lines and mass production developed. The third is caused by new computer and communication technologies, which some say are replacing human labor.

7. **Understand the arguments of those who hold that new technology will de-job workers and those who maintain that new technology will create more jobs than it destroys, as history has shown.** One argument is that the third industrial revolution will abolish blue-collar workers and result in an elite group that controls the technology and everyone else without a job. But lessons from the first and second revolutions are that new technology creates more jobs than it destroys.

8. **Explain digital or soft factories.** Digital or soft factories use software and computer networks that emphasize human skills to shorten production time. A result is to blur traditional boundaries by tying production to both suppliers and customers.

9. **Explain why successful managers must sometimes relinquish control in a world out of control, as exemplified by Internet.** The high-performance workplace, the third industrial revolution, and soft factories are moving business organizations away from traditional hierarchical control practices toward cooperation, encouragement, and incentives. Successful leaders will have to relinquish control and honor error because a breakthrough may at first be indistinguishable from a mistake.

KEY WORDS

- subsidiaries   696
- affiliates   696
- subsidiary detriment   698
- de-jobbing   703

- hierarchy   703
- third industrial revolution   703
- digital or soft factories   704

QUESTIONS

1. In determining whether decisions will be made by the parent company or by its subsidiaries, what are the considerations when equipment and products are standardized worldwide rather than tailored to individual national circumstances and markets?

2. *a.* In an IC, what are some decisions that could result in detriment for a subsidiary but greater benefit for the enterprise?

   b. In such circumstances, where will the decision be made—at IC headquarters or at the affected subsidiary?

3. What measures can be utilized to control subsidiaries that are less than 100 percent owned by the firm or joint venture partners in which the firm has no ownership?

4. What are the roles of reporting in multinational controls?

5. Why are rich-world firms being forced more and more to compete on quality rather than price, variety rather than volume, and after-sales service rather than quantity?

6. Explain the argument that the world is de-jobbing.

7. What is causing the movement away from the traditional hierarchical organization of the workforce?

8. What is replacing the hierarchy, and how are workers trained and encouraged?

9. What are digital or soft factories, and why are they creating work?

10. Explain the statement that leaders will have to relinquish control.

MINICASE 22–1   Competition within the IC

Worldwide (W) is an IC with subsidiary manufacturing plants in several countries around the world. W has just won a very large contract to supply locomotives to Paraguay, which is modernizing its entire railway system with financing from the World Bank.

W's home country is the United States, and it could manufacture parts of or the complete locomotives in its U.S. plants. W subsidiary companies in Spain, Argentina, and Australia could also manufacture parts or the locomotives. The managers of all those subsidiaries know about the big, new contract, and each is eager to get the work involved in performing it.

A meeting of the subsidiary chief executive officers (CEOs) is called at W's headquarters in New York to discuss which plant or plants will get the work. The manager of the American locomotive division is also at the meeting, and she makes a strong case that her plant needs the work. It has laid off 3,000 workers, and this big job would permit it to recall them. In addition, the American factory has all the latest technology, some of which has not been shared with the subsidiaries.

Each CEO argues that there is unemployment in their host country, and as responsible citizens, they must hire more local people. That, moreover, would reduce hostility in the host country and give them defenses against left-wing attacks on foreign-owned companies. One subsidiary CEO suggests that each subsidiary and the American division enter competitive bids and let Paraguayan Railways make the decision.

You are the CEO of W and have the responsibility to allocate parts of or all the work to one or more of the plants. List and explain the considerations that will govern your decisions.

The Evolution of Ogre Mills

This is a case involving the evolution of Ogre Mills (OM) from a Soviet enterprise in the Latvian Republic of the U.S.S.R. to a private company in an independent Latvia.

The Name "Ogre Mills"

It is given that OM has begun to acquire raw materials in Western countries—Australia and New Zealand are named—and wishes to sell its products internationally. The two named countries are English-speaking and probably some markets will also use English.

We don't know what "Ogre" means in Latvian, but in English it is a "fabled, man-eating giant or monster." (We suppose it wouldn't discriminate and would eat women also, given the opportunity). Another definition is "one who is particularly cruel, brutish, or hideous." Now, we submit that that's not a cheerful or pleasant or even a neutral name. Students are invited to suggest a change in OM's name.

Fundamentals

The communist state (the U.S.S.R. of which Latvia was a part) began by seizing private property. When Latvia became an independent country, fundamental principles were rediscovered, of which among the most important were the crucial role of private ownership and the linkage between legality, democracy, and prosperity. The restitution of private property and privatization of state-owned assets have been at the heart of the transition to a law-based, multiparty market economy and society.

Privatization itself has not created enterprise, capital, or managerial enterprise. It has generated the need for efficient banks, stock markets, and investment funds, and sparked off a hunt for foreign equity investments and managerial skills. The distance from the old command economy is already large. Governments have learned that foreign investment brings more than capital; it also provides technology, managerial skills, and access to world markets.

Among central and eastern European countries and former Soviet republics, some have made more progress than others, and the decline in production that followed market reform and the COMECON market collapse is over. Latvia and the other Baltic states, the Czech Republic, Hungary, Poland, Slovakia, and Slovenia, have made the most progress.

The Bottom Line Is: What's the Bottom Line?

The three areas of Western expertise most needed are in finance and accounting, sales and marketing, and general management. Frequently, Western investors don't even try to teach management techniques at first. Instead they try to teach employees what a market is—what it means, for example, to have customers who actually can refuse your products because someone else's are better.

Part of the problem was the definition of sales. The tendency was to equate sales figures with production figures. It was common to hear that 10,000 units had been sold when 7,000 were still in the warehouse waiting to be bought. Another big problem is keeping machinery repaired. Accustomed to delays and parts shortages, repair people don't believe in speed; getting something fixed can take weeks.

Home Boys Help—Or Do They?

Eastern Europe's émigrés are flooding back—straight into some of the "old countries'" top posts. As bureaucrats, military men, and even cabinet ministers, "reémigrés" are shaping Europe's emerging democracies controversially.

Several top officials at the Latvian central bank are Latvians who have returned home from abroad, including one on secondment from the U.S. Treasury. For the most part, central and eastern Europe's fledgling democracies, short of money, contacts, and technical skills, benefit from the return of such émigrés. They are, as one Hungarian put it, like a generation sent abroad for on-the-job training.

Some émigrés help by donating to educational institutions. Others are busy demolishing the demand economy. Privatization requires skills not common in centrally planned economies, and they have to be imported. So, the privatization agency in Estonia (next door to Latvia) is run by a man who made his fortune managing the pop group, ABBA, while living in Sweden. A Polish-American banker helped design and will run Poland's privatization program.

Yet, despite the benefits they can bring, returning émigrés are controversial. Their countrymen receive them with a combination of awe, envy, and resentment. Skills and sophistication do not compensate for the fact that, having lived abroad, they did not endure the hardship of communism. And now they get the best jobs.

And, of course, there are a few duds whose main qualifications are well-cut suits and clean teeth. One young Lithuanian-Canadian parlayed a tenuous diploma in marketing to promote himself from his job as a barman in Toronto to chief European officer at Lithuania's Ministry of International Economic Relations. He has since been removed from his lofty post. Others compete with each other in elections for political offices, and one managed the successful campaign of a communist in beating a candidate who was a fellow reémigré of the campaign manager.

The Communists Are Coming

The reemergence of communism, usually with new names, is troubling businesspeople and governments of the West. Among reasons given for this are:

- The West vastly underestimated the psychological damage inflicted by decades of communism.

- The communist officials who controlled vast sectors of the economy and the military never relinquished influence over politics and economies.

- While the communist officials maintained solidarity, the democratic, anticommunist movements frequently splintered and fell to fighting each other.

But the communists may not get our OM

Out of the 22 states in Central and Eastern Europe, there are only five in which the communists, by whatever name, do not hold power or significantly share in government. One of the five is Latvia. The others are Albania, Armenia, the Czech Republic, and Estonia.

OM's Future

In attempting to become a successful international company, should OM seek assistance? If not, why not? If yes, what sorts of assistance from whom? Should it reorganize, privatize, or both?

Three Diversified Cases

In closing, we offer three cases, each quite different than the others. They present factual situations, problems, and the solutions decided on by the people involved. You might want to consider whether you would have approached and solved them the same ways.

The first case shows how badly most, but not all, of Perrier's management handled the company's benzene crisis. The second is about how three companies set up operations in Germany. The third case is about how political policy change can affect business plans.

CASE I

Oh No, No Eau

Until January last year, laboratory workers at the Mecklenburg County Environmental Protection Department in Charlotte, North Carolina, made a regular pilgrimage to their local supermarket to buy two or three bottles of Perrier, a leading brand of sparkling mineral water. The scientists needed purified water to dilute substances they were testing for hazardous chemicals; buying Perrier was simpler than making their own. But on January 19, a biologist at the laboratory spotted an unusual reading on his mass spectrometer: something was corrupting his sample.

As Perrier had been an unfailingly reliable source, James Ward, the laboratory's director, was sure his equipment was to blame. But after spending two days checking everything from the spectrometer to utensils, the scientists went shopping for Perrier again. Another eight bottles were tested. Each one contained minute quantities of benzene, an industrial solvent—and a carcinogen. It was a discovery that was to prove costly to Source Perrier, the mineral water's French manufacturer. Within weeks it had withdrawn every bottle from worldwide circulation—160 million in all—at a total cost now estimated at up to $200 million.

Perrier did not get to hear of the problem until the Mecklenburg laboratory's findings had been confirmed by both American state and federal officials. There seemed little cause for haste. The concentrations of benzene found in the Perrier varied between 12.3 and 19.9 parts per billion—well above the limit of five parts per billion specified by America's Food and Drug Administration (FDA), but far below the sort of levels that might endanger health. A cup of non-freeze-dried decaffeinated coffee contains more benzene.

Nonetheless, when Perrier Group of America was told of the problem in early February 1990, it moved fast, recalling over 70 million bottles from North American shops and restaurants. But it also broke the first rule of crisis management: don't play the problem down. Before it even knew the source of the benzene contamination, Perrier's American arm was confidently announcing that the contamination was limited to North America.

In France, however, Source Perrier was making more far-reaching errors. At first, it reacted decisively, halting global bottling of the sparkling water that made up 14 percent of its FFr13.6 billion ($2.5 billion) sales in 1990 (all told, Perrier water and the company's other mineral waters—from different springs—accounted for 60 percent of Source Perrier's 1990 revenues). But then it started breaking every rule in the book.

On February 11, two days after the crisis had broken, a Source Perrier spokesman announced that the source of the benzene was a cleaning fluid mistakenly used on the bottling line that served the North American market; the machine in question had now been cleaned and repaired. Independent tests, said Perrier, showed that the natural source of Perrier water, at Vergèze in the south of France, was unaffected by any pollutants. This was a claim that was later to return to haunt Perrier.

It was also, to say the least, a little disingenuous: in reality, Source Perrier still had no idea where the contamination at its 36-hectare Vergèze plant was coming from. Less than three days later it discovered the real cause. Company employees had failed to replace charcoal filters used to screen out impurities in the natural gas that was present in the Perrier spring. Six months worth of production was affected, covering Perrier's entire global market. The firm had to change its story.

In Paris, Source Perrier still did not seem to have grasped the enormity of its problem. A press conference called for February 14—five days after the story broke—was held in a room too small to hold the hordes of journalists covering the story. With refreshing tactlessness, Perrier water was served. Gustave Leven, the firm's 75-year-old chairman, announced a global withdrawal of the water, but was at pains to make light of the problem. When asked why Perrier had expanded its recall, Leven, in a reference to one of Perrier's French ads, quipped, "Perrier is crazy!"

"All this publicity helps build the brand's renown," chipped in Frederik Zimmer, president of Perrier's international division. More worryingly, Zimmer observed that Perrier water "naturally contains several gases, including benzene. Those have to be filtered out." But if the company was actively filtering benzene, surely the filtration plant was the obvious place to look for contamination?

The revelation that benzene was present in the spring was a disaster. Mineral water is an odd product. As with petrol (which is only two-thirds the price of Perrier), most consumers have difficulty telling one brand from another. With such weak product differentiation, the strength of the brand is everything.

Perrier's brand, the world leader, was—like rival brands—built on purity. In the health-conscious 1980s, the supposed purity of mineral waters—whether sparkling or still—was the main reason the world market for bottled water grew at 30 to 40 percent a year. As Tom Pirko, president of Bevmark, an American drinks consultancy, put it at the time Perrier's troubles began: "The last possible thing that Perrier can afford to have happen is for the public to think there is benzene in their spring, whether it gets filtered out or not." Particularly in America, where the company's advertising slogan was, "It's perfect. It's Perrier."

Oh No, No Eau

From the outset, Perrier's was an odd sort of corporate crisis. Although it was only the second

global withdrawal of a brand (the first was Johnson & Johnson's withdrawal of its Tylenol painkiller in 1986 when, for the second time, some capsules were deliberately laced with cyanide), it was the first not to be caused by malicious tampering. But as Stephen Greyser, a professor at Harvard Business School, points out, when a product problem is of a firm's own making—as Perrier's was—consumers can be less forgiving. Second, unlike the Tylenol incidents in 1982 and 1986, which resulted in a total of eight deaths, Perrier's problem posed no real health risk.

To a Perrier drinker who did not read newspapers, watch television, or listen to the radio, Perrier's response to the crisis would have seemed perfect: it withdrew the product swiftly, cleared up the problem, and reintroduced the product within weeks. But because Source Perrier in France fumbled its initial explanations so badly, the company got rotten press worldwide. Could it have done better?

Source Perrier need not have looked far for an exemplar. Wenche Marshall Foster, Norwegian-born chairman of Perrier's British subsidiary, had realized years earlier that Perrier would stand or fall by its brand's purity and quality; she had also been horrified by the Tylenol scare. So in 1985, she put together a four-strong crisis-management team: Daphne Barrett, head of Infoplan, a public-relations agency; Peter Thomas, Perrier (UK) marketing director; Richard Wheatly, chairman of Leo Burnett, Perrier's British advertising agency; and herself. In the event of a crisis, only these four were to talk to Perrier's "constituents" (employees, customers, shareholders, regulators, and suppliers), the media, and other affected parties.

While Source Perrier in Paris got its relations with the outside world dreadfully wrong in the first few days of the nightmare, Perrier (UK) stuck doggedly to its crisis-management plan. The team was to be found in Perrier's London offices for days after the saga began, talking to everyone affected by the problem. No press conference was held: Marshall Foster talked to journalists individually. Until the team was sure of the cause of the contamination, it candidly confessed that it did not know what had happened—rule two in the crisis-management handbook. Journalists covering the story say they were impressed with the firm's candor.

Perrier (UK) also twigged at an early stage that the presence of a carcinogen in its water, no matter how small its quantity, would frighten customers. To reassure Perrier drinkers, the company took out full-page advertisements in the British press, stating that there was "no hazard to health." But there was no international coordination: in no other markets did Perrier run explanatory advertisements. Nor did it, in any market, apologize to its customers. Only when Perrier started running global relaunch ads, in March 1990, did a halfhearted hint of contrition creep in: American relaunch ads conceded that "for a product known for purity, [the problem] was definitely a mistake."

It was a mistake that would run and run. Once a product crisis has broken, the company concerned tends to be put under the microscope—as Perrier soon discovered. After the initial shock of discovering benzene in its water, Perrier was beset by aftershocks. In Britain, finding herself with 40 million unwanted bottles of mineral water to dispose of, Marshall Foster spent days arranging for the glass to be recycled. Eventually she triumphantly announced that half of the bottles would be recycled—only to be pilloried by Friends of the Earth for not recycling the other half. After a further struggle she arranged for all 40 million bottles (along with caps and other packaging) to be recycled, a tall order in Britain, where there is little call for green glass. The water was—after local authorities were reassured about its safety—simply poured away.

Nor was Perrier's staggered relaunch, starting in early March 1990, without incident. In mid-April, a week before Perrier was due back on sale in America, the FDA ruled that the claim on the mineral water's label that it was "naturally sparkling" was false, on the grounds that the gas and the water were taken out of the ground separately; the carbonation, said the FDA, was thus artificial. The FDA also objected to the label's claim that Perrier was "calorie free"—water, after all, usually is. Perrier gave in on both counts. Then, on the eve of Perrier's American relaunch, New York's Center for Environmental Health objected to the term "sodium free" on Perrier's label, on the grounds that some bottles, when tested, had marginally exceeded FDA limits.

Perrier's $25 million American relaunch ad campaign (four times the amount the firm spent on advertising in America in the whole of 1989) also came in for criticism. Its radio ads, featuring "Jill Purity," a fictional reporter for the "Perrier News Network," were castigated for making light of the benzene incident. Terry Hill, a director of Burson-Marsteller, the PR agency that helped develop the campaign, predictably took a differ-

ent view when interviewed at the time: "This is just not serious. It's nothing that's going to cause widows." But Perrier might have done better to take the advice of *Adweek* magazine and go for a more direct relaunch campaign. *Adweek's* suggestion—"Perrier. The benzene's gone."—was at least to the point.

The Sleau Road Back

In a booming market that it had largely created, Perrier's share was being squeezed by old rivals and newcomers alike well before the benzene crisis broke. Because the market was growing so rapidly, however, Source Perrier's sales were still rising steadily, reaching FFr16.7 billion in 1989. Last year's 18 percent fall in turnover was accompanied by a 21 percent decline in the group's operating profits, to FFr1.1 billion. Source Perrier's share price was also battered by the crisis, falling by one-third by the end of 1990. The mishandling of the early days of the incident cost the aging Leven, Source Perrier's chairman and founder, his job. In June 1990, he was replaced by Jacques Vincent, the company's vice chairman.

But the lasting legacy of the benzene affair shows up most clearly in Perrier's withered market shares. Deprived of Perrier for at least six weeks, water drinkers started to discover other brands—and found they were little different. In America, Perrier's biggest overseas market, a 13 percent pre-crisis share of the take-home market for sparkling waters has been cut to 9 percent. In Britain Perrier's take-home market share has tumbled from 49 percent to under 30 percent. Only in France has Perrier held on to its pre-crisis market share of around 38 percent. Last year that dipped slightly, to 34 percent.

Perrier reckons it has learned several (costly) lessons from the affair. Foremost is a need for coordination the instant a crisis breaks. Perrier's biggest mistake in the days immediately after the benzene story hit the headlines was the inconsistency in—and lack of credibility of—the stories it was telling the media. Perrier admits to being staggered by the speed with which the affair spiraled out of the company's control—many of its trade customers found out about the benzene scare from the press. That allowed rumors to spread about the cause of the contamination.

Perrier had prided itself on being a highly decentralized company, with each of its subsidiaries operating autonomously. That is still true, but it has now put an international marketing strategy in place and says it is "working on" an international crisis-management strategy—although Perrier (UK) is hanging on to its own crisis-management team for now.

Perrier says it is pleased with the way its brand has withstood the crisis: without this underlying strength—what Marshall Foster describes as "public warmth" towards the Perrier brand—the company would have been sunk. That Perrier, like "Hoover" and "Walkman," had become something like a generic brand (consumers often ask for a Perrier when what they really want is any sparkling water) helped it weather the storm. But the crisis may have damaged Perrier's long-term ability to remain the Hoover of mineral water.

If what Perrier should have done in the first days of the crisis now seems so clear, why was it so hard to do at the time? Writing in *Prism*, a journal published by Arthur D. Little, a management-consulting firm, Ashok Kalelkar and John Magee point out one key reason: managers tend to be wrong-footed by corporate crises because they are used to shaping events, not to having events grasp control and shape them. Once it had regained control of the affair—a week-long struggle—Perrier did most things right. But it would all have been a lot easier had each part of the company been pouring from the same bottle at the outset.

Source: Adapted from "When the Bubble Burst," *The Economist*, August 3, 1991, pp. 67–68.

CASE 2

Three Foreign Companies Move into Germany—Differently

You are the head of a company that wants to expand abroad, and your eyes have lit eagerly on Western Europe's biggest market.

With a population of 79 million, Germany seems an obvious magnet for your operation and an ideal route for deeper export penetration. Its hardworking, prosperous people demand the best in what they buy and are prepared to pay for it.

But wait a moment. Isn't the German language one of Western Europe's most difficult? And what about the infuriating German thoroughness and addiction to rules and bureaucracy? Then there are the country's tightly hedged labor laws—making it hard to fire people whose work is not up to scratch—and its high wages.

Are you ready to cope with all this?

When you have weighed these aspects, you can consider whether your product or service will really appeal to fussy German consumers, how

you can find this out, and how you should get your message across. Clearly, you will need to think long and hard about setting up in Germany.

Once the decision has been made, however, the results can be well worth the effort. For as well as being the world's biggest exporter, the Federal Republic is also a sizable importer. Its flourishing export surpluses have added hugely to purchasing power, though Germans are also champion savers.

When talking to companies that have recently established themselves in Germany and to those who advise them, several things become apparent. Although it may not seem easy at first glance, forming a subsidiary need not be that difficult. Follow the rules—there are plenty of them—use all the expert help you can get, and the way becomes smoother.

"Compared with other countries, it's not that difficult to establish subsidiaries here," says Patrick Manon, commercial attaché at the French consulate in Frankfurt. "It's easier than in France. It's a matter of will." This is important, as psychological brick walls can easily appear in Germany.

Setting up and surviving in Germany can be a bit of a shock, particularly for the unprepared small firm, according to Roger Thomas, U.K. commercial consul in the city. Such preparation can be made much easier by seeking help from consulates, local development bodies, or specialist advisers.

He warns: "The rules, regulations, and procedures for buying a car, getting a resident's permit, setting up a business, or even opening a bank account and obtaining credit are all quite normal to German citizens who have grown up with the system, but they can be quite horrific for the easygoing Brit who is used to doing all that in an afternoon back home."

Although Germans are mostly helpful and friendly as well as diligent, they are not, as a rule, easygoing.

For this case, the experiences of three very different companies have been looked at: Psion, a small but fast-growing U.K. maker of hand-held personal computers; Toys "R" Us, a big U.S. toy retailer that is expanding worldwide; and Cisi, a French software concern specializing in defense, electronics, and aerospace applications.

Looking back, all admit that getting started in Germany took some effort but was ultimately worthwhile. There is no substitute for actually being in the market. "The name of the game is to think German, act German, and above all, be in Germany," asserts Thomas.

The market can be both tough and rewarding. It can be a mistake for companies to think they can simply transfer their product and marketing from their home market to Germany.

"The German market is completely different," believes Rolf Kannenberg, Psion's general manager in Germany. "It is even different from Austria and Switzerland. It is certainly different from France and Belgium and much more different from operating in the English-speaking area."

Germans tend to be perfectionists. "There's no doubt," says David Elder, Psion's export manager in London, "that Germans require everything working and perfect from day one. In the U.K. and France, you can get away with 90 percent."

Thus, out of a total staff of 10 in Germany, it has 3 technical people rather than the 2 it might need elsewhere. One works on a full-time hotline service to ensure a rapid follow-up to problems.

"You have to invest in technical support," says Elder. "You have to carry that overhead earlier than you would otherwise have done." Also, no matter how good the product—and Psion's business is growing in Germany, with a planned annual turnover of up to DM5 million—people will not buy it if the marketing is not right.

So Kannenberg has made a determined assault on large, specialized dealers and distributors, aiming to line up around 30 across the country. These, in turn, serve local outlets.

Previously, its business was handled by a Hanover-based dealer, whose reach was too small for Psion's ambitions in Germany. The specialized trade dealers are the most important sales route for Psion, says Kannenberg, followed by individual firms or retailing groups like Computerland, and then by store chains like Kaufhof and Karstadt and mail-order concerns. A portable Psion computer costs nearly DM500 in Germany, excluding add-on equipment.

Potential buyers with specific professional needs want to be convinced of the product's value and will feel best served by a specialized dealer who can explain and demonstrate its advantage fully.

"People are more critical here," notes Kannenberg. "They're more demanding on quality and the price-performance relationship."

The challenges Psion faces now in Germany are those of a company on the move. Getting started was another matter. Like many other foreign—mainly British and U.S.—companies, it used the services of Lairco, which specializes in helping foreign businesses start up in Germany. Lairco provides space, telephones, secretaries, and friendly advice at a cost much lower than the expenses of setting up a new office alone.

This is where Psion began, with Sheila Hartley, now office manager, as its first employee. "Without Lairco, Psion in England would have had to invest a lot more money. They couldn't have just started with me." Lairco, run by an American husband-and-wife team, Alexander and Bernadine Lairo, charges around DM45,000 ($24,300) a year, including 500 hours of secretarial use, for one of its offices—compared to an estimated DM150,000 for a company starting with no local support.

"They helped with translators and things like letterheads; they even found us a butcher to supply a party when we left them," says Hartley. Today, Psion operates from smart new offices in Bad Homburg. This enables it to skirt another potential snag—high city rents. Being just outside Frankfurt, its rents are only DM19 a square meter, compared with DM45 in central Frankfurt.

Once out of the Lairco fold, she found the biggest hurdle was the bureaucracy. "I saw it as a challenge. I took it in my stride. All the requirements have got to be adhered to, and it is important to do them correctly. It became a matter of egoism."

Actually establishing the subsidiary—the most common form is the GmbH (Gesellschaft mit beschrankter Haftung), a limited company—is the least of the obstacles. That requires a minimum capital of DM50,000 ($27,000) and can be done, with the necessary lawyers' signatures and official registration, in under two months.

More frustrating are practical matters like telephones, accommodation, furniture, cars, and, not least, staff.

Here Hartley has a few words of warning. Furniture can take up to 10 weeks to arrive, because suppliers work to orders. "So at first, it was a bit sparse here." For cars, too, the German practice can be frustrating. The leasing company insisted on bank guarantees for Psion's first three cars.

Taking on staff may also be a headache. A top bilingual secretary can cost DM5,000 a month. "Just hiring a secretary can be such an important first step," says Alexander Lairo. "Some look for foreign companies because they know how to take advantage of them."

Under strict labor laws, inefficient staff cannot easily be fired. On the other hand, many Germans are skeptical about working for foreign, especially small, companies—wondering how long they will last.

"We employ people at the start of each quarter," says Hartley. This is normal German practice. "In England, people tend to come and go." In Germany, most employees want security and are thinking of their pension rights at a young age. "We wanted to employ one woman as a secretary, and her husband wanted to know all about our parent and its activities." In the end, she decided the job was too risky.

To guard against disappointments on both sides, a probationary period of three months is usual for most staff, with six for managers. Also, employees expect to be paid a 13th month, though this does not necessarily mean the total sum is any different from what they would receive on a 12-month basis.

Germans are also used to better working conditions that those existing in many other countries. Comments John Brennan, head of Access Business Services, a similar operation to Lairco: "Germans expect bigger offices than maybe their chairman would occupy in the United States."

That may be the least of the differences, however. At the German headquarters of Toys "R" Us in Cologne, Joseph Baczko, president of its international division, explains how a raft of objections was thrown up by outsiders when the group considered coming to Germany: "We were told the Germans like wooden toys and are keen on technical things. Well, we sell a lot of plastic, we are self-service, and we sell both technical and nontechnical items."

Some local manufacturers also thought Toys "R" Us would be better advised to go for 5,000 square feet instead of its usual 45,000-square-foot stores. It ignored this. "We were told we wouldn't get the permission," adds Baczko, "Our management has to come face to face with the conventional wisdom every day and challenge it." The U.S. concern has done so to the extent that it now has 12 stores in Germany. Its goal is 50.

Because busy young German mothers are used to hypermarkets and supermarkets, says Baczko, they have taken to the all-embracing Toys "R" Us concept, where a host of products is offered all year round and not just at Christmas.

Even the limited shopping hours in Germany are not seen as a hindrance, though Baczko does not regard them as immutable. "We didn't come to Germany just to get market share. We aim to be number one, and we will be. In that way, restrictive trading practices work in our favor. We are the point of convenience for the customer."

To obtain the edge-of-town sites it requires, Toys "R" Us is prepared to argue with local authorities for as long as it takes. "There's not one site yet that we've abandoned." Where sites are not zoned for retailing, the company has to do a lot of badgering, especially where local competitors have strong influence. "We have to fight; we continue to do that every day."

Within the company, Toys "R" Us strives for harmony and informality. All staff have stock options, which is unusual in Germany—"a bit of sweet equity underscores the entrepreneurial drive," says Baczko.

Staff are also encouraged to call each other by first names, definitely a rarity in German operations where titles and surnames are used. "To us, the culture is very important. If they're all going to be entrepreneurs, you can't have that type of hierarchy."

With typical American energy, Toys "R" Us has managed to both work with the German system and implant its own concept onto the retail landscape. "There's been nothing put forward as an obstacle or as a reason for not being here that has not proved to be false," insists Baczko.

Its managers clearly have to be untypical, gung-ho types. Speaking as distant revelers rolled through Cologne's streets, he concluded: "If you're not ready to be here on carnival day in Cologne, you probably don't belong here."

Few newcomers have the resources or the fiercely can-do approach of Toys "R" Us. But all face basically the same problems in Germany. Dieter Glotzel, general manager of Cisi Engineering, part of Cisi Software of France, agrees with Psion that distribution is a major hurdle, especially for specialized products and services. So is finding the right staff, blending both technical and sales expertise. He reckons French engineers are much better educated in information technology than Germans are.

Overcoming many Germans' aversion to risk taking is also not easy. "A lot of people strive for security and would never join a small firm. Others have the pioneer spirit, and those are the ones we want." Cisi is still small in Germany, with turnover of around DM1 million. But like Toys "R" Us at the other end of the scale, it is breaking new ground in a market that can pay handsome dividends if well nurtured.

Source: Adapted from *The Financial Times*, March 15, 1989, p. 19.

CASE 3

New Government Demands Quick Profit

The postal services of Durbania were not as efficient as they should have been—mail was delayed and sometimes lost—and it was running seven-digit losses, which were increasing. In desperation, the minister for postal services turned to the private sector for a management and organization expert and hired Jason McNab, one of the best. McNab took over as chairman of postal services.

He found the following state of affairs. The equipment was old, out of date, and subject to frequent malfunction. As with all postal services, this one is required to pick up and deliver mail throughout the whole country, including the sparsely populated mountains and rural areas. It cannot shut down those loss-causing services and concentrate on the profitable business and urban customers.

Competition was growing from such profitable, private communications methods as electronic mail, facsimile transmission, and UPS-type services. Durbania's postal service offered none of those services.

After two years in the job, McNab had ended the long history of increasing postal service losses, and they were stable along with the government subsidy necessary to keep services going. He was well along with a multimillion-dollar investment program that was on track to make postal services break even within five years.

At this time, Durbania held elections, and the Reform party won in a landslide over the Labor party, which had governed for eight years. McNab expected a period of uncertainty followed by a cost-saving exercise that would pay lip service to promises to lower inflation and speed up privatization of public services.

To his surprise, the Reformers acted quickly, as the central bank raised discount rates 2 percent as an inflation-fighting measure. That would make the financing for his modernization of the postal service equipment more expensive.

Then, barely a week after the new postal minister's appointment, McNab was summoned to her office. She got straight to the point by announcing to a stunned McNab that his government subsidy would be withdrawn at the end of the next fiscal year, which was only 20 months in the future. "We've got to reduce public spending next year, and I don't think we can afford you. We

should see a return on assets—perhaps 2 percent—in three years," she told McNab. Her goal was to privatize the postal service before the end of Reform's four-year term.

McNab explained his schedule, which projected an end of losses and at least a break-even in five years. He pointed out that higher interest rates were already hampering his modernization efforts and how difficult it would be to cut costs sufficiently to offset loss of the subsidy.

"That's your problem," said the minister. "If you don't think you can meet the new government's goals, then I'm sure we'll be able to find someone who can."

Poor McNab rushed back to his office and called a must meeting of the top postal service managers for that night. He had no time to spare. They worked through the night and until noon the next day; when the meeting ended, they were tired but enthusiastic. They had decided on the only strategy bold enough to have any reasonable chance of success.

They decided they must increase revenue and cut unit costs, which are the only ones that reasonably can be cut back given the large fixed-cost base of the postal system. They must maintain output if revenue is to rise.

The revenue increases required to have any chance of profitability in three years must come from the high-income parts of the market. These are premium services for which customers are willing to pay for quality service. The postal service must move into competition with private companies and offer electronic mail, facsimile, and UPS-types of services.

Its fixed assets, which it must maintain to remain a postal service for all the people, will give it excellent bases from which to offer the premium services. They decided they could not afford to cut the investment program. Not only will it increase quality of services, it will also result in a more salable asset at privatization time.

Source: Adapted from "Dilemma & Decision," *International Management*, December 1988, p. 22.

Endnotes

Chapter 1

1. 1—Philips (Dutch), 2—Unilever (Dutch-English), 3—Electrolux (Swedish), 4—Unilever (Dutch-English), 5—Grand Metropolitan (English), 6—Polly Peak International (English), 7—Michelin (French), 8—Bass PLC (English), 9—Bass PLC (English), 10—American, 11—American, 12—American, 13—Continental (German), 14—Cadbury Schweppe (English), 15—Accor (French), 16—Grand Metropolitan (English).

2. A. Coskin Samli, Richard Still, and John S. Hill, *International Marketing* (New York: Macmillan, 1993), p. 210; and Thomas Hout, Michael E. Porter, and Eileen Rudden, "How Global Companies Win Out," *Harvard Business Review,* September–October, 1982, pp. 98–110.

3. Sumantra Ghoshal and Nitin Nohria, "Horses for Courses," *Sloan Management Review,"* Winter 1993, p. 26.

4. "The Growth of Global Industry," *The Wheel Extended,* no. 4, 1989, p. 11.

5. Mira Wilkins, *The Maturing of the Multinational Enterprise, 1914–1970* (Cambridge, MA: Harvard University Press, 1974), pp. 1–83.

6. "American Business Abroad," *Financial World,* June 25, 1991, p. 45.

7. Christopher Tungendhat, *The Multinationals* (New York: Random House, 1972), p. 12.

8. "Kodak Is Close to Announcing Buyer of L&F," *The Wall Street Journal,* August 8, 1994, p. A3.

9. George S. Yip, "Global Strategy in a World of Nations," *Sloan Management Review,* Fall 1991, pp. 29–39.

10. Division on Transnational Corporations and Investment, *World Investment Report 1994* (New York: United Nations, 1994), p. 419.

11. Ibid., p. 419.

12. Ibid., pp. 1–18.

13. *Japan 1995,* (Tokyo: Keizai Koho Center, 1995), pp. 43–45.

14. *The World Bank Atlas 1994* (Washington, DC: World Bank, 1994), pp. 18–19; and "The World's Largest Corporations," *Fortune,* July 25, 1994, pp. 143–52.

15. Michael Minor, *Changes in Developing Country Regimes for Foreign Investment* (Greenville: University of South Carolina, 1990), p. 15.

16. "The World's Largest Industrial Corporations," *Fortune,* July 25, 1994, pp. 138–54; and "The Largest Industrial Companies in the World," *Fortune,* August 10, 1981, pp. 205–18.

17. "Multinational Reshuffle," *Europe,* May–June 1982, pp. 12–15; and "A Guide to the Global 500," *Fortune,* July 25, 1994, pp. 142–52.

18. "Global 500," *Fortune,* July 25, 1994, p. 184–95.

19. "Mini-Nationals Are Making Maximum Impact," *Business Week,* September 6, 1993, p. 66.

Appendix A

1. "Breaking through the Job Market Catch-22," *The European,* March 25–31, 1994, p. 21.

2. Donald A. Ball and Wendell McCulloch, Jr., "International Business Education Programs in American and Non-American Schools: How They are Ranked by the Academy of International Business," *Journal of International Business Studies,* Summer 1988, pp. 295–99.

3. "Getting a Global M.B.A.," *U.S. News & World Report,* November 11, 1991, p. 87.

Chapter 2

1. Programme on Transnational Corporations, *World Investment Report 1993* (New York: United Nations, 1993), pp. 20 and 25.

2. The Programme on Transnational Corporations uses the stock of foreign direct investment as a measure of the productive capacity of international corporations in foreign countries, Washington, DC: International Monetary Fund, p. 13.

3. International Monetary Fund, *Balance of Payments Yearbook* 1993, p. 36.

4. Yukio, Ohnuma, "Trading Their Way to the Top," *Japan Update,* October 1992, pp. 20–21; and "Sogo-Shosha Begin Global Metamorphosis," *Japan Update,* December 1992, pp. 22–23.

5. *Monthly Bulletin of Statistics* (New York: United Nations, June 1994), p. 259.

6. "The International Investment Position in the United States in 1993," *Survey of Current Business,* June 1994, p. 69.

7. Ibid., p. 70.

8. Ibid., p. 69.

9. "U.S. Business Enterprises Acquired or Established by Foreign Direct Investment in 1993," *Survey of Current Business,"* May 1994, p. 50.

10. Ibid., p. 50.

11. "Technical Notes," *World Development Report 1994* (Washington, DC: World Bank, 1994), p. 231.

12. Ibid., p. 232.

13. Ibid., p. 163.

14. "Hunting Heads in the Global Village," *International Management,* May 1990, pp. 52–54.

15. "The Pitfalls of Global Restructuring," *Dun's Business Month,* June 1988, p. 41.

16. Warner-Lambert, *Annual Report 1990*, p. 25.

17. Bristol-Myers Squibb, *Annual Report 1993*, p. 3.

18. "International Performance Outshines Domestic Results," *Business International*, September 29, 1986, p. 305.

19. "The 100 Largest U.S. Multinationals," *Forbes*, July 18, 1994, p. 276.

20. "U.S. Concerns Seek Inspiration for Products from Overseas," *The Wall Street Journal*, September 29, 1988, p. 15.

21. "A Hard Row for Auto Parts Makers," *Fortune*, March 7, 1983, p. 110.

22. "Honda, Is It an American Car?" *Business Week*, November 1991, pp. 105–12.

23. "Toyota's Camry: Made in the USA—Sort of," *Business Week*, November 22, 1993, p. 6.

24. "Mitsubishi Bank to Open Office," *Columbus Dispatch*, March 20, 1987, p. 12.

25. "Kodak Will Open Its First Plant in Japan," *Modesto Bee*, October 18, 1985, p. B5.

26. Zenith to Shift TV Assembly Work out of U.S. Plant," *The Wall Street Journal*, October 31, 1991, p. A13.

27. "Maquila Scoreboard," Twin Plant News, September 1994, p. 41.

28. "Maquilas Face Uncertainty Under NAFTA," *McAllen Monitor*, August 17, 1994, p. 1C.

29. "New Trends in the Maquilas," *Twin Plant News*, August 1994, p. 28.

30. "Who Made Your Underwear?" *Forbes*, July 25, 1988, pp. 56–58.

31. *Guidebook to the Andean Trade Preference Act* (Washington, DC: Department of Commerce, July 1992), pp. 1–6.

32. "Growth Triangle Cooperatives Make Progress," *Indonesia Development News Quarterly*, Autumn 1993/Winter 1994, p. 13; and Asian Development Bank, *ADB Quarterly Review*, January 1994, p. 13.

33. *Handy Facts on U.S.–Japan Economic Relations* (Tokyo: JETRO, 1993), p. 3.

34. "As Recession Bites, Many Multinationals Get Lift from Abroad," *The Wall Street Journal*, July 23, 1980, p. 1.

35. "Taking the Sting out of the Plunging Dollar," *Business Week*, December 7, 1987, pp. 72–73.

36. "U.S. Companies See 1992 as Opportunity," *San Jose Mercury News*, March 26, 1989, p. 1.

37. "The Selling of America," *Fortune*, May 23, 1988, p. 61.

38. "Japanese Firms Hunt Big Foreign Game," *The Wall Street Journal*, November 10, 1988, p. A20.

39. "Ford and VW Split Up Venture in Latin America," *The Wall Street Journal*, December 2, 1994, p. A8.

40. "Europe Cooks Up a Cereal Brawl," *Fortune*, June 3, 1991, pp. 175–79.

41. "Merck Has an Ache in Japan," March 18, 1985, pp. 42–48.

42. "Van Heusen-Polgat JV First to Take Advantage of U.S.–Israel FTA," *Business International*, August 18, 1986, p. 262.

43. One of the writers, who was employed by the Mexican affiliate of an American company, which held 33 percent equity in the affiliate, was asked by the Mexican secretary of commerce why the Mexican plant was not exporting to Guatemala. The reason, which he could not disclose, was that the company served the Guatemalan market from wholly owned plants in the United States and thus kept all the profits. A hurried call to Akron gave him permission to do some exporting to Guatemala to appease the Mexican government, but he was asked "not to try too hard."

44. Telephone conversation with Pfizer executive, April 6, 1989.

45. "The Great Patent Plague," *Forbes ASAP*, September 1993, pp. 59–66.

46. "U.S. International Transactions," *Survey of Current Business*, June 1994, p. 94.

47. "Two Makers of Microchips Broaden Ties," *The Wall Street Journal*, November 21, 1991, p. B4.

48. "Toshiba-Westinghouse JV Tunes into U.S. Tube Market," *Business International*, February 17, 1986, pp. 49–51.

49. "Stake in TV-Tube Venture Sold to Japan's Toshiba," *The Wall Street Journal*, November 1, 1988, p. A27.

50. "Making Global Alliances Work," *Fortune*, December 17, 1990, pp. 121–26.

51. "Is U.S. Business Giving Away Its Technology—Again?" *Fortune*, September 11, 1989, p. 10.

Chapter 3

1. "The Rhythm of the Future," *The Economist*, December 14, 1991, p. 19.

2. Government administrators involved in project evaluation are increasingly applying socioeconomic rather than purely financial criteria. For example, social rates of discount and opportunity costs are considered rather than the pure costs of borrowing money. Although marketing managers do not have to be development economists any more than they need to be specialists in marketing research, they should have a knowledge of the basic concepts.

3. "Fortress of Mercantilism," *Insight*, July 18, 1988, pp. 15–17.

4. David Ricardo, "The Principles of Political Economy and Taxation," in *International Trade Theory: Hume to Ohlin*, ed. William R. Allen (New York: Random House, 1965), pp. 62–67.

5. The idea that only hours of labor determine production costs is known as the *labor theory of value*. In fairness to Ricardo, we must admit that he included the cost of capital as "embodied labor" in his labor costs. Actually, as shown in the section "Introducing Money," the theory of comparative advantage can be explained by the cost of all factors of production.

6. Eli F. Heckscher, "The Effect of Foreign Trade on the Distribution of Income," *Economisk Tidskrift*, XXI, 1919, pp. 497–512; and Bertil Ohlin, *Interregional and International Trade* (Cambridge, MA: Harvard University Press, 1933).

7. The economist, Bela Belassa, in his *Stages Approach to Comparative Advantage*, published by the World Bank in 1977, found in a study of 26 developed and developing nations that "the intercountry differences in the structure of exports are in a large part explained by differences in physical and human capital endowments."

8. J. Sachs and H. Shatz, "Trade and Jobs in U.S. Manufacturing," cited in *The Economist*, October 1, 1994, p. 19.

9. "While Toyota Loses Its Hold," *Business Week*, April 26, 1993, p. 28.

10. Louis Wells, "A Product Life Cycle for International Trade," *Journal of Marketing*, July 1968, pp. 1–6.

11. Many new products come not from the manufacturer's laboratories but from its suppliers of machinery and raw materials.

12. Belassa, *Stages Approach to Comparative Advantage,"* pp. 26–27.

13. Richard B. Chase and Nicholas J. Aquilano, *Production and Operations Management*, 6th ed. (Burr Ridge, IL: Richard D. Irwin, 1995), pp. 320–23.

14. Dennis R. Appleyard and Alfred J. Field, *International Economics* (Homewood, IL: Richard D. Irwin, 1992), pp. 226–29.

15. John H. Dunning, *The Globalization of Business* (London: Routledge, 1993), p. 106.

16. "Footwear Industry Tells Congress 'Shoe Gap' Threatens U.S. Defense," *The Wall Street Journal*, August 24, 1984, p. 21.

17. "Mexican Labor's Hidden Costs," *Fortune*, October 17, 1994, p. 32.

18. "Brie and Hormones," *The Economist*, January 7, 1989, pp. 21–22.

19. *Report on United States Barriers to Trade and Investment* (Brussels: Services of the European Commission, April 1994), p. 79.

20. "E.C. Imposes Antidumping Duties on Japanese Printers," *Europe*, October 1988, p. 42.

21. "The Jumbo War," *The Economist*, June 15, 1991, p. 65.

22. "The New Rules of Trade," *National Review*, April 18, 1994, pp. 40–44.

23. "The Jumbo War," *The Economist*, June 15, 1991, pp. 65–66.

24. "Draped in Import Quotas," *Seattle Times*, February 27, 1994, p. D1.

25. "Voluntary Export Restraints," *Finance & Development*, December 1987, p. 2.

26. "Honda Studies Output Boost," *Columbus Dispatch*, July 15, 1994, p. 1E; and "Japanese Fear Car Production Shifts to U.S.," *The Columbian*, November 7, 1993, p. F8.

27. "A Hidden Tax on All Our Houses," *US News & World Report*, March 21, 1988, pp. 51–52.

28. "U.S. Share of Japanese Chip Market Hits 21.9%," *McAllen Monitor*, September 15, 1994, p. C1.

29. "Producer Subsidy Equivalents," *Agricultural Policies, Markets, and Trade* (Paris: OECD, 1993), Table II.1.

30. "EC Threatens Trade Sanctions to Counter U.S.," *The Wall Street Journal*, February 3, 1993, p. A17.

31. "The New Face of American Power," *Fortune*, July 26, 1993, p. 72.

32. "Nissan Wins Tariff Appeal," *McAllen Monitor*, September 8, 1994, p. B1.

33. "India Calls Rayon Skirt Recall Order a Protectionist Move by U.S." *Dallas Morning News*, August 16, 1994, p. 10D.

34. "News/Trends," *Fortune*, July 26, 1993, p. 13.

35. "Analysis," *International Business Chronicle,"* June 25–July 8, 1990, p. 14.

36. "The Fanjuls of Palm Beach: The Family with a Sweet Tooth," *Forbes*, May 14, 1990, pp. 56–59.

37. The OECD published *Costs and Benefits of Protection*, which evaluates a wide range of studies on import restrictions of manufactured goods in OECD countries.

38. Yam-yann, Twu, "Taking Stock of the NICs Success," *Economic Eye*, September 1988, pp. 28–32. Professor Twu Jaw-yann writes that the "term *newly industrializing countries* has generally given way to *newly industrialized countries* (or *economies*), which is used almost exclusively to refer to the Asian tigers." See also "The Asian NIEs: Trends in Exchange Rates and Trade Patterns," *Tokyo Financial Review*, August 1988, pp. 1–6. The term NIE is used for the four Asian tigers.

39. "Working in the Shadows," *The Economist*, February 12, 1994, p. 75.

40. "Everybody's Doing It," *International Management*, July–August 1987, p. 27.

41. "Mexico's Underground Economy," *The Wall Street Journal*, October 9, 1991, p. A10.

42. "Technical Notes," *World Development Report 1994*, (New York: Oxford University Press, 1994), p. 231.

43. Ibid.

44. Charles Kindleberger and Bruce Herrick, *Economic Development* (New York: McGraw-Hill, 1977), p. 1.

45. *Human Development Report 1990* (New York: UNDP, 1990), p. 110–11.

46. "New UN Index Measures Wealth as Quality of Life," *The New York Times*, May 23, 1993, p. A6.

47. Charles Kindleberger, *American Business Abroad* (New York: Yale University Press, 1969), pp. 43–44.

48. Stephen Hymer, *The International Operations of International Firms: A Study in Direct Investment* (Cambridge, MA: MIT Press, 1976).

49. Ricard Caves, "International Corporations: The Industrial Economics of Foreign Investment," *Economica*, February 1971, pp. 5–6.

50. F. T. Knickerbocker, *Oligopolistic Reaction and Multinational Enterprise* (Boston: Harvard Business School, 1973).

51. E. M. Graham, "Transatlantic Investments by Multinational Firms: A Rivalistic Phenomenon," *Journal of Post-Keynesian Economics*, Fall 1978, pp. 82–99.

52. Buckley and M. Casson, *The Future of Multinational Enterprise* (New York: Macmillan, 1976).

53. R. Z. Aliber, "A Theory of Direct Investment," *The International Corporation* (Cambridge, MA: MIT Press, 1970), pp. 17–34.

54. A. Rugman, *International Diversification and the Multinational Enterprise* (Lexington, MA: Lexington Books, 1979).

55. John H. Dunning, *International Production and the Multinational Enterprise* (London: George Allen & Unwin, 1981), pp. 109–10.

Chapter 4

1. "United Nations Sea of Blue," *The Economist*, April 30, 1994, p. 52.

2. "Shamed Are the Peacekeepers," *The Economist*, April 30, 1994, pp. 15–16.

3. Brian Crozier, "Closing Time for the UN?" *National Review*, May 13, 1991, pp. 44–45.

4. "A Case for Emergency Treatment," *The Economist*, December 2, 1989, pp. 23–26.

5. Crozier, "Closing Time?" p. 45.

6. Alec Cairncross, *The International Bank for Reconstruction and Development*, Princeton University Essays in International Finance, no. 33 (March 1949), p. 27.

7. Maurice Wolf and Eiting Arnold, *Doing Business with the International Development Organizations in Washington* (Washington, DC: Tax Management, Inc., Bureau of National Affairs, 1982), pp. 20–88.

8. Article I of the Articles of Agreement of the International Finance Corporation (Washington, DC), June 20, 1956), p. 3.

9. IFC General Policies (Washington, DC: IFC, 1970).

10. "The Young Stock Markets," *The Economist*, June 1, 1991, p. 77.

11. Nancy Dunne, "NIB Chief Lindback to Lead World Bank Arm," *Financial Times*, June 28, 1993, p. 4.

12. Antonia Sharpe, "IFC Emerges from the World Bank's Shadows," *Financial Times*, September 13, 1993, p. 23.

13. Simon Holberton, "Soros Joins $1 Billion Fund Investing in Asia, *Financial Times*, February 8, 1994, p. 25.

14. "Hey, Big Lender," *The Economist*, April 23, 1994, pp. 81–82.

15. Michael Prowse, "IDA to Sharpen Focus on Poverty," *Financial Times*, January 14, 1993, p. 5.

16. Melanie Tammen, "Privatize the World Bank," *The Wall Street Journal*, May 17, 1991, p. A14.

17. Ibid.

18. *United Nations Monetary and Finance Conference, Bretton Woods, New Hampshire, July 1 to 22, 1944*, Department of State Publication 287, Conference Series 55 (Washington, DC: Department of State, 1944).

19. A. Acheson et al., *Bretton Woods Revisited* (Toronto: University of Toronto Press, 1972).

20. Oscar L. Altman, "Quotas in the International Monetary Fund," *International Monetary Fund Staff Papers 5*, no. 2 (1956).

21. Leland M. Goodrich and Edward Hambro, *Charter of the United Nations: Commentary and Documents*, rev. ed. (Boston: World Peace Foundation, 1949), p. 349.

22. For a discussion of how surveillance is working, see G. G. Johnson, "Enhancing the Effectiveness of Surveillance," *Finance & Development*, December 1985, pp. 2–5.

23. Art Pine, "IMF Becomes Leader," *The Wall Street Journal*, January 11, 1983, p. 56.

24. Robert Preston and Jimmy Burns, "EBRD Spends More on Itself than It Lends Out in Loans," *Financial Times*, April 13, 1993, p. 1.

25. Anthony Robinson, "Quiet Revolution Pays Dividends for EBRD," *Financial Times*, April 19, 1994, p. 2.

26. "The EBRD: Economy Class," *The Economist*, April 23, 1994, p. 81.

27. Leslie Crawford, "Chaotic Bank Threatens Africa Soft Loans," *Financial Times*, May 9, 1994, pp. 1 and 16; "Mounting Arrears Weigh on African Bank," *Financial Times*, May 10, 1994, p. 4; and "African Bank Meeting Runs into the Sands," *Financial Times*, May 13, 1994, p. 4.

28. Richard Gourlay, "A Time for Critical Self-Study at the ADB," *Financial Times*, February 22, 1988, p. 3; and Cheah Cheng Hye, "ADB Goes Begging for Borrowers," *The Asian Wall Street Journal*, February 10, 1986, p. 5.

29. Cynthia Owens, "ADB Still Drawing Flack on Private-Sector Finance," *The Asian Wall Street Journal*, May 7, 1990, p. 24.

30. "Development Bank Develops Markets," *Euromoney Supplement*, September 1992, p. 27.

31. "More Money in the Bank," *The Economist*, March 26, 1994, p. 40; and Alexander Nicoli, "ADB Tightens Lending Policies," *Financial Times*, April 20, 1994, p. 4.

32. "Bank Ends Pivotal Four-Year Period," *The IDB*, March 1994, p. 8.

33. Klaus Engelen, "New Money, New Initiatives and New Partnerships," *The European*, April 22–28, 1994, p. 19.

34. "Latin America: More for More," *The Economist*, April 16, 1994, pp. 48 and 50.

35. "The Bank for International Settlements: A Profile of an International Institution," CH 4002 Basel, June 1990, pp. 1–8.

36. Peter Marsh, "New East Meets Old West at Central Bankers' Bank," *Financial Times*, July 9, 1991, p. 2.

37. Richard N. Gardner, *Sterling-Dollar Diplomacy* (New York: Oxford University Press, 1956).

38. Gerard Curzon, *Multilateral Commercial Diplomacy* (New York: Praeger, 1965).

39. Bernard Norwood, "The Kennedy Round: A Try at Linear Trade Negotiations," *Journal of Law and Economics*, October 12, 1966, pp. 297–319; Ernest M. Preeg, *Traders and Diplomats* (Washington, DC: Brookings Institution, 1970); John W. Evans, *The Kennedy Round in American Trade Policy: The Twilight of GATT?* (Cambridge, MA: Harvard University Press, 1971); Sidney Golt, *The GATT Negotiations, 1973–1974: A Guide to the Issues* (London, Washington, and Ottawa: British–North America Committee, 1974); and B. Balassa and M. E. Dreinin, "Trade Liberalization under the Kennedy Round: The Static Effects," *Review of Economics and Statistics*, May 1967, pp. 125–37.

40. "GATT Comes Right," *The Economist*, December 18, 1993, pp. 13–14.

41. Louis S. Richman, "What's Next after GATT's Victory?" *Fortune*, January 10, 1994, pp. 66–71.

42. Joe Cobb, "A Guide to the New GATT Agreement," *Backgrounder*, no. 497, The Heritage Foundation, May 5, 1994.

43. Perez Alfonze, "The Organization of Petroleum Exporting Countries," (Caracas) *Monthly Bulletin*, no. 2 (1966). See also John B. Judis, "Time for an American Industrial Policy," *The Wall Street Journal*, February 14, 1991, p. A13; and Kevin L. Kearns, "Behind Those Shrinking Trade Deficit Numbers," *The Wall Street Journal*, July 25, 1991, p. A15.

44. Wendell H. McCulloch, Jr., notes of interviews and conversations with OPEC employees and others in Geneva.

45. *International Petroleum Encyclopedia*, 1979, pp. 194–95, table 6.

46. Luis Vallenilla, *Oil: The Making of a New Economic Order* (New York: McGraw-Hill, 1975).

47. James Cook, "Comeuppance," *Forbes*, May 9, 1983, pp. 55–56.

48. Bhushan Bahree and James Tanner, "OPEC's Efforts to Regain Control of Oil Pricing Are Being Hampered by Russia's Huge Reserves," *The Wall Street Journal*, April 4, 1994, p. C8.

49. "The Impact of Lower Oil Prices," *IMF World Economic Outlook*, May 1994, pp. 20–21.

50. Victor Smart, "Tycoon Who Is Scourge of Eurocrats," *The European*, April 29–May 5, 1994, p. 9.

51. Wendell H. McCulloch, Jr., "United States of Europe?" *Backgrounder*, no. 706, The Heritage Foundation, May 5, 1989.

52. "Fortress Europe: Poor Men at the Gate," *The Economist*, April 16, 1994, p. 60; and "European Union: A Touch of Eastern Promise," *The Economist*, March 26, 1994, p. 58.

53. "The European Un-union," *The Economist*, March 5, 1994, p. 20.

54. Joel Haveman, "EC Racked by Fields of Fraud, *Los Angeles Times*, August 31, 1993, pp. H1 and 4.

55. Lucy Walker and Rory Watson, "EC Frauds Are Costing $7 Billion," *The European*, October 1–7, 1993, pp. 1 and 2; and Rory Watson, "EC Plugs Fraud Loophole," *The European*, October 22–26, 1993, p. 1.

56. See "A Death in the Family," *The Wall Street Journal*, October 13, 1993, p. A16; and Rebecca Hallerstein, "Is the Single Market Doomed?" *Global Competitor*, Spring 1994, pp. 11–13.

57. McCulloch, "United States," p. 4.; and see Karen Elliott House, "Europtimism Dies," *The Wall Street Journal*, May 9, 1991, p. A14; Lucy Walker, "Rome Blots Its Market Copybook," *The European*, June 2, 1991, p. 4; "Laws unto Themselves," *The Economist*, June 22, 1991, p. 76; and Mark M. Nelson, "EC Summit Indicates Coming Months Will Be Both Divisive and Unpredictable," *The Wall Street Journal*, July 1, 1991, p. A10.

58. David Gardner, "EEA Links 17 nations in World's Largest Free Trade Zone," *Financial Times*, January 1–2, 1994, pp. 1 and 22; and "EEA Up and Running!" *EFTA News*, January–February 1994, pp. 1 and 2.

59. "Third Countries Still High on the EFTA Agenda," *EFTA Bulletin*, May 1993. "Asean Members Agree to Create Free Trade Area," *Indonesia Development News Quarterly*, Spring 1992, pp. 3 and 8.

60. "ASEAN Launches Free Trade Area," *Indonesia Development News Quarterly*, Winter 1993, pp. 1, 8, and 12.

61. Wendell H. McCulloch, Jr., and Donald A. Ball, "Canada–United States Free Trade Agreement: Add Mexico?" *Proceedings of the International Trade and Finance Association Annual Meeting*, May 30–June 2, 1991, Volume 1, pp. 1–14.

62. Bob Ortega, "Some Mexicans Charge North in NAFTA's Wake," *The Wall Street Journal*, February 22, 1994, p. B1.

63. Leslie Crawford, "Chile Makes U.S. Free Trade Pact a Top Priority," *Financial Times*, April 16, 1991, p. 3.

64. "South American Common Market," *Review of the Economic Situation of Mexico*, Banamex, June 1991, pp. 259–63; "The Caracas Act," *Venezuelan News and Views*, June 1991, p. 9; "U.S. Signs Trade Pact with Four Latin Nations," *The Wall Street Journal*, June 21, 1991, p. B9.

65. John Urquhart, "Canadian Trade Minister Says NAFTA Should Be Opened Up to Other Nations," *The Wall Street Journal*, May 31, 1994, p. B7.

66. OECD, *International Investment and Multinational Enterprises*, adopted June 21, 1976, OECD Doc. 21 (76)4/I (1976).

Chapter 5

1. Charles N. Henning, William Pigott, and Robert Haney Scott, *International Financial Management* (New York: McGraw-Hill, 1978), p. 149.

2. Albert C. Whitaker, *Foreign Exchange*, 2nd ed. (New York: Appleton-Century-Crofts, 1933), p. 157.

3. Jacques Rueff, *The Wall Street Journal*, June 5, 1969, pp. 6 and 9.

4. John Mueller, "The Reserve Currency Curse," *The Wall Street Journal*, September 4, 1986, p. 26.

5. "Sell Some Gold," *The Wall Street Journal*, September 4, 1986, p. 26.

6. "Taking in the Biscuits," *The Economist*, May 11, 1991, p. 79.

7. K. K. Sharma and R. C. Murthy, "India Sends 25 Tonnes of Gold to London," *Financial Times*, July 9, 1991, p. 3.

8. *Articles of Agreement, International Monetary Fund* (Washington, DC: IMF, 1944), Article I.

9. Robert Z. Aliber, *The Future of the Dollar as an International Currency* (New York: Praeger Publishers, 1966).

10. For a discussion of how the pars were set, see Henning, et al., *International Financial Management*, pp. 108, 218.

11. Theodore Sorenson, *Kennedy* (New York: Harper & Row, 1965), p. 408. See also *Maintaining the Strength of the United States Dollar in a Strong Free World Economy* (Washington, DC: U.S. Treasury Department, January 1968), p. xi; and *Economic Report of the President*, January 1964, p. 139.

12. *Federal Reserve Bulletin*, September 1969 and January 1974.

13. Ibid., December 1971 and January 1974.

14. Ibid., January 1974, p. A75.

15. This was perceived by the French economist Jacques Rueff, who also forecast the results; see endnote 3.

16. William Safire, *Before the Fall* (New York: Belmont City Books, 1975), p. 514. The size of the British request has been questioned; see Charles Coombs, *The Arena of International Finance* (New York: John Wiley & Sons, 1976), p. 218, where Coombs says that the Bank of England request was for cover of only US$750 million.

17. Wilson E. Schmidt, "The Night We Floated," International Institute for Economic Research, Original Paper 9, October 1977.

18. Ibid., p. 7.

19. For detailed accounts of the international monetary system during the 1971–73 period, see Coombs, *Arena of International Finance*, chap. 12; and Robert Solomon, *The International Monetary System* (New York: Harper & Row, 1977), chaps. 12–15.

20. For discussions of the varieties and methods of clean or dirty floats plus comparisons of float versus peg, see, for example, Weir M. Brown, *World Afloat: National Policies Ruling the Waves*, Essays in International Finance, no. 116 (Princeton, NJ): International Finance Section, Department of Economics, Princeton University, May 1976); Harry G. Johnson, *Further Essays in Monetary Economics* (Winchester, MA: Allen & Unwin, 1972); Anthony M. Lanyi, *The Case for Floating Exchange Reconsidered*, Essays in International Finance, no. 72 (February 1976); Raymond F. Mikesell and Henry M. Goldstein, *Rules for a Floating Regime*, Essays in International Finance, no. 109 (March 1975); and "Economics Brief: To Fix to Float," *The Economist*, January 9, 1988, pp. 66–67.

21. Wendell H. McCulloch, Jr., "American Exports: Why Have They Lagged?" A Study for the Subcommittee on Trade, Productivity, and Economic Growth of the Joint Economic Committee, Congress of the United States, May 14, 1985.

22. Peter Norman, "Adjusting to a New Climate," *Financial Times*, April 29, 1991, section IV, p. 1.

23. Jose de la Torre, "International Finance Has Become the Dog-Wagging Tail of 90s," *Los Angeles Times*, March 20, 1994, p. D2.

24. Stanley W. Black, *Floating Exchange Rates and National Economic Policy* (New Haven: Yale University Press, 1977), pp. 23–26, 49–50, 129–30, 149–50, 154–56, and 173–74.

25. Charles N. Stabler, "Banks and Their Foreign Loans," *The Wall Street Journal*, January 29, 1976, p. 16.

26. Geoffrey Bell, "The International Financial System and Capital Shortages," in *The World Capital Shortage*, ed. Alan Heslop (Indianapolis: Bobbs-Merrill, 1977), pp. 35–57.

27. Juanita Darling, "Dollar Holding Strong against Mexico's Peso," *Los Angeles Times*, July 7, 1994, p. D2.

28. Craig Turner, "The Buck Hops Here," *Los Angeles Times*, July 7, 1994, p. D1.

29. Peter Marsh, "They're Breathing Down London's Neck," *Financial Times*, May 26, 1993, p. IV.

30. Jim McCallum, "Big Three Battle It Out," *Financial Times*, April 29, 1991, section III, p. 4.

31. Peter Kenen, "Techniques of Central International Reserves." Paper presented at the J. Marcus Flemming Memorial Conference, International Monetary Fund, November 12, 1976.

32. *IMF Survey*, October 1993, pp. 9–11.

33. Philip Revzin, "Fathers of Europe's Monetary System Push Creation of a Joint Central Bank," *The Wall Street Journal*, February 23, 1988, p. 20.

34. Peter Norman, "EMU Hinges on Political Will," *Financial Times*, June 2, 1994, p. III.

35. Peter Norman, "Embryo Central Bank Faces Credibility Battle," *Financial Times*, January 10, 1994, p. 14.

36. "The Definition of the ECU," *Economic and Financial Prospects Supplement*, Swiss Bank Corporation, February–March 1989, pp. 2–3.

37. "A Fistful of ECUs," *The Economist*, July 13, 1991, p. 83.

38. Ibid.

39. Giscard d'Estaing, "The ECU and the European Monetary System," *Bulletin, Swiss Banking Magazine*, November 1989, pp. 11–13.

40. Gary Humphreys, "Institutions Stay Cool on the ECU," *Euromoney*, August 1993, pp. 75–80.

41. John Evans, "Lisbon's Bond Gives ECU Fresh Life," *The European*, February 11–17, 1994, p. 21.

Chapter 6

1. Discussed by Robert Z. Aliber, *The International Money Game*, 2nd ed. (New York: Basic Books, 1976), pp. 189–90.

2. Samuel I. Katz, " 'Managed Floating' as an Interim International Exchange Rate Regime, 1973–1975," *New York University Bulletin*, 1975–3 (New York: Center for the Study of Financial Institutions, New York University, 1975), pp. 13–14.

3. Vermont Royster, "Thinking Things Over, 'A Thrice-Told Tale,' " *The Wall Street Journal*, May 10, 1978, p. 18.

4. "Latin America: Real Output and Inflation," *Bank for International Settlements 64th Annual Report, April 1, 1993–March 31, 1994*, June 13, 1994.

5. Georg Junge and Max Schieler, "The Real Choices Facing the Debtor Countries," *Economic and Financial Prospects*, April–May 1990, pp. 1–5.

6. "Life under Brady," *Barclays Economic Review*, August 1990, pp. 30–35.

7. Stephen Fidler, "A Market Transformed," *Financial Times*, April 5, 1991, p. 28.

8. Brian Bollen, "Debt Traders Look to Eastern Europe," *Euromoney*, November 1993, pp. 50–52.

9. Ben Edwards, "The Age of the Exotic Sovereign Borrower," *Euromoney*, March 1994, pp. 127–30.

10. Stephen Fidler, "Brady Plan for Reducing Debt Makes Good Progress," *Financial Times*, September 13, 1990, p. 16; Peter Truell, "Paris Club Pact to Forgive Half of Polish Debt," *The Wall Street Journal*, March 15, 1991, p. A3; and Leslie Crawford, "The Happy Passing of a Debt Negotiator," *Financial Times*, March 22, 1991, p. 3.

11. Leslie Crawford, "Senegal in 'Debt for Children' Swap," *Financial Times*, December 18–19, 1993, p. 3.

12. Alan Abelson, "Do the Wrong Thing, Young Bankers," *Barron's*, September 25, 1989, pp. 1 and 53.

13. Alfred L. Malabre, Jr., "Low Savings Also May Slow Expansion," *The Wall Street Journal*, April 5, 1993, p. A1.

Chapter 7

1. "And Now, the Home-Brewed Forecast," *Fortune*, January 20, 1986, pp. 53–54.

2. Many of these factors also affect domestic firms, but multinational firms are generally more vulnerable and usually must act more quickly.

3. If management is interested in a country as a possible site for investment, it will require the same detailed information as it does for an area where the firm is already doing business.

4. *International Bibliography, Information, Documentation (IBID)*, an excellent bibliography, is published quarterly by UNIPUB. It includes abstracts of publications and studies containing economic and demographic data.

5. You can make your own table for countries not listed in Table 7–6 by first getting the average hourly earnings in national currency from the U.S. Department of Labor, Bureau of Statistics, *Handbook of Labor Statistics*. However, the data in this publication lag considerably, so you then go to the latest issue of *International Financial Statistics*, published monthly by the IMF. Here, for each country listed in the *Handbook*, you can find a very recent index of average hourly costs. Multiplying a ratio of the IMF's index values by the latest value in national currency in the *Handbook*, you can derive more recent values in local currency. Then you go back to the IMF publication and select the average exchange rates for the years you are comparing and convert national currencies to dollars. You will find differences between *Business Europe's* figures and the results you obtain by this method. We're not sure why, but obviously *Business Europe* either used different exchange rates or obtained different values expressed in national currency (probably the exchange rates). This illustrates the problem in expressing any national statistic in dollars.

6. "Preliminary Overview of the Economy of Latin America and the Caribbean, 1993," *Notas Sobre la Economia y el Desarrollo* (Santiago, Chile: CEPAL, December 1993), p. 24.

7. "How the Debt Crisis Is Battering Multinationals," *Business Week*, July 25, 1983, p. 52.

8. "Viva las Pampas," *Forbes,* October 28, 1991, p. 106.

9. "Latin America's New Currency," *The Economist,* October 29, 1988, p. 87.

10. "Hidden Horrors," *The Economist,* October 22, 1994, p. 95.

11. Developed nations are not immune. France, the Netherlands, and Belgium have faced this problem.

12. *World Development Report 1994* (Washington, DC: World Bank, 1994), pp. 212–13.

13. "Whirlpool Jumps into the Global Market," *The European,* November 1–3, 1991, p. 25; "Planning for Global Expansion at Whirlpool," *Business International,* April 15, 1991; and "Whirlpool Is Gathering a Global Momentum," *The New York Times,* April 23, 1989, p. 10.

14. *World Development Report 1984* (Washington, DC: World Bank, 1984), p. 134.

15. "Population Policy: Country Experience," *Finance & Development,* September 1984, p. 19.

16. *World Development Report 1993* (Washington, DC: World Bank, 1993), p. 289.

17. "The Silvering of Japan," *The Economist,* October 7, 1989, p. 81.

18. "The Coming World Labor Shortage," *Fortune,* April 9, 1990, p. 72; and "Death and Taxes," *The Economist,* August 13, 1994, pp. 19–21.

19. "Japan's Struggle to Restructure," *Fortune,* June 28, 1993, pp. 84–88.

20. There are three distinct measures for the dependency ratio: (1) retirees per 100 workers, (2) people aged 65 or 60 and over per 100 people aged between 15 and 64, and (3) number of people aged 14 and under and 65 and over per 100 people aged between 15 and 64. We use the third measure in the text.

21. *World Development Report 1994,* pp. 162–63.

22. Ibid., pp. 222–23.

23. "Airing the Ethnic Message, *Canada Reports,* Fall 1987, p. 11.

Chapter 8

1. Robert Bartels, ed., *Comparative Marketing: Wholesaling in 15 Countries* (Homewood, IL: Richard D. Irwin, 1963), p. 4.

2. "Austria as a Business Location," *Report* (Vienna: Bank Austria, June 1994), pp. 12–13.

3. "The Challenge of Enlargement: Commission Opinion on Finland's Application for Membership," *Bulletin of the European Communities,* June 1992, p. 47.

4. "The Challenge of Enlargement: Commission Opinion on Austria's Application for Membership," *Bulletin of the European Communities,* April 1992, pp. 10–11.

5. OECD, *Monthly Bulletin of Statistics,* June 1994, pp. 44–52.

6. When a sales engineer from Madrid and one of the writers went to Barcelona, the Detroit of Spain, on a business trip, we were accompanied on our visits to customers by our salesman from Barcelona. Our meetings with customers always followed the same pattern. The Barcelona salesman would begin the meeting by telling the customer we were from Madrid and did not speak Catalan, the local language. The meeting would proceed in Spanish until either the customer or our local salesman, in searching for a word in Spanish, would use the more familiar (to him) word in Catalan. This would trigger the other to begin speaking in Catalan (completely unintelligible to anyone speaking only Spanish), and the sales engineer and the writer would be completely in the dark as to what was being discussed. After a moment, the local salesman and the customer would realize what they were doing and apologize. The discussions in Spanish would be resumed, and then the switch to Catalan would be repeated. If our local salesman had not been present to smooth over these lapses and provide the necessary empathy with the customer, these meetings would have been disastrous.

7. "Basques Fight Back," *Europe,* December 1993–January 1994, pp. 42–43.

8. World Bank, *World Development Report, 1994* (New York: Oxford University Press, 1994), p. 223.

9. Australia has no north-south railway mainly because there is little population and economic activity in the center of the country to support one. There is an east-west coastal system in the more populous southern region that was completed partly because the federal government feared the western states might secede from the Australian union. The system, however, has the same problems as those of other large developing nations, such as India and Brazil. There are three different gauges along its length, with a few disconnected feeder lines going inland from the ports to mining and farm districts. Goods in transit between Sydney and Perth take 14 days when, because of the distance, they should take 5. Some unification has been done, but it is not complete. Goods and passengers still must be transferred at some state borders.

10. *World Development Report, 1994,* p. 163.

11. "South America May Go Back to Its Trade Roots," *Financial Times,* August 4, 1992, p. 5.

12. "Estudian Establecimiento de un Corredor Bioceánico," *El Mercurio,* Santiago, Chile, September 13, 1994, p. B3.

13. Rhoads Murphey, *The Scope of Geography,* 2nd ed. (Skokie, IL: Rand McNally, 1973), pp. 188–89.

14. Ibid., p. 119.

15. Andrew M. Karmack, *The Tropics and Economic Development* (Washington, DC: World Bank, 1976), p. 5.

16. Joseph H. Butler, *Economic Geography* (New York: John Wiley & Sons, 1980), p. 108.

17. "Atco, Sun Co. Units Sign Pact to Develop Cogeneration Plant," *The Wall Street Journal,* January 27, 1993, p. B8.

18. "Canadian Tar Sands Come of Age," *Financial Times,* June 1, 1993, p. 16.

19. "Dakota Gasification Builds Its Chemical Business," *Chemical Week,* July 27, 1964, pp. 38–39.

20. "The New Prize," *The Economist,* June 18, 1994, p. 13.

21. "Conoco Venture Places Russian Oil Field on Line," *Oil & Gas Journal,* September 5, 1994, pp. 38–40.

22. "Texaco-Led Consortium Nears Russian Oil Agreement," *The Wall Street Journal,* November 30, 1994, p. B4.

23. "The New Prize," p. 5.

24. "The Sun Shines Brighter on Alternative Energy," *Business Week,* November 8, 1993, pp. 94; and "The New Prize," p. 4.

25. "The Sun Shines Brighter," p. 94.

26. "Deep-Six the Law of the Sea," *The Wall Street Journal,* July 28, 1994, p. A14.

724

27. "World Law of Sea Goes into Effect," *McAllen Monitor*, November 17, 1994, p. 11A.
28. "Fill 'Er Up, Please—With Hydrogen," *Newsweek*, March 5, 1990, p. 42.
29. "Brazil Balks at International Pressure," *The Wall Street Journal*, February 13, 1989, p. A7B.
30. "Luxury, Calm, and Speed: It's the Chunnel Train," *Business Week*, November 14, 1994, p. 143; and "On the Right Track," *International Management*, July–August 1994, p. 19.
31. "Seto Ohashi Bridge," *Japan Update*, Winter 1989, pp. 10–11.
32. "Union Carbide, India Reach $470 Million Settlement," *The Wall Street Journal*, February 15, 1989, p. B12.
33. "Indian Gassing Victims Endure Another Disaster—No Aid," *San Antonio Express-News*, November 29, 1994, p. 4A.
34. "The Blotch on the Rhine," *Newsweek*, November 24, 1986, pp. 58–60; and "Suddenly a Deathwatch on the Rhine," *Business Week*, November 24, 1986, p. 52.
35. "Beyond the Spill on the Rhine," *World Press Review*, January 1987, p. 50.
36. "Alaska Oil Spill," *Management Review*, April 1990, pp. 13–14.
37. "Exxon Is Told to Pay $5 Billion for Valdez Spill," *The Wall Street Journal*, September 19, 1994, p. A2.
38. "Lakes of Spilled Oil Plunge Kuwait into Ever-Deeper Mess," *The Wall Street Journal*, August 12, 1991, p. A8.
39. "Persian Gulf War Leaves Behind Ecologically Ravaged Landscape," *San Antonio Express-News*," November 12, 1994, p. 9A.
40. "Mopping Up the Tundra," *The Economist*, October 29, 1994, p. 62.
41. "Anderson Reflects on Managing Bhopal," *Industry Week*, October 13, 1986, p. 21.

Chapter 9

1. "How to Win Friends and Influence Clients," *The European*, January 21–27, 1994, p. 11.
2. Ibid.
3. I. Brady and B. Isaac, *A Reader in Cultural Change*, vol. 1 (Cambridge, MA: Schenkman Publishing, 1975), p. x.
4. V. Barnouw, *An Introduction to Anthropology* (Homewood, IL: Dorsey Press, 1975), p. 5.
5. E. T. Hall, *Beyond Culture* (Garden City, NY: Doubleday, 1977), p. 16.
6. Vern Terpstra and K. David, *The Cultural Environment of International Business* (Cincinnati: South-Western Publishing, 1985), p. 7.
7. Hall, *Beyond Culture*, p. 54.
8. "After Early Stumbles, P&G Is Making Inroads Overseas," *The Wall Street Journal*, February 6, 1989, p. B1; "Slow and Steady," *The Wall Street Journal*, September 21, 1989, p. A1; "They Didn't Listen to Anybody," *Forbes*, December 15, 1986, pp. 168–69; and "P&G Rewrites the Marketing Rules," *Fortune*, November 6, 1989, pp. 34–46.
9. "Monsieur Mickey," *Time*, March 25, 1991, p. 48–49.
10. "National versus Corporate Culture: Implications for Human Resource Management," *Human Resource Management*, Summer 1988, pp. 232–45.
11. One of the writers installed in a Spanish factory new production equipment that was to replace old but still serviceable machinery. Before leaving for a week's work in Madrid, he tested the equipment, trained some workers to use it, and advised the supervisor that it was ready. On his return, he was surprised to find that the new equipment was not being utilized. The supervisor explained that the old machinery was working well and he didn't want to "disrupt production." Actually, the new equipment was easier to use and would greatly increase output. Realizing that drastic action was called for, the writer grabbed a sledgehammer and make a token effort to destroy the old equipment. Only then did the supervisor get the message. Admittedly, the action was unorthodox, but it did bring immediate results. Not wanting to replace a still serviceable object with a new object, even when the new object is superior, is a quite common attitude in many countries.
12. "Mouse Trap," *The Wall Street Journal*, March 10, 1994, p. A12.
13. This classification depends in part on M. J. Herskovits, *Man and His Works* (New York: Alfred A. Knopf, 1952). p. 634. It was embellished by anthropologists at the University of South Alabama.
14. "Tire Maker Says Tread Designs Were Not Meant to Offend Allah, *Columbus Dispatch*, July 26, 1992, p. 6A.
15. Herskovits, "Man and His Works, p. 414.
16. "The Middle East Mirage," *International Management*, April 1989, p. 21.
17. John A. Reeder, "When West Meets East: Cultural Aspects of Doing Business with Asia, *Business Horizons*, January–February 1987, pp. 18–22.
18. "Middle East Mirage," p. 23.
19. Thomas E. Maher and Yim Yu Wong, "The Impact of Cultural Differences on the Growing Tensions Between Japan and the United States," *SAM Advanced Management Journal*, Winter 1994, p. 45; and "Blunders Abroad," *Nation's Business*, March 1989, p. 54.
20. "German View: You Americans Work Too Hard—and for What?" *The Wall Street Journal*, July 14, 1994, p. B1.
21. "Leisure Time in Japan," *Sumitomo Corporation News*, May 1992, p. 12.
22. It is difficult to translate adequately the connotations of the two words. No one proudly says he is an *obrero* even if he earns more than the *empleado* who is a file clerk.
23. "How the Japanese Are Changing," *Fortune*, Pacific Rim, 1990, pp. 15–22.
24. "Asia Conjures Wind and Water to Boost Business," *International Management*, July–August 1987, pp. 57–60.
25. "Some Chinese Won't Make a Move without Fung Shui," *The Wall Street Journal*, December 19, 1983, p. 1.
26. "World Wire," *The Wall Street Journal*," January 10, 1995, p. A17; Kenneth L. Woodward, "Religions in Asia," *Modern Maturity*, December 1984–January 1985, pp. 75–78; and "Islam: Seeking the Future in the Past," *U.S. News & World Report*, July 6, 1987, pp. 33–36.
27. "Islam's Arrow of Death," *The Economist*, March 11, 1989, p. 41.
28. "Salman Rushdie Visits White House," *The Oregonian*, November 25, 1993, p. A13.
29. "French Government Backs Down on Rebuff of Writer," *McAllen Monitor*, October 8, 1994, p. 10A.

30. "Mahfouz Urges Defeat of Islamic Extremism," *McAllen Monitor*, October 16, 1994, p. 10A.

31. "Iran, Iraq Engage in Power Struggle to Select Spiritual Leader of Shiites," *The Wall Street Journal*, February 11, 1994, p. A12.

32. "Malaysian Malady: When the Spirit Hits, a Scapegoat Suffers," *The Wall Street Journal*, March 3, 1980, p. 1.

33. "Compaq to Shift Some Computer Output to its Houston Facility from Singapore," *The Wall Street Journal*, February 25, 1994, p. B4; and "Moving the Lab Closer to the Marketplace," *Business Week*, Reinventing America, 1992, p. 168.

34. "Where Technology Is the Appropriate Word," *The Economist*, April 18, 1987, p. 83.

35. "How to Sell Soap in India," *The Economist*, September 10, 1988, p. 82.

36. "Weak in Technology, South Korea Seeks Help from Overseas," *The Wall Street Journal*, January 7, 1986, p. 1.

37. Programme on Transnational Corporations, *World Investment Report 1993* (New York: United Nations, 1993), p. 85.

38. This is one of three accepted definitions, and its application is subject to qualifiers in a number of countries. From "Technical Notes," *World Development Report 1994* (Washington, DC: World Bank, 1994), p. 232.

39. "Let Open Doors Swing Both Ways," *The Wall Street Journal*, June 15, 1988, p. 12.

40. "Costly Brain Drain, *Development Forum* (Geneva: United Nations, March 1982), p. 12.

41. "Costly Export," *The Wall Street Journal*, April 18, 1989, p. A1.

42. "South Korea to Recruit 110 Top Scientists during 1992," *The McAllen Monitor*, February 8, 1992, p. 23.

43. "Return of the Natives," *The Wall Street Journal*, May 24, 1993, p. R14; and "Train 'em Here, Keep 'em Here," *Forbes*, May 27, 1991, p. 110.

44. "Have Skills, Will Travel—Homeward," *Business Week*, 21st Century Capitalism, 1994, p. 164; and "Bringing It All Back Home, " *Business Week*, December 7, 1992, p. 133.

45. "Costly Export," p. A1.

46. "What's Worrying the Swiss?" *Bulletin* (Zurich: Crédit Suisse, April 1988), pp. 4–5.

47. "Do the Swiss Want to Join the EU after All?" *Bulletin* (Zurich: Crédit Suisse, January 1995), pp. 10–12.

48. To avoid using English as the link language in India, Hindi was declared the official language. As late as 1986, Tamil-speaking students from the south were rioting against the imposition of Hindi, which was spoken by 30 percent of the population, mainly in the north. The students wanted English to be the link language. From *Los Angeles Times*, December 11, 1986, part I, p. 5.

49. "Europe's Youth Votes for English," *The European*, November 15–17, 1991, p. 2.

50. "Pulling Down the Language Barrier," *International Management*, July–August 1994, p. 44.

51. "Why Speaking English Is No Longer Enough," *International Management*, November 1986, p. 42.

52. This mistake was caught before it was published locally, but an incident happened to one of the writers, newly arrived in Brazil, that did go all over the country. The ad manager, a Brazilian, brought him a campaign empha-sizing that car owners should maintain 24 pounds per square inch in their tires to get maximum wear. To really get the point across, life-size figures of a tire company salesman were made up, with the name of the company and a large "24" printed across his chest. Care was taken to get these figures out to the dealers, who were to set them up on a "D day." The writer, sitting in his São Paulo office, proud of the unusually good coordination of the campaign, began receiving calls from competitors asking what type of people worked in his company. Over the laughter came the message—24 in Brazilian Portuguese means homosexual.

53. " 'Stupid' Translations Include Menu Items Hardly Digestible," *The Columbus Dispatch*, December 23, 1994, p. C1.

54. "What's the Bon Mot? France Steps Up Battle against Use of English," *The Oregonian*, March 15, 1994, p. A6; and *Crossborder Monitor*, July 20, 1994, p. 3.

55. "Wal-Mart Again Runs into Language-Law Trouble," *The Wall Street Journal*, June 24, 1994, p. A4.

56. "Well, Excuse Moi! English Suffers Kick in Derriere," *The Wall Street Journal*, February 24, 1994, p. A12; and "Firm Cultural Ownership Rules Wanted by Minister but Not Cabinet," *Vancouver (Canada) Sun*, April 30, 1994, p. B12.

57. "A Little Bad English Goes a Long Way in Japan's Boutiques," *The Wall Street Journal*, May 5, 1993, p. A1.

58. "Watch Your Body Language," *International Management*, May 1990, p. 84; and "Taking Cues from Body Language," *Management Review*, June 1989, pp. 59–60.

59. E. T. Hall, *The Hidden Dimension* (Garden City, NY: Doubleday, 1969), pp. 134–35.

60. One of the writers, who lived in Latin America for 15 years, was surprised to read this statement in *The Silent Language in Overseas Business* by E. T. Hall. His Mexican wife, who had lived on both sides of the border, absolutely refuted it, so when he went to Ecuador recently as a consultant, he was careful to observe conversational distances. In no instance did he note any appreciable difference.

61. Roger E. Axtell, ed., *Do's and Taboos around the World*, 2nd ed. (New York: John Wiley & Sons, 1990), pp. 113–47.

62. Neil H. Jacoby, Peter Nehemkis, and Richard Eells, *Bribery and Extortion in World Business* (New York: Macmillan, 1977), pp. 174–75.

63. Interestingly, the Foreign Corrupt Practices Act of 1977 permits grease to be paid when its sole purpose is to expedite nondiscretionary official actions.

64. "New Agency Girds to Fight Corruption, Picks Ecuador as Early Battleground," *The Wall Street Journal*, May 21, 1993, p. A8; and "The Destructive Costs of Greasing Palms," *Business Week*, December 6, 1993, pp. 133–38.

65. Herskovits, *Man and His Works*, p. 303.

66. "Europe's Women Unite to Throw Off Their Chains," *International Management*, July–August 1987, pp. 42–49.

67. "Sexes' Equality a Myth," *U.S. News & World Report*, July 8, 1985, p. 40.

68. Geert Hofstede, "Cultural Dimensions in Management and Planning," *Asia Pacific Journal of Management*, January 1984, p. 83.

69. Ibid., p. 83.

70. Lisa Hoecklin, *Managing Cultural Differences* (Wokingham, England: Addison-Wesley Publishing, 1995), pp. 28–30.

71. Ibid., p. 31.
72. Rose Knotts and Sheryann Tomlin, "A Comparison of TQM Practices in U.S. and Mexican Companies," *Production and Inventory Management Journal*, First Quarter, 1994, p. 54.
73. Hofstede, p. 85.
74. Hoecklin, pp. 31–32.
75. Ibid., pp. 31 and 36.
76. Hofstede, pp. 81 and 84.

Chapter 10

1. Ian Brownlie, *Principles of Public International Law* (Oxford, England: Oxford University Press, 1966), pp. 435–36.
2. "Why Planned Economies Fail," *The Economist*, June 25, 1988, p. 67. See also, "Wounded Pride: Why Communism Fell," *The Economist*, May 25, 1991, pp. 98–99.
3. Jack Lowenstein, "Ready to Join the Big League?" *Euromoney*, October 1990, pp. 66–73.
4. Murray Seeger, "Italy Takes Prize for Its Corporate Octopus," *Los Angeles Times*, November 1, 1979, part 1, p. 12.
5. Now "Abolish Yourself," *The Economist*, June 4, 1994, p. 67.
6. Robert Graham, "Quick Comeback for Former Chief of IRI," *Financial Times*, July 28, 1994, p. 2.
7. Charles C. Tillinghast, Jr., "Competing against State-Owned Companies," paper presented at the Academy of International Business Annual Meeting, 1979.
8. Richard L. Holman, "EC Widens Business Control," *The Wall Street Journal*, July 25, 1991, p. A10.
9. "Thatcher's Sales," *Business Week*, December 10, 1990, p. 26.
10. Jill Leovy, "Lockheed Looks to Expand Its Airport Business," *Los Angeles Times*, May 31, 1994, pp. D1 and 6.
11. Martin Dickson, "America's Sale of the Century," *Financial Times*, June 1, 1992, p. 12.
12. Frederick Studemann, "German Postal Sell-Off Nearer as Parties Agree," *The European*, February 11–17, 1994, p. 16.
13. Gekko, "Random Walk: Wall Street," *National Review*, June 27, 1994, p. 26.
14. Mary Shirley, "The Experience with Privatization," *Finance & Development*, September 1988, pp. 34–35.
15. Felix Kessler, "France's Erratic Policies on Investment by Foreigners Confuse Many U.S. Firms," *The Wall Street Journal*, April 7, 1980, p. 24.
16. "Italy's Ever-Growing Monster," *The Economist*, July 27, 1991, pp. 43–44.
17. Henrik Bering-Jensen, "The Dirty Secrets of State Terror," *Insight*, August 6, 1990, pp. 34–35; and Jonas Bernstein, "When in Need, Terrorist Groups Turned Eastward," *Insight*, January 21, 1991, pp. 18–21.
18. David G. Hubbard, "Lilliput Revisited: A Data-Based Critique of Corporate Captivity in Connection with Kidnapping and Terrorist Threat," in *The International Essays for Business Decision Makers*, vol. 4, ed. Mark B. Winchester (Dallas: Center for International Business, 1979), pp. 19–31.
19. Brian O'Reilly, "Business Copes with Terrorism," *Fortune*, January 6, 1986, pp. 47–55.
20. Peter Almond with Bill Whalen, "Insurance against Terrorists an Emerging Growth Industry," *Insight*, March 17, 1986, pp. 52–54.
21. Robin Wright, "U.S. Hoping to Turn Corner in Terrorism War," *Los Angeles Times*, August 18, 1991, pp. A1 and 10–11.
22. "Germany's Latest Victim," *The Wall Street Journal*, April 4, 1991, p. A14.
23. Michael Bond, "Europe Alert over Threat of Nuclear Terrorism," *The European*, March 10–24, 1994, pp. 1 and 2.
24. Steven Emerson, "Diplomacy That Can Stop Terror," *The Wall Street Journal*, July 22, 1994, p. A10.
25. Everett G. Martin, "Playing It Cool in Bolivia," *The Wall Street Journal*, June 3, 1976, p. 14.
26. *The Wall Street Journal*, April 11, 1977, p. 12.
27. Winston Moore, "Rich in Natural Resources," *Financial Times*, April 11, 1994, p. IV.
28. William Colby, "Bolivia," *Colby Report*, July 11, 1994, p. 1.
29. Shirley Hobbs Scheibla, "McNamara's Band Sour," *Barron's*, December 3, 1979, pp. 9, 26, and 27.
30. Barbara Linehan, "The European Community, Its Legislation and Where to Find It," *The California International Practitioner* 2, no. 2, 1990–91, pp. 22–28.
31. For a good discussion of the powers that an MNE can use, see Stefan H. Robock and Kenneth Simmonds, *International Business and Multinational Enterprises* (Homewood, IL: Richard D. Irwin, 1989), chap. 15.
32. See Table 1–3.
33. "Come Back Multinationals," *The Economist*, November 26, 1988, p. 73.
34. For several good discussions of various aspects of CRA, see Jerry Rogers, ed., *Global Risk Assessments: Issues, Concepts, and Applications*, book 2 (Riverside, Calif.: Global Risk Assessments, 1986).
35. Monua Janah, "Rating Risk in the Hot Countries," *The Wall Street Journal*, September 20, 1991, p. R4.
36. Ibid.

Chapter 11

1. David Dreier, "Cut the Capital-Gains Tax to Get Money Flowing and Create Jobs," *Los Angeles Times*, March 25, 1994, p. B7.
2. George Graham, "UK Still Unhappy with California Tax Proposals" and "Unitary v. Water's Edge: Seeking a Company Tax Deal, *Financial Times*, August 21–22, 1993, p. 2.
3. Chris Endean, "Italians Urged to Shop Tax-Dodging Friends," *The European*, June 2, 1991, p. 4.
4. Jonathan Schwarz, "Stimuli for Freer Trade," *Financial Times*, May 20, 1994, p. II.
5. Richard L. Holman, "EC Antitrust Efforts Boosted," *The Wall Street Journal*, March 20, 1991, p. A17; and "EC Court Reinforces Commission's Antitrust Clout," *Eurecom*, April 1991, p. 1.
6. Andrew Hill, "Predatory Pricing Judgment Confirmed, *Financial Times*, July 5, 1991, p. 2.
7. Andrew Hill, "Tera Pak: Swiss Precision in Seeing Off Its Competitors," *Financial Times*, July 21, 1991, p. 2; and Martin Du Bois and Brian Coleman, "EC Blocks Sale of a Boeing Unit to French-Italian Joint Venture," *The Wall Street Journal*, October 3, 1991, p. A14.

8. Emma Tucker, "Price-Fixing Cartel Given Record Fine by Brussels," *Financial Times*, July 14, 1994, pp. 1 and 18.

9. Raymond Hughes, law courts correspondent, "Partial Victory for Adams in Commission Case," *Financial Times of London*, July 12, 1985, p. 2.

10. *The Economist*, June 9, 1979, pp. 91–92.

11. "Touched for the Very First Time," *The Economist*, October 30, 1993, p. 70.

12. *The Economist*, December 10, 1977, pp. 77–78.

13. Joel Haveman, "EC Getting Close to a Joint Antitrust Policy," *Los Angeles Times*, February 12, 1991, p. H3.

14. Joe Davidson, "U.S. Decides to Enforce Antitrust Laws against Collusion by Foreign Concerns," *The Wall Street Journal*, April 6, 1992, p. C10.

15. "Japan's Fair Trade Commission, Pussycat," *The Economist*, October 23, 1993, pp. 85–86.

16. Thomas G. Donlan, "Not So Free Trade: U.S. Preaches What It Doesn't Always Practice," *Barron's*, June 27, 1988, pp. 70–71.

17. "The American Car Industry's Own Goal," *The Economist*, February 6, 1988, p. 69. For a good discussion of protectionism, see Robert Z. Lawrence and Robert E. Litan, "Why Protectionism Doesn't Pay," *Harvard Business Review*, May–June 1987, pp. 60–67.

18. Sandra N. Hurd and Frances E. Zollers, "Desperately Seeking Harmony: The European Community's Search for Uniformity in Product Liability Law," *American Business Law Journal 30* (1992) pp. 35–68.

19. Ibid.

20. Barbara Crutchfield George, "The Legislative Process of the European Union: Its Social and Cultural Dimension," *Rocky Mountain Regional Academy of Legal Studies in Business Conference*, September 16, 1994.

21. Barbara Crutchfield George and Linda McCallister, "The Effect of Cultural Attitudes on Product Liability Laws," *Southwestern Association of Administrative Disciplines*, March 4, 1993.

22. Carolyn Lochhead, "Strict Liability Causing Firms to Give up on Promising Ideas," *The Washington Times*, August 22, 1988, p. B5.

23. Steven P. Galante, "American Insurance Crisis Begins to Hurt European Firms with Operations Here," *The Wall Street Journal*, December 29, 1985, p. 12; and Patrick Cockburn, "The Tricky Waters of U.S. Liability Insurance," *Financial Times*, March 29, 1990, p. 21.

24. Tom Dunkel, "Saving Hapless Americans Abroad," *Insight*, March 26, 1990, pp. 47–49.

25. Mark A. Goldstein, "The UN Sales Convention," *Business America*, November 21, 1988, pp. 12–13.

26. Lucy Kellaway, "EC Legal Convention on Contracts Approved," *Financial Times*, January 30, 1991, p. 7.

27. "Firms Specify Arbitration for International Fights," *The Wall Street Journal*, July 29, 1994, p. A4.

28. Michael Moser, "A Good Place to Make Peace," *Euromoney*, July 1991, special supplement, pp. 50–54.

29. A. H. Herman, "Growth in International Trade Law," *Financial Times*, March 30, 1989, p. 10.

30. "Merchandise exports, 1993," *The Economist*, April 16, 1994, p. 115.

31. Jonathan Peterson, "U.S. Trades In on Its Know-How," *The Wall Street Journal*, February 28, 1994, pp. A1 and 12.

32. Frances Williams, "GATT joins battle for right to protect," *Financial Times*, July 7, 1994, p. 7.

33. "Japanese firm in South-East Asia," *The Economist*, May 7, 1994, pp. 75–76.

34. Alan W. Lepp, "Intellectual Property Rights Regimes in Southeast Asia," *Journal of Southeast Asia Business*, Fall 1990, pp. 28–40.

35. "Digital Banditry in China," *The Economist*, April 23, 1994, p. 70.

36. Malcolm Baldrige, "Rx for Export Woes: Antitrust Relief," *The Wall Street Journal*, October 15, 1985, p. 32. See also, Thomas M. Jorde and David J. Teece, "To Keep U.S. in the Chips, Modify the Antitrust Laws," *Los Angeles Times*, July 24, 1989, part II, p. 5.

37. *The Wall Street Journal*, April 14, 1978, p. 14.

38. "When We Wear the Black Hats," *The Wall Street Journal*, March 22, 1990, p. A16.

39. John S. Estey and David W. Marston, "Pitfalls (and Loopholes) in the Foreign Bribery Law," *Fortune*, October 9, 1978, pp. 182–88.

40. Barbara Crutchfield George, "The U.S. Foreign Corrupt Practices Act: The Price Business Is Paying for the Unilateral Criminalization of Bribery," *International Journal of Management*, September 1987, pp. 391–402; and "Some Guidelines on Dealing with Graft," *Business International*, February 25, 1983, p. 62.

41. Wendell H. McCulloch, Jr., interviews conducted in Europe during July and August 1979.

42. Robert Keatley, "U.S. Campaign against Bribery Faces Resistance from Foreign Governments," *The Wall Street Journal*, February 4, 1994, p. A10.

43. Jerry Landauer, "Proposed Treaty against Business Bribes Gets Poor Reception Overseas, U.S. Finds," *The Wall Street Journal*, March 28, 1977, p. 26.

44. *The Wall Street Journal*, October 31, 1985, p. 32.

45. Keatley, "U.S. Campaign against Bribery," p. A10.

46. George, "The U.S. Foreign Corrupt Practices Act," p. 400.

47. *The Economist*, September 2, 1978, p. 101.

48. Thomas M. Burton, "How Baxter Got off the Arab Blacklist, and How It Got Nailed," *The Wall Street Journal*, March 26, 1993, pp. A1 and 5.

49. "American Express's Bank Unit Is Fined in Arab Boycott Case," *The Wall Street Journal*, August 17, 1993, p. A5.

50. *The Wall Street Journal*, April 3, 1978, p. 6.

51. Eduardo Lochia, "U.S. Law Successfully Blocks Arab Bid to Keep American, Israeli Firms Apart," *The Wall Street Journal*, July 14, 1984, p. 28.

52. David Ignatius, "Catch 22: Trading with Iraq," *The Wall Street Journal*, March 25, 1982, p. 22.

Chapter 12

1. Barry Newman, "Unwelcome Guests," *The Wall Street Journal*, May 9, 1983, pp. 1, 22.

2. Bromwen Maddox, "UN warns of world's creaking cradle," *Financial Times*, August 18, 1994, p. 3.

3. Birna Helgadottir, "Diminutive Giant of Japan, Sadako Ogata, UN High Commissioner for Refugees," *The European*, 4–10 February, 1994, p. 10.

4. Tim Carrington, "Central Europe Borders Tighten as Emigres Flood in from East," *The Wall Street Journal*,

February 8, 1991, p. A10; and Richard Gwyn, "Fortress Europe on Horizon: Tidal Wave," *The Toronto Star*, October 14, 1990, p. H1.

5. Lara Marlowe, "Guest Workers Say Their Farewells to Saudi Arabia," *Financial Times*, September 25, 1990, p. 2.

6. Margareta Pagano, "Problems Go Skin Deep," *The European*, September 13–15, 1991, p. 19; and George Graham, "Newcomers Hit by Left, Right, Centre," *Financial Times*, August 8, 1991, p. 11.

7. Haig Simonian, "Charged with a Gentle Closing of the Door," *Financial Times*, May 1, 1991, p. 2; and "A Different Sort of Docksider," *The Economist*, August 17, 1991, p. 42.

8. Yaroslav Trofinov, "Israel recruits east European guest workers," *The European*, April 22–28, 1994, p. 18.

9. Anthony Ramirez, "Making It," *The Wall Street Journal*, May 20, 1980, pp. 1 and 27.

10. Joseph Spiers, "Women Chill Out," *Fortune*, June 27, 1994, p. 20.

11. Michael C. Jensen, "A Revolution Only Markets Could Love," *The Wall Street Journal*, January 3, 1994, p. 6.

12. Mark French and Peter Jarrett, "The United States Restoring Productivity Growth," *The OECD Observer*, December 1993–January 1994, pp. 46–48.

13. William J. Baumol, "A Modest Decline Isn't All That Bad," *The New York Times*, February 15, 1987, p. 14.

14. Alfred L. Malabre, Jr., "Low Savings Also May Slow Expansion," *The Wall Street Journal*, April 5, 1993, p. A1.

15. *Los Angeles Times*, February 27, 1980, part 1, p. 2; see also The Cost of Caste," *The Economist*, February 16, 1980, pp. 46–47.

16. "Japan's Women Executives Finding Progress Painful," *Asian Wall Street Journal*, December 13, 1982, p. 11.

17. John Thor Dahlburg, "Closing the Education Gap for Women," *Los Angeles Times*, April 12, 1994, pp. H1 and 5.

18. Ethan Bronner, "Summit seeks end to female mutilation," *Press Telegram*, September 11, 1994, pp. A1 and 4.

19. "Brussels for the boys," *The Economist*, May 7, 1994, p. 57.

20. Gerard O'Dwyer, "The Fair Sex Gets the Fairest Deal in Scandinavia," *The European*, June 2, 1991, p. 3.

21. Daniel Wattenberg, "Internationalism Turns Ugly with Attacks on Africans," *Insight*, January 30, 1989, pp. 28–30.

22. See the discussion of employee attitudes and motivation in Sincha Ronen, *Comparative and Multinational Management* (New York: John Wiley & Sons, 1986), chap. 5.

23. Everett M. Kassalow, *Trade Unions and Industrial Relations: An International Comparison* (New York: Random House, 1969).

24. Michiyo Nakamoto, "Japan's Unions Faced with a Dwindling Role," *Financial Times*, March 31, 1994, p. 6.

25. Noemi Trevino, "The Struggle for European Unions," *International Management*, December 1990, pp. 70–75.

26. Harry Bernstein, "Democracy Moves into Workplace," *Los Angeles Times*, October 23, 1980, part 1, pp. 1 and 14–15.

27. "Doug Fraser's Conflicts," *The Wall Street Journal*, September 22, 1982, p. 28.

28. Jesus Sanchez and Donald Wontat, "Chrysler to Drop Union President's Spot on Its Board," *Los Angeles Times*, March 14, 1991, p. D1.

Chapter 13

1. Kenichi, Ohmae, *Triad Power: The Coming Shape of Global Competition* (New York: Free Press, 1985).

2. "Doing It, Earning It," *The Economist*, February 26, 1994, pp. 35–36; and "Korea Is Overthrown as Sneaker Champ," *The Wall Street Journal*, October 7, 1993, p. A14.

3. "Competitiveness: Getting It Back," *Fortune*, April 27, 1987, pp. 217–23.

4. Kenneth M. Davidson, "Fire Sale on America?" *Journal of Business Strategy*, September–October 1989, p. 11.

5. "Waiting for the Yen to Stop Pummeling Profits," *Business Week*, June 1, 1987, pp. 58–59.

6. "U.S. Plans Sanctions Move as Talks with Japan Fail," *The Wall Street Journal*, February 14, 1994, p. A3.

7. "U.S., Japan Differ over Significance of Cellular Pact as Trade-Talk Model," *The Wall Street Journal*, March 15, 1994, p. A20.

8. "Copy to Come," *The Economist*, January 7, 1995, pp. 51–52; "Counterfeit Goods Stall China's Effort to Enter Global Trading Community," *The Wall Street Journal*, December 27, 1994, p. A12; and "Will China Scuttle Its Pirates?" *Business Week*, August 15, 1994, pp. 40–41.

9. "China's Hurdles to Making U.S. Accord a Success Spur Worries Among Analysts," *The Wall Street Journal*, February 28, 1995, p. A4.

10. "Battle Fatigue," *Far Eastern Economic Review*, March 17, 1994, p. 56; and "Clinton Renews Trade Measure Aimed at Japan," *The Wall Street Journal*, March 4, 1994, p. A3.

11. "Singled Out," *The Wall Street Journal*, May 26, 1989, p. A1.

12. "Why Washington Backed Down at the Midnight Hour," *Newsweek*, October 17, 1994, p. 46; and "Clinton's High-Risk Trade Tactics," *Fortune*, May 16, 1994, pp. 73–74.

13. "An Appropriate Corporate and Financial Strategy for Successfully Investing in the Japanese Market," *Business Economics*, July 1994, pp. 50–55; and "Learning from Japan," *Business Week*, January 27, 1992, pp. 52–60.

14. "Inside the Charmed Circle," *The Economist*, January 5, 1991, p. 54.

15. "Japan Auto Makers Buy More U.S. Parts," *The Wall Street Journal*, August 24, 1993, p. A2.

16. "Why Japan Keeps on Winning," *Fortune*, July 15, 1991, p. 76.

17. "Panelists Compete to Pinpoint Faults in Competitiveness," *The Wall Street Journal*, March 5, 1992, p. A6.

18. "Love Thy Competitor as Thyself," *U.S. News & World Report*, June 5, 1989, p. 12.

19. "Airbus Subsidies Are Invisible to Radar," *The Wall Street Journal*, March 4, 1994, p. A14.

20. "If Clinton Is Aiming at Airbus, Why Is Boeing Whining?" *Business Week*, March 15, 1993, p. 30.

21. "Boeing to Give Airbus a Role on Superjumbo," *The Wall Street Journal*, March 4, 1994, p. A7.

22. "Why Washington Is Anointing Flat Panels," *Business Week*, May 16, 1994, pp. 36–37; and "Road toward Success at 'Flat Screens' Is Full of Bumps," *The Wall Street Journal*, April 29, 1994, p. B4.

23. Council on Competitiveness, *Critical Technologies Update 1994* (Washington, DC: Council on Competitiveness, 1994), p. 4.

24. *Survey of Current Business,* July 1994, p. 168.

25. Robert B. Reich, "Who Is Us?" *Harvard Business Review,* January–February 1990, pp. 54, 56, and 63.

26. Dennis J. Encarnation, *Rivals beyond Trade* (Ithaca, NY: Cornell University Press, 1992), p. 215.

27. "Panelists Compete to Pinpoint Faults," p. A6.

28. "American Business Forges Ahead," *The Economist,* January 15, 1994, pp. 65–66.

29. Council on Competitiveness, *Competitiveness Index 1994,* p. 17.

30. "Invest or Die," *Fortune,* February 22, 1993, p. 52.

31. "Why America Needs Unions," *Business Week,* May 23, 1994, p. 71.

32. "Trying to Rev Up," *Business Week,* January 24, 1994, p. 32.

33. "Competitiveness," *Fortune,* April 18, 1994, p. 55.

34. "Advantage, Mitsubishi" *Forbes,* March 18, 1991, p. 100.

35. "The New American Century," *Fortune,* Special Issue, Spring–Summer 1991, p. 22; and *Critical Technologies Update, 1994,* p. 3.

36. "Toppled," *The Economist,* September 10, 1994, p. 7.

37. "Unequal Partnership," *The Banker,* January 1990, p. 40.

38. "The European Community," *The Economist,* July 3, 1993, p. 9.

39. "European Labour Costs Hold Steady," *Business Europe,* September 19–25, 1994, p. 2.

40. *International Comparisons of Hourly Compensation Costs for Production Workers in Manufacturing, 1993* (Washington, DC: U.S. Department of Labor, 1994), p. 9.

41. "Europe's Diminishing Competitiveness," *Business Europe,* March 15–21, 1993, pp. 1–2.

42. "1994 Manufacturing Futures Survey," *The Economist,* October 29, 1994, p. 74.

43. "Europe's Shakeout," *Business Week,* September 14, 1992, pp. 42–45.

44. "Issues and Challenges for European and Japanese Car Manufacturers in European Market," *The JAMA Forum,* December 1994, pp. 7–11.

45. "Getting Tough with the Japanese," *Fortune,* April 20, 1992, pp. 149–55.

46. "Now Japan's Autos Push into Europe," *Fortune,* January 29, 1990, p. 96.

47. "Choppy Water," *The Economist,* December 10, 1994, p. 66; and "The European Car Industry and the EC–Japan Agreement," *Economic & Financial Outlook* (Frankfurt am Main: Deutsche Bank Research, March 2, 1992), pp. 1–7.

48. "The Rising Sun in the Old World," *Europe,* June 1993, p. 32.

49. "Turning Japanese," *Journal of European Business,* September–October 1993, p. 33.

50. "The Latest from Japan," *International Management,* March 1991, pp. 29–32.

51. "Europe's Software Debacle," *The Economist,* November 12, 1994, pp. 77–78.

52. "How Not to Catch Up," *The Economist,* January 9, 1993, pp. 19–21.

53. "You Want EC Business? You Have Two Choices," *Business Week,* October 19, 1992, p. 59.

54. "Teamwork Pays Off for the Firm," *Quality Progress,* May 1994, pp. 53–59; and "The Last Barrier to the European Market," *The Wall Street Journal,* October 7, 1991, p. A14.

55. "Drive to Attract Asian Investors," *Asian Business,* July 1994, p. 54.

56. "Kia to Make Vans in Germany," *The Wall Street Journal,* January 19, 1995, p. A12.

57. "Asian Tigers Are on the Prowl in Europe," *The Wall Street Journal,* October 26, 1994, p. A17; and "Daewoo, Samsung, and Goldstar: Made in Europe?" *Business Week,* August 24, 1992, p. 43.

58. "Unemployment in Japan Hits a 7-Year High," *The Wall Street Journal,* August 31, 1994, p. A9.

59. "More Concerns in Japan Shift Work Overseas," *The Wall Street Journal,* August 23, 1994, p. A9.

60. "New Realism," *Fortune,* October 31, 1994, pp. 117–36.

61. "Japan's White Collar Blues," *Fortune,* March 21, 1994, p. 97.

62. "New Realism," p. 122.

63. "What? Everyday Bargains? This Can't Be Japan," *Business Week,* September 6, 1993, p. 41.

64. "Shopping Lessons," *The Wall Street Journal,* December 31, 1993, p. 1.

65. "Bull in the Japan Shop," *Forbes,* January 31, 1994, pp. 41–42; and *Crossborder Monitor,* February 8, 1994, p. 1.

66. "Making Inroads," *The Wall Street Journal,* April 15, 1994, p. A1.

67. "Apple's Man in Japan Steps Up the Mac Attack," *Business Week,* October 31, 1994, p. 117.

68. "NEC Cuts Prices as Much as 45% on Computers," *The Wall Street Journal,* November 12, 1993, p. A9A.

69. Telephone calls to Ford, General Motors, and Chrysler on February 16 and 17, 1995.

70. "Asian Promise," *The Economist,* June 12, 1993, p. 77.

71. "Korea's Export Boom Is Hurting—and Helping—Japan," *Business Week,* August 8, 1994, p. 16.

72. "The Sun Rises in the East," *Global Competitor,* Spring 1994, pp. 27–31.

73. Ibid., p. 30.

74. "Japanese Giants Losing Grip," *Asian Business,* January 1994, pp. 42–44.

75. "Samsung on the Cutting Edge of Chip Technology," *Business Korea,* September 1994, p. 32.

76. "Microchip Challenge," *Far Eastern Economic Review,* March 3, 1994, p. 42.

77. "Seller Beware," *Forbes,* October 25, 1993, p. 170.

78. "Copyright Law Removes 3 Million Tapes," *Indonesia Development News,* July–August 1988, p. 5.

79. "U.S. Warns Thailand against Pirated Sales," *McAllen Monitor,* February 18, 1995, p. 11A.

80. "Copy to Come," *The Economist,* January 7, 1995, p. 51.

81. "Trade War Erupts as U.S., China Fire Off Sanctions," *San Antonio Express-News,* February 5, 1995, p. 1A; and "U.S., China Resume Negotiations in Effort to Avert a Trade War," *The Wall Street Journal,* February 16, 1995, p. A13.

82. "Ontario Air, Two Executives Plead Guilty to Supplying Fraudulent Aircraft Parts," *The Wall Street Journal,* May 19, 1994, p. A10.

83. "A Really Nasty Business," *Business Week*, November 5, 1990, pp. 36–43.

84. "Group: Illegal Software Users Cost Firms Around $12 Billion," *McAllen Monitor*, June 4, 1993, p. C1.

85. "Mata Hari?" *Financial World*, Fall 1994, pp. 44–46; "GM Says It Accused Former Executive Linked to Lopez," *The Wall Street Journal*, May 18, 1994, p. A10; and "Why Jose's Dream-Car Matters," *The Economist*, July 24, 1993, p. 65.

86. "Countering the Threat of Espionage," *Security Management*, May 1994, pp. 35–37.

87. "Lost Secrets = Lost Profits," *Risk Management*, July 1994, p. 96.

88. "French Suspected of Spying," *McAllen Monitor*, April 18, 1993, p. C1.

89. "Industrial Spys Come in for the Gold," *Business Mexico*, August 1994, p. 6.

90. "CI Systems Take Root at U.S. Firms—but Slowly," *Business International*, November 18, 1991, p. 389.

91. "How to Snoop on Your Competitors," *Fortune*, May 14, 1984, pp. 28–33.

92. "George Smiley Joins the Firm," *Newsweek*, May 2, 1988, pp. 46–47.

93. "Still a Distant Second," *Across the Board*, November 1991, pp. 42–47; and "The New Face of Japanese Espionage," *Forbes*, November 12, 1990, p. 96.

94. "What Ronald McDonald, Mickey Mouse Taught Nissan," *Business International*, February 22, 1993, pp. 57–58.

95. "A Backstage View of World-Class Performers," *The Wall Street Journal*, August 26, 1991, p. A10.

96. "Revolution in Japanese Retailing," *Fortune*, February 7, 1994, pp. 143–46.

97. *Japan 1995* (Tokyo: Keizai Koho Center, December 1994), Table 4–18, p. 45.

98. "A Bargain Basement Called Japan, *Business Week*, June 27, 1994, p. 42.

99. "What? Everyday Bargains? This Can't Be Japan," *Business Week*, September 6, 1993, p. 41.

100. " 'Shop Till You Drop' Hits Europe," *Business Week*, November 29, 1993, pp. 58–59.

101. "Now, Japan Is Feeling the Heat from the Gray Marketeers," *Business Week*, March 14, 1988, p. 50.

102. "A Red-Letter Day for Gray Marketeers," *Business Week*, June 13, 1988, p. 30.

Chapter 14

1. Ram Subramanian, Nirmala Fernandes, and Earl Harper, "Environmental Scanning in U.S. Companies: Their Nature and Their Relationship to Performance," *Management International Review* 33, 1993, p. 271; and J. F. Preble, P. A. Rau, and A. Reichel, "The Environmental Scanning Practices of U.S. Multinationals in the Late 1980s," *Management International Reports*, April 1988, pp. 4–13.

2. R. W. Walvoord, "Export Market Research," *American Export Bulletin*, May 1980, pp. 82–91. Robinson Peterson, "Screening Is First Step in Evaluation," *Marketing News*, June 1990, p. 13, captures the idea we are describing.

3. Regression analysis is a statistical technique employing the least squares criterion to determine the relationship between a dependent variable and one independent variable or more. For an in-depth explanation of regression analysis, see any statistics text.

4. Susan P. Douglas and C. Samuel Craig, *International Marketing Research* (Englewood Cliffs, NJ: Prentice Hall, 1983), pp. 259–73.

5. Commonly, public utilities, mineral extraction, banking, and communications are reserved either for the government or its citizens. Many of the developing countries tend to limit foreign participation to 49 percent generally and even less in certain industries.

6. "Promoting Exports to Europe," *International Trade Forum*, April–June 1992, pp. 16–17.

7. Secondary data and some primary data will be gathered on the field trip, but the visitor rarely has the time or the ability to conduct a complete research study.

8. "New Record," *The European*, August 2–4, 1991, p. 11.

9. While living in São Paulo, one of the authors wanted to call Santos (an hour's drive away). The assistant to his secretary, whose main job was to dial for an outside line, had tried to place the call all morning. Finally, at noon he drove to Santos, completed his business, and returned to the office to find his assistant still dialing.

10. "Third World Research Is Difficult, but It's Possible," *Marketing News*, August 26, 1987, p. 51.

11. "Data Collection Methods Hold Key to Research in Mexico," *Marketing Today*, April 1994, p. 28.

12. "Market Research Wins Fans in India," *Advertising Age*, January 26, 1987, p. 57.

Chapter 15

1. "Multinational, Not Global," *The Economist*, December 24, 1988, p. 99.

2. "Nestlé Shows How to Gobble Markets," *Fortune*, January 16, 1989, p. 75.

3. "U.S. Firms Are Letting Saudi Market Slip," *The Wall Street Journal*, November 30, 1989, p. A10.

4. One of the authors went to pick up his car in a repair shop and asked the mechanic whether he had test-driven it after finishing the repair. Much to his surprise, the mechanic answered he had not—he didn't know how to drive!

5. When General Tire was an American company, it used to do a good business in the United States selling tires for antique cars. The company imported the tires from its foreign subsidiaries, where they were in regular production to supply the old cars still on the roads in those countries.

6. "Consumer Nondurables," *Business International*, June 16, 1986, p. 10.

7. "Hired Guns Packing High-Powered Know-how," *Business Week/21st Century Capitalism*, 1994, p. 94.

8. Ibid.

9. "Pick a Card," *The Wall Street Journal*, February 15, 1994, p. A1.

10. "Call It Worldpool," *Business Week*, November 29, 1994, pp. 98–99; and "Whirlpool Is Expanding in Europe Despite the Slump," *The Wall Street Journal*, January 1, 1994, p. B4.

11. "A Global Comeback," *Advertising Age*, August 20, 1987, p. 146.

12. "Belgium's Strong Drinks," *International Management*, June 1992, p. 65.

13. "Tough Sale," *The Wall Street Journal*, July 29, 1994, p. A1; and "Major Chains Look to Mexico for Growth Opportunities," *Stores*, August 1994, pp. 33–34.

14. "Some Companies Look North to Benefit from Devaluation," *McAllen Monitor*, January 29, 1995, p. 1F.

15. Gillette, *Annual Report 1994*, p. 38; and "Keys Sales to Third World Tastes," *The Wall Street Journal*, January 23, 1986, p. 36.

16. "How to Be a Global Manager," *Fortune*, March 14, 1988, pp. 52–53.

17. Warren J. Keegan, "Multinational Product Planning: Strategic Alternatives," *Journal of Marketing*, January 1969, pp. 58–62, combines these alternatives to formulate five product and promotional strategies.

18. "World's Top 50 Advertising Organizations," *Advertising Age*, January 3, 1994, p. 22.

19. "Remixing the Message," *Business Asia*, February 15, 1993, p. 4.

20. "Ad Agencies Take on the World," *International Management*, April 1994, pp. 50–52.

21. Ibid.

22. "Selling to the World," *The Wall Street Journal*, August 27, 1992, p. A1.

23. "Regional Commonalities Help Global Ad Campaigns Succeed in Latin America," *Business International*, February 17, 1992, pp. 47–48.

24. "Pay TV Goes South," *Business Week*, December 6, 1994, pp. 174–75; "MTV Quits Star to Launch Own Asia Channels," *The Wall Street Journal*, May 2, 1994, p. A11; and "TV Is Exploding All over Asia," *Fortune*, January 24, 1994, pp. 98–101.

25. "Western-Style News, Entertainment Is Dished Out to Arab Viewers Via MBC," *The Wall Street Journal*, March 5, 1992, p. A12.

26. *International Marketing Data & Statistics* (London: Euromonitor, Ltd., 1995), p. 390.

27. "Videotapes Are Common throughout Middle East," *International Advertiser*, February 1986, p. 31.

28. Various annual reports.

29. "Selling to the World," p. A1.

30. "PepsiCo's New Campaign to Knock Rival Coca-Cola," *Financial Times*, January 19, 1995, p. 12; and "Pepsi-Cola Challenged on Italian Knocking Advert," *Business Europe*, May 24, 1991, p. 3.

31. "No Women, No Alcohol: Learning Saudi Taboos before Placing Ads," *International Advertiser*, February 1986, pp. 11–12.

32. "Robert S. Trebus, "Can a Good Ad Campaign Cross Borders?" *Advertising World*, Spring 1978, pp. 6–8.

33. "Ad Agencies Take on the World," p. 52.

34. "World Brands," *Advertising Age*, February 2, 1992, p. 33.

35. "Gillette Builds on Its Success," *Business Europe*, February 8–14, 1993, pp. 6–7; and "Gillette's Panregional Approach," *Business International*, February 20, 1989, p. 51.

36. D. Peebles, J. Ryan, and I. Vernon, "Coordinating International Advertising," *Journal of Marketing*, January 1978, pp. 28–34; and "Centralized International Advertising," *International Advertiser*, September 1986, pp. 35–36.

37. "The Avon Lady of the Amazon," *Business Week*, October 24, 1994, p. 93.

38. "Europe's PC Market Thrives Despite Weak Economics," *The Wall Street Journal*, February 18, 1993, p. B4; "Japan's PC Market Bows to U.S. Makers as NEC Stronghold Continues to Loosen," *The Wall Street Journal*, February 15, 1995, p. B4; and "Dell: Mail Order Was Supposed to Fail," *Business Week*, January 20, 1992, p. 89.

39. "Fishing Only Where the Fish Swims," *Business Europe*, April 26, 1991, p. 3.

40. "Global Coupon Use Up: U.K., Belgium Tops in Europe," *Marketing News*, August 5, 1991, p. 5.

41. "After the Dust Has settled," *Financial Times*, April 28, 1994, p. 9; "Hoover Free Flight Offer Cost Company 48.2m," *Financial Times*, April 21, 1994, p. 6; and "It Sucks," *The Economist*, April 3, 1993, p. 66.

42. "Number Fever Leaves Pepsi Drinkers Cold," *Financial Times*, June 2, 1994, p. 8; "Pepsi in the Philippines," *Business Asia*, March 14, 1994, pp. 6–7; and "PepsiCo Is Facing Mounting Lawsuits from Botched Promotion in Philippines," *The Wall Street Journal*, July 28, 1993, p. B6.

43. "U.S. Philanthropy in Japan," *Fortune*, March 11, 1991, p. 13.

44. "Warner-Lambert Brings Its Image-Building Program to Latin America," *Business Latin America*, July 15, 1991, p. 227–30.

45. "IBM Lobbies for Freer European Market," *The Wall Street Journal*, April 20, 1988, p. 18.

46. "EU Penalizes 16 Steel Firms over Pricing," *The Wall Street Journal*, February 17, 1994, p. A12.

47. "Who Pays $25,000 for a Fax Machine? You," *Business Week*, March 21, 1994, p. 8.

48. "IRS Sets Up Crack Team to Fight Plague of Cross-Border Tax Cheats," *The Wall Street Journal*, January 25, 1994, p. B7.

49. "Balladur Halts March of the Hypermarchés," *International Management*, June 1993, p. 24.

50. "Guess Who's Selling Barbies in Japan Now?" *Business Week*, December 9, 1991, p. 72.

51. "Toy Joy," *The Economist*, January 4, 1992, p. 62.

52. "Change at the Checkout," *The Economist*, March 4, 1995, pp. 1–15; and "U.S., European Retailers Are Becoming More Transnational," *Europe*, January–February 1989, pp. 20–54.

53. The idea for this matrix came to one of the writers when he was working on the first edition of this book. It is a kind of checklist to help those working on the standardization of an element of the marketing mix to remember the impact of the uncontrollable forces. He wishes he had such a tool when he was an international marketing manager.

Chapter 16

1. William A. Delphos, ed., *The World Is Your Market* (Washington, DC: Braddock Communications, 1990), p. 6.

2. David Burch, "Trading Places," *Inc.*, April 1988, p. 43.

3. *The World Is Your Market*, p. 6.

4. Telephone conversation with Ford International representative.

5. "Selling Abroad," *U.S. News & World Report*, March 2, 1992, p. 64.

6. *National Trade Data Bank User's Guide* (Washington, DC: U.S. Department of Commerce, July 1991), p. 1.

7. "U.S. Government Overseas Export Activities, *Business America*, 1991 World Trade Week Edition, pp. 18–19.

8. *The Trade Point Global Network* (Geneva: United Nations, October 1994), pp. 1–7; "The New Trading Gateway," *Global Trade Talk*, July–August 1994, pp. 6–7; and "Trade Partnership to Be Formed," *The Columbus Dispatch*, March 5, 1994, p. 1C.

9. "Export Financing at the State Level," *Business America*, November 15, 1993, pp. 2–5.

10. These and other terms have been codified in *INCO-TERMS, 1990* by the International Chamber of Commerce, which has been adopted by the U.S. Chamber of Commerce, the National Council of American Exporters, and the National Foreign Trade Council. The point at which title and risk pass from the seller to the buyer is specified, as are the duties of each party.

11. "Innovative Export Financing: Factoring and Forfaiting," *Business America*, January 11, 1993, pp. 12–14.

12. "Financing and Insurance Programs for U.S. Exporters," *Business America*, World Trade Week Edition, 1993, pp. 15–16.

13. "Foreign Sales Corporations," *D&B Reports*, July–August 1993, pp. 54–55.

14. "Duty Drawback," *Foreign Trade*, September 1994, p. 53; and "How to Take Advantage of Duty Drawbacks," *Traffic Management*, September 1990, p. 59.

15. "Sales of Japan's Nine Sogo Shosha (FY1993)," *Japan 1995*, December 15, 1994) p. 45.

16. "New Tariff Code Streamlines Global Trading System," *Business America*, November 23, 1987, pp. 2–5.

17. Discussion with Customs officials Gilbert Medina and Carlos Barajas at Hidalgo, Texas, on March 10, 1995.

Chapter 17

1. "Fiddling with the Taps," *The Economist*, July 16, 1994, p. 58.

2. Ibid.

3. Klaus Engelen, "Can't Pay, Won't Pay," *The European*, September 16–22, 1994, p. 18.

4. "Still in the Red," *The Economist*, September 17, 1994, p. 85.

5. Jonathon Peterson and James R. Wilburn, "Transforming an Economy," *Los Angeles Times*, September 10, 1991, p. H4.

6. Alan Murray, "Harvard, to the Dismay of U.S. Conservatives, May Replace Communism as Soviets' Planner," *The Wall Street Journal*, August 27, 1991, p. A14.

7. Carey Goldberg, "Joint Ventures Failing to Lift Soviet Economy," *Los Angeles Times*, May 26, 1991, pp. D1 and 16; and "Russian Roulette with Six Bullets," *The Economist*," January 12, 1991, pp. 64–65.

8. Carl F. Tey, "Important Design Characteristics for Russian-Foreign Joint Venture Success," *Academy of International Business Conference*, November 3–6, 1994.

9. "Free Markets, Soviet Style," *Fortune*, September 9, 1991, p. 188.

10. John Lloyd, "Russian Trade Turns Westward," *Financial Times*, November 24, 1994, p. 4.

11. Nicholas Denton and Richard Lapper, "Privatization Lures Cash to Russia," *Financial Times*, November 28, 1994, p. 15.

12. Richard W. Judy, "From Anarchy to Zhirinovsky?" *National Review*, March 21, 1994, pp. 49–52.

13. "Death in Russia Booming," *The Economist*, July 9, 1994, pp. 50–52.

14. "Bet on Russian Reform," *Colby Report for International Business*, July 11, 1994, pp. 1–2.

15. Donald Woutat, "East Europe's Realities Put Chill on Investment Climate, *Los Angeles Times*, July 9, 1991, pp. A1 and 6.

16. Ibid.

17. "Investing in Eastern Europe: The Money Pit," *The Economist*, June 22, 1991, pp. 74–75.

18. Charles T. Powers, "Levi Strauss Sews Up Enthusiastic Support for Factory in Polish City," *Los Angeles Times*, July 9, 1991, p. A6.

19. Anthony Robinson, "EU Policies 'Main Threat to Eastern Europe Exports,'" *Financial Times*, October 20, 1994, p. 3.

20. Ibid.

21. Tony Paterson, "The Time Bomb They Left Behind," *The European*, October 11–13, 1991, p. 12.

22. "China: Wolf or Sheep?" *The Economist*, January 22, 1994, p. 34.

23. Robert Thompson, "China's Row with the U.S. Reveals Discord in Beijing," *Financial Times*, October 4, 1991, p. 8.

24. "Joint Ventures in China: A Trickle or a Flood?" *The Economist*, August 6, 1994, pp. 56–57.

25. Vigor Keung Fung, "Chinese Are Eager to Take the Plunge," *The Asian Wall Street Journal*, November 17, 1986, p. 22.

26. Peter Ellingsen, "China Shuts Door on Rapid Reform," *Financial Times*, March 20, 1989, p. 26.

27. Joseph Kahn, "What Revolution? China Gets Rich Instead," *The Wall Street Journal*, September 21, 1994, p. A14.

28. "The South China Miracle," *The Economist*, October 5, 1991, pp. 19–22.

29. James McGregor, "China's Conundrum," *The Wall Street Journal*, September 24, 1991, p. A1.

30. Robert Thompson, "What Price Ideology?" *Financial Times*, October 18, 1991, p. 22.

31. Louise Lucas, "World Waits for the Second Chinese Wave, *Financial Times*, March 2, 1994, p. 20.

32. "China Business," *The Wall Street Journal*, November 18, 1994, p. A18; "China's Bad Debts: Red Ink," *The Economist*, November 19, 1994, p. 88; and Joseph Kahn and Neil Behrmann, "China Balks at Paying Its Trading Debts," *The Wall Street Journal*, November 25, 1994, p. A6.

33. Mark Skousen, "Bureaucratic Nightmare," *Forecasts & Strategies*, April 1989, p. 7.

34. Lynne Curry, "Trading in China is not for the lighthearted," *Financial Times*, April 24, 1991, p. VI.

35. Tony Walker, "Long March to a Private Bathroom," *Financial Times*, November 27–28, 1993, p. 9.

36. "Big," *The Economist*, April 30, 1994, p. 78.

37. Joann S. Lublin and Craig S. Smith, "U.S. Companies Struggle with Scarcity of Executives to Run Outposts in China," *The Wall Street Journal*, August 23, 1994, p. B1.

38. Peter Stein, "Foreign Businesspeople Find Dissidents Aren't Only Ones China Puts in Jail," *The Wall Street Journal*, May 25, 1994, p. A10.

39. "Summary of External Debt," *World Economic Outlook*, International Monetary Fund, October 1994, p. 173.

40. John Thornhill, "Russia Seeks More Time to Repay Its £51 Billion Debt," *Financial Times*, 27–28 August, 1994, p. 24.

41. Dana Milbank, "New Competition," *The Wall Street Journal*, September 21, 1994, pp. A1 and 7.

42. "Cocom: Controlling a Deadly Trade," *The Economist*, March 26, 1994, pp. 52 and 56.

43. William Dawkins, "Soviet Union Faces EC Probe on Chemical Pricing," *Financial Times*, August 1, 1989, p. 6.

44. Benjamin A. Sharman, in an interview reported in *Contemporary Perspectives in International Business*, ed. Harold W. Berkman and Ivan R. Vernon (Skokie, IL: Rand McNally, 1979), p. 142.

45. "Every Step Hurts," *The Economist*, January 14, 1988, pp. 44–45.

46. Peter Gumbel, "Soviet Trade Awaits the Next Revolution," *The Wall Street Journal*, February 21, 1989, p. A14.

47. Robert McCluskey, "The Bottom Line," *International Management*, July 1986, pp. 49–50.

48. Nancy Yoshihara, "China to Open Office to Aid U.S. Firms," *Los Angeles Times*, April 13, 1986, pt. 4, p. 4.

Chapter 18

1. David Holley, "Lifetime Employment Fading Fast in Japan," *Los Angeles Times*, January 24, 1994, p. D3; Andrew Fisher, "The End of a Tradition," *Financial Times*, July 20, 1994, p. 10; and Sara Olkon, "More Jobs Eliminated in Japan," *The Wall Street Journal*, December 29, 1994, p. A6.

2. David Holley, "Pink Slip in Japan: A Trip into Psychological Abyss," *The Los Angeles Times*, January 2, 1994, pp. A1 and 10.

3. Jathon Sapsford, "Unemployment in Japan Hits a 7-Year High," *The Wall Street Journal*, August 31, 1994, p. A7.

4. David Marsh, "A Crossroad of Frustrations," *Financial Times*, February 28, 1994, p. 13.

5. John-Thor Dahlburg, "Trading with Tiny Hands," *Los Angeles Times*, July 12, 1994, pp. H1 and 4.

6. Hugh Williamson, "Mixed Feelings," *Far Eastern Economic Review*, July 28, 1994, p. 20.

7. Manning Nash, "The Interplay of Culture and Management in a Guatemalan Textile Plant," in *Culture and Management*, ed. Ross A. Webber (Homewood, IL: Richard D. Irwin, 1969), pp. 317–24.

8. "How Regulation Kills New Jobs," *The Economist*, November 15, 1994, p. 78.

9. Amanda Bennett, "U.S. Concerns Topped European Firms in Job Creation in 1980s, Study Shows," *The Wall Street Journal*, November 18, 1994, p. A7A.

10. Peter Norman, "A 60-Point Strategy for Putting People Back to Work," *Financial Times*, June 8, 1994, p. 4.

11. *Business International*, July 2, 1983, pp. 209 and 211.

12. *Business International*, July 22, 1983, pp. 228–29.

13. Lisa Wood, "Search for Worldly-Wide Company Executives," *Financial Times*, April 9, 1991, p. 15.

14. Shawn Tully, "Europe: Best Business Schools," *Fortune*, May 23, 1988, pp. 106–10; see also Shawn Tully, "The Hunt for the Global Manager," *Fortune*, May 21, 1990, pp. 140–44.

15. Amanda Bennett, "Women's Job Contacts May Hold Them Back," *The Wall Street Journal*, September 4, 1991, p. B1.

16. Lesli Hicks, "Women Confront Gender Barriers South of the Border," *McAllen Monitor*, November 2, 1994, p. 1C.

17. "Women Chill Out," *Fortune*, June 27, 1994, p. 20; and Richard Donkin, "Women 'Opting Out' of Careers in Management," *Financial Times*, May 3, 1994, p. 8.

18. "Women on the Move—with Husbands in Tow," *Fortune*, October 17, 1994, p. 20.

19. John Frankenstein, "Training Experts to Manage in China," *The Asian Wall Street Journal*, August 26, 1985, p. 17.

20. Fortunat F. Mueller-Maerkl, "Dos and Don'ts in Selecting Managers for Foreign Operations," in *U.S.-German Economic Survey* (New York: German/American Chamber of Commerce, 1984), pp. 123–25.

21. Amanda Bennett, "Good Managers Share Same Skills Worldwide," *The Wall Street Journal*, September 4, 1991, p. B1.

22. Some writers regard paid home leave as an allowance, but our experience convinces us that it is a bonus, because ICs consistently give more frequent or longer home leaves to employees working in less desirable assignments.

23. Joann S. Lublin, "Employee Stock Plans Run into Foreign Snags," *The Wall Street Journal*, September 16, 1991, p. B1.

24. Joann S. Lublin, "Firms Woo Executives from Third Countries," *The Wall Street Journal*, September 16, 1991, p. B1.

25. G. W. Hallmark and Charles W. Rogers III, "The Challenge of Providing Benefit and Compensation Programs for Third-Country Nationals," in *The International Essays for Business Decision Makers*, vol. 3, ed. Mark W. Winchester (New York: AMACOM for the Center for International Business, 1978).

26. *Handbook for Employees Transferring to France*, Ernst & Whinney, International Series, March 1980; *to the United States*, March 1980; *to Belgium*, April 1980; *to the United Kingdom*, April 1980; *to Italy*, June 1980; *to Hong Kong*, October 1980; *to Luxembourg*, October 1980; *to Denmark*, October 1980; *Abroad*, November 1980; and more. They are updated periodically.

Chapter 19

1. "A Guide to Global Sourcing," *Journal of Business Strategy*, March–April 1991, pp. 21–25.

2. "Sales by Nonbank U.S. Parents and Foreign Affiliates," *Survey of Current Business*, June 1994, Table 8, p. 51.

3. "Total U.S. Trade and Merchandise Trade of Nonbank Affiliates, 1992," *Survey of Current Business*, July 1994, Table 14, p. 168.

4. Richard B. Chase and Nicholas J. Aquilano, *Production and Operations Management*, 7th ed. (Burr Ridge, IL: Richard D. Irwin, 1995), p. 716.

5. "Global Sourcing at Second Glance," *Global Competitor*, Summer 1994, pp. 70–74.

6. "U.S. Companies Come Back Home," *Fortune*, December 30, 1991, pp. 106–12.

7. "Du Pont Sets Up S.A. Site," *San Antonio Express-News*, October 27, 1994, p. 1F.

8. Lloyd Dobyns and Clare Crawford-Mason, *Quality or Else* (Boston: Houghton Mifflin, 1991), pp. 10–17.

9. *Production and Operations Management*, 6th ed., p. 229.

10. *Quality or Else*, p. 18.

11. Shigeo Shingo, *Non-Stock Production: The Shingo System for Continuous Improvement* (Cambridge, MA: Productivity Press, 1988), p. 36.

12. *Production and Operations Management*, 7th ed., p. 240.

13. "Innovation," *Business Week*, Special Issue, June 1989, p. 107.

14. "New Work Order," *The Economist*, April 9, 1994, p. 76.

15. "Motivation Systems for Small-Group Quality Control Activities," *Japan Economic Journal*, June 28, 1983, pp. 33–35.

16. *Production and Operations Management*, 7th ed., p. 240.

17. Franklin Strier, "Quality Circles in the United States: Fad or Fixture?" *Business Forum*, Summer 1984, pp. 19–23.

18. *Production and Operations Management*, 5th ed., pp. 736–68.

19. "Installing Successful Factories in Developing Countries," *International Management*, September–October 1990, p. 29.

20. *Production and Operations Management*, 6th ed., p. 908.

21. Ibid., p. 913.

22. "Digital Factory," *Fortune*, November 14, 1994, pp. 93–108.

23. "Ringing the Changes," *International Management*, September 1994, p. 59.

24. "Herr Lazarus," *The Economist*, March 18, 1995, pp. 63–64.

25. "Lean, Mean, and Mobile," *The Journal of European Business*, July–August 1993, pp. 53–56.

26. "An Eastern Breeze in the Med," *Financial Times*, June 25, 1991, p. 18.

27. "A Select Few Poised to Lead Business in the 90s," *The Wall Street Journal*, Centennial Edition, June 23, 1989, p. A3.

28. "Crunch at Chrysler," *The Economist*, November 12, 1994, pp. 93–94.

29. "How AVCO's Quality System Boosts Profits Worldwide," *Business International*, January 18, 1988, pp. 9–11.

30. "The Export of a Japanese Idea," *The Economist*, April 25, 1987, p. 68.

31. "The Winds of Change Blow Everywhere," *Business Week*, October 17, 1994, pp. 92–93.

32. "French Quality Circles Multiply," *International Management*, December 1986, p. 31.

33. " 'Just-in-Time' Inventories Putting Australian Firms on More Competitive Footing," *Business Asia*, November 9, 1987, p. 360.

34. "How to Win the Baldrige Award," *Fortune*, April 23, 1990, pp. 101–16.

35. *Production and Operations Management*, 6th ed., pp. 229 and 237.

36. "Ford Tests Just-in-Time Parts Delivery at German Plant," *Automotive News*, October 17, 1988, p. 40.

37. Conversation with Ford International representatives, June 19, 1989.

38. D. J. Teece, "Technology Transfer by Multinational Firms," *Economic Journal*, June 1977, pp. 242–61.

39. A highly automated machine might make only one or two sizes or types of a product, whereas a general-purpose machine may be capable of producing not only all sizes of a product but other products as well. Its output, however, may be as little as 1 percent of that of a specialized machine.

40. The skill level required of general-purpose machine operators is much higher than that required of operators attending automated machinery, but it is lower than that needed to set up and maintain this equipment.

41. This does not mean that unit production costs are lower in the small plants, and certainly the coordination of their activities will be formidable. The example does illustrate the extreme range of possibilities when capital costs are a primary consideration. From Colin Norman, *Soft Technology, Hard Choice* (Washington, DC: Worldwatch Institute, June 1978), p. 14.

42. *Transnational Corporations in World Development* (New York: United Nations, 1988), p. 170.

43. Louis T. Wells, *Technology and Third World Countries*, ILO Working Paper, Geneva, 1982.

Chapter 20

1. There is almost always some cost for protection, and an important management function is to compare the magnitude of the risk with the cost of protection against it.

2. If you were dealing in a currency more actively traded than the krone, such as the British, Canadian, French, Japanese, Swiss, or German currency, you would use the 180-day futures quotation for that currency.

3. Covered positions are also referred to as "square" or "perfect" positions.

4. In every IC, there is one central company at the top of the organization. That company is called the parent company. The other companies are referred to as affiliated or subsidiary companies.

5. The power of ICs to control the timing and currencies of payment and of asset accumulation has not been ignored by governments. In furtherance of their tax and exchange control policies, most countries have legal limits on acceleration, delays, and intra-IC netting.

6. Currencies may be fixed in value in terms of each other by international agreement; if there are no such agreements, they are said to float.

7. The Netherlands and Belgium are both members of the European Monetary System.

8. Jeff Madura, *International Financial Management*, 3rd ed. (St. Paul, MN: West Publishing Company, 1992), p. 341.

9. Ibid., p. 621.

10. A blocked-currency situation arises either because there is no satisfactory market for the currency or because of a country's laws.

11. In such circumstances, the equivalent amount is subject to some negotiation because a blocked, nonconvertible currency does not have a free market spot or other exchange rate, which would be used when dealing with two convertible currencies.

12. When equity securities (stock) are issued, part of the ownership is being sold. No money is being borrowed that must be repaid, as is the case when debt securities (bonds) are issued.

13. The international, or Euro-type, capital market has been created by national currencies being traded, borrowed, and lent outside their countries of origin. Thus, U.S. dollars outside the United States are Eurodollars, and German deutsche marks outside Germany are Euromarks.

14. "What Do They Mean by That?" *Financial Times*, November 16, 1994, p. V.

15. "A Risky Old World," *The Economist*, October 1, 1994, pp. 18–20.

16. *Mitsui Trade News*, March–April 1987, pp. 1–4.

17. John-Thor Dahlburg, "PepsiCo to Swap Cola for Soviet Vodka and Ships," *Los Angeles Times*, April 10, 1990, pp. A1 and 18.

18. Michael McCarthy, Jr., "Pepsi Seeking to Boost Sales to Ukrainians," *The Wall Street Journal*, October 23, 1992, p. A10.

19. Shelley Neumeier, "Why Countertrade Is Getting Hot," *Fortune*, June 29, 1992, p. 25.

20. Richard L. Holman, "World Trade Volume Grows," *The Wall Street Journal*, March 26, 1991, p. A18; and "World Trade Growth Sputters," *The Wall Street Journal*, March 18, 1992, p. A10.

21. Stephen S. Cohen and John Zysman, "Countertrade Deals Are Running out of Control," *Los Angeles Times*, March 23, 1986, part 4, pp. 3 and 7.

22. "Countertrade: Avoiding Problems with Suppliers," *Business Eastern Europe*, May 16, 1988, p. 155.

23. Alan Spence, "East-West Countertrade Entering New Era of Complexity," *Financial Times*, December 13, 1988, p. 38.

24. Ibid.

25. Ronald E. Hayt, "East-West Trade Growth Potential for the 1980s," *Columbia Journal of World Business*, Spring 1978, p. 63.

26. *The Economist*, December 13, 1986, p. 84.

Chapter 21

1. Wroe Alderson, *Dynamic Marketing Behavior* (Homewood, IL: Richard D. Irwin, 1965), pp. 75–97. In the late 1970s, McCarthy and other writers of "principles of marketing" texts discussed the use of the transvection as a unit of analysis.

2. "Rethinking Vision and Mission," *Planning Review*, September–October 1994, pp. 9–11.

3. Pfizer, *Annual Report*, 1993, inside front cover.

4. Du Pont, *Annual Report*, 1992, inside front cover and p. 1.

5. Grand Metropolitan, *Annual Report*, 1993, inside front cover.

6. Goodyear Tire & Rubber, *Annual Report*, 1994, pp. 2–4.

7. Ibid., p. 2.

8. Paul Shrivastava, "Integrating Strategy Formulation with Organizational Culture," *Journal of Business Strategy*, November–December 1985, pp. 103–11.

9. Pepsico, *Annual Report*, 1989, pp. 12–13.

10. P. J. Shoemaker, "Multiple Scenario Development: Its Conceptual and Behavioral Foundation," *Strategic Management Journal*, March 1993, p. 195.

11. "Scenario-Based Planning: Decision Model for the Learning Organization," *Planning Review*, March–April 1994, p. 7.

12. "Managing the Management Tools," *Planning Review*, September–October 1994, pp. 20–24.

13. "Who Should Be Responsible for Business Strategy?" *Journal of Business Strategy*, November–December 1988, pp. 40–41.

14. "The New Breed of Strategic Planner," *Business Week*, September 17, 1984, p. 62.

15. Ibid., p. 62.

16. Ibid., p. 64.

17. Ibid., p. 66.

18. P. W. Beck, "Corporate Planning for an Uncertain Future," *Long-Range Planning*, August 1982, p. 14.

19. Frederick W. Gluck, "A Fresh Look at Strategic Management," *Journal of Business Strategy*, Fall 1985, p. 6.

20. Christopher A. Bartlett, "MNCs: Get Off the Reorganization Merry-Go-Round," *Harvard Business Review*, March–April 1983, p. 138.

21. Ford, *Ford around the World*, 1994, p. 4; and IBM, *Annual Report*, 1994, p. 6.

22. "Seven Organizational Alternatives for MNCs in the 1990s," *Business International*, February 13, 1989, p. 46.

23. Arthur A. Thompson and A. J. Strickland, *Crafting and Implementing Strategy*, 6th ed. (Burr Ridge, IL: Richard D. Irwin, 1995), p. 276.

24. "Barons Swept Out of Fiefdoms," and "End of a Corporate Era," *Financial Times*, March 30, 1995, p. 15.

25. "The Virtual Corporation," *Business Week*, February 8, 1993, pp. 98–103.

26. "The Horizontal Corporation," *Business Week*, December 20, 1993, pp. 76–81.

27. "Jack Welch Reinvents General Electric Again, *The Economist*, March 30, 1991, p. 59.

28. Richard D. Daft, *Organization Theory and Design*, 4th ed. (St. Paul, MN: West Publishing, 1992), pp. 226–28.

29. "Is Big Still Good?" *Fortune*, April 20, 1992, p. 52.

30. Ibid., p. 60.

Chapter 22

1. Louise Kehoe, "Radical Change of IBM Format," *Financial Times*, November 21, 1991, p. 27.

2. Richard L. Hudson and Joann S. Lublin, "Power at Multinationals Shifts to Home Office," *The Wall Street Journal*, September 9, 1994, pp. B1 and 3.

3. Teresa Watanabe, "IRS Seeks More Power to Probe Foreign Firms," *Los Angeles Times*, February 22, 1991, pp. D1 and 12.

4. Richard L. Hudson, ". . . Power . .," *The Wall Street Journal*, September 9, 1994, p. B1.

5. Wendell W. McCulloch, Jr., "Japan's Trade and Investment with the Less-Developed Countries," *The Wall Street Journal*, October 3, 1980, p. 19.

6. Richard Thomas Cupitt, "Foreign Political Risk Assessment," *The International Trade Journal*, Summer 1990, pp. 341–56.

7. Richard F. Janssen, "U.S. Lenders Taking New Looks at Risks from Political, Social Upheavals Abroad," *The Wall Street Journal*, March 13, 1979, p. 7.

8. "New Work Order," *The Economist*, April 9, 1994, p. 76.

9. William Bridges, "The End of the Job," *Fortune*, September 19, 1994, pp. 62–74.

10. Robert Taylor, "Apocalyptic Vision of a Near-Workless World," *Financial Times*, January 1, 1995, p. 20. This is a review of Jeremy Rifkin, *The End of Work: The Decline of the Global Labor Force, and the Dawn of the Post-Market Era* (New York: G. P. Putnam's Sons, 1995).

11. "Technology and Unemployment," *The Economist*, February 11, 1995, pp. 21–23.

12. Gene Bylinsky, "The Digital Factory," *Fortune*, November 14, 1994, pp. 92–110.

13. "Mess.com," *The Economist*, October 15, 1994, p. 82.

14. Rick Tetzeli, "Managing in a World out of Control," *Fortune*, September 5, 1994, p. 111.

Glossary

absolute advantage The advantage enjoyed by a country because it can produce a product at a lower cost than can other countries.

accidental exposure Export business obtained through no effort of the exporter.

accounting exposure The total net of accounting statement items on which loss could occur because of currency exchange rate changes.

adjustment assistance Financial and technical assistance to workers, firms, and communities to help them adjust to import competition.

ad valorem tariff or duty Literally "according to the value." A method in which customs duties or tariffs are established and charged as a percentage of the value of imported goods.

advertising, paid Nonpersonal presentation of ideas, goods, or services by an identified sponsor.

advising bank The bank that notifies the beneficiary of the opening of a letter of credit. The advising bank makes no payment commitment.

aesthetics A culture's sense of beauty and good taste.

affiliated company May be a subsidiary or a company in which an IC has less than 100 percent ownership.

A.G. Aktien-Gesellschaft. A joint stock company in Germany.

agency office An office of a foreign bank in the United States that cannot accept domestic deposits. It seeks business for the bank when U.S. companies operate internationally.

air waybill For goods shipped by air, performs the functions of a bill of lading in land surface transport or of a marine bill of lading in water transport.

allowance Extra payments to expatriate employees to meet the higher costs they incur abroad.

American depository receipt (ADR) Stock of a foreign corporation is deposited at an American bank. The bank issues an ADR, not the corporation's stock certificate, to an American investor who buys shares of that corporation. The stock certificate is kept at the bank.

antiboycott law An American law against complying with the Arab countries' boycott of Israel.

antitrust laws Laws to prevent business from engaging in such practices as price-fixing or market sharing.

appreciation An increase in the value of one asset in terms of another.

apprenticeship program Enables a person to learn a job skill by working with a skilled worker.

appropriate technology The technology—advanced, intermediate, or primitive—that most fits the society using it.

arbitrage The simultaneous purchase and sale of something in two (or more) markets at a time when it is selling (being bought) at different prices in the markets. Profit is the price differential minus the cost.

arbitration The settlement of a dispute between parties by a third, presumably unbiased, party, not a court of law.

arm's-length transaction A transaction between two or more unrelated parties. (A transaction between two subsidiaries of an IC would not be an arm's-length transaction.)

associations Social units based on age, sex, or common interest, not on kinship.

back-to-back letter of credit (L/C) A paying bank that will pay the exporter opens a back-to-back L/C based on the underlying L/C the exporter's supplier (a manufacturer, for example) may be paid.

back-to-back loans A unit of one IC lends to a unit of a second IC; and at the same time and in equivalent amounts, another unit of the second IC lends to another unit of the first.

backward vertical integration Establishing facilities to manufacture inputs used in the production of a firm's final products.

balance of payments (BOP) A financial statement that compares all reported payments by residents of one country to residents of other countries with payments to domestic residents by foreign residents. If more money has been paid out than received, the BOP is in deficit. If the opposite condition exists, the BOP is in surplus.

banker's acceptance A draft drawn, for example, by an exporter on an importer's bank. If the bank accepts the draft, the bank has agreed to pay in accordance with its terms.

bank swaps To avoid currency exchange problems, a bank in a soft-currency country will lend to an IC subsidiary there. The IC or its bank will make hard currency available to the lending bank outside the soft-currency country.

barter The exchange of goods or services for goods or services. No money is used.

bill of exchange (draft) An unconditional written order calling on the party to whom it is addressed to pay on demand or at a future date a sum of money to the order of a named party or to the bearer. Examples are acceptances or the commercial bank check.

bill of lading (B/L) A receipt given by a carrier of goods received and contract for their delivery. Usually a B/L is made to the order of someone and is negotiable. The B/L is also a document of title with which the holder may claim the goods from the carrier.

blocked account Financial assets that cannot be transferred into another currency or out of the country without the government's permission.

bonded warehouse Warehouse authorized by customs authorities for storage of goods on which payment of import duties is deferred until the goods are removed.

bonds: (1) Eurobond A long-term bond marketed internationally in countries other than the country of the currency in which it is denominated. The issue is not subject to national restrictions. (2) **zero-coupon bonds** Pay no periodic interest (hence their name), so the total yield is obtained entirely as capital gain on the final maturity date. (3) **dual-currency bonds** Denominated in one currency but pay interest in another currency at a fixed rate of exchange. Dual-currency bonds can also pay redemption proceeds in a different currency than the currency of denomination. (4) **floating-rate bonds** The most commonly issued instrument, the interest coupons on which are adjusted regularly according to the level of some base interest rate plus a fixed spread.

bonuses Extra payments to expatriates because of hardships and inconveniences encountered in some foreign postings.

boomerang effect Refers to the fact that technology sold to companies in another nation may be used to produce goods that will then compete with those of the seller of the technology.

bottleneck Operation in production system whose output sets limit for entire system's output.

bottom-up planning Planning process that begins at the lowest level in the organization and continues upward.

brain drain The loss by a country of its most intelligent and best educated people.

branch office An office or department of a company at a location away from headquarters. It is a part of the company and not a separate legal entity, as is a subsidiary, an affiliate, or a joint venture.

Bretton Woods A resort in New Hampshire at which bank and treasury officials of the major Allied powers met near the end of World War II. There they estab-

lished the International Monetary Fund, the World Bank, and an international monetary system.

bribes Gifts or payments to induce the receiver to do something illegal for the giver.

buffer stock A supply of a commodity that the executive of a commodity agreement tries to accumulate and hold so that when the price of the commodity begins to rise above desirable levels, sales can be made from that stock to dampen the price rise.

Canadian Shield A massive land area of bedrock covering one-half of Canada's landmass.

capital intensive Describes processes that require a high concentration of capital relative to labor per unit of output and products produced by such processes. The opposite is labor intensive.

capitalism All possible activities are performed by private business or persons rather than by a government.

cartel An organization of suppliers that controls the supply and price of a commodity. To be successful, a cartel should have relatively few members who control most of the export supply of the commodity; the members must observe the cartel rules; and the commodity must be a necessity with a price-inelastic demand.

caste system An aspect of Hinduism by which the entire society is divided into four groups plus the outcasts, and each is assigned a certain class of work.

central banks Government institutions with authority over the size and growth of the national monetary stock. Central banks frequently regulate commercial banks and usually act as the government's fiscal agent.

centrally planned economy Governments plan and direct almost all economic activity and usually own the factors of production.

centrally planned markets Markets in which there is almost no free market activity and the government owns all major factors of production, controls labor, and tries to plan all activity.

central reserve assets Gold, SDRs, ECUs, or hard foreign currencies held in a nation's treasury.

certificate of review Legal document issued by U.S. Department of Commerce that grants immunity from state and federal antitrust prosecution to export trading companies.

chaebol Large South Korean conglomerates, mostly family-owned and directed, that have succeeded worldwide in such fields as microchips, electronics, construction, and shipbuilding. Korean law prohibits banks from being part of chaebol.

CIF (cost, insurance, and freight) A term used in the delivery of goods from one party to another. The price includes the costs of the goods, the maritime or other appropriate transportation, the insurance premium, and the freight charges to the destination.

climate The meteorological conditions, including temperature, precipitation, and wind, that prevail in a region.

cluster analysis Statistical technique dividing objects into groups so that the objects within each group are similar.

COCOM Voluntary group of most NATO nations that administers a common set of export controls to prevent transfer of sensitive goods to hostile nations.

codetermination A system in which representatives of labor participate in the management of a company.

collection documents All documents submitted to a buyer for the purpose of receiving payment for a shipment.

collective bargaining Bargaining between an employer and a labor union about employee wages and working conditions.

commodity agreement An agreement between the producers and consumers of a commodity (for example, tin, cocoa, or rubber) to regulate the production, price, and trade of the commodity.

common external tariff Under an agreement reached by a group of nations, such as the EU, the same level of tariffs is imposed by these nations on all goods imported from other nations.

communism A theory of a classless society conceived by Marx. Lenin, Stalin, and others developed it differently.

comparative advantage Unless a country has the same absolute advantage in producing all goods and services, there would be some goods and services in which it had less relative advantage. It would gain by importing those and exporting the ones in which it had an absolute advantage, or the greatest relative advantage.

compensation A form of countertrade involving payment in goods and cash.

compensatory financing A program to assist countries in financial difficulties due to drops in export earnings because of natural causes, such as drought, or because of international market price decreases. The IMF and the EU have compensatory financing programs.

compensatory trade Any transaction that involves asset transfer as a condition of purchase.

competitive alliance Cooperation between competitors for specific purposes.

competitive analysis Process in which principal competitors are identified and their objectives, strengths, weaknesses, and product lines are assessed.

competitor intelligence system Procedure for gathering, analyzing, and disseminating information about a firm's competitors.

compound duty A form of import duty consisting of an ad valorem duty and a specific duty.

confirm Act of a correspondent bank in the seller's country by which it agrees to honor the issuing bank's letter of credit.

confirmed letter of credit (L/C) An L/C confirmed by a bank other than the opening bank. Thus, it is an obligation of more than one bank.

confiscation Seizure by a government of foreign-owned assets that is not followed by prompt, effective, and adequate compensation.

Confucian work ethic Same as the Protestant work ethic. The term is used in Asian nations where Confucianism is a major religion.

conservative In American political usage, a conservative advocates minimum government activity.

contingency plan Plan for the best- or worst-case scenarios or for critical events that could have a severe impact on the firm.

contract manufacturing Manufacturing of a product or component by one company for another company. The two companies may or may not be related by stock ownership, common parent, or otherwise.

controllable forces The forces internal to the firm that management administers to adapt to changes in the uncontrollable environmental forces.

convertible currencies Currencies that may be changed for or converted into other currencies, at least for current account payments, without government permission.

cooperative exporters Established international manufacturers who export other manufacturers' goods as well as their own.

coproduction A form of industrial cooperation in which two or more factories produce components for a final product.

corporate strategy Action plan to enable an organization to reach its objectives.

cottage industry Production away from a central factory, typically in the worker's own home or cottage. Workers are paid on a piece-rate basis, or so much for each unit produced.

counterfeiting Illegal use of a well-known manufacturer's brand name on copies of the firm's merchandise.

countertrade A transaction in which goods are exchanged for goods. Payment by a purchaser is entirely or partially in goods instead of hard currencies for products or technology from other countries.

countervailing duty An additional amount of tariff levied on an import that is found to have benefited from an export subsidy.

country risk assessment Evaluating the risks before lending or investing in a country.

covered investment or interest arbitrage Investment in a second currency that is "covered" by a forward sale of that currency to protect against exchange rate fluctuations. Profit depends on interest rate differentials minus the discount or plus the premium on a forward sale.

covering Buying or selling foreign currencies in amounts equivalent to future payments to be made or received. A means of protection against loss due to currency exchange rate fluctuations.

credit or money market hedge Hedging by borrowing the currency of risk, converting it immediately to the ultimately desired currency, and repaying the loan when payment is received.

cross investment Foreign direct investment made by oligopolistic firms in each other's home country as a defense measure.

cross rate The direct exchange rate between two non-U.S. dollar currencies. It is determined by observing the U.S. dollar exchange rate for each of the other two currencies and, from those rates, computing their direct exchange rate.

culture The rules, techniques, institutions, and artifacts that characterize human populations.

currency area The group of countries whose currencies are pegged to any one DC currency. Many LDCs peg the value of their currency to that of their major DC trading partner.

currency exchange controls A government's controls over how much foreign currency its residents or visitors can have and how much they must pay for it.

currency swap The exchange of one currency into another at an agreed rate and a reversal of that exchange at the same rate at the end of the swap contract period.

customhouse broker Independent business that handles import shipments for compensation.

customs union An arrangement between two or more countries whereby they eliminate tariffs and other import restrictions on one another's goods and establish a common tariff on the goods from all other countries.

debt capital Money raised by selling bonds, the principal and interest on which must be repaid.

debt default When a debtor fails or refuses to pay a debt.

debt rescheduling Defaulted debt is renegotiated, giving the debtor a longer time to pay, a lower interest rate, or both.

delayering Removing levels of middle management.

demonstration effect The result of having seen others with desirable goods.

demurrage Charge assessed by a carrier on an exporter or an importer for excess time taken to unload or load a vessel.

depreciation of a currency A decline in the value of a currency in terms of another currency or in terms of gold. *Depreciation* and *devaluation* are used interchangeably.

derivatives A contract, the value of which changes in concert with the price movements in a related or underlying commodity or financial instrument. The term covers standardized exchange-traded futures and options as well as over-the-counter swaps, options, and other customized instruments.

devaluation Depreciation of a currency by official government action.

developed A classification for all industrialized nations; that is, those that are more developed technically.

developed countries (DCs) Industrialized countries.

developing A classification for the world's lower-income nations that are less technically developed.

development banks Banks that aid less developed countries (LDCs) in economic development. They may lend or invest money and encourage local ownership. They may be worldwide, regional, or national.

direct exporting The exporting of goods and services by the firm that produces them.

direct investment Sufficient investment to obtain at least some voice in management. The U.S. government considers 10 percent or more equity in a foreign company to be direct investment.

dirty float A currency that floats in value in terms of other currencies but is not free of government intervention. Governments intervene to "smooth" or "manage" fluctuations or to maintain desired exchange rates.

discretionary income The amount of income remaining after paying taxes and making essential purchases.

disposable income The amount of income remaining after taxes.

distributors Independent importers who buy for their own account for resale.

district export councils Groups of volunteer businesspeople in every state that are appointed by the U.S. Department of Commerce to assist exporters.

documentary drafts Drafts accompanied by such documents as invoices, bills of lading, inspection certificates, and insurance papers.

domestication Term used to indicate process in which a host government brings pressure to force a foreign owner to turn over partial ownership to the host country government or host country citizens.

domestic environment All the uncontrollable forces originating in the home country that surround and influence the firm's life and development.

domestic international sales corporation (DISC) A subsidiary corporation of a U.S. company that is incorporated in a state of the United States for the purpose of exporting from the United States. DISCs are given certain tax advantages. Generally, they have been superseded by foreign sales corporations.

drafts (bills of exchange) Orders drawn by a drawer that order a second party, the drawee, to pay a sum of money to a payee. The payee may be the same party as the drawer.

drawback The reimbursement of the tariff paid on an imported component that is later exported. When a component is imported into the United States, a tariff is levied on it and paid by the importer. If that component is later exported, the exporter is entitled to get 99 percent of the tariff amount from U.S. Customs.

drawee See drafts.

drawer See drafts.

dumping Selling abroad at prices lower than those charged in the home or other markets.

duties (tariffs) Amounts charged when goods are imported into a country. If such duties are based on the values of the goods, they are called ad valorem. If they are based on the number of items imported, they are called specified.

earned income Income derived from efforts, labor, sales, or active participation in business. Salaries, wages, bonuses, and commissions are examples. Un-earned income is a return on investment of money or time. Examples are interest, dividends, and royalties. The distinction is important for purposes of U.S. taxation of American residents abroad.

East-West trade Trade between the centrally planned economies of the communist block (East) and the more market-oriented economies of the OECD nations (West). Recent developments, such as the breakup of the Soviet Union and the end of the COMECON trade bloc that it dominated, have reduced the number of avowedly communist countries. Many of those countries are trying to achieve market economies and democracy, but progress is slow and difficult at best.

Edge Act corporation A subsidiary of a U.S. commercial bank that operates in a foreign country. The Edge subsidiary, operating abroad, is free of restraints of U.S. law and may perform whatever services and functions are legal in the countries where it operates.

employee facilities Schools, cafeterias, housing, recreation, or other employer-provided facilities.

environment All the forces surrounding and influencing the life and development of the firm.

environmental scanning Procedure in which a firm scans the world for changes in the environmental forces that might affect it.

equity capital Money raised by selling corporate stock that represents ownership of the corporation.

equity-related bonds Bonds that are convertible at the option of the holder into other securities of the issuer, usually common stock-type equity. Called *convertibles* in the United States.

escape clause A legal provision concerning products whose tariffs have been reduced. If, thereafter, imports increase and threaten the domestic producers of those products, the escape clause permits the tariffs to be put back up.

estimation by analogy Using a market factor that is successful in one market to estimate demand in a similar market.

ethnocentricity A belief in the superiority of one's own ethnic group.

Eurobonds Bonds that are issued outside the restriction applying to domestic offerings and are syndicated and traded mostly from London. Most of these bonds are denominated in U.S. dollars.

Eurocurrency A currency being used or traded outside the country that issued it.

Eurodollar The U.S. dollar is the most widely used Eurocurrency.

European Currency Unit (ECU) A currency unit established by the European Monetary System. Its value is determined by reference to the value of a "basket" of currencies. The currencies in the basket are those of the system's member-countries.

European Economic Area The European Free Trade Area consisting of the EU and EFTA.

European Monetary Cooperation Fund (EMCF) Lends assistance to EMS member-countries that have difficulties in keeping their currencies within the agreed value relationships.

European Monetary System (EMS) A system, established in 1979, under which West European countries agreed to keep their currency values within an established range in relation to one another.

exchange rate The price of one currency stated in another currency.

exchange rate risk In activities involving two or more currencies, the risk that losses can occur as a result of changes in their relative value.

Eximbank (Export-Import Bank) Principal federal government agency that aids American exporters by means of loans, guarantees, and insurance programs.

export bill of lading Contract of carriage between shipper and carrier. Straight bill of lading is nonnegotiable; an endorsed "to-order" bill gives the holder claim on merchandise.

export draft An unconditional order drawn by the seller on the buyer to pay the draft's amount on presentation (sight draft) or at an agreed future date (time draft) that must be paid before the buyer receives shipping documents.

export incentives Subsidies or tax rebates paid by governments to companies to encourage them to export.

export licenses A government document that permits the exporter to export designated goods to certain destinations. In the United States, the export license will be either a general export license or a validated export license.

export management company A company that acts as the export department for other companies. It performs all export-related services for its customers except supplying the product.

export processing zones Specific and limited areas into which imported components may be brought for further processing. The finished product must be reexported to avoid payment of import duties.

export trading company A firm established principally to export domestic goods and services and help unrelated companies export their products.

exposure netting An open position in two or more currencies whose strengths and weaknesses are thought to balance one another.

expropriation Seizure by a government of foreign-owned assets. Such seizure is not contrary to international law if it is followed by prompt, adequate, and effective compensation. If not, it is called confiscation.

extended family Includes relatives beyond the parents and children.

extortion The demand for payments to keep the receiver from causing harm to the payer.

extraterritorial application of laws Attempts by a government to apply its laws outside its territorial borders

factor A buyer, at a discount, of a company's receivables with short-term maturities of no longer than a year.

factor endowment A country is or is not endowed with one or more of the factors of production, capital, labor, and natural resources.

factoring Discounting without recourse an account receivable.

factory door cost The production cost of a good or service to which marketing and general administrative costs have not been added.

firm surveillance The IMF has the power to monitor the exchange rate policies of member-nations.

fiscal policies Government policies about the collection and spending of money.

fixed exchange rates A system under which the values of currencies in terms of other currencies are fixed by intergovernmental agreement and by governmental intervention in the currency exchange markets.

fixed interest rate An interest rate that is set when a loan is made and remains the same for the life of the loan regardless of whether other interest rates rise or fall.

floating exchange rates A system in which the values of currencies in terms of other currencies are determined by the supply of and demand for the currencies in currency markets. If governments do not intervene in the markets, the float is said to be *clean*. If they do intervene, the float is said to be *dirty*.

floating interest rates A loan situation in which the interest rate set when a loan is made may rise or fall as the interest rates of some reference, such as LIBOR or the prime rate, vary. Sometimes called *variable rates*.

floating-rate notes or bonds Debt instruments with floating or variable interest rates. The interest rates are pegged to a fluctuating interest rate, such as the six-month LIBOR rate.

fluctuating exchange rates See *floating exchange rates*.

Foreign Corrupt Practices Act of 1977 An American law against making questionable payments when American companies do business abroad.

foreign exchange The exchanges of the currency of one country for that of another country.

foreign exchange rates Prices of one currency in terms of other currencies.

foreign exchange reserves Gold, SDRs, U.S. dollars, and other convertible currencies held in a nation's treasury.

foreign financing Occurs when a foreign company or other borrower comes to a nation's capital market and borrows in the local currency; for example, when an Italian company borrows U.S. dollars in New York or French francs in Paris.

foreign freight forwarder Independent business that handles export shipments for compensation.

foreign national pricing Local pricing in another country.

foreign sales corporation (FSC) A corporation provided for in the Tax Reform Act of 1984. The FSC replaces the domestic international sales corporation (DISC) as a tax incentive for exporters.

foreign tax credit The credit an American taxpayer may take against American income tax for tax levied on the same income by a foreign government.

foreign trade zone (FTZ) American version of a free trade zone. In an FTZ, goods may be imported and manufactured or handled and changed in any way. No tariff need be paid unless and until the goods are removed from the FTZ into the country where the FTZ is located.

forfaiting Has the same purposes and procedures as factoring, which is the sale by an exporter of its accounts receivable for immediate cash. However, there are two important differences: (1) factoring involves credit terms of no more than 180 days, while forfaiting may involve years; (2) factoring does not usually cover political and transfer risks, while forfaiting does.

forward contract A contract to exchange one currency for another currency at an agreed exchange rate at a future date, usually 30, 90, or 180 days. May be used to hedge. See *forward rate*.

forward rate The cost today for a commitment by one party to deliver to or take from another party an agreed amount of a currency at a fixed future date. This rate is established by the forward contract.

Fourth World The poorest of the world's countries.

franchising A franchisee pays a franchisor for the right to use the franchisor's logo, procedures, materials, and advertising.

free trade zones An area designated by the government of a country for duty-free entry of any nonprohibited goods.

friendship, commerce, and navigation (FCN) treaties The basic agreements between nations about such matters as treatment of each others' citizens or companies.

fringe benefits Payments or other benefits given to employees over and above base wages.

futures contract An agreement between a buyer and a seller to exchange a particular good for a particular price at a specified future date.

general export license Any export license covering export commodities for which a validated license is not required. No formal application is required.

generalized systems of preference (GSP) An agreement under the auspices of WTO under which many products of developing nations are provided duty-free access to developed nations.

general trading companies Exist in many countries, including the United States, though the Japanese versions of these companies, called *sogo shosha* in Japanese, are the best known. For many years, the sogo shosha have imported and distributed commodities and products for use by Japanese industries and consumers, sought foreign customers for Japanese companies, and exported to other companies.

geocentric As used in this book, hiring and promoting employees because of their abilities without reference to their nationality or race.

gilts Technically, British and Irish government securities, though the term also includes issues of local British authorities.

global company A company that markets a standardized product worldwide and allows only minimum adaptations to local conditions and tastes from country to country. Its financial, marketing, and advertising strategies are global with little differentiation among countries or areas as to product. Other authors, particularly when writing about the automobile industry, mean the company's ability to source parts and components from subsidiaries in several countries for assembly in the market country or area.

GmbH Gesellschaft mit beschrankter Haftung (organization with limited ability). A German form of business organization.

GNP/capita The gross national product of a nation divided by its population (an arithmetic mean).

gold exchange standard The system established at Bretton Woods whereby the value of one currency (the U.S. dollar) was set in terms of gold. The United States held gold and agreed that when another country accumulated U.S. dollars, it could exchange them for gold at the set value.

gold standard A system under which currency values are set in terms of gold and each country agrees that if a second country accumulates more of a first country's currency than it wants for other purposes, the second country can exchange the first country's currency for that amount of the first country's gold.

gold tranche The amount of gold paid by a country as its contributed capital in the International Monetary Fund.

gray market Where goods are sold, that are either legal but unauthorized imports bearing domestic manufacturers' trade names or are exports diverted to the domestic market.

gross domestic product (GDP) The market value of a country's output attributable to factors of production located in the country's territory. It differs from GNP by the exclusion of net factor income payments, such as interest and dividends received from, or paid to, the rest of the world. See *gross national product (GNP)*.

gross national product (GNP) The market value of all the final goods and services produced by a national economy over a period of time, usually a year.

Group of 5 The term used for meetings of the finance ministers and central bank governors of France, the Federal Republic of Germany, Japan, the United Kingdom, and the United States.

Group of 7 The Group of 5 plus Canada and Italy.

Group of 10 The Group of 7 plus Belgium, the Netherlands, and Sweden.

Group of 77 Had its origins in the caucus of 75 developing countries that met in 1964 to prepare for UNCTAD. After the first UNCTAD meeting, the caucus grew to 77.

groups (*grupos* in Spanish-speaking countries) Conglomerates or a number of firms that together form a vertically integrated marketing and production system. Groups are common in Europe and Latin America. Frequently owned by immediate family members or a small investment combine. See chaebol.

guest workers Foreign workers who are brought into a country by legal means to perform needed labor.

hard currency A currency that is freely convertible into other currencies.

hard loans Loans that must be repaid in a hard currency at market interest rates.

hedging Selling forward currency exchange, borrowing, or using other means to protect against losses from possible currency exchange rate changes that affect the values of assets and liabilities.

hierarchy A system in which there are several layers of authority between the lowest rank (say, the peasants or untouchables) to the highest rank (say, king, commissar, or brahmin).

hit list or Super 301 Refers to Section 301 of the U.S. 1988 Trade Act, which requires the U.S. trade representative to prepare a list of countries that systematically restrict access of American products to their markets.

hollowing out Refers to the practice of firms that close their production facilities and become marketing organizations for other producers, mostly foreign.

home country The country where the parent company's headquarters are located.

horizontal organizations A form of organization characterized by lateral decision processes, horizontal networks, and a strong corporate-wide business philosophy.

host country The country in which foreign investment is made.

human needs approach A way to economic development that includes the elimination of poverty and unemployment as well as an increase in income.

hybrid organization A structure organized by more than one dimension at the top level.

hypermarkets Huge combination supermarkets and discount stores where soft and hard goods are sold.

import substitution An industrialization policy followed by some developing nations by which the government encourages the local production of substitutes for imported goods. High import duties protect local producers from import competition.

incentive pay plans Plans that pay employees more for achieving certain goals.

income distribution A measure of how a nation's income is apportioned among its people. It is commonly reported as the percentage of income received by population quintiles.

INCOTERMS A publication of the International Chamber of Commerce setting forth recommended standard definitions for the major trade terms used in international trade.

indexing Taking into account the effect of inflation on assets and liabilities and adjusting the amounts of these items to preserve their original relationships.

indicative planning Planning done by governments in collaboration with industry. It is essentially a forecast of the direction the economy is expected to take. An indicative plan does not control economic activity as in centrally planned economies, and firms are free to make their own decisions.

indirect exporting The exporting of goods and services through various types of home-based exporters.

industrial cooperation A long-term relationship with a company in a DC in which an LDC produces products for its own market, exports to the West, or both.

industrial espionage Stealing trade, process, customer, pricing, or technology secrets from a business.

industrial targeting Government practice of assisting selected industries to grow.

information glut There is too much information to absorb or it is not properly classified or organized.

infrastructure The fundamental underpinnings of an economy—roads, railroads, communications, water supplies, energy supplies, and so forth.

in-house training programs Programs provided by an employer on its own property.

instability As used in this book, occurs when a government is likely to be overthrown by a revolution or coup.

insurance certificate Evidence that marine insurance has been obtained to cover stipulated risks during transit.

interest arbitrage Lending in another country to take advantage of higher interest rates. Such arbitrage tends to equalize interest rates.

interest rate swap A transaction in which two parties exchange interest payment streams of differing character based on an underlying principal amount. The three main types are coupon swaps (fixed rate to floating rate in the same currency), basis swaps (one floating rate index to another floating rate index in the same currency), and cross-currency interest rate swaps (fixed or floating rate in one currency or fixed or floating rate in another currency).

intermediate technology Production method between capital- and labor-intensive methods.

internalization theory An extension of the market imperfection theory, which claims that to obtain a higher return on its investment, a firm will transfer its superior knowledge to a foreign subsidiary rather than sell it on the open market.

international division A division in the organization that is at the same level as the domestic division in the firm and is responsible for all non-home-country activities.

international environment The interaction between the domestic and foreign environmental forces.

international finance center A multinational's or global's office that handles most of the international money transactions for all the firm's units.

international financing Occurs when a borrower raises capital in the Eurocurrency or Eurobond markets, outside the restrictions that are applied to domestic or foreign offerings. See *foreign financing*.

international law A body of principles and practices that have been generally accepted by countries in their relations with other countries and with citizens of other countries.

international management information system Organized process of gathering, storing, processing, and disseminating information about international operations to managers to assist them in making business decisions.

international monetary system The agreements, practices, laws, customs, and institutions that deal with money (debts, payments, investments) internationally.

international product life cycle A theory that helps explain both trade flows and foreign direct investment on the basis of a product's position in the four stages of (1) exports of an industrialized nation, (2) beginning of foreign production, (3) foreign competition in export markets, and (4) import competition in the country where the product was introduced originally.

international status Confers extra perquisites and privileges on a multinational's top employees.

internet A global web of computer networks with some 5 million host computers. It has created a new form of communication but is neither organized by any organization nor regulated by any government or agency.

intervention currency A currency bought or sold by a country (not necessarily the one issued by it) to influence the value of its own currency.

intraenterprise transaction A transaction between two or more units of the same IC.

irrevocable letter of credit (L/C) A letter of credit that cannot be canceled.

Islam A religion found primarily in North Africa and the Middle East. Moslems believe the future is ordained by Allah (God). The Koran, a collection of Allah's revelations to Muhammad, the founder of Islam, is accepted as God's eternal word.

iterative planning Repetition of the bottom-up or top-down planning process until all differences are reconciled.

J curve A curve illustrating the theory that immediately after a country devalues its currency, its imports become more expensive and its exports cheaper, thus worsening a BOP deficit. As the country's exports increase, it earns more money and the deficit bottoms out and becomes a surplus up the right side of the J.

joint venture May be (1) a corporate entity between an IC and local owners, (2) a corporate entity between two or more ICs that are foreign to the area where the joint venture is located, or (3) a cooperative undertaking between two or more firms for a limited-duration project.

just-in-time delivery A balanced system in which there is little or no delay time or inventory.

key currencies Those held extensively as foreign exchange reserves.

labor force composition The different sorts of available laborers, differentiated in terms of skill, age, race, or gender.

labor intensive Describes products whose production requires a relatively large amount of labor and a relatively small amount of capital. Also describes the manufacturing process.

labor market The labor available in an area.

labor mobility The movement of labor from one location to another.

labor productivity How much a labor force produces in a given time period.

labor quality The skill and industriousness of labor.

labor quantity The number of available laborers.

labor unions Organizations of laborers that represent and negotiate for workers.

lags As used in this book, delaying conversion when payment is to be made in another currency in the belief the other currency will cost less when needed.

landlocked Refers to a nation bordered on all of its frontiers by land.

LASH Specially designed oceangoing vessel for carrying barges.

leads As used in this book, converting immediately when payment is to be made in another currency in the belief the other currency will cost more when needed.

left wing Extremely liberal, in the American sense of the word.

less developed countries (LDCs) Countries with low per capita income, low levels of industrialization, high illiteracy, and usually political instability.

letter of credit (L/C) A letter issued by a bank indicating that the bank will accept drafts (make payments) under specified circumstances.

liberal In American political usage, a liberal advocates extensive government intervention in business and society.

licensing A contractual arrangement in which one firm, the licensor, grants access to its patents, trademarks, or technology to another firm, the licensee, for a fee, usually called a royalty.

lingua franca A foreign language used to communicate among diverse cultures that speak different languages.

linkage In international marketing, the creation of demand in a second national market by movement of the product or the customer into that market.

Lombard rate The interest rate that a central bank charges other banks on loans secured by government and other selected securities.

Lomé convention An agreement between 69 African, Caribbean, and Pacific states and the EU by means of which 99.2 percent of the former group's exports are admitted duty-free to the EU.

London Interbank Offered Rate (LIBOR) The interest rate the most creditworthy banks charge one another for loans of Eurodollars overnight in the London market. LIBOR is a cornerstone in the pricing on money market issues and other short-term debt issues by both government and business borrowers. Interest is often stated to be LIBOR plus a fraction.

long position The position taken when a party buys something for future delivery. This may be done in the expectation that the item bought will increase in value. It may also be done to hedge a currency risk.

managed float See *floating exchange rates. Managed* is a more decorous word than *dirty.*

managed trade Trade managed in some way by governments.

management contract An agreement by which one firm provides management in all or specific areas to another company for a fee.

management information system (MIS) The computerized system through which multinational or global executives get timely, relevant information about all the company's units.

manufacturers' agents Independent sales representatives of various noncompeting suppliers.

manufacturing rationalization Division of production among a number of production units, enabling each to produce components for all of a firm's assembly plants.

maquiladora (in-bond plant) Introduced by the Mexican government to create jobs for its people.

Plants along the Mexican-American border cooperate, with the plant on the American side doing the capital-intensive work and the Mexican plant doing the labor-intensive production.

market economies Economies characterized by a relatively large, free (nongovernmental) market sector. There is no such thing as a totally free market; all governments regulate, tax, and intervene in various ways.

market factors Economic data that correlate highly with market demand for a product.

market indicators Economic data used to measure relative market strengths of countries or geographical areas.

market method to correct BOP deficit Deflate the economy and devalue the currency.

market screening A version of environmental scanning in which the firm identifies desirable markets by using the environmental forces to eliminate the less desirable markets.

Marshall Plan The U.S. aid program that helped European countries reconstruct after World War II. Cooperation among the European countries was a forerunner of the EC.

material culture Refers to all man-made objects and is concerned with how people make things (technology) and who makes what and why (economics).

matrix organization An organizational structure composed of one or more organizational structures superimposed over one another in an attempt to mesh product, regional, functional, and other expertise.

matrix overlay An organization whose top-level divisions are required to heed input from a staff composed of experts of another organizational dimension. It attempts to avoid the double-reporting difficulty of a matrix organization but still mesh two or more dimensions.

mercantilism The economic philosophy that equates the possession of gold or other international monetary assets with wealth. It also holds that trade activities should be directed or controlled by the government.

merchant banks Combine long- and short-term financing with the underwriting and distributing of securities.

minorities As used in this book, a group of people of one race or religion living in an area populated by a larger number of people of a different race or religion.

mission statement A broad statement defining an organization's scope.

mitbestimmung German for *codetermination*. The Germans pioneered codetermination, and their word for it is frequently used.

monetary policies Government policies regulating whether the country's money supply grows and, if so, how fast.

money markets Places where currencies are traded or capital is raised.

monopolistic advantage theory The idea that foreign direct investment is made by firms in oligopolistic industries that possess technical and other advantages over indigenous firms.

most favored nation (MFN) The policy of nondiscrimination in international commercial policy, extending to all nations the same customs and tariff treatments as are extended to the most favored nation.

multinational economic union A group of nations that have reduced barriers to intergroup trade and are cooperating in economic matters.

multinational, company or enterprise (MNC or MNE) Terms used by some authors to mean an organization consisting of a parent company in a home country that owns relatively autonomous subsidiaries in various host countries.

national (macro) competition Ability of a nation's producers to compete successfully in the world markets and with imports in their own domestic markets.

national economic plans Plans prepared by governments that state their economic goals and means for reaching them for periods of usually up to five years.

nationalism A strong attachment to and support of one's country.

nationalization Government takeover of private property.

national tax jurisdiction Taxation on the basis of nationality regardless of where in the world taxpayer's income is earned or where the activities of the taxpayer take place.

natural resources Anything supplied by nature on which people depend.

net negative international investment position Residents of a country have less investments abroad than nonresidents have in the country.

neutralizing the balance sheet Having the assets in a given currency approximate the liabilities in that currency.

newly industrializing countries (NICs) A group of middle-income nations with high growth in manufacturing. Much of their production goes to high-income, industrialized nations.

newly industrialized economies (NIE) The 4 Asian tigers—Hong Kong, South Korea, Taiwan, and Singapore.

nonmarket economy The World Bank designation for a communist nation.

nonmarket measures Use of currency controls, tariffs, or quotas to correct a BOP deficit.

nonrecourse financing Financing in which the factor assumes the full responsibility and all the risk of collecting from a third party. See *forfaiting*.

nonrevenue tax purpose Use of a tax to encourage some perceived socially desirable end such as home ownership, or to discourage something undesirable, such as tobacco.

nontariff barriers (NTBs) Constraints on imports other than import duties, such as quotas, product standards, orderly marketing arrangements, customs and administrative procedures, and government participation in trade.

note issuance facility (NIF) Medium-term arrangements that enable borrowers to issue paper, typically of three- or six-months' maturity, in their own names. A group of underwriting banks guarantees the availability of funds to the borrower by purchasing any unsold notes or by providing standby credit.

off-premises training The employer sends workers away from its property to a school or other site to be trained.

offshore banking The use of banks located in other countries, particularly tax havens like the Caymans and the Bahamas.

offshore funds Investment funds whose shares are usually denominated in U.S. dollars but located and sold outside the United States. There are tax and securities-registration reasons for such funds.

on-the-job training Employees learn a job by performing it under supervision.

opening bank The bank that opens a letter of credit (L/C). This bank will honor (pay) drafts drawn under the L/C if specified conditions are met.

orderly marketing agreements (OMAs) Compacts negotiated between two or more nations under whose terms the exporting nation or nations agree to limit exports of specified goods to the importing nation. They are sometimes called *voluntary export agreements (VEAs)*.

Overseas Private Insurance Corporation (OPIC) A U.S. government corporation that offers American investors in developing countries insurance against expropriation, currency inconvertibility, and damages from wars and revolutions.

overvalued currency A currency whose value is kept higher by government action than it would be in a free market.

paper gold See *special drawing rights (SDRs)*.

parallel importing The importing of a product by an independent operator that is not part of the manufacturer's channel of distribution. The parallel importer may compete with the authorized importer or with a subsidiary of the foreign manufacturer that produces the product in the local market.

parent company A company that owns subsidiary companies.

par value The value that a government, by agreement or regulation, sets on its currency in terms of other currencies. At Bretton Woods, other currencies were assigned par values in terms of the U.S. dollar.

paternalism A system in which a chief, sheik, or other authority figure cares for all the people as if he were their father.

pegged exchange rate An exchange rate in which a country's currency is fixed in terms of another country's currency. Frequently, the other country is a major trading partner or a country with which there was a colonial relationship.

peril point In U.S. law, a point below which a tariff cannot be lowered without causing or threatening serious injury to U.S. producers of competitive products.

physical product The basic physical product produced by a firm's production system. It does not include attributes added after production, such as packaging, brand name, service, or financing.

political risks The risks to a business and its employees that stem from political unrest in an area. As a result of such unrest, the markets or supplies of the business may be disrupted or the business may be nationalized and its employees may lose their jobs or be kidnapped, injured, or even killed.

population density A measure of the number of inhabitants per area unit (inhabitants per kilometer or mile).

population distribution A measure of how the inhabitants are distributed over a nation's area.

polymetallic deposits Deposits that contain a number of metals.

portfolio investment The purchase of stocks and bonds to obtain a return in the money invested. The investors are not interested in assuming control of the firm.

preindustrial societies A designation that can signify anything from traditional societies through societies in the early stages of agricultural and industrial organization.

preventive maintenance (planned maintenance) Maintenance done according to plan, not when a machine breaks down.

price and wage controls Government limits on prices that may be charged and wages that may be paid.

privatization When a government transfers ownership, operation, or both of a government-owned enterprise to private owners/operators.

product liability Liability of a product's manufacturer for damage caused by the product.

pro forma invoice Exporter's formal quotation containing a description of the merchandise, price, delivery time, method of shipping, terms of sale, and points of entry.

programmed-management approach A middle-ground advertising strategy between globally standardized and entirely local programs.

promotion All forms of communication between a firm and its publics.

promotional mix A blend of the promotional methods a firm uses to sell its products.

Protestant work ethic The duty of Christians to glorify God by hard work and the practice of thrift.

public relations Various methods of communicating with the firm's publics to secure a favorable impression.

purchasing power parity The relative ability of one unit of two countries' currencies to purchase similar goods. From this relative ability is derived an indication of what the market exchange rate between the two currencies should be.

quality circles (quality control circles) Small work groups that meet periodically to discuss ways to improve their functional areas in the firm and the quality of the products.

questionable or dubious payments Bribes.

quota (1) A limitation on imports by number or by weight; for example, only so many of a given item or only so many pounds or kilos may be imported. (2) At the IMF, each member-nation has a quota that determines the amount of its subscription and how much it can borrow.

reengineering A radical redesign of business processes to achieve dramatic improvements in critical measures of performance, such as cost, quality, service, or speed.

regional dualism A situation in which some regions of a nation have high productivity and high incomes while other regions of the same country have little economic development and lower incomes.

regression analysis Statistical technique that utilizes a linear model to establish relationships between independent variables and the dependent variable.

reinvoicing Centralizing all international invoicing by an IC. The reinvoicing center decides which currencies should be used and where, how, and when.

repatriation The transfer home of assets held abroad.

representative office An office of an out-of-state or foreign bank that is not permitted to conduct direct banking functions. The purpose of such an office is to solicit business for its parent bank, where it can conduct such functions.

restrictive trade practices legislation The European versions of American antitrust laws.

revaluation of a currency An increase in a currency's value in terms of other currencies. See *devaluation*.

reverse engineering Dismantling a competitor's product to learn everything possible about it.

reverse imports Products made by a multinational's overseas subsidiaries that are exported to the home country.

revocable letters of credit (L/Cs) L/Cs that the opening bank may revoke at any time without notice to the beneficiary.

Rhine waterway A system of rivers and canals that is the main transportation artery of Europe.

right wing Extremely conservative politically.

robotics Machines, usually computer controlled, doing work previously done by human workers.

RO-RO Specially designed oceangoing vessel that permits any equipment on wheels to be rolled on board.

rural-to-urban shift Describes the movement of a nation's population from rural areas to cities.

S.A. Société Anonyme, Sociedad Anomina, or Societa Anomina. Joint-stock companies (in French, Spanish, and Italian, respectively).

safe haven The currency of a country that is politically secure is called a *safe haven currency*.

sales company A corporate entity established in a foreign country by the parent company to sell goods or services imported from the parent company and other foreign affiliates.

sales promotion Selling aids, including displays, premiums, contests, and gifts.

S.A.R.L. Société à Responsibilité Limitée.

scenario Description of a possible future. Managers often use most likely, worst, and best cases for the purpose of planning.

securitization The term is most often used to mean the process by which traditional bank assets, mainly loans or mortgages, are converted into negotiable securities. More broadly, refers to the development of markets for a variety of new negotiable instruments.

self-reference criterion Unconscious reference to one's own cultural values when judging behavioral actions of others in a new and different environment.

shale A fissile (capable of being split) rock composed of laminated layers of claylike, fine-grained sediment.

short position The position of a party when it has sold something it does not own. This is for future delivery in the expectation that the item sold will decrease in price. It is also done to hedge a currency risk.

sight draft A bill of exchange that is payable immediately on presentation or demand. A bank check is a sight draft.

skilled labor Employees trained in needed skills.

Smithsonian agreement New agreements on currency par values, the value of gold, and tariffs reached by the major trading countries at the Smithsonian Institution in Washington, DC, in December 1971. When the United States closed the "gold window" in August 1971, the world currency exchanges were thrown into turmoil, and such agreements became necessary.

snake During the 1970s, several West European countries agreed to keep the values of their currencies within established ranges in terms of one another. The currencies would all float in value in terms of other currencies for example, the U.S. dollar and the Japanese yen.

socialism A theory of society in which the government owns or directs most of the factors of production.

soft currency A currency that is not freely convertible into other currencies. Such a currency is usually subject to national currency controls.

soft loans Loans like those granted by the IDA. These loans may have grace periods during which no payments need be made; they may bear low or no interest; and they may be repayable in a soft currency.

sogo shosha The Japanese term for general trading companies.

sovereign debt The debt of a national government.

sovereign immunity The immunity of a government from lawsuits in the courts of its own country or other countries unless it submits voluntarily. Such immunity is particularly likely to exist if the government limits itself to governmental functions as opposed to economic ones.

sovereignty The power of each national government over the land within its borders and over the people and organizations within those borders.

special drawing rights (SDRs) Accounting entries at the IMF. SDRs are treated as reserve assets and are credited or debited to member-countries' accounts. Sometimes called *paper gold*, they permit liquidity to be created by agreement at the IMF rather than having it depend on the U.S. BOP deficit.

specific tariff or duty A method of measuring customs duties or tariffs by number or weight instead of by value. Thus, the amount of the tariff or duty is based on how many units or how many pounds or kilos are imported, regardless of their value. See *ad valorem tariff or duty*.

spot rate or spot quotation The rate of exchange between two currencies for delivery, one for the other within two business days.

stability As used in this book, occurs when a government is not likely to be overturned by a revolution or a coup.

standardization of the marketing mix The utilization of the same pricing, product, distribution, and promotional strategies in all markets where the firm does business.

straight bonds or notes Issues with a fixed, not floating, coupon or interest rate.

strategic business unit (SBU) Business entity with a clearly defined market, specific competitors, the ability to carry out its business mission, and a size appropriate for control by a single manager.

subcontracting Prime manufacturers purchase of components from other suppliers. Used in industrial cooperation.

subsidiaries Companies owned by another company, which is referred to as the parent company.

subsidiary detriment A subsidiary is deprived of a potential advantage so that the IC as a whole may enjoy a greater advantage.

subsidies, export Financial encouragement to export. Such subsidies can take the form of lower taxes, tax rebates, or direct payments.

superstores Name given to hypermarkets in Japan and in some parts of Europe and the United States.

swaps Are of two basic kinds: interest rate swaps and currency swaps. Interest rate swaps typically exchange fixed-rate for floating-rate payments. Currency swaps are accords to deliver one currency against another currency at certain intervals.

swing In a bilateral trade agreement, the leeway provided for mutual extension of credit.

switch trade A type of countertrade utilized when a country lacks sufficient hard currency to pay for its imports. When it can acquire from a third country products desired by its creditor country, it switches shipment of those products to the creditor country. Its debt to the creditor country is thereby paid.

synchronous production An entire manufacturing process with unbalanced operations. Total system performance is emphasized.

takeoff A phase in the development of an LDC when its infrastructure has been sufficiently developed, enough interacting industries have been established, and domestic capital formation exceeds consumption so that the country's own momentum carries the development process onward.

tariff quota A tariff that has a lower rate until the end of a specified period or until a specified amount of the commodity has been imported. At that point, the rate increases.

tariffs See *duties*.

tax haven A country that has low or no taxes on income from foreign sources or capital gains.

tax incentives The tax holidays that LDCs sometimes give companies and their managements if they will invest in the country, or that DCs sometimes give them to induce investment in an area of high unemployment or to encourage exports.

tax treaty A treaty between two countries in which each country usually lowers certain taxes on residents who are nationals of the other, and the countries agree to cooperate in tax matters like enforcement.

Taylor's scientific management system A system based on scientific measurements that prescribes a division of work whereby planning is done by managers and plan execution is left to supervisors and workers.

technological dualism The presence in a country of industries using modern technology while others employ more primitive methods.

terms of sale Conditions of a sale that stipulate the point where all costs and risks are borne by the buyer.

terms of trade The real quantities of exports that are required to pay for a given amount of imports.

territorial tax jurisdiction The levying of tax on taxpayers while living and working in the territory of the taxing government. Income earned while living and working elsewhere is not taxed or is taxed at a lower rate.

terrorism The use by nongovernment forces of murder, kidnapping, and destruction to publicize or gain political goals or money.

third country nationals Citizens of neither the home country nor the host country who work in a host country affiliate.

Third World The Eastern-bloc countries that were dominated by the U.S.S.R. were considered one world. The countries of the West, primarily the OECD countries, were considered another world. All other countries are sometimes referred to as the Third World countries.

tied loans or grants Loans or grants that the borrower or recipient must spend in the country that made them.

time draft An unconditional order drawn by the seller on the buyer to pay the draft's amount at an agreed future date.

top-down planning Planning process that begins at the highest level in the organization and continues downward.

topography The surface features of a region, such as mountains, deserts, plains, and bodies of water.

total product What the customer buys; it includes the physical product, brand name, after-sale service, warranty, instructions for use, the company image, and the package.

total quality control system A system that integrates the development, maintenance, and improvement of quality among all functional areas of the firm.

trade acceptance A draft similar to a banker's acceptance, the difference being that no bank is involved. The exporter presents the draft to the importer for its acceptance to pay the amount stated at a fixed future date.

trade bloc A group of countries with special trading rules among them, such as the EU.

trade deficit/surplus A trade deficit is an excess of merchandise imports over exports. A trade surplus is the opposite.

trade fair A large exhibition generally held periodically at the same place and time at which companies maintain booths to promote the sale of their products.

trade mission Group of businesspeople, government officials (state and federal), or both that visits a foreign market in search of business opportunities.

trading at a discount When a currency costs less in the forward market than the spot cost.

trading at a premium When a currency costs more in the forward market than the spot cost.

trading companies Firms that develop international trade and serve as intermediaries between foreign buyers and domestic sellers, and vice versa.

traditional economy An area in a most rudimentary state. In such an economy, the people are typically nomadic, agriculture is at a bare subsistence level, and industry is virtually nonexistent.

traditional hostilities When nations, races, or religions have been in conflict for long periods.

transaction risk The risk run in international trade that changes in relative currency values will cause losses.

transfer price The price charged by one unit of an IC for goods or services that it sells to another unit of the same IC.

translation risk The apparent losses or gains that can result from the restatement of values from one currency into another, even if there are no transactions, when the currencies change in value relative to each other. Translation risks are common with long-term foreign investments as foreign currency values are translated to the investor's financial statements in its home currency.

transnationals Used by the UN and some others to connote organizations variously called global, multinational, worldwide companies, or IC.

Treaty of Rome Established the EU.

trend analysis Statistical technique by which successive observations of a variable at regular time intervals are analyzed for the purpose of establishing regular patterns used for establishing future values.

twin plants Along the Mexican-American border, the plant on the U.S. side does the high-tech, capital-intensive part of production, while the Mexican plant, also called *maquiladoras*, does the labor-intensive part.

unbalanced growth theory The idea that economic growth can be attained by deliberately creating an imbalance in the economy through investment in an industry that will require further investment in supporting industries to reduce the imbalance.

uncontrollable environmental forces The external forces in the domestic and foreign environments over which management has no direct control.

underground economy The part of a nation's income that, underreported or unreported, is not measured by official statistics.

undervalued currency A currency that has been oversold because of emotional selling, or a currency whose value a government tries to keep below market to make its country's exports less expensive and more competitive.

unit labor costs The labor cost to produce one unit of output.

unskilled labor Employees without needed skills.

unspoken language Nonverbal communication, such as gestures and body language.

untouchables Lowest-caste Indians. Mahatma Gandhi called them *harijans*, the children of God.

Uruguay Round The round of GATT negotiations that held its first meeting in Uruguay in 1986.

validated export license A required document issued by the U.S. government authorizing the export of specified commodities.

value-added tax (VAT) A tax levied at each stage in the production of a product. The tax is on the value added to the product by that stage.

variable levy Import duties set at the differences between world market prices and local government-supported prices. Used by the European Union on grain imports to ensure that they have no price advantage over locally grown grains.

vehicle currency A currency used in international transactions to make quotes and payments. The U.S. dollar is the currency most often used.

venture capital Money invested, usually in equity, in a new, relatively high-risk undertaking.

vertical mobility An individual's opportunities to move upward in a society to a higher caste or a higher social status.

virtual corporation A temporary group of independent companies including manufacturers, marketers, suppliers, customers, and competitors, connected by a computer network, for the purpose of designing, manufacturing and marketing a product.

voluntary export agreements (VEAs) See *orderly marketing agreements.*

watch list List containing items of interest concerning uncontrollable variables of special interest to the firm.

Webb-Pomerene Act Exempts from U.S. antitrust laws those associations among business competitors engaged in export trade. They must not restrain trade within the United States or the trade of any other U.S. competitors.

World Trade Organization (WTO) The organization that succeeded the General Agreement on Tariffs and Trade (GATT) as a result of the successful completion of the Uruguay Round of GATT negotiations.

worldwide companies Used by some authors to connote the organizations referred to by others as globals, multinationals, transnationals, or ICs.

zaibatsu Centralized, family-dominated, monopolistic economic groups that dominated the Japanese economy until the end of World War II, at which time they were broken up. As time passed, however, the units of the old zaibatsu drifted back together, and they now cooperate within the group much as they did before their dissolution.

zero-coupon bonds Bonds that are issued at a heavy discount and pay no interest but are redeemable at par at a future date.

Indexes

NAME INDEX

COMPANY INDEX

SUBJECT INDEX